BY APPOINTMENT
TO H.M. QUEEN ELIZABETH
THE QUEEN MOTHER
BRITISH LEYLAND UK LIMITED
LEYLAND CARS
MANUFACTURERS OF DAIMLER, JAGUAR,
ROVER CARS AND LAND ROVERS,
BIRMINGHAM AND COVENTRY

Jaguar

XJ6
SERIES 2

Daimler

SOVEREIGN
SERIES 2

Repair Operation Manual

Publication Part No. E188/4

INTRODUCTION

The purpose of this Manual is to assist skilled mechanics in the efficient repair and maintenance of Jaguar and Daimler vehicles. Using the appropriate service tools and carrying out the procedures as detailed will enable the operations to be completed in the time stated in the 'Repair Operation Times'.

Indexing
For convenience, the Manual is divided into a number of sections. Pages 01-01 to 01–18 give an alphabetical index of operations contained in each section.

Operation Numbering
A master index of numbered operations has been compiled for universal application to all vehicles manufactured by the British Leyland Motor Corporation and, therefore, because of the different specifications of various models, continuity of the numbering sequence cannot be maintained throughout this manual.

Each operation described in the Manual is allocated a number from the master index and cross-refers with an identical number in the 'Repair Operation Times'. The number consists of six digits arranged in three pairs.

Each instruction within an operation has a sequence number and, to complete the operation in the minimum time, it is essential that the instructions are performed in numerical sequence commencing at 1 unless otherwise stated. Where applicable, the sequence numbers identify the relevant components in the appropriate illustration.

Service Tools
Where performance of an operation requires the use of a service tool, the tool number is quoted under the operation heading and is repeated in, or following, the instruction involving its use. An illustrated list of all necessary tools is included in Section 99.

References
References to the left- or right-hand side in the Manual are made when viewing from the rear. With the engine and gearbox assembly removed, the 'timing cover' end of the engine is referred to as the front. A key to abbreviations and symbols is given on page 04–1.

REPAIRS AND REPLACEMENTS

When service parts are required it is essential that only genuine Jaguar or Unipart replacements are used.

Attention is particularly drawn to the following points concerning repairs and the fitting of replacement parts and accessories.

Safety features embodied in the car may be impaired if other than genuine parts are fitted. In certain territories, legislation prohibits the fitting of parts not to the vehicle manufacturer's specification. Torque wrench setting figures given in the Repair Operation Manual must be strictly adhered to. Locking devices, where specified, must be fitted. If the efficiency of a locking device is impaired during removal it must be renewed. Owners purchasing accessories while travelling abroad should ensure that the accessory and its fitted location on the car conform to mandatory requirements in their country of origin. The car warranty may be invalidated by the fitting of other than genuine Jaguar parts. All Jaguar or Unipart replacements have the full backing of the factory warranty.
Jaguar Distributors and Dealers are obliged to supply only genuine service parts.

SPECIFICATION

Purchasers are advised that the specification details set out in this Manual apply to a range of vehicles and not to any one. For the specification of a particular vehicle, purchasers should consult their Distributor or Dealer.

The Manufacturers reserve the right to vary their specifications with or without notice, and at such times and in such manner as they think fit. Major as well as minor changes may be involved in accordance with the Manufacturer's policy of constant product improvement.

Whilst every effort is made to ensure the accuracy of the particulars contained in this Manual, neither the Manufacturer nor the Distributor or Dealer, by whom this Manual is supplied, shall in any circumstances be held liable for any inaccuracy or the consequences thereof.

COPYRIGHT

Contents

INDEX

CAUTION: Maintenance operations which must be carried out on cars built to Federal Specifications are detailed on pages 10–2 and 10–3.

continued

FUEL SYSTEM

ELECTRONIC FUEL INJECTION

continued

ELECTRONIC FUEL INJECTION – continued

COOLING SYSTEM

MODEL 12 AUTOMATIC TRANSMISSION

MODEL 65 AUTOMATIC TRANSMISSION

PROPELLER AND DRIVE SHAFTS

FINAL DRIVE

continued

FRONT SUSPENSION

REAR SUSPENSION

continued

REAR SUSPENSION – continued

WARNING: IF CAR IS FITTED WITH A POWR-LOK DIFFERENTIAL, UNDER NO CIRCUMSTANCE MUST ENGINE BE RUN WITH CAR IN GEAR AND ONE REAR WHEEL OFF THE GROUND. IF IT IS FOUND NECESSARY TO TURN TRANSMISSION WITH CAR IN GEAR, BOTH WHEELS MUST BE RAISED.

BRAKES

BODY

continued

BODY – continued

HEATING AND VENTILATION

AIR CONDITIONING

ELECTRICAL

continued

ELECTRICAL – continued

INSTRUMENTS

Section No.

SECTION 44 – AUTOMATIC TRANSMISSION

SECTION 51 – FINAL DRIVE

SECTION 57 – STEERING

SECTION 60 – FRONT SUSPENSION

STANDARDISED ABBREVIATIONS AND SYMBOLS IN THIS MANUAL

Term	Abbreviation or Symbol
Across flats (bolt size)	A.F.
After bottom dead centre	A.B.D.C.
After top dead centre	A.T.D.C.
Alternating current	a.c.
Amperes	A
Ampere-hour	Ah
Atmospheres	Atm
Before bottom dead centre	B.B.D.C.
Before top dead centre	B.T.D.C.
Bottom dead centre	B.D.C.
Brake horse power	b.h.p.
Brake mean effective pressure	b.m.e.p.
British Standards	B.S.
Carbon monoxide	CO
Centigrade (Celsius)	C
Centimetres	cm
Cubic centimetres	cm^3
Cubic inches	in^3
Cycles per minute	c/min
Degree (angle)	deg. or °
Degree (temperature)	deg. or °
Diameter	dia.
Direct current	d.c.
Fahrenheit	F
Feet	ft
Feet per minute	ft/min
Fifth	5th
Figure (illustration)	Fig.
First	1st
Fourth	4th
Gallons (Imperial)	gal.
Gallons (U.S.)	U.S. gal.
Grammes (force)	gf
Grammes (mass)	g
High compression	h.c.
High tension (electrical)	h.t.
Horse power	hp
Hundredweight	cwt
Inches	in.
Inches of mercury	inHg
Independent front suspension	i.f.s.
Internal diameter	i.dia.
Kilogrammes (force)	kgf
Kilogrammes (mass)	kg
Kilogramme centimetre	kgf cm
Kilogramme metres	kgf m
Kilogrammes per square centimetre	kgf/cm^2 or kg/cm^2
Kilometres	km
Kilometres per hour	km/h
Kilovolts	kV
King pin inclination	k.p.i.
Left hand	L.H.
Left hand steering	L.H. Stg.
Left hand thread	L.H. Thd.
Low compression	l.c.
Low tension	l.t.
Maximum	max.
Metres	m
Miniature Edison Screw	MES
Miles per gallon	m.p.g.
Miles per hour	m.p.h.
Millimetres	mm
Millimetres of mercury	mmHg
Minimum	min.
Minus (of tolerance)	–
Minute (of angle)	
Negative (electrical)	–
Newton metres	Nm
Number	No.
Ounces (force)	ozf
Ounces (mass)	oz
Ounce inch (torque)	ozf in
Outside diameter	o.dia.
Overdrive	O/D
Paragraphs	para.
Part Numbers	Part No.
Percentage	%
Pints (Imperial)	pt
Pints (U.S.)	U.S. pt
Plus or minus	±
Plus (tolerance)	+
Positive (electrical)	+
Pounds (force)	lbf
Pounds (mass)	lb
Pounds feet (torque)	lbf ft
Pounds inches (torque)	lbf in
Pounds per square inch	lbf/in^2 or lb/in^2
Radius	r
Ratio	:
Reference	ref.
Revolutions per minute	rev/min
Right hand	R.H.
Right hand steering	R.H.Stg.
Second (angle)	"
Second (numerical order)	2nd
Single carburetter	SC
Society of Automobile Eng.	S.A.E.
Specific gravity	sp.gr.
Square centimetres	cm^2
Square inches	in^2
Standard	std.
Standard wire gauge	s.w.g.
Synchroniser/synchromesh	synchro.
Third	3rd
Top dead centre	T.D.C.
Twin carburetters	TC
United Kingdom	UK
Volts	V
Watts	W
Screw Threads	
American Standard Taper Pipe	N.P.T.F.
British Association	B.A.
British Standard Fine	B.S.F.
British Standard Pipe	B.S.P.
British Standard Whitworth	B.S.W.
Unified Coarse	U.N.C.
Unified Fine	U.N.F.
Metric	M (e.g. M20)

GENERAL SPECIFICATION DATA

Final Drive Unit

Type	Hypoid, with normal differential "Powr Lok" differential available as optional extra
Ratio (standard)	3.54 : 1 (46/13) for all 3.4 litre cars and manual transmission 4.2 litre cars
The following alternative ratios are also supplied	3.07 : 1 (43/14), 3.31 : 1 (43/13) for 4.2 litre automatic transmission cars

Automatic Gearbox

	Early Cars	Later Cars
Make and Type	Borg Warner Model 12	Borg Warner Model 65
Ratios	First gear 2.40 : 1	First gear 2.39 : 1
	Second gear 1.46 : 1	Second gear 1.45 : 1
	Third gear 1.00 : 1	Third gear 1.00 : 1
	Reverse 2.00 : 1	Reverse 2.09 : 1
	Torque Converter 2.00 : 1 max.	Torque Converter 2.3 : 1 max.

4-speed Manual Gearbox

Type	4 Speed with baulk-ring synchromesh on all forward gears
Ratios	First gear Early cars 2.933 : 1
	Later cars 3.238 : 1
	Second gear 1.905 : 1
	Third gear 1.389 : 1
	Fourth gear 1.00 : 1
	Reverse Early cars 3.378 : 1
	Later cars 3.428 : 1

Overdrive (on all 4-speed Manual Gearbox Cars)

Make and Type	Laycock de Normanville "Compact 'A' Type"
Ratio	0.778 : 1 giving overall ratio of 2.753 : 1

Cooling System

Water pump – Type	Centrifugal
– Drive	Belt
No. of cooling fans	1 – 12 blade, belt driven through 'Holset' coupling
Cooling system and control	Thermostat
Filler cap pressure rating	13 lb/in^2 (0,91 kg/cm^2)
Filler cap – Make	AC Delco

Fuel System
A – For North American Market only

Carburetters

Make and reference No.	Zenith Stromberg
	1974 3598R (Front) 3598L (Rear)
with automatic choke	1975 3737R (Front) 3737L (Rear)
	1976-7 3848RH (Front) 3848LH (Rear)
Needles	1974 B1CG (Fixed Orifice E.G.R.)
	1974 **B2AZ** (Variable Orifice E.G.R.)
	1975-6-7 B2BC
Spring colour	Natural

B – For all Markets except North America

Carburetters
(Early cars, up to engine No. 8L 26203 (4.2L) and 8A 5098 (3.4L)

Make and reference No. – 4.2 Litre	SU HS8 AUD 397 (R.H. Stg.) AUD 538 (L.H. Stg.)
– 3.4 Litre	SU HS8 AUD 710
Needles – 4.2 Litre	BAW (no intake temp. control)
	BBK (i.t.c., up to 7L.80999)
	BCC (i.t.c., after 7L.81000)
– 3.4 Litre	BCX
Spring colour	Red/Green

(Later cars, from engine No. 8L 26204 (4.2L) and 8A 5099 (3.4L)

Make and reference No. – 4.2 Litre	SU HIF7 1049F (Front) 1049R (Rear)
– 3.4 Litre	SU HIF7 FZX1053 F (Front) FZX1053 R (Rear)
Needles – 4.2 Litre	BDN (internal vent) BDY (external vent)
– 3.4 Litre	BDW
Spring colour (all carburetters)	Red

Fuel Pumps

Operation	Electrical
Make and Type	Two SU AUF 301 (early cars)
	Two AC Delco submerged 0363 LH (later 0364 RH cars)

Braking System

Front Brakes – Make and Type	Girling; ventilated discs, bridge type calipers
Rear Brakes – Make and Type	Girling; damped discs, bridge type calipers incorporating handbrake friction pads
Handbrake – Type	Mechanical, operating on rear discs
Disc diameter – Front	11.18 in. (284 mm.)
– Rear	10.375 in. (263,5 mm.)
Disc thickness – Front	0.95 in. (24,13 mm.)
– Rear	0.50 in. (12,7 mm.)
Master cylinder bore dia.	0.875 in. (22,23 mm.)
Brake operation	Hydraulic
Hydraulic fluid	Castrol/Girling Universal Brake & Clutch Fluid – exceeding specification S.A.E. J.1703/D
Main brake friction pad material	Ferodo 2430 Slotted
Hand brake friction pad material	**Mintex M.68/1**
Servo unit refs. R.H.D. cars	Girling 64049669
L.H.D. cars	Girling 64049668

Front Suspension

Type	Independent – coil spring
Castor angle	2¼° ± ¼° positive
Camber angle	½° ± ¼° positive
Front wheel alignment	1/16 in. to 1/8 in. (1,6 mm. to 3,2 mm.) toe-in
Dampers	Telescopic, gas filled

Rear Suspension

Type	Independent – coil springs, co-axial with dampers
Camber angle	¾° ± ¼° negative
Rear wheel alignment	Parallel ± 1/32 in. (±0,08 mm.)
Dampers	Telescopic, gas filled

Power Assisted Steering

Type	Rack & Pinion
Number of turns, lock to lock	3.31
Turning circle, kerb to kerb	
2-door cars	37 ft. (11,3 m.) L. & R.
4-door cars	38 ft. (11,6 m.) L. & R.

Electrical Equipment

Battery – Make and Type	Lucas CP11 (R.H.D. cars) or CP11/8 (L.H.D. cars)
Voltage	12V
No. of plates per cell	11
Capacity at twenty hour rate	66 Ah

Alternator

Make and Type	
(a) All air conditioned cars; also non-air conditioned cars for Malaysia and Hong Kong	Lucas 20 ACR or Lucas 25 ACR or Motorola 9AR 2512P
(b) Non-air conditioned cars	Lucas 18 ACR
Nominal voltage	12V
Cut in voltage	13.5V at 2100 r.p.m. (Motorola 14V at 1050 r.p.m.)
Earth polarity	Negative
Maximum output	66A (20 ACR) (Motorola 70A) 45A (18 ACR)
Maximum operating speed	12,400 r.p.m.
Rotor winding resistance	3.2 ohms (18 ACR) @ 20°C 3.6 ohms (20 ACR)
Brush spring pressure	9-13 oz. (255-368 g)

Starter Motor

Make and Type	3.4L and 4.2L Lucas 3M100 Pre-engaged 2.8L Man. Lucas 3M100 inward engaging 2.8L Auto. Lucas 3M100 outward engaging
Lock torque	29 lbf. ft. (4,01 kgfm) at 940 amps
Torque at 1000 rev/min	13 lbf. ft. (1,80 kgfm) at 535 amps
Light running current	100A at 5000 to 6000 rev/min

Distributor

Make and Type	4.2L Lucas 22D/6, 45D/6, 45 DE6 3.4L Lucas 45D/6 2.8L Lucas 25D/6 45D/6

Windscreen Wiper Motor

Make and Type	Lucas 16W
Light running speed, rack disconnected (after 60 seconds from cold)	Normal – 46-52 rev/min High – 60-70 rev/min
Light running current (after 60 seconds from cold)	Normal – 1.5 A High – 2.0 A

LAMP BULBS

LAMP	LUCAS BULB NO.	WATTS	APPLICATION
Headlamp RHD Outb'd Main and dip		60/45	United Kingdom (sealed beam)
Headlamp RHD Outb'd Main and dip		50/37.5	Japan (sealed beam)
Headlamp LHD Outb'd Main and dip		37.5/50	U.S.A. (sealed beam)
Headlamp LHD Outb'd Main and dip	411	45/40	France (yellow bulb)
Headlamp LHD Outb'd Main and dip		60/50	All other countries (sealed beam)
Headlamp inboard (main beam only)		37.5	Japan (sealed beam)
Headlamp inboard (main beam only)		37.5	U.S.A. (sealed beam)
Headlamp inboard (main beam only)	411	45	France (yellow bulb)
Headlamp inboard (main beam only)		50	All other countries (sealed beam)
Front flasher and side lamp	380	21-6	Double filament – Italy and North America only
Front flasher	382	21 }	All other countries
Side lamp	989	6 }	
Reverse lamps (festoon bulbs)	273	21	All countries except France
Reverse lamps (festoon bulbs)	267	15	France only
Number plate lamp	989	6	
Sidemarker lamp	989	6	Export only
Side flash repeater (capless)	601	5	Special order only
Red tail/flasher	380	21-6	N. America, Greece & Portugal
Stop/tail	380	21-6 }	U.K. and Europe
Rear flasher	382	21 }	
Map light (festoon bulb)	254	6	
Roof lamp (festoon bulb)	272	10	2-door cars only (Hella lamps)
Pillar lamps (festoon bulbs)	272	10	
Luggage compartment light	989	6	
Clock illumination (M.E.S.)	987	2.2	
Flasher warning light		1.2 }	
Hazard warning light		1.2 }	Miniature capless bulbs
Ignition warning light		1.2 }	Smith 40-621-109-86
Handbrake/brake fluid warning light		1.2 }	or Thorn 21-2130
Oil pressure warning light		1.2 }	
Instrument panel illumination	281	2	
Instrument cluster (M.E.S.)	987	2.2	
Opticell unit light	6253	6	AAU 9276 bulb (Wotan)
Console lights	987	2.2	
Cigar lighter (miniature bayonet)		2.2	Vitality bulb No. G.70112
Push-push switch illumination	280	1.5	
Speedometer illumination (M.E.S.)	981	2.2	
Rev. counter illumination (M.E.S.)	981	2.2	
Choke warning light	987	2.2	Emission control cars only
Choke handle illumination	281	2	Emission control cars only
Headlight warning light	987	2.2	
Safety belt warning light	987	2.2	
Heater control panel illumination	280	1.5	
Switch indicator strip	281	2	
Automatic transmission indicator	281	2	
Fog lamp (Cibié)	Cibié H2	55	
Spot lamp (Cibié)	Cibié H2	55	

TYRE PRESSURES

N.B. Check pressures with tyres cold, and not when they have attained their normal running temperature.

Tyre Type ER.70 VR 15 SP Sport

	PRESSURE Front	Rear
For normal use up to 100 m.p.h. (160 km./hr.) with driver and two passengers	27 lb./in.^{2} 1,90 kg./cm.^{2}	26 lb./in.^{2} 1,83 kg./cm.^{2}
For normal use up to 100 m.p.h. (160 km./hr.) with full load (inc. luggage) of 904 lb. (410 kg.)	27 lb./in.^{2} 1,90 kg./cm.^{2} 1,86 Bars	30 lb./in.^{2} 2,11 kg./cm.^{2} 2,07 Bars
For speeds above 100 m.p.h. (160 km./hr.) with full load (inc. luggage) of 904 lb. (410 kg.)	33 lb./in.^{2} 2,32 kg./cm.^{2} 2,27 Bars	36 lb./in.^{2} 2,53 kg./cm.^{2} 2,48 Bars

Tyre Replacement and Wheel Interchanging

When replacement of tyres is necessary, it is preferable to fit a complete car set. Should either front or rear tyres only show a necessity for replacement, new tyres must be fitted to replace the worn ones. No attempt must be made to interchange tyres from front to rear or vice-versa as tyre wear produces characteristic patterns depending upon their position and if such position is changed after wear has occurred, the performance of the tyre will be adversely affected. It should be remembered that new tyres require to be balanced.

The DUNLOP radial ply tyres specified are designed to meet the high speed performance of which this car is capable.

Only tyres of identical specification as shown under "GENERAL DATA" must be fitted as replacements and, if of different tread pattern, should not be fitted in mixed form.

UNDER NO CIRCUMSTANCES SHOULD CROSS-PLY TYRES BE FITTED.

RECOMMENDED SNOW TYRES

The following table is intended to assist in the correct choice of snow tyres and it must be emphasised that the tyres mentioned are the only snow tyres recommended by Jaguar Cars.

Special inner tubes stamped with the tyre size and the words "WEATHERMASTER ONLY" are available and must **ALWAYS** be fitted when using 185/15 SP M. & S. Tyres.

TYRE DESIGNATION	RECOMMENDED FITMENT	ROAD SPEED AND TYRE PRESSURES	REMARKS
1. **E.70 15 SP.44 Weathermaster** (Tubeless)	Complete sets only	Up to 85 m.p.h. (137 km/h) **FRONT** 27 lbf/in^2, 1,90 kgf/cm^2, 1,86 bar **REAR** 26 lbf/in^2, 1,83 kgf/cm^2, 1,76 bar From 85 m.p.h. (137 km/h) up to a maximum of 100 m.p.h. (161 km/h) **FRONT** 35 lbf/in^2, 2,5 kgf/cm^2, 2,4 bar **REAR** 34 lbf/in^2, 2,49 kgf/cm^2, 2,36 bar	1. Snow chains **MUST NOT** be fitted. 2. Tyres may be fitted with studs providing maximum speed does not exceed 75 m.p.h. (121 km/h)
2. **Weathermaster 185/15 SP M. & S.** (Tubed)	Complete sets only	As above / As above	1. Snow chains may be fitted to rear wheels only. 2. Tyres may be fitted with studs providing maximum speed does not exceed 75 m.p.h. (121 km/h)

ENGINE TUNING DATA – 3.4 LITRE

General Data

Number of cylinders	6 (in line)
Bore	3.2677 in. (83,0 mm.)
Stroke	4.1732 in. (106,0 mm.)
Cubic capacity	3441.2 cc (210 cu. in.)
Compression ratio	8.4 : 1
Ignition timing (static)	8° B.T.D.C.
Firing order	1 5 3 6 2 4 (No. 1 cyl. at rear)

Cylinder Block

Material	Chromium cast iron
Type of cylinder liner	Dry (used for salvage only)
Material (liners)	Cast iron
Liner interference fit	0.0025 to 0.0045 in. (0,064 to 0,114 mm.)

Bore diameters after honing — Piston

Grade	max in	mm	min in	mm
F	3.2676	82,997	3.2673	82,989
G	3.2680	83,007	3.2677	83,000
H	3.2684	83,017	3.2681	83,010

NOTE: 'S' grade pistons are 3.2675 to 3.2685 in. (82,995 to 83,020 mm.) dia. across bottom of skirt at right angles to gudgeon pins. Honed diameter of bore for these pistons must be 0.0007 to 0.0013 in. (0,018 to 0,133 mm.) greater than measured diameter of piston at this position.

Outside diameter of liners	3.3945 to 3.3955 in. (86,220 to 86,246 mm.)
Line bore for main bearings	2.9165 to 2.9170 in. (74,08 to 74,09 mm.)

Cylinder Head

Material	Aluminium alloy
Valve seat angle – inlet	45°
– exhaust	45°

Crankshaft

Material	BS 970 - 709M 40/T (EN 19 T) or BS 970 - 605M 36/T (EN 16 T)
Number of main bearings	7
Main bearing type	Vandervell VP2C or Glacier SL (P)
Journal diameter	2.7502 to 2.7497 in. (69,855 to 69,842 mm.)
Journal length, over 0.095 in. (2,4 mm.) radii	Front 1.562 ± 0.010 in. (39.675 ± 0.254 mm.) Centre 1.3755 to 1.3760 in (34,938 to 34,950 mm.) Intermediate 1.217 to 1.221 in. (30,912 to 31,013 mm.) Rear 1.67 in. (42,4 mm.)
Thrust taken	Centre bearing thrust washers
Thrust washer thickness	0.091 to 0.093 in. (2,311 to 2,362 mm.) or 0.095 to 0.097 in. (2,413 to 2,464 mm.)
Permissible end float	0.004 to 0.006 in. (0,10 to 0,15 mm.)
Width of main bearing	Front 1.360 to 1.375 in. (34,544 to 34,925 mm.) Centre 1.115 in. to 1.130 in. (28,321 to 28,702 mm.) Rear 1.360 to 1.375 in. (34,544 to 34,925 mm.) Intermediate 0.985 to 1.00 in. (25,019 to 24,400 mm.)
Diametrical clearance	0.0008 to 0.025 in. (0,020 to 0,064 mm.)
Crankpins – diameter	2.0861 to 2.0865 in. (52,987 to 52,974 mm.)
length	1.1867 to 1.1887 in. (30,142 to 30,193 mm.)
Regrind undersizes	0.010, 0.020 in. (0,25 mm., 0,51 mm.)
Min. dia. for regrind	- 0.020 in. (- 0,51 mm.)

Connecting Rods

Length between centres	7.75 in. (196,85 mm.)
Big end bearing type	Vandervell VP2C or Glacier SL (P)
Bore for big end bearing	2.2330 to 2.2335 in. (56,718 to 56,731 mm.)
Width of big end bearing	0.960 to 0.975 in. (24,38 to 24,77 mm.)
Big end diametrical clearance	0.0010 to 0.0027 in. (0,025 to 0,069 mm.)
Big end side clearance	0.052 to 0.0092 in. (0,132 to 0,234 mm.)
Small end bush material	Vandervell VP10
Bore for small end bush	0.9995 to 1.0005 in. (25,387 to 25,413 mm.)
Width of small end bush	1.06 to 1.08 in. (26,92 to 27,43 mm.)
Bore dia. of small end bush	0.87525 to 0.87540 in. (22,231 to 22,235 mm.)

Pistons

Type	Solid skirt
Skirt clearance (measured midway down bore across bottom of piston skirt)	0.0007 to 0.0013 in. (0,018 to 0,033 mm.)

Piston Rings

Number of compression rings	2
Number of oil control rings	1
Top compression ring width	0.0615 to 0.0625 in. (1,562 to 1,588 mm.)
Second compression ring width	0.0772 to 0.0782 in. (1,961 to 1,986 mm.)
Oil control ring width	Self expanding ring
Top compression ring thickness	0.124 to 0.130 in. (3,150 to 3,302 mm.)
Second compression ring thickness	0.124 to 0.130 in. (3,150 to 3,302 mm.)
Side clearance of top compression ring in groove	0.0015 to 0.0035 in. (0,038 to 0,089 mm.)

Side clearance of second compression ring in groove	0.0015 to 0.0035 in. (0,038 to 0,089 mm.)
Side clearance of oil control ring in groove	Self expanding ring; groove width 0.1578 to 0.1588 in. (4,008 to 4,034 mm.)
Top compression ring gap in bore	0.013 to 0.018 in. (0,33 to 0,46 mm.)
Second compression ring gap in bore	0.009 to 0.014 in. (0,23 to 0,36 mm.)

Gudgeon Pins

Type	Fully floating
Length	2.830 to 2.845 in. (71,882 to 72,263 mm.)
Outside diameter – marked Red	0.8751 to 0.8752 (22,228 to 22,230 mm.)
– marked Green	0.8750 to 0.8751 in. (22,225 to 22,228 mm.)

Camshafts

Number of journals	4 per shaft
Number of bearings	4 per shaft (8 half bearings)
Type of bearings	White metal steel backed, Vandervell D2 Bimetal or Glacier steel and L2 White metal
Journal diameter	0.999 to 0.9995 in. (25,375 to 25,387 mm.)
Diametrical clearance	0.0005 to 0.0022 in. (0,013 to 0,056 mm.)
Thrust taken	Front ends of shaft

Valves and Valve Springs

Inlet valve material	Silico chrome steel
Exhaust valve material	Austenitic steel
Inlet valve head diameter	1.745 to 1.755 in. (44,32 to 44,58 mm.)
(fuel injection engines)	1.870 to 1.880 in (47,50 to 47,75 mm)
Exhaust valve head diameter	1.620 to 1.630 in. (44,15 to 41,40 mm.)
Valve stem diameter – inlet and exhaust	0.310 to 0.3125 in. (7,87 to 7,94 mm.)
Valve lift	0.375 in. (9,53 mm.)
Inlet valve clearance	0.012 to 0.014 in. (0,305 to 0,356 mm.)
Exhaust valve clearance	0.012 to 0.014 in. (0,305 to 0,356 mm.)
Outer valve spring free length	2.103 in. (53,42 mm.)
Inner valve spring free length	1.734 in. (44,04 mm.)

Valve Guides and Seats

Valve guide material	Cast iron (Brico Alloy 2 or BS. 1452/12)
Inlet valve guide length	1.86 in. (47,24 mm.)
Exhaust valve guide length	1.95 in. (49,53 mm.)
Outside diameter (both guides)	
Standard	0.501 to 0.502 in. (12,725 to 12,751 mm.)
First oversize	0.503 to 0.504 in. (12,776 to 12,802 mm.)
Second oversize	0.506 to 0.507 in. (12,852 to 12,878 mm.)
Third oversize	0.511 to 0.512 in. (12,979 to 13,005 mm.)
Interference fit in cylinder head	0.0005 to 0.0022 in. (0,013 to 0,056 mm.)
Valve seat material	Sintered iron (Brico AO25/M)
Inlet valve seat outside diameter	Standard 1.852 to 1.8525 in. (47,041 to 47,054 mm.)
Interference fit in cylinder head	0.003 in. (0,0762 mm.)
Exhaust valve seat outside diameter	Standard 1.6955 to 1.6960 in. (43,066 to 43,078 mm.)
Interference fit in cylinder head	0.003 in. (0,0762 mm.)

Tappets

Tappet material	Chilled cast iron
Outside diameter of tappet	1.3738 to 1.3742 in. (34,895 to 34,905 mm.)
Tappet guide interference fit	0.0073 to 0.0087 in. (0,185 to 0,221 mm.)
Diametrical clearance of tappet in guide	0.0008 to 0.0019 in. (0,020 to 0,048 mm.)

Lubricating System

Oil pump	Hobourn Eaton rotor type
Oil filter	Full flow, renewable element or disposable canister

Timing Chains and Sprockets

Type	Duplex
Pitch	3.8 in. (9,5 mm.)
Number of pitches – lower chain	82
– upper chain	100
Crankshaft sprocket – teeth	21
Intermediate sprocket (outer) teeth	28
Intermediate sprocket (inner) teeth	20
Camshaft sprockets – teeth	30

Spark Plugs

Make	Champion
Type	N12Y
Gap	0.025 in. (0,64 mm.)

4.2 LITRE

General Data

Number of cylinders	6 (in line)
Bore	92,07 mm. (3.625 in.)
Stroke	106 mm. (4.173 in.)
Cubic capacity	4235 cc (258.43 cu. in.)
Compression ratio	'S' or 'L'
Ignition timing (static)	8° B.T.D.C.
Firing order	1 5 3 6 2 4 with No. 1 cyl. at REAR

Cylinder Block

Material (cylinder block)	Chromium cast iron
Type of cylinder liner	Interference fit, dry liner
Material (liners)	Brivadium
Liner intereference fit	0.003 in. to 0.005 in. (0,076 to 0,127 mm.)

Bore diameters after honing

Grade	max in	mm	min in	mm
F	3.6253	92,083	3.6250	92,075
G	3.6257	92,093	3.6254	92,085
H	3.6261	92,103	3.6258	92,095

NOTE: 'S' grade pistons are 3.6252 to 3.6262 in. (92,080 to 92,105 mm.) dia. across bottom of skirt at right angles to gudgeon pins. Honed diameter of bore for these pistons must be 0.0007 to 0.0013 in. (0,018 to 0,033 mm.) greater than measured diameter of piston at this position.

Outside diameter of liners	3.766 in. max. 3.765 in. min. (95,66 mm. max. 95,63 mm. min.)
Line bore for main bearings	2.9165 to 2.9170 in. (74,08 to 74,09 mm.)

Cylinder Head

Material	Aluminium alloy
Valve seat angle – inlet	45°
– exhaust	45°

Crankshaft

Material	En 16, 18 or 111
Number of main bearings	7
Main bearing type	Vandervell VP2C or Glacier SL (P)
Journal diameter	2.7500 in. to 2.7505 in. (69,85 to 69,86 mm.)
Journal length (Over 3/32 in. radii)	Front: 1.562 ± 0.10 in. (39,69 ± 0,254 mm.) Centre: 1.375 + 0.001 − 0.0005 (34,925 + 0.025 − 0.013 mm.) Intermediate: 1.2188 ± 0.002 in. (30,96 ± 0,051 mm.) Rear: 1.6875 in. (42,86 mm.)
Thrust taken	Centre main bearing cap, half washers
Thrust washer thickness	0.091 to 0.093 in. (2,31 to 2,36 mm.)
Permissible end float	0.004 to 0.006 in. (0,10 to 0,15 mm.)
Width of main bearing	Front: 1.360 to 1.375 in. (34,54 to 34,93 mm.) Centre: 1.115 to 1.130 in. (28,32 to 28,70 mm.) Intermediate: 0.985 to 1.00 in. (24,81 to 25,40 mm.) Rear: 1.360 to 1.375 in. (34,54 to 34,93 mm.)
Diametrical clearance	0.0008 to 0.0025 in. (0,0203 to 0,0635 mm.)
Crankpins – diameter	2.0860 to 2.0866 in. (52,984 to 53,00 mm.)
– length	1.1873 to 1.1882 in. (30,158 to 30,181 mm.)
Regrind undersize	0.010 in. 0.020 in. (0,25 mm. 0,51 mm.)
Minimum diameter for regrind	−0.02 in. (−0,51 mm.)

Connecting Rods

Length between centres	7.75 in. (196,85 mm.)
Big end bearing type	Vandervell VP2C or Glacier SL(P)
Bore for big end bearing	2.2330 to 2.2335 in. (56,72 to 56,73 mm.)
Width of big end bearing	0.960 to 0.975 in. (24,38 to 24,77 mm.)
Big end diametrical clearance	0.0010 to 0.0027 in. (0,025 to 0,069 mm.)
Big end side clearance	0.0058 to 0.0087 in. (0,147 to 0,221 mm.)
Small end bush material	Vandervell VP10
Bore for small end bush	1.0 ± 0.0005 in. (25,4 ± 0,013 mm.)
Width of small end bush	1.060 to 1.080 in. (26,92 to 27,43 mm.)
Bore diameter of small end bush	0.87525 + 0.00015 − 0.000 in. (22,23 + 0,0038 − 0,000 mm.)

Pistons

Type	Solid skirt
Skirt clearance (measured midway down bore across bottom of piston skirt)	0.0007 to 0.0013 in. (0,018 to 0,033 mm.)

Piston Rings

Number of compression rings	2
Number of oil control rings	1
Top compression ring width	0.0781 in. noml. (2 mm. noml.)
Second compression ring width	0.0781 in. noml. (2 mm. noml.)
Oil control ring width	Self expanding
Top compression ring thickness	0.171 to 0.188 in. (4,35 to 4,60 mm.)
Second compression ring thickness	0.171 to 0.188 in. (4,35 to 4,60 mm.)
Side clearance of top compression ring in groove	0.0015 to 0.0035 in. (0,038 to 0,089 mm.)
Side clearance of second compression ring in groove	0.0015 to 0.0035 in. (0,038 to 0,089 mm.)
Side clearance of oil control ring in groove	Self expanding
Top compression ring gap in bore	0.015 to 0.020 in. (0,38 to 0,51 mm.)

Second compression ring gap in bore	0.009 to 0.014 in. (0,23 to 0,35 mm.)
Oil control ring gap in bore	0.015 to 0.045 in. (0.38 to 1,14 mm.)

Gudgeon Pins

Type	Fully floating
Length	2.990 to 3.000 in. (75,95 to 76,2 mm.)
Outside diameter marked RED	0.8751 to 0.8752 in. (22,228 to 22,230 mm.)
marked GREEN	0.8750 to 0.8751 in. (22,225 to 22,228 mm.)

Camshafts

Number of journals	4 per shaft
Number of bearings	4 per shaft (8 half bearings)
Type of bearings	White metal steel backed, Vandervell
Journal diameter	0.9995 to 0.9990 in. (25,387 to 25,375 mm.)
Diametrical clearance	0.0005 to 0.002 in. (0,013 to 0,051 mm.)
Thrust taken	Front end of shafts

Valves and Valve Springs

Inlet valve material	Silico chrome steel
Exhaust valve material	Austenitic steel
Inlet valve head diameter	1.745 to 1.755 in. (44,32 to 44,58 mm.)
(fuel injection engines)	1.870 to 1.880 in (47,50 to 47,75 mm)
Exhaust valve head diameter	1.620 to 1.630 in. (41,15 to 41,40 mm.)
Valve stem diameter – inlet and exhaust	0.310 to 0.3125 in. (7,87 to 7,94 mm.)
Valve lift	0.375 in. (9,53 mm.)
Inlet valve clearance	0.012 to 0.014 in. (0,305 to 0,356 mm.)
Exhaust valve clearance	0.012 to 0.014 in. (0,305 to 0,356 mm.)
Outer valve spring free length	1.938 to 2.00 in. (49,21 to 50,80 mm.)
Inner valve spring free length	1.656 to 1.719 in. (42,07 to 43,66 mm.)

Valve Guides and Seats

Valve guide material	Cast iron (Brico Alloy 2 or BS.1452/12
Inlet valve guide length	1.86 in. (47,24 mm.)
Exhaust valve guide length	1.95 in. (49,53 mm.)
Outside diameter (both guides)	
Standard	0.501 to 0.502 in. (12,725 to 12,751 mm.)
First oversize	0.503 to 0.504 in. (12,776 to 12,802 mm.)
Second oversize	0.506 to 0.507 in. (12,852 to 12,878 mm.)
Third oversize	0.511 to 0.512 in. (12,979 to 13,005 mm.)
Interference fit in cylinder head	0.0005 to 0.0022 in. (0,013 to 0,056 mm.)
Valve seat material	Sintered iron (Brico AO25/M)
Inlet valve seat outside diameter	Standard 1.852 to 1.8525 in. (47,041 to 47,054 mm.)
Interference fit in cylinder head	0.003 in. (0,0762 mm.)
Exhaust valve seat outside diameter	Standard 1.6955 to 1.6960 in. (43,066 to 43,078 mm.)
Interference fit in cylinder head	0.003 in. (0,0762 mm.)

Tappets

Tappet material	Chilled cast iron
Outside diameter of tappet	1.3738 to 1.3742 in. (34,895 to 34,905 mm.)
Tappet guide intereference fit	0.0073 to 0.0087 in. (0,185 to 0,221 mm.)
Diametrical clearance of tappet in guide	0.0008 to 0.0019 in. (0,020 to 0,048 mm.)

Lubricating System

Oil pump	Hobourn Eaton rotor type
Oil filter	Full flow, renewable element

Timing Chains and Sprockets

Type	Duplex
Pitch	3/8 in. (9,5 mm.)
Number of pitches – lower chain	82
– upper chain	100
Crankshaft sprocket – teeth	21
Intermediate sprocket (outer) – teeth	28
Intermediate sprocket (inner) – teeth	20
Camshaft sprockets – teeth	30

Spark Plugs

Make	Champion
Type	N11Y (N10Y – fuel injection engines)
Gap	0.035 in. (0,89 mm.) – fuel injection engines 0.025 in. (0,63 mm.) – carburetter engines

TORQUE WRENCH SETTINGS

NOTE: Set torque wrench to the mean of figures quoted unless otherwise specified.

ITEM	DESCRIPTION	lbf ft	kgf m
ENGINE			
Cylinder head	7/16 in. UNF nut	54.2 max.	7,48 max.
Main bearing caps	1/2 in. UNF bolt	72.0 max.	9,96 max.
Con. rod big end	3/8 in. UNF bolt	37.5	5,20
Flywheel	7/16 in. UNF nut	66.6 max.	9,22 max.
Crankshaft	3/4 in. UNF bolt	125–150	17,3–20,7
Camshaft cap	5/16 in. UNF nut	9.0 max.	1,24 max.
Torque converter	3/8 in. UNF bolt	35 max.	4,83 max.
P.A.S. pump to mtg. bracket	3/8 in. UNC nut	37 max.	5,12 max.
Oil filter canister (renewable element type)	3/8 in. UNC Special bolt	15–20	2,09–2,76
Cam cover (domed nuts)	1/4 in. UNF	5–6	0,70–0,83
Flex. hose for clutch slave cylinder	7/16 in. UNF nut	11.7–14.1	1,62–1,95
Distributor clamp } Alternatives	Rotating nut	2.5 max.	0,35 max.
Distributor clamp } Alternatives	Trapped nut	4.2 max.	0,58 max.
Idler pulley arm securing nut	5/16 in. UNF nut	9–11	1,24–1,52
Disposable canister oil filter	1 in. UNF thread	6–8	0,83–1,10
ENGINE MOUNTINGS			
Rear mounting bracket to body fixing	5/16 in. UNF bolt	14–18	1,94–2,48
Rear mounting bracket to body fixing	3/8 in. UNF bolt	27–32	3,74–4,42
Front bracket to beam	5/16 in. UNF nut	14–18	1,94–2,48
Rear mounting peg	1/2 in. UNF nut	25–30	3,46–4,14
Rear rubbers	3/8 in. UNF nut	27–32	3,74–4,42
Tie bolt	1/2 in. UNF nut	25–30	3,46–4,14
EXHAUST AND HEAT SHIELDS			
Front down pipes to manifold	3/8 in. UNF nut	22–26	3,05–3,59
'U' bolt clips	5/16 in. UNF nut	11–13	1,53–1,79
Coupling flange	5/16 in. UNF nut	11–13	1,53–1,79
Vibration damper	5/16 in. UNF nut	11–13	1,53–1,79
Clip, outer exhaust pipe	5/16 in. UNF nut	11–13	1,53–1,79
Exhaust mtg. ring assy. to crossbeam	5/16 in. UNF nut	14–18	1,94–2,48
Tail pipe mtg. assy. to body	5/16 in. UNF nut	8–10	1,10–1,38
Tail pipe grub screw	1/4 in. UNF	6–7	0,83–0,96
Heat shield to manifold	No. 10 UNF nut	2–2.5	0,28–0,34
Mtg. bar assy. to over axle pipe assy.	3/8 in. UNF nut	10–13	1,40–1,79
Grass shield to exhaust pipe	1/4 in UNF bolt	6–7	0,83–0,96

ITEM	DESCRIPTION	lbf ft	kgf m
ENGINE COOLING SYSTEM			
Radiator to front cross member	3/8 in. UNF nut	22–26	3,05–3,59
Retainer to radiator cross member	5/16 in. UNF nut	14–18	1,94–2,48
Fan cowl upper bracket to body	1/4 in. UNF nut	6–7	0,83–0,96
Expansion tank to valance	5/16 in. UNF nut	8–10	1,10–1,38
Engine oil cooler pipes	1 1/16 in. UNS nut	40–45	5,53–6,22
Deflector and bracket to cowl	1/4 in. UNF bolt	6–7	0,83–0,96
Lower bracket to cowl	1/4 in. UNF nut	4.5–5.5	0,62–0,76
Lower cowl bracket to body	1/4 in. UNF bolt	6–7	0,83–0,96
FUEL SYSTEM			
Fuel tank mounting	5/16 in. UNF bolt	14–18	1,94–2,48
Drain plug on fuel tank – small	3/8 in. UNF bolt	22–26	3,05–3,59
Drain plug on fuel tank – large	1 1/4 in. gas plug	25–28	3,46–3,87
Filter guard to bracket } early cars	1/4 in. UNF bolt	6–7	0,83–0,96
Filter bracket to body } early cars	5/16 in. UNF bolt	14–18	1,94–2,48
Fuel pump to floor } early cars	1/4 in. UNF bolt	6–7	0,83–0,96
Carbon storage canister to body	3/8 in. UNF bolt	14–18	1,94–2,48
Fuel pipe unions	5/16 in. pipe dia.	6.3–7	0,87–0,96
Fuel pipe unions	3/8 in. pipe dia.	11–13	1,53–1,79
Fuel pipe unions	1/2 in. pipe dia.	20–25	2,76–3,46
Fuel tank connector	9/16 in. x 24 TPI	8–10	1,10–1,38
Fuel gauge (special tool required)	–	4–10	0,56–1,38
Banjo bolts for fuel pipes	–	22–26	3,05–3,59
Carbon canister (Bolt, brkt. to rad. post)	5/16 in. UNF nut	14–18	1,94–2,48
(Bolt, brkt. assy.)	5/16 in. UNF nut	14–18	1,94–2,48
TRANSMISSION			
Mounting plate to body	1/4 in. UNF bolt	6–7	0,83–0,96
Selector lever return spring	No. 10 UNF locknut	4–4.5	0,56–0,62
Reverse switch	5/8 in. special	14–18	1,94–2,48
Adjusting ball end to gearbox lever	1/4 in. UNF nut	6–7	0,83–0,96
Cable to adjustable ball end (collet)	7/16 in. UNF nut	11–13	1,53–1,79
Inhibitor switch	1/4 in. UNF nut	3.5–4.5	0,49–0,62
Cable abutment bracket to selector gate	1/4 in. UNF nut	6–7	0,83–0,96
Cable to bracket	5/16 in. UNF bolt	14–18	1,94–2,48
Bracket to trans. unit	3/8 in. UNF nut	22–26	3,05–3,59
Cable to abutment bracket	5/8 in. UNF nut	14–18	1,94–2,48
Front and rear propeller shaft assy.	3/8 in. UNF nut	27–32	3,74–4,42
Rubber mtg. to prop. shaft flange	5/16 in. UNF nut	14–18	1,94–2,48
Rubber mtg. to mounting bracket	1/4 in. UNF bolt	6–7	0,83–0,96
Mounting bracket to body bracket	1/4 in. UNF nut	4.5–5.5	0,62–0,76
Carrier plate to base plate	1/4 in. UNF nut	4.5–5.5	0,62–0,76
Mounting to body brackets	5/16 in. UNF nut	14–18	1,94–2,48
Base plate to body	5/16 in. UNF bolt	14–18	1,94–2,48
Cable to location block lower	5/16 in. UNF bolt	14–18	1,94–2,48
Centre bearing to mounting plate (1 piece bearing)	5/16 in. UNF bolt	14–18	1,94–2,48

ITEM	DESCRIPTION	lbf ft	kgf m
MODEL 12 AUTOMATIC TRANSMISSION			
Pump to gear case	bolt	17–22	2,35–3,04
Front servo to gear case	bolt	30–35	4,15–4,84
Rear servo to gear case	bolt	40–50	5,53–6,91
Centre support to gear case	bolt	20–25	2,76–3,46
Valve body to gear case	1/4 in. bolt	5–8	0,69–1,11
Valve body to gear case	5/16 in. bolt	17–20	2,35–2,76
Extension housing to gear case	bolt	28–33	3,87–4,56
Oil pan to gear case	bolt	10–13	1,38–1,80
Pressure check point	plug	13–17	1,80–2,35
Filler tube	nut	20–25	2,76–3,46
Rear band adjusting screw	locknut	40–44	5,53–6,08
Gear case to bell housing	bolt	58–65	8,02–8,98
Manual lever attachment	nut	35–40	4,84–5,53
Front pump cover attachment	screw	2–3	0,28–0,42
Governor inspection cover attachment	screw	5–6	0,69–0,83
Governor valve body to counterweight	bolt	4–5	0,55–0,69
Governor valve body cover	screw	2–2.5	0,28–0,35
Valve and body strainer	screw	2–2.5	0,28–0,35
Vacuum control unit		13–17	1,80–2,35
Rear seal cover to extension housing	bolt	30–35	4,15–4,84
Nut – dipstick tube to oil pan	1 1/16 in. UNS nut	34–38	4,70–5,25
MODEL 65 AUTOMATIC TRANSMISSION			
Transmission case to converter hsg.	M.10 x 30 (1.5P)	25	3,46
	M.12 x 30 (1.75P)	40	5,53
Oil pan to transmission case	M.6 x 15 (1.O P)	5.75	0,80
Front servo cover	M.8 x 25 (1.25 P)	19	2,63
Rear servo cover	M.8 x 25 (1.25 P)	19	2,63
Oil pump adaptor to oil pump housing	10–24 UNC x 2A x 5/8	2.5	0,35
	5/16 in. – 18 UNC 2A x 7/8	19.5	2,70
Oil pump adaptor to transmission case	M.8 x 25 (1.25 P)	19	2,63
Pressure point on transmission case	1/8 in. 27 Dryseal N.P.T.F.	7	0,97
Oil pan drain plug	3/8 in. 24 x 3/8 in.	10.5	1,45
Upper valve body to lower valve body	10–24 UNC 2A x 5/8 in.	2.1	0,29
Lower valve body to upper valve body	10–24 UNC 2A x 15/16 in.	2.1	0,29
Lower valve body to upper valve body	10–24 UNC 2A x 1 3/8 in.	2.1	0,29
Suction tube assy. to lower valve body	10–24 UNC 2A x 3/8 in.	2.1	0,29

ITEM	DESCRIPTION	lbf ft	kgf m
Oil tube plate to lower valve body	10–24 UNC 2A x 5/8 in.	2.1	0,29
	10–24 UNC 2A x 15/16 in.	2.1	0,29
End plate to lower valve body	10–24 UNC 2A x 5/8 in.	2.1	0,29
End plate to upper valve body	10–24 UNC 2A x 3/8 in.	2.1	0,29
Lower valve body to transmission case	1/4 in. – 20 UNC 2A x 1 1/4 in.	6.75	0,93
Lower valve body to transmission case	1/4 in. – 20 UNC 2A x 2 in.	6.75	0,93
Lower valve body to cam bracket	10–32 UNF 2A x 1 7/16 in.	2.6	0,36
Tube location plate	M5 x (6.8P)	1.75	0,24
Detent spring to lower valve body (200)		2.1	0,29
Front servo adjusting screw locknut	9/16 in. – 12 UNC 2A	35	4,84
Rear servo adjusting screw locknut	9/16 in. – 12 UNC 2A	35	4,84
Oil cooler pipe unions	1/4 in. – 18 Dryseal	21	2,90
Extension housing to transmission case	7/16 in. – 14 UNC x 1 3/8 in.	42.5	5,88
Parking brake cam plate to trans. case	M6 x 12 (1.0 P)	5.25	0,73
Output flange bolt (04 00 149 008D)	M20 (1.5 P)	35–50	4,84–6,90
Governor to output shaft	M24 x 2 –6g	16.5	2,28
Nut – dipstick tube to oil pan	7/8 in. UNS nut	28–32	3,87–4,42
Abutment bracket to gearbox	5/16 in. UNF bolt	14–18	1,94–2,48
4 SPEED MANUAL GEARBOX			
Top cover	5/16 in. bolt & setscrew	12–14	1,66–1,93
Rear cover	5/16 in. nut	12–14	1,66–1,93
Clutch housing	7/16 in. bolt & setscrew	40–44	5,53–6,09
Slave cylinder to clutch housing	3/8 in. nut	22–25	3,04–3,45
Filler plug	3/8 in. B.S.P.	25–27	3,46–3,73
Drain plug	3/8 in. B.S.P.	25–27	3,46–3,73
Coupling flange	3/4 in. nut	100–120	13,85–16,60
Propeller shaft	3/8 in. nut	27–32	3,74–4,43
Reverse lever	3/8 setscrew	22–25	3,04–3,45
Gear lever securing nut	5/16 in. UNF nut	12–14	1,66–1,93
Constant pinion nut	1 1/2 in. – 20 UNS	140–160	19,36–22,12
Mainshaft nut – rear	1 3/8 in. – 20 UNS	140–160	19,36–22,12
Mainshaft nut – front	1 1/2 in. – 20 UNS	140–160	19,36–22,12

ITEM	DESCRIPTION	lbf ft	kgf m
FRONT SUSPENSION			
Stub axle to vertical link	5/8 in. UNF nut	80–90	11,1–12,4
Tie-rod lever to vertical link (early cars)	7/16 in. UNF bolt	49–55	6,8–7,60
Tie-rod lever to vertical link (later cars)	Metric M12 bolt	50–55	6,91–7,60
Front disc to hub, pressed spoke wheel	7/16 in. UNF bolt	30–36	4,2–4,97
Caliper to vertical link (early cars)	7/16 in. UNF bolt	50–60	6,91–8,29
Caliper to vertical link (later cars)	Metric M12 bolt	50–60	6,91–8,29
Ball socket cap to vertical link	5/16 in. UNF bolt	15–20	2,08–2,76
Lower ball pin to lower wishbone	9/16 in. UNF nut	45–55	6,23–7,60
Upper ball pin to vertical link	1/2 in. UNF nut	35–50	4,84–6,91
Fulcrum shaft upper wishbone	1/2 in. UNF nut	45–55	6,23–7,60
Fulcrum shaft lower wishbone	9/16 in. UNF nut	32–50	4,43–6,91
Upper ball joint to wishbone	3/8 in. UNF nut	26–32	3,60–4,42
Upper fulcrum to cross member	7/16 in. UNF nut	49–55	6,78–7,60
Clamp and shield to vertical link	1/4 in. UNF nut	4.5–5.5	0,62–0,76
Spring pan bolts	3/8 in. UNF bolt	27–32	3,74–4,42
Damper mounting bracket	3/8 in. UNF nut	27–32	3,74–4,42
Damper – front upper	3/8 in. UNF nut	27–32	3,74–4,42
Damper – front lower	7/16 in. UNF nut	32–36	4,43–4,97
Rubbers to spring pan	5/16 in. UNF nut	8–10	1,1–1,38
Rebound rubbers to upper wishbone	5/16 in. UNF bolt	8–10	1,1–1,38
Anti-roll bar bracket to body	3/8 in. UNF nut	27–32	3,74–4,42
Anti-roll bar to link	3/8 in. UNF nut	14–18	1,94–2,48
Link to lower wishbone	3/8 in. UNF nut	14–18	1,94–2,48
Wheel nuts (set spanners to 45 lbf.ft.)	1/2 in. UNF nut	40–60	5,54–8,29
Clamp bolt, front mounting	1/2 in. UNF nut	25–30	3,46–4,14
Front mounting bolt	3/4 in. UNF nut	95–115	13,14–15,91
Vee mounting to body	3/8 in. UNF bolt	22–26	3,05–3,59
Vee mounting to beam (Cleveloc nut)	3/8 in. UNF nut	14–18	1,94–2,48
REAR SUSPENSION AND MOUNTINGS			
Bottom plate to cross beam and inner fulcrum mounting	5/16 in. UNF nut & bolt	14–18	1,94–2,48
Inner fulcrum mounting to drive unit	7/16 in. UNC bolt	60–65	8,30–8,98
Drive unit to crossbeam	1/2 in. UNC bolt	70–77	9,68–10,64
Caliper to drive unit flanges	7/16 in. UNF bolt	49–55	6,78–7,60
Fulcrum pin (inner)	1/2 in. UNF nut	45–50	6,23–6,91
Outer pivot pin	5/8 in. UNF nut	97–107	13,41–14,80
Drive unit to drive shaft (Cleveloc nut)	7/16 in. UNF nut	49–55	6,78–7,60
Half shaft to hub carrier (bearing)	3/4 in. UNF nut	100–120	13,83–16,60
Radius rods to wishbones	1/2 in. UNF bolt	60–70	8,30–9,68
Safety strap and radius rods to body	7/16 in. UNF bolt	40–45	5,54–6,22
Safety strap to floor panel	3/8 in. UNF bolt	27–32	3,74–4,42
Rear damper upper	7/16 in. UNF nut	32–36	4,43–4,97
Rear damper lower	7/16 in. UNF nut	32–36	4,43–4,97
Vee mounting to body	3/8 in. UNF nut	27–32	3,74–4,42
Vee mounting to beam	5/16 in. UNF nut	14–18	1,94–2,48
Bump stop rubber to body	5/16 in. UNF nut	8–10	1,10–1,38
Wheel nuts (set spanners to 45 lbf ft)	1/2 in. UNF nut	40–60	5,54–8,29

ITEM	DESCRIPTION	lbf ft	kgf m
STEERING COLUMN, RACK AND FIXINGS			
Pinion housing cover plate	5/16 in. UNF nut	14–18	1,94–2,48
Rack to ball end of track rod	13/16 in. UNF nut 1 1/8 in. UNF locknut	45–55	6,22–7,60
Track adjustment (hold track rod end by spanner flats)	5/8 in. UNF nut	60–70	8,30–9,68
Track rod end ball joint	1/2 in. UNF locknut	45–50	6,22–6,91
Bolt in tie-rod end assembly	1/4 in. UNF bolt	6–7	0,83–0,96
Mounting bolts	5/16 in. UNF nut	14–18	1,94–2,48
Universal joints	5/16 in. UNF nut	14–18	1,94–2,48
Column transverse strut to body	5/16 in. UNF nut	8–10	1,10–1,38
Steering wheel to shaft	5/8 in. UNF nut	25–32	3,46–4,42
Column to lower bracket	5/16 in. UNF bolt	14–18	1,94–2,48
Column to upper bracket	5/16 in. UNF nut	14–18	1,94–2,48
Locknut–collet adaptor retaining screw	1/4 in. UNF nut	6–7	0,83–0,96
Longitudinal strut to body	5/16 in. UNF nut	11–13	1,53–1,79
Vertical strut to body	5/16 in. UNF bolt	14–18	1,94–2,48
Vertical strut to longitudinal strut	5/16 in. UNF nut	8–10	1,10–1,38
P.A.S. feed hose	1/2 in. UNF pipe nut	14–16	1,94–2,21
P.A.S. return hose	5/8 in. UNF pipe nut	18–20	2,48–2,76
Rack locking bolt	3/8 in. UNF bolt	27–32	3,74–4,42
Adaptor (rack)	7/16 in. UNF	49–55	6,78–7,60
Rack hydraulic connections	nuts	8–9	1,10–1,24
Clamp bolt, steering wheel	1/4 in. UNF nut	10–12	1,40–1,65
P.A.S. Hose assy. valve to pump	5/8 in. UNF pipe nut	18–20	2,48–2,76
P.A.S. Hose assy. valve to pump	1/2 in. UNF pipe nut	14–16	1,94–2,21
Horizontal strut to vertical bracket	5/16 in. UNF nut	8–10	1,10–1,38
BRAKE AND CLUTCH SYSTEMS			
Brake pedal box to body	5/16 in. UNF nut	11–13	1,53–1,79
Brake pedal box to body	5/16 in. UNF bolt	11–13	1,53–1,79
Clutch master cylinder to pedal box (Manual transmission only)	5/16 in. UNF nut	11–13	1,53–1,79
Clutch pedal box to body (Manual transmission only)	5/16 in. UNF nut	11–13	1,53–1,79
Brake pedal pivot pin	3/8 in. UNF nut	14–18	1,94–2,48
Brake pedal lever shaft locking pin	1/4 in. UNC bolt	2–2.5	0,28–0,34
Brake reservoir to bracket	1/4 in. UNF nut	2–2.5	0,28–0,34
Hydraulic connections	nuts UNF & M10	6.3–7	0,83–0,96
Hydraulic connections	M12 nuts	12–14	1,66–1,94
Master cylinder to booster	M10 nuts	15.5–19.5	2,14–2,70
Booster to pedal box	M8 nuts	8–10	1,10–1,38
P.D.W.A. to body	1/4 in. UNF nut	6–7	0,83–0,96
Front double-ended union to body	M10 nut	10–12	1,40–1,65

ITEM	DESCRIPTION	lbf ft	kgf m
Front & Rear 3 way connections	1/4 in. UNF nut	6–7	0,83–0,96
Front and Rear flex hoses to brackets	M10 nut	10–12	1,40–1,65
Hose mounting bracket R.H.	5/16 in. UNF bolt	11–13	1,53–1,79
Hose mounting bracket L.H.	1/4 in. UNF bolt	6–7	0,83–0,96
Vacuum hose to top of bell housing	5/16 in. UNF bolt	14–18	1,94–2,48
Clutch cover plate	1/4 in. UNF nut	6–7	0,83–0,96
Handbrake cable locknut	11/16 in. x 16 UNF nut	7–10	0,97–1,38
Handbrake switch locknut	1/4 in. UNF nut	3.5–4.5	0,48–0,62
Handbrake to body	1/4 in. UNF bolt	6–7	0,83–0,96
Long lever pivot	3/8 in. UNF bolt	22–26	3,05–3,59
Fork end assy.	1/4 in. UNF nut	6–7	0,83–0,96
Cable guide	No. 10 UNF bolt	4–4.5	0,56–0,62
Abutment to body	1/4 in. UNF bolt	6–7	0,83–0,96
Tipping valve retaining nut		35–40	4,84–5,53
Front double ended union to body	M10 nut	10–12	1,40–1,65
Brake light switch to bracket	1/4 in. UNF bolt	3.5–4.5	0,48–0,62
Rear cable to relay lever	1/4 in. UNF nut	6–7	0,83–0,96
Brake cable support plate to body	No. 10 UNF bolt	4–4.5	0,56–0,62
Cable guide to plate	No. 10 UNF nut	4–4.5	0,56–0,62
Clutch pedal plate to pedal lever	5/16 in. UNF nut	8–10	1,10–1,38
ACCELERATOR AND CHOKE CONTROLS			
Accelerator pedal mtg. brkt. to floor	1/4 in. UNF bolt	6–7	0,83–0,96
Pedal to mounting plate	1/4 in. UNF nut	4.5–5.5	0,62–0,76
Accelerator lever carrier assy. to body	1/4 in. UNF nut	6–7	0,83–0,96
Accelerator cable to body	5/16 in. UNF nut	8–10	1,10–1,38
Accelerator stop	5/16 in. UNF nut	14–18	1,94–2,48
Outer choke cable pivot	No. 10 UNF bolt	2–2.5	0,28–0,34
Retainer plate	1/4 in. UNF bolt	6–7	0,83–0,96
Choke bracket to body	1/4 in. UNF nut	6–7	0,83–0,96

ITEM	DESCRIPTION	lbf ft	kgf m
AIR CONDITIONING SYSTEM (when fitted)			
Pipe connection nuts on air conditioned cars (includes 'O' ring fittings)	3/8 in. dia. pipe	11–13	1,53–1,79
	5/8 in. dia. pipe	21–27	2,91–3,73
Gasket to drier bottle bracket	No. 10 UNF nut	2–2.5	0,28–0,34
Drier bottle bracket to body	1/4 in. UNF bolt	6–7	0,83–0,96
Evap. hose to engine brkt.	1/4 in. UNF bolt	4–4.5	0,56–0,62
Condenser mountings	1/4 in. UNF nut	6–7	0,83–0,96
Top distribution duct to dash rail	1/4 in. UNF bolt	4–4.5	0,56–0,62
Demist ducts to dash rail	1/4 in UNF nut	4–4.5	0,56–0,62
Air cond./heater assy. and heatshields to body (tube nuts)	5/16 in. UNF nut	14–18	1,94–2,48
Stay to heater volute and air cond. unit	1/4 in. UNF bolt	6–7	0,83–0,96
Stay to body	1/4 in. UNF nut	6–7	0,83–0,96
Volute to choke bracket	1/4 in. UNF nut	6–7	0,83–0,96
Heater valve to mounting bracket	No. 10 UNF nut	4–4.5	0,56–0,62
Heater valve bracket to dash upper panel	No. 10 UNF nut	4–4.5	0,56–0,62
Upper mounting bracket to condenser	1/4 in. UNF nut	4.5–5.5	0,56–0,62
Condenser brkt. to upper rad. cross member	1/4 in. UNF bolt	6–7	0,83–0,96
Spacing brkt. (or oil cooler) to rad. brkt.	5/16 in. UNF bolt	14–18	1,94–2,48
Hose (receiver drier to evaporator) to R.H. brace tube	1/4 in. UNF nut	6–7	0,83–0,96
Hose (heat exchanger to compressor) to engine breather front cover	No. 10 UNF nut	4–4.5	0,56–0,62
Hose (evaporator to heat exchanger) to L.H. brace	No. 10 UNF nut	4–4.5	0,56–0,62
Vacuum tank mtg. brkt. to valance	1/4 in. UNF pan head bolt	6–7	0,83–0,96
Vacuum tank heater control to vacuum tank brkt.	1/4 in. UNF pan head bolt	6–7	0,83–0,96
Vacuum hose to dash to tunnel reinforcement	1/4 in UNF bolt	6–7	0,83–0,96
Hose clips – air cond. hoses to pipes	Worm drive clips	3.7–4.1	0,52–0,57
Securing plates and hoses to rear of compressor	3/8 in. UNF bolt	22–26	3,05–3,59

GENERAL FITTING INSTRUCTIONS

Precautions against damage

1. Always fit covers to protect wings before commencing work in engine compartment.
2. Cover seats and carpets, wear clean overalls and wash hands or wear gloves before working inside car.
3. Avoid spilling hydraulic fluid or battery acid on paint work. Wash off with water immediately if this occurs. Use polythene sheets in boot to protect carpets.
4. Always use a recommended Service Tool, or a satisfactory equivalent, where specified.
5. Protect temporarily exposed screw threads by replacing nuts or fitting plastic caps.

Safety Precautions

1. Whenever possible use a ramp or pit when working beneath car, in preference to jacking. Chock wheels as well as applying handbrake.
2. Never rely on a jack alone to support car. Use axle stands or blocks carefully placed at jacking points to provide rigid location.
3. Ensure that a suitable form of fire extinguisher is conveniently located.
4. Check that any lifting equipment used has adequate capacity and is fully serviceable.
5. Inspect power leads of any mains electrical equipment for damage and check that it is properly earthed.
6. Disconnect earth (grounded) terminal of car battery.
7. Do not disconnect any pipes in air conditioning refrigeration system, if fitted, unless trained and instructed to do so. A refrigerant is used which can cause blindness if allowed to contact eyes.
8. Ensure that adequate ventilation is provided when volatile de-greasing agents are being used.
   CAUTION: Fume extraction equipment must be in operation when trichlorethylene, carbon tetrachloride, methylene chloride, chloroform, or perchlorethylene are used for cleaning purposes.
9. Do not apply heat in an attempt to free stiff nuts or fittings; as well as causing damage to protective coatings, there is a risk of damage to electronic equipment and brake lines from stray heat.
10. Do not leave tools, equipment, spilt oil etc., around or on work area.
11. Wear protective overalls and use barrier creams when necessary.

Preparation

1. Before removing a component, clean it and its surrounding areas as thoroughly as possible.
2. Blank off any openings exposed by component removal, using greaseproof paper and masking tape.
3. Immediately seal fuel, oil or hydraulic lines when separated, using plastic caps or plugs, to prevent loss of fluid and entry of dirt.
4. Close open ends of oilways, exposed by component removal, with tapered hardwood plugs or readily visible plastic plugs.
5. Immediately a component is removed, place it in a suitable container; use a separate container for each component and its associated parts.
6. Before dismantling a component, clean it thoroughly with a recommended cleaning agent; check that agent is suitable for all materials of component.
7. Clean bench and provide marking materials, labels, containers and locking wire before dismantling a component.

Dismantling

1. Observe scrupulous cleanliness when dismantling components, particularly when brake, fuel or hydraulic system parts are being worked on. A particle of dirt or a cloth fragment could cause a dangerous malfunction if trapped in these systems.
2. Blow out all tapped holes, crevices, oilways and fluid passages with an air line. Ensure that any O-rings used for sealing are correctly replaced or renewed, if disturbed.
3. Mark mating parts to ensure that they are replaced as dismantled. Whenever possible use marking ink, which avoids possibilities of distortion or initiation of cracks, liable if centre punch or scriber are used.
4. Wire together mating parts where necessary to prevent accidental interchange (e.g. roller bearing components.
5. Wire labels on to all parts which are to be renewed, and to parts requiring further inspection before being passed for reassembly; place these parts in separate containers from those containing parts for rebuild.
6. Do not discard a part due for renewal until after comparing it with a new part, to ensure that its correct replacement has been obtained.

Inspection – General

1. Never inspect a component for wear or dimensional check unless it is absolutely clean; a slight smear of grease can conceal an incipient failure.
2. When a component is to be checked dimensionally against figures quoted for it, use correct equipment (surface plates, micrometers, dial gauges, etc.) in serviceable condition. Makeshift checking equipment can be dangerous.
3. Reject a component if its dimensions are outside limits quoted, or if damage is apparent. A part may, however, be refitted if its critical dimension is exactly limit size, and is otherwise satisfactory.
4. Use 'Plastigauge' 12 Type PG-1 for checking bearing surface clearances; directions for its use, and a scale giving bearing clearances in 0.0001 in. (0,0025 mm.) steps are provided with it.

Ball and Roller Bearings

NEVER REPLACE A BALL OR ROLLER BEARING WITHOUT FIRST ENSURING THAT IT IS IN AS-NEW CONDITION.

1. Remove all traces of lubricant from bearing under inspection by washing in petrol or a suitable de-greaser; maintain absolute cleanliness throughout operations.
2. Inspect visually for markings of any form on rolling elements, raceways, outer surface of outer rings or inner surface of inner rings. Reject any bearings found to be marked, since any marking in these areas indicates onset of wear.
3. Holding inner race between finger and thumb of one hand, spin outer race and check that it revolves absolutely smoothly. Repeat, holding outer race and spinning inner race.
4. Rotate outer ring gently with a reciprocating motion, while holding inner ring; feel for any check or obstruction to rotation, and reject bearing if action is not perfectly smooth.
5. Lubricate bearing generously with lubricant appropriate to installation.
6. Inspect shaft and bearing housing for discoloration or other marking suggesting that movement has taken place between bearing and seatings. (This is particularly to be expected if related markings were found in operation 2.) If markings are found, use 'Loctite' in installation of replacement bearing.
7. Ensure that shaft and housing are clean and free from burrs before fitting bearing.

8. If one bearing of a pair shows an imperfection it is generally advisable to renew both bearings; an exception could be made only if the faulty bearing had covered a low mileage, and it could be established that damage was confined to it.
9. When fitting bearing to shaft, apply force only to inner ring of bearing, and only to outer ring when fitting into housing.

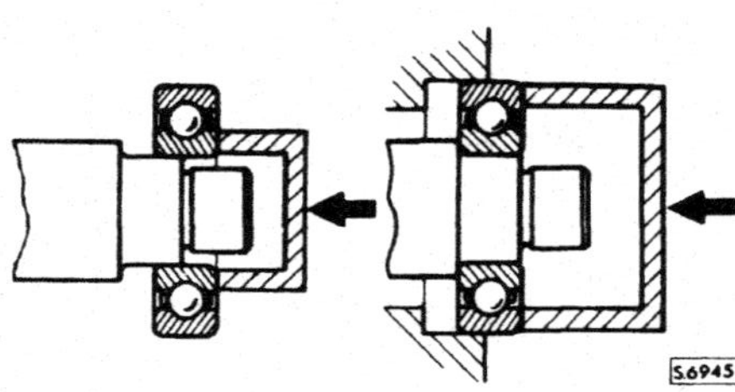

10. In the case of grease-lubricated bearings (e.g. hub bearings) fill space between bearing and outer seal with recommended grade of grease before fitting seal.
11. Always mark components of separable bearings (e.g. taper roller bearings) in dismantling, to ensure correct re-assembly. Never fit new rollers in a used cup.

Oil Seals

1. Always fit new oil seals when re-building an assembly. It is not physically possible to replace a seal exactly when it has bedded down.
2. Carefully examine seal before fitting to ensure that it is clean and un-damaged.
3. Smear sealing lips with clean grease; pack dust excluder seals with grease, and heavily grease duplex seals in cavity between sealing lips.
4. Ensure that seal spring, if provided, is correctly fitted.
5. Place lip of seal towards fluid to be sealed and slide into position on shaft, using fitting sleeve when possible to protect sealing lip from damage by sharp corners, threads or splines. If fitting sleeve is not available, use plastic tube or adhesive tape to prevent damage to sealing lip.

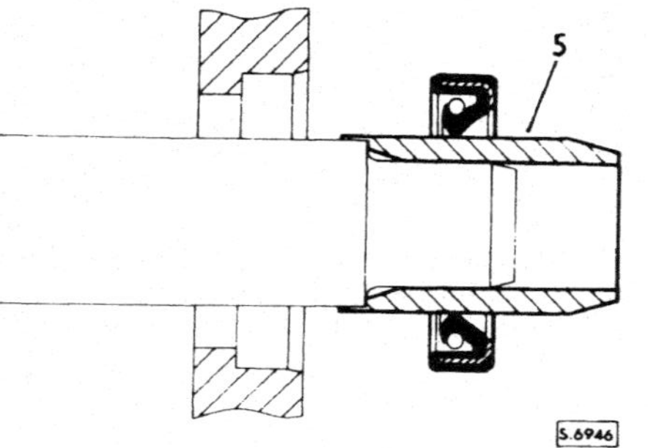

6. Grease outside diameter of seal, place square to housing recess and press into position, using great care and if possible a 'bell piece' to ensure that seal is not tilted. (In some cases it may be preferable to fit seal to housing before fitting to shaft.) Never let weight of unsupported shaft rest in seal.

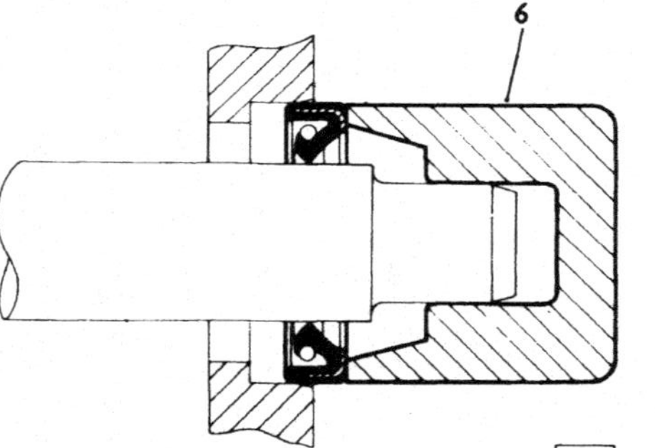

7. If correct service tool is not available, use a suitable drift approximately 0.015 in (0,4 mm) smaller than outside diameter of seal. Use a hammer **VERY GENTLY** on drift if a press is not suitable.
8. Press or drift seal in to depth of housing if housing is shouldered, or flush with face of housing where no shoulder is provided.
   NOTE: Most cases of failure or leakage of oil seals are due to careless fitting, and resulting damage to both seals and sealing surfaces. Care in fitting is essential if good results are to be obtained.

Joints and Joint Faces

1. Always use correct gaskets where they are specified.
2. Use jointing compound only when recommended. Otherwise fit joints dry.
3. When jointing compound is used, apply in a thin uniform film to metal surfaces; take great care to prevent it from entering oilways, pipes or blind tapped holes.
4. Remove all traces of old jointing materials prior to reassembly. Do not use a tool which could damage joint faces.
5. Inspect joint faces for scratches or burrs and remove with a fine file or oil stone; do not allow swarf or dirt to enter tapped holes or enclosed parts.
6. Blow out any pipes, channels or crevices with compressed air, renewing any O-rings or seals displaced by air blast.

Flexible Hydraulic Pipes, Hoses

1. Before removing any brake or power steering hose, clean end fittings and area surrounding them as thoroughly as possible.
2. Obtain appropriate blanking caps before detaching hose end fittings, so that ports can be immediately covered to exclude dirt.
3. Clean hose externally and blow through with airline. Examine carefully for cracks, separation of plies, security of end fittings and external damage. Reject any hose found faulty.
4. When refitting hose, ensure that no unnecessary bends are introduced, and that hose is not twisted before or during tightening of union nuts.
5. Containers for hydraulic fluid must be kept absolutely clean.
6. Do not store hydraulic fluid in an unsealed container. It will absorb water, and fluid in this condition would be dangerous to use due to a lowering of its boiling point.
7. Do not allow hydraulic fluid to be contaminated with mineral oil, or use a container which has previously contained mineral oil.
8. Do not re-use fluid bled from system.
9. Always use clean brake fluid to clean hydraulic components.
10. Fit a blanking cap to a hydraulic union and a plug to its socket after removal to prevent ingress of dirt.
11. Absolute cleanliness must be observed with hydraulic components at all times.
12. After any work on hydraulic systems, inspect carefully for leaks underneath the car while a second operator applies maximum pressure to the brakes (engine running) and operates the steering.

Metric Bolt Identification

1. An **ISO** metric bolt or screw, made of steel and larger than 6 mm in diameter can be identified by either of the symbols **ISO M** or **M** embossed or indented on top of the head.
2. In addition to marks to identify the manufacture, the head is also marked with symbols to indicate the strength grade e.g. 8.8, 10.9, 12.9 or 14.9, where the first figure gives the minimum tensile strength of the bolt material in tens of kg/sq mm.

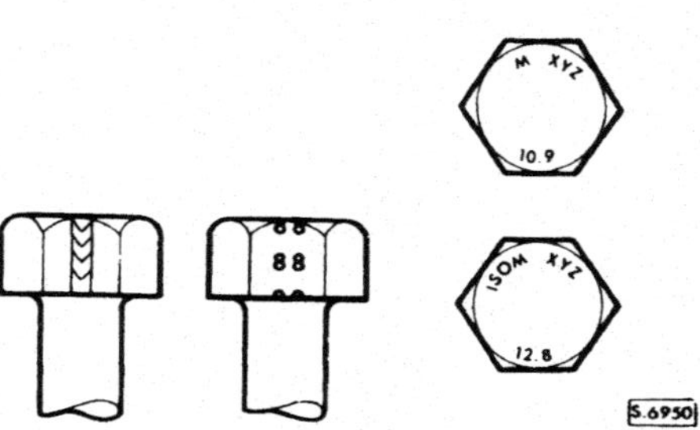

3. Zinc plated ISO metric bolts and nuts are chromate passivated, a greenish-khaki to gold-bronze colour.

Metric Nut Identification

1. A nut with an ISO metric thread is marked on one face or on one of the flats of the hexagon with the strength grade symbol 8, 12 or 14. Some nuts with a strength 4, 5 or 6 are also marked and some have the metric symbol **M** on the flat opposite the strength grade marking.
2. A clock face system is used as an alternative method of indicating the strength grade. The external chamfers or a face of the nut is marked in a position relative to the appropriate hour mark on a clock face to indicate the strength grade.
3. A dot is used to locate the 12 o'clock position and a dash to indicate the strength grade. If the grade is above 12, two dots identify the 12 o'clock position.

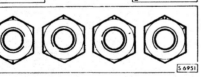

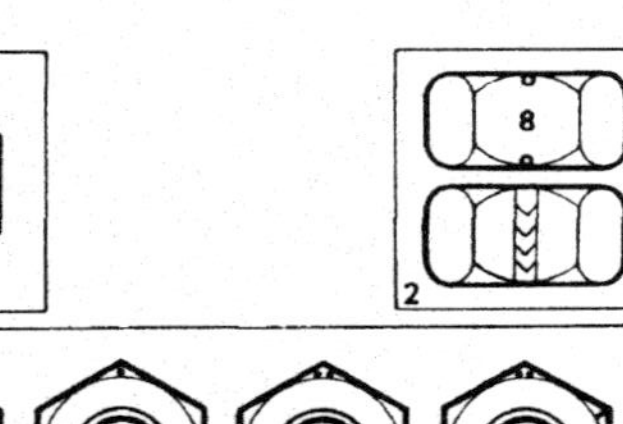

Hydraulic Fittings – Metrication

WARNING: Metric and Unified threaded hydraulic parts. Although pipe connections to brake system units incorporate threads of metric form, those for power assisted steering are of UNF type. It is vitally important that these two thread forms are not confused, and careful study should be made of the following notes.

Metric threads and metric sizes are being introduced into motor vehicle manufacture and some duplication of parts must be expected. Although standardisation must in the long run be good, it would be wrong not to give warning of the dangers that exist while UNF and metric threaded hydraulic parts continue together in service. Fitting UNF pipe nuts into metric ports and vice-versa should not happen, but experience of the change from BSF to UNF indicated that there is no certainty in relying upon the difference in thread size when safety is involved.

To provide permanent identification of metric parts is not easy but recognition has been assisted by the following means.

1. All metric pipe nuts, hose ends, unions and bleed screws are coloured black.
2. The hexagon area of pipe nuts is indented with the letter 'M'.
3. Metric and UNF pipe nuts are slightly different in shape.

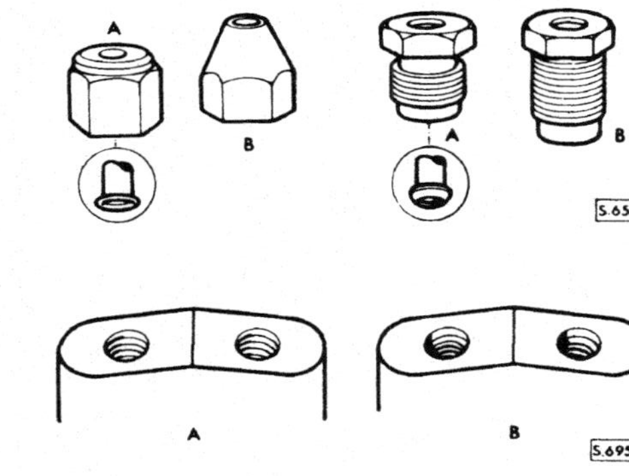

The metric female nut is **always** used with a trumpet flared pipe and the metric male nut is **always** used with a convex flared pipe.

4. All metric ports in cylinders and calipers have no counterbores, but unfortunately a few cylinders with UNF threads also have no counterbore. The situation is, all ports with counterbores are UNF, but ports not counterbored are most likely to be metric.
5. The colour of the protective plugs in hydraulic ports indicates the size and the type of the threads, but the function of the plugs is protective and not designed as positive identification. In production it is difficult to use the wrong plug but human error must be taken into account.

The Plug colours and thread sizes are:

	UNF
RED	$\frac{3}{8}$" x 24 UNF
GREEN	$\frac{7}{16}$" x 20 UNF
YELLOW	½" x 20 UNF
PINK	$\frac{7}{8}$" x 18 UNF
	METRIC
BLACK	10 x 1 mm
GREY	12 x 1 mm
BROWN	14 x 1.5 mm

6. Hose ends differ slightly between metric and UNF.

Gaskets are not used with metric hoses. The UNF hose is sealed on the cylinder or caliper face by a copper gasket but the metric hose seals against the bottom of the port and there is a gap between faces of the hose and cylinder.

Pipe sizes for UNF are $\frac{3}{16}$ in, ¼ in, and $\frac{5}{16}$ in outside diameter.

Metric pipe sizes are 4.75 mm, 6 mm and 8 mm

4.75 mm pipe is exactly the same as $\frac{3}{16}$ in pipe. 6 mm pipe is .014 in smaller than ¼ in pipe. 8 mm pipe is .002 in larger than $\frac{5}{16}$ in pipe.

Convex pipe flares are shaped differently for metric sizes and when making pipes for metric equipment, metric pipe flaring tools must be used.

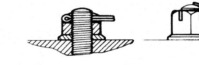

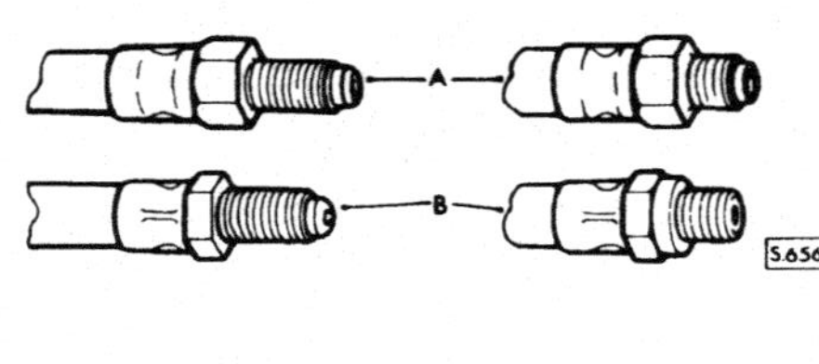

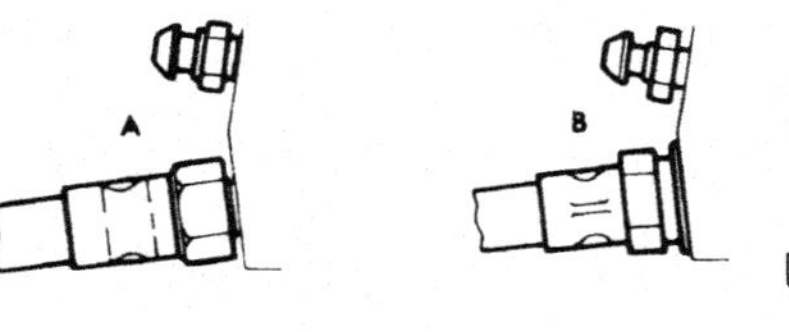

The greatest danger lies with the confusion of 10 mm and $\frac{3}{8}$ in UNF Pipe nuts used for $\frac{3}{16}$ in (or 4.75 mm) pipe. The $\frac{3}{8}$ in UNF pipe nut or hose can be screwed into a 10 mm port but is very slack and easily stripped. The thread engagement is very weak and cannot provide an adequate seal. The opposite condition, a 10 mm nut in a $\frac{3}{8}$ in port, is difficult and unlikely to cause trouble. The 10 mm nut will screw in 1½ or two turns and seize. It has a crossed thread 'feel' and it is impossible to force the nut far enough to seal the pipe. With female pipe nuts the position is of course reversed.

The other combinations are so different that there is no danger of confusion.

Keys and Keyways

1. Remove burrs from edges of keyways with a fine file and clean thoroughly before attempting to refit key.
2. Clean and inspect key closely; keys are suitable for refitting only if indistinguishable from new, as any indentation may indicate the onset of wear.

S.6948

Split Pins

1. Fit new split pins throughout when replacing any unit.
2. Always fit split pins where split pins were originally used. Do not substitute spring washers: there is always a good reason for the use of a split pin.
3. All split pins should be fitted as shown unless otherwise stated.

Tab Washers

1. Fit new washers in all places where they are used. Never replace a used tab washer.
2. Ensure that the new tab washer is of the same design as that replaced.

Nuts

1. When tightening up a slotted or castellated nut **never slacken it back to** insert split pin or locking wire except in those recommended cases where this forms part of an adjustment. If difficulty is experienced, alternative washers or nuts should be selected, or washer thickness reduced.
2. Where self-locking nuts have been removed it is advisable to replace them with new ones of the same type.
   NOTE: Where bearing pre-load is involved nuts should be tightened in accordance with special instructions.

Locking Wire

1. Fit new locking wire of the correct type for all assemblies incorporating it.
2. Arrange wire so that its tension tends to tighten the bolt heads, or nuts, to which it is fitted.

Screw Threads

1. Both UNF and Metric threads to ISO standards are used. See below for thread identification.
2. Damaged threads must always be discarded. Cleaning up threads with a die or tap impairs the strength and closeness of fit of the threads and is not recommended.
3. Always ensure that replacement bolts are at least equal in strength to those replaced.
4. Do not allow oil, grease or jointing compound to enter blind threaded holes. The hydraulic action on screwing in the bolt or stud could split the housing.
5. Always tighten a nut or bolt to the recommended torque figure. Damaged or corroded threads can affect the torque reading.
6. To check or re-tighten a bolt or screw to a specified torque figure, first slacken a quarter of a turn, then re-tighten to the correct figure.
7. Always oil thread lightly before tightening to ensure a free running thread, except in the case of self-locking nuts.

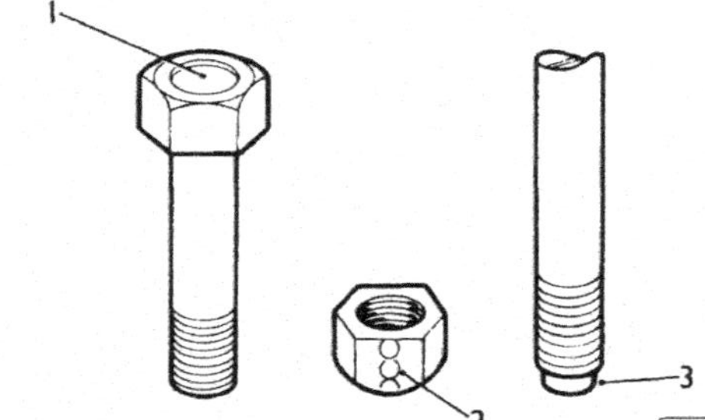

Unified Thread Identification

1. **Bolts**
   A circular recess is stamped in the upper surface of the bolt head.
2. **Nuts**
   A continuous line of circles is indented on one of the flats of the hexagon, parallel to the axis of the nut.
3. **Studs, Brake Rods, etc.**
   The component is reduced to the core diameter for a short length at its extremity.

JACKING, LIFTING AND TOWING

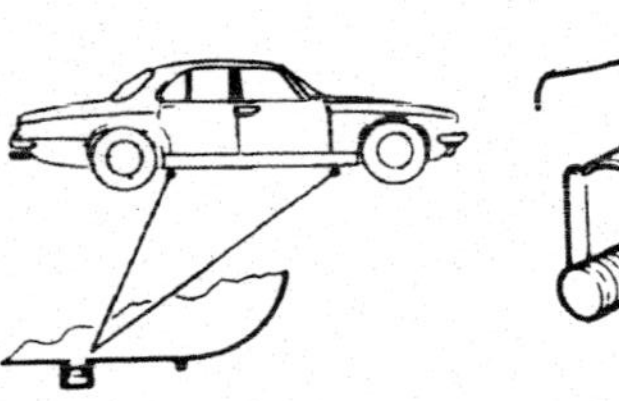

JACKING POINT

Four jacking points are provided beneath the body side members, in front of each rear wheel and behind each front wheel. They consist of downward-facing spigots designed to engage the lifting head of the tool kit jack.
Ensure that jack head is fully engaged with spigot before lifting car, and that wheels on side opposite to that being lifted are chocked, as well as checking handbrake application.

STANDS

When carrying out any work which requires a wheel to be raised (apart from a simple wheel change) always replace tool kit jack by a stand engaging jacking spigot, to provide secure support.

WORKSHOP JACK

Front – one wheel
Place jack head under lower spring support pan, interposing a suitable wooden block before raising wheel. Place a stand in position at adjacent spigot and remove jack before working on car.

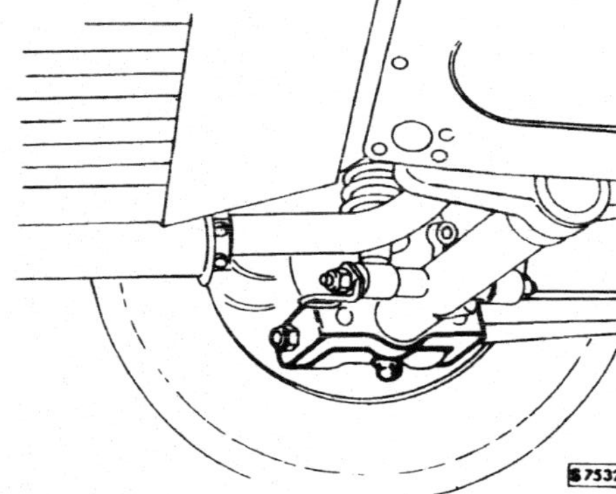

Rear – one wheel
Place jack head under outer fork of wishbone at wheel to be jacked; interpose suitable wooden block between jack head and wishbone, ensuring that aluminium alloy hub carrier and its grease nipple will not be contacted by block as wheel is raised. Place a stand in position at adjacent spigot and remove jack before working on car.

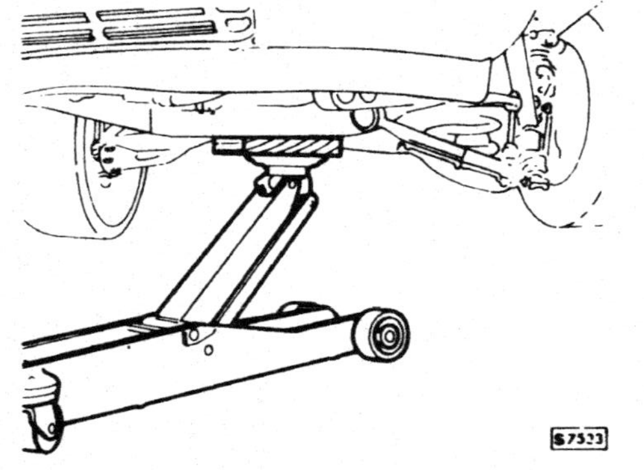

Front – both wheels
Place jack, with a shallow wooden block on its head, centrally beneath front cross-member, between lower wishbones. Raise car, then lower it on to two stands engaging front jacking spigots; remove jack before working on car.

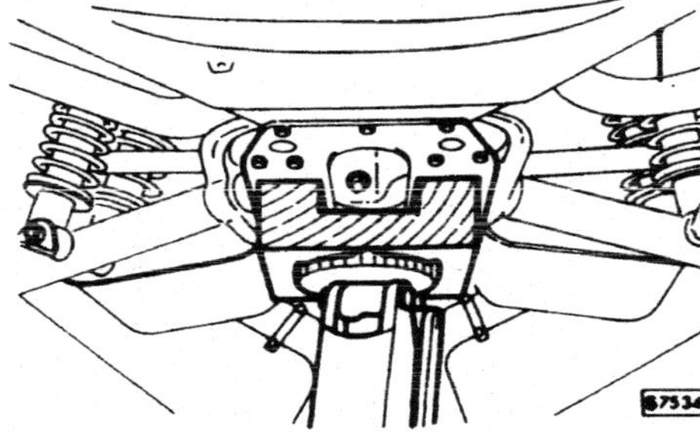

Rear – both wheels
Place jack head centrally under plate below final drive unit, and interpose a wooden block between jack head and plate, the block being shaped to prevent load being applied to plate flanges. Raise rear end of car, then lower on to two stands engaging rear jacking spigots; remove jack before working on car.

LIFTING

Locate lifting pads at the four jacking spigots

TOWING

Two towing eyes are provided on all cars, located adjacent to the front cross-member forward attachments, for use in towing from the front. Tie-down lugs at rear damper lower attachments are NOT suitable for rear towing.
When towing an automatic transmission car, it is essential to carry out the following operations:–

A. With automatic transmission functioning correctly:–

1. Add three pints (1.7 litres) of correct automatic transmission fluid (Type 'F' M2C 33F) to transmission, via under-bonnet filler tube.
2. Place selector lever at 'N'.
3. Check that ignition key is in place, and turn it to 'ACC'.
4. Tow car at a speed not exceeding 30 m.p.h. (48 km/h) for not more than 30 miles (48 km).
5. After completing tow, remove sufficient fluid from transmission to restore correct reading on dipstick.

CAUTION

It must be remembered that steering is no longer power-assisted when engine is not running, and that brake servo will become ineffective after a few applications of the brakes. Be prepared therefore, for relatively heavy steering and the need for increased pressure on the brake pedal. This applies to manual transmission cars as well as to those with automatic transmission.

B. With automatic transmission defective, either tow car with rear wheels clear of ground, or disconnect propeller shaft at final drive input flange and firmly secure rear end of shaft to one side of flange. Restrictions on towing distance do not apply when output shaft of gearbox is not being turned, but it is still essential that ignition key is turned to 'ACC' and the cautionary note above still applies.
Manual transmission cars require no special precautions in towing, but it is essential that the ignition key is turned to 'ACC' and the cautionary note above must be remembered.

TRANSPORTING

Automatic transmission cars only.

CAUTION

WHEN VEHICLE IS BEING TRANSPORTED SELECTOR LEVER MUST BE IN 'N' OR 'D', NEVER IN 'P', TO OBVIATE POSSIBILITY OF DAMAGE TO PAWL MECHANISM. HAND BRAKE SHOULD BE APPLIED.

Notes

RECOMMENDED LUBRICANTS, FLUIDS, FUEL CAPACITIES AND DIMENSIONS

RECOMMENDED LUBRICANTS – U.S.A.

ENGINE CARBURETTERS, DISTRIBUTOR AND OIL CAN	MANUAL GEARBOX AND FINAL DRIVE (NORMAL DIFFERENTIAL)	POWR-LOK DIFFERENTIAL	AUTO TRANSMISSION AND POWER ASSISTED STEERING	GREASE POINTS
RECOMMENDED SAE VISCOSITY RANGE/ AMBIENT TEMPERATURE SCALE °C -30 -20 -10 0 10 20 30 40 °F -20 -10 0 10 20 30 40 50 60 70 80 90 100 Use a well known brand of oil to BLSO.OL.02, MIL–L–2104B or API.SE specification with a viscosity band spanning the temperature range of locality in which the car is used.	E.P.90 (MIL–L–2105B)	NOTE: For re-fill, use only approved brands of fluid specially formulated for Powr-Lok For topping up ONLY, EP 90 can be used	Specification type 'F' (M2C 33F)	Multipurpose Lithium Grease (N.L.G.I. Consistency No. 2)

RECOMMENDED LUBRICANTS – U.K. and OTHER COUNTRIES

ENGINE CARBURETTERS, DISTRIBUTOR AND OIL CAN		MANUAL GEARBOX AND FINAL DRIVE (NORMAL DIFFERENTIAL)	POWR-LOK DIFFERENTIAL	AUTO TRANSMISSION AND POWER ASSISTED STEERING	GREASE POINTS
RECOMMENDED SAE VISCOSITY RANGE/ AMBIENT TEMPERATURE SCALE °C -30 -20 -10 0 10 20 30 40 °F -20 -10 0 10 20 30 40 50 60 70 80 90 100 Use a well-known brand of oil to BLSO.OL.02, MIL–L–2104B or API.SE specification with a viscosity band spanning the temperature range of locality in which the car is used.		E.P.90 (MIL–L 2105B)	NOTE: For refill, use only approved brands of fluid specially formulated for Powr-Lok For topping up ONLY, EP 90 can be used	Specification type 'F' (M2C 33F)	Multipurpose Lithium Grease (N.L.G.I. Consistency No. 2)
EXAMPLES OF APPROVED BRANDS AVAILABLE IN U.K.	Castrol GTX Shell Super Oil BP Super Visco-static Mobiloil Super Duckhams Q motor oil Texaco Havoline Esso Uniflo Fina Supergrade	Castrol Hypoy Shell Spirax 90EP BP Gear oil 90EP Mobilube HD 90 Duckhams Hypoid 90 Texaco Multi-gear EP90 Esso Gear oil GX 90/140 Fina Pontonic MP 90	Castrol Hypoy L.S. Shell S8096B BP Limslip 90/1 Mobilube 46 Duckhams Hypoid 90 DL Texaco 3450 Gear oil Esso GX 90/140 Fina Pontonic Plus SAE 90	Castrol T.Q.F. Shell Donax T7 BP Autran B Mobil ATF 210 Duckhams Q-Matic Texaco Type F Esso Glide Fina Purfimatic 33F	Castrol L.M. Shell Retinax A BP Energrease L.8 MP Super Duckhams Texaco – Martak Esso Multi-purpose 11 Fina Marson HTL2

RECOMMENDED HYDRAULIC FLUID

Braking System and Clutch Operation

Castrol-Girling Universal Brake and Clutch fluid. This fluid exceeds S.A.E. J1703/D specification. NOTE: Check all pipes in the brake system at the start and finish of each winter period for possible corrosion due to salt and grit used on the roads.

ANTI FREEZE

COMPONENT	ADDITIVE
Cooling system	1. Bars leak inhibitor (Jaguar Part No. 12953). 1 sachet per car. 2. Marston SQ.36M Corrosion Inhibitor – 4% solution (1 part SQ.36M to 24 parts water) in tropical countries. 3. Unipart Universal, B.P. Type H21 or Prestone 2 Anti-freeze – 55% concentration (5 parts anti-freeze to 4 parts water). United Kingdom 40% concentration (4 parts anti-freeze to 5 parts water).
Windscreen Washer	Windscreen washer anti-freeze fluid (proprietary brands).

IMPORTANT NOTES:

1. **CHANGE COOLANT EVERY TWO YEARS.** In places where Unipart Universal is not available, drain the Cooling system, flush and refill with a solution of BP Type H21 or Union Carbide UT 184 (marketed as Prestone Anti-freeze, Prestone UT 184 or Prestone 2).
2. **ALWAYS** top up the Cooling system with recommended strength of anti freeze **NEVER WITH WATER** only.
3. **ALL AIR CONDITIONED CARS**, regardless of operating conditions, require the continued use of the correct minimum concentration of anti freeze as indicated above.

TOTAL COOLANT FILL

In countries where anti freeze is not in general use, and if there is doubt about water quality, a total coolant fill can be used. It is important that cooling systems be thoroughly flushed with water before such coolant is used. Total coolants must not be mixed with any other mixture, or diluted. If in doubt consult your Distributor or Dealer.

CARBUROL FORLIFE (formerly 'Radmaster'). This coolant fulfils Jaguar Cars (BLUK) Ltd. requirements and is comparatively widely available. If difficulty is experienced in obtaining Carburol Forlife, consult your Distributor or Dealer.

FUEL REQUIREMENTS

Only cars with 'S' compression ratio engines require 97 octane fuel.
Cars with 'L' compression ratio engines should use 94 octane fuel.
In North America use 'regular' grade fuel.

In the United Kingdom use '4 STAR' FUEL

If, of necessity, the car has to be operated on lower octane fuel do not use full throttle otherwise detonation may occur with resultant piston trouble.

CAPACITIES

	Pint	U.S. Pint	Litres
Engine (refill including filter)	14.5	17.4	8,2
Manual gearbox and overdrive	4.5	5.4	2,5
Model 65 Automatic transmission	12.8	15.3	7,3
Model 12 Automatic transmission	16.5	19.8	9,4
Cooling system	32	38.5	18,2
	gal.	**U.S. gal.**	**litres**
Fuel tank, right hand	10.5	12.6	47,75
Fuel tank, left hand	10.5	12.6	47,75
Boot volume	17 cu. ft.		0.48 cu. m.

DIMENSIONS AND WEIGHTS

CAR TYPE	FOUR DOOR CARS	EARLY FOUR DOOR AND ALL TWO DOOR CARS
Wheelbase Track – Front – Rear	113.1 in.(2,873 m.) 58.0 in.(1,473 m.) 58.6 in.(1,488 m.)	109.1 in. (2,771 m.) 58.0 in. (1,473 m.) 58.6 in. (1,488 m.)
1. Overall length Overall width Overall height	194.7 in. (4,945 m.) 69.7 in. (1,760 m.) 54.1 in. (1,374 m.)	190.7 in. (4,844 m.) 69.7 in. (1,760 m.) 54.1 in. (1,374 m.)
2,3 Kerb weight (approx.) (European spec^{n}.) (N. American spec^{n}.)	3907 lb. (1772 kg) –	3879 lb (1759 kg) 4086 lb. (1853 kg)
Gross vehicle weight (European spec^{n}.) (N. American spec^{n}.)	4832 lb. (2192 kg) –	4654 lb. (2110 kg) 4861 lb. (2205 kg)
Turning circle Ground clearance (mid-laden)	38 ft. (11,6 m.) 6 in. (152 mm.)	36 ft. 9 in. (11,2 m.) 6 in. (152 mm.)

Notes:
1. Add 4.2 in. (107 mm.) to this dimension to N. American cars for special bumpers.
2. Weights are for cars with Model 65 Automatic transmission.
3. Deduct 65 lb. (29,5 kg.) if air conditioning is not fitted.

SUMMARY CHART – NOT U.S.A.

Item No.	OPERATION	10.10.06	10.10.12	10.10.24
	Operation Number	10.10.06	10.10.12	10.10.24
	Interval in Miles x 1000	3	6	12
	Interval in Kilometres x 1000	5	10	20
	PASSENGER COMPARTMENT			
	(Clean hands or fit gloves when carrying out items 1 to 8)			
	Fit seat cover, place protective cover on carpets	x	x	x
	Drive car on lift (ramp)	x	x	x
1	Check function of original equipment i.e. interior and exterior lamps, indicators, horns and warning lights	x	x	x
2	Check operation of window controls	x	x	x
3	Check handbrake operation	x	x	x
4	Check footbrake operation	x	x	x
5	Check clock is running and set to time	x	x	x
6	Check windscreen washers and wipers for correct operation and that jets are clear and correctly positioned	x	x	x
7	Check condition and security of seats and seat belts	x	x	x
8	Check rear view mirrors for cracks and crazing	x	x	x
	EXTERIOR AND LUGGAGE COMPARTMENT			
9	Check door locks for correct operation	x	x	x
10	Check luggage compartment light for correct operation	x	x	x
11	Renew fuel filter			x
12	Check/adjust tyre pressures including spare	x	x	x
13	Check that tyres comply with manufacturers specification	x	x	x
14	Check tyres for tread depth, visually for cuts in fabric, exposure of ply or cord structure, lumps or bulges	x	x	x
15	Check tightness of road wheel fastenings and that spare is correctly stowed	x	x	x
16	Check for fuel leaks at filter, pumps and pipes; ensure all connections are tight	x	x	x
17	Check front wheel alignment		x	x
18	Lubricate all locks and hinges (not steering lock)		x	x
19	Check, if necessary renew windscreen wiper blades	x	x	x
20	Check/adjust headlight alignment	x	x	x
	ENGINE COMPARTMENT			
21	Open bonnet, fit wing covers	x	x	x
22	Check/top up engine oil	x		
23	Top up carburetter piston dampers	x	x	x
24	Check/top up cooling system	x	x	x
25	Check/top up windscreen washer reservoir	x	x	x
26	Check/top up brake fluid reservoir	x	x	x
27	Check/top up clutch fluid reservoir	x	x	x
28	Check/top up fluid in power steering reservoir	x	x	x
29	Check/top up automatic gearbox fluid		x	x
30	Check distributor points. Adjust or renew		x	x
31	Clean/adjust spark plugs		x	
32	Renew spark plugs			x
33	Lubricate distributor		x	x
34	Lubricate accelerator control linkage and check operation		x	x
35	Clean engine breather filter			x
36	Clean A.E.D. unit filter	x	x	x
37	Renew air cleaner element and seal			x
38	Check/adjust torque of cylinder head nuts			x
39	Check/adjust torque of exhaust manifold nuts			x
40	Check/adjust ignition timing and distributor characteristics using electronic equipment		x	x
41	Check/adjust carburetter idle speed		x	x
42	Check/adjust driving belts	x	x	x
43	Check/top up battery electrolyte; clean and grease terminals	x	x	x
44	Check cooling and heating systems for leaks	x	x	x
45	Check visually hydraulic pipes and unions for chafing, leaks and corrosion	x	x	x
46	Check visually all joints for petrol, oil or air leaks	x	x	x
47	Check exhaust system for leakage and security	x	x	x
	UNDERBODY			
	Raise ramp	x	x	x
48	Renew engine oil and filter		x	x
49	Check/top up gearbox oil – Cars fitted with manual transmission only		x	x
50	Check/top up final drive oil		x	
51	Renew final drive oil			x
52	Check/adjust clutch push rod free travel } Cars fitted with manual transmission only		x	x
53	Lubricate clutch linkage } Cars fitted with manual transmission only		x	x
54	Lubricate automatic gearbox exposed selector linkage		x	x
55	Lubricate handbrake mechanical linkage and cable		x	x
56	Lubricate all grease points excluding hubs		x	x
57	Lubricate all grease points including hubs			x
58	Inspect brake pads for wear and discs for condition	x	x	x
59	Check security of engine and suspension fixings			x
60	Check exhaust system for leakage and security	x	x	x
61	Check engine, power assisted steering, gearbox and final drive for oil leaks	x	x	x
62	Check condition and security of steering unit joints and gaiters	x	x	x
63	Check cooling and heating systems for leaks		x	x
64	Check visually hydraulic pipes and unions for chafing, leaks and corrosion	x	x	x
65	Check visually all joints for petrol, oil or air leaks	x	x	x
	Lower ramp	x	x	x
66	Remove wing covers, close bonnet and check bonnet for correct operation	x	x	x
	ROAD OR DYNAMOMETER TEST			
	(Clean hands before carrying out following items)			

Ensure seat cover and protective cover on carpets are in place . .	x	x	x
Drive car off lift (ramp)	x	x	x
67 Carry out road/roller test and check function of all instrumentation. Check safety harness inertia reel mechanism	x	x	x
68 Remove seat cover and protective cover from carpets . .	x	x	x

LUBRICATION	A	B	C	D
Lubricate all grease points (excluding hubs)			x	x
* Renew engine oil	x		x	x
* Renew engine oil filter	x		x	x
Check level of fluid in: brake, clutch reservoir, battery, engine, rear axle, transmission, cooling system, power steering and windshield washer		x	x	x
* Lubricate accelerator control linkage and pedal pivot: check operation	x			x
Lubricate all locks and hinges (not steering lock)		x	x	x

MAINTENANCE SUMMARY – U.S.A. 1978 – 1979

Weekly

Check/top up engine oil.
Check/top up brake and clutch fluid reservoirs, and automatic transmission.
Check/top up battery electrolyte.
Check/top up cooling system.
Check/top up washer reservoir.
Check function of original equipment i.e. exterior lamps, wipers and warning indicators.
Check tyres for tread depth, visually for external cuts in fabric, exposure of ply or cord structure, lumps or bulges.
Check/adjust tyre pressures including spare.

Check tightness of road wheel fastenings–maximum 50 lb.ft. (6,9 kg.m.).

MINIMUM MAINTENANCE SCHEDULES

NOTE: The maintenance schedules are based on an annual mileage of 12,500 miles. Should the vehicle complete substantially less miles than this, then it is recommended that a lubrication service is completed at six month intervals and a major service annually.

ENGINE	A	B	C	D
* Check all driving belts – adjust or renew as necessary	x			x
Check brake servo and cooling system hoses for condition and tightness	x	x	x	x
* Check/rectify crankcase breathing and evaporative system hoses, pipes and restrictors for blockage, security and deterioration				x
* Clean crankcase breather filter				x
* Check/adjust torque of cylinder head nuts and bolts	x			
* Renew air cleaner element				x
* Check security of all vacuum pipes	x			x

FUEL SYSTEM	A	B	C	D
* Renew fuel line filter	x			x
* Check fuel system for leaks	x	x	x	x
* Check condition of fuel filler cap seal				x
* Renew charcoal canister 25,000 miles only				

SERVICE	MILEAGE x 1000																
	1	3	6	9	12.5	16	19	22	25	28	31	34	37.5	41	44	47	50
A	x																
B		x		x		x		x		x		x		x		x	
C			x				x				x				x		
D					x				x				x				x

OSCILLOSCOPE AND COMBUSTION CHECK	A	B	C	D
* Check ignition wiring for fraying, chafing and deterioration	x			x
* Clean distributor cap, check for cracks and tracking				x
* Lubricate distributor				x

* These items are emission related.

OSCILLOSCOPE AND COMBUSTION CHECK (continued)	A	B	C	D
* Renew spark plugs				X
* Check coil performance on oscilloscope				X
* Check operation of distributor vacuum unit	X			X
* Check/adjust ignition timing using electronic equipment	X			X
* Check/adjust throttle disc gap	X			X
* Check/adjust idle speed	X			X
* Check/adjust CO at idle	X			X
* Check exhaust system for security and leaks	X	X	X	X
Check charging system output			X	X
* Renew oxygen sensor and reset the counter				X

SAFETY	A	B	C	D
Check condition and security of steering unit joints and gaiters			X	X
Check security of suspension fixings			X	X
Adjust front hub bearings end-float			X	X
Check visually hydraulic pipes and unions for leaks, chafing and corrosion			X	X
Inspect brake pads for wear and discs for condition		X	X	X
Check/adjust headlamp alignment			X	X
Check/adjust front wheel alignment				X
Check/adjust tyre pressures (including spare)			X	X
Check tyres visually for tread depth, cuts in fabric, exposure of ply or construction, lumps or bulges		X	X	X
Check/adjust foot and handbrake			X	X
Check operation of all door locks and window controls				X
Check condition, security and operation of seats, seat belts/interlock				X
Check, if necessary renew, wiper blades				X
Check for fuel leaks at filter, pumps and pipes; ensure all connections are tight	X	X	X	X

ROAD TEST	A	B	C	D
Ensure that operation of vehicle is satisfactory and report all items requiring attention.	X	X	X	X

BRAKES

At 19,000 and 37,500 miles brake fluid in the hydraulic brake system should be renewed. All hydraulic seals and hoses in the brake system should be renewed at 37,500 miles.

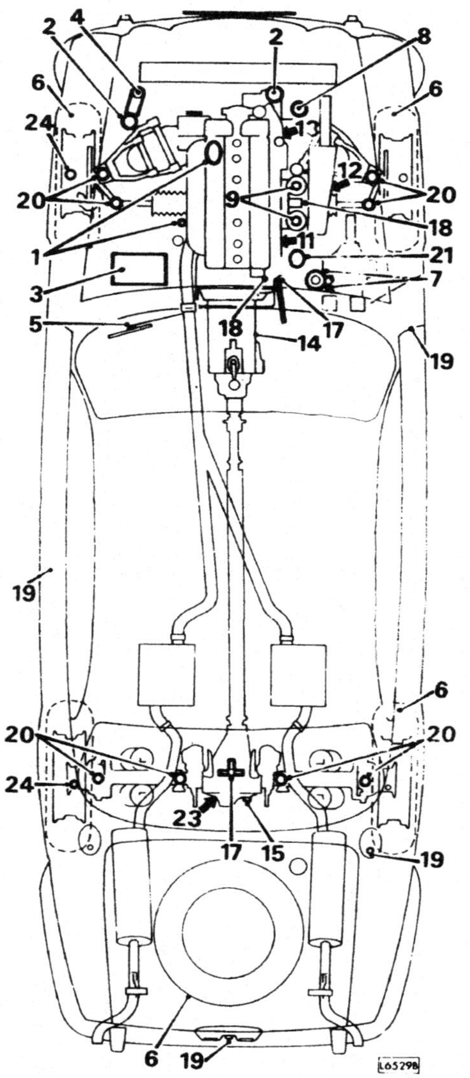

LUBRICATION CHART

Daily

1 Engine – check oil level and top up with recommended oil if necessary.
2 Cooling system – check level and top up if necessary with correct coolant.

Weekly

3 Battery – check electrolyte level and top up with distilled water if necessary.
4 Windscreen washer – check fluid level in reservoir and top up with suitable fluid if necessary.
5 Windscreen wiper blades – inspect and clean.
6 Tyres – check pressures and inspect for damage; adjust to correct pressures (including spare) if necessary.

Every 3,000 miles (5,000 Km.)

7 Brake fluid reservoir and clutch fluid reservoir (if fitted) – check fluid level and top up with Castrol – Girling brake fluid.
8 Power assisted steering – check fluid level in reservoir, and top up with recommended fluid if necessary.
9 Carburetters – top up piston dampers with clean engine oil.

Every 6,000 miles (10,000 Km.)

10 Carry out operations 7 to 9.
11 Engine – drain and refill sump.
12 Engine – renew oil filter element.
13 Distributor – lubricate with two or three drops of clean engine oil on rotor carrier shaft oil pad.
14 Gearbox – check oil level and top up with recommended lubricant if necessary.
15 Final drive unit – check oil level and top up with recommended lubricant if necessary.
16 Gearbox selector linkage – lubricate exposed parts with engine oil.
17 Handbrake – lubricate mechanical linkage and cable with engine oil.
18 Accelerator linkage – lubricate with engine oil.
19 Lubricate bonnet, boot, door locks, hinges and petrol filler flap locks.
20 Grease all points excluding wheel hubs.

Every 12,000 miles (20,000 Km.)

21 Fuel filter – renew.
22 Carry out operations 10 to 14 and 16 to 20.
23 Final drive unit – drain and refill with recommended oil.
24 Grease all points including wheel hubs.

3,000 mile (5,000 Km) Service 10.10.06

NOTE: Before undertaking any operation which involves access to the interior of passenger or luggage compartments, operators must wear gloves, or ensure that their hands are clean. Fit seat cover and place protective covers on carpets and steering wheel; these covers are to remain in place until completion of service. Drive car on lift (ramp) or over pit.

PASSENGER COMPARTMENT

1 Check function of original equipment i.e. interior and exterior lamps, indicators, horns and warning lights. Report any faults.
2 Check operation of window controls; check electrically operated windows for smoothness of operation and complete closure.
3 Check operation of handbrake; if a normal hand load causes the brake handle to move more than 5 inches, adjustment is necessary; proceed as follows:–

Early Cars

1 Set handbrake fully off.
2 Slacken front yoke locknut.
3 Remove split pin, flat washer and clevis pin securing yoke to bellcrank lever.
4 Check handbrake calipers are "fully off".
5 Turn back yoke on adjuster rod, to a point that, when the yoke is connected to the handbrake lever, a slight amount of slack is apparent in the cable.

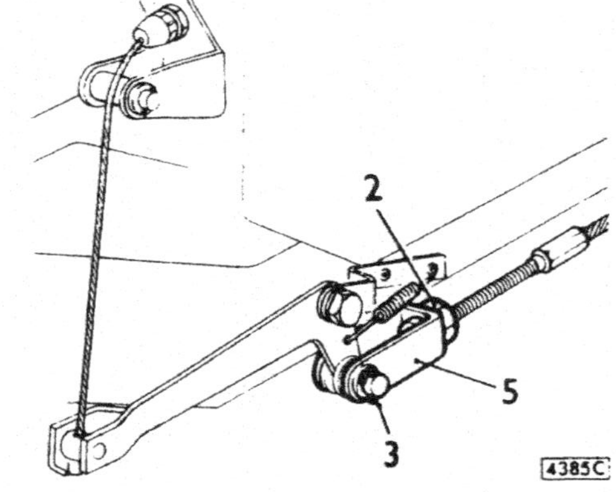

NOTE: Should cable be adjusted so that all slack is removed, binding of the handbrake caliper may result.

6 Replace clevis pin in bellcrank and yoke and secure with a new split pin.
7 Tighten yoke locknut.

Check footbrake operation and action of servo; refer also to item 30.

Later Cars

1 Set handbrake fully off.
2 Slacken locknut.
3 Remove clevis pin; discard split pin.
4 Ensure that levers at calipers are fully off by pressing them towards calipers.
5 Adjust cable by unscrewing cable end to a point just short of where caliper levers start to move.
6 Refit clevis pin; use a new split pin.
7 Tighten locknut.
8 Ensure that brakes do not bind.

4 Check that clock is running and set to time; reset if necessary, by means of the small knob adjacent to the dial.
5 Check operation of windscreen washers and wipers; ensure that jets are clean and reposition if necessary for optimum efficiency.

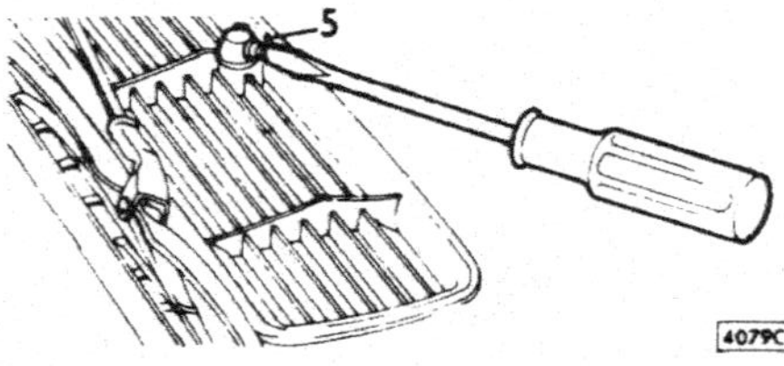

6 Check condition and security of seats and seat belts; check seat adjustment mechanisms for smooth operation, and inertia reels and buzzer alarm (if fitted) for function.
7 Check rear view mirrors for cracks and crazing; check operation of dipping lever and of door mirror remote control (if fitted).

EXTERIOR AND LUGGAGE COMPARTMENT

8 Check door locks for correct operation; do not overlook "child proof" safety catches on rear doors of four door cars. If door closing requires noticeable effort, or is in any other way unsatisfactory, refer to operation 76.37.01.

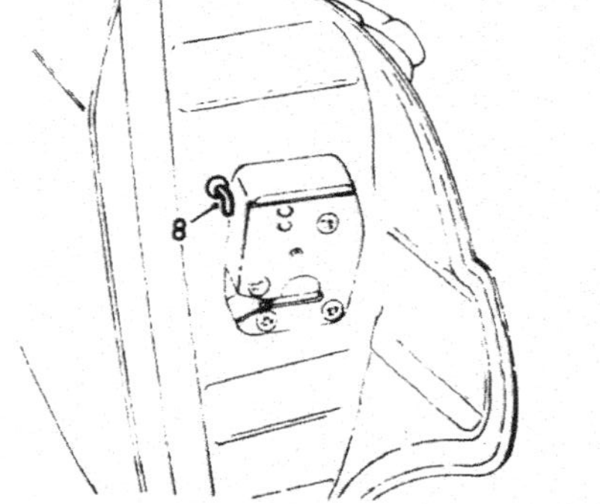

9 Check luggage compartment light for correct operation; if a failure to operate is not corrected by bulb replacement, and the lead to the unit is "live", the automatic switch, which is an integral part of the light assembly, must be replaced. See operation 86.45.16.
10 Check/adjust tyre pressures including spare; this operation must only be carried out if the tyres are cool. Tyre type and pressure data are quoted in General Specification Data, Section 04.
11 Check that tyres fitted to the car are as specified in the tyre data. Report if tyres are not to specification.
12 Measure the minimum depths of tread in the tyres and examine visually for any cuts in the tread or fabric of the tyres, for exposure of the ply or cord structure, for any lumps or bulges in the sidewalls, and for signs of uneven wear which could indicate uneven braking or faulty wheel alignment. Report any faults.

continued

13 Check that the wheel nuts are tightened to the recommended torque of 40 to 50 lbf.ft. (5,54 to 5,9 kgf.m.), and if necessary correct with a torque wrench set to 45 lbf.ft. (6,23 kgf.m.). Check also that the spare wheel is correctly stowed.

14 Examine windscreen wiper blades for damage or wear, and check their wiping efficiency; renew blades if necessary.

15 Check headlight beam pattern and alignment, using approved beam setting equipment; adjust if necessary; See operation 86.40.18.

ENGINE COMPARTMENT

16 Open the bonnet and fit wing covers.

17 Check oil level as shown by dipstick and top up if necessary with an approved engine oil.

18 Unscrew the caps from the tops of the carburetter suction chambers, and top up the hollow piston spindles with clean engine oil.

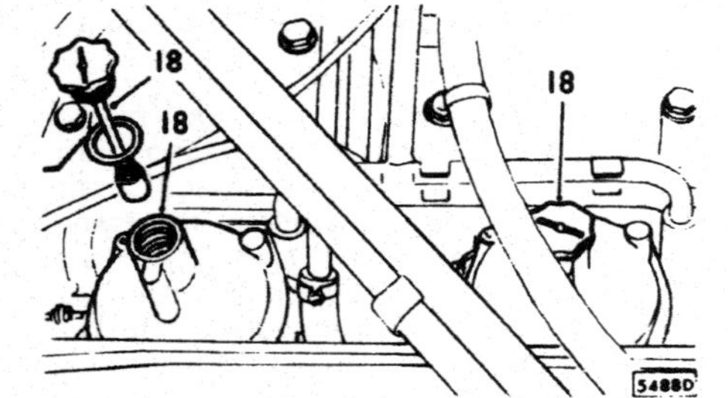

19 Ensure that the engine is cold and remove the plain coolant filler cap from the header tank 'B'. Should coolant be present in the header tank, system does not require topping up. Remove the second pressure relief coolant filler cap from the expansion tank 'A' and check that the tank is at least approximately half full, adding coolant if necessary. Replace both

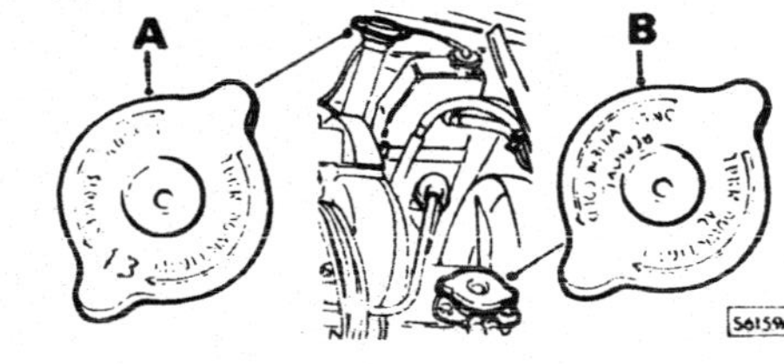

caps securely, taking care that they are not reversed. If the coolant level is below that specified, and the tank is less than half full, a coolant leak must be suspected; while if the tank is full, or nearly so, and the level in the system is low, a leakage exists, permitting air to be drawn into the system while it is cooling down.

In either case the leak must be located and rectified before topping up. To top up, add the specified coolant slowly to the header tank, with the cap of the expansion tank also removed, until the level reaches the bottom of the filler neck. Replace the filler caps securely.

CAUTION: If more than 4 pints (4.8 U.S. pints, or 2,3 litres) of coolant are required to replenish the system, a complete cold refill procedure must be carried out. See operation 26.10.01.

NOTE: When the system contains anti-freeze ensure that the specific gravity of the coolant is maintained.

20 Inspect the level of fluid in the windscreen washer reservoir, and top up if necessary.

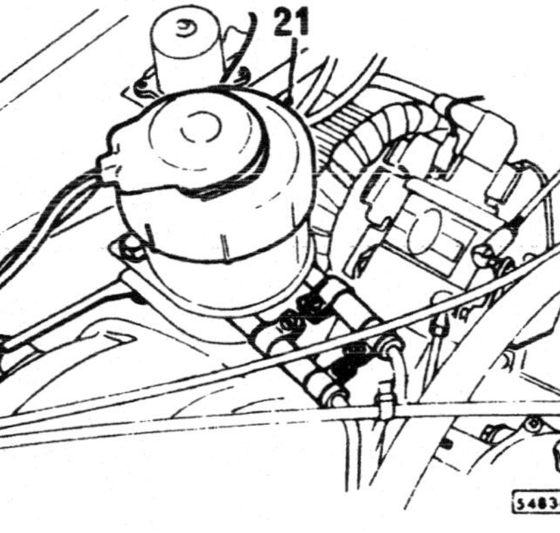
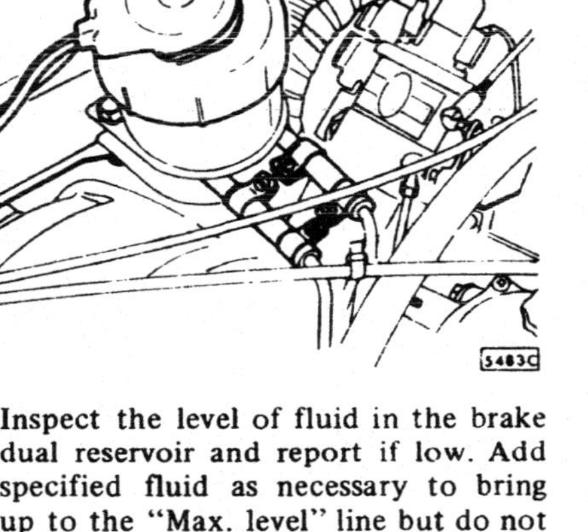
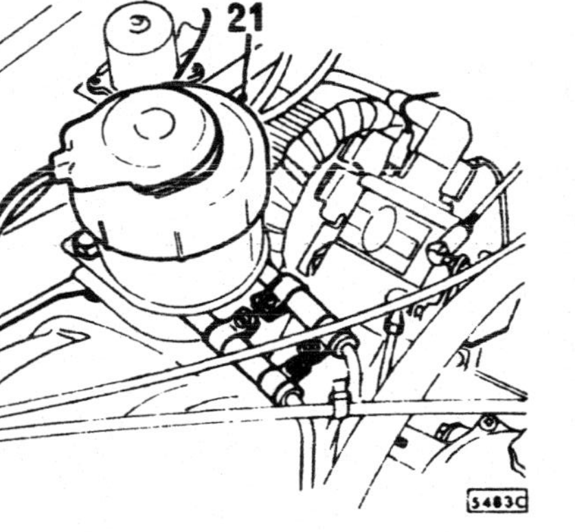

21 Inspect the level of fluid in the brake dual reservoir and report if low. Add specified fluid as necessary to bring up to the "Max. level" line but do not overfill.

22 **Manual Transmission cars only**. Remove cap from clutch fluid reservoir and report if low. Top up if necessary, with specified fluid to the bottom of the filler neck.

23 Remove the filler cap from the power steering oil reservoir; take great care to prevent any foreign matter from entering the reservoir. Inspect the oil level shown on the dipstick and top up if necessary, with the recommended fluid. The level must be to the "Full" mark when the oil is warm.

24 Check the tension of all drive belts to the following data, which quote the deflection caused in the longest run of the belt when a specified load is applied at right angles to the belt. Adjust as necessary to obtain the correct deflection.

25 Remove the filler manifold cover from the battery by lifting at both ends, and inspect the electrolyte level in the six tubes exposed. If liquid is visible in all the tubes, replace the manifold cover. If liquid is not visible in some or all of the tubes, add distilled water slowly to the manifold until all six tubes are filled. Replace the manifold cover. Wipe off any surplus water and clean and grease the battery terminals.

26 Inspect all pipes and joints in the engine cooling and car heating systems which are visible from above for leaks and security of connections and attachments. Report findings.

27 Inspect all visible hydraulic pipes and unions for signs of chafing, leaks or corrosion. Report any faults.

28 Inspect all visible joints for evidence of petrol, oil or air leaks. Report findings.

29 Check exhaust system for security of manifold mountings and gaskets, and for signs of leakage. Report findings.

Driving belt for:	Deflecting force lb.	kg.	Deflection ins.	mm.	Location of adjustment data
P.A.S. pump & water pump	6.4	2,9	0.17	4,30	57.20.01
Alternator (18 ACR) Alternator (20 ACR)	3.2	1,45	0.15	3,80	86.10.05
Air Pump	3.2	1,45	0.18	4,60	17.25.13
Compressor	6.4	2,9	0.17	4,30	82.10.01

UNDERBODY

30 Raise ramp. Inspect brake pads and discs for wear and condition; the minimum thickness permitted for the brake pads is 1/8 in. (3,18 mm.). If less than this the pads must be renewed. See operations 70.40.02 and 03 (footbrake pads) and 70.40.04 (handbrake pads). The discs should be free from deep scoring and signs of distortion or uneven wear.

31 Check mountings and joints of under-car exhaust system for security, and inspect for evidence of leakage and damage, or corrosion.

32 Inspect carefully for oil leaks from engine, power assisted steering, gearbox and final drive; report findings.

33 Check condition and security of steering joints; examine gaiters carefully for splits, cracking or damage, and ensure that they are firmly fixed in position.

34 Carefully inspect all visible brake pipes and unions for leaks, chafing or corrosion, and for possible damage to *flexible pipes*.

35 Check all joints in external pipes for evidence of damage and of petrol, oil or air leaks.

Lower ramp

36 Remove wing covers, close bonnet and check all three bonnet catches for correct operation.

ROAD OR DYNAMOMETER TEST

(Clean hands or wear gloves before carrying out the following items.)
Ensure that protective covers are still in place on seats and carpets. Remove steering wheel cover. Drive car off lift (ramp) or pit.

37 Carry out road or roller test and check that all instruments and controls are functioning correctly. Check that footbrake performance exceeds the requirements of current regulations, and will provide a retardation of 10 ft./sec.^{2} (3 m./s^2), with a pedal load not exceeding 30 lbf. (13,5 kgf). Check that the handbrake holds the car securely on a hill, facing up or down, and that the retardation it provides as an emergency brake meets legal requirements with a hand load not exceeding 88 lbf. (40 kgf).
Check that brake servo performance is consistent, and that there is no evidence of air leakage into the vacuum system.

38 Remove protective covers from seats and carpets, ensure that steering wheel, controls and car interior have not been marked, and complete Passport to Service.

6,000 mile (10,000 Km.) Service 10.10.12

1 Carry out items ref. 1 to 9 – See operation 10.10.06.

2 Change fuel filter element in boot on early cars.

NOTE: Later cars are fitted with a disposable filter, located in engine bay and changed at 12,000 mile (20,000 km.) Service. See 10.10.24 operations 10 to 16.

Removing

WARNING: A CERTAIN AMOUNT OF FUEL SPILLAGE IS UNAVOIDABLE DURING THIS OPERATION, IT IS THEREFORE IMPERATIVE THAT ALL DUE PRECAUTIONS ARE TAKEN AGAINST FIRE AND EXPLOSION.

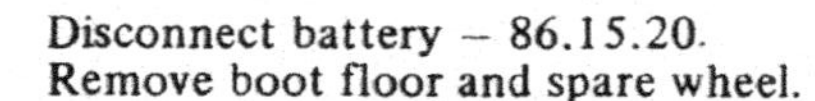

3 Disconnect battery – 86.15.20.

4 Remove boot floor and spare wheel.

5 Fit clamp on inlet pipe to fuel filter head.

6 Place shallow tray, lined with rag, beneath fuel filter bowl.

7 Remove centre bolt securing filter bowl.

Refitting

8 Clean out filter bowl thoroughly and replace with new element and seals; fit element with larger hole upwards.

9 Tighten centre bolt to secure filter bowl. DO NOT OVERTIGHTEN.

10 Remove pipe clamp and tray.

11 Reconnect battery.

12 Start engine and check for fuel leaks at filter, pumps and pipes; ensure that all connections are tight.

13 Replace spare wheel and boot floor. Carry out items 10 to 13 – See operation 10.10.06.

14 Check front wheel alignment using approved equipment.
Correct figures are 1/16 in. to 1/8 in. (1,6 mm. to 3,2 mm.) toe-in, measured at the rims. Refer to operation 57.65.01.

15 Lubricate door bonnet and boot locks and hinges, using engine oil. Do not lubricate steering lock, and ensure that all surplus oil is removed.
Carry out items 14 to 16 – See operation 10.10.06.
Carry out items 18 to 23 – See operation 10.10.06.

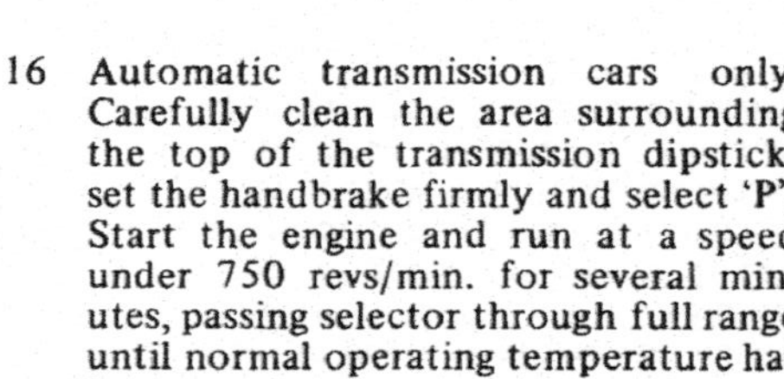

16 **Automatic transmission cars only.** Carefully clean the area surrounding the top of the transmission dipstick, set the handbrake firmly and select 'P'. Start the engine and run at a speed under 750 revs/min. for several minutes, passing selector through full range until normal operating temperature has been reached.
With engine still idling, remove the dipstick, wipe with clean paper or non-fluffy rag, replace fully and immediately withdraw. The fluid level indicated should be at the "Full" or "High" mark. Top up if necessary, using one of the specified fluids, with the engine still idling. Do not overfill. Report quantity of fluid required.

Non Federal Cars Only

17 Remove the distributor cap, inspect the contact breaker points and, if pitted, clean with fine carborundum stone or very fine emery cloth; if badly pitted fit a replacement unit. Set gap of points to 0.014 in. to 0.016 in. (0,36 mm. to 0,41 mm.)

18 Lubricate distributor; lift off rotor arm and:–

continued

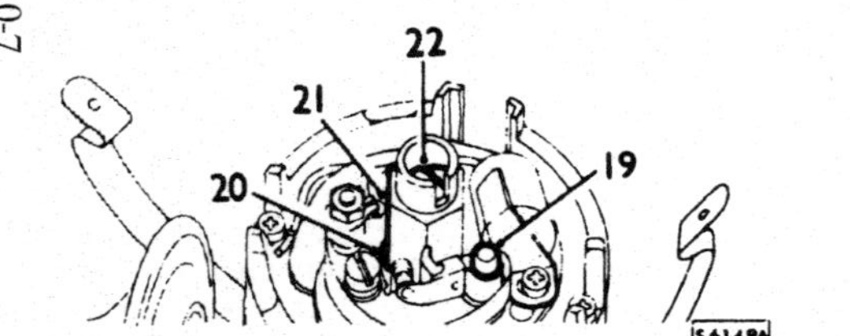

19 Apply one drop of engine oil to the pivot post.
20 Inject a few drops of engine oil through the aperture at the edge of the contact breaker base plate, to lubricate the centrifugal advance mechanism.
21 Lightly smear the cam with Mobilgrease No. 2 or clean engine oil.
22 Apply a few drops of engine oil at the central screw.
Replace rotor arm and distributor cap.
23 Remove all spark plugs. Check that they are to specification, clean on an approved plug cleaning machine and set the points to a gap of 0.025 in. (0,64 mm.). Refit plugs.
24 Lubricate, with engine oil, all pivots and joints in the throttle control linkage. Check that operation is smooth, that throttles close correctly, and that full opening is obtained (before 'Kick-down') where applicable.
25 Check ignition timing characteristics, using electronic equipment. The static setting is 8° (crankshaft) B.T.D.C. Advance characteristics are:–

Distributor rev/min	Advance of decelerating speeds, degrees of distributor rotation (vac. pipe disconnected)				
	4.2 L, No. Emission Control	4.2 L, 'B' Emission Control	4.2 L, 'A' Emission Control	4.2 L, 'A Calif' Emission Control	3.4 L, 'B' Emission Control
2800	12–14	12–14	11–13	11–13	13–15
2500			11–13	11–13	
2200	11.5–13.5	11.5–13.5	10–12	10–12	
1600					13–15
1500	9–11	9–11			
1250			7–9	7–9	10–12
900	7–9	7–9	4.5–7	4.5–7	5.5–7.5
700	3–5	3–5	1–3.5	1–3.5	
600					1.5–3.5
550	0–2	0–2			
450	0		0		
400	0	0	0	0	
325	0	0	0	0	0

26 Check engine idling speed, which should be 650 to 750 rev./min. with engine warm.
Adjust carburetter settings if necessary. Refer to operation 19.15.02.
Carry out items 24 to 29 – See operation 10.10.06.
27 Remove plug (1) and washer (2) from automatic enrichment device, withdraw filter element (3) and wash clean in petrol. Refit element and plug, using new sealing washer; do not overtighten plug.

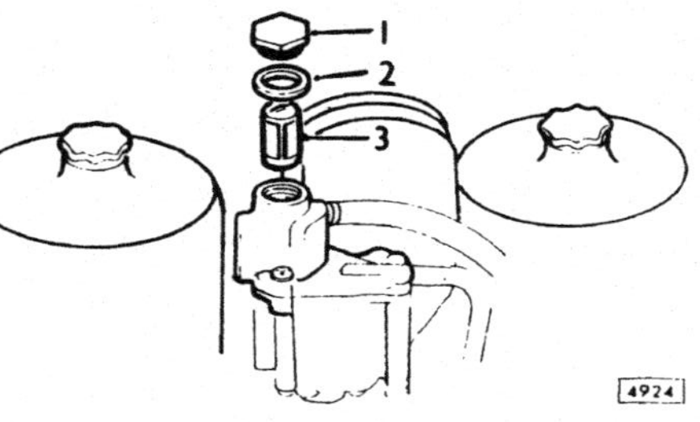

Underbody – Raise ramp
28 Clean area of engine sump around drain plug and remove plug. Drain oil into a container of at least 2 gallons (9 litres) capacity. Discard sealing washer. On Early Cars unscrew central bolt securing oil filter canister, withdraw canister with bolt sealing ring and filter element. Discard filter and sealing ring and wash canister and bolt in clean petrol.

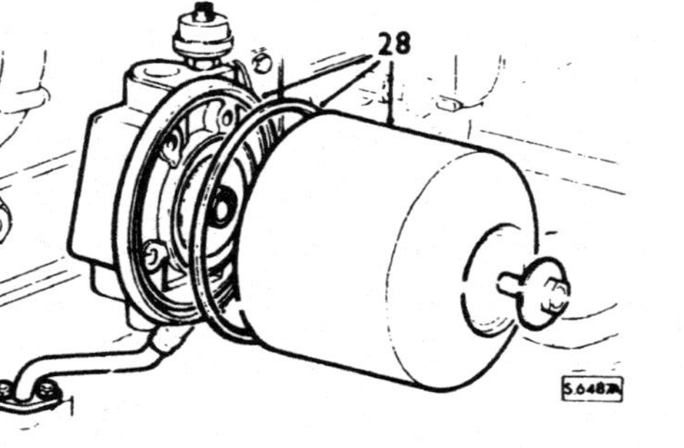

Re-assemble filter with new element and sealing ring, and top up sump with specified oil to the "full" mark on dipstick. Run engine at a fast tick-over for 2 to 3 minutes, stop and re-check oil level, adding further oil if necessary to bring the oil level to the "full" mark.
On Later Cars, fitted with disposable canister filter, remove air cleaner cover and element to improve access to filter, unscrew canister and discard canister and seal. Ensure new seal is correctly located on new canister, smear with engine oil and screw into place by hand only. DO NOT OVERTIGHTEN. Top up sump and run engine as above.
29 **Manual transmission cars only.** Clean the gearbox around the filler/level plug on the right hand side of the box, and remove the plug.
Top up slowly to bottom of the plug hole with one of the recommended SE.90 oils, taking great care to ensure absolute cleanliness; this is essential since the overdrive unit uses gearbox oil in its hydraulic system. Report the quantity of oil used.
30 Clean the area of the final drive rear cover around the filler/level plug, and remove the plug. The oil level should be up to the bottom of the thread. If topping up is necessary, use Hypoid oil of the correct grade and brand. If the brand of oil present in the final drive is not known, it is preferable to drain and refill rather than introducing another oil which may not mix satisfactorily.

Note that different grades of oil are specified for normal and "Powr-Lok" differentials, which are fitted to some 6 cylinder cars. See 09-1 and item 10 of operation 10.10.24.

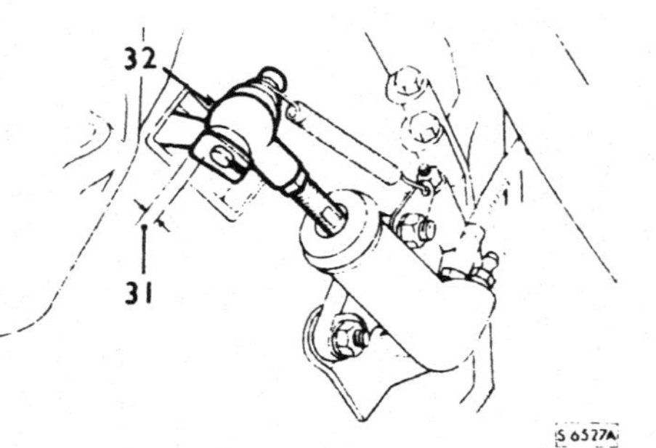

31 **Manual transmission cars only** – clutch operation. Check the free movement of the clutch operating rod, which should be 1/16 in. (1,5 mm.) on the rod which couples the slave cylinder to the clutch withdrawal level. Adjust if necessary by slackening the locknut, turning the operating rod until the required free movement is obtained and retightening the locknut. Free travel is increased by screwing the rod into the knuckle joint. Replace the return spring, if disturbed, after adjustment.

32 **On manual transmission cars,** lightly lubricate, with engine oil, the end joint of the clutch operating rod.

33 **On automatic transmission cars,** lubricate the joints of the exposed selector linkage with engine oil.

34 Lubricate, with engine oil, the joints, pivots and cable of the handbrake mechanism.

35 Using one of the approved greases, lubricate front wheel swivel joints (4 nipples) steering tie-rods (2 nipples), steering pinion housing, rear suspension outer bearings, (2 nipples), rear suspension inner bearings (4 nipples) and rear axle universal joints (4 nipples). Access to these joint nipples is obtained by removing rubber plugs from the joint covers. Ensure that the plugs are correctly refitted after greasing. Before greasing the outer suspension bearings, ensure that the bleed holes, diametrically opposite to the grease nipples, are clear; when sufficient grease has been applied to the joints the excess will appear at the bleed holes.
Carry out items 30 to 33 See operation 10.10.06.

36 Inspect all pipes and joints in cooling and heating systems for leaks.
Carry out items 34 to 38 – See operation 10.10.06.

12,000 mile (20,000 Km.) Service 10.10.24

1 Carry out items 1 to 22 as applicable – see operation 10.10.12.

2 Remove all spark plugs and replace with new plugs with the spark gaps set to .025 in. (0,64 mm.). The correct plugs are Champion N11Y.
Carry out item 24 – See operation 10.10.12.

3 Clean engine breather filter.

4 Disconnect the breather pipe from the cover on the front of the engine. Remove pipe.

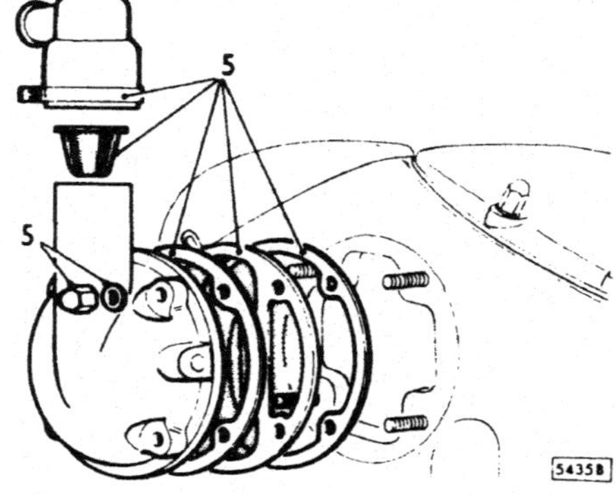

5 Remove four nuts securing the cover and detach cover, two gaskets and the flame trap gauze.

6 Wash gauze, gaskets, cover and tube in petrol. Examine all parts and renew where necessary.

7 Refit by reversing items 4 and 5, and check all clamps for tightness.

8 Check the tightness of the cylinder head nuts by applying a tightening torque of 54.2 lbf.ft. (650 lbf.ins. or 7,48 kgf.m.).

9 Check that all exhaust manifold nuts are securely tightened.

10 Change fuel filter in engine bay on later cars. It is located in a fuel line adjacent to carburetters.

Removing

WARNING: A CERTAIN AMOUNT OF FUEL SPILLAGE IS UNAVOIDABLE DURING THIS OPERATION. IT IS THEREFORE IMPERATIVE THAT ALL DUE PRECAUTIONS ARE TAKEN AGAINST FIRE AND EXPLOSION.

11 Disconnect battery.

12 Disconnect hose clips clamping hoses to filter casing, collecting fuel released from filter and pipes.

13 Remove and discard filter unit.

Refitting

14 Insert new filter in fuel line, with arrow moulded on casing pointing in direction of fuel flow.

15 Tighten hose clips to not more than 6 lbf.in. (0,07 kgf.m.).

16 Reconnect battery.
Carry out items 25 to 29 – See operation 10.10.12.

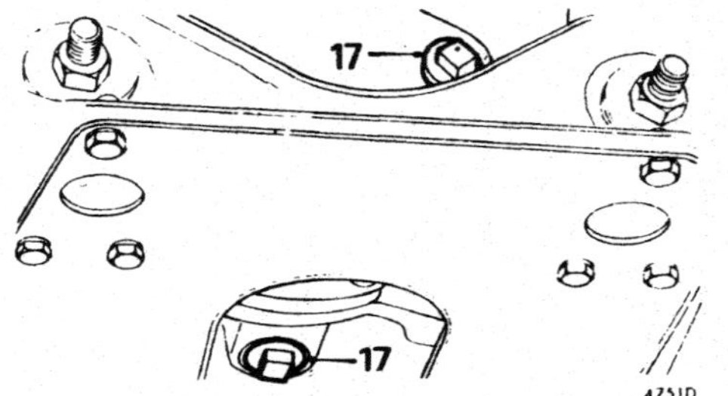

17 Remove oil filler plug and drain plug from final drive unit, and empty oil into a suitable receptacle. This is preferably done after a run, while the oil in the final drive unit is warm.
Replace the drain plug and refill with a specified oil, noting that different oils are specified for normal and "Powr-Lok" differentials.

continued

"Powr-Lok" differentials, when fitted, can be identified by a tab stamped "PL" fitted to the bottom left hand cover attachment setscrew. Fill the differential case slowly until the oil reaches the bottom of the filler thread. Replace plug and tighten securely. Carry out items 31 to 35 – See operation 10.10.12.

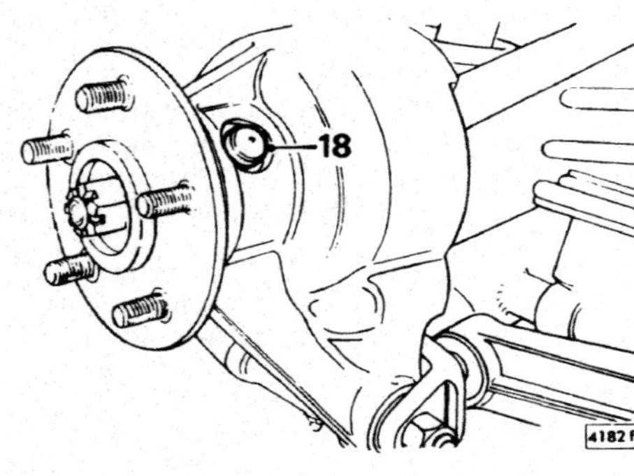

18 Lubricate front and rear hubs. Remove the front wheel nave plates, exposing grease nipples. Inject specified lubricant until it appears at the bleed holes at the hub centres.

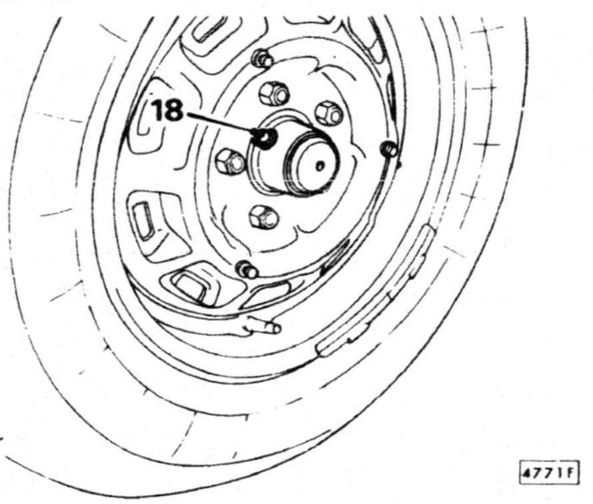
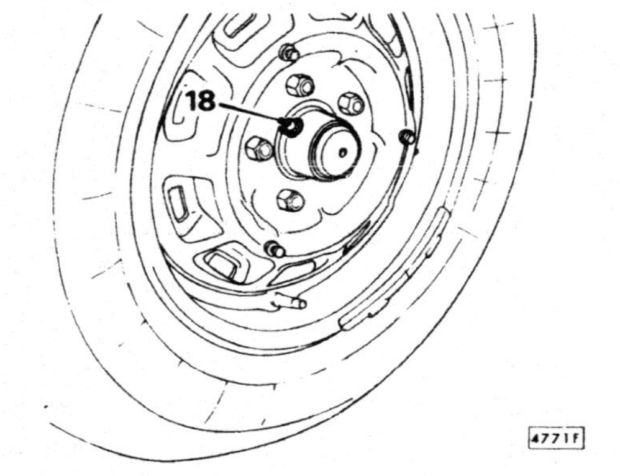

Remove the rear wheels, exposing holes in the hub carriers closed by dust caps. Clean the caps, and the area surrounding them, and prise them out of the nub carriers. Inject a specified grease into the hubs until no more will enter; do not build up pressure in the hubs. Clear the vent holes in the dust caps and replace them. Replace the rear wheels.

19 Clean areas surrounding engine mountings and front and rear cross beam and suspension attachments. Inspect rubber mountings and bushes carefully for signs of deterioration or distortion and check all fixing bolts and nuts for security; torque spanner settings are quoted in Section 06.
Carry out items 30 to 33 – See operation 10.10.06.
Carry out item 36 – See operation 10.10.12
Carry out items 34 to 38 – See operation 10.10.06.

20 Carry out any additional services as applicable – see page 10–3.

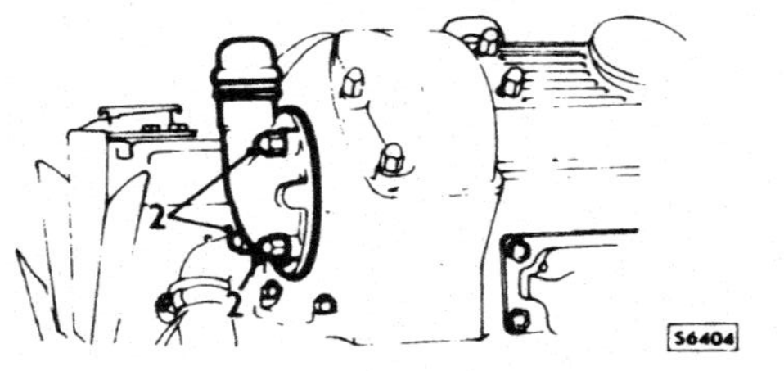

CAMSHAFT

Remove and refit – Left hand or Right hand **12.13.01**

Service tools: Top timing chain adjuster tool JD.2B; Valve timing gauge C.3993.

Removing
1 Remove camshaft covers – 12.29.42.
2 Remove nuts securing breather housing to front of cylinder head and withdraw housing.
3 Slacken nut on idler sprocket shaft.
4 Knock down tabs and remove two camshaft sprocket retaining bolts.

5 Rotate engine until valve timing gauge can be fitted to slot in camshaft; remove remaining camshaft bolts.
6 Use Service tool JD.2B, turned in a clockwise direction, to slacken camshaft chain.
CAUTION: Do not rotate engine with camshafts disconnected.
7 Slide sprocket up support bracket.
NOTE: Mark 'fit' holes in adjuster plates.
8 Progressively slacken camshaft bearing cap nuts starting with centre cap and working outwards; lift off bearing caps. Note mating marks on each bearing cap.
NOTE: If same shell bearings are being refitted, note location to ensure they are fitted in original position.
9 Lift camshaft from cylinder head.

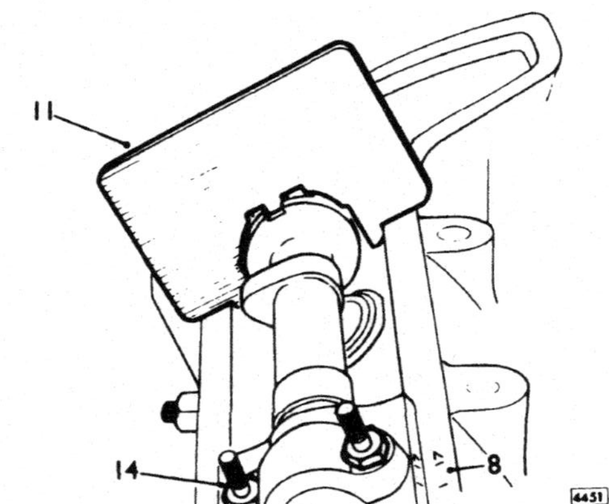

Refitting
10 Fit camshaft shell bearings.
11 Fit camshaft in bearings so that keyway in front flange is located by valve timing gauge C.3993.
12 Fit bearing caps to their respective positions and fit 'D' washers, spring washers and nuts.
13 Tighten down bearing caps evenly, commencing with the centre cap.
14 Tighten nuts to torque of 9 lbf.ft (1,24 kg.m.).
15 Locate camshaft sprocket on camshaft and ensure 'fit' holes line up. Fit one bolt on lock plate.
NOTE: If all preceding instructions have been followed, valve timing will be correct.
16 Check tappet adjustment – 12.29.48.
17 Rotate engine and fit remaining bolts to camshaft sprocket. Turn up tabs.
18 Using tool JD.2B tension top timing chain until slight flexibility remains in chain on both outer sides of camshaft sprockets. Chain MUST NOT be dead tight.
19 Securely tighten locknut.
20 Reverse operations 1 and 2.

CAMSHAFT BEARINGS

Remove and refit **12.13.13**

Follow procedure detailed under Camshaft Remove and refit – 12.13.01.

PISTON AND CONNECTING ROD

Remove and refit – engine set **12.17.01**

Service tool – Piston ring clamp 38.U3.

Removing
1 Remove engine and gearbox assembly – 12.37.01.
2 Remove cylinder head – 12.29.11.
3 Remove oil sump – 12.60.44, operations 2 to 16 inclusive.
4 Remove nuts from connecting rod bolts.

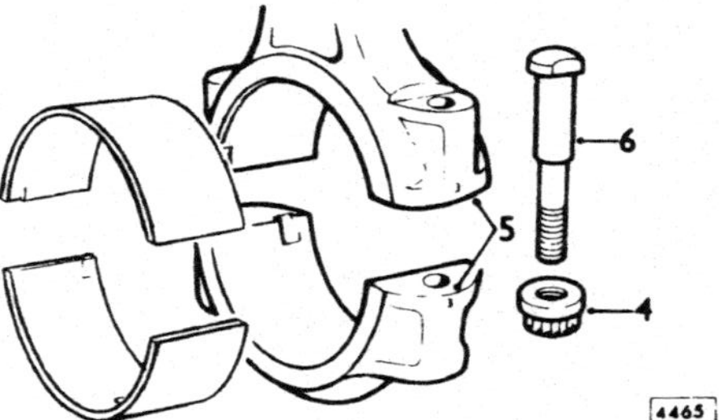

5 Remove connecting rod cap noting corresponding cylinder numbers on connecting rod and cap. Number 1 cylinder at rear of engine.
6 Remove connecting rod bolt and withdraw piston and connecting rod from top of cylinder bore.
7 Repeat operations 4 to 6 inclusive on each cylinder then continue with operation 8.

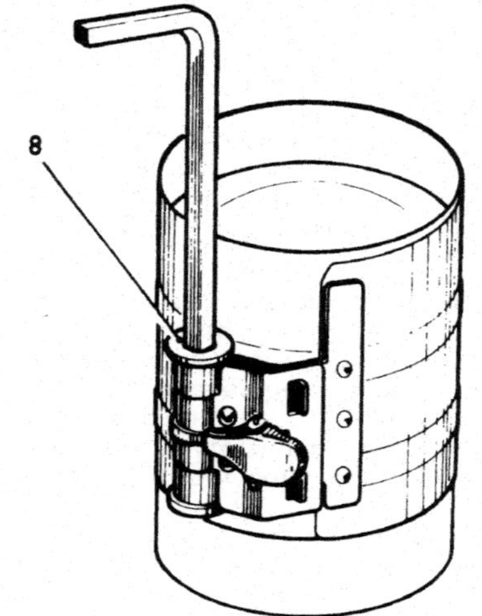

Refitting
NOTE: If original pistons and connecting rods are being fitted, they must be replaced in the cylinder bore from which they were removed.
If new pistons and connecting rods are being fitted they should be stamped with the number of the bore in which they are to be installed. Number 1 cylinder is at the rear of the engine.
8 Fit Service tool 38.U3 to a piston, and fully compress piston rings.
9 Enter piston into cylinder bore, ensuring that stamped 'FRONT' on piston is towards front of engine.
10 Fit bearing shells to connecting rod and cap, liberally coating them with clean engine oil.
11 Fit cap to connecting rod, ensuring that cylinder numbers stamped on each part are on the same side.
12 Tighten connecting rod nuts to a torque of 37.5 lb.ft. (5,2 kg.m.).
13 Repeat operations 8 to 12 inclusive on each cylinder in turn.
14 Refit oil sump.
15 Refit cylinder head.
16 Refit engine and gearbox assembly.

PISTON AND CONNECTING ROD

Overhaul **12.17.10**

NOTE: Pistons are supplied complete with gudgeon pins. As pins and pistons are matched assemblies it is not permissible to interchange component parts.

Overhaul

1 Remove piston and connecting rods – 12.17.01.
2 Remove circlips.
3 Push gudgeon pin out of piston.
4 Withdraw connecting rod.

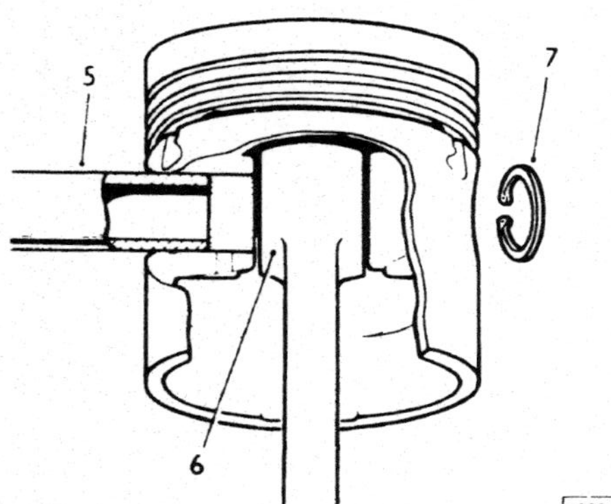

Refitting

5 Fit gudgeon pin in piston.
CAUTION: Connecting rods must be refitted to pistons in such a way that when installed in engine word 'FRONT' on piston crown faces front of engine and chamfer on big end eye faces crank pin radius.
6 Align small end with end of gudgeon pin and push pin home.
7 Use new circlips to retain gudgeon pin.
NOTE: Gudgeon pin is a push fit in piston at 20 deg. C (68 deg. F). Fit will vary with ambient temperature.

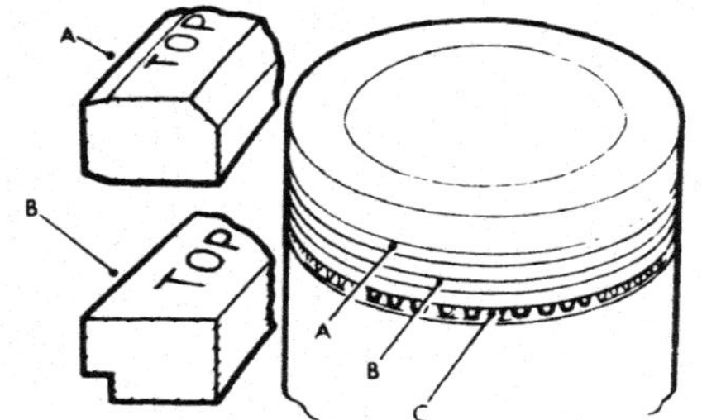

Three piston rings are fitted, they are as follows:

A. Top ring – Compression.
B. Second ring – Compression.
C. Bottom ring – Oil control.

Both top and second rings have tapered peripheries and are marked 'TOP' to ensure correct fitting. In addition, the top ring has a chrome plated periphery and is also cargraph coated. This coating is coloured RED and must not be removed. The bottom ring consists of an expander sandwiched between two rails, the assembly being held together by an adhesive.

8 Check piston ring gap in bore. Push ring to a point midway down bore, check that ring is square and measure gap – See Engine data group 05.
9 Fit bottom ring ensuring that expander ends are not overlapping.
10 Fit second and top rings ensuring that they are fitted the correct way up.
11 Position rings so that gaps are staggered around periphery of piston.
12 Check side clearance of rings in piston groove. See Engine data group 05.
13 Check connecting rods for alignment on a suitable jig.
14 Check bore of small end bush – See Engine data group 05.
CAUTION: If small end bush is worn beyond acceptable limits, a service exchange connecting rod must be fitted. It is NOT advisable to renew bushes as specialised equipment is needed to hone bushes to finished size.
15 Refit pistons and connecting rods.

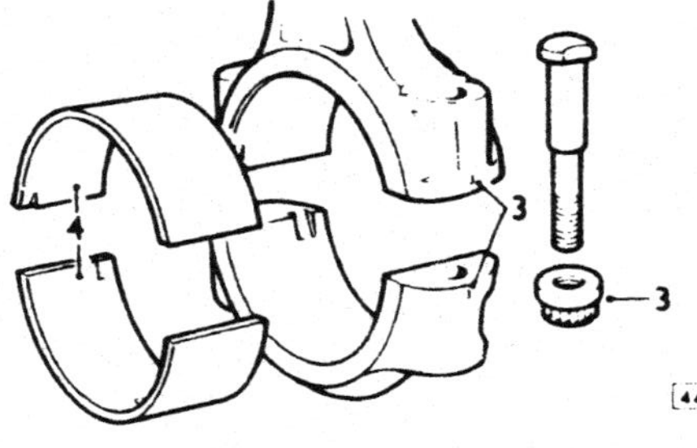

CONNECTING ROD BEARINGS

Remove and refit (Set) – Engine in situ **12.17.16**

Removing

1 Remove oil sump – 12.60.44.
2 Turn engine until one big-end bearing is at bottom dead centre.
3 Remove connecting rod cap noting that corresponding cylinder number on connecting rod and cap are on the same side.
4 Lift connecting rod from crank pin and withdraw bearing shells.

Inspection

Check crank pin for signs of overheating, scoring or transfer of bearing metal. If crank pin is suspect in any way, engine must be removed and crankshaft rectified or renewed as necessary.

Refitting

5 Liberally coat replacement bearing shells with clean engine oil and locate in connecting rod and cap.
6 Secure connecting rod cap, ensuring marks coincide.
7 Tighten connecting rod nuts to a torque of 37.5 lb.ft. (5,2 kg.m.).
8 Repeat operations 2 to 7 inclusive on remaining five journals then proceed with operation 9.
9 Refit oil sump.

CRANKSHAFT DAMPER AND PULLEY

Remove and refit **12.21.01**

Removing

1 Remove four plain nuts and shakeproof washers securing fan and torquatrol unit to water pump pulley. Remove unit.
2 Remove steering pump belt – 57.20.02.
3 Remove compressor belt – 82.10.02 – cars fitted with air conditioning only.

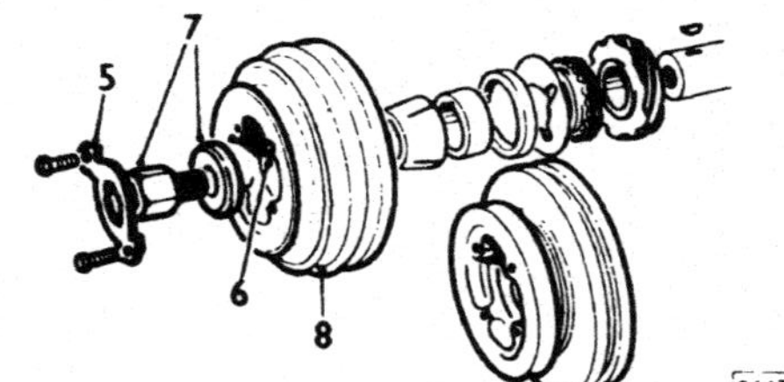

4 Remove alternator belt – 86.10.03.
5 Knock back locking tabs on pulley bolts.
6 Remove four bolts securing crankshaft pulley to torsional damper. Recover locking ring.
7 Remove large bolt securing torsional damper and recover large plain washer.
8 Strike damper with hide mallet and remove it from crankshaft.

Inspection

9 Examine rubber portions of damper for signs of deterioration and if necessary, fit a new damper.
10 Examine pulley and damper grooves for wear. Drive belts must not bottom in grooves.

Refitting

11 Reverse operations 1 to 7 inclusive.

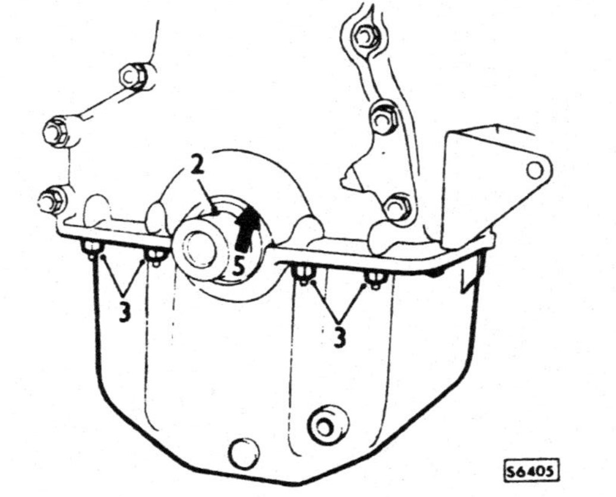

CRANKSHAFT FRONT OIL SEAL

Remove and refit 12.21.14

Removing

1 Remove crankshaft damper and pulley - 12.21.01.
2 If cone has not drawn clear with torsional damper, prise slot open and draw from crankshaft. Recover Woodruff key.
3 Remove oil sump – 12.60.44.
4 Draw distance piece from crankshaft.
5 Prise oil seal from front timing cover recess, taking great care not to damage surface of crankshaft or oil seal recess.

Refitting

6 Liberally coat new oil seal with clean engine oil and locate in timing cover recess, open side inwards.
7 Check 'O' ring seal in distance piece, fit distance piece on to crankshaft.
8 Fit oil sump.
9 Fit Woodruff key in crankshaft and fit cone.
10 Fit crankshaft damper and pulley.

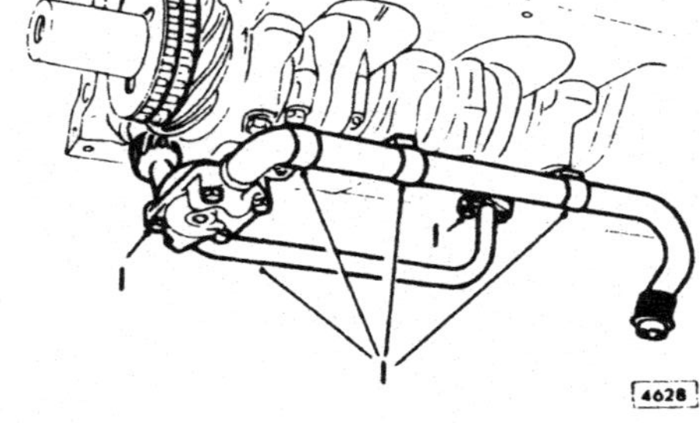

MAIN BEARINGS

Remove and refit (set) – Engine in situ 12.21.39

Removing

1 Remove oil pump and pipes – 12.60.26.
2 Withdraw bolts securing rear main bearing cap and discard washers. Note corresponding numbers on bearing cap and crankcase.

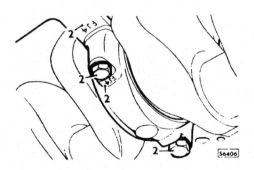

3 Withdraw upper half of bearing shell
4 Liberally coat replacement bearing shells with clean engine oil and locate in crankcase and bearing cap. Ensure lugs on bearing shell locate correctly.
5 Secure bearing cap using bolts and new flat washer.
6 Tighten bolts to torque of 72 lb.ft. (9,96 kg.m.).
7 Repeat operations 2 to 6 inclusive on the four intermediate main bearing caps. Continue with operation 8.
8 Remove bolts securing centre main bearing cap. Discard bearing shells and thrust washers.

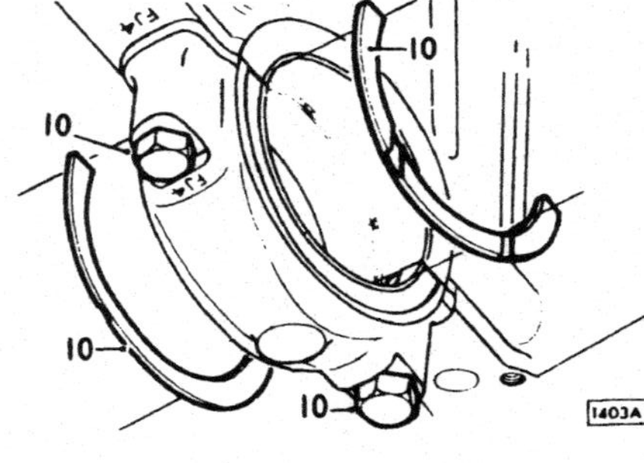

9 Liberally coat replacement bearing shells and two new thrust washers with clean engine oil and locate shells in crankcase and bearing cap. Ensure lugs on bearing shell locate correctly.
10 Locate thrust washers on either side of bearing cap, white metal side outwards and secure cap using bolts and new flat washers.
11 Tighten bolts to torque of 72 lb.ft. (9,96 kg.m.).
12 Set crankshaft to T.D.C. No. 6 cylinder (front) firing, and remove distributor cap.
13 Remove setscrew and remove distributor.

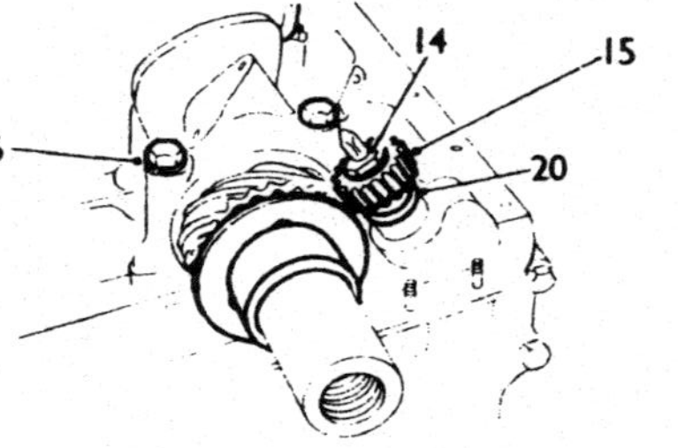

14 Beneath engine, flatten tab washer and slacken nut securing distributor shaft drive gear four or five turns, but DO NOT remove.
15 Tap distributor drive shaft up through gear, then draw gear and shaft downwards. Ensure gears do not come out of mesh.
16 Remove bolts securing front main bearing cap and manoeuvre cap clear. Discard bearing shells.
17 Liberally coat replacement bearing shells with clean engine oil and locate shells in crankcase and bearing cap. Ensure lugs on bearing shell locate correctly.
18 Secure bearing cap using bolts and new flat washers.
19 Tighten bolts to torque of 72 lb.ft. (9,96 kg.m.).
20 Tighten distributor drive gear nut, ensuring thrust washer locates correctly. Secure lockwasher.
21 Reverse operation 1.

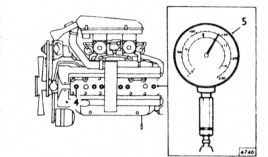

CYLINDER PRESSURES

Check 12.25.01

1 Set transmission selector at 'P' – automatic transmission cars only.
2 Run engine until normal operating temperature is reached. Switch off engine.
3 Remove H.T. cable from ignition coil.
4 Remove all sparking plugs.
5 Fit approved pressure gauge at one plug hole and with throttle held fully open, crank engine with starter motor. Note highest steady pressure reading achieved and repeat at each plug hole in turn.
The reading taken at each cylinder must not differ from the reading taken at any other cylinder by more than 5 lb./in.^{2} (0,35 kg./cm.^{2}).

CYLINDER HEAD GASKET

Remove and refit 12.29.02

Removing

Follow procedure given for removing cylinder head – 12.29.11. Check cylinder head and faces of cylinder block and liners for damage that caused, or was the result of, gasket failure; rectify as necessary.

CYLINDER HEAD

Remove and refit 12.29.11

Service tools: Top timing chain adjuster tool JD2B; Valve timing gauge C.3993.

Removing

1 Disconnect battery – 86.15.20.
2 Drain coolant and conserve in a clean receptacle.
3 Remove both wing valance stays. Unclip pressure pipe from wing valance stays – air conditioned cars only.
4 Remove air cleaner – 19.10.01.
5 Detach inner and outer throttle cables from abutment and linkage brackets. Detach kickdown cable from linkage and abutment – automatic transmission Model 65 only.
6 Slacken clip at heater hose to water valve.

Cars fitted with air conditioning only

WARNING: ON NO ACCOUNT MUST ANY PORTION OF THE AIR CONDITIONING SYSTEM BE DISCONNECTED BY ANYONE OTHER THAN A QUALIFIED REFRIGERATION ENGINEER. BLINDNESS CAN RESULT IF THE GAS CONTAINED WITHIN THE SYSTEM COMES INTO CONTACT WITH THE EYES.

7 Release inlet and outlet petrol pipe union nuts at heat exchanger. Plug inlet petrol pipe to prevent fuel syphon.
8 Release clips securing air conditioning suction pipe to engine. Remove screws and lay heat exchanger at left hand side of engine compartment.

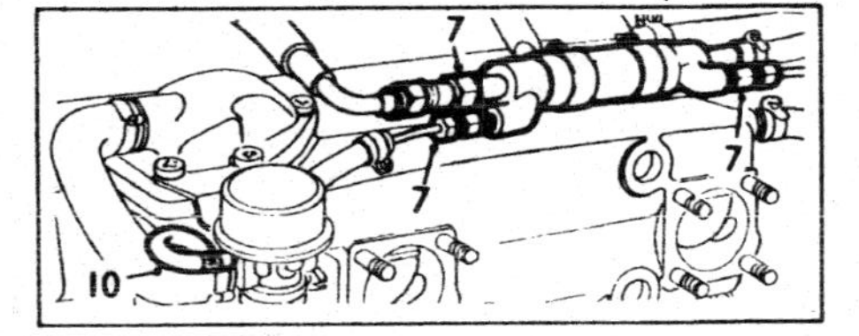

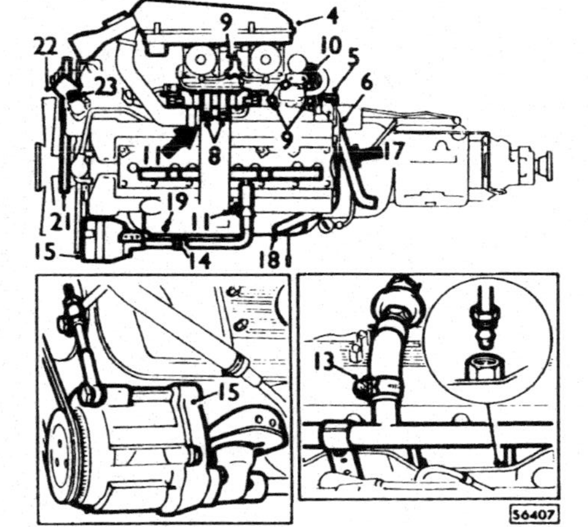

Cars fitted with emission control to Federal specification only

9 Release union nut at E.G.R. system 'Y' piece – fixed orifice system only. Remove four screws and carefully separate cover from secondary throttle housing. Pull vacuum pipe from valve – variable orifice E.G.R. system only.
10 Pull anti run-on system vacuum pipe 'H' from tee piece at gulp valve.
11 Remove two cross head screws and detach air duct – **all emission control cars.**
12 Pull float chamber and carburetter breather cross-over pipes from rubber connector pieces and plastic clips, and lay them at left hand side of engine compartment.
13 Slacken pipe clip at air injection rail check valve.
14 Remove nut, bolt and spacer securing air supply pipe clip, and pull pipe from air pump and air rail.
15 Remove air pump.
16 Remove air pump bracket.
17 Remove setscrew at rear of cylinder block securing E.G.R. system supply pipe.
18 Release union nut securing E.G.R. system pipe to exhaust manifold adaptor. Restrain adaptor while releasing union nut; lay E.G.R. pipe across bell housing. Unscrew adaptor.
19 Remove setscrew and lift heat shield from exhaust manifolds – **all emission control cars.**
20 Remove three nuts and bolts securing heat shield to exhaust manifold – left hand drive cars only.

All Cars

21 Remove steering pump drive belt – 57.20.02, and swing pump away from engine.
22 Release pipe clip and pull radiator top hose from header tank.
23 Release pipe clips and pull remote header and radiator bleed pipes from header tank.
24 Release pipe clip to free coolant hose to water pump.
25 Release pipe clip and free secondary throttle housing heater pipe – emission control cars to Federal specification only.
26 Note connections and pull all vacuum pipes and wires from beneath inlet manifold.
27 Remove sixteen nuts securing exhaust manifolds to cylinder head. Draw manifolds from cylinder head and remove gaskets.
28 Disconnect two camshaft oil pipes at rear of cylinder head.

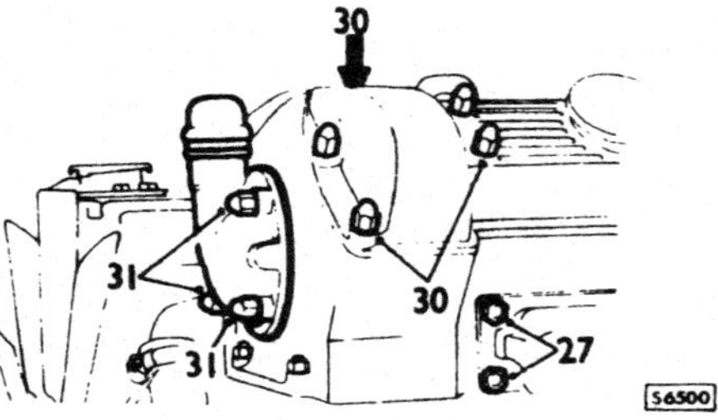

29 Remove distributor cap, H.T. leads and spark plugs.
30 Remove dome nuts and countersunk screws securing camshaft covers and lift off covers.
31 Remove nuts securing breather housing to front of cylinder head and withdraw housing.
32 Slacken locknut on idler sprocket shaft.

33 Use Service tool JD2B to slacken top timing chain tension by pressing on to serrated adjuster plate and rotating tool in a clockwise direction.
34 Knock down tabs and remove two camshaft sprocket retaining bolts from each camshaft.
35 Rotate engine until remaining two bolts are accessible.
36 Remove remaining two bolts.

CAUTION: The engine MUST NOT be rotated while camshaft sprockets are disconnected and cylinder head is in place.

37 Draw sprockets from camshafts and slide sprockets up support brackets. **NOTE**: Mark 'fit' holes in adjuster plates.
38 Remove fourteen cylinder head dome nuts and six nuts securing front of cylinder head, working out from centre. Recover two lifting brackets.

39 Carefully lift cylinder head assembly from cylinder block.
NOTE: As the valves in the fully open position protrude below the cylinder head joint face, the cylinder head **MUST NOT** be placed joint face downwards directly on a flat surface; support the cylinder head on wooden blocks, one at each end.

40 Thoroughly clean joint faces of cylinder head and block.

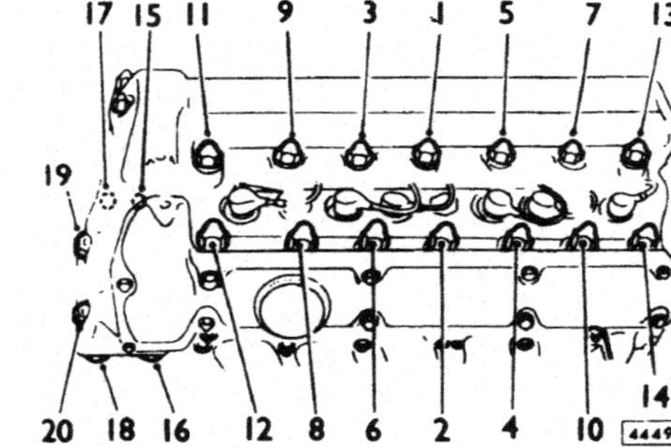

Refitting

41 Fit new gasket, dry, on cylinder block ensuring side marked 'TOP' is uppermost.

42 Rotate crankshaft to set No. 6 cylinder (front) to T.D.C. position, with distributor rotor arm pointing approximately forward along engine.

43 Rotate camshafts until timing gauge C.3993 can be located in slots in front flanges.
CAUTION: Ensure inlet and exhaust valves do not foul each other.

44 Lower cylinder head into position on cylinder block.

45 Fit sparking plug lead bracket and lifting brackets to appropriate cylinder head studs.

46 Place washers on cylinder head studs and fit fourteen large cylinder head dome nuts.

47 Fit six nuts and washers to secure forward end of cylinder head.

48 Tighten large nuts, in order shown, to torque of 54 lbs.ft. (7.5 kg.m.).

49 Fully tighten six small nuts.
CAUTION: Do not rotate engine or camshaft until camshaft sprockets have been connected.

50 Locate sprockets on camshaft flanges and ensure both holes in each flange are in alignment with 'fit' holes in adjuster plates.
NOTE: If necessary remove circlip, disengage serrations and re-position adjuster plate as necessary. Refit circlip.

51 Secure each adjuster plate to camshaft using two bolts and lockplates.

52 Rotate engine until remaining holes on each camshaft are accessible and fit bolts. Turn up tabs.

53 Tension timing chain by using Service tool JD2B rotated in an anti-clockwise direction.
NOTE: When correctly tensioned there should be slight flexibility on both outer sides of chain.

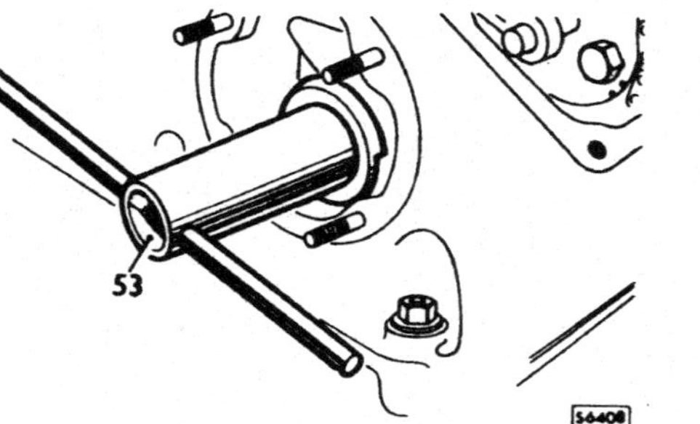

54 Securely tighten locknut.

55 Ensure No. 6 cylinder is at T.D.C. firing (with pointer opposite 'O' on timing scale) and recheck position of camshafts using gauge C.3993.

56 Use operations 1 to 32, as appropriate, in reverse order to complete reassembly.

57 Re-check ignition timing as appropriate.

58 Carry out an exhaust emission check – exhaust emission cars only.

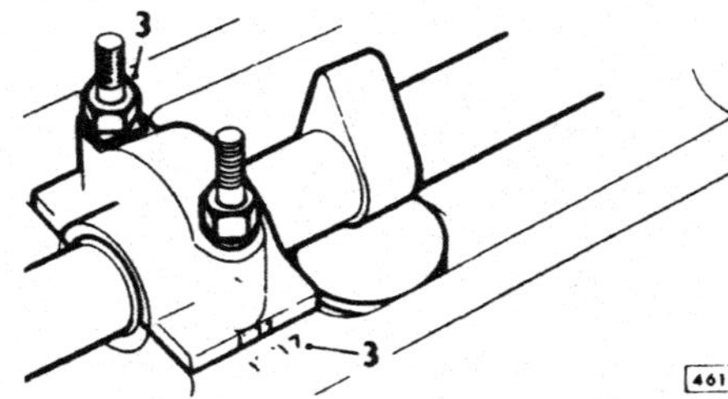

CYLINDER HEAD

Overhaul 12.29.19

Service Tool: Valve spring compressor JD.6118C. Valve timing gauge C.3993

1 Remove cylinder head 12.29.11.

Dismantling

2 Remove inlet manifold from cylinder head. Discard gasket and thoroughly clean mating faces taking great care not to damage castings.

3 Remove four bearing caps from each camshaft. Note mating marks on each bearing cap.

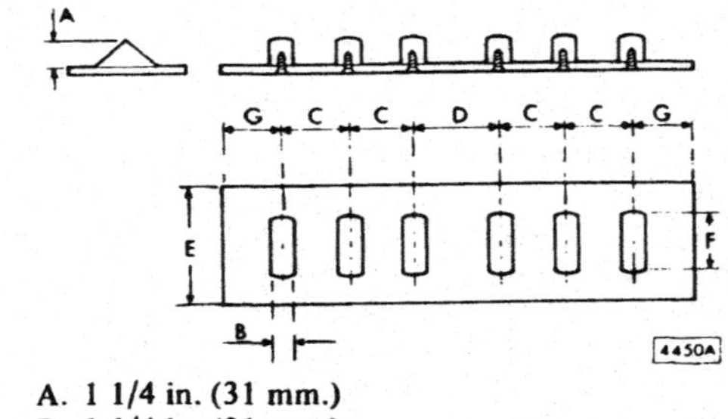

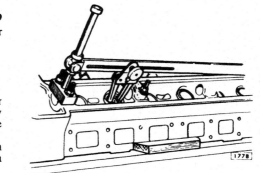

A. 1 1/4 in. (31 mm.)
B. 1 1/4 in. (31 mm.).
C. 3 25/32 in. (96,04 mm.)
D. 4 3/8 in. (111,1 mm.)
E. 6 in. (152 mm.)
F. 3 in. (76 mm.)
G. 8 in. (203 mm.)

4 Withdraw tappets and lay out in order to ensure correct replacement.

5 Remove adjusting pads from each valve stem, and place with their respective tappets.

6 Make up wooden block to dimensions given and use to support valves.

7 Compress valve spring using service tool JD.6118C and extract cotters.

8 Remove collars, valve springs and spring seats. Repeat for remaining five cylinders.
NOTE:
(a) Remove oil seal from stem of inlet valves before removing spring seat.
(b) Valves are numbered and must be replaced in original locations No. 1 cylinder being at flywheel end of engine.

9 Remove all traces of carbon from combustion chambers, and deposits from induction and exhaust ports. Great care must be taken to avoid damaging head, use worn emery cloth and paraffin only.

Valve guides

10 Check clearance between valve guide and stem; this should be .001 in. to .004 in. (,025 mm. to ,10mm.). When removing a worn guide, care must be taken to identify each individual guide to its bore in the cylinder head.
Replacement guides are available in the three following sizes, and have identification grooves machined in the shank as noted below.
NOTE: Valve guides, when fitted during initial engine assembly, are to the following dimensions and may be fitted in mixed form.

Standard (No identification)
.501 in. to .502 in. (12,73 mm. to 12,75 mm.).
1st Oversize (One machined groove)
.503 in. to .504 in. (12,78 mm. to 12,80 mm.).
2nd Oversize (Two machined grooves)
.506 in. to .507 in. (12,85 mm. to 12,88 mm.).
3rd Oversize (Three machined grooves)
.511 in. to .512 in. (12,98mm. to 13,00 mm.).

When new guides are to be fitted, they should always be one size larger than the old guide. Standard and 1st Oversize valve guides may be replaced in the following manner:

11 Immerse head in boiling water for 30 minutes.
12 Using a piloted drift, drive the guide out of head from combustion chamber end.
13 Coat new valve guide with graphite grease and refit circlip.
14 Heat cylinder head.
15 Using a piloted drift, drive in guide from top until circlip is seated in groove.
CAUTION: **This procedure is not recommended owing to the difficulty of establishing truth with the centre of the valve seat; it should not be attempted unless comprehensive machine shop facilities are available. A replacement cylinder head should be considered as an alternative.**
NOTE: If a 2nd Oversize guide is to be replaced the cylinder head bore must be reamed to the following dimension.
.510 in. + .0005 in. – .0002 in.
(12,95 mm. + ,012 mm. – ,005 mm.).

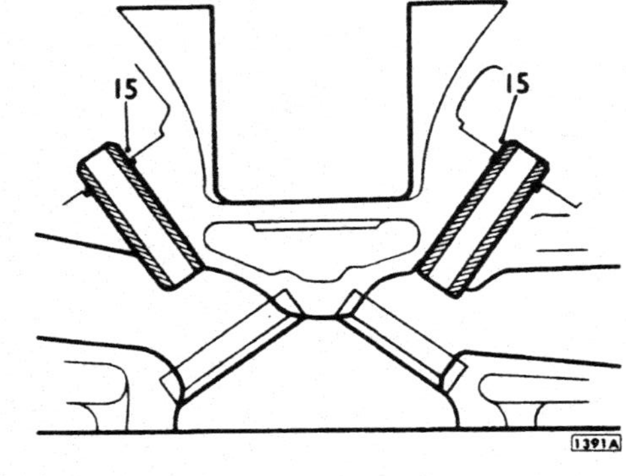

Valve seats

Examine valve seats for pitting or excess wear. If seats are damaged past reclamation by approved refacing procedures, the seat inserts may be replaced.
CAUTION: **This procedure is not recommended owing to the difficulty of removing old valve seat and risk of damage to cylinder head; it should not be attempted unless comprehensive machine shop facilities are available. A replacement cylinder head should be considered as an alternative.**

17 Remove inserts by machining, leaving approximately .010 in. (,025 mm.) of metal which can easily be removed by hand without damaging cylinder head.
18 Measure diameter of insert recess in cylinder head.
19 Grind down outside diameter of new insert to a dimension .003 in. (,08 mm.) larger than insert recess.
20 Heat cylinder head for half an hour from cold at a temperature of 150 deg. C. (300 deg. F).
21 Fit insert ensuring that it beds evenly in the recess.

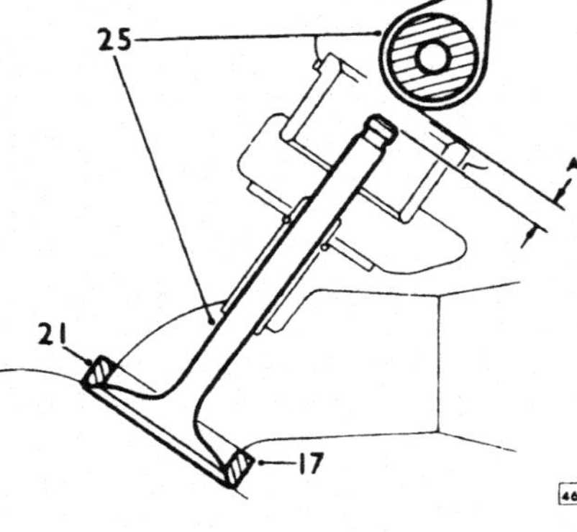

22 Renew or reface valves as necessary. Correct valve seat angles are:

Inlet	Exhaust
44½ deg.	44½ deg.

Valves

23 Check valve stems for distortion or wear, renew valves with stems worn in excess of .003 in. (,08 mm.) see group 05.
24 Using a suitable suction tool, grind valves into their respective seats.
25 If new valve inserts have been fitted, the clearance 'A' between valve stem and cam must be checked; this should be .320 in. (8,13 mm.) plus the valve clearance. The dimension must be taken between valve stem and back of cam. Should this dimension not be obtained, metal must be ground from valve seat of insert.
NOTE: Only suitable grinding equipment should be used.

Tappet guides

26 Examine tappets and tappet guides for wear. The diametrical clearance between the tappet and tappet guide should be .0008 in. to .0019 in. (,02 mm. to ,05 mm.).
CAUTION: **The following procedure is not recommended owing to the difficulty of removing old tappet guide and risk of damage to cylinder head; it should not be attempted unless comprehensive machine shop facilities are available. A replacement cylinder head should be considered as an alternative.**

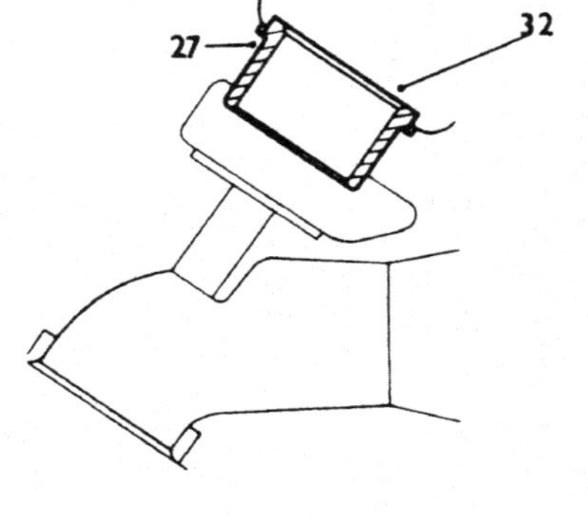

27 Remove old tappet guide by boring out until guide collapses. Take great care not to damage guide bore in cylinder head.
28 Carefully measure diameter of tappet guide bore at room temperature 68 deg. F. (20 deg. C.).
29 Grind down outside diameter of replacement tappet guide to a dimension .003 in. (,08 mm.) larger than tappet guide bore diameter measured in operation 28.
30 Grind same amount from 'lead-in' at bottom of tappet guide. The reduction in diameter from the adjacent diameter should be .0032 in. to .0057 in. (,08 mm. to ,14 mm.).
31 Heat cylinder head in oven for half an hour from cold at a temperature of 300 deg. F. (150 deg. C.).
32 Fit tappet guide, ensuring that lip at top of guide beds evenly in recess in top of cylinder head.
33 Allow cylinder head to cool then ream tappet guide bore to diameter of:
1,375 in. + .0007 in. – .0000 in.
(34,925 mm. + ,018 mm. – ,000 mm.).
It is essential that, when reamed, tappet guide bore is concentric with valve guide bore.

Adjusting pads
34 Examine adjusting pads for signs of indentation.
35 Renew, if necessary, with appropriate size when making valve clearances adjustment on re-assembly.

Valve springs
36 Test valve springs for pressure either by checking against Valve spring data – 05 or checking against a new spring.

Re-assembling
37 Examine valves for pitting, burning or distortion, and reface or renew valves as necessary. Also reface valve seats in cylinder head and grind valves to their respective seats using a suction valve tool. When refacing valves or seat inserts do not remove more metal than is necessary to clean up facings.
38 Refit valves in order removed and place cylinder head on the wooden blocks.
39 Refit valve spring seats, refit inlet valve guide oil seals.
40 Refit springs and collars.
41 Compress springs using Service tool JD.6118C and fit split cotters. Tap valve stems to ensure cotters seated.
42 Fit adjusting pads and tappets to their respective valves.
CAUTION: Camshafts must not be rotated independently.

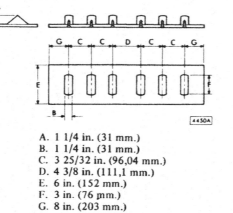

A. 1 1/4 in. (31 mm.)
B. 1 1/4 in. (31 mm.)
C. 3 25/32 in. (96,04 mm.)
D. 4 3/8 in. (111,1 mm.)
E. 6 in. (152 mm.)
F. 3 in. (76 mm.)
G. 8 in. (203 mm.)

43 Fit camshaft shell bearings, locate one camshaft and secure bearing cap nuts working from centre outwards. Tighten nuts to torque of 9 lb.ft. (1,24 kg.m.).
44 Check tappet adjustment.
45 Remove camshaft fitted in operation 43 and fit remaining camshaft.
46 Check tappet adjustment.
47 Fit adjustment pads as required and fit camshafts, lining each up using Service Tool C.3993.

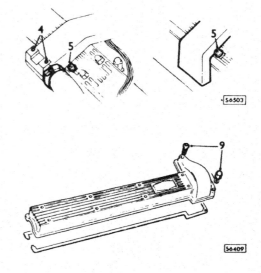

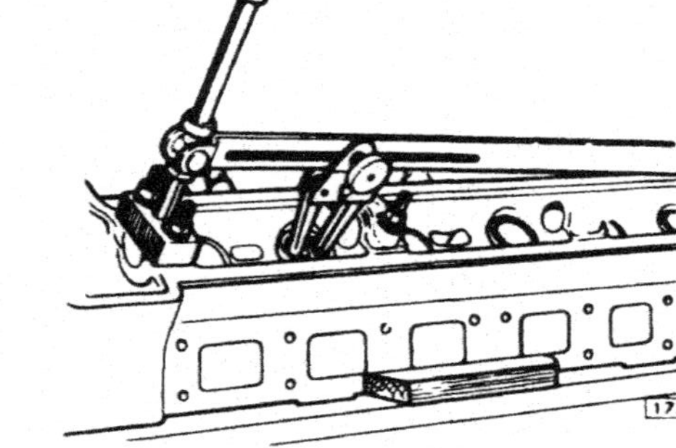

CAMSHAFT COVER

Remove and refit 12.29.42

Removing
1 Disconnect battery – 86.15.20.
2 Remove distributor cap – right hand cover only.

Cars fitted with air conditioning only

WARNING: ON NO ACCOUNT MUST ANY PORTION OF THE AIR CONDITIONING SYSTEM BE DISCONNECTED BY ANYONE OTHER THAN A QUALIFIED REFRIGERATION ENGINEER. BLINDNESS CAN RESULT IF THE GAS CONTAINED WITHIN THE SYSTEM COMES INTO CONTACT WITH THE EYES.

3 Release inlet and outlet petrol pipe union nuts at heat exchanger. Plug inlet petrol pipe to prevent fuel syphon.
4 Release clips securing air conditioning suction pipe to engine. Remove screws and lay heat exchanger at left hand side of engine compartment.

Cars fitted with emission control only
5 Remove two crosshead screws and detach air duct.
6 Pull float chamber and carburetter breather cross-over pipes from rubber connector pieces and plastic clips, and lay them at left hand side of engine compartment – cars to Federal specification only.
7 Pull carburetter balance and engine breather pipe from clips and engine breather filter housing.
8 Release clips and pull air injection supply pipe from valve – cars to Federal specification only – left hand cover only.

All cars
9 Remove dome headed nuts and two setscrews securing camshaft covers.

Refitting
Reverse operations 1 to 9 inclusive, using new gaskets and rear seals.

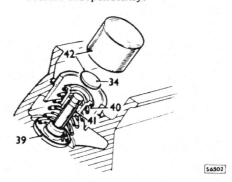

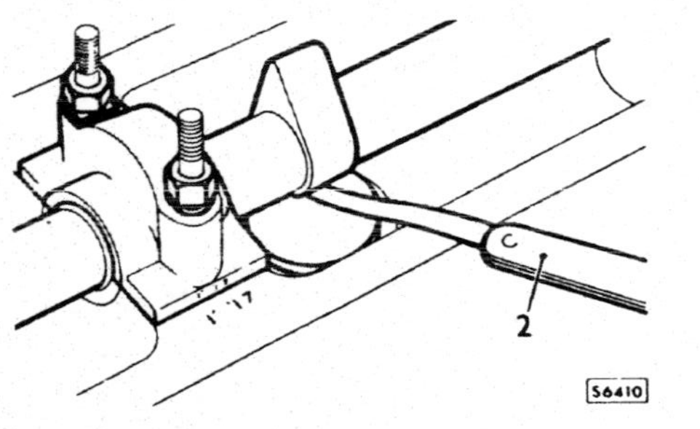

TAPPETS

Adjust 12.29.48

Service Tool: Valve timing gauge C.3993.

CAUTION: If checking valve clearances with cylinder head removed from engine, the camshafts must be fitted and checked one at a time. If one camshaft is rotated while the other is in position fouling is likely between inlet and exhaust valves.

1 If necessary remove camshaft covers.
2 Rotate camshafts and record clearance between back of each cam in turn, and the respective tappet. Clearance to be as detailed in group 05. If adjustment necessary, proceed with operations 2 to 12 inclusive, as appropriate.
3 If cylinder head is on engine, before removing last securing bolt, rotate engine until valve timing gauge C.3993 can be located in front flange of each camshaft.

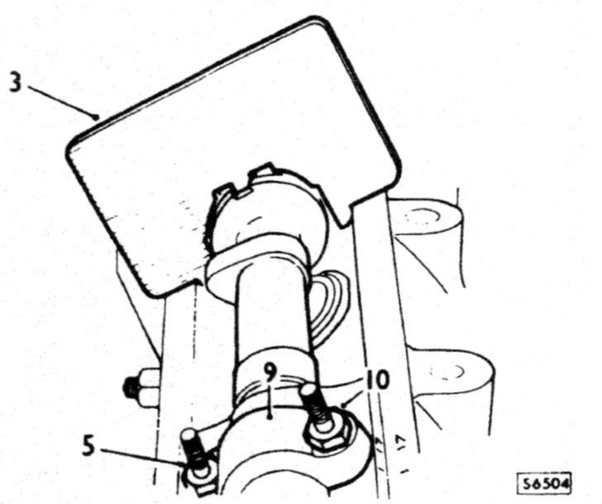

4 If necessary, disconnect sprockets from camshafts.
CAUTION: Do not rotate engine while camshaft sprockets are disconnected.
5 Remove camshaft bearing caps and lift camshaft clear.
6 Remove each tappet taking careful note of location. Remove and check adjusting pad.
NOTE: Subtract appropriate valve clearance from dimension obtained in operation 2, and select suitable adjusting pads **which equal this new dimension.** Adjusting pads are available rising in .001 in. (.03 mm.) sizes from .085 in. to .110 in. (2.16 mm. to 2.79 mm.) and are etched on the surface with letter 'A' to 'Z' each letter indicating an increase in size of .001 in. (.03 mm.).
7 Fit selected adjusting pads.
8 Fit tappets.
9 Fit camshaft, bearing caps and nuts.
NOTE: If cylinder head on engine, locate camshaft using gauge C.3993 before tightening bearing cap nuts.
10 Tighten bearing cap nuts to torque of 9 lb.ft. (1,2 kg.m.).
11 Connect camshaft sprockets.
12 If necessary fit camshaft covers and complete assembly.

ENGINE AND GEARBOX ASSEMBLY

Remove and refit 12.37.01

Service tool: Engine support tool MS.53(A)

Removing
1 Remove bonnet – 76.16.01.
2 Remove battery – 86.15.01.

Cars fitted with air conditioning only
3 Depressurise air conditioning system – 82.30.05.
4 Unclip air conditioning suction and pressure hoses.
NOTE: Ensure suitable clean, dry male and female sealing plugs are to hand.
5 Remove setscrew and spring washer securing shipping plate to rear of air conditioning compressor and remove suction and pressure unions. IMMEDIATELY seal all connection orifices using clean dry plugs.
6 Remove inlet and outlet petrol pipes at heat exchanger. Plug inlet pipe to prevent siphon.
7 Remove inlet pipe from clips, draw clear of engine and secure to valance.
8 Remove two cross head screws securing heat exchanger.
9 Secure compressor suction and delivery hoses back from engine.
10 Beneath right hand wheel arch, remove two setscrews securing receiver/drier clip, and secure receiver/drier and delivery hose back from engine.

All cars
11 Remove wing valance stays.
12 Remove air cleaner – 19.10.01.
13 Remove coolant radiator – **26.40.01**.
14 Disconnect coolant pipes to expansion tank and radiator at engine end. Note locations to assist replacement.
15 Reach in on either side of engine and remove nut, plain and spring washers securing engine mounting to engine bracket.
16 Extract fluid from power assisted steering pump reservoir.
17 Disconnect feed and return pipes from power assisted steering pump.

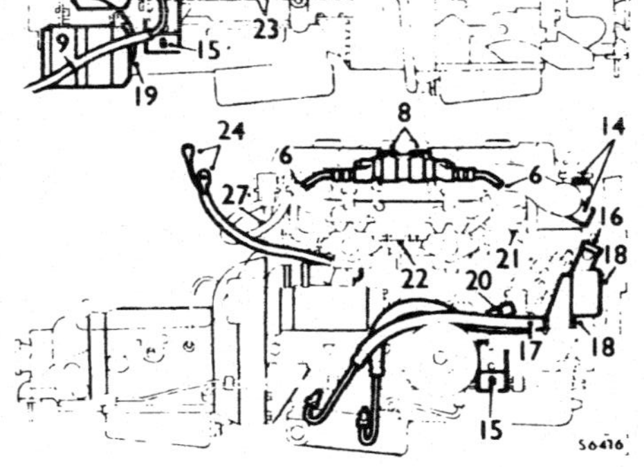

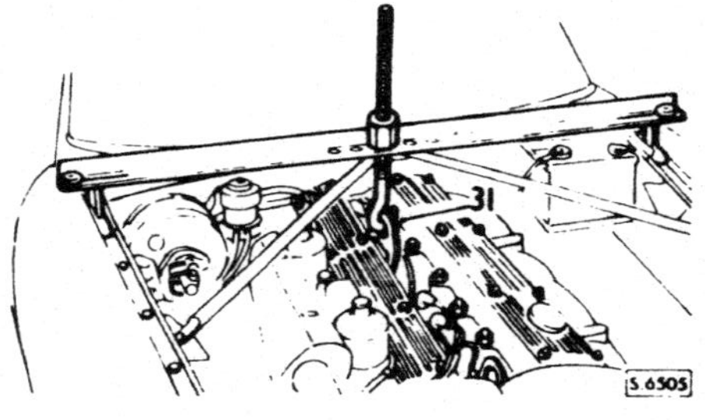

18 Slacken pump mounting bolts, and push pump as close to engine as possible.
19 Pull connectors from rear of alternator.
20 Separate connector plug of engine harness.
21 Disconnect brake vacuum pipe at manifold, and secure back from engine.
22 Release pipe clip and pull heater/air conditioning operating vacuum pipe from non-return valves. Secure back from engine.
23 Remove eight nuts securing exhaust pipes to exhaust manifolds.
24 Remove starter motor main feed from terminal post, and pull solenoid cable from lucar connector.

25 Remove two screws securing steering universal joint heat shield – right hand drive cars only.
26 Remove heater matrix hoses at bulkhead unions.
27 Disconnect inner and outer throttle cables and secure back from engine.
28 Disconnect choke cables from carburetters and secure back from engine. Disconnect hoses from carbon canister pipes – cars to Federal emission control specification only.
29 Remove banjo bolt at clutch master cylinder reservoir, release hose from clip and secure across engine – left hand drive manual transmission cars only.
30 Remove nuts and washers securing clutch slave cylinder. Draw slave cylinder from push rod and secure to side of transmission tunnel – right hand drive manual transmission cars only.
31 Locate tool MS53(A) across rear engine lifting eye and fit hook to support engine.
NOTE: If car fitted with manual transmission, position on hoist or on blocks to increase ground clearance by approximately 1 foot (30 cm.).
32 Remove overdrive switch from gear lever knob and remove gear lever knob from lever – cars fitted with manual transmission only.
33 Remove nut at centre of rear gearbox mounting. Remove two nuts and washers securing strengthening bracket – cars fitted with Model 65 gearbox only.
34 Remove fastenings securing heatshield.
35 Locate jack to support mounting plate and release four setscrews and washers.
36 Lower jack and remove mounting plate. Recover spring washers and rubber rings.

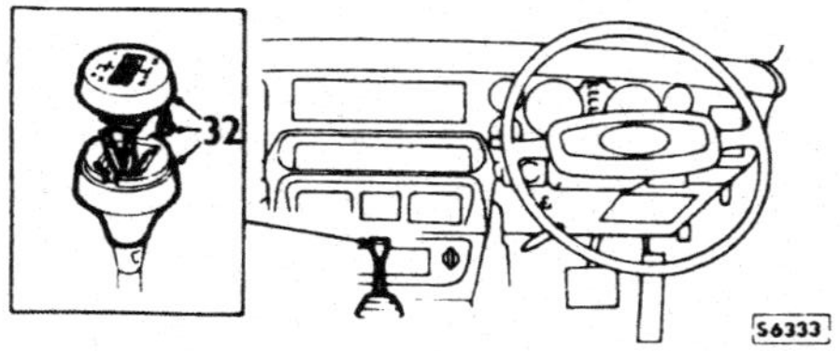

32

S6333

37 Remove special nuts securing propeller shaft to output flange.
38 Separate gearbox harness at snap connectors – cars fitted with manual transmission only.
39 On transmission unit selector lever, remove nut to release ball peg on inner selector cable – cars fitted with automatic transmission only.
40 Remove setscrew and spring washer securing outer selector cable abutment clamp – cars fitted with automatic transmission only.
41 Disconnect speedometer cable at gearbox.
42 From front of car, position trolley jack to support assembly beneath gearbox/transmission unit oil sump.
43 Support engine on lifting tackle located in rear lifting eye.
44 Remove support tool MS.53(A).

Cars fitted with manual transmission only
45 Carefully lower rear of engine and raise front – taking great care not to damage air conditioning expansion valve (if fitted) – until gear lever is clear of transmission tunnel draught excluders.

All cars
46 Withdraw engine forwards and upwards.

Refitting
47 Fit insulating material across transmission.

Cars fitted with manual transmission only
48 Ensure gearbox switches correctly connected.
49 Position car on hoist or on blocks to increase ground clearance by approximately 1 foot (30 cm.).

All cars
50 From front of car, position trolley jack beneath engine compartment.
51 Lift engine with tackle located in rear lifting eye.
52 Lower engine into engine compartment to locate transmission unit sump on trolley jack.

Cars fitted with manual transmission only
53 Manoeuvre engine rearwards to locate gear lever below transmission tunnel draught excluder.
54 Using lifting tackle and trolley jack, raise assembly to pass gear lever up into car.

All cars
55 Locate engine on front mountings and raise rear to approximately fitted position.
56 Position tool MS.53(A) across rear engine lifting eye, and fit hook to take weight of engine.
57 Remove lifting tackle and trolley jack.
58 Fit nuts and spring washers to secure engine to front mountings.
59 Connect speedometer drive cable.
60 Fit inner and outer transmission selector cable to lever and abutment, in that order.
61 Fit gearbox harness to snap connectors – cars fitted with manual transmission only.
62 Secure propeller shaft to output flange.
63 Position rubber rings, washers and spring into rear mounting plate and raise into position. Secure using setscrews, special washers and spacers.
64 Remove tool MS.53(A) from engine lifting eye.
65 Fit nut and washers to rear mounting centre bolt. Refit strengthening bracket – cars fitted with Model 65 gearbox only.
66 Re-locate and secure heat shield.
67 Refit clutch hydraulic hose on slave cylinder – cars fitted with manual transmission only.
68 Reconnect choke cables and carbon canister hoses – emission control cars to Federal specification only.
69 Reconnect throttle cables.
70 Fit heater hoses to matrix at bulkhead unions.
71 Fit starter motor main feed to connector post, and fit solenoid cables.
72 Secure exhaust pipes to exhaust manifolds using eight special nuts.
73 Fit steering column universal joint shield – right hand drive cars only.
74 Fit brake and air conditioning/heater system vacuum pipes beneath manifold.

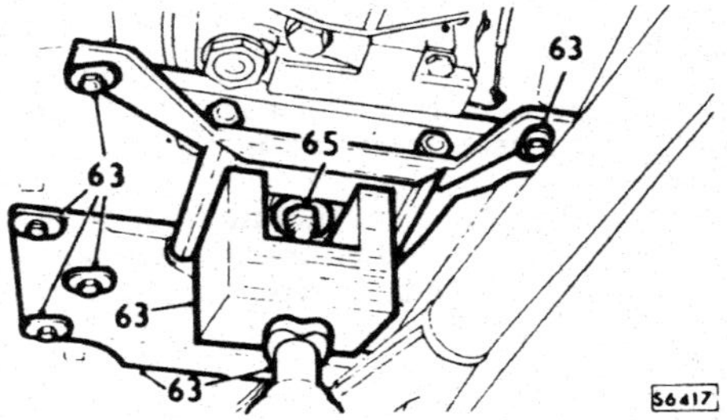

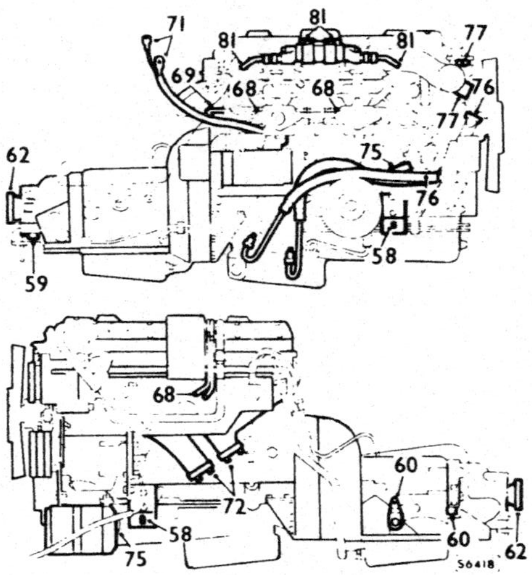

63 63 65 63 63 63

S6417

71 81 81 81 77 69 68 68 76 77 75 62 76 59 58

68 60 72 58 60 75 62

S6418

75 Fit connectors to rear of alternator and connect engine harness.
76 Reconnect feed and return pipes to power assisted steering pump. **Top up pump reservoir using specified fluid.**
77 Fit coolant radiator and connect pipes between expansion tank, engine header tank and radiator.

Cars fitted with air conditioning only
78 Fit receiver/drier and locate pipes.

All Cars
79 Fit air cleaner.
80 Fit wing valance stays.

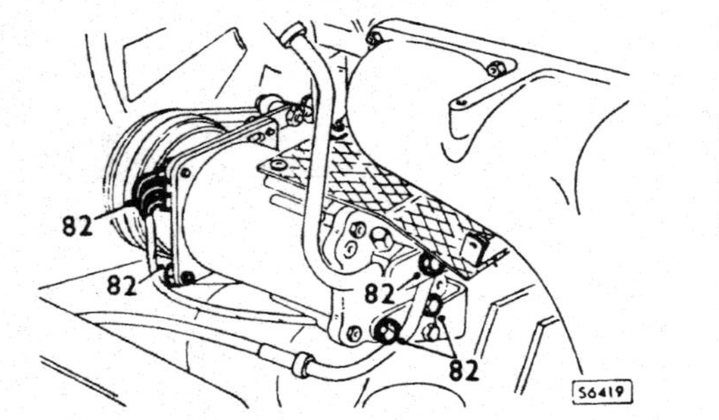

Cars fitted with air conditioning only
81 Locate and secure heat exchanger, connect petrol pipe.
82 Locate suction and pressure unions at compressor and connect compressor clutch cables and earth wire.
83 Clip all air conditioning hoses.

All Cars
84 Fit and connect battery.
85 Fill cooling system.

Cars fitted with air conditioning only
86 Charge air conditioning system – 82.30.08.

All Cars
87 Adjust throttle cable to fit without moving throttle linkage from stop.
88 Adjust engine fast idle speed – if manual choke fitted – 19.15.02.
89 Adjust kickdown cable – 44.30.02 – cars fitted with Model 65 automatic transmission only.
90 Adjust kickdown switch – 44.30.12 – cars fitted with Model 12 automatic transmission only.
91 Bleed clutch hydraulic system – cars fitted with manual transmission only – 33.15.07.
92 Bleed power assisted steering system by turning steering from lock to lock with engine running.
Check fluid and top up if necessary.
93 Fit bonnet.
94 If components referred to in Emission Control Section 17, have been disturbed, carry out the relevant emission control checks.

ENGINE

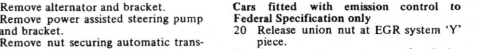

Dismantle and reassemble 12.41.05

Service tools: Oil seal pre-sizing tool JD.17B. Timing chain adjuster tool JD.2B. Piston ring compressor 38U3. Valve timing gauge C.3993.

1 Drain engine oil.
2 Remove torque converter – cars fitted with automatic transmission only – 44.17.07.
3 Remove clutch assembly – cars fitted with manual transmission only – 33.10.01.

Dismantling
4 Remove distributor cap, pull vacuum pipe from capsule.
5 Remove ignition coil bracket from engine.
6 Note connection and remove engine cable harness.
7 Slacken clips on coolant pipes at front of engine.
8 Cut clip and pull automatic transmission vacuum reference pipe from manifold – cars fitted with Model 12 transmission only.
9 Remove two screws securing hot air duct.

Cars fitted with emission control to Federal specification only
10 Remove nut, bolt and washer securing air supply pipe to exhaust manifold heat shield.
11 Slacken clip at air rail and pull air supply pipe from air rail and pump.
12 Slacken air pump belt adjustment and trunnion nuts.
13 Remove bolt securing air pump adjustment link to air pump.
14 Remove three setscrews securing air pump bracket.

All Cars
15 Remove four plain nuts and spring washers securing fan and torquatrol unit to water pump pulley.
16 Remove air conditioning compressor and bracket – cars fitted with air conditioning only.

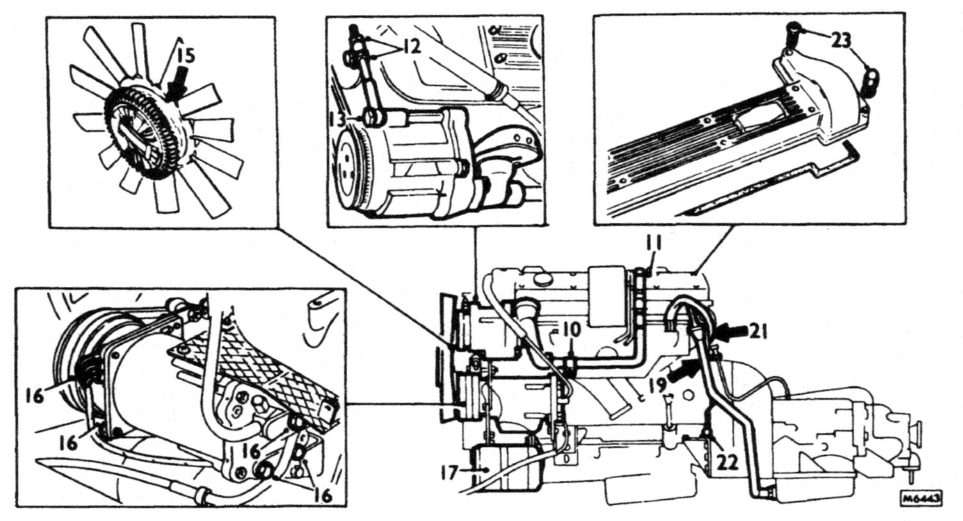
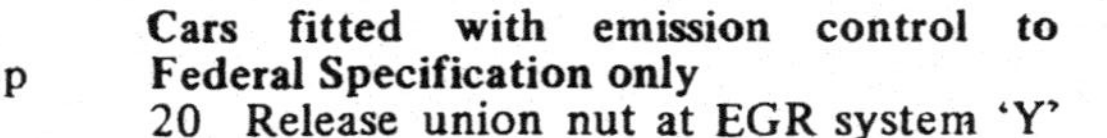

17 Remove alternator and bracket.
18 Remove power assisted steering pump and bracket.
19 Remove nut securing automatic transmission unit filler tube bracket – cars fitted with automatic transmission only.

Cars fitted with emission control to Federal Specification only
20 Release union nut at EGR system 'Y' piece.
21 Remove setscrew at rear of cylinder block securing EGR system supply pipe.

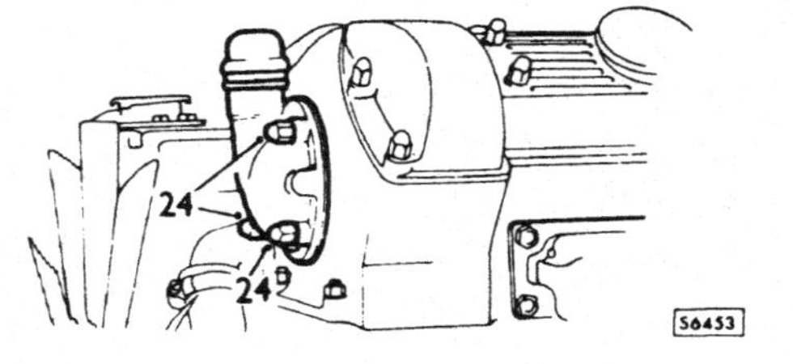

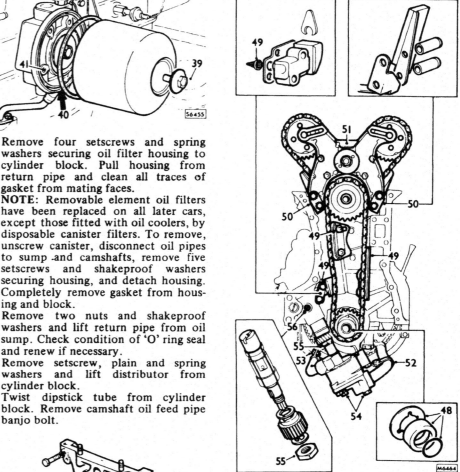

All Cars

22 Remove camshaft oil feed pipe banjo bolts.

23 Remove ten dome head nuts and two cross head screws securing each camshaft cover.

24 Remove dome head nuts securing crankcase breather.

25 Slacken locknut and use tool JD.2B to slacken top timing chain. Rotate tool in a clockwise direction.

26 Knock down tabs at camshaft sprockets and remove two bolts from each.

27 Rotate engine to gain access to remaining bolts and remove.

CAUTION: Engine MUST NOT be rotated with camshaft sprockets disconnected and cylinder head in place.

28 Draw sprockets from camshafts and slide sprockets up support brackets. **NOTE**: Mark 'fit' holes in adjuster plates.

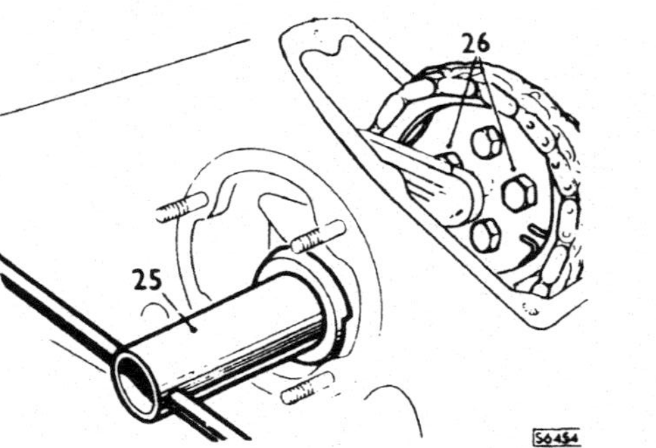

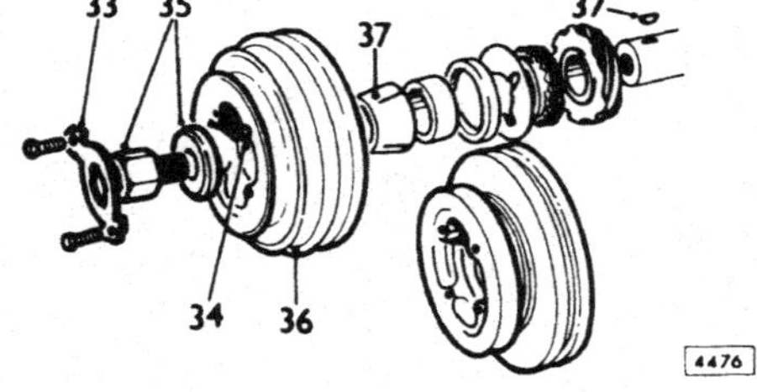

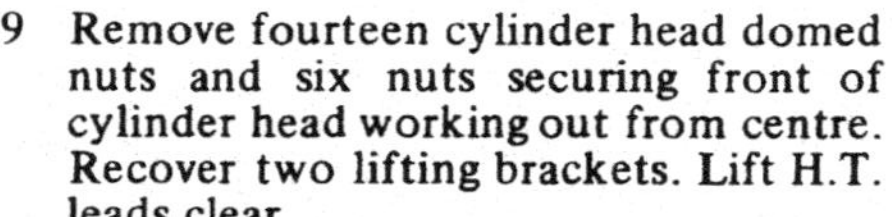

29 Remove fourteen cylinder head domed nuts and six nuts securing front of cylinder head working out from centre. Recover two lifting brackets. Lift H.T. leads clear.

30 Carefully lift cylinder head assembly from cylinder block. **NOTE**: As the valves in the fully open position protrude below the cylinder head joint face, the cylinder head **MUST NOT** be placed joint face downwards directly on a flat surface; support the cylinder head on wooden blocks, one at each end.

31 Remove and discard gasket, clean face of block.

32 On flywheel – manual transmission cars – or drive plate – automatic transmission cars – tap down lock plate tabs and remove bolts. Remove drive plate/flywheel from crankshaft using draw bolts through dowels.

33 Knock back locking tabs on crankshaft pulley bolts.

34 Remove four bolts securing pulley(s) to torsional damper. Recover locking ring.

35 Remove large bolt securing torsional damper and recover large plain washer.

36 Strike damper with hide mallet to break taper, and remove it from crankshaft.

37 Remove cone and extract Woodruff key from crankshaft.

38 Remove bolts, nuts and spring washers securing water pump. Remove water pump and clean all traces of gasket from mating faces.

39 Remove centre bolt securing oil filter bowl and remove element.

40 Slacken hose clips on oil return pipe to sump.

41 Remove four setscrews and spring washers securing oil filter housing to cylinder block. Pull housing from return pipe and clean all traces of gasket from mating faces.
NOTE: Removable element oil filters have been replaced on all later cars, except those fitted with oil coolers, by disposable canister filters. To remove, unscrew canister, disconnect oil pipes to sump and camshafts, remove five setscrews and shakeproof washers securing housing, and detach housing. Completely remove gasket from housing and block.

42 Remove two nuts and shakeproof washers and lift return pipe from oil sump. Check condition of 'O' ring seal and renew if necessary.

43 Remove setscrew, plain and spring washers and lift distributor from cylinder block.

44 Twist dipstick tube from cylinder block. Remove camshaft oil feed pipe banjo bolt.

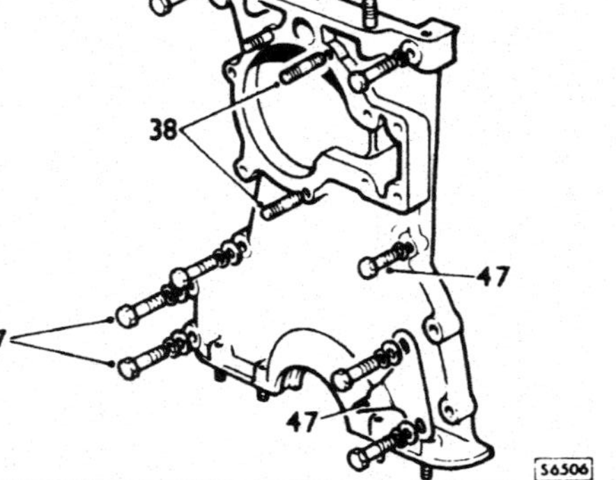

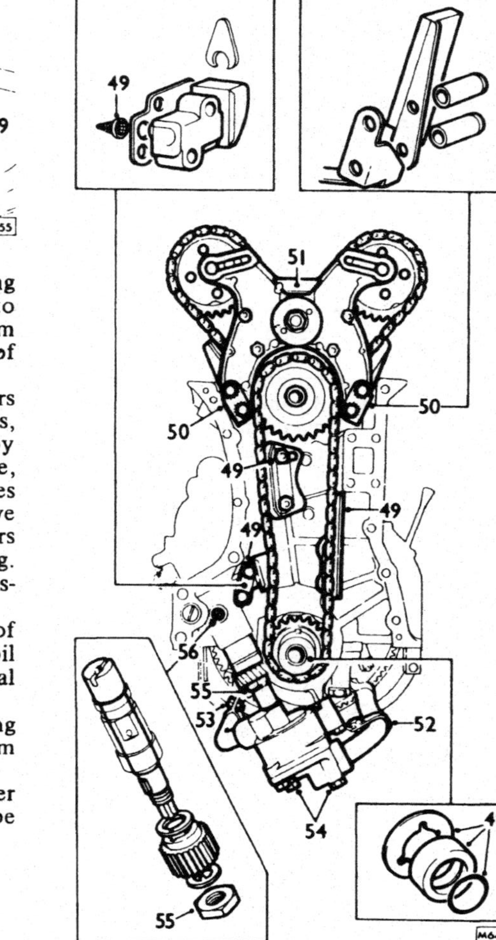

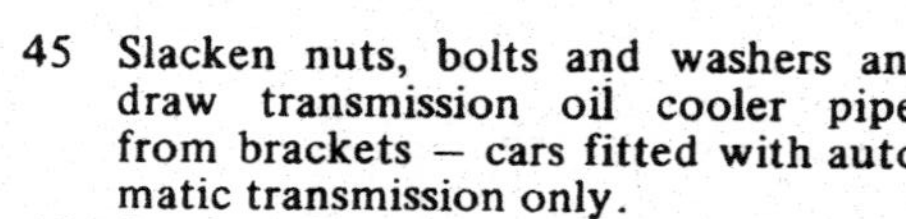

45 Slacken nuts, bolts and washers and draw transmission oil cooler pipes from brackets – cars fitted with automatic transmission only.

46 Remove four nuts and spring washers, and all setscrews and spring washers securing oil sump. Note location of cooler pipe brackets – cars fitted with automatic transmission only.

47 Remove setscrews and special washers and carefully prise timing chain cover from engine. Recover timing pointer. Remove and discard gasket and crankshaft oil seal.
48 Draw distance piece from crankshaft, check condition of 'O' ring seal and renew if necessary. Recover oil thrower.
49 Remove setscrews securing lower timing chain tensioner and chain guides. Recover conical filter behind tensioner.
50 Slacken four setscrews and shakeproof washers securing upper timing chain assembly. Do not remove setscrews at this stage.
51 Withdraw crankshaft timing gear and chain assembly carry out overhaul – 12.65.14 operations 7 to 24.
52 Remove self locking nuts, bolts and washers and pull suction pipe from oil sump.
53 Knock down tabs, remove self locking nut washer and bolt, and pull delivery pipe from oil pump.
54 Knock down tabs and remove three bolts securing oil pump. Draw oil pump clear and recover drive coupling.
55 Knock down tab washer and remove nut securing distributor drive gear. Draw gear and thrust washer from shaft; remove shaft and key.
56 If necessary, remove locating grub screw and drift distributor drive shaft bush downwards from cylinder block.
57 Remove special nuts securing connecting rod bearing caps; remove caps together with shell bearings. Remove big end bolts.

S6465

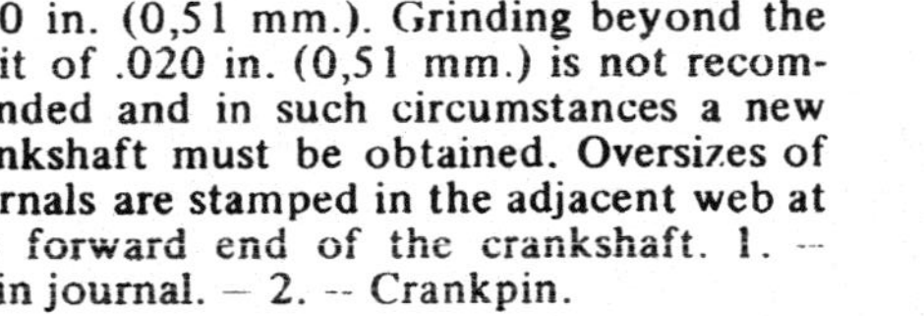

58 Pass pistons up through bores.
59 Remove crankshaft rear oil seal assembly cap screws. Remove and discard oil seal.
60 Remove main bearing bolts and washers, noting position of oil pipe brackets. Remove bearing caps.
61 Remove two Allen screws securing lower half of rear oil seal. Prise out seal.
62 Remove three Allen screws securing upper half of rear oil seal. Prise out seal.
63 Lift crankshaft from cylinder block. Recover bearing shells.

Inspection
CAUTION: Ensure that all components are scrupulously clean, blow out all oil galleries in crankcase, crankshaft and camshaft with clean dry compressed air.

(a) **Crankshaft** Regrinding of the crankshaft is generally recommended when wear or ovality in excess of .003 in. (,08 mm.) is found. Grinding may be undertaken in two steps of .010 in. (,25 mm.) to a limit of

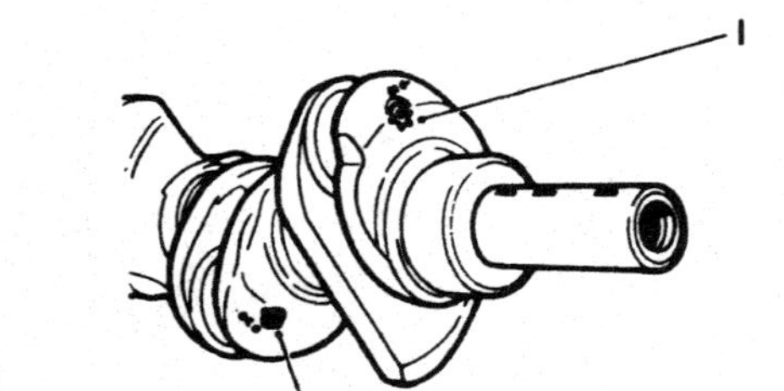
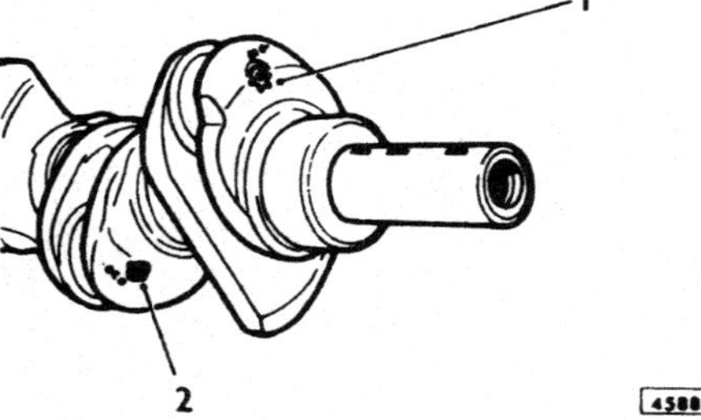

.020 in. (0,51 mm.). Grinding beyond the limit of .020 in. (0,51 mm.) is not recommended and in such circumstances a new crankshaft must be obtained. Oversizes of journals are stamped in the adjacent web at the forward end of the crankshaft. 1. – Main journal. – 2. – Crankpin.

(b) **Cylinder Block** Check the top face of the cylinder block for truth. Check that the main bearing caps have not been filed and that the bearing bores are in alignment. Should the caps show damage or the bearing housing misaligned, the caps must be re-machined and the bearing housings line bored.
Remove the cylinder head studs (1). Check area around the studs holes for flatness (2). Skim any raised areas flush with the joint face to ensure a perfectly flat surface. Reboring is normally recommended when the bore wear exceeds .006 in. (0,15 mm.). Reboring beyond the limit of .020 in. (0,51 mm.) is not recommended. Oversize pistons are available of this size, see group 05. If the bores will not clean out at .020 in. (0,51 mm.) new liners and standard size pistons should be fitted.

1 4 2 6 5 7
4642

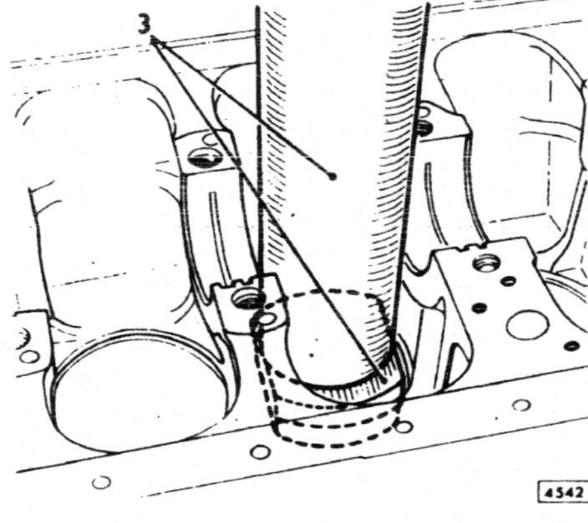

Press out the worn liners (3) from below, using the illustrated stepped block. Before fitting a new liner, lightly smear the cylinder walls with jointing compound to a point halfway down the bore and also smear the top outer surface of the liner (4). Press in the new liners flush with the top face of the cylinder block (5). Dry liners are fitted in engine manufacture to all 4.2 L blocks, but not normally to 3.4 L blocks.
Bore out and hone the liners to suit the grade of pistons to be fitted. (See piston grades below).
Following reboring, the blanking plugs in the main oil gallery (6) should be removed and the cylinder block oilways and crankcase interior thoroughly cleaned.
When dry, coat the interior of the crankcase with an oil and heat resisting paint.
Check all core plugs (7) fitted to the cylinder block and renew any which show signs of leaking.

(c) **Piston and connecting rod**

Piston Grades
The following selective grades are available in standard size pistons only. When ordering standard size pistons the identification letter of the selective grade should be clearly stated. Pistons are stamped on the crown with the letter identification and the cylinder block is also stamped on the top face adjacent to the bores.

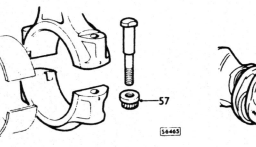

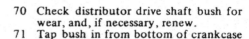

Grade Identification

Letter	For cylinder bore size 3.4 L	4.2 L
F	3.2673–3.2676 in (82,989 82,997 mm.)	3.6250–3.6253 in. (92,075–92,0826 mm.)
G	3.2677–3.2680 in. (83,000–83,007 mm.)	3.6254–3.6257 in. (92,0852–92,0928 mm.)
H	3.2681 3.2684 in. (83,010 83,017 mm.)	3.6258–3.6261 in. (92,0953–92,1029 mm.)

'S' pistons are 3.2675 to 3.2685 in. (82,995 to 83,020 mm.) dia. across bottom of skirt for 3.4 L engines and 3.6252 to 3.6262 in. (92,080 to 92,105 mm.) dia. across bottom of skirt for 4.2 L engines.

Measure exact dimension, at right angles to gudgeon pin, and hone bores to 0.0007 to 0.0013 in. (0,018 to 0,033 mm.) more than this measured dimension when fitting 'S' pistons.

When actually removing or refitting the gudgeon pin, the operation should be effected by immersing the piston, gudgeon pin and connecting rod small end in a bath of hot oil. When the piston and the small end have reached a sufficient temperature, 230 deg. F. (110 deg. C.) the gudgeon pin can be moved into position. Always use new circlips on assembly.

Gudgeon pins are graded by colour coding (red or green). For identification purposes the colour coding is also indicated on the gudgeon pin hole boss on the pistons.

Oversize Pistons

Oversize pistons are available in +.020 in. (0,51 mm.) only.

There are no selective grades in oversize pistons as grading is necessary purely for factory production methods. For reboring the cylinder see the instructions given above.

If connecting rods have been in use for a very high mileage, or if bearing failure has been experienced, it is desirable to renew the rod(s) owing to the possibility of fatigue.

The connecting rods fitted to an engine should not vary one with another by more than 2 drams (3.5 grammes). The alignment should be checked on an approved connecting rod alignment jig.

If alignment incorrect, an exchange rod should be fitted.

The big end bearings are of the precision shell type and under no circumstances should they be hand scraped or the bearing cap filed.

The small ends are fitted with steel-backed phosphor-bronze bushes which are a press fit in the connecting rod. After fitting, the bush should be bored, reamed and honed to a diameter of .875 in. to .8752 in. (22,225 to 22,23 mm.). Always use new connecting bolts and nuts at overhauls.

Before fitting new big end bearings, the crankpins must be examined for damage or the transfer of bearing metal.

When a new connecting rod is fitted, although the small end bush is reamed to the correct dimensions, it may be necessary to hone the bush to achieve the correct gudgeon pin fit.

(d) **General** Remove oil suction strainer in sump and clean thoroughly. Inspect all components for damage.

Reassembling

NOTE: Before refitting the crankshaft the rear oil seal must be offered up and sized correctly. Before fitting seal halves into housing grooves, brush a thin coat of red Hermetite into both grooves for 1 inch (25 mm) from joint face on opposite halves (from leading edge of seal on both).

64 Carefully tap new rear oil seal halves on side face to narrow section and press into grooves in seal housings. Use hammer handle to roll seal into housing until ends do not protrude, **DO**

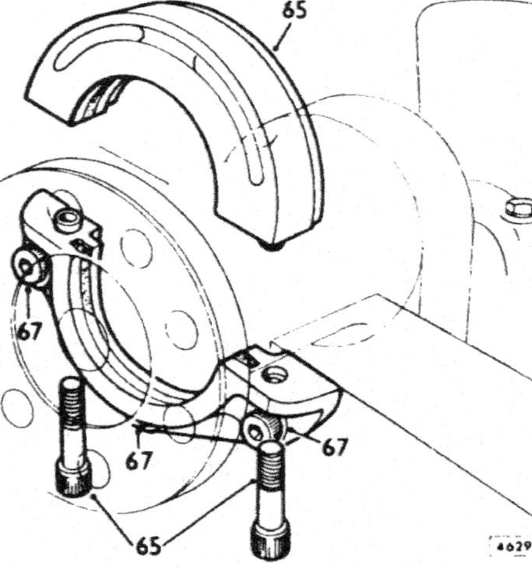

NOT cut ends of seal. Use knife or similar tool to ensure no loose strands are proud.

65 Assemble two halves of seal and secure using two socket head screws.

66 Fit rear main bearing cap without bearings and tighten bolts to torque of 72 lb.ft. (9,96 kg.m.).

67 Assemble rear oil seal housing to cylinder block using three socket head screws.

68 Smear small quantity of colloidal graphite around inside surface of oil seal and insert sizing tool JD.17B. Press tool inwards and rotate it until fully home. Withdraw tool by pulling and twisting at same time.

69 Remove and separate rear main bearing oil seal housing and remove rear main bearing cap.

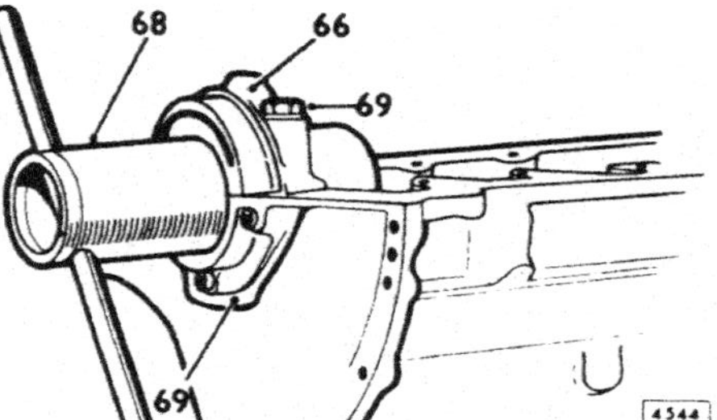

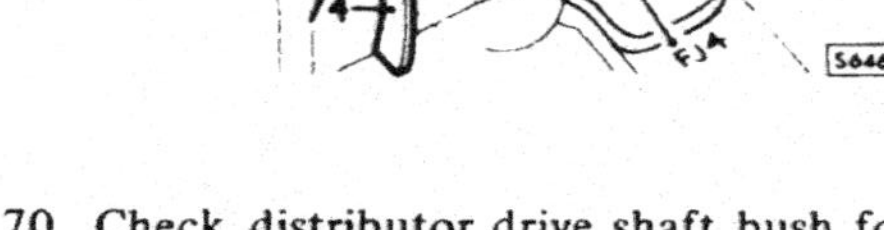

70 Check distributor drive shaft bush for wear, and, if necessary, renew.

71 Tap bush in from bottom of crankcase ensuring location holes line up.

72 Fit locating peg.

73 Fit main bearing shells in cylinder block, lay crankshaft in position and fit rear oil seal housing.

74 Fit new thrust washers to centre main bearing cap, white metal side outwards. Fit cap to cylinder block.

75 Check crankshaft endfloat, which should be .004 in. to .006 in. (,10 mm. to ,15 mm.).

NOTE: Thrust washers are supplied in two sizes, standard and .004 in. (,10 mm.) oversize and should be selected to bring the endfloat within required limits. Oversize washers are stamped .004 on the steel face.

76 Fit main bearing shells and caps with numbers on caps corresponding with numbers on cylinder block.

77 Fit main bearing bolts, locating oil pipe brackets as noted, and lock washer and tighten to torque of 72 lb.ft. (9,96 kg.m.).

78 Test crankshaft for free rotation.

79 Fit Woodruff key to inner slot and tap oil pump/distributor drive gear into position.

80 Fit pistons and connecting rods to cylinder bores and secure to crankshaft using special nuts. Check crankshaft for free rotation.

CAUTION: Ensure pistons fitted with 'FRONT' on each crown towards front of cylinder block.

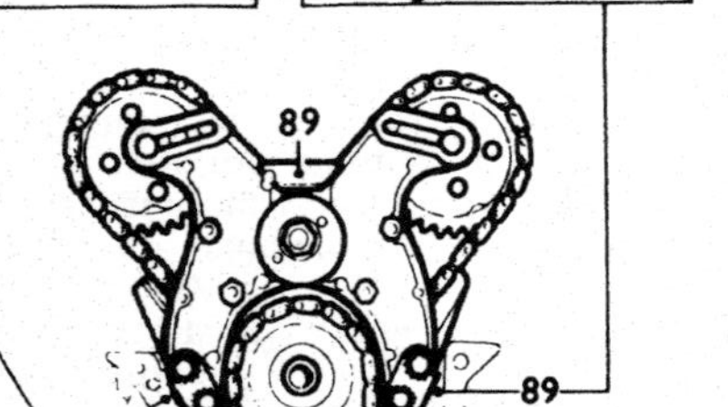
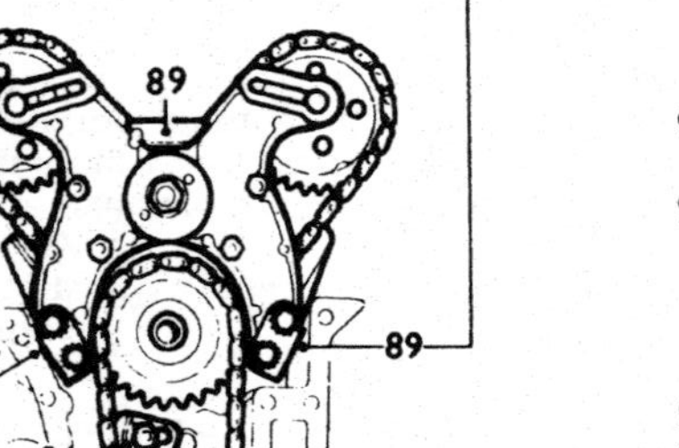

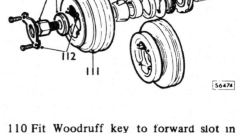

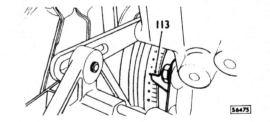

81 Turn crankshaft to accurately set pistons 1 and 6 to T.D.C.
82 Place distributor drive shaft in position with offset slot as shown.
83 Slightly withdraw shaft and fit Woodruff key, thrust washer and drive gear on shaft.
84 Maintaining correct slot position press shaft into gear ensuring that keyway engages correctly.
85 Fit pegged tab washer and secure with plain nut.
86 Check endfloat of shaft. Clearance should be .004 in. – .006 in. (,10 mm. – ,15 mm.). If no clearance exists renew drive gear. In emergency, thrust washer can be reduced.
87 Locate lower timing chain dampers and loosely fasten.
88 Fit Woodruff key to second slot.
89 Offer top and bottom timing chain assembly and chain sprockets into position and secure using four setscrews and locking washers.
90 Position damper in light contact with chain and secure.
91 Screw slipper of chain tensioner into body casting. Fit slip gauge or distance card supplied with new tensioner to maintain a clearance of .125 in. (3,17 mm.) between slipper and body.
92 Locate conical filter in cylinder block.
93 Secure chain tensioner to cylinder block using two setscrews and lockwashers. Fit shims as required to ensure slipper runs central on chain.
94 Set adjustable damper into light contact with chain and secure.
95 Remove slip gauge or distance card.
96 Locate coupling on oil pump and secure to front main bearing cap. Fit lockplates and pipe bracket.
97 Ensure 'O' ring seal fitted in oil pump suction and delivery ports.
98 Use new gasket and fit delivery pipe between oil pump and cylinder block. Secure pipe clip.
99 Fit oil suction pipe and secure pipe clips.
NOTE: Locate pipe on main bearing cap brackets so that intake end is on centre line of engine.
100 Fit oil thrower at timing chain sprocket.
101 Use new gaskets smeared with grease and fit timing cover. Fit ignition timing pointer.
102 Liberally coat new front oil seal with engine oil and locate in timing cover recess, open side inwards.
103 Check 'O' ring seal in distance piece and fit on to crankshaft.
104 Use new gaskets smeared with grease and fit oil sump. Locate transmission oil cooler pipe brackets – cars fitted with automatic transmission only.

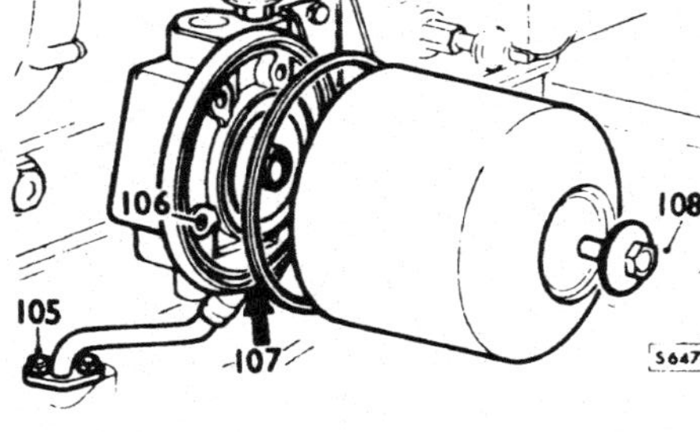
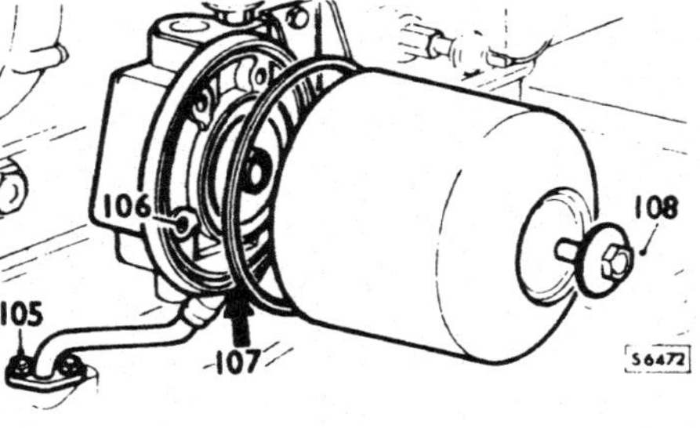
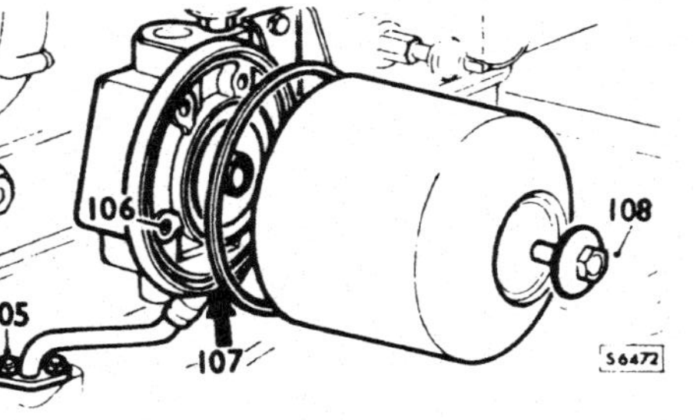

CAUTION: Ensure short setscrew fitted at front right hand corner.
105 Fit new 'O' ring seal on oil return pipe and secure to sump using two plain nuts and spring washers.
106 Using new gasket lightly smeared with grease, fit oil filter housing. Locate oil return pipe hose, oil feed pipe to camshafts and oil cooler hoses, if fitted. Secure housing to block using four setscrews and shakeproof washers.
107 Tighten hose clips and replace oil pressure transmitter and pedestal.
108 Fit oil filter element and cover, using new seals kit.
NOTE: Removable-element oil filters have been replaced on all later cars, except those fitted with oil coolers, by disposable canister filters. Refit filter housing using new gasket lightly smeared with grease, secure with five setscrews and shakeproof washers and reconnect oil pipes to sump and camshafts. Smear seal of new canister with engine oil and screw into place by hand only. DO NOT OVERTIGHTEN.
109 Fit water pump omitting lower right hand bolt if car to Federal emission control specification.

110 Fit Woodruff key to forward slot in crankshaft and fit damper cone.
111 Fit Woodruff key in damper cone and fit torsional damper. Secure with large bolt on plain washer.
112 Fit crankshaft pulley(s) and secure using four setscrews and lockplate.

113 Accurately set No. 1 and No. 6 pistons at T.D.C. and adjust position of ignition timing pointer.
114 Locate flywheel/drive plate on crankshaft and tap dowels through. Secure using ten bolts on new lockplate.

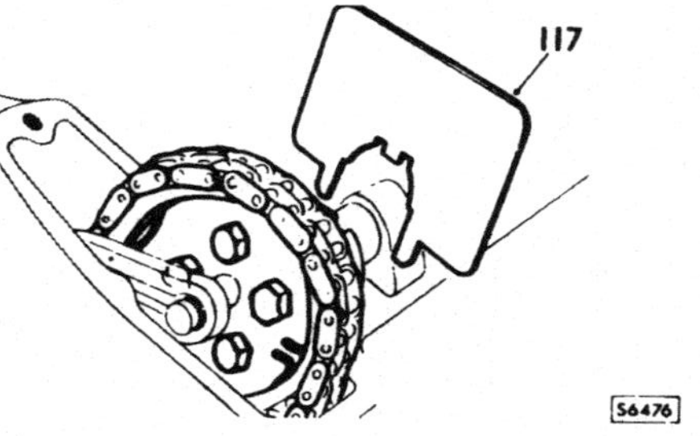

115 Fit new cylinder head gasket, dry, ensuring that side marked 'TOP' is uppermost.
116 Check No. 6 (front) cylinder at T.D.C.
117 Carefully rotate camshafts and set with gauge C.3993.
CAUTION: Ensure valves do not foul each other.
118 Fit cylinder head, complete with manifolds, to cylinder block.
CAUTION: Engine **MUST NOT** be rotated until camshaft sprockets are connected.
119 Fit spark plug lead carrier brackets and lifting eyes to appropriate studs and fit plain washers to rest.
120 Fit and tighten fourteen large dome head nuts, to torque of 54.2 lbs.ft. (7,48 kg.m.). See item 48 operation 12.29.11.
121 Fit six nuts and spring washers across front of cylinder head.

122 Locate camshaft sprockets on camshafts, remove circlips and pull adjuster plates forward to disengage serrations.
123 Rotate adjuster plates until 'fit' holes line up exactly with tapped holes in camshafts.
124 Fit one bolt at each camshaft.
125 Rotate engine to afford access to remaining holes and fit bolts. Lock bolts at both camshafts.
126 Tension top timing chain using special tool JD.2B until there is slight flexibility on outer sides of chain. Tighten locknut.
127 Complete reassembly by reversing operations 1 to 24 inclusive.

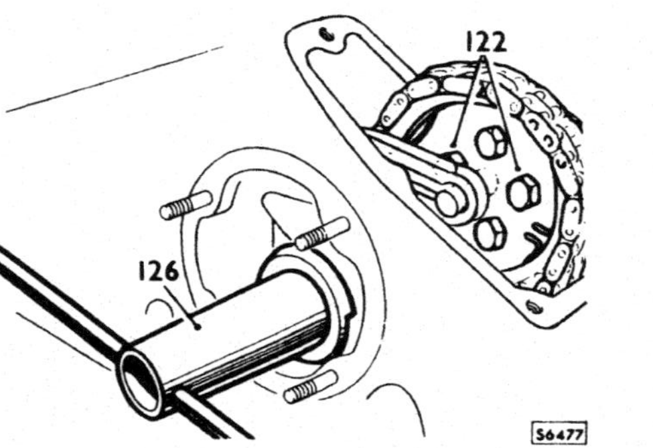

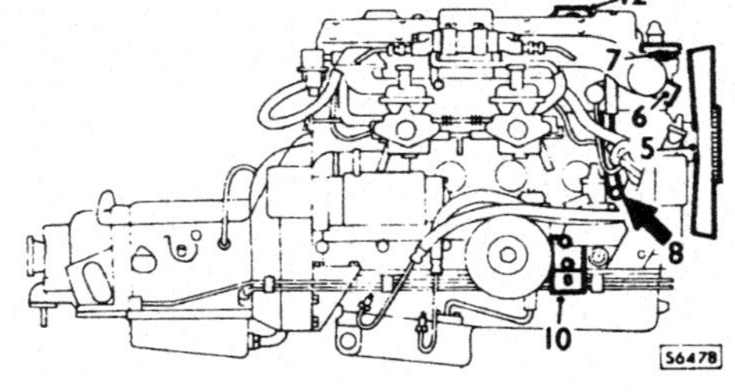

ENGINE MOUNTING –FRONT SET

Remove and refit **12.45.04**

Removing

1 Disconnect battery – 86.15.20.
2 Remove right hand wing valance stay.
3 Remove air cleaner element – 19.10.08.
NOTE: On cars to European and Federal emission control specification, detach vacuum pipe from flap valve servomotor.
4 Drain coolant – 26.10.01.
5 Remove nuts and spring washers securing fan and torquatrol unit to water pump pulley. Allow unit to rest forward clear of studs.
6 Slacken clips and pull top hose from radiator.
7 Slacken clips and pull radiator bleed and expansion tank pipes from engine header tank.
8 Slacken clip and pull brake servo non-return valve from hose coupling.
9 Detach left hand horn – early cars fitted with emission control only.
10 Remove self locking nuts and plain washers at top and bottom of both front engine mounts.
11 Remove exhaust front pipe heat shield.
CAUTION: On air conditioned cars ensure that engine does not foul expansion valve.
12 Use hoist on engine front lifting eye to raise engine sufficient to clear mountings.
13 Remove mountings.

Refitting

14 Ensure fibre discs fitted on top surface of replacement mountings and manoeuvre into position.
15 Reverse operations 1 to 12 inclusive.

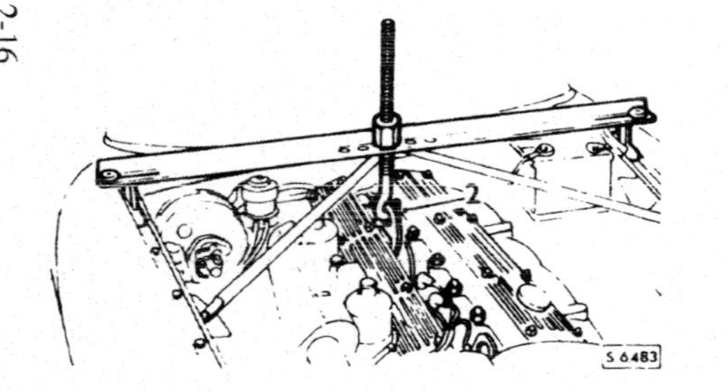

ENGINE MOUNTING – REAR CENTRE

Remove and refit 12.45.08

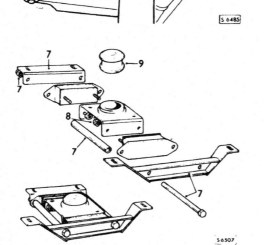

Service tool: Engine support tool MS.53(A).

Removing

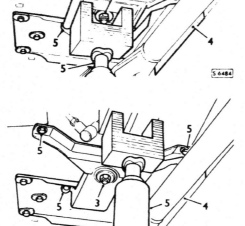

1 Disconnect battery – 86.15.20.
2 Position service tool MS.53(A) across rear engine lifting eye and set hook to support engine.
3 Remove nut at centre of mounting and recover plain washer. Remove nuts and washers securing forward end of strengthening plate to rear of transmission casing – cars fitted with Model 65 transmission.
4 Remove fastenings securing heat shield.
5 Locate jack to support mounting plate and release four setscrews and washers.
6 Lower jack and remove mounting plate. Recover spring washers, spacers and rubber rings.
NOTE: Continue with operations 7 and 8 for mountings removed from cars fitted with manual or Model 65 transmission.
7 Remove locknuts from bolts securing forward and rear brackets of mounting, and recover spacing tubes.
8 Remove locknuts securing mounting rubbers to centre bracket.
9 Check all bushes and rubber rings and renew if necessary.

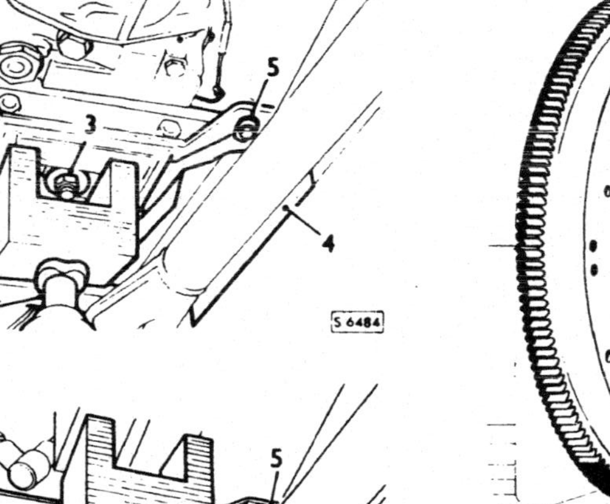

Refitting

Reverse operations 1 to 9 as appropriate.

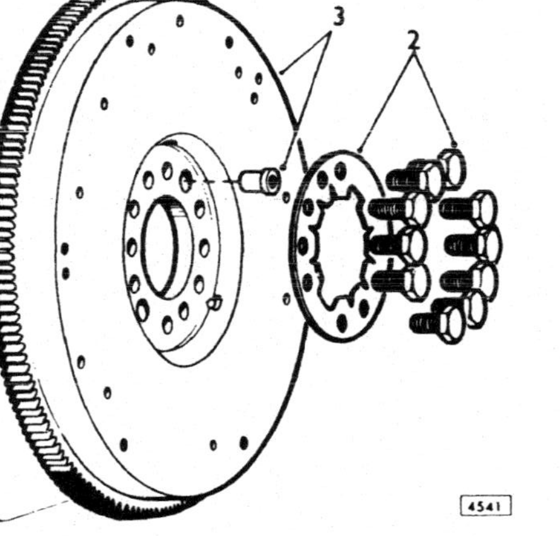

FLYWHEEL

Remove and refit 12.53.07

Removing

1 Remove clutch assembly – 33.10.01.
2 Knock down locking plate tabs and remove ten bolts.
3 Remove flywheel from crankshaft using draw bolts through dowels.

Refitting

4 Locate dowels in crankshaft and tap fully home through flywheel.
5 Fit locking plate and secure flywheel using ten bolts. Tighten to torque of 66.6 lbs.ft. (9,22 kg.m.). Turn up tabs.
6 Refit clutch assembly.

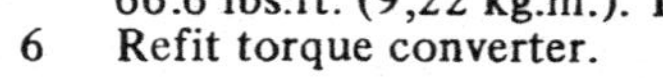

DRIVE PLATE

Remove and refit 12.53.13

Removing

1 Remove torque converter – 44.17.07.
2 Knock down locking plate tabs and remove ten bolts.
3 Remove drive plate from crankshaft using draw bolts through dowels.

Refitting

4 Locate dowels in crankshaft and tap fully home through drive plate.
5 Fit locking plate and secure drive plate using ten bolts. Tighten to torque of 66.6 lbs.ft. (9,22 kg.m.). Turn up tabs.
6 Refit torque converter.

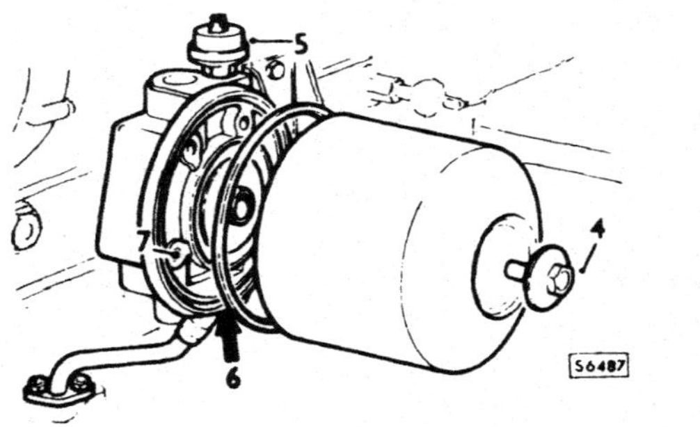

OIL FILTER ASSEMBLY (EARLY CARS)

Remove and refit **12.60.01**

Removing

1 Disconnect battery – 86.15.20.
2 Remove right hand wing valance stay – cars fitted with emission control only.
3 Remove air cleaner element. Pull vacuum pipe from flap valve servo motor – emission control cars only.
4 Unscrew centre bolt in oil filter canister. Lift element clear.
5 Remove oil pressure gauge transmitter.
6 Slacken hose clip at top of oil return pipe.
7 Remove four setscrews and lock washers and pull housing from cylinder block.
8 Pull housing upwards from oil return pipe.
9 Remove all traces of gasket from cylinder block and oil filter housing.
10 Thoroughly clean canister and housing, and renew all seals on centre bolt.

Refitting

11 Reverse operations 1 to 9 inclusive, using new gasket between housing and cylinder block and new seal in housing. If necessary, transfer relief valve to replacement housing.
12 Run engine and check for oil leaks.
13 Check oil level and top up to correct level.

OIL FILTER ASSEMBLY (LATER CARS)

Remove and refit (disposable canister type filter) **12.60.01**

Removing

1 From beneath car, separate filter housing from pipe to sump by releasing two hose clips. Catch spilled oil.
2 Release nut connecting camshaft oil feed to filter housing.
3 Unscrew and withdraw five setscrews securing filter housing to crankcase casting.
4 Withdraw filter and housing.
5 Remove and discard gasket.
6 Detach canister and thoroughly clean housing.

Refitting

7 Fit new gasket and reverse operations 1 to 4.
8 Fit new canister, smearing seal with engine oil and screwing into place by hand only.
9 Run engine and check for oil leaks.
10 Check oil level and top up as necessary.

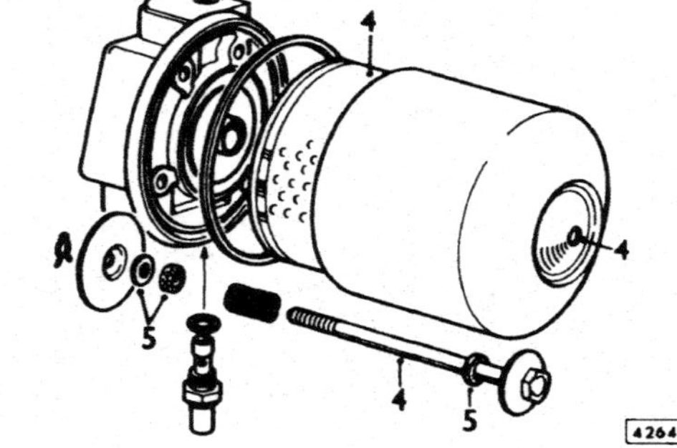

OIL FILTER ELEMENT (EARLY CARS)

Remove and refit **12.60.02**

Removing

1 Disconnect battery – 86.15.20.
2 Remove right hand wing valance stay – cars fitted with emission control only.
3 Remove air cleaner element. Pull vacuum pipe from flap valve servo motor – emission control cars only.
4 Unscrew centre bolt in oil filter canister. Lift element clear.
5 Thoroughly clean canister and fit new seals on centre bolt.

Refitting

6 Use new seal in filter housing and secure filter canister with centre bolt. Tighten to torque of 17.5 lbs.ft. (2,42 kg.m.).
7 Reconnect battery.

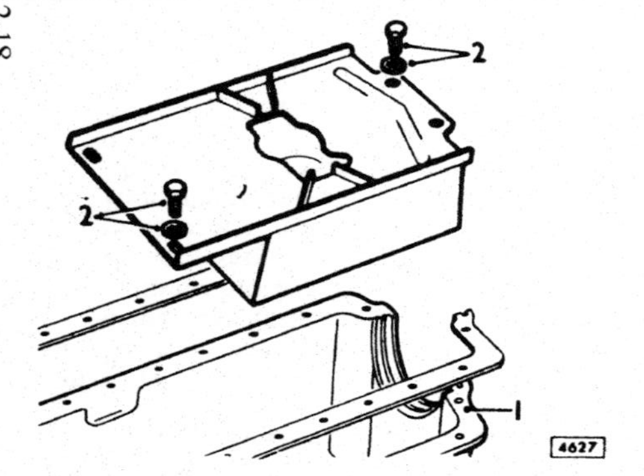

OIL PICK-UP STRAINER

Remove and refit 12.60.20

Removing
1 Remove oil sump – 12.60.44.
2 Remove four setscrews and spring washers securing strainer box.

Clean
3 Wash suction strainer gauze in clean paraffin or petrol, and dry thoroughly.
4 Clean out sump.

Refitting
5 Secure strainer box in position using four setscrews and spring washers.
6 Refit oil sump.

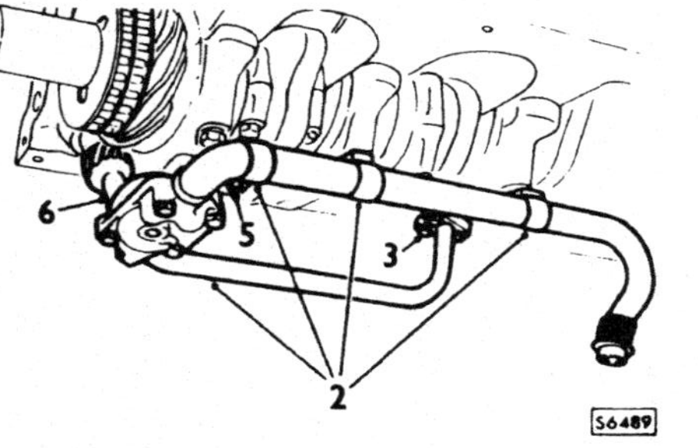

OIL PUMP

Remove and refit 12.60.26

Removing
1 Remove oil sump – 12.60.44.
2 Detach suction and delivery pipe clips from brackets.
3 Knock back tabs and remove setscrews securing delivery pipe.
4 Pull both pipes from oil pump.
5 Knock back tabs and remove setscrews securing oil pump.
6 Recover pipe bracket and drive coupling.

Refitting
7 Check condition of 'O' ring seals and, if necessary, fit new.
8 Locate drive coupling on oil pump and secure pump using three setscrews, tab washer and pipe bracket. Turn up tabs.
9 Fit delivery pipe on new gasket, turn up tabs.
10 Locate suction pipe and secure clips to brackets. Ensure pipe intake on centre line of engine.
11 Refit oil sump.

OIL PUMP

Overhaul 12.60.32

Dismantling
1 Remove oil pump – 12.60.26.
2 Unscrew four bolts and detach bottom cover.
3 Withdraw inner and outer rotors from oil pump body.
NOTE: Do not attempt to separate inner rotor from shaft.

Inspection
4 Thoroughly clean all components.
5 Check that clearance between lobes of inner and outer rotors does not exceed .006 in. (,15 mm.).
6 Check that clearance between outer rotor and pump body does not exceed .010 in. (,25 mm.).
7 Check that endfloat of rotors does not exceed .0025 in. (,06 mm.).
NOTE: If necessary outer rotor and/or body may be lapped on surface plate to rectify.
8 Examine all components for signs of scoring or wear.
9 Ensure inner rotor tight on drive shaft.
NOTE: Inner rotor drive shaft and outer rotor are only available as an assembly.
10 Renew 'O' ring seals in pump body.

Reassembling
11 Assemble inner rotor to body.
12 Assemble outer rotor to body ensuring that chamfered end inserted first.
13 Secure bottom cover using four bolts and lock washers.
14 Fit oil pump.

5
4470

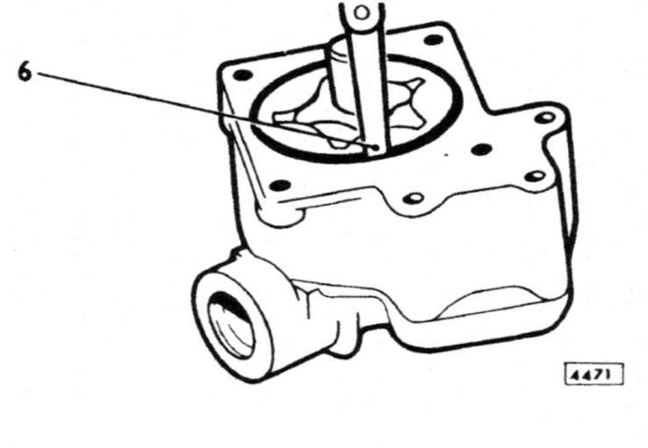

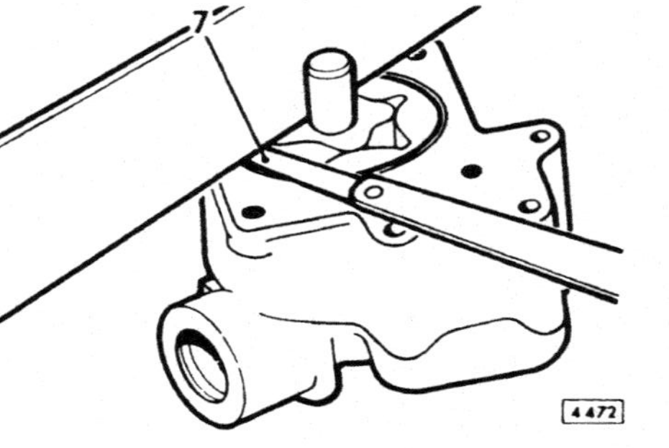

OIL SUMP

Remove and refit **12.60.44**

Removing

1 Remove front suspension – 60.35.05.
2 Drain engine oil.
3 Remove two nuts and lockwashers securing oil return pipe.
4 Remove nuts, bolts and washers securing transmission oil cooler pipe clips – cars fitted with automatic transmission only.
5 Remove setscrews and lockwashers, and four nuts and lockwashers securing oil sump.
6 Remove four setscrews and washers securing intake strainer box. Clean out sump pan and strainer.
7 Thoroughly clean all traces of gaskets and seals from sump, taking great care not to damage alloy surfaces.
8 Thoroughly clean mating surface of cylinder block.

Refitting

9 Fit strainer box and secure using four setscrews and lockwashers.
10 Ensure 'O' ring seal fitted to oil return pipe.
11 Lightly coat new oil seal with grease and locate in groove in sump. **DO NOT** trim ends but press seal into groove until ends flush.
12 Lightly grease new gaskets and locate on sump.
13 Offer sump into position and secure using twenty-six setscrews – short setscrew at front right hand corner – four nuts and spring washers.

NOTE:

(a) Ensure oil return pipe locates in sump. Secure using two nuts and lockwashers.
(b) Ensure front oil seal locates correctly in groove.
(c) Locate transmission oil cooler pipe brackets on relevant setscrews – cars fitted with automatic transmission only.

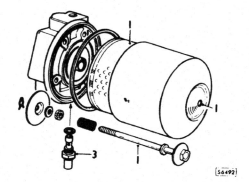

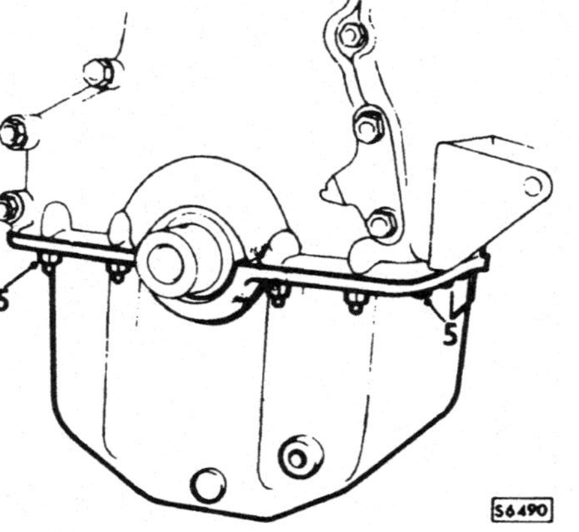

S6491

14 Refit front suspension.
15 Pour 14.5 Imp. pints (8,25 litres) of recommended oil into engine.
16 Run engine, check oil level and adjust as necessary.

OIL PRESSURE SWITCH

Remove and refit **12.60.50**

See 88.25.08/2.

OIL PRESSURE RELIEF VALVE

Remove and refit – early right hand drive cars only **12.60.56**

Removing

1 Remove oil filter element – 12.60.02.
2 Slacken nuts securing transmission oil cooler pipes to brackets – cars fitted with automatic transmission only.
3 Unscrew oil pressure relief valve.

Refitting

4 Fit new seal and screw relief valve into oil filter housing.
5 Retighten cooler pipe clips.
6 Refit oil filter element.

OIL PRESSURE RELIEF VALVE

Remove and refit – all later cars and early left hand drive cars 12.60.56

Removing

1 Slacken nuts securing transmission oil cooler pipes to brackets – cars fitted with automatic transmission only.
2 Unscrew oil pressure relief valve.

Refitting

3 Fit new seal and screw relief valve into oil filter housing.
4 Retighten cooler pipe clips.

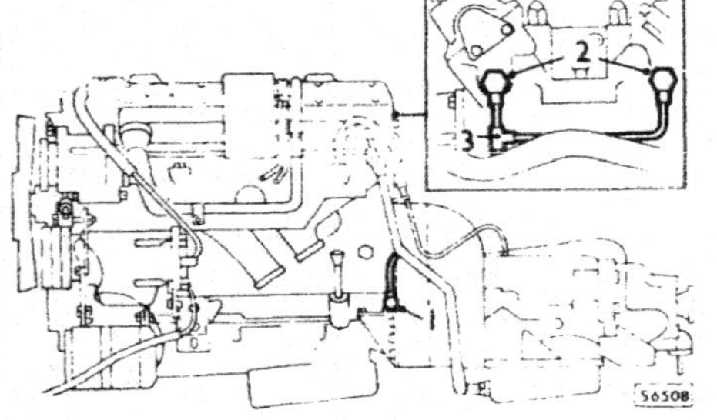

CAMSHAFT OIL FEED PIPE

Remove and refit 12.60.83

Removing

1 Remove banjo bolt at oil gallery on crankcase or union nut at oil filter housing on later cars.
2 Remove banjo bolts at rear of each camshaft.
3 Manoeuvre oil feed pipe clear.
4 Thoroughly clean out pipe.

Refitting

5 Ensure copper seals are in good condition and refit banjo bolts.

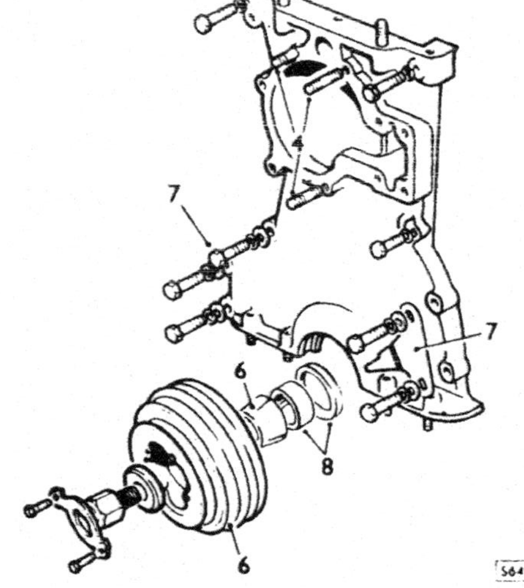

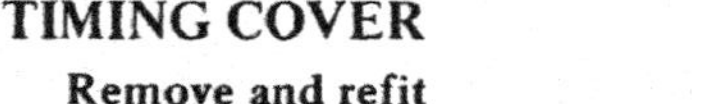

TIMING COVER

Remove and refit 12.65.01

Removing

1 Remove engine and gearbox assembly – 12.37.01.
2 Remove cylinder head, using operations from Cylinder head – remove and refit – 12.29.11., as appropriate.
3 Remove oil sump, using operations from Oil Sump – remove and refit – 12.60.44., as appropriate.
4 Remove water pump – 26.50.01.
5 Remove crankcase breather.
6 Remove torsional damper, cone and crankshaft Woodruff key.
7 Remove timing gear cover and recover timing pointer.
8 Recover distance piece and front oil seal.

Refitting

9 Thoroughly clean mating faces, taking care not to damage alloy casting.
10 Reverse operations 1 to 7 inclusive, using new gaskets, 'O' rings and seals.

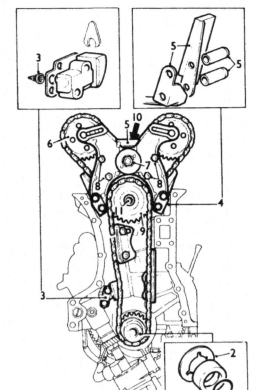

TIMING CHAINS

Remove and refit 12.65.14

Removing

1 Remove timing cover – 12.65.01.
2 Remove oil thrower from crankshaft.
3 Remove setscrews securing bottom timing chain tensioner and chain guides. Recover conical filter behind tensioner.
4 Slacken four setscrews and shakeproof washers securing top timing chain assembly. Do not remove setscrews at this stage.
5 Withdraw crankshaft timing sprocket and chain assembly. Recover distance pieces, top timing chain dampers and top timing chain retainer.
6 Disengage camshaft sprockets from top chain.
7 Remove nut and serrated washer from idler shaft and withdraw serrated plate, plunger and spring.
8 Remove four nuts and serrated washers securing front mounting bracket to rear mounting bracket. Separate brackets.
9 Remove timing chains from intermediate and idler sprockets.
10 Draw idler shaft, idler sprocket and bush from rear mounting bracket.
11 Remove circlip and press intermediate shaft from rear mounting bracket. Recover intermediate sprockets, bush and shim.

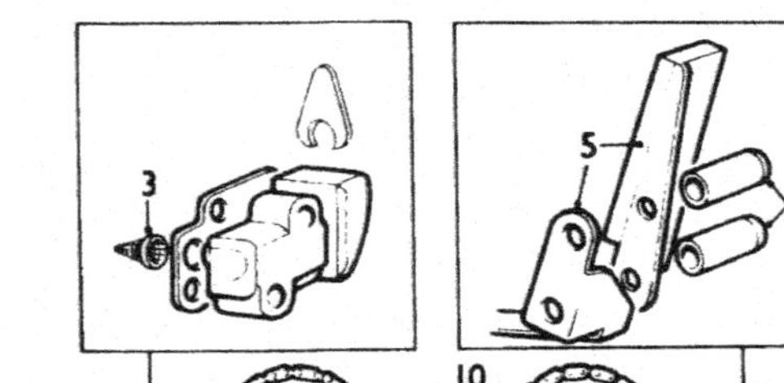
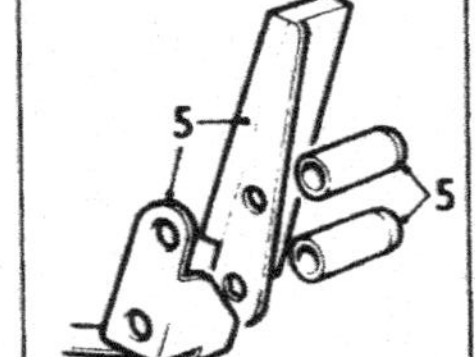
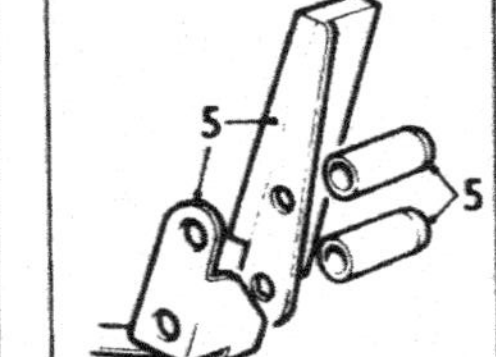
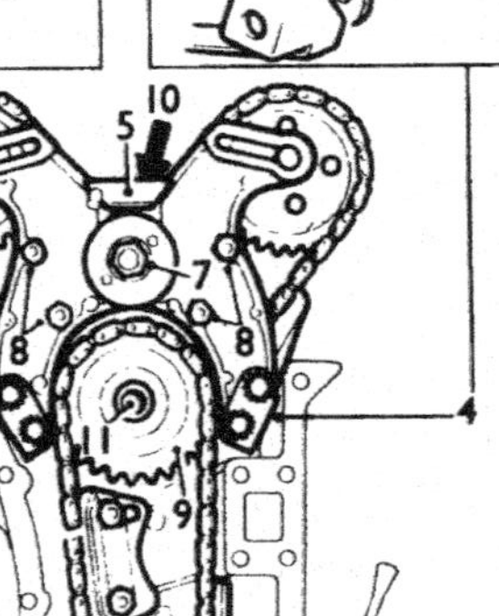

Inspection

12 Examine timing chains for signs of damage or wear.
13 Examine all sprockets for signs of damage or wear.
14 Examine all dampers and chain tensioner for signs of damage or excessive wear.
15 Examine idler sprocket bush and intermediate sprocket bush for signs of wear.

NOTE: If timing chains or sprockets show signs of excessive wear or are damaged in any way, all sprockets and the chains should be renewed.

Refitting

16 Fit eccentric idler shaft to hole in front mounting bracket.
17 Fit spring and plunger in bracket and locate serrated plate on shaft. Loosely secure using serrated washer and nut.
18 Fit idler sprocket (21 teeth) to idler shaft.
19 Fit intermediate sprocket, large gear forward, on intermediate shaft; fit shim in rear mounting bracket, ensuring that roll pin engages in slot, and retain shaft with circlip.
20 Locate top timing chain (longer) on small intermediate sprocket, and lower timing chain on large sprocket.
21 Loop top chain beneath idler sprocket and secure top mounting bracket to rear mounting bracket using four nuts and serrated washers.
22 Fit four long setscrews and spring washers to front mounting bracket and fit dampers, chain support plate and distance pieces to setscrews.
23 Equalize loops of top timing chain, and locate camshaft sprockets in loops.
24 Rotate eccentric idler shaft to lift idler sprocket to highest position between camshaft sprockets.
25 Ensure Woodruff key fitted to crankshaft.
26 Locate crankshaft sprocket on shaft, but do not slide fully home at this stage.
27 Loop bottom timing chain beneath crankshaft sprocket, tap sprocket fully home and locate assembly.
28 Tighten four setscrews to retain assembly.
29 Fit bottom timing chain guides but do not tighten setscrews at this stage.
30 Fit conical filter in hole in cylinder block.
31 Screw slipper into tensioner until dimension of .125 in. (3,17 mm.) exists between slipper and body.
32 Locate tensioner on shims as necessary to ensure slipper runs central on chain and secure using two setscrews and lockplate.

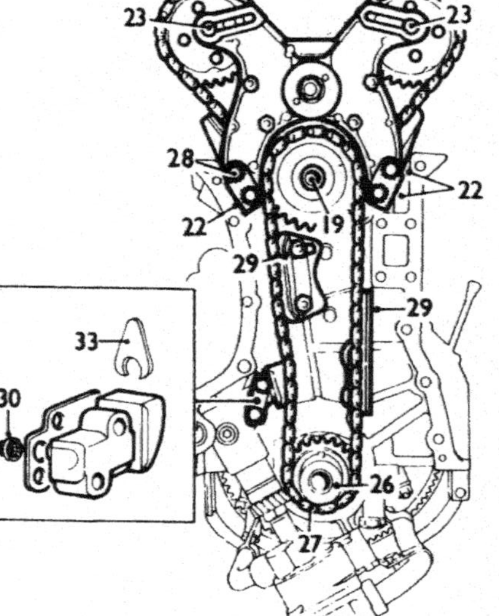

33 Place slip gauge or distance card supplied with new tensioner between slipper and body of tensioner to maintain dimension of operation 31 and adjust intermediate damper to touch chain. Tighten setscrews and turn up tabs of lockplate.
34 Remove slip gauge and top chain or tensioner slipper to release ratchet.
35 Position oil thrower on crankshaft.
36 Refit timing cover.

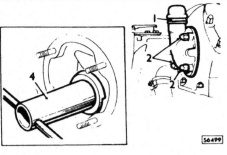

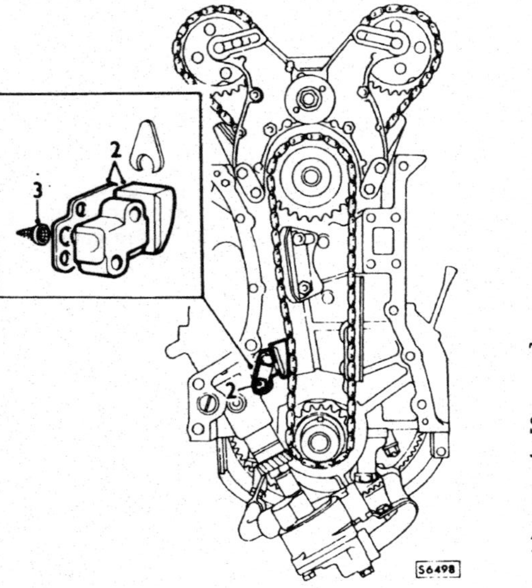

TIMING CHAIN TENSIONER

Remove and refit 12.65.28

Removing

1 Remove timing cover – 12.65.01.
2 Remove setscrews and locking plate securing tensioner. Recover tensioner and shim.
3 Remove conical filter from cylinder block.

Refitting

4 Thoroughly clean conical filter and fit to cylinder block.
5 Screw slipper into tensioner and fit distance card supplied with new tensioner or .125 in. (3,17 mm.) slip gauge between slipper and body.
6 Locate tensioner on shims as necessary to ensure slipper runs central on chain and secure using two setscrews and lockplate.
7 Slacken setscrews securing intermediate damper and set into light contact with chain. Tighten screws and relock.
8 Remove slip gauge and tap chain or tensioner slipper to release ratchet.

S6499

TIMING CHAIN

Adjust 12.65.44

Service tool: Timing chain adjuster tool JD.2B.

1 Release clip securing crankcase breather pipe to breather.
2 Remove dome head nuts securing breather housing. Note position of clips and brackets fitted.
3 Withdraw breather housing and filter gauze.
4 Slacken locknut and use tool JD.2B to tension top chain. Rotate tool in an anti-clockwise direction and **DO NOT** use undue force.
5 Tighten locknut and refit breather housing and all brackets and clips removed.
6 If necessary, re-tension air pump drive belt – cars fitted with emission control to Federal specification only – 17.25.13.

EMISSION CONTROL SYSTEM

Description 17.00.01

Cars are fitted with certain of the following components as necessary to comply with local legislation.

The emission control system is of the air injection type and comprises the following major components. The components act upon the engine, and interact with each other, as detailed below.

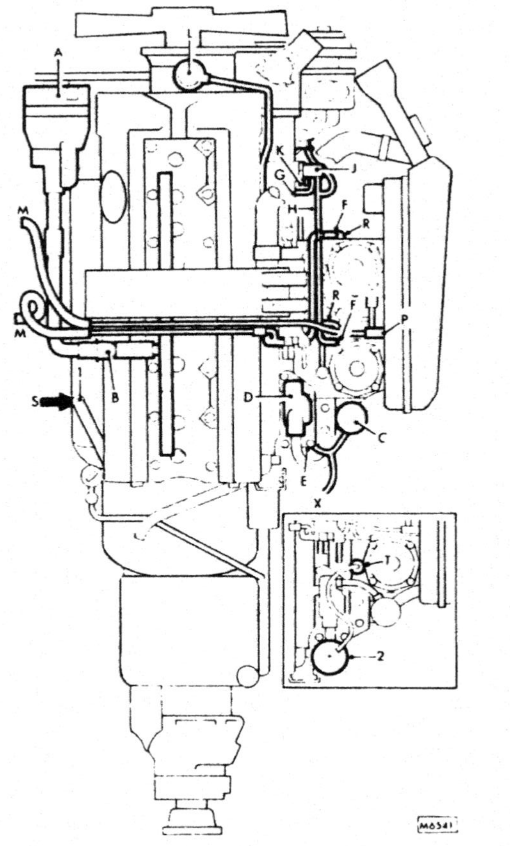

An air delivery pump, 'A', supplies air under pressure, air being passed through a non-return valve, 'B', to the exhaust ports just above the exhaust valve heads. This air combines with the exhaust gases to continue the oxidisation process in the exhaust system. The non-return valve prevents reverse flow in the air injection rails when exhaust gas pressure exceeds air supply pressure.

The gulp valve 'C' operates in response to an abrupt fall in manifold pressure, i.e. sudden closure of the throttle, and provides a quantity of air to the induction manifold 'D'. This additional air compensates for the evaporation of residual fuel from the induction tract walls by forming a weaker mixture that will burn in the cylinders. The gulp valve is actuated by manifold pressure via rubber pipe, 'E', connected to a tapping beneath the inlet manifold.

A throttle by-pass valve, 'F', is incorporated in both carburetters. The valve is operated by a specific range of manifold pressures sensed at a tapping 'G', beneath the inlet manifold. The valves open to provide a mixture that will ensure complete combustion under conditions of closed throttle over-run. The valves in both carburetters are actuated via a small bore rubber tube 'H', to ensure balanced performance.

In addition to normal centrifugal advance the distributor is fitted with an opposing vacuum retard mechanism actuated by manifold pressure. Manifold pressure is sensed, via the thermostatic vacuum switch 'J', at tapping 'G' beneath the inlet manifold.
The thermostatic vacuum switch provides overheating protection for the engine made necessary by the large degree of vacuum retard used.
The switch isolates the distributor vacuum retard capsule from its reference point if the engine coolant temperature rises above a specific level. The capsule is then referenced to atmospheric pressure at 'K' leaving the distributor subject only to centrifugal advance.
The thermostatic vacuum switch simultaneously inhibits operation of the throttle by-pass valves. These would otherwise open due to the change in manifold pressure

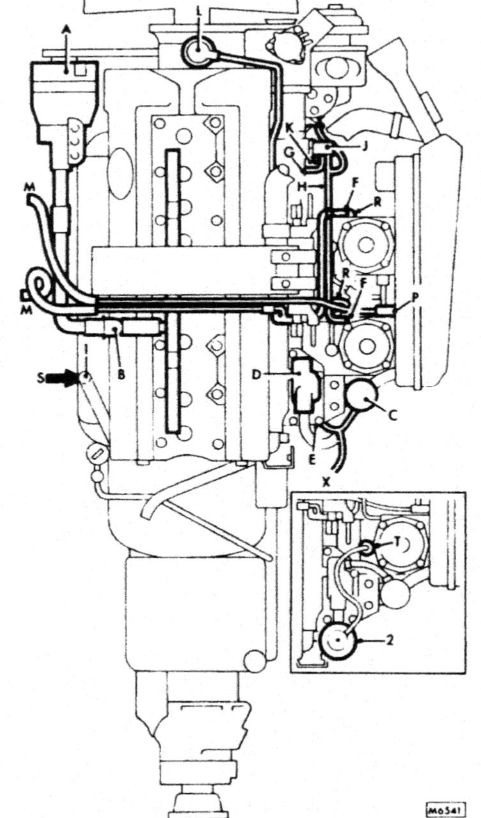

resulting from the change in distributor retard angle. The by-pass valve tube 'H' is vented to atmosphere via port 'K'.

A positive crankcase ventilation system is fitted to all cars. Fumes from the crankcase breather 'L', are drawn into the engine by the carburetter balance pipe while the engine is running.

An evaporative emission control system is also fitted on cars to Federal specification. The system utilizes canister 'M', containing activated carbon, to retain fumes given off by the engine crankcase assembly 'L', the fuel tank 'N', and carburetter float chambers 'P', while the engine is at rest. When the engine is running, a stream of air is drawn through the air pipe 'Q' and canister 'M' by the carburetter balance and breather system 'R' carrying the adsorbed fumes into the engine and purging the canister.
Engines to Federal specification are fitted with an exhaust gas recirculation system (EGR) that taps off a specific proportion of exhaust gas from a point 'S' between No. 1 and No. 2 cylinders, and re-introduces it into the carburetter induction tract.
Early engines are fitted with a restrictor '1' to control the proportion of gas recirculated. On later cars the proportion of gas recirculated is metered by a valve '2' controlled by manifold pressure. The pressure is sensed at a throttle edge tapping 'T'.
The valve is calibrated so that no gas is recirculated when the throttle butterfly valve is closed, or when the manifold pressure is below a specific figure.
If it is required to remove the exhaust manifold heat shield, the union nut securing the EGR pipe must be released before the adaptor securing the heat shield is moved. Restrain the adaptor while loosening the union nut.

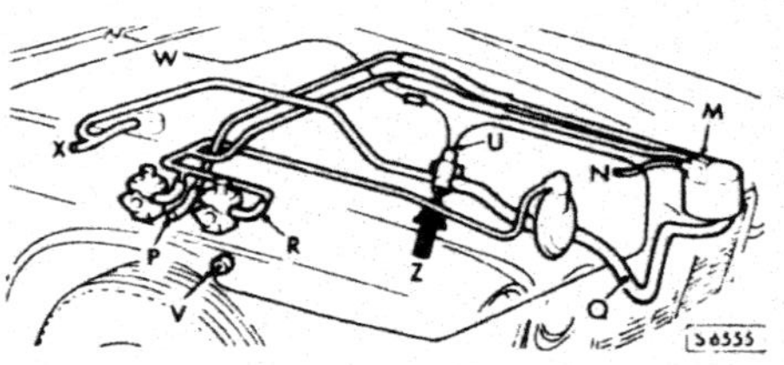

To prevent any tendency of the engine to run-on when the ignition is switched off, an anti run-on system is fitted. The system comprises a solenoid valve 'U', an additional oil pressure switch 'V', and an extra contact in the ignition switch 'W'.
When the ignition switch is turned off, a voltage is applied to a solenoid valve in the evaporative loss canister purge pipe. The solenoid valve is connected electrically in series with an oil pressure switch that is closed while oil pressure exists, and therefore operates to close the purge pipe to atmosphere. The solenoid valve simultane-

ously applies manifold pressure, 'X', via the evaporative loss canister, to the interior of the carburetter float chambers 'P'. This equalizes pressures on both sides of the carburetter jet and prevents fuel flow past the metering needle.
When the engine stops, lubricating oil pressure falls and opens the pressure switch; this removes the electrical supply from the solenoid which relaxes and re-opens the purge pipe to atmospheric pressure at 'Z'.

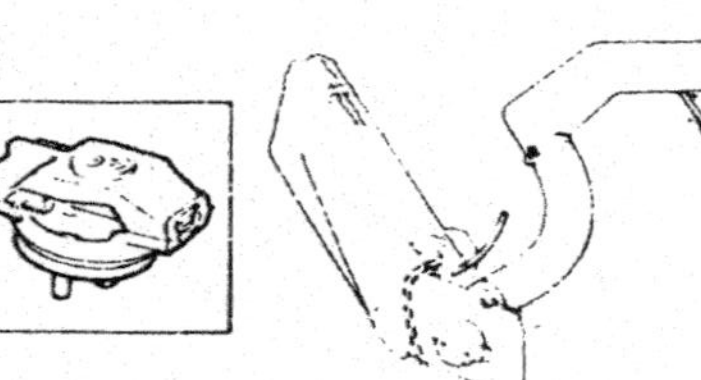

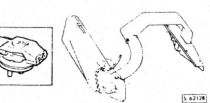

An air intake temperature control system is fitted as the carburetters are adjusted to operate most efficiently when the air intake temperature is approximately 40°C. (105°F.).
To maintain the induction air temperature at this level, a temperature sensor unit is fitted in the air cleaner backplate, and a flap valve is fitted in the intake system tuned stage.
Manifold pressure to operate the flap valve servo motor in the air cleaner is sensed at a tapping beneath the induction manifold.
The temperature sensor varies the manifold pressure applied to the flap valve vacuum motor, and therefore varies the position of the flap valve. The flap valve then mixes cold air – from the induction ram pipe – and hot air – from the cowl around the exhaust manifolds – in the proportions required by the temperature sensor to maintain the correct intake air temperature.

The emission control system fitted to this engine is designed to keep emissions within legislated limits providing ignition timing and carburetter settings are correctly maintained and the engine is in sound mechanical condition.
It is essential that routine maintenance operations detailed in the Manual are carried out by your Distributor or Dealer at the specified mileage intervals.

Testing
In order that engine exhaust emissions are kept within legislated limits an exhaust emission test MUST be carried out after completing certain operations. The following table lists these operations together with the type of emission test required.

CAUTION: CO content MUST not exceed 4½% with air delivery pipe hose disconnected. It is essential that the equipment used for testing purposes is of the following type.

1 An infra-red CO exhaust gas analyser.
2 Engine and ignition diagnostic equipment.
3 A carburetter balance meter.

OPERATION	EMISSION TEST REQUIRED
Carburetters – Remove and refit	1 Engine and ignition diagnostic check 2 Carburetters tuned and balanced 3 Exhaust gas CO content analysed
Air delivery pump – Remove and refit	1 Check that pump delivers air
Carburetters – Tune and adjust	1 Check that pump delivers air 2 Exhaust gas CO content analysed
Crankcase breather and/or pipe	1 Check thimble filter for obstruction 2 Exhaust gas CO content analysed

To prevent air pollution by vapours from the fuel tank and carburetter vents, the control equipment stores the vapour in a charcoal-filled vanister while the engine is stopped and disposes of it via the engine crankcase ventilation system when the engine is running.
The fuel tank venting is designed to ensure that vapours are vented through the control system even when the car is parked on an inclined surface.
A capacity-limiting device in the fuel tank ensures sufficient free capacity is available after filling to accommodate fuel which would otherwise be displaced as a result of large temperature rise.

Fuel Tank Evaporative Loss Control System

Cars have a fuel tank evaporative system fitted as standard equipment to meet U.S. Federal requirements. The system operates as follows:
Interconnected tubing attached to the air vents in both fuel tanks conveys petrol vapour to the carburetters via a sealed storage canister and a flame trap incorporated in the breather housing on the cylinder head.
The system is completely sealed and no 'Routine Maintenance' is necessary with the exception of the carbon canister which should be renewed at the recommended periods.

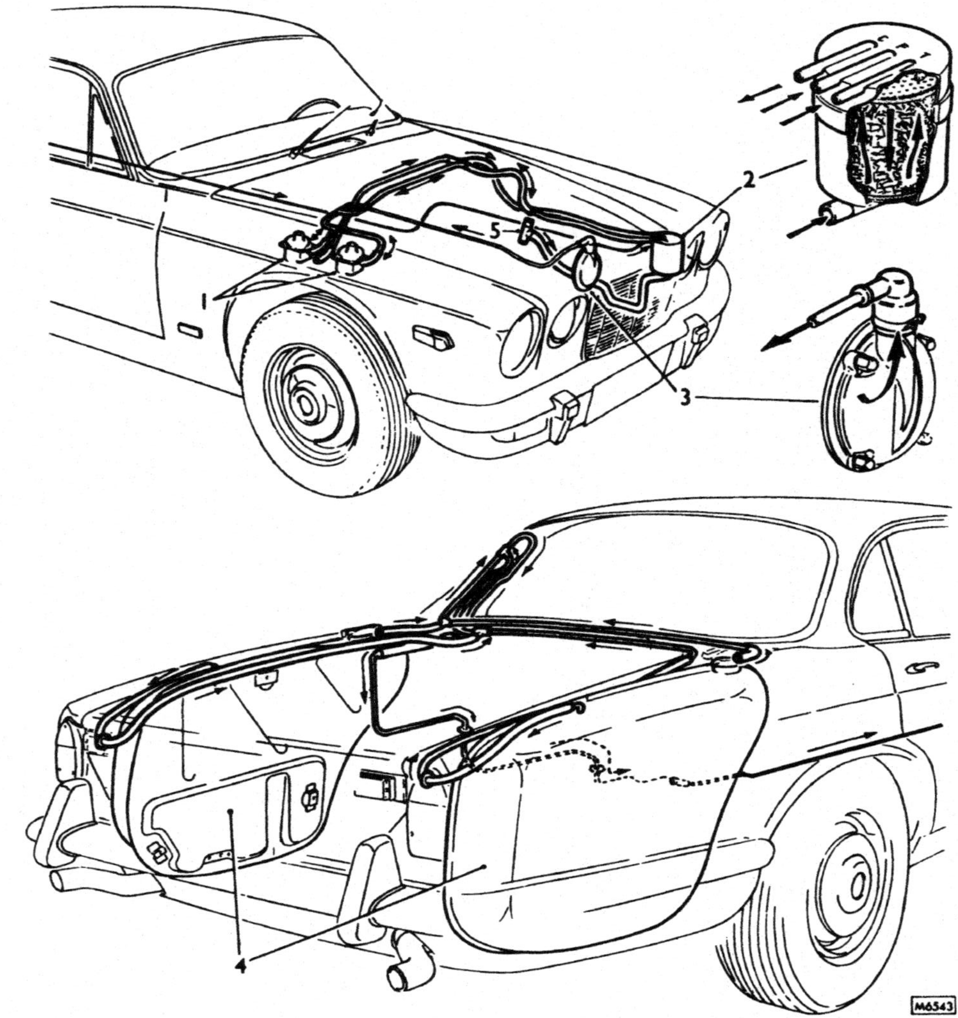

1 Carburetters
2 Carbon canister
3 Crankcase breather
4 Fuel tanks
5 Anti run-on valve

Fault Finding

CAUTION: The checks and procedures covered in the fault finding chart must be carried out on both carburetters if satisfactory results are to be obtained.

SYMPTOM	CAUSE	CURE
Erratic or Poor Idling; Excessively High Idling Speed	1 Float height incorrect	1 Check float height; rectify if necessary
	2 Dirty or worn needle valve	2a Wash valve in petrol; check filter gauze is clean 2b Renew needle valve if sticking or worn
	3 Piston sticking	3 Clean piston and rod, lubricate with clean engine oil. Top up piston rod to correct level
	4 Carburetter inlet obstructed	4 Check that air cleaner and case are correctly fitted and that gaskets are not causing obstruction
	5 Diaphragm damaged	5 Check for splits in diaphragm; renew if necessary
	6 Temperature compensator not operating correctly	6 Refer to operation 17.20.07 items 22 and 23
	7 Leakage at induction manifold joints	7 Check all joints for leakage and renew gaskets as necessary
	8 Leakage from vacuum pipe connections	8 Check all vacuum pipe connections for security and rectify as necessary
	9 Carburetters not tuned correctly	9 Carry out operation 19.15.02
Hesitation or Flat Spot	1 Check items 1 to 9 enumerated above	1 If trouble still persists proceed to 2 below 2 Check that piston return spring is not broken and that spring colour coded RED is fitted
Air delivery pump inoperative or amount of air pump delivers is low	1 Driving belt tension	1 Carry out operation 17.25.13
	2 Poor hose connections	2 Check all connections for tightness; rectify as necessary
	3 Symptoms persist after checking 1 and 2	3 Replace pump
Engine will not start	1 Anti run-on valve sticking	1 Change anti run-on valve
Flat battery or burnt out anti run-on valve	1 Pressure switch short circuited	1 Check pressure switch and wiring. Change pressure switch if necessary

CAUTION: It is essential that an exhaust emission check is carried out immediately after completing any operation detailed in this section.

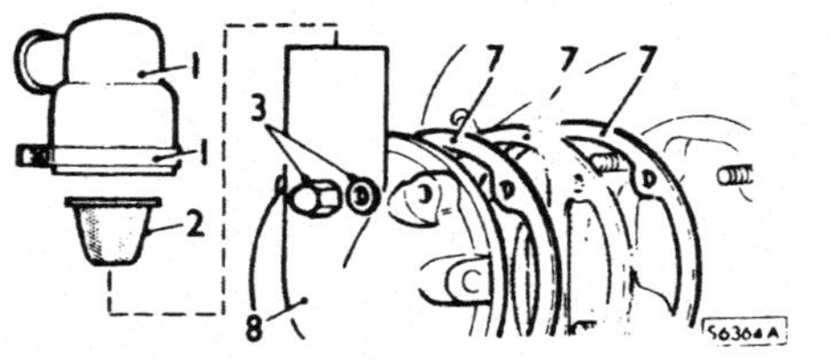

ENGINE BREATHER FILTER AND GAUZE

Remove and refit 17.10.02

Removing
1 Remove clip securing rubber elbow to breather housing; lift off elbow.
2 Remove dome-head nuts and washers securing breather housing.
4 Slacken nuts and release tension of air pump driving belt.
5 Pull tensioner bracket clear of studs.
6 Remove all traces of old gaskets and wash filter gauze and housing in clean petrol. Dry using clean, dry compresse air.

Refitting
7 Locate new gasket over studs, followed by gauze baffle and another new gasket.
8 Locate breather housing.
9 Locate air pump belt tensioner bracket – if fitted.
10 Locate hose brackets – if fitted.
11 Secure breather housing using four dome-head nuts and washers.
12 Fit filter into breather housing.
13 Locate rubber elbow and secure clip.

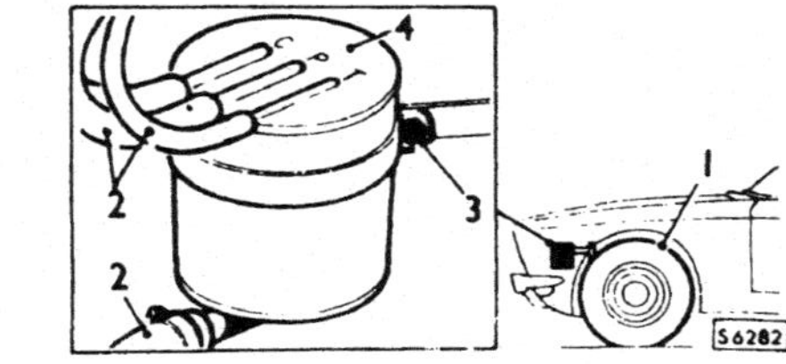

ADSORPTION CANISTER

Remove and refit 17.15.13

Removing
1 Remove left hand front wheel.
2 Note location of inlet and outlet pipes and detach from canister.
3 Remove bolt and self locking nut securing clamp.
4 Pull canister from clamp ring.

Refitting
Reverse operations 1 to 4.

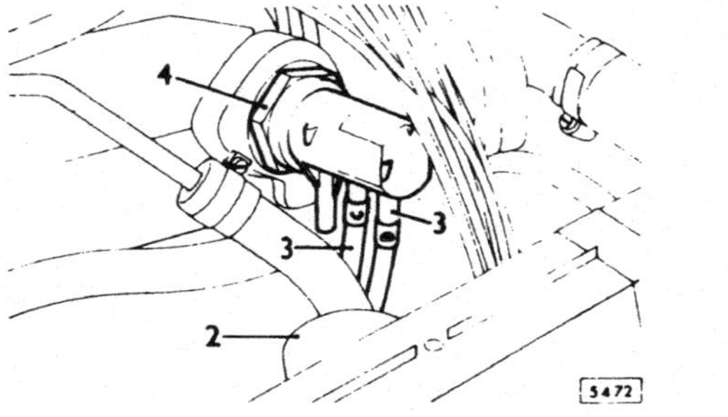

THERMOSTATIC VACUUM SWITCH

Remove and refit **17.20.31**

Removing

1 Open radiator drain tap and partially drain coolant.
2 Slacken clip and disconnect flexible hose from air cleaner.
3 Disconnect vacuum pipes from switch.
4 Slacken union nut and remove switch from inlet manifold.

Refitting

Reverse operations 1 to 3; NOTE switch MUST be fitted in position shown and to enable this to be done, switch may be turned independently of union nut.

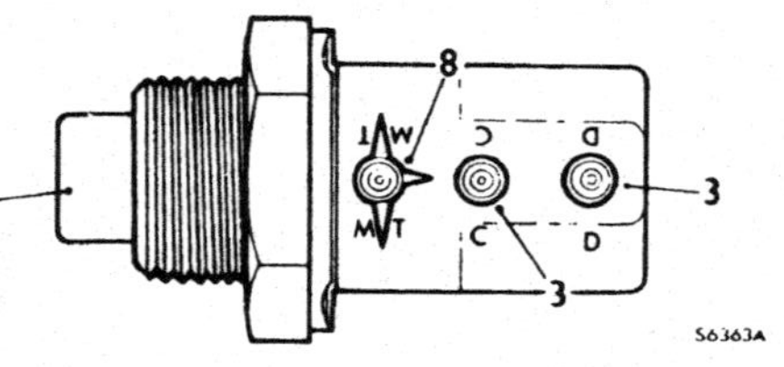

THERMOSTATIC VACUUM SWITCH

Test **17.20.32**

1 Remove switch – 17.20.31.
2 Connect suitable lengths of tubing to tappings 'C' and 'D'.
3 Blow down pipe 'D', air should be ejected from pipe 'C'.
4 If air is not ejected from pipe 'C', switch must be renewed.
5 If, however, air is ejected from pipe 'C', proceed with items 6 to 9.
6 Immerse switch bulb in bath of oil.
7 Heat oil to a temperature of 220°F. (104.4°C.).
8 Blow down pipe 'D' air should be ejected from tapping 'MT' this indicates that switch is satisfactory.
9 If, however, air is not ejected from tapping 'MT' or if it is ejected from pipe 'C', switch must be renewed.
10 Clean all traces of oil from switch before refitting.

SECONDARY THROTTLE HOUSING (REPLACED ON LATER CARS BY WATER HEATED SPACERS)

Remove and refit **17.20.36**

Removing

1 Remove radiator header tank cap.
2 Open radiator drain tap and drain off approximately 1 U.S. gallon of coolant. **NOTE**: Conserve coolant if anti-freeze is in use.
3 Remove EGR valve – 17.25.35 (variable orifice system only).
4 Remove carburetters – 19.15.11.
5 Disconnect inlet manifold hose from gulp valve.
6 Slacken clip and disconnect water inlet hose.
7 Note which hole in spring anchor brackets secondary throttle return springs are secured; detach return springs.
8 Slacken clip and disconnect water outlet hose.
9 Remove nuts and spring washers securing secondary throttle housing and spring anchor brackets to inlet manifold.
10 Withdraw secondary throttle housing together with gulp valve and anchor brackets; remove and discard gaskets.

Refitting

11 Reverse operations 1 to 10; use new gaskets between secondary throttle housing and inlet manifold.
12 Check and if necessary adjust throttle linkage – 19.20.05.
13 Set secondary housing throttle stops to just keep butterfly valves open.

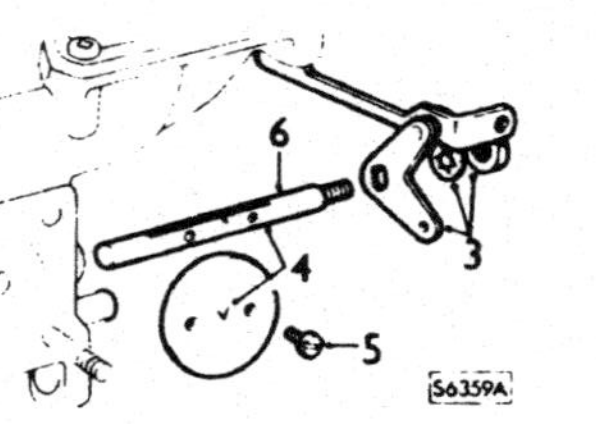

SECONDARY THROTTLE HOUSING

Overhaul **17.20.37**

Dismantling

1 Remove secondary throttle housing – 17.20.36.
2 Slacken nut on front throttle spindle then remove nut and washer securing bellcrank to front secondary throttle spindle; withdraw bellcrank.
3 Slacken nut on rear throttle spindle, then remove nut and washer securing bellcrank to rear secondary throttle spindle; withdraw bellcrank.
4 Mark relative position of each throttle disc to spindle and each spindle to secondary throttle housing.
5 Remove screws securing throttle discs to spindles, rotate spindles and withdraw discs.
6 Withdraw spindle from secondary throttle housing.
7 Prise throttle spindle seals out of spindle bush; discard seals.

Inspection and cleaning

8 Remove all deposits from inside top cover and delivery pipe – EGR variable orifice system only.

Reassembling

9 Press new throttle spindle seals into spindle bush.
10 Check by means of straight edge that throttle spindles are not bent or distorted; spindles found to be damaged in this way must be renewed.
11 Fit spindles into housing.
12 Position throttle discs in spindles, fit securing screws but do not tighten at this stage.
13 Adjust position of discs until they close fully; tighten securing screws.
14 Fit bellcranks to throttle spindle; do not overtighten securing nuts.
15 Refit secondary throttle housing.

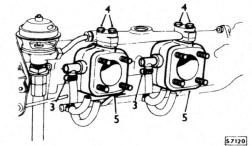

WATER HEATED SPACERS

Remove and refit **17.20.40**

Removing

1 Remove coolant filler cap.

2 Place container under drain tap and drain off approximately 1 gallon (5 litres) of coolant. Retain coolant for refill.
3 Remove carburetters, withdrawing water supply pipes from spacers.
4 Remove four setscrews securing E.G.R. balance pipe to spacers.
5 Slide spacers off studs. Discard gaskets between spacers and manifold.

Refitting
6 Fit new gaskets and reverse operations 3 to 5.
7 Refill coolant and replace cap.
8 Check operation of throttle and adjust linkage if necessary.

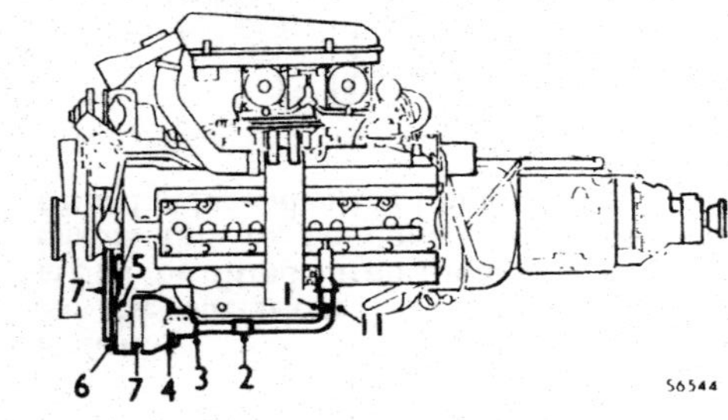

AIR DELIVERY PUMP

Remove and refit 17.25.07

Removing
1 Slacken jubilee clip on air pump delivery pipe.
2 Remove nut, washer, spacer and bolt securing air delivery pipe to exhaust manifold heat shield.
3 Extract air delivery pipe from pump outlet elbow.

WARNING: On no account must the outlet pipe from the air conditioning compressor pump be disconnected as the gas contained within the system can cause blindness.

4 Remove bolts and washers securing outlet elbow to pump; lift off elbow.
5 Remove bolts, washers and spacers from trunnion.
6 Remove retaining nut and washer on pump mounting bolt.
7 Swing pump towards engine and disengage drive belt.
8 Withdraw pump mounting bolt, collecting spacers and washers; lift out pump.

Refitting
9 Reverse operations 1 to 8, use new gasket on pump outlet elbow and 'O' ring inside outlet elbow.
10 Adjust drive belt -- 17.25.13.
11 Slacken clip securing air delivery pipe to check valve inlet.
12 Start engine and check that pump delivers air.
13 Tighten clip.
CAUTION: No servicing or overhaul of the air delivery pump is possible. In the event of failure, service exchange unit MUST be fitted.

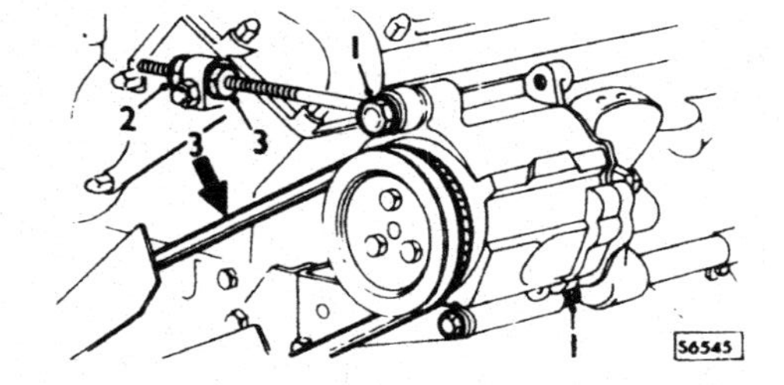

AIR DELIVERY PUMP DRIVE BELT

Tensioning 17.25.13

1 Slacken air pump mounting bolts.
2 Slacken off adjuster locknut.
3 Tighten adjusting nut to obtain a belt tension as follows:
A load of 3.2 lb. (1,45 kg.) applied on upper and midway portion of belt will give a deflection of .18 in. (4,6 mm.).
4 Retighten adjuster locknut and mounting bolts.

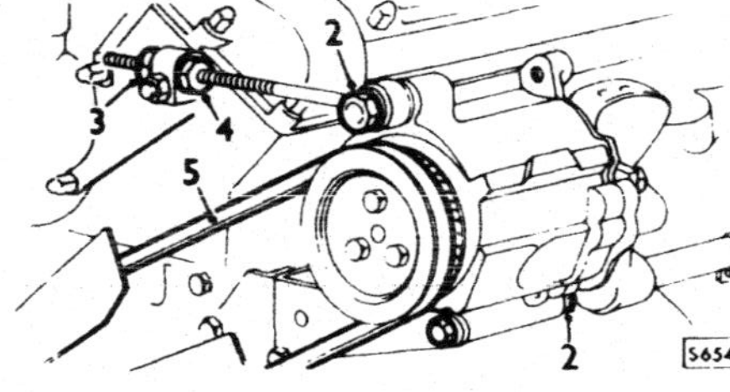

AIR DELIVERY PUMP DRIVE BELT

Remove and refit 17.25.15

Removing
1 Remove steering pump drive belt – 57.20.02.
2 Slacken air pump mounting bolts.
3 Slacken off adjuster locknut.
4 Wind back adjusting nut.
5 Remove drive belt.

Refitting
6 Manoeuvre replacement belt into position.
7 Set drive belt tension, operations 3 and 4 – 17.25.13.
8 Refit steering pump drive belt.

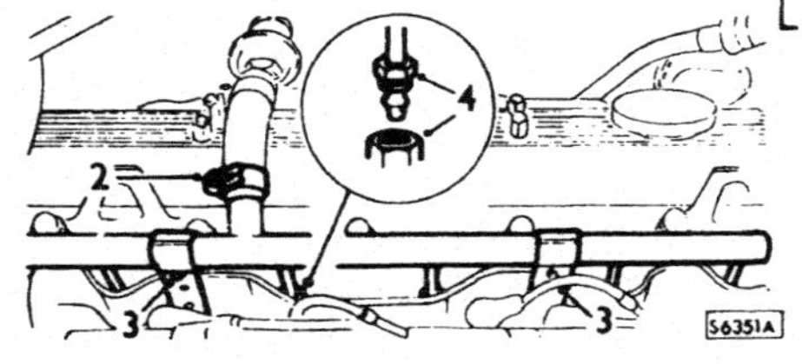

AIR RAIL

Remove and refit 17.25.17

Removing
1 Remove hot air duct -- 17.30.30.
2 Slacken clip securing check valve hose to air rail.
3 Remove nuts and spring washers securing air delivery pipe to steady brackets.
4 Unscrew union nuts securing air pipe to cylinder head; disengage air rail from steady brackets and withdraw.

Refitting
Reverse operations 1 to 4.

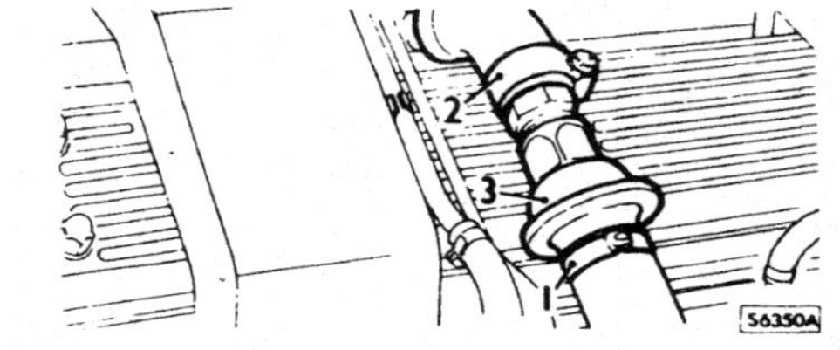

CHECK VALVE

Remove and refit 17.25.21

Removing
1 Remove clip securing air delivery pipe hose to check valve inlet.
2 Slacken jubilee clip securing check valve outlet to air delivery pipe rail; lift out check valve.

Refitting
Reverse operations 1 and 2.
NOTE: Use new clips to secure air delivery pipe hose.

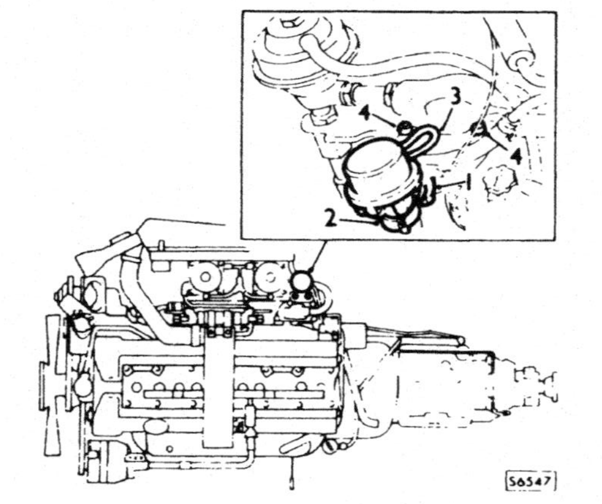

GULP VALVE

Remove and refit **17.25.30**

Removing

1. Remove clip securing throttle housing air delivery hose to gulp valve outlet.
2. Remove clip securing air delivery hose to gulp valve inlet.
3. Detach operating sensor tube at gulp valve.
4. Remove two Phillips head screws and plain washers securing gulp valve mounting bracket.
5. Lift off gulp valve and bracket.

Refitting

Reverse operations 1 to 5.
NOTE: Use new hose clips.

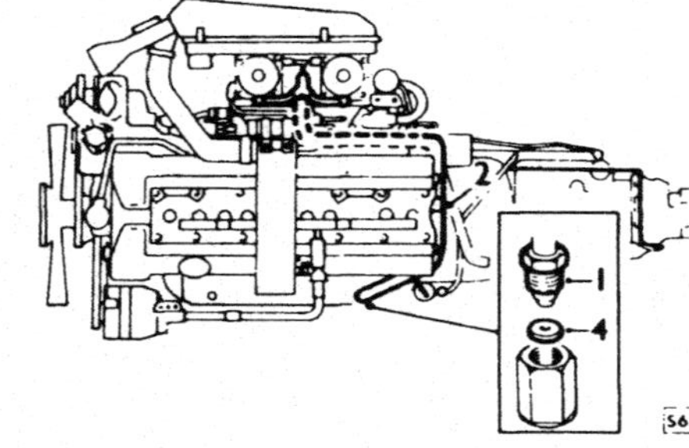

EGR RESTRICTOR AND 'Y' PIECE (Fixed orifice only)

Decarbonise **17.25.32**

1. Unscrew union nut securing outlet pipe to adaptor.
2. Release setscrew and clip at rear of cylinder block.
3. Remove carburetters -- 19.15.11.
4. Withdraw restrictor from adaptor.
5. Clean 'Y' piece, pipes and restrictor with a suitable wire brush; blow all pipes through with dry, clean compressed air.
6. Inspect both carburetters.
7. Reverse operations 1 to 4.
   NOTE: Should restrictor be inadvertently misplaced, replacements are available from your Dealer.
   CAUTION: The engine MUST NOT, under any circumstances, be run with the restrictor not in position.

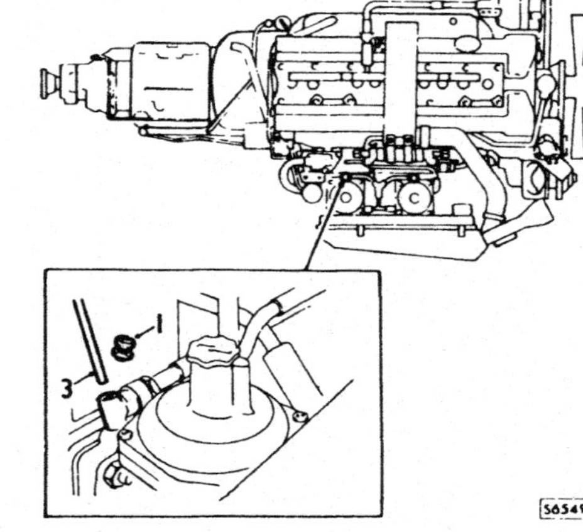

EXHAUST GAS RECIRCULATION INLET DRILLING (Fixed orifice only)

Decarbonise **17.25.33**

1. Remove blanking screw from top of left hand carburetter mounting flange.
2. Hold throttle fully open.
3. By means of a mild steel rod 8 in. (203 mm.) long x 1/8 in. (3,2 mm.) diameter, carefully remove carbon deposits from inlet drilling.
4. Refit blanking screw.
5. Carry out operations 1 to 4 on remaining carburetter.

AIR INTAKE TEMPERATURE CONTROL SYSTEM

Testing **17.30.01**

1. Disconnect hot air intake flexible pipe.
2. With engine cold and NOT running, flap valve must be in a position parallel to intake ram pipe.
3. With engine cold and running, with choke lever fully off, flap valve must move to "hot air" position, i.e. closing ram pipe and opening hot air duct.
4. Reconnect flexible pipe.
5. With engine hot and running, under bonnet temperature approximately 50°C., flap valve must be in "cold air" position, i.e. parallel to ram pipe and closing hot air duct.

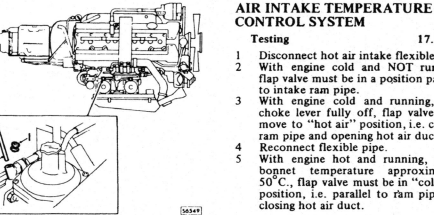

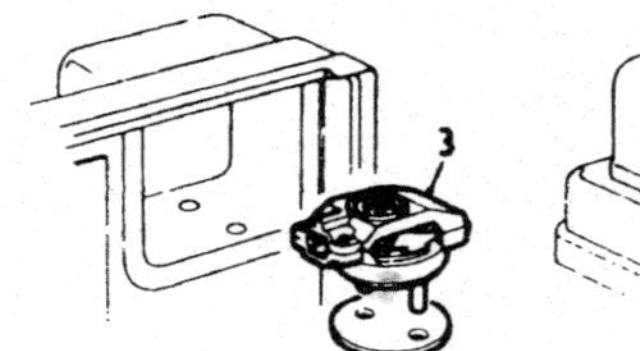

TEMPERATURE SENSOR UNIT

Remove and refit **17.30.10**

Removing

1. Remove air cleaner – 19.10.01.
2. Carefully prise spring clip off vacuum pipes.
3. Lift out temperature sensor unit.

Refitting

Reverse operations 1 to 3.

FLAP VALVE SERVO MOTOR

17.30.15

It is not possible to remove or repair the flap valve servo motor. Failure of this component therefore necessitates renewal of the air cleaner cover.

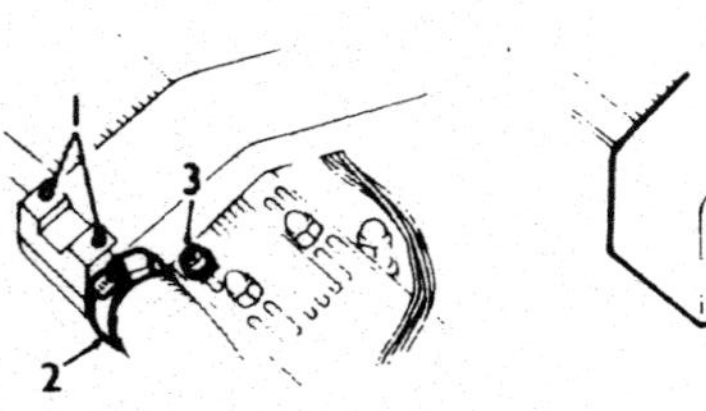

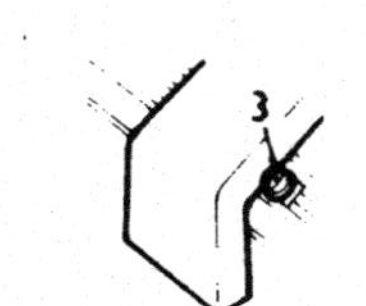

HOT AIR DUCT

Remove and refit **17.30.30**

Removing

Cars fitted with air conditioning only –

1 Remove screws and spire nuts securing heat exchanger to air duct.
2 Slacken clip securing air delivery pipe to air duct.
3 Remove screws, spring washers and plain washers securing air duct to camshaft covers.

Refitting

Reverse operations 1 to 3 as appropriate.

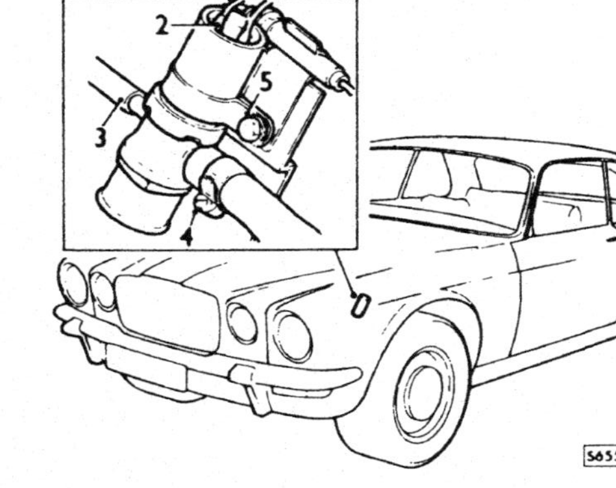

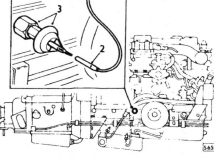

ANTI RUN-ON VALVE

Remove and refit **17.40.01**

Removing

1 Disconnect battery – 86.15.20.
2 Pull electrical connectors from solenoid.
3 Pull rubber manifold pressure tube from valve.
4 Release clip securing evaporative loss canister purge pipe to valve.
5 Slacken setscrews securing clip and remove valve downwards.

Refitting

Reverse operations 1 to 5; do not overtighten setscrew.

ANTI RUN-ON PRESSURE SWITCH

Remove and refit **17.40.10**

Removing

1 Disconnect battery – 86.15.20.
2 Beneath car pull connector from pressure switch.
3 Restrain adaptor and unscrew pressure switch.

Refitting

4 Fit new pressure switch on new copper washer.
5 Fit connector.
6 Reconnect battery, start engine and check for leaks.
7 Switch off engine.

ANTI RUN-ON SYSTEM

Testing **17.40.14**

If it is suspected that the anti run-on system is inoperative, carry out the following tests in the order given.

1 With engine running at idle speed, use finger to raise plunger and hold. If engine does not stop, continue with operation 2 and 3. If engine does stop, continue with operation 4 to 8 inclusive.
2 Check vacuum tube between inlet manifold and anti run-on valve on wing valance. Resecure or renew as necessary.

3 Check security of float chamber vent pipe, carburetter balance pipe, fuel tank vent pipe, and canister purge pipe, at canister and engine. Check for splits. Resecure or renew as necessary.
4 Check in line fuse adjacent to valve. If fuse is faulty fit replacement, if not, continue with operation 5.
5 Pull cable from oil pressure switch to rear of oil filter bowl.
6 Start engine. Short oil pressure switch cable to block and switch engine off. If engine does not run on, renew oil pressure switch, remake connections. If engine does run on, continue with operation 7.
7 Check security of all electrical connections in system, and ensure 12 V present at anti run-on valve and pressure switch with ignition switch off. If all satisfactory, renew valve.
8 Refit all electrical connectors and air pipes.

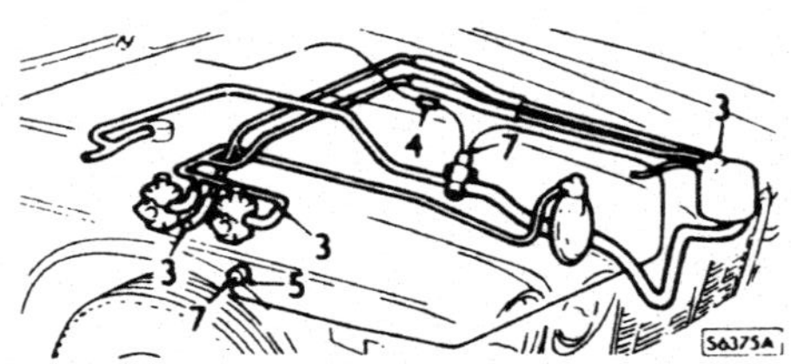

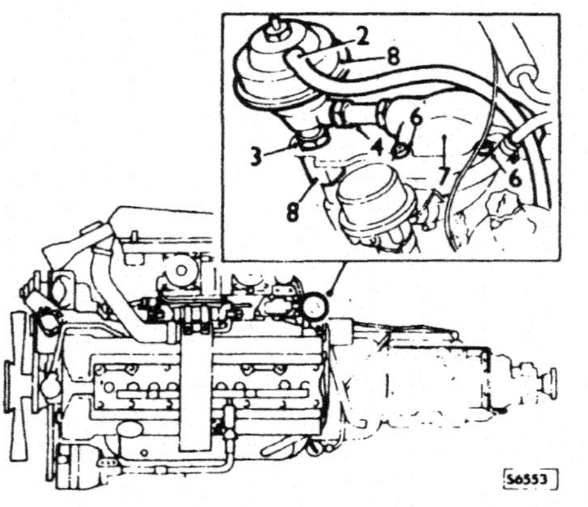

EXHAUST GAS RECIRCULATION VALVE
(Variable orifice system)

Remove and refit 17.45.01

Removing
1 Disconnect battery – 86.15.20.
2 Pull vacuum pipe from EGR valve.
3 Slacken locknut on top of EGR valve bracket.
4 Unscrew union nut at EGR valve delivery port.
5 Separate gulp valve inlet elbow from air cleaner backplate.
6 Remove four crosshead screws securing secondary throttle housing cover to housing.
7 Carefully separate cover from housing and move delivery pipe from EGR valve.
8 Restrain EGR pipe and screw valve from tube nut.
9 Check condition of housing cover gasket and, if necessary, renew.

Refitting
10 Ensure locknut fitted to EGR valve at top of thread.
11 Locate bracket over thread and screw valve into EGR pipe nut; offer secondary throttle housing cover into position and screw valve into nut until delivery pipe lines up with delivery port.
12 Secure cover, gulp valve bracket and EGR valve bracket into position using four crosshead screws and spring washers.
13 Secure delivery pipe tube nut.
14 Restrain EGR pipe and tighten locknut.
15 Fit vacuum pipe to EGR valve.
16 Fit gulp valve intake elbow to air cleaner backplate.
17 Reconnect battery.

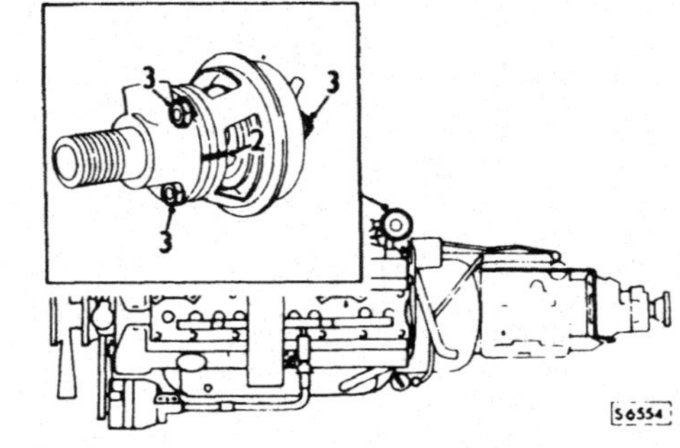

EXHAUST GAS RECIRCULATION VALVE
(Variable orifice system)

Overhaul 17.45.02

Dismantling
1 Remove EGR valve - 17.45.01.
2 Mark across diaphragm unit/valve body joint to ensure correct re-assembly.
3 Remove three nuts and separate diaphragm unit from body.
CAUTION: The adjustment screw and locknut on top of the diaphragm unit MUST NOT BE MOVED.

Cleaning
4 Thoroughly clean diaphragm unit using stiff brush and petrol. Dry with shop airline.
5 Scrape accumulated deposits from valve, valve seat and shaft, and body. Ensure all particles removed and wash body in petrol. Dry with shop airline.

Inspection
6 Check valve head, shaft and seat for excessive wear or pitting.
7 Check diaphragm for signs of wear or damage.
NOTE: The EGR valve must be renewed if either of the above checks are not satisfactory.

Reassembling
8 Offer valve into body and secure diaphragm unit, orientated correctly, using three nuts.
9 Refit EGR valve.

EMISSION CONTROL SYSTEM

Description 17.00.00

The emission control system fitted is designed to comply with local legislative requirements. Some or all of the following components may be fitted depending on those requirements. The description that follows refers to cars with an emission control system that complies with North American Federal specification.

Crankcase Breather System

To ensure that piston blow-by gas does not escape from the crankcase to atmosphere, a depression is maintained in the crankcase under all operating conditions. This is achieved by connecting the crankcase breather housing, located at the front of the cylinder head, to the air intake system between the air-flow meter and the throttle housing where a depression exists under all engine operating conditions.

Fuel Evaporative Loss Control

The fuel tank venting is designed to ensure that vapours are vented through the control system even when the car is parked on an inclined surface.
A capacity limiting device in the fuel tanks ensures sufficient free volume is available after filling to accommodate fuel which would otherwise be displaced as a result of high temperature rise.
Cars have a fuel tank evaporative loss control system fitted as standard equipment to meet U.S. Federal and Californian requirements.
The system operates as follows:
Interconnected tubing attached to the air vents in both fuel tanks conveys petrol vapour via a sealed storage canister to the throttle body.
The system is completely sealed. However, it is essential that routine maintenance operations detailed in this supplement are carried out by your Dealer **at the specified mileage intervals.**

Catalytic Converters

A catalytic converter is fitted into the exhaust system in order to reduce emissions of carbon monoxide, hydrocarbons, and oxides of nitrogen.

Catalytic Converter Precautions

1 In order to maintain the efficiency of the emission control system it is essential to use UNLEADED gasoline only; this fuel minimizes spark plug fouling thereby sustaining engine performance.

2 **DO NOT** tamper with the engine settings; they have been established to ensure that the vehicle will comply with stringent exhaust emission regulations. Incorrect engine settings could cause unusually high catalytic converter temperatures and thus result in damage to the converter and vehicle. If adjustment to the settings is considered necessary, this should be performed by a British Leyland Dealer or other qualified service facility.

3 A correctly tuned engine optimises exhaust emissions performance and fuel economy and it is recommended that the vehicle is maintained as outlined under **'MAINTENANCE SUMMARY'** of this Manual.

4 **DO NOT** continue to operate the vehicle if any engine malfunction is evident; malfunctions should be rectified immediately. For instance, misfire, loss of engine performance or engine run-on may lead to unusually high catalytic converter temperature and may result in damage to the converter and car.

5 **NEVER** leave the vehicle unattended with the engine running.

6 The use of a catalytic converter increases exhaust system temperatures (particularly under engine malfunction); therefore do not operate or park the vehicle in areas where combustible materials such as dry grass or leaves may come into contact with the exhaust system.

7 The vehicle is designed for normal road use. Below are examples of abuse which could damage the catalytic converters and car and may lead to a dangerous condition due to excessively high catalytic converter temperatures:
- a Competition use
- b Off roadway use
- c Excessive engine revolutions
- d Overloading the vehicle
- e Excessive towing loads
- f Switching off the engine and coasting in gear.

8 **DO NOT** run the engine with either a spark plug lead disconnected or a spark plug removed.
DO NOT use any device that requires an insert into a spark plug hole in order to generate air pressure (e.g. tyre pump, paint spray attachment, etc.), as this could also result in catalytic converter damage.

9 **DO NOT** push or tow the vehicle to start it; this could damage the catalytic converters. It is recommended that jumper leads are used.

10 Heavy impact on the converter casing must be avoided as it contains ceramic material which is easily damaged.

Fuel Filler Caps

Unleaded fuel **MUST** be used on catalyst-equipped cars, and labels to indicate this are displayed on the fuel gauge and the tank filler caps. The filler caps are designed to accommodate unleaded fuel pump nozzles only. The anti-surge flap prevents leaded fuel from being added to the fuel tanks because it does not open when a leaded fuel pump nozzle is entered into the filler neck up to the position of the restrictor and the pump is switched on.

Misfiring

If the engine misfires, the cause must be immediately rectified to prevent catalytic converter damage.

The emission control system fitted to this engine is designed to keep emissions within legislated limits providing ignition timing and fuel injection settings are correctly maintained and the engine is in sound mechanical condition.
It is essential that routine maintenance operations detailed in this Manual are carried out by your Dealer at the specified mileage intervals.

Exhaust Emission – Testing

In order that exhaust emissions are kept within the legislated limits an idle exhaust emission test MUST be carried out after any unscheduled service operations which might affect the emission control system.
CAUTION: CO content must not exceed 1.5% or be less than 0.5% with the electrical lead to the oxygen sensor disconnected.
It is essential that the equipment used for testing purposes is of the following type:
1 An infra-red CO exhaust gas analyser.
2 Engine and ignition diagnostic equipment.
3 Lucas 'EPITEST' fuel injection diagnostic equipment.

ENGINE BREATHER FILTER

Remove and refit 17.10.02

Removing
1 Remove hose clip securing rubber cover to breather housing.
2 Disconnect breather pipe from rubber cover.
3 Remove rubber cover.
4 Lift out filter.

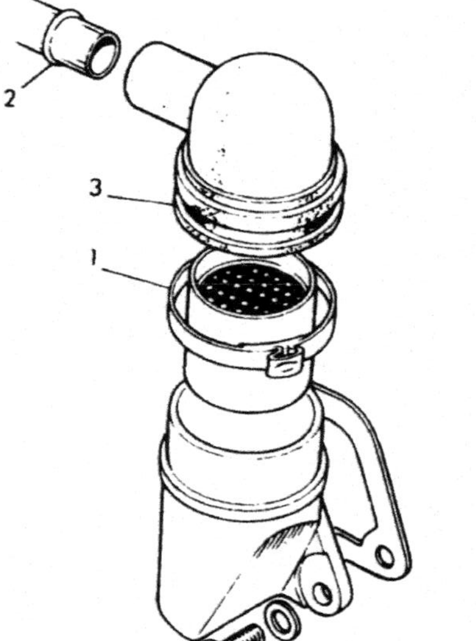

Refitting
Reverse operations 1 to 4.

ADSORPTION CANISTER

Remove and refit 17.15.13

Removing
1 Remove front right-hand road wheel.
2 Detach pipes from canister.
3 Remove nut, spring washer, plain washer and bolt securing canister clamp to mounting strap.
4 Withdraw canister.

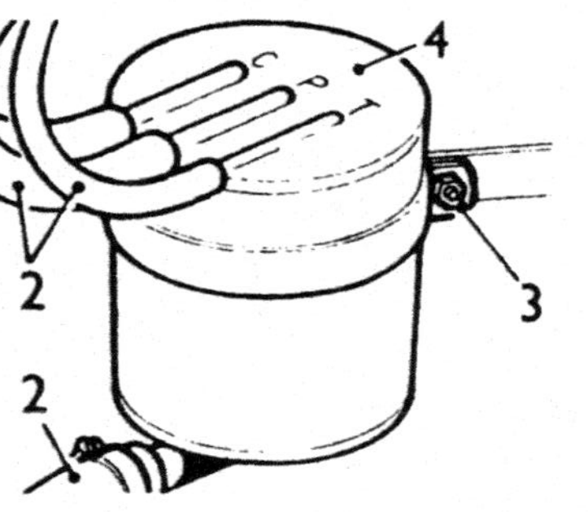

Refitting
5 Position replacement canister in clamp.
6 Reverse operations 1 to 3.

CATALYTIC CONVERTER

Remove and refit 17.50.01

Removing
1 Raise the vehicle on a ramp.
2 Remove nuts, plain washers and bolts securing flanges, separate intermediate pipe from down-pipe. Ensure intermediate pipe is adequately supported.
3 Remove nuts and plain washers securing heatshield and down-pipe to exhaust manifolds; withdraw heatshield.
4 Withdraw down-pipe/catalyst.

Refitting
Reverse operations 1 to 4. Coat all joints with Holt's Firegum. Tighten down-pipe and clamping flange fixing by diagonal selection to avoid distortion.

Fuel tank evaporative loss control system
An evaporative emission control system is fitted to cars to U.S. Federal and Australian design rule specifications. The system utilizes a canister containing activated charcoal to retain fumes given off the engine crankcase assembly and the fuel tank while the engine is at rest.
When the engine is running, a stream of air is drawn through the air pipe by means of connections to the throttle edge tappings on the inlet manifold throttle bodies carrying the adsorbed fumes into the engine and purging the canister.

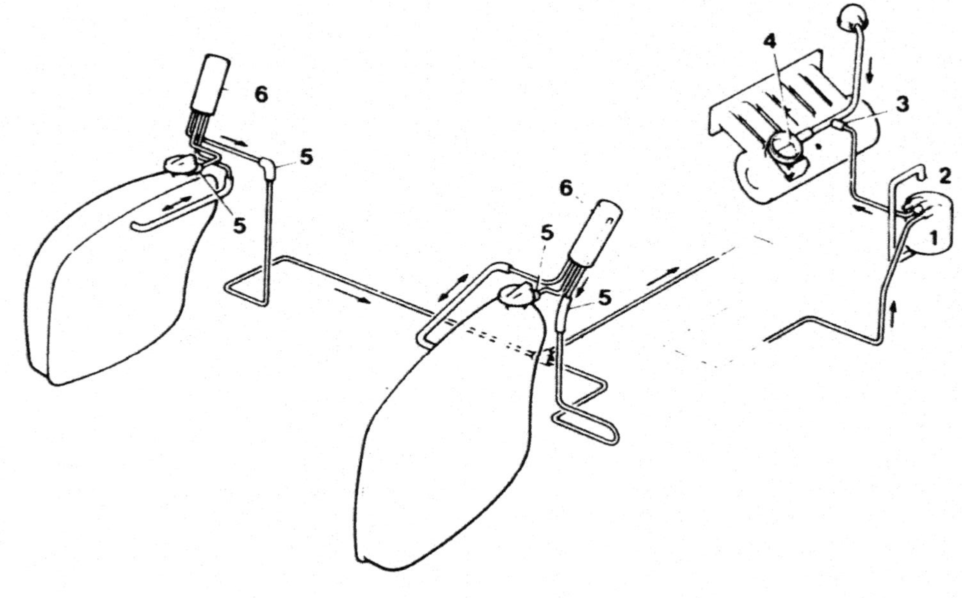

1. Charcoal canister
2. Purge air inlet
3. Restrictor
4. Purge port
5. Restrictor
6. Vapour separator

FAULT FINDING

This chart indicates the possible areas of the cause of the faults. Perform checks and remedial action shown in the order given, until the fault is rectified.

Details of the checks and remedial action are given on the respective area charts.

Extra checks shown in brackets refer only to the specific condition shown in brackets after the symptom.

SYMPTOM	POSSIBLE CAUSES IN ORDER OF CHECKING
Will not start (warm engine)	B1, B2, D1, D2, A1, A13, (A5), A5, A3, A6, A7, C1, C2, C3, A20, A8, A18.
Poor or erratic idle (cold engine)	D1, D2, A1, A12, A6, (A5), A3, C4, C6, C3, C5, A10, A11, B4, B3, B6, (A13), E1, E3, E4, E5, A21, A7, A8, A18.
Hesitation or flat spot (cold engine)	D1, D2, A1, A4, (A5), A9, A3, A6, B5, (A13), C4, C6, C3, C5, A15, B4, B3, B6, E1, E3, E4, E5, A7, A8, A18.
Excessive fuel consumption	D3, A4, A5, B5, B4, B3, B6, B8, B7, E1, E3, E4, E5, A21, A7, A19, A8, A18.
Lack of engine braking or high idle speed	A2, A16, A9, A12, A3, A13, A10, C3, A11, B5, A14, B6.
Lack of engine power	D1, D2, A1, A4, A5, A17, A3, B5, A15, A6, C4, C6, C3, C5, B4, B3, B6, E1, E3, E4, E5, A8, A18.
Engine overheating	B7, B8, C4.
Engine cuts out or stalls (at idle)	D1, D2, A1, A7, (A12), (A5), A5, A15, (A3), B4, A6, C4, C6, C3, C5, (A11), B6, E1, E3, E4, E5, B3, A8, A18.
Engine misfires	D1, D2, A1, A5, A6, A3, C4, C6, C3, C5, A15, B4, A11, B3, B6, E1, E3, E4, E5, A21, A8, A18.
Fuel smells	D3, A5, E4, E2, E3, E5, A11, A15, A19, A21, A8, A18.
Engine runs on	D1, A12, A16, A10, E4, E3, B7, B8, C3, C5.
Engine knock or pinking	D1, C3, C5, B7, B8.
Arcing at plugs	C4, C6.
Lean running (low CO)	A1, A14, A4, A2, A7, D1, D2, B6, E1, E3, E4, E5, A8, A18.
Rich running (excess CO)	A5, A11, E5, A19, A21, A8, A18.
Backfiring in exhaust	D1, D2, A1, A15, B4, B6, C3, E1, A8, A18.

ELECTRONIC PETROL INJECTION SYSTEM CHECKS

	POSSIBLE CAUSE	CHECK AND REMEDIAL ACTION
A1	Connections	Ensure all connector plugs are securely attached. Ensure electronic control unit (ECU) multi-pin connector is fully made. Ensure all ground connections are clean and tight.
A2	Air leaks	The engine will run weak because air leaking into the manifold is not monitored by the air-flow metering device. Ensure all hose and pipe connections are secure. Check all joints for leakage and re-make as necessary.
A3	Sticking air flap	Ensure that the air-flow meter flap moves freely. If the flap sticks the air-flow meter should be replaced.
A4	Throttle switch	Check function of full load switch.
A5	Cold start system inoperative	Check function of cold start system.
A6	Trigger	Check function of trigger unit.
A7	Temperature sensors	Check sensors for open and short circuit.
A8	ECU	As a last resort the ECU should be checked by substitution.
A9	Throttle butterfly adjustment	Reset as per operation 19.20.11.
A10	Throttle by-pass valve	The valve should be suitably adjusted until fault has been rectified and re-check function.
A11	Incorrect idle mixture	Check CO level and adjust to specified levels using the screw under the black dust cover on the air-flow meter. The oxygen sensor should be disconnected for this operation.
A12	Incorrect idle speed	This should be adjusted by means of the screw on the air distribution block.
A13	Auxiliary air valve inoperative	Test in accordance with operation 19.20.17.
A14	Throttle spindle leaks	Check seals, bearings and spindles for wear. Renew as required.
A15	Air cleaner blocked	Inspect element and renew as necessary.
A16	Throttle sticking	Lubricate, check for wear and reset.
A17	Throttle inhibited	Check and remove obstructions of free movement of throttle mechanism through total travel. If no obstructions apparent, reset.
A18	Air-flow meter	As a last resort the air-flow meter should be checked by substitution.
A19	Oxygen sensor	The oxygen sensor should be checked by substitution.
A20	Power resistors	The power resistors should be checked by substitution.
A21	Injector faults	Check function of injectors.

BASIC ENGINE CHECKS

	POSSIBLE CAUSE	CHECK AND REMEDIAL ACTION
B1	Low battery condition	Check battery condition with hydrometer. Re-charge, clean and secure terminals, or renew as necessary. (If battery is serviceable but discharged, trace and rectify cause of flat battery, e.g. short circuit or insufficient chart from alternator.)
B2	Start system deficient	If starter fails to turn engine briskly, check engagement circuit and connections. Check and clean main starter circuit and connections.
B3	Poor compressions	Check compressions with proprietary tester. If compressions are low or uneven, check/adjust valve clearances and re-test. If compressions are still unsatisfactory, remove cylinder head for further examination and rectification.
B4	Exhaust system leaking or blocked	Check and rectify as necessary.
B5	Faults on areas of vehicle other than engine	Check for binding brakes, slipping clutch, etc.
B6	Air leaks at inlet manifold	Check inlet manifold/cylinder head joint. Re-make with new gasket if necessary. Check manifold tappings for leaks--seal as necessary.
B7	Cooling system blocked or leaking	Flush system and check for blockage. Check hoses and connections for security and leakage. Renew as necessary. Check thermostat, and renew if faulty.
B8	Cylinder head gasket leaking	Check cylinder block/head joint for signs of leakage. Renew gasket if necessary.

IGNITION SYSTEM CHECKS

	POSSIBLE CAUSE	CHECK AND REMEDIAL ACTION
C1	H.T. circuit faults	Disconnect king lead at distributor and position the end approximately 3/16 in (5 mm) from earthed metal. Switch on ignition, disconnect white/blue lead and check for spark at king lead end each time white/blue lead is disconnected. If spark is non-existent or weak, renew king lead and re-test. If spark is satisfactory, check H.T. leads for fraying, deterioration and security, distributor cap for cracks, tracking, dirt or condensation, distributor rotor for deterioration and spark plugs. Renew leads, cap, rotor or plugs as necessary. With distributor cap removed, crank engine and check that distributor shaft rotates.
C2	L.T. power faults	Ensure ignition switch on and check supply voltage. If less than 9 volts, check ignition switch, wiring and connections. If more than 9 volts, check voltage at coil '+ve' terminal. If this is not in the range 4 to 8 volts, renew the ballast resistance wire and re-test. If satisfactory, check voltage at coil '–ve' terminal. If this is more than 2 volts, check the drive resistor (9 to 11 ohms) and renew if necessary, ensure that the distributor body is earthed and, as a last resort, renew the distributor complete. If the coil '–ve' terminal voltage is less than 2 volts, disconnect the white/blue lead and re-check the coil '–ve' terminal voltage. If this is now more than 9 volts, check the coil by substitution and as a last resort, renew the distributor complete. If less than 9 volts, disconnect coil '–ve' lead and again check voltage on coil '–ve' terminal. If the voltage is 9 volts, check the coil by substitution. If more than 9 volts, renew the distributor.
C3	Ignition timing incorrect	Check ignition timing and adjust as necessary.
C4	System deterioration	Check ignition wiring for fraying, chafing and deterioration. Check distributor cap for cracks and tracking and rotor condition. Renew leads, cap or rotor as necessary.
C5	Advance system faults	Disconnect vacuum pipes and check operation of advance mechanism against advance figures, using stroboscopic timing light. Lubricate or renew as necessary. Re-connect vacuum pipes and check operation of advance unit. Renew or secure vacuum pipes if necessary.
C6	Spark plug faults	Remove spark plugs, clean, reset gap and test on proprietary spark plug testing machine. Renew if in doubt.

FUEL SYSTEM CHECKS

	POSSIBLE CAUSE	CHECK AND REMEDIAL ACTION
D1	Insufficient, incorrect or contaminated fuel	Ensure that the fuel tank has an adequate level of the correct grade of fuel. If dirt or water contamination is suspected, drain and flush the fuel tank, flush the system and renew the fuel line filter before filling with clean fuel.
D2	Fuel starvation	Check fuel pressure according to operation 19.45.12. If not satisfactory, check fuel feed pipes for leaks or blockage. Renew connectors if damaged or deteriorated. If contamination of fuel is discovered, flush fuel system and renew line filter. If necessary, renew fuel line filter, pressure regulator or fuel pump to rectify.
D3	Leaking fuel	Check fuel system for leaks and rectify as necessary. Renew any doubtful connectors.

EVAPORATIVE AND CRANKCASE VENTILATION SYSTEM CHECKS

	POSSIBLE CAUSE	CHECK AND REMEDIAL ACTION
E1	Engine oil filter cap loose or leaking	Check cap for security. Renew cap if seal is deteriorated.
E2	Fuel filler cap defective	Check seal for condition – renew if deteriorated. Check filler cap for security – rectify or renew as necessary.
E3	Restrictors missing or blocked	Check and clear or renew as necessary.
E4	Hoses blocked or leaking	Check and clear as necessary. Renew any deteriorated hoses.
E5	Charcoal canister restricted or blocked	Inspect and renew if necessary.

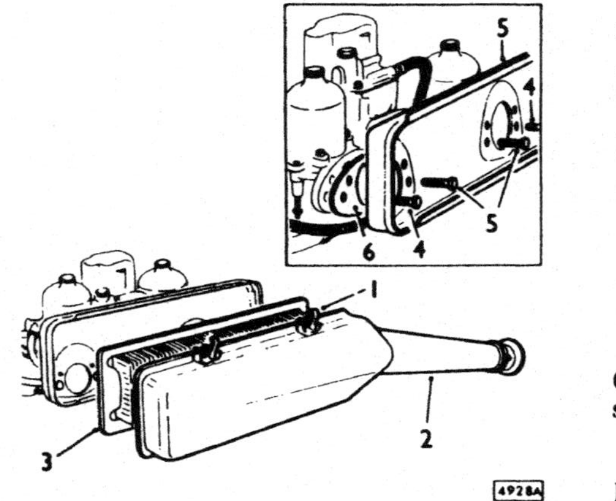

AIR CLEANER

Remove and refit **19.10.01**

Non emission control cars only

Removing
1. Release toggle clips securing air cleaner cover to backplate.
2. Lif off cover.
3. Remove element.
4. Remove outer pair of nuts and bolts securing backplate to carburetter flanges.
5. Support A.E.D. unit and remove inner pair of nuts and bolts; lift off backplate.
6. Remove carburetter flange gaskets and discard.

Refitting
Reverse operations 1 to 6; use new carburetter flange gaskets.

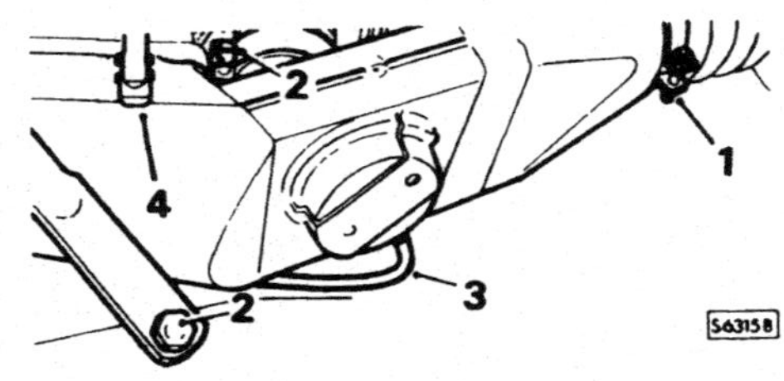

Remove and refit

Cars to European emission control specification with H.I.F. 7 carburetters only

Removing
1. Slacken clip and disconnect flexible inlet pipe.
2. Slacken clip and disconnect air duct flexible pipe.
3. Pull vacuum pipe from flap valve servo motor.
4. Release hose clip securing vent hose to stub pipe on inner face of back plate.
5. Release toggle clips and withdraw air cleaner cover.
6. Lift out filter element.
7. Remove outer pair of nuts and bolts securing backplate to carburetter flanges and spacers.
8. Support A.E.D. unit and remove inner pair of nuts and bolts. Collect spacers.
9. Move backplate away from carburetters and disconnect vacuum pipe from temperature sensor unit and vent hose from stub.
10. Lift out backplate; remove and discard gaskets.

Refitting
Reverse operations 1 to 10, using four new gaskets. Ensure that air cleaner cover is correctly fitted.

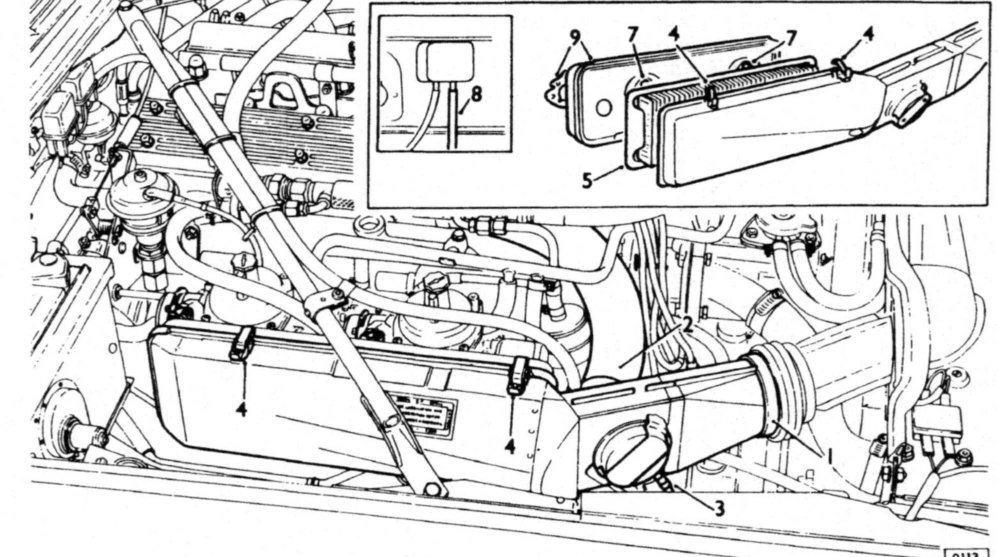

Remove and refit

Cars to U.S. Federal emission control specification only

Removing
1. Slacken clip and disconnect flexible inlet pipe.
2. Slacken clip and disconnect air duct flexible pipe.
3. Pull vacuum pipe from flap valve servo motor.
4. Release toggle clips and withdraw air cleaner cover.
5. Lift out filter element.
6. Carefully prise gulp valve hose (where fitted) from backplate; slacken clip on float chamber vent pipe, between carburetters.
7. Remove bolts and spring washers securing backplate to carburetter flanges.
8. Move backplate away from carburetters and disconnect vacuum pipe from temperature sensor unit.
9. Lift out backplate; remove and discard gaskets.

Refitting
Reverse operations 1 to 8; use new gasket between air cleaner and carburetters. Ensure air cleaner cover is correctly fitted.

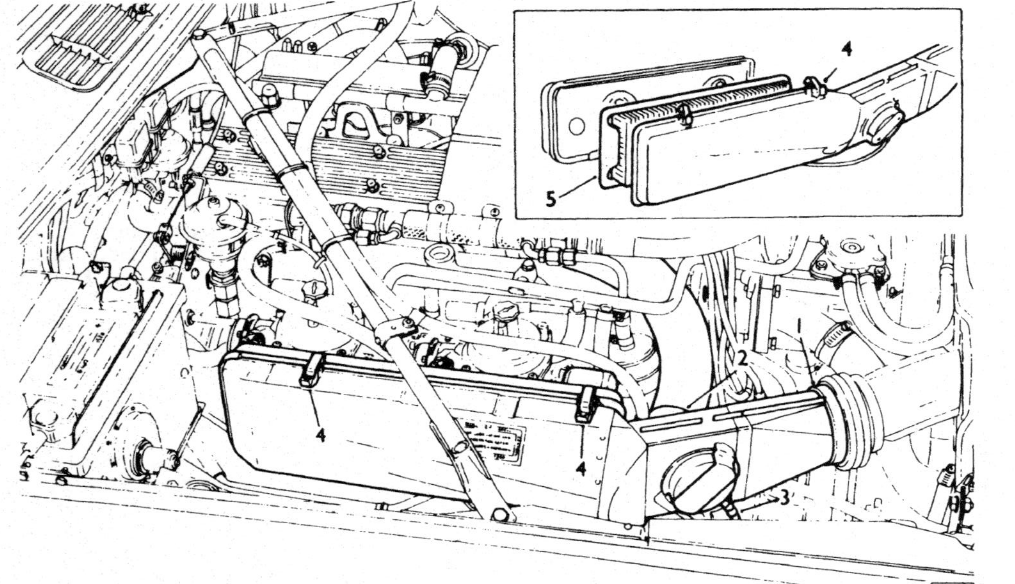

AIR CLEANER

Renew Element **19.10.08**

Non emission control cars only

Removing

1 Release toggle clips securing air cleaner cover to backplate.
2 Lift off cover.
3 Remove element.

Refitting

Reverse operations 1 to 3 inclusive, and ensure cover fitted correctly.

Renew element

Cars to European and U.S. Federal emission control specification only

Removing

1 Slacken clip and disconnect flexible inlet pipe.
2 Slacken clip and disconnect air duct flexible pipe.
3 Disconnect vacuum pipe from flap valve servo motor.
4 Release toggle clips and withdraw air cleaner cover.
5 Lift out filter element.

Refitting

Reverse operations 1 to 5 inclusive, and ensure cover fitted correctly.

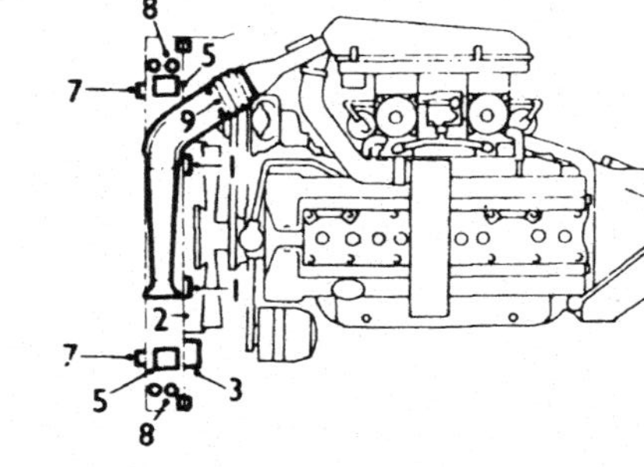

RAM TUBE

Remove and refit **19.10.21**

Cars to European and U.S. Federal emission control specification only

Removing

1 Remove nuts, bolts and washers securing expansion tank pipe and radiator bleed pipe clips. Retain cable harness clips.
2 Remove set screws, washers and locknuts securing fan cowl brackets.
3 Remove two self tapping screws securing headlamp relay.
4 Note connections and pull connectors from headlamp relay.
5 Note connections and pull connectors from headlamp fuse boxes.
6 Carefully pull cable harness from top rail grommet.

Cars fitted with air conditioning only

7 Remove Phillips head screws, washers and rubber bushes securing condenser unit. Support condenser using suitable padding.

All cars

8 Remove six setscrews and two nuts, bolts and washers securing radiator top rail.
9 Release clip securing flexible inlet pipe.
10 Lift ram tube and radiator top rail assembly from car.
11 Release clips and remove fuse boxes from top rail.

Refitting

Reverse operations 1 to 11.

CARBURETTERS

Description **19.15.00**

Cars built to U.S. federal emission control requirements are fitted with Zenith-Stromberg carburetters, early cars having manual choke controls, replaced on later cars by automatic chokes controlled by coolant temperature. No work may be carried out on these carburetters unless equipment is available for carrying out an exhaust emission test after completing the work.

Other cars are fitted with two S U carburetters and an A.E.D. (automatic enrichment device) to provide rich mixture for cold starting and initial running. Early cars have H.S.8 carburetters but they are replaced after engine No. 8L 26204 (4.2 L engines) and 8A 5098 (3.4 L engines) by H.I.F. 7 units. These carburetters provide an additional automatic adjustment of mixture strength according to changes in fuel temperature and assist in achieving the precise control of emissions required to meet current regulations. Being of more compact design than the H.S. carburetters they also provide improved access to adjacent equipment and have the advantage of concentric float chambers.

DATA

Needle type 4.2 cars, B.D.N.
3.4 cars, B.D.W.
Spring (4.2 and 3.4) RED.
A.E.D. unit type (4.2 and 3.4) TZX 1002

Introduction

The HIF (Horizontal Integral Float-Chamber) carburetter is functionally similar to preceding S.U. designs and operates on the variable choke/constant depression principle. This instrument has been designed as part of a carburation system which can achieve the precise induction of mixture required to control exhaust emissions to within statutory limits.

The HIF employs the familiar suction chamber/piston assembly together with a single jet-needle fuel metering system.

Main design changes are to be found in the position and layout of the float chamber, the incorporation of a fuel temperature compensating device and the arrangement for mixture setting.

Float Chamber Design
The float chamber is integral with the main body casting. Access to the chamber is obtained by removing the bottom cover plate. The moulded float is shaped so that it surrounds the jet tube and is pivoted along a line parallel to the inlet flange. The float is retained by a spindle which screws into the body casting.

Entry of fuel into the float chamber is through a brass tube in the side of the carburetter body via a needle valve assembly.

The jet is pressed into the top of an aluminium tube which is in turn pressed into a plastic moulding. This hollow moulding known as the jet head is open at the lower end allowing fuel to enter the jet tube.

Mixture Adjustment
The jet tube is moved in the vertical plane to provide mixture adjustment only.

Fuel Temperature Compensation
This device alters the jet position in relation to the metering needle to compensate for changes in fuel viscosity which take place with changes in fuel temperature.

The jet head is attached to a bi-metal blade. This bi-metal is immersed in fuel in the float chamber and will move in the vertical plane in response to changes in fuel temperature. The jet will be raised to a weaker position on the jet needle when the fuel temperature rises and will be lowered to a richer position when the temperature falls.

From this is will be seen that once the jet position has been selected by adjusting the mixture screw, alterations of fuel temperature will bring about slight alterations in jet position to compensate for the change in fuel viscosity.

The effect of this device is that driveability is improved over wide ranges of temperature, and exhaust emissions kept within closer limits during cold starting and warm up period. Temperature compensation also allows carburetters to have the mixture setting pre-set and sealed before a vehicle is delivered.

CARBURETTERS – CAR SET

Tune and adjust **19.15.02**
(H.S.8 carburetters)

Non emission control and cars to European specification only

Adjust
NOTE: Before tuning the carburetters, check sparking plug gaps, contact breaker gap, distributor centrifugal advance mechanism and ignition timing. Adjust as necessary. The mixture adjusting screws 'A' are pre-set during manufacture and SHOULD ON NO ACCOUNT BE DISTURBED.

1 Remove air cleaner cover and element – 19.10.08.
2 Run engine until it attains normal operating temperature.
3 Check that mixture delivery pipe is warm.

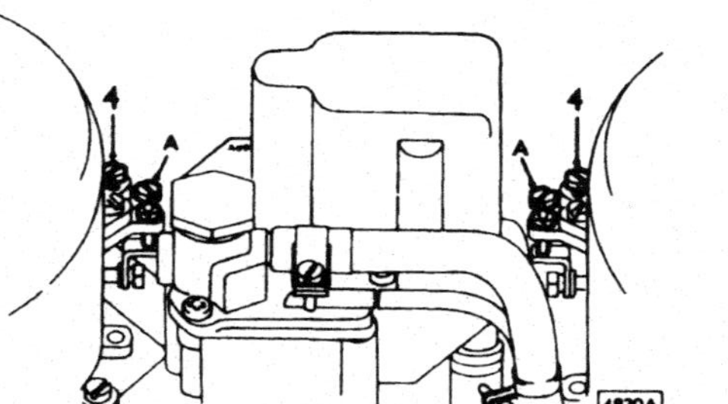

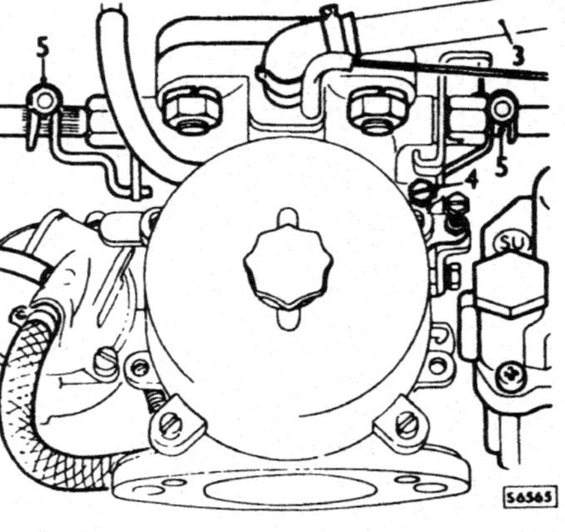

4 Screw back throttle adjusting screws until they no longer contact throttle levers.
5 Slacken clamp bolts at both sides or rear carburetter.
6 Ensure that butterfly valve in each carburetter is fully closed.
7 Screw throttle adjusting screws until they just contact throttle levers, then screw in a further 1½ turns.
8 Start engine and compare intensity of intake 'hiss' on both carburetters. Alter throttle adjusting screws until 'hiss' is the same on both carburetters.

NOTE: Correct idling speed is 750 rev/min.

9 Stop engine.
10 Adjust position of forward clamp so that tongue on clamp rests against **BOTTOM** edge of yoke without operating rear carburetter; tighten clamp bolt – cars fitted with manual transmission only.
Cars fitted with automatic transmission **MUST** have tongue at TOP edge of yoke so that there is absolutely NO BACKLASH between carburetters.

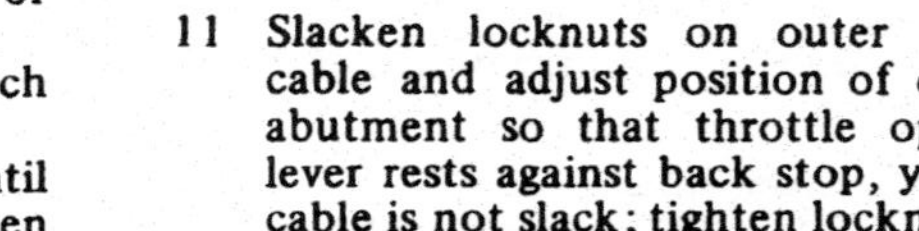

11 Slacken locknuts on outer throttle cable and adjust position of cable in abutment so that throttle operating lever rests against back stop, yet inner cable is not slack; tighten locknuts.
12 Tighten bolt of rearmost clamp.
13 Check operate throttle pedal; cable should pick up linkage immediately pedal is moved.
14 Slacken locknut and wind back operating lever stop screw.
15 Press operating lever to fully open butterfly valves and wind stop screw to contact lever. Tighten locknut.
16 Depress throttle pedal and ensure that operating lever moves to touch stop screw with pedal at end of its travel. Adjust pedal stop so that cable is not under undue strain when pedal fully depressed.
17 Check operation of kickdown cable – 44.30.02 – cars fitted with Model 65 automatic transmission only.
18 Check operation of kickdown switch – 44.30.12 – cars fitted with Model 12 automatic transmission only.
19 Refit air cleaner.

CARBURETTERS – CAR SET

Tune and adjust (H.I.F. 7 Carburetters) **19.15.02**

NOTE: Carburetter mixture adjustment is pre-set and sealed and should not normally be altered. The only adjustment that should be made are to idle speed setting and throttle controls.
Before making any adjustment to carburetters or throttle controls, check and if necessary rectify spark plug conditions and gaps, contact breaker gap, ignition timing, distributor centrifugal advance mechanism and compression pressures. Check tappet clearances if compression pressures are uneven.
If satisfactory results are not achieved by carrying out the procedure detailed below it will be necessary to refer to mixture controls, adjust and reset. See 19.15.06.

NOTE: These operations may not be undertaken unless suitable C.O. metering equipment is available for emission testing, and it is a legal requirement for cars first registered on or after 1st October 1976 in Europe and Switzerland, or on or after 1st April 1977 in the United Kingdom that the tamper-proofing seals fitted to the carburetters of these cars may not be removed unless such equipment is provided. Tamper-proof seals, if fitted, **MUST** be renewed after current emission regulations have been met in test.

1 Remove air cleaner element. See 19.10.08.
2 Unscrew damper cap of one carburetter.

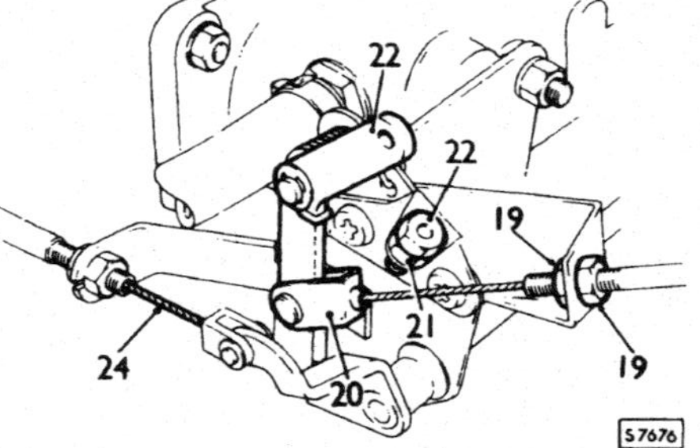

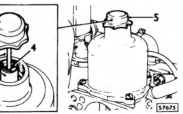

CAUTION: It is essential that in lifting cap, damper retainer clip fitted below it is not displaced from its position in piston rod. If retainer is inadvertently displaced it must be refitted by pressing fully into piston rod.

3 Carefully withdraw damper, by raising cap, until piston and damper **TOGETHER** reach limit of upward travel, and inspect oil level in damper retainer clip.
4 If oil is not visible in retainer add engine oil (preferably SAE 20) to recess in retainer until it is just visible at bottom of retainer recess. Move damper GENTLY up and down to 'pump' any trapped air out of reservoir.
5 Replace cap and tighten firmly by hand.
6 Repeat operations 2 to 5 on second carburetter.
7 Check that throttle linkage and cable to pedal operate smoothly.

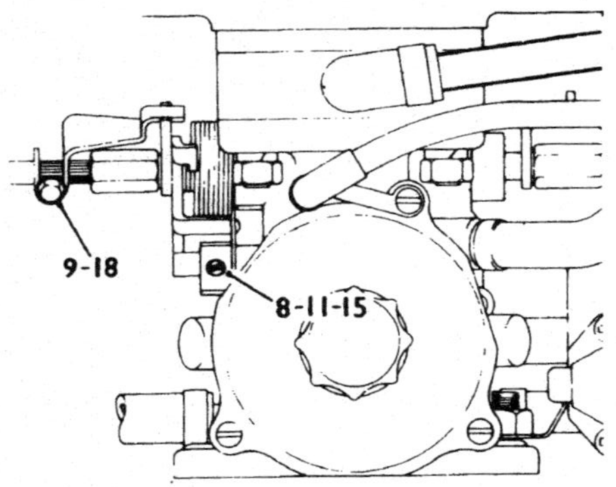

8 Remove lids of tamper proof caps (if fitted) over slow running adjusting set screws. Detach setscrews, remove tamper proof seals and replace with new seals. Refit adjusting screws, and screw in until they almost contact throttle levers. DO NOT close lid on this operation.

NOTE: If tamper proof cap is not fitted, unscrew slow running adjusting screws until they no longer contact throttle levers.

9 Slacken nuts of clamp bolts on throttle operating spindles on both sides of rear carburetter.
10 Raise piston in each carburetter with finger and, using mirror, inspect to check that both butterfly valves are fully closed and that over-run valves are correctly seated.
11 Screw down both adjusting screws until they just contact throttle levers, then screw down another one turn.
12 Start engine and run until it reaches normal operating temperature, stop engine.
13 Check that mixture pipe from AED unit is warm.
14 Start engine again and using rubber tube as "listening tube" compare intensity of hiss of air entering each choke. Alter setting of adjusting screws until hiss is the same on both carburetters.
NOTE: This operation may, if preferred be carried out using a balance meter to maker's instructions.
15 Alter settings of both adjusting screws by the same amount to achieve correct idling speed, i.e. 750 rev/min.
16 When correct idling speed is achieved, recheck balance of carburetters by repeating operation 14; alter settings of adjusting screws if necessary to secure correct balance and idling speed.
17 Stop engine.
18 Retighten clamp bolts on throttle operating rods to secure correct opening characteristics on throttle. On automatic transmission cars there should be no backlash between tongue and upper arm of yoke behind rear carburetter, or between tongue and lower arm of yoke between carburetters; both butterflies should start to open as soon as throttle cable is moved. On manual transmission cars there should be a gap of up to 0.036 in. (0,9 mm.) between tongue and lower arm of yoke between carburetters, so that rear butterfly opens by up to 3° before front butterfly starts to open.
There should be no backlash between tongue and upper arm of yoke behind rear carburetter.

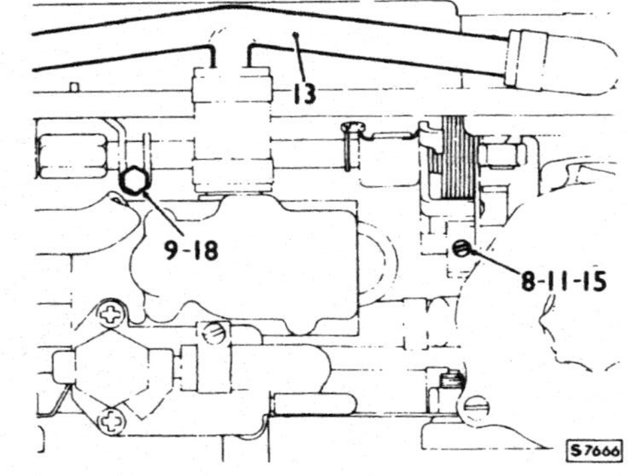

19 Slacken locknuts on outer throttle cable and adjust position of cable in abutment so that throttle operating lever rests against back stop, yet inner cable is not slack; tighten locknuts.
20 Check operate throttle cable; cable should pick up linkage immediately pedal is moved.
21 Slacken locknut and wind back operating lever stop screw.
22 Press operating lever to open butterfly valves fully and turn stop screw to contact lever. Tighten locknut.
23 Depress throttle pedal and ensure that operating lever moves to touch stop screw with pedal at end of its travel. Adjust pedal stop so that cable is not under undue strain when pedal is fully depressed.
24 Check operation of kickdown cable on cars fitted with automatic transmission. See 44.30.02.
25 Refit air cleaner element. See 19.10.08.
26 Check CO emissions, using approved equipment, and correct if necessary to bring within current requirements.
27 Secure lids of tamper proof caps, if fitted, over slow running adjustment set screws.

CARBURETTERS – CAR SET

Tune and adjust 19.15.02

Cars to U.S. Federal emission control specification only

Adjust
It is impossible to tune carburetters successfully unless engine timing, spark plug gaps and tappet clearances are correctly set.

If carburetters are to be re-set, either following removal or as a result of unsatisfactory performance, the quality of fast and slow idling must first be adjusted.

If it is found impossible to achieve satisfactory results by other adjustment, and there is reasonable certainty that mixture strength is at fault, the procedure detailed under **Mixture – check and adjust** may be carried out.

Under normal circumstances mixture adjustment is not necessary as carburetters are pre-set by the manufacturer, any adjustment made will, therefore, be due to either a fault condition or unauthorised tampering.

It is stressed that owing to the difficulty of satisfactory balancing, the needle adjustment **must not** be tampered with unless fully skilled personnel and adequate test equipment are available.

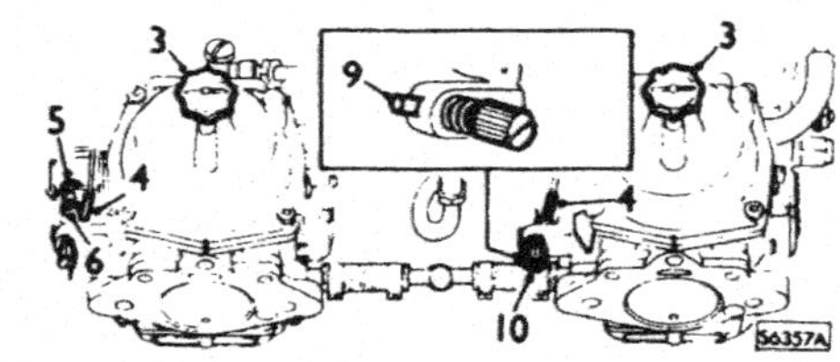

Slow idle setting
1 Remove air cleaner cover and filter element – 19.10.08.
2 Run engine until it reaches normal operating temperature.
3 Top up carburetter piston dampers with clean engine oil.
4 Slacken off idle trim screw on each carburetter until it no longer contacts throttle lever.
5 Slacken off choke inner cable clamping bolts; ensure each choke is fully closed; retighten clamping bolts.
6 Slacken throttle spindle clamping bolts, ensure throttles are fully closed.
7 Screw in idle trim screw on both carburetters until contact is just made with throttle lever, then further 1½ turns.
8 Start engine and adjust idle screws to give idle speed of 750 r.p.m.
NOTE: Selector lever MUST be in 'P' position.
9 Check synchronisation of carburetters by means of a balance meter and adjust idle screws as necessary.
10 Tighten clamp bolts.
11 Check the secondary throttle butterfly valve adjustment screws are in contact with induction housing and holding valves slightly open.
12 If necessary, check and adjust engine fast idle speed.
13 Refit air cleaner filter element and cover.
14 Carry out an exhaust gas CO content analysis.

Fast Idle setting
1 Remove air cleaner cover and filter element – 19.10.08.
2 Run engine until it reaches normal operating temperature.
3 Top up carburetter piston dampers with clean engine oil.
4 Slacken off choke inner cable clamping bolts, push choke control knob fully closed, ensure each choke is fully closed and retighten clamping bolts.

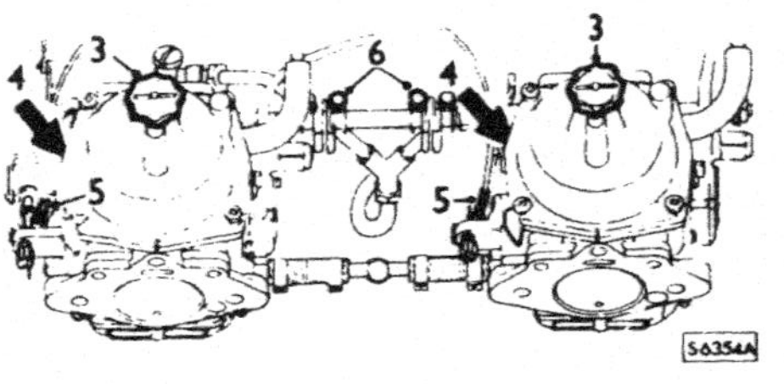

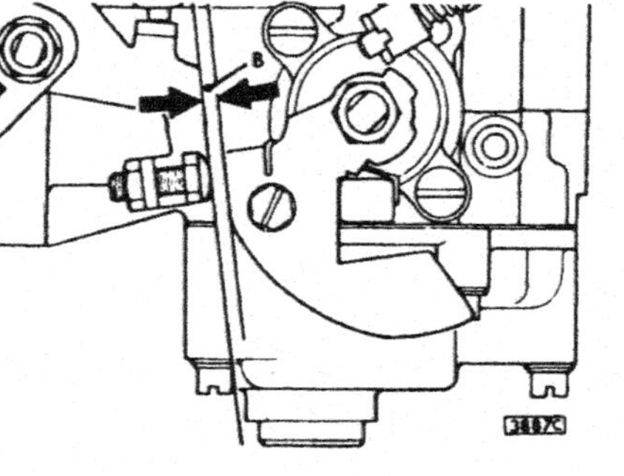

5 Slacken locknut on rear carburetter fast idle adjustment screw.
6 Turn fast idle adjustment screw until gap between head of screw and choke cam 'B' is .067 in. (1,6 mm.).
7 Tighten locknut and recheck gap.
8 Refit air cleaner filter element and cover.

To adjust for Summer or Winter operation:
NOTE: A control on both front and rear carburetters enables the choke to be varied for summer and winter operation.

9 Note position of pin; if lying in horizontal slot in casting, choke is set for winter running.
10 Depress plunger and turn through 90° for summer running.
11 Repeat operations 9 and 10 on other carburetter.

Mixture – Check and adjust
Service tools – Carburetter adjusting tool S.353: Sampling meter (CO).

1 Disconnect air injection system on air pump side of non-return valve, and block valve inlet.
2 Insert probe of a CO sampling meter fully into each exhaust tail pipe in turn. Note CO levels indicated. The CO content of the exhaust gases must be within the range 3% to 4½%.
3 If adjustment is required proceed with operations 4 to 20.

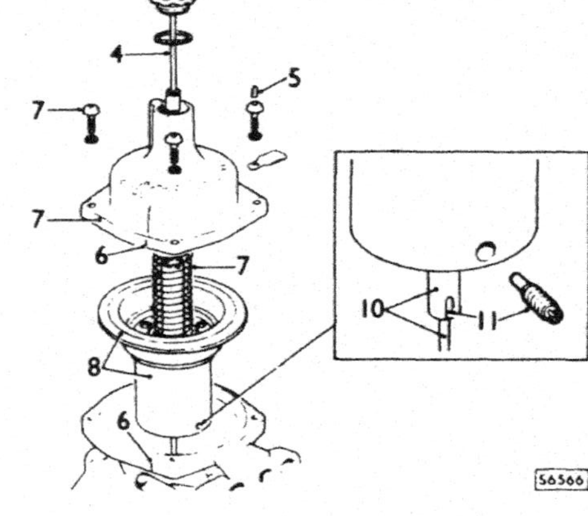

NOTE: Carry out operations 4 to 14 on both carburetters.

4 Remove carburetter damper.
5 Remove lead plug from carburetter cover securing screw.
6 Mark relative position of cover to carburetter body.
7 Remove cover securing screws; lift off cover and remove piston return spring.
8 Withdraw piston and diaphragm assembly.
9 Check condition of diaphragm.
10 Check whether needle bias spring is intact. If broken, needle housing must be renewed.
11 Remove needle retaining screw and check plunger spring intact. Refit if satisfactory, renew if not. Fully tighten screw to locate plunger in keyway of needle housing.
12 Press needle housing into air valve while rotating inner tool S.353 clockwise until plug engages.
13 Turn tool clockwise until Delrin disc on needle is flush with needle housing guide tube.
14 Reverse operations 4 to 8 on both carburetters, ensuring lug on diaphragm locates in body.
15 Repeat operation 2. If adjustment is still necessary proceed with operations 16 to 20.

16 Remove carburetter dampers and slowly insert carburetter adjusting tool, S.353 into dashpot until outer tool engages in lugs in air valve and inner tool engages hexagon in needle adjuster plug.

WARNING: MOVEMENT OF THE INNER TOOL MUST NOT EXCEED A THREE QUARTER TURN IN EITHER DIRECTION.

17 Hold outer tool firmly and turn inner tool clockwise to enrich mixture (increase CO content) or anti-clockwise to weaken mixture (decrease CO content).
18 When satisfactory results are achieved remove Service tool and stop engine.
19 Check and, if necessary, regulate oil level in carburetter dashpots and refit dampers.
20 Refit air cleaners.
21 Refit air delivery pipe after unblocking valve inlet.

CARBURETTERS

Mixture control on SU H.I.F. 7 carburetters.

Adjust and reset **19.15.06**

NOTE: Do not adjust mixture control on carburetters until all other possible factors which could cause faulty carburation have been eliminated; control setting has been correctly set and sealed before delivery, and should not require alteration.
Resetting mixture controls necessitates a check of emissions, using an exhaust gas analyser; regulation regarding emissions must be strictly adhered to. Ensure that equipment required for emission check is available before commencing mixture adjustment, and proceed as follows:
1 If possible, choose a location with an ambient temperature of between 15° and 26°C (60° to 80°F) to carry out job. Place selector at P on automatic transmission cars.
2 Remove air cleaner. See 19.10.01.

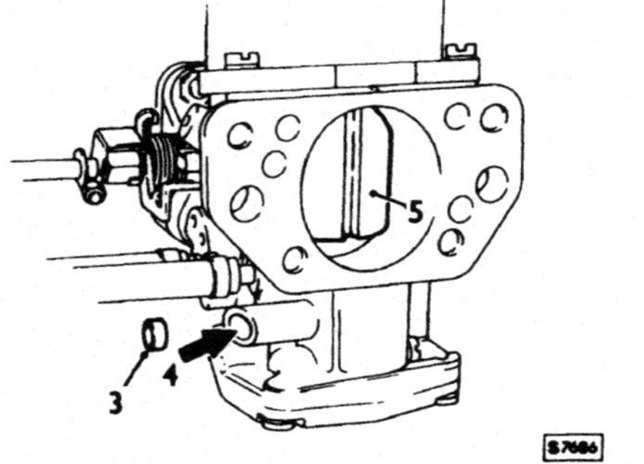

3 Remove plugs and sealant from both carburetter jet adjustment screws.
4 Turn jet adjusting screws clockwise, if necessary, (to lower jets) until jets are below level of transverse bridges in carburetter bores.
5 Lift one carburetter piston by hand and insert straight edge approximately 13 mm. (0.5 in.) wide alongside needle in a vertical plane.
6 Turn adjusting screw anti-clockwise until jet just contacts steel rule. Jet is then accurately positioned level with carburetter bridge.
7 Screw in adjusting screw 3 2/3 turns, bringing jet 0.117 in. (2,97 mm.) below carburetter bridge. This is the datum position at 20°C (68°F) from which final adjustments are to be made.
8 Repeat operations 5, 6 and 7 on second carburetter.
9 Check oil level in carburetter piston bores – See 19.15.02 operations 2 to 5.
10 Start engine and run until fully warm, for at least five minutes after thermostat opens.
11 Run engine at approximately 2500 rev/min for one minute; stop engine.

**NOTE: Adjustment may now be carried out for three minutes, then engine must be run again for one minute at 2500 rev/min before any further adjustment is made.
This cycle of operations – run for one minute, adjust for three – may be repeated as often as necessary.**

12 Check that idling speed is 750 rev/min and if not adjusted to this figure – See 19.15.02 operations 9 to 18.
13 Turn each jet adjusting screw clockwise to enrich mixture or anti-clockwise to weaken, turning each screw by the same small amount until fastest idling speed is indicated.
14 Turn each screw anti-clockwise, each by the same amount until engine speed just begins to fall.
15 Turn each screw clockwise by the same very small amount until maximum speed is regained.
16 Readjust tickover, if necessary, to achieve figure obtained in operation 12.
17 Connect a suitable exhaust gas analyser to vehicle exhaust and allow it to stabilise for at least one minute before checking C O emission.
18 If necessary adjust mixture screws further to bring emissions just within current regulation limit.
19 Seal mixture setting screws and close aperture with red plug.
20 Refit air cleaner.

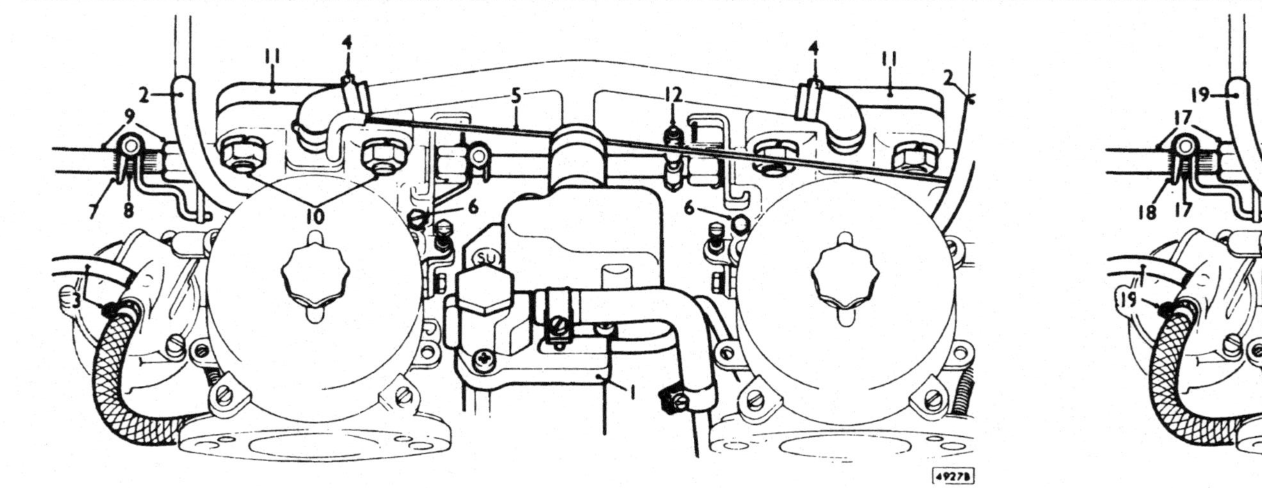

CARBURETTERS – CAR SET

Remove and refit 19.15.11

Non emission control and cars to European specification only, with S.U. H.S.8 carburetters

Removing
1 Remove A.E.D. Unit – 19.15.38.
2 Disconnect crankcase breather pipe from carburetters.
3 Disconnect fuel inlet and overflow pipes from float chambers. Plug fuel inlet pipe.
4 Disconnect mixture delivery pipes.
5 Disconnect vacuum pipe from rear carburetter.
6 Slacken off slow running adjustment screws until they no longer contact throttle levers.
7 Mark relative position of throttle rod to clamping bracket.
8 Slacken off clamping bolt and slide clamping bracket along throttle rod until it is disengaged from carburetter linkage.
9 Withdraw throttle rod from hollow nut by gently pushing rod in direction of bulkhead.
10 Remove nuts and spring washers securing carburetters to inlet manifold; lift off carburetters together with throttle lever return springs and brackets.
11 Remove carburetter flange gaskets and discard.
12 Slacken off clamping bolt and withdraw front carburetter from throttle linking rod.

Refitting
13 Insert throttle linking rod into hollow nut on front carburetter throttle spindle DO NOT tighten clamping bolt at this stage.
14 Position new carburetter flange gaskets on mounting studs.
15 Fit carburetters together with throttle lever return springs and brackets; tighten retaining nuts by diagonal selection.
16 Ensure that both throttle butterflies are in closed position and tighten clamping bolt.
17 Position throttle rod in hollow nut and engage clamping bracket with carburetter linkage.
18 By means of a spanner on hollow nut, hold throttle butterflies closed; rotate throttle rod until reference marks on rod and clamping bracket are in alignment; tighten clamping bolt.
19 Reverse operations 1 to 5.
20 Tune carburetters – 19.15.02.

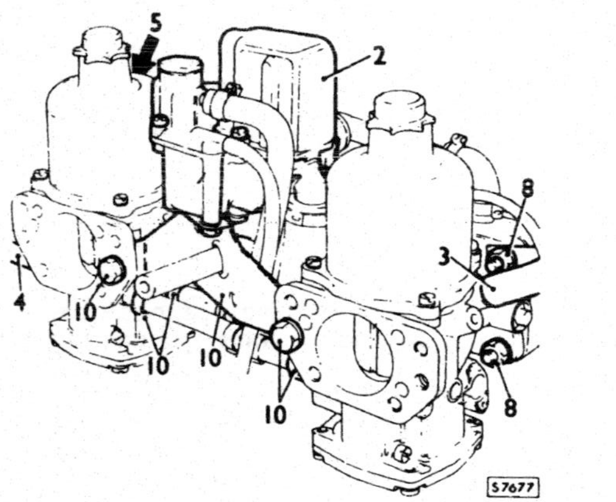

CARBURETTERS – CAR SET

Remove and refit **19.15.11**

Cars to Europe specification with S.U. H.I.F. 7 Carburetters only

Removing

1 Remove air cleaner – See 19.10.01.
2 Remove A.E.D. unit – See 19.15.38.
3 Disconnect crankcase breather pipes from carburetters.
4 Disconnect fuel pipes from carburetters and plug fuel supply pipe.
5 Disconnect vacuum pipe from rear carburetter.

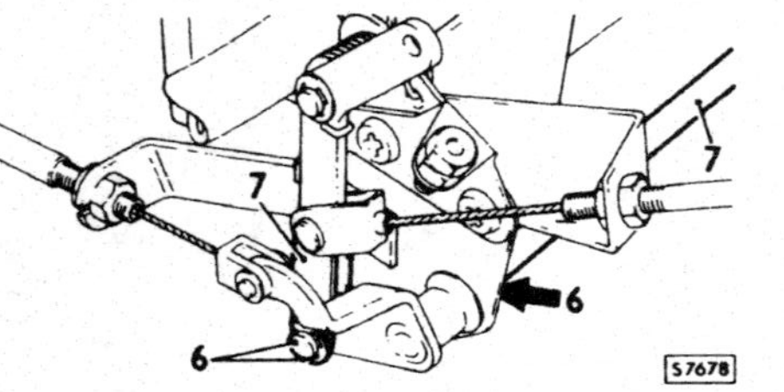

6 Release external circlips from throttle rod and lower pin in linkage. Withdraw pin.
7 Disengage links from lever on rod and draw rod back until its forward end disengages from nut on rear carburetter spindle.
8 Remove eight nuts and spring washers securing carburetters to manifold, and slide carburetters off studs.
9 Discard flange gaskets but replace two nuts on studs, to retain adaptors and insulating spacers in their original positions.
10 Release clips of fuel and vent pipes, remove A.E.D. bracket and draw front carburetter with throttle linking rod away from rear carburetter.

Refitting

11 Slide new O-clips over fuel and vent hoses and fit hoses over stubs on carburetters. Do not tighten clips at this stage.
12 Engage rear end of throttle linking rod with hollow nut on front of rear carburetter spindle and engage tongue of clamping bracket with yoke.
13 Remove nuts (fitted in operation 10 to retain adaptors) from manifold studs, place new gaskets in position and offer up carburetters to studs.
14 Fit spring washers and retaining nuts and tighten nuts by diagonal selection.
15 Ensure that fuel and vent hoses between carburetters are not twisted or distorted and secure O-clips retaining them to stubs.
16 Move throttle rod forward, engaging its ball end with hollow nut on rear throttle spindle, and tongue of clamping bracket with yoke.
17 Replace link pin and circlips.

NOTE: Ensure that circlips are replaced on rod and pin. They are not interchangeable.

18 Check that both throttle butterflies are in fully closed position.
19 Reverse operations 2 to 6.
20 Tune and adjust carburetters – See 19.15.02, operations 2 to 23.
21 Refit air cleaner – See 19.10.01.

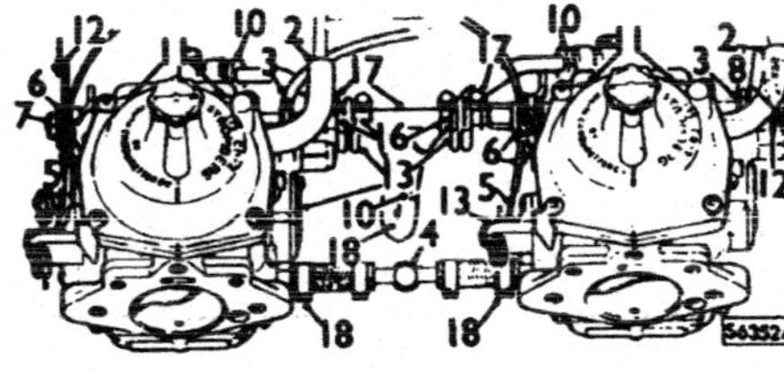

CARBURETTERS – CAR SET

Remove and refit **19.15.11**

Cars to U.S. Federal emission control specification only

Removing

1 Remove air cleaner – 19.10.01.
2 Disconnect crankcase breather pipe from each carburetter.
3 Disconnect vacuum pipe from each by-pass valve.
4 Slacken clip and disconnect fuel inlet pipe from tee-piece. Plug fuel inlet pipe.
5 Slacken clamp bolts and withdraw inner choke cables, where fitted.
6 Disconnect outer choke cables from clips, if fitted.
7 Remove nut at rear of throttle spindle and recover shakeproof washer, plain washer and brass bushes from both levers. Note fitting of bushes.
8 Remove nut at forward end of throttle spindle on cars with secondary throttles and recover shakeproof washer, plain washer and brass bush from secondary throttle lever. Recover operating arm.

Cars fitted with Model 65 automatic transmission only

9 Release spring clip and disconnect kickdown cable from throttle lever and abutment.

All cars

10 Pull throttle edge pipe from rear carburetter – variable orifice EGR system only.
Release union nut at EGR pipe – fixed orifice EGR system only.
11 Remove nuts and spring washers securing carburetters to secondary throttle housing or water heated spacer.
12 Withdraw carburetters slightly and disconnect front and rear throttle levers from connecting links.
13 Lift off carburetters taking care not to bend throttle spindle connecting clamps.
14 Remove and discard carburetter flange gaskets.
15 Place carburetters on a flat surface.
16 Mark relative position of throttle spindles to connecting rod.
17 Slacken bolts on each connecting clamp and remove coupling rod.
18 Remove clips securing tee-piece to carburetters and remove petrol pipe; carburetters may now be separated.

Refitting

19 Reverse operations 1 to 18; use new carburetter flange gaskets and tee-piece clips.
20 Check choke and accelerator controls for correct operation.
21 Carry out an engine and ignition diagnostic check.
22 Tune carburetters – 19.15.02.
23 Carry out an exhaust gas CO content analysis check.

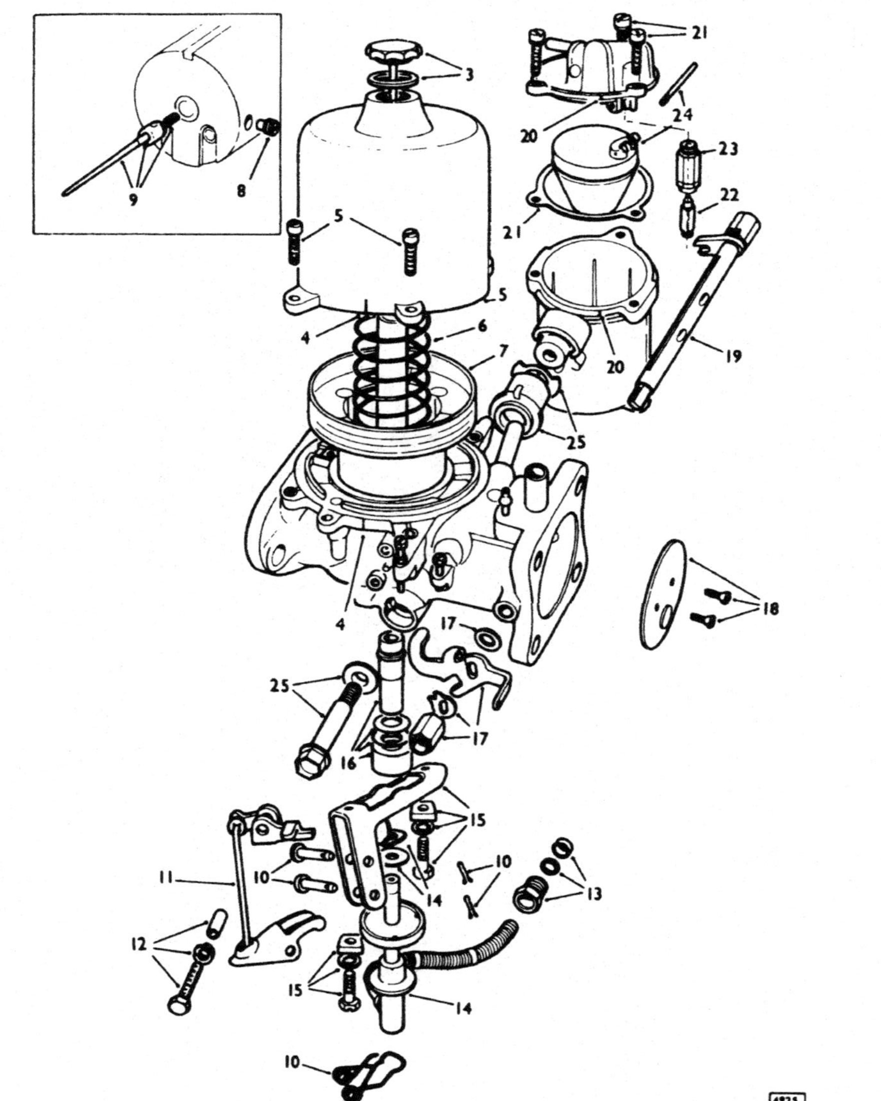

CARBURETTER

Overhaul **19.15.17**

Non emission control and cars to European specification only, with SU HS8 carburetters. For carburetter overhaul to U.S. Federal specification see EMISSION CONTROL – 17.20.07.

Dismantling

NOTE: Overhaul procedure is given for rear carburetter. Front carburetter differs only in levers and plates attached to throttle spindle.

1 Remove carburetters – 19.15.11.
2 Thoroughly clean outside of carburetter.
3 Remove damper and washer.
4 Mark relative positions of suction chamber and carburetter body.
5 Remove suction chamber securing screws. Lift off chamber.
6 Lift off piston spring.
7 Carefully withdraw piston and needle assembly.
8 Remove needle locking screw.
9 Withdraw needle from piston together with bias sleeve and spring.
10 Remove split pins retaining jet spring anchor pin and jet fork pivot pin; withdraw pins and spring.
11 Withdraw jet fork from bracket.
12 Remove bolt, washer and bush securing link arm to carburetter body.
13 Unscrew nut securing flexi-pipe to float chamber, withdraw pipe followed by washer and gland.
14 Withdraw jet assembly together with bi-metal sensor, washer and spacer.
15 Remove bolts, washers and spacers securing fork bracket to carburetter body.
16 Withdraw jet bearing together with spacer and concave washers.
17 Bend back tabs and unscrew throttle lever securing nut, withdraw lever followed by plain washer.
18 Remove and discard screws securing throttle butterfly to spindle, withdraw butterfly.
19 Push spindle out of carburetter body.
20 Mark relative positions of float chamber lid and float chamber.
21 Remove float chamber lid retaining screws; lift off lid together with gasket.
22 Withdraw float needle from lid.
23 Unscrew needle seating.
24 Withdraw float hinge pin, lift out float.
25 Remove bolt securing float chamber to carburetter body; detach float chamber together with rubber distance piece and steel backing washer.

Inspection

CAUTION: Any component showing signs of unserviceability or wear MUST be renewed.

26 Check float for damage.
27 Check float needle and seating for wear.
28 Check that there is not excessive clearance between butterfly spindle and carburetter body.
29 Check that jet assembly is free to move in jet bearing.
30 Check flexi-pipe for cracks or obstructions.

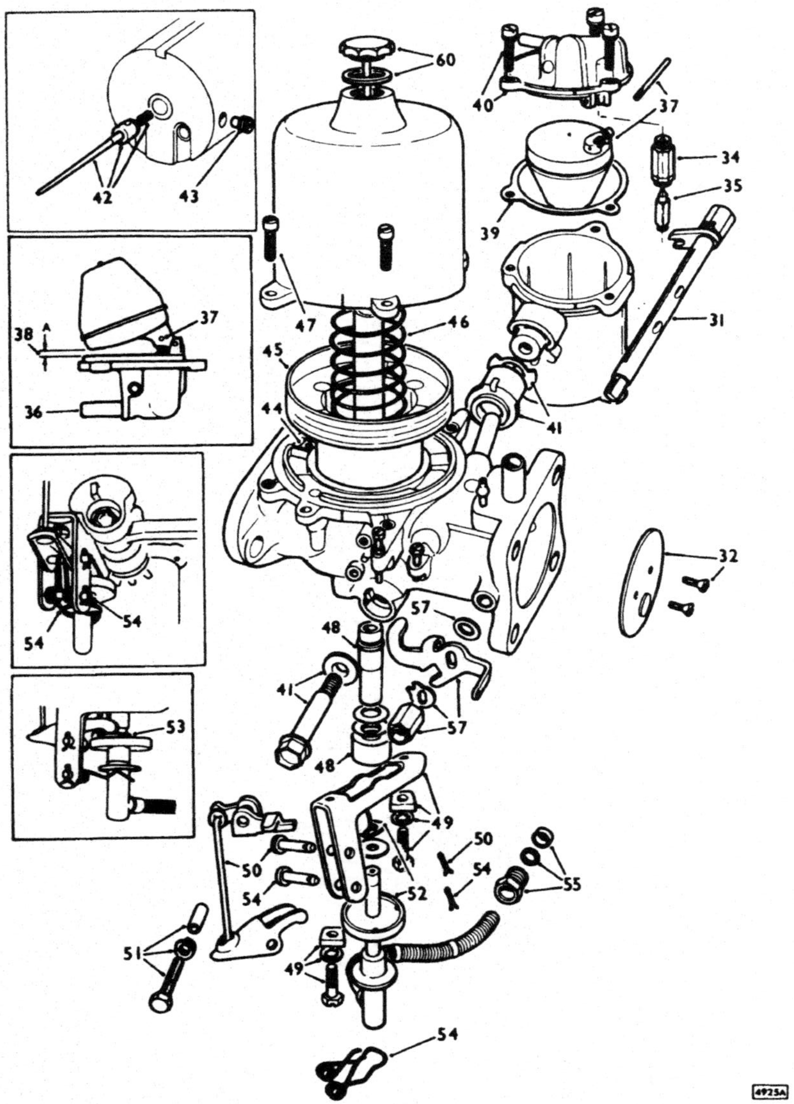

Reassembling

31 Insert throttle spindle into carburetter body.

32 Insert butterfly into slot in spindle, fit two new securing screws but do not tighten at this stage.

33 Adjust position of butterfly until it closes fully; tighten and spread split end of screws to prevent turning.

34 Screw needle seating into float chamber lid; do not overtighten.

35 Refit needle, coned end first.

36 Hold needle in closed position, apply LOW pressure air to fuel inlet and check that no leakage occurs past needle. If leakage is evident, needle and/or seating must be replaced.

37 Refit float followed by hinge pin.

38 Invert float chamber lid assembly and allow float to rest on needle. Check that gap 'A' is 1/8 in. to 3/16 in. (3,2 mm. to 4,7 mm.). If this dimension is not obtained, a new float and/or needle must be fitted.

39 Fit a new gasket to lid.

40 Fit float chamber lid and gasket to float chamber in the position, marked during dismantling. Tighten securing screws diagonally to prevent distorting lid.

41 Insert float chamber bolt into carburetter body; refit rubber distance piece, steel washer and float chamber.

42 Fit bias sleeve and spring to needle in position shown.

43 Fit needle securing screw and tighten; check that needle is free to move.

44 Check that piston key is securely fitted.

45 Lightly oil periphery of piston and fit piston in carburetter body.

46 Fit piston spring.

47 Fit suction chamber to carburetter body in position marked during dismantling; tighten screws by diagonal selection.

48 Fit jet bearing together with concave washers and spacer.

49 Fit fork bracket, spacers and bolts.

50 Position jet fork in bracket, insert pivot pin and secure with new split pin.

51 Position bush in link arm, secure with bolt and double spring washer.

52 Position bi-metal sensor, copper washer and spacer on jet assembly and slide assembly into jet bearing.

53 Position spacer as shown.

54 Fit jet spring, insert anchor pin and secure with new split pin.

55 Slide nut on to flexi-pipe followed by steel washer and new gland.

56 Position flexi-tube in bottom of float chamber, fit nut; DO NOT overtighten.

57 Fit plain washer, throttle lever, new tab washer and nut to butterfly spindle, hold butterfly closed whilst tightening nut; bend over tabs to secure nut.

58 Refit carburetters to car.

59 Top up piston damper with S.A.E. 20 engine oil.

60 Fit damper and washer.

61 Tune carburetters – 19.15.02.

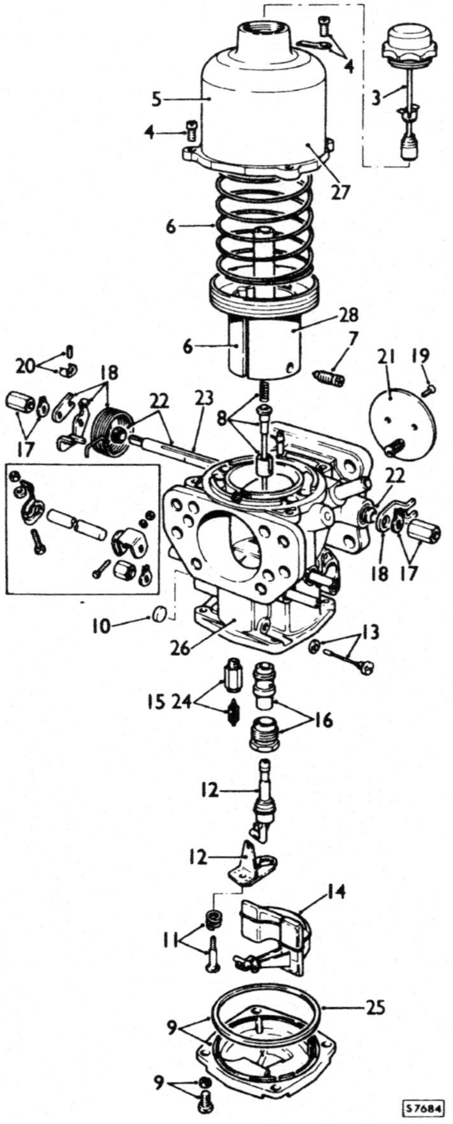

CARBURETTER

Overhaul **19.15.17**

Cars to European specification with S.U. H.I.F. 7 carburetters only.

Dismantling

NOTE: Overhaul procedure is given for rear carburetter. Front carburetter differs in fuel supply and vent pipe connections, throttle spindle details, and in absence of vacuum take-off stub.

Service tools: Refitting piston ball cage retainer tool.

1 Remove carburetters. See 19.15.11.
2 Thoroughly clean outside of carburetter.
3 Unscrew cap of suction chamber, lift until resistance is felt, support piston (with finger through intake) at top of its travel and pull cap firmly upwards to release damper retainer from piston rod. Remove damper.
4 Unscrew suction chamber retaining screws and remove identity tag.
5 Slightly rotate suction chamber to free it and lift vertically from body without tilting.
6 Remove spring, lift out piston and needle assembly and empty oil from piston rod.
7 Mark lower face of piston to locate position of V-mark on needle guide for correct reassembly and remove needle guide locking screw. Discard screw.
8 Withdraw needle with guide and spring.
9 Remove bottom cover plate retaining screws and spring washers and detach cover plate with sealing ring.
10 Only if it is essential to remove jet adjusting screw, remove plug and sealing from its counterbore and withdraw screw; an O-ring is carried in a groove in its head.
11 Remove jet adjusting lever retaining screw. Collect spring.
12 Withdraw jet and adjusting lever together and separate lever from jet.
13. Unscrew and remove float pivot spindle. Collect washers from between pin head and carburetter body.
14 Withdraw float.
15 Remove needle valve and unscrew valve seat.
16 Unscrew jet bearing locking nut and withdraw jet bearing.
17 Bend back lockwasher tabs and unscrew nut retaining throttle levers and return spring. Note location of levers and spring.
18 Remove yoke, lever and return spring.
19 Remove throttle disc retaining screws.
20 Remove slow running adjustment grub screw, tamper-proof cap, if fitted, and spring clip.
21 Close throttle and mark position of throttle disc in relation to carburetter flange. Do not mark the disc in vicinity of over-run valve. Open throttle and carefully withdraw disc from throttle spindle, taking care not to damage over-run valve.
22 Withdraw throttle spindle and remove its seals, noting the way it is fitted in relation to carburetter body to ensure correct reassembly.

Inspection

23 Examine throttle spindle and its bearings in carburetter body; check for excessive play, and renew parts as necessary.
24 Examine float needle and seating for damage and excessive wear; examine nylon body of needle for cracks; renew both needle and seat if necessary.
25 Examine all rubber seals and 'O' rings for damage or deterioration; renew as necessary. The cover-plate sealing ring must be renewed.
26 Examine carburetter body for cracks and damage and for security of brass connections and piston key.
27 Clean inside of suction chamber and piston rod guide with fuel or methylated spirit (denatured alcohol) and wipe dry. Abrasives must not be used.
28 Examine suction chamber and piston for damage and signs of scoring.

29 Check that all balls are in piston ball race (2 rows 6 per row).
Fit piston into suction chamber, without damper and spring, hold assembly in a horizontal position and spin piston. Piston should spin freely in suction chamber without any tendency to stick.

Reassembling

30 Fit new seals to carburetter body and replace spindle. Press seals just inside spindle housing bosses.
31 Insert throttle disc in spindle, ensuring that it is positioned as marked in operation 20.
32 Fit two new throttle disc retaining screws. Ensure that throttle closes correctly before tightening screws fully, and spread their slotted ends sufficiently to secure. Do not over-spread.
33 Replace return spring, lever and yoke on throttle spindle.
34 Fit new lockwasher and replace nut on throttle spindle. Tighten to 37 lbf in. (0,43 kgf m.) and secure by bending over tabs.
35 Replace slow-running adjusting grub screw, with new spring clip and tamper-proof cover, if fitted. DO NOT CLOSE LID OF COVER.
36 Replace jet bearing and tighten locking nut to 10 to 12 lbf ft. (1,38 to 1,65 kgf m.).
37 Replace needle valve seat and refit needle.
38 Replace float and spindle with washer and tighten to 6 lbf in.min. (0,07 kgf m.min.).

39

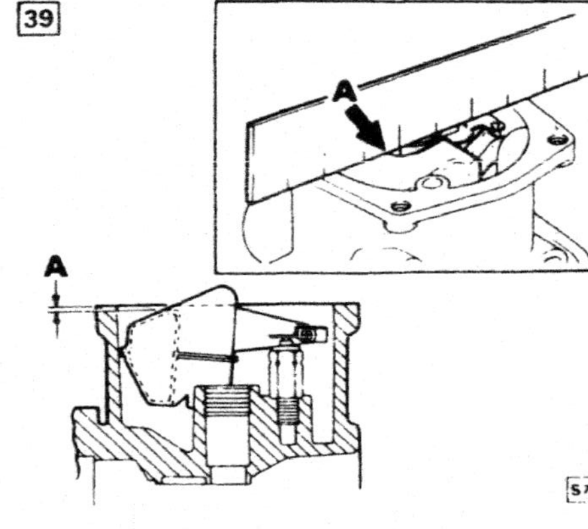

39 Invert carburetter so that needle valve is held on seat by weight of float. Check that lowest point, indicated on float as A in illustration, is 0.04 ± 0.02 in. (1,0 ± 0,5 mm.) below level of float chamber face. Adjust if necessary by carefully bending brass arm. Check that float pivots correctly about spindle.
40 Assemble jet and adjusting lever and plate in position in body, engaging forked end of lever with reduced diameter of adjusting screw. Fit retaining screw and spring, but tighten finger tight only, initially.
41 Check that jet head is free to move in cut-out in adjusting lever and slides easily in jet bearing. Fully tighten retaining screw.
42 If adjusting screw has been removed, fit new O-ring to it and insert carefully, ensuring that its reduced tip diameter engages slot of adjusting lever. Screw in until jet is flush with bridge of body, then screw in a further 3 2/3 turns, to bring jet 0.117 in. (3,0 mm.) below bridge.
43 Fit new sealing ring to bottom cover-plate and refit as marked. Replace four retaining screws and spring washers and tighten screws.
44 Refit spring to needle, ensuring that spring is located in its groove.
Slide needle guide over needle (with open end of slot adjacent to projection in flange) and insert in piston as marked in operation 7.
45 Insert NEW needle retaining screw in piston, position needle guide flush with bottom face of piston and tighten screw to 12 to 15 lbf in. (0,14 to 0,17 kgf m.).
46 Carefully replace piston and needle assembly in carburetter body.
47 Replace spring on piston, and lower suction chamber carefully over spring, avoiding turning the chamber as it compresses the spring (to prevent the spring from twisting the piston).
48 Fit three screws and identity tag.
49 Insert damper piston in bore of piston rod and using tool, press damper retainer fully into top of rod.
50 Fill bore of piston rod with engine oil, preferably SAE 20, up to bottom of damper retainer and tighten suction chamber cap firmly by hand.
51 Replace carburetters. See 19.15.11.

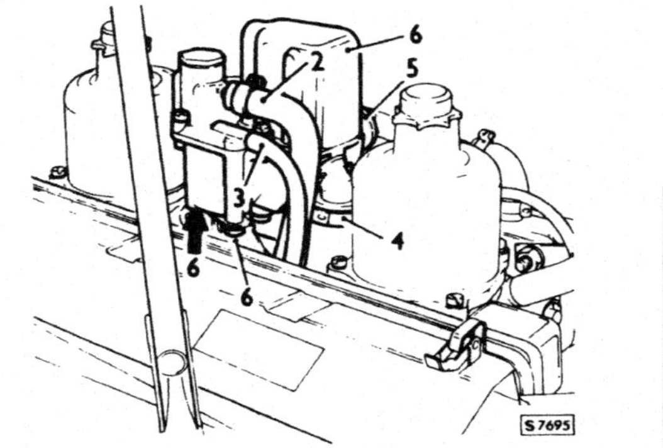

AUTOMATIC ENRICHMENT DEVICE (A.E.D.)

Remove and refit **19.15.38**

Non emission control and cars to European specification only

Removing
1 Disconnect battery – 86.15.20.
2 Disconnect fuel inlet pipe.
3 Disconnect fuel overflow pipe.
4 Disconnect air delivery pipe.
5 Disconnect mixture delivery pipe.

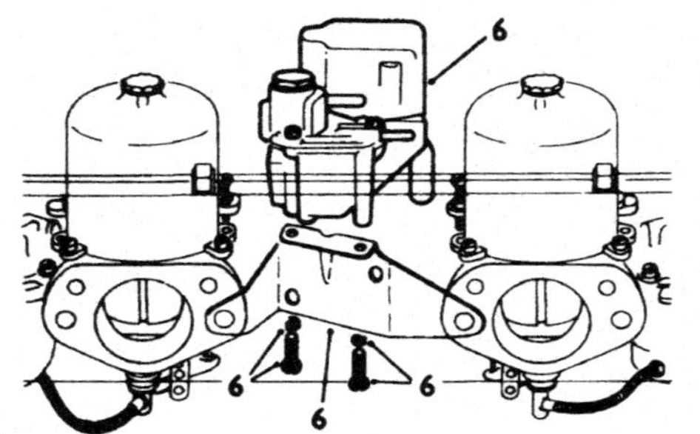

6 Remove bolts and spring washers securing A.E.D. unit to mounting bracket; lift off A.E.D. unit.

Refitting
7 Reverse operations 1 to 6, use new clips on hot air inlet and mixture delivery pipes.

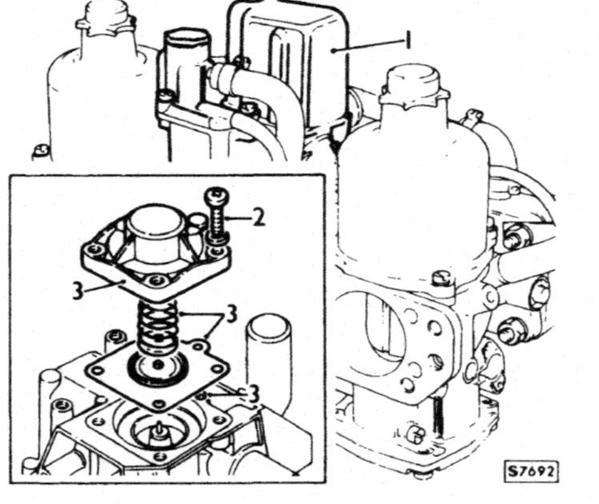

DIAPHRAGM

Remove and refit **19.15.40**

Removing
1 Remove A.E.D. unit – 19.15.38. and invert.
2 Remove four screws and spring washers securing diaphragm cover.
3 Withdraw cover, spring, diaphragm and locating dowel.

Refitting
4 Ensure bore of locating dowel is clean.
5 Push dowel into hole in A.E.D. unit.
6 Locate diaphragm on A.E.D. unit. **NOTE**: Rivet head **must** face toward A.E.D. unit.
7 Insert spring in diaphragm cover.
8 Position diaphragm cover and spring squarely over diaphragm ensuring spring is seated in diaphragm plate.
9 Push cover down, ensuring that locating dowel enters hole in cover.
10 Reverse operations 1 and 2.

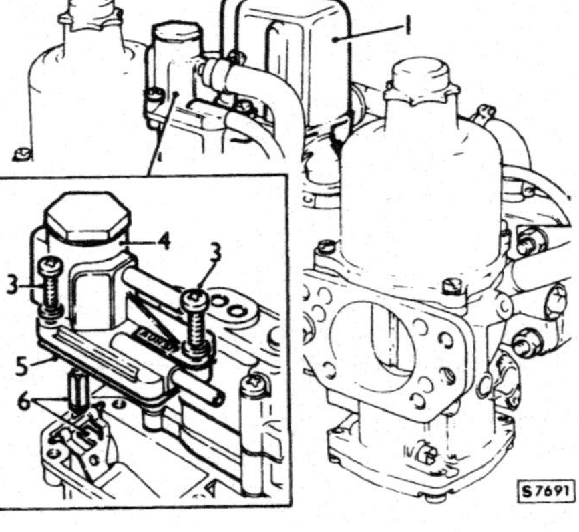

NEEDLE VALVE

Remove and refit **19.15.42**

Removing
1 Remove A.E.D. unit – 19.15.38.
2 Carefully prise insulation cover from A.E.D. unit.
3 Remove three screws and spring washers securing float chamber cover.
4 Lift off cover.
CAUTION: DO NOT MOVE COVER SIDEWAYS.
5 Remove and discard gasket.
6 Unclip needle valve from float arm.

Refitting
7 Lift float from chamber.
8 Position needle valve in recess in cover.
9 Clip needle valve to float arm.
10 By means of a steel rule, hold float against cover.
11 Position new gasket on A.E.D. body – Do not use jointing compound or grease.
12 Lower cover on to A.E.D. unit ensuring that float and needle valve are not displaced.
13 Ensure float hinge pin is correctly located.
14 Reverse operations 1 to 3.

A.E.D. FILTER

Remove, clean and refit **19.15.43**

Removing
1 Disconnect battery – 86.15.20.
2 Remove plug and aluminium washer.
3 Withdraw filter element.

Cleaning
4 Wash filter element in petrol and dry using clean, dry compressed air.

Refitting
5 Locate element and secure using plug and new aluminium washer.

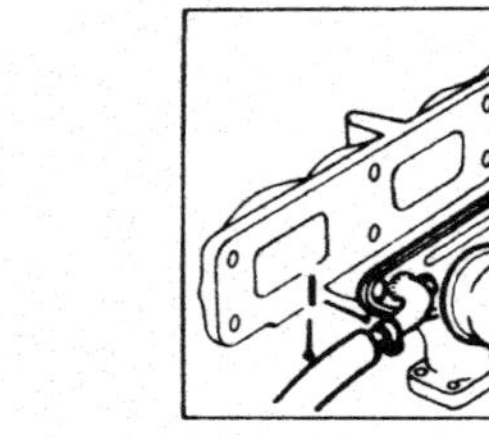

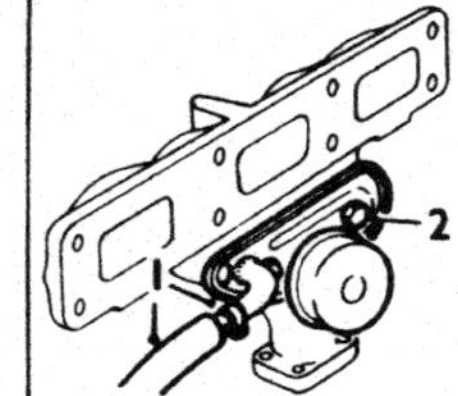

4933

HOT AIR PICK-UP UNIT

Remove and refit 19.15.44

Removing

1 Slacken clamping bolt and withdraw air delivery pipe from outlet tube.
2 Remove bolts securing pick-up unit to exhaust manifold, withdraw pick-up unit together with air filter.

Refitting

Reverse operations 1 and 2.

HOT AIR DELIVERY PIPE

Remove and refit 19.15.45

Removing

1 Slacken clamping bolt and withdraw air delivery pipe from outlet tube.
2 Remove nut and bolt securing pipe clip to support bracket.

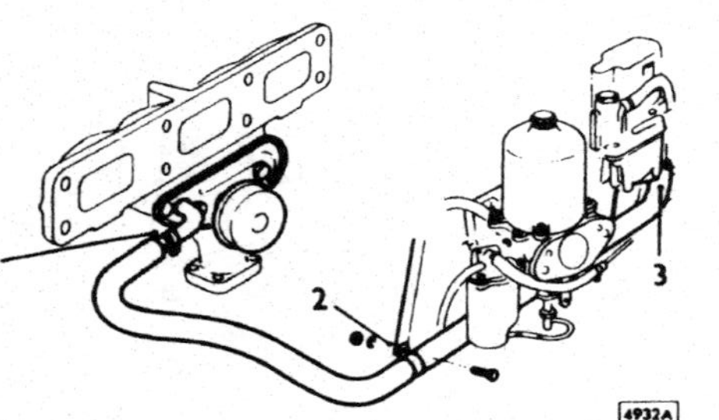

4932A

3 Disconnect delivery pipe from A.E.D. unit.

Refitting

Reverse operations 1 to 3; use new clip to secure delivery pipe to A.E.D. unit.

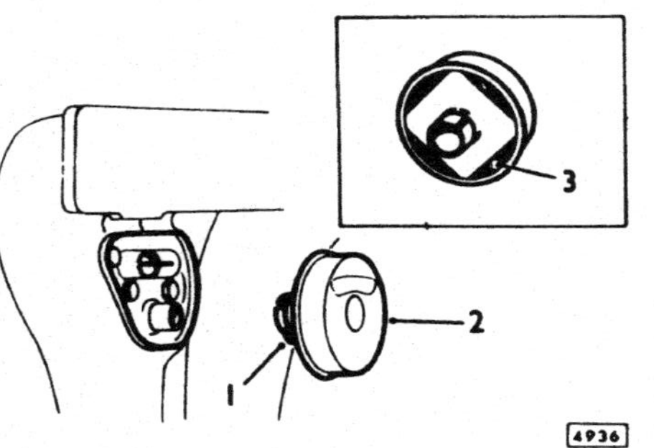

4936

HOT AIR FILTER

Remove, clean and refit 19.15.46

Removing

1 Slacken off clamping bolt.
2 Move filter towards cylinder block and withdraw.

Cleaning

3 Wash filter in petrol and dry with compressed air.
4 Lightly oil filter gauze with engine oil.

Refitting

Reverse operations 1 and 2.

AUTOMATIC CHOKE

Remove and refit 19.15.63

Cars to U.S. Federal emission control specification only.

Removing

1 Remove carburetters from engine.
2 Open throttle and prevent from closing with suitable temporary stop (piece of plastic tube or soft wood) in throttle bore.
3 Remove three screws securing choke unit to carburetter body. Remove choke unit and gasket, discard gasket.
4 Remove throttle stop screw and locknut.

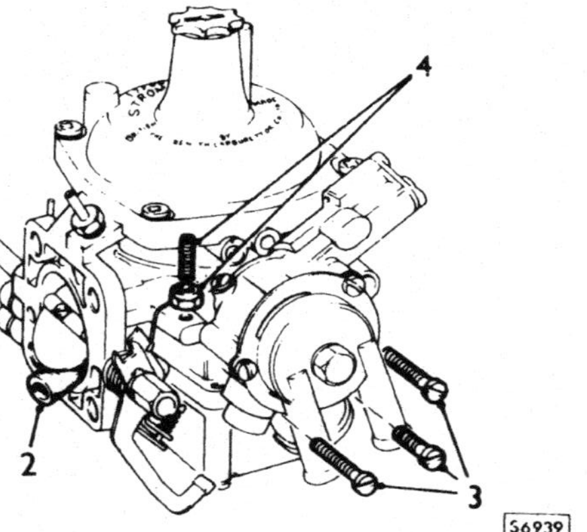

S6939

Refitting

5 Clean face of carburetter to which choke unit is fitted.
6 Remove central bolt, washer, water jacket and sealing ring from choke unit.
7 Remove three screws and washers securing clamp ring to choke unit, lift off clamp ring.

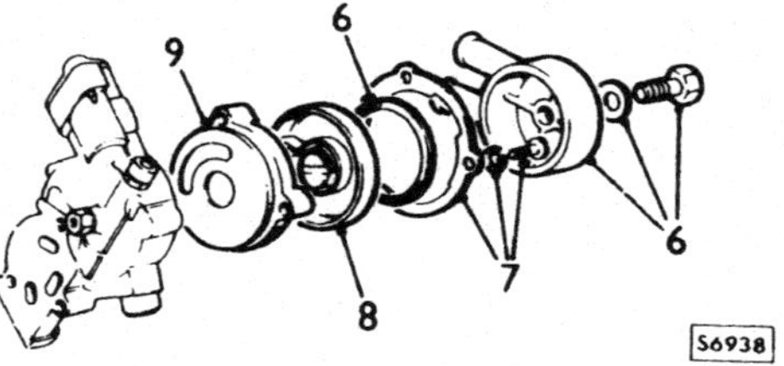

S6938

8 Carefully remove finned aluminium heat mass ensuring temperature sensitive coil attached is not strained.
9 Remove heat insulator.
10 Fit new gasket to carburetter, do not use sealing compound.
11 Fit new choke unit to carburetter tightening the three screws progressively and evenly to a torque of 40-45 lbf. in. (46-52 kgf. cm.).
12 Fit new throttle stop screw and locknut.
13 Check clearance between fast idle pin and base circle of cam is 0.045 to 0.055 in. (1.14 to 1.27 mm.) as follows:
Open throttle and remove temporary stop, allow throttle to close normally. Screw down idle speed screw until the clearance between the lugs is 0.10 in. (2.5 mm.) minimum. Lightly rotate thermostat lever with finger in an anti-clockwise direction to the fully 'off' position.

14
13
13
1517

14 If necessary adjust throttle stop screw until correct clearance is obtained. Using the nut, lock the throttle stop screw securely and recheck the clearance as detailed above.
15 Replace heat insulator with thermostat arm protruding through slot provided.

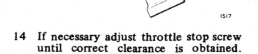

16 **Replace finned aluminium heat mass ensuring proper engagement of thermostat arm with rectangular loop** of temperature sensitive coil. To check **engagement** rotate heat mass 30° to 40° only in both directions. In each case the unit should spring back to its original position.
CAUTION: On no account should the heat mass be rotated more than 30° to 40° as the coil could be permanently damaged.

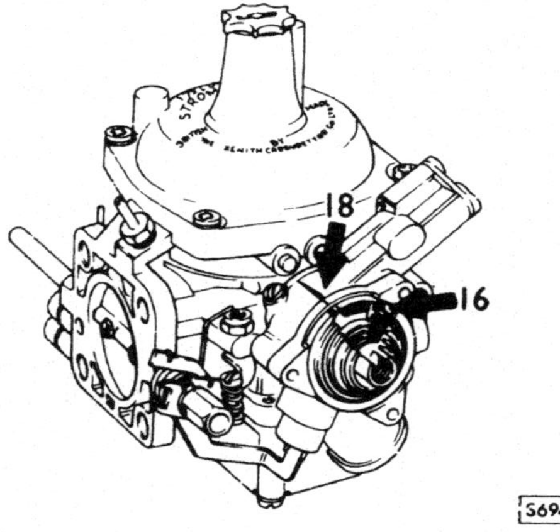

17 Replace clamp ring and three screws and washers, do not tighten.
18 Rotate heat mass in anti-clockwise direction until index mark on outer edge is aligned with datum mark on body of choke unit.
19 Hold heat mass with index mark correctly aligned and tighten three screws securing clamp plate to a torque of 8-10 lbf. in. (9-11.5 kgf. cm.).
20 **Replace sealing ring and water jacket, ensuring that water pipe connections correctly orientated.**
21 **Replace central bolt and aluminium washer and tighten to a torque of** 65-75 lbf. in. (72-84 kgf. cm.).
22 **Reset idle speed screw.**
23 **Repeat on other carburetter.**
24 **Refit carburetters to engine.**

AUTOMATIC CHOKE

Check and adjust 19.15.66

Cars to U.S. Federal emission control specification only.

NOTE: Prior to removal of a faulty choke unit the following checks should be carried out on the vehicle.

1 **Check alignment of datum mark on side of heat mass with datum mark on choke unit body.**
2 **Open throttle and check that head of fast idle pin is flush with outer edge of guard.**
3 **Check three screws securing choke unit to carburetter body for tightness.** 40-45 lbf. in. (46-52 kgf. cm.).
If trouble still persists proceed as follows:
4 **Remove carburetters from engine.**
5 **Open throttle and prevent from closing with suitable temporary stop (piece of plastic tube or soft wood) in throttle bore.**
6 **Remove central bolt, washer, water jacket and sealing ring from choke unit.**

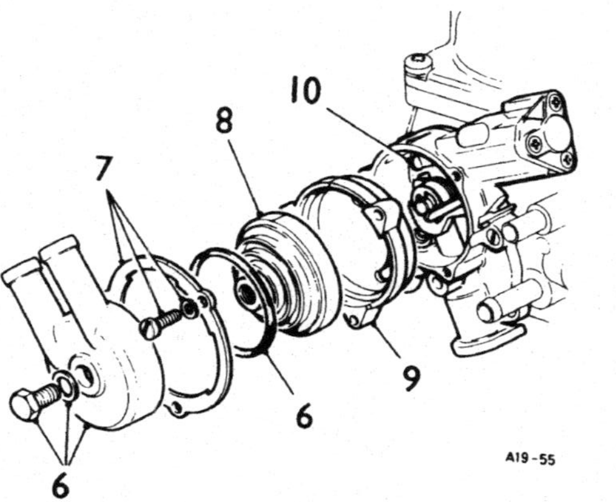

7 **Remove three screws securing clamp ring to choke unit, lift off clamp ring.**
8 **Carefully remove finned aluminium heat mass ensuring temperature sensitive coil attached is not strained.**
9 **Remove heat insulator.**
10 **Check vacuum kick piston and rod for full and free movement in guide bush.**

11 **Ensure fast idle cam and thermostat lever free to move on pivot and that torsion spring retains the cam against the lever.**
NOTE: Rotation of this mechanism also actuates vacuum kick piston and rod, and metering needle.
12 **Carry out operations 13–24 as detailed in operation 19.15.63.**

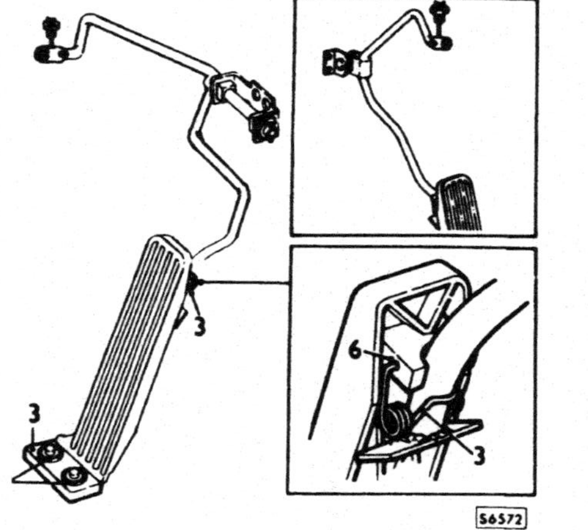

THROTTLE PEDAL

Remove and refit 19.20.01

Removing
1 Fold carpet away from base of throttle pedal.
2 Remove nuts and washers securing base of pedal to mounting plate.
3 Pull base of pedal away from mounting plate and disengage spring from pedal.
4 Examine spring for wear and renew if necessary.

Refitting
5 Engage rod with pedal.
6 Position spring on pedal.
7 Push base of pedal towards bulkhead and locate on mounting studs.
8 Reverse operations 1 and 2.

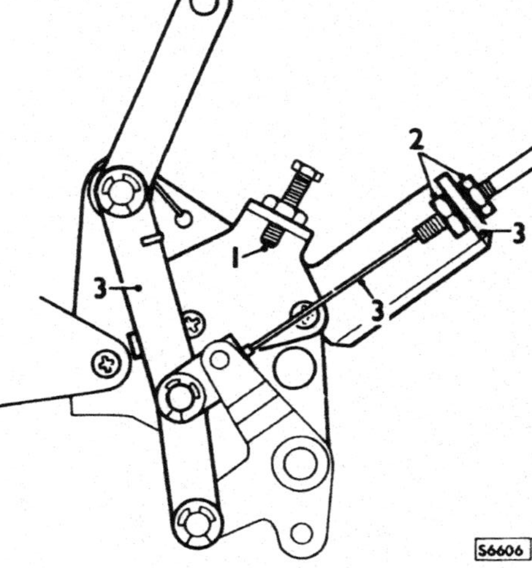

THROTTLE LINKAGE

Check and adjust 19.20.05

Check
1 Fully depress throttle pedal and ensure butterfly valve operating lever comes to a position just touching operating lever stop screw. If lever does not touch stop screw, **and linkage was initially correctly set up,** proceed with operations 2, 3 and 4. To carry out complete adjustment of throttle linkage, see Carburetter Car Set – Tune and adjust – 19.15.02.

Adjust
2 Slacken locknuts at outer throttle cable abutment.
3 Adjust position of outer cable in abutment to place inner cable under light tension but **NOT** to move throttle operating lever, and secure locknuts.
4 Re-check operation 1.

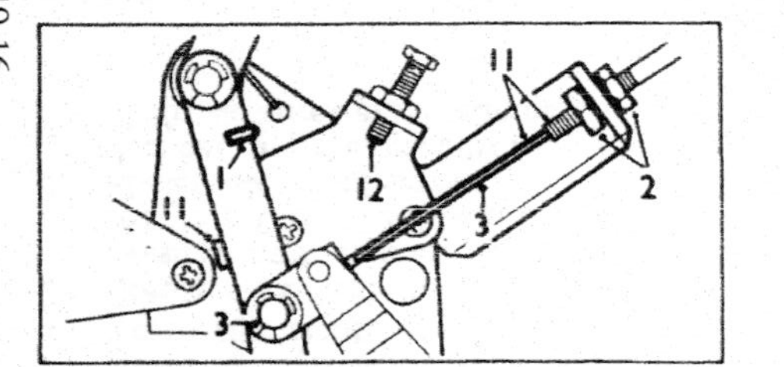

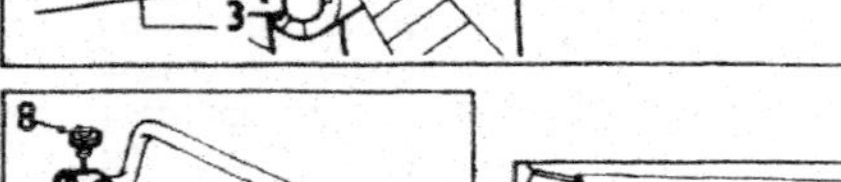

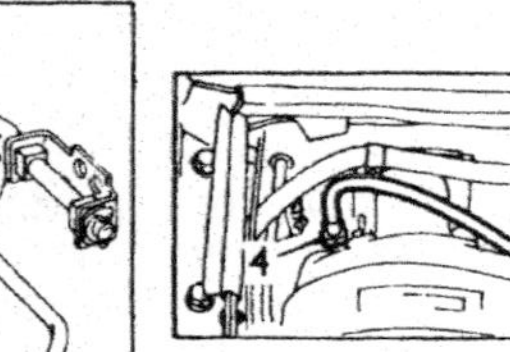

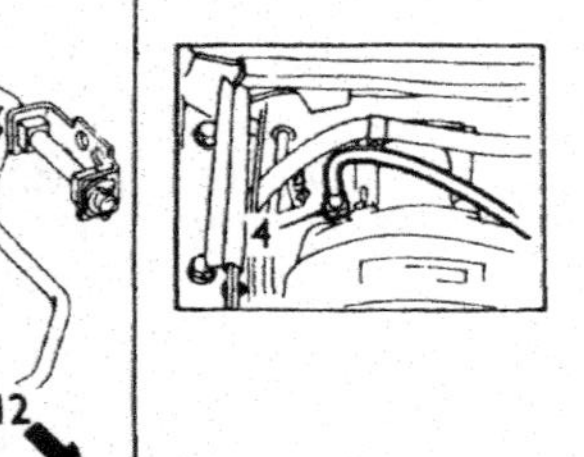

THROTTLE CABLE

Remove and refit **19.20.06**

Removing
1 Disengage throttle return spring from throttle operating lever.
2 Slacken locknuts at outer throttle cable abutment and draw cable clear.
3 Remove 'C' clip securing cable yoke clevis pin and detach inner cable from operating lever; temporarily replace clevis pin.
4 Slacken locknut on top surface of footwell.
5 Remove under scuttle casing.
6 Remove split pin at top end of operating rod.
7 Disengage sleeve and nipple from rod.
8 Remove nut from cable sheath and draw cable assembly into engine compartment. Recover operating rod abutment plate.

Refitting
9 Examine grommets for wear and renew as necessary.
10 Reverse operations 1 to 8. Apply sealing compound around thread on top surface of footwell.
11 Slacken locknuts on outer throttle cable and adjust position of cable in abutment so that throttle operating lever rests against back stop, yet inner cable is not slack; tighten locknuts.
12 Depress throttle pedal and ensure that operating lever moves to touch stop screw with pedal at end of its travel. Adjust pedal stop so that cable is not under undue strain when pedal fully depressed.
13 Check operation of kickdown switch – 44.30.12 – cars fitted with Model 12 automatic transmission only.
14 Check operation of kickdown cable – 44.30.02 – cars fitted with Model 65 automatic transmission only.

THROTTLE OPERATING ROD BUSHES

Remove and refit **19.20.10**

Removing
1 Remove throttle pedal – 19.20.01.
2 Remove under scuttle casing.
3 Prise spring clips from steering column universal joint cover; detach covers and padding – left hand drive cars only.

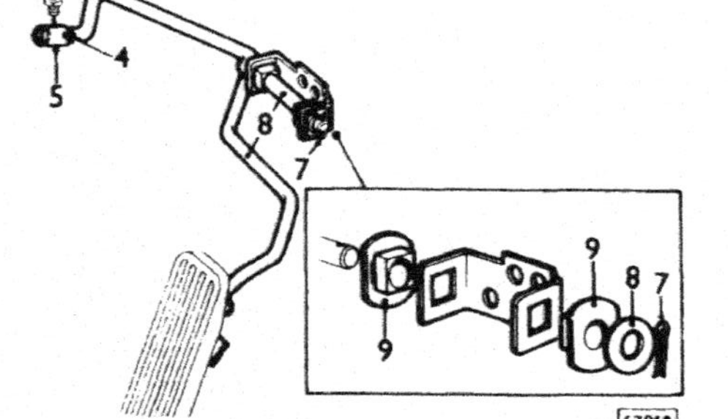

4 Remove split pin at top end of operating rod.
5 Disengage sleeve and nipple from rod.
6 Remove two self locking nuts and draw pedal arm from studs – right hand drive cars only.
7 Remove split pin from operating rod pivot.
8 Pull rod from pivot. Recover plain washer.

Refitting
9 Remove worn bushes and fit new.
10 Reverse operations 1 to 8; use new split pins.

CHOKE CABLE – ASSEMBLY

Remove and refit **19.20.13**

Early cars to U.S. Federal emission control specification only

Removing
1 Remove air cleaner – 19.10.01.

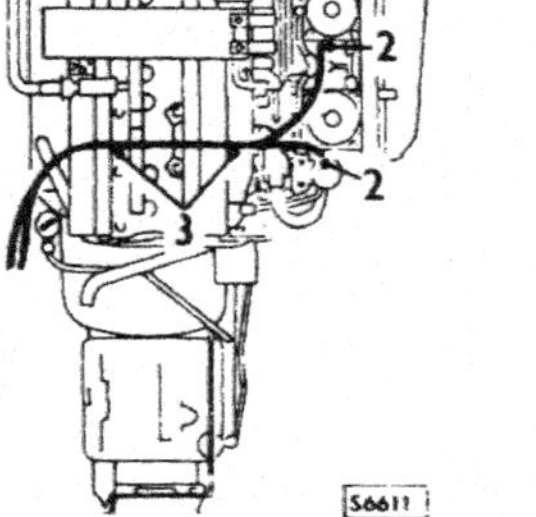

2 Beneath bonnet, disconnect choke cable inner and outer from front and rear carburetters.
3 Withdraw cables from clips.
4 Remove dash liner – 76.46.11.
5 Slacken two pinch bolts on choke lever.
6 Slacken pinch bolt and press cable assembly from pivot block abutment.
7 Withdraw cable assembly rearward through bulkhead into car.

Refitting
8 Examine grommets for damage and renew as necessary.
9 Reverse operations 1 to 7.
10 Check choke control for smoothness of operation; re-route cables if control feels stiff.
11 Check fast idle setting – 19.15.02.

CHOKE CABLE – INNER

Remove and refit **19.20.14**

Early cars to U.S. Federal emission control specification only

Removing
1 Remove air cleaner – 19.10.01.

2 Beneath bonnet disconnect choke cable inner and outer from carburetter.
3 Release cables from clips.
4 Remove dash liner – 76.46.11.
5 Slacken pinch bolt of cable to be removed, and draw cable from sheath into engine compartment.

Refitting
6 Reverse operations 1 to 5, entering inner cable from engine compartment end.
7 Check fast idle setting – 19.15.02.

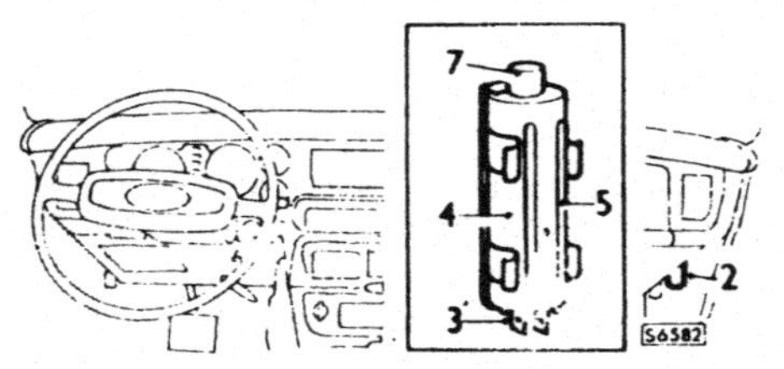

FUEL CUT-OFF INERTIA SWITCH

Remove and refit 19.22.09

Removing

1 Disconnect battery – 86.15.20.
2 Remove screws securing switch cover at passenger side of facia.
3 Pull connectors from switch.
4 Pull switch from spring clip.

Refitting

5 Press switch into spring clips, ribs towards rear of car and terminals at bottom.
NOTE: Ensure switch is raised in clips to abut on top lip of bracket.
6 Fit connectors to switch, polarity is unimportant.
7 Press in plunger at top of switch.
8 Fit switch cover and secure.
9 Reconnect battery.

FUEL SYSTEM

Fuel Main Filter

Description 19.25.00

An in-line disposable canister fuel filter is fitted to all later cars.
Located in engine compartment, it is situated ahead of front carburetter on air-conditioned cars and behind or below rear carburetter on other cars.

FUEL MAIN FILTER

Remove and refit (early cars) 19.25.02

Removing

WARNING: A CERTAIN AMOUNT OF FUEL SPILLAGE IS UNAVOIDABLE DURING THIS OPERATION. IT IS THEREFORE IMPERATIVE THAT ALL DUE PRECAUTIONS ARE TAKEN AGAINST FIRE AND EXPLOSION.

1 Disconnect battery – 86.15.20.
2 Remove spare wheel.

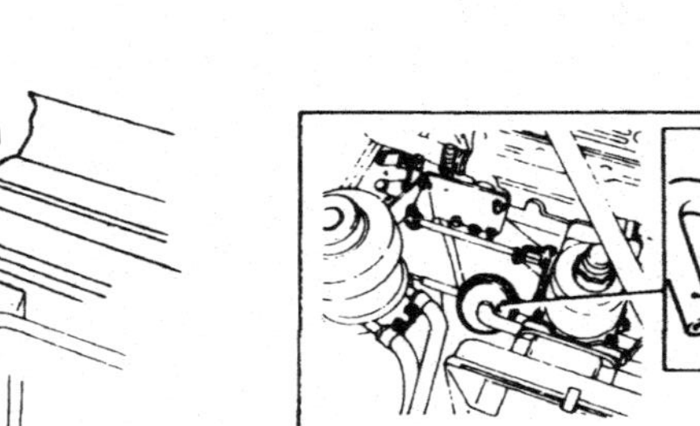

3 Fit clamp on inlet pipe to fuel filter head.
4 Place shallow tray, lined with rag, beneath fuel filter bowl.
5 Release inlet pipe union from filter head.
6 Release outlet pipe union from filter head; restrain adaptor and turn union nut.
7 Remove two setscrews and washers securing filter to side of wheel well.

Refitting

Reverse operations 1 to 7.

FUEL FILTER

Remove and refit (later cars) 19.25.02

Removing

WARNING: TAKE ALL DUE PRECAUTIONS AGAINST FIRE OR EXPLOSION WHEN CARRYING OUT THE FOLLOWING OPERATIONS.

1 Disconnect battery earth lead.
2 Slacken clips securing hoses to filter.
3 Disconnect top hose from filter.
4 Withdraw filter from bottom hose.
WARNING: HOLD BOTTOM HOSE AS HIGH AS POSSIBLE TO PREVENT FUEL SPILLAGE.

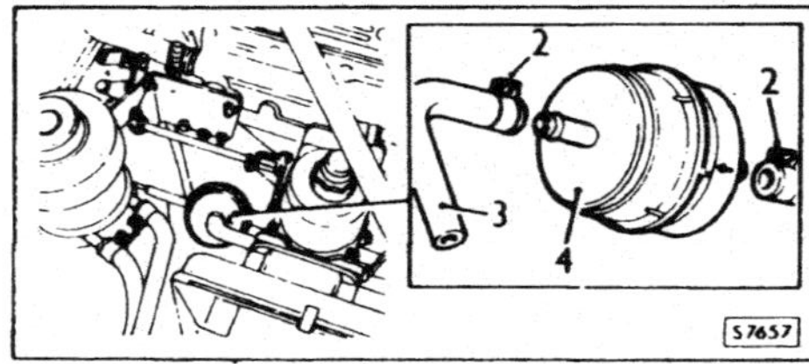

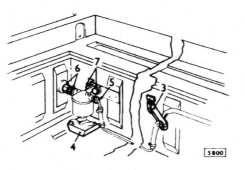

Refitting

5 Reverse operations 1 to 4 ensuring that arrow on side of filter body points in direction of fuel flow. Tighten hose clips to 6 lbf. in. (0,07 kgf. m.).

FUEL MAIN FILTER ELEMENT

Remove and refit (early cars) 19.25.07

Removing

WARNING: A CERTAIN AMOUNT OF FUEL SPILLAGE IS UNAVOIDABLE DURING THIS OPERATION. IT IS THEREFORE IMPERATIVE THAT ALL DUE PRECAUTIONS ARE TAKEN AGAINST FIRE AND EXPLOSION.

1 Disconnect battery – 86.15.20.
2 Remove spare wheel.

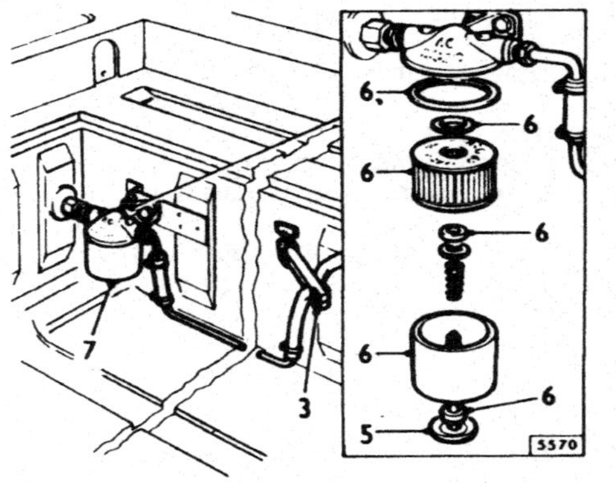

3 Fit clamp on inlet pipe to fuel filter head.
4 Place shallow tray, lined with rag, beneath fuel filter bowl.
5 Remove centre bolt securing filter bowl.

Refitting

6 Ensure filter bowl thoroughly cleaned out, fit new element and seals. Fit element large hole upwards.
7 Tighten centre bolt to secure filter bowl. DO NOT OVERTIGHTEN.
8 Remove pipe clamp and tray.
9 Reconnect battery.
10 Start engine and check filter for leaks.
11 Replace spare wheel.

S6591

FUEL PIPE ARRANGEMENT

Description 19.40.00

The system utilizes two fuel pump assemblies and draws from two fuel tanks fitted in the rear wings.
When the left hand tank is selected on the instrument panel switch, voltage is applied to the left hand fuel pump and fuel is passed, via the filter, to the two carburetter float chambers.

Selection of the right hand tank energises the right hand fuel pump.

The outlet non-return valve of the inoperative pump prevents fuel passing from one tank to the other.

On later cars the two SU pumps, indicated in the diagram, are replaced by 'submerged' pumps, located in the fuel tanks. Separate non-return valves are fitted in the flexible hoses near the tanks.

Later air conditioned cars are equipped with fuel coolers, attached to the hot air duct near the carburetters.

Special precautions, detailed below, must be taken before working on the fuel cooler.

FUEL COOLER

Remove and refit 19.40.40

Removing

WARNING: EXPOSURE TO REFRIGERANT GAS, WHICH IS RELEASED IF A REFRIGERANT HOSE IS DETACHED FROM THE COOLER, CAN CAUSE BLINDNESS. IT IS THEREFORE ESSENTIAL TO DEPRESSURISE THE AIR CONDITIONING SYSTEM BEFORE DISCONNECTING A REFRIGERANT HOSE. SEE 82.30.05.

FIRE PRECAUTIONS ARE ALSO ESSENTIAL AS FUEL MAY BE SPILLED WHEN FUEL HOSES ARE DISCONNECTED.

1 Disconnect battery – 86.15.20.
2 Depressurise air conditioning system – 82.30.05.
3 Disconnect refrigerant inlet and outlet hoses from cooler.
4 Clamp fuel hoses.
5 Disconnect fuel hoses.
6 Remove two self-tapping screws and washers securing fuel cooler. Collect mounting clips and insulating sleeve.

Refitting

Fit insulating sleeve and clips to replacement cooler, reverse operations 3 to 6 and charge air conditioning system – 82.30.08.

FUEL PUMP

Remove and refit (early cars) 19.45.08

Removing

1 Disconnect battery – 86.15.20.
2 Remove spare wheel.
3 Remove seven self tapping screws securing fuel pump cover.
NOTE: Do not remove centre screw at front edge of cover.

4 Fit a clamp to suction pipe at pumps.
5 Release both banjo bolts on pump.
6 Remove strapping around pump and hose.
7 Detach setscrew and serrated washers securing earth strap to pump body.
8 Remove one setscrew and washer securing pump clamp.
9 Lift pump clear and separate electrical connector.
10 Remove insulation from pump body.

Refitting

Reverse operations 1 to 10, ensuring that seals at banjo connectors are in good condition.

FUEL PUMP (SUBMERGED TYPE)

Remove and refit (either side) 19.45.08

Removing
1 Place car on ramp NOT over pit.
2 Disconnect battery earth lead.
3 Remove rear wheel adjacent to pump to be removed.
4 Drain fuel tank – 19.55.02.

WARNING: TAKE ALL DUE PRECAUTIONS AGAINST FIRE AND EXPLOSION WHEN DRAINING FUEL.

5 Remove four screws securing circular cover plate to rear vertical wall of wheel arch. Withdraw cover along flexible hose.
6 Disconnect electrical leads from pump.
7 Release hose clip and detach flexible hose from pump.
8 Turn locking flange anti-clockwise to release pump and withdraw pump and sealing washers, taking care to avoid damage to filter as pump is removed. Discard sealing washer.
9 Remove all sealant from pump, mounting flange and tank.

Refitting
10 Ensure that mounting faces of pump flange and fuel tank are clean, and that correct pump assembly is being refitted. C45442 is R.H. pump and C45443 is L.H. pump.
11 Fit new sealing washer and introduce pump carefully into tank, securing in position with locking flange.
12 Refit flexible hose to pump outlet pipe and tighten hose clip screw to not more than 6 lbf in. (0,07 kgf m.).
13 Fit electrical connections and smear terminals with waterproof grease.
14 Replace cover plate and secure with four screws.
15 Make good sealing around cover and screw leads by coating with "Flintkote" or similar protective covering.

NOTE: If it is found necessary to detach forward end of flexible hose, or to fit new hose, it is most important that a non-return valve, fitted in forward end of flexible hose, is correctly installed. Purpose of the non-return valve is to prevent fuel from draining into lower tank when car is tilted, and therefore ball must be at rear, or tank, end of fitting, as shown in illustration at 'A'.

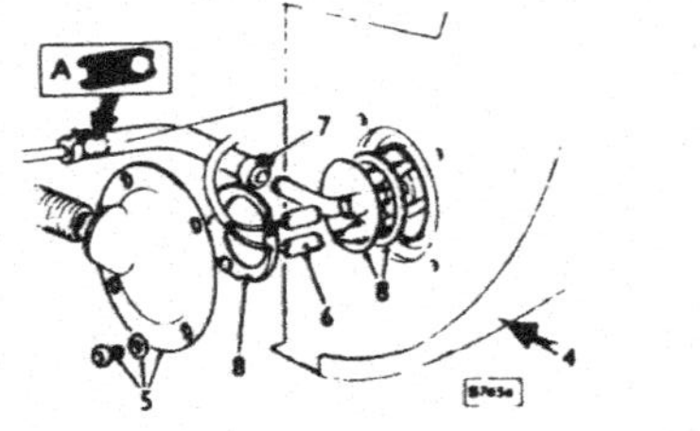

FUEL PUMP

Overhaul (early cars) 19.45.16

1 Remove fuel pumps – 19.45.08.

Dismantling
2 Mark relative positions of coil housing and pump body.
3 Remove screws securing coil housing to pump body; lift off housing, remove and discard gasket.
4 Remove tape and sealing ring from cover.
5 Remove polythene sleeve from terminal stud.
6 Remove nut, terminal tag and lock-washer.
7 Lift off cover.
8 Unscrew diaphragm assembly and withdraw from coil housing.

CAUTION: Diaphragm and spindle are serviced as a complete assembly and no attempt should be made to separate them.

9 Remove armature spring and rubber impact washer from spindle.
10 Remove nylon centralising guide.
11 Remove screw securing terminals and contact blade to pedestal; lift off contact blade.
12 Remove screw securing condenser terminal, earth terminal and pedestal to coil housing.
13 Remove remaining pedestal securing screw and lockwasher.
14 Move pedestal away from coil housing.

CAUTION: Unless pedestal is to be renewed, it is not advisable to remove terminal from terminal stud.

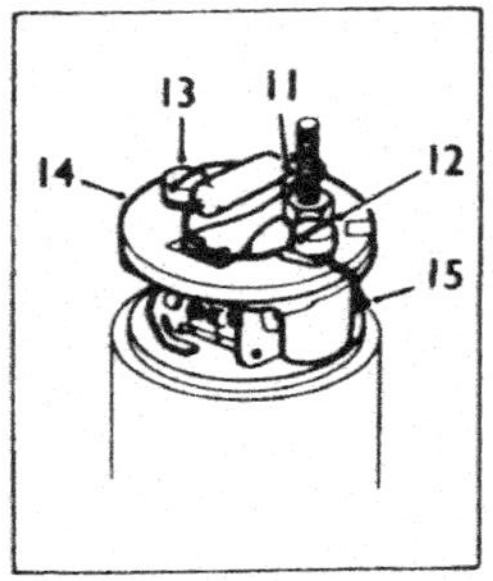

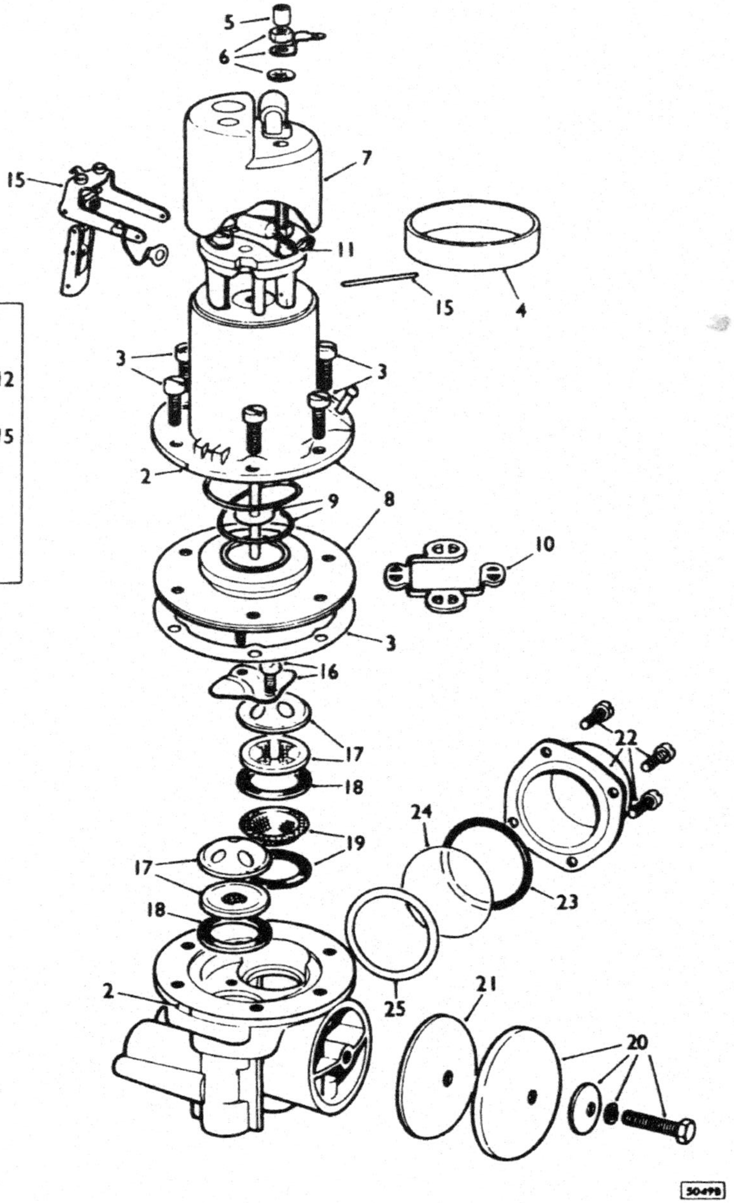

15 Withdraw rocker assembly pivot pin; remove rocker assembly.
16 Remove screws securing valve clamping plate to body; lift out clamping plate.
17 Note which way valves face, remove valve caps and withdraw valves.
18 Remove and discard neoprene sealing rings.
19 Remove filter gauze from inlet valve seat, remove and discard neoprene sealing ring.
20 Remove bolt, spring and plain washers securing air bottle cover to body.
21 Prise cork seal out of cover; discard seal.
22 Remove screws securing flow smoothing valve cover to body; lift off cover.
23 Remove and discard 'O' ring.
24 Remove diaphragm.
25 Remove and discard sealing washer.

Inspecting components

CAUTION: If gum formation has occurred in fuel, pump components which have been in contact with this fuel will have become coated with a varnish like substance. Metal components which have become contaminated can be cleaned by boiling in a 20 per cent solution of caustic soda, dipped in a strong nitric acid solution and finally washed in boiling water. Light alloy components must be cleaned by soaking in denatured alcohol (methylated spirits).

26 Clean pump body and inspect for cracks and damage.
27 Examine valves for damage, check operation by blowing and sucking with the mouth.
28 Check that tongue on each valve cage is not distorted and allows a valve lift of approximately 0.062 in. (1,6 mm.). Tongues may be bent slightly to achieve this dimension.
29 Examine flow smoothing valve diaphragm for damage; renew if necessary.
30 Examine valve recesses in body for pitting, corrosion or damage; if excessive, body must be renewed.
31 Examine contact breaker points for signs of burning or pitting, if this is evident, rocker assembly and contact blade must be renewed.
32 Examine pedestal for cracks or damage, particular attention should be paid to the narrow ridge on which contact blade rests. Renew pedestal if damaged.
33 Check that ball in non-return vent is free to move.
34 Examine diaphragm for splits or distortion. If damaged, diaphragm and spindle must be renewed as a complete assembly.
35 Check that nylon centralising guide is not split or distorted, renew if damaged.

Reassembling

36 Ensure all components are thoroughly clean.
37 Fit new sealing washer in body.
38 Position diaphragm in body; concave side must face inwards.
39 Fit new 'O' ring followed by flow smoothing valve cover.
40 Tighten securing screws by diagonal selection to avoid distorting cover.
41 Position new cork seal in air bottle cover.
42 Fit air bottle cover, do not overtighten securing bolt.
43 Fit new neoprene sealing rings in valve recesses.
44 Fit filter gauze and neoprene sealing ring in inlet valve recess.
45 Fit inlet and outlet valves followed by valve caps.
46 Fit valve clamp plate; do not overtighten securing screws.
47 Position rocker assembly in pedestal, insert pivot pin.
48 Position pedestal on coil housing, fit pedestal retaining screw and lockwasher; do not tighten screw at this stage.
49 Position condenser and earth terminals on remaining pedestal retaining screw, tighten both retaining screws.
50 Fit nylon centralising guide to diaphragm assembly.
51 Fit rubber impact washer followed by spring.
52 Insert spindle in coil housing.
53 Screw threaded end of spindle into rocker assembly trunnion.

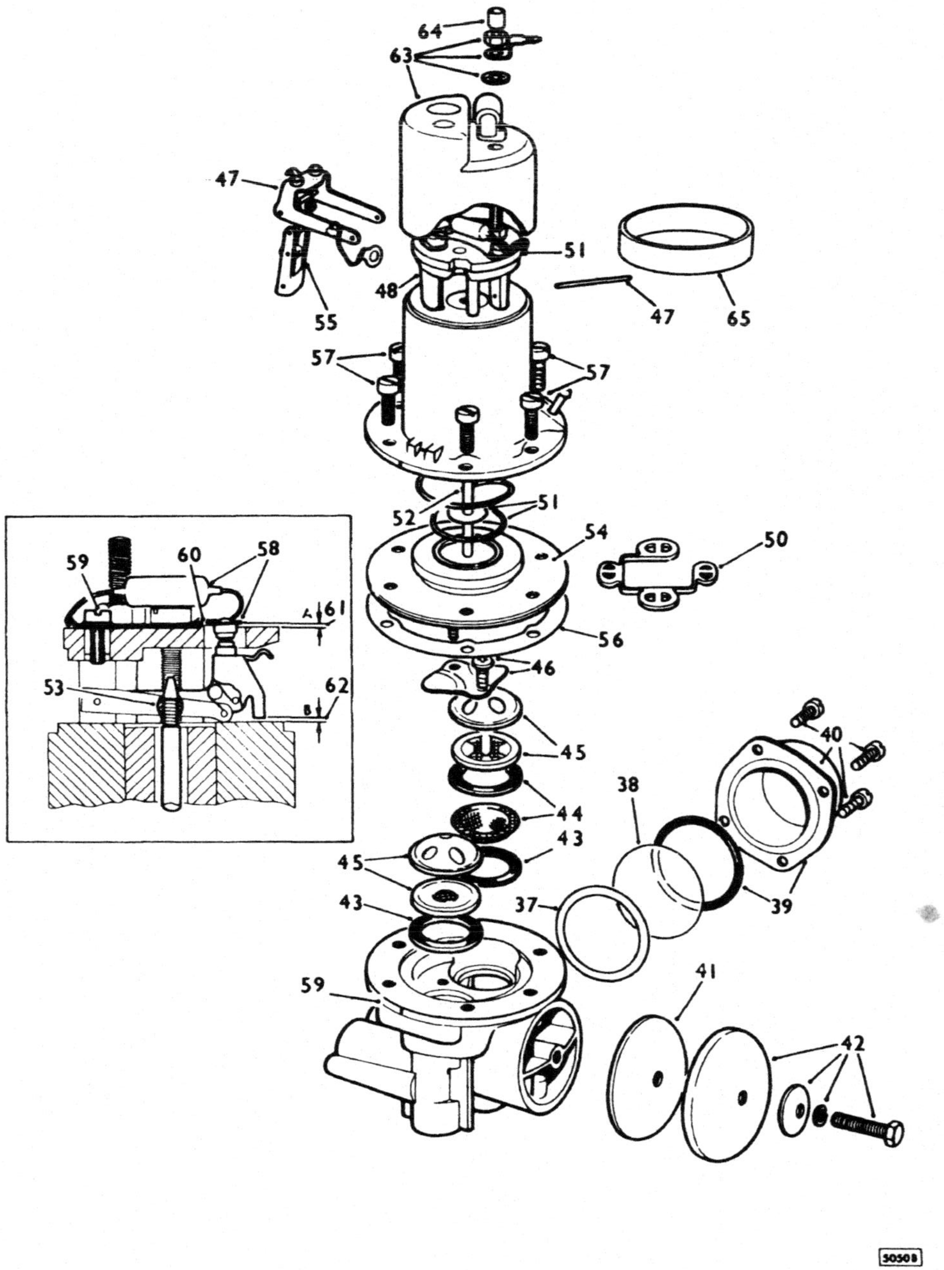

54 Screw in diaphragm until rocker no longer "throws over".
55 Unscrew diaphragm until rocker just "throws over", continue unscrewing until holes are in alignment then unscrew a further two thirds of a turn (four holes).
56 Position new gasket on body.

CAUTION: Gasket must be fitted dry; do not use jointing compound or grease.

57 Fit coil housing to body ensuring reference marks made during dismantling are in alignment. Tighten securing screws by diagonal selection to avoid distorting flange.
58 Fit contact blade, condenser and coil leads to screw; do not fully tighten screws at this stage.
59 Manoeuvre contact blade until contact points on blade and rocker assembly are in alignment; tighten securing screw.
60 Check that with points in open position, contact blade rests on narrow ridge on pedestal, contact blade may be bent slightly to achieve this.
61 Hold points in closed position and check that gap 'A' = .035 in. (,9 mm.). If necessary, bend stop finger on rocker assembly until correct dimension is obtained.
62 With rocker assembly stop finger resting on coil housing check that gap 'B' = .070 in. (1,8 mm.). If necessary bend stop finger until correct dimension is obtained.
63 Fit end cover, lockwasher, terminal tag and nut.
64 Fit polythene sleeve to stud.
65 Fit sealing ring and tape.

FUEL PUMP (SUBMERGED TYPE)

Overhaul **19.45.16**

The immersed fuel pumps are only supplied as complete units, which are fitted in the event of malfunction. See 19.45.08.

FUEL TANK

Remove and refit – either **19.55.01**

Removing

1 Drain fuel tank – 19.55.02.
2 Disconnect battery – 86.15.20.
3 Remove side section of rear bumper – 76.22.13.
4 Remove crosshead screws and washers securing rear quarter fuel tank cover.
5 Remove setscrews and plain nuts, spring and plain washers securing rear quarter fuel tank cover. Remove cover.
6 Remove self tapping screw securing forward end of luggage boot side casing. Remove casing.
7 Remove four screws and shakeproof washers securing flange of fuel tank filler cap.
8 Taking great care to avoid damaging paintwork, prise flange from body.
9 Pull vent pipe from stub – emission control cars to U.S. Federal specification only.
10 Remove gasket and 'O' ring seal.
11 Remove bolt, special washer and shakeproof washer at side panel of luggage boot.
12 Release fuel pipe connector at base of tank. Separate connection and push pipe carefully inwards flush with panel.
13 Remove two bolts, special washers and shakeproof washers in silencer tunnel and recover wedges.
14 Release nyloc nut at hanger bolt.
15 Carefully lower fuel tank, note connections and detach cables from tank unit.

Cars fitted with emission control to U.S. Federal specification only

16 Lower tank until vent pipe is accessible and detach pipe from stub.

NOTE: On later cars, fitted with submerged fuel pumps, omit operation 12 above, and reach up between rear of tank and tail/stop/flasher light units to detach leads from fuel gauge tank unit. (Submerged pump replaces gauge unit in forward tank aperture.) Detach leads and flexible hose from pump before withdrawing tank.

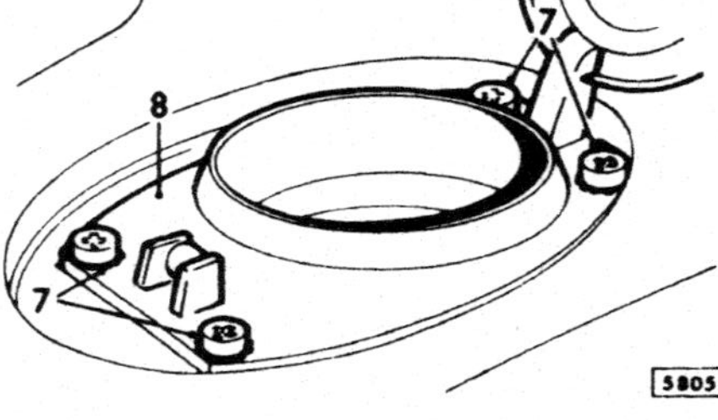

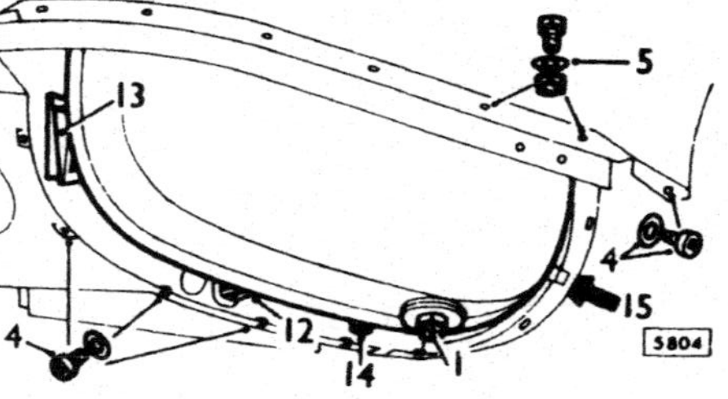

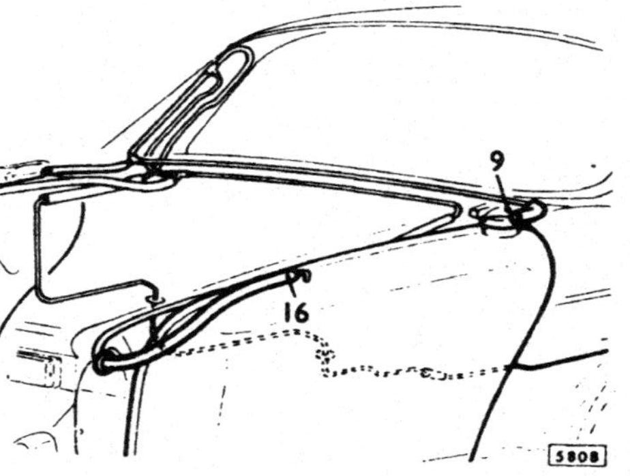

Refitting

Cars fitted with emission control to U.S. Federal specification only

17 Offer tank up and attach vent pipe to stub.

All cars

18 Lift tank and connect cables to tank unit and submerged pump on later cars.
19 Lift tank and engage hanger bolt in bracket, secure with nyloc nut.
20 Fit bolts, special and shakeproof washers at upper and forward location. Do not tighten at this stage.
21 Fit bolt, special and shakeproof washer at rear location. Fit wedges between fuel tank and side panel. Do not tighten at this stage.
22 Fit new 'O' ring seal in fuel tank neck.
23 Press vent pipe on to filler neck stub – emission control cars to U.S. Federal specification only.
24 Use new gasket at petrol filler cap flange and secure using four screws and shakeproof washers.
25 From beneath, firmly press fuel tank up to locate on filler cap flange spigot and tighten rear mounting bolt on wedges.
26 Secure hanger bolt nut. Do not overtighten.
27 Tighten remaining two mounting bolts.
28 Secure supply pipe union to tank; connect hose to pump on later cars with submerged pumps.
29 Pour 2-3 gallons Imp. (9-13 litres) of specified fuel into tank.
30 Connect battery.
31 Switch on ignition and select fuel tank that has been changed.
32 Check to ensure no leaks at unions and that fuel gauge registers. Switch off ignition.
33 Fit and secure rear quarter fuel tank cover.
34 Fit and secure side section of rear bumper.

FUEL TANK

Drain **19.55.02**

WARNING: PETROL (GASOLINE) MUST NOT BE EXTRACTED OR DRAINED FROM A VEHICLE STANDING OVER A PIT.

Petroleum or gasoline vapour is highly flammable, and in confined spaces is also very explosive and toxic.

When petrol/gasoline evaporates it produces 150 times its own volume in vapour, which when diluted with air becomes an ignitable mixture. The vapour is heavier than air, and will always fall to the lowest level and it can readily be distributed throughout a workshop by air currents. Even a small spillage of petrol or gasoline is potentially very dangerous.

Extracting or draining petrol (gasoline) from a vehicle fuel tank must be carried out in a well-ventilated area, preferably outside the workshop. All forms of ignition must be extinguished or removed, any hand lamps used must be flameproof and kept clear of any spillage. The receptacle used to contain the petrol drained or extracted must be more than adequate to receive the full amount to be drained.

1 Open fuel tank filler cap.
2 Place suitable receptacle beneath fuel tank drain plug.
3 Remove drain plug.
4 Check condition of sealing washer and replace plug. Do not overtighten.

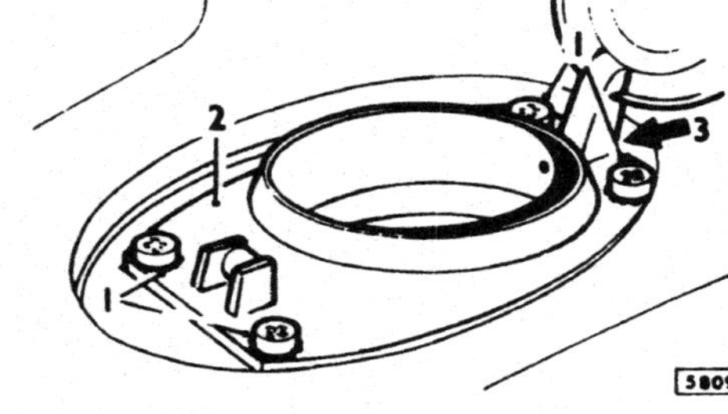

FUEL FILLER CAP ASSEMBLY

Remove and refit **19.55.08**

Removing

1 Remove four screws and shakeproof washers securing flange of fuel tank filler cap.
2 Taking great care to avoid damaging paintwork, prise flange from body.
3 Pull vent pipe from stub -- emission control cars to U.S. Federal specification only.
4 Remove gasket and 'O' ring seal.

Refitting

Reverse operations 1 to 3, using new gasket and 'O' ring seal.

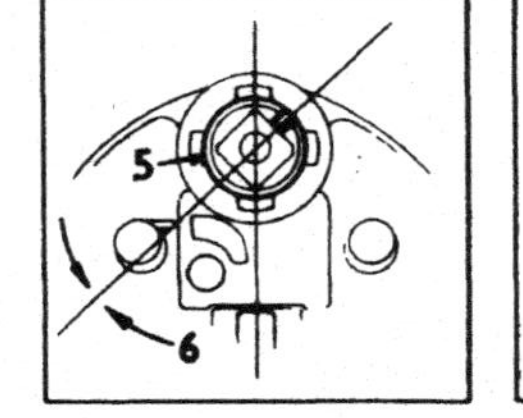

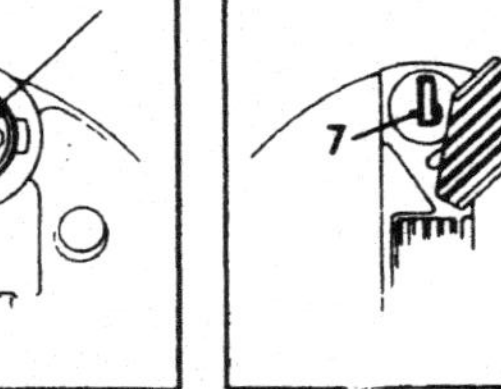

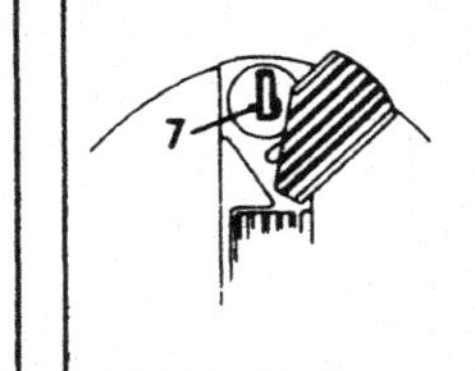
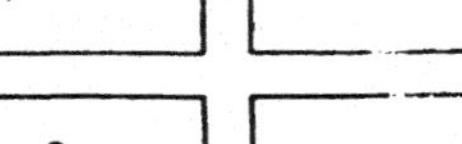
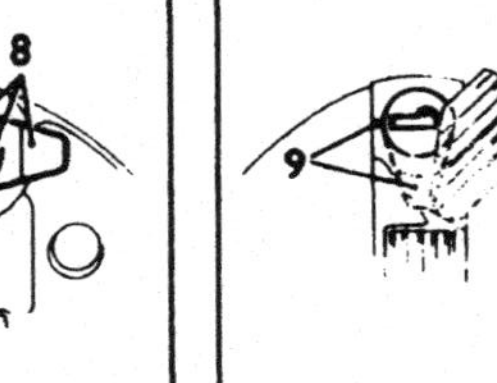

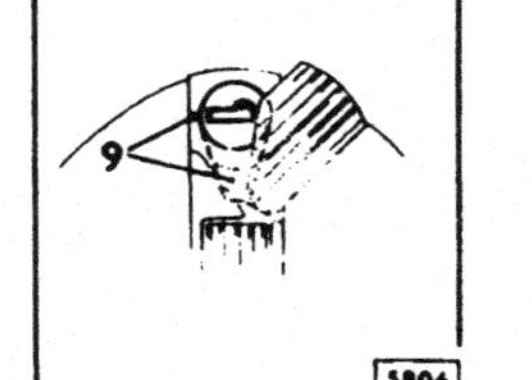

FUEL FILLER LOCK

Remove and refit **19.55.09**

Removing

1 Open filler cap lid.
2 Cover filler hole with rag or adhesive tape.
3 Remove screw and washer securing ward to lock barrel.
4 If key is available, insert in lock, and press barrel from inside to out.
5 If key is not available, insert a piece of stiff wire to lift tumblers and turn barrel to mid position.
6 Keep barrel in this angular position and press from lid.

Refitting

7 Insert key in barrel of replacement lock and offer into lid. Remove key.
8 Secure ward to barrel using screw and washer.
9 Test operate lock and ensure that ward turns to a position in line with, and facing, the lid catch. Unlock.
10 Remove obstruction from filler hole and close lid.

ELECTRONIC FUEL INJECTION

Description
The electronic fuel injection system can be divided into two separate systems interconnected only at the injectors.
The systems are:

1 A fuel system delivering to the injectors a constant supply of fuel at the correct pressure.
2 An electronic sensing and control system which monitors engine operating conditions of load, speed, temperature (coolant and induction air) and throttle movement. The control system then produces electrical current pulses of appropriate duration to hold open the injector solenoid valves and allow the correct quantity of fuel to flow through the nozzle for each engine cycle.

As fuel pressure is held constant, varying the pulse duration increases or decreases the amount of fuel passed through the injector to comply precisely with engine requirements.

Pulse duration, and therefore fuel quantity, is also modified to provide enrichment during starting and warming-up and at closed throttle, full throttle and while the throttle is actually opening.

All the injectors are simultaneously operated by the Electronic Control Unit (ECU) twice per engine cycle.

The induction system is basically the same as that on a carburetted engine: tuned ram pipe, air cleaner, plenum chamber and induction ports. The air is drawn through a paper element cleaner to a single throttle butterfly valve and to individual ports for each cylinder leading off the plenum chamber. The injectors are positioned at the cylinder head end of each port so that fuel is directed at the back of each inlet valve.

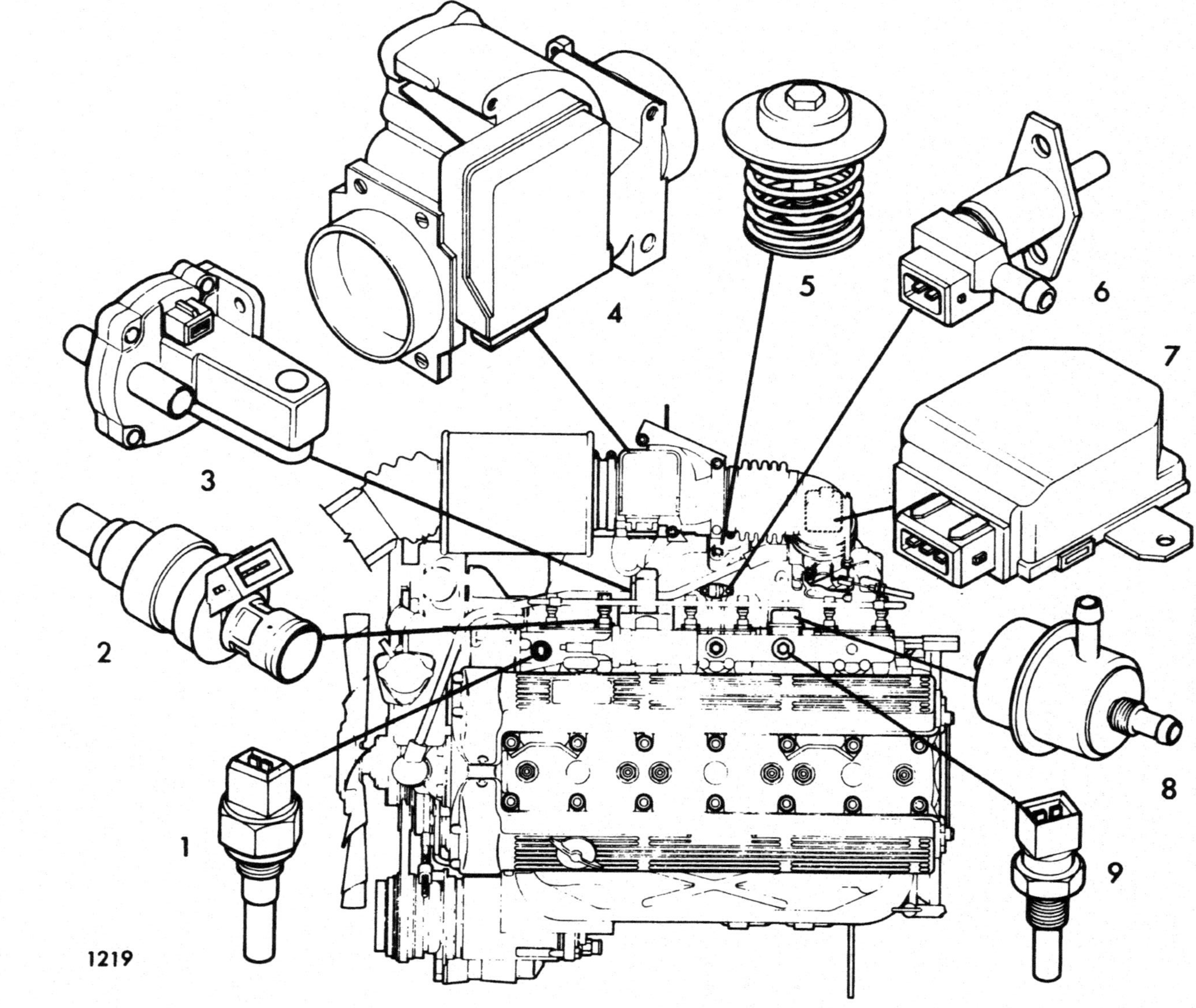

1. Thermotime switch
2. Fuel injectors
3. Auxiliary air valve
4. Air flow meter
5. Overrun valve
6. Cold start injector
7. Throttle switch
8. Fuel pressure regulator
9. Water temperature sensor

FUEL SYSTEM

Fuel Supply

Fuel is drawn from the tanks (1) at rear of the car by a fuel pump (3) via a solenoid operating change-over valve (2) to a fuel rail, through an in-line filter (5) and a pressure regulator (7). Fuel is controlled so that the pressure drop across the injector nozzle is maintained at a constant 2.5 bars (36.25 lbf/in^2). Excess fuel is returned to the tank from which it was drawn via a fuel cooler (4) – on air-conditioned cars only – and a solenoid operated shut-off valve. The six fuel injectors (8) are connected to the fuel rail (6) and are electro-mechanically operated to inject into each inlet port. Fuel is also supplied to a cold start injector (9) which is only operated during the starting of a cold engine.

0473

1. Fuel tank
2. Change over valve
3. Fuel pump
4. Fuel cooler
5. Fuel filter
6. Fuel rail
7. Fuel pressure regulator
8. Injectors
9. Cold start injector
10. Air bleed valve and non return valve

AIR INTAKE SYSTEM

Air is drawn from the air cleaner, through the air meter and throttle into the engine. The air passing through the air meter deflects the flap inside against a spring to a position dependent on the rate of air-flow. A potentiometer connected to the flap spindle converts the flap angular position to a voltage. This voltage is transmitted to the ECU as a measure of air flow.

ELECTRONIC SYSTEM

The Electronic Control Unit (ECU) receives information from sensors placed about the engine. It computes the quantity of fuel required and therefore the time for which the injectors must remain open. An ignition L.T. circuit switch triggers all injectors simultaneously at every third spark. The injectors open twice per engine cycle, each time delivering half the fuel requirement of each cylinder.

Temperature Sensors

The temperature of the air being taken into the engine through the inlet manifold, and the temperature of the coolant in the cylinder block are constantly monitored. The information is fed directly to the ECU.
The air temperature sensor has a small effect on the injector pulse width, and should be looked upon as a trimming rather than a control device. It ensures the fuel supplied is directly related to the weight of air drawn in by the engine. Therefore, as the weight (density) of the air charge increases with falling temperature, so the amount of fuel supplied is also increased to maintain optimum fuel/air ratio.
The coolant temperature sensor has a much greater degree of control although its main effect is concentrated while the engine is initially warming-up. The coolant temperature sensor operates in conjunction with the cold start system and the auxiliary air valve to form a completely automatic equivalent to a carburetter choke.

Flooding Protection System

With the ignition switched on, the pump will not operate until the engine is cranked. The system prevents flooding should an injector, or injectors, become faulty (remain in the open position), and the ignition is left switched on.

Auxiliary Air Valve

The auxiliary air valve consists of a variable orifice controlled by a bi-metal element. The unit is mounted on the water rail and also responds to coolant temperature. A heater is fitted round the bi-metal element to speed up the bi-metal response. The heater is connected in parallel with the fuel pump and so is energized as long as the engine is running.

Cranking Enrichment

The ECU provides an increased pulse duration during engine cranking in addition to any enrichment due to the coolant temperature sensor or the cold start injectors. The additional signal reduces slightly when cranking stops, but does not fall to normal level for a few seconds. This temporary enrichment sustains the engine during initial running.

Throttle Switch

The throttle switch, mounted on the throttle spindle, signals the position of the throttle to the ECU.
In addition to a richer air/fuel mixture during cold starting and warm-up, a slight additional amount of fuel is required during idle. The ECU supplies this additional amount of fuel on European cars in response to the closed throttle contact on the throttle switch. This contact is fitted, but not used, on cars to the USA and certain other countries.
Fuel return valves are situated in the left-hand and right-hand rear wheel arches, in line with the rearmost edge of the tyres. Care must be taken when changing them as they are NOT interchangeable, side for side.
The left-hand valve has a fixing bracket spot-welded to it that prevents it being incorrectly fitted (it would foul the wheel). It has an arrow showing direction of fuel flow (towards the rear).

Cold Start
For cold starting, additional fuel is injected into the inlet manifold by the cold start injector. This is controlled by the cold start relay and Thermotime switch. The Thermotime switch senses coolant temperature, and depending on the temperature it senses, interrupts or completes the ground connection for the relay. When the starter is operated the cold start relay is energized with its circuit completed via the Thermotime switch. The Thermotime switch also limits the length of time for which the relay is energized, to a maximum of 12 seconds under conditions of extreme cold. This enrichment is in addition to that provided by the coolant temperature sensor.
If the coolant temperature is above 35°C the switch does not operate at all, no starting enrichment additional to cranking enrichment being required.

Fuel Pressure Regulator
The fuel pressure regulator operates to maintain a constant pressure drop across the injector nozzles. It is connected one side to manifold depression and is operated by a spring-loaded diaphragm. Excess fuel is returned to the tank from which it was drawn via a solenoid-operated shut-off valve.

Ballast Resistor
In order to open and close the injectors a fairly high current drive is needed, about 1.5 amps per injector. The ECU has an output stage designed to deliver this current, but to protect the output transistors of the ECU from injector faults and short circuits there is a ballast resistor wired in series with each injector. These resistors will limit fault current to a safe value, thus protecting the ECU. The ballast resistors for each injector are housed in a single unit which is secured to the right-hand front engine valance by two screws.

Idle Speed Adjustment
The idle speed adjusting screw is located in the air distribution block and controls air flow to the auxiliary air valve.

Oxygen Sensor – Cars to USA only
The sensor measures the free oxygen concentration in the exhaust gases. This unconverted oxygen is a measure of the balance of the gases in the exhaust system. Excessive free oxygen over a certain proportion indicates a weak mixture and insufficient free oxygen indicates a rich mixture. A voltage is fed back to the electronic control unit to compensate for variations by revising the applied pulse width of the input signal.

GOOD PRACTICE

The following instructions must be strictly observed:

1 Always disconnect the battery before removing any components.
2 Always depressurize the fuel system before disconnecting any fuel pipes, see 19.50.02.
3 When removing fuelling components always clamp fuel pipes approximately 1.5 in (38 mm) from the unit being removed. Do not overtighten clamp.
4 Ensure rags are available to absorb any spillage that may occur.
5 When reconnecting electrical components, always ensure that good contact is made by the connector before fitting the rubber cover. Always ensure that ground connections are made on to clean bare metal, and are tightly fastened using correct screws and washers.

WARNING

1 **Do not let the engine run without the battery connected.**
2 **Do not use a high-speed battery charger as a starting aid.**
3 **When using a high-speed charger to charge the battery, the battery MUST be disconnected from the rest of the vehicle's electrical system.**
4 **When installing, ensure that battery is connected with correct polarity.**
5 **No battery larger than 12V may be used.**

MAINTENANCE
There is no routine maintenance procedure laid down for the electronic fuel injection system other than that, at all service intervals, the electrical connectors must be checked for security.
The fuel filter must be discarded and a replacement component fitted at 12,000 mile (20 000 km) intervals, when the air cleaner element must also be renewed.

AIR CLEANER

The air cleaner element is of the paper type and is situated between the air intake trumpet and the air-flow meter.

Remove and refit **19.10.08**

Removing
To renew the element, proceed as follows:

1 Slacken clips securing inlet and outlet hoses.
2 Slide air cleaner assembly forwards until bracket is clear of mounting spigots.
3 Release spring clips securing front cover.

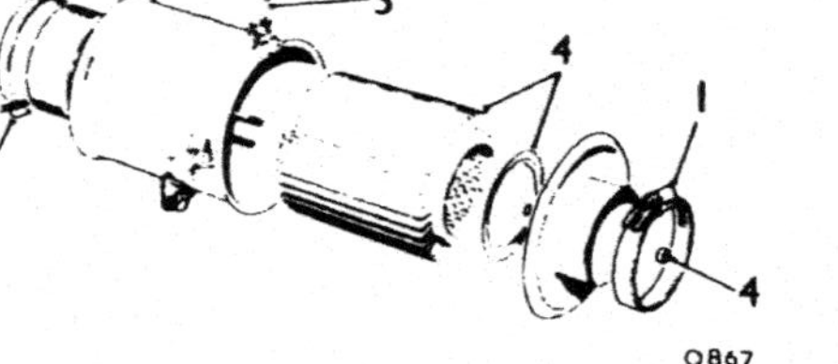

4 Remove Nyloc nut securing end-plate, withdraw end-plate and filter element.

Refitting

5 Remove dirt, grease etc., from air cleaner casing; reverse operations 1 to 4.
Do not overtighten Nyloc nut.

THROTTLE PEDAL

Remove and refit **19.20.01**

Removing

1 Fold carpet away from base of throttle pedal.
2 Remove nuts and washers securing base of pedal to mounting plate.
3 Pull base of pedal away from mounting plate and disengage spring from pedal.
4 Examine spring for wear, and renew if necessary.

3 2 3 6 3 3
S6572

Refitting

5 Engage rod with pedal.
6 Position spring on pedal.
7 Push base of pedal towards bulkhead and locate on mounting studs.
8 Reverse operations 1 and 2.

THROTTLE LINKAGE

Check and adjust 19.20.05

Check
1 Ensure throttle return springs correctly secured and that throttle moves freely, resting against closed stop when released.
2 Ensure that throttle butterfly closed stop screw has not been moved. If signs of tampering are present, check and if necessary, adjust.

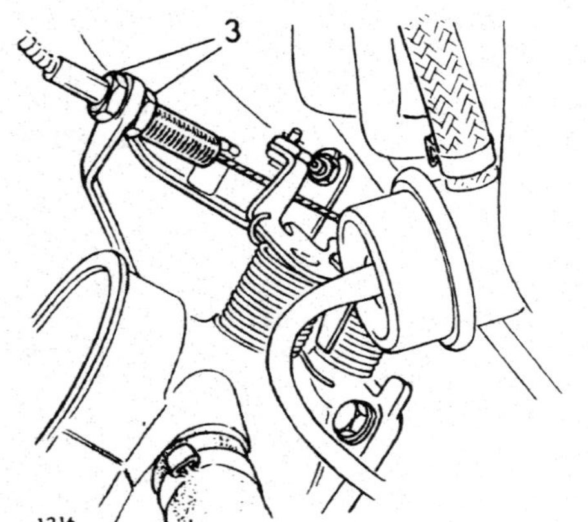

Adjust
3 Slacken locknuts at, outer throttle cable abutment.
4 **Adjust position of outer cable in abutment to place inner cable under light tension but NOT to move throttle operating lever, and secure locknuts.**
5 **Re-check operation 1.**

THROTTLE CABLE

Remove and refit 19.20.06

Removing
1 Disengage throttle return spring from throttle operating lever.
2 Slacken locknuts at outer throttle cable abutment and draw cable clear.
3 Remove 'C' clip securing cable yoke clevis pin and detach inner cable from operating lever; temporarily replace clevis pin.
4 Slacken locknut on top surface of footwell.
5 Remove underscuttle casing.
6 Remove split pin at top end of operating rod.
7 Disengage sleeve and nipple from rod.
8 Remove nut from cable sheath and draw cable assembly into engine compartment. Recover operating rod abutment plate.

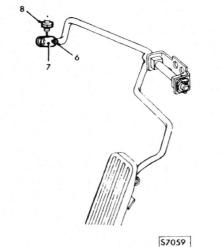

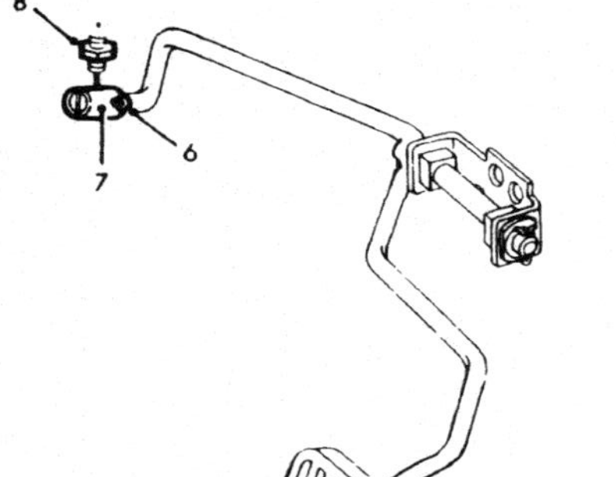

Refitting
9 Examine grommets for wear, and renew as necessary.
10 Reverse operations 1 to 8. Apply sealing compound around thread on top surface of footwell.

THROTTLE BUTTERFLY VALVE

Adjust 19.20.11

1 Remove the elbow and the convolute hose to expose the throttle body.
2 Slacken locknut on throttle butterfly stop screw. Wind back screw.
3 Ensure throttle butterfly valve closes fully.
4 Insert 0.002 in (0,05 mm) feeler gauge between top of valve and housing to hold valve open.
5 Set stop screw to just touch stop arm and tighten locknut with feeler in position.
6 Press stop arm against stop screw and withdraw feeler.
7 Seal threads of adjusting screws and locknuts using a blob of paint.
8 Refit the elbow and convolute hose.
9 Check throttle linkage adjustment, see 19.20.05.
10 Check operation of throttle switch, see 19.22.37.
11 Check kickdown switch adjustment, see 44.30.12.

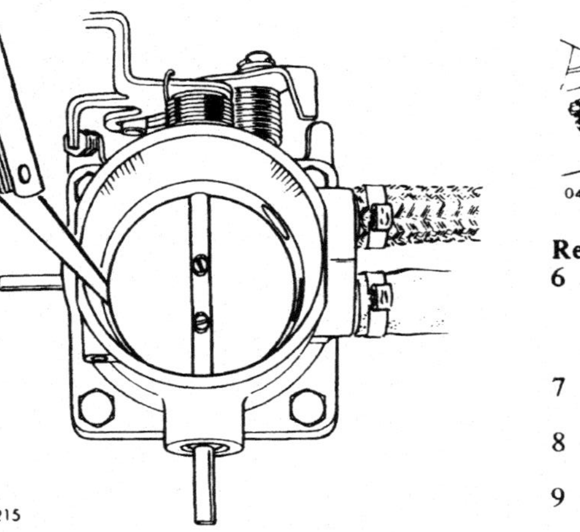

AUXILIARY AIR VALVE

Description

The auxiliary air valve is mounted on the water outlet rail and is controlled by coolant temperature. The valve opens to pass additional air into the inlet manifold under cold start and cold idle conditions.

AUXILIARY AIR VALVE

Remove and refit 19.20.16

Removing
CAUTION: The procedure **MUST ONLY** be carried out on a cold or cool engine.
1 Disconnect battery, see 86.15.20.
2 Carefully remove pressure cap from remote expansion tank to release any cooling system residual pressure. Replace cap tightly.
3 Slacken clips securing air hoses to auxiliary air valve. Pull hoses clear.
4 Remove two screws and washers securing auxiliary air valve to coolant pipe and lift clear.
5 Clean all traces of gasket from coolant pipe, taking care not to damage seating area.

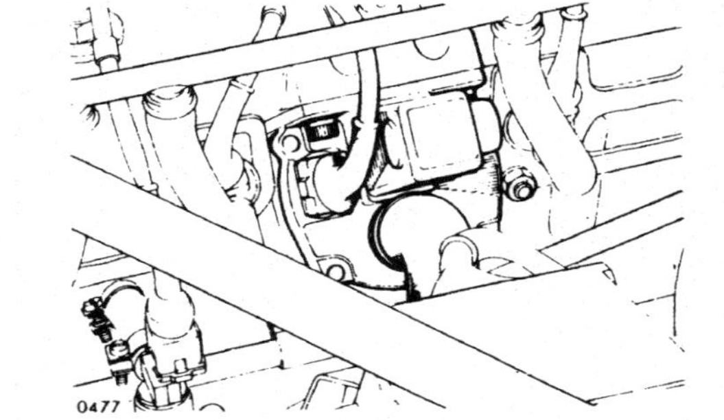

Refitting
6 Coat new gasket with suitable non-hardening sealing compound and locate valve, orientated correctly, on coolant pipe.
7 Secure valve using two screws and washers.
8 Fit air hoses and secure clips. Re-connect battery.
9 Check coolant level at remote header tank, and if necessary, top up.

AUXILIARY AIR VALVE

Test 19.20.17

1 Remove the electrical connector from the auxiliary air valve.
2 Connect a voltmeter across the terminals of the connector.
3 Crank the engine over; battery voltage should be obtained. If there is no voltage there is a fault in the electrical system and the wires should be checked for leakage and deterioration. When it has been established that power is reaching the auxiliary air valve, the heating coils resistance should be checked.
4 Connect an ohmmeter between the terminals of the air valve. A resistance of 33 ohms should be obtained. If there is no resistance the air valve should be replaced.
5 Remove the auxiliary air valve mounting plate from the water rail, see 19.20.16.
6 Immerse the air valve in cold water, being careful not to get water into the electrical terminals or into the by-pass channel. The blocking plate should fully expose the by-pass orifice.
7 Immerse the air valve mounting plate in hot water. The blocking plate should gradually close off the by-pass orifice.

IDLE SPEED

Adjust 19.20.18

1 Ensure engine is at normal operating temperature.
2 Check throttle linkage for correct operation, and that return springs are secure and effective.
3 Start engine and run for two to three minutes.
4 Set idle speed adjustment screw to achieve 750 rev/min.

NOTE: If it proves impossible to reduce idle speed to specified level proceed as detailed in operations 5 to 9.

5 Check **ALL** pipes and hoses to inlet manifold for security and condition.
6 Check security of injectors and cold start injectors.
7 Ensure that all joints are tight, and that inlet manifold to cylinder head fastenings are tight.
8 Ensure that throttle butterfly closed stop shows no signs of tampering; if it does, adjust throttle butterfly valve.
9 Check operation of over-run valve.
10 If operations 5 to 9 do not reduce the idle speed, check operation of auxiliary air valve.

OVER-RUN VALVE – Cars fitted with Emission Control

Description

An over-run valve is fitted beneath the air distributor block. The valve is calibrated to open and limit manifold depression under conditions of closed throttle over-run. This ensures that air is available to maintain a combustible air/fuel ratio under all conditions.

OVER-RUN VALVE

Test 19.20.21

1 Slacken the hose clip securing the over-run valve air feed hose to the throttle body.
2 Block off the hose.
3 Start the engine; idle speed should remain correct.
4 If the idle speed is not correct, renew the over-run valve.

OVER-RUN VALVE

Remove and refit 19.20.22

Removing
1 Disconnect battery, see 86.15.20.
2 Remove air-flow meter, see 19.22.25.
3 Slacken the clip securing the auxiliary air hose (to the air distribution block) and pull the hose off.
4 Slacken the clip securing the hose from the throttle butterfly housing.
5 Remove the three screws securing the air distribution block to the inlet manifold.
6 Lift the air distribution block from the inlet manifold and pull off the air hose.
7 Withdraw the over-run valve.

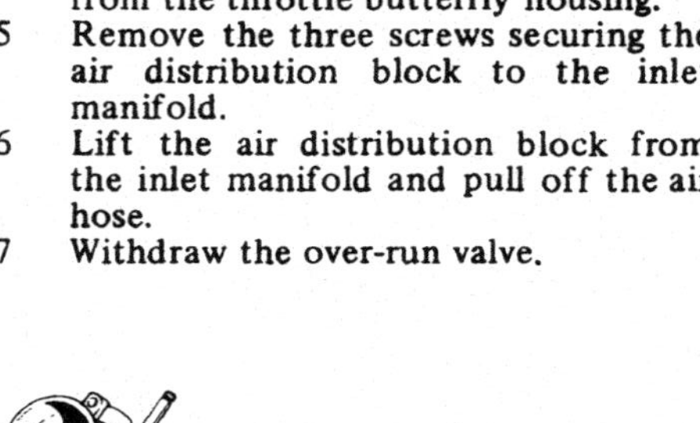

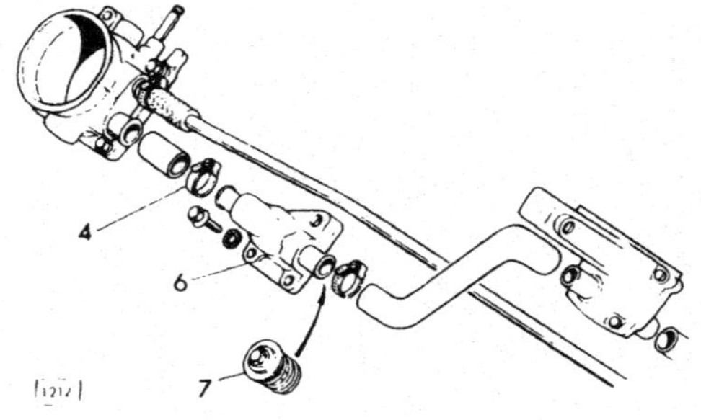

Refitting
8 Reverse operations 1 to 7.

FUEL CUT-OFF INERTIA SWITCH

Remove and refit 19.22.09

Removing
1 Disconnect battery, see 86.15.20.
2 Remove screws securing switch cover at passenger side of fascia.
3 Pull connectors from switch.
4 Pull switch from spring clips.

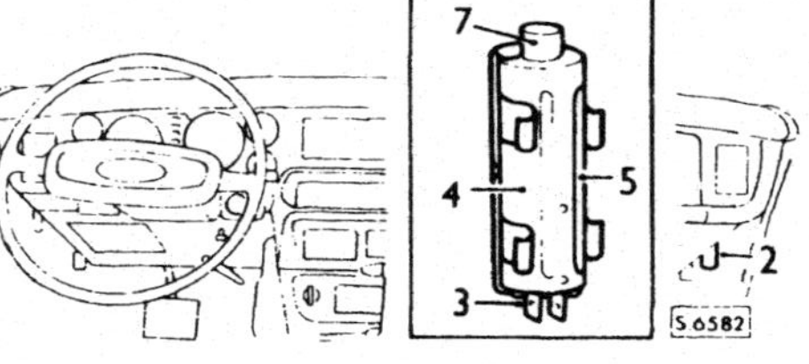

Refitting
5 Press switch into spring clips, ribs towards rear of car and terminals at bottom.
NOTE: Ensure switch is raised in clips to abut on top lip of bracket.
6 Fit connectors to switch; polarity is unimportant.
7 Press in plunger at top of switch.
8 Fit switch cover and secure.
9 Re-connect battery.

OXYGEN SENSOR

Description

The oxygen sensor is located in the exhaust down-pipe. The sensor monitors the oxygen content in the exhaust and sends a proportional signal to the ECU thus maintaining close air/fuel ratio control under all operating conditions.

OXYGEN SENSOR

Remove and refit. 19.22.16

Removing
1 Disconnect the battery, see 86.15.20.
2 Disconnect the electrical connector on the oxygen sensor.
3 Remove the oxygen sensor.
4 Clean the sensor sealing face.

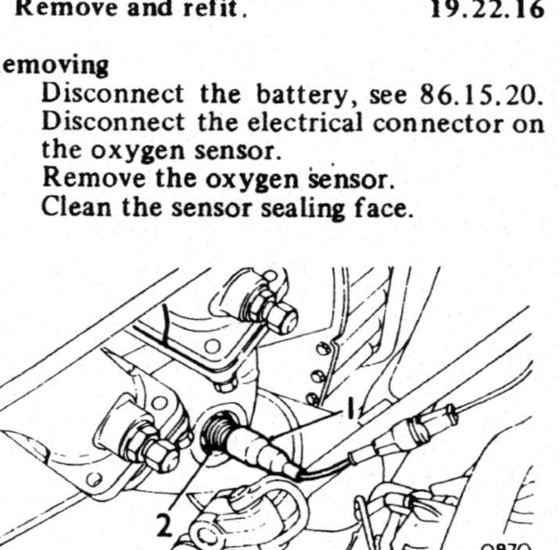

Refitting
5 Replace with a new oxygen sensor.
6 Re-connect the electrical connector.
7 Re-connect the battery.

COOLANT TEMPERATURE SENSOR

Description

The coolant temperature sensor is located at the rear of the water rail.
The sensor comprises a temperature-sensitive resistor with a negative temperature coefficient, that is, the electrical resistance decreases with increasing temperature. The sensor provides the ECU with a coolant temperature parameter that controls the injector signal pulse with respect to engine temperature. Practically, the sensor establishes a rich level of fuelling at low temperature, and a weaker level at high temperature. In conjunction with the auxiliary air valve the coolant temperature sensor forms an equivalent to a carburetter automatic choke.

COOLANT TEMPERATURE SENSOR

Remove and refit 19.22.18

Removing
NOTE: This procedure **MUST ONLY** be carried out on a cold or cool engine.

1 Disconnect battery, see 86.15.20.
2 Pull connector from coolant temperature sensor.
3 Carefully remove pressure cap from remote header tank to release any cooling system residual pressure. Replace cap tightly.

NOTE: The replacement component is prepared at this point, and the transfer made as quickly as possible.

4 Ensure sealing washer located on replacement temperature sensor and coat threads with suitable sealing compound.
5 Remove temperature sensor from the water rail.

Refitting
6 Screw replacement temperature sensor into position.
7 Refit electrical connector.
8 Re-connect battery.
9 Check coolant level at remote header tank. If necessary, top-up.

COOLANT TEMPERATURE SENSOR

Test 19.22.19

1 Disconnect battery, see 86.15.20.
2 Pull connector from temperature sensor.
3 Connect suitable ohmmeter between terminals, note resistance reading. The reading is subject to change according to temperature, and should closely approximate to the relevant resistance value given in the table.
4 Disconnect ohmmeter.
5 Check resistance between each terminal in turn and body of sensor. A very high resistance reading (open circuit) must be obtained.
6 Re-connect cable.
7 Re-connect battery.

Coolant Temperature (°C)	Resistance (kilohms)
– 10	9.2
0	5.9
+ 20	2.5
+ 40	1.18
+ 60	0.60
+ 80	0.325

THERMOTIME SWITCH

Description

The Thermotime switch is located at the front of the water rail. The switch comprises a bi-metallic contact opened and closed by coolant temperature and, in addition, auto-excited by a heating element. The switch controls the cold start injector through the cold start relay and is energised by operation of the starter motor. While the start system is in operation a voltage is applied to the bi-metallic switch contact heating element which then tends to open the contact and isolate the relay and injector. The length of time that this takes depends upon the initial temperature of the bi-metallic element up to a maximum of eight seconds under conditions of extreme cold. It can be deduced, therefore, that when the engine is warm, or at normal operating temperature, there will be no fuel supplied by the cold start injector.

THERMOTIME SWITCH

Remove and refit 19.22.20

Removing
NOTE: This procedure **MUST ONLY** be carried out on a cool or cold engine.
1 Disconnect battery, see 86.15.20.
2 Pull connector from Thermotime switch.
3 Carefully remove pressure cap from remote header tank to release any cooling system residual pressure. Replace cap tightly.
4 Ensure new sealing washer located on replacement Thermotime switch and coat threads with suitable sealing compound.
5 Remove Thermotime switch from the front of the water rail.

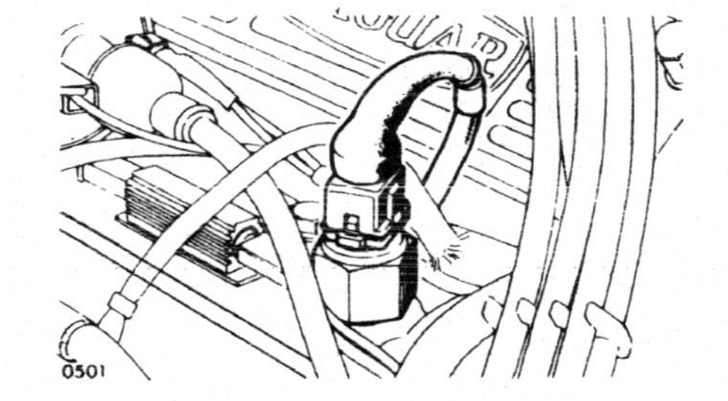

Refitting
6 Screw replacement Thermotime switch in position.
7 Refit electrical connector.
8 Reconnect battery.
9 Check coolant level at remote header tank, and top-up if necessary.

THERMOTIME SWITCH

Test 19.22.21

Equipment required: Stop watch, ohmmeter, single-pole switch, jump lead for connecting switch to battery and Thermotime switch, and a thermometer.

NOTE: Check coolant temperature with thermometer and note reading before carrying out procedures detailed below. Check rated value of Thermotime switch (stamped on body flat).

1 Disconnect battery earth lead.
2 Pull electrical connector from Thermotime switch.

'A' Coolant temperature higher than switch rated value
3 Connect ohmmeter between terminal 'W' and earth. A very high resistance reading (open circuit) should be obtained.
4 Renew switch if a very low resistance reading (short circuit) is obtained.

'B' Coolant temperature lower than switch rated value

5 Connect ohmmeter between terminal 'W' and earth. A very low resistance reading (closed circuit) should be obtained.
6 Connect 12V supply via isolating switch to terminal 'G' of Thermotime switch.
7 Using stop watch, check time delay between making isolating switch and indication on ohmmeter changing from low to high resistance. Delay period must closely approximate to time indicated in table, see table for specific coolant temperature (noted above).
8 Renew Thermotime switch if necessary.
9 Re-connect Thermotime switch.
10 Re-connect battery earth lead.

Coolant Temperature	Delay
– 20°C	8 sec.
0°C	4½ sec.
+ 10°C	3½ sec.
+ 35°C	0

AIR TEMPERATURE SENSOR

Description

The air temperature sensor is an integral part of the air flow meter.
The sensor provides information to the ECU relating to the ambient air density and temperature, thus maintaining an optimum fuel/air ratio.

AIR TEMPERATURE SENSOR

Test 19.22.23

1 Disconnect the battery, see 86.15.20.
2 Remove the multi-pin electrical connector from air-flow meter.
3 Connect a suitable ohmmeter between terminals 6 and 27 of the air-flow meter.

Ambient Air Temperature (°C)	Resistance (kilohms)
– 10	9.2
0	5.9
+ 20	2.5
+ 40	1.18
+ 60	0.60

4 Note the resistance reading. The reading is subject to change according to the temperature and should closely approximate to the relevant resistance value given in the table above.
5 Disconnect the ohmmeter.
6 Re-connect the multi-pin connector.
7 Re-connect the battery.

AIR-FLOW METER

Description

The air-flow meter is located between the air cleaner and the inlet manifold mounted throttle butterfly. The flap in the air-flow meter is opened when air is drawn into the engine. The ECU uses the flap angle to compute fuel requirements.

AIR-FLOW METER

Remove and refit 19.22.25

Removing

1 Disconnect the battery, see 86.15.20.
2 Slacken the two hose clips which secure the air intake hoses on each side of the air-flow meter.
3 Disconnect the electrical connector from the air-flow meter.
4 Remove the three screws which secure the air-flow meter to its mounting bracket.
5 Remove the air-flow meter from the mounting bracket and withdraw the air intake hoses.

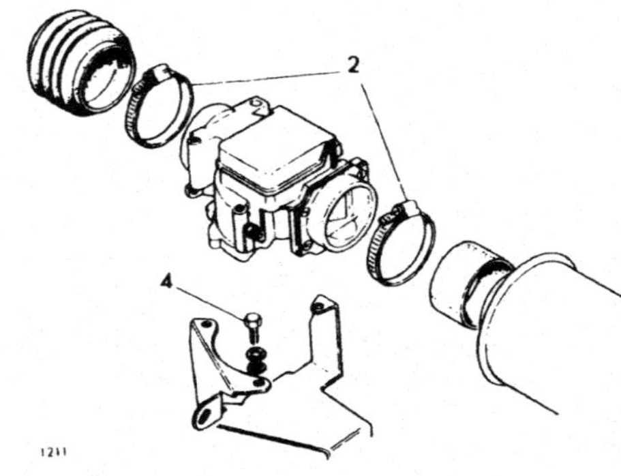

Refitting

6 Reverse operations 1 to 5.

COLD START SYSTEM

Test 19.22.32

WARNING: THIS TEST RESULTS IN FUEL VAPOUR BEING PRESENT IN THE ENGINE COMPARTMENT. IT IS THEREFORE IMPERATIVE THAT ALL DUE PRECAUTIONS ARE TAKEN AGAINST FIRE AND EXPLOSION.

1 Remove the electrical connector from the cold start injector.
2 Connect a volt-meter across the terminals of the connector.
3 Crank the engine over; battery voltage should be obtained.
4 Remove the setscrew and washer securing cold start injector to inlet manifold. Remove cold start injector.
5 Arrange container to collect sprayed fuel, and refit connector removed in operation 1.
6 Check for fuel leaking past the nozzle.
7 When the engine is cold, crank the engine over.
8 The cold start injector should spray fuel out for a few seconds until the Thermotime switch switches off the injector. When the engine is warm the injector should not spray fuel during engine cranking.

ELECTRONIC CONTROL UNIT (ECU)

Description

The ECU is mounted in the luggage compartment against the front bulkhead. The ECU receives all electrical input signals from various sensors. This information is used to determine the correct period of time for which the injectors are held open in each engine cycle. A control knob on the ECU adjusts idle CO level and **MUST NOT** normally be moved.

ELECTRONIC CONTROL UNIT (ECU)

Remove and refit 19.22.34

Removing

1 Disconnect battery, see 86.15.20.
2 At forward end of luggage compartment, remove ECU cover.
3 Remove retainer band.
4 Remove cable clamp clip.
5 Unclip end cover.
6 Locate handle on harness plug and withdraw plug.

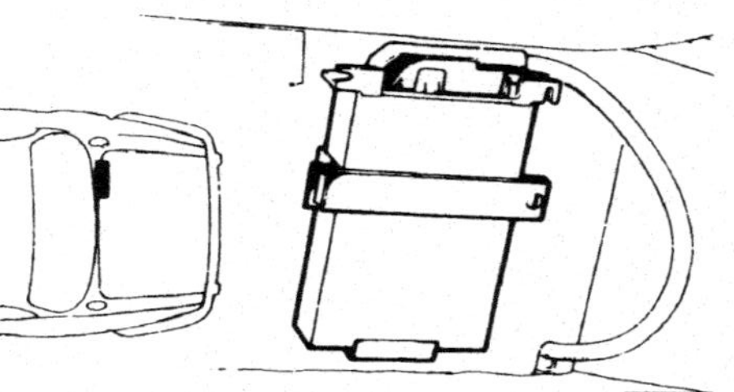

Refitting

CAUTION: THE IDLE FUELLING POTENTIOMETER IS PRESET AND MUST NOT BE MOVED.

7 Reverse operations 1 to 6.
8 Check idle CO level.

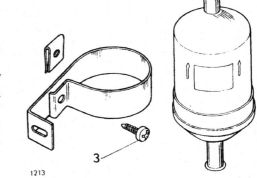

THROTTLE SWITCH

Description

The throttle switch is located on the end of the throttle spindle. The switch closes when the throttle nears the wide-open position and provides information to the ECU of fuel quantity required by the injector for maximum power output at full throttle.

THROTTLE SWITCH

Remove and refit 19.22.36

Removing
1 Disconnect the battery, see 86.15.20.
2 Pull the electrical connector from the throttle switch.
3 Remove the two screws, plain and shakeproof washers securing the throttle switch and lift the switch from the spindle.

0474

Refitting
4 Locate the switch on the spindle.
5 Secure the switch with the two screws, plain and shakeproof washers.

THROTTLE SWITCH

Test 19.22.37

NOTE: Before commencing the following tests ensure that the throttle butterfly valve and throttle linkage are correctly adjusted, see 19.20.11.

1 Disconnect the battery, see 86.15.20.
2 Remove the electrical connector from the throttle switch.
3 Connect a powered test lamp between terminals 3 and 18 of the throttle switch.
4 Open the throttle; the bulb should light up when the throttle nears the wide open position.
6 If the bulb does not light, replace the throttle switch.
7 Refit the electrical connector to the switch.
8 Re-connect the battery.

COLD START/PUMP RELAY

Description

The double relay is mounted on the engine rear bulkhead next to the vehicle battery. When the ignition key is turned, one half of the relay is activated connecting the battery circuit to the ballast resistors and the injectors. The double relay also allows current to flow to the ECU and the pump switch on the air-flow meter.
When the engine is cranked for starting the second half of the relay is activated and thus energizes the auxiliary air valve, the cold start system and the fuel pump.

COLD START/PUMP RELAY

Remove and refit

Cold start relay 19.22.31
Pump relay 19.22.39

Removing
1 Disconnect battery, see 86.15.20.
2 Note connections and pull electrical connectors from relay.
3 Remove securing screw.

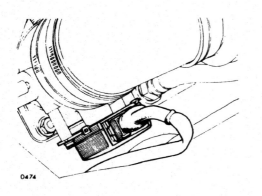

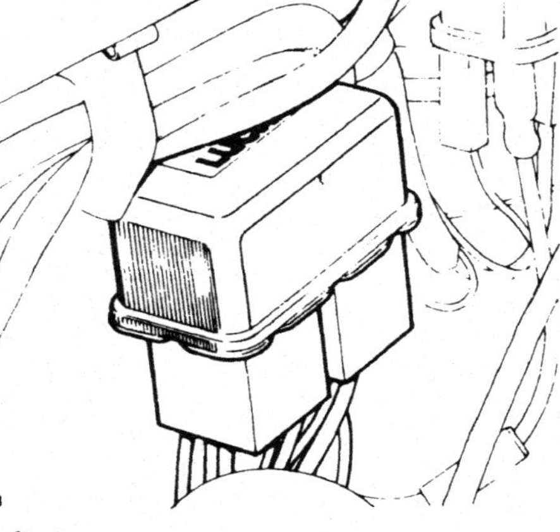

Refitting
Reverse operations 1 to 3.

FUEL LINE FILTER

Remove and refit 19.25.01

WARNING: A certain amount of fuel spillage is unavoidable during this operation. It is therefore imperative that all due precautions are taken against fire and explosion.

The fuel filter is located in the engine compartment mounted on the right-hand valance under the air cleaner.

Removing
1 Disconnect the battery, see 86.15.20.
2 Remove air cleaner.
3 Remove bolt securing filter and draw filter clear of clamp.
4 Clamp inlet and outlet pipes.
5 Slacken pipe clips on either side of the filter.
6 Remove filter unit and discard.

3

1213

Refitting
7 Fit new filter unit.
8 Tighten pipe clips.
9 Remove pipe clamps.
10 Locate filter in clamp and secure.
11 Replace air cleaner.
12 Re-connect battery.
13 Run engine and check for leaks.

FUEL TANK CHANGE-OVER VALVE

Description

The change-over valve is located in the luggage compartment adjacent to the fuel pump. When energized by the change-over switch, the valve opens the outlet pipe from the right-hand fuel tank.

FUEL TANK CHANGE-OVER VALVE

Remove and refit 19.40.31

Removing
1 Disconnect battery, see 86.15.20.
2 Remove spare wheel.
3 Clamp inlet and outlet pipes.
4 Release pipe clips and pull pipes from change-over valve.
5 Disconnect cable to valve.
6 Remove screws securing valve clamp to boot floor.

S7033

Refitting
Reverse operations 1 to 6, securing ground lead beneath one foot of clamp.

FUEL TANK CHANGE-OVER VALVE

Test 19.40.32

1 Disconnect battery, see 86.15.20.
2 Remove spare wheel.
3 Clamp inlet and outlet pipes.
4 Release pipe clips and pull pipes from change-over valve.
5 Disconnect cable to valve.
6 Push a suitable length of rubber pipe on to centre inlet port of valve.
7 Blow through rubber pipe. Air should flow from outlet union through body of solenoid.
8 Apply 12V d.c. to valve cable.
9 Blow through rubber pipe. Air should flow from outlet union towards opposite side.
10 If results satisfactory, reverse operations 1 to 7.
11 If results not satisfactory, replace valve.

FUEL COOLER

Remove and refit 19.40.40

Removing
WARNING: REFRIGERANT GAS CAN CAUSE BLINDNESS. IT IS THEREFORE ESSENTIAL TO DEPRESSURIZE THE AIR CONDITIONING SYSTEM PRIOR TO DISCONNECTING REFRIGERANT HOSE TO FUEL COOLER. SEE OPERATION 82.30.05.

1 Depressurize fuel system, see 19.50.02.
2 Depressurize air conditioning system, see 82.30.05.
3 Disconnect refrigerant inlet and outlet hoses.
4 Clamp fuel hoses.
5 Disconnect fuel hoses.
6 Remove two setscrews, washers and spire nuts securing fuel cooler to air cleaner brackets.

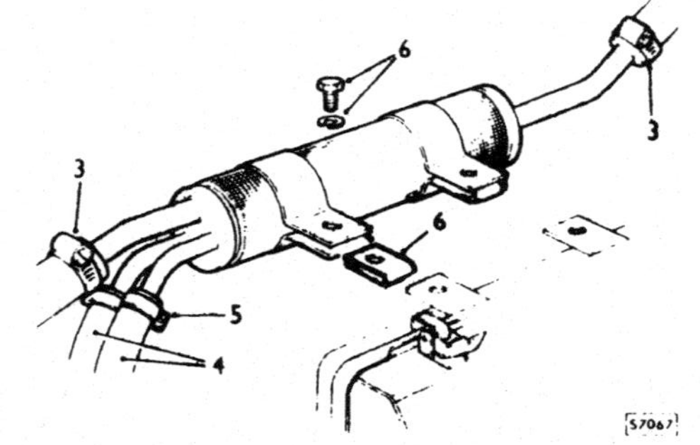
S7067

Refitting
Reverse operations 1 to 6.

FUEL PUMP

Description

The fuel pump is located beneath the luggage compartment floor. It is flexibly mounted and secured using noise- and shock-absorbing material. The pump is a roller-type machine delivering a continuous flow of fuel.

FUEL PUMP

Remove and refit 19.45.08

Removing
1 Disconnect the battery, see 86.15.20.
2 Remove spare wheel.
3 Clamp inlet and outlet pipes of pump.
4 Release pipe clips and pull pipes from pump unions.
5 Remove electrical connector.
6 Remove screws securing pump mounting bracket.
7 Remove clamp securing nuts and draw pump from clamp.

S7031

Refitting
8 Clean pump bracket around earth connecting screw.
9 Reverse operations 1 to 7, locating earth wire on bright metal beneath one securing screw.

FUEL PRESSURE REGULATOR

Description

The fuel pressure regulator is mounted on the inlet manifold and is connected to the fuel rail on one side and inlet manifold depression on the other. The regulator maintains fuel pressure in the fuel rail at the correct value.

FUEL PRESSURE REGULATOR

Remove and refit 19.45.11

Removing
1 Depressurize fuel system, see 19.50.02.
2 Disconnect battery, see 86.15.20.
3 Remove two setscrews and washers securing pressure regulator mounting bracket and carefully pull regulator and bracket upwards. Note orientation of regulator in bracket.
4 Clamp inlet and outlet pipes of regulator.
5 Release pipe clips and pull pipes from regulator unions.
6 Remove nut and washer and release regulator from bracket.

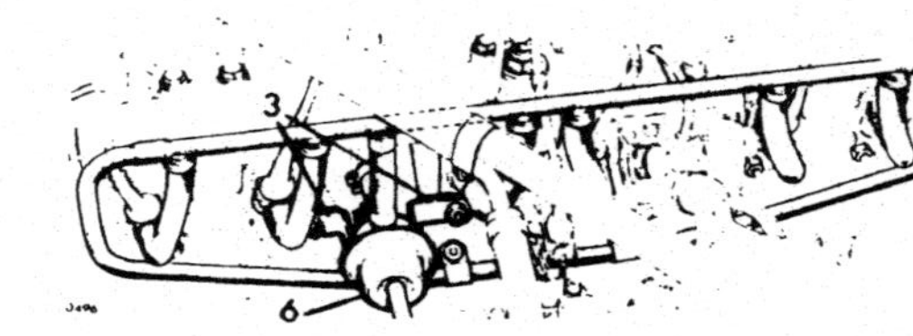

Refitting
7 Locate regulator in bracket orientated as noted in operation 3 and secure using nut and spring washer.
8 Push inlet and outlet pipes on to regulator and secure pipe clips ensuring that pipes are not kinked or twisted.
9 Remove pipe clamps.
10 Carefully press regulator and bracket into position and secure with two setscrews and washers.
11 Re-connect battery.

FUEL PRESSURE REGULATOR

19.45.12

Check

1. Depressurize fuel system, see 19.50.02.
2. Slacken pipe clip securing cold start injector supply pipe to fuel rail and pull pipe from rail.
3. Connect pressure gauge pipe to fuel rail and tighten pipe clip.
   CAUTION: Pressure gauge must be checked against an approved standard at regular intervals.
4. Pull '–ve' L.T. lead from ignition coil and switch ignition on.
   Check reading on pressure gauge; reading must be 36.25 ± 0.725 lbf/in^2 (2,55 ± 0,05 kgf/cm^2)
   NOTE: The pressure reading may slowly drop through either the regulator valve seating or the pump non-return valve. A slow steady drop is permissible; a rapid fall **MUST** be investigated.
5. Operate fuel change-over switch on centre dash panel.
6. Re-check pressure gauge reading.
   NOTE: If satisfactory results have been obtained, depressurize fuel system and continue with operations 8 to 11. If satisfactory results have not been obtained replace the regulator with a new unit.
7. Slacken pipe clip and remove pressure gauge from fuel rail.
8. Re-connect cold start injector supply pipe and secure pipe clip.
9. Re-connect the '–ve' L.T. lead to ignition coil.
10. Switch ignition on and check for leaks.
11. Switch ignition off.

FUEL SYSTEM

Depressurize 19.50.02

CAUTION: The fuel system MUST always be depressurized before disconnecting any fuel system components.

1. Remove spare wheel.
2. Remove the fuel pump earth lead.
3. Switch on and crank engine for a few seconds.
4. Switch the ignition off and re-connect the pump to earth.

Pressure test see 19.45.12.

INJECTORS

Description

The 6 injectors are mounted on the induction ram pipes, so that the fuel jet is directed on to the back of each inlet valve. The injectors are solenoid-operated valves which are controlled by the ECU.

INJECTORS

Remove and refit 19.60.01

Removing

1. Depressurize fuel system, see 19.50.02.
2. Disconnect battery, see 86.15.20.
3. Clamp fuel inlet pipe between filter and fuel rail.
4. Pull electrical connector from injector(s) to be removed.
5. Remove two setscrews securing fuel rail to inlet manifold.
6. Release clips securing supply rail to return rail.
7. Pull manifold pressure pipe from inlet manifold.
8. Remove 6 nuts and spring washers securing injector clamps to induction ram pipes.
9. Carefully lift fuel rail complete with injectors sufficient for injectors to clear induction ram pipes. Ensure adequate rag to hand to absorb spilled fuel.
10. Suitably plug or cover injector holes in ram pipes to prevent ingress of dirt or foreign matter.
11. Slacken pipe clip(s) of injector(s) to be removed.
12. Note orientation of electrical sockets, and pull injector(s) from fuel rail.
13. Remove two rubber sealing 'O' rings from **ALL** injectors and discard.
    CAUTION: Sealing rings MUST be renewed each time the injectors are removed from the manifold.

Refitting

14. Locate new sealing 'O' rings at **ALL** injectors.
15. Press replacement injector(s), orientated correctly, on to fuel rail stub(s).
16. Secure pipe clip(s) at replacement injector(s).
17. Locate fuel rail complete with injectors into position and secure injector clamps with 6 nuts and spring washers.
18. Reverse operations 2 to 8.

INJECTORS – SET

Injector winding check 19.60.02

1. Use ohmmeter to measure resistance value of each injector winding, which should be 2.4 ohms at 20°C (68°F).
2. Check for short-circuit to earth on winding by connecting ohmmeter probes between either injector terminal and injector body. Meter should read ∞ (infinity).
   If any injector winding is open-circuited or short-circuited, replace the injector.

FUEL RAIL

Remove and refit 19.60.04

Removing

1. Depressurize fuel system, see 19.50.02.
2. Disconnect battery, see 86.15.20.
3. Pull manifold pressure pipe from the inlet manifold.
4. Clamp fuel pipe between filter and supply fuel rail.
5. Release clips securing return fuel rail to supply rail.
6. Release clips securing return fuel rail to regulator outlet hoses and fuel return pipe. Pull hoses from rail.
7. Release clips securing supply fuel rail to filter, main fuel rail, cold start injector and regulator inlet hoses. Pull hoses from supply rail.
8. Remove supply and return fuel rails.
9. Pull electrical connectors from injectors and cold start injector.
10. Remove 6 nuts and spring washers securing injector clamps to induction ram pipe.
11. Carefully lift fuel rail complete with injectors from induction ram pipes. Ensure adequate rags to hand to absorb spilled fuel.
12. Suitably plug or cover injector holes in ram pipes to prevent ingress of dirt or foreign matter.
13. Slacken clips securing injectors to fuel rail stubs, pull injectors from fuel rail.
    NOTE: If necessary, transfer clips and insulation to replacement fuel rail.

Refitting

14 Press injectors on to fuel rail stubs; tighten pipe clips.
15 Locate new sealing 'O' rings at **ALL** injectors.
18 Manoeuvre fuel rail and injectors into position and secure injector clamps using 6 nuts and spring washers.
17 Reverse operations 5 to 9.
18 Remove pipe clamp at filter.
19 Refit manifold pressure pipe.
20 Re-connect battery.
21 Switch ignition on and check for leaks. Switch ignition off.

COLD START INJECTOR

Description

A cold start injector is mounted in inlet manifold, aligned to spray a finely atomized mist of fuel towards the throttle butterfly valve. The injector is controlled by the cold start side of the double relay and the Thermotime switch and is only operative during the first few seconds of a cold engine starting cycle.

COLD START INJECTOR

Remove and refit 19.60.06

Removing

1. Depressurize fuel system, see 19.50.02.
2. Disconnect battery, see 86.15.20.
3. Fit clamp on supply pipe to injector.
4. Pull electrical connector from injector.
5. Slacken pipe clips and pull pipe from injector.
6. Remove two setscrews securing injector to inlet manifold.
7. Check condition of gasket and renew as necessary.

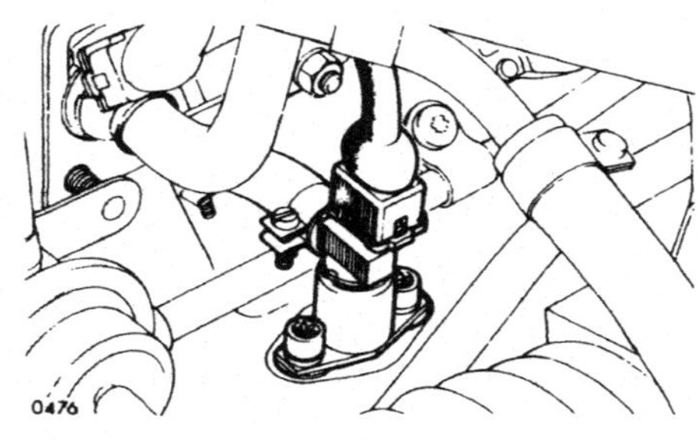

Refitting
Reverse operations 1 to 7.

Test 19.60.07

See 'Cold start system–test', 19.22.32.

FAULT-FINDING

The fault-finding procedures are divided into two sections. The first section covers the procedures necessary to rectify the engine failure to start. The second section covers rectification procedures should the engine cut out, run unevenly or lose power. The procedures follow a logical sequence which must be adhered to until the 'Action' instruction is to 'drive away' or 'consult Distributor or Dealer'.

It is assumed that the vehicle has sufficient fuel in the tanks, and that purely engine functions, e.g. ignition timing, valve timing, and the ignition system as a whole are operating satisfactorily. If necessary, these functions must be checked by following the relevant procedures in the Repair Operations Manual before the fuel injection system is suspected.

For further information relating to electronic fuel injection refer to the 'Lucas Epitest' operating instructions and test procedures.

0502

COMPONENT LOCATION

1	Thermotime Switch	6	Over-run Valve	11	1 Spark Plug Lead
2	Fuel Injectors	7	Throttle Switch	12	Double Relay
3	Auxiliary Air Valve	8	Fuel Rail	13	Convolute Hose
4	Air Flow Meter	9	Fuel Pressure Regulator	14	Induction Elbow
5	Cold Start Injector	10	Coolant Temperature Sensor	15	Ignition Coil

SECTION 1. ENGINE FAILS TO START

	PROCEDURE	RESULT	ACTION
	If the engine fails to crank.	Engine does not turnover.	Check battery leads for security and cleanliness; battery, for state of charge.
B	Ignition ON. Attempt to start engine.	Engine starts.	Go to N.
		Engine fails to start.	Go to C.
C	Check that coolant temperature sensor No. 10 is correctly connected.	Connected.	Go to D.
		Disconnected.	Re-connect sensor. Start engine and drive away.
D	Check for spark at No. 1 spark plug lead. Disconnect lead from plug and hold end approx. 1/8" from bare metal of engine block and crank engine.	Good spark.	Go to E.
		No spark.	Check ignition system.
E	Ignition ON. Check fuel tank contents.	Fuel in both tanks.	Go to G.
		Fuel in RIGHT HAND TANK ONLY.	Go to F.
F	Select left hand tank. Add fuel as necessary. Crank engine.	Engine starts.	Drive away. Inform Distributor or Dealer as soon as possible.
		Engine fails to start.	Go to G.
G	Ensure fuel cut off inertia switch is closed. (Located above footwell fresh air selector knob on passenger side of car.)	Switch closed.	Go to H.
		Switch open.	Close switch by pressing button on top of switch. Start engine and drive away.
H	Switch ignition OFF. Switch ignition ON. Crank engine and listen in boot for fuel pump running.	Pump does not run.	Go to I.
		Pump runs.	Go to K.
I	Switch ignition OFF. Remove cover from inertia switch and ensure cables are connected. If cables secure, disconnect and short together. Switch ignition ON. Pump should run when engine cranked.	Pump does not run.	Go to J.
		Pump runs.	Secure cables together and make safe with insulating tape etc. Start engine and drive away. Contact Dealer or Distributor as soon as possible.
J	Re-connect inertia switch. Ensure fuel injection system 12 volt cable is connected to the battery post. Check connections at double relay No. 12 (situated on bulkhead).	Loose or detached connections.	Secure connections. Start engine and drive away.
		All connections secure.	Contact Dealer or Distributor.
K	Crank engine in neutral gear position. Listen carefully to ensure all injectors click.	Injectors click.	Go to M.
		Injectors do not click.	Go to L.
L	Check electrical connections to double relay No. 12 ignition coil No. 15 check multi-pin connectors to E.C.U. and air meter No. 4.	Loose or disconnected connectors or wires.	Reconnect, secure connectors and drive away.
		Connectors secure.	Go to M.
M	Check for possible air leakage into manifold. Through convolute hose, No. 13. Through induction elbow, No. 14. Through auxiliary air valve, No. 3. Top and bottom hose.	Loose or disconnected.	Secure. Start engine and drive away.
		Connections secure.	Go to O. Contact Dealer or Distributor.

	PROCEDURE	RESULT	ACTION
N	Engine starts and runs.	Normally.	Drive away.
		Unevenly.	Check following connections for condition and security. Coolant temperature sensor No. 10, Auxiliary air valve No. 3, Throttle switch No. 7, and all injector plugs. If all in order go to section 2.
O	Check for free movement of air meter control flap after removing convolute hose at rear of air meter.	Operates normally.	Contact Dealer or Distributor.
		Sticking.	Free flap. Drive away. Contact Dealer or Distributor.

SECTION 2. ENGINE CUTS OUT, RUNS UNEVENLY OR LOSES POWER

	PROCEDURE	RESULT	ACTION
A	Vehicle operating normally.	Engine cuts out.	Pull to side of road, switch OFF ignition. Go to C of section '1'.
		Engine runs unevenly or loses power.	Pull to side of road, leave engine running. Go to B.
B	Engine running, car at standstill. Ensure manual transmission cars are in neutral, automatic cars have either N or P selected and handbrake applied.	Engine idles normally.	Go to D.
		Engine idles unevenly.	Go to C.
C	Ignition OFF. Check—Spark plug leads. Injector connectors. Start engine.	Engine runs normally.	Drive away.
		Engine runs unevenly.	Go to F and return if necessary to C. Stop engine. Check for excessive oil fumes at breather or exhaust. Contact Distributor or Dealer as soon as possible.
D	Apply pressure to throttle pedal and increase engine revolutions slowly.	Engine runs normally.	Go to E.
		Engine runs unevenly.	Go to F.
E	Engage forward gear and drive at moderate speed.	Engine runs unevenly.	Go to F.
		Engine runs normally.	Fuel filter or supply pipe probably obstructed. Drive away, contact Distributor or Dealer as soon as possible.
F	Check for possible air leakage into manifold. 1. Convolute hose No. 13. 2. Induction elbow No. 14. 3. Auxiliary air valve, top No. 13 and bottom hose.	Loose or disconnected.	Secure. Start engine and drive away.
		Connections secure.	Return to C.

POSSIBLE CAUSES IN ORDER OF CHECKING

SYMPTOMS

Will not start* Difficult cold start Difficult hot start

Starts but will not run Misfires and cuts out Runs rough

Idle speed too fast Hunting at idle Low power and top speed

High fuel consumption

* Before proceeding with checks, hold throttle fully open and attempt a start. If the engine then starts and continues to run, no further action is necessary.

PROCEDURES FOR RECTIFICATION OF CAUSES SHOWN IN TABLE

Battery: Battery depleted, giving insufficient crank speed or inadequate spark. Check battery condition with hydrometer. Recharge, clean and secure terminals, or renew as necessary.

Connections: Ensure all connector plugs are securely attached. Pull back rubber boot and ensure plug is fully home. While replacing boot press cable towards socket. Ensure Electronic Control Unit (ECU) multi-pin connector is fully made. Ensure all ground connections are clean and tight.

Ignition System: Check ignition system as detailed in electrical section of Repair Operations Manual.

Fuel System: Open filler cap of fuel tank being used. Change tank being used. Check for fuel pipe failure (strong smell of fuel) and retention of in-line fuel pressure. Check inertia switch closed. If necessary, clear fuel tank vents or supply pipe.

Cold Start System: Fault conditions could cause cold start system to be inoperative on a cold engine, or operative on a hot engine. If engine is either very hot, or cold, these particular faults will cause the engine to run very rich. Check cold start system, see 19.22.32.

ECU/Amplifier: If the ECU is faulty it is possible that injectors will be inoperative. The ECU may also be responsible for any degree of incorrect fuelling. Before suspecting the ECU for fuelling problems, however, all other likely components should be proved good.

Air Leaks: Ensure all hose and pipe connections are secure. Engine is, however, likely to start more easily with air leaks if cold, as air leaking augments that through the auxiliary air valve. A leak, or failed air valve is shown up, however, by a very high idle speed when engine is warm and air valve main passage should be closed.

Temperature Sensors: If either sensor is short-circuited, starting improves with higher engine temperature. Engine will run very weak, improving as temperature rises, but still significantly weak when fully hot. If a sensor is open-circuit, or disconnected, engine will run very rich, becoming worse as temperature rises. Engine may not run when fully hot, and will almost certainly not restart if stalled. Effect of air temperature sensor will be less marked than coolant temperature sensor.

Auxiliary Air Valve: Check opening throttle. If engine immediately starts, unscrew idle speed adjustment, and re-check start with closed throttle. Re-set idle speed when engine hot. Check cold start. Check throttle return springs and linkage for sticking or maladjustment as a sticking throttle may have enforced incorrect idle speed adjustment on a previous occasion.

Throttle Switch: Check operation of throttle switch. Incorrect function or sequence of switching will give this fault.

Throttle Butterfly: Check adjustment of the throttle butterfly valve, ensure return springs correctly fitted, and throttle not sticking open.

Over-run Valve: Check operation of over-run valve.

Compression: Low compressions; a general lack of engine tune could cause this fault. Check engine timing, ignition timing, and function of ignition system complete. If necessary, check valve condition.

Idle Fuel Control Setting: Check exhaust gas CO level. If necessary, adjust idle fuelling trim control on ECU. **CAUTION**: This knob MUST NOT be moved unless correct test equipment and skilled personnel are in attendance to monitor changes made.

Air Filters: Remove air filters and check for choked filter element.

Throttle Linkage: Check throttle linkage adjustment and ensure that throttle butterfly valves can be fully operated.

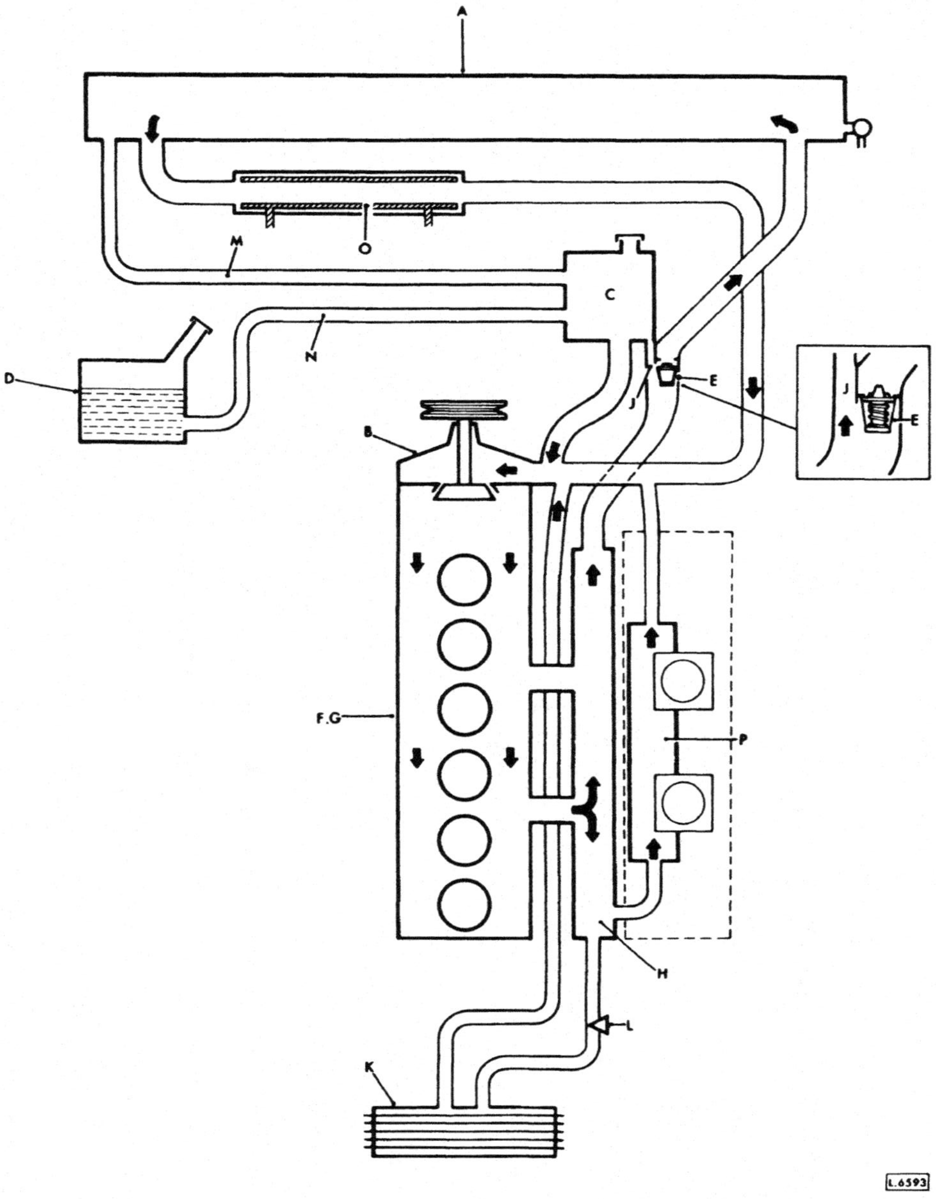

COOLING SYSTEM

Description 26.00.01

The cooling system consists of a radiator matrix, A, a water pump, B – belt driven by the engine crankshaft – a header tank C, and a remote header (or expansion) tank D.
A thermostatic valve, E, is fitted to ensure rapid warm-up from cold.
Later air-conditioned cars are fitted with twin electric fans, mounted in front of the condenser and radiator, in addition to the engine driven fan. The electric fans are thermostatically controlled and it is possible, in very hot conditions, for them to continue to operate after the engine has been switched off. They will switch off automatically when the coolant temperature drops to 92°C.
Under cold start conditions (see inset) coolant is forced by the water pump through the cylinder block, cylinder head and induction manifold (F, G and H) to the thermostatic valve housing. The valve is closed and coolant is therefore returned via a by-pass drilling, J, to the water pump suction inlet.
The heater matrix, K, is purged during this phase by opening the heater water control valve, L, at the matrix inlet and allowing pump suction to remove trapped air. The radiator has a vent pipe, M, through which, during initial cold filling, the radiator is vented.
When the engine temperature rises to a predetermined level the thermostatic valve opens and allows hot coolant to flow into the top of the radiator. Full pump suction then draws coolant from the base of the radiator and starts the full cooling circuit; coolant expansion due to temperature rise is accommodated by the expansion tank, D, via tube N.
Cars fitted with automatic transmission have a cooling tube O, included in the centre section of the radiator bottom hose. The tube is connected in series with the automatic transmission fluid circulation.
Cars fitted with exhaust emission control to U.S.A. Federal specification are fitted with a water heated secondary throttle housing, P, on early cars and with water heated spacers between carburetters and inlet manifolds on later cars; water pipes connect the spacers with automatic chokes fitted to the latest carburetters.

ANTIFREEZE

We use and recommend Unipart Universal Antifreeze which should be used at the specified concentration whenever the cooling system is refilled. For topping up purposes, only reputable brands of antifreeze, formulated and approved for 'mixed metal' engines may be used.
If Unipart Universal Antifreeze is unobtainable, B.P. Type H21 or Union Carbide UT.184 (marketed as Prestone Antifreeze, Prestone UT.184 or Prestone II) may be used as approved alternatives.
Important Note: The concentration of antifreeze must not be allowed to fall greatly below the recommended strength as sediment may be formed in the cooling system by certain types of antifreeze at low concentrations.
A 40% solution by volume in the United Kingdom (55% U.S.A./Canada and all other countries) of all antifreeze must be used at all times, either when topping up or replenishing the cooling system. For maximum corrosion protection, the concentration should never be allowed to fall below 25%. Always top up with recommended strength of antifreeze, NEVER WITH WATER ONLY.
In countries where it is unnecessary to use antifreeze, Marston SQ 36 Corrosion Inhibitor must be used in the cooling system in the proportion of 1 part SQ 36 to 24 parts water. CHANGE COOLANT EVERY TWO YEARS.
An alternative coolant known as CARBUROL FORLIFE is recommended where temperatures below –10°C. (14°F.) are NOT encountered. Before Carburol Forlife is used, the coolant already present in the system must be drained out and the system flushed before filling with Carburol Forlife. Once in use the system should be topped up with Carburol Forlife only, and a label giving this information should be affixed in an appropriate and prominent position.

COOLANT

Drain and refill 26.10.01

NOTE: A procedure for topping up is given at the end of this operation.

Draining
1 When engine is cold, remove pressure cap at expansion tank and sealing cap at engine header tank.
2 Open radiator drain tap and remove drain plug on cylinder block.
3 Remove drain plug in radiator bottom hose pipe.
4 If it is required to empty expansion tank, loosen pipe clip and pull pipe from base of tank. Refit pipe.
5 Insert water hose pipe into engine header tank and regulate flow until engine and radiator are kept full without excessive spillage.
6 Run engine at fast idle (1,000 r.p.m.) until water from drain points runs clear.
7 Switch off engine, but **DO NOT** turn off water hose pipe for a further minute.
8 Fit drain plugs and close radiator drain tap.

Refilling
9 Slowly pour recommended coolant mixture into engine header tank.
10 When coolant fills tank, fit sealing cap.
11 Pour coolant into expansion tank to base of filler neck. Fit pressure cap.
12 Set heater control to 'DEF' (and 'HI' non-air conditioned cars only).
13 Start engine and run at fast idle (1,000 r.p.m.) for 3 minutes.
14 Switch off engine.
15 Carefully remove expansion tank pressure cap and, if necessary, add coolant to bring level to base of filler neck.
NOTE: It is not important if coolant is above this level as excess liquid will be ejected through vent pipe.

TOPPING UP AND GENERALLY CHECKING COOLANT LEVEL

NOTE: This procedure must only be carried out when engine is cold.

1 Remove expansion tank pressure cap.
2 If coolant is below base of neck of tank add specified coolant mixture to correct level.
3 Fit pressure cap.

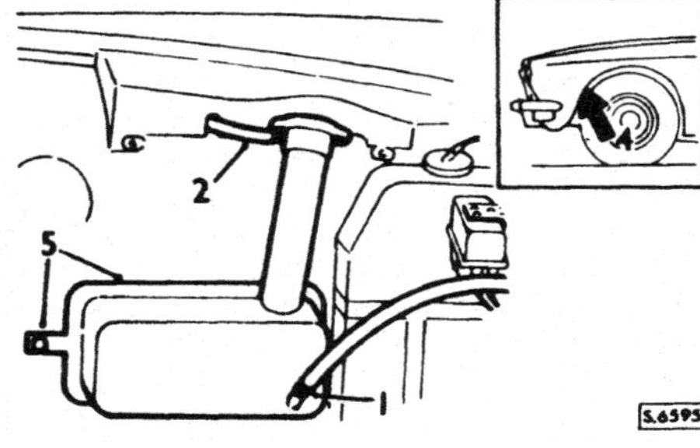

REMOTE HEADER TANK (EXPANSION TANK)

Remove and refit 26.15.01

Removing
1 Slacken clip on pipe at base of tank; remove pipe and secure, pointing upwards, as high as possible.
2 Pull vent pipe from filler neck.
3 Apply full left hand steering lock.
4 Beneath wheel arch, remove two nyloc nuts and plain washers securing front of expansion tank (and adsorption canister – emission control cars to U.S.A. Federal specification only).
5 Remove setscrew, washers and nyloc nut securing rear of tank. Lift tank clear.

Refitting
6 Fit tank and secure using nuts, washers and setscrews.
7 Fit pipe at base of tank and secure pipe clip.
8 Fit vent pipe to filler neck.
9 Fill tank to base of filler neck with specified coolant.

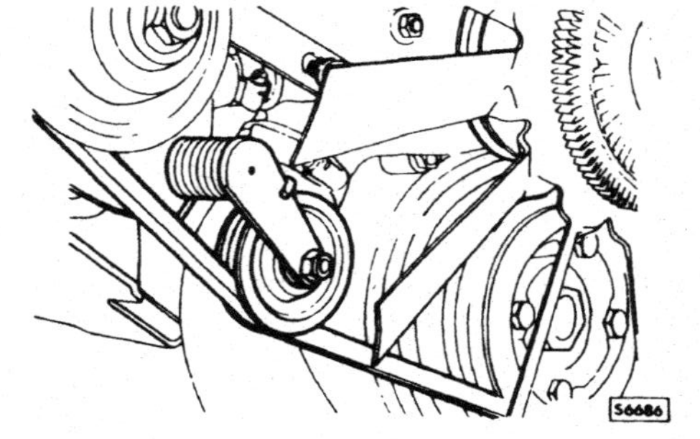

FAN/STEERING PUMP BELT

Adjust 26.20.01

The belt tension is automatically adjusted by means of a spring loaded jockey pulley and routine adjustment is not necessary.

FAN/STEERING PUMP BELT

Remove and refit 26.20.07

Removing
1 Slacken adjustment bolt in support strap.
2 Press steering pump towards engine and remove belt.

Refitting
3 Press jockey pulley against spring and fit belt over pulleys.
4 Pull steering pump away from engine and tighten support strap bolt.

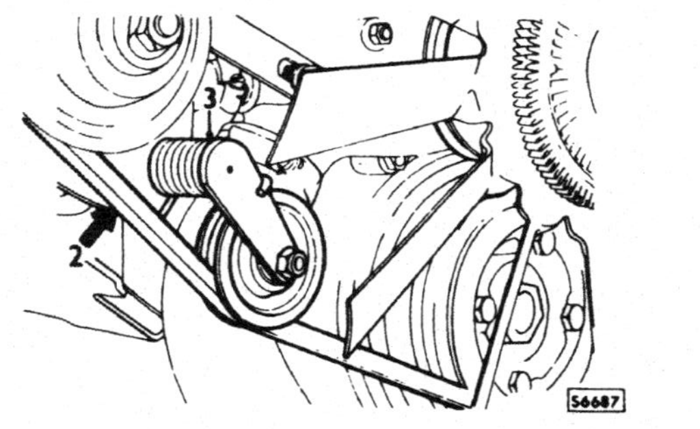

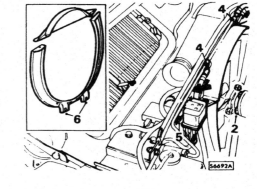

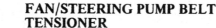

FAN/STEERING PUMP BELT TENSIONER

Remove and refit **26.20.15**

Removing

1 Remove steering pump – 57.20.14.
2 Remove self locking nut and limiting stop arm.
3 Draw jockey pulley arm and spring from bracket.

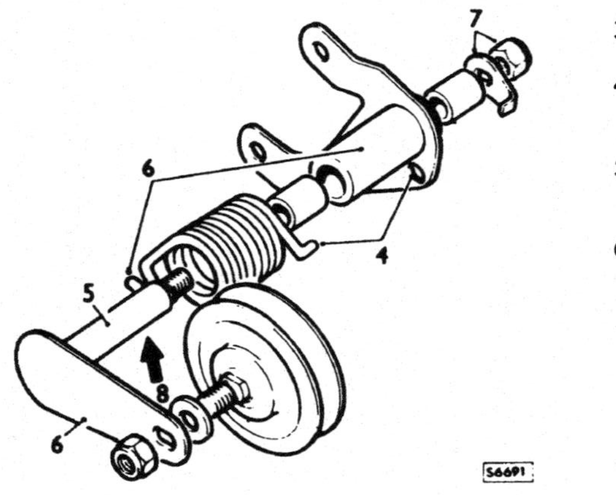

Refitting

4 Fit spring over pivot bush on bracket and engage straight arm in hole.
5 Smear spindle with suitable waterproof grease.
6 Fit jockey pulley arm spindle into bearing bushes and rotate arm anticlockwise to engage hooked end of spring on arm.
7 Offer limiting stop arm on to spindle and start nyloc nut on to threads.
8 Twist jockey pulley arm anticlockwise, viewed from front of steering pump, until limiting stop arm engages on flats of spindle.
9 Fully tighten nyloc nut.
10 Fit steering pump.

FAN/STEERING PUMP BELT TENSIONER

Overhaul **26.20.16**

Dismantling

1 Remove fan/steering pump belt tensioner – 26.20.15.
2 Check jockey pulley bearing for excessive play. If movement is considered too great or if roughness is felt, jockey pulley must be replaced – operations 3 and 4.
3 Remove self locking nut and remove jockey pulley from arm.
4 Fit plain washer to replacement pulley and bearing assembly and secure using new self locking nut.
5 Remove locknut and stop arm and check jockey arm spindle surface for scoring or signs of wear.
6 Check bearing bushes in jockey pulley arm bracket for scoring or signs of wear. If bearing bushes or arm spindle worn, both components must be replaced by following instructions detailed in operations 7 to 13 inclusive. If bushes in good condition, proceed to operation 14.

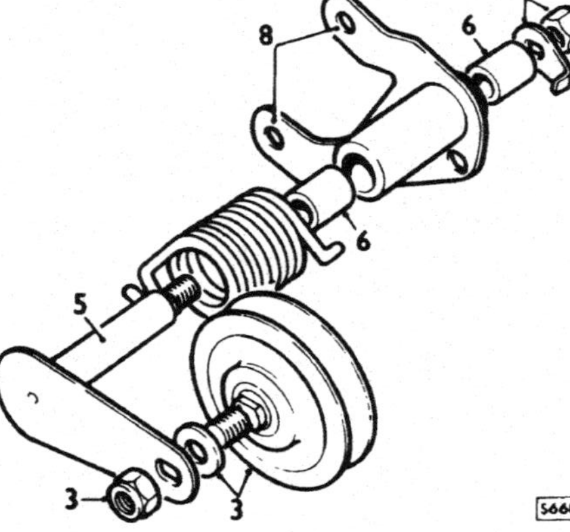

7 Remove tabwasher and nut, and withdraw steering pump pulley.
8 Remove two setscrews and lock washers securing jockey arm bracket to steering pump.
9 Using suitable mandrel press bearing bushes from bracket.
10 Press a replacement bearing bush into tube from each end until bush is recessed 1/16 in. (1,59 mm.) from end face.
11 If necessary lightly ream bushes, using replacement spindle to size.

Assembling

12 Secure bracket to steering pump using two setscrews and washers.
13 Fit steering pump pulley. **DO NOT** drift pulley on to shaft, draw on using nut and washers.
14 Fit fan/steering pump belt tensioner – 26.20.15.

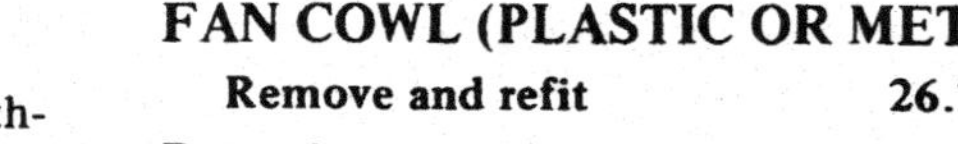

FAN COWL (PLASTIC OR METAL)

Remove and refit **26.25.11**

Removing

1 Disconnect battery – 86.15.20.
2 Remove fan and torquatrol unit – 26.25.21.
3 Remove two self tapping screws securing headlamp relay to radiator top rail.
4 Remove nuts, bolts and washers securing radiator vent pipe clips.
5 Remove two setscrews, washers and self locking nuts securing fan cowl to radiator top rail.
6 Beneath car remove self locking nuts and plain washers securing fan cowl to brackets.
7 Remove setscrews and shakeproof washers securing brackets to lower crossmember.
8 Lift fan cowl clear.

Refitting

Reverse operations 1 to 8 inclusive.

FAN MOTORS – SET

Remove and refit 26.25.20

NOTE: Air conditioned cars intended for use in hot climates are fitted with twin electric fans located in front of refrigerant condenser and radiator. These fans, additional to the engine driven fan, are controlled by a thermostatic switch sensing coolant temperature, and operate when this exceeds 96°C (205°F), being switched off when temperature drops to 92°C (198°F).

Removing
1 Disconnect battery – 86.15.20.
2 Remove bonnet – 76.16.01.
3 Remove radiator front lower grille – 76.55.06.
4 Disconnect positive leads from horns, and separate snap connectors in fan motor leads.
5 Remove bolt securing horn post steady bracket to front flange of lower cowl.
6 Remove four bolts and nuts securing fan mounting crossbeam to brackets at its ends.
7 Lift out crossbeam sub-assembly and transfer to workbench.

Refitting
8 Reverse operations 1 to 7.
9 Apply 12V. supply, with correct polarity, to fan motors and check that rotation is correct and that fans or motors do not foul lower grille or cowls.
10 Test drive, checking operation of air conditioning system and thermal switching of fans.

NOTE: If fans are operating when engine is switched off they will continue to run until coolant temperature drops to 92°C (198°F).

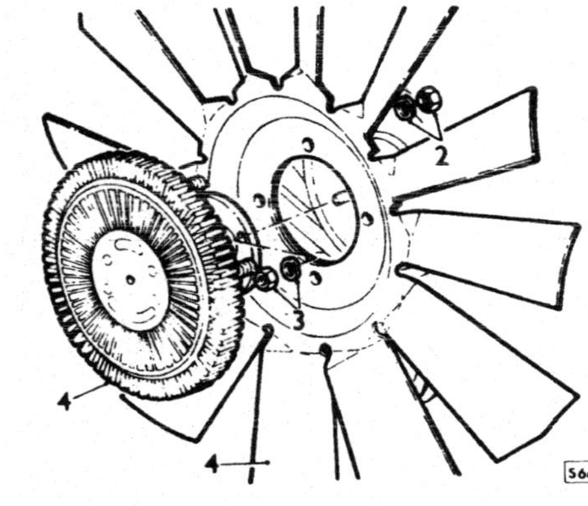

FAN AND TORQUATROL UNIT (Early Cars)

NOTE: Torquatrol flange secured to water pump pulley with four plain nuts.

Remove and refit 26.25.21

Removing
1 Slacken adjustment bolt in support of steering pump.
2 Remove four plain nuts and washers securing fan to torquatrol unit.
3 Remove four plain nuts and washers securing torquatrol unit to water pump pulley.
4 Manoeuver fan and torquatrol unit clear.

Refitting
Reverse operations 1 to 4 inclusive.

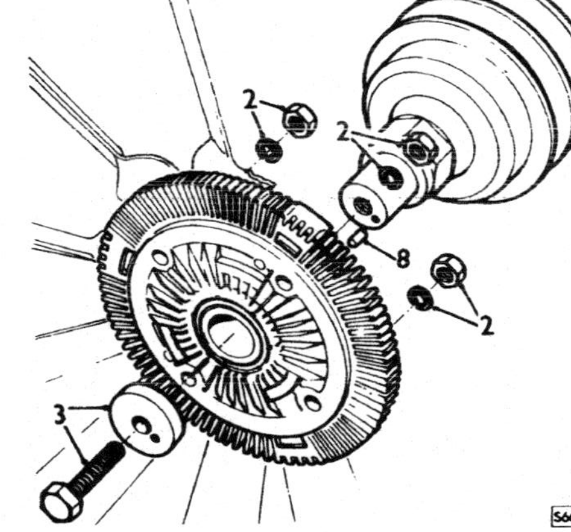

FAN AND TORQUATROL UNIT (Later Cars)

NOTE: Hexagonal nose to water pump pulley.

Remove and refit 26.25.21

Removing
1 Remove setscrews securing top section of fan cowl.
2 Remove four nuts and washers securing fan to torquatrol unit.
3 Restrain pulley and remove centre bolt from torquatrol unit, recover special washer.
4 Gently tap torquatrol unit forward from pulley spigot.
5 Lift fan from fan cowl.

Refitting
6 Locate four bolts in torquatrol unit.
7 Locate fan over pulley nose.
8 Ensure locating pin in position in pulley spigot and lightly grease spigot.
9 Offer torquatrol on to pulley.
10 Secure torquatrol unit to pulley using centre bolt and special washer.
NOTE: Ensure special washer locates on pin in pulley spigot before tightening bolt.
11 Secure fan to torquatrol unit using spring washers and plain nuts.
12 Refit top section of fan cowl.

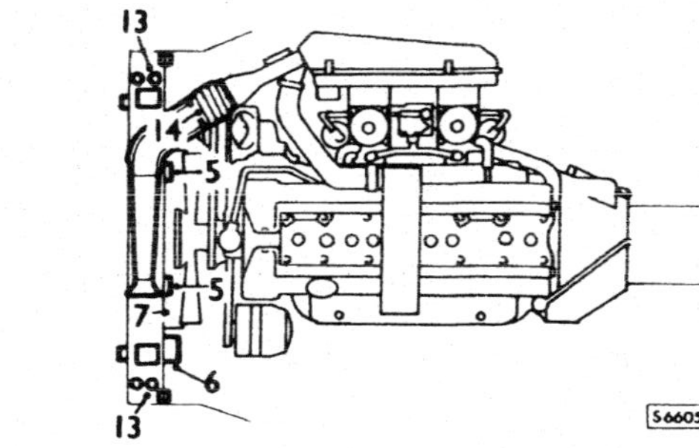

RADIATOR BLOCK

Remove and refit 26.40.04

Removing
1 Drain coolant – 26.10.01.
2 Disconnect battery – 86.15.20.
3 Remove bonnet – 76.16.01.

Cars fitted with air conditioning only

WARNING: UNDER NO CIRCUMSTANCE MUST ANY PORTION OF THE AIR CONDITIONING SYSTEM BE DISCONNECTED BY ANY ONE OTHER THAN A QUALIFIED REFRIGERATION ENGINEER. BLINDNESS CAN RESULT IF THE GAS CONTAINED WITHIN THE SYSTEM COMES INTO CONTACT WITH THE EYES.

4 Remove condenser unit – 82.15.07 – and receiver drier unit if fitted to radiator top rail.

All Cars
5 Remove nuts, bolts and washers securing cooling system vent pipe clips. Retain cable clips.
6 Remove screws securing headlamp relay to radiator top rail, release cable harness from clips.
7 Remove two setscrews, washers and self locking nuts securing fan cowl to radiator top rail.
8 Release clip and pull top hose from radiator.
9 Release clip and pull vent pipe from radiator.

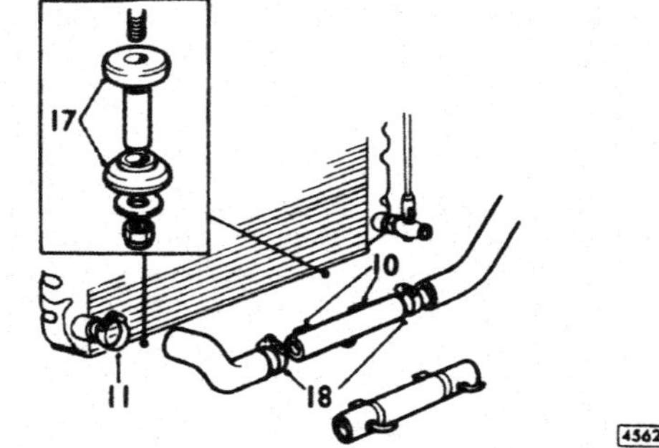

10 Remove two self tapping screws securing centre section of bottom hose to cross member.
11 Release clip and pull bottom hose from radiator.
12 Remove two nyloc nuts and special washers from radiator locating studs.
13 Remove six setscrews, plain and spring washers, and two nuts, bolts and washers securing radiator top rail.

Cars to European and U.S.A. Federal emission control specification only
14 Release clip and separate coupling from air intake ram pipe.

All Cars
15 Lift radiator top rail clear. Recover two distance pieces.
16 Lift radiator from car. Recover foam padding.
17 Check conditions of radiator locating stud bushes and if necessary renew.
18 Ensure centre section of bottom hose clean and free from scale or sludge.

Refitting
Reverse operations 1 to 17 inclusive, ensuring special plain washer fitted on top of bush.

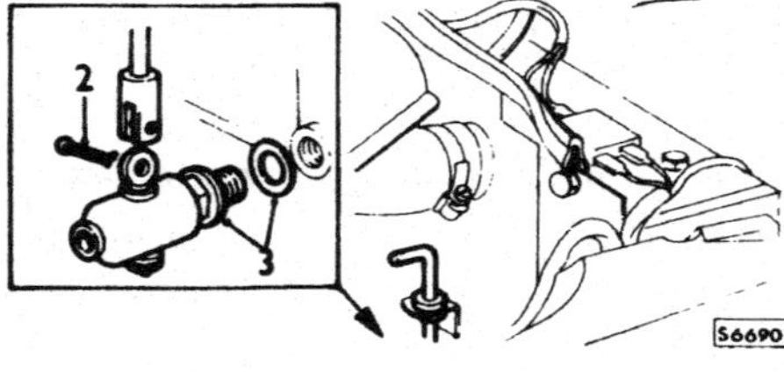

RADIATOR DRAIN TAP

Remove and refit **26.40.10**

Removing
1 Drain coolant – 26.10.01.
2 Pull split pin from fork end of control rod.
3 Unscrew tap from radiator block. Discard seals.

Refitting
4 Lightly coat threads of tap with non hardening sealing compound, and screw home on new seals to locate beneath control rod.
5 Couple control rod to tap, orientated correctly, and secure using new split pin.
6 Check operate tap.
7 Refill with coolant.

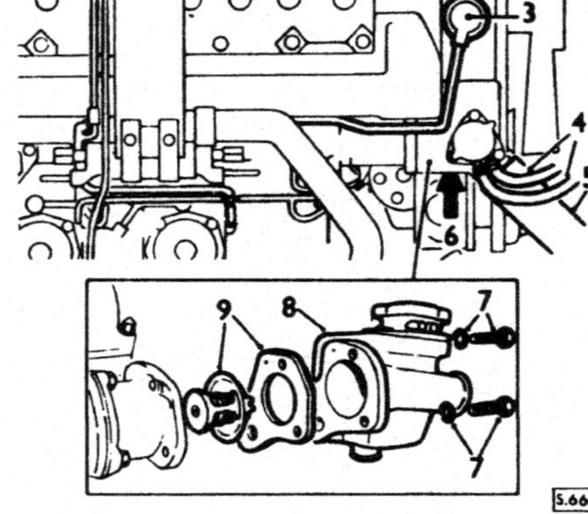
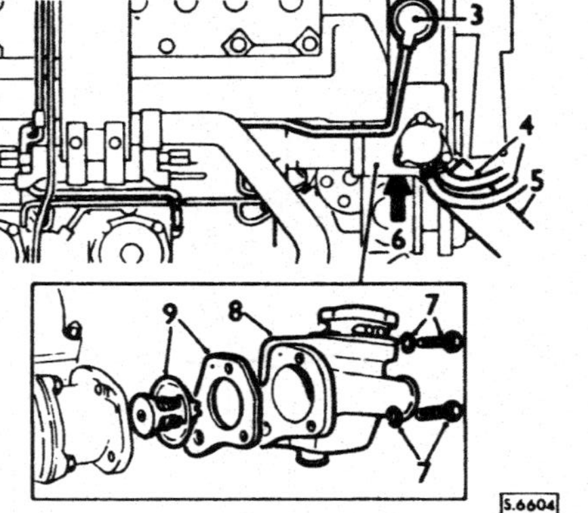

THERMOSTAT

Remove and refit **26.45.01**

Removing
1 Disconnect battery – 86.15.20.
2 Partially drain coolant.
3 Pull carburetter breather pipe from clips and from rubber boot of crankcase breather.
4 Slacken pipe clips and pull vent pipes from filler neck.
5 Slacken hose clips at both ends of radiator top hose and pull from radiator and header tank.
6 Slacken clip at top end of hose to water pump.
7 Remove three setscrews and spring washers securing header tank to thermostat housing.
8 Carefully break joint and pull header tank upwards from water pump hose.
9 Remove thermostat from thermostat housing. Discard old gasket.
10 Clean mating faces of header tank and thermostat housing.
11 Remove any sludge or scale present.

Refitting
Reverse operations 1 to 11 inclusive, using new gasket.

THERMOSTAT

Test **26.45.09**

1 Remove thermostat – 26.45.01.
2 Thoroughly clean thermostat.

3 Place thermostat in a container of water together with a thermometer.
4 Heat water and observe if thermostat operates in accordance with data given in Group 04.

WATER PUMP

Remove and refit **26.50.01**

Removing
1 Drain coolant – 26.10.01.
2 Remove fan cowl – 26.25.11.
3 Remove fan/steering pump belt – 26.20.07.
4 Remove support strap bolt at water pump.

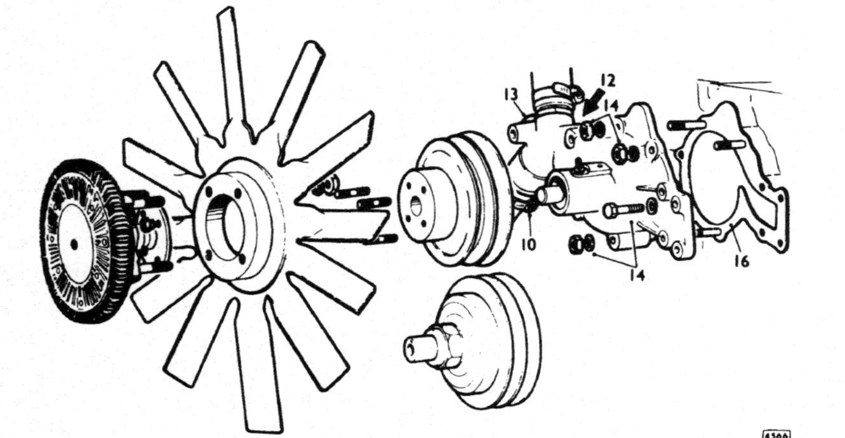

Cars fitted with emission control to U.S.A. Federal specification only

5 Remove nut, bolt and washers at exhaust manifold cowl, and release air pump delivery pipe. Pull pipe from air pump.

6 Slacken air pump belt adjuster nuts and remove air pump belt.

7 Remove bolt securing adjuster to air pump and recover spacer.

8 Remove setscrews and locking washers securing air pump bracket to cylinder block and lift air pump and bracket clear.

All Cars

9 Remove header tank – 26.45.01, operations 5 to 8 inclusive.

10 Slacken clip securing bottom hose.

11 Remove distributor cap.

12 Slacken clip securing heater supply pipe.

Cars fitted with emission control to U.S.A. Federal specification only

13 Slacken clip securing secondary throttle housing outlet pipe when fitted.

All Cars

CAUTION: **On certain engines the torsional damper overlaps the lower edge of the water pump. In these cases, the damper must be detached – 12.21.01, and the cross head setscrew removed before attempting to release the water pump.**

14 Remove bolts and nuts securing water pump to cylinder block. Note location of long and short bolts.

15 Carefully break seal and draw water pump from cylinder block.

Refitting

16 Reverse operations 1 to 15 inclusive, using new gasket coated with suitable sealing compound.

17 Check tension of drive belts and adjust if necessary.

18 Refill with coolant.

WATER PUMP

Overhaul **26.50.06**

1 Remove water pump – 26.50.01.

Dismantling

2 Use suitable extractor and draw pulley from water pump (early cars). Use

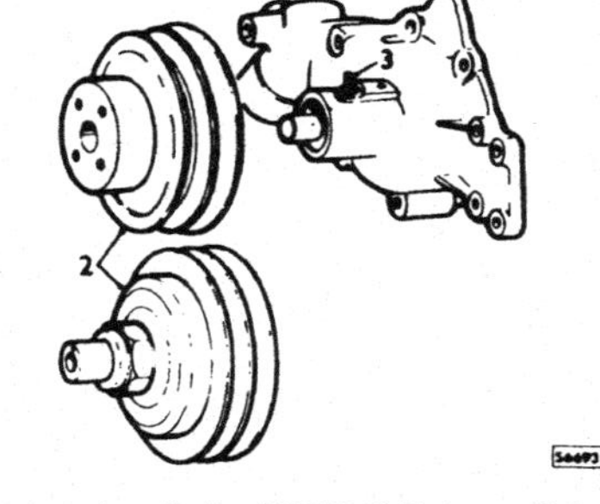

extractor bolt (UFB 3/8 in. x 2 in.) on later cars.

3 Slacken locknut and remove bearing lockscrew.

4 Support body of pump on press bed close around impeller.

5 Using suitable mandrel acting against **case of bearing** press bearing/spindle and impeller assembly from body of pump.

6 Press bearing/spindle assembly from impeller.

Inspection

7 Thoroughly clean all parts of pump **except** bearing/spindle assembly in suitable cleaning solvent.

8 Inspect bearing for excessive play and remove any burrs, rust or scale from the shaft using fine emery cloth.
NOTE: Wrap bearing in cloth to prevent contamination by emery dust.

9 If signs of wear or corrosion are evident in bearing bore or on face in front of impeller, body of pump must be replaced.

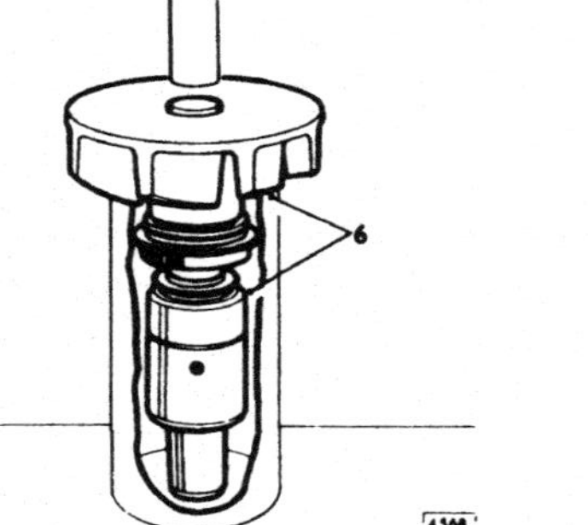

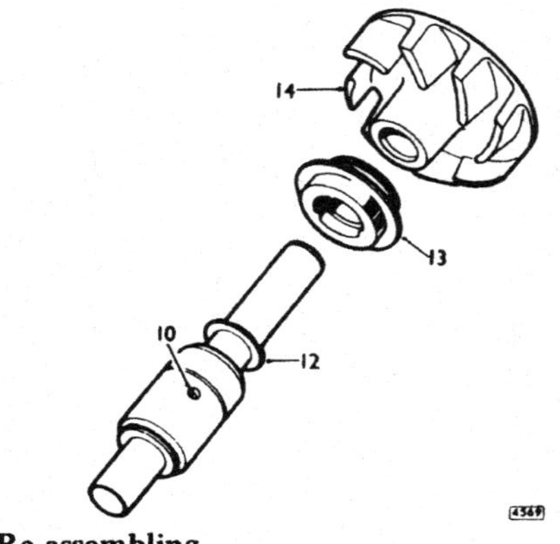

Re-assembling

10 Align location hole in bearing with tapped hole in pump body and press bearing/spindle assembly into body until holes coincide.

11 Fit bearing lockscrew and secure using locknut.

12 Fit rubber water thrower in groove in spindle (early cars only).
NOTE: Later cars have thrower permanently fitted to spindle.

13 Coat outside of brass seal housing with a suitable sealing compound, and fit into recess in pump body.

14 Carefully press impeller on to spindle to dimension shown on illustration.

15 Press pulley on to spindle taking care to ensure that impeller is not moved from dimensions given in operation 14.

It will simplify removal if joints except front pipe/intermediate pipe joint are first heated with a welding torch. Every precaution must be taken when working near petrol and brake piping to prevent damage to components.

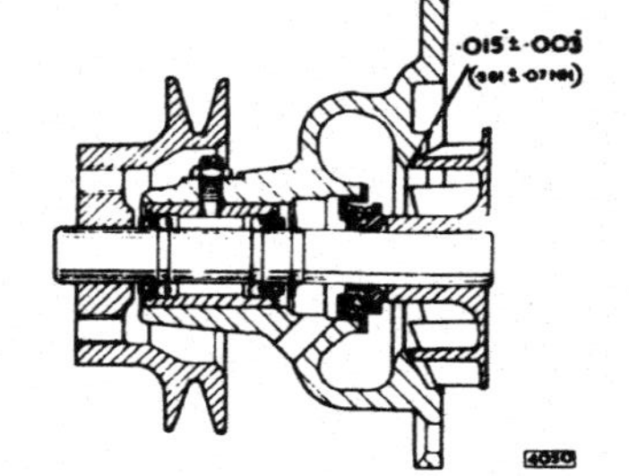

EXHAUST SYSTEM COMPLETE

Remove and refit **30.10.01**

Removing

1 In luggage boot, remove two self locking nuts securing each rear silencer mounting.
2 Remove three nuts, bolts and washers securing front pipe/intermediate pipe flange.
3 Release clamp at rear of forward silencer assembly.
4 Separate intermediate pipe and forward silencer assemblies from rear intermediate pipes, taking care to avoid damage to catalyst unit, if fitted.
5 Release clamp at tail pipe and silencers.
6 Separate tail pipe and silencers from rear intermediate pipes.
7 Draw rear intermediate pipes rearwards from mounting rubbers and suspension unit.
8 Remove self tapping screws and separate trim from tail pipe and silencers.
9 Draw tail pipe and silencer forwards from body.
10 Remove three nuts, bolts and washers securing heat shield at exhaust manifold/front pipe joint.
11 Remove four special nuts and plain washers at each exhaust manifold and draw front pipe downwards. Recover heat shield brackets.
CAUTION: Take great care to avoid damaging steering rack gaiter.
12 Check condition of mounting rubbers in rear suspension unit and mounting brackets and renew as necessary.

Refitting

13 Offer rear intermediate pipes into rear suspension and locate on mountings.
14 Position rear mounting brackets and secure each using two self locking nuts.
15 Offer tail pipes and silencers into position and locate in mounting rubbers.
16 Coat joint with FIREGUM, mate up and secure with clamp.
17 Complete re-assembly, using new seals and gaskets, by reversing operations 1 to 11 as necessary.

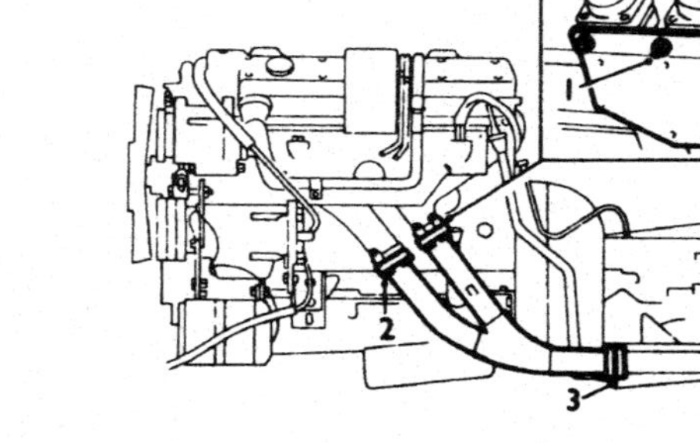

FRONT PIPE

Remove and refit **30.10.09**

Removing

1 Remove three nuts, bolts and washers securing heat shield at exhaust manifold/front pipe joint.
2 Remove four special nuts and plain washers at each exhaust manifold.
3 Beneath car remove three nuts, bolts and washers securing front pipe/intermediate pipe flange.
4 Draw front pipe downwards and remove.
CAUTION: Take great care to avoid damaging steering rack gaiter.

Refitting

Reverse operations 1 to 4 using new seals. Apply FIREGUM at front pipe/intermediate pipe joint.

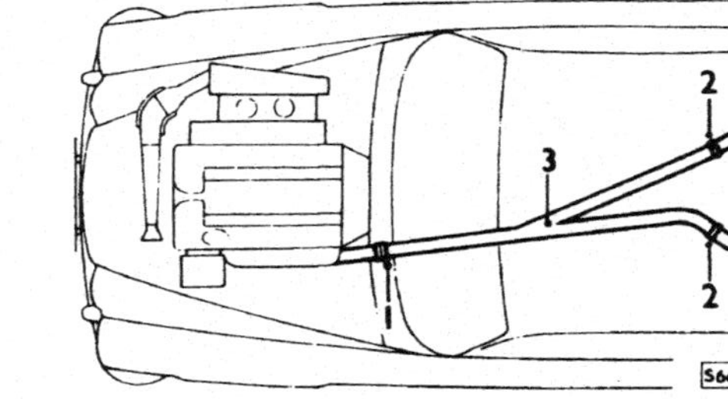

INTERMEDIATE PIPE

Remove and refit **30.10.11**

Removing

1 Remove three nuts, bolts and washers securing flange.
2 Release clamp at front end of both forward silencer assemblies.
3 Remove pipe, taking care to avoid damage to catalyst unit, if fitted.

Refitting

Reverse operations 1 to 3 inclusive, using FIREGUM to seal joint to silencer and front pipe. Use new seal at front pipe/intermediate pipe flange.

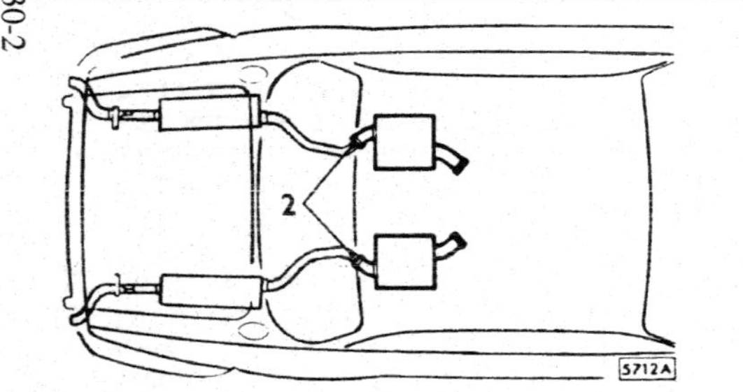

SILENCER ASSEMBLY

Remove and refit Left Hand – 30.10.15
Right Hand – 30.10.16

Removing
1 Remove intermediate pipe – 30.10.11.
2 Slacken clamp and draw silencer from rear intermediate pipe.

Refitting
Reverse operations 1 and 2 using FIREGUM to seal joints.

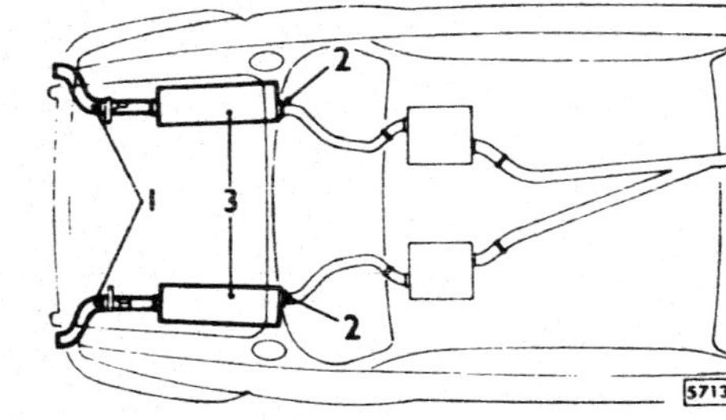

TAIL PIPE AND SILENCER

Remove and refit
Left or Right Hand – 30.10.22

Removing
1 Remove Allen grub screw and separate trim from tail pipe.
2 Release clamp to rear intermediate pipe and separate.
3 Draw tail pipe and silencer, forwards down through tunnel to clear mounting rubber.
4 Check condition of mounting and renew as necessary.

Refitting
5 Locate tail pipe and silencer in mounting.
6 Coat joint with FIREGUM, fit clamp and secure to rear intermediate pipe.
7 Fit exhaust trim, check alignment and secure with Allen grub screw.
NOTE: Cars to U.S.A. Federal specification **must** have a distance of 1.5 in. (38 mm.) between top surface of exhaust trim and lower surface of energy absorbing beam.

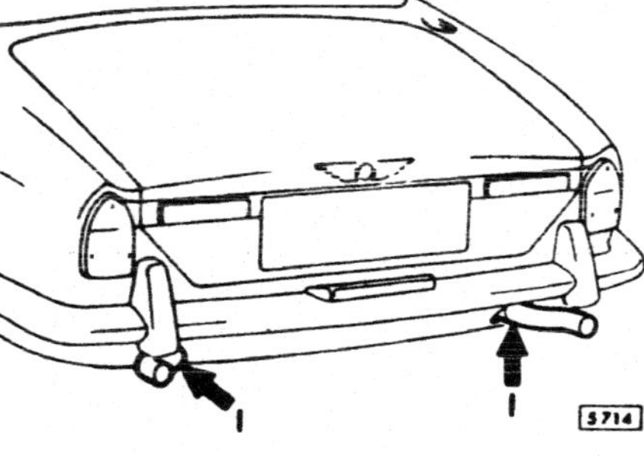

EXHAUST TRIM

Remove and refit **30.10.23**

Removing
1 Remove grub screw using Allen key, and separate trim from tail pipe and silencer.

Refitting
Use **FIREGUM** to seal joint.
NOTE: Cars to U.S.A. Federal specification must have a distance of 1.5 in. (38 mm.) between top surface of exhaust trim and lower surface of energy absorbing beam.

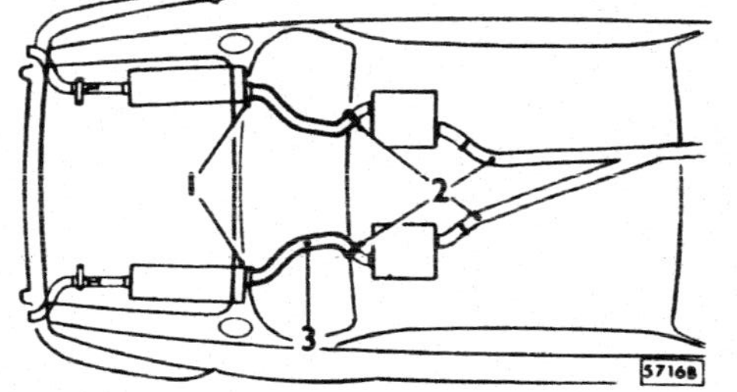

REAR INTERMEDIATE PIPE

Remove and refit Left Hand – 30.10.24
Right Hand – 30.10.25

Removing
1 Release clamp to tail pipe and silencer and separate.
2 Support intermediate pipe, release clamp to silencer and separate.
3 Draw rear intermediate pipe from suspension unit.
4 Check condition of mounting rubber and renew as necessary – 30.20.02.

Refitting
Reverse operations 1 to 3, use FIREGUM to seal joints.

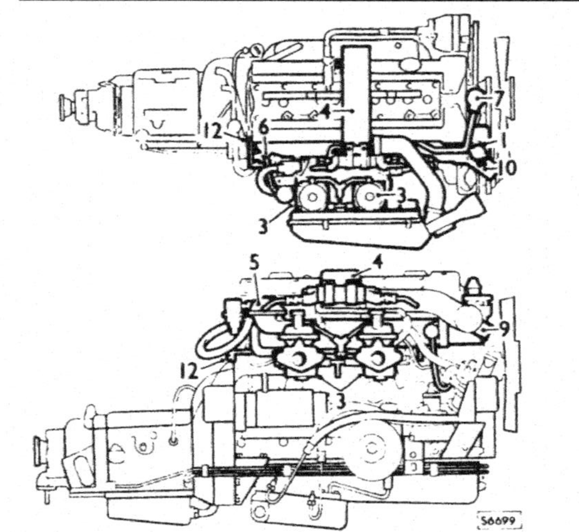

INDUCTION MANIFOLD

Remove and refit **30.15.02**

Removing
1 Remove radiator header tank cap.
2 Open radiator drain tap and drain off approximately 1 gallon of coolant. **NOTE**: Conserve coolant if anti-freeze is in use.
3 Remove carburetters – 19.15.11.

Cars fitted with emission control only
4 Remove hot air duct – 17.30.30.

Cars to U.S.A. Federal specification only
5 Remove secondary throttle housing – 17.20.36 or water heated spacers on later cars – 17.20.40.

All Cars
6 Slacken clip and disconnect water outlet hose.
7 Spring crankcase breather pipe out of retaining clips; withdraw pipe from rubber elbow.
8 Disengage H/T leads from retaining clip.

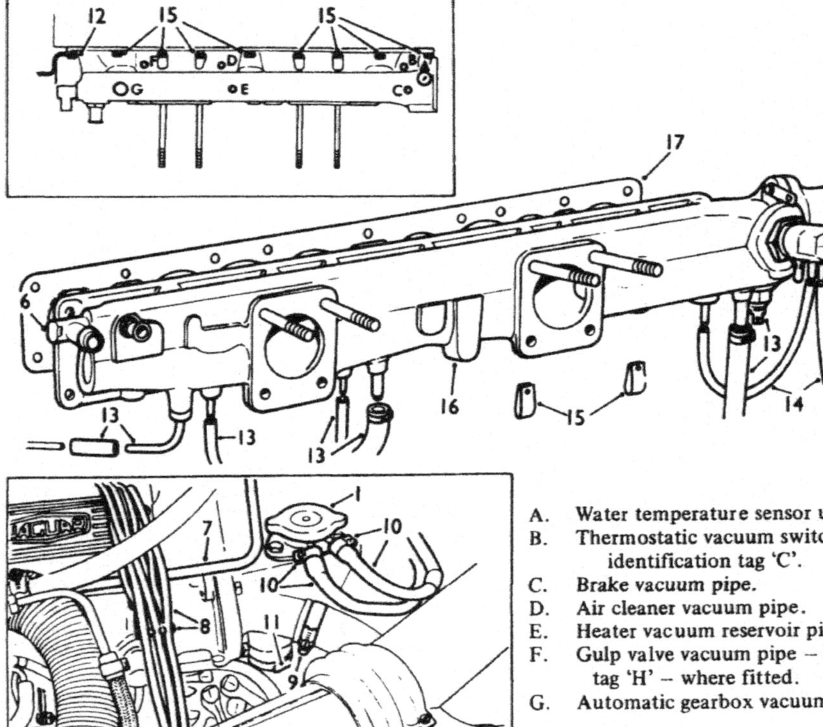

A. Water temperature sensor unit wire.
B. Thermostatic vacuum switch pipe – identification tag 'C'.
C. Brake vacuum pipe.
D. Air cleaner vacuum pipe.
E. Heater vacuum reservoir pipe.
F. Gulp valve vacuum pipe – identification tag 'H' – where fitted.
G. Automatic gearbox vacuum servo pipe.

9 Slacken clip and disconnect radiator top hose.
10 Slacken clips and disconnect hoses from header tank filler neck.
11 Slacken clip securing water pump hose to header tank.
12 Remove three nuts and spring washers securing throttle linkage; withdraw linkage and support in frame.
13 Disconnect pipes and water temperature transmitter wire from underside of inlet manifold.
14 Disconnect pipes from thermostatic switch – cars to U.S.A. Federal specification only.
15 Remove nuts and spring washers securing inlet manifold to cylinder head; note fitted positions of two pipe clips and remove.
16 Withdraw inlet manifold from studs, disconnect water pump hose from underside of header tank; lift out inlet manifold.
17 Remove gaskets and discard.

Refitting
Reverse operations 1 to 17 as appropriate; use new gaskets.

EXHAUST MANIFOLD

Remove and refit **30.15.10**

Removing

Cars fitted with emission control only
1 Remove two cross head screws and washers securing hot air duct to camshaft covers.
2 Pull hot air duct from exhaust manifold heat shield.

Cars to U.S.A. Federal specification only
3 Remove nut, washers, spacer and bolt securing air delivery pipe clip to exhaust manifold heat shield.
4 Pull air delivery pipe from air pump outlet elbow.
5 Slacken lock nuts on air pump belt adjustment, remove air pump belt from pulley and draw pump as far as possible away from cylinder head.
6 Restrain adaptor and release nut securing E.G.R. pipe.

Rear manifold only on cars with S.U. carburetters
7 Slacken pipe clip and pull hot air pipe from A.E.D. hot air pick-up unit.

Left hand drive cars only

8 Remove three 2 BA nuts, bolts and washers securing steering pinion heat shield.

All Cars

9 Remove setscrews/adaptor and washers securing exhaust manifold heat shield to exhaust manifolds.
NOTE: Do not mislay restrictor from E.G.R. adaptor (fixed orifice system only).

Cars fitted with air conditioning only

10 Remove compressor heat shield.

All Cars

11 Remove eight nuts and washers securing exhaust manifolds to exhaust front pipes.
12 Remove eight nuts and washers securing each exhaust manifold to cylinder head.
13 Remove three screws securing hot air pick-up unit to rear exhaust manifold.
14 Clean all traces of gaskets from joint faces.

Refitting

Reverse operations 1 to 14 as appropriate, using new gaskets and seals throughout.
NOTE: After loosely securing exhaust manifolds to cylinder head, locate exhaust front pipe on studs before finally tightening manifold nuts.

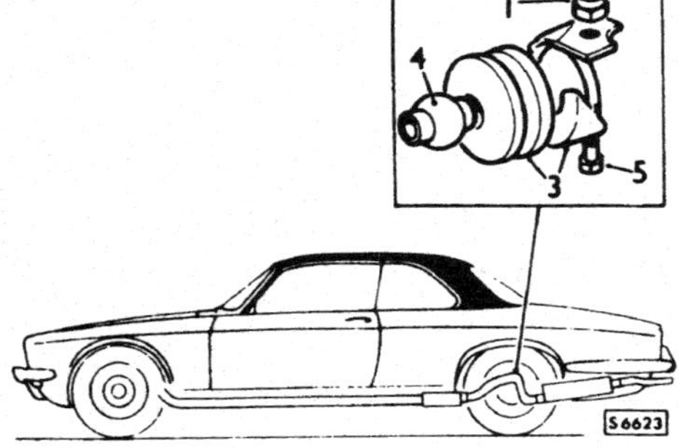

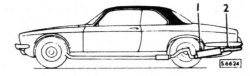

MOUNTING RUBBER – FRONT

Remove and refit **30.20.02**

Removing

1 Reach over rear suspension unit and release self locking nut and bolt securing rear mounting bracket.
2 Slide bracket from spigot on rear intermediate pipe and remove.

Refitting

3 Locate replacement mounting rubber in bracket ring.
NOTE: Brackets are handed.
4 Smear bush with soft soap and press into mounting rubber.
5 Locate bush on spigot and secure using bolt from below and self locking nut.

MOUNTING RUBBER – REAR

Remove and refit **30.20.04**

Removing

1 Remove tail pipe and silencer – 30.10.22.
2 In luggage boot, remove two self locking nuts securing rear mounting.

Refitting

3 Fit replacement mounting rubber and bracket and secure using two self locking nuts.
4 Fit tail pipe and silencer.

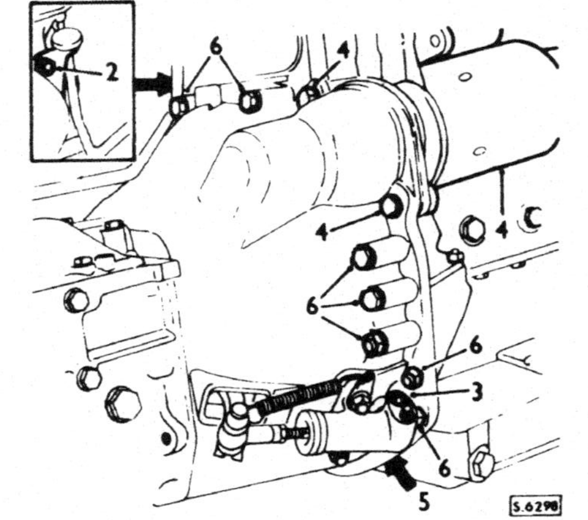

CLUTCH ASSEMBLY

Remove and refit **33.10.01**

Removing

1 Remove engine and gearbox assembly – 12.37.01.
2 Remove bolts securing gearbox breather pipe to rear exhaust manifold.
3 **Left hand drive cars only** Disconnect fluid pipe from slave cylinder; plug or tape broken connections to prevent ingress of dirt.
4 Remove two bolts, spacers and spring washers securing starter motor. Withdraw motor from bell housing.
5 Remove bolts and spring washers securing flywheel cover to bell housing.
6 Remove bolts securing bell housing to cylinder block, noting positions of long and short bolts.
NOTE: Some recent cars are fitted with an additional tie plate, connecting bases of sump and bellhousing. Remove four bolts and detach tie plate.

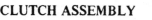

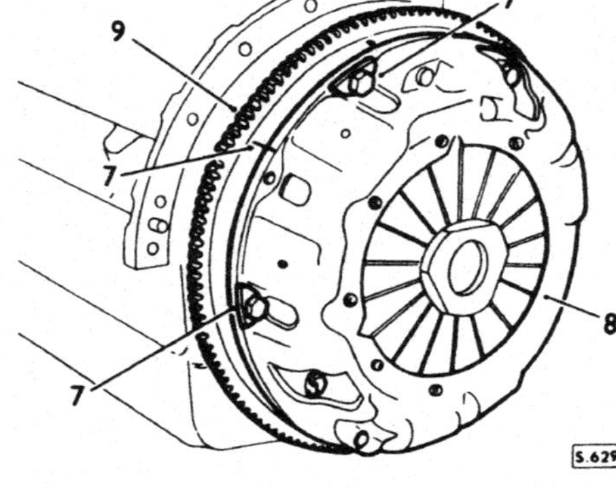

7 Mark relative positions of clutch cover to flywheel and balance weights to clutch cover.
8 Remove bolts and spring washers securing clutch cover to flywheel; withdraw cover together with clutch plate.
9 Examine flywheel face for scoring. If scoring is excessive, flywheel must be renewed.
10 Examine clutch plates for oil contamination or evidence of slipping. If oil contamination is evident, crankshaft rear oil seal should be examined and, if necessary, replaced.

CAUTION: It is always advisable when renewing clutch to fit a new release bearing. To do this, proceed as follows, see also operation 33.25.12 items 7 and 8.

11 Release spring clips securing release bearing to withdrawal lever.
12 Disengage lugs from withdrawal lever.

Refitting

13 Position lugs of release bearing in withdrawal lever.
14 Fit spring clips; ensure that lips are correctly seated in recesses.

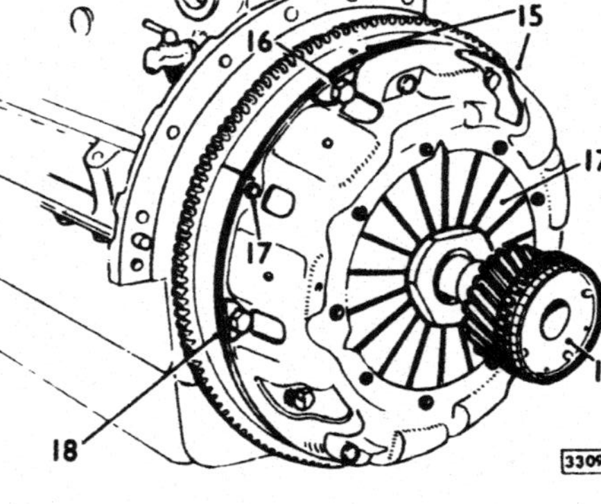

15 Position clutch plate and cover on flywheel, ensure reference marks made during dismantling are in alignment.
16 Fit balance weights, bolts and washers; do not tighten bolts at this stage.
17 Using dummy shaft, align clutch plate, ensure clutch cover is correctly located on dowels.
18 Tighten bolts by diagonal selection.
19 Reverse operations 1 to 6. Replace tie plate, if fitted, with its flanges downwards, and secure with four bolts, plain and spring washers.
20 Check slave cylinder push rod adjustment – 33.10.03.

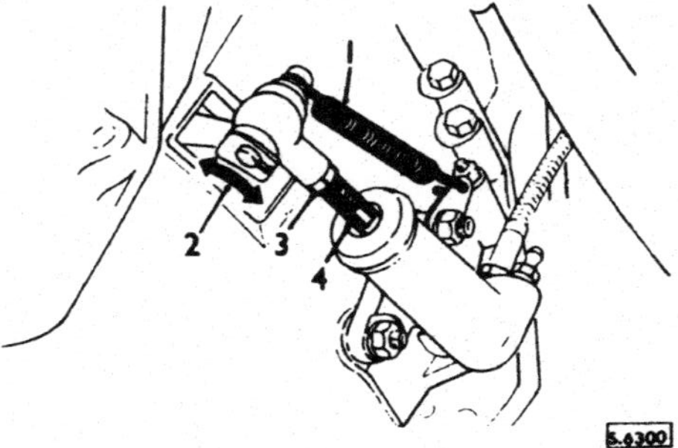

CLUTCH SLAVE CYLINDER PUSH ROD

Check and adjust **33.10.03**

Checking

1 Release return spring.
2 Move push rod backwards and forwards, measure total free movement of rod which, when correctly adjusted is .125 in. (3,2 mm.).

Adjusting

3 Slacken locknut.
4 Screw push rod in or out of trunnion until correct amount of free movement is obtained.
NOTE: Flats are machined on shank of push rod to enable spanner to be used.
5 Tighten locknut.
6 Reconnect return spring.
7 Operate clutch pedal several times and recheck amount of free travel.

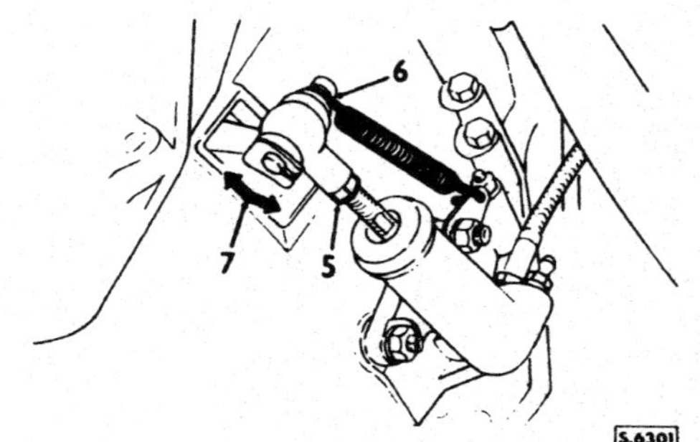

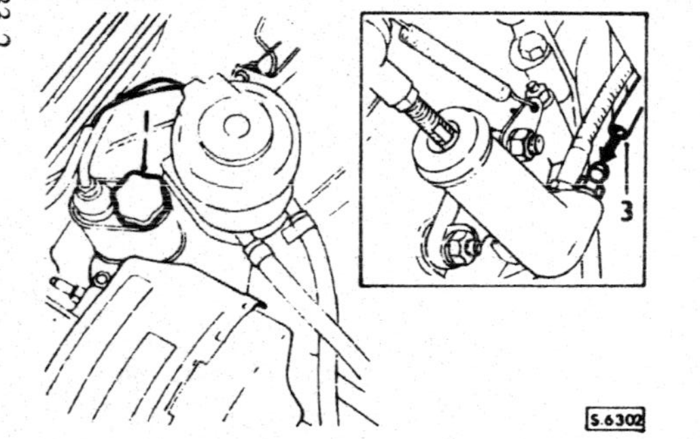

HYDRAULIC SYSTEM

Bleed 33.15.01

WARNING: ONLY CASTROL/GIRLING UNIVERSAL BRAKE FLUID MAY BE USED IN THE CLUTCH HYDRAULIC SYSTEM. (THIS FLUID EXCEEDS SAE J.1703/C.)

Bleeding

1 Remove reservoir filler cap.
2 Top up reservoir to correct level with hydraulic fluid.
3 Attach one end of a bleed tube to slave cylinder bleed nipple.
4 Partially fill a clean container with hydraulic fluid.
5 Immerse other end of bleed tube in fluid.
6 Slacken slave cylinder bleed nipple.
7 Pump clutch pedal slowly up and down, pausing between each stroke.
8 Top up reservoir with fresh hydraulic fluid after every three pedal strokes.
9 Pump clutch pedal until pedal becomes firm, tighten bleed nipple.
10 Top up reservoir.
11 Refit filler cap.
12 Apply working pressure to clutch pedal for two to three minutes and examine system for leaks.

WARNING: DO NOT USE FLUID BLED FROM SYSTEM FOR TOPPING UP PURPOSES AS THIS WILL CONTAIN AIR. IF FLUID HAS BEEN IN USE FOR SOME TIME IT SHOULD BE DISCARDED. FRESH FLUID BLED FROM SYSTEM MAY BE USED AFTER ALLOWING IT TO STAND FOR A FEW HOURS TO ALLOW AIR BUBBLES TO DISPERSE.

FLUID HOSE

Remove and refit
– Right hand drive cars only – 33.15.13

Removing

1 Remove setscrews and washers securing clip to heat shield.
2 Release union nut securing master cylinder pipe to flexible hose.
3 Slacken union nut at master cylinder end plug.
4 Restrain hose union at bracket and remove locknut and shakeproof washer.
5 Beneath car remove bleed nipple from slave cylinder.
6 Unscrew flexible hose from slave cylinder; plug or tape broken connections to prevent ingress of dirt.

Refitting

7 Reverse operations 1 to 6 inclusive.
8 Bleed hydraulic system – 33.15.01.

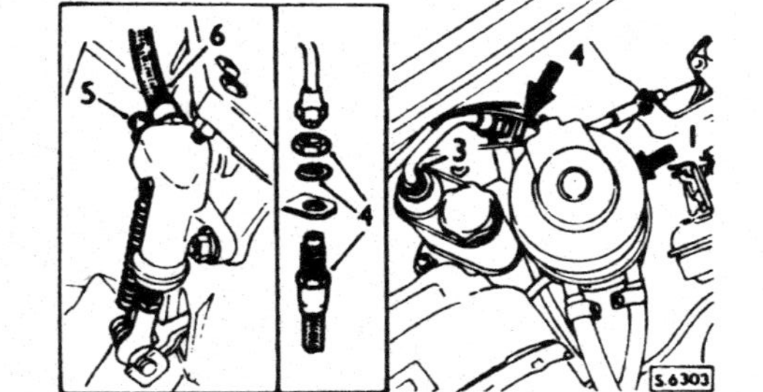

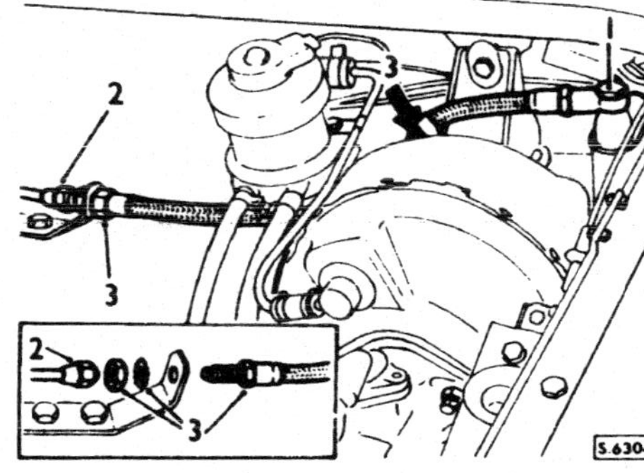

FLUID HOSE

Remove and refit
– Left hand drive cars only – 33.15.13

Removing

1 Remove banjo bolt and washer securing hose to master cylinder.
2 Disconnect bundy pipe at bracket.
3 Restrain hose union and remove locknut and shakeproof washer; remove clip securing hose to brake servo mounting stud. Withdraw hose together with clip.
4 Plug or tape broken connections to prevent ingress of dirt.

Refitting

5 Reverse operations 1 to 4.
6 Bleed hydraulic system – 33.15.01.

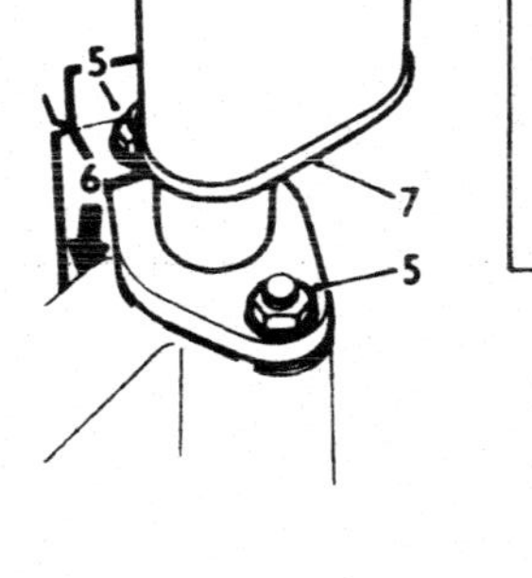

MASTER CYLINDER

Remove and refit 33.20.01

Removing

1 Remove pedal box – 70.35.03.
2 Note fitted position of return spring; disconnect spring from pedal.
3 Remove and discard split pin.
4 Withdraw clevis pin, recover plain washer.
5 Remove nuts and spring washers securing master cylinder to pedal box.

Right hand drive cars only

6 Remove setscrew, nut and washers securing brake fluid reservoir bracket to pillar.
7 Withdraw brake fluid reservoir bracket; lift off master cylinder and shims.

Refitting

Reverse operations 1 to 5 or 7.

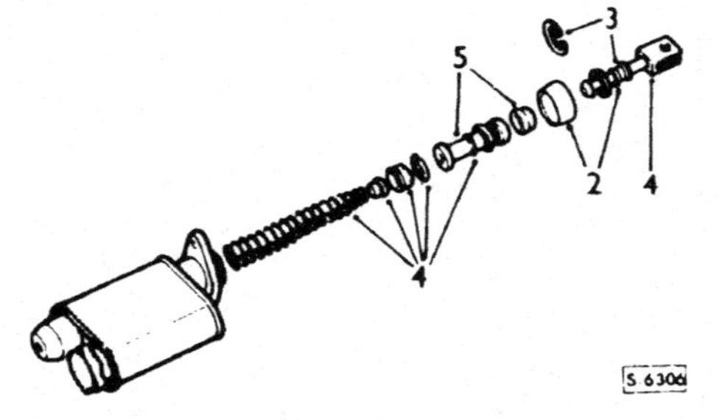

MASTER CYLINDER

Overhaul 33.20.07

WARNING: USE ONLY CLEAN BRAKE FLUID OR GIRLING CLEANING FLUID FOR CLEANING. ALL TRACES OF CLEANING FLUID MUST BE REMOVED BEFORE REASSEMBLY. ALL COMPONENTS SHOULD BE LUBRICATED WITH CLEAN BRAKE FLUID AND ASSEMBLED USING THE FINGERS ONLY.

Dismantling

1 Remove master cylinder 33.20.01.
2 Detach rubber boot from end of barrel and move boot along push rod.
3 Depress push rod and remove circlip.
4 Withdraw push rod, piston, piston washer, main cup, spring retainer and spring.
5 Remove secondary cup from piston.

Inspection

6 Examine cylinder bore for scores.
7 Thoroughly wash out reservoir and ensure by-pass hole in cylinder bore is clear. Dry using compressed air or lint-free cloth.
8 Lubricate replacement seals with clean brake fluid.

Reassembling

9 If necessary, fit end plug on new gasket.
10 Fit spring retainer to small end of spring. If necessary, bend over retainer ears to secure.
11 Insert spring, large end leading, into cylinder bore; follow with main cup, lip foremost. Ensure lip is not damaged on circlip groove.
12 Using fingers only, stretch secondary cup on to piston with small end towards drilled end and groove engaging ridge. Gently work round cup with fingers to ensure correct bedding.
13 Insert piston washer into bore, curved edge towards main cup.
14 Insert piston in bore, drilled end foremost.
15 Fit rubber boot to push rod.
16 Offer push rod to piston and press into bore until circlip can be fitted behind push rod stop ring.
CAUTION: It is important to ensure circlip is correctly fitted in groove.
17 Locate rubber boot in groove.

NOTE: Early cars have 0.75 in. dia. bore master cylinders, Part Nos. C45859 and C45860. Later cars have 19 mm. dia. bore master cylinders, Part Nos. CAC1028 and CAC1029.

RELEASE BEARING

Remove and refit 33.25.12

Removing

1 Remove engine and gearbox assembly from car – 12.37.01.
2 Remove two bolts, spacers and spring washers securing starter motor; withdraw motor from bell housing.

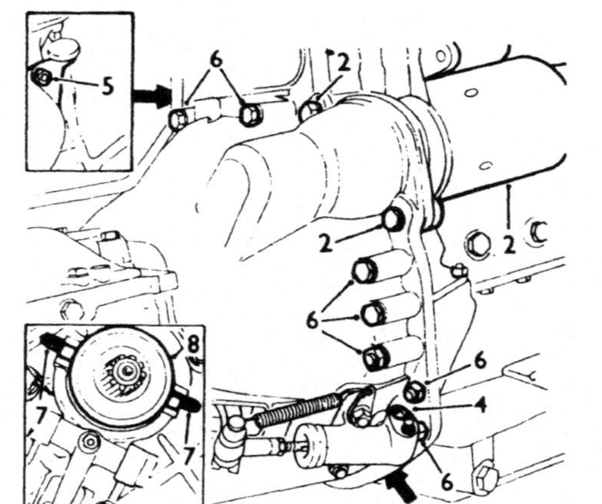

3 Remove bolts and spring washers securing flywheel cover to bell housing.
4 **Left hand drive cars only** – Disconnect fluid pipe from slave cylinder; plug or tape broken connections to prevent ingress of dirt.
5 Remove nut securing gearbox breather to rear exhaust manifold stud.
6 Remove remaining bolts securing bell housing to cylinder block noting positions of long and short bolts.
7 Release spring clips securing release bearing to withdrawal lever.
8 Disengage lugs from withdrawal lever.

Refitting

Reverse operations 1 to 8 inclusive.

RELEASE ASSEMBLY

Remove and refit 33.25.12

Removing

1 Remove release bearing – 33.25.12 (above).
2 Remove spring clip from slave cylinder push rod and remove return spring and clevis pin.
3 Slacken locknut and remove locating screw from withdrawal lever.
4 Press shaft downwards from bushes and withdrawal lever.
5 Manoeuver withdrawal lever clear of bell housing.

Refitting

Reverse operations 1 to 5 inclusive.

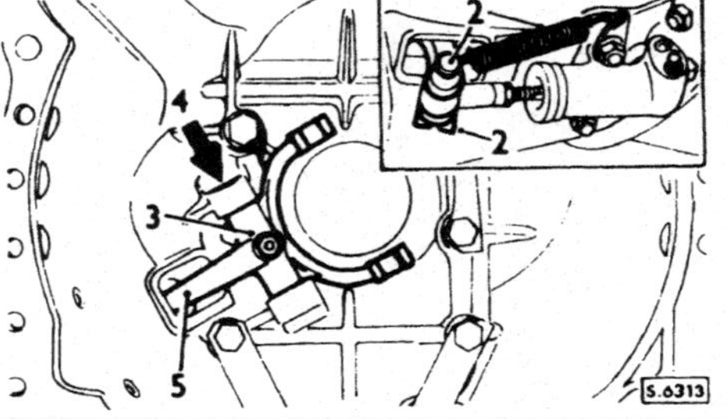

RELEASE ASSEMBLY

Overhaul 33.25.17

1 Remove release assembly – 33.25.12.
2 Check bearing bushes and pivot shaft for wear.
3 If replacement bearing bushes are necessary, use suitable pieces of tube for mandrels and press new bushes into position to displace the old.
4 Lightly ream to size, using pivot shaft for gauge.

CLUTCH PEDAL

Remove and refit 33.30.02

Removing

1 Remove pedal box – 70.35.03.
2 Use large screwdriver to disengage return spring from pedal.
3 Remove split pin, washer and clevis pin securing pedal arm to master cylinder push rod.
4 Remove locating pin.
5 Tap clutch shaft from pedal box casting and recover pedal return spring and washers.

Refitting

6 Locate return spring on pedal boss.
7 Smear clutch shaft with suitable grease
8 Tap clutch shaft through casting – locating groove to outside edge – positioning a washer at either side of pedal boss.
9 Fit pedal arm to master cylinder push rod and secure using clevis pin, plain washer and new split pin.
10 Fit pedal box.
11 Bleed hydraulic system – 33.15.01.

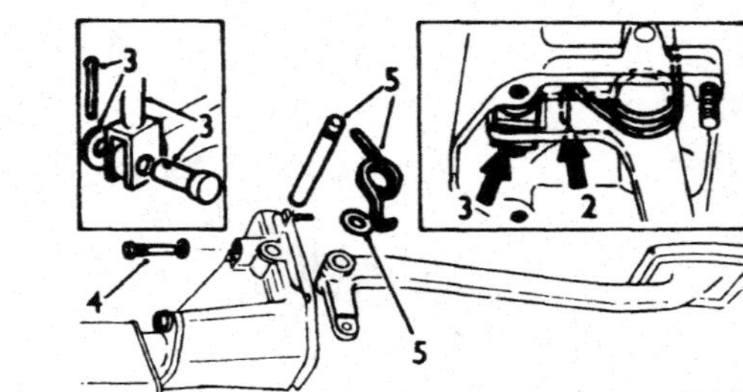

CLUTCH PEDAL

Overhaul **33.30.07**

Dismantling
1 Remove clutch pedal – 33.30.02.
2 Using suitable mandrel, press bearing bushes from pedal boss.

Reassembling
3 Using suitable mandrel press new bearing bushes in from each side. Press until bushes are flush with sides of pedal.
4 Lightly ream bearing bushes to size using pedal shaft to check fit.
5 Smear bushes with suitable grease.
6 Fit clutch pedal.

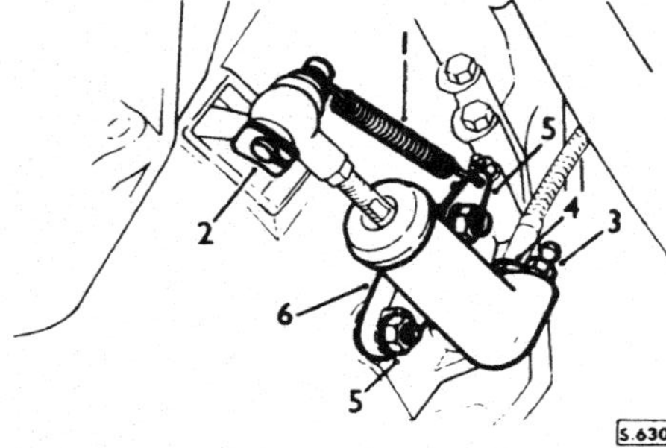

SLAVE CYLINDER

Remove and refit
– Right hand drive cars only – 33.35.01

Removing

NOTE: If removal of push rod is not required, omit operation 2 but slide rubber boot away from slave cylinder.

1 Release return spring.
2 Remove spring clip; withdraw push rod clevis pin.
3 Remove bleed nipple.
4 Slacken union but DO NOT attempt to remove flexible hose.
5 Note fitted position of return spring anchor plate and remove nuts and spring washers securing slave cylinder; withdraw slave cylinder.
6 Restrain hose union, screw **slave cylinder** off union; plug or tape broken connections to prevent loss of fluid and ingress of dirt.

Refitting
7 Restrain hose and screw slave cylinder on to union.
8 Reverse operations 1 to 5 but check tightness of hose union before fitting bleed nipple.
9 Bleed clutch – 33.15.01.
10 Check push rod adjustment – 33.10.03.

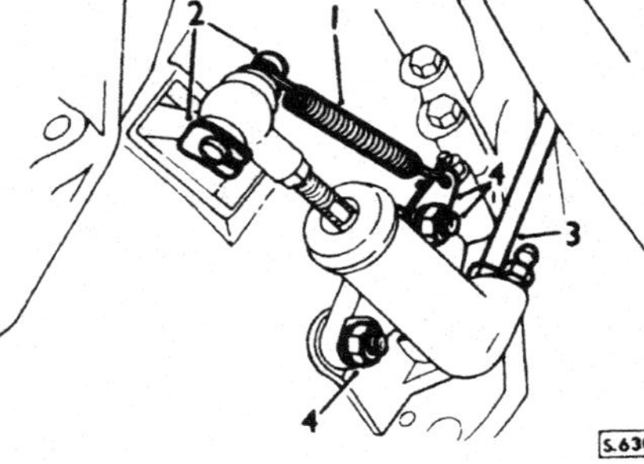

SLAVE CYLINDER

Remove and refit
–Left hand drive cars only – 33.35.01

Removing
NOTE: If removal of push rod is not required, omit operation 2 but slide rubber boot away from slave cylinder.

1 Release return spring.
2 Remove spring clip and push rod clevis pin.
3 Disconnect hydraulic pipe; plug or tape broken connections to prevent loss of fluid and ingress of dirt.
4 Note fitted position of return spring anchor plate and remove nuts and spring washers securing slave cylinder; withdraw slave cylinder.

Refitting
5 Reverse operations 1 to 4.
6 Bleed clutch – 33.15.01.
7 Check push rod adjustment – 33.10.03.

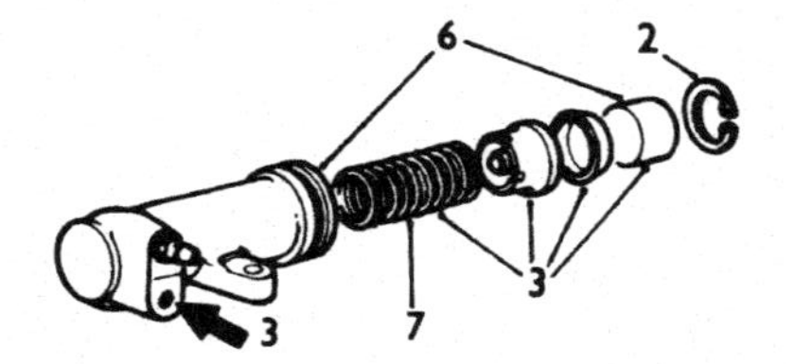

SLAVE CYLINDER

Overhaul **33.35.07**

WARNING: USE ONLY CLEAN BRAKE FLUID OR GIRLING CLEANING FLUID FOR CLEANING. ALL TRACES OF CLEANING FLUID MUST BE REMOVED BEFORE REASSEMBLY. ALL COMPONENTS SHOULD BE LUBRICATED WITH CLEAN BRAKE FLUID AND ASSEMBLED USING THE FINGERS ONLY.

Dismantling
1 Remove slave cylinder – 33.35.01.
2 Remove circlip.
3 Apply low air pressure to inlet port and expel piston, cup, cup filler and spring.
4 Discard cup.

Inspecting components
5 Wash all components in denatured alcohol (methylated spirits) and dry using clean, lint free cloth.
6 Examine piston and slave cylinder bore for signs of scoring. Should scoring be evident, components must be renewed.
7 Examine spring for signs of distortion, renew if necessary.
8 Check condition of rubber boot on push rod. If distorted or perished in any way, boot must be renewed.

Reassembling
Reverse operations 1 to 4; use new cup.

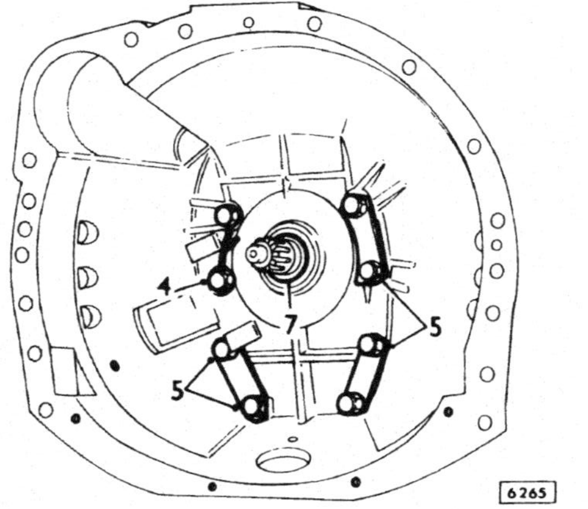

BELL HOUSING

Remove and refit 37.12.07

Removing
1 Remove engine and gearbox – 12.37.01.
2 Remove clutch assembly – 33.10.01.
3 Remove withdrawal assembly – 33.25.12.
4 Remove and discard locking wire.
5 Knock back locking tabs and remove setscrews securing bell housing to gearbox; discard locking tabs.
6 Remove bell housing; remove and discard gasket.
7 Remove and discard oil seal.

Refitting
8 Smear new oil seal with clean engine oil.
9 Push oil seal into bell housing with lip of seal towards gearbox.
10 Smear new gasket with grease; position gaskets on front of gearcase.
11 Cover splines of first motion shaft with adhesive tape to prevent damage to oil seal.
12 Slide bell housing over first motion shaft; use new lock plates when refitting setscrews.
13 Tighten setscrews by diagonal selection.
14 Turn up tabs of lock plates and wire lock setscrews.
15 Reverse operations 1 to 3.

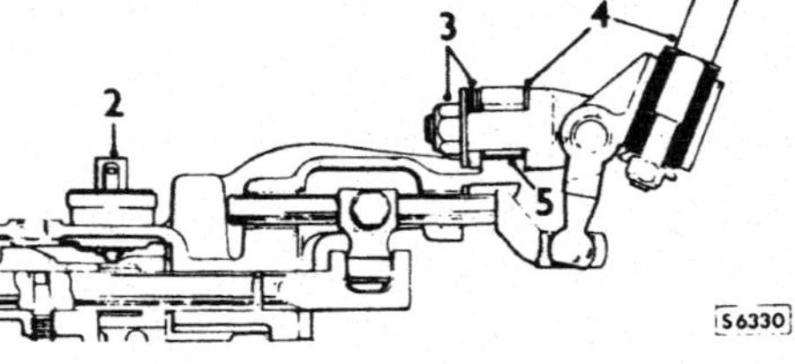

TOP COVER

Remove and refit 37.12.16

Removing
1 Remove engine and gearbox – 12.37.01.
2 Slacken hose clip securing breather pipe to elbow; disconnect pipe.
3 Disconnect overdrive cable at snap connector.
4 Remove nuts securing cable clips to overdrive unit.
5 Place gear lever in neutral.
6 Note fitted position of top cover securing bolts; remove bolts and detach cable clips.
NOTE: Top cover is dowelled to gearbox case.
7 Lift top cover off gear case; remove and discard gasket.

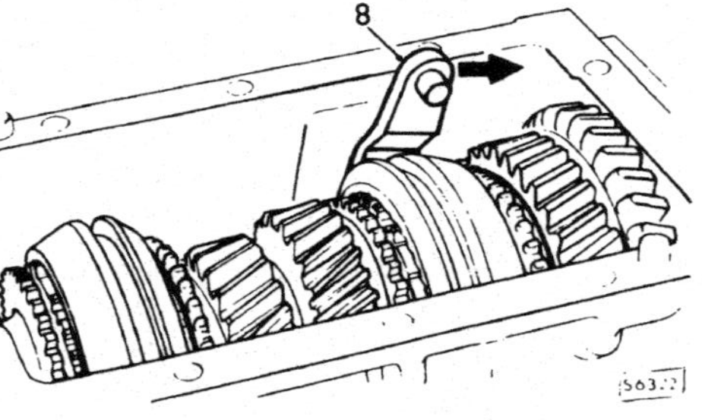

Refitting.
8 Ensure reverse idler gear is out of mesh by pushing lever towards rear of gearbox.
9 Reverse operations 1 to 7 ensuring selector levers are correctly engaged.

Use a new gasket when fitting top cover.

NOTE: Later cars are fitted with a modified operating finger engaging with modified selector shafts, to reduce gear lever lateral movement; ensure that correct replacement is fitted if renewing top cover assembly.

TOP COVER

Overhaul 37.12.19

Dismantling
1 Remove top cover – 37.12.16.
2 Note fitted positions of cable; disconnect cables from overdrive and reverse switches.
3 Remove self locking nut, remove coil spring, plain and fibre washer securing gear lever to top cover.
4 Withdraw gear lever together with harness; recover second fibre washer.
5 Press bush from pivot jaw housing.
6 Remove locking wire and remove retaining screws from selector forks and locating arm.
7 Withdraw 3rd/top selector rod and collect selector fork, spacing tube and interlock ball.
8 Withdraw 1st/2nd selector rod and collect selector fork, spacing tube and loose interlock pin in rod.
9 Withdraw reverse selector rod, fork and locating arm.
NOTE: Collect reverse rod detent plunger, ball and spring. Collect interlock ball.
10 Release locknut on reverse selector, and slacken setscrew.
11 Recover detent plunger, stop spring, detent ball and spring.

Inspection
12 Examine all components for scores and undue wear. Examine ball bearings for pitting. Check springs for length against new items.
13 Remove 'O' ring seals from selector rods, and fit new. Examine gear change lever spigot bush for wear and renew if necessary.

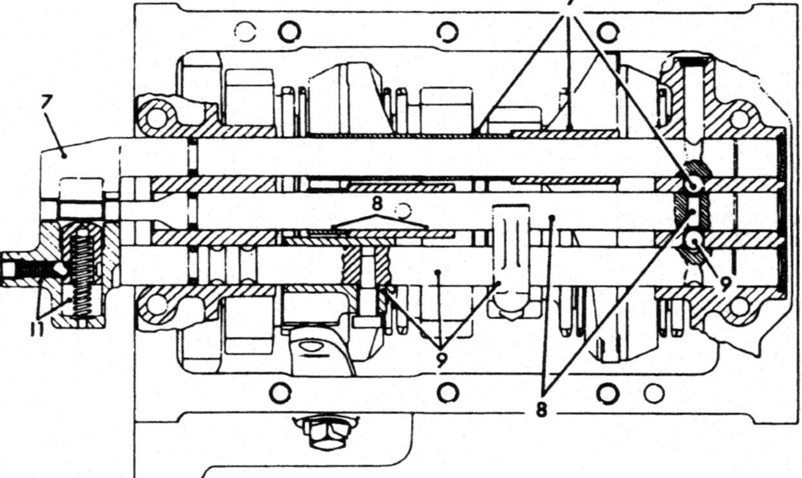

Reassembling

14 Fit detent plunger and spring to reverse selector rod.
15 Fit detent ball, spring setscrew and lock-nut.
16 Press detent plunger fully home, and tighten setscrew to lock plunger.
17 Slowly slacken setscrew until plunger is released and detent ball engages in groove.
18 Restrain setscrew and tighten locknut.
19 Place reverse selector rod detent spring, plunger and ball in its housing. Depress plunger and fit selector rod.
20 Fit selector fork and locating arm to reverse selector rod.
21 Fit retaining screws.
22 Fit 1st/2nd selector rod into cover far enough to collect selector fork and spacing tube.
23 Place top cover on its side, reverse selector rod downwards, and carefully push an interlock ball through 1st/2nd selector rod hole at front of top cover. Locate ball in hole in casting, against groove in reverse selector rod.
24 Push 1st/2nd selector rod into hole to retain ball in groove.

NOTE: Take care not to push ball ahead of rod.

25 Fit retaining screw to 1st/2nd selector fork.
26 Check interlock by ensuring selector rods will not move together, and that moving one locks the other.
27 Carefully place interlock plunger through 3rd/top selector rod hole at front of top cover. Gently manipulate 1st/2nd rod until plunger drops through.
28 Ensure reverse and 1st/2nd selector rods level and carefully push second interlock ball through 3rd/top hole to rest in hole in casting.
29 Pass 3rd/top selector rod through hole in top cover and fit selector fork and spacing tube.
30 Push 3rd/top selector rod into hole to retain ball in groove.
NOTE: Take care not to push ball ahead of rod.
31 Fit locating screw.
32 Check interlock by ensuring selector rods will not move together, and that moving one locks both the others.

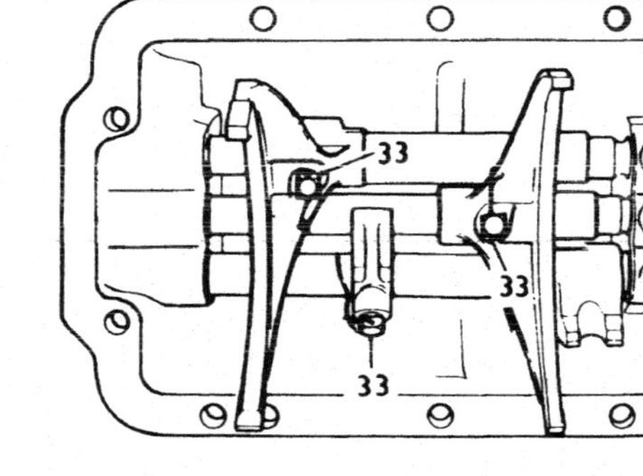

33 Check tighten locating screws and wirelock each to its fork.
34 Fit new bush to pivot jaw housing. Lightly ream to size, using jaw pivot pin as a gauge.
35 Fit fibre washer to gear selector pivot jaw pin.
36 Push pin through bush in top cover and secure with fibre washer, flat washer, coil spring and self locking nut.
37 Refit top cover.

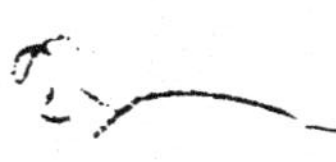

GEAR CHANGE LEVER ASSEMBLY

Remove and refit **37.16.04**

Removing
1 Remove console – 76.25.01.
2 Remove gear change lever knob – 37.16.11.

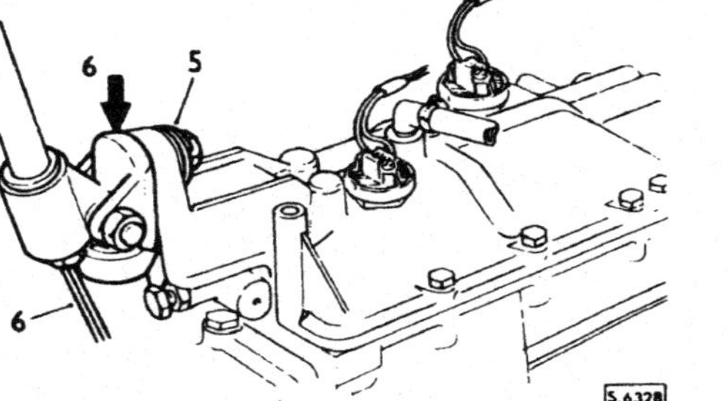

3 Remove draught excluder – 37.16.05.
4 **Carefully** cut insulation pad away from vicinity of gear lever.
5 Remove self locking nut and recover coil spring, plain and fibre washers securing gear lever to top cover.
6 Withdraw assembly feeding overdrive cables through shank of gear lever. Recover second fibre washer.

Refitting
Reverse operations 1 to 6, repair insulation pad with suitable petroleum based adhesive.

GEAR CHANGE LEVER DRAUGHT EXCLUDER

Remove and refit **37.16.05**

Removing
1 Remove console – 76.25.01.
2 Remove gear knob – 37.16.11.
3 Remove screws securing retaining ring.
4 Withdraw draught excluder.

Refitting
Reverse operations 1 to 4; take care not to damage draught excluder.

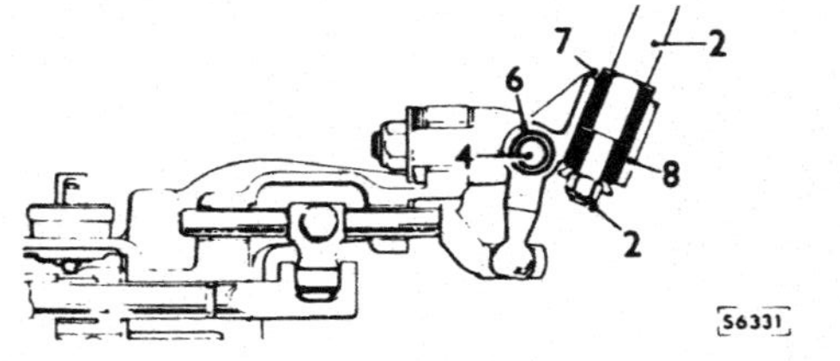

GEAR CHANGE LEVER ASSEMBLY

Overhaul **37.16.10**

Dismantling
1 Remove gear change lever assembly – 37.16.04.
2 Remove self locking nut and press gear lever out of selector lever.
3 Remove self locking nut securing pivot pin.
4 Tap pivot pin out of pivot jaw taking care not to damage threads.
5 Recover one spring and two fibre washers.
6 Using a suitable mandrel, press pivot pin bushes out of pivot jaw.
7 Prise upper bush out of pivot jaw.
8 Using a suitable mandrel, press lower bush out of pivot jaw.

Reassembling
9 Press new lower bush into pivot jaw pressing in from underside until rubber is flush with bottom of jaw.
10 Press new upper bush into pivot jaw. **CAUTION: Ensure lower bush is not displaced during this operation.**
11 Press new pivot pin bushes in pivot jaw.
12 Using a piloted reamer, lightly ream bushes using pivot pin as a gauge.
13 Reverse operations 1 to 5.

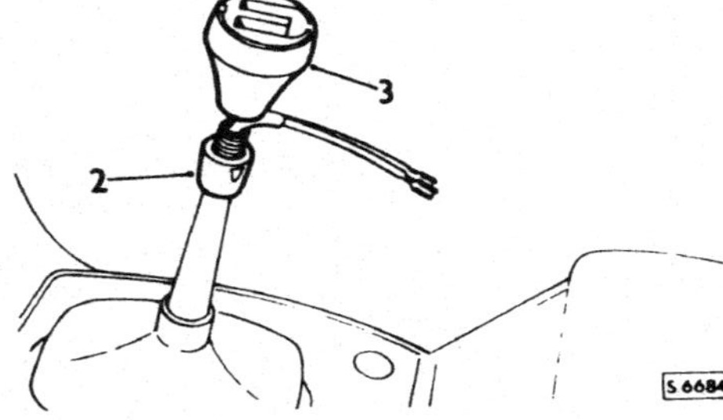

GEAR CHANGE LEVER KNOB

Remove and refit **37.16.11**

Removing
1 Remove overdrive switch – 40.24.01.
2 Slacken ferrule locking gear knob in position.
3 Unscrew gear knob.

Refitting
Reverse operations 1 to 3.

GEAR CHANGE SELECTORS

Remove and refit **37.16.31**

Follow procedure given in operation 37.12.19 – Top Cover Overhaul.

GEARBOX

Remove and refit **37.20.01**

Removing
1 Remove bell housing – 37.12.07.
2 Remove overdrive unit – 40.20.07.

Refitting
Reverse operations 1 and 2.

GEARBOX

Overhaul **37.20.04**

Dismantling
1 Remove engine and gearbox – 12.37.01.
2 Remove overdrive unit – 40.20.07.
3 Remove bell housing – 37.12.07.
4 Remove top cover – 37.12.16.
5 Remove bolts securing adaptor plate, withdraw plate; remove and discard gasket.
6 Move synchro sleeves away from each other to engage gears.
7 Knock back tab washer and remove rear bearing nut; discard tab washer.
8 Withdraw countershaft, collect Woodruff key.
CAUTION: Ensure rear thrust washer (pegged to casing), drops down in a clockwise direction, viewed from rear of casing, as countershaft is withdrawn. This will prevent washer being trapped by reverse gear when mainshaft is driven forward.
9 Remove and discard fibre plug from front of countershaft.
10 Rotate first motion shaft until cutaway portions of driving gear are facing top and bottom of casing.
11 Using two levers, ease first motion shaft and front bearing forward until assembly can be withdrawn.
12 Recover spacer ring and top gear synchro ring.
13 Remove bearing from inside first motion shaft.
14 Knock back tab washer and remove nut, tab washer, and oil thrower; discard tab washer.
15 Tap shaft sharply against a metal plate to dislodge bearing.
16 Tap reverse idler shaft out of rear of gearbox, collect Woodruff key.
17 Knock back tab washer and remove bolt securing reverse lever; discard tab washer.
18 Withdraw reverse lever.
19 Rotate mainshaft until one of the large cutaway portions of third/top synchro hub is in line with countershaft gear.

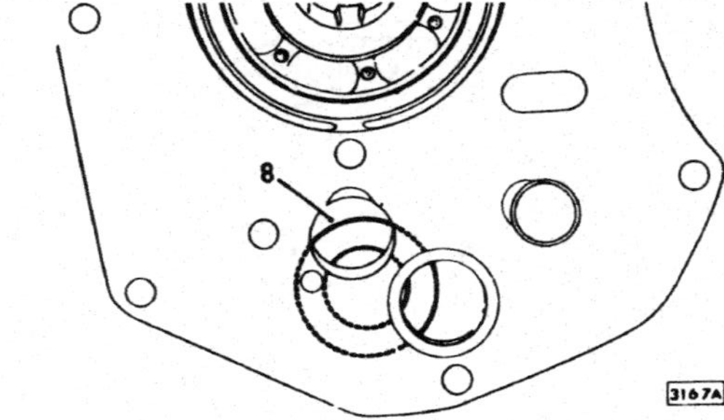

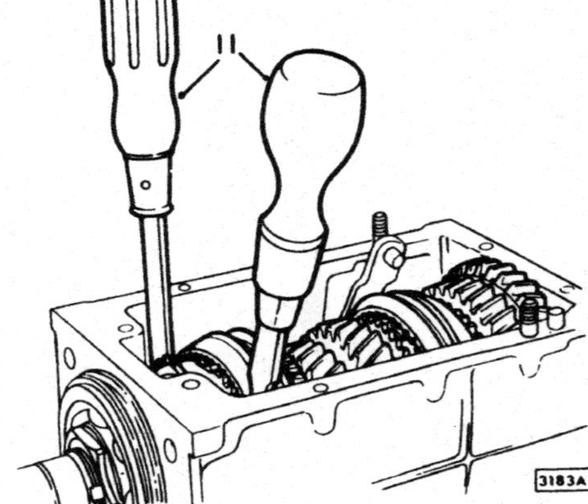

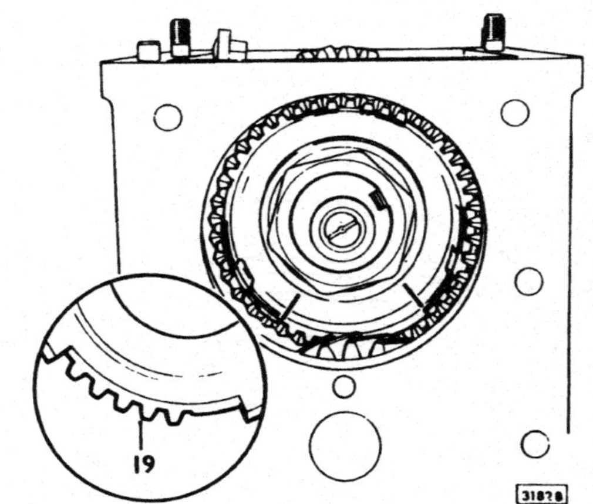

20 Tap mainshaft forward through rear bearing ensuring that reverse gear is kept pressed against first gear.
21 Withdraw rear bearing from casing and fit hose clip to mainshaft to prevent reverse gear from sliding off as mainshaft is withdrawn.
22 Lift out mainshaft and gears.
23 Lift out reverse idler gear.
24 Lift out countershaft gears and collect needle rollers, inner and outer thrust washers and retaining rings. Discard thrust washers.
CAUTION: Needle rollers are graded by size. If it is necessary to replace any rollers, complete sets MUST be obtained and old rollers discarded.
25 Remove hose clip retaining reverse gear; withdraw gear.
NOTE: To assist in identifying components, mainshaft is shown in position.
26 Withdraw first speed gear; collect needle rollers, spacer and sleeve.
27 Note fitted position of first/second synchro assembly to rings, remove synchro assembly and collect loose rings.
28 Withdraw second speed gear, collect needle rollers, remove narrow spacer.

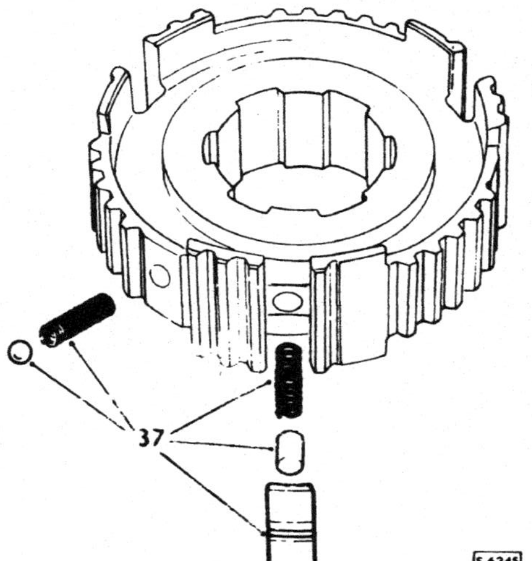

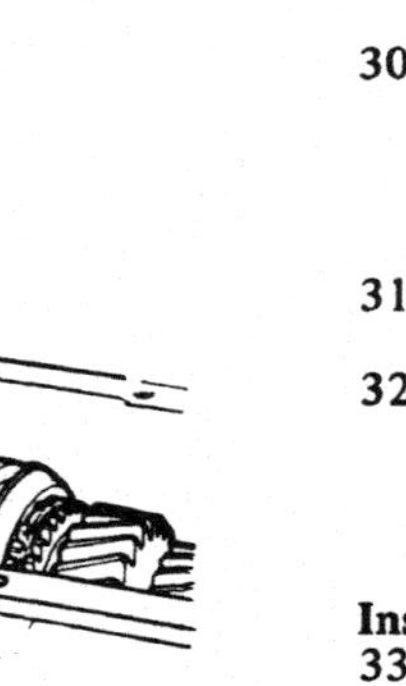

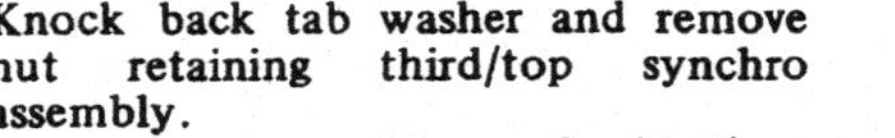

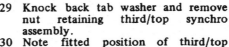

29 Knock back tab washer and remove nut retaining third/top synchro assembly.
30 Note fitted position of third/top synchro assembly to rings, remove synchro assembly and collect loose rings; remove and discard thrust washer.
31 Withdraw third speed gear, collect needle rollers; remove wide spacer.
32 Push synchro hub from operating sleeve, collect detent balls and springs, thrust members, plungers and springs.

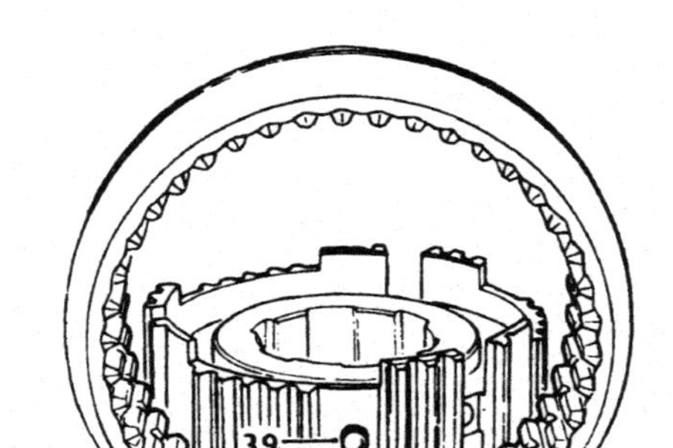

Inspection
33 Check all components for signs of damage, undue wear, overheating, scoring or excessive clearances.
34 Check that oil-ways in mainshaft are unobstructed.
CAUTION: Needle rollers are graded by size. If any rollers are displaced or damaged, all rollers MUST be renewed. It is advisable to renew synchro assemblies especially if gearbox has seen considerable service. It is, however, permissible to re-use hubs and sleeves providing no damage is evident but springs, balls, plungers and thrust members MUST always be renewed.

Reassembling
35 Assemble synchro hub to operating sleeve with wide boss of hub on opposite side to wide chamfer end of sleeve.
NOTE: Hub should slide smoothly over sleeve with no trace of binding.
36 Line up hub so that holes for balls and springs are exactly level with top of operating sleeve.
37 Fit three springs, plungers and thrust members in synchro hub.
NOTE: These springs are colour coded red.
38 Ensure lip on each thrust member is facing outwards; press thrust members down as far as possible.
39 Assemble three balls and springs in line with operating sleeve teeth having three detent grooves.
NOTE: These springs have no colour coding.

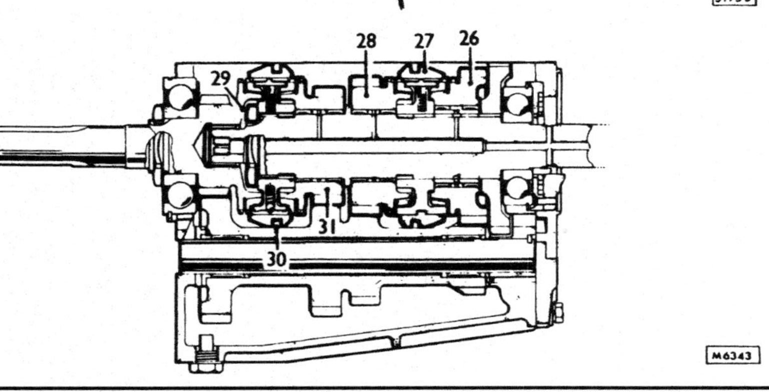

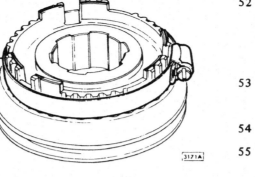

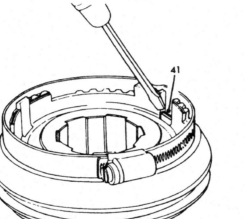

40 Compress springs with large hose clip or piston ring clamp.
41 Depress hub slightly and push thrust members down until they engage neutral groove in operating sleeve.
42 Tap hub down using a hide or lead hammer until balls can be heard and felt to engage with neutral groove (second click).
43 Repeat operations 35 to 42 on remaining synchro assembly.
44 Fit one retaining ring in front (large gear) end of cluster gear.
45 Fit needle rollers and inner thrust washer; retain rollers with grease. **CAUTION: Ensure peg on washer locates in groove in cluster gear.**
46 Fit a retaining ring, needle rollers and second retaining ring in rear of cluster gear; retain rollers with grease.
47 Position new pegged rear thrust washer on boss; retain washer with grease.
48 Position new outer thrust washer on front of cluster gear; retain washer with grease.
49 Thoroughly clean interior and exterior of gearbox casing.
50 Carefully lower cluster gear into position, large gear to front of casing and insert dummy countershaft.
51 Tap countershaft backwards and forwards to ensure that it is seated correctly.

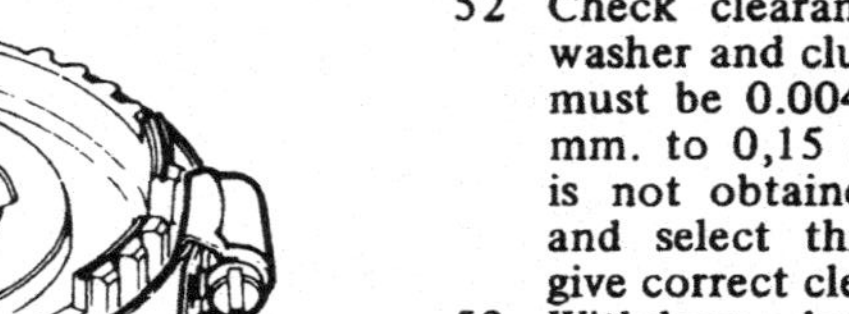

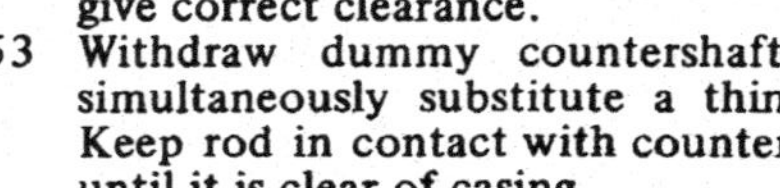

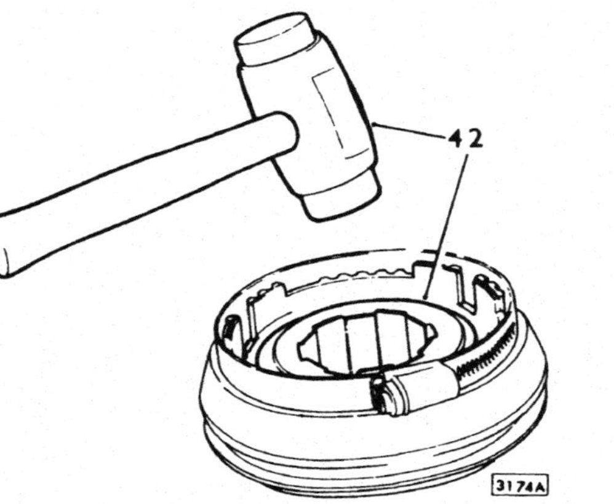

52 Check clearance between rear thrust washer and cluster gear. Dimension 'A' must be 0.004 in. to 0.006 in. (0,10 mm. to 0,15 mm.). If this dimension is not obtained, remove cluster gear and select thrust washer which will give correct clearance.
53 Withdraw dummy countershaft and simultaneously substitute a thin rod. Keep rod in contact with countershaft until it is clear of casing.
54 Place Woodruff key in reverse idler shaft.
55 Fit reverse idler gear, lever and idler shaft. DO NOT fit retaining bolt at this stage.
56 Fit bearing race in rear of first motion shaft.
57 Position oil thrower on first motion shaft with raised centre portion of thrower facing upwards towards bearing.
58 Fit snap ring in groove in front bearing.
59 Press bearing on first motion shaft ensuring that it is square to shoulder of gear.
60 Fit new tab washer and nut; turn up tab.
61 Reverse operations 25 to 32, retain needle rollers with grease; use new tab washer.
62 Enter mainshaft assembly through top of casing and pass rear of shaft through bearing aperture; remove hose clip.
63 Smear a new gasket with grease and position it on front of gearcase.
64 Position synchro ring to locate on front face of third/top synchro hub.
65 Enter first motion shaft through front of casing with cutaway portions of driving gear at top and bottom.
66 Tap first motion shaft into position ensuring that spigot on mainshaft enters bearing.
67 Fit snap ring in groove in rear bearing.
68 Hold first motion shaft in position and with a hollow drift, tap rear bearing into position. Ensure bearing is seated correctly.

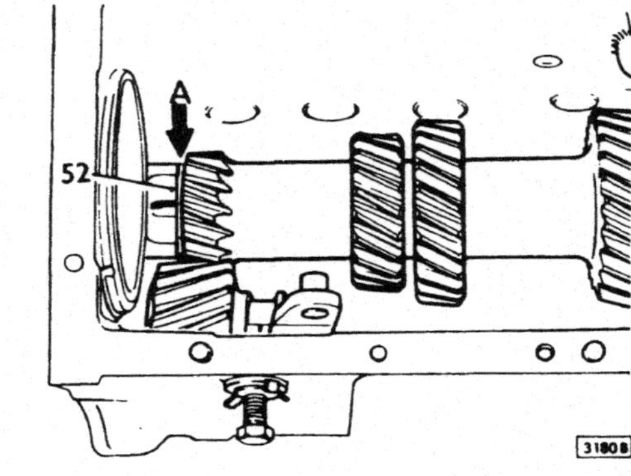

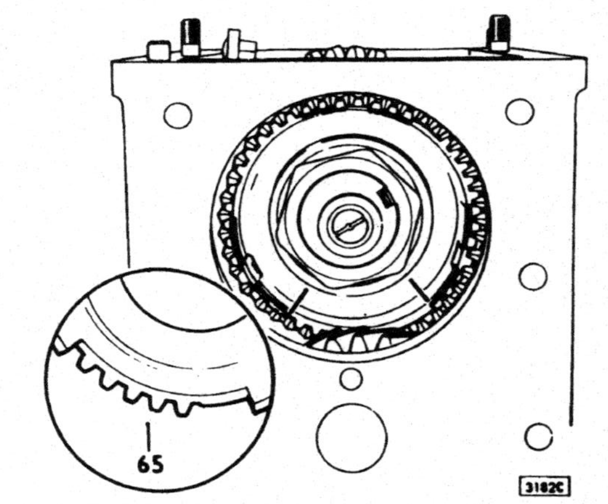

69 Withdraw thin rod and simultaneously substitute dummy countershaft.
CAUTION: Ensure that gasket is not damaged and needle rollers are not displaced.

70 Place Woodruff key in countershaft.

71 Enter countershaft through hole in rear of gearcase. Tap countershaft home at the same time withdrawing dummy shaft.
CAUTION: Ensure that gasket is not damaged and needle rollers are not displaced.

72 Fit new fibre plug at front of countershaft.

73 Fit reverse lever bolt; use a new tab washer.

74 Fit rear bearing nut; use a new tab washer.

75 Reverse operations 1 to 5; use a new gasket between adaptor plate and gearbox and adaptor plate and overdrive unit.

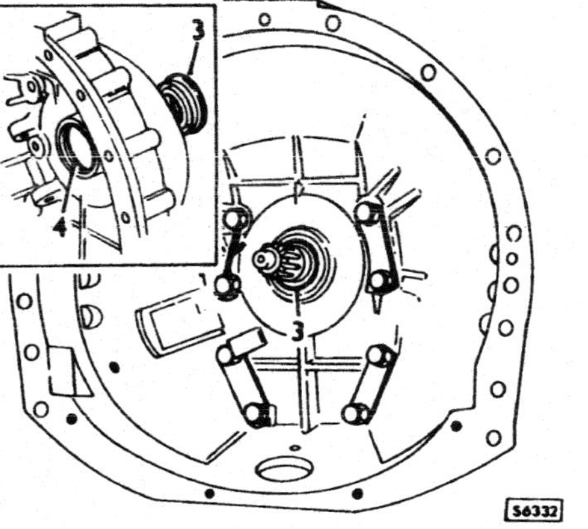

FRONT OIL SEAL

Remove and refit **37.23.06**

Removing

1 Remove engine and gearbox – 12.37.01.
2 Remove bell housing – 37.12.07.
3 Remove and discard oil seal.
4 Ensure oil seal recess is perfectly clean.

Refitting

5 Smear new oil seal with clean engine oil.
6 Push oil seal into bell housing with lip of seal towards gearbox.
7 Reverse operations 1 and 2; cover splines of first motion shaft with adhesive tape to prevent damage to oil seal.

OVERDRIVE UNIT

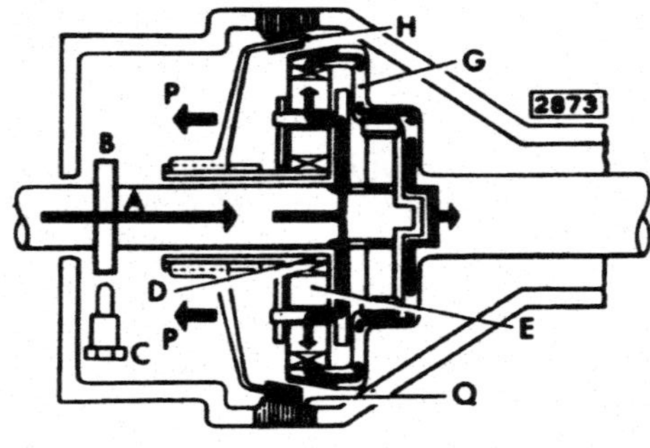

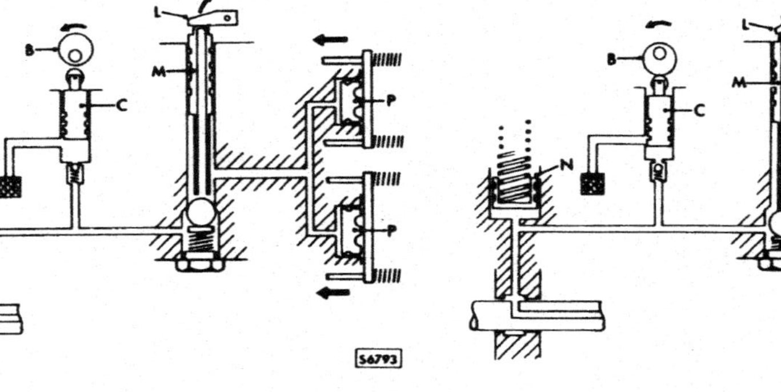

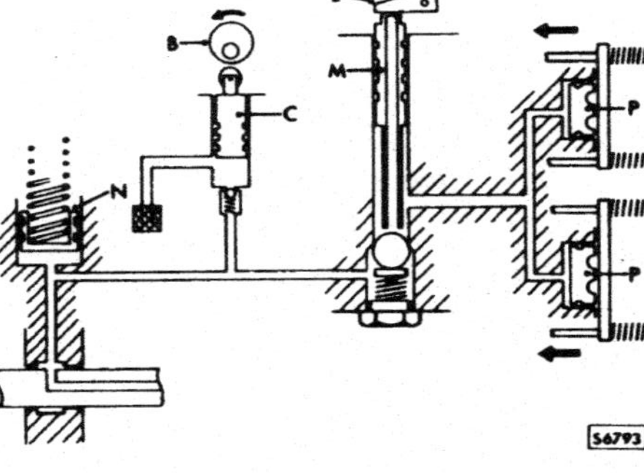

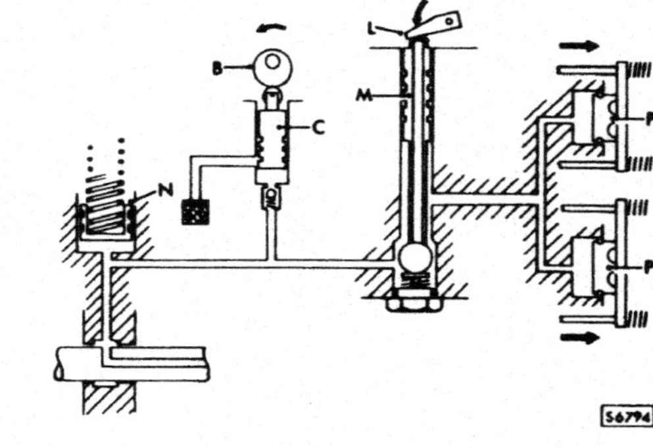

Description 40.00.00

The Laycock de Normanville overdrive unit consists of a hydraulically controlled epicyclic gear housed in a casing at the rear of the gearbox.
When engaged, the overdrive reduces the engine speed in relation to the road speed, thus permitting high road speeds with low engine revolutions. Consequently, the use of the overdrive results in fuel economy and reduced engine wear. The overdrive is operated by an electric solenoid controlled by a switch mounted on the gear lever knob. The solenoid is fused at the main fuse block.
Overdrive can only be engaged when the car is in top gear.

Power input

The power input enters the overdrive unit through the extension of the gearbox driven shaft 'A' and by means of a cam 'B' operates the plunger-type hydraulic pump 'C'. This, in turn, builds up pressure against the spring loaded piston in the accumulator cylinder placed vertically in the main casing. The output of the oil pump and accumulator is also used to supply high pressure lubricating oil for the gearbox.

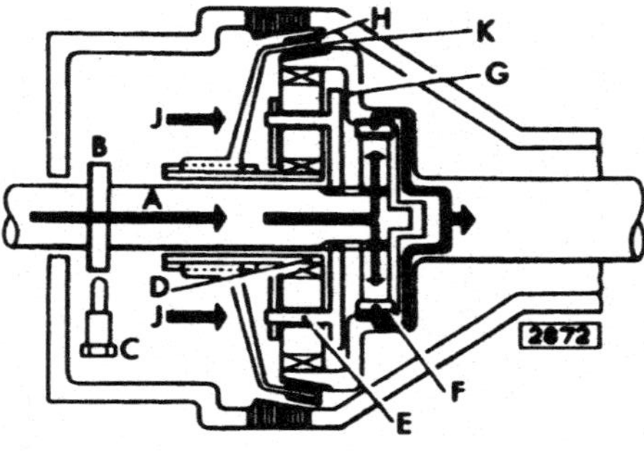

The sun wheel

The sun-wheel 'D' is integral with a sliding member which is free to rotate on the input shaft. Immediately behind the sun-wheel and splined to the gearbox driven shaft is the planetary carrier 'E' in which are mounted the three planet wheels.

The uni-directional clutch 'F'

This operates from the input shaft on to which is splined the inner member. The other components of this clutch are the rollers and the outer member which is attached to the combined annulus and output shaft 'G'. The drive is transmitted from the input shaft through the clutch inner member and the rollers which are forced up the inner members' inclined faces wedging the whole clutch solid. The clutch then drives the annulus output shaft.

The cone clutch

The cone clutch 'H' is mounted on the sliding member on which it is free to slide. The cone clutch springs 'J' which hold the inner lining 'K' in contact with the corresponding cone of the annulus, maintain the clutch in the direct drive position. This prevents a free-wheel condition when the car tries to overrun the engine. Engine braking, therefore, is always available.
When the reverse gear is engaged, power is transmitted by way of the cone clutch, inner lining and the annulus, as the uni-directional clutch is inoperative.

Hydraulic operation

Overdrive is brought into operation by rotating the operating shaft 'L', thus depressing the operating valve 'M'. This action allows the stored hydraulic pressure in the accumulator 'N' to be applied to the two pistons, 'P'.
The pistons move the clutch forward away from the annulus. During the forward movement of the clutch the drive from the engine to the wheels is maintained by the roller clutch. The hydraulic operation causes the outer lining of the cone clutch to contact the brake ring 'Q' bringing the sunwheel and sleeve to rest.
This action is effected without shock as the clutch is oil immersed. The input drive now passes from the gearbox driven shaft to the planet carrier and the rotation of the planet wheels around the stationary sun-wheel causes both the annulus and the output shaft to be driven faster than the input shaft. In this condition the outer member of the roller clutch over-runs the inner member.
Because the sun-wheel can move neither backwards or forwards, there is always engine braking available in overdrive gear.

FAULT DIAGNOSIS

When an overdrive unit does not operate properly it is advisable to check the level of the gearbox oil. If below the low level, top up with fresh oil and test the unit again before making any further investigations.
Faulty units should be checked for defects in the order listed below.
If the electrical control does not operate, the electrical circuit should be checked from the diagram.

CAUTION: Before removing any of the valve plugs it is essential to operate the solenoid several times in order to release all hydraulic pressure from the system. To do this, engage top gear, switch on the ignition and operate the overdrive control switch several times.

PROBLEM		CHECKS ON UNIT
Overdrive does not engage	(a)	Insufficient oil in gearbox.
	(b)	Solenoid not operating due to fault in electric system.
	(c)	Solenoid operating lever out of adjustment.
	(d)	Insufficient hydraulic pressure due to pump non-return valve incorrectly seating (probably dirt on seat).
	(e)	Insufficient hydraulic pressure due to worn accumulator.
	(f)	Pump not working due to choked filter.
	(g)	Pump not working due to damaged pump roller or cam.
	(h)	Leaking operating valve due to dirt on ball seat.
	(i)	Damaged parts within the unit requiring removal and inspection.
Overdrive does not disengage	(a)	Fault in electrical control system.
	(b)	Solenoid sticking.
CAUTION: If the overdrive does not release, do NOT reverse the car, otherwise extensive damage will be caused.	(c)	Blocked restrictor jet in operating valve.
	(d)	Solenoid operating lever incorrectly adjusted.
	(e)	Sticking clutch.
	(f)	Damaged gears, bearing or sliding parts within the unit.
Clutch slip in overdrive	(a)	Insufficient oil in gearbox.
	(b)	Solenoid lever out of adjustment.
	(c)	Insufficient hydraulic pressure due to pump non-return valve incorrectly seating (probably dirt on the seat).
	(d)	Insufficient hydraulic pressure due to worn accumulator.
	(e)	Operating valve incorrectly seated.
	(f)	Worn or glazed clutch lining.
Clutch slip in reverse or free wheel condition in overdrive	(a)	Solenoid operating lever out of adjustment.
	(b)	Partially blocked restrictor jet in operating valve.
	(c)	Worn or burnt inner clutch lining.
Change into top gear noisy when overdrive already selected	(a)	Check adjustment of isolator switch – 40.24.04.

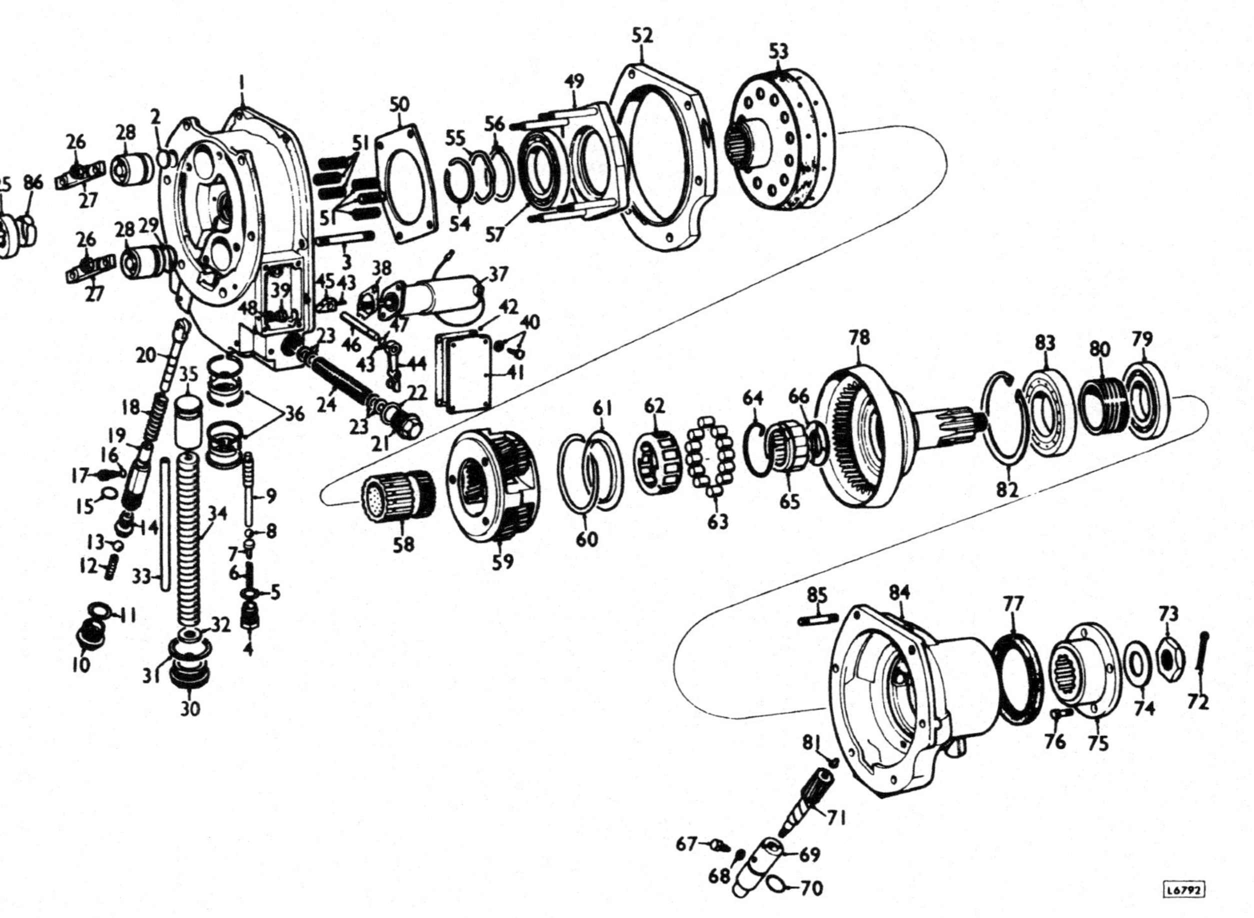

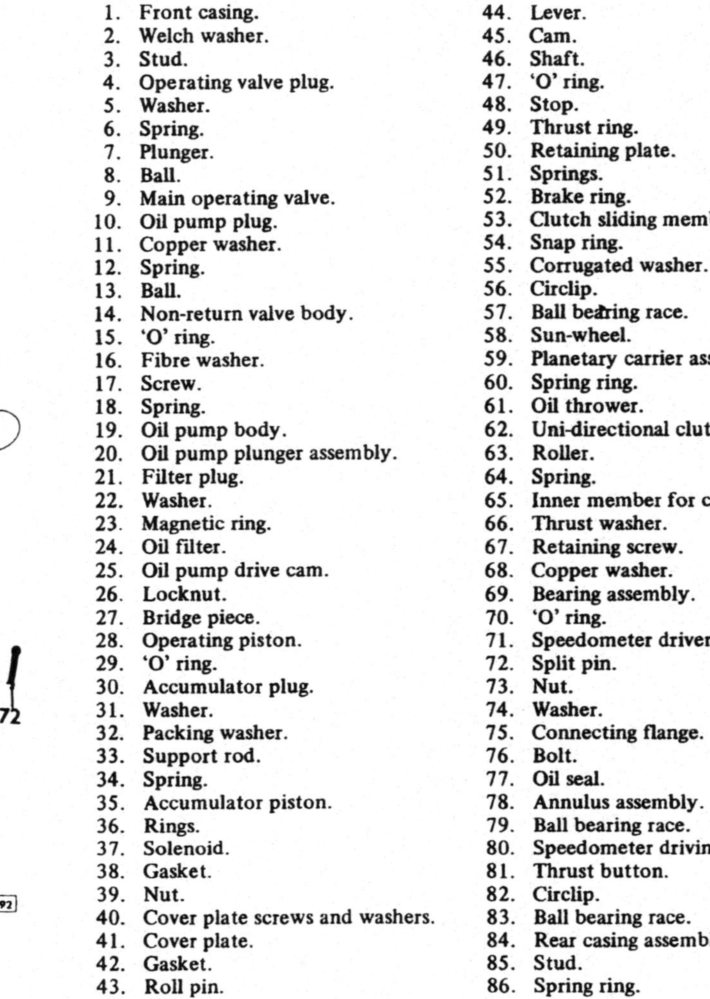

1. Front casing.
2. Welch washer.
3. Stud.
4. Operating valve plug.
5. Washer.
6. Spring.
7. Plunger.
8. Ball.
9. Main operating valve.
10. Oil pump plug.
11. Copper washer.
12. Spring.
13. Ball.
14. Non-return valve body.
15. 'O' ring.
16. Fibre washer.
17. Screw.
18. Spring.
19. Oil pump body.
20. Oil pump plunger assembly.
21. Filter plug.
22. Washer.
23. Magnetic ring.
24. Oil filter.
25. Oil pump drive cam.
26. Locknut.
27. Bridge piece.
28. Operating piston.
29. 'O' ring.
30. Accumulator plug.
31. Washer.
32. Packing washer.
33. Support rod.
34. Spring.
35. Accumulator piston.
36. Rings.
37. Solenoid.
38. Gasket.
39. Nut.
40. Cover plate screws and washers.
41. Cover plate.
42. Gasket.
43. Roll pin.
44. Lever.
45. Cam.
46. Shaft.
47. 'O' ring.
48. Stop.
49. Thrust ring.
50. Retaining plate.
51. Springs.
52. Brake ring.
53. Clutch sliding member.
54. Snap ring.
55. Corrugated washer.
56. Circlip.
57. Ball bearing race.
58. Sun-wheel.
59. Planetary carrier assembly.
60. Spring ring.
61. Oil thrower.
62. Uni-directional clutch cage.
63. Roller.
64. Spring.
65. Inner member for clutch.
66. Thrust washer.
67. Retaining screw.
68. Copper washer.
69. Bearing assembly.
70. 'O' ring.
71. Speedometer driven gear.
72. Split pin.
73. Nut.
74. Washer.
75. Connecting flange.
76. Bolt.
77. Oil seal.
78. Annulus assembly.
79. Ball bearing race.
80. Speedometer driving gear.
81. Thrust button.
82. Circlip.
83. Ball bearing race.
84. Rear casing assembly.
85. Stud.
86. Spring ring.

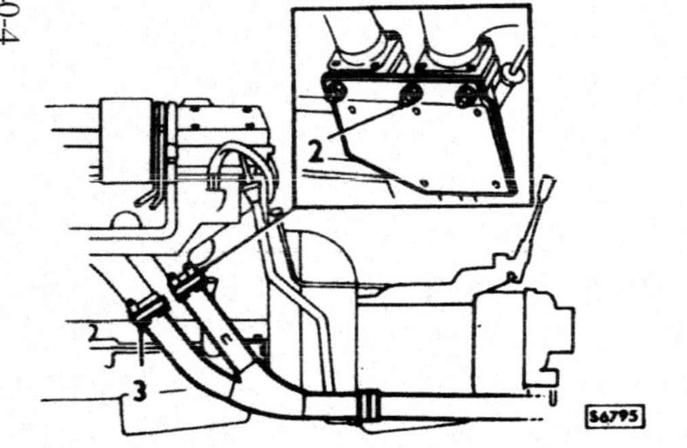

SUMP FILTER

Remove and refit **40.10.01**

Removing

CAUTION: Scrupulous cleanliness must be observed throughout the following operation. Use lint-free cloth.

1 Disconnect battery – 86.15.20.
2 Remove three 2 BA nuts securing steering pinion heat shield – left hand drive cars only.
3 Remove eight nuts securing exhaust front pipe to exhaust manifolds, and allow exhaust pipe to rest on steering rack.
4 Beneath car, remove plug situated immediately below solenoid cover plate.
5 Drain oil into suitable container.
6 Withdraw cylindrical gauze filter.
7 Recover two magnetic rings.
NOTE: Take care not to displace magnetic rings in recess in casing.

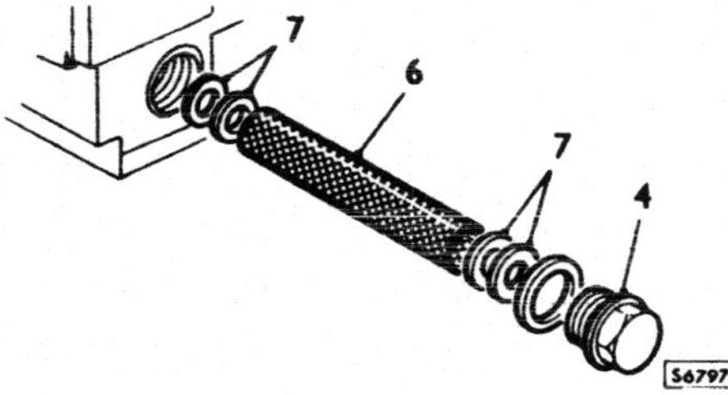

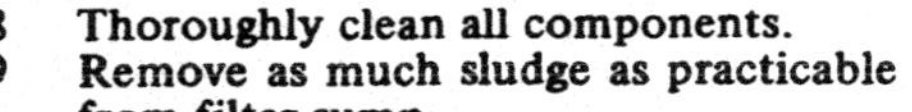

8 Thoroughly clean all components.
9 Remove as much sludge as practicable from filter sump.

Refitting
10 Locate magnetic rings and filter gauze and fit plug. If necessary use new washer.
NOTE: Ensure washer correctly located on plug before tightening.
11 Top up gearbox oil – 37.20.03.
12 Reverse operations 1 to 3 as applicable.

REAR OIL SEAL

Remove and refit **40.15.01**

Service tool: Engine support bracket MS.53(A).

Removing
1 Disconnect battery – 86.15.20.
2 Drain gearbox oil.
3 Remove three 2 BA nuts retaining exhaust pipe heat-shield.
4 Remove eight nuts securing exhaust front pipe to exhaust manifold.
5 Support rear of engine using engine support bracket MS.53(A).

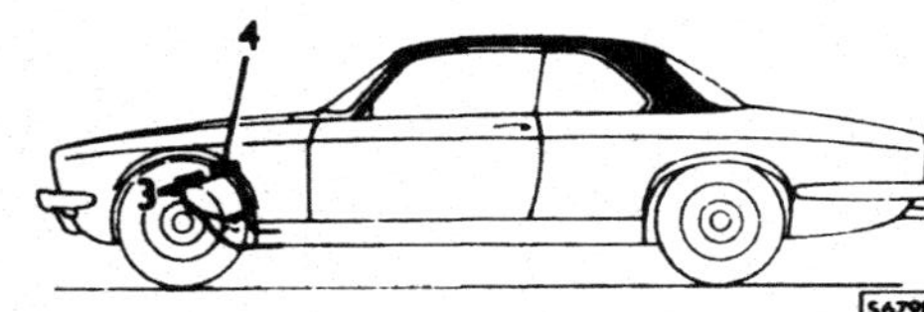

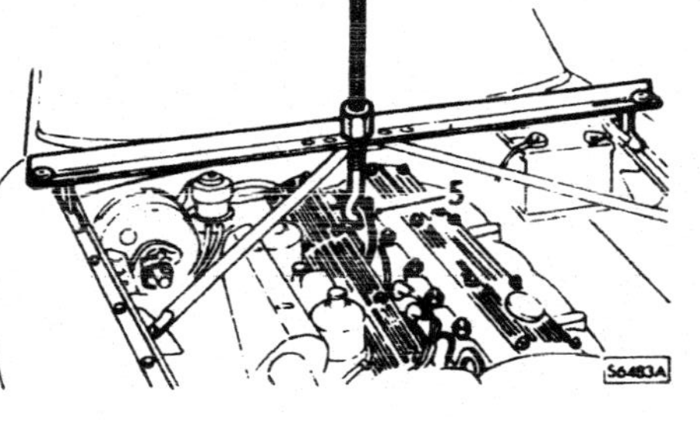

6 Remove self tapping screw securing intermediate heat shield.
7 Support rear engine mounting with jack and remove four special bolts, plain and spring washers and spacers securing engine mounting bracket to body and base plate.
8 Slowly lower jack to release spring tension.
9 Remove nut and washers securing centre bolt of rear engine mounting and recover springs, plain washers and rubber rings.
10 Remove self tapping screw securing rear heat shield to engine mounting base plate.
11 Remove eight setscrews, spring and special washers securing mounting base plate to body.
12 Disconnect speedometer angle drive from overdrive unit.
13 Remove nuts securing propeller shaft drive flange to overdrive unit output flange.
14 Support rear of engine using chains or jack.

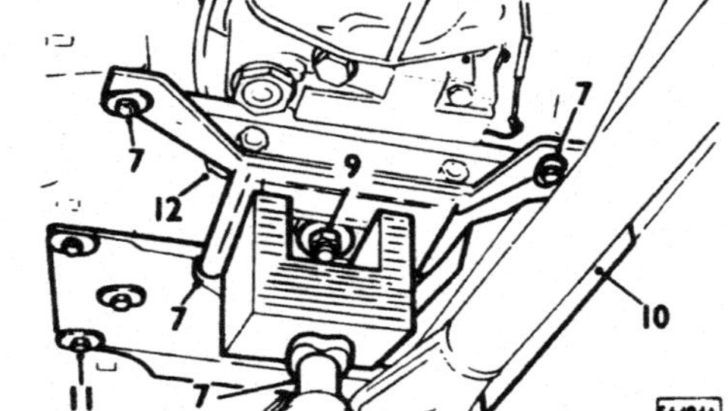

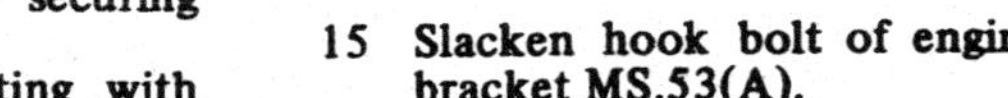
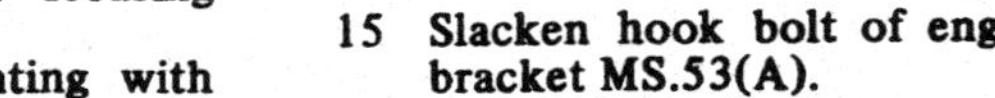

15 Slacken hook bolt of engine support bracket MS.53(A).
CAUTION: Engine must not be allowed to rest on steering rack or on air conditioning unit expansion valve (if fitted) or heater water valve.
16 Carefully lower rear of engine as far as possible without allowing it to rest on steering rack. Observe air conditioning system expansion valve (if fitted) and heater water valve throughout this operation. Ensure clutch cylinder flexible hose is not stretched or kinked.
17 Remove split pin from output flange nut and, using spanners working in opposition, remove flange nut.
18 Recover plain washer, and tap output flange from overdrive unit.
19 Prise oil seal from overdrive unit rear casing.

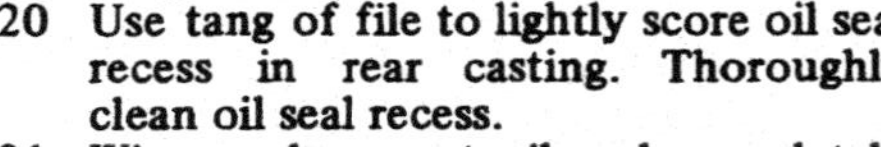

Refitting
20 Use tang of file to lightly score oil seal recess in rear casting. Thoroughly clean oil seal recess.
21 Wipe replacement oil seal completely dry and tap, square, fully into recess.
22 Fit four propeller shaft bolts to output flange, lubricate oil seal with clean new gearbox oil and tap flange onto splines.
23 Fit castellated nut on plain washers to secure output flange. Secure using new split pin.
24 Complete re-assembly by reversing operations 1 to 16 inclusive.

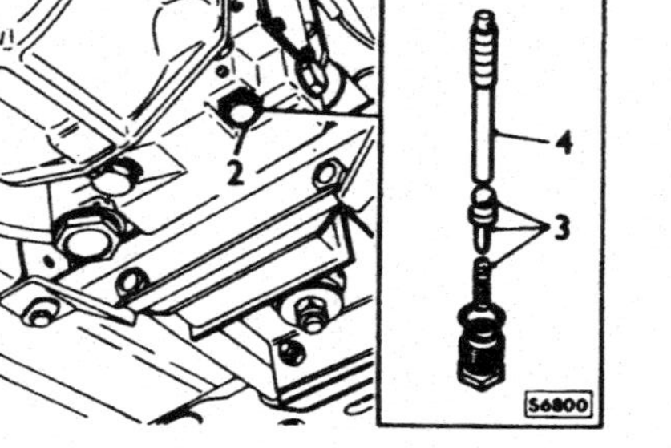

OPERATING VALVE

Remove and refit **40.16.01**

Removing

CAUTION: Before proceeding with this operation ensure overdrive accumulator is exhausted by switching on ignition, engaging top gear and operating the overdrive switch 10-12 times.

1 Disconnect battery – 86.15.20.
2 Beneath car, remove operating valve plug.
3 Remove spring, plunger and ball.
4 Withdraw operating valve by inserting a piece of stiff wire and drawing it down.
CAUTION: Take care to avoid damaging seating at bottom of valve.
5 Thoroughly clean all components and check for signs of damage to valve seating and valve ball. Renew damaged components.
NOTE: Ensure small hole near top of valve is not clogged.

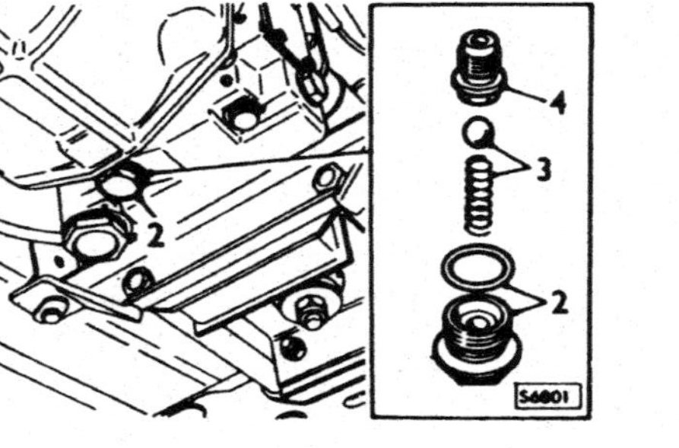

NON–RETURN VALVE

Remove, reseat and refit **40.16.10**

Service tools: Pump non-return valve key L.213.

Removing

CAUTION: Before proceeding with this operation ensure overdrive accumulator is exhausted by switching on ignition, engaging top gear and operating the overdrive switch 10-12 times.

1 Disconnect battery – 86.15.20.
2 Beneath car, remove pump non-return valve plug and washer.
3 Remove spring and 7/32 in. (5,56 mm.) ball.
4 Using pump non-return valve key, L.213, unscrew non-return valve body.
5 Thoroughly clean all components, and check for signs of damage to ball valve or spring.
6 Seat ball to non-return valve body by locating ball on seat, and lightly tapping ball with a copper drift.

Refitting
7 Using Service tool L.213 screw non-return valve body into pump body.
8 Fit ball, spring, copper washer and plug.
NOTE: Ensure washer correctly located on plug before tightening.
9 Check level of gearbox oil, and if necessary, top up using recommended lubricant.
10 Reconnect battery.

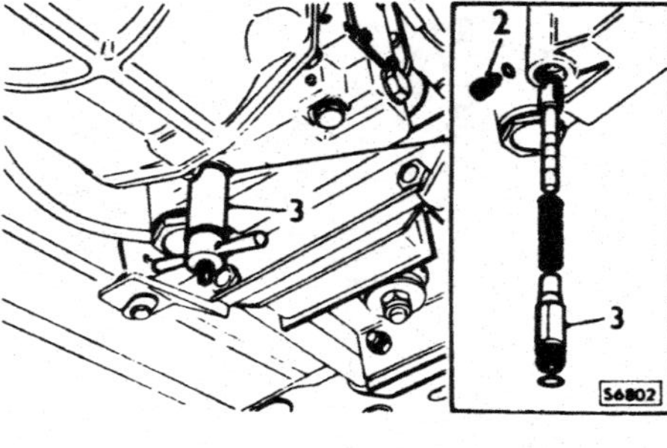

OIL PUMP

Remove and refit **40.18.01**

Service tools: Oil pump body remover handle L.183A, Adaptor L.183A-2. Pump barrel remover L.183-3.

Removing

CAUTION: Before proceeding with this operation, ensure overdrive accumulator is exhausted by switching on ignition, engaging top gear and operating the overdrive switch 10-12 times.

1 Remove non-return valve – 40.16.10.
2 Remove locating screw.
3 Using Service tools L.183A, L.183A-2 and L.183-3, remove pump body. Plunger and spring will also come out when body is withdrawn.
4 Thoroughly clean all components and check pump plunger, cam follower roller, spring and pump bore for wear.

Refitting
5 Assemble pump plunger and spring to pump body.
6 Offer pump body into overdrive casing, so that flat on pump plunger is towards rear of overdrive unit.
7 Tap pump body into casing until annular groove on pump body lines up with locating hole in overdrive casing.
NOTE: Use piece of welding wire as feeler.
8 Fit fibre washer to locating screw and, ensuring that dowel seats into pump body annular groove, tighten screw.
9 Fit non-return valve and complete re-assembly.
NOTE: Ensure washer correctly located on plug before tightening.

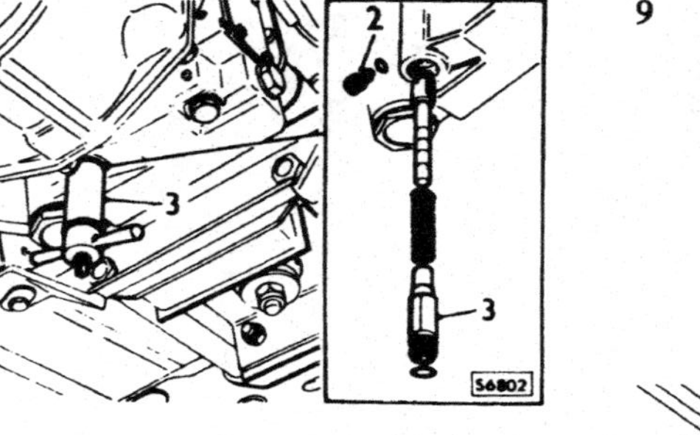

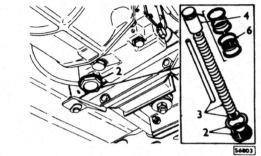

ACCUMULATOR PISTON

Remove and refit **40.18.08**

Service tools: Accumulator piston replacer tool – L.304.

Removing

CAUTION: Before proceeding with this operation ensure overdrive accumulator is exhausted by switching on ignition, engaging top gear and operating the overdrive switch 10-12 times.

1 Disconnect battery – 86.15.20.
2 Beneath car remove accumulator plug. Plug is long enough to relax spring.
NOTE: Oil will drain from overdrive unit.
3 Recover spring and spring support pin. Note whether packing rings fitted beneath spring.
4 Withdraw accumulator piston using piece of stiff wire hooked in internal groove.

Inspection
5 Thoroughly clean piston using petrol

and a stiff brush. Dry using a shop airline.
6 Check condition of piston rings and renew if necessary.

Refitting
7 Lubricate piston with clean gearbox oil.
8 Locate accumulator piston fitting tool L.304 into overdrive unit body.
9 Enter piston into tool, ringed end first, and holding fitting tool firmly into body, tap piston home.
10 Locate sealing washer on plug and locate any packing rings removed in operation 3 within plug.
11 Locate spring and spring support pin and screw in plug.
NOTE: Ensure washer correctly seated before tightening plug.
12 Check level of oil in gearbox and top up.
13 Run engine in top gear with rear wheels lifted clear of ground for 1-2 minutes. Stop engine.
14 Immediately check oil level in gearbox and top up as necessary.

OVERDRIVE UNIT

Hydraulic pressure test 40.20.01

Service tool: Hydraulic test equipment L.188.

Testing

CAUTION: Before proceeding with this operation, ensure overdrive accumulator is exhausted by switching on ignition, engaging top gear and operating the overdrive switch 10-12 times.

1 Check, and if necessary, top up gearbox level.
2 Jack up rear of car and place body securely on stands.
3 Remove operating valve plug and in its place fit test gauge L.188. Ensure spring, plunger and ball fitted above union.
4 Start engine, release handbrake, engage top gear and run up to 20 m.p.h., (32 k.p.h.) indicated on speedometer.

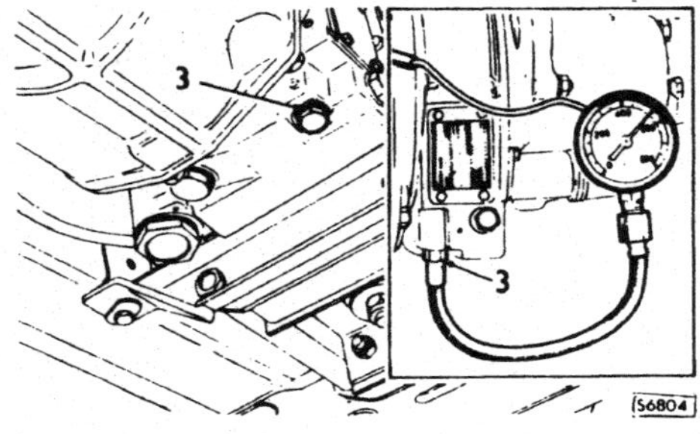

5 Record pressure indicated on gauge. Pressure should be 490 to 510 lb./sq.in. (34,5 to 35,8 kg./sq.cm.).
6 Operate overdrive switch on gear lever. Record pressure indicated on gauge. Pressure should be 490 to 510 lb./sq.in. (34,5 to 35,8 kg./sq.cm.).
7 If pressure recorded in operation 5 is low, operating valve may require cleaning and re-seating.
8 If pressure recorded in operation 6 is low, pump non-return valve may require cleaning and re-seating.
9 If unit fails to operate after re-seating valves, oil pump may not be priming or spring may be broken. To check accelerate engine to approximately 4000 rpm. If pump does still not deliver oil, switch off engine and proceed with operation 10.
10 Operate overdrive switch several times with ignition ON and top gear selected to ensure accumulator exhausted. Switch OFF ignition.
11 Remove test pressure gauge and retain spring, plunger and operating valve ball.
12 Place clean receptacle to catch waste oil.
13 Start engine, engage top gear, and with engine running slowly, watch for oil being pumped into valve chamber. If none appears, stop engine and check pump for damage. See operation – 40.18.01.
14 Refit operating valve ball, plunger spring, washer and plug.
NOTE: Ensure washer correctly seated on plug before tightening.
15 Check and if necessary, top up gearbox oil level.

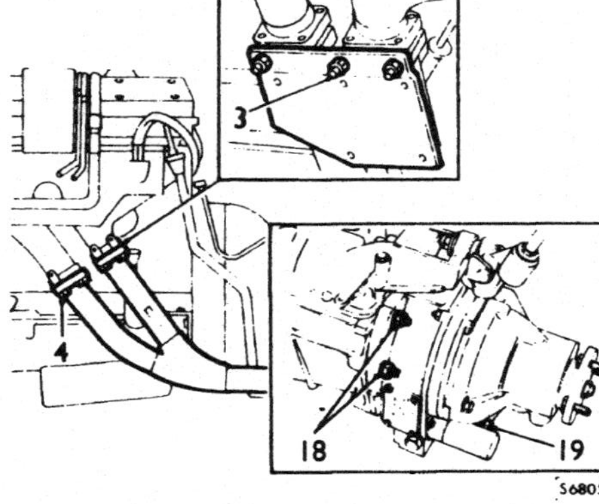

OVERDRIVE UNIT

Remove and refit 40.20.07

Service tool: Engine support bracket MS.53(A), Dummy drive shaft L.185A.

Removing
1 Disconnect battery – 86.15.20.
2 Drain gearbox oil.
3 Remove three 2 BA nuts retaining steering pinion heat-shield – left hand drive cars only.
4 Remove eight nuts securing exhaust front pipe to exhaust manifold.
5 Support rear of engine using engine support bracket MS.53(A).
6 Remove self tapping screw securing intermediate heat shield.
7 Support rear engine mounting with jack and remove four special bolts, plain and spring washers and spacers securing engine mounting bracket to body and base plate.

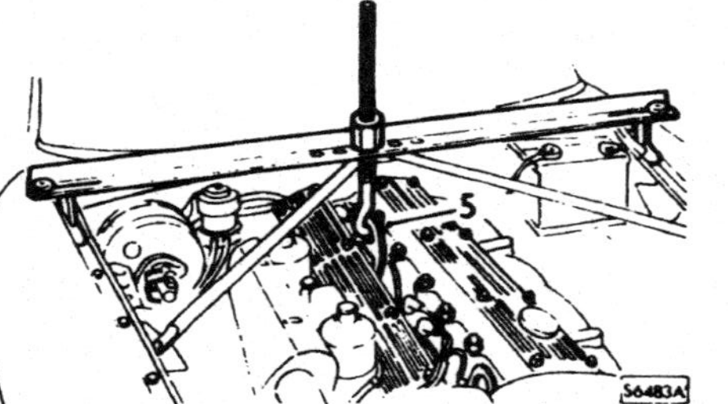

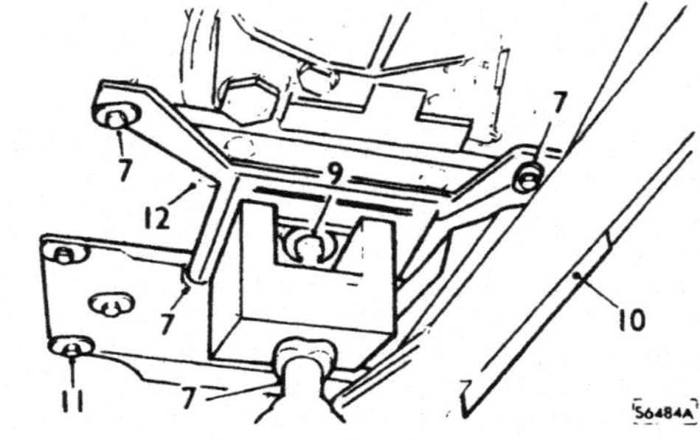

8 Slowly lower jack to release spring tension.
9 Remove nut and washers securing centre bolt of rear engine mounting and recover springs, plain washers and rubber rings.
10 Remove self tapping screw securing rear heat shield to engine mounting base plate.
11 Remove eight setscrews, spring and special washers securing mounting base plate to body.
12 Disconnect speedometer angle drive from overdrive unit.
13 Remove nuts securing propeller shaft drive flange to overdrive unit.
14 Support rear of engine using chains or jack.
15 Slacken hook bolt of engine support bracket MS.53(A).
CAUTION: Engine must not be allowed to rest on steering rack or on air conditioning unit expansion valve (if fitted).
16 Carefully lower rear of engine as far as possible without allowing it to rest on steering rack. Observe air conditioning system expansion valve (if fitted) throughout this operation. Ensure clutch supply flexible hose is not stretched or kinked.
17 Separate electrical connector to overdrive solenoid.
18 Remove four nuts and spring washers securing overdrive unit to gearbox adaptor plate.
19 Remove lower two nuts and spring washers securing overdrive unit rear casing to gearbox adaptor plate long studs.

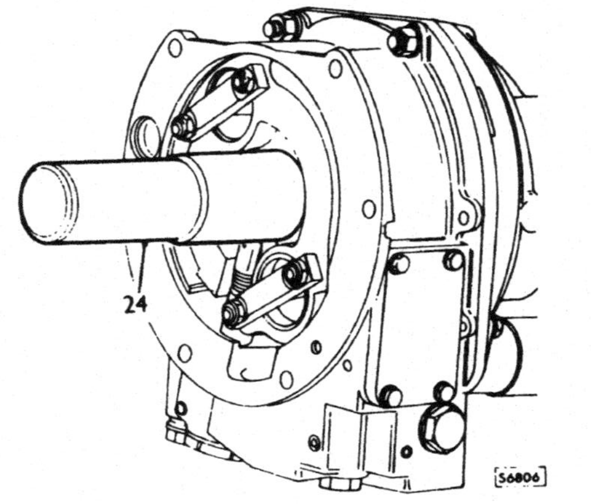

WARNING: OVERDRIVE UNIT IS HEAVY.

20 Carefully slide overdrive unit rearwards from long studs and gearbox output shaft splines.
21 Recover overdrive unit oil pump driving cam from gearbox output shaft.
22 Clean all traces of old gasket from mating faces of overdrive unit and adaptor plate.

Refitting

23 Engage 1st gear on gearbox. Do not turn gearbox again until overdrive in position.
24 Ensure internal splines of overdrive unit are lined up using dummy drive shaft L.185A. **DO NOT** move overdrive output flange after dummy drive shaft has been withdrawn.
25 **Fit oil pump drive cam to gearbox output shaft** so that lobe of cam is uppermost.
26 Check condition of spring ring on gearbox output shaft splines. Ring must not protrude above splines.
27 Fit new paper gasket to overdrive unit front flange, after lightly coating both sides of gasket with suitable sealing compound.

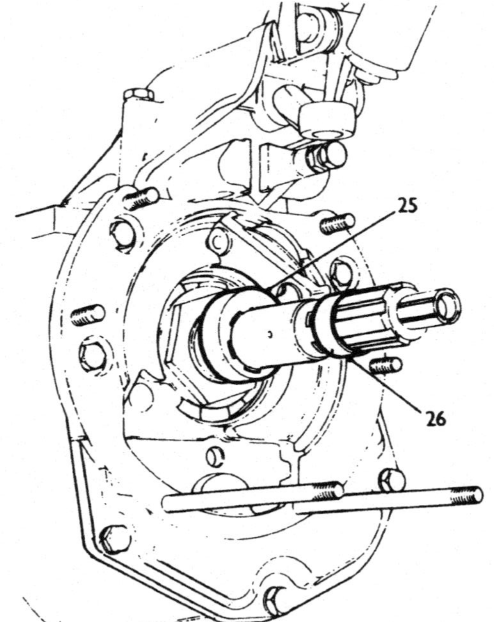

28 Offer overdrive unit onto gearbox output shaft and long studs, and **carefully** slide forward until flanges mate up. **NOTE: If overdrive unit front flange will not meet adaptor plate by approximately 5/8 in. (16 mm.) DO NOT FORCE UNIT FURTHER** as splines have become misaligned. Overdrive unit must be removed, splines realigned using a long screwdriver, dummy mainshaft inserted to confirm and overdrive unit again offered up until flanges mate correctly.
29 Reverse operations 1 to 19, inclusive, to complete re-assembly.

OVERDRIVE UNIT

Overhaul **40.20.10**

Service tools: Dummy drive shaft L.185A, Pump Body remover – main tool L.183A, Pump body remover adaptor L.183A-2, Pump barrel remover L.183-3, Unidirectional clutch assembly ring L.178, Annulus bearing replacer L.303, Accumulator piston replacer L.304, Pump non-return valve key L.213.

1 Remove overdrive unit – 40.20.07.

Dismantling

CAUTION: Scrupulous cleanliness must be maintained through all the following operations. Even minute particles of dust, dirt or lint from cleaning cloths may cause damage or prevent correct operation of the unit.

2 Set overdrive unit, front casing upwards, between soft jaws of vice.
3 Remove four setscrews and detach solenoid cover plate.
4 Remove two screws and carefully detach solenoid from front casing. **Undo self locking nut and remove solenoid plunger.**
5 Release four nuts retaining operating piston bridge pieces.

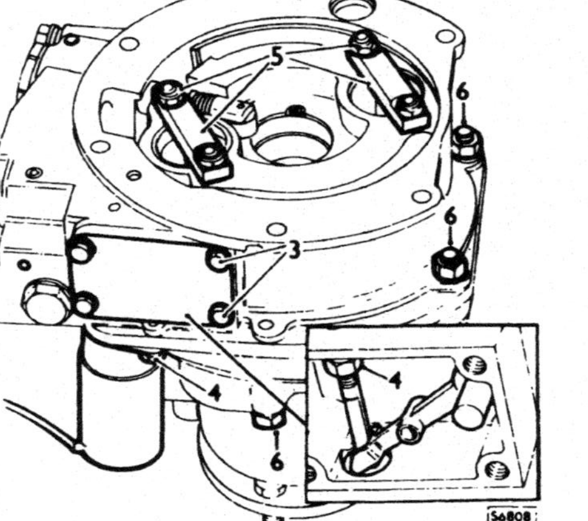

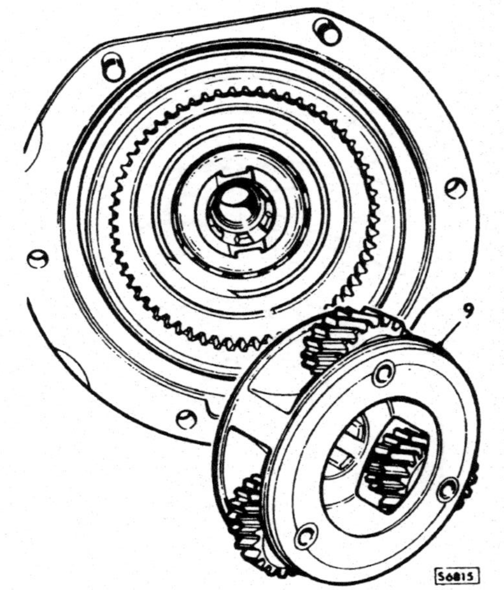

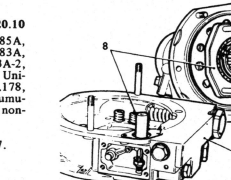

6 Remove four nuts and spring washers securing front casing to rear casing.
7 Separate two casings using hide mallet. **NOTE**: Brake ring is spigotted into both casings and may remain attached to either. Remove brake ring.
8 Lift out clutch sliding member complete with thrust ring, bearing and sun wheel. Recover retaining plate and return springs.
9 Lift out planet carrier assembly.

9
S6815

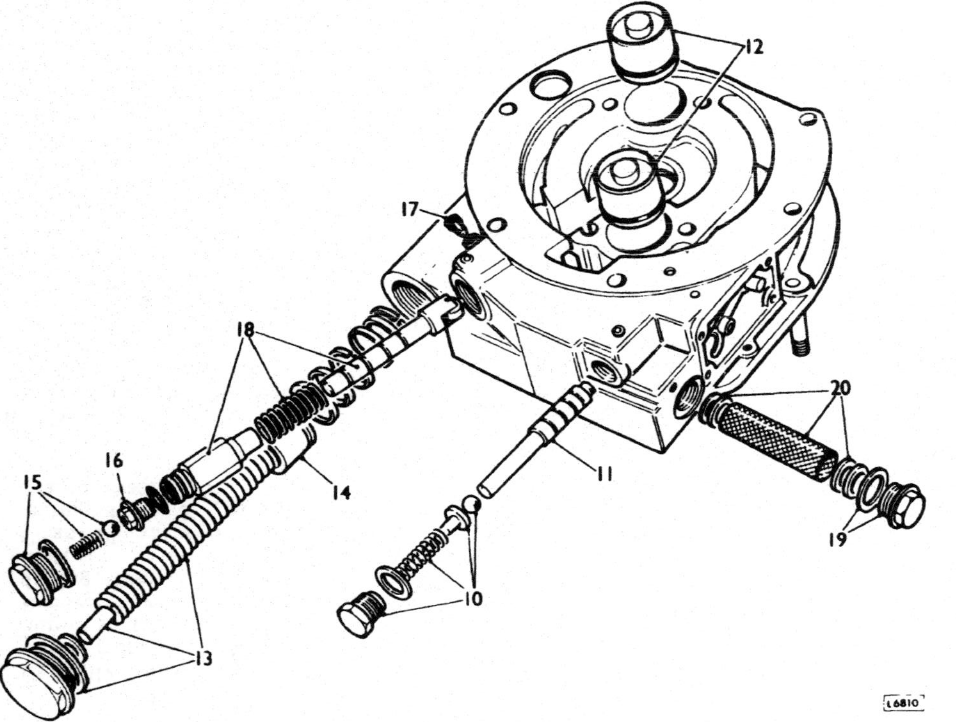

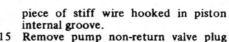

10 From front casing remove operating valve plug and washer. Recover spring, plunger and ball valve.

11 Remove operating valve using a piece of stiff wire.

12 Remove operating pistons by gripping boss in a pair of pliers and exerting a rotary pull.

13 Remove accumulator plug and washer. Plug thread is long enough to relax accumulator spring. Remove spring and spring support pin.

14 Withdraw accumulator piston using a piece of stiff wire hooked in piston internal groove.

15 Remove pump non-return valve plug and washer and recover spring and ball valve.

16 Withdraw non-return valve body using special tool L.213.

17 Remove pump locating screw.

18 Using special tools L.183A, L.183A-2 and L.183-3, withdraw oil pump body. Plunger and spring will come with pump body.

19 Unscrew oil filter plug and remove washer.

20 Withdraw four magnetic washers and cylindrical filter gauze.

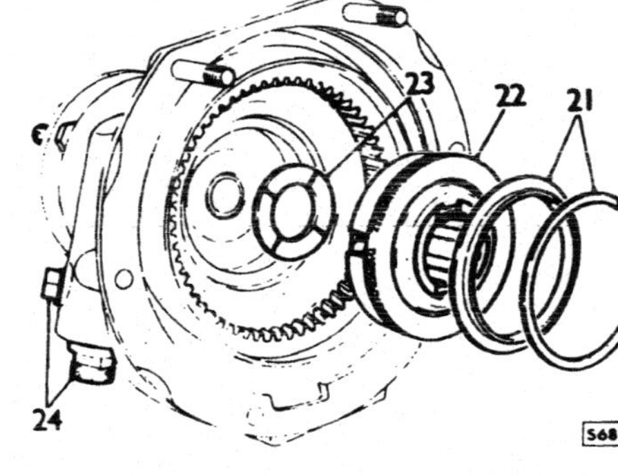

21 Remove spring ring and oil thrower from annulus.

22 Place special tool L.178 over uni-directional clutch and lift clutch assembly complete from annulus. This ensures that rollers do not fall out of cage.

23 Remove bronze thrust washer from annulus.

24 Remove speedometer drive pinion bush dowel screw and withdraw bush and pinion.

25 Remove split pin, castellated nut, washer and coupling flange.

26 Press annulus forward from rear casing.

27 Remove oil seal.

28 Drift out rear bearing. Recover speed-ometer drive gear and thrust button.

29 Remove circlip and drive out front bearing.

30 Remove circlip from sun wheel and withdraw corrugated washer and sliding member. Withdraw sun wheel.

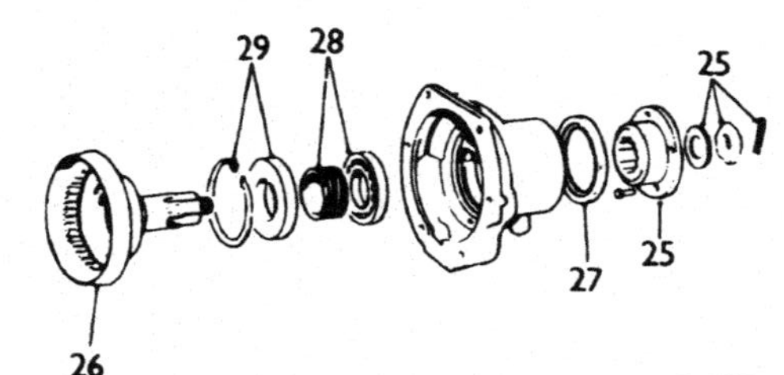

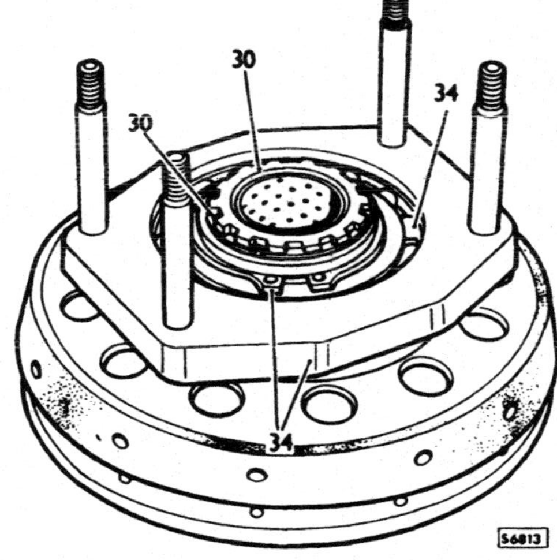

Inspection

31 Thoroughly clean and dry all components. Ensure all oil passages and jets are clear.

32 Inspect all components for damage to gear teeth, rollers, bearings and clutch faces.

33 Examine all hydraulic components for scores or signs of wear on valves, ball valves and all bores.

34 Inspect sliding member ball bearing race. Damage to this component will cause noise in direct drive. To renew bearing race remove circlip and draw thrust ring from sliding member.

35 Clutch assembly must be renewed if clutch faces are damaged or burnt.

36 Clutch return springs must be of equal length and undamaged. If necessary they must be changed as a set.

37 If sun wheel assembly bush is worn, complete assembly must be renewed; it is not possible to rebush.

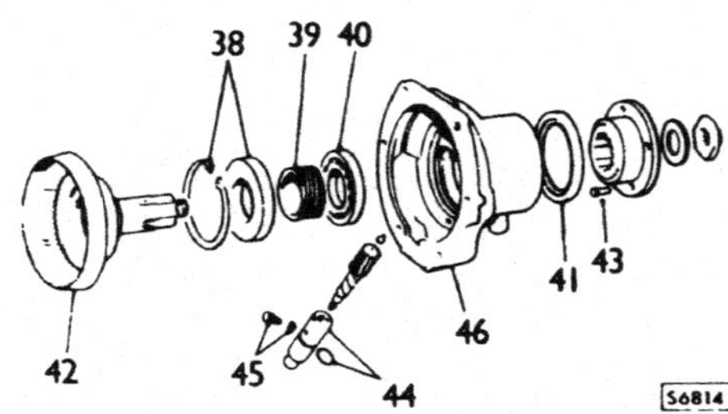

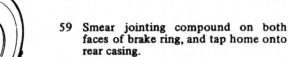

Reassembling

38 Assemble rear casing front bearing race to casing and fit circlip.
39 Ensure speedometer drive pinion thrust button is in position.
40 Enter speedometer drive gear into rear casing and press rear ball bearing race into position using tool L.303.
41 Fit oil seal.
42 Press annulus into rear casing.
43 Fit four bolts to drive flange, locate flange on annulus shaft and secure with plain washer, castellated nut and split pin.
44 Ensure 'O' ring seal on speedometer drive pinion bush is in good condition and fit pinion to bush.
45 Ensure locating holes are lined up and press bush into rear casing. Fit dowel screw and washer to retain pinion.
46 Place rear casing, drive flange downwards, between soft jaws of vice.
47 Locate bronze thrust washer, slots upwards, in centre of annulus.
48 Assemble spring into roller cage of uni-directional clutch.
49 Fit inner member into cage and engage on other end of spring.
NOTE: Engage slots of inner member with tongues of roller cage so that when rollers are fitted they will be propelled up the inclined faces of inner member ramps. Cage is loaded anti-clockwise when viewed from front (cage) end.

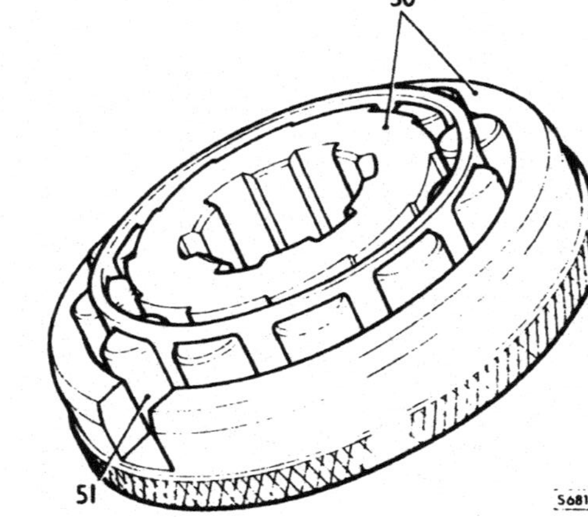

50 Place assembly in special tool L.178 front face downwards.
51 Fit rollers through slot in tool, turning clutch clockwise until all rollers are in place.
52 Pick up tool and assembled clutch complete, and locate in annulus. Remove tool.
53 Fit oil thrower and spring ring.

WARNING: IT IS MOST IMPORTANT THAT THE FOLLOWING OPERATION IS FOLLOWED EXACTLY.

54 Turn each gear of the planet carrier assembly until a dot marked on one tooth of the larger gear is radially outwards.
55 Insert sunwheel assembly to mesh with gears, ensuring that dots remain in the same position. Insert sunwheel and planet carrier assembly into annulus.
56 If necessary, press thrust bearing into thrust ring and press this assembly onto clutch sliding member. Retain by fitting circlip to hub of sliding member.
57 Slide this assembly onto sunwheel assembly splines until inner clutch surface of sliding member contacts annulus. Retain using corrugated washer and circlip on sunwheel.
58 Fit retaining plate over bolts of thrust ring bearing assembly.

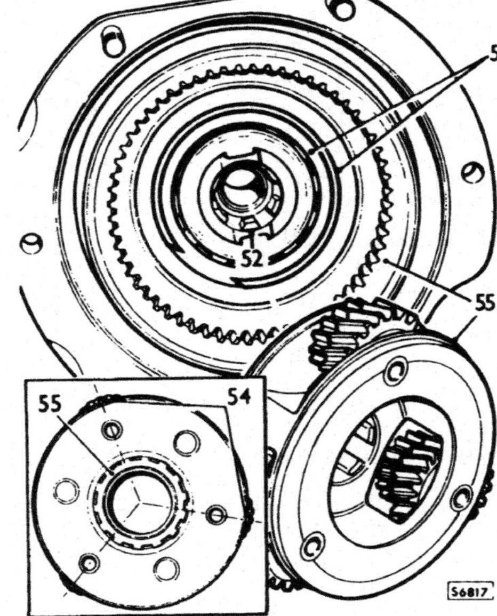
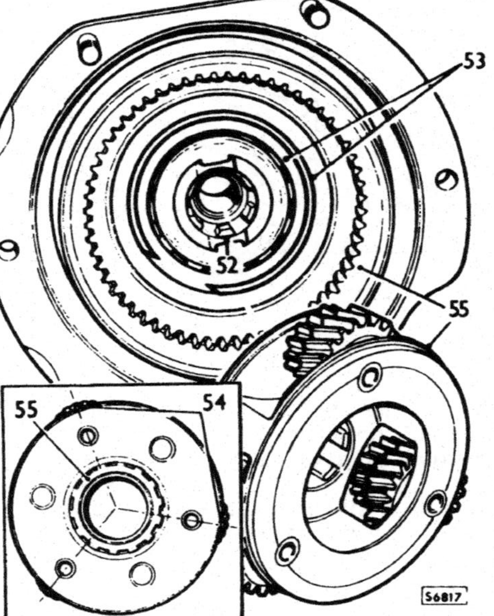
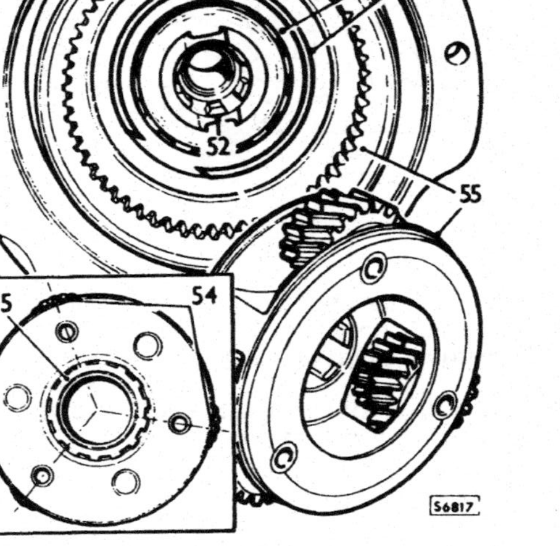

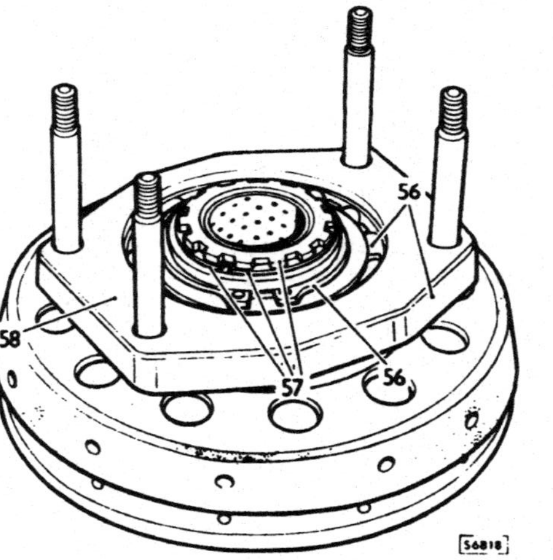
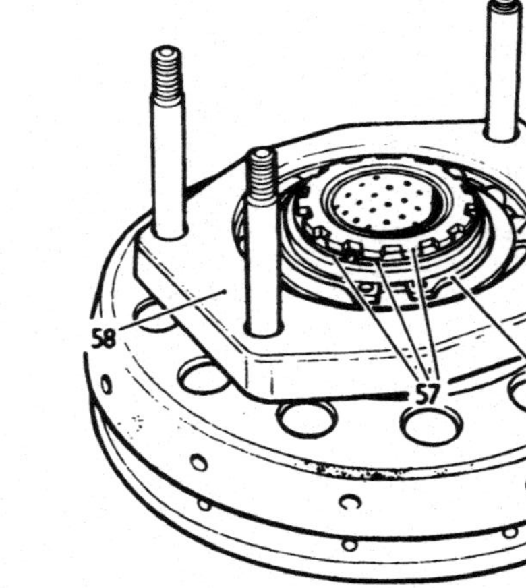

59 Smear jointing compound on both faces of brake ring, and tap home onto rear casing.
60 Offer front casing into position and rotate thrust ring until bolts line up with four holes. Remove front casing.
61 Using blob of grease, retain clutch springs in front casing. Offer front casing onto brake ring so that four bolts pass through holes without binding.

62 Fit four nuts and spring washers to studs at rear casing. Progressively tighten nuts to compress clutch springs.
63 Fit operating pistons, boss outwards, in operating cylinders, taking great care not to damage 'O' ring seals.
64 Fit bridge pieces to thrust ring bolts and retain using new self locking nuts.
65 Fit gasket to solenoid and locate plunger in fork of operating lever. Secure solenoid using two setscrews and washers.
66 Ensure rings of accumulator piston are in good condition, and fit piston to front casing using Service tool L.304.
67 Fit spring, spring support and any packing removed, retain with plug and washer.
NOTE: Ensure washer correctly located before tightening plug.
68 Fit oil pump and non-return valve. Fit plug and washer on ball and spring.
69 Fit operating valve, ball valve plunger and spring and retain with plug and washer.
70 Locate magnetic rings in front casing and oil filter plug and fit cylindrical filter gauze.
71 Adjust solenoid – 40.22.01.
72 Refit overdrive unit to gearbox.

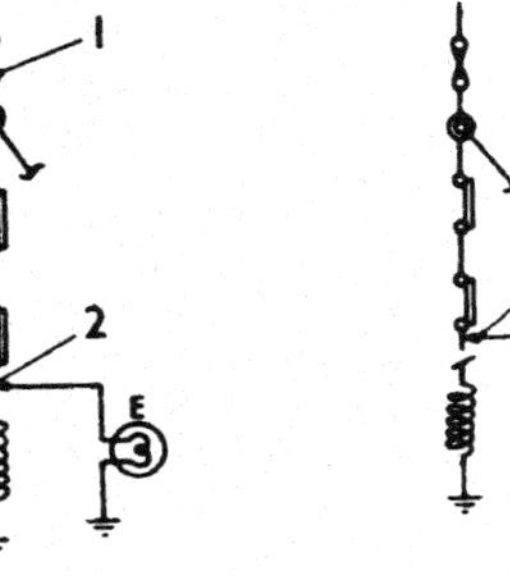

A. Fuse No. 6 main block.
B. Gearbox isolator switch.
C. Gear lever overdrive switch.
D. Overdrive solenoid.
E. Test lamp.

SOLENOID

Test and adjust 40.22.01

Test: If it is suspected that the solenoid is not operating, proceed as follows:

NOTE: As many operational failures are due to corroded terminals and faulty wiring, wiring and connections should be checked first.
Good earth connections are essential on all earthed components. This applies particularly to the solenoid because of the heavy current passed momentarily each time the overdrive is engaged. Incorrect adjustment of the solenoid, resulting in the failure of the main winding contacts to open, may cause damage to the solenoid. Select top gear and switch on ignition before commencing tests.

Test

1 Check that fuse has not blown (this fuse is located No. 6 on the main fuse block). Replace with an 8 amp fuse if necessary.
2 If fuse has not blown, check that current is available at solenoid. Partly disconnect cable at solenoid junction and connect a test lamp in parallel. Switch on overdrive. If current is available as indicated by test bulb illumination, renew solenoid unit – 44.22.05.
3 If current is not available, reconnect solenoid and prise overdrive switch from gear lever.
4 Pull yellow cable from switch and connect test lamp between switch terminal and a good earth. Operate switch to ensure voltage present.
5 If voltage is not present, detach green/yellow cable and use test lamp to check voltage on cable. If voltage present, renew gear lever switch – 40.24.01.
6 If voltage not present on green/yellow cable, check and if necessary renew isolator switch on gearbox – 40.24.04.
7 Position gear lever in neutral and switch off ignition.

Adjust

1 Beneath car, remove rectangular cover plate, secured by four setscrews and spring washers.
2 Move solenoid lever to right until a 3/16 in. dia. (4,76 mm.) pin pushed through hole in lever engages in hole in casing.

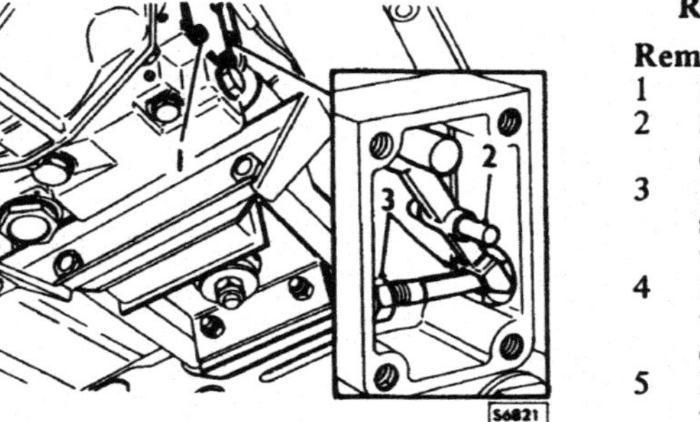

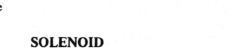

3 Screw nut on plunger until a point is reached where plunger is pushed right home in solenoid and nut just contacts fork of lever.
4 Remove pin.
5 Connect 0-30 ampere ammeter in series with solenoid supply cable and energise solenoid.
6 Current consumption should be 1 ampere.

NOTE: If current consumption is between 15 and 20 amperes, the plunger is not moving far enough to isolate operating coil. Repeat operations 2 and 3 until a satisfactory result is obtained. **This is important as high current will cause solenoid failure.**

7 Refit rectangular cover on new gasket and secure using four setscrews and spring washers.

SOLENOID

Remove, refit and adjust lever 40.22.05

Remove

1 Disconnect battery – 86.15.20.
2 Separate in-line connector in solenoid cable.
3 Remove rectangular cover plate secured by four setscrews and spring washers.
4 Remove two setscrews and spring washers and draw solenoid from overdrive unit.
5 If necessary, restrain plunger and remove locknut.

Refitting
6 Offer plunger into solenoid hole and fit locknut on opposite side of lever fork.
7 Assemble solenoid, on new gasket, to overdrive unit front case, and secure with two setscrews and spring washers.
8 Connect in-line connector to supply cable.
9 Move solenoid lever to right until a 3/16 in. dia. (4,76 mm.) pin pushed through hole in lever engaged in hole in casing.
10 Screw nut on plunger until a point is reached where plunger is pushed right home in solenoid and nut just contacts fork of lever.
11 Remove pin.
12 Connect 0-30 ampere ammeter in series with solenoid supply cable, and energise solenoid.
13 Current consumption should be 1 ampere.
NOTE: If current consumption is between 15 and 20 amperes, the plunger is not moving far enough to isolate operating coil. Repeat operations 2 and 3 until a satisfactory result is obtained. This is important as high current will cause solenoid failure. Remove ammeter and secure connector.
14 Refit rectangular cover on new gasket and secure using four setscrews and spring washers.

SELECTOR SWITCH

Remove and refit **40.24.01**

Removing
1 Disconnect battery – 86.15.20.
2 Carefully prise knob cover from top of gear selector lever.

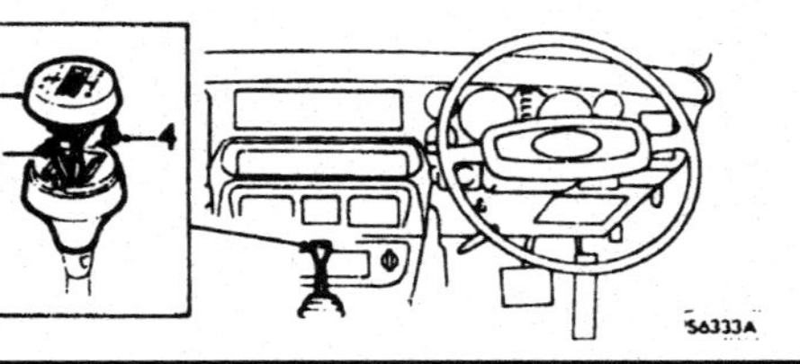

3 Disconnect switch.
4 Remove two screws and detach switch from knob cover.

Refitting
Reverse operations 1 to 4.

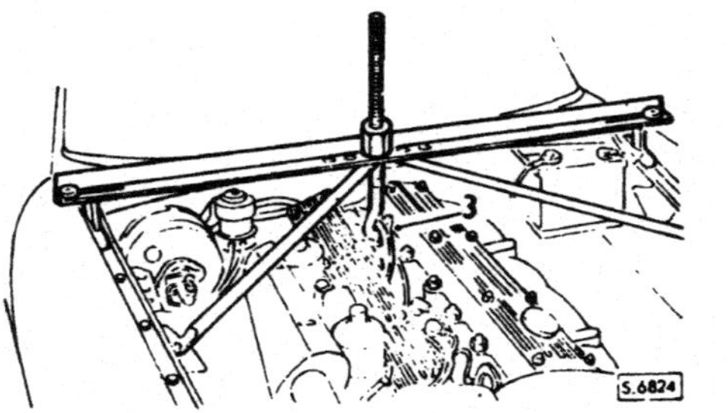

ISOLATOR SWITCH

Remove and refit **40.24.04**

Service tool: Engine support bracket MS.53(A).

Removing
1 Disconnect battery – 86.15.20.
2 Remove transmission tunnel cover – 76.25.07.
3 Locate engine support bracket MS.53(A) across rear of engine and secure to lifting eye.
4 Remove four special screws securing rear engine mounting bracket.

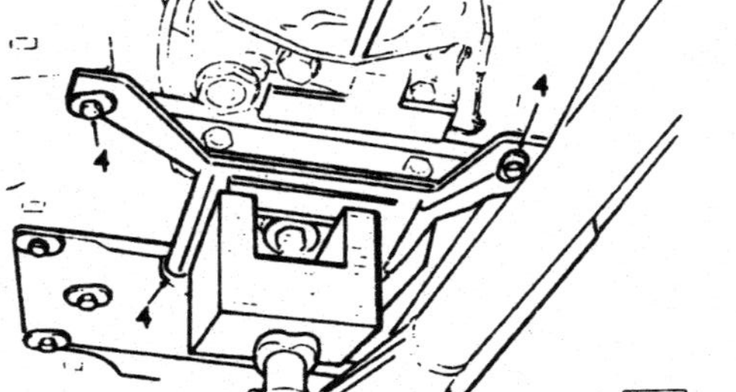

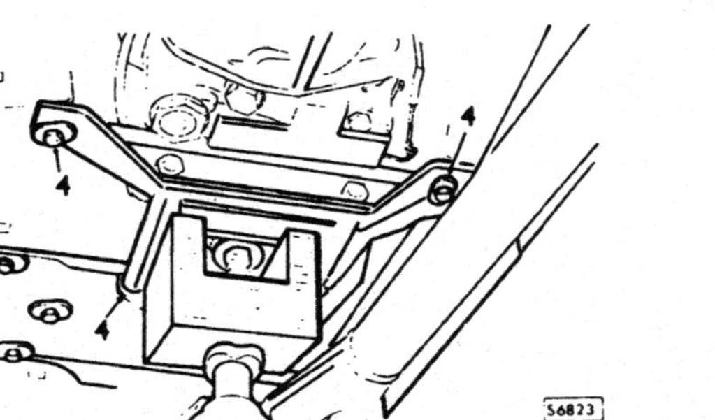

5 Carefully lower rear of engine 1-2 inches (25 to 50 mm.).
6 Draw insulation material up from either side of gearbox and from gear lever.
7 Release cables from switch at front left hand side of gearbox.
8 Unscrew switch from gearbox. Retain gasket washers.

Refitting
NOTE: Switch must be adjusted until contacts are open when gear lever is in neutral and close immediately gear lever is pressed towards top gear.
9 Screw replacement switch into top cover of gearbox on washers removed in operation 8.
10 Connect a continuity meter between switch terminals.
11 Place gear lever in neutral, meter should show open circuit (very high resistance).
12 Press gear lever towards top gear, meter should indicate short circuit **immediately** gear lever moves.
13 Add or remove washers to achieve the requirements of operations 11 and 12.
NOTE: Removing washers brings changeover point forward.
14 Disconnect continuity meter.
15 Reverse operations 1 to 7 inclusive.

Notes

BORG-WARNER MODEL 12 AUTOMATIC TRANSMISSION (Fitted to Early Cars Only)

DESCRIPTION

TORQUE CONVERTER

The torque converter is of the three element, single phase type. The three elements are: Impeller, connected to the engine crankshaft; Turbine, connected to the gearbox input shaft, and Stator, mounted on a one-way clutch on the stator support projecting from the gearbox case. The converter provides torque multiplication of from 1:1 to 2:1 and the speed range during which this multiplication is obtained varies with the accelerator position.

Torque converter – principle of operation

GEAR SET

The planetary gear set consists of two sun gears, two sets of pinions, a pinion carrier and a ring gear.
Power enters the gear set via the two sun gears, the forward sun gear driving in forward gears, the reverse sun gear driving in reverse gear. The ring gear, attached to the output shaft, is the driven gear. The planet wheels connect driving and driven gears, two sets of planet wheels being used in forward gears and one set in reverse.
The planet carrier locates the planet wheels relative to sun and ring gears, also serving as a reaction member.

CLUTCHES

The gearbox input shaft is connected to the torque converter turbine at the front end and is therefore known as the turbine shaft. The rear end of the shaft is connected to the front and rear clutches, (the clutches are of the multi disc type operated by hydraulic pressure). Engagement of the front clutch connects the turbine shaft to the forward sun gear. Engagement of the rear clutch connects the turbine shaft to the reverse sun gear.

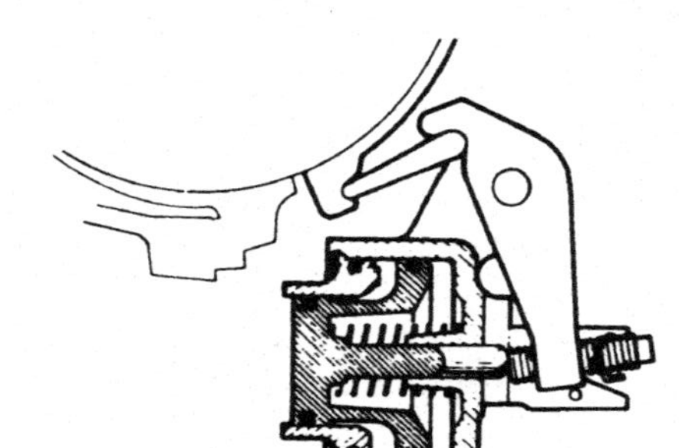

Front servo operation

Rear servo operation

BRAKE BANDS

The brake bands operated by hydraulic servos, are used to hold drive train components stationary in order to obtain low, intermediate and reverse gears. The front band is clamped around the rear clutch outer drum to hold the reverse sun gear stationary. The rear band is clamped around the planet carrier to hold the planet carrier stationary.

ONE WAY CLUTCH

The "one-way" clutch is situated between the planet carrier and the gearbox case. Rotation of the planet carrier against engine direction is prevented so providing the reaction member for low gear (drive). Rotation of the planet carrier in engine direction is allowed (free-wheeling) providing smooth changes from low to intermediate and intermediate to low gears.

MECHANICAL POWER FLOWS

Neutral and Park

In neutral the front and rear clutches are off, and no power is transmitted from the converter to the gear set. The front and rear bands are also released. In 'P' the Rear Servo circuit is pressurised while the engine is running, so that the rear band is applied.

First Gear ('D' selected)

The front clutch is applied, connecting the converter to the forward sun gear. The one-way clutch is in operation, preventing the planet carrier from rotating anti-clockwise. When the vehicle is coasting the one-way clutch over-runs and the gear set freewheels.

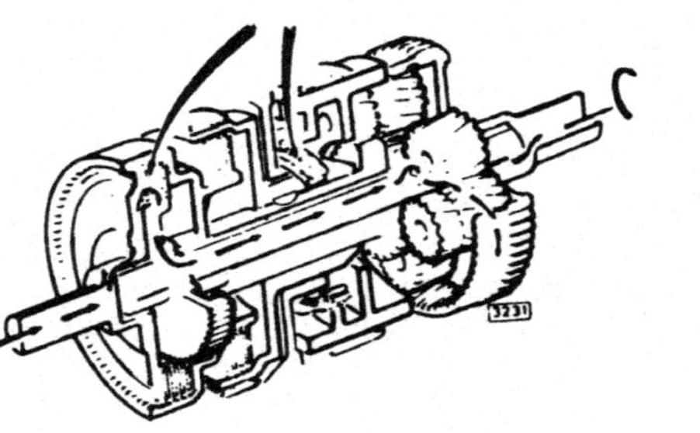

'D' selected; first gear

First Gear ('1' selected)

The front clutch is applied, connecting the converter to the forward sun gear. The rear band is applied, holding the planet carrier stationary. The reverse sun gear rotates freely in the opposite direction to the forward sun gear.

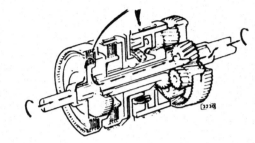

'1' selected; first gear

Second Gear ('2' or 'D' selected)

Again the front clutch is applied, connecting the converter to the forward sun gear. The front band is applied, holding the reverse sun gear stationary.

'2' or 'D' selected; second gear

Third Gear ('D' selected)
Again the front clutch is applied, connecting the converter to the forward sun gear. The rear clutch is applied, connecting the converter also to the reverse sun gear; thus both sun gears are locked together and the gear set rotates as a unit, providing a ratio of 1 : 1.

'D' selected; third gear

Reverse Gear ('R' selected)
The rear clutch is applied, connecting the converter to the reverse sun gear. The rear band is applied, holding the planet carrier stationary.

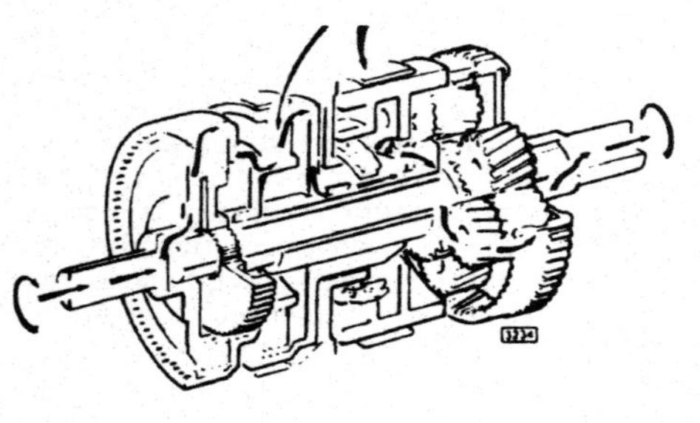

'R' selected; reverse gear

	A	B	C	D	E
1 (first gear)	●			●	
D (first gear)	●				●
2&D (sec.gr.)	●		●		
D (third gear)	●	●			
R (rev.gear)		●		●	

4610A

Clutch and band application chart

A Front Clutch
B Rear Clutch
C Front Band
D Rear Band
E One Way Clutch

GENERAL DATA

Gear Train End Float .... 0.008 to 0.44 in. (0,20 to 1,12 mm.)
Pinion End Float .... 0.010 to 0.020 in. (0,25 to 0,51 mm.)
Minimum Rear Clutch Plate Coning .... 0.010 in. (0,25 mm.)
One Way Clutch Spring to Lever Clearance .... 0.125 to 0.188 in. (3,2 to 4,8 mm.)
Thrust Washer Sizes .... 0.061 to 0.063 in. (1,55 to 1,60 mm.)
0.067 to 0.069 in. (1,70 to 1,75 mm.)
0.074 to 0.076 in. (1,88 to 1,93 mm.)
0.081 to 0.083 in. (2,08 to 2,11 mm.)
0.092 to 0.094 in. (2,34 to 2,39 mm.)
0.105 to 0.107 in. (2,67 to 2,72 mm.)
Control Pressure at 9 to 10 in. (23 to 25 cm) Hg ... $75 {}^{+20}_{-5}$ lb./in.^{2} ($5{,}27 {}^{+1{,}40}_{-0{,}35}$ kg./cm^2)
Stall speed (Normal) .... 1,600 to 1,700 r.p.m.

GEAR CHANGE SPEEDS

3.31 : 1 axle ratio

Throttle position		Upshifts 1 to 2	Upshifts 2 to 3	Downshifts 3 to 2	Downshifts 2 to 1
Minimum	M.P.H.	6 to 10	14 to 18		
Full	M.P.H.	39 to 45	73 to 82		
Full throttle Kickdown	M.P.H.			63 to 73	13 to 17
Zero	M.P.H.				7 to 17
Part	M.P.H.			20 to 26 max.	
Minimum	K.P.H.	9 to 16	22 to 29		
Full	K.P.H.	62 to 72	117 to 132		
Full throttle Kickdown	K.P.H.			101 to 117	21 to 27
Zero	K.P.H.				11 to 27
Part	K.P.H.			32 to 42 max.	

3.07 : 1 axle ratio

Throttle position		Upshifts 1 to 2	Upshifts 2 to 3	Downshifts 3 to 2	Downshifts 2 to 1
Minimum	M.P.H.	7 to 11	16 to 20		
Full	M.P.H.	45 to 51	85 to 94		
Full throttle Kickdown	M.P.H.			73 to 83	15 to 19
Zero	M.P.H.				9 to 19
Part	M.P.H.			23 to 29 max.	
Minimum	K.P.H.	11 to 18	25 to 32		
Full	K.P.H.	72 to 82	136 to 151		
Full throttle Kickdown	K.P.H.			117 to 133	24 to 30
Zero	K.P.H.				14 to 30
Part	K.P.H.			37 to 47 max.	

NOTE: The figures in this table are theoretical and actual figures may vary slightly from those quoted due to such factors as tyre wear, pressures etc.

The following spring-identification table is given to assist in identifying valve springs when overhaul work is being carried out. When valve block is dismantled, springs should be compared with dimensions given. Any spring which is distorted or coil bound MUST be replaced.

DESCRIPTION	LENGTH	DIAMETER	NUMBER OF COILS	COLOUR
Primary regulator valve	2.032 in. (51,6 mm)	.740 – .750 in. (18,8 – 19,0 mm)	9	Orange
Primary regulator valve (inner)	1.557 in. (39,6 mm)	.640 – .650 in. (16,3 – 16,5 mm)	6	Plain
Throttle modulator valve	1.338 in. (34,0 mm)	.463 – .473 in. (11,7 – 12,1 mm)	9	Red
Secondary regulator valve	1.000 in. (25,4 mm)	.228 – .238 in. (5,7 – 6,0 mm)	15	Orange
Modulator valve (governor)	1.310 in. (33,3 mm)	.458 in. (11,6 mm)	11	Plain
Orifice control and throttle valve	.686 in. (17,4 mm)	.175 – 185 in. (4,4 – 4,6 mm)	12	Pink
Downshift valve	.812 in. (20,6 mm)	.178 – 1.88 in. (4,5 – 4,7 mm)	17	Plain
Governor safety valve	.638 in. (16,2 mm)	.220 – .240 in. (5,6 – 6,1 mm)	10	Yellow
1–2 Shift valve	1.781 in. (45,2 mm)	.627 in. (15,9 mm)	6	Light green
2–3 Shift valve (inner)	1.352 in. (34,4 mm)	.280 – .290 in. (7,1 – 7,4 mm)	14	Plain
2–3 Shift valve (outer)	1.31 in. (33,3 mm)	.440 – .450 in. (11,1 – 11,4 mm)	9	Plain
Servo regulator valve	1,730 in. (44,0 mm)	.580 – .590 in. (14,7 – 15,0 mm)	9	Plain
Manual valve detent	1.667 in. (42,2 mm)	.357 – .367 in. (9,1 – 9,3 mm)	17	Plain

KEY TO COMPONENTS SHOWN ON HYDRAULIC CHARTS

A Torque Converter
B Pump
C Front Clutch
D Rear Clutch
E One-Way Clutch
F Front Servo
G Rear Servo
H Primary Regulator
J Secondary Regulator
K Downshift Valve
L Throttle Valve
M Manual Valve
N Throttle Modulator Valve
P Orifice Control Valve
Q 2-3 Shift Valve
R 1-2 Shift Valve
S Servo Regulator Timer
T Throttle Modulator Cut-Back Valve
U Governor Modulator Valve
V Servo Regulator
W Governor

KEY TO HYDRAULIC CHART CODE

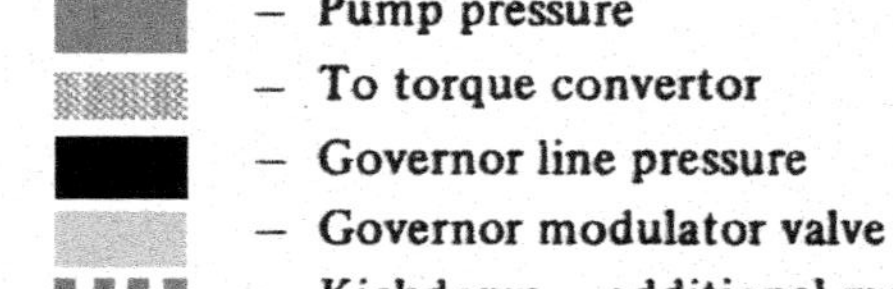

– Pump pressure
– To torque convertor
– Governor line pressure
– Governor modulator valve
– Kickdown – additional modulator throttle pressure.

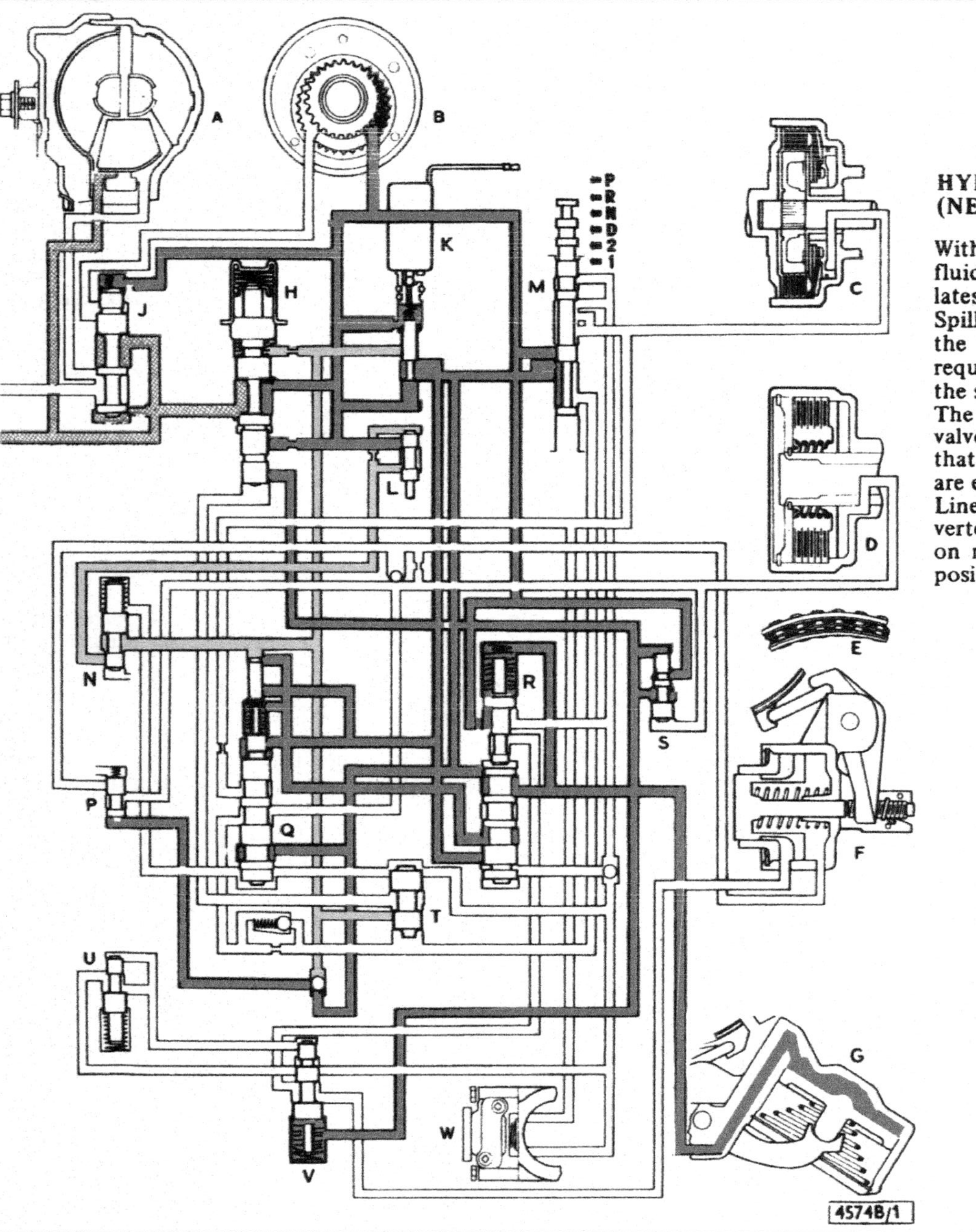

HYDRAULIC OPERATION IN 'N' (NEUTRAL)

With the engine running, the pump supplies fluid to the primary regulator which regulates line pressure.
Spill from the primary regulator supplies the torque converter and lubrication requirements. This supply is regulated by the seondary regulator.
The line pressure supplied to the manual valve is blocked by a land on the valve so that neither governor, clutches nor servos are energised.
Line pressure at the throttle valve is converted to throttle pressure, dependent on manifold depression, i.e. throttle pedal position.

HYDRAULIC OPERATION IN 'P' (PARK)

Coupled to the manual valve operating lever is a linkage incorporating a pawl; movement of this lever to the 'Park' position engages the pawl with the toothed outer surface of the ring gear, so locking the output shaft to the transmission case. The rear servo is energised in 'P' selection but, as both the front and rear clutches are not energised, drive is impossible and the transmission remains inoperative.

KEY TO HYDRAULIC CHART CODE

- Pump pressure
- To torque convertor
- Governor line pressure
- Governor modulator valve
- Kickdown – additional modulator throttle pressure.

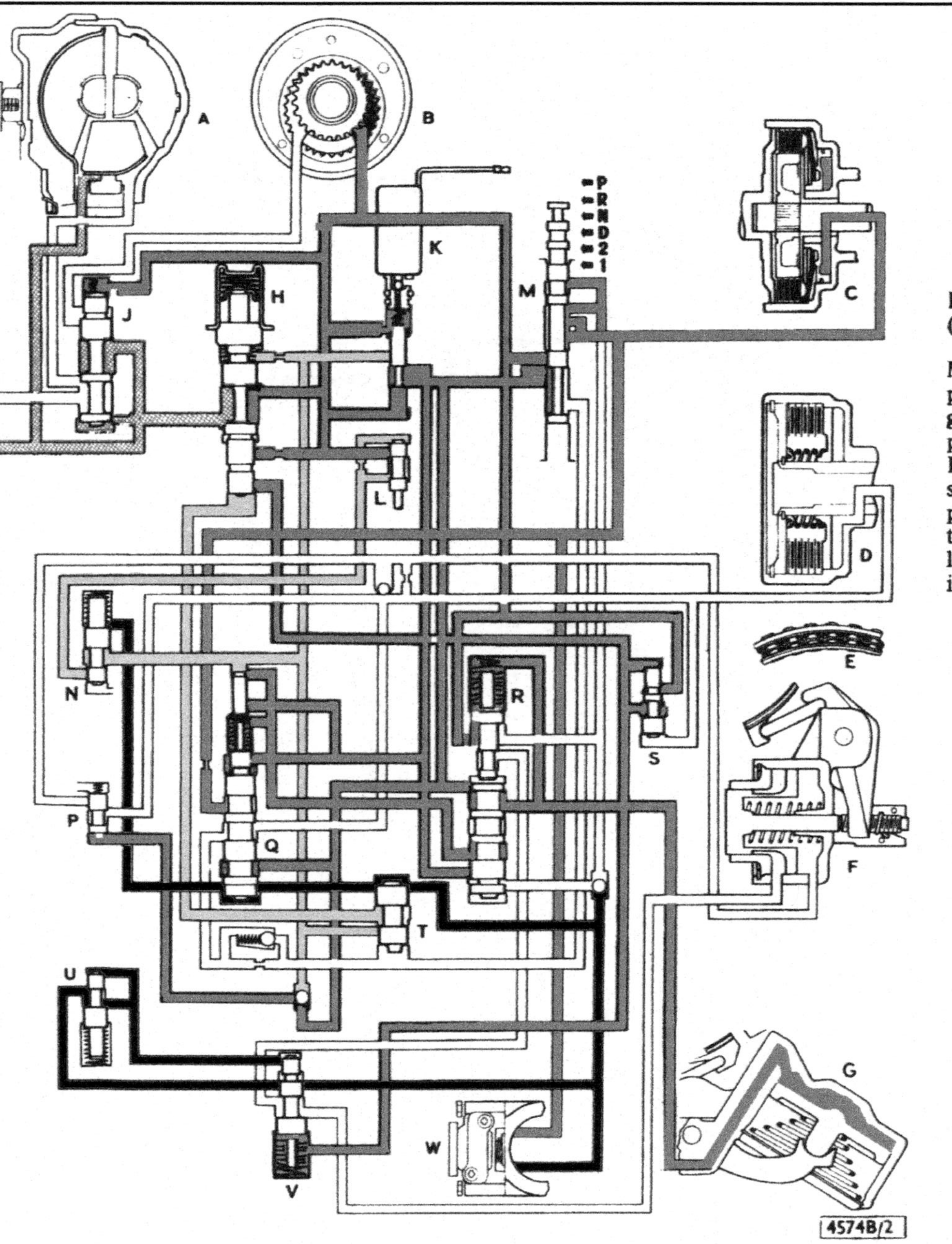

HYDRAULIC OPERATION IN 'D' (FIRST GEAR)

Movement of the manual valve to the 'D' position opens the front clutch and governor to line pressure. No other component is required to engage first gear.
Line pressure is supplied to the top of the secondary regulator to control converter pressure. Throttle pressure is applied to the top and bottom of the primary regulator to modulate line pressure in the interests of shift quality.

HYDRAULIC OPERATION IN '1' (FIRST GEAR)

Application of the front clutch and rear servo are required in '1' (Manual) selection. The rear band is applied to provide engine braking. Line pressure applied to the lands of the 1-2 shift valve opposes governor pressure. There is, therefore, no upshift and the transmission remains in '1' (Low) ratio.

KEY TO HYDRAULIC CHART CODE

- Pump pressure
- To torque convertor
- Governor line pressure
- Governor modulator valve
- Kickdown – additional modulator throttle pressure.

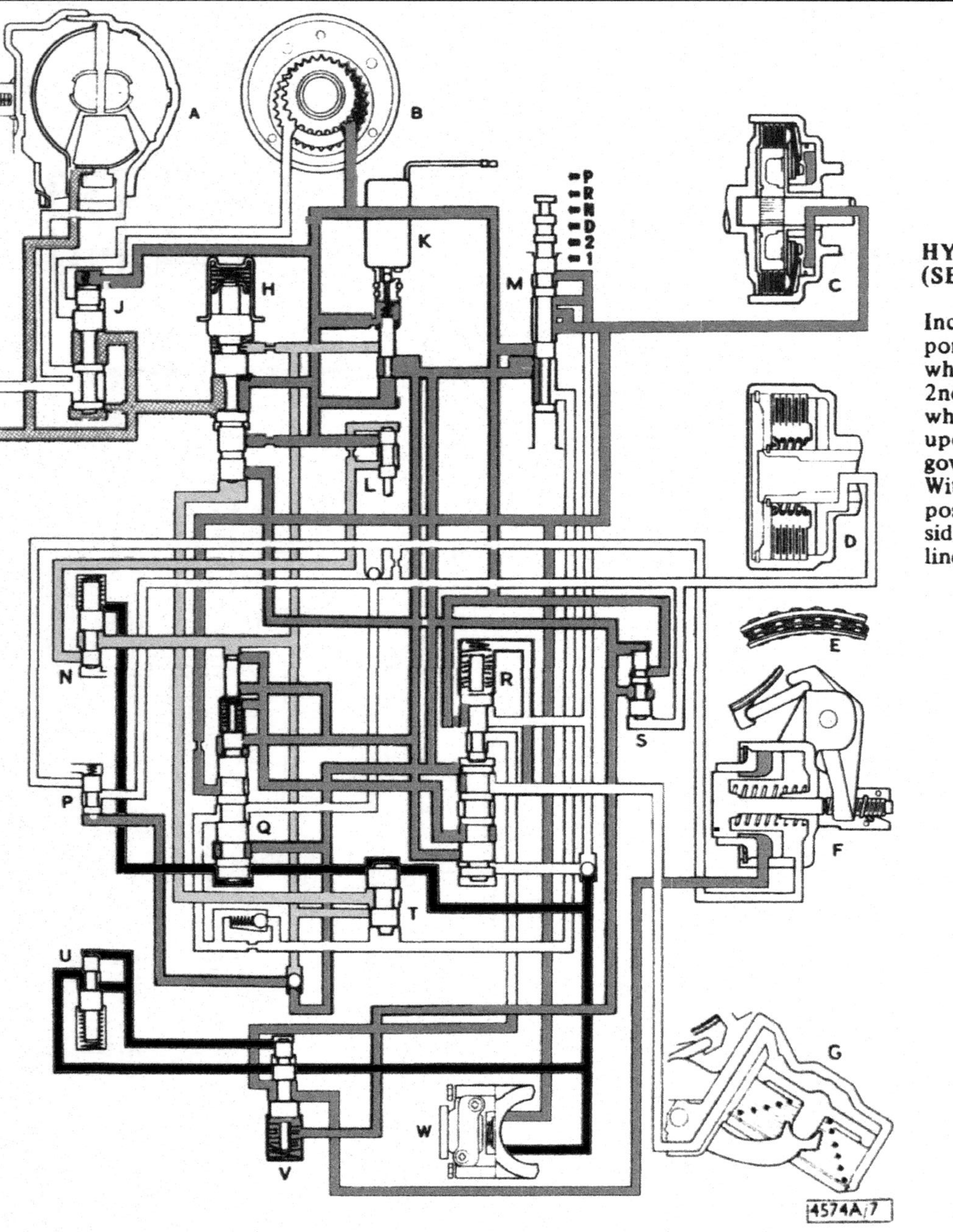

HYDRAULIC OPERATION IN 'D' (SECOND GEAR)

Increasing road speed results in a corresponding increase in governor pressure which will move the 1-2 shift valve to the 2nd gear position. The exact speed at which this change takes place is dependent upon the throttle pressure opposing governor pressure at the 1-2 shift valve.
With the 1-2 shift valve in the 2nd gear position, the line to the front servo apply side, through the servo regulator, is open to line pressure and the front band is applied.

HYDRAULIC OPERATION IN '2' (SECOND GEAR)

Once '2' (Manual) is engaged, there are n upshifts or downshifts. If either are required, a change to '1' (Manual) or 'D' must be made. Movement of the manual valve to the '2' (Manual) position allows line pressure to flow to a ball valve where it closes the governor line and introduces line pressure to the base of the 1-2 shift valve to retain it in the '2' (Intermediate) ratio.

KEY TO HYDRAULIC CHART CODE

- Pump pressure
- To torque convertor
- Governor line pressure
- Governor modulator valve
- Kickdown – additional modulator throttle pressure.

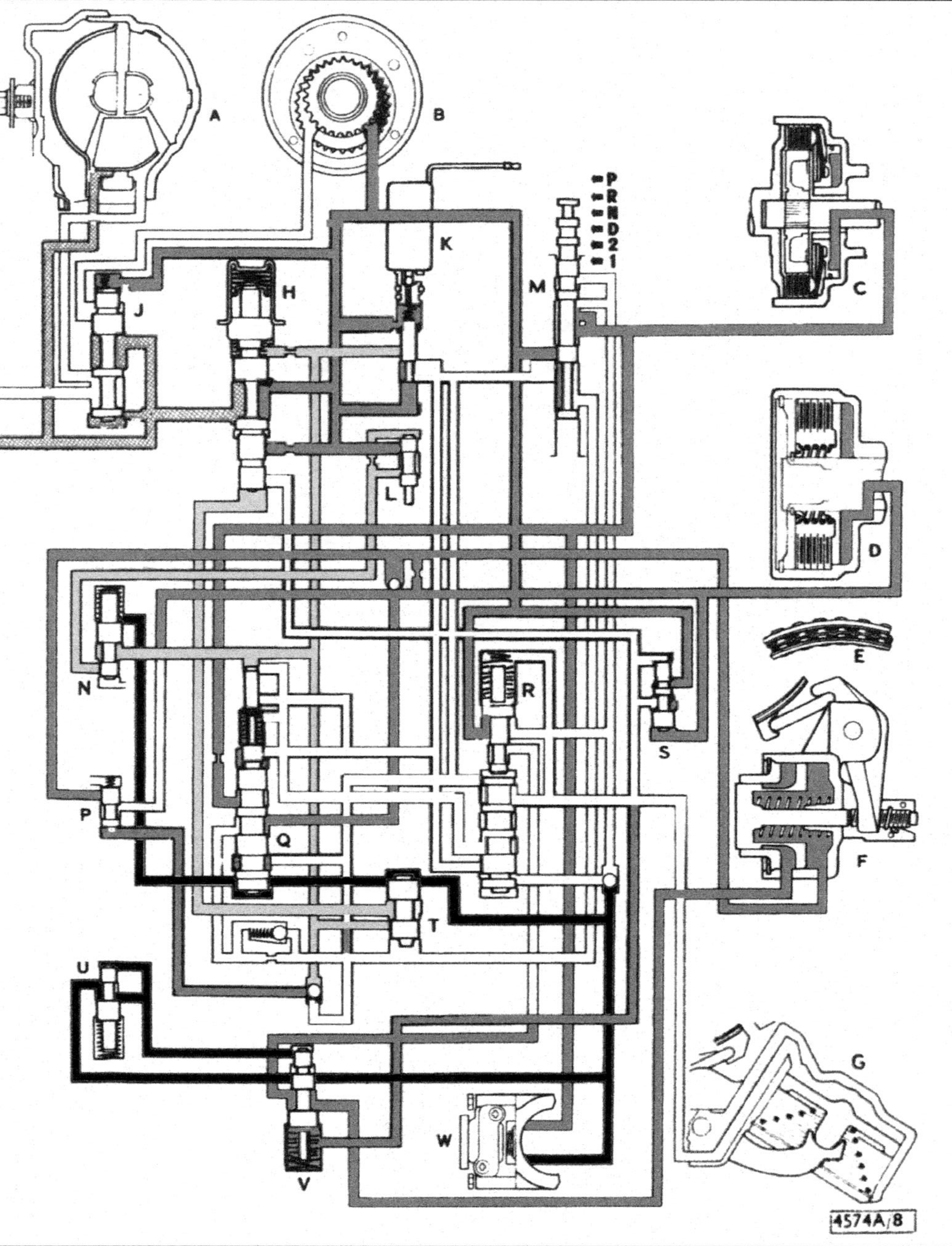

HYDRAULIC OPERATION IN 'D' (THIRD GEAR)

In order to change to third gear, the front band must be released and the rear clutch applied. With the movement of the 2-3 shift valve to the third gear position the lines to the front servo release and the rear clutch are open to line pressure.
The lines now supplied with line pressure are the front clutch, rear clutch, front servo apply and front servo release. As the front servo release has a greater area than the apply side, the front band is released, therefore the front and rear clutches remain applied.

KEY TO HYDRAULIC CHART CODE

- Pump pressure
- To torque convertor
- Governor line pressure
- Governor modulator valve
- Kickdown – additional modulator throttle pressure.

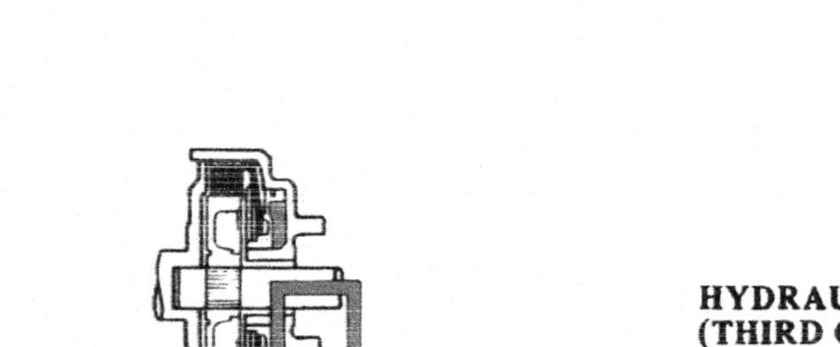

HYDRAULIC OPERATION IN 'D' (THIRD GEAR TO SECOND GEAR) KICKDOWN

Depression of the accelerator to the kick-down position actuates the kickdown switch to energise the kickdown solenoid at the valve block. With the solenoid energised, the plunger is lifted, allowing line pressure to escape past the ball valve. This sudden pressure drop allows the line pressure at the base of the downshift valve to move the valve upwards so introducing extra modulated throttle pressure to the 2-3 shift valve. This extra pressure opposing governor pressure at the 2-3 shift valve assists in overcoming governor pressure so returning the shift valve to the 2nd gear position.

KEY TO HYDRAULIC CHART CODE

- Pump pressure
- To torque convertor
- Governor line pressure
- Governor modulator valve
- Kickdown – additional modulator throttle pressure.

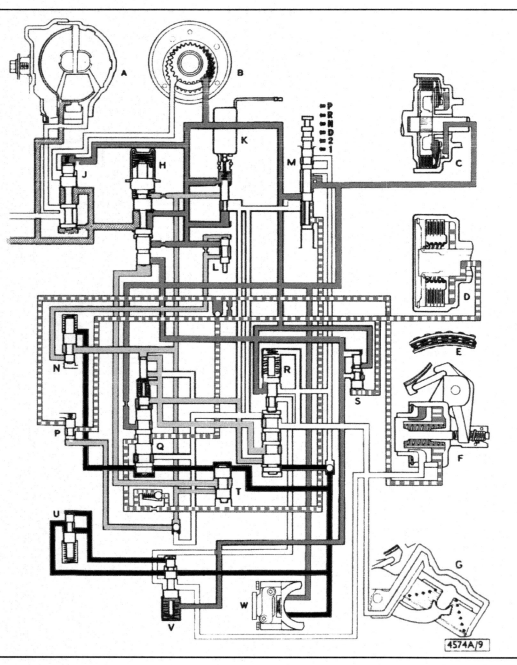

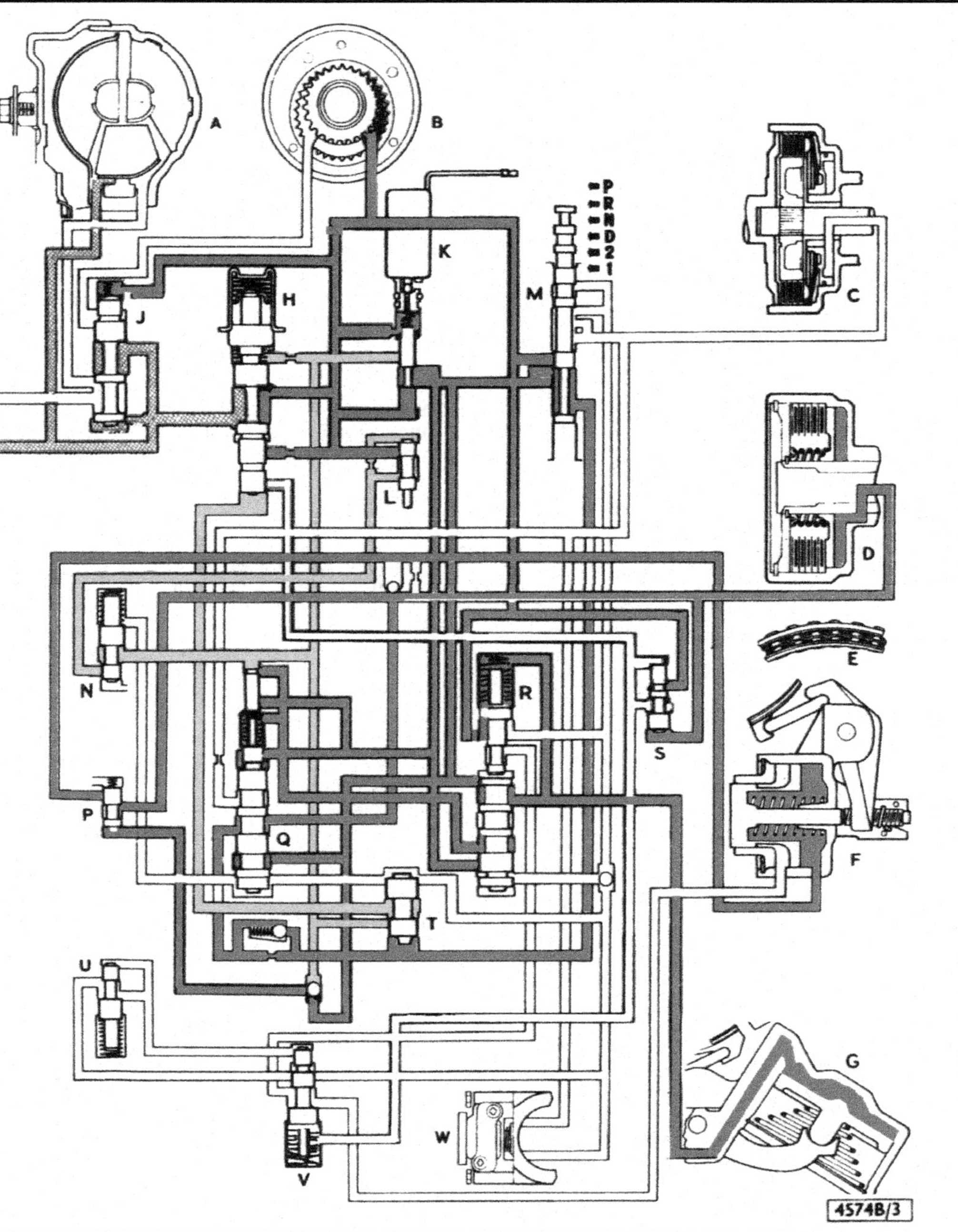

HYDRAULIC OPERATION IN 'R'

Movement of the manual valve to the reverse position closes the lines to the front clutch and governor. The rear clutch and rear servo are energised so reversing the direction of rotation of the output shaft. As the front servo release and rear clutch are interconnected, the front servo release will also be energised. This has no effect on the operation of reverse gear.

KEY TO HYDRAULIC CHART CODE

- Pump pressure
- To torque convertor
- Governor line pressure
- Governor modulator valve
- Kickdown – additional modulator throttle pressure.

ROAD TEST AND FAULT DIAGNOSIS 44.00.00

The following points should be checked before proceeding with the road test.

1 Fluid level.
2 Engine idle speed.
3 Manual lever adjustment.
4 Manifold vacuum of 9 to 10 in. (23 to 25 cm) Hg.

ROAD TEST

The road speed figures for the tests listed below are to be found under "GENERAL DATA – GEAR CHANGE SPEEDS".

Road testing should follow the complete sequence detailed below. Transmission should be at normal working temperature, i.e. after being driven on road or rollers.

1 With brakes applied and engine idling, move selector from:
'N' to 'R'
'N' to 'D'
'N' to '2'
'N' to '1'
Engagement should be felt with each selection.
2 Check stall speed.
3 Select 'D' accelerate with minimum throttle opening and check speed of first gear to second gear shift.
4 Continue with minimum throttle and check speed of second gear to third gear shift.
5 Select 'D', accelerate with maximum throttle opening (kickdown) and check speed of first gear to second gear shift.
6 Continue with maximum throttle and check speed of second gear to third gear shift.
7 Check for kickdown shift third gear to second gear.
8 Check for kickdown shift second gear to first gear.
9 Check for kickdown shift third gear to first gear.
10 Check for "roll-out" downshift with minimum throttle, second gear to first gear.
11 Check for part throttle downshift, third gear to second gear.

Should a fault be apparent during road test, first identify the problem from the list printed in the Fault Diagnosis Chart. The reference numbers shown opposite each fault may be translated by reference to the page headed "Transmission Fault Key".

FAULT DIAGNOSIS

Problem	Checks in Vehicle	Checks on Bench
Engagements		
Harsh	A1, A3, A4, A5, M2, V1, V2, V3, V4	T4 (in revers only)
Soft or delayed	M1, A2, A3, A4, A5, V1, V2, V3, V9	T14
None in all Positions	V16, M1, A2, V2, C3	T9, T10, C2
No forward		
in 1 position	V16, M1, A2, V1, V2	T1, T4, T7, T14
in 2 position	V16, M1, A2, T16, T13, V1, V2, V10	T1, T4, T14
in D position	V16, M1, A2, V1, V2, A5	T1, T4, T7, T14
in all positions	V16, M1, A2, V1, V2	C2, T9, T10, T14
No reverse	V16, M1, A2, A5, T15, T6, V1, V5, V6	T2, T3, T14
Jumps in forward	A2, A3, A4, A5	T4, T7
Jumps in reverse	A2, A3, A4, A5	T2, T3
No neutral	A2, V1, V16	T2
Upshifts		
No 1-2	M1, A2, A4, G1, T5, T13, T16, V1, V2, V4, V5	T14
No 2-3	M1, A2, G1, T13, V1, V2, V4, V5, V6	T3, T14
Shift points too high	A1, A2, M2, G1, V1, V2, V4, V5, V8, V12, V14	T14
Shift points too low	A1, M3, G1, M4, V1, V5, V6, V12, V14	T14
Upshift Quality		
1-2 slips or runs-up	M1, A1, A2, M3, G1, T13, V1, V2, V4, V9, V10, V5	T10, T5, T14
2-3 slips or runs-up	M1, A1, A2, A4, M3, G1, T13, V1, V2, V4, V5, V6, V9, V10, V12	T10, T5, T14
1-2 harsh	A1, A2, A4, A5, M2, V1, V2, V3, V4, V5, V9	T1, T7, T8
2-3 harsh	A1, A2, A4, M2, V1, V2, V4, V9	T4
1-2 ties-up or grabs	A4, A5, V1, V5, T16	T4, T7, T8
2-3 ties-up or grabs	A2, A4, T13, V17, T15	

Problem	Checks in Vehicle	Checks on Bench
Downshifts		
No 2-1	A1, A2, A6, M3, M4, G1, V1, V5, V14	T7
No 3-2	A1, A2, A6, M4, G1, V1, V6, V14, T13	T4
Shift points too high	A1, A2, M2, G1, V1, V4, V5, V6, V12	T14
Shift points too low	A1, A2, M3, G1, V1, V4, V5, V6, V12	T14
Downshift Quality		
2-1 slides	T5, A1, A2, A4, T13, G1, V1, V2, V4, V9, V11	T7
3-2 slides	A1, A2, A4, T13, G1, V1, V2, V4, V9, V11, T5	
2-1 harsh	A1, A2, A4, A5, M2, V1, V2, V3, V4, V9	T1, T7, T14
3-2 harsh	A1, A2, A4, G1, V1, V2, V3, V4, V9	T3, T4
Reverse		
Slips or chatters	M1, A1, A2, A5, T6, V1, V2, V4, V10	T14, T2, T3
Line Pressure		
Low idle	M1, A1, A2, A3, T13, V1, V2, G1	T10, T14
High idle	A1, M2, V1, V2, V3, V4	
Low stall	M1, A1, M3, M4, T13, G1, V1, V2, V4, V14	T10
High stall	A1, V1, V2, V3	
Stall speed		
Too low (200 rpm or more below)		C1
Too high (200 rpm or more above)	M1, A1, A2, A4, T13, V1, V4	T14, T1, T3, T6, T7, T9, T10
Others		
Transmission overheats	M1, A4, A5, V2, V3, M5, T13, V1	T1, T2, T3, T4, T5, T6, T7, T10, T14
Drag in neutral	A2, A3	T2, T4
Poor Acceleration	M1, V2, V3	C1
Noisy in neutral	V13	T2, T4, V15
Noisy in park	V13, V15	T10

Problem	Checks in Vehicle	Checks on Bench
Noisy in all gears	V13, C3, V15	T10, C1, C2
Noisy during coast (30-20 mph)		T12
Park brake does not hold	A2, T11	
Ties up in 1 or low	A4, T15, T13, V1	T4, T14
Ties up in 2 or intermediate ratio D or 2 selected	A5, T16, A2, V1	T4, T14, T8
Ties up in direct drive	A5, T16, A2, V1, A4, T15, T12	T17, T14, T8
Poor acceleration	M6, A1, A2, A4, M1, T15, T16, V1, V2	C1, T10, T14
Oil out breather	T18, M1, G1, T13, V1	T14
Oil out fill tube	T18, M1, G1, T13, M7	T14

TRANSMISSION FAULT KEY

Adjustments
- A1 Vacuum control adjustment.
- A2 Manual control adjustment.
- A3 Engine idle speed.
- A4 Front band adjustment.
- A5 Rear band adjustment.
- A6 Kickdown switch adjustment.

Miscellaneous
- M1 Fluid level.
- M2 Vacuum leak.
- M3 Vacuum line restricted.
- M4 Broken kickdown wire or blown fuse.
- M5 Oil cooler, lines and connections.
- M6 Engine tune-up.
- M7 Breather plugged.

Converter
- C1 Converter blading or one-way clutch failed.
- C2 Pump drive tangs on converter hub broken.
- C3 Broken converter drive plate.

Governor
- G1 Governor, sticking, leaking or incorrectly assembled.

Transmission
- T1 Front clutch slipping due to worn or faulty parts.
- T2 Front clutch seized or plates distorted.
- T3 Rear clutch slipping due to worn plates or faulty parts.
- T4 Rear clutch seized or plates distorted.
- T5 Front band slipping due to a faulty servo, broken or worn band.
- T6 Rear band slipping due to a faulty servo, broken or worn band.
- T7 One-way clutch slipping or incorrectly installed.
- T8 One-way clutch seized.
- T9 Broken input shaft.
- T10 Front pump worn or defective.
- T11 Parking linkage.
- T12 Planetary assembly.
- T13 Oil tubes missing or broken.
- T14 Sealing rings missing or broken and other oil leaks.
- T15 Front band locked in the applied condition.
- T16 Rear band locked in the applied condition.
- T17 Rear clutch piston ball check valve leaking.
- T18 Dipstick length.

Valve Body
- V1 Valve body improperly assembled or screws missing.
- V2 Primary valve sticking.
- V3 Secondary valve sticking.
- V4 Throttle valve sticking.
- V5 1-2 shift valve sticking.
- V6 2-3 shift valve sticking.
- V7 Governor modulator valve sticking.
- V8 Throttle modulator valve sticking.
- V9 Cutback valve sticking.
- V10 Servo regulator valve sticking.
- V11 Orifice control valve sticking.
- V12 2-3 shift valve plug sticking.
- V13 Regulator valve buzz.
- V14 Defective solenoid.
- V15 Dirty oil Screen.
- V16 Manual valve not connected to shift control.
- V17 Ball check valve stuck.

GEAR SELECTOR CABLE

Remove and refit 44.15.08

Removing
1. Remove console – 76.25.01.
2. Place quadrant selector lever in '1'.
3. Unscrew gear selector knob.
4. Remove screws securing selector indicator; withdraw indicator over selector lever.
5. Remove split pin and washer securing cable to selector lever; detach cable.
6. Unscrew front locknut securing cable to abutment bracket.
7. Lift carpet from left hand side of transmission tunnel.
8. Remove screws securing cable shroud to transmission tunnel; withdraw shroud.
9. Withdraw cable from abutment bracket.

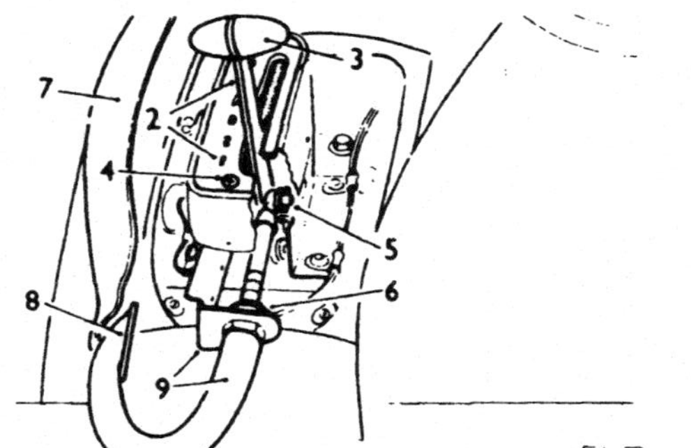

10. Remove screws securing access panel to transmission tunnel.
11. Withdraw panel, clean off old sealing compound.
12. Ensure gearbox selector lever is in '1'.
13. Remove nut securing selector cable to gearbox selector lever; detach cable.
14. Remove bolt and spring washer securing trunnion block.
15. Withdraw cable.

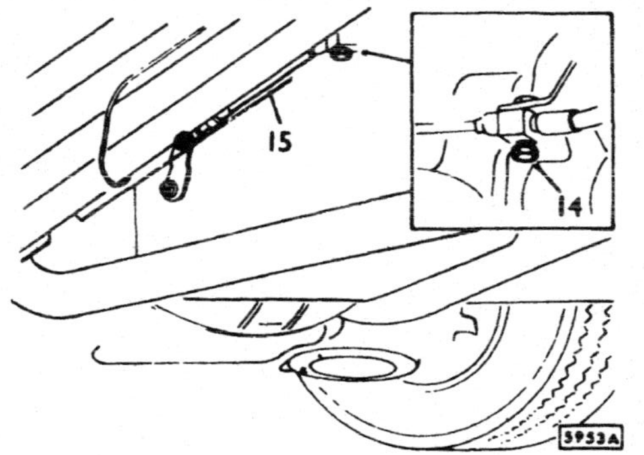

Refitting

16. Reverse operations 7 to 15, seal access panel and hole in cable shroud with suitable non-hardening sealing compound.
17. Fit front locknut to cable but do not tighten at this stage.
18. Ensure gearbox selector and quadrant selector levers are in '1'.
19. Adjust front and rear locknuts until cable can be connected to quadrant lever without either quadrant or gearbox lever being disturbed.
20. Tighten locknuts, secure cable with new split pin.
21. Reverse operations 1 to 4.

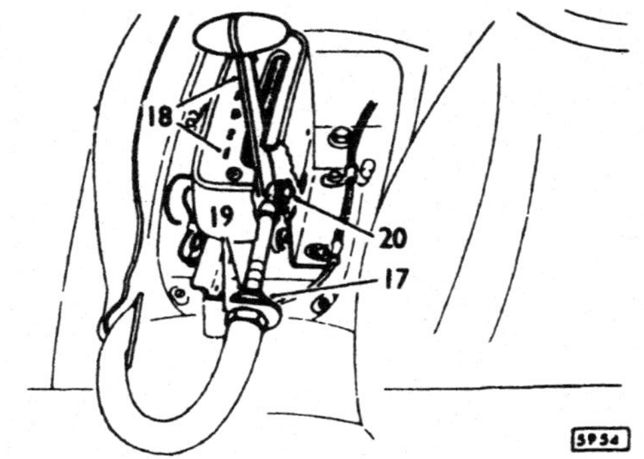

STARTER INHIBITOR SWITCH

Check and adjust 44.15.18

Adjusting
1 Disconnect battery – 86.15.20.
2 Unscrew gear selector knob.
3 Carefully prise electric window switch panel away from centre console; do not disconnect window switches.
4 Remove screws securing control escutcheon; withdraw escutcheon slightly to obtain access to cigar lighter and door lock switch terminals.
5 Note fitted position of cigar lighter and door lock switch terminals; detach terminals and withdraw escutcheon.
6 Detach feed cable from inhibitor switch.
7 Connect a test lamp and battery in series with switch.
NOTE: Switch is in earthed position.
8 Place selector lever in 'N' position.
9 Slacken locknuts securing switch and adjust position of switch until lamp lights.
10 Tighten locknuts, check that lamp remains on with lever in 'P' position and is off with lever in drive position.
11 Remove battery and test lamp, reconnect feed cable to switch.
12 Reverse operations 1 to 5.
13 Check operation of window switches, door lock switch and cigar lighter.

STARTER INHIBITOR SWITCH

Remove and refit 44.15.19

Refer to operation 86.65.28.

REVERSE LIGHT SWITCH

Check and adjust 44.15.21

Refer to operation 86.65.20.

REVERSE LIGHT SWITCH

Remove and refit 44.15.22

Refer to operation 86.65.20.

KICKDOWN SWITCH

Remove and refit 44.15.23

Removing
1 Note location of input and output wires; disconnect wires from switch.
2 Remove bolts securing switch; withdraw switch.

Refitting
3 Reverse operations 1 and 2.
4 Check switch adjustment – 44.30.12.

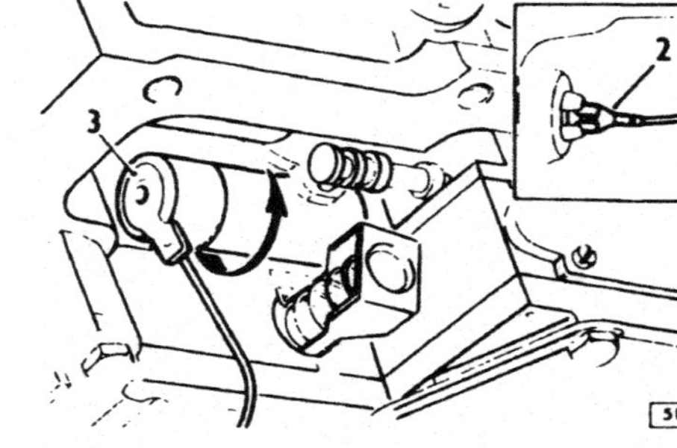

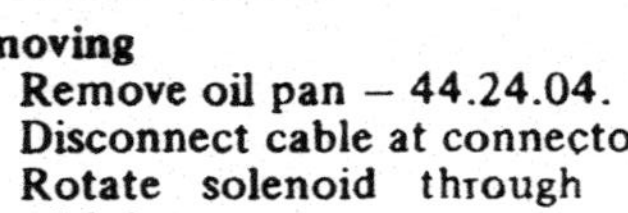

KICKDOWN SOLENOID

Remove and refit 44.15.24

Removing
1 Remove oil pan – 44.24.04.
2 Disconnect cable at connector.
3 Rotate solenoid through 180° and withdraw.

Refitting
Reverse operations 1 to 3, lubricate 'O' ring on solenoid prior to refitting.

VACUUM UNIT

Remove and refit 44.15.27

Removing
1 Disconnect hose from vacuum unit.
2 Unscrew vacuum unit.
3 Withdraw push rod.

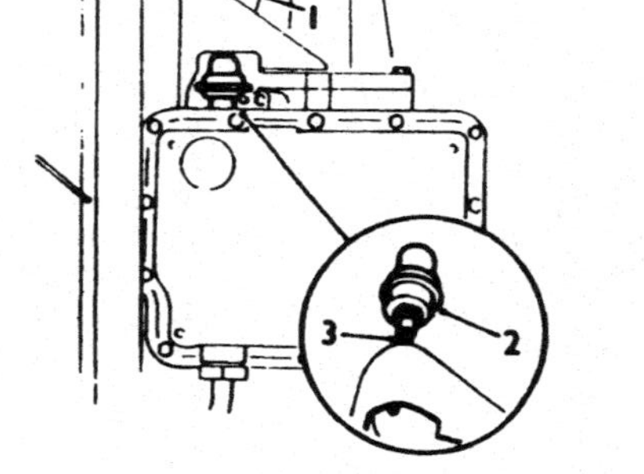

Refitting
4 Reverse operations 1 to 3.
5 If new vacuum unit has been fitted carry out operation 44.30.05.

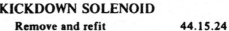

CONVERTER HOUSING

Remove and refit 44.17.01

Removing
1 Remove engine and transmission assembly – 12.37.01.
2 Remove transmission unit – 44.20.01.
3 Remove bolts and spring washers securing starter motor; support or withdraw starter motor.
4 Remove bolts and washers securing front cover to converter housing; withdraw cover.
5 Remove bolts and lockwashers securing converter housing to cylinder block; withdraw housing.

Refitting
Reverse operations 1 to 5, securing converter housing to transmission before refitting assembly to engine.

CONVERTER

Remove and refit **44.17.07**

Removing
1 Remove engine and transmission assembly, see 12.37.01.
2 Remove transmission unit, see 44.20.01.
3 Remove converter housing, see 44.17.01.
4 Remove starter motor, see 86.60.01.
5 Remove four setscrews, accessible through starter motor mounting aperture, securing torque converter to drive plate; withdraw converter.

Refitting
Reverse operations 1 to 5, refitting torque converter to transmission unit before assembling transmission unit and converter housing to the engine. Tighten bolts to a torque of 35 lb.ft. (4,8 kg.m).
CAUTION: The torque converter is a sealed unit and no overhaul is possible. In the event of a defect arising, the assembly must be replaced.

WARNING: TORQUE CONVERTERS SHOULD NOT BE CLEANED EITHER EXTERNALLY OR INTERNALLY WITH FLAMMABLE LIQUIDS.

TRANSMISSION UNIT

Remove and refit **44.20.01**

Removing
1 Remove engine and transmission assembly – 12.37.01.
2 Disconnect oil cooler pipes, plug pipes and unions to prevent ingress of dirt.
3 Pull breather pipe off stub pipes.
4 Withdraw dipstick; disconnect oil filler tube at oil pan.
5 Drain and discard fluid.
6 Pull vacuum pipe off vacuum unit.
7 Remove nuts, bolts and washers securing vacuum pipe clips; recover clips.
8 Remove four nuts and lockwashers securing gearbox to torque converter housing withdraw gearbox.
CAUTION: Do not allow gearbox to hang on input shaft.

Refitting
9 Reverse operations 1 to 8; ensure torque converter and gearbox input splines are correctly aligned when fitting gearbox.
10 When engine and gearbox assembly is refitted, refer to operation 44.24.02 items 4 to 9.

TRANSMISSION ASSEMBLY

Overhaul **44.20.06**

Service Tools: Bench cradle CWG.35; Mainshaft end float gauge CBW.33; Circlip pliers 7066; Clutch spring compressor CWG.37; Clutch spring compressor adaptor CBW.37A; Torque screwdriver CBW.548; Screwdriver bit adaptors CBW.547A-50-5 and CBW.548-1; Torque wrench CBW.547A-50; Rear clutch piston replacer CWG.41; Front clutch piston replacer CWG.42; Front servo adjuster adaptor CBW.548-2A; Gauge block CBW.34.

Dismantling
1 Thoroughly clean gearbox casing.
2 Fit bench cradle CWG.35.
3 Remove bolts and washers securing oil pan, lift off oil pan; remove and discard gasket.
4 Remove magnet from rear servo mounting bolt.
5 Unscrew vacuum control unit, remove and discard 'O' ring.
6 Withdraw push rod.
7 Disconnect cable from connector.

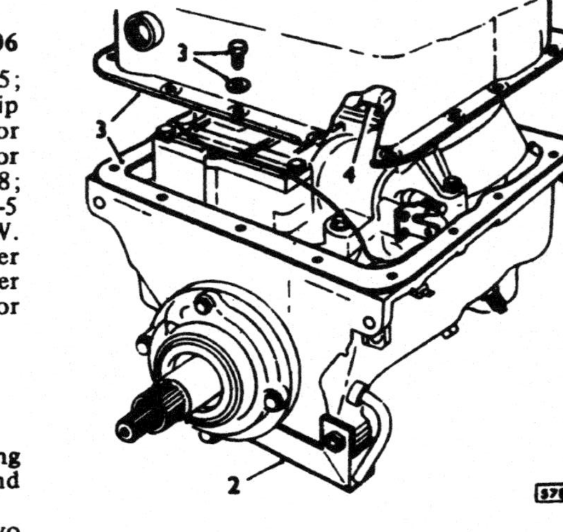

8 Compress retaining lugs and withdraw connector; remove and discard 'O' ring.

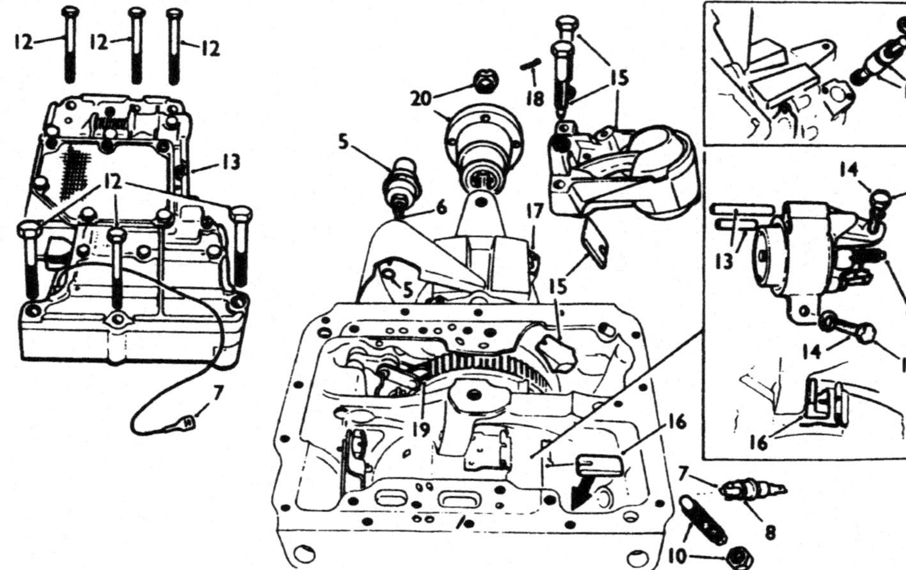

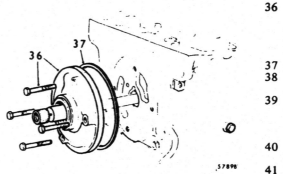

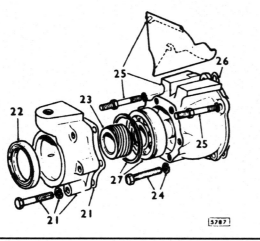

9 Slacken off front servo adjusting screw. **CAUTION: This screw has a left hand thread.**
10 Slacken off rear servo adjusting screw locknut; remove screw.
11 Slacken off, but do not remove front servo retaining bolts.
12 Remove six valve body retaining bolts; note relative sizes and fitted positions of bolts.
13 Lift valve body clear of transmission case and withdraw servo tubes.
14 Remove front servo retaining bolts, carefully lift off servo at the same time noting fitted positions of brake band struts.
15 Remove rear servo retaining bolts, carefully lift off servo at the same time noting fitted positions of brake band struts.
16 Recover front and rear brake band struts from transmission case.
17 Remove speedometer driven gear housing together with driven gear; remove and discard 'O' ring.
18 Remove and discard split pin locking output flange securing nut.
19 Move manual lever until parking pawl engages ring gear.
20 Remove output flange securing nut; withdraw flange.

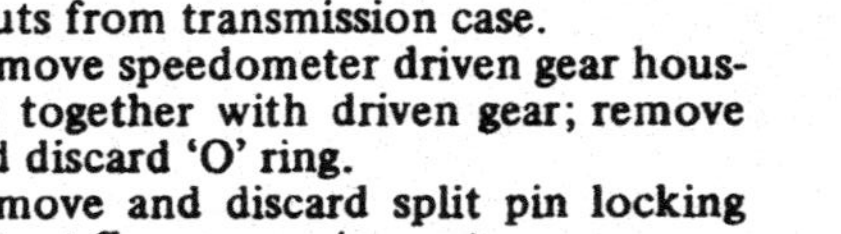

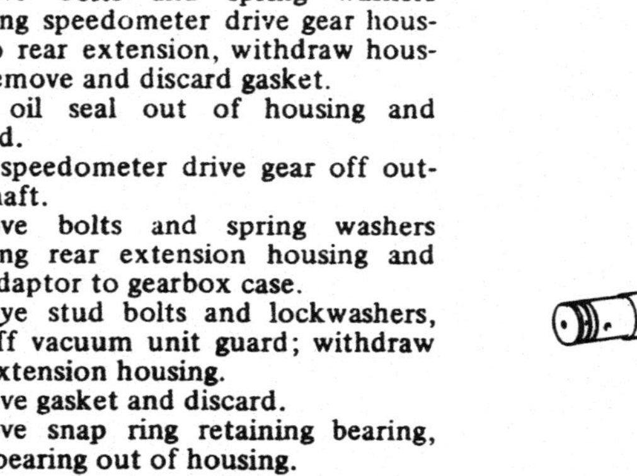

21 Remove bolts and spring washers securing speedometer drive gear housing to rear extension, withdraw housing; remove and discard gasket.
22 Prise oil seal out of housing and discard.
23 Slide speedometer drive gear off output shaft.
24 Remove bolts and spring washers securing rear extension housing and rear adaptor to gearbox case.
25 Remove stud bolts and lockwashers, lift off vacuum unit guard; withdraw rear extension housing.
26 Remove gasket and discard.
27 Remove snap ring retaining bearing, push bearing out of housing.
28 Remove snap ring retaining governor, slide governor off output shaft; recover drive ball.
29 Withdraw rear adaptor, remove and discard gasket.
30 Hold rear clutch drum steady and withdraw output shaft and ring gear assembly.
31 Remove selective thrust washer and discard.
32 Remove snap ring and withdraw output shaft from ring gear.
33 Hold forward sun gear shaft steady and withdraw planet carrier assembly.
34 Remove needle thrust bearing and steel backing washer.
35 Note fitted position of rear brake band; compress and withdraw brake band.

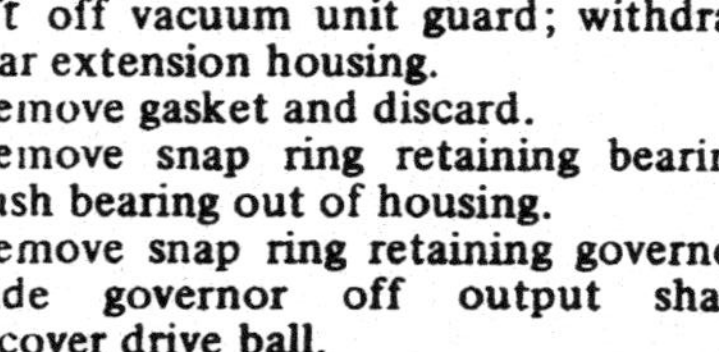

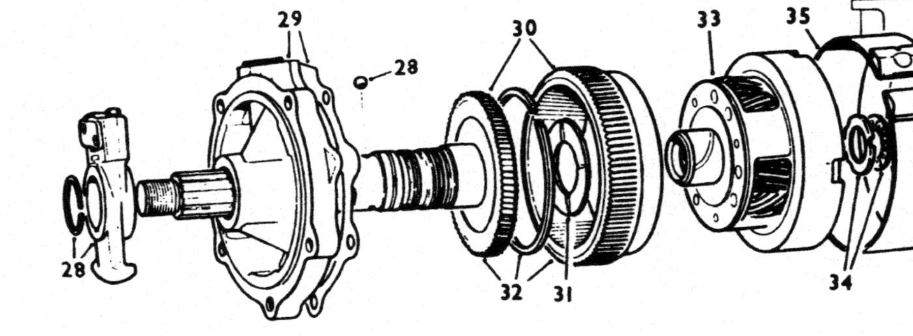

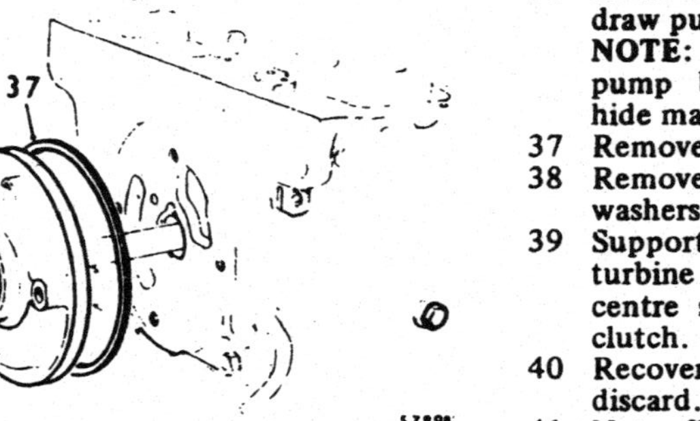

36 Remove pump mounting bolts; withdraw pump.
NOTE: It may be necessary to free pump by tapping pump body with hide mallet.
37 Remove and discard sealing ring.
38 Remove centre support bolts and lockwashers.
39 Support forward sun gear shaft, push turbine shaft rearwards and withdraw centre support, rear clutch and front clutch.
40 Recover steel thrust washer and discard.
41 Note fitted position of front brake band; compress and withdraw brake band.

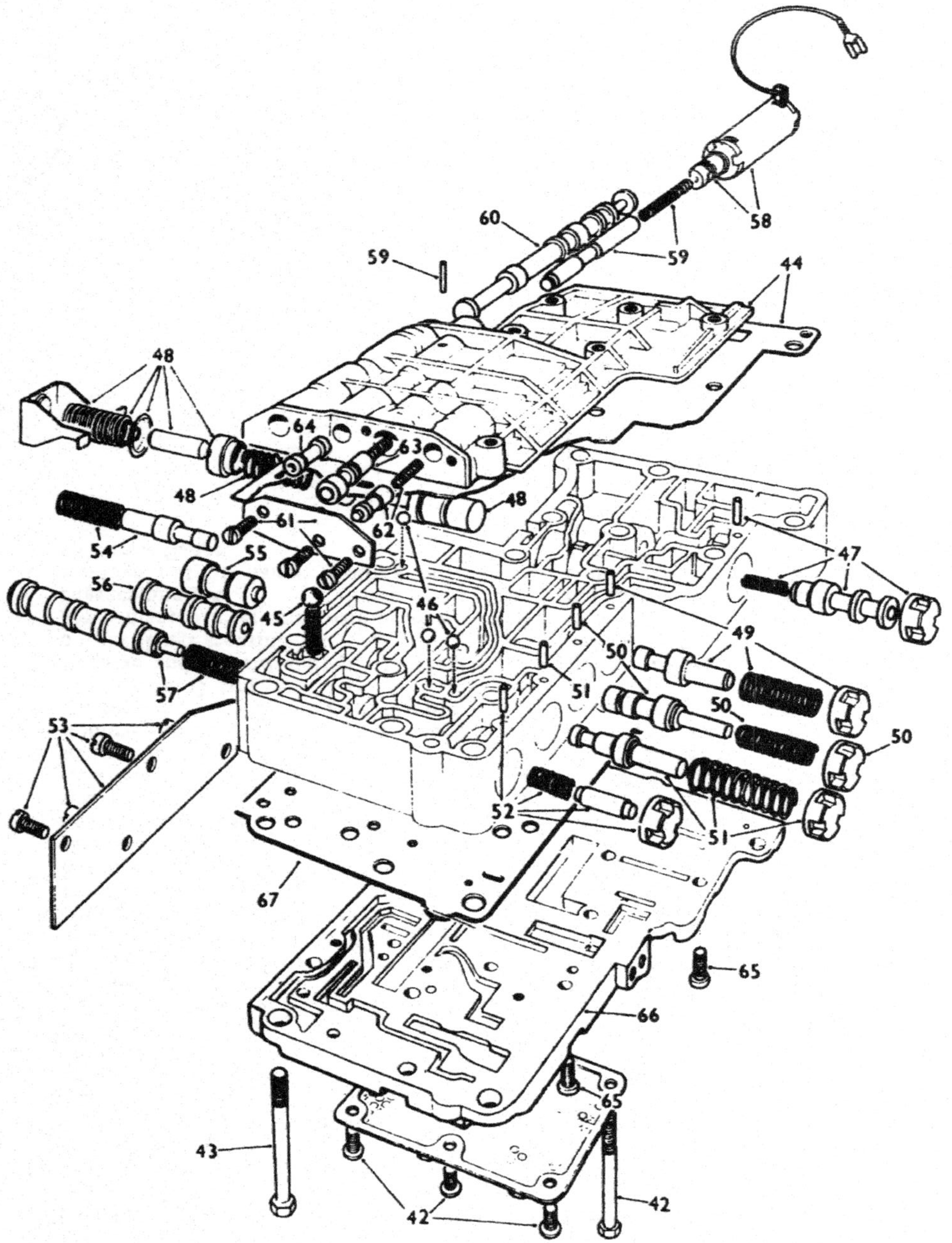

VALVE BLOCK

Overhaul

CAUTION: Ensure that all working surfaces are clean. Use only lint free cloth and clean transmission fluid for cleaning and lubricating.

Dismantling

42 Remove three pan head screws and three ¼ UNC x 2.25 in. (57 mm) bolts: lift off filter screen.
43 Remove one ¼ UNC x 2.00 in. (50,8 mm.), one ¼ UNC x 2.75 in. (60 mm.) and four ¼ UNC x 2.25 in. (57 mm.) bolts securing upper valve body to valve block.
CAUTION: **Do not allow components to separate at this stage.**
44 Holding upper valve body and valve block together, invert assembly and carefully lift off upper valve body and separator plate.
CAUTION: Governor safety valve ball is spring loaded and is retained by the separator plate; great care should, therefore, be exercised when removing separator plate to ensure that ball is not misplaced.
45 Recover governor safety valve ball and withdraw spring.
46 Invert valve body and recover three nylon ball valves.
47 Remove retaining pin and extract plug, secondary regulator valve and spring.
48 Remove spring retainer, seat and spring. Extract plug sleeve, primary regulator valve and spring.
49 Remove retaining pin and extract plug, governor modulator valve and spring.
50 Remove retaining pin, extract plug, spring and servo regulator valve.
51 Remove retaining pin, extract plug, spring and 1-2 shift valve.
52 Remove retaining pin, extract plug, 2-3 shift valve and spring.
53 Remove four 10 UNF x .375 in. (9,5 mm.) cheese head screws and detach valve body end plate.
54 Extract modulator spring and valve.
55 Extract throttle modulator cut back valve.
56 Extract 1-2 shift valve.
57 Extract 2-3 shift valve and spring.
58 Rotate kickdown solenoid through 180° and withdraw, remove and discard 'O' ring.
59 Withdraw retaining pin, extract spring and downshift valve.
60 Extract manual valve.
61 Remove three 10 UNF x .375 in. (9,5 mm.) cheese head screws and detach upper valve body end plate.
62 Extract orifice control valve and spring.
63 Extract servo regulator timer and spring.
64 Extract throttle valve.
65 Remove three 10 UNF x .56 in. (14,3 mm.) cheese head and two 10 UNF x .56 in. (14,3 mm.) pan head screws securing lower valve body to valve block.
66 Lift off lower valve body.
67 Remove separator plate.
68 Renew any valves showing signs of scoring or burrs.
69 Check springs with data shown in spring identification table, see 44.00, Page 00; renew springs which are distorted or shorter than specified length.
70 Check ball valves for wear or signs of damage; renew if necessary.
71 Thoroughly clean all components and lubricate with clean transmission fluid of the correct specification.

Reassembling

Reverse operations 42 to 67, use new 'O' ring for kickdown solenoid.
CAUTION: **Tightening torque figures must be adhered to, see group 06.**

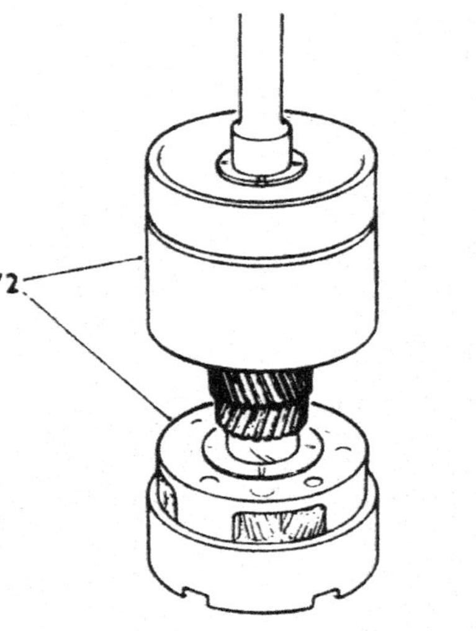

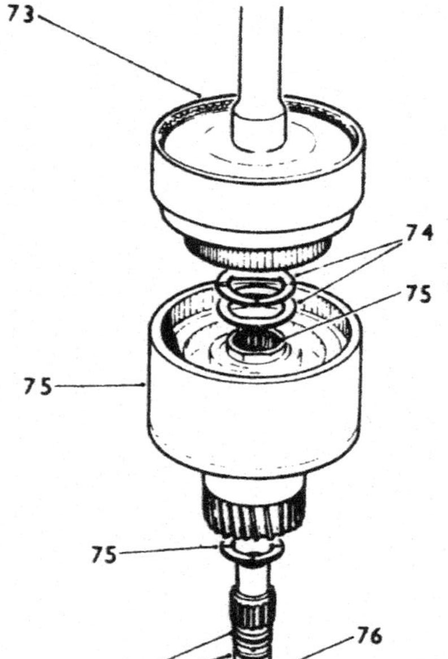

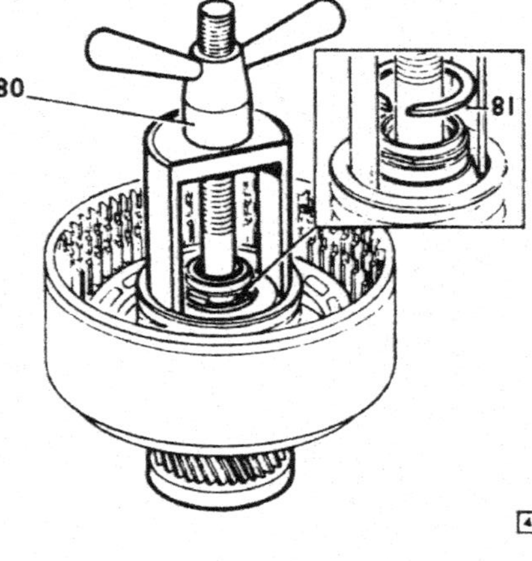

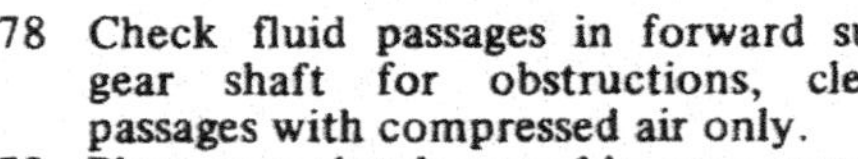

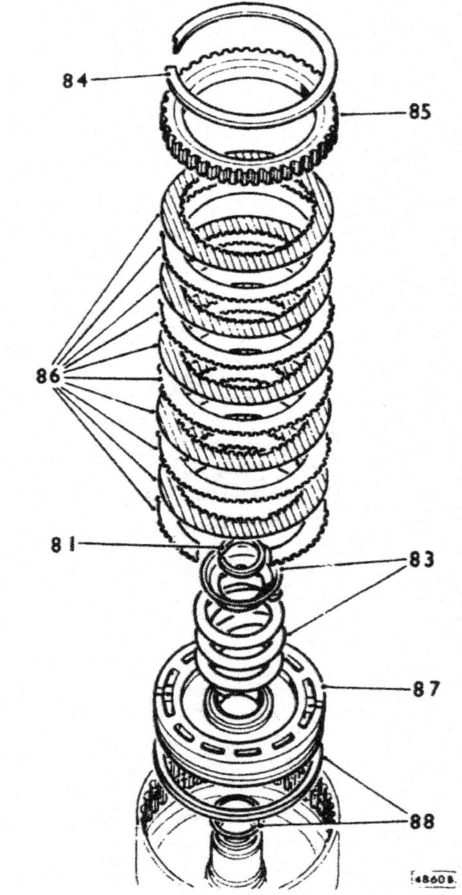

REAR CLUTCH

Overhaul

Dismantling

CAUTION: The clutch units as removed from the gearcase are assembled together with the forward sun gear shaft. To facilitate separation of front and rear clutch assemblies a suitable stand is required and the planet carrier should be used for this purpose.

72 Insert rear end of forward sun gear shaft in planet carrier.
73 Carefully lift front clutch assembly off forward sun gear shaft.
74 Remove steel thrust washer and backing plate; discard thrust washer.
75 Carefully lift rear clutch assembly off forward sun gear shaft; recover needle roller bearings and bronze thrust washer.
76 Remove forward sun gear shaft from planet carrier.
77 Remove and discard sealing rings.
78 Check fluid passages in forward sun gear shaft for obstructions, clear passages with compressed air only.
79 Place rear clutch assembly over central splindle of clutch spring compressor CWG.37, reverse sun gear down.
80 Fit spring compressor CBW.37A over spindle.
81 Compress spring and remove spring ring.
82 Slowly release pressure and remove compressor.
83 Remove retainer and spring.
84 Remove spring ring retaining pressure plate.
85 Remove pressure plate.
86 Remove inner and outer clutch plates.
87 Remove piston by applying air pressure to supply hole in centre bore.
88 Remove and discard piston ring and 'O' ring.

continued

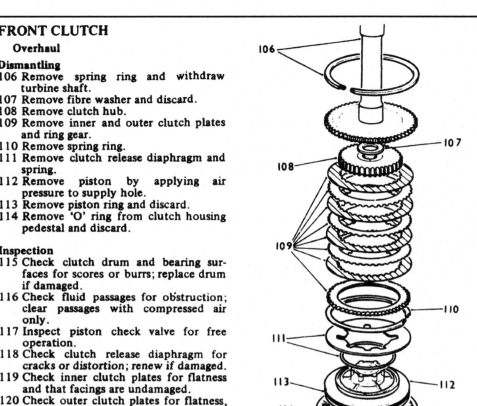

Inspection

89 Check clutch drum and bearing surfaces for scores or burrs; replace drum if damaged.

90 Check fluid passages for obstructions, clear passages with compressed air only.

91 Inspect piston check valve for free operation.

92 Check clutch release spring for distortion, renew if distorted.

93 Check inner clutch plates for flatness and that facings are undamaged.

94 Check that coning on outer clutch plates is **not less** than .010 in. (,25 mm.).

95 Check outer clutch plates for scores or burrs; renew if damaged. Minor scores or burrs may however be removed with a very fine abrasive.

Reassembling

96 Fit new sealing rings on forward sun gear shaft.

97 Insert rear end of forward sun gear shaft in planet carrier.

98 Fit new bronze thrust washer.

99 Fit needle rollers; retain rollers with light grease.

100 Lubricate piston ring and 'O' ring with petroleum jelly.

101 Fit piston ring and 'O' ring.

102 Position rear clutch piston replacer tool CWG.41 in clutch drum.

103 Lubricate piston and install; remove replacer tool.

104 Reverse operations 79 to 86.
CAUTION: Outer clutch plates must be assembled with cones facing same direction.

105 Position rear clutch assembly on forward sun gear shaft; refit steel backing plates followed by new steel thrust washer.
CAUTION: Do not remove rear clutch assembly and forward sun gear shaft from planet carrier.

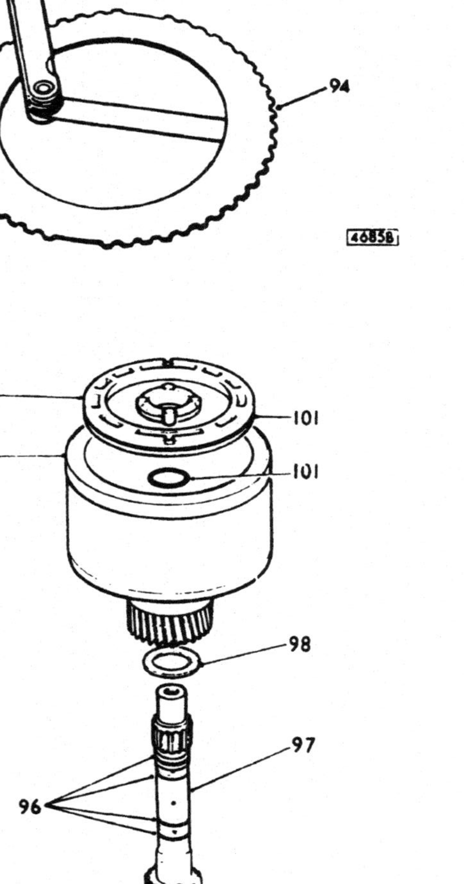

FRONT CLUTCH

Overhaul

Dismantling

106 Remove spring ring and withdraw turbine shaft.

107 Remove fibre washer and discard.

108 Remove clutch hub.

109 Remove inner and outer clutch plates and ring gear.

110 Remove spring ring.

111 Remove clutch release diaphragm and spring.

112 Remove piston by applying air pressure to supply hole.

113 Remove piston ring and discard.

114 Remove 'O' ring from clutch housing pedestal and discard.

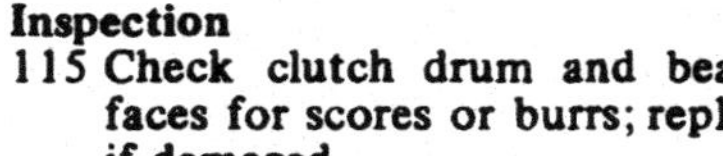

Inspection

115 Check clutch drum and bearing surfaces for scores or burrs; replace drum if damaged.

116 Check fluid passages for obstruction; clear passages with compressed air only.

117 Inspect piston check valve for free operation.

118 Check clutch release diaphragm for cracks or distortion; renew if damaged.

119 Check inner clutch plates for flatness and that facings are undamaged.

120 Check outer clutch plates for flatness, scores or burrs, renew if damaged. Minor scores or burrs may, however, be removed with a very fine abrasive.

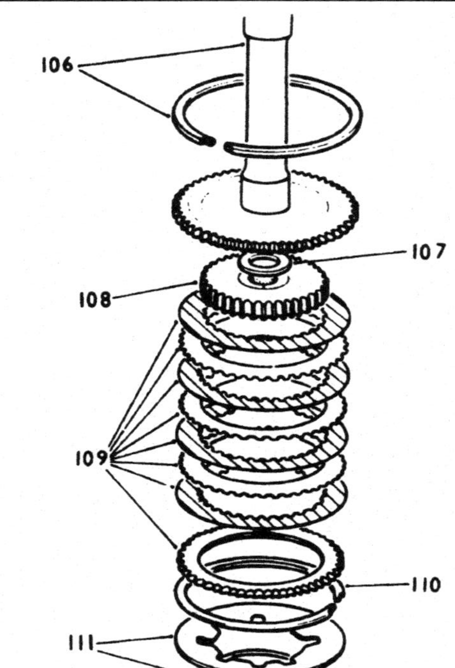

Reassembling

121 Lubricate piston ring and 'O' ring with petroleum jelly.
122 Fit 'O' ring to clutch housing pedestal.
123 Fit piston ring.
124 Position front clutch piston replacer tool CWG.42 in clutch drum.
125 Lubricate piston and install; remove replacer tool.
126 Fit release diaphragm and spring.
127 Fit spring ring; ensure ring is correctly seated in groove.
128 Fit backing plate and new steel thrust washer.
129 Carefully lower front clutch over forward sun gear shaft and into rear clutch.
130 Ensure that front clutch is fully seated in rear clutch.
131 Fit ring gear.
132 Fit inner and outer clutch plates.
133 Check to ensure that teeth of inner clutch plates are in alignment.
134 Fit clutch hub.
135 Place new fibre washer over forward sun gear shaft.
136 Fit turbine shaft and spring ring; ensure spring ring is correctly seated in groove.
CAUTION: On no account should front and rear clutch assemblies be separated as damage to sealing rings on forward sun gear shaft will result.
137 Fit new steel thrust washer.

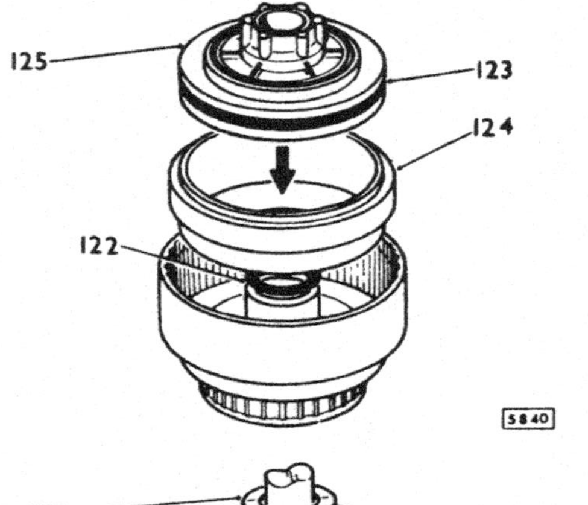

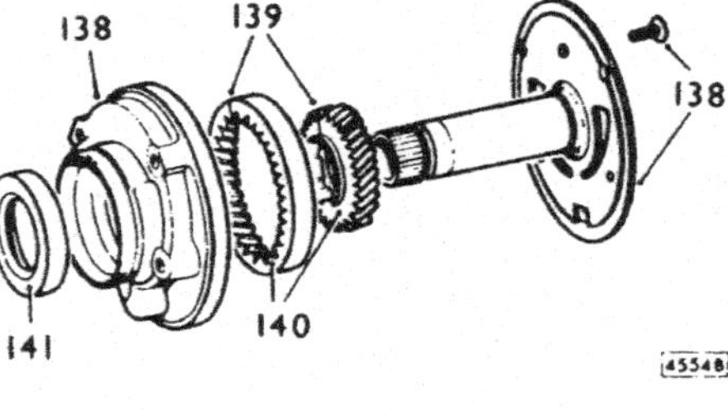

PUMP

Overhaul

Dismantling

138 Remove locking screw, separate pump halves.
139 Mark mating surfaces of gears with die marker.
140 Remove gears from pump body.
141 Prise oil seal out of pump body; discard seal.

Inspection

142 Check bearing surfaces, gear teeth and splines for wear or damage; renew if necessary.
CAUTION: If gears are damaged or worn, they must be renewed as a set, individual gears must not be fitted.

Reassembling

143 Soak new oil seal in clean transmission fluid and press carefully into pump body; ensure seal is squarely seated.
144 Reverse operations 138 to 140.

FRONT SERVO

Overhaul

Dismantling

145 Depress piston and sleeve, remove spring ring.
146 Withdraw piston and stop plate, collect spring.
147 Remove setscrew, lockwasher and plain washer.
148 Drift piston out of stop plate and piston sleeve.
149 Withdraw stop plate from piston sleeve.
150 Remove and discard sealing rings.
151 Drive out hinge pin by tapping at opposite end to grooves.
152 Remove operating lever and adjusting screw.
NOTE: Adjusting screw has left hand thread.

Inspection

153 Check that hinge pin is a tight fit in servo body.
154 Check servo body for cracks or scoring: renew if necessary.
155 Check spring for distortion; renew if necessary.
156 Check fluid passages for obstruction; clear passages with compressed air only.

Reassembling

Reverse operations 145 to 152, coat new sealing rings with petroleum jelly prior to fitting.

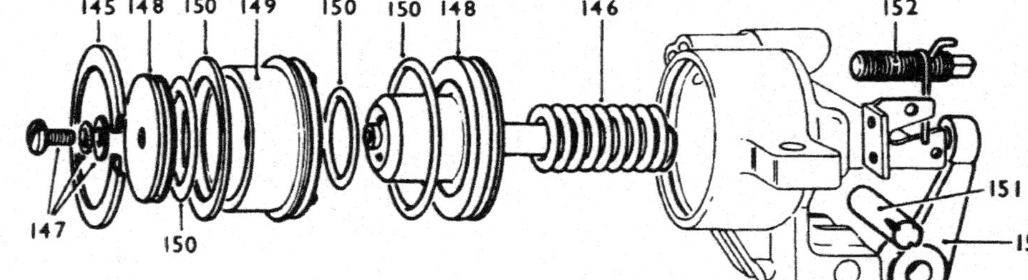

REAR SERVO

Overhaul

Dismantling

157 Drive roll pin out of hinge pin with a .125 in. (3 mm.) punch.

158 Remove hinge pin and operating lever, collect thrust washers and needle rollers.

159 Compress piston return spring by pressing down on cover plate.

160 Note fitted positions of spring ring and cover plate; remove spring ring.

161 Slowly release pressure on cover plate; remove plate, return spring and piston.

162 Remove and discard piston sealing ring.

Inspection

163 Check servo body for cracks or scoring; renew if damaged.

164 Check piston return spring for distortion; renew if distorted.

165 Check hinge pin for scoring, burrs or ovality. Light scoring or burrs may be removed with a fine abrasive; pins showing signs of ovality must be renewed.

166 Check fluid passage plug for tightness.

167 Check fluid passages for obstruction; clear passages with compressed air only.

Reassembling

168 Reverse operations 159 to 162; coat piston sealing ring with petroleum jelly prior to fitting.

169 Position hinge pin in one side of servo body and fit thrust washer.

170 Lightly smear needle rollers with grease and position in operating lever.

171 Position operating lever in servo body and carefully push hinge pin half way through, ensuring that needle rollers are not displaced.

172 Fit remaining thrust washer.

173 Push hinge pin through operating lever thrust washer and servo body.

174 Fit roll pin.

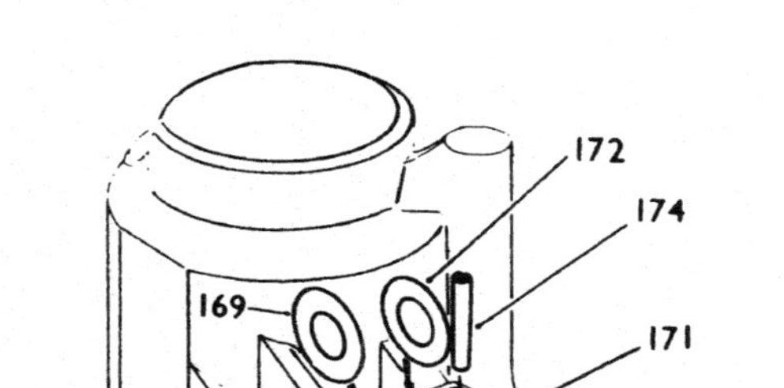

GOVERNOR

Overhaul

Dismantling

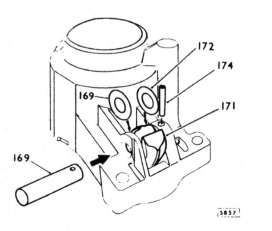

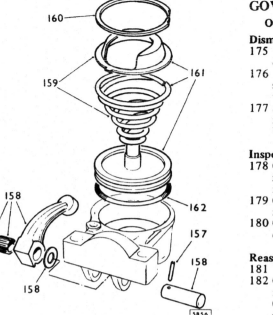

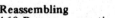

175 Remove screws securing cover plate; detach cover plate.

176 Remove bolts and spring washers securing body assembly to counterweight.

177 Slide retaining plate off weight; remove spring, valve and weight from body.

Inspection

178 Check weight and valve body for scoring or burrs. Minor scoring or burrs may be removed with a fine abrasive.

179 Check spring for distortion; renew if necessary.

180 Check fluid passages for obstruction; clear passages with compressed air.

Reassembling

181 Reverse operations 175 to 177.

182 Check weight and valve for free movement.

CAUTION: If weight or valve show signs of sticking governor body assembly must be renewed.

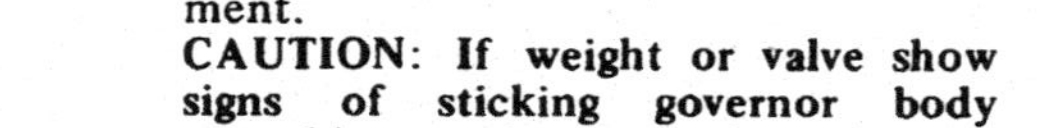

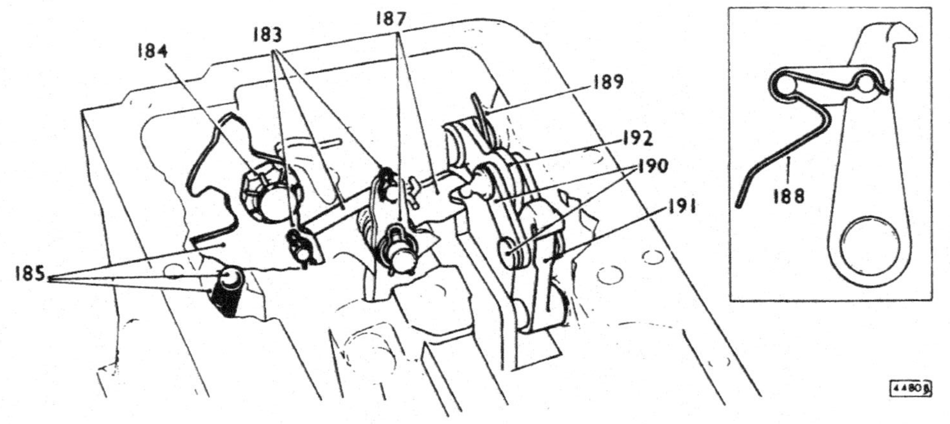

PARKING BRAKE PAWL ASSEMBLY

Overhaul

Dismantling
183 Remove clips retaining link rod; withdraw rod.
184 Remove nut securing manual shaft lever; withdraw lever.
185 Remove lever detent, ball and spring.
186 Withdraw and discard seal.
187 Remove retaining clip, washer and torsion lever.
188 Note fitted position of pawl return spring.
189 Withdraw pawl return spring and retaining clip.
190 Remove toggle link and pins.
191 Move pawl back and forth until pin protrudes, then withdraw pin and pawl.
192 Drive toggle lever towards gearbox casing; withdraw toggle lever pivot pin and toggle lever.

Inspection
193 Check components for excess wear, renew if necessary.
194 Check springs for distortion; renew if necessary.
195 Check pawl tooth for signs of chipping or uneven wear, renew if damaged.

Reassembling
196 Lightly grease all pivots and pins.
197 Reverse operations 183 to 192.

BRAKE BANDS

Inspection
198 Check front and rear brake bands for damage or distortion.
199 Check linings for uneven, excess wear or damage.
CAUTION: Should doubt exist as to condition of brake bands or bands show any of the conditions detailed above, they must be renewed.

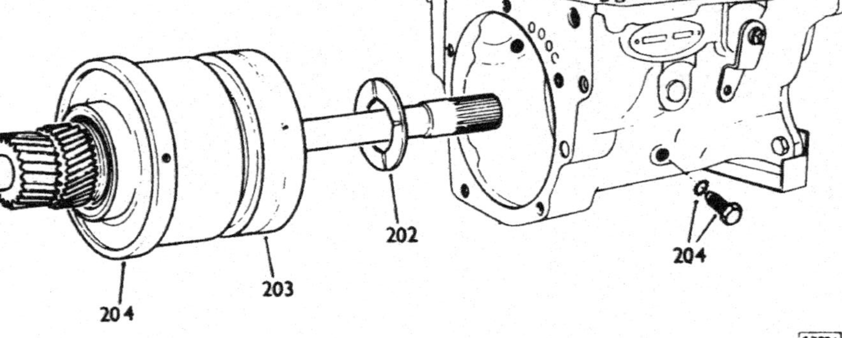

TRANSMISSION ASSEMBLY

Reassembling
200 Thoroughly clean gearcase; blow all oil holes through with dry, clean compressed air.
201 Position front brake band in transmission case.
202 Ensure that thrust washer, fitted in operation 137 is correctly positioned on turbine shaft.
203 Hold front and rear clutch assemblies firmly together and enter them into gearcase through rear aperture; fit needle thrust bearing and steel backing washer.
CAUTION: On no account must clutch assemblies be allowed to separate as damage to sealing rings on forward sun gear shaft will result.
204 Position centre support in gearcase, fit two side retaining bolts and lockwashers; DO NOT tighten bolts at this stage.

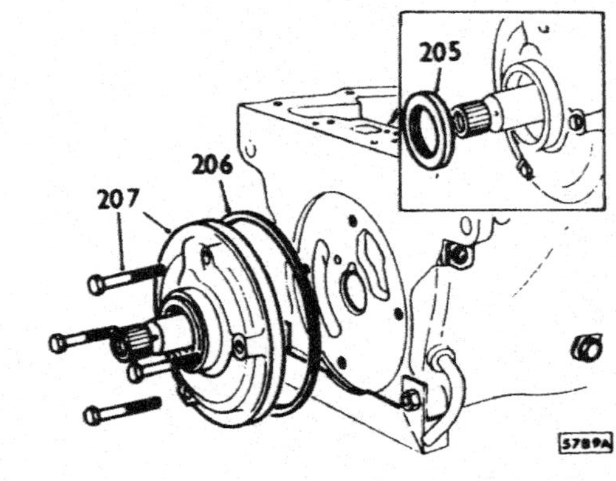

205 Smear new oil pump oil seal with clean transmission fluid; press oil seal into pump body using hand pressure only.

continued

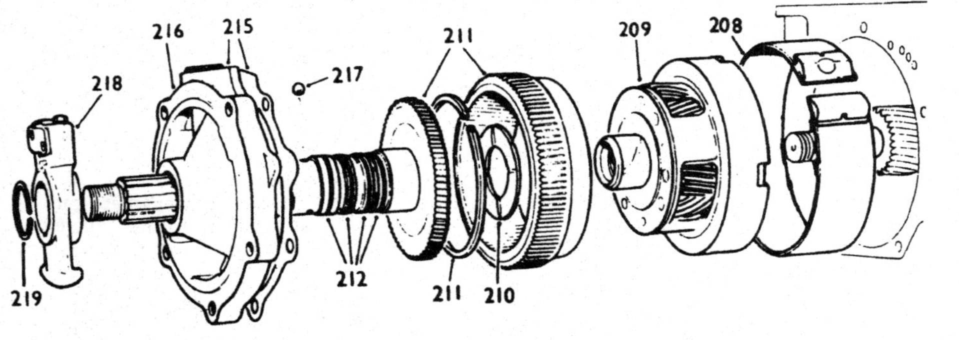

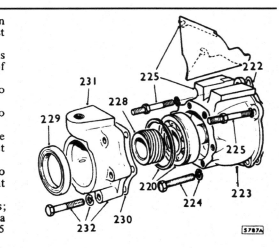

206 Lightly grease new oil pump sealing ring with petroleum jelly; position ring in recess in gearcase.
207 Position oil pump assembly on gearcase; tighten bolts evenly to a torque of 17 to 22 lb.ft. (2,35 to 3,0 kg/m.).
208 Position rear brake band in gearcase.
209 Fit planet gear carrier.
NOTE: If one way clutch has been removed, it must be refitted with lip on periphery of clutch facing towards gears.
CAUTION: The thrust washer located between the planet ge.ır carrier and output shaft is selective to enable correct end float to be obtained after reassembly. Available selective thrust washer sizes are as follows:

	Inches	Millimetres
1.	.061 – .063	1,55 – 1,60
2.	.067 – .069	1,70 – 1,75
3.	.074 – .076	1,88 – 1,93
4.	.081 – .083	2,06 – 2,11
5.	.092 – .094	2,34 – 2,39
6.	.105 – .107	2,67 – 2,72

Experience has shown that if thrust washer number 4 – .081–.083 ins. (2,06–2,11 mm.) is selected, correct end float of .008 in. to .040 in. (,20 to 1,01 mm.) is usually obtained and it is recommended that this washer be used.
210 Fit thrust washer.
211 Position output shaft in ring gear; fit snap ring ensuring that it is correctly located in groove.
212 Fit new sealing rings on output shaft.
213 Fit output shaft and ring gear assembly.
214 Position sealing rings so that gaps are staggered.
215 Lightly grease new rear adaptor gasket and position on rear adaptor.
216 Fit rear adaptor ensuring that holes in gearcase and adaptor are in alignment.
217 Position governor drive ball in **blind** hole in output shaft; retain drive ball with a smear of grease.
218 Slide governor on to output shaft with oil holes in governor towards gearcase.
219 Fit snap ring; ensure that it is correctly located in groove.
220 Fit snap ring on rear extension housing bearing; ensuring snap ring is correctly located in groove.
221 Lightly grease bearing.
222 Lightly grease new rear extension housing gasket; position gasket on housing.
223 Fit rear extension housing ensuring that holes in housing and rear adaptor are in alignment.
224 Fit securing bolts and lockwasher; do not tighten bolts at this stage.
225 Fit vacuum unit guard, stud bolts and lockwashers; do not tighten stud bolts at this stage.
226 Push bearing into rear extension housing until snap ring abuts against housing.
227 Tighten securing bolts and stud bolts by diagonal selection to a torque of 28 33 lb.ft. (3,9–4,5 kg.m.).
228 Slide speedometer drive gear on to output shaft.
229 Lightly oil new seal and press into speedometer drive gear housing.
230 Lightly grease new speedometer drive gear housing gasket; position gasket on housing.
231 Fit speedometer drive gear housing to rear extension housing ensuring that bolt holes are in alignment.
232 Fit securing bolts and spring washers; tighten bolts by diagonal selection to a torque of 28–33 lb.ft. (3,9–4,5 kg.m.).
233 Slide output flange on to output shaft; fit castellated nut.
234 Move manual lever until parking pawl engages ring gear.
235 Tighten output flange securing nut; ensure that split pin hole in output shaft is in alignment with one of the castellations in the nut. **DO NOT** fit split pin at this stage.
236 Assemble end float gauge CBW.33 to gearcase with stylus contacting end of turbine shaft; insert a suitable lever between front clutch and front of gearcase. Ease gear train to rear of gearcase and zero end float gauge.
237 Insert lever between ring gear and rear clutch and ease gear train to front of gearcase.
238 Note reading on gauge which should be between .008–.040 in. (,20 mm.–1,01 mm.).
CAUTION: If end float is not within above limits, reverse operations 213 to 235 and select thrust washer which will bring end float within limits. For example: if end float exceeds .040 in. (1,01 mm.) select a thicker thrust washer, number 5 or 6. If, however, end float is less than .008 in. (,20 mm.) select a thinner washer, number 1, 2 or 3. Repeat operations 213 to 238.

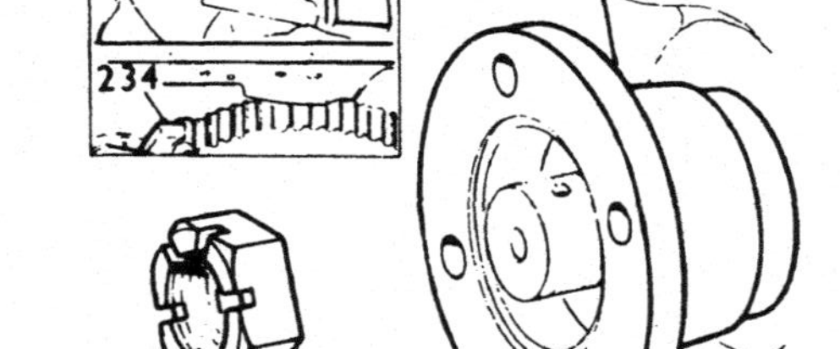

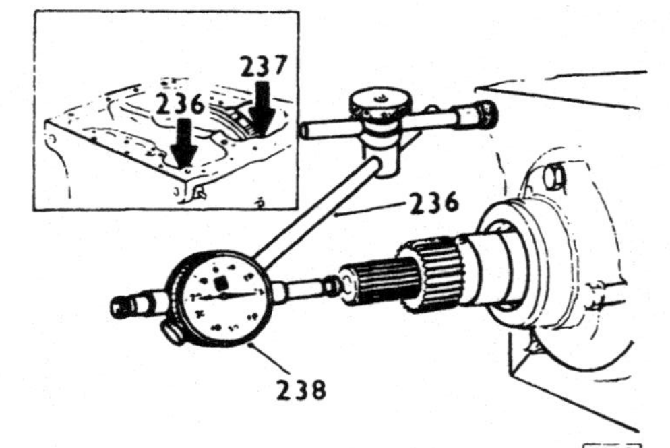

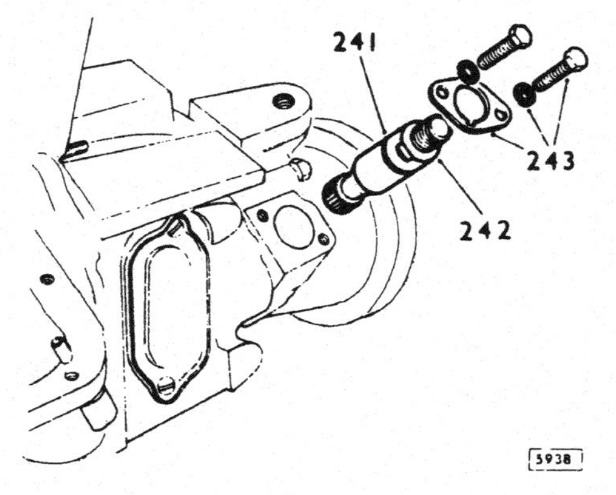

239 Remove end float gauge.
240 Fit new split pin to lock output flange nut.
241 Lubricate new 'O' ring with petroleum jelly and fit to speedometer driven gear shaft.
242 Fit speedometer driven gear ensuring that gear meshes correctly with drive gear.
243 Fit cover and securing bolts and spring washers.
244 Locate rear servo adjusting screw in tapped hole in gearcase; turn screw until ball end protrudes into gearcase.
245 Fit adjusting screw locknut but do not tighten at this stage.
246 Position cast brake band strut on ball end of rear servo adjusting screw and rotate rear brake band until it is in contact with strut; ensure that staking on brake band locates in slot in strut.
247 Position steel brake band strut on rear servo operating lever.
NOTE: Strut should be retained in position with a smear of grease.
248 Position rear servo on gearcase ensuring that staking on rear brake band locates in slot in strut.
249 Fit servo retaining bolts and spring washers but do not tighten at this stage.
250 Screw in rear servo adjusting screw until finger tight.
251 Ensure that steel brake band strut has not been displaced and tighten securing bolts to a torque of 40–50 lb.ft. (5,5–6,9 kg.m.).
252 Tighten two centre support side bolts to a torque of 20–25 lb.ft. (2,8–3,45 kg.m.).
253 Position front brake band upper strut in gearcase ensuring that spigot on rear of strut is located in hole in gearcase.
254 Fit remaining brake band strut to front servo ensuring that staking on servo operating lever locates in slot in strut.
NOTE: Strut should be retained in position with a smear of grease.
255 Position front servo on gearcase and compress front brake band slightly until strut can be fitted under lip of brake band.
256 Fit servo retaining bolts and spring washers but do not tighten at this stage.
257 Ensure that brake band strut has not been displaced.
258 Lubricate new 'O' ring with petroleum jelly and fit to cable connector.
259 Insert cable connector into gearcase.
260 Slide servo tubes into holes in front servo.
261 Move manual lever to 'R' position.
262 Position valve block on gearcase and insert servo tubes.
263 Ensure that spigot on detent lever is located in groove in manual valve.
264 Fit valve block retaining bolts. Tighten, working from centre outwards, to a torque of ¼ U.N.F. bolts 5–8 lb.ft. (0,7–1,1 kg.m.) and 5/16 U.N.F. bolts 17–20 lb.ft. (2,3–2,7 kg.m.).
265 Tighten front servo retaining bolts to a torque of 30–35 lb.ft. (4,15–4,8 kg.m.).
266 Connect kickdown solenoid valve to connector.

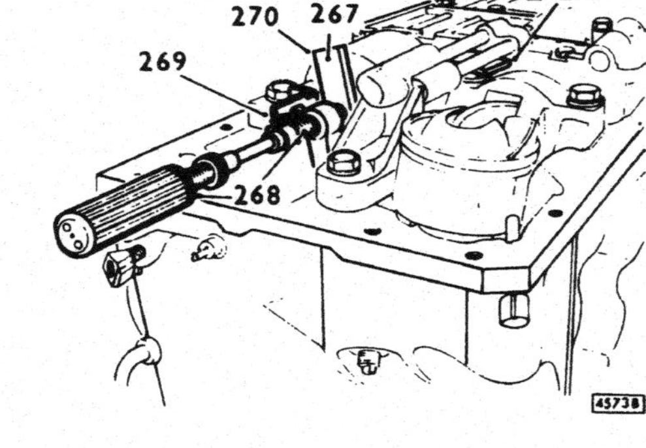

267 Pull front servo operating lever back and insert gauge block CBW.34 between adjusting screw and piston pin.
268 Using torque screwdriver CBW.548 and adaptors CBW.547A-50-5 and CBW.548-1, tighten adjusting screw to 10 lb.inches (,12 kg.m.).
CAUTION: Adjusting screw has a left hand thread.
269 Ensure that locking spring is located in retaining slot.
270 Remove gauge block.
271 Place magnet on rear servo mounting bolt.
272 Insert vacuum unit push rod through gearcase and into valve block.
273 Lubricate new 'O' ring with petroleum jelly and fit on to vacuum unit.
274 Insert end of push rod in vacuum unit; screw unit into gearcase. DO NOT overtighten.

continued

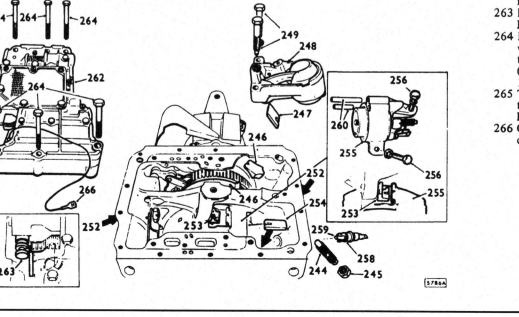

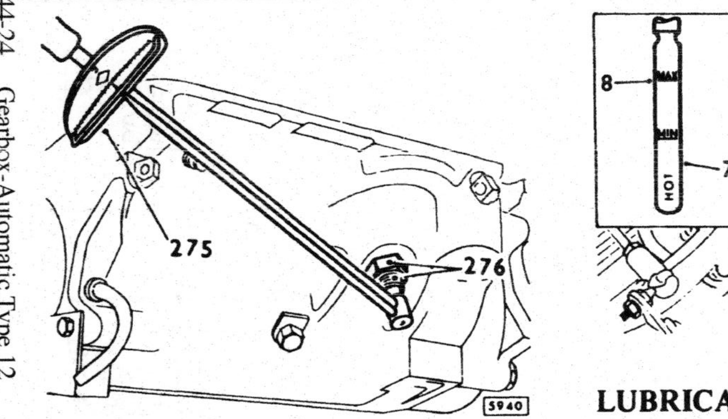

275 Tighten rear servo adjusting screw to a torque of 10 lb.ft. (1,4 kg.m.).

276 Loosen adjusting screw 1.25 turns and tighten locknut.

CAUTION: Ensure screw does not turn when tightening locknut as severe damage to transmission unit will result if screw is not backed off exactly 1.25 turns.

277 Lightly grease new oil pan gasket and position on gearcase.

278 Fit oil pan retaining bolts and spring washers. Tighten bolts progressively to a torque of 10–13 lb.ft. (1,4–1,8 kg.m.).

279 Remove bench cradle.

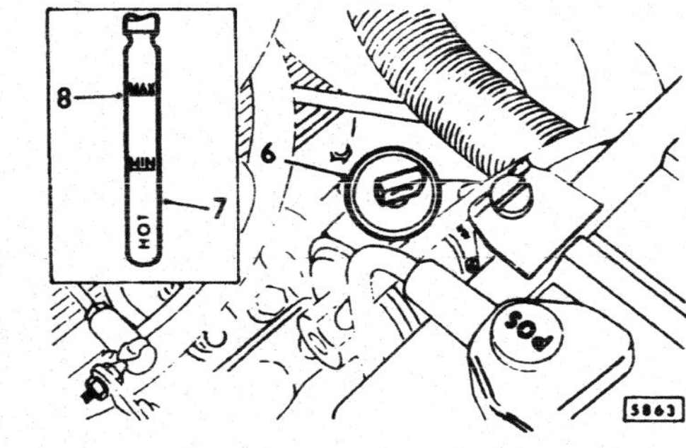

LUBRICATION SYSTEM

Drain and refill **44.24.02**

CAUTION: Due to method of construction, it is not possible to completely drain transmission fluid, and this should be taken into account when transmission is being refilled. As it should only be necessary to carry out the following operations preparatory to carrying out work on the transmission which will involve removal of oil pan, the following procedure should be followed. It is possible, however, to drain a smaller amount of fluid by removing dipstick/filler tube.

Draining
1 Remove oil pan – 44.24.04.
2 Discard fluid.

Refilling
3 Refit oil pan, fill transmission to 'MAX' mark on dipstick.
4 Apply handbrake and select 'P' position.
5 Run engine until it reaches normal operating temperature.
6 With engine still running, withdraw dipstick, wipe clean and replace.
7 Immediately withdraw dipstick and note reading on 'HOT' side of dipstick.
8 If necessary, add fluid to bring level on dipstick to 'MAX'.

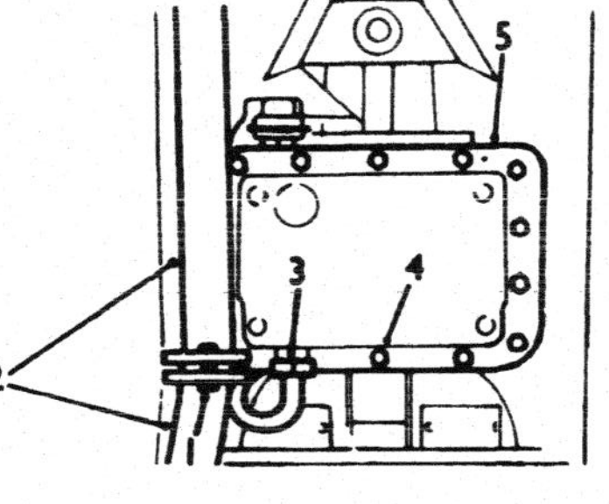

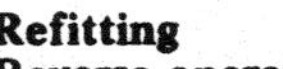

OIL PAN

Remove and refit **44.24.04**

Removing
1 Remove nuts and bolts securing intermediate exhaust pipe clamp.
2 Separate intermediate exhaust pipe from down pipe.
3 Unscrew union nut securing dipstick/filler tube to oil pan, withdraw tube.
4 Remove bolts and spring washers securing oil pan to transmission case.
5 Lower oil pan; remove and discard gasket.
6 Discard fluid.

Refitting
7 Reverse operations 1 to 5, use new gasket.
8 Refill transmission – See operation 44.24.02.

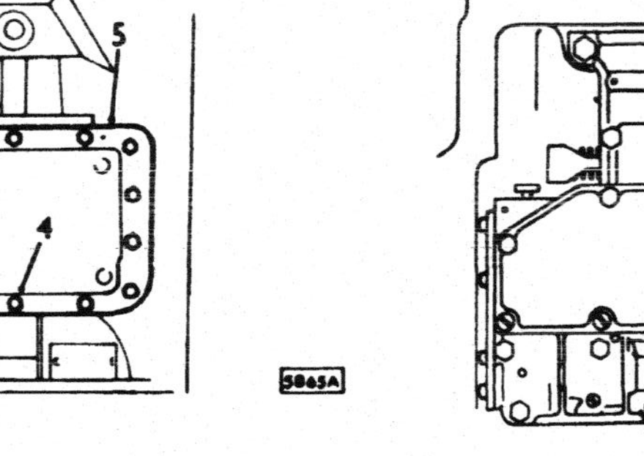

OIL STRAINER

Remove and refit **44.24.07**

Removing
1 Remove oil pan – 44.24.04.
2 Remove pan head screws and bolts securing strainer to valve block; detach strainer.
3 Thoroughly clean strainer.

Refitting
Reverse operations 1 and 2.

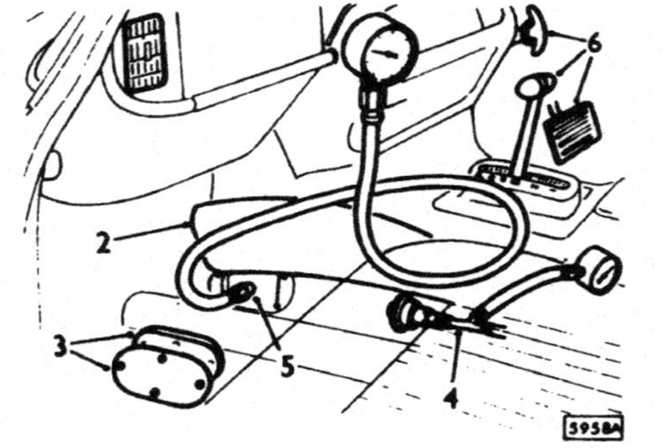

VACUUM CONTROL UNIT

Line pressure check and adjustment **44.30.05**

Special tools – Pressure gauge CBW.1A-642; Adaptor STN.5752.

1 Check engine tune i.e. cylinder compressions, spark plugs, ignition timing.
2 Lift carpet from left hand side of gearbox housing.
3 Remove access plate.
4 Disconnect pipe from vacuum control unit. Insert 'T' piece union and reconnect pipe. Connect a vacuum gauge to centre junction.
5 Remove the .125 in. (3,2 mm.) plug at gear case front left-hand side and connect the pressure gauge CBW.1A-642 using adaptor STN.5752.
6 With engine and transmission at normal running temperature select 'D', apply hand and foot brakes.
7 Accelerate engine until vacuum gauge reads 9–10 in. (23–25 cm.) Hg at 1,200 r.p.m.
8 Check reading of line pressure gauge which should be:
$75 {}^{+20}_{-5}$ lb/in^2 ($5{,}27 {}^{+1{,}40}_{-0{,}35}$ Kg/cm^2)
NOTE: Pressure reading below 70 p.s.i. (4,9 kg/cm^2) at 1,200 r.p.m. will result in possible clutch slip and damage to transmission.
9 To gain access to vacuum control unit control screw, remove vacuum hose.
10 Insert screwdriver and turn clockwise to increase line pressure and anti-clockwise to decrease line pressure.
CAUTION. Approximately two full turns on screw will vary pressure about 10 lb./in.^{2} (0,7 kg./cm^2). THERE IS NO LOCKNUT ON THE SCREW. Therefore, when all feel of loading on screw has been removed, it must be turned clockwise half-a-turn to ensure contact with the servo actuating rod. If contact is not maintained, a rapid knocking noise will be evident between 600 to 800 r.p.m.
11 After each adjustment replace vacuum hose and re-check line pressure as before.
CAUTION: To avoid over-heating of transmission, do not stall for more than 10 seconds at a time or for a total of one minute in any half hour period.
12 Remove vacuum gauge, refit hose.
13 Remove pressure gauge, refit plug.
14 Refit access plate.
15 Refit carpet.

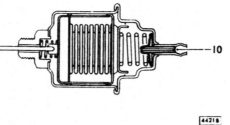

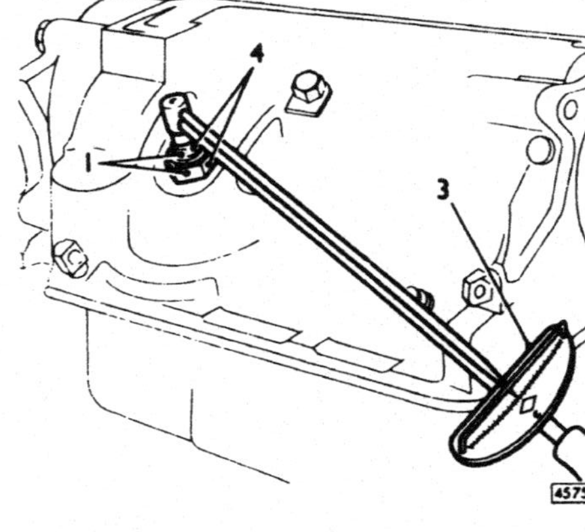

FRONT BRAKE BAND

Adjustment **44.30.07**

Service Tools: Torque screwdriver CBW.548; Screwdriver bit adaptors CBW.547A-50-5 and CBW.548-1; Gauge block CBW.34.

1 Remove oil pan – 44.24.04.
2 Slacken adjusting screw until it no longer contacts piston pin.
CAUTION: Adjusting screw has a left hand thread.
3 Pull front servo operating lever back and insert gauge block CBW.34 between adjusting screw and piston pin.
4 Using torque screwdriver CBW.548 and adaptors CBW.547A-50-5 and CBW.548-1, tighten adjusting screw to 10 lb. inches (,12 kg.m.).
CAUTION: Adjusting screw has a left hand thread.
5 Ensure that locking spring is located in retaining slot.
6 Remove gauge block.
7 Refit oil pan.

VACUUM CONTROL UNIT DIAPHRAGM

The presence of a rupture in the diaphragm will be indicated by one or all of the following:
1 Engine exhaust will show increased smoking due to oil being drawn from gearbox, through diaphragm up to inlet manifold.
2 Low oil level in transmission.
3 Rough gear changes.

Test **44.30.09**

1 Remove vacuum unit – 44.15.27.
2 Couple control unit to a suitable vacuum source.
3 If control unit can hold 18 in. (46 cm.) Hg. diaphragm is satisfactory. If, however, vacuum falls below this figure diaphragm is damaged and unit MUST be replaced.
4 Refit vacuum unit.

REAR BRAKE BAND

Adjustment **44.30.10**

Service Tool: Torque wrench CBW.547A-50.

1 Slacken locknut on adjusting screw.

continued

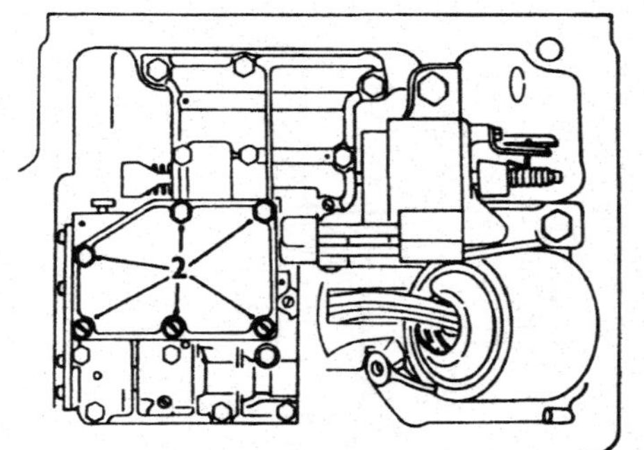

2 Loosen adjusting screw approximately two full turns.
3 Tighten adjusting screw to a torque of 10 lb.ft. (1,4 kg.m.).
4 Loosen adjusting screw 1.25 turns and tighten locknut.
CAUTION: Ensure screw does not turn when tightening locknut as severe damage to transmission unit will result if screw is not backed off exactly 1.25 turns.

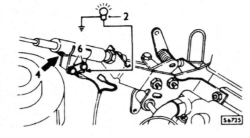

KICKDOWN SOLENOID

Test 44.30.11

1 Disconnect solenoid wire at connector.
2 With jumper lead, momentarily connect battery positive to connector.
3 Solenoid should operate with an audible click if functioning correctly.
4 Refit wire to connector.

KICKDOWN SWITCH

Check and adjust 44.30.12

1 Switch on ignition and check that current is available at input terminal (cable coloured green).
2 Connect earthed test lamp to output terminal (cable colour black/red).
3 Fully depress throttle pedal.
4 If lamp does not light, release throttle pedal and gently depress switch arm.
5 If lamp still does not light, renew switch; see operation 44.15.23. If, however, lamp lights, proceed as follows:
6 Slacken securing bolts and move switch towards cable until at full throttle opening, lamp lights.
7 Tighten securing bolts and recheck.

STALL SPEED

Test 44.30.13

The results of this test indicate condition of gearbox and converter.
Stall speed is maximum engine revolutions recorded whilst driving impeller against stationary turbine. Stall speed will vary with both engine and transmission conditions so before attempting a stall speed check, engine condition must be determined. Engine and transmission must be at normal operating temperature before commencing check.

1 Apply handbrake.
2 Apply footbrake.
3 Start engine.
4 Select 'D'.
5 Fully depress accelerator.
6 Note tachometer reading.
CAUTION: To avoid overheating of transmission do not stall for more than 10 seconds at a time or for a total of one minute in any half hour period.

R.P.M.	CONDITION INDICATED
Under 1,000	Stator free wheel slip
1,600 to 1,700	Normal
Over 2,100	Clutch slip

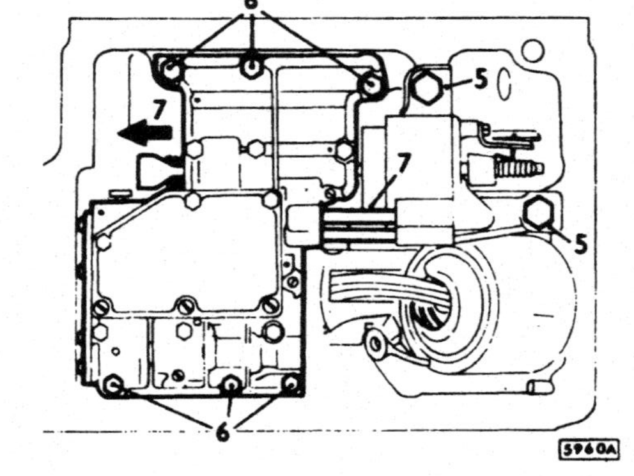

VALVE BLOCK

Remove and refit 44.40.01

Removing
1 Remove oil pan – 44.24.04.
2 Remove kickdown solenoid – 44.15.24.
3 Remove vacuum unit and pushrod – 44.15.27.
4 Select 'R' on transmission selector.
5 Slacken, BUT DO NOT REMOVE front servo retaining bolts.
6 Remove bolt securing valve block to transmission.
7 Slide valve block sideways, withdraw servo tubes; lower valve block.
CAUTION: Ensure manual valve is not displaced.

Refitting
Reverse operations 1 to 7, ensure that spigot on detent lever is located in groove in manual valve.
Tighten fixing bolts from centre outwards to a torque of:
¼ U.N.F. bolts 5–8 lb.ft. (0,7–1,1 kg.m.).
5/16 U.N.F. bolts 17–20 lb.ft. (2,3–2,7 kg.m.).

BORG-WARNER MODEL 65 AUTOMATIC TRANSMISSION

DESCRIPTION

TORQUE CONVERTER
The torque converter is of the three element, single phase type. The three elements are: Impeller, connected to the engine crankshaft; Turbine, connected to the gearbox input shaft, and Stator, mounted on a one-way clutch on the stator support projecting from the gearbox case. The converter provides torque multiplication of from 1 : 1 to 2.3 : 1 and the speed range during which this multiplication is obtained varies with the accelerator position.

GEAR SET
The planetary gear set consists of two sun gears, two sets of pinions, a pinion carrier and a ring gear.
Power enters the gear set via the two sun gears, the forward sun gear driving in forward gears, the reverse sun gear driving in reverse gear. The ring gear, attached to the output shaft, is the driven gear. The planet wheels connect driving and driven gears, two sets of planet wheels being used in forward gears and one set in reverse.
The planet carrier locates the planet wheels relative to sun and ring gears, also serving as a reaction member.

CLUTCHES
The gearbox input shaft is connected to the torque converter turbine at the front end and is therefore known as the turbine shaft. The rear end of the shaft is connected to the front and rear clutches, (the clutches are of the multi disc type operated by hydraulic pressure). Engagement of the front clutch connects the turbine shaft to the forward sun gear. Engagement of the rear clutch connects the turbine shaft to the reverse sun gear.

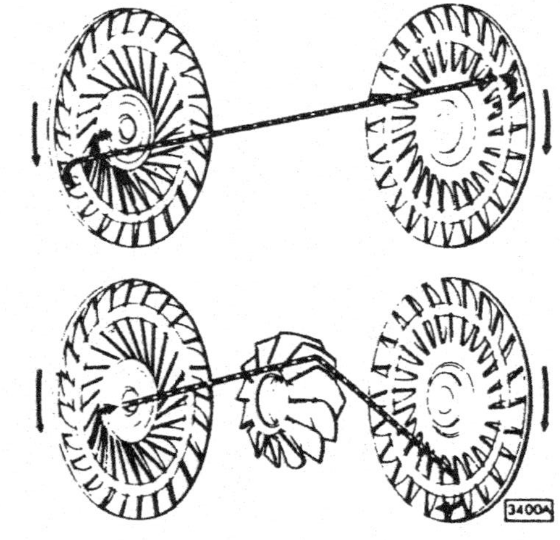

BRAKE BANDS
The brake bands operated by hydraulic servos, are used to hold drive train components stationary in order to obtain low, intermediate and reverse gears. The front band is clamped around the rear clutch outer drum to hold the reverse sun gear stationary. The rear band is clamped around the planet carrier to hold the planet carrier stationary.

ONE-WAY CLUTCH
The "one-way" clutch is situated between the planet carrier and the gearbox case. Rotation of the planet carrier against engine direction is prevented so providing the reaction member for low gear (drive). Rotation of the planet carrier in engine direction is allowed (free-wheeling) providing smooth changes from low to intermediate and intermediate to low gears.

MECHANICAL POWER FLOWS

Neutral and Park
In neutral the front and rear clutches are off, and no power is transmitted from convertor to the gear set. The front and rear bands are also released. In 'P' the rear servo circuit is pressurised while the engine is running, so that the rear band is applied.

First Gear ('D' selected)
The front clutch is applied, connecting convertor to forward sun gear. The one-way clutch is in operation, preventing the planet carrier from rotating anti-clockwise. When the vehicle is coasting the one-way clutch over-runs and the gear set freewheels.

First Gear ('1' selected)
The front clutch is applied, connecting convertor to forward sun gear. The rear band is applied, holding the planet carrier stationary. Planet pinions drive ring gear and reverse sun gear rotates freely in the opposite direction to the forward sun gear.

Second Gear ('D', '2' or '1' selected)
Again the front clutch is applied, connecting convertor to forward sun gear. The front band is applied, holding the reverse sun gear stationary. Combined rotation of planet pinions and carrier drive the ring gear.

Third Gear ('D' selected)
Again the front clutch is applied, connecting convertor to forward sun gear. The rear clutch is applied, connecting the convertor also to the reverse sun gear; thus both sun gears are locked together and the gear set rotates as a unit, providing a ratio of 1 : 1.

Reverse Gear ('R' selected)
The rear clutch is applied, connecting convertor to reverse sun gear. The rear band is applied, holding planet carrier stationary. Planet pinions drive ring gear in an opposite direction to engine rotation.

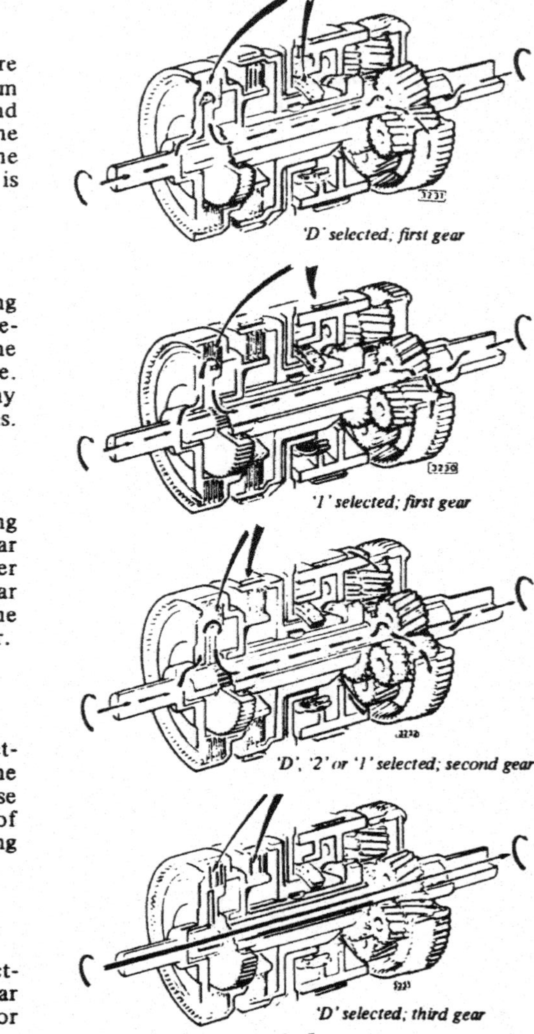

'D' selected; first gear

'1' selected; first gear

'D', '2' or '1' selected; second gear

'D' selected; third gear

'R' selected; reverse gear

	A	B	C	D	E
1 (first gear)	●			●	
D (first gear)	●				●
2&D (sec.gr.)	●		●		
D (third gear)	●	●			
R (rev.gear)		●		●	

4610A

Clutch and band application chart

A Front Clutch
B Rear Clutch
C Front Band
D Rear Band
E One Way Clutch

KEY TO COMPONENTS SHOWN ON HYDRAULIC CHARTS

A Torque Convertor
B Front Clutch
C Rear Clutch
D Front Servo
E Rear Servo
F Governor
G Pump
H Primary Regulator
J Secondary Regulator
K 2-3 Shift Valve
L 1-2 Shift Valve
M Servo Orifice Control Valve
N Manual Valve
P Downshift Valve
Q Throttle Valve
R Modulator Valve

KEY TO HYDRAULIC CHART CODE

– Pump pressure
– To torque convertor
– Governor line pressure
– Governor modulator valve
– Pump suction

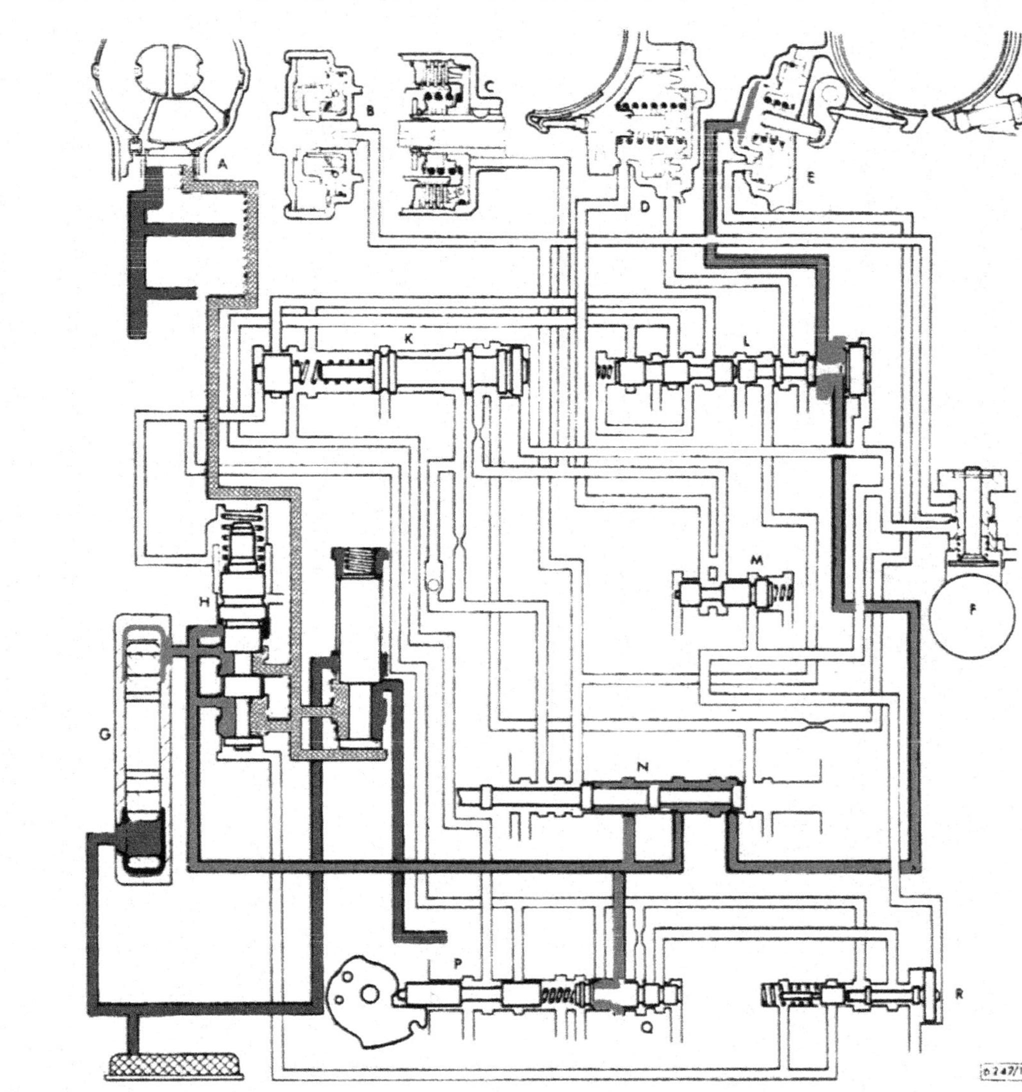

HYDRAULIC OPERATION IN 'P' (PARK)

Coupled to the manual valve operating lever is a linkage incorporating a pawl; movement of this lever to the 'Park' position engages the pawl with the toothed outer surface of the ring gear, so locking the output shaft to the transmission case. The rear servo is energised in 'P' selection but, as both the front and rear clutches are not energised, drive is impossible and the transmission remains inoperative.

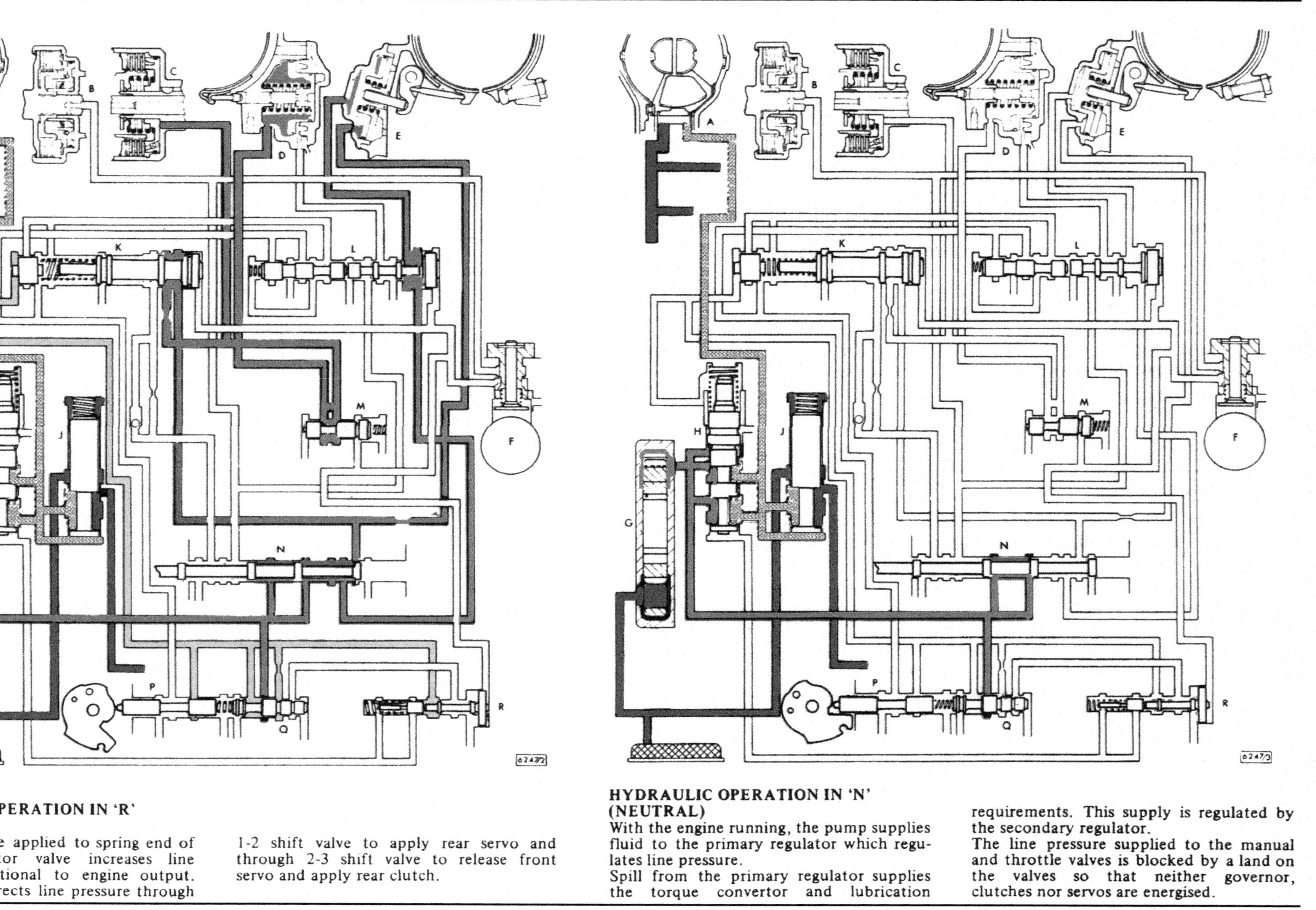

HYDRAULIC OPERATION IN 'R' (REVERSE)

Throttle pressure applied to spring end of primary regulator valve increases line pressure proportional to engine output. Manual valve directs line pressure through 1-2 shift valve to apply rear servo and through 2-3 shift valve to release front servo and apply rear clutch.

HYDRAULIC OPERATION IN 'N' (NEUTRAL)

With the engine running, the pump supplies fluid to the primary regulator which regulates line pressure.

Spill from the primary regulator supplies the torque convertor and lubrication requirements. This supply is regulated by the secondary regulator.

The line pressure supplied to the manual and throttle valves is blocked by a land on the valves so that neither governor, clutches nor servos are energised.

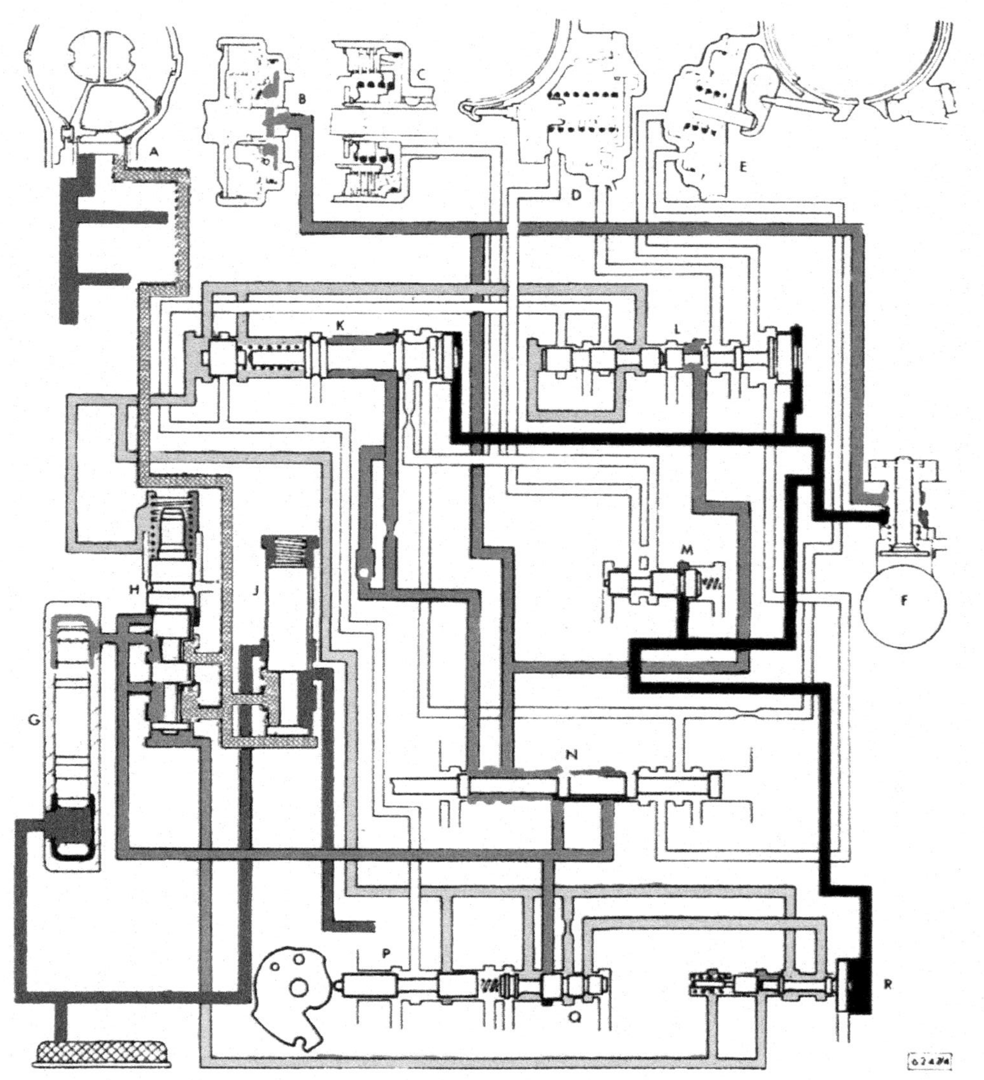

HYDRAULIC OPERATION IN 'D' (FIRST GEAR)

Throttle pressure is applied to spring end of primary regulator valve. When throttle valve is in full throttle position, modulator valve plug applies regulated line pressure to other end of primary regulator valve thereby controlling shift quality.

Manual valve directs line pressure to apply front clutch thereby enabling vehicle to move off in first gear.

Manual valve also directs line pressure to governor feed and to 1-2, 2-3 shift valves for subsequent upwards gearshifts.

HYDRAULIC OPERATION IN 'D' (SECOND GEAR)

Pressure control by primary regulator valve functions as described in 'D' (First gear).
When governor pressure exceeds throttle pressure, 1-2 shift valve moves and directs line pressure to front servo which applies front brake band. Front clutch being applied, transmission operates in second gear.
When downshift valve is in forced throttle (kickdown) position, forced throttle pressure acts upon 1-2 and 2-3 shift valves thereby delaying upshifts or, if governor pressure is low, causes a 2-1 downshift.

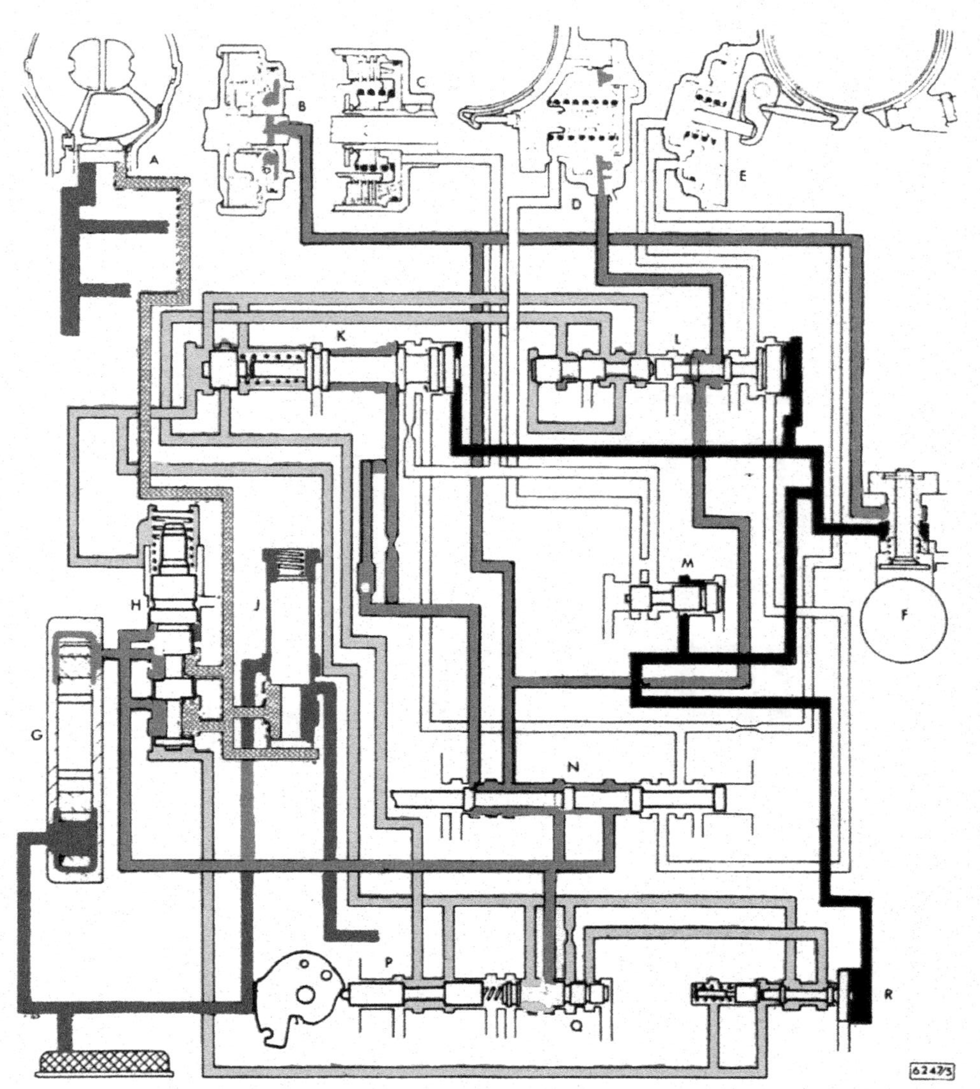

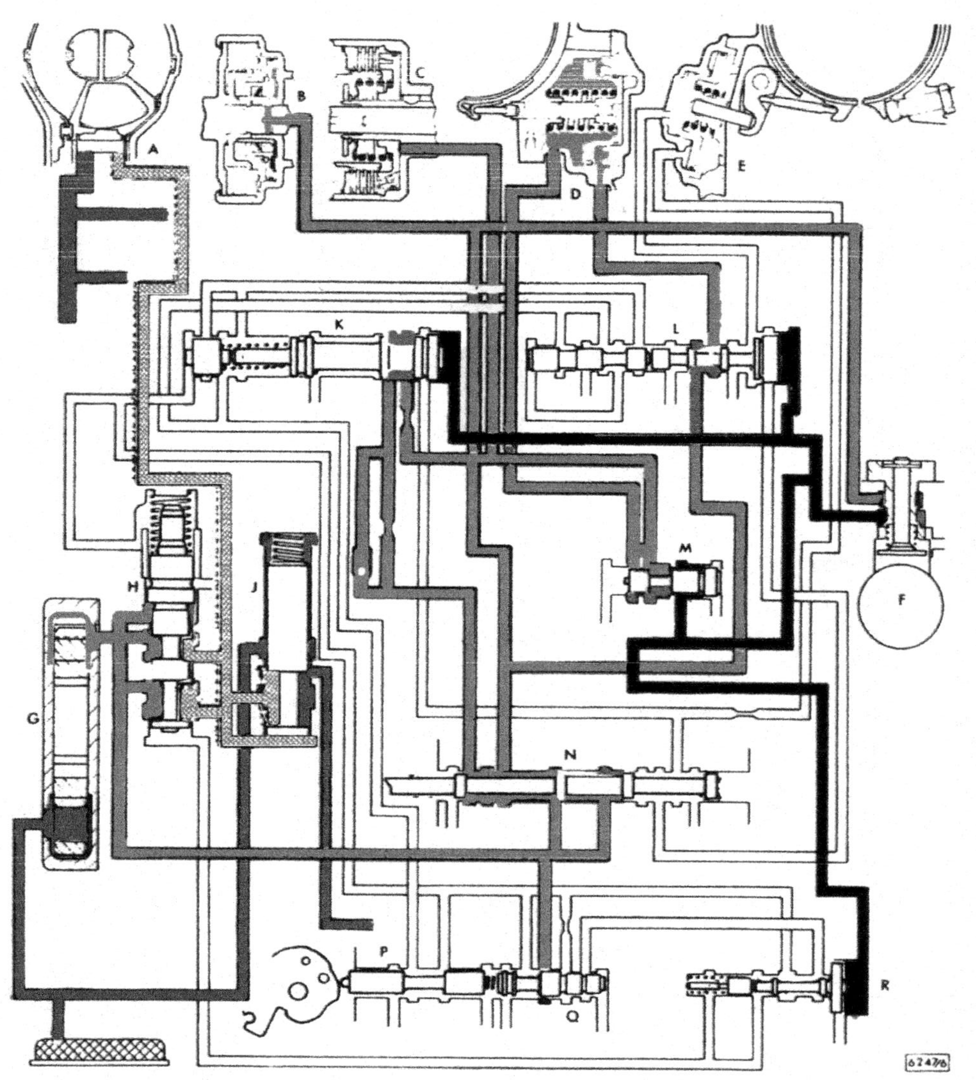

HYDRAULIC OPERATION IN 'D' (THIRD GEAR)

Pressure control by primary regulator valve functions as described in 'D' (First gear).

2-3 shift occurs early at light throttle or late at full throttle depending upon balance between governor and throttle pressure. When governor pressure exceeds throttle pressure, 2-3 shift valve directs line pressure to rear clutch and also to "release" side of front servo via servo orifice control valve.

The timed relationship between rear clutch "apply" and front servo "release" is dependent on governor pressure which in turn is controlled by road speed. A high governor pressure closes servo orifice control valve so directing front servo "release" fluid through a restrictor thereby delaying front servo "release" in relation to rear clutch "apply"

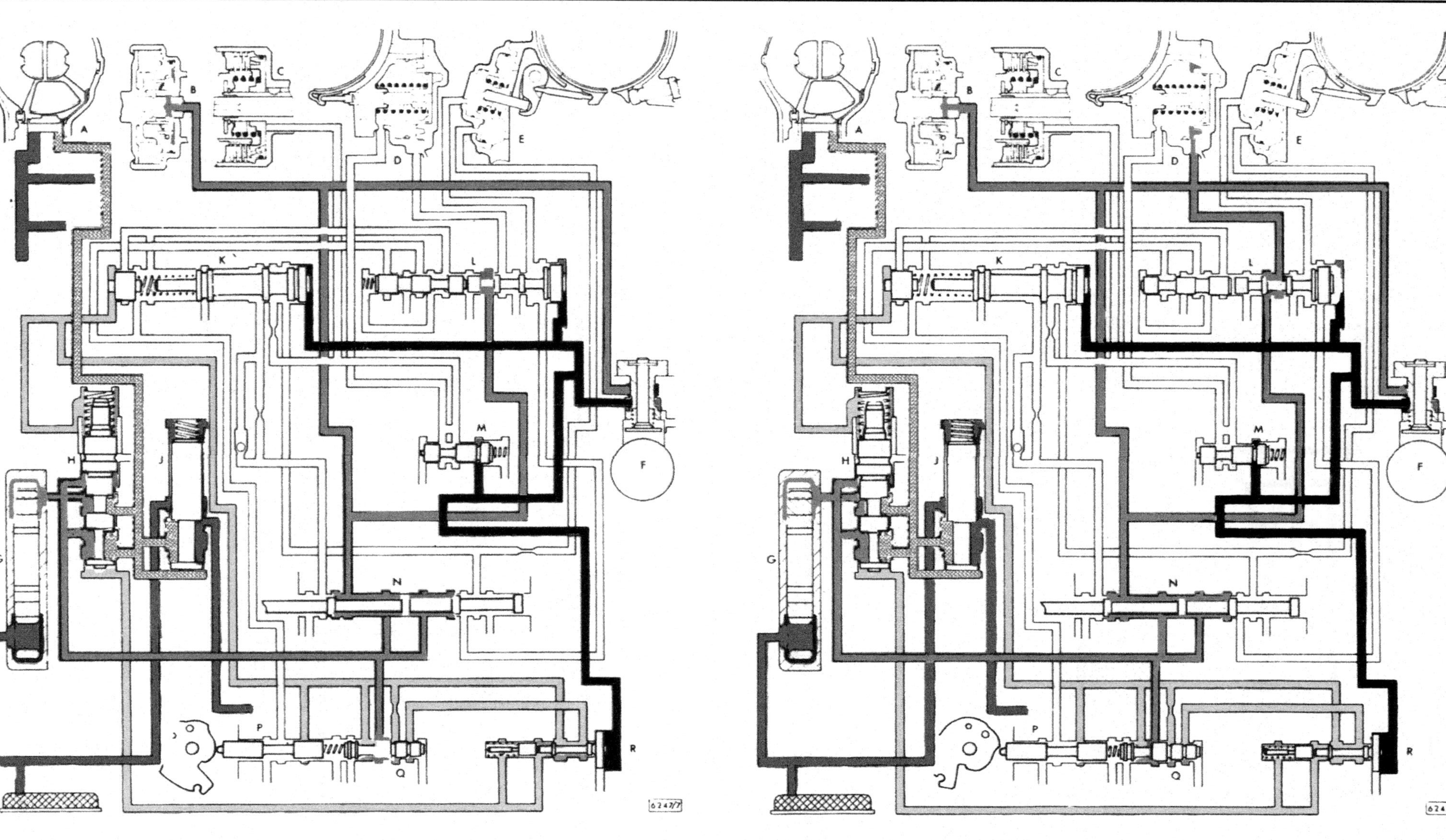

HYDRAULIC OPERATION IN '2' (LOW GEAR)

Pressure control by primary regulator valve functions as described in 'D' (First gear). Front clutch is applied but as engine speed is low, governor pressure causes 1-2 shift valve to remain closed thereby blocking feed from modulator valve.

HYDRAULIC OPERATION IN '2' (SECOND GEAR)

Front clutch is still applied and as engine speed increases, governor pressure rises and moves 1-2 shift valve. This allows pressure from manual valve to front servo "apply".

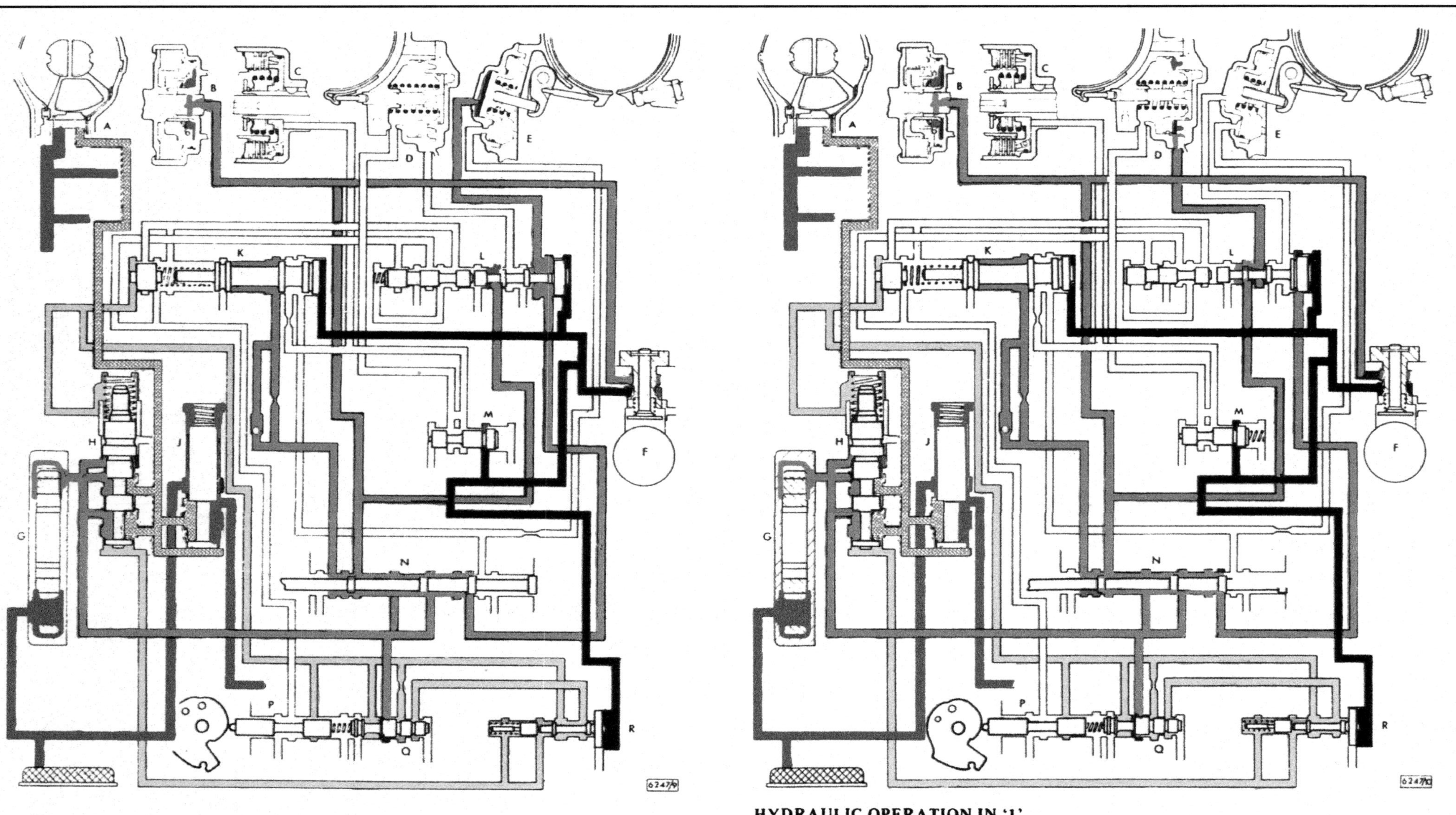

HYDRAULIC OPERATION IN '1' (LOW GEAR)

Pressure control by primary regulator valve functions as described in 'D' First gear. Manual valve directs line pressure to front clutch, governor feed and 1-2 shift valve.

Pressure is also directed to enlarged end of 1-2 shift valve so opposing governor pressure and hydraulically locking the valve. Rear servo is also applied and no upshift can occur.

HYDRAULIC OPERATION IN '1' (SECOND GEAR)

When selector lever is moved to position '1' at speed, front servo is released and a downshift from high to intermediate gear occurs. A further downshift to low gear occurs when vehicle speed falls sufficiently.

ROAD TEST AND FAULT DIAGNOSES

44.00.00

The following points should be checked before proceeding with the road test.

1. Fluid level.
2. Engine idle speed.
3. Manual lever adjustment.

ROAD TEST

The road speed figures for the tests listed below are to be found under "GENERAL DATA – GEAR CHANGE SPEEDS".

Road testing should follow the complete sequence detailed below. Transmission should be at normal working temperature, i.e. after being driven on road or rollers.

1 With brakes applied and engine idling, move selector from:
  'N' to 'R'
  'N' to 'D'
  'N' to '2'
  'N' to '1'
  Engagement should be felt with each selection.
2 Check stall speed.
3 Select 'D', accelerate with minimum throttle opening and check speed of first gear to second gear shift.
4 Continue with minimum throttle and check speed of second gear to third gear shift.
5 Select 'D', accelerate with maximum throttle opening (kickdown) and check speed of first gear to second gear shift.
6 Continue with maximum throttle and check speed of second gear to third gear shift.
7 Check for kickdown shift third gear to second gear.
8 Check for kickdown shift second gear to first gear.
9 Check for kickdown shift third gear to first gear.
10 Check for "roll-out" downshift with minimum throttle, second gear to first gear.
11 Check for part throttle downshift, third gear to second gear.

Should a fault be apparent during road test, first identify the problem from the list printed in the Fault Diagnosis Chart. The reference numbers shown opposite each fault may be translated by reference to the page headed "Transmission Fault Key".

FAULT DIAGNOSIS

	ACTION
STATIONARY TEST FINDINGS	
Starter will not operate in 'P' or 'N' or operates in all positions	22
Faulty operation of reverse lights	22
Excessive bump on engagement of 'D', '1' and 'R'	3, 4
Drives in 'N' also giving judder or no drive in 'R' depending on degree of front clutch seizure	2, 9
STALL TEST FINDINGS	
Stall test shows over 2,100 rpm (transmission slip), with possible squawk in '1' and 'R'	4
a. only in '1'	9
b. only in 'R'	6, 8, 10, 21, 15
Stall test shows under 1,300 rpm (slipping stator)	20
DRIVING TEST FINDINGS	
Selection faults	
Incorrect selection of all positions except 'P'	2
Parking pawl does not hold vehicle	16
Ratio faults	
No drive in 'D', '2', '1' or 'R' but 'P' operates	1, 2, 4
No drive in 'D', '2' or '1'	12, 13, 9
No drive in 'D' 1st ratio	17
No drive in '1' and transmission binding during shift from '1' to 'D'	23
No second ratio	5, 7, 11
No D3 (Reverse indicating rear clutch normal)	11
Drag in 'D'	6
Drag in 'D', '1' and reverse	5
No engine braking in '1' and no drive in reverse ratio	6, 8, 15
Moves off in 2nd ratio in 'D' and '1' and no drive in reverse or engine braking in '1'	11
Shift point faults	
Incorrect or erratic "kickdown" and/or light throttle shift points	4, 12, 13
1-2 shift only incorrect	11
2-3 shift only incorrect	11
No up-shifts	12, 13
Lack of 'up-shifts' and no reverse ratio	11
Moves off with possible transmission slip	12
Reduced maximum speed in all ratios, more so in 'D', and severe convertor overheating	20
Shift quality faults	
Bumpy and possibly delayed shifts	4
Slip (engine "flare-up") shifting into and out of second ratio	5, 7, 11, 14
Slip (engine "flare-up") on 2-3 and 3-2 shifts	10, 11, 21
Noise faults	
Whining noise from convertor area, continuous whenever the engine is running	18
Irregular (possibly grating) noises from gearbox but not in 'D'	19
Whine from convertor, for short period following engine starting after vehicle has been standing for, say, not less than 12 hours	24

TRANSMISSION FAULT KEY

ACTIONS	
1	Check fluid level.
2	Check manual selector/adjustment.
3	Reduce engine idle speed.
4	Check down-shift throttle cable/adjustment. If pressure cannot be corrected, dismantle and clean valve bodies. For low pressure also check strainer, alloy suction pipe, 'O' ring and pump.
5	Check front brake band adjustment.
6	Check rear brake band adjustment.
7	Check front servo seals and fit of pipes.
8	Check rear servo seals and fit of pipe.
9	Examine front clutch, support housing and forward sun gear shaft seals.
10	Check rear clutch feed pipe.
11	Strip valve bodies and clean.
12	Strip governor valve and clean.
13	Examine output shaft rings and governor pressure tube seals.
14	Check front brake band for wear.
15	Check rear brake band for wear.
16	Adjust/examine parking pawl, linkage, and gear.
17	Renew one-way clutch.
18	Examine pump gears and convertor nose bush.
19	Strip and examine gear train.
20	Replace torque convertor.
21	Examine rear clutch and sealing rings.
22	Test inhibitor switch, circuit, and check for operation.
23	Check one-way clutch (possibly fitted backwards).
24	Ball check valve in forward sun gear shaft faulty, no detriment to performance.

GENERAL DATA

Gear train end float . . . . 0.008 to 0.029 in. (0,21 to 0,73 mm.)
Pinion end float . . . . 0.010 to 0.020 in. (0,25 to 0,51 mm.)
Minimum clutch plate coning . . . . 0.010 in. (0,25 mm.)
Thrust washer sizes . . . . Std: 0.068 in. (1,72 mm.)
Alternative: 0.080 in. (2,03 mm.)
Control pressure . . . . 60 to 90 lb/in^2 (4,2 to 6,33 kg/sq.cm.)
Stall speed (normal) . . . . 1,950 to 2,100 r.p.m.

GEAR CHANGE SPEEDS

4.2 L

Throttle Position		Upshifts 1 to 2	Upshifts 2 to 3	Downshifts 3 to 2	Downshifts 3 to 1	Downshifts 2 to 1
Minimum	M.P.H.	8–12	13–18			
Full	M.P.H.	41–51	73–81			
Full throttle Kickdown	M.P.H.			63–73	25–35	
Closed throttle downshift (Roll out)	M.P.H.					5–10
Part throttle Kickdown	M.P.H.			32–42		
Minimum	K.P.H.	13–19	21–29			
Full	K.P.H.	66–82	117–130			
Full throttle Kickdown	K.P.H.			101–117	40–56	
Closed throttle downshift (Roll out)	K.P.H.					8–16
Part throttle Kickdown	K.P.H.			51–67		

3.4 L

Throttle Position		Upshifts 1 to 2	Upshifts 2 to 3	Downshifts 3 to 2	Downshifts 3 to 1	Downshifts 2 to 1
Minimum	M.P.H.	7–10	16–18			
Full	M.P.H.	34–38	60–66			
Full throttle Kickdown	M.P.H.			60–65	34–37	
Closed throttle downshift (Roll out)	M.P.H.			10–11		5–7
Part throttle Kickdown	M.P.H.			44–46		
Minimum	K.P.H.	11–16	25–29			
Full	K.P.H.	55–60	96–106			
Full throttle Kickdown	K.P.H.			96–105	55–60	
Closed throttle downshift (Roll out)	K.P.H.			16–18		8–11
Part throttle Kickdown	K.P.H.			70–74		

NOTE: The figures in these tables are theoretical and actual figures may vary slightly from those quoted due to such factors as tyre wear, pressures etc.

VALVE SPRING IDENTIFICATION

The following spring identification table is given to assist in identifying valve springs when overhaul work is being carried out. **When valve block is dismantled, springs should be compared with dimensions given. Any spring which is distorted or coil bound MUST be** replaced.

DESCRIPTION	LENGTH	DIAMETER	NUMBER OF COILS	COLOUR
Secondary regulator valve	2,593 in. (65,8 mm.)	.480–.490 in. (12,2–12,4 mm.)	23	Blue
Primary regulator valve	2.94 in. (74,6 mm.)	.604–.610 in. (15,3–15,5 mm.)	14	Blue
Servo orifice control valve	1.005 in. (25,5 mm.)	.198–.208 in. (5,0–5,3 mm.)	17	Yellow
2-3 Shift valve	1.59 in. (40,4 mm.)	.275–.285 in. (6,9–7,2 mm.)	22.5	Yellow
1-2 Shift valve	1.094 in. (27,7 mm.)	.230–.240 in. (5,8–6,1 mm.)	13	Plain
Throttle return valve	.807 in. (20,5 mm.)	.136–.146 in. (3,4–3,7 mm.)	28	Yellow
Modulator valve	1.069 in. (27,1 mm.)	.150–.160 in. (3,8–4,1 mm.)	19	Plain
Throttle valve	1.175–1.185 in. (29,8–30,1 mm.)	.230–.240 in. (5,8–6,1 mm.)	18	Green
Dump ball valve	.70 in. (17,7 mm.)	.210–.230 in. (5,3–5,8 mm.)	16	Plain or White

DOWNSHIFT CABLE

Remove and refit **44.15.01**

Service Tool: Downshift cable remover tool CBW.62.

Removing

1 Remove oil pan – 44.24.04.
2 Disconnect cable from cam.
3 Position cable remover tool CBW.62 on plastic ferrule, push tool upwards until ferrule, together with cable, is pressed out of transmission case.
4 Remove split pin, washer and clevis pin securing clevis to throttle linkage; discard split pin.
5 Slacken locknut; withdraw downshift cable.

Refitting

6 If old cable is being refitted, renew 'O' ring on ferrule.
7 Lubricate ferrule with clean transmission fluid.
CAUTION: Do not lubricate inner cable.
8 Press ferrule into gearcase; connect cable to cam.
9 Connect clevis to throttle linkage; use a new split pin.
10 With accelerator pedal released and throttle levers resting on idle speed screws, adjust cable until heel of downshift cam just makes contact with downshift valve.
11 With accelerator pedal depressed, check that lobe of cam fully depresses downshift valve.
12 Reverse operation 1.
13 Carry out downshift cable pressure check – 44.30.03.

5
4
S6768

GEAR SELECTOR CABLE

Renew and refit **44.15.08**

Removing

1 Remove console – 76.25.01.
2 Place quadrant selector lever in '1'.
3 Unscrew gear selector knob.
4 Remove screws securing selector indicator; withdraw indicator over selector lever.
5 Remove split pin and washer securing cable to selector lever; detach cable.
6 Unscrew front locknut securing cable to abutment bracket.
7 Lift carpet from left hand side of transmission tunnel.
8 Remove screws securing cable shroud to transmission tunnel; withdraw shroud.
9 Withdraw cable from abutment bracket.
10 Remove screws securing access panel to transmission tunnel.
11 Withdraw panel clean off old sealing compound.
12 Ensure gearbox selector lever is in '1'.
13. Remove nut securing selector cable to gearbox selector lever; detach cable.
14 Remove bolt and spring washer securing trunnion block.
15 Withdraw cable.

Refitting

16 Reverse operations 7 to 15, seal access panel and hole in cable shroud with suitable non-hardening sealing compound.
17 Fit front locknut to cable but do not tighten at this stage.
18 Ensure gearbox selector and quadrant selector levers are in '1'.
19 Adjust front and rear locknuts until cable can be connected to quadrant lever without either quadrant or gearbox lever being disturbed.
20 Tighten locknuts, secure cable with new split pin.
21 Reverse operations 1 to 4.

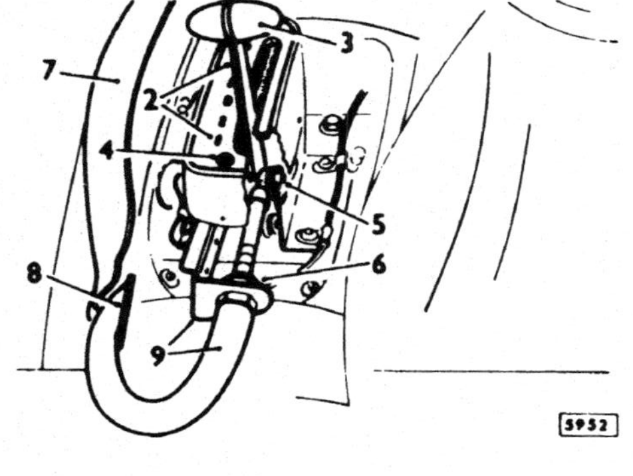

15
14
5953A

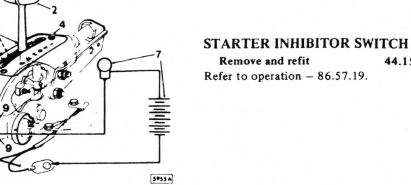

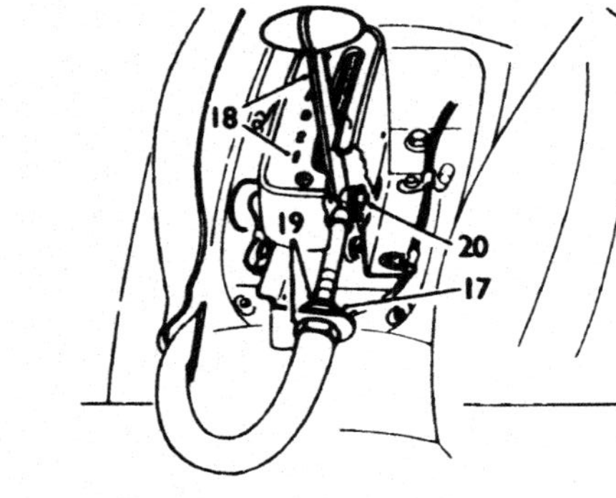

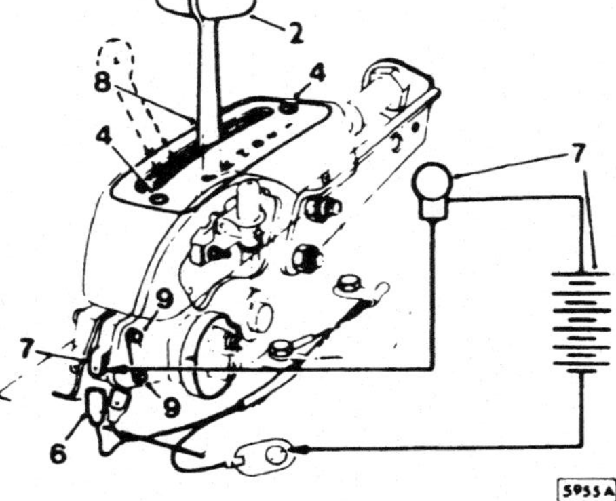

STARTER INHIBITOR SWITCH

Check and adjust **44.15.18**

Adjusting

1 Disconnect battery – 86.15.20.
2 Unscrew gear selector knob.
3 Carefully prise electric window switch panel away from centre console; do not disconnect window switches.
4 Remove screws securing control escutcheon; withdraw escutcheon slightly to obtain access to cigar lighter and door lock switch terminals.
5 Note fitted position of cigar lighter and door lock switch terminals; detach terminals and withdraw escutcheon.
6 Detach feed cable from inhibitor switch.
7 Connect a test lamp and battery in series with switch.
NOTE: Switch is in earthed position.
8 Place selector lever in 'N' position.
9 Slacken locknuts securing switch and adjust position of switch until lamp lights.
10 Tighten locknuts, check that lamp remains on with lever in 'P' position and is off with lever in drive position.
11 Remove battery and test lamp, reconnect feed cable to switch.
12 Reverse operations 1 to 5.
13 Check operation of window switches, door lock switch and cigar lighter.

STARTER INHIBITOR SWITCH

Remove and refit **44.15.19**

Refer to operation – 86.57.19.

REVERSE LIGHT SWITCH

Check and adjust **44.15.21**

Refer to operation – 86.65.20.

REVERSE LIGHT SWITCH

Remove and refit **44.15.22**

Refer to operation – 86.65.20.

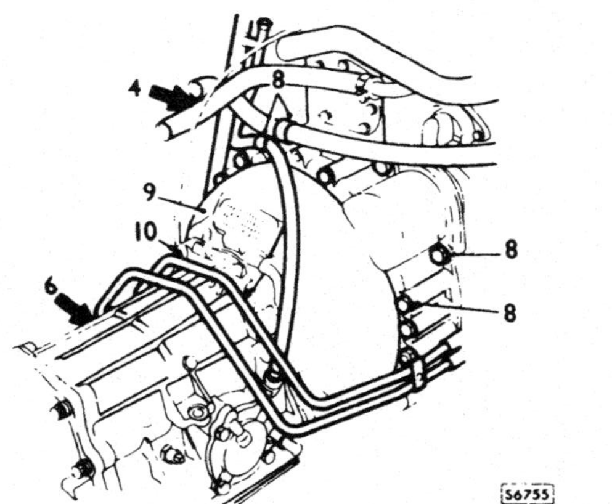

CONVERTER HOUSING

Remove and refit 44.17.01

Removing

1 Remove engine and transmission assembly – 12.37.01.
2 Remove split pin, washer and clevis pin securing downshift cable; discard split pin.
3 Slacken locknut, withdraw downshift cable from retaining bracket.
4 Remove bolt and washer securing dipstick tube.
5 Remove bolts and washers securing front cover to converter housing; withdraw cover.
6 Disconnect oil cooler pipes from gearcase; plug or tape broken connections to prevent ingress of dirt.
7 Note fitted position of earth strap and convertor housing fixings.
NOTE: Some recent cars are fitted with an additional tie plate, connecting bases of sump and converter housing. Remove four set bolts and detach tie plate.
8 Remove nuts, bolts and washers securing converter housing, withdraw starter motor.
9 Withdraw converter housing together with transmission assembly.
CAUTION: Transmission must be adequately supported during this operation.
10 Remove bolts securing converter housing to gearcase; withdraw housing.

Refitting

Reverse operations 1 to 10, attaching converter housing to gearcase before refitting assembly to engine. Replace tie plate, if fitted, with its flanges, downwards, and secure with four bolts, plain and spring washers.

CONVERTER

Remove and refit 44.17.07

Removing

1 Remove engine and transmission assembly – 12.37.01.
2 Remove split pin, washer and clevis pin securing downshift cable; discard split pin.
3 Slacken locknut, withdraw downshift cable from retaining bracket.
4 Remove bolt and washer securing dipstick tube.
5 Remove bolts and washers securing front cover to converter; withdraw cover.
6 Disconnect oil cooler pipes from gearcase; plug or tape broken connections to prevent ingress of dirt.
7 Note fitted position of earth strap and converter housing fixings.
8 Remove nuts, bolts and washers securing converter housing; withdraw starter motor.
9 Withdraw converter housing together with transmission.
CAUTION: Transmission must be adequately supported during this operation.
10 Rotate engine until setscrew securing converter is accessible through hole in starter motor aperture; remove setscrew.
11 Repeat operation 10 until four setscrews have been removed; withdraw converter.
CAUTION: The torque converter is a sealed unit and no overhaul is possible. In the event of a defect arising, the assembly must be replaced.

WARNING: TORQUE CONVERTERS SHOULD NOT BE CLEANED EITHER EXTERNALLY OR INTERNALLY WITH FLAMMABLE LIQUIDS.

Refitting

Reverse operations 1 to 11, refitting converter and replacing converter housing before bolting assembly of transmission unit and converter housing to engine; tighten converter securing bolts to a torque of 35 lbf ft (4,8 kgf m).

TRANSMISSION UNIT

Remove and refit 44.20.01

Removing

1 Carry out procedure detailed under operation, 44.17.01.

TRANSMISSION ASSEMBLY

Overhaul 44.20.06

Service Tools: Mainshaft end float gauge CBW.33; Circlip pliers 7066; Clutch spring compressor CWG.37; Clutch spring compressor adaptor CBW.37A; Torque screwdriver CBW.548; Screwdriver bit adaptors CBW.547A-50-5 and CBW.548-1; Torque wrench CBW.547A-50; Rear clutch piston replacer CBW.41A; Front clutch piston replacer CBW.42A; Kickdown cable ferrule remover CBW.62.

Dismantling

1 Remove torque converter housing, see 44.17.01.
2 Thoroughly clean exterior of gearcase.

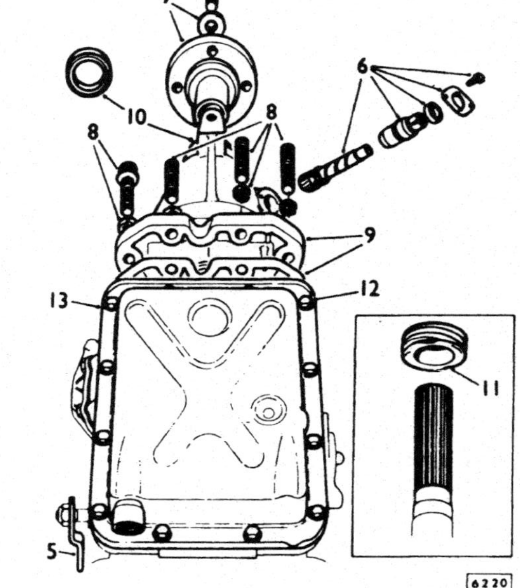

3 Remove dipstick tube and breather assembly; drain fluid from gearbox.
4 Invert transmission.
5 Position selector lever in 'P' (Park).
6 Remove speedometer driven gear housing together with driven gear, remove and discard 'O' ring.
7 Remove bolt and plain washer securing output flange; withdraw flange.
8 Note fitted position of bolts, stud bolts and spacers. Remove bolts, stud bolts, plain washers and spacers securing rear extension housing to transmission case.
9 Withdraw rear extension housing, remove and discard gasket.
10 Remove and discard oil seal.
11 Slide speedometer drive gear off output shaft.
12 Remove bolts and spring washers securing oil pan to transmission case.
13 Lift off oil pan; remove and discard gasket.

continued

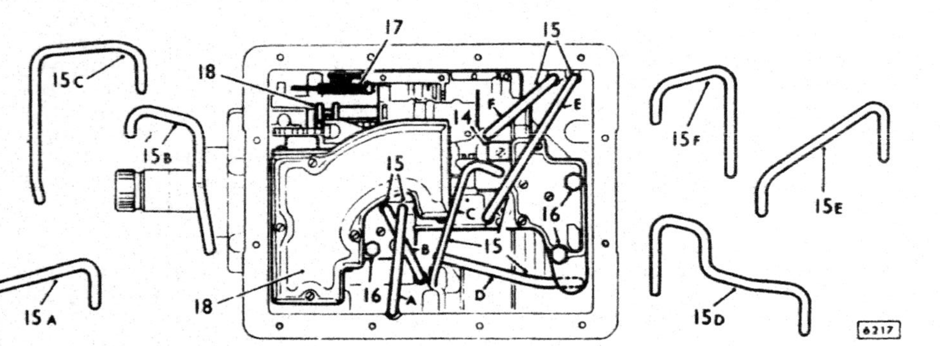

14 Remove magnet from valve block.
15 Note fitted positions of oil tubes and using a suitable screwdriver, carefully lever tubes, with the exception of tube 15D, out of transmission.
16 Remove bolts and spring washers securing valve block noting that shortest bolt is fitted at front of valve block.
17 Disconnect kickdown cable from cam.
18 Lift off valve block taking care that manual valve is not displaced; remove tube 15D as described in operation 15.
19 Carefully lever oil cooler tube from transmission.
20 Remove bolts retaining oil tube retaining plate; withdraw plate.
21 Using suitable long nosed pliers; withdraw pump inlet tube; remove and discard 'O' ring.
22 Withdraw pump outlet pipe.
23 Withdraw converter feed tube.
24 Scribe alignment marks on transmission case and oil pump.
25 Remove bolts and wave washers securing oil pump to transmission case.
26 Support stator tube and withdraw oil pump.

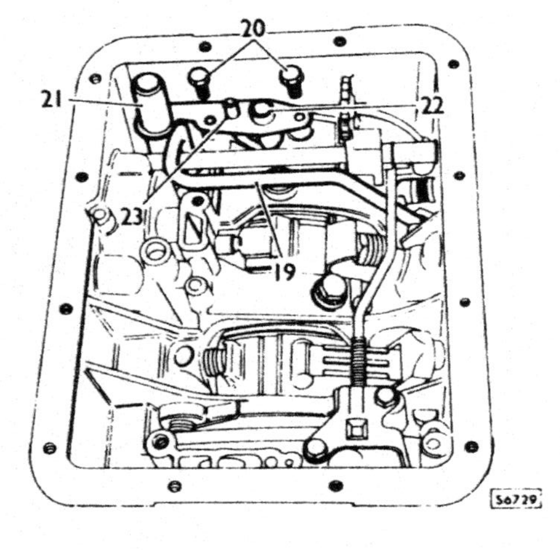

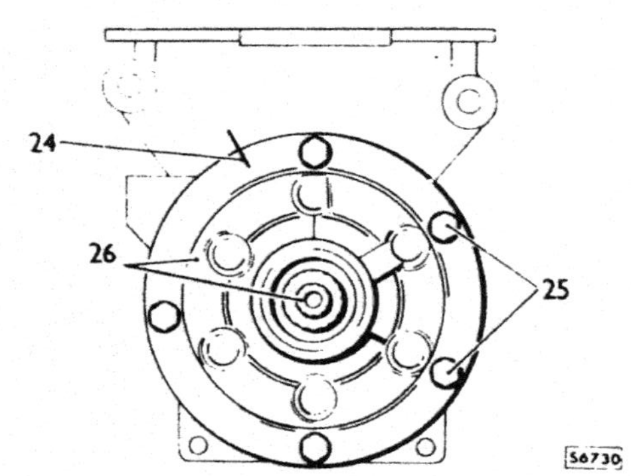

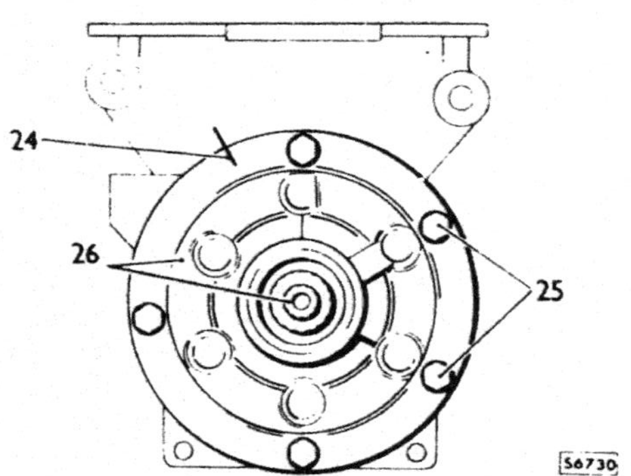

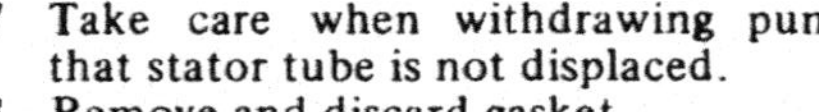

27 Take care when withdrawing pump that stator tube is not displaced.
28 Remove and discard gasket.
29 Remove and discard bronze thrust washer.
30 Remove plug and spring washer securing governor on output shaft.
31 Note fitted position of governor; slide governor off output shaft.
32 Carefully lever governor feed tube, governor return tube and lubrication tube out of transmission case.
33 Slacken locknut and unscrew front brake band adjuster screw; recover brake band strut.
34 Slacken locknut and unscrew rear brake band adjuster screw; recover brake band strut.

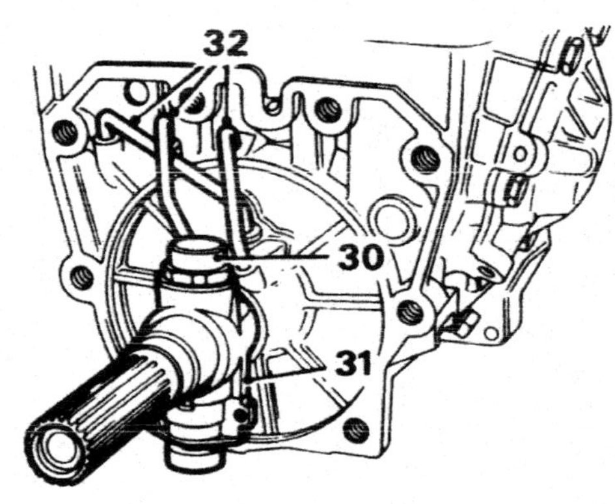

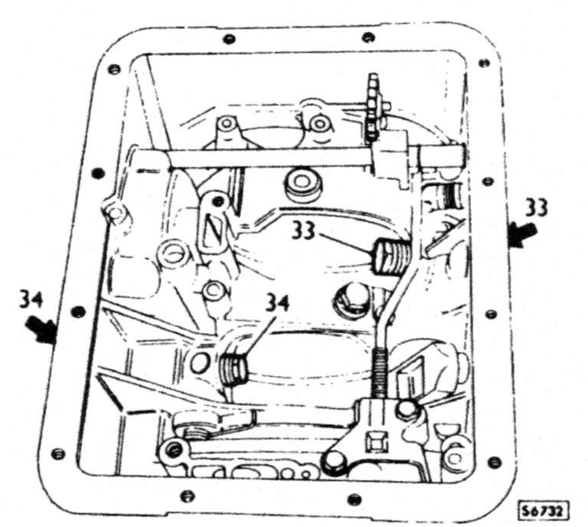

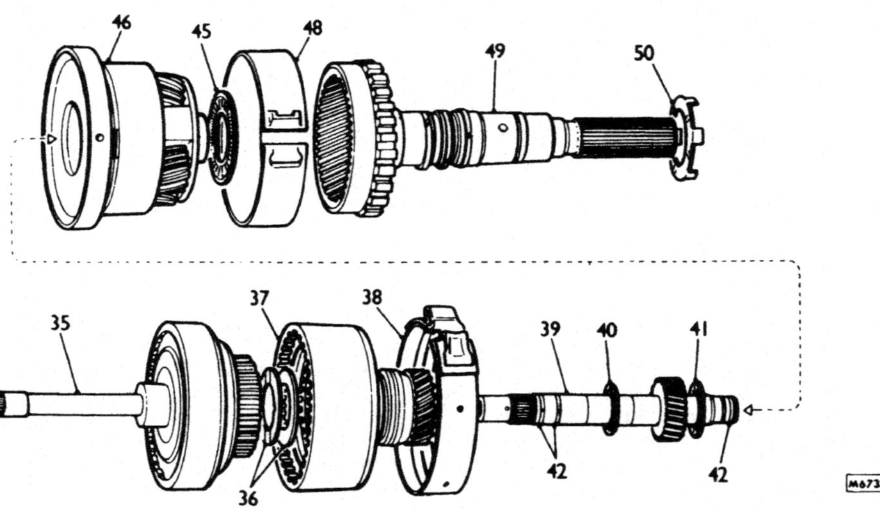

35 Withdraw front clutch assembly together with input shaft.
36 Remove steel backing washer and bronze thrust washer; discard thrust washer.
37 Withdraw rear clutch assembly; remove and discard sealing rings.
38 Note fitted position of front brake band; compress and withdraw brake band.
39 Withdraw forward sun gear shaft.
40 Remove small needle roller bearing from input end of shaft.
41 Recover flanged backing washer and large needle roller bearing from output end of shaft.
NOTE: These components may remain in sun gear assembly but should still be removed.
42 Remove and discard two sintered metal sealing rings from input end and one fibre sealing ring from output end of shaft.

43 Remove bolts and lockwashers securing centre support.
44 Push output shaft forwards to displace centre support and sun gear assembly.
45 Withdraw centre support and sun gear assembly from transmission case; remove needle roller bearing from input end of sun gear assembly.
46 Separate centre support from sun gear assembly.
47 Pull output shaft rearwards.
48 Note fitted position of rear brake band; compress and withdraw brake band.
49 Withdraw output shaft and ring gear assembly.
50 Remove and discard bronze thrust washer.

51 Remove bolts securing front servo to transmission case.
52 Withdraw front servo, operating rod and spring; remove and discard gasket.
53 Scribe alignment marks on rear servo and transmission case.
54 Remove bolts securing rear servo to transmission case.
55 Withdraw rear servo together with operating rod and spring; remove and discard 'O' rings and gasket.
56 Remove bolts securing plate retaining parking brake pawl and rear servo operating lever pivot pin; remove plate.
57 Withdraw pivot pin and rear servo operating lever.

continued

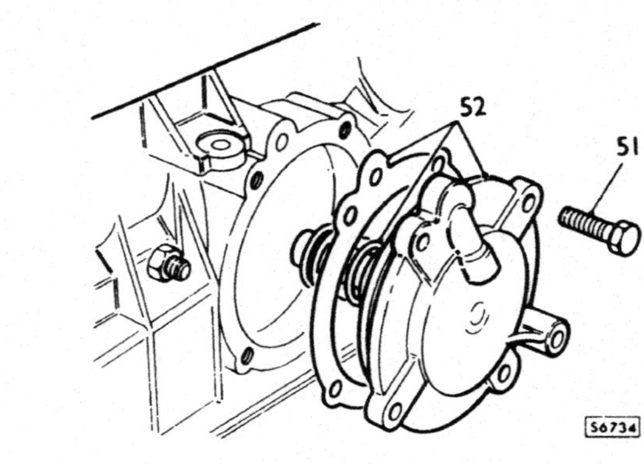

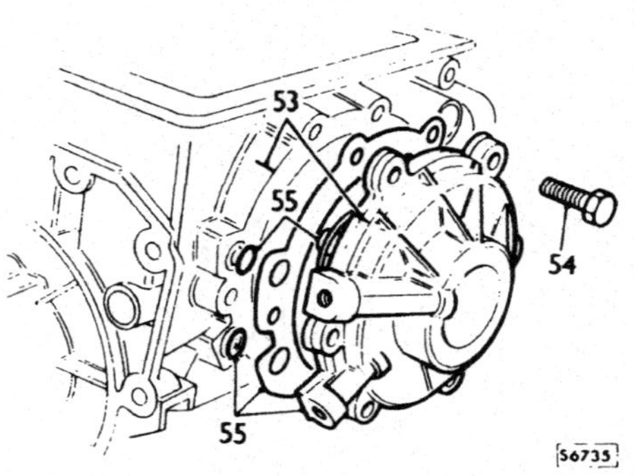

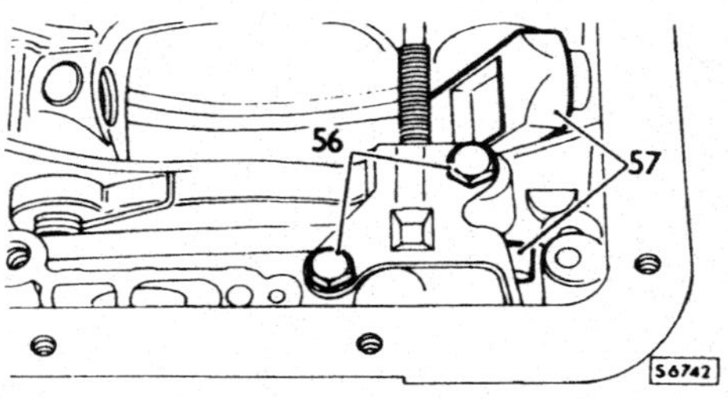

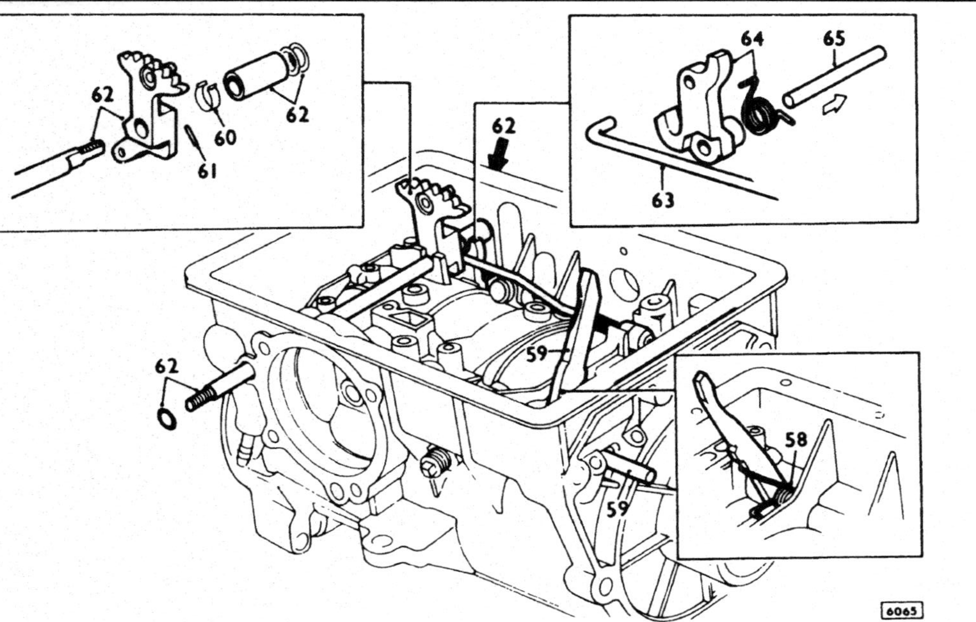

If it is found necessary to dismantle parking pawl assembly, carry out items 58 to 65 inclusive.

58 Note fitted position of parking pawl torsion spring, release spring from pawl.
59 Withdraw parking pawl pivot pin; collect pawl and torsion spring.
60 Release clip locating manual valve lever.
61 Withdraw pin locating manual valve lever.
62 Withdraw detent shaft, collect manual valve lever, spacer and plain washers; remove and discard 'O' ring and oil seal.
63 Release parking brake rod assembly from parking pawl.
64 Note fitted position of parking brake rod operating lever and torsion spring, release spring from lever.
65 Using suitable punch, drive out operating lever pivot pin; withdraw lever and spring.

If it is found necessary to remove kick-down cable assembly, carry out items 66 and 67.

66 Using Service Tool CBW.62 compress lugs of cable retaining plug.
67 Withdraw kickdown cable assembly; remove and discard 'O' ring.
CAUTION: It is not possible to remove retaining plug from kickdown cable assembly and if lugs are broken, cable assembly must be renewed.

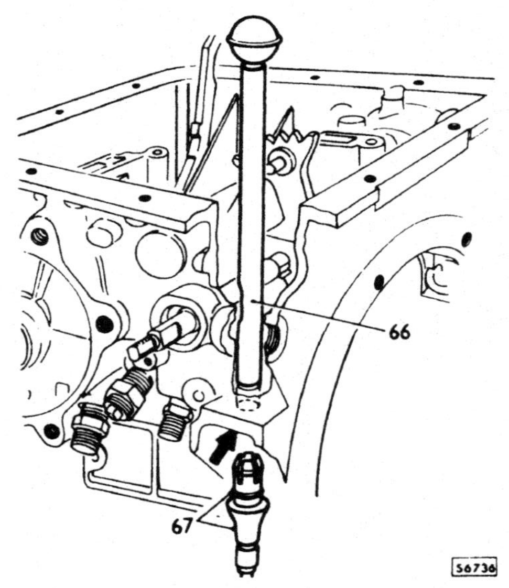

VALVE BLOCK

Overhaul

CAUTION: Ensure that all working surfaces are clean. Use only lint free cloth and clean transmission fluid for cleaning and lubricating.

Dismantling

68 Withdraw manual valve.
69 Remove screws securing suction tube assembly to lower valve body.
70 Lift off tube assembly; remove and discard gasket.
71 Remove six upper valve body securing screws from lower valve body.
72 Invert valve body and remove four screws securing upper valve body and cam mounting arm; remove mounting arm.
73 Extract downshift valve and spring.
74 Lift off upper valve body.
75 Remove screws securing both end plates to upper valve body; carefully remove end plates.
76 Extract spring, 1-2 shift valve and plunger.
77 Extract 2-3 shift valve, spring and plunger.
78 Remove eight screws securing collector plate to lower valve body; lift off collector plate.
79 Slacken, but do not remove four screws securing governor line plate.
80 Hold separator plate in contact with valve body, remove governor line plate securing screws and lift off governor line plate.
81 Note fitted position of ball valve and carefully slide separator plate off valve body.
CAUTION: Ball valve is spring loaded; ensure ball is not displaced during this operation.
82 Remove ball valve; extract spring.
83 Note fitted position of check valve (if fitted), remove valve.
84 Withdraw retainer, extract spring and servo orifice control valve.
85 Withdraw retaining pin, extract plug, modulator valve and spring.
86 Withdraw throttle valve spring retainer.
87 Withdraw throttle valve retainer.
88 Extract spring and throttle valve.
89 Remove screw securing detent spring and roller assembly, detach assembly; collect spacer.
NOTE: Roller arm may be peened to valve body. If so, swing arm clear of screws securing regulator valve retaining plate.
90 Remove screws securing regulator valve retaining plate; remove plate slowly until spring loading is no longer felt.
91 Extract spring, sleeve and primary regulator valve.
92 Extract spring and secondary regulator valve.

Inspection

93 Check springs with data shown in spring identification table, see page 44–37; renew springs which are distorted or shorter than specified length.
94 Check all valves for burrs or scoring. Check that valves move freely in valve bodies.
CAUTION: In the event of valves and/or valve bodies being damaged, valve block assembly MUST be renewed.

Reassembling

Reverse operations 68 to 92 ensure all components are scrupulously clean and that tightening torque figures (See Group 06) are adhered to.

CAUTION: A new gasket must be used when refitting suction tube assembly.

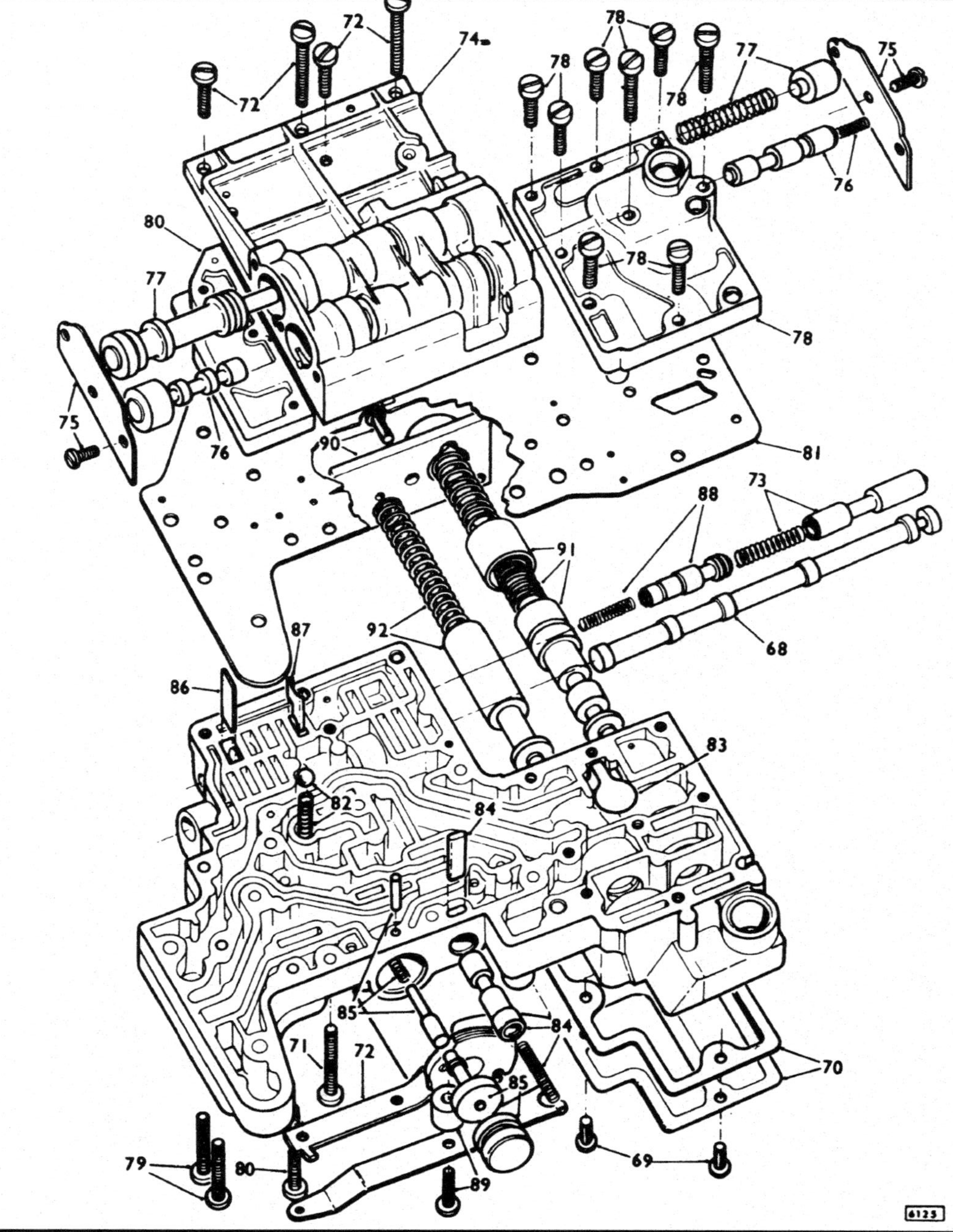

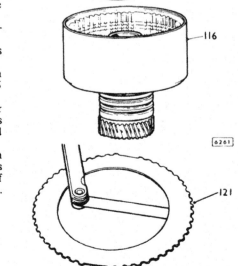

PLANET CARRIER

CAUTION: No overhaul of planet carrier is possible. In event of any of the following defects being discovered, planet carrier assembly must be renewed.

Inspection
95 Check gear teeth for chipping or scoring. light scoring may be disregarded.
96 Check that end float of gears is not excessive and that gears turn smoothly when spun by hand.
97 Check bush for scores or evidence of metal transfer.

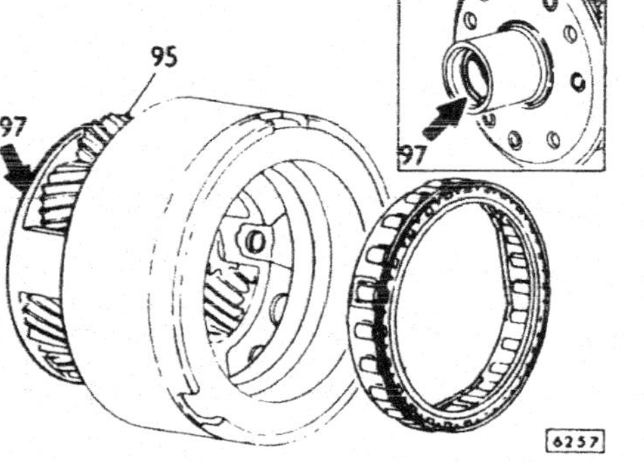

ONE WAY CLUTCH

CAUTION: No overhaul of one way clutch is possible. In the event of any of the following defects being discovered, one way clutch must be renewed.

Dismantling
98 Note fitted position of one way clutch.
99 Withdraw clutch from planet carrier.

Inspection
100 Check sprag faces for flat spots indicating wear.
101 Check sprag faces for flat spots indicating wear.

Reassembling
102 Push one way clutch into planet carrier, ensure that lip faces outwards and that clutch is fully seated in recess.

FORWARD SUN GEAR SHAFT

Inspection
103 Check drillings in shaft for obstruction; clear with compressed air only.
104 Check splines, sealing ring grooves and gear teeth for burrs or signs of damage; renew if damaged. Minor burrs may, however, be removed with a very fine abrasive.
105 Examine large and small needle roller bearings; renew if either show signs of wear or damage.

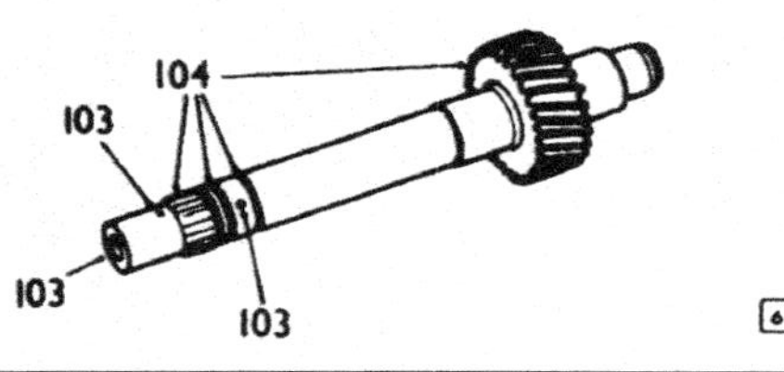

REAR CLUTCH

Overhaul

Dismantling
106 Place rear clutch assembly over central spindle of clutch spring compressor CWG.37, reverse sun gear down.
107 Fit spring compressor CBW.37A over spindle.
108 Compress spring and remove snap ring.
109 Slowly release pressure and remove compressor.
110 Remove retainer and spring.
111 Remove snap ring retaining pressure plate.
112 Remove pressure plate.
113 Remove inner and outer clutch plates.
NOTE: Five outer and five inner clutch plates are fitted.
114 Remove piston by applying air pressure to supply hole in clutch housing pedestal.
115 Remove and discard piston seal.

Inspection
116 Check clutch drum and bearing surfaces for scores or burrs; replace drum if damaged.
117 Check fluid passages for obstructions, clear passages with compressed air only.
118 Inspect piston check valve for free operation.
119 Check clutch release spring for distortion, renew if distorted.
120 Check inner clutch plates for flatness and that facings are undamaged.
121 Check that coning on outer clutch plates is not less than .010 in. (,25 mm.).
122 Check outer clutch plates for scores or burrs, renew if damaged. Minor scores or burrs may however be removed with a very fine abrasive.
123 Check needle bearings and bush in clutch housing for signs of wear, scores or evidence of metal transfer. If damaged, clutch hub must be renewed.

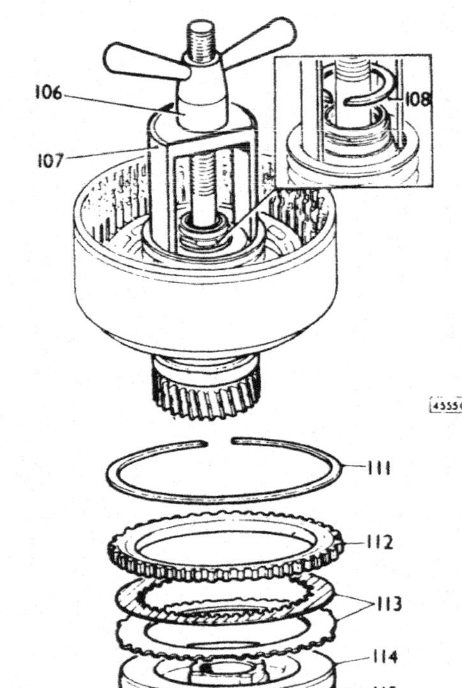

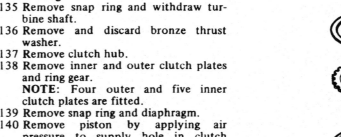

Reassembling

124 Smear new piston seal with petroleum jelly and fit to piston.

125 Position rear clutch piston replacer tool CBW.41A in clutch drum.

126 Lubricate piston and replacer tool with clean transmission fluid.

127 Install piston; remove tool.

128 Reverse operations 106 to 113.
CAUTION: Outer clutch plates must be assembled with cones facing in same direction.

129 Smear large needle bearing with petroleum jelly and position it on output end of forward sun gear shaft.

130 Position backing washer, flange leading in planet carrier.

131 Insert forward sun gear shaft in planet carrier; fit new fibre sealing ring on output end of shaft.

132 Position centre support in planet carrier.

133 Smear small needle roller bearing with petroleum jelly and position it on forward sun gear shaft.

134 Position rear clutch assembly on forward sun gear shaft; fit new sintered sealing rings on input end of shaft. Ensure gaps in sealing rings are staggered.
CAUTION: Do not remove rear clutch assembly and forward sun gear shaft from planet carrier.

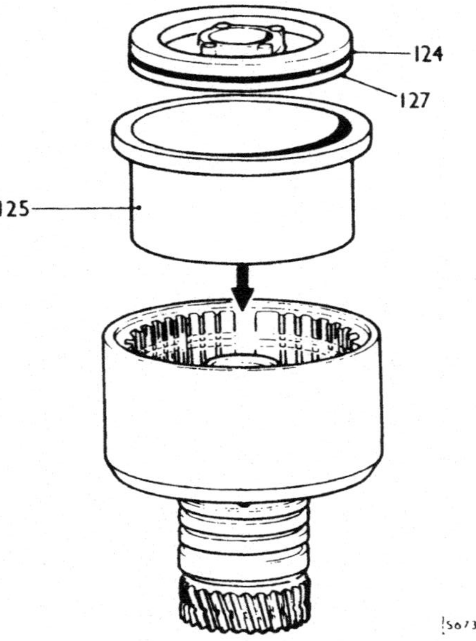
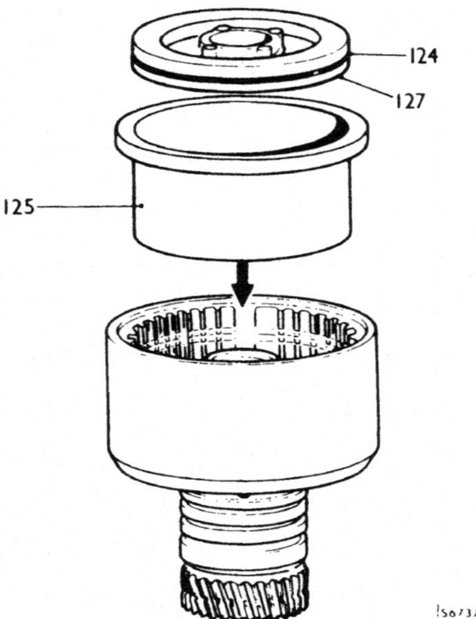
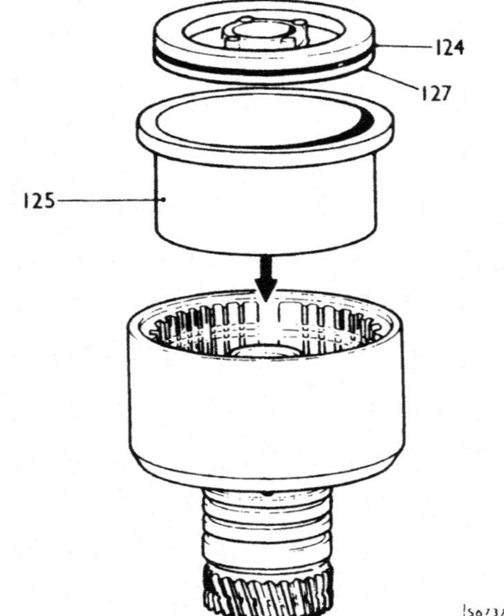

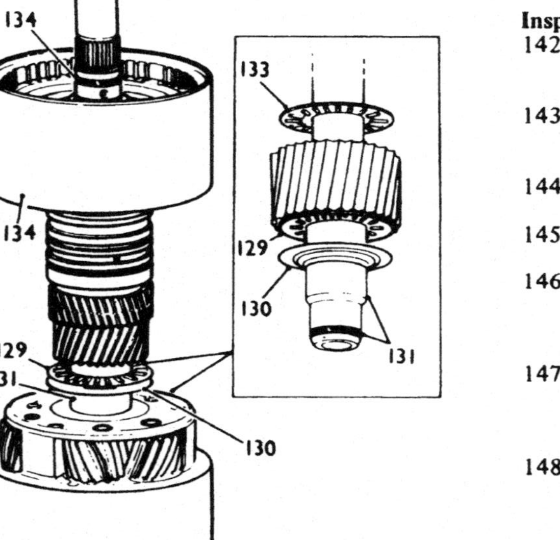

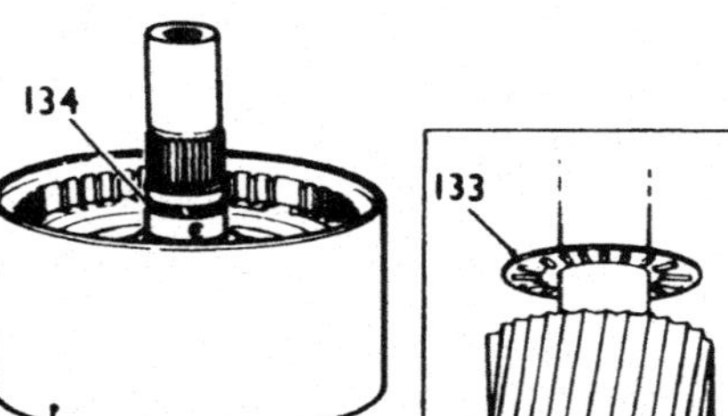
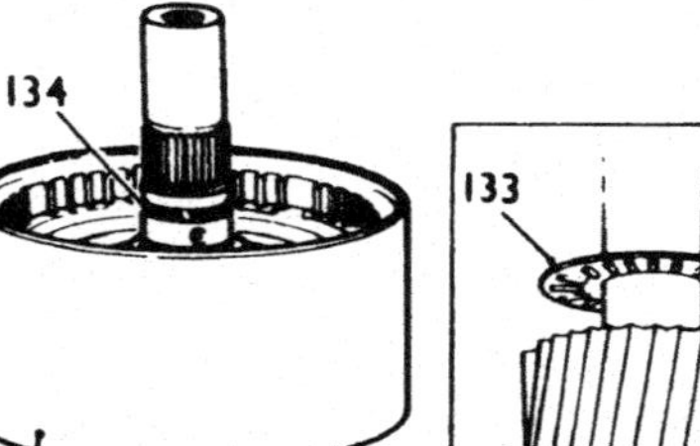
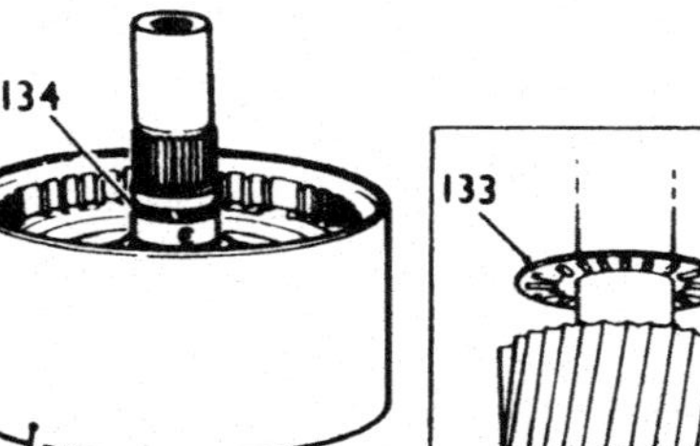
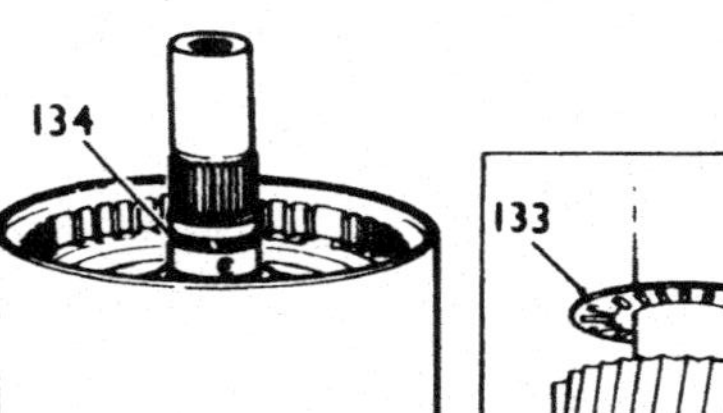
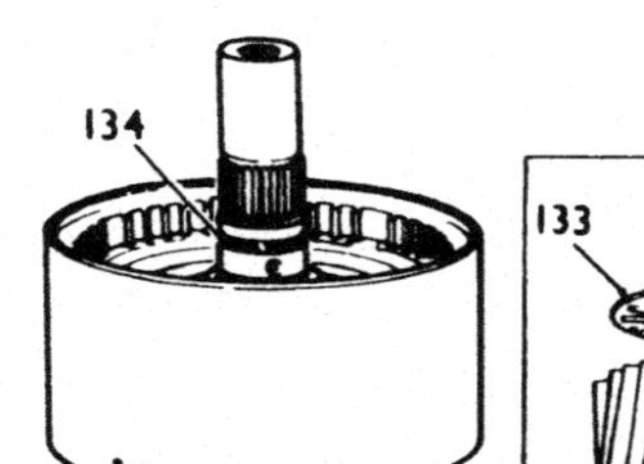

FRONT CLUTCH

Overhaul

Dismantling

135 Remove snap ring and withdraw turbine shaft.

136 Remove and discard bronze thrust washer.

137 Remove clutch hub.

138 Remove inner and outer clutch plates and ring gear.
NOTE: Four outer and five inner clutch plates are fitted.

139 Remove snap ring and diaphragm.

140 Remove piston by applying air pressure to supply hole in clutch housing pedestal.

141 Remove plain and belleville washers; remove and discard seal and 'O' ring.

NOTE: On later cars, six belleville washers are used, with no plain washer.

Inspection

142 Check clutch drum and bearing surfaces for scores or burrs; replace drum if damaged.

143 Check fluid passages for obstruction; clear passages with compressed air only.

144 Inspect piston check valve for free operation.

145 Check clutch release diaphragm for cracks or distortion; renew if damaged.

146 Check inner clutch plates for flatness and that facings are undamaged.
NOTE: There is no coning on clutch plates.

147 Check outer clutch plates for flatness, scores or burrs, renew if damaged. Minor scores or burrs may, however, be removed with a very fine abrasive.

148 Check bush in turbine shaft for scores or evidence of metal transfer. If damaged, turbine shaft must be renewed.

135
136
137
138
139
144
140
141
141
141
6234

continued

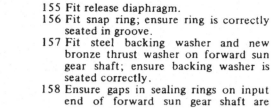

Reassembling

149 Smear new 'O' ring with petroleum jelly and fit to piston.

150 Position belleville and plain washers in piston, retain washers with a smear of petroleum jelly.
NOTE: Later cars are fitted with six belleville washers and no plain washers. Replace these in three opposing pairs, the inner diameters of the washers in each pair being in contact. This washer arrangement may be used to replace the earlier assembly, but if this is done the plain washer originally fitted must be discarded.

151 Soak new oil seal in clean transmission fluid and insert in piston.
NOTE: Open end of seal faces outwards.

152 Position front clutch piston replacer tool CBW.42A in clutch drum.

153 Lubricate piston and replacer tool with clean transmission fluid.

154 Install piston; remove tool.

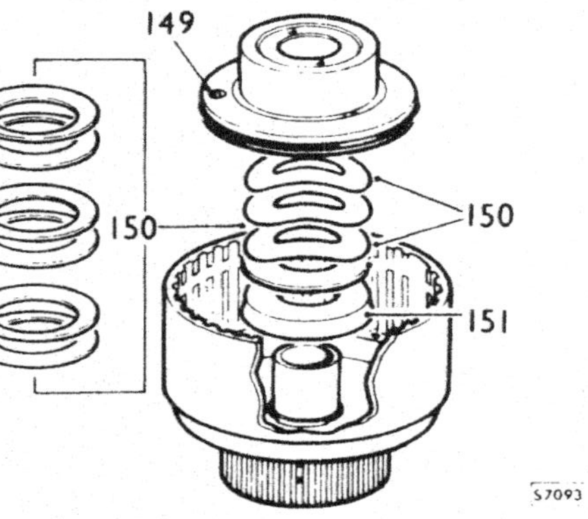

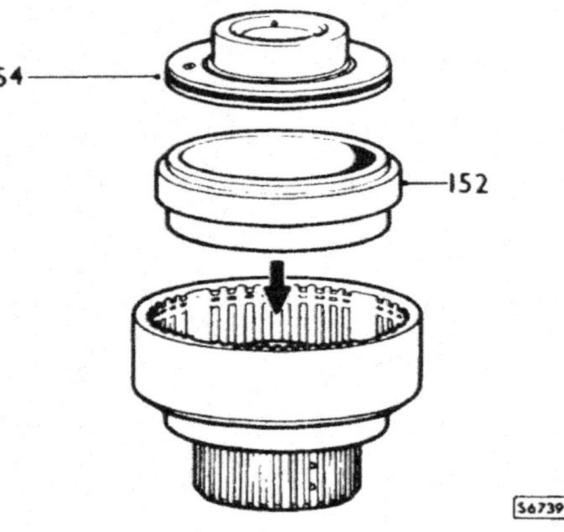

155 Fit release diaphragm.

156 Fit snap ring; ensure ring is correctly seated in groove.

157 Fit steel backing washer and new bronze thrust washer on forward sun gear shaft; ensure backing washer is seated correctly.

158 Ensure gaps in sealing rings on input end of forward sun gear shaft are staggered.

159 Check to ensure that teeth of rear clutch inner plates are in alignment.

160 Carefully lower front clutch hub and piston assembly over shaft and into rear clutch.
NOTE: To facilitate engagement of gear with rear clutch plates, front clutch should be moved backwards and forwards slightly.

161 Fit ring gear.

162 Position inner and outer clutch plates in clutch drum.
NOTE: For identification purposes, two pairs of teeth at 180° have been omitted on outer clutch plates.

163 Check to ensure that teeth of inner clutch plates are in alignment.

164 Fit clutch hub; ensure hub fully engages all clutch plates.

165 Position new bronze thrust washer in recess in clutch hub.

166 Fit turbine shaft and snap ring; ensure snap ring is correctly seated in groove.
CAUTION: On no account should front and rear clutch assemblies be separated as damage to sealing rings on forward run gear shaft will result.

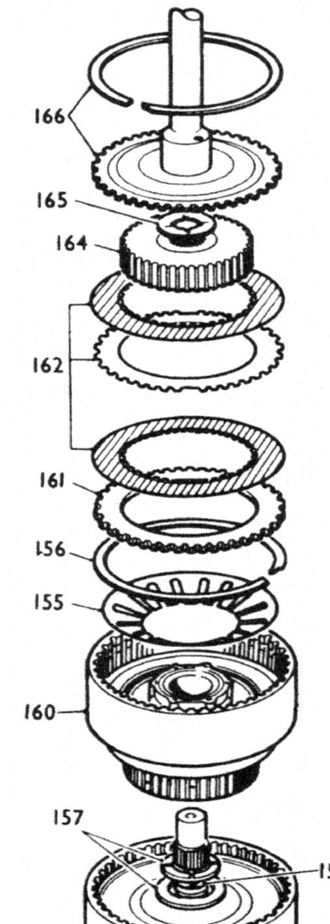

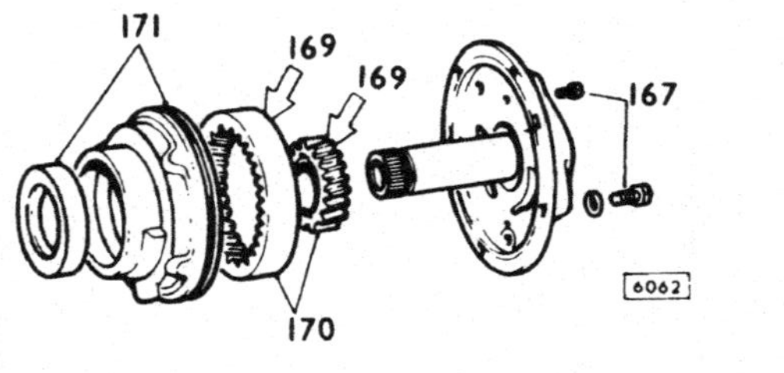

PUMP

Overhaul

Dismantling

167 Remove bolts, screw and spring washers securing pump adaptor to pump body.

168 Hold pump body and using a hide mallet, gently tap convertor tube.
CAUTION: Take care that gears are not displaced when adaptor and body separate.

169 Mark mating surfaces of gears with die marker, **DO NOT** use a punch or scriber.

170 Remove gears from pump body.

171 Remove and discard 'O' ring and oil seal.

Inspection

172 Check bearing surfaces, gears, splines and bushes for damage or wear. Should any component show signs of damage etc., oil pump assembly must be renewed.

Reassembling

173 Soak new oil seal in clean transmission fluid and press carefully into pump body; ensure seal is squarely seated.

174 Soak new 'O' ring in clean transmission fluid and position in groove in periphery of pump body.

175 Reverse operations 167 to 170 ensuring reference marks on gears, adaptor and body are in alignment.

176 Progressively tighten bolts to a torque of 2.5 lb.ft. (,35 kg.m.).

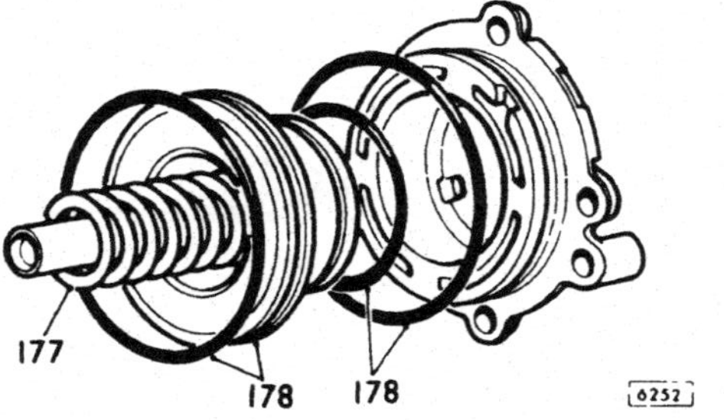

FRONT SERVO

Overhaul

Dismantling

177 Remove piston return spring.

178 Withdraw piston from servo body; remove and discard 'O' rings.

Inspection

179 Check return spring for distortion; renew if necessary. Check fluid passage for obstruction; clear passage with compressed air only.

Reassembling

Reverse operations 177 and 178; coat new 'O' rings with petroleum jelly prior to fitting.

REAR SERVO

Overhaul

Dismantling

180 Withdraw piston from servo body; remove and discard 'O' rings.

Inspection

181 Check return spring, removed during operation 55, for distortion; renew if necessary.

182 Check fluid passages for obstruction; clear passages with compressed air only.

Reassembling

Reverse operation 180; coat new 'O' rings with petroleum jelly prior to fitting.

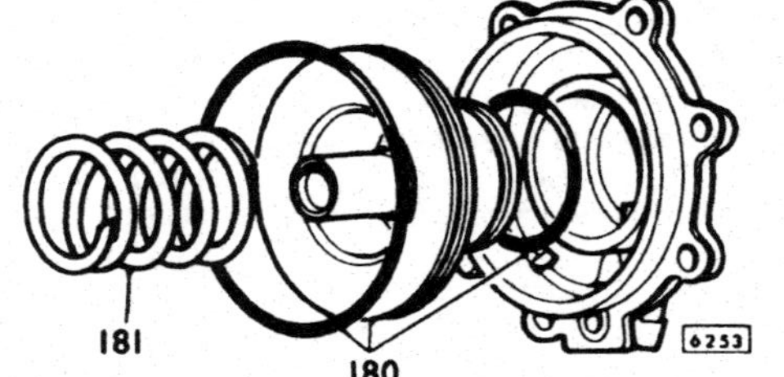

GOVERNOR

Overhaul

Dismantling

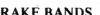

183 Depress governor weight stem to expose circlip.

184 Remove circlip and weight, discard circlip.

185 Withdraw stem, spring and valve from governor body.

Inspection

186 Check all components for signs of damage and additionally, check spring for distortion. In the event of any component being found unsatisfactory, governor assembly must be removed.

Reassembling

187 Reverse operations 183 to 185; use a new circlip.

188 Check weight stem for free movement.
CAUTION: If weight stem shows signs of sticking, governor assembly must be renewed.

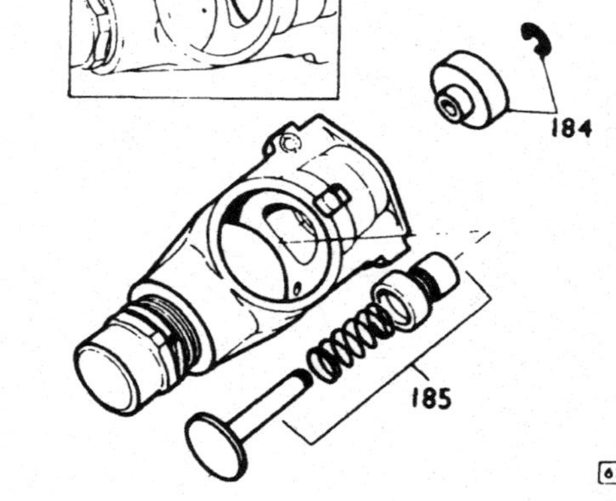

BRAKE BANDS

Inspection

189 Check front and rear brake bands for damage or distortion.

190 Check linings for uneven or excess wear.
CAUTION: Bands must be renewed if any of the defects detailed above are apparent or if doubt exists as to their condition.

OUTPUT SHAFT AND RING GEAR

Overhaul

Dismantling

191 Remove and discard sealing rings from output shaft.

192 Remove snap ring retaining output shaft; withdraw shaft.

Inspection

193 Check drillings in output shaft for obstruction; clear with compressed air only.

194 Check splines, sealing ring grooves and gear teeth for burrs or signs of damage; renew if damaged. Minor burrs may however be removed with a very fine abrasive.

195 Check bush for scores or evidence of metal transfer. Should damage be evident, output shaft must be renewed.

Reassembling

Reverse operations 191 and 192.

CAUTION: Ensure gaps in sealing rings are staggered.

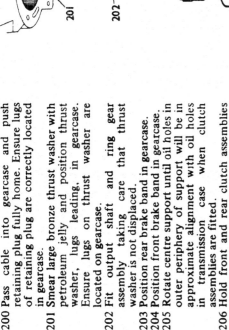

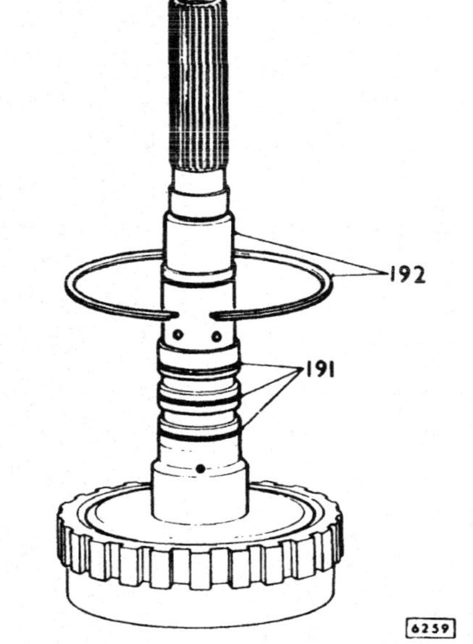

GEAR CASE

Inspection

196 Remove oil cooler return union together with non-return valve assembly (if fitted).

197 By means of a piece of thin wire, check operation of ball valve. Valve should operate smoothly and seat fully. Check bush in gear case for scores, burrs or transfer of metal.
NOTE: Smear threads of union with Loctite Grade AV before refitting.

198 Reverse operations 56 to 65 as applicable, lightly smearing manual lever shaft and its bore in servo housing with lithium-based grease.

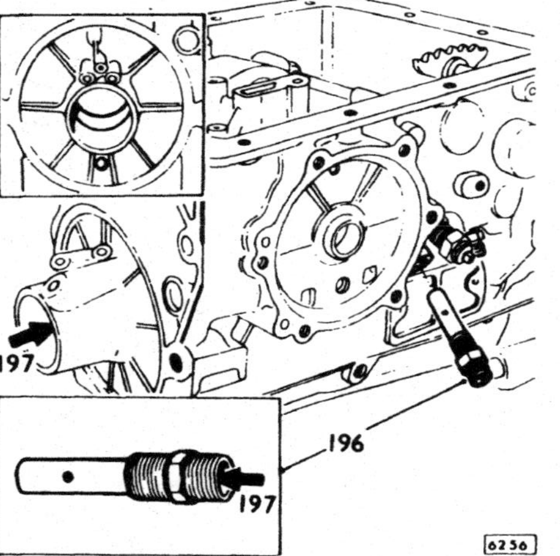

TRANSMISSION ASSEMBLY

Reassembling

199 If kickdown cable was removed, smear new 'O' ring with petroleum jelly; position 'O' ring on retaining plug.

200 Pass cable into gearcase and push retaining plug fully home. Ensure lugs of retaining plug are correctly located in gearcase.

201 Smear large bronze thrust washer with petroleum jelly and position thrust washer, lugs leading, in gearcase. Ensure lugs on thrust washer are located on gearcase.

202 Fit output shaft and ring gear assembly taking care that thrust washer is not displaced.

203 Position rear brake band in gearcase.

204 Position front brake band in gearcase.

205 Rotate centre support until oil holes in outer periphery of support will be in approximate alignment with oil holes in transmission case when clutch assemblies are fitted.

206 Hold front and rear clutch assemblies firmly together and checking alignment between oil holes in centre support and gearcase, enter assembly into gearcase through rear aperture.
CAUTION: On no account allow clutch assemblies to separate as this will cause damage to sealing rings on forward sun gear shaft.

207 Ensure planet carrier gears are fully engaged with output shaft ring gear.

208 Rotate centre support, ensuring that alignment of oil holes is correct, until securing bolts and lockwashers can be fitted. Tighten securing bolts evenly.

209 Position new bronze thrust washer on oil pump; ensure that lugs on washer face towards pump.
NOTE: This thrust washer is selective and determines amount of gear train end float. Two thrust washers of different thickness are available and experience has shown that if the thinner of the two washers is selected, correct end float is usually obtained. It is recommended therefore that this washer be used.

210 Smear new oil pump gasket with grease, position gasket on oil pump.

211 Fit oil pump ensuring that stator tube is not displaced. **Do not** tighten oil pump securing bolts at this stage.

212 Position new 'O' ring on oil pump inlet tube; smear 'O' ring with clean transmission fluid.

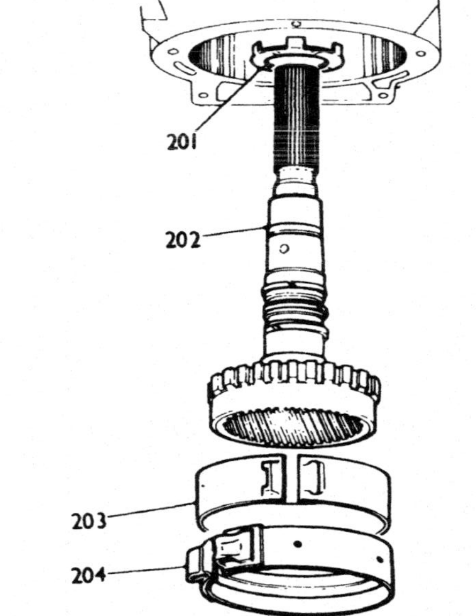

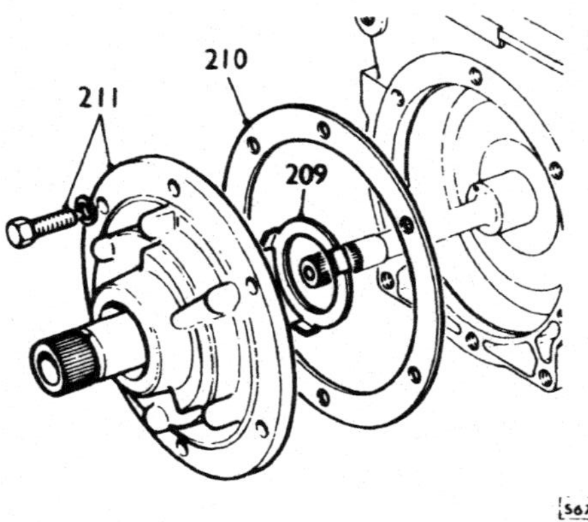

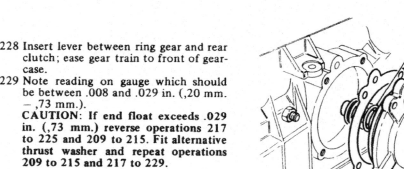

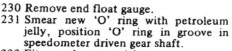

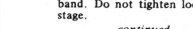

213 Fit oil pump inlet and outlet tubes; also convertor feed tube. Ensure tubes are correctly seated.
NOTE: Oil pump may be rotated slightly to achieve this.
214 Fit oil tube retaining plate; tighten bolts to a torque of 1.75 lbf.ft. (0,24 kgf/m.).
215 Tighten oil pump securing bolts by diagonal selection to a torque of 19 lbf.ft. (2,63 kgf/m.).
216 Fit governor feed tube, governor return tube and lubrication tube into transmission case; ensure tubes are correctly seated.
CAUTION: Do not use undue force when pushing tubes into oil holes.
217 Slide governor on to output shaft, fit plug and spring washer, ensure plug enters BLIND hole in output shaft. Tighten plug to 16.5 lbf.ft. (2,28 kgf/m.).
218 Slide speedometer drive gear on to output shaft.
219 Coat new oil seal with clean transmission fluid; press seal into recess in extension case. Ensure seal is correctly seated.
220 Smear new extension case gasket with grease; position gasket on extension case ensuring holes in gasket and case are in alignment.
221 Fit extension case ensuring that splines of output shaft do not damage oil seal and that extension case does not foul oil pipes.
222 Fit bolts, stud bolts, washers and spacers. Tighten bolts by diagonal selection to a torque of 42.5 lbf.ft. (5,88 kgf.m.).
223 Slide output flange on to output shaft; fit plain washer and nut. Do not tighten nut at this stage.
224 Move selector lever until parking pawl engages with ring gear.
225 Tighten output flange securing bolt to a torque of 40–50 lbf.ft. (5,53–6,90 kgf.m.).
226 Assemble end float gauge CBW.33 to gearcase with stylus contacting end of turbine shaft.
227 Insert a suitable lever between front clutch and front of gearcase. Ease gear train to rear of gearcase and zero end float gauge.

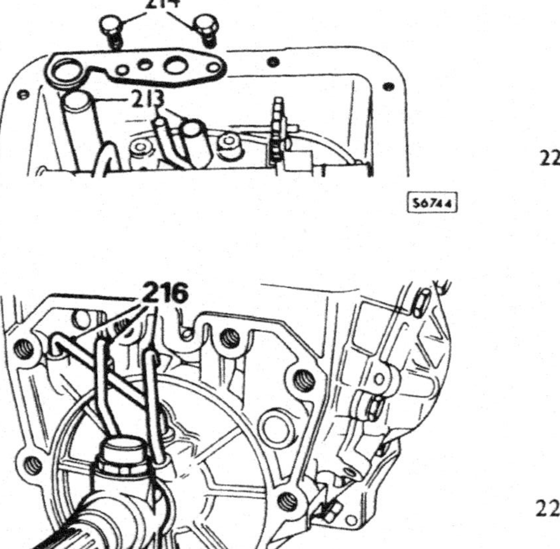

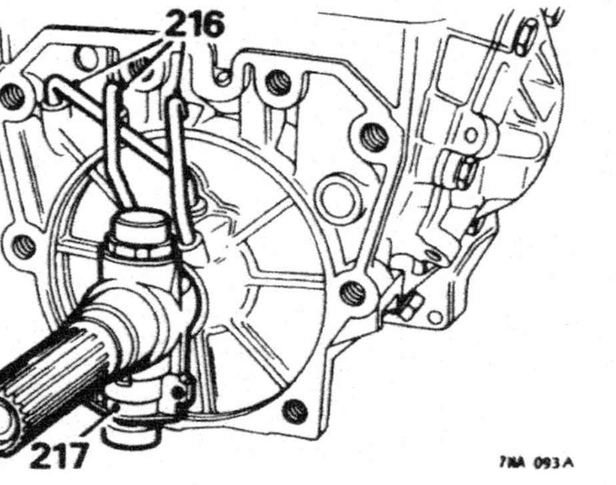

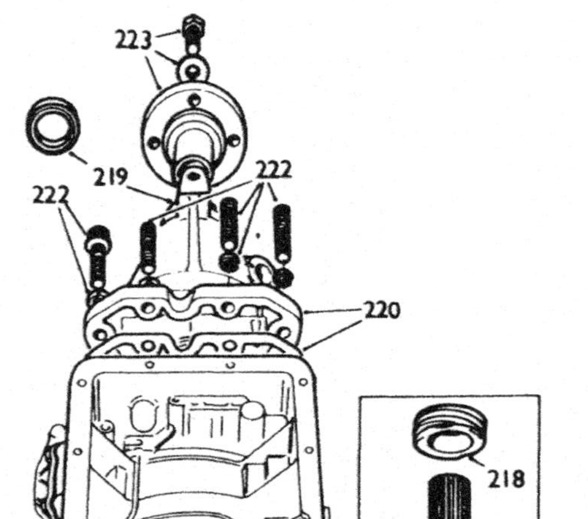

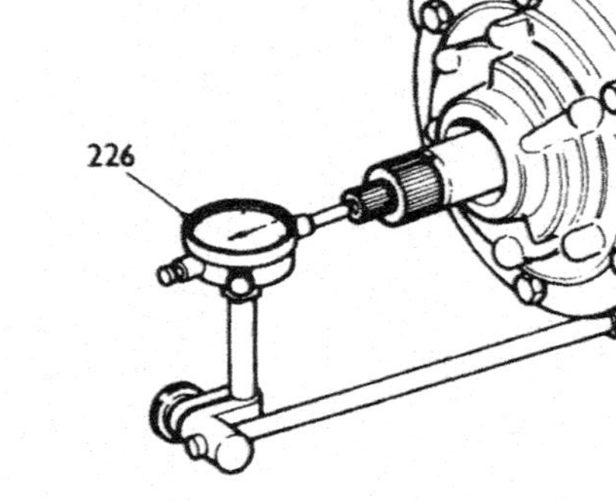

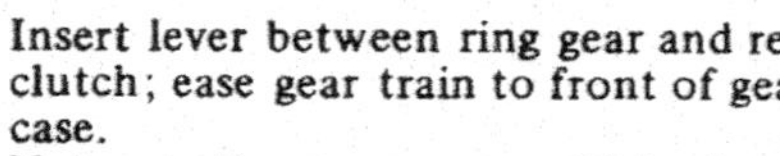

228 Insert lever between ring gear and rear clutch; ease gear train to front of gearcase.
229 Note reading on gauge which should be between .008 and .029 in. (,20 mm. – ,73 mm.).
CAUTION: If end float exceeds .029 in. (,73 mm.) reverse operations 217 to 225 and 209 to 215. Fit alternative thrust washer and repeat operations 209 to 215 and 217 to 229.

230 Remove end float gauge.
231 Smear new 'O' ring with petroleum jelly, position 'O' ring in groove in speedometer driven gear shaft.
232 Fit speedometer driven gear; ensure driven gear meshes with drive gear; do not overtighten securing bolts.
233 Smear new front servo gasket with grease; position gasket on servo body.
234 Fit front servo and spring. Tighten bolts by diagonal selection to a torque of 19 lbf.ft. (2,63 kgf.m.).
235 Position front brake band strut in gearcase. Ensure spigot on strut is located in detent in servo rod and that brake band is correctly positioned.
236 Screw in front brake band adjusting screw until contact is made with brake band. Do not tighten locknut at this stage.

continued

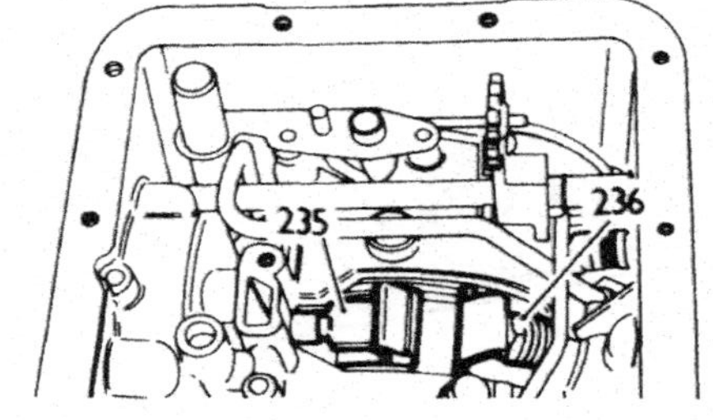

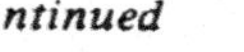

237 Smear new 'O' rings with clean transmission oil; position 'O' rings in rear servo body oil holes.
238 Smear new rear servo gasket with grease, position gasket on servo body.
239 Position servo operating rod and spring in servo.
240 Fit servo assembly ensuring that operating rod is located in detent in operating lever. Do not tighten securing bolts at this stage.
241 Position rear brake band strut in gearcase; ensure brake band is correctly positioned.
242 Screw in rear brake band adjusting screw until contact is made with brake band. Do not overtighten locknut at this stage.
243 Tighten rear servo securing bolts by diagonal selection to a torque of 19 lbf.ft. (2,63 kgf.m.).
244 Fit tube 15D, do not use undue force.
245 Position valve block in transmission case, ensure that spigot on detent lever is located in groove in manual valve and that valve body fits on oil tubes.
246 Fit valve block securing bolts noting that shortest bolt is fitted at front of valve block.
247 Tighten valve block securing bolts to a torque of 6.75 lbf.ft. (0,93 kgf.m.).
248 Connect kickdown cable to cam.
249 Fit oil tubes; see operation 15. Do not use undue force when fitting tubes.
250 Position magnet on valve block in position shown.
251 Smear new oil pan gasket with grease; position gasket on gearcase.
252 Fit oil pan; tighten bolts by diagonal selection to a torque of 5.75 lbf.ft. (0,80 kgf.m.).
253 Reverse operations 1, 3 and 4, but do not fill gearbox with fluid.
254 Tighten front and rear brake band adjusting screws to a torque of 5 lbf.ft. (0,7 kgf.m.), and then back off screws ¾ of a turn.
255 Tighten each adjusting screw locknut to a torque of 35 lbf.ft. (4,8 kgf.m.).
CAUTION: Ensure screws do not move during this operation.

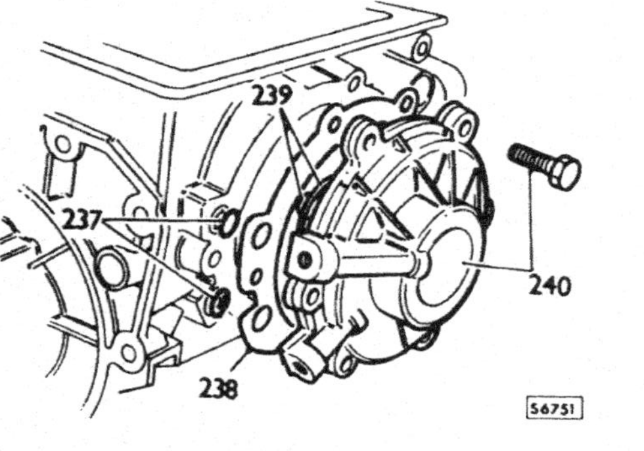

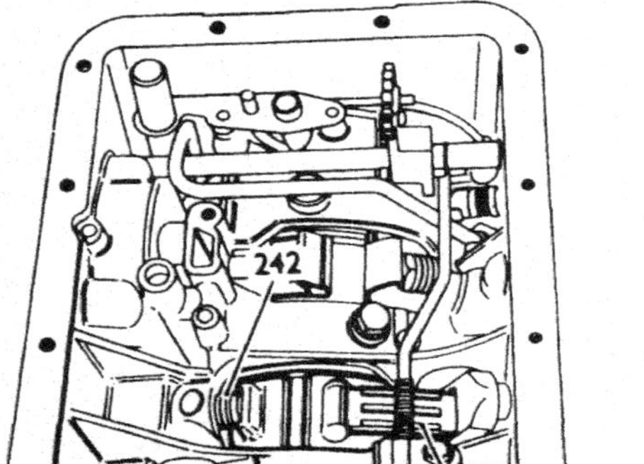

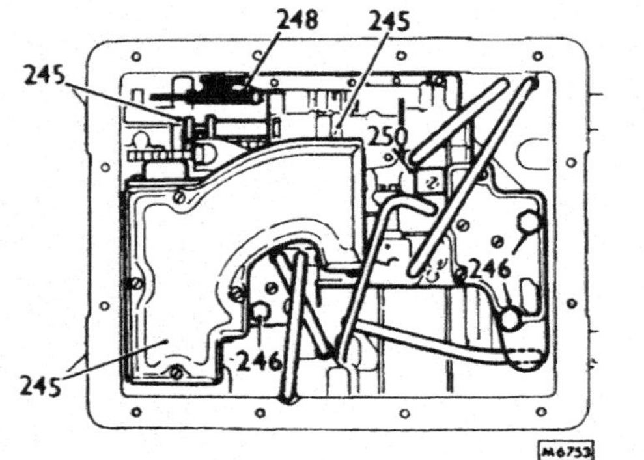

REAR EXTENSION HOUSING

Remove and refit **44.20.15**

Service Tool: Torque wrench – CBW.547 A-50.

Removing

1. Remove rear engine mounting – 12.45.08.
2. Remove screw securing intermediate heat shield; withdraw shield.
3. Remove screw securing rear heat shield to rear engine mounting support plate.
4. Remove six bolts and special washers securing rear engine mounting support plate to floor pan.
5. Remove bolts and special washers securing rear engine mounting support plate to transmission tunnel.
6. Remove self locking nuts and bolts securing propeller shaft to gearbox output flange; swing propeller shaft to one side.
   NOTE: This operation will be greatly facilitated if one rear wheel (both wheels if 'Powr-Lok' differential is fitted) is raised and gear selector placed in 'N' (Neutral) thereby enabling propeller shaft to be rotated.

WARNING: CHOCK BOTH FRONT WHEELS TO PREVENT VEHICLE MOVING.

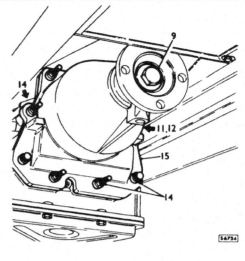

7. Using engine support tool fitted in operation 1, lower rear of engine slightly.
   CAUTION: Ensure engine does not foul heater water valve.
8. Place selector lever in 'P' (Park).
9. Remove bolt and plain washer securing gearbox output flange; withdraw flange.
10. Disconnect speedometer right angle drive.
11. Remove bolts securing speedometer drive retaining plate; withdraw plate.
12. Withdraw speedometer driven gear; remove and discard 'O' ring.
13. Remove bolt securing selector cable trunnion to mounting bracket.
14. Note fitted position of stud bolts, bolts and nuts. Remove these fixings, withdraw trunnion mounting bracket and remove two further stud bolts and spacers.
15. Withdraw rear extension; remove and discard gasket.
16. Prise oil seal out of rear extension housing; discard oil seal.

Refitting

17. Lightly score oil seal recess in rear extension housing.
18. Smear new oil seal with clean transmission fluid and gently tap seal into recess. Ensure seal is fully seated.
19. Reverse operations 14 and 15, use new gasket between rear extension and gearcase.
20. Tighten rear extension fixings to a torque of 42.5 lbf ft (5,88 kgf m).
21. Reverse operations 9 to 13, use a new 'O' ring on speedometer driven gear. Tighten output flange securing bolt to a torque of 40–50 lbf ft (5,53–6,90 kgf m).
22. Reverse operations 1 to 8.
23. Top up lubrication system, see operation 44.24.02.

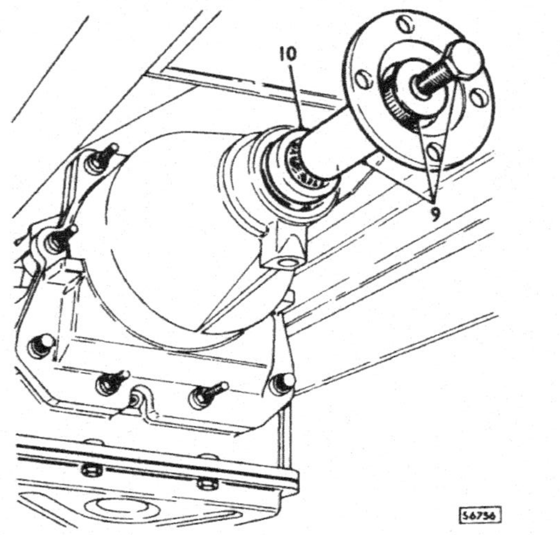

REAR EXTENSION HOUSING OIL SEAL

Remove and refit 44.20.18

Removing

WARNING: CHOCK BOTH FRONT WHEELS TO PREVENT VEHICLE MOVING.

1 Remove rear engine mounting – 12.45.08.
2 Remove screw securing intermediate heat shield; withdraw shield.
3 Remove screws securing rear heat shield to rear engine mounting support plate.
4 Remove six bolts and special washers securing rear engine mounting support plate to floor pan.
5 Remove bolts and special washers securing rear engine mounting support plate to transmission tunnel.
6 Remove self locking nuts and bolts securing propeller shaft to gearbox output flange; swing propeller shaft to one side.
NOTE: This operation will be greatly facilitated if one rear wheel (both wheels if 'Powr-Lok' differential is fitted) is raised and gear selector placed in 'N' (Neutral), thereby enabling propeller shaft to be rotated.
7 Using engine support tool fitted in operation 1, lower rear of engine slightly.
CAUTION: Ensure engine does not foul heater water valve.
8 Place selector lever in 'P' (Park).
9 Remove bolt and plain washer securing gearbox output flange; withdraw flange.
10 Prise oil seal out of rear extension housing, discard seal.

Refitting

11 Lightly score oil seal recess in rear extension housing.
12 Smear new oil seal with clean transmission fluid and gently tap seal into recess. Ensure seal is fully seated.
13 Reverse operations 1 to 9; tighten output flange securing bolt to a torque of 40 to 50 lbf ft (5,53 to 6,90 kgf m).
14 Top up lubrication system, see operation 44.24.02.

GOVERNOR

Remove and refit 44.22.01

Removing

1 Remove rear extension housing – 44.20.15.
2 Slide speedometer drive gear off output shaft.
3 Position selector lever in 'N' (Neutral).
4 If necessary, rotate output shaft to gain access to governor securing plug.
5 Note fitted position of governor and remove plug and spring washer securing governor to output shaft.
6 Slide governor off output shaft.
NOTE: If governor is to be overhauled, carry out items 183 to 188, operation 44.20.06.

Refitting

7 Slide governor on output shaft noting location of blind hole in shaft.
8 Fit governor securing plug and spring washer, ensure domed end of plug enters blind hole in output shaft. Tighten plug to a torque of 16.5 lbf ft (2,28 kgf m).
9 Reverse operations 1 and 2.

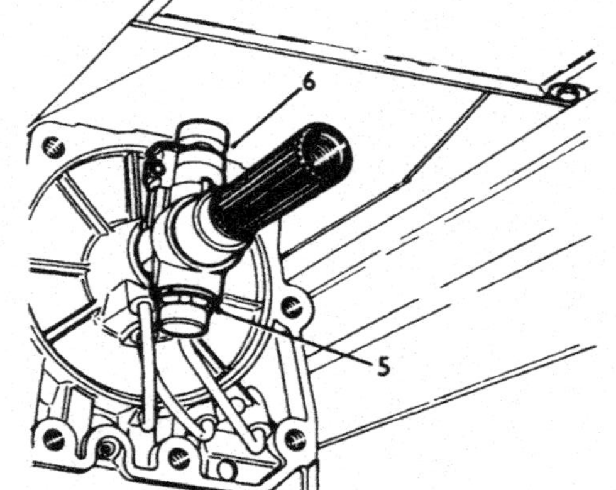

LUBRICATION SYSTEM

Drain and refill 44.24.02

CAUTION: Due to method of construction, it is not possible to completely drain transmission fluid, and this should be taken into account when transmission is being refilled. As it should only be necessary to carry out the following operations preparatory to carrying out work on the transmission which will involve removal of oil pan, the following procedure should be followed. It is possible, however, to drain a smaller amount of fluid by removing dipstick/filler tube.

Draining

1 Remove oil pan – 44.24.04.
2 Discard fluid.

Refilling

3 Refit oil pan, fill transmission to 'MAX' mark on dipstick.
4 Apply handbrake and select 'P' position.
5 Run engine until it reaches normal operating temperature.
6 With engine still running, withdraw dipstick, wipe clean and replace.
7 Immediately withdraw dipstick and note reading on 'HOT' side of dipstick.
8 If necessary, add fluid to bring level on dipstick to 'MAX'.
NOTE: Difference between 'MAX' and 'MIN' marks on dipstick represents approximately 1½ pints (2 U.S. Pints, 0,75 litre).

OIL PAN

Remove and refit 44.24.04

Removing

1 Unscrew union nut, withdraw dipstick tube; drain and discard fluid.
2 Remove bolts and plain washers securing oil pan to transmission case.
3 Lower oil pan, remove and discard gasket.

Refitting

4 Reverse operations 1 to 3, smear new gasket with grease prior to fitting. Tighten bolts by diagonal selection to a torque of 5.75 lbf ft (0,80 kgf m).
5 Refill transmission, see operation 44.24.02.

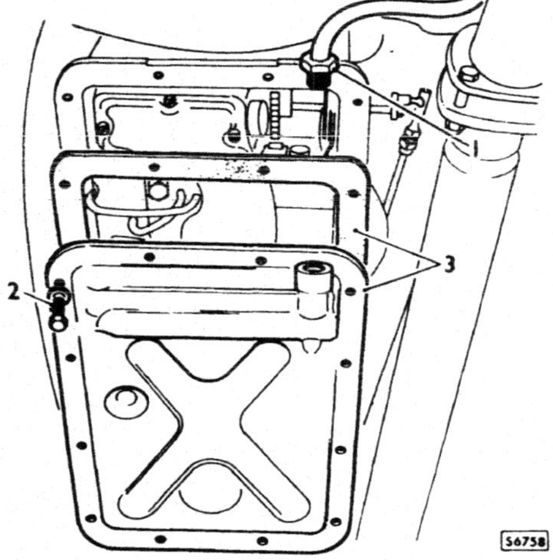

OIL FILTER

Remove and refit 44.24.07

Service Tools: Torque screwdriver CBW.548; Screwdriver bit adaptor CBW.548-1.

Removing

1 Remove oil pan – 44.24.04.
2 Remove screws securing suction tube to valve block.
3 Lower suction tube, remove and discard gasket, extract filter.

Refitting

4 Reverse operations 1 to 3, use a new gasket. Ensure that brass strainer, part No. AAU 7085, is fitted, NOT steel strainer.
NOTE: Gasket must be smeared with clean transmission fluid prior to fitting.
5 Using torque screwdriver CBW.548 and adaptor CBW.548-1, tighten securing screws to a torque of 2.1 lbf ft (0,30 kgf m).

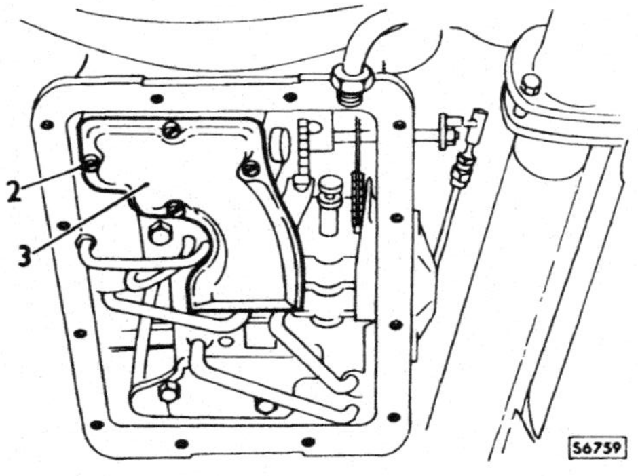

DOWNSHIFT CABLE

Check and adjust 44.30.02

For details of this operation, refer to 44.30.03, downshift cable pressure check.

DOWNSHIFT CABLE

Pressure check 44.30.03

Service tools:
Gearboxes prior to Serial No. 015 2153:
Pressure gauge CBW.1A or 1B or lightweight pipe and pressure gauge CBW.1C; gearbox adaptor CBW.1B/2 and hose adaptor 18G 677B.

Gearboxes after Serial No. 015 2153:
Pressure gauge CBW.1A or 1B or lightweight hose and pressure gauge CBW.1C; gearbox adaptor CBW.1C-5.

1 Check engine tune i.e. cylinder compressions, spark plugs, ignition timing, carburetters.
2 Lift carpet from left hand side of transmission tunnel.
3 Remove screws securing access plate; withdraw plate.
4 Clean any traces of sealing compound off access plate and transmission tunnel.
5 Using a suitable Allen key, remove blanking plug from gearcase.
CAUTION: On later cars, a bracket is fitted between gearbox and rear mounting. Access to blanking plug is through hole in bracket and under no circumstances may bracket be removed.
6 Connect pressure gauge to gearbox using appropriate adaptor.
CAUTION: Do not over tighten adaptor.
7 Feed gauge and hose through aperture in transmission tunnel ensuring that hose is kept clear of exhaust pipe.
8 Run engine until it reaches normal operating temperature.
9 Chock wheels and apply hand and foot brakes.
10 Select 'D', pressure gauge should read 60 to 75 lbf/in^2 (4,2 to 5,3 kgf/cm^2) at idling speed.
11 Increase engine speed to 1200 r.p.m., gauge should read 75 to 115 lbf/in^2 (5,3 to 8,1 kgf/cm^2).
If above readings are not obtained, proceed as follows:

WARNING: ENGINE MUST BE SWITCHED OFF AND SELECTOR LEVER IN 'N' BEFORE CARRYING OUT ADJUSTMENT.

12 Slacken locknut on downshift cable.
13 By means of abutment nut on outer cable, adjust length of cable to alter pressure.
NOTE: Increasing length of cable causes an increase in pressure; decreasing length of cable causes a decrease in pressure. Ferrule crimped on inner cable should be approximately 0.010 in. (0,4 mm.), from threaded portion of outer cable (Dimension 'A').
14 When pressure is correct, tighten locknut.
15 Reverse operations 2 to 11, use new sealing compound, on access plate; do not overtighten blanking plug.
16 Check gearbox fluid level, see 44.24.02, items 4 to 8.
17 Road test car, see 44.00.00, pages 44–35 and 44–36.

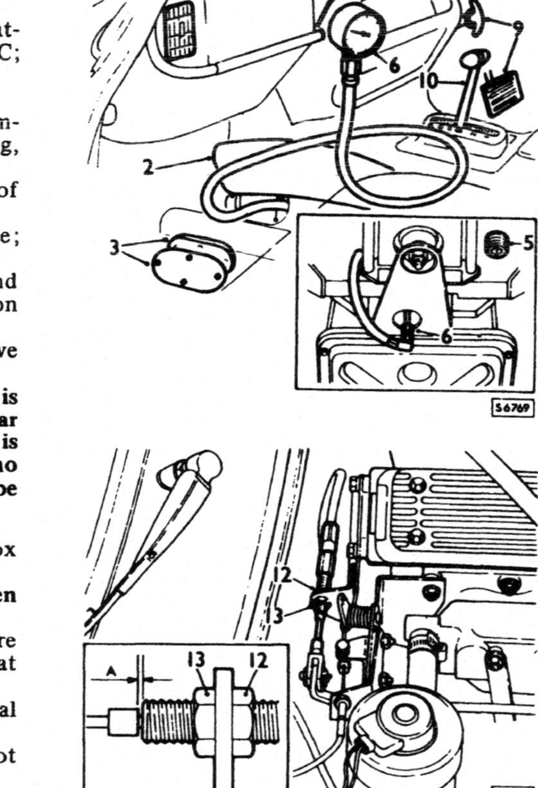

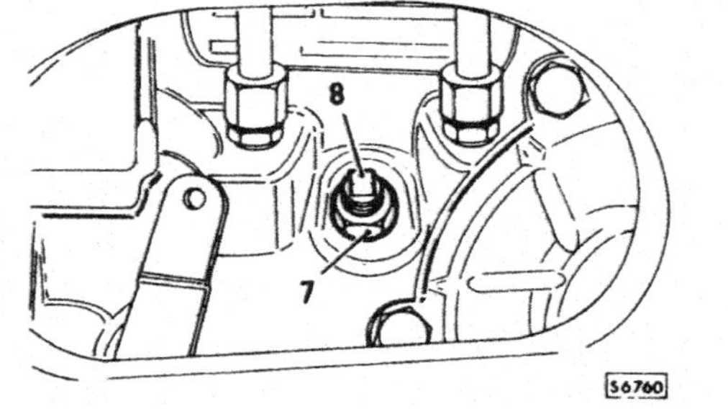

FRONT BRAKE BAND

Adjustment **44.30.07**

Service tools: Torque wrench CBW.547A-50; Adaptor CBW.547-50-2A.

1 Remove self locking nut securing selector lever to selector shaft; withdraw lever.
2 Push left hand seat fully rearwards.
3 Lift carpet from left hand footwell.
4 Remove console side casing – 76.25.02.
5 Remove four screws securing access plate to transmission tunnel.
6 Withdraw access plate, clean off old sealing compound.
7 Slacken locknut securing brake band adjuster screw.
8 Slacken adjuster screw two or three turns.
9 Using torque wrench CBW.547A-50, suitable 3/8 in. drive straight extension and adaptor CBW.547A-50-2A, tighten brake band adjuster screw to a torque of 5 lbf./ft. (,80 kgf./m.) and then back off screw 3/4 of a turn.
10 Tighten locknut to a torque of 35 lbf./ft. (4,8 kgf./m.).
CAUTION: Ensure adjuster screw does not turn during this operation.
11 Reverse operations 1 to 6, seal access plate with suitable sealing compound.

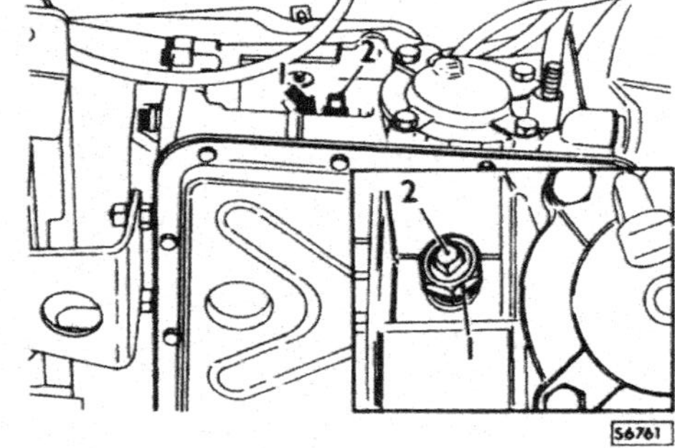

REAR BRAKE BAND

Adjustment **44.30.10**

Service Tools: Torque wrench CBW. 547A-50; Adaptor CBW.547A-50-2A.

1 Slacken locknut securing brake band adjuster screw.
2 Slacken adjuster screw two or three turns.
3 Using torque wrench CBW.547A-5 and Adaptor CBW.547A-50-2A, tighten brake band adjuster screw to a torque of 5 lbf./ft. (,80 kgf./m.) and then back off screw 3/4 of a turn.
4 Tighten locknut to a torque of 35 lbf./ft. (4,8 kgf./m.).
CAUTION: Ensure adjuster screw does not turn during this operation.

STALL SPEED

Test **44.30.13**

The results of this test indicate condition of gearbox and converter.
Stall speed is maximum engine revolutions recorded whilst driving impeller against stationary turbine. Stall speed will vary with both engine and transmission conditions so before attempting a stall speed check, engine condition must be determined. Engine and transmission must be at normal operating temperature before commencing check.

1 Apply handbrake.
2 Apply footbrake.
3 Start engine.

4 Select 'D'.
5 Fully depress accelerator.
6 Note tachometer reading.

CAUTION: To avoid overheating of transmission do not stall for more than 10 seconds at a time or for a total of one minute in any half hour period.

R.P.M.	CONDITION INDICATED
Under 1300	Stator free wheel slip
1950 to 2100	Normal
Over 2,500	Clutch slip

FRONT SERVO

Remove and refit **44.34.07**

Service Tool: Torque wrench CBW. 547A-50.

Removing
1 Remove valve block – 44.40.01.
2 Remove bolts securing servo to transmission case.
3 Withdraw servo together with push rod and spring.
4 Remove and discard gasket.
5 Recover brake band strut.
NOTE: If front servo is to be overhauled, carry out operation 44.20.06, items 177 to 179.

Refitting
6 Smear new gasket with grease, position gasket on servo body.
7 Position brake band strut in transmission case ensuring that strut is correctly located on brake band.
8 Insert servo push rod and spring in transmission ensuring that spigot on brake band strut is located in hole in push rod.
9 Position servo on transmission case ensuring that push rod and spring are correctly located.
10 Fit and tighten servo securing bolts by diagonal selection to a torque of 19 lbf./ft. (2,64 kgf./m.).
11 Reverse operation 1.
12 Adjust front brake band – 44.30.07.

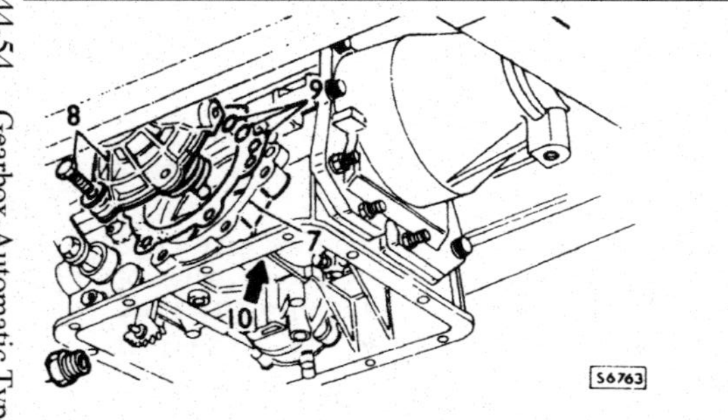

REAR SERVO

Remove and refit 44.34.13

Service Tool: Torque wrench CBW 547A-50.

Removing

1. Remove valve block – 44.40.01.
2. Remove nuts, bolts and washer securing intermediate exhaust pipe to front pipe.
3. Separate intermediate pipe from front pipe; remove and discard joint.
4. Remove screws and special washers securing left hand heat shield to body, withdraw heat shield.
5. Remove bolt and spring washer securing gear shift cable trunnion block to mounting bracket.
6. Remove self-locking nut securing selector lever to selector shaft; withdraw lever and selector cable assembly.
7. Mark relative position of rear servo body to transmission case.
8. Remove bolts securing servo to transmission case, withdraw servo, push rod and spring.
9. Remove and discard gasket and two 'O' rings.
10. Collect brake band strut if strut should be displaced.
    NOTE: If rear servo is to be overhauled, carry out operation 44.20.06, items 180 to 182.

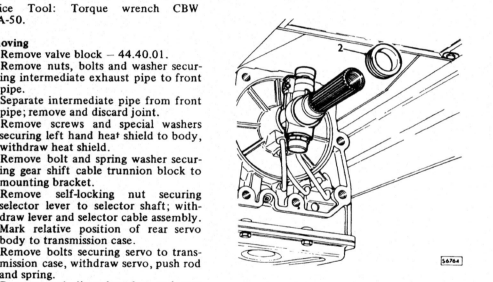

Refitting

11. Smear new 'O' rings with clean transmission fluid, position 'O' ring in each recess in servo body.
12. Smear new gasket with grease, position gasket on servo body.
13. Position brake band strut (if removed) in transmission case ensuring that strut is correctly located.
14. Reverse operations 1 to 8, tighten servo securing bolts by diagonal selection to a torque of 19 lbf./ft. (2,64 kgf./m.). Coat new exhaust joint with Firegum prior to refitting.
15. Adjust rear brake band – 44.30.10.

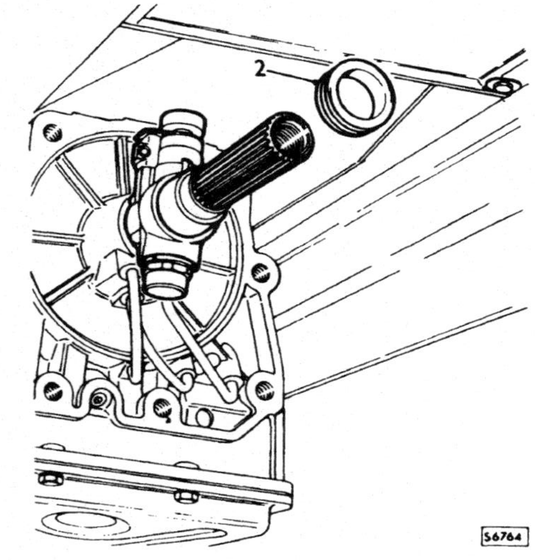

SPEEDOMETER DRIVE GEAR

Remove and refit 44.38.07

Removing

1. Remove rear extension housing – 44.20.15.
2. Slide speedometer drive gear off output shaft.

Refitting

Reverse operations 1 and 2.

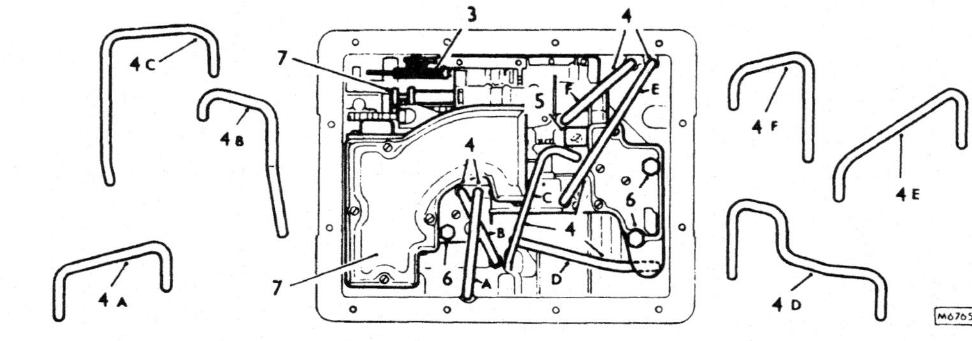

VALVE BLOCK

Remove and refit 44.40.01

Service Tool: Torque wrench CBW. 547A-50.

Removing

1. Position selector lever in 'P' (Park).
2. Remove oil pan – 44.24.04.
3. Disconnect kickdown cable from cam.
4. Note fitted position of oil tubes. See Operation – 44.20.06 item 15 and using a suitable screwdriver, lever tubes out of transmission.
5. Note fitted position of magnet; withdraw magnet.
6. Remove bolts securing valve block to transmission noting that shortest bolt is fitted at front.
7. Pull valve block downwards ensuring that manual valve is not displaced.
   CAUTION: Extreme care must be taken to ensure that action of removal does not damage converter feed, pump feed or pump outlet pipes.
   NOTE: If valve block is to be overhauled, carry out operation 44.20.06, items 68 to 94.

Refitting

8. Ensure convertor feed, pump feed and pump outlet pipes are not damaged; push each pipe upwards to ensure correct location is maintained.
9. Locate valve block in transmission case ensuring that tubes detailed in operation 8 are correctly located in valve block.
   NOTE: Valve block may be tapped **gently** with a hide mallet to ensure correct location is obtained.
10. Ensure that spigot on detent lever engages with groove machined in manual valve.
11. Reverse operations 1 to 6 ensuring that oil pipes are correctly fitted. Tighten valve block securing bolts to a torque of 6.75 lbf./ft. (,93 kgf./m.).

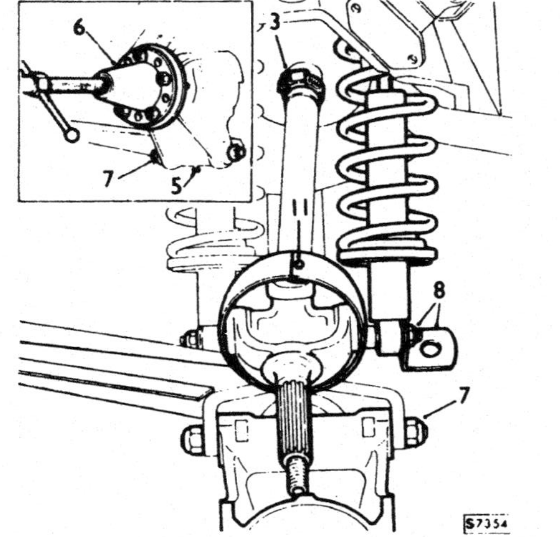

DRIVE SHAFT

Remove and refit – Left or right hand **47.10.01**

Service tool: Hub remover JD.1D.

Removing

1 Jack up rear of vehicle and support on stands.
2 Remove wheel.
3 Slacken inner shroud clip and slide shroud away from flange. Remove nuts.
4 Withdraw split pin and remove castellated nut and plain washer from drive shaft in hub. Discard split pin.
5 Remove grease nipple from hub carrier.
6 Fit hub puller JD.1D to hub and secure. Withdraw hub assembly from splined shaft and remove puller.
7 Pivot hub assembly on fulcrum shaft.
8 Remove nut at damper mounting, detach lash down bracket, drift pin forward and release lower end of damper.
9 Remove drive shaft assembly; collect shims fitted between flange and brake disc.
NOTE: If new drive shaft assembly is to be fitted it is now necessary to detach shrouds and remove oil seal track and spacer for fitting to replacement shaft; carry out operations 10 to 14. If the same shaft is to be refitted these operations may be omitted, and the shrouds, spacer and oil seal track left in position.
10 Remove phosphor bronze spacer and inner oil seal track from splined shaft.
11 Drill out pop rivets from shrouds, remove clips and collect halves of shrouds.
12 Place shroud halves on replacement shaft, line up holes and pop rivet halves together.
13 Seal shroud joints with underseal, fit clips, place outer shroud in position and tighten clip.
14 Fit inner oil seal track (note that chamfer clears radius on drive shaft) and spacer to splined shaft.

Refitting

15 Clean and refit camber shims, place flanged end of shaft in position and refit nuts but do not tighten at this stage.
16 Refit damper to lower mounting pin, replace lash down bracket and tighten nut to 32 to 36 lbf.ft. (4,43 to 4,98 kgf.m.).

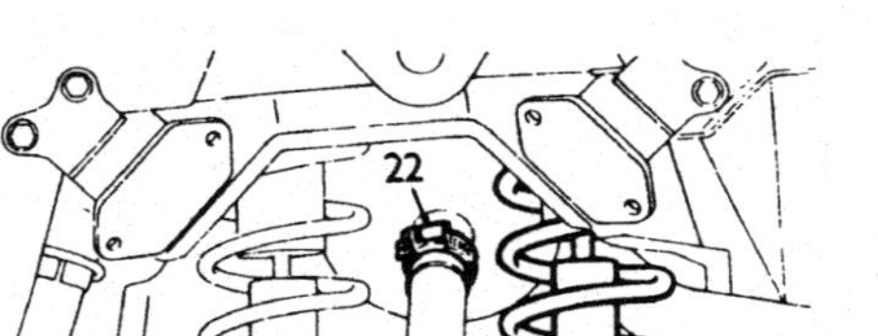
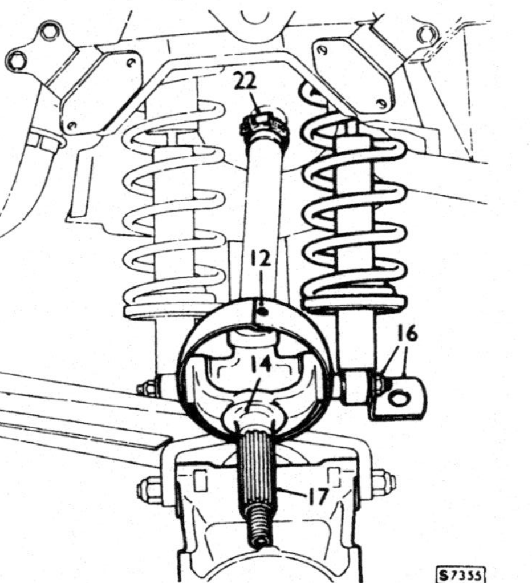

17 Apply Loctite to splines, check that spacer and oil seal track are installed, raise hub carrier and enter splined shaft into hub.
18 Tap hub home on splines, replace washer, tighten nut to 100 to 120 lbf.ft. (13,83 to 16,60 kgf.m.) and fit split pin.
19 Check hub bearing end float, see 64.15.13.
20 Refit fulcrum grease nipple in hub carrier.
21 Tighten drive shaft nuts to 49 to 55 lbf.ft. (6,7 to 7,60 kgf.m.).
22 Slide inner shroud into position and tighten clip.
23 Replace wheel.
24 Remove car from stands.
25 Check and if necessary adjust camber angle of rear wheel, see 64.25.18.

DRIVE SHAFT

Overhaul **47.10.08**

1 Remove drive shaft, see 47.10.01, operations 1 to 9.

Dismantling

2 Remove grease nipples.
3 Place shaft in vice and remove two opposed circlips.
NOTE: Tap bearings slightly inwards to assist removal of circlips.
4 Tap one bearing inwards to displace opposite bearing.
5 Trap displaced bearing in vice and remove shaft and joint from bearing.

6 Replace shaft in vice, displace second bearing by tapping joint spider across and extract second bearing.
7 Remove two grease seals from spider.
8 Detach spider, with end section of shaft, from centre section of shaft.
9 Place end section of shaft in vice and repeat operations 3 to 7.
10 Remove spider from end section of shaft.
11 Repeat operations 3 to 10 on opposite end of shaft.

Inspection

12 Wash all parts in petrol.
13 Check splined yoke for wear of splines.
14 Examine bearing races and spider journals for signs of looseness, load markings, scoring or distortion.
NOTE: Spider or bearings should not be renewed separately, as this will cause premature failure of the replacement.
It is essential that bearing races are a light drive fit in yoke trunnion.

Reassembling

15 Remove bearing assemblies from one replacement spider; if necessary, retain rollers in housings with petroleum jelly. Leave grease shields in position.

continued

3 8 7 2 7 4 3
S7356

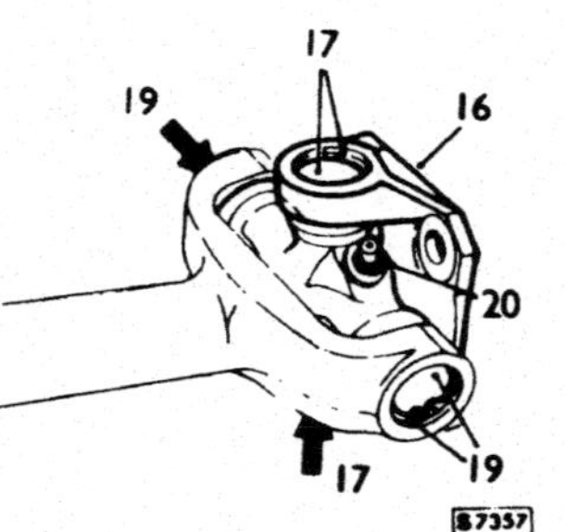

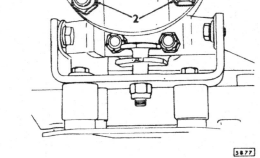

16 Fit spider to one end section of shaft.
17 Fit two bearings and circlips in end section trunnions. Use a soft round drift against bearing housings.
18 Insert spider in trunnions of centre section of shaft.
19 Fit two bearings and circlips in centre section trunnions.
20 Fit grease nipple to spider.
21 Repeat operations 15 to 20 on opposite end of drive shaft.
22 Grease joints with hand grease gun.
23 Refit drive shaft, see 47.10.01, operations 15 to 25.

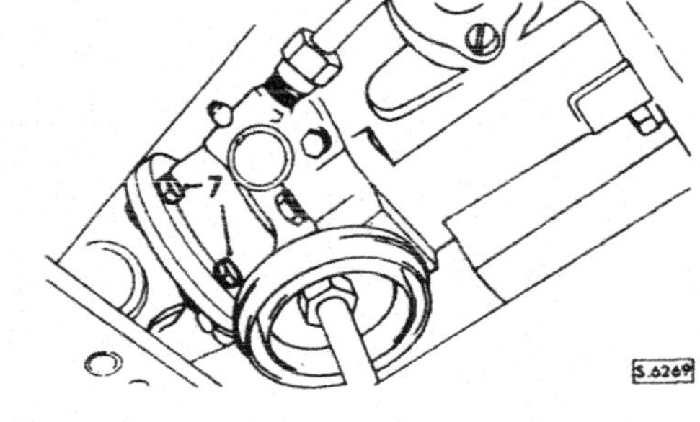

PROPELLER SHAFT ASSEMBLY

Remove and refit **47.15.01**

Service tools: Engine support tool – MS.53(A).

Removing

1 Fit engine support tool, MS.53(A), to rear lifting eye of engine.
2 Remove exhaust intermediate pipe – 30.10.11.
3 Remove fastenings securing rear and intermediate heat shields.
4 Remove setscrews, plain and spring washers and spacers (if fitted) securing rear engine mounting plate.

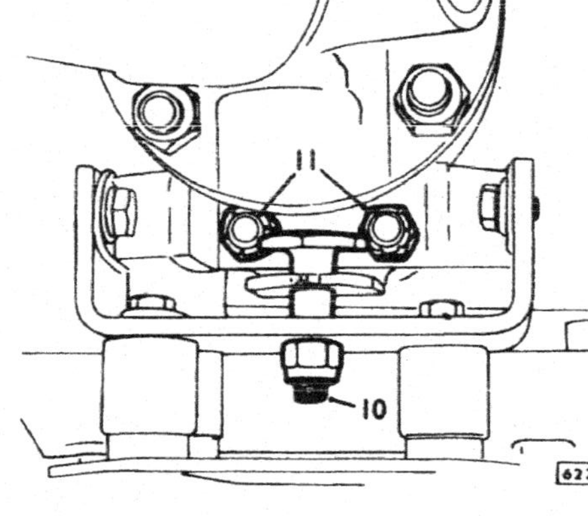

5 Place jack and suitably formed block of wood beneath gearbox and release self locking nut and washers securing rear engine mount.
CAUTION: On cars fitted with automatic transmission, wood must be positioned under casting, not oil pan.
6 Remove nuts securing bracket (if fitted) to gearcase. Remove engine mounting plate, mounting spring and plain washers.
7 Remove four nuts and bolts securing propeller shaft drive flange to gearbox.
NOTE: This will be greatly facilitated if rear wheel (both wheels if "Powr Lok" differential is fitted) is raised.

WARNING: CHOCK BOTH FRONT WHEELS TO PREVENT VEHICLE MOVING.

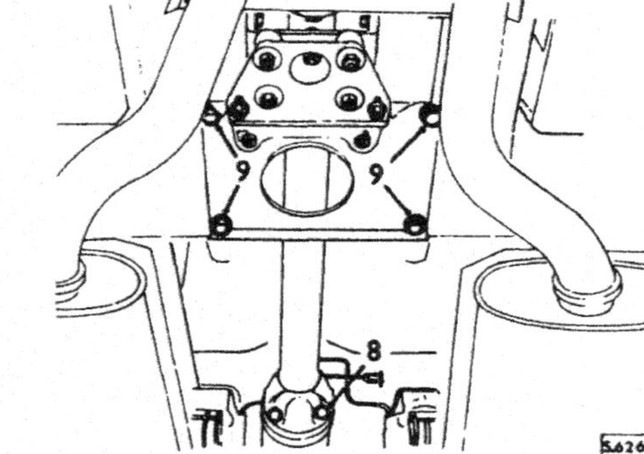
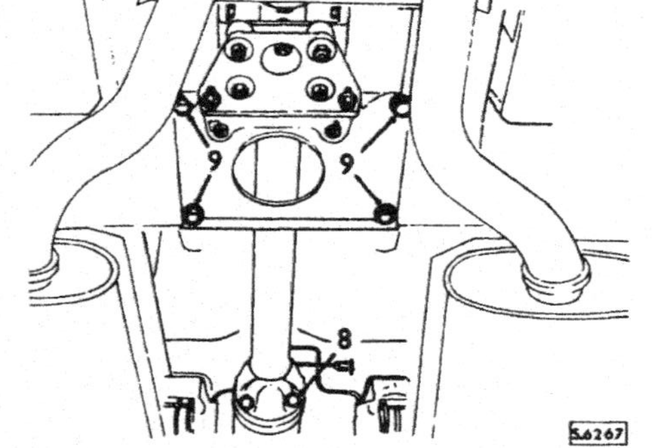

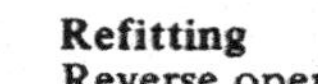

8 Remove four nuts and bolts securing propeller shaft drive flange to final drive unit.
9 Remove bolts, plain and spring washers securing centre bearing base plate, remove propeller shaft assembly from car.
10 Remove self locking nut and bolt from centre bearing carrier.
11 Remove self locking nuts securing centre bearing ring to rubber mounting bracket.

Refitting

Reverse operations 1 to 11.

PROPELLER SHAFT – FRONT

Remove and refit **47.15.02**

Removing

1 Remove propeller shaft – 47.15.01.
2 Remove four nuts and bolts securing front propeller shaft drive flange to rear propeller shaft.

Refitting

3 Fit front propeller shaft, sliding joint towards front, to rear propeller shaft drive flange.
4 Reverse operation 1.

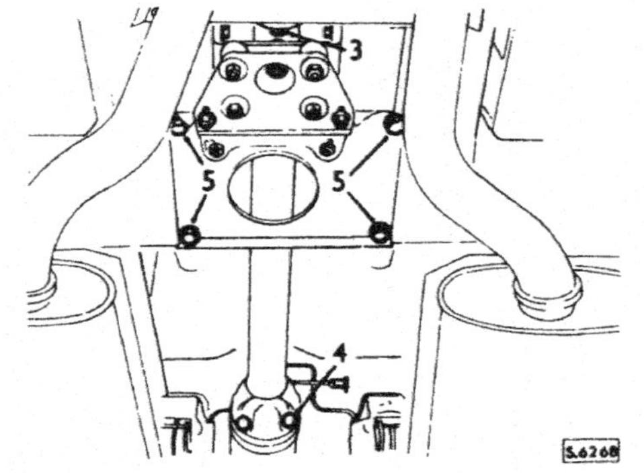

PROPELLER SHAFT – REAR

Remove and refit **47.15.03**

Removing

1 Remove exhaust *intermediate pipe* – 30.10.11.
2 Remove fixings securing rear heat shield.
3 Remove four nuts and bolts securing rear propeller shaft drive flange to front propeller shaft.
4 Remove four nuts and bolts securing rear propeller shaft drive flange to final drive unit.

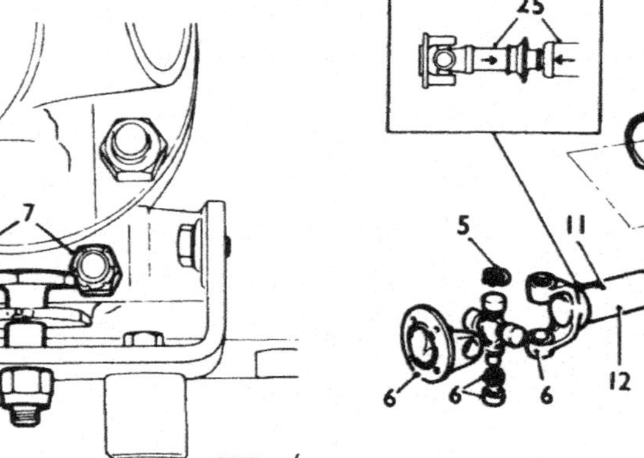

5 Remove bolts, plain and spring washers securing centre bearing base plate, remove rear propeller shaft assembly from car.
6 Remove self locking nut and safety bolt from centre bearing carrier.
7 Remove self locking nuts securing centre bearing ring to rubber mounting bracket.

Refitting

Reverse operations 1 to 7.

PROPELLER SHAFTS

Overhaul **47.15.10**

1 Remove propeller shaft assembly – 47.15.01.
2 Remove four nuts and bolts securing front propeller shaft to rear propeller shaft.
3 Check condition of four grommets in centre bearing carrier and renew as necessary.
CAUTION: Ensure spacer tubes are removed and fitted in replacement grommets.

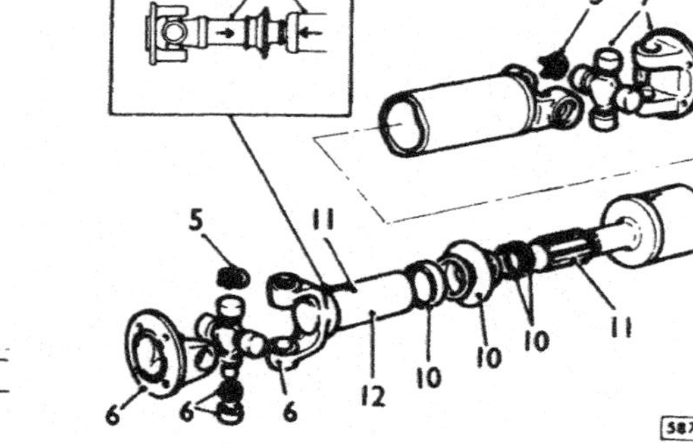

Dismantling

4 Clean paint and dirt from all universal joints.
5 Remove snap rings from grooves.
NOTE: If snap ring is difficult to remove, tap bearing inwards to relieve pressure on ring.
6 Hold flanged yoke in hand and tap lug with soft faced hammer. Bearing will gradually emerge and can finally be removed with the fingers.
7 Repeat operation for opposite bearing and remove flanged yoke.
8 Rest exposed trunnions on wood or lead blocks, and tap yoke to remove remaining two bearings.
9 Repeat operations 6 to 8 inclusive on opposite end of shaft.

Front propeller shaft only

10 Remove metal and plastic clips from gaiter and withdraw gaiter along shaft.
11 Partially withdraw sleeve yoke from splined shaft. Examine spline for wear. If there is more than .004 in. (0,1 mm.) circumferential movement measured on the outside diameter of spline, renew complete propeller shaft.
12 Withdraw sleeve yoke from splined shaft.

Inspection

13 Wash all parts in petrol.
14 Examine bearing races and spider journals for signs of looseness, load markings, scoring or distortion.
15 Spider or bearings should not be renewed separately, as this will cause premature failure of the replacement. It is essential that bearing races are a light drive fit in yoke trunnion.

Reassembling

16 Fit new cork gaskets and gasket retainers to spiders.
17 Fit needle rollers in bearing housings. Retain, if necessary, with petroleum jelly during assembly.
18 Insert two spider journals in a yoke, and using a soft round drift .031 in. (0,8 mm.) smaller in diameter than hole in yoke, tap bearings into position.
19 Fit two spider journals to shaft yoke and assemble bearing as in operations 16, 17 and 18.
20 When four bearings are assembled to joint, fit new snap rings to retain bearing housings.
21 If joint appears to bind, tap it lightly with a soft faced hammer and exercise it until free.
22 Complete assembly of opposite end of propeller shaft.

Front propeller shaft only

23 Fit gaiter and plastic and metal clips to sleeve yoke.
24 Lubricate splines using recommended grease.
25 Fit sleeve yoke to shaft splines, ensuring that alignment arrows coincide.
26 Secure clips.
27 Connect front and rear propeller shafts, using four nuts and bolts.
28 Reverse operation 1.

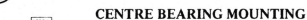

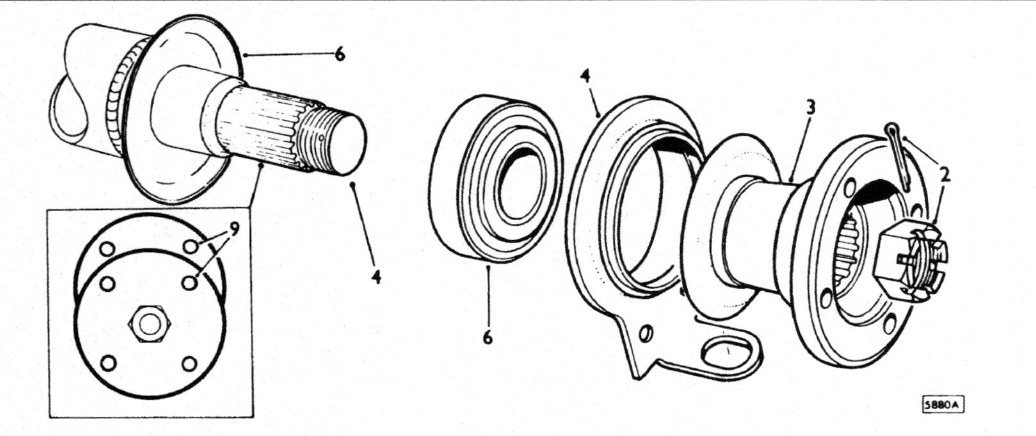

CENTRE BEARING

Remove and refit **47.15.32**

Removing

1 Remove rear propeller shaft – 47.15.03.
2 Remove split pin and castellated nut.
3 Draw drive flange from propeller shaft.
4 Support bearing ring in a vice and drive propeller shaft downwards to remove bearing ring.
5 Using hammer and sharp cold chisel, raise dust exclude ring from bearing.
6 Drift bearing from shoulder on propeller shaft.

Refitting.

7 Using tubular drift acting on centre ring of bearing, drift centre bearing on to propeller shaft shoulder.
8 Tap bearing ring on to bearing outer race until shoulder in ring seats on bearings. DO NOT USE EXCESSIVE FORCE.
9 Clean shaft splines and coat sparingly with loctite.
CAUTION: Ensure correct relationship is maintained between drive flanges at each end of propeller shaft.
10 Ensure dust excluder is fitted to drive flange and tap flange on to splines.
11 Secure with castellated nut and new split pin.
12 Carefully re-form rearmost dust excluder using suitable hammer.
13 Reverse operation 1.

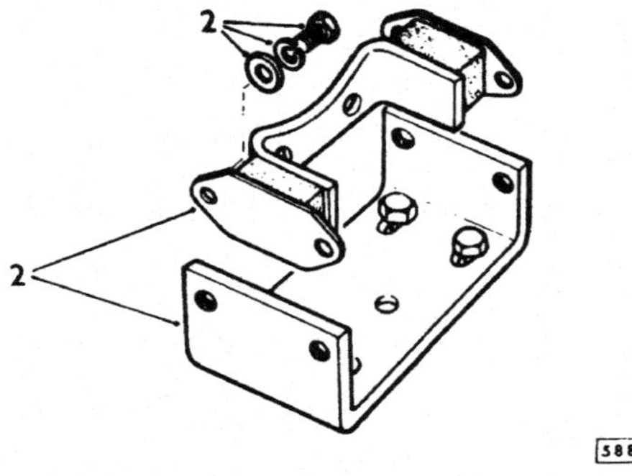

CENTRE BEARING MOUNTING

Remove and refit **47.15.33**

Removing

1 Remove rear propeller shaft – 47.15.03.
2 Remove setscrews, plain and shakeproof washers securing centre bearing mounting to centre bearing carrier.

Refitting

Reverse operations 1 and 2.

DESCRIPTION

51.00.00

The standard transmission unit is a Salisbury 4HU final drive, incorporating a 'Powr Lok' differential when specified.
The unit is rigidly attached to a fabricated sheet steel crossbeam which is flexibly mounted to the body structure by four rubber and metal sandwich mountings.
Noises coming from the vicinity of the final drive unit usually originate from incorrect meshing of drive gear and pinion, or from bearings on differential or pinion shafts developing play. Operation procedures for the correction of these noise sources are fully covered in section 51.25.19, but a noise occurring at low speeds only, under braking, could be caused by loss of pre-load in the output shaft bearings. Bearing inspection involves the removal and renewal of an oil seal before resetting pre-load, and is covered in 51.20.04, while if inspection indicates that bearing renewal is advisable this is detailed in 51.10.22.

OUTPUT SHAFT ASSEMBLY

Remove and refit (one side) 51.10.20

Removing
1 Remove brake disc attached to flange of shaft, see 70.10.11. Collect and retain separately any shims fitted at inner and outer faces of disc.
2 Cut locking wire and remove five set bolts securing caliper mounting bracket to final drive casing.
3 Withdraw output shaft assembly. Discard 'O' ring.

Refitting
NOTE: Before fitting replacement output shaft assembly check length of shaft on replacement unit against that removed, and ensure that four disc attachment bolts are in position in flange.
4 Fit new 'O' ring seal into groove in bearing housing.
5 Lightly oil splines and outside of bearing housing and replace assembly in final drive casing.
6 Fit five setbolts with spring washers to secure caliper mounting bracket to final drive and tighten to 60 to 69 lbf.ft. (8,3 to 9,5 kgf.m.).
7 Secure setbolts by wire-locking bolt heads together; arrange wire tension to pull bolt heads in a clockwise direction.
8 Replace brake disc, see 70.10.11, ensuring that shims are correctly replaced on both sides of disc.
9 Check camber angle of rear wheels and adjust if necessary, see 64.25.18.

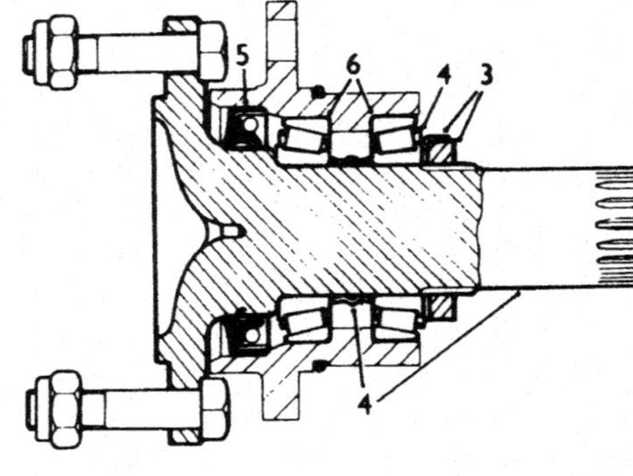

OUTPUT SHAFT BEARINGS

Remove and refit 51.10.22

Service tools: Torque screwdriver CBW.548, Adaptor, Spanner SL.15 or 15A, Output shaft bearing remover/replacer SL.47.

Removing
1 Remove output shaft assembly incorporating bearing to be removed, see 51.10.20 operations 1 to 3.
2 Clean assembly and clamp caliper mounting bracket between suitably protected jaws of vice.
3 Turn down tabs of lock washer and remove nut from shaft, using spanner SL.15. Remove and discard lock washer.
4 Withdraw output shaft from caliper mounting bracket. Collect inner bearing and cone. Discard collapsed spacer.
NOTE: If outer bearing remains on shaft and pushes oil seal out of caliper mounting bracket on withdrawal, remove it from shaft using tool SL.47.
5 Prise oil seal from caliper mounting bracket. Collect outer bearing and cone. Discard oil seal.
6 Using a brass drift, gently tap bearing cups out of housing.
7 Remove caliper mounting bracket from vice and carefully clean internally.

NOTE: When bearings are to be renewed, always replace complete bearings. Never fit new cone and roller assemblies into used cups. Pack bearings with No. 2 grease (preferably with E.P. additive) before fitting.

Refitting
8 Press cups of replacement bearings into housing, using suitable press and adaptors to ensure that cups are pressed fully home in housing.
9 Place roller and cone assembly of outer bearing (already greased) in position.
10 Press replacement oil seal into position, ensuring that spring-loaded sealing edge is adjacent to bearing. Load seal with grease between sealing edges.
11 Clamp caliper mounting bracket between protected jaws of vice.
12 Check that four special bolts for brake disc are in position in output shaft flange and enter shaft through seal and outer bearing.
13 Fit new collapsible spacer, roller and cone assembly of inner bearing and new lock washer on to shaft.
14 Place nut on shaft, grease face next to washer and tighten finger-tight only.
15 Using torque screwdriver CBW.548 and suitable adaptor, check torque required to turn shaft in caliper mounting bracket against resistance of oil seal. Record torque.
NOTE: Set screwdriver initially to 4 lbf.in. (0,05 kgf.m.). Setting should then be progressively increased until torque figure is established at the point when shaft commences to turn.
16 Using spanner SL.15 and a tommy-bar at disc attachment bolts to oppose torque, tighten nut on shaft just sufficiently to almost eliminate play from bearings. Repeat operation 15. Torque required to turn shaft should be unchanged; if it has increased, slacken nut very slightly and re-check.

continued

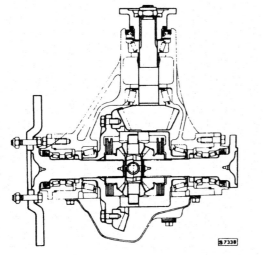

17 Tighten nut very slightly further (not more than a thirty-second of a turn – about 3/16 in. (5 mm.) at perimeter of nut) and re-check torque required to turn shaft. If this torque exceeds by between 4½ and 5½ lbf.in. (0,052 and 0,063 kgf.m.) the torque recorded in operation 15, correct bearing pre-load has been achieved. Otherwise, continue to tighten nut in very small increments, measuring torque after each increment, until correct figure is reached.
CAUTION: If torque required to turn shaft exceeds by more than 6 lbf.in. (0,007 kgf.m.) torque recorded in operation 15, it is necessary to dismantle assembly, discard collapsed spacer and rebuild with new collapsible spacer. It is not permissible to slacken back nut after collapsing spacer as bearing cones are then no longer rigidly clamped.
18 Turn down tab washers in two places to lock nut and remove assembly from vice.
19 Refit output shaft assembly to final drive unit, see 51.10.20, operations 4 to 10.

PINION BEARINGS

Remove and refit 51.15.19

Pinion bearing replacement entails stripping of final drive assembly and resetting of mesh of pinion and drive gear. Refer, therefore, to Final Drive – Overhaul, 51.25.19.

DIFFERENTIAL ASSEMBLY (POWR LOK)

Overhaul 51.15.30

Refer to 51.25.19.

DRIVE FLANGE

Remove and refit 51.15.36

CAUTION: In order that correct pinion bearing pre-load is obtained, carry out operation 51.20.01.

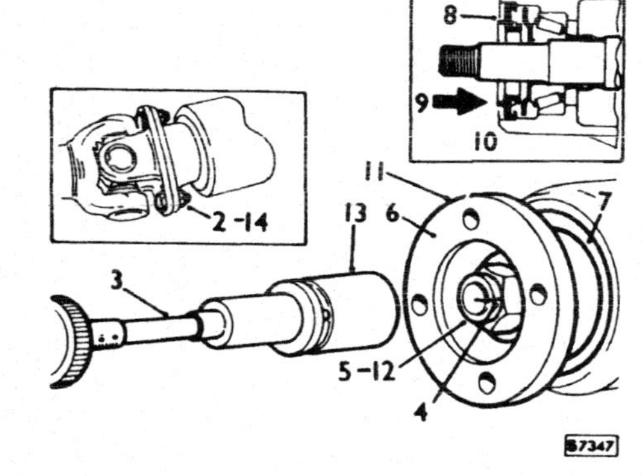

DRIVE PINION SHAFT OIL SEAL

Remove and refit 51.20.01

Service tool: Torque screwdriver CBW.548, Hand press SL.Γ4 with adaptor.

Removing
1 Place car on ramp, set handbrake, chock wheels and raise ramp.
2 Remove nuts securing propeller shaft flange to final drive flange; remove bolts and disconnect propeller shaft.
3 Using torque screwdriver CBW.548, suitable adaptor and socket, check and record torque required to turn final drive flange clockwise through backlash movement.
NOTE: Set screwdriver initially to 15 lbf.in. (0,17 kgf.m.) and increase setting progressively until torque figure is reached at which flange commences to move. Flange **MUST** be turned fully anti-clockwise through backlash between each check.
4 Mark nut and pinion shaft so that in refitting, nut may be returned to its original position on shaft.
5 Unscrew nut and remove washer and place both washer and nut aside for refitting.
6 Draw flange off pinion shaft using extractor.
7 Prise oil seal out of final drive casing.

Refitting
8 Thoroughly clean splines on pinion shaft and flange, removing all old Loctite. Clean oil seal recess and coat internally with Welseal liquid sealant.
9 Using suitable 'bell-piece' tap new oil seal squarely into position with sealing lip facing to rear. Smear sealing lip with grease.
10 Apply Loctite grade A.V.V. to outer two thirds of pinion shaft splines.
11 Lightly tap flange back on pinion shaft, using wooden mallet.
12 Refit washer and nut removed in operation 5 and tighten nut until it exactly reaches position marked in operation 4.
13 Repeat operation 3. Torque required to turn pinion shaft through backlash should exceed by 5 to 10 lbf.in. (0,06 to 0,12 kgf.m.) the torque recorded in operation 3. If torque is below 25 lbf.in. (0,29 kgf.m.), tighten flange nut further until torque figures is between 25 and 30 lbf.in. (0,29 and 0,35 kgf.m.). If, however, torque required to turn pinion shaft exceeds 45 lbf.in. (0,52 kgf.m.), final drive overhaul, operation 51.25.19 **MUST** be carried out.
14 Lift propeller shaft into position, replace bolts, fit and tighten nuts to 27 to 32 lbf.ft. (3,73 to 4,42 kgf.m.).
15 Check oil level in final drive unit and top up if necessary.
16 Remove car from ramp and road test. If final drive is noisy, overhaul procedure 51.25.19 **MUST** be carried out.

OUTPUT SHAFT OIL SEAL

Remove and refit (later cars) 51.20.04

Service tools: Torque screwdriver CBW.548, Adaptor, Spanner SL.15 or SL.15A.

Removing
1 Remove output shaft assembly, see 51.10.20, operations 1 to 3.
2 Clean assembly and clamp caliper mounting bracket between suitably protected jaws of vice.
3 Turn down tabs of lock washer and remove nut from shaft, using spanner SL.15. Remove and discard lock washer.
4 Withdraw output shaft from caliper mounting bracket. Collect inner bearing and cone and mark for correct reassembly. Discard collapsed spacer.
5 Prise oil seal from caliper mounting bracket and discard. Collect outer bearing and cone.
6 Remove caliper mounting bracket from vice and thoroughly clean internally.

NOTE: Carefully inspect taper roller bearing components before refitting. If any fault is found in either bearing, replace both complete bearings. Refer to 50.10.22, operations 6 and 8 to 19. Never fit new cone and roller assemblies into used cups. If bearings are satisfactory, grease with Silkolene grade 904 petroleum grease or if this is not available, final drive oil.

Refitting
7 Place roller and cone assembly of outer bearing (already greased) in position.
8 Press replacement oil seal into position, ensuring that spring-loaded sealing edge is adjacent to bearing. Load seal with grease between sealing edges.
9 Clamp caliper mounting bracket between protected jaws of vice.
10 Check that four special bolts for brake disc are in position in output shaft flange and enter shaft through seal and outer bearing.
11 Fit new collapsible spacer, followed by marked roller and cone assembly for inner bearing and new lock washer.

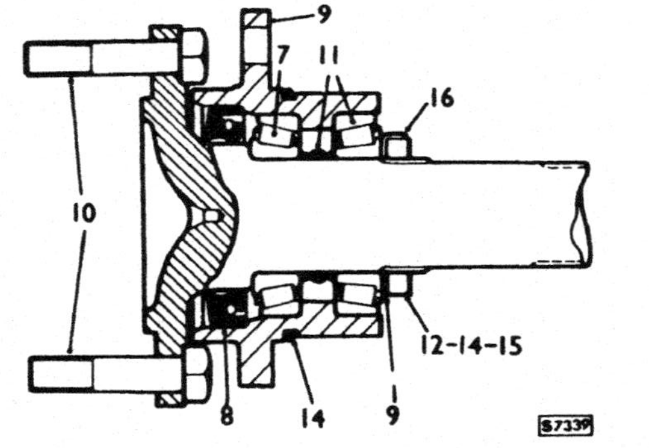

12 Place nut on shaft, grease face next to washer and tighten finger-tight only.
13 Using torque screwdriver CBW.548 and adaptor check torque required to turn shaft in caliper mounting bracket against resistance of oil seal. Record torque.
NOTE: Set screwdriver initially to 4 lbf.in. (0,05 kgf.m.). Setting should then be progressively increased until torque figure is established at the point when shaft commences to turn.
14 Using spanner SL.15 and a tommy-bar at disc attachment bolts to oppose torque, tighten nut on shaft just sufficiently to almost eliminate play from bearings. Repeat operation 13. Torque required to turn shaft should be unchanged; if it has increased, slacken nut very slightly and recheck.
15 Tighten nut very slightly further (not more than a thirty-second of a turn – about 3/16 in. (5 mm.) at perimeter of nut and recheck torque required to turn shaft. If this torque exceeds 2½ to 3 lbf.in. (0,03 and 0,035 kgf.m.) the torque recorded in operation 13, correct bearing pre-load has been achieved; otherwise continue to tighten nut in very small increments, measuring torque after each increment, until correct figure is reached.
CAUTION: If torque required to turn shaft exceeds more than 4 lbf.in. (0,045 kgf.m.) torque recorded in operation 13, it is necessary to dismantle assembly, discard collapsed spacer and rebuild with new collapsible spacer. It is not permissible to slacken back nut after collapsing spacer as bearing cones are then no longer rigidly clamped.
16 Turn down tab washers in two places to lock nut and remove assembly from vice.
17 Refit output shaft assembly to final drive unit, see 51.10.20, operations 4 to 9.

HYPOID CASING REAR COVER GASKET

Remove and refit **51.20.08**

Removing
1 Place car on ramp, set handbrake, chock wheels and raise ramp.
2 Remove 14 bolts and setscrews securing bottom tie plate to crossbeam and inner fulcrum brackets.
3 Remove drain plug and collect oil in suitable container. Discard oil.
4 Remove 10 setscrews securing rear cover. Retain identification tabs carried by three screws.
5 Detach rear cover and remove gasket.
6 Clean faces of final drive casing and cover.

Refitting
7 Smear both faces of new gasket with grease and place on final drive casing.
8 Place cover over gasket and insert two screws and spring washers to retain, coating threads with Loctite.
9 Replace remaining 8 setscrews, coating threads with Loctite and replacing spring washers and tabs.
10 Tighten screws by diagonal selection to 18 to 20 lbf.ft. (2,49 to 2,77 kgf.m.).
11 Refit drain plug.
12 Remove filler plug from cover and fill with recommended lubricant until oil escapes from filler hole.
NOTE: Car must be level for lubricant replenishment.
13 Refit filler plug.
14 Replace bottom tie plate and tighten bolts and setscress to 14 to 18 lbf.ft. (1,94 to 2,49 kgf.m.).
15 Remove car from ramp.

DRIVE SHAFT OIL SEAL

Remove and refit
(Early cars only) **51.20.19**

The drive shaft oil seal is integral with the caliper mounting bracket and cannot be renewed separately.

Removing
1 Remove drive shaft – 47.10.01.
2 Remove locking wire and withdraw two bolts and lockwashers securing brake caliper to final drive unit.
3 Remove discs, noting number of shims removed between brake disc and drive shaft flange.
4 Remove locking wire and remove five bolts securing caliper mounting bracket.
5 Withdraw drive shaft, together with caliper mounting bracket shims, ball bearing and square section oil seal.
6 Turn down tab washer and remove nut from drive shaft.
7 Remove ball bearing and caliper mounting bracket from drive shaft.

Refitting
8 Lightly oil new square section seal, position carefully, and press squarely to fully seat in final drive case groove.
CAUTION: Under no circumstances must the protruding portion of oil seal, A, be removed. This induces a metal contact between mounting bracket and bearing, and completely destroys the seal properties.
9 Coat oil seal with hypoid gear oil, fit four special flange bolts and position caliper mounting bracket and oil seal *assembly over drive shaft.*
NOTE: Brackets are handed.
10 Slide a ball bearing on to drive shaft followed by a new tab washer and nut.
11 Ensure bearing seats square to drive shaft shoulder. Tighten nut to 90 to 110 lb.ft. (12,44 to 14,2 kg.m.) and turn up tab washer.
12 Lightly oil drive shaft splines and fit shaft into differential casing.
13 Fit five bolts and spring washers to retain mounting bracket. Screw up until finger tight.
NOTE: Allowance has been made when calculating shimming required for .003 in. (,076 mm.) squash of the oil seal when fully tightened.
14 Using feeler gauges, measure dimension between inside face of caliper mounting bracket and differential housing. The measurement obtained determines shimming required to give correct degree of nip on outer ball bearing race and oil seal flange.
Shims are available in the following thicknesses: .003 in., .005 in., .010 in. and .030 in. (,076 mm., ,127 mm., ,254 mm. and ,762 mm.).

continued

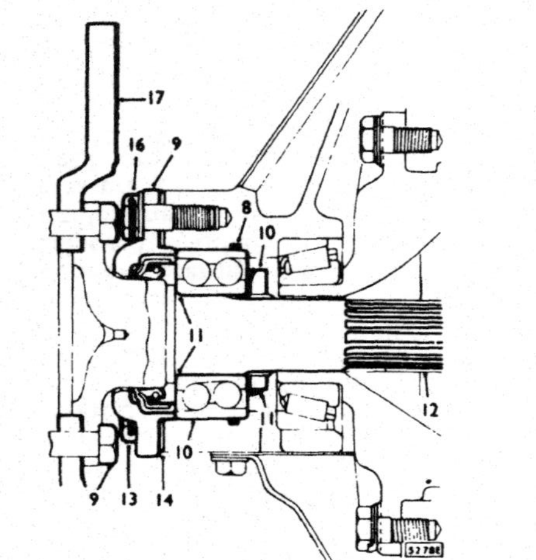

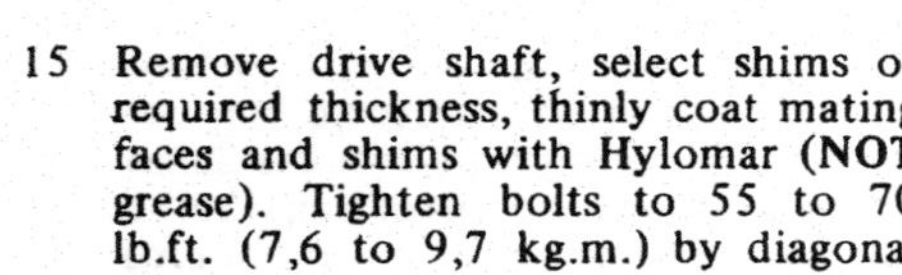

15 Remove drive shaft, select shims of required thickness, thinly coat mating faces and shims with Hylomar (**NOT** grease). Tighten bolts to 55 to 70 lb.ft. (7,6 to 9,7 kg.m.) by diagonal selection.
16 Wire lock five securing bolts to tension in clockwise direction.
17 Fit discs to drive shaft flanges, using shims removed in operation 3 between disc and flange.
18 Fit caliper to mounting bracket using two bolts and lockwashers.
19 Fit distance tubes (oversize nuts) to disc studs and secure using four nuts. Use feeler gauges to ensure disc central between jaws of caliper. If necessary add to or remove from shim pack between drive flange and disc.
20 Reverse operations 1 and 2.

FINAL DRIVE UNIT

Remove and refit 51.25.13

Service tool: Dummy shaft JD.14.

Removing
1 Removing rear suspension unit, see 64.25.01.
2 Invert unit and place on workbench.

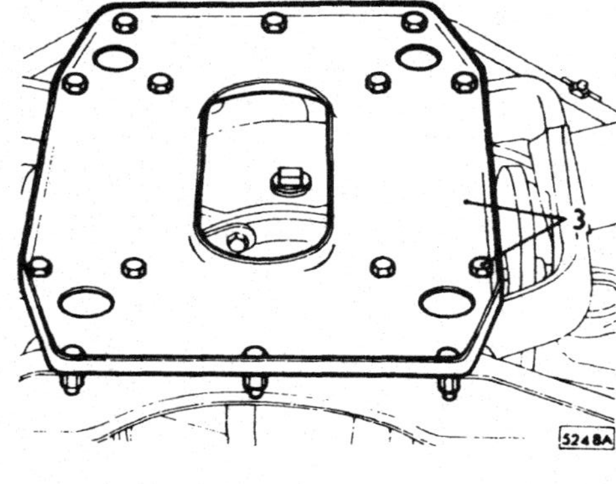

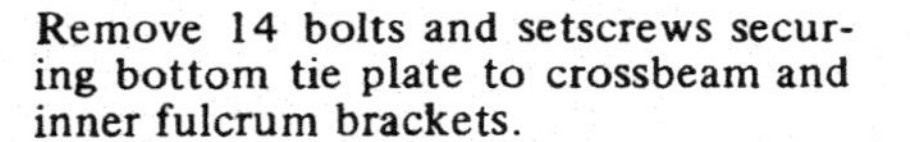

3 Remove 14 bolts and setscrews securing bottom tie plate to crossbeam and inner fulcrum brackets.
4 Remove nuts and washers securing dampers to wishbone.
5 Drift out damper mounting pins; recover spacers and tie-down brackets.
6 Slacken clips securing inner universal joint shrouds and displace shrouds outwards.
7 Remove four self locking nuts securing drive shaft inner universal joint to brake disc and output flange on one side.
8 Remove nut from inner wishbone fulcrum shaft.
9 Drift out shaft, collecting spacers, seals and bearings for wishbone pivots.
10 Remove drive shaft, hub and wishbone assembly from rear suspension.
11 Remove camber shims from drive shaft flange studs at brake disc.
12 Repeat operations 7 and 11 on opposite side assembly.
13 Tap spacer tubes from between lugs of fulcrum brackets.
14 Turn suspension assembly over on bench.
15 Disconnect brake feed pipes at calipers. Seal ports and ends of pipes.
16 Release brake return springs at handbrake levers.
17 Cut locking wire and remove bolts attaching final drive to crossbeam.
18 Lift suspension crossbeam off final drive unit.

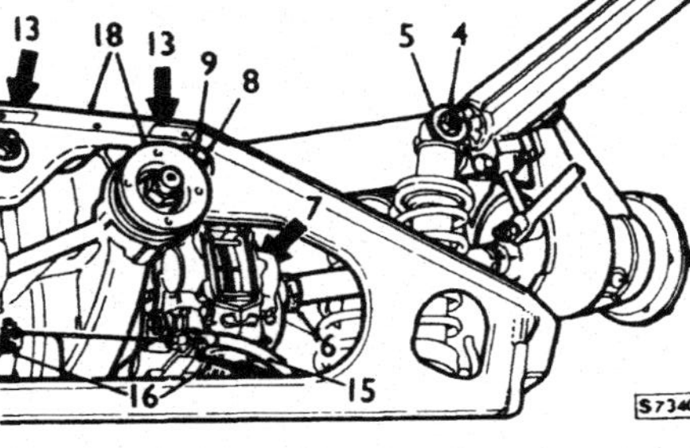

19 Invert final drive unit.
20 Remove locking wires from setscrews securing fulcrum brackets to final drive unit. Remove setscrews and remove brackets, noting position and number of shims at each attachment point.
21 Cut locking wires from caliper mounting bolts; remove bolts and calipers.
22 Remove brake discs, noting number of shims between discs and flanges.

Refitting
23 Replace shims and disc on one drive shaft flange; secure with two nuts.
24 Replace caliper, tighten mounting bolts and check centering and run-out of disc.
25 Correct centering of disc, if necessary, to within ± 0.010 in. (0,25 mm.) by transferring shims from one side of disc to the other.
26 Tighten caliper bolts to 49 to 55 lbf.ft. (6,77 to 7,60 kgf.m.) and wire lock.
27 Repeat operations 24 to 27 on opposite side.
28 Remove nuts from both discs.
29 Place crossbeam over final drive, align, replace bolts, tighten to 70 to 77 lbf.ft. (9,68 to 10,64 kgf.m.) and wire lock.
30 Slacken brake feed pipes at centre union.
31 Unseal brake pipes and ports, align pipes and tighten union nuts to 6.3 to 7 lbf.ft. (0,88 to 0,96 kgf.m.).
32 Replace handbrake lever return springs.
33 Invert assembly on bench.
34 Position fulcrum brackets against final drive unit and locate each bracket loosely with two setscrews.
35 Replace shims removed in operation 20 between brackets and final drive unit.
36 Tighten setscrews to 60 to 65 lbf.ft. (8,30 to 8,98 kgf.m.) and wire lock.
37 Refit camber shims, removed in operation 11, to drive shaft studs on one side.
38 Replace drive shaft on studs, and fit nuts loosely, then tighten to 49 to 55 lbf.ft. (6,78 to 7,60 kgf.m.).
39 Replace spacer tube between lugs of fulcrum bracket.
40 Clean, inspect and grease wishbone bearings, thrust washers etc. Refit with new oil seals.
41 Offer up wishbone fulcrum bracket lugs and locate with dummy shafts, tool No. JD.14. Take great care not to displace any component during this operation.
42 Drift dummy shafts from fulcrum bracket with fulcrum shaft. Restrain dummy shafts to prevent spacers or thrust washers dropping out of position.
43 Tighten fulcrum shaft nut to 45 to 50 lbf.ft. (6,23 to 6,91 kgf.m.).
44 Reposition and secure drive shaft shroud.
45 Line up damper lugs with wishbone bosses and replace damper shaft, including spacer and tie-down bracket. Tighten nuts to 32 to 36 lbf.ft. (4,43 to 4,97 kgf.m.).
46 Repeat operations 31 to 39 on opposite side.
47 Replace bottom tie plate and tighten bolts and setscrews to 14 to 18 lbf.ft. (1,94 to 2,48 kgf.m.).
48 Replace rear suspension unit, see 64.25.01.
49 Check rear wheel camber, see 64.25.18.
50 **Bleed brakes**, see 70.25.02.
51 Check final drive oil level and top up as necessary.

FINAL DRIVE UNIT

Overhaul 51.25.19

Service tools: Puller SL.14, SL.14/1, SL.14/3, Gauge mount SL.3, Pinion oil seal replacer SL.4, Gauge block 4 HA, Press tool SL.550/4, Handle 550.

CAUTION: The following procedure covers 'Powr-Lok' and non 'Powr-Lok' differential units and care should be taken to ensure that relevant instructions are followed.

Dismantling

1 Support unit in vice.
2 Remove rear cover; discard gasket.
3 Remove locking wire and remove five bolts securing caliper mounting bracket.
4 Withdraw drive shaft, together with caliper mounting bracket shims, ball bearing and square section oil seal. Turn down tab washer, remove nut and withdraw ball bearing and caliper mounting bracket from drive shaft.
5 Carry out operations 3 and 4 on second drive shaft.
6 Remove two bolts holding each differential bearing cap.
7 Lift caps out of differential housing.
8 Using two levers, suitably padded to prevent damage to differential carrier, prise out differential unit, crownwheel and bearing assembly.

Items 9 and 10 refer to non 'Powr-Lok' differential units

9 Remove peening and drift pinion shaft lock pin out of carrier.
10 Withdraw gears, shaft and shims from carrier.
11 Remove drive pinion nut and washer.
12 Withdraw flange.
13 Using a suitable press, extract pinion from housing.
14 Remove oil seal, oil thrower and outer bearing cone.
15 Examine inner and outer bearing cups for wear. If replacement is required, extract cups using Tools No. SL.14 and SL.14/1.
NOTE: Extraction may be eased by **gently** heating final drive case in area of bearing cups.

Items 16 to 35 refer to 'Powr-Lok' differential units only

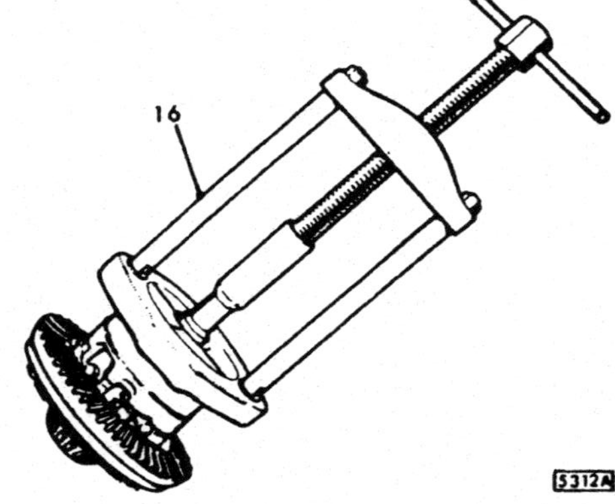

16 Remove differential side bearings using Tools No. SL.14 and SL.14/3.

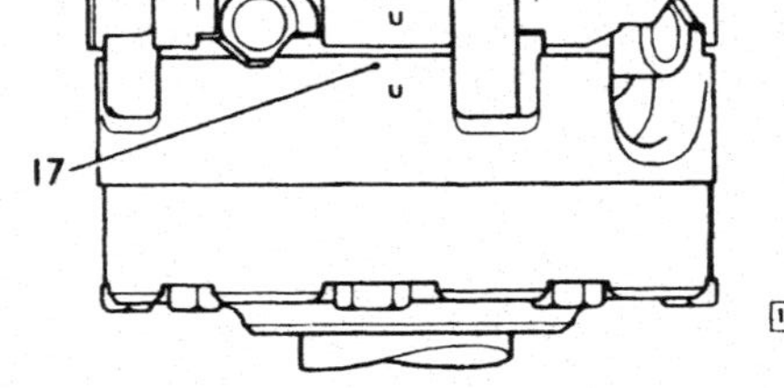

17 In the absence of any alignment marks, scribe a line across both halves of differential casing to facilitate reassembly.

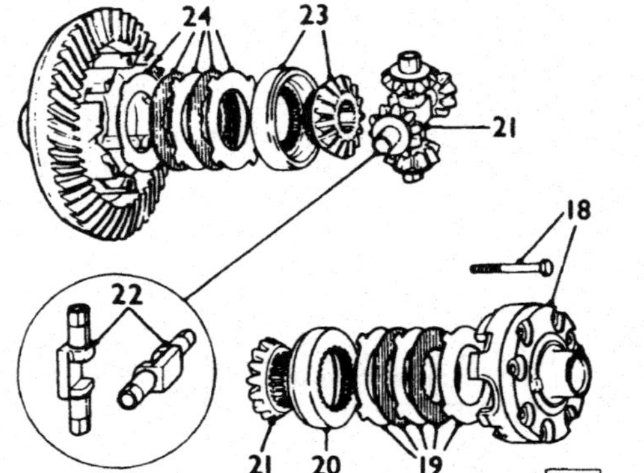

18 Remove eight bolts securing both halves of differential casing.
19 Split casing and remove clutch discs and plates from one side.
20 Remove differential side ring.
21 Remove pinion side gear and pinion cross shafts complete with gears.
22 Separate cross shafts.
23 Remove remaining side gear and ring.
24 Extract remaining clutch discs and plates.
NOTE: Only early cars have discs and plates arranged as shown here. On rebuild, all units should be reassembled as shown in illustration accompanying operations 25 to 33.

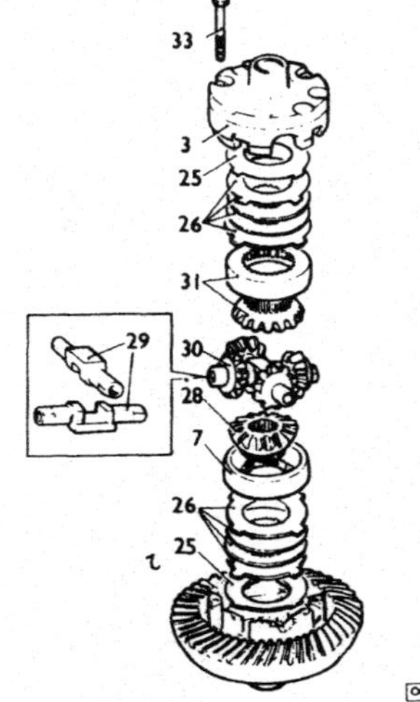

Reassembling

25 Refit two Belleville clutch plates so that convex sides are against differential casing.
26 Refit clutch plates and discs as shown into each half of the casing.
27 Fit side ring.
28 Position one side gear into ring recess.
29 Fit cross shafts.
30 Refit pinion mating cross shafts complete with pinion gears ensuring that ramps on the shafts coincide with the mating ramps in the differential case.
31 Assemble remaining side gear and ring.
32 Offer up R.H. half of differential case to flange half in accordance with identification marks and position clutch friction plate tongues so that they align with grooves in differential case.
33 Assemble R.H. half to flange half of differential case using eight bolts, but do not tighten at this stage.
34 Check alignment of splines by inserting two drive shafts.

continued

35 Tighten eight bolts to a torque of 35 to 46 lb.ft. (4,84 to 6,36 kg.m.) while drive shafts are in position. With one drive shaft locked, the other drive shaft must not turn radially more than .75 in. (19 mm.) measured on a 6 in. (152 mm.) radius.

Item 36 refers to non 'Powr-Lok' differential units only

36 Fit pinion shaft, shims and gears into differential carrier; secure lock pin by peening.

Thickness of shims required in the installation of the differential side bearings is determined as follows:

37 Fit differential side bearings, without shims, on the differential case, making sure that bearings and housing are perfectly clean.
38 Place the differential assembly, with the bearings in their housing, within the gear carrier, the pinion not being assembled.

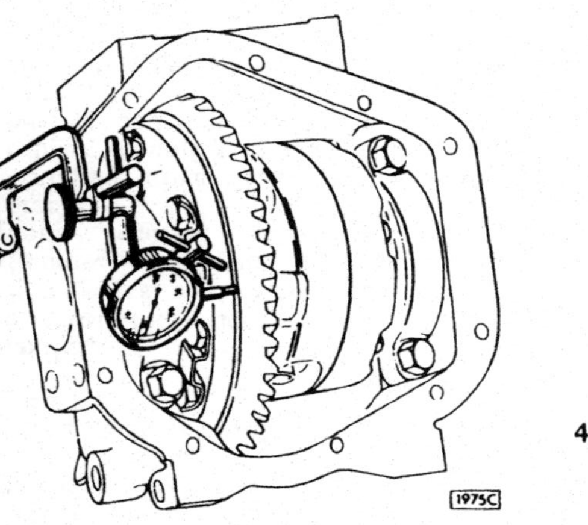

39 Install dial indicator gauge (tool No. SL.3), setting the button against back face of drive gear.
40 Inserting two levers between housing and the bearing cups, move the differential assembly to one side of the carrier.
41 Set the dial indicator to zero.
42 Move the assembly to the other side and record indicator reading, giving total clearance between bearings, as now assembled, and abutment faces of the gear carrier housing.
NOTE: Add .009 in. (,20 mm.) more to the clearance reading to give preload: This thickness of shims to be used in the installation of the differential bearings, the shims being divided to give the gear position with correct backlash.
43 Remove differential assembly from the gear carrier.

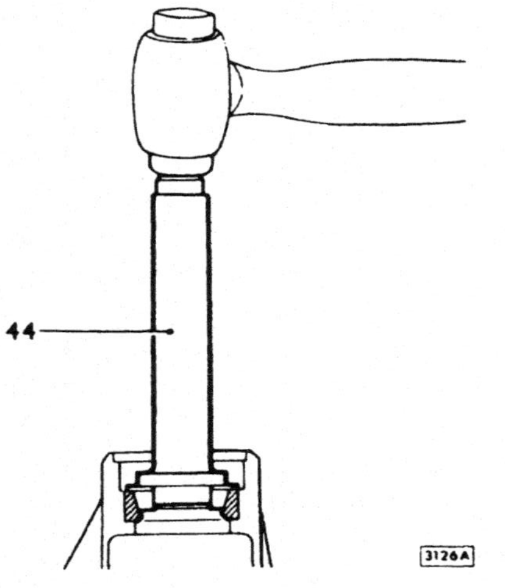

44 Re-install the pinion outer bearing cup using tool No. SL.550/4 with 550 Handle.
NOTE: Insertion may be eased by **gently** heating final drive case in area of bearing cups.
45 Fit inner bearing cup adjusting shims and install inner bearing cup.
46 Press inner bearing cone on to pinion using an arbor press and length of tube contacting the inner race only. Do not press on roller retainer.

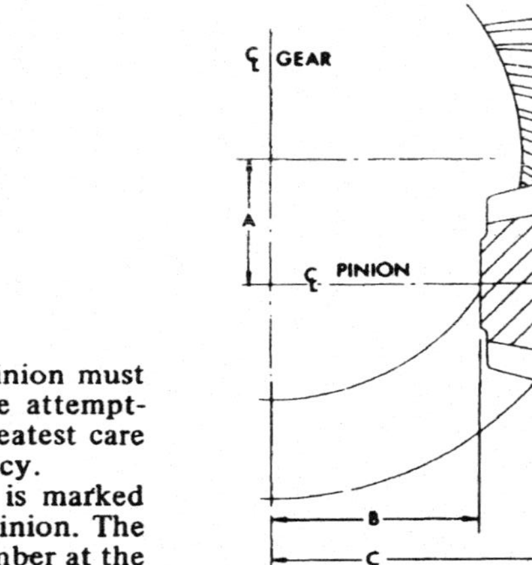

NOTE: The hypoid drive pinion must be correctly adjusted before attempting further assembly, the greatest care being taken to ensure accuracy.
The correct pinion setting is marked on the ground end of the pinion. The matched assembly serial number at the top is also marked on the drive gear, and care should be taken to keep similarly marked gears and pinions in their matched sets as each pair is lapped together before despatch from the factory. The letter on the left is a production code letter and has no significance relative to assembly or servicing of any axle. The letter and figure on the right refer to the tolerance on offset or pinion drop dimension, which is stamped on the cover facing of the gear carrier housing.
The number at the bottom gives the cone setting distance of the pinion and may be Zero (0), Plus (+) or Minus(–).
When correctly adjusted a pinion marked Zero will be at the zero cone setting distance dimension which is 2.625 in. (66,67 mm.) (i.e. from the centre line of the gear to the face on the small end of the pinion. A pinion marked Plus two (+2) should be adjusted to the nominal (or Zero) cone setting plus .002 in. (,0508 mm.) and a pinion marked Minus two (–2) to the cone setting distance minus .002 in. (,0508 mm.). Thus for a pinion marked Minus two (–2) the distance from the centre of the drive gear to the face of the pinion should be 2.623 in. i.e. 2.625–.002 (66,619 mm. i.e. 66,67–,0508 mm.) and for a pinion marked Plus three (+3) the cone setting distance should be 2.628 in. (66,746 mm.).

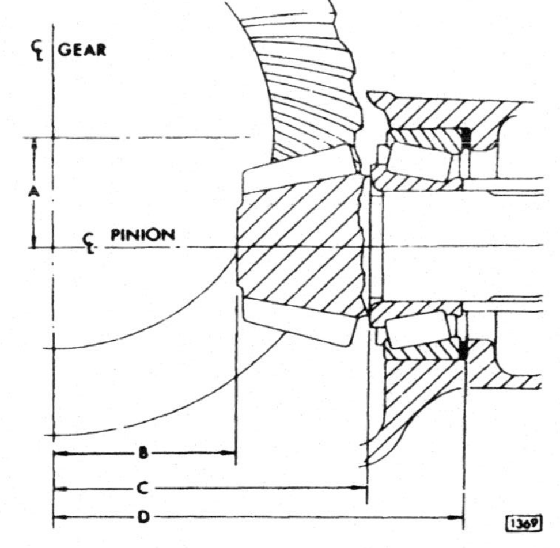

A Pinion drop 1.5 in. (38,1 mm.)
B Zero cone setting 2.625 in. (66,67 mm.)
C Mounting distance 4.312 in. (108,52 mm.)
D Centre line to bearing house 5.495 in. (139,57 mm.) to 5.505 in. (139,83 mm.)

47 Place pinion, together with inner bearing cone, into gear carrier.
48 Turn carrier over and support pinion with a suitable block of wood for convenience before attempting further assembly.
49 Fit pinion outer bearing cone, companion flange, washer and nut only, omitting the collapsible spacer, oil thrower and oil seal, and tighten nut.

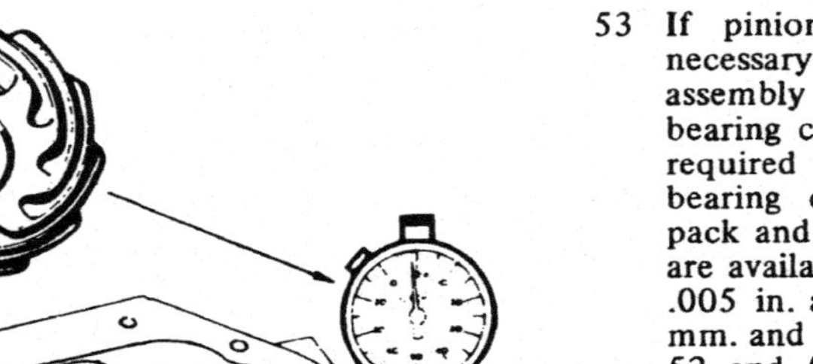

50 Check pinion setting distance by means of gauge, tool No. SL.3.

51 Adjust bracket carrying dial indicator using 4 H.A. setting block and set dial face to zero.

52 Check pinion setting by taking a dial indicator reading on the differential bearing bore with the assembly firmly seated on the ground face of the pinion. The correct reading will be the minimum obtained; that is, when the indicator spindle is at the bottom of the bore. Slight movement of the assembly will enable the correct reading to be easily ascertained. The dial indicator shows the deviation of the pinion setting from the zero cone setting and it is important to note the direction of any such deviation as well as the magnitude.

53 If pinion setting is incorrect it is necessary to dismantle the pinion assembly and remove pinion inner bearing cup. Add or remove shims as required from the pack locating the bearing cup and re-install the shim pack and bearing cup. Adjusting shims are available in thicknesses of .003 in., .005 in. and .010 in. (,076 mm., ,127 mm. and ,254 mm.). Repeat operations 52 and 53 until satisfactory result is obtained.

54 Extract pinion shaft from gear carrier sufficiently far to enable the outer bearing cone to be removed from the pinion.

55 Fit the collapsible spacer to the pinion ensuring that it seats firmly on the machined shoulder on the pinion shaft.

56 Insert pinion into gear carrier.

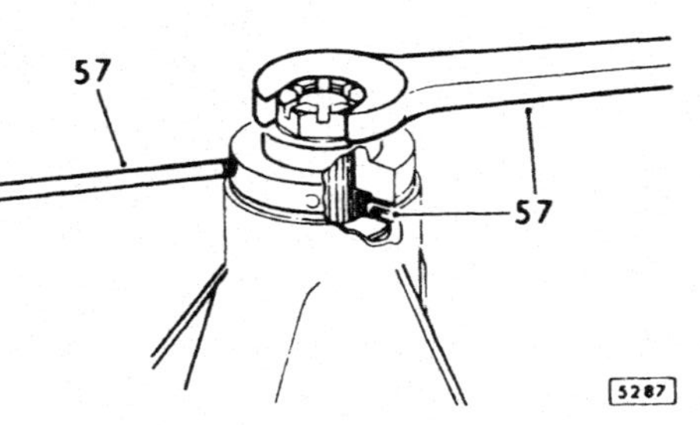

57 Refit outer-bearing cone, oil thrower and oil seal.

58 Lightly grease splines of pinion shaft and fit flange.

59 Fit new washer, convex side facing towards the end of the shaft.

60 Fit the nut but DO NOT tighten at this stage.

61 Place differential assembly complete with side bearings but less shims, in the housing. Ensure that bearings and housing are perfectly clean.

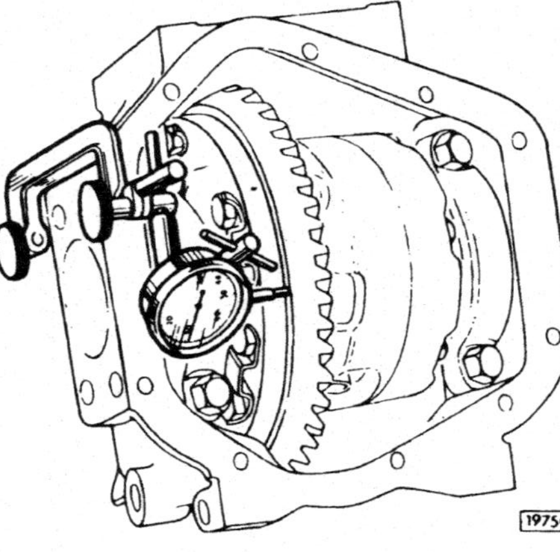
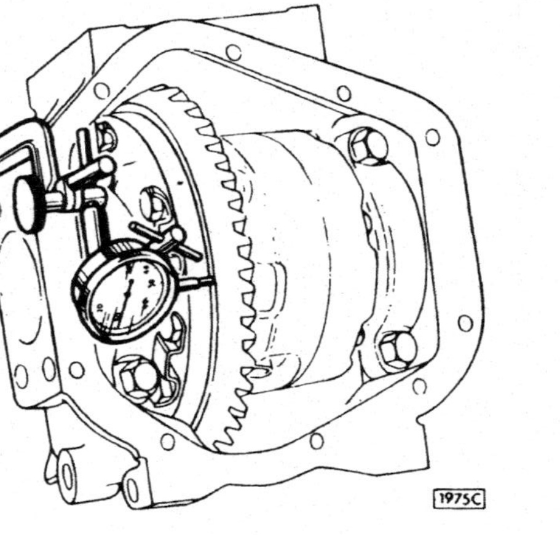

62 Install a dial indicator on the housing with button on back face of drive gear.

63 Insert two small levers between housing and side bearing. Move differential case and drive gear assembly away from pinion until opposite side bearing is seated against housing.

64 Set dial indicator to zero, then move differential assembly towards pinion until drive gear is in metal to metal contact, and deeply in mesh with pinion.
NOTE: The indicator reading now obtained (i.e. clearance between drive gear and pinion) minus the backlash allowance etched on the drive gear (e.g. **B/L** .007) denotes the thickness of shims (in inches) to be placed between the differential case and the side bearing on the drive gear side of the differential.

65 Install thickness of shims determined in operation 64, on drive gear side of differential, taking shims from pack determined previously in operation 42.

66 Install balance of total shims required on opposite side of differential case.
NOTE: As an example of differential and drive gear adjustment, assume that the total indicator reading obtained in operation 42 is .080 in. (2,030 mm.). This figure plus .009 in. (0,23 mm.) for the recommended preload, equals .089 in. (2,26 mm.) which denotes the total thickness of shims to be used. Also assuming the clearance between drive gear and pinion to be .042 in. (1,067 mm.) determined as in operations 61 to 64, subtract the backlash as etched on the gear, say .007 in. (,178 mm.) from the .042 in. (1,067 mm.) clearance. The .035 in. (,889 mm.) difference denotes the thickness of shims to be placed between the differential case and side bearing on the drive gear side of the differential. Then subtract the thickness of shims .035 in. (,889 mm.) inserted on the drive gear side of the differential case from 0.089 in. (2,26 mm.) and the 0.054 in. (1,37 mm.) difference denotes the thickness of shims to be installed on the opposite side of the case.

67 Lower differential assembly into position lightly tapping the bearings home with a hide hammer.
NOTE: Ensure that gear teeth are led into mesh with those of the pinion. Careless handling at this stage may result in bruising the gear teeth. Removal of the consequent damage can only be partially successful and will result in inferior performance.

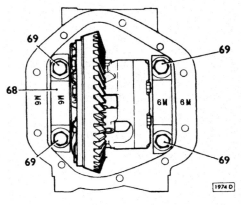

68 When refitting side bearing caps, ensure that position of the numerals marked on gear carrier housing face and side bearing cap coincide.

69 Tighten caps to a torque of 60 to 65 lb.ft. (8,3 to 9,0 kg.m.).

continued

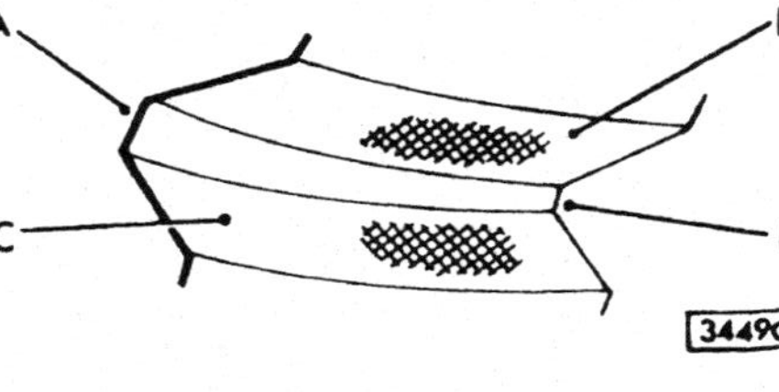

1975C

70 Mount a dial indicator on gear carrier housing with the button against back face of gear as for operation 62.

71 Turn pinion by hand and check run out on back face of gear. Run out should not exceed .005 in. (,13 mm.). If run out excessive, strip the assembly and rectify by cleaning the surfaces locating the drive gear Any burrs on these surfaces must be removed.

72 Remount dial indicator on gear carrier housing with button tangentially against one of drive gear teeth.

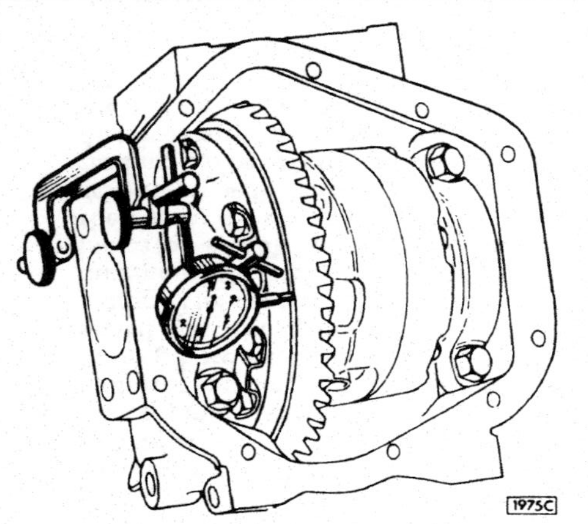

1973C

73 Move drive gear by hand to check backlash which should be as etched on the gear. If backlash is not to specification, transfer the necessary shims from one side of the differential case to the other to obtain the desired setting.
NOTE: To increase backlash remove shims from the drive gear side of the differential and install on the opposite side. To decrease backlash transfer shims to the drive gear side from the opposite side of the differential case.

74 After setting backlash to required figure use a small brush to sparingly paint eight or ten of the drive gear teeth with a stiff mixture of marking raddle or with engineers blue. Move painted gear teeth in mesh with pinion until a good impression of the total contact is obtained. The result should conform with ideal impression given. Correction procedure of poor meshing is also given.

75 The ideal tooth bearing impression on the drive and coast sides of the gear teeth is evenly distributed over the working depth of the tooth profile and is located nearer to the toe (small end) than the heel (large end). This type of contact permits the tooth bearing to spread towards the heel under operating conditions when allowance must be made for deflection.
NOTE: If 'ideal' impression obtained, proceed with operation 80, otherwise continue with operation 76, 77, 78 or 79 as applicable.
Nomenclature referring to gear teeth is as follows:

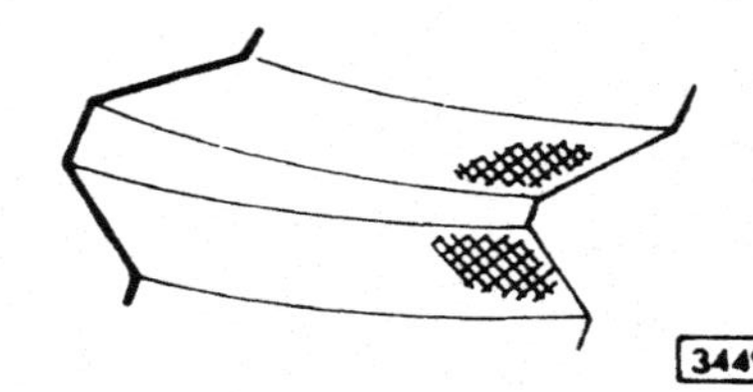

3449a

The HEEL is the large or outer end of the tooth (see 'A').
The TOE is the small or inner end of the tooth (see 'B').
The DRIVE side of the drive gear tooth is CONVEX (see 'C').
The COAST side of the drive gear tooth is CONCAVE (see 'D').

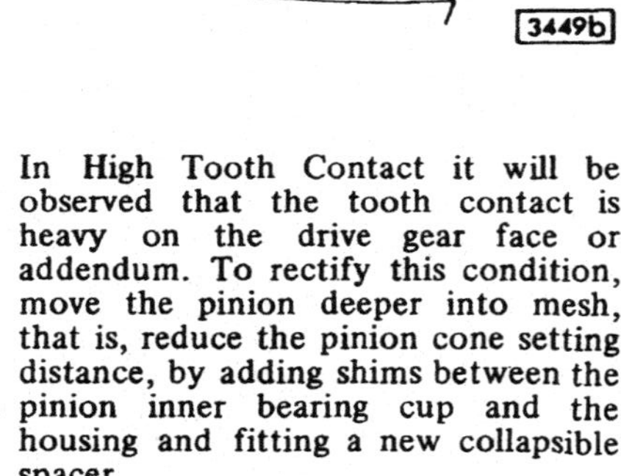

3449b

76 In High Tooth Contact it will be observed that the tooth contact is heavy on the drive gear face or addendum. To rectify this condition, move the pinion deeper into mesh, that is, reduce the pinion cone setting distance, by adding shims between the pinion inner bearing cup and the housing and fitting a new collapsible spacer.
This correction has a tendency to move the tooth bearing towards the toe on drive and heel on coast, and it may therefore be necessary after making this change to adjust the drive gear as described in operations 78 and 79.

3449c

77 In Low Tooth Contact it will be observed that the tooth contact is heavy on the drive gear flank or dedendum. This is the opposite condition from that shown in 76 and is therefore corrected by moving the pinion out of mesh, that is, increase the pinion cone setting distance by removing shims from between the pinion inner bearing cup and housing and fitting a new collapsible spacer.
This correction has a tendency to move the tooth bearing towards the heel on drive and toe on coast, and it may therefore be necessary after making this change to adjust the drive gear as described in operations 78 and 79.

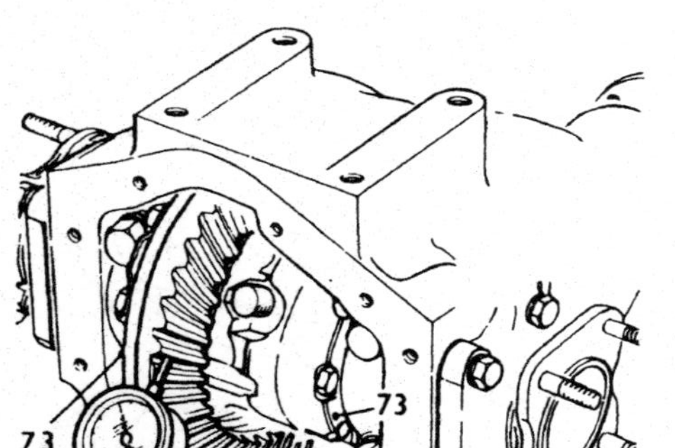

3449d

78 Toe Contact occurs when the bearing is concentrated at the small end of the tooth. To rectify this condition, move the drive gear out of mesh, that is, increase backlash, by transferring shims from the drive gear side of the differential to the opposite side.

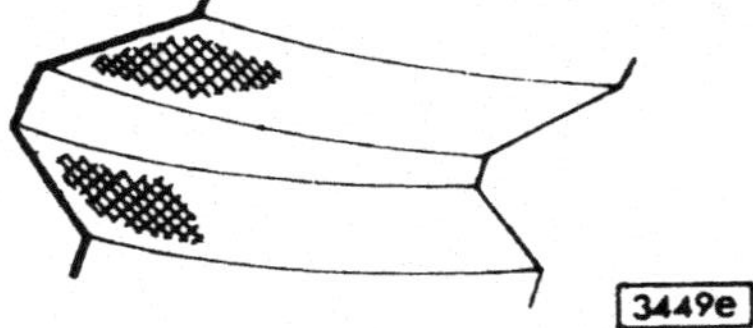
3449e

79 Heel Contact is indicated by the concentration of the bearing at the large end of the tooth. To rectify this condition move the drive gear closer into mesh, that is, reduce backlash, by adding shims to the drive gear side of the differential and removing an equal thickness of shims from the opposite side.
NOTE: It is important to remember when making this adjustment to correct a heel contact that sufficient backlash for satisfactory operation must be maintained. If there is insufficient backlash the gears will at least be noisy and have a greatly reduced life, whilst scoring of the tooth profile and breakage may result. Therefore, always maintain a minimum backlash requirement of .004 in. (,10 mm.).

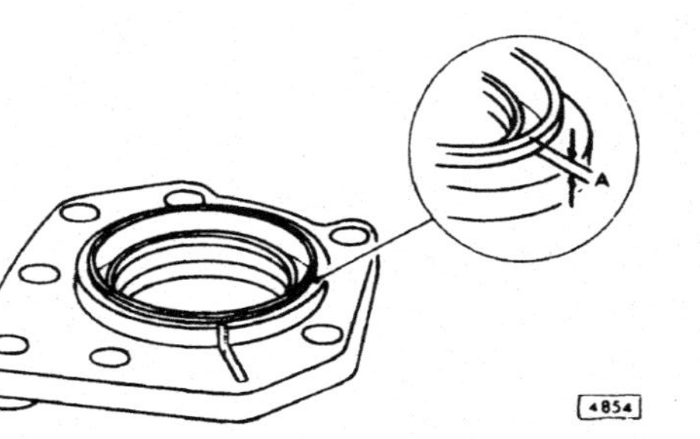

4854

80 Lightly oil new square section seal, position carefully, and press squarely to fully seat in final drive case groove.
CAUTION: **Under no circumstance must the protruding portion of oil seal, A, be removed. This induces a metal to metal contact between mounting bracket and bearing, and completely destroys the seal properties.**

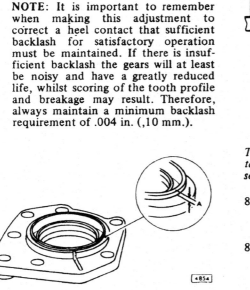

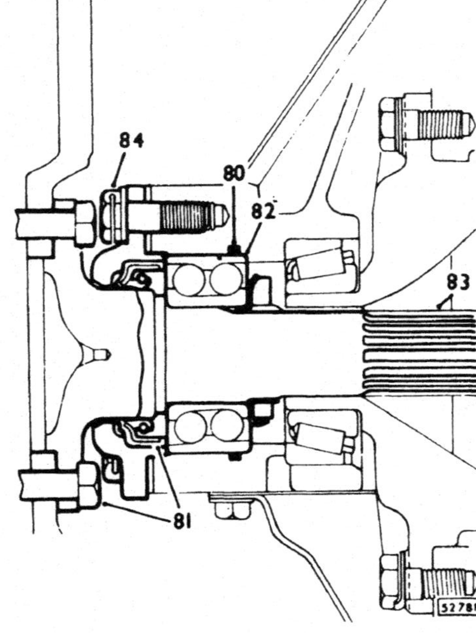

5278F

This does not apply to later units, in which taper roller bearings replace the ball races, see 51.10.20, operations 4 to 7.

81 Coat oil seal with hypoid gear oil, fit four special flange bolts and position caliper mounting bracket and oil seal assembly over drive shaft.
82 Slide a ball bearing on to drive shaft followed by new tab washer and nut. Ensure bearing seats square to drive shaft shoulder. Tighten nut to 90 to 110 lb.ft. (12,44 to 14,2 kg.m.) and turn up tab washer.
83 Lightly oil drive shaft splines and fit shaft into differential casing.
84 Fit five bolts and spring washers to retain mounting bracket. Screw up until finger tight.
NOTE: Allowance has been made when calculating shimming required for .003 in. (,076 mm.) squash of the oil seal when fully tightened.

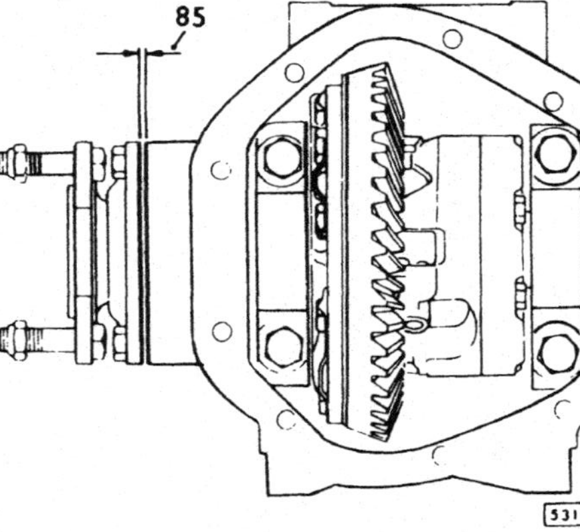

5311

85 Using feeler gauges, measure dimension between inside face of caliper mounting bracket and differential housing. The measurement obtained determines shimming required to give correct degree of nip on outer ball bearing race and oil seal flange.
Shims are available in the following thicknesses: .003 in., .005 in., .010 in. and .030 in. (,076 mm., ,127 mm., ,254 mm. and ,762 mm.).
86 Remove drive shaft, select shims of required thickness. Thinly coat mating faces and shims with Hylomar (NOT grease). Fit four special flange bolts and refit drive shaft. Tighten bolts to 49 to 55 lb.ft. (6,8 to 7,6 kg.m.) by diagonal selection.
87 Wire lock five securing bolts to tension in clockwise direction.
CAUTION: Exercise the greatest care when torqueing companion flange nut as overtightening will necessitate almost complete dismantling of final drive unit to replace collapsible spacer.
88 Tighten companion flange securing nut to 120 to 140 lb.ft. (16,6 to 19,355 kg.m.). During tightening operation, the companion flange should be rotated periodically to ensure correct seating of the taper roller bearings.
Should the nut be inadvertently overtightened, a new collapsible spacer must be fitted. On no account must the nut be slackened off and retorqued, as this will result in incorrect preloading of drive pinion bearings.

89 Using new gasket coated with Hylomar fit rear cover. Fit axle ratio tab beneath securing bolts.
90 Refit final drive unit to rear suspension unit.

Notes

SYMPTOM AND DIAGNOSIS CHART

SYMPTOM	CAUSE	CURE
External oil leaks from steering rack unit.	Damaged or worn seals Loose unions. Damaged union sealing washers.	Replace seals. Tighten unions. Replace sealing washers.
Oil leak at pump shaft.	Damaged shaft seal.	Replace shaft seal.
Oil leak at high pressure outlet union.	Loose or damaged union. Damaged pipe end.	Tighten union. Replace pipe.
Oil leak at low pressure inlet connection.	Loose or damaged hose connection.	Remove and refit or renew hose and clip.
Oil overflowing reservoir cap.	Reservoir overfull. Sticking flow control valve (closed).	Reduce level in reservoir. Remove valve, renew and refit.
Oil leak at reservoir edge.	Damaged 'O' ring.	Replace 'O' ring.
Noise from hydraulic system.	Air in system.	Bleed system, 57.15.02.
Noise from pump.	Slack drive belt (squealing). Internal wear and damage.	Adjust drive belt tension, 57.20.01. Overhaul pump, 57.20.20.
Noise from rack (rattling).	Worn rack and pinion gears. Worn inner ball joints. Universal joint loose.	Adjust rack damper, 57.10.13. Replace inner ball joints, 57.55.03. Tighten clamping bolts.
Steering veering to left or right.	Unbalanced tyre pressures. Incorrect tyres fitted. Incorrect geometry. Steering unit out of trim.	Inflate to correct pressure. Fit tyres of correct specification. Reset geometry to correct specification. Replace valve and pinion assembly, 57.10.19.
Heavy steering when driving.	Low tyre pressures. Tightness in steering column. Tightness in steering joints.	Inflate to correct specification. Grease or replace. Grease or renew joints.
Heavy steering when parking.	Low tyre pressures. Tightness in steering column. Tightness in steering joints. Slack drive belt (squealing). Restricted hose. Sticking flow control valve. (open). Internal leaks in steering unit.	Inflate to correct specification. Grease or replace. Grease or renew joints. Adjust drive belt tension, 57.20.01. Replace hose. Remove and renew valve. Replace seals.
Steering effort too light.	Valve torsion bar dowel pins worn. Valve torsion bar broken.	Replace valve assembly. Replace valve assembly.

WARNING: IT IS ABSOLUTELY ESSENTIAL THAT THE HIGHEST STANDARDS OF CLEANLINESS ARE MAINTAINED IN ANY OPERATIONS INVOLVING ACCESS TO COMPONENTS IN CONTACT WITH FLUID, SINCE STEERING ASSISTANCE CAN BE SERIOUSLY AFFECTED BY THE PRESENCE OF DIRT IN THE SYSTEM.

POWER ASSISTED STEERING (P.A.S.) UNIT

Remove and refit **57.10.01**

Service tools: Ball joint separator JD.24. Steering rack checking fixture JD.36. Rack centralising tool Jaguar Part No. 12297.

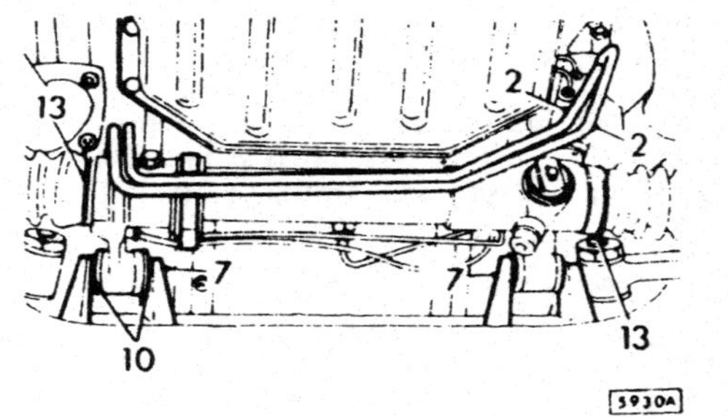

Removing

1 Place car on ramp or over pit.
2 Disconnect both unions from pinion housing; collect escaping oil in a suitable container.
3 Blank off ports and pipes to prevent entry of dirt.
4 Remove nuts and washers from ball pins in hub steering arms.
5 Extract ball pins, using Service tool JD.24.
6 Remove pinch bolt, nut and washer clamping lower universal joint to pinion shaft.
7 Remove three self locking nuts and washers and withdraw three mounting bolts.
8 Withdraw rack assembly downwards collecting steel/rubber bonded washers from two lugs, stiffener from lugs at pinion housing and shim washers from single lug.

continued

Refitting

9 Offer up rack to mounting brackets and pinion shaft to universal joint.

10 Select shim washers to centralise single lug between crossbeam brackets. The assistance of a second operator is desirable for this item.

11 Fit selected shim washers between metal faces of thrust washers and crossbeam brackets; and check that a gap of 0.10 to 0.12 in. (2,54 to 3,05 mm.) exists between rubber faces of thrust washers and single lug.

12 Insert pinch bolt in universal joint and mounting bolts in lugs; do not fully tighten self locking nuts.

13 Remove inner locking wires securing gaiters to rack housing and withdraw both gaiters from rack.

14 Locate two attachment brackets of Service tool JD.36 on two large hexagon heads of lower wishbone fulcrum shafts.

15 Release looking screw on forward arm of tool, and move slide until its slot engages with front weld flange of crossbeam. Tighten locking screw.

16 Lift two coupled checking levers until one or both levers touch rack shaft. Adjust position of rack, if necessary, to bring both levers into contact. Tighten nuts of three mounting bolts to secure rack in this position.

17 Remove checking tool.

18 Replace gaiters and renew locking wire.

19 Reverse items 1 to 6.

20 Refill system with recommended fluid and bleed - 57.15.02.

21 Check wheel alignment – 57.65.01.
NOTE: (a) It is important that distance between rubber faces of thrust washers and adjacent rack lug should in no case be less than 0.1 in. (2,5 mm.) to allow adequate "rack compliance" in either direction. (b) If a replacement rack unit is to be fitted it may be necessary to detach lower column from upper column at universal joint to obtain correct centralisation.
Refer to 57.40.25.

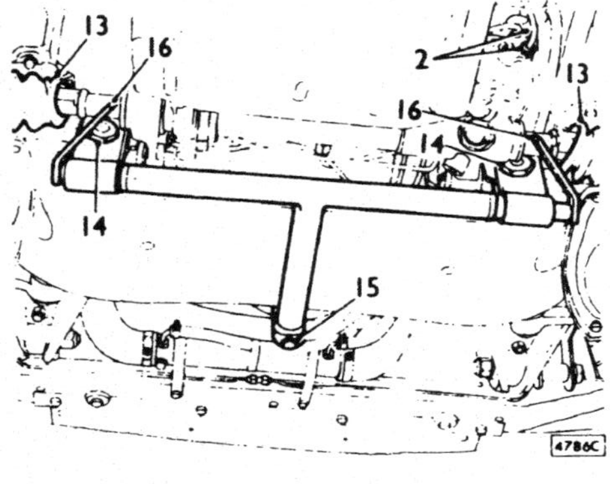

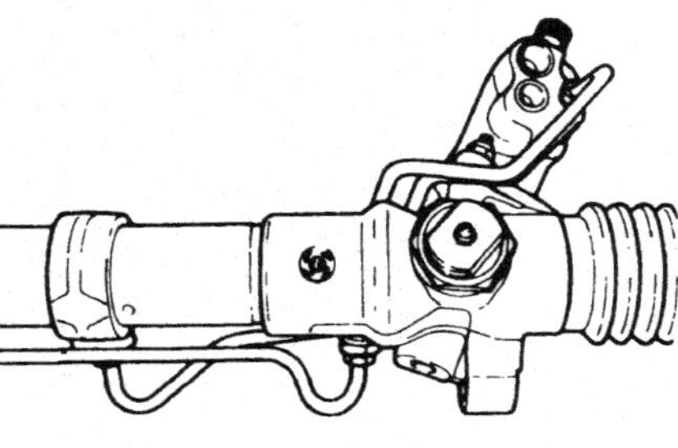

A

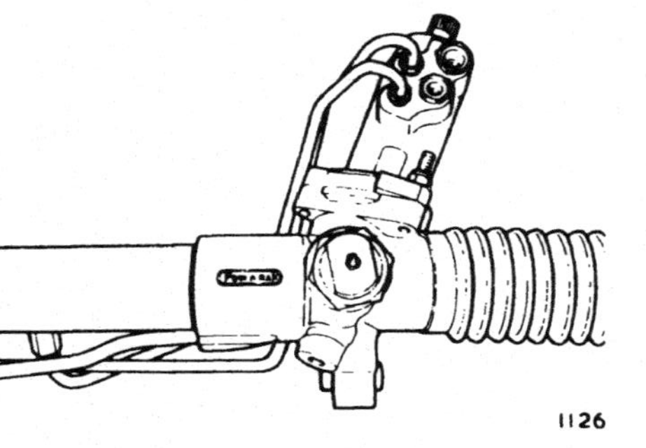

B

1126

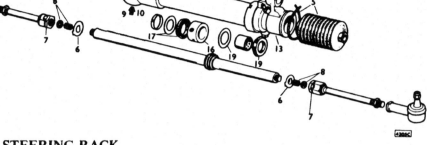

A Alford and Alder rack
B Adwest rack

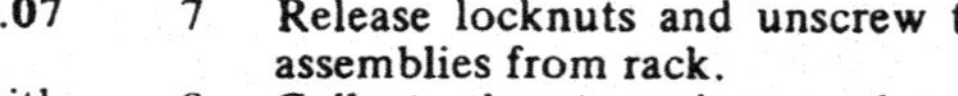

POWER STEERING RACK

Overhaul (Adwest rack) 57.10.07

NOTE: Early cars are all fitted with Adwest racks, but from 1974 a similar Alford and Alder rack became alternative equipment on R.H.D. cars. Instructions below apply to Adwest racks, those for Alford and Alder racks following them.

Dismantling

1 Remove rack assembly – 57.10.01.

2 Clean exterior of rack and pinion housings.

3 Remove external pipes.

4 Remove valve and pinion assembly – 57.10.19.

5 Remove wire retaining clips and fold back gaiters to expose inner ball joints.
NOTE: Do not disturb outer ball joints unless replacement is necessary. If joints are to be renewed, measure accurately, and record total length of both tie-rods, before releasing locknuts.

6 Knock back tabwashers situated inboard of locknuts.
CAUTION: **Do not disturb lock-washers between locknuts and ball pin housing.**

7 Release locknuts and unscrew tie rod assemblies from rack.

8 Collect thrust springs and packing washers.

9 Remove locknut securing rack damper.

10 Remove nut, screwed plug, spring and rack damper pad.

11 Remove air transfer pipe from both end caps.

12 Unscrew ring nut from end cap.

13 Remove end cap with bush, seal, retaining washer and 'O' ring.

14 Withdraw rack and piston.

15 Remove union adaptor and bonded seal washer from centre of housing.

16 Extract centre pipe fitting from bore of rack housing.

17 Withdraw seal and retaining washer located behind centre fitting. Discard seal.

18 Renew cracked or damaged pipe union seals – 57.10.24.

19 Remove retaining washer and seal from end cap. Discard seal.

Reassembling

20 Protect seal from damage by sharp corners of rack teeth, by covering teeth with a thin walled plastic tube, or with thin plastic adhesive tape.

21 Slide centre pipe fitting 'D', new seal 'C' from seal kit, and retaining washer 'B' over protected teeth on to plain portion of rack bar.
NOTE: 'Open' side of seal must face towards centre pipe fitting.

22 Remove protective covering from rack teeth.

23 Inspect piston ring and replace if scored or damaged.

24 Inspect housing bore and replace housing if bore is deeply scored or damaged. Light axial score marks can be permitted.

25 Enter rack bar into housing, rack end first; check that threaded hole in centre pipe fitting registers with hole in housing.

26 Secure centre pipe fitting with centre pipe adaptor fitted with bonded seal washer; tighten fully.

27 Place end seal cap retaining washer 'E' over plain end of rack.

28 Fit seal 'F' over plain end of rack, with its 'Open' side towards washer 'E'.

29 Slide housing 'G' on to rack, pushing seal back into position, and secure with ring nut.

30 Refit air transfer pipe.

31 Refit damper pad assembly by reversing item 10. Do not adjust at this stage.

32 Refit valve and pinion assembly – 57.10.19.

33 Reverse operations 5 to 8. Tighten locknuts fully and secure with tab washers. Renew gaiters if damaged – 57.10.27. Coat both rack ball housings with 1½ to 2 oz. (45 to 55 g.) of a recommended grade of grease before refitting gaiters.

34 Adjust rack damper – 57.10.13.

35 Apply grease gun to nipple in damper screwed plug and inject 1 oz. (28 g.) of a recommended grade of grease. Do not over-lubricate to extent where gaiters become distended.

36 Refit external pipes.

37 Refit rack assembly.

38 Refill with a recommended fluid and bleed system – 57.15.02.

39 Check wheel alignment – 57.65.01.

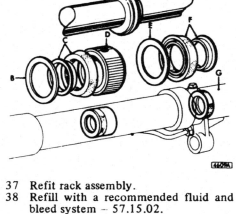

POWER STEERING RACK

Overhaul (Alford and Alder rack) **57.10.07**

Service tools: 18G 1321, 18G 1322, 18G 1323, 18G 1327

Dismantling

1 Remove the power steering rack – 57.10.01.

2 Thoroughly clean the outside of the unit.

3 Eject the oil from the unit by moving the rack through its full stroke in each direction.

4 Note the position of the valve housing porting face relative to the pinion housing, also the position of the two valve to cylinder pipes.

5 Hold the unit at the pinion end of the cylinder in a soft-jawed vice.

6 Break the wire ties and slide the gaiters along the tie-rods to expose the inner ball joints.

7 Extend the rack and hold the unit across the rack teeth in a soft-jawed vice.

8 Remove the tie-rod assemblies by unscrewing the inner ball joints and shearing the lock washer tabs.

9 Hold the unit at the pinion end of the cylinder in a soft-jawed vice.

10 Remove the air transfer pipe.

11 Remove the valve to cylinder pipes.

12 Hold the end housing in a soft-jawed vice and slacken the retaining nut using service tool 18G 1327.

13 Hold the unit at the pinion end of the cylinder in a soft-jawed vice.

14 Slacken the locknut and unscrew the threaded plug to release the plunger spring load.

15 Remove the three locknuts and withdraw the valve assembly, gently tapping the housing if necessary. Do not separate the pinion from the valve housing.

16 Unscrew the retaining nut and remove the end housing.

17 Withdraw the rack and pinion assembly.

18 Remove the porting adaptor and slide the porting ring along the cylinder to expose the feed hole.

19 Using a scriber or similar pointed tool press the point into the seal expander ring (visible through the feed hole) and lever the seal towards the open end of the cylinder until it is turned sideways across the cylinder bore taking care to avoid damaging the feed hole seating. Withdraw the seal from the cylinder using a length of wire with one end turned to form a hook.

20 Remove the locknut, threaded plug, spring and plunger from the pinion housing.

21 Thoroughly wash and dry the cylinder assembly and rack assembly. Do not remove the piston ring.

22 Remove the 'O' ring and abutment washer from the end housing.

23 Remove the seal from the end housing by gripping the seal expander ring with thin-nosed pliers.

24 Wash and dry the end housing.
NOTE: Do not allow the housing to soak in a degreasing agent as this may wash out the lubricant from the sintered iron rack bush.

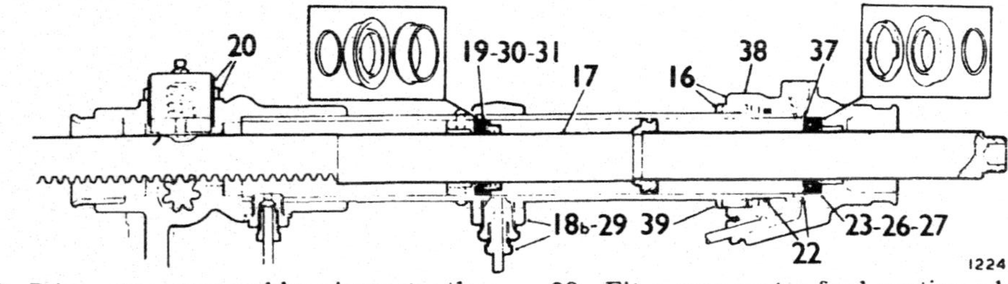

25 Prior to reassembly inspect the undermentioned components as follows:

a Pipes – Renew if pipe or end fittings are damaged. Nuts with cracked or heavily flared seatings can cause damage on assembly.

b Rack – Check ground surfaces for longitudinal scratch lines. Scratches that can be felt by a 'fingernail test' should be removed with super fine emery cloth used across the scratch lines. Wash the rack thoroughly after such work.

c Rack and cylinder ends – Check for burrs or sharp edges and remove with an oil stone.

d Rack teeth – Check for damage and excessive wear.

e Ball joints (inner and outer) – Check for free play.

f Gaiters – Remove all grease and oil and renew if damaged.

g Control valve – Renew seal and gasket if oil leakage from the control valve is apparent. See operation 57.10.23.

Reassembling

26 Lightly oil the rubber part of the end housing rack seal. Select the narrower expander ring from the kit and fit it into the seal body.

27 Position the anti-extrusion ring in the end housing and fit the seal ensuring that it is pressed fully against the abutment face (load applied to the expander ring). Ensure that the anti-extrusion ring engages correctly with the seal body.

28 Lubricate the 'O' ring and fit it into the housing groove.

29 Fit a new centre feed porting adaptor into the porting ring. Position the ring to allow the conical seating on the adaptor to engage with the seating on the cylinder. Tighten to 22 to 25 lbf ft (3,05 to 3,46 kgf m).

30 Lightly oil the rubber part of the rack seal. Select the wider expander ring from the kit and fit it into the seal body.

31 Assemble the rack seal on service tool 18G 1323 and pass the tool over the toothed section of the rack to bring the seal up to the piston. Lightly oil the anti-extrusion ring and engage it with the recess in the back of the seal.

32 Hold the pinion end of the cylinder in a soft-jawed vice.

33 Oil the bore of the cylinder at the open end and grease the rack directly behind the teeth (plunger contact area). Fit service tool 18G 1322 onto the cylinder and carefully enter the rack and piston assembly into the cylinder, using a firm, steady pressure to push the seal down the cylinder until it contacts the abutment face. As the piston ring enters the bore, ensure that the ring collapses and is carefully guided into the cylinder.

34 Fit a new gasket to the valve mounting face of the pinion housing.

35 Liberally grease the pinion small journal, pinion teeth and ball race and fit the control valve on the pinion housing ensuring correct valve port positioning. Fit the three locknuts and tighten progressively to 10 to 14 lbf ft (1,40 to 1,94 kgf m).

36 Smear the end housing, bush and seal bores with grease.

37 Smear the inner face of the abutment washer with grease and locate it in the housing.

50 44 43 50 35

1223

38 Fit service tool 18G 1321 onto the end of the rack and carefully align and fit the end housing.

39 Screw the locking ring into the end housing sufficiently to hold the mounting feet in parallel alignment.

40 Hold the end housing in a soft-jawed vice with the cylinder vertical.

41 Using service tool 18G 1327 tighten the locking ring to 80 to 90 lbf ft (11,1 to 12,4 kgf m).
Re-check alignment of the mounting feet and reset if necessary.

42 Hold the unit in a soft-jawed vice at the pinion end of the cylinder so as not to obstruct pipe runs.

43 Fit the plunger spring, threaded plug and locknut. Tighten the threaded plug whilst moving the rack through its full stroke in each direction until hard mesh is achieved, then back off the threaded plug just sufficiently to achieve a smooth traverse (normally one-eighth of a turn). Tighten the locknut without allowing the adjusting screw to move. Re-check action of the unit.
NOTE: Excessive plunger lift resulting in the unit 'knocking' in service will occur if the threaded plug is backed off excessively.

44 Fit the air transfer pipe (housing end first).

45 Fit the valve to cylinder pipes and tighten to 10 to 14 lbf ft (1,40 to 1,94 kgf m).

46 Fit a lock washer over the inner ball joints and run up the ball joints onto the rack ends ensuring correct engagement of the lock washer tabs in the slots across the rack ends.

47 Extend the rack at the toothed end sufficiently to grip the rack teeth in a soft-jawed vice. Tighten the inner ball joints to 66 to 81 lbf ft (9,13 to 11,20 kgf m).
NOTE: Do not tighten the ball joints using the pinion to prevent rotation.

48 Remove the unit from the vice and support the inner ball joint housing on a firm base. Using a drift, tap over the lock washer skirt onto each of the six flats on the ball housing. Repeat for the other inner ball joint. Move the rack through its full stroke in each direction to ensure that the crimped lock washer clears the recess in each housing.

49 Hold the unit at the pinion end of the cylinder in a soft-jawed vice and extend the rack at the end housing end. Smear this section of the rack with grease.

50 Place approximately 1 to 2 oz (28 to 56 grammes) of grease in each gaiter and secure the gaiters with a wire tie to each housing.

51 Remove the plug and fit a grease nipple to the tapped hole in the threaded plug. Charge the unit with approximately five strokes of a hand grease gun. Do not overgrease.

52 Remove the grease nipple and replace the plug.

NOTE: To facilitate front wheel alignment it is advisable to slacken the locknuts on the tie-rod outer ball joints and the clips on the bellows prior to refitting the power steering rack.

53 Refit the power steering rack 57.10.01.

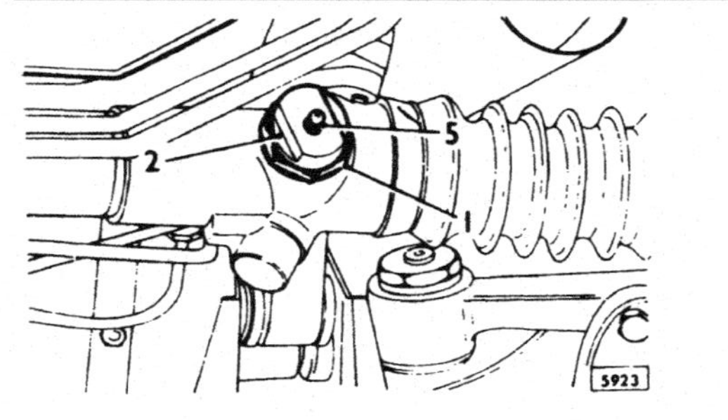

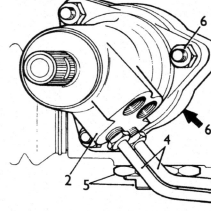

POWER STEERING RACK

Adjust (both racks) **57.10.13**

Service tool: Ball joint separator JD.24.

NOTE: The following adjustment for rack rattle, usually apparent when travelling on rough surfaces, can be carried out from underneath the car.

1 Release locknut securing screwed rack damper plug.
2 Screw in plug until a firm resistance is felt, and back off 60° (1/6 of a turn).
3 Remove nut and washer from ball pin in hub steering arm nearest to rack damper.
4 Using tool JD.24, remove ball pin from steering arm.
5 Remove grease nipple from screwed plug and insert a dial gauge, ensuring that its stem passes through spring and plunger to contact back of rack.
6 Grip tie-rod firmly and pull towards screwed plug until adjuster spring resistance is felt. By pulling rack against spring, total play at the rack can be measured. This should not exceed .01 in. (,25 mm.).
Correct minimum clearance should allow smooth operation of unit without binding at any point throughout full travel.
7 Complete adjustment by securing locknut and reversing items 3 to 5.
8 Check wheel alignment – 57.65.01.

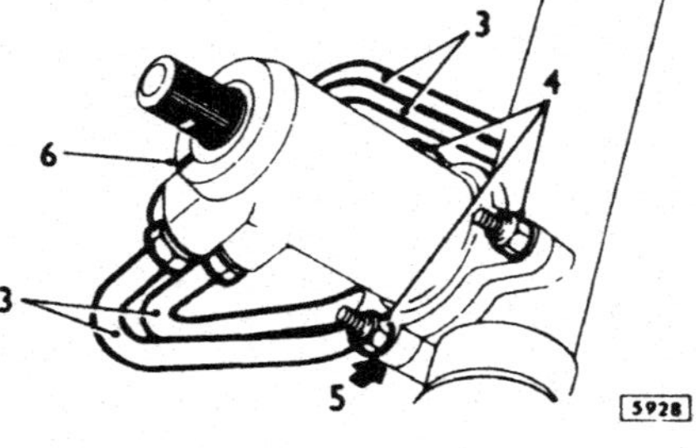

CONTROL VALVE AND PINION

Remove and refit (Adwest) **57.10.19**

Removing
1 Remove lower steering column – 57.40.05.
2 Clean pinion housing and adjacent rack housing. Prise off heatshield, if fitted to pinion shaft.
3 Detach all pipes from valve housing. Collect and dispose of spilled fluid.
4 Remove three self locking nuts from studs securing pinion and valve housing to rack unit.
5 Release rack adjuster locknut and back off adjuster screwed plug.
6 Mark location of pinch bolt recess in pinion shaft in relation to housing (for reference in refitting).
7 Withdraw valve and pinion housing. Discard joint gasket.
CAUTION: Do not move road wheels or turn steering column after pinion has been withdrawn.

Refitting
8 Reverse operations 3 to 7 using new joint gasket; ensure that pinch bolt recess is correctly placed relative to housing before connecting universal joint.
9 Adjust rack adaptor screwed plug – 57.10.13.
10 Remove car from ramp or pit.
11 Bleed system – 57.15.02.

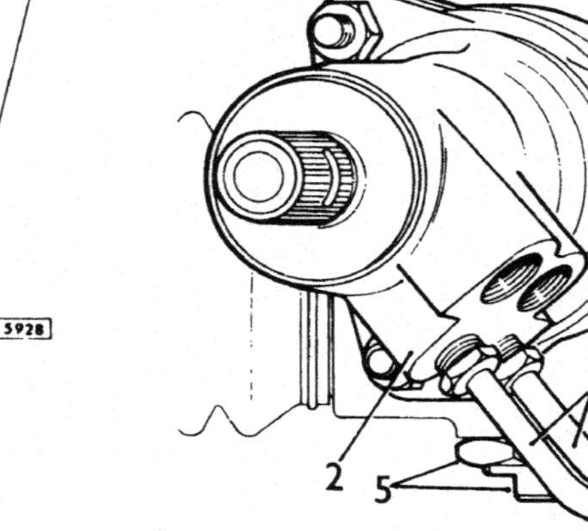

CONTROL VALVE AND PINION

Remove and refit (Alford and Alder) **57.10.19**

Removing
1 Remove the power steering rack – 57.10.01.
2 Note the position of the valve housing porting face relative to the pinion housing, also the position of the two valve to cylinder pipes.
3 Hold the unit at the pinion end of the cylinder in a soft-jawed vice.
4 Remove the two valve to cylinder pipes.
5 Slacken the locknut and unscrew the threaded plug to release the plunger spring load.
6 Remove the three locknuts and withdraw the valve assembly, gently tapping the housing if necessary. Discard the gasket.

Refitting
7 Reverse instructions 1 to 6, using a new valve housing gasket.

CONTROL VALVE AND PINION

Test **57.10.20**

Faults developing in control valve and pinion assembly as indicated in following test or as shown under 'Symptoms and Diagnosis' will necessitate renewal of control valve and pinion. No adjustment or repair is permissible to the Adwest unit, but an internal seal may be renewed on the Alford and Alder control valve, see 57.10.22.
Check tyres, tyre pressure and steering geometry before testing.

1 Fit a 100 lb./in.^{2} (7 kg./cm.^{2}) pressure gauge in feed line from p.a.s. pump, start engine and allow to idle. Gauge should register 40 lb./in.^{2} (2,8 kg./cm.^{2}) approximately.
2 Turn steering wheel slightly to right or left.
CAUTION: Do not turn steering excessively, as this will produce high pressure resulting in irreparable damage to gauge.
Pressure should increase by an equal amount irrespective of direction of steering wheel rotation. Any unbalance will be indicated by a slight fall in pressure on either side before rising.
3 Stop and restart engine and check that steering does not kick to one side.

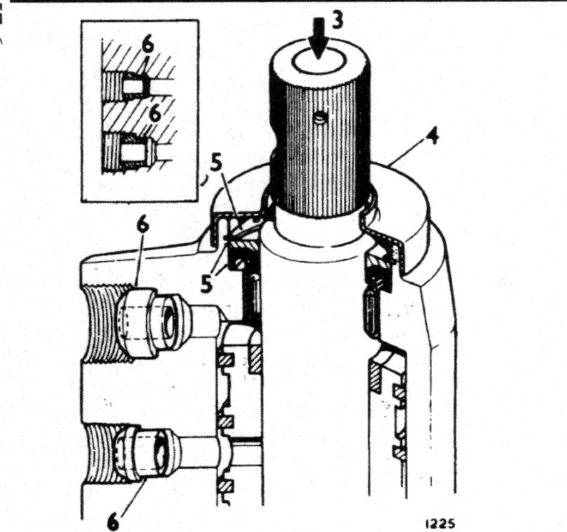

CONTROL VALVE AND PINION

Overhaul (Alford and Alder unit only) **57.10.22**

Service Tools: 18G 257 N, 18G 1259, 18G 1320

Dismantling

1 Remove the power steering rack – 57.10.01.
2 Remove the control valve and pinion – 57.10.19.
3 Hold the valve housing and tap the end of the splined input shaft on a firm base to separate the housing and the valve/pinion assembly.
4 Carefully lever off the top cover from the valve housing and wipe the grease from the top of the seal.
5 Using service tool 18G 257 N, remove the circlip, lift out the back-up ring and carefully lever out the top valve seal. Discard the back-up ring and top valve seal.
6 Using an 'Easi-Out' extractor, withdraw the inserts from the valve housing.
7 Check the condition of the four tapped holes in the valve porting face for damage, and rectify as necessary. ($\frac{5}{8}$ in U.N.F. return, ½ in U.N.F. feed and $\frac{7}{16}$ in U.N.F. cylinder).
8 Wash and dry the housing.

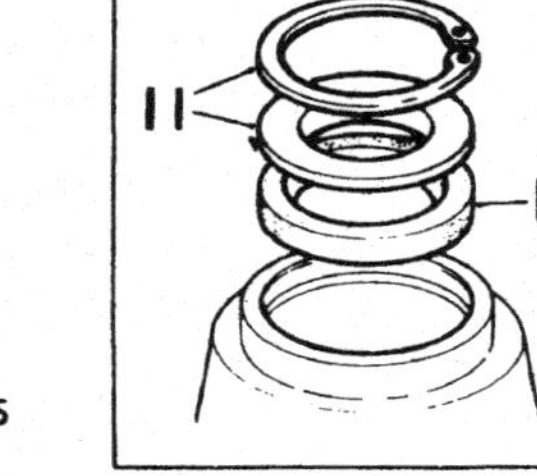
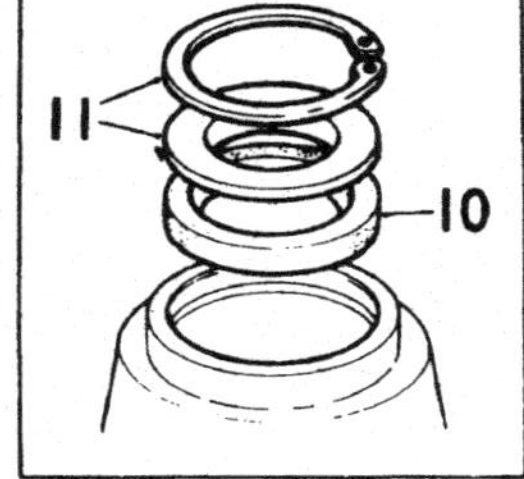
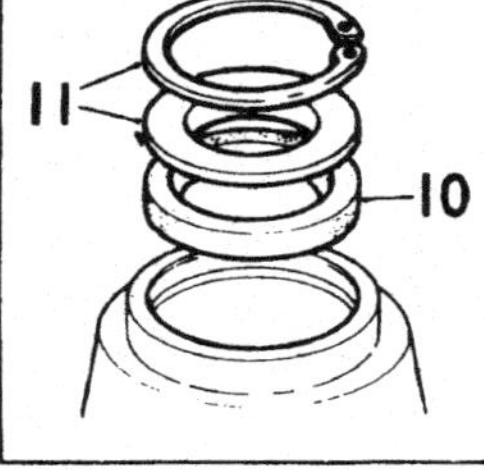

Reassembling

9 Fit new inserts in the feed and return ports. Tap the inserts into position with a drift.
10 Grease the outside of a new top valve seal and fit the seal in the housing using service tool 18G 1320.
11 Fit a new back-up ring and refit the circlip.
12 Remove the Nu-lip seal from the pinion.
13 Check the rotor spline and pinion teeth for damage and excessive wear.
14 Wash the valve/pinion assembly in a clean solvent and either blow dry or leave to dry.
NOTE: Do not wipe dry with a cloth as this may leave fibres likely to cause valve malfunction.
15 Oil or grease a new Nu-lip seal and fit it on the pinion.
16 Fit a protection sleeve (service tool 18G 1259) over the pinion splines. Oil the surfaces of the sleeve, the exposed rotor shaft, valve sleeve seals and pinion seal.
17 Fit the valve/pinion assembly into the housing. Lightly tap the end of the pinion on a firm base to engage the ball race in the housing.
18 Grease the cavity in the top of the housing and refit the housing top cover.
19 Refit the control valve and pinion – 57.10.19.
20 Refit the power steering rack – 57.10.01.

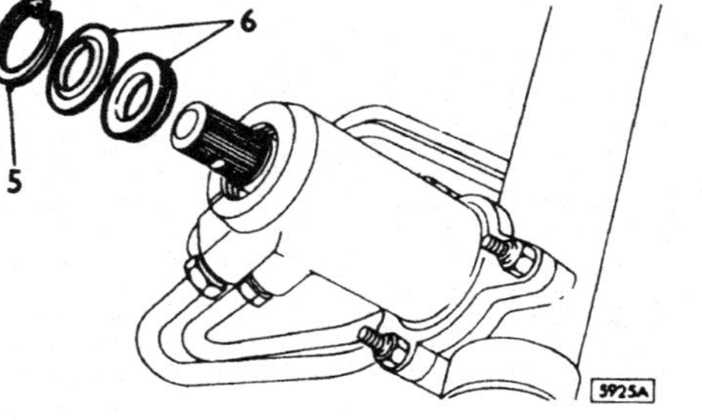

PINION SEAL

Remove and refit (both racks) **57.10.23**

Service tool: Pinion Seal Replacer 18G 1319 (for Alford & Alder racks only)

Removing

1 Place car on ramp or over pit.
2 Thoroughly clean shaft end of pinion housing.
3 Remove lower steering column – 57.40.05.
4 Clean off dirt from splines of pinion housing.
5 Remove circlip from valve housing.
6 Withdraw seal and retainer.
CAUTION: Do not move road wheels or turn steering while joint is disconnected.

Refitting

7 Reverse operations 3 to 6.
8 Remove car from ramp or pit.

PORT INSERTS

Remove and refit **57.10.24**

Removing

1 Tap a suitable thread in bore of seat, and insert a setscrew with attached nut, washer and distance piece.
2 Tighten nut and withdraw seat.

Refitting

Insert seat, and tap home squarely with a soft mandrel.

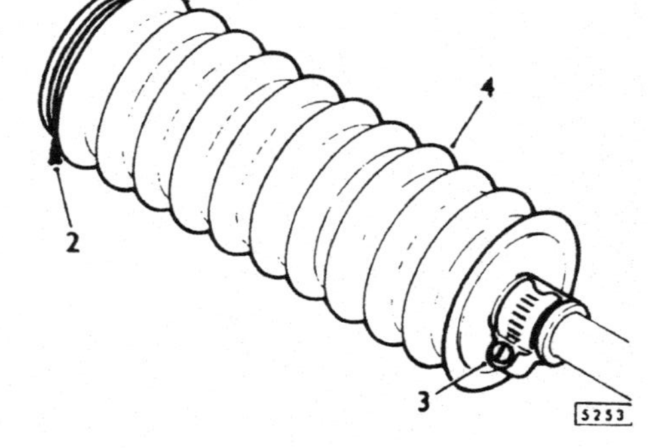

POWER STEERING RACK GAITERS

Remove and refit **57.10.27**

Removing

1 Remove outer ball joint – 57.55.02.
2 Remove wire clip.
3 Slacken clip securing gaiter to tie rod.
4 Withdraw gaiter; clean grease from inner joints.

Refitting

Reverse operations 1 to 4. Coat each inner ball joint with 1½ to 2 oz. (45 to 55 g.) of recommended grade of grease before attaching gaiter to rack housing. Do not omit check of wheel alignment – 57.65.01.

NOTE: It is permissible, in emergency, to replace a damaged gaiter from an Adwest rack with one supplied for an Alford and Alder rack, or vice versa, if the correct replacement is not available.

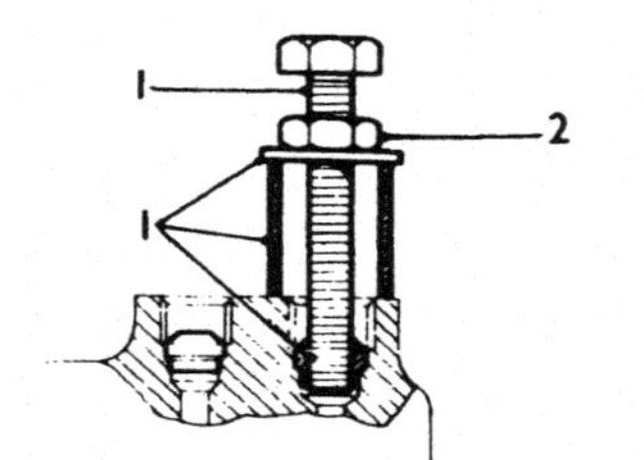

SYSTEM TESTING

57.15.01

Service Tool: Tap JD.10.2.

Faults in system can be caused by inefficiences in the hydraulic system, see 'Fault Finding Chart'. The following test may be carried out without removing any components from the car. Before commencing work fluid should be checked for correct level and freedom from froth.

Pump Blow Off Pressure

1 Fit pressure gauge reading to 1500 lb./in.^{2} (100 kgf./cm.^{2}) in pressure line from pump.
2 Start engine and allow to run at idling speed.
3 Turn steering to full lock and continue to increase steering effort until pressure recorded on gauge ceases to rise.
4 Check that recorded pressure lies between 1100 and 1200 lb./in.^{2} (77,5 kgf./cm.^{2} and 84,4 kgf./cm.^{2}).
NOTE: If pressure is below 1100 lb./in.^{2} (77,5 kgf./cm.^{2}) at tickover, but rises to correct figure with increased engine speed the reason is a defective control valve in pump, or excessive internal leakage in rack and pinion unit. Carry out following test to establish location.
5 Fit tap JD.10-2 between pump and pressure gauge, arranging connections as shown, so that pressure gauge is at all times connected to pump, but rack unit can be isolated from it.
6 With tap OPEN, start engine and allow to run at idling speed.
7 Turn steering to full lock.
8 Check that gauge reading exceeds 1100 lb./in.^{2} (77,5 kgf./cm.^{2}).
9 If pressure does not reach this figure, CLOSE TAP AT ONCE, noting gauge reading as tap reaches 'OFF' position.
CAUTION: Tap must not remain closed for more than 5 seconds when engine is running.

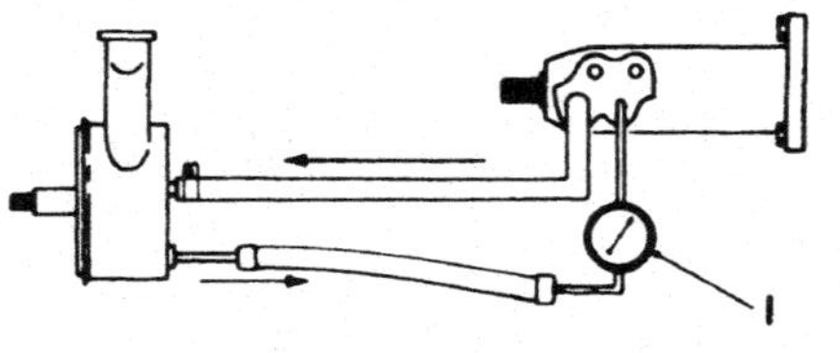

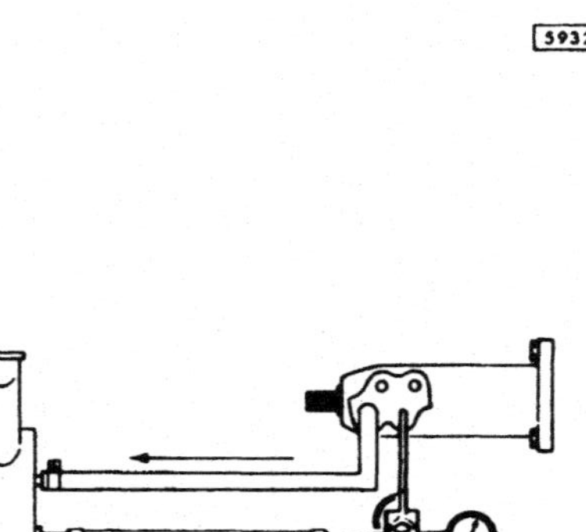

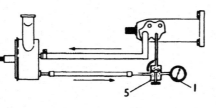

If reading of pressure gauge increases to at least 1100 lb./in.^{2} (77,5 kgf./cm.^{2}) when tap is turned off, leaks are confined to steering unit, which must be overhauled – See 57.10.07.

If pressure reading exceeds 1200 lb./in.^{2} (84,4 kgf./cm.^{2}) remove pump discharge port, withdraw valve assembly located behind it, and inspect a small hemispherical gauze filter carried at its inner extremity, which may be found to be blocked. Clean filter by airline or other means, and replace valve and discharge port.

POWER STEERING SYSTEM

Bleed **57.15.02**

1 Fill reservoir to 'Full' mark on dipstick with recommended grade of fluid.
2 Start engine and turn steering wheel from lock to lock a few times to expel any air which may be present in system. This is shown by all 'lumpiness' disappearing.
3 Check fluid level and top up with correct fluid only.
CAUTION: Feed and return hoses differ in length and details of rigid ends between Adwest and Alford and Alder racks on all cars built prior to 1978 model year, and must not be interchanged. When renewing a hose check replacement against hose removed to ensure that correct part is being fitted.

STEERING RACK FEED HOSE

Remove and refit **57.15.21**

Removing

1 Remove air cleaner – 19.10.01.
2 Place car on ramp or over pit.
3 On L.H.D. cars only; remove five clips securing both flexible hoses to the crossbeam.
4 Detach small union nuts on pump and valve body; plug orifices to prevent loss of fluid and entry of dirt.
5 Remove pipes and flexible hose.

Refitting

6 Reverse operations 1 to 5.
7 Top up system with recommended fluid and bleed.

STEERING RACK RETURN HOSE

Remove and refit **57.15.22**

Removing

1 Remove air cleaner – 19.10.01.
2 Place car on ramp or over pit.
3 On L.H.D. cars only; remove five clips securing both flexible hoses to crossbeam.
4 Detach hose clip at pump and large union nut at valve body; plug orifices to prevent loss of fluid and entry of dirt.
5 Remove pipe and flexible hose.

Refitting

6 Reverse operations 1 to 5.
7 Top up system with recommended fluid and bleed.

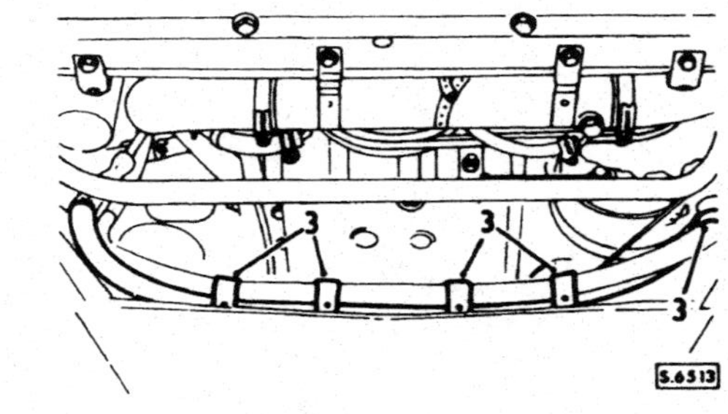

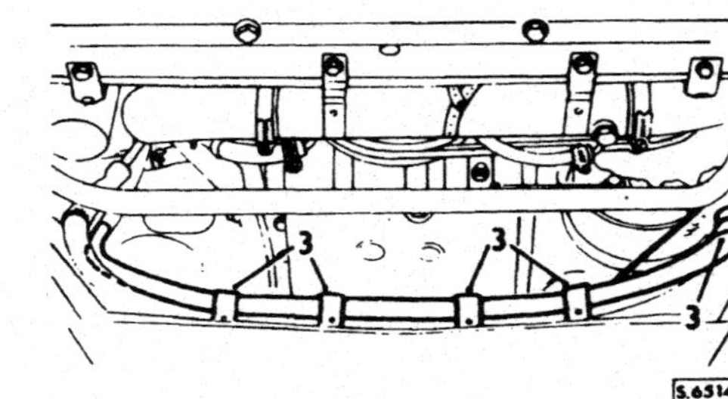

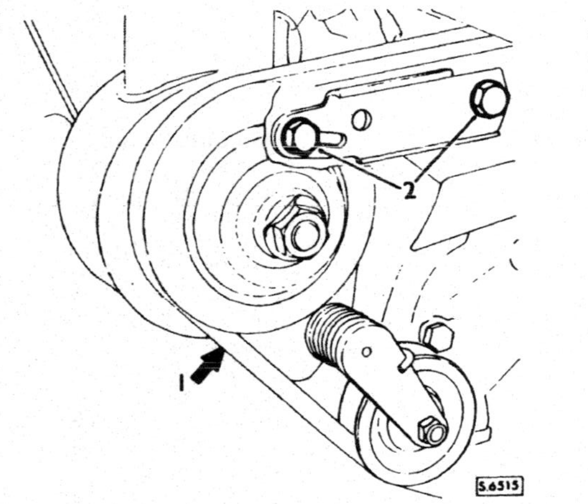

STEERING PUMP DRIVE BELT

Adjust **57.20.01**

This belt is automatically tensioned by a spring-loaded jockey pulley; adjustment therefore, should seldom be necessary. If, however, it is needed, proceed as follows:

1 Slacken nut of pump mounting pivot bolt.
2 Slacken two setbolts attaching horizontal link to steering pump and water pump casting.
3 Carefully lever pump and mounting outwards until desired belt tension is obtained.
4 Retighten setbolts and nut.

STEERING PUMP DRIVE BELT

Remove and refit **57.20.02**

Removing
1 Slacken nut of pump mounting pivot bolt.
2 Slacken setbolts attaching horizontal link to water pump casting and steering pump.
3 Push steering pump towards engine, lift jockey pulley against its spring and remove belt.

Refitting
Reverse operations 1 to 3.

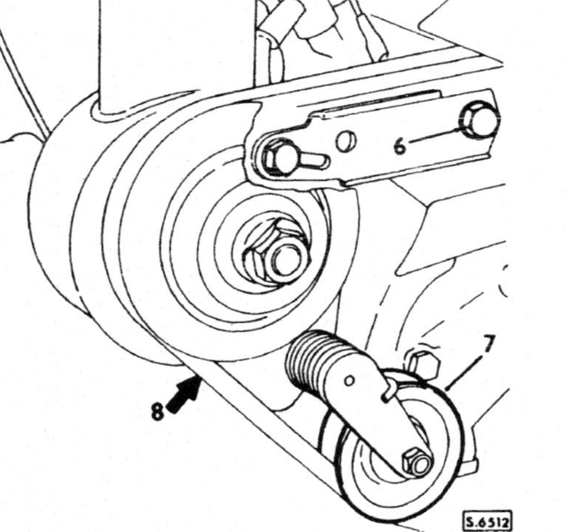

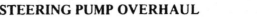

STEERING PUMP

Remove and refit **57.20.14**

Removing
1 Remove cover from air cleaner – refer to 19.10.08.
2 Slacken hose clip securing return hose to rear of reservoir.
3 Detach hose, and insert plugs to prevent entry of dirt into hose or reservoir.
4 Remove union nut attaching feed hose to union on reservoir.
5 Detach feed hose and insert plugs.
6 Remove setbolt attaching horizontal link to water pump casting; collect washer and distance piece.
7 Push steering pump inwards, lift jockey pulley against spring and remove belt.
8 Remove nut from front of pivot bolt and withdraw bolt, collecting washers.
9 Lift pump with horizontal link and mounting bracket from engine compartment.

Refitting
10 Reverse items 1 to 9.
11 Refill system with recommended fluid and bleed – 57.15.02.

STEERING PUMP OVERHAUL

Dismantling and reassembling **57.20.20**

Service tool: Power Steering Pump Pulley Remover/Replacer 18G 1326

Dismantling
1 Remove pump – 57.20.14.
2 Remove plugs and drain oil from pump and reservoir.
3 Bend back tabwasher, remove nut and draw off pump pulley, using an extractor reacting on pump shaft.
NOTE: Latest cars are fitted with flanged pulley carriers pressed on to shaft, to which pulley is attached by 3 setscrews secured by spring washers. Remove setscrews to detach pulley, clean out tapped hole in pump shaft and fit reaction screw for Saginaw-approved removal tool, 18G 1326, screwing it fully into shaft. Engage body of extractor with recessed diameter of carrier and remove carrier by tightening extractor screw. Remove reaction screw before next operation.
4 Remove two nuts attaching pump to cast mounting bracket.
5 Remove setscrew securing link to pump; note number and position of spacing washers.
NOTE: Before dismantling further, thoroughly clean exterior.
6 Remove high pressure outlet union and two mounting studs.
7 Detach reservoir from pump body. Remove 'O' ring from body.
8 Remove three 'O' rings from recesses in pump body.
9 Insert suitable pin punch in hole in pump body. Push retaining ring away from groove.
10 Lever out ring with screwdriver.

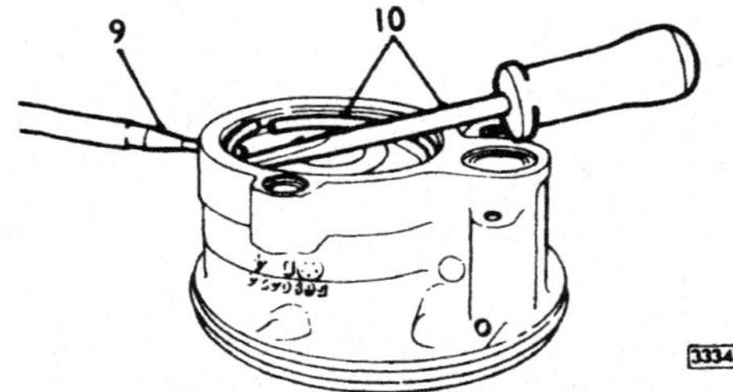

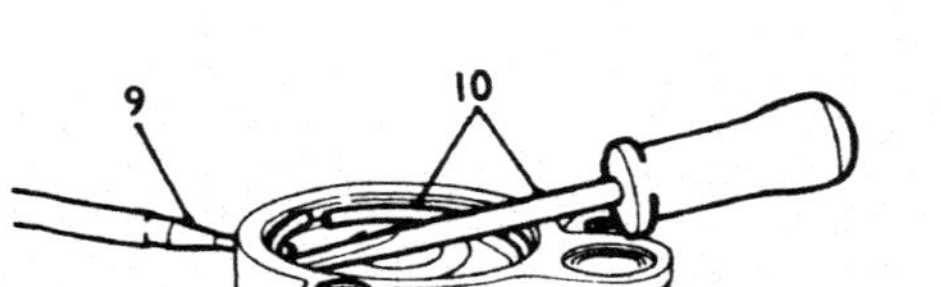

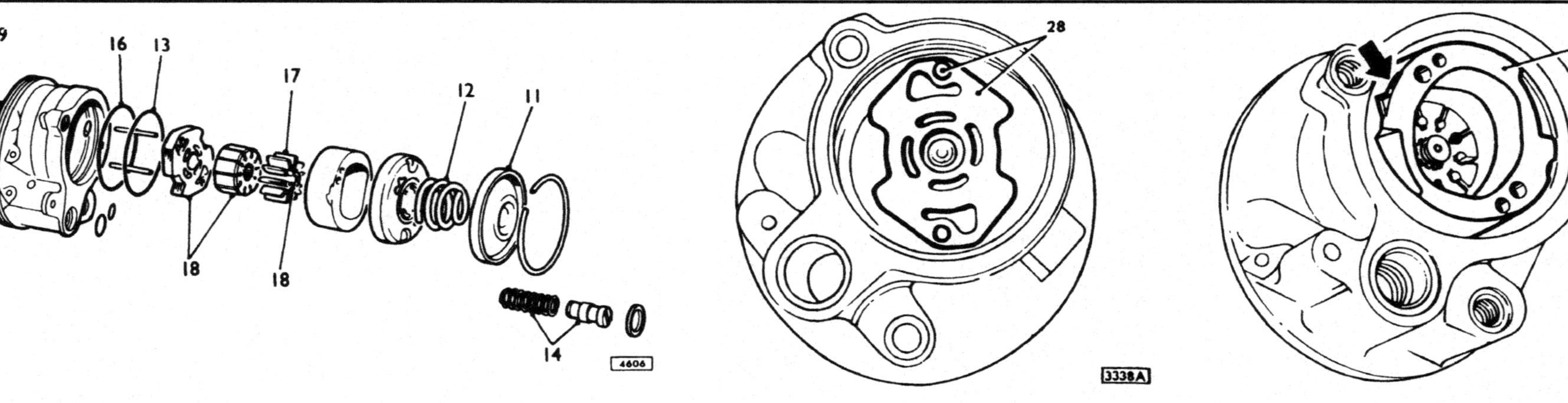

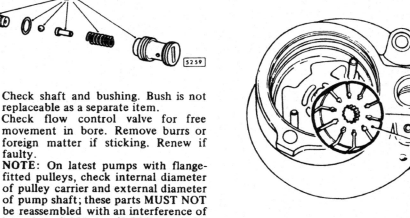

11 Remove end plate.
NOTE: If end plate sticks in pump body a light tap will free it.
12 Remove spring.
13 Remove end plate 'O' ring from internal recess in pump body.
14 Withdraw flow control valve and spring.
15 Remove drive key and tap shaft and rotor assembly rearwards through pump body.
NOTE: Drive key is not fitted to latest pumps with pulley mounted on carrier.
16 Remove pressure plate 'O' ring from pump body.
17 Separate rotor assembly components taking care not to damage pump rotor vanes.
18 Remove circlip and withdraw rotor and thrust plate.
19 Remove drive shaft oil seal.

Inspection

20 Clean all parts in solvent. Renew all 'O' rings and shaft seal. Seal kit No. 10992.
NOTE: Do not immerse new seals in solvent.
21 Check pressure plate, thrust plate and rotor. Light scoring can be removed by lapping.
22 Check contour surface for extreme wear. Scuff marks and uniform wear are not detrimental. Renew pump ring and vanes if chatter marks and grooves exist. Repair kit No. 11653.

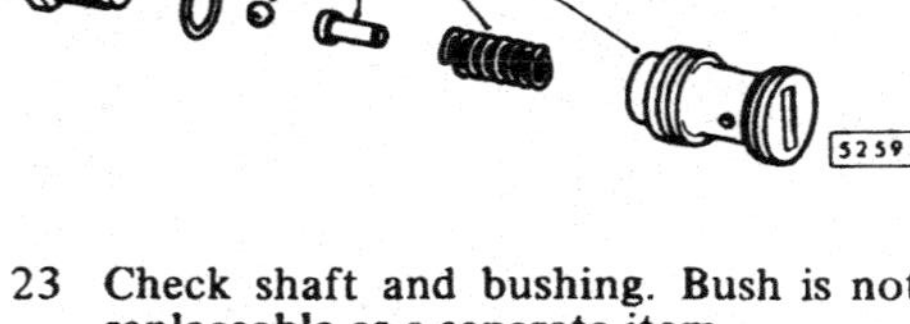

23 Check shaft and bushing. Bush is not replaceable as a separate item.
24 Check flow control valve for free movement in bore. Remove burrs or foreign matter if sticking. Renew if faulty.
NOTE: On latest pumps with flange-fitted pulleys, check internal diameter of pulley carrier and external diameter of pump shaft; these parts MUST NOT be reassembled with an interference of less than 0.001 in. (0,025 mm.), or more than 0.0026 in. (0,066 mm.).

28

3338A

31

3337A

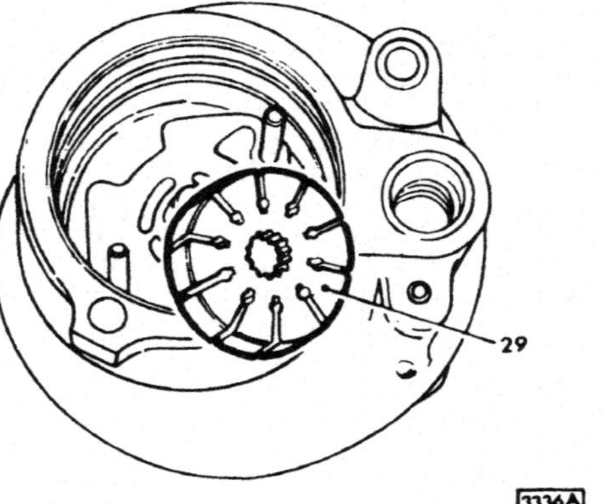

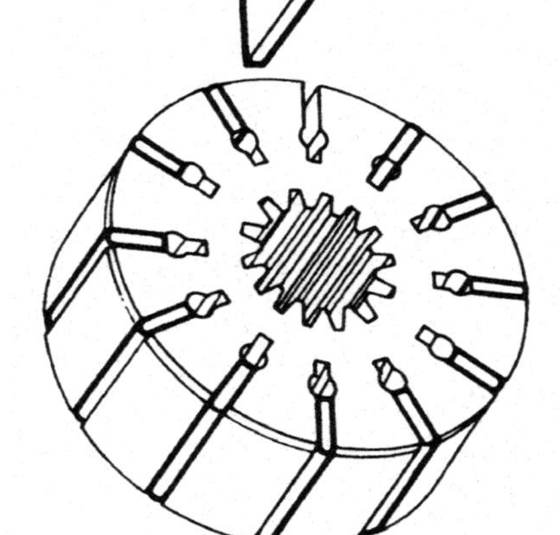

Reassembling

25 Lubricate shaft seal with petroleum jelly and fit to pump body.
26 Insert drive shaft, splined end first.
27 Insert dowel pins in pump body.
28 Fit thrust plate over dowel pins, ported face uppermost.
29 Fit rotor on splines with counterbored side towards thrust plate.
30 Fit retaining clip.
31 Fit pump ring over dowel pins, rotation arrow uppermost.
32 Insert vanes in rotor slots, radiused edges outwards.

continued

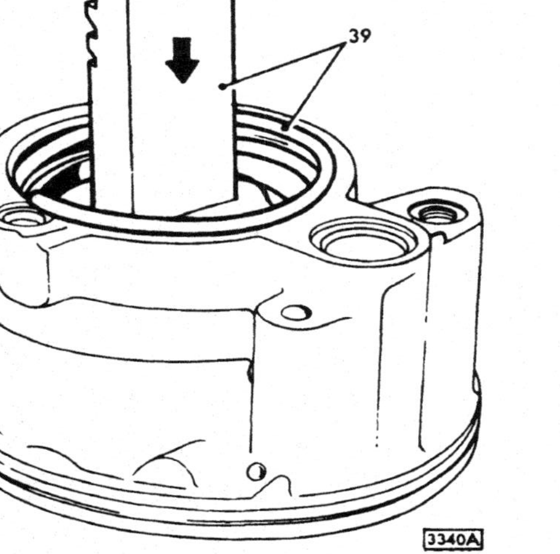

33 Lubricate pressure plate 'O' ring and insert in lower groove.
34 Lubricate periphery of pressure plate and fit over dowel pins with recess for spring uppermost.
35 Push plate down firmly and squarely to engage 'O' ring.
NOTE: Do not tap into position.
36 Lubricate end plate 'O' ring and insert in groove in pump body.
37 Fit spring in circular recess in pressure plate.
38 Lubricate periphery of end plate. Place in position with retaining ring. Ensure that gap in ring is not opposite removal hole in pump body.
39 Place assembly under a press. Apply pressure until retaining ring can be sprung into groove.
40 Place control valve spring in bore.
41 Insert control valve.
42 Fit new 'O' rings for retaining studs and outlet union.
43 Lubricate reservoir sealing ring and fit to pump body.
44 Fit reservoir, secure with retaining studs and outlet union.
45 Fit drive key, pulley, tab washer and nut.
NOTE: On latest pumps with flange-mounted pulleys it is essential to use a Saginaw-approved tool, 18G 1326, to refit carrier to shaft. Place carrier on tool with its flange adjacent to 3/8 in.

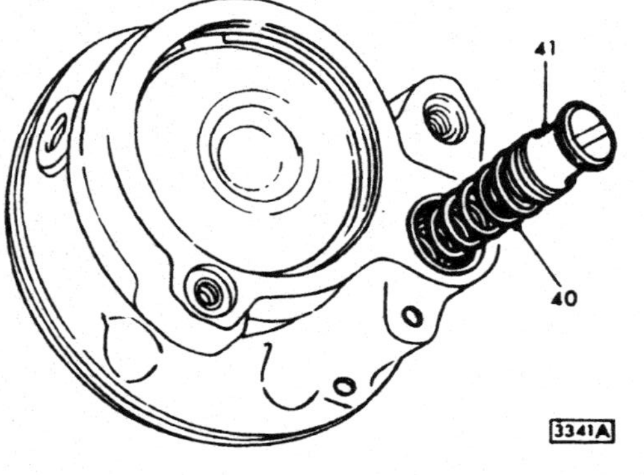

U.N.C. thread of tool. Screw this threaded stud into tapped hole in pump shaft until it bottoms then, still holding spindle of tool with spanner, screw body of installer down spindle until face of carrier is flush with end of pump shaft. Unscrew tool from pump shaft; (the tapped hole in pump shaft is provided solely to suit installation and removal tools).

UPPER STEERING COLUMN

Remove and refit **57.40.02**

Removing
1 Disconnect battery – 86.15.20.
2 Remove steering wheel – 57.60.01.
3 Remove speedometer – 88.30.01.
4 Remove tachometer – 88.30.21.
5 Remove trim panel below upper steering column – 76.46.11.
6 Disconnect electrical switchgear on upper column by separating three plug and socket connections.
7 Remove horn feed cable from its contact on upper steering column.
8 Detach self locknut and remove pinch bolt securing upper universal joint to lower steering column.
9 Slacken two setscrews securing lower end of upper column to its mounting strut.
10 Working through speedometer and tachometer apertures, remove two nuts securing top mounting of upper column to body; supporting this end of column with one hand, collect bolts, rubber washers and any packing washers fitted.
11 Still supporting column, detach two setscrews already slackened, at lower mounting; collect any packing fitted.
12 Remove upper column from car, complete with universal joint and switchgear.
NOTE: Excessive force must not be used in separating universal joint from lower column.

Overhaul
No repair or adjustment of any description is permitted on upper steering columns. If damage is suspected, remove adjusting clamp – 57.40.07 – mark its position, remove universal joint and measure overall length of inner column, which must be between 21.565 and 21.695 in. (547,74 and 551,04 mm.). Any column outside these limits must be renewed; renew also in all cases of doubt. If column is to be renewed, refer to section 86.65 for details of removal and refitting of electrical equipment.

Refitting
13 If universal joint has been removed, refit it to its marked location and replace its securing bolt, washer and self locking nut. Tighten nut to 14–18 lbf.ft. (2,0–2,5 kgf.m.).
14 Refit adjusting clamp if removed – 57.40.07.
15 Reverse operations 1 to 12.
16 Check that 3/8 in. (9,5 mm.) clearance exists axially in lower universal joint; if less, move upper universal joint further along lower column to increase clearance.
17 Check that direction indicators on both sides self-cancel correctly, when steering wheel is returned to straight ahead position; if not, proceed as follows:
18 Detach lower switch cover by removing three screws.
19 Check that lower dogs on fixed portion of switch engage correctly with cutaways on outer (fixed) column, and that a dog on collet adaptor enters slot in movable section of switch.
20 Turn steering wheel to bring clamp bolt of column adaptor to horizontal, below axis of column; self-cancelling switch will then function correctly.
21 Remove steering wheel, rotate it to straight ahead position and refit to splined column with minimum of rotation. Refer to 57.60.01.
22 Replace lower switch cover.

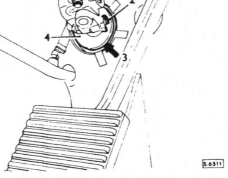

LOWER STEERING COLUMN

Remove and refit 57.40.05

Removing

1 Place car on ramp and raise ramp.
2 Remove pinch bolt securing lower universal joint to pinion shaft. Collect heat shield fitted to pinion shaft on later cars.
3 Lower ramp.
4 Detach lower parcel shelf – 76.67.03.
5 Remove both pinch bolts securing upper universal joint to upper and lower columns.
6 Release two lower mounting screws of upper column.
7 Release lower column from upper universal joint.
8 Raise ramp.
9 Remove lower universal joint from pinion shaft and withdraw lower column.
10 Lower ramp.

Refitting

No repairs are permissible. Faulty or damaged columns must be renewed. Reverse operations 1 to 10. Check that upper column and road wheels are centralised before reconnecting splines, and tighten pinch bolt nuts to 14–18 lbf.ft. (2,0–2,5 kgf.m.). Ensure that a gap of 3/8 in. (10 mm.) exists between sections of lower universal joint.

CAUTION: Excessive force, which may damage nylon shear plugs, must not be used when withdrawing and refitting columns. Burrs on splines should be removed with a fine file.

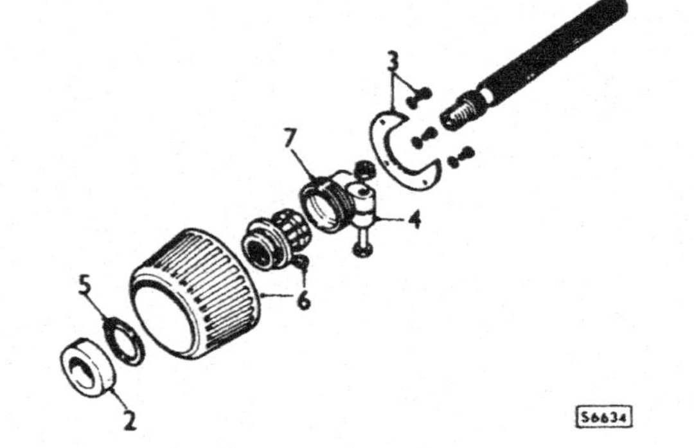

STEERING COLUMN ADJUSTING CLAMP

Remove and refit 57.40.07

Removing

1 Remove steering wheel – 57.60.01.
2 Remove impact rubber from steering wheel shaft.
3 Remove three small cheese head screws from beneath hand locknut, and collect retaining plate.
4 Unscrew collet adaptor completely and remove from shaft.
5 Remove collet circlip from within upper side of hand locknut.
6 Withdraw hand locknut, collecting stop button.
7 Slide split collet off shaft.

Refitting

8 Clean thoroughly and inspect all parts; remove any small burrs with a fine file.
9 Lightly lubricate all enclosed metal parts with engine oil.
10 Reverse operations 1 to 7.

STEERING COLUMN – LOWER – SEAL

Remove and refit 57.40.15

Removing

1 Remove upper steering column – 57.40.02.
2 Slacken hose clip attaching upper sealing sleeve to lower column; remove clip and sleeve.
3 Remove three setscrews securing gaiter retainer to bulkhead; slide gaiter, retainer and sealing sleeve up and off lower column.

Refitting

4 Fit assembly of sealing sleeve, gaiter and retainer over end of lower column, taking care not to damage gaiter or flanged face of sleeve.
5 Insert and tighten three setscrews securing retainer to bulkhead.
6 Carefully slide second sealing sleeve, flanged end first, over lower column as far as first sealing sleeve; replace its hose clip but do not tighten.
7 Move second sealing sleeve approximately ¼ in. (6 mm.) towards bulkhead, to pre-load it against first sleeve; secure it with its hose clip in this position.
8 Refit upper steering column – 57.40.02.

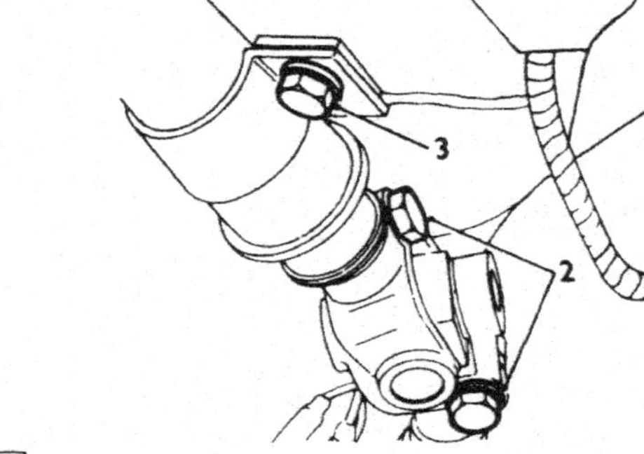

STEERING COLUMN UNIVERSAL JOINT

Remove and refit 57.40.25

Removing

1 Detach lower parcel shelf – 76.67.04.
2 Remove both pinch bolts securing upper universal joint to upper and lower columns.
3 Remove two lower mounting screws of upper column.
4 Remove upper universal joint from upper column, then from lower column.

Refitting

Reverse operations 1 to 4. Ensure that the two universal joints are correctly aligned with each other, and tighten pinch bolt nuts to 14–18 lbf.ft. (2,0–2,5 kgf.m.).
NOTE: Lower universal joint is integral with lower steering column and removed with it – 57.40.05.

STEERING COLUMN LOCK

Remove and refit **57.40.31**

Removing

1 Remove upper column – 57.40.02.
2 Remove retaining bolts by forming centre-punch indentations near edges of heads and unscrewing with light drift.
3 Withdraw lock.
NOTE: If lock is to be returned to manufacturer under warranty, include key number on material return label.

Refitting

4 Refit lock to column.
5 Insert new shear bolts parallel to steering column and tighten until heads are sheared away.
6 Reverse operation 1.

OUTER TIE-ROD BALL JOINT

Remove and refit **57.55.02**

Service tool: Ball joint separator JD.24.

Removing

1 Remove wire clip and detach gaiter from rack housing.
2 Remove outer ball joint from steering arm with tool JD.24.
3 Check exact length of tie-rod between ball centres and record.
4 Release locknut and unscrew ball joint from tie-rod.

Refitting

Reverse operations 1 to 4. Ensure that tie-rod is assembled to exact length as noted in operation 3. Check wheel alignment – 57.65.01.

INNER TIE-ROD BALL JOINT

Remove and refit **57.55.03**

Removing

NOTE: Replacement inner ball joints will only be supplied complete with tie-rods, less outer ball joints, as an assembly. No adjustment or repair is permissible.

1 Remove outer ball joint – 57.55.02.

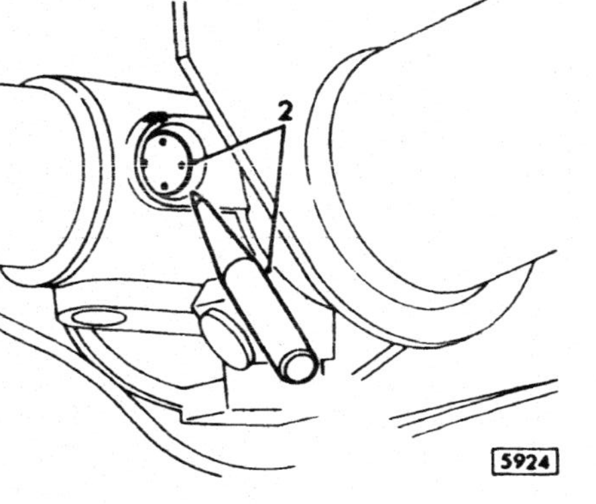
5924

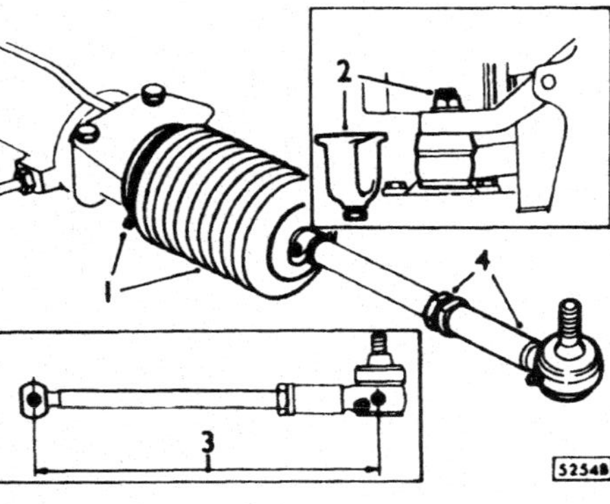
5254B

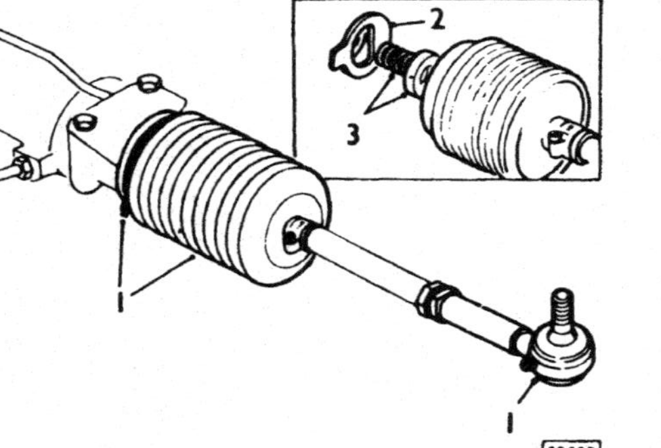
5255B

2 Knock back tab washer and release locknut securing ball joint to rack shaft.
3 Remove tie-rod and ball joint; collect spring and spacer.

Refitting

4 Reverse operations 1 to 3. Secure nut with new tab washer.
5 Coat inner ball joint with 2 oz. (60 g.) of a recommended grade of grease before attaching gaiter to rack housing.
6 Check wheel alignment – 57 61 01.

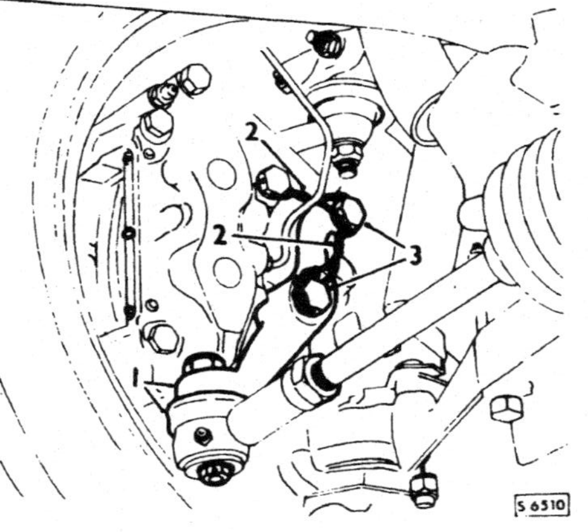
S 6510

STEERING LEVERS

Remove and refit **57.55.29**

Service tool: Ball joint separator JD.24.

Removing

1 Remove outer tie-rod ball joint with Churchill Tool No. JD.24.
2 Remove locking wire from lower set-screw attaching steering arm to vertical link.
3 Remove both setscrews and withdraw lever. Note number and location of shim washers, (if any), fitted between steering lever and lugs on vertical link and caliper.

Refitting

4 Reverse operation 3; ensure shims are correctly replaced.
5 Tighten setscrews to 49 to 55 lb./ft. (6,8 to 7,6 kgf.m.).
6 Lock setscrews with new locking wire.
7 Replace tie rod outer ball joint.
8 Check wheel alignment – 57.65.01.

STEERING WHEEL

Remove and refit **57.60.01**

Removing

1 Centralise front wheels and mark steering wheel to record its position. Do not turn front wheels again.
2 Remove three screws securing lower switch cover, and detach cover.
3 Working from below, remove clamp bolt securing collet adaptor to steering column.
4 Slacken locknut of grubscrew in collet adaptor and unscrew grub screw two turns.
5 Withdraw steering wheel, complete with hand locknut, impact rubber, collet adaptor and shaft.

Dismantling

6 Unscrew two self tapping screws from lower face of steering wheel boss and lift off padded horn contact.
7 Unscrew nylon nut from top of steering wheel shaft and remove it carefully withdrawing horn contact tube with it.
8 Remove self locking nut and plain washer securing steering wheel.
9 Carefully draw the steering wheel from its splined shaft, collecting both halves of split cone.

Reassembly

10 Clean thoroughly and remove any burrs with a fine file.
11 Lightly lubricate all enclosed metal parts with engine oil.
12 Reverse operations 6 to 9.

Refitting

13 Reverse operations 1 to 5, taking care to replace horn contact tube correctly, (enclosing end of contact rod), and to replace wheel in its straight ahead position, with front wheels still centralised. Tighten grub screw finger tight, tighten its locknut and tighten clamp bolt to 10–12 lbf.ft. (1,4–1,65 kgf.m.).

FRONT WHEEL ALIGNMENT

Check and adjust **57.65.01**

Service Tool: Rack Centralising Tool Jaguar Part No. 12297.

Check

1 Inflate tyres to correct pressures.
2 Set front wheels in straight ahead position.
3 Remove grease nipple from rack adjuster pad.
4 Insert centralising tool (Jaguar part number 12297) and adjust position of rack until reduced tip of tool enters locating hole in rack.
5 Check alignment by using light beam equipment or an approved track setting gauge.
NOTE: As a front wheel alignment check is called for in each 6,000 mile (10,000 km.) service, very little variation from specified figures for wheel alignment is to be expected; if, however, a discrepancy of as much as 1/8 in.(3 mm.) from specified limits of 1/16 in. to 1/8 in. (1,6 mm. to 3,2 mm.) toe-in is recorded, accidental damage to a steering lever may have occurred and following further check must be carried out, on both levers.
6 Remove steering levers – 57.55.29.
7 Accurately check dimensions of each lever against those quoted in illustration.
8 Reject for scrap and replace any lever with dimensions outside limits quoted.

WARNING: IT IS ABSOLUTELY FORBIDDEN TO ATTEMPT TO RECTIFY A REJECTED LEVER BY BENDING.

If both steering levers are within limits, a discrepancy in alignment figures may be due to distortion of upper or lower wishbones, or end of stub axle carriers (vertical links). Dimensioned drawings of these parts for checking purposes, are given in Group 60.

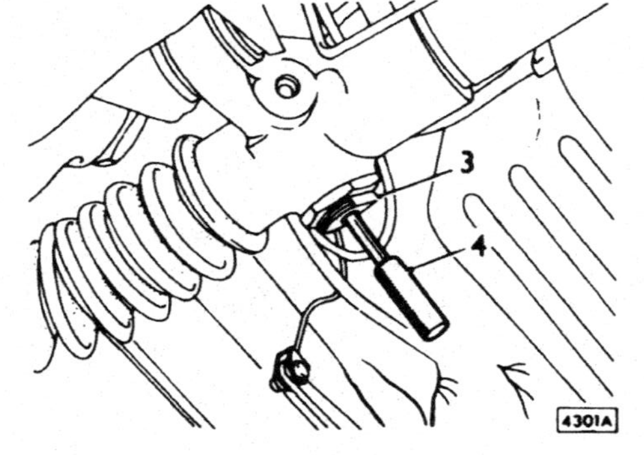

Adjust

9 Slacken locknuts at outer ends of each tie-rod.
10 Release hose clips securing outer ends of gaiters to tie-rods.
11 Turn tie-rods by an equal amount until alignment of wheels is correct.
12 Tighten locknuts to 60–70 lbf.ft. (8,30–9,68 kgf.m.) while holding track rod end by spanner flats.
13 Re-check alignment.
14 Ensure that gaiters are not twisted and retighten clips.
15 Remove centralising tool and refit grease nipple.

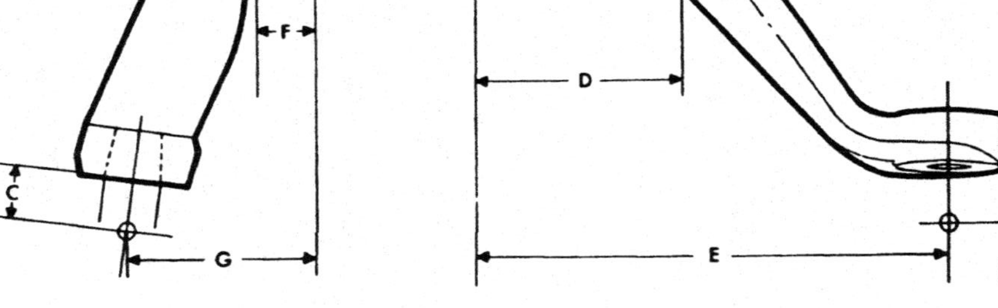

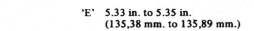

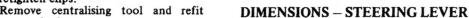

DIMENSIONS – STEERING LEVER

'A' 3,248 in. to 3.252 in. (82,5 mm. to 82,6 mm.)

'B' 4.01 in. to 4.03 in. (101,85 mm. to 102,36 mm.)

'C' 0.875 in. (22,23 mm.)

'D' 2.32 in. to 2.34 in. (58,93 mm. to 59,44 mm.)

'E' 5.33 in. to 5.35 in. (135,38 mm. to 135,89 mm.)

'F' 0.70 in. to 0.71 in. (17,78 mm. to 18,03 mm.)

'G' 2.14 in. to 2.16 in. (54,36 mm. to 54,86 mm.)

CASTOR ANGLE

Check and adjust **57.65.04**

Service tool: Suspension links JD.25.

Check

CAUTION: Before checking castor angle, examine all rubber/steel bushes for deterioration or distortion. Check upper and lower wishbone ball joints for excessive play: check shock absorbers and mountings.

1 Ensure that car is standing on level ground and inflate tyres to correct pressure; check that standing heights are equal on both sides of car.
2 Make up two suspension setting tubes to dimensions shown.
3 Compress front suspension and insert setting tubes under upper wishbones adjacent to rebound stop rubbers, and over brackets welded to bottom of 'turrets' as shown. This locks front suspension in mid-laden condition.
4 Lock rear suspension in mid-laden condition by compressing suspension, hooking links JD.25 through lower holes in rear mountings, and passing looped ends of links over rear pivot nuts, as shown.
5 Check castor angle by normal methods, using an approved gauge; correct angle is 2¼ deg. ± ¼ deg.

Adjust

6 Slacken two bolts on each side securing upper wishbone members to upper ball joints.
7 Transpose shims, which can now be lifted out, from front to rear or vice versa, to reduce or increase castor, respectively. Transposing one shim 1/16 in. (1,6 mm.) thick will alter castor angle by approximately ¼ deg.
8 After adjusting castor to correct figure, retighten four bolts slackened in operation 6, to 26–32 lbf.ft. (3,60–4,42 kgf.m.).
9 Recheck front wheel alignment and adjust if necessary – 57.65.01.

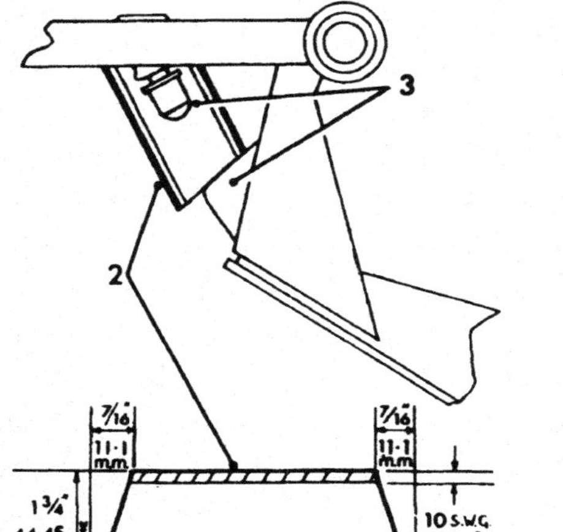

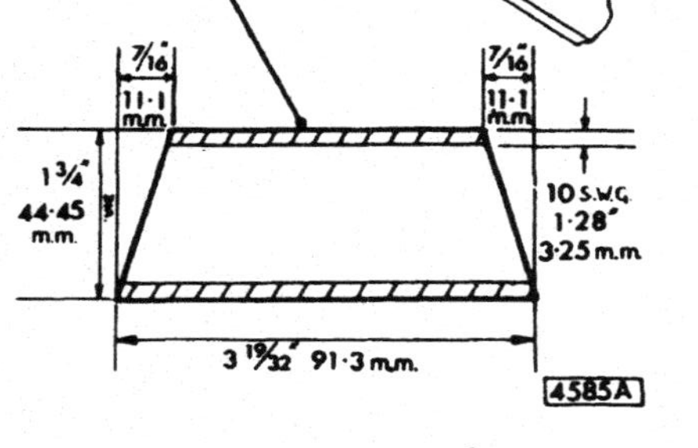

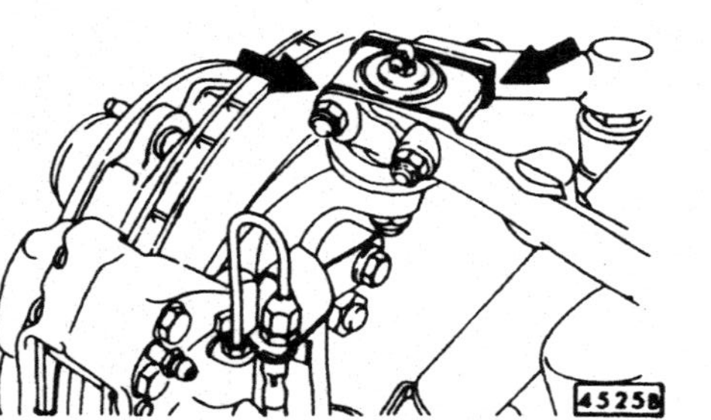

CAMBER ANGLE

Check and adjust **57.65.05**

Check

1 Set up car in mid-laden condition – 57.65.04 operations 1 to 4.
2 Line up wheel to be checked in straight ahead position and check camber angle with an approved gauge. Correct camber is ½ deg. positive ± ¼ deg. and the two front wheels must be within ¼ deg. of each other.
3 Rotate wheels through 180 deg. and re-check camber angle.

Adjust

4 Release nuts from bolts securing upper wishbone inner pivots to cross member turrets.
5 Add or remove shims between pivot shafts and cross member turrets to reduce or increase camber angle. Shims are available in 1/32 in. (,8 mm.), 1/16 in. (1,6 mm.) and 1/8 in. (3,2 mm.) thickness, and a change of 1/16 in. (1,6 mm.) in shims will alter camber angle by approximately ¼ deg. **NOTE**: It is necessary to partly withdraw bolts to change shims, so only one bolt of a pair should be shimmed at a time. It is important that an equal thickness of shims should be changed on front and rear bolts, as otherwise castor angle will be affected.
6 Re-tighten nuts to 45–55 lbf.ft. (6,23–7,60 kgf.m.).
7 Check new camber angle on both wheels.
8 Check front wheel alignment and adjust if necessary – 57.65.01.

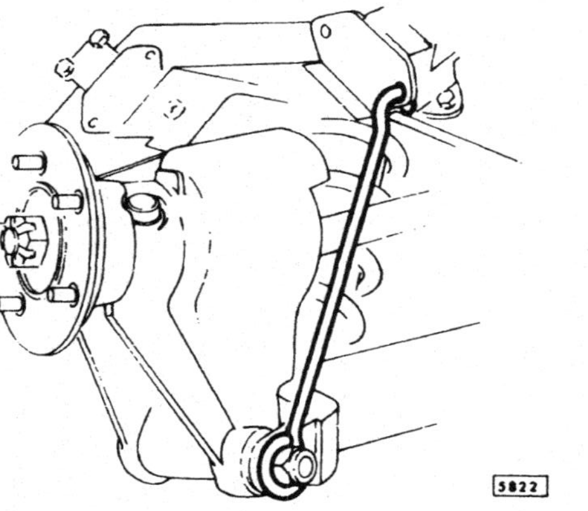

ACCIDENTAL DAMAGE

The dimensional drawings are provided to assist in assessing accidental damage. A component suspected of being damaged should be removed from the car, cleaned off and the dimensions checked and compared with those given in the appropriate illustration.

Components found to be dimensionally inaccurate, or damaged in any way MUST be scrapped and NO ATTEMPT made to straighten and re-use.

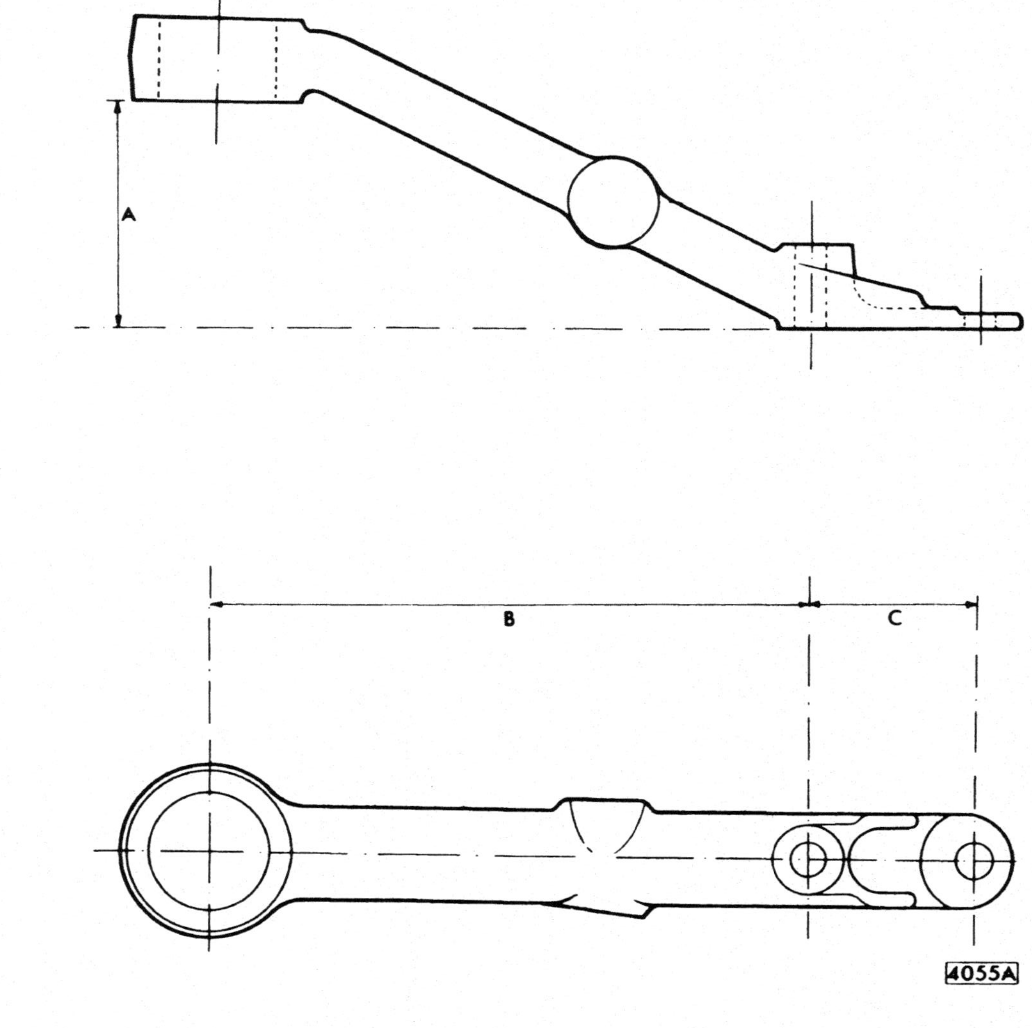

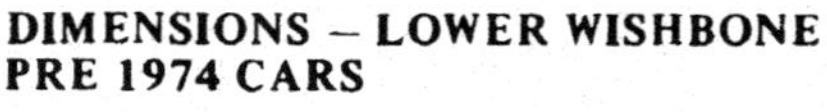

DIMENSIONS – LOWER WISHBONE – PRE 1974 CARS

A. 14.0 in. (35,5 cm.)
B. 0.91 in. (23,11 mm.)
C. 1.06 in. (27,0 mm.)
D. 0.84 in. (21,35 mm.)
E. 1.375 in. (34,9 mm.)
F. 8.88 in. (22,57 cm.)
G. 9.625 in. (24,45 cm.) nominal

DIMENSION – UPPER WISHBONE ARM – FRONT – PRE 1974 CARS

A. 2.38 in. (6,04 cm.)
B. 6.36 in. (16,15 cm.)
C. 1.75 in. (4,45 cm.)

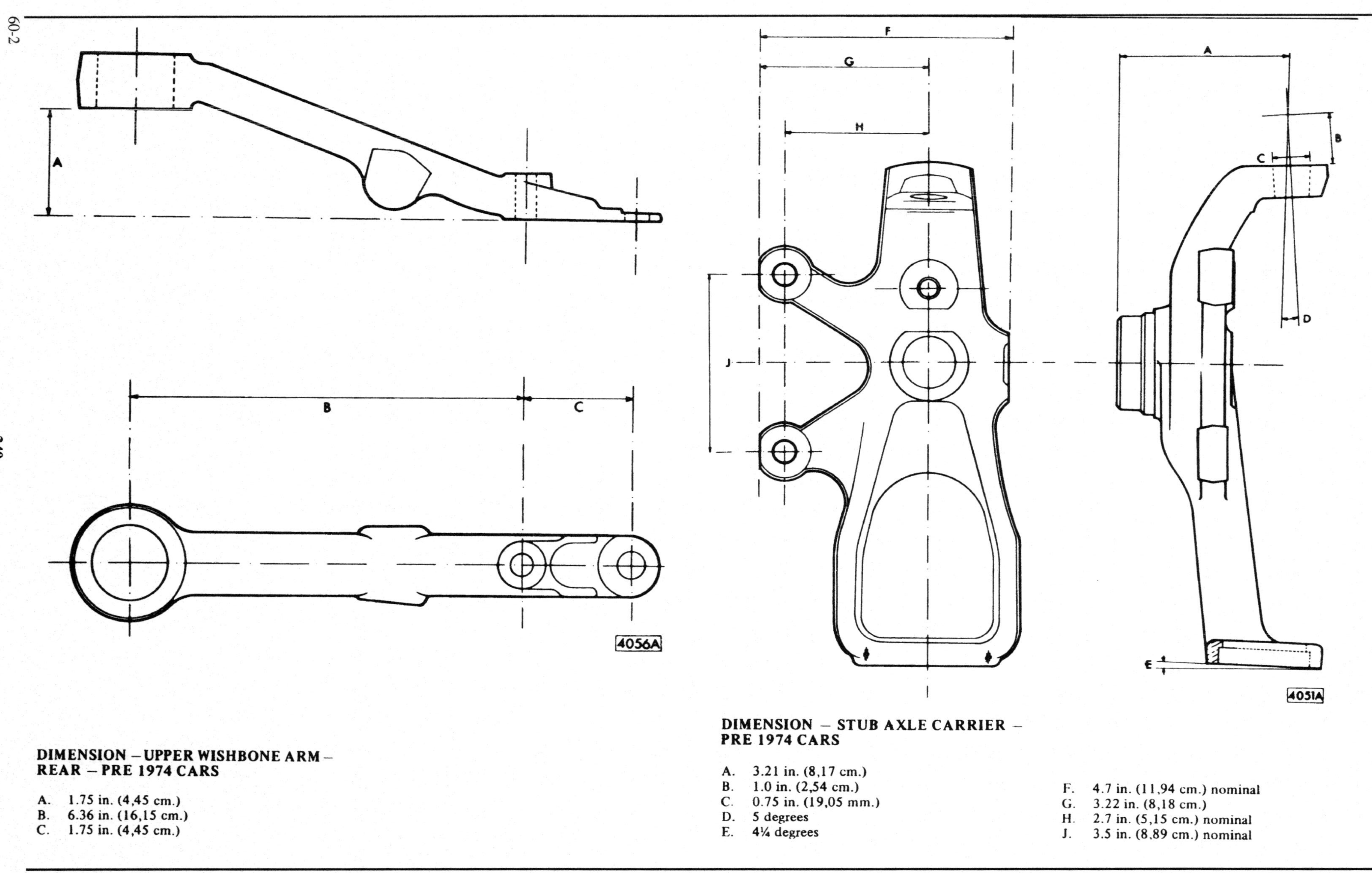

DIMENSION – UPPER WISHBONE ARM – REAR – PRE 1974 CARS

A. 1.75 in. (4,45 cm.)
B. 6.36 in. (16,15 cm.)
C. 1.75 in. (4,45 cm.)

DIMENSION – STUB AXLE CARRIER – PRE 1974 CARS

A. 3.21 in. (8,17 cm.)
B. 1.0 in. (2,54 cm.)
C. 0.75 in. (19,05 mm.)
D. 5 degrees
E. 4¼ degrees
F. 4.7 in. (11,94 cm.) nominal
G. 3.22 in. (8,18 cm.)
H. 2.7 in. (5,15 cm.) nominal
J. 3.5 in. (8,89 cm.) nominal

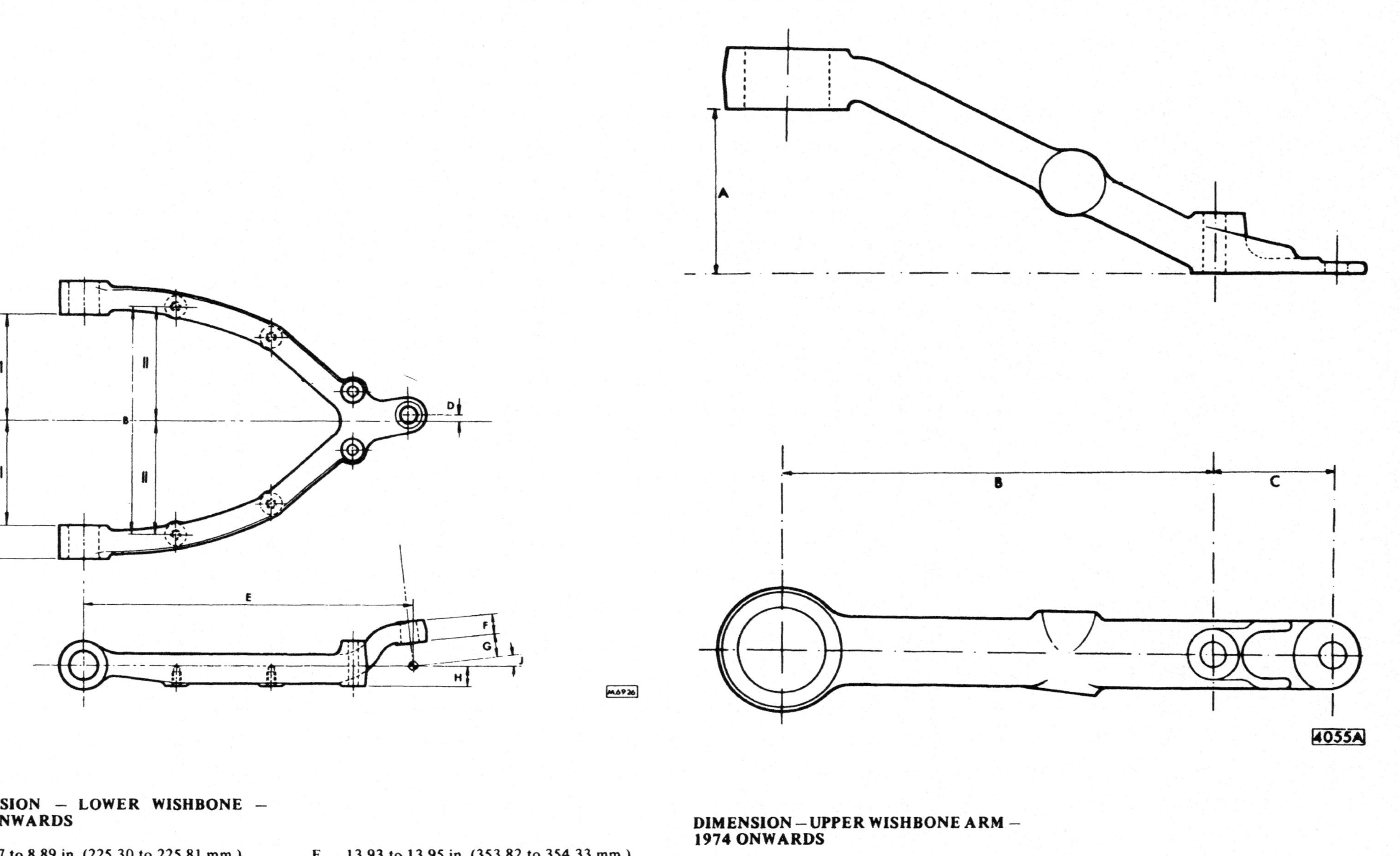

DIMENSION – LOWER WISHBONE – 1974 ONWARDS

A. 8.87 to 8.89 in. (225,30 to 225,81 mm.)
B. 9,62 to 9.63 in. (244,35 to 244,60 mm.)
C. 1.365 to 1.385 in. (34,67 to 35,18 mm.)
D. 0.23 to 0.25 in. (5,84 to 6,35 mm.)
E. 13.93 to 13.95 in. (353,82 to 354,33 mm.)
F. 0.90 to 0.92 in. (22,86 to 23,37 mm.)
G. 1.05 to 1.07 in. (26,67 to 27,18 mm.)
H. 0.83 to 0.85 in. (21,08 to 21,59 mm.)

DIMENSION – UPPER WISHBONE ARM – 1974 ONWARDS

A. 2.10 in. (5,3 cm.)
B. 6.30 in. (16,0 cm.)
C. 1.75 in. (4,45 cm.)

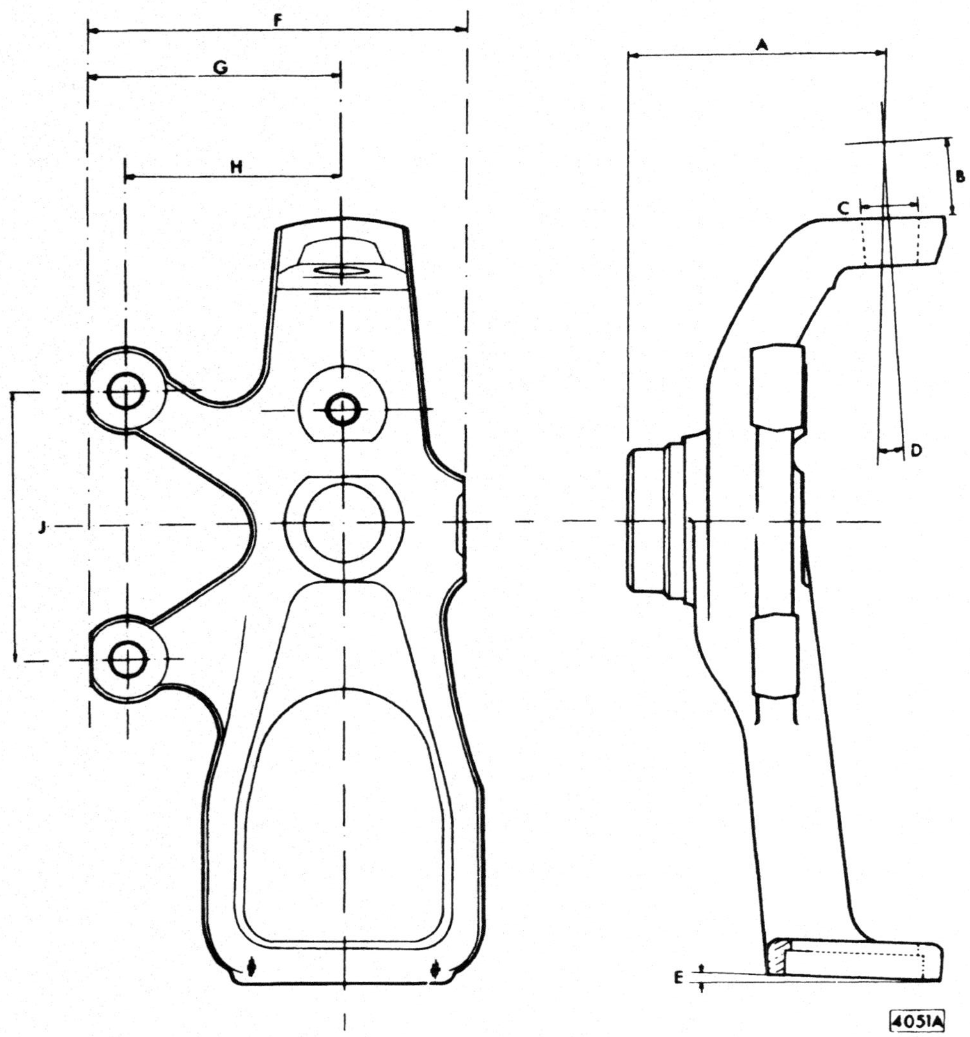

DIMENSION – STUB AXLE CARRIER – 1974 ONWARDS

A. 3.21 in. (8,17 cm.)
B. 1.0 in. (2,54 cm.)
C. 0.75 in. (19,05 mm.)
D. 5 degrees
E. 2 degrees
F. 4.48 in. (113,9 mm.) nominal
G. 2.80 in. (5,1 cm.)
H. 2.33 in. (5,92 cm.) nominal
J. 3.5 in. (8,89 cm.) nominal

ANTI-ROLL BAR

Remove and refit 60.10.01

Removing

1 Jack up front of car and rest on stands.
2 Remove both front wheels.
3 Remove self locking nut, special washer and rubber pad securing each end of anti-roll to anti-roll bar links.
4 Remove four self locking nuts and setscrews securing keeper plates to sub frame members.
5 Detach anti-roll bar and recover split bushes.
6 Remove nut and release one steering tie-rod ball joint.
7 Manoeuvre anti-roll bar clear of car.

Refitting

NOTE: Fitting of bushes will be greatly facilitated if a proprietary rubber lubricant or a solution of twelve parts water to one part of liquid soap is used.

8 Manoeuvre anti-roll bar into position across car.
9 Lubricate bushes and position them on anti-roll bar adjacent to keeper plate locations, split towards rear of car.
10 Fit keeper plates and loosely secure to subframe using four setscrews – from top – and four self locking nuts.
CAUTION: All nuts and setscrews must be tightened with full weight of car on suspension; premature failure of rubber bushes may occur if this precaution is not taken.
11 Ensure spacer tube fitted on anti-roll bar link and locate anti-roll bar on link at both sides of car.
12 Fit rubber pads, special washers and self locking nuts to anti-roll bar links.
13 Refit tie rod ball joint.
14 Fit wheel and lower car.
15 With weight of car on road wheels, fully tighten all fastenings.

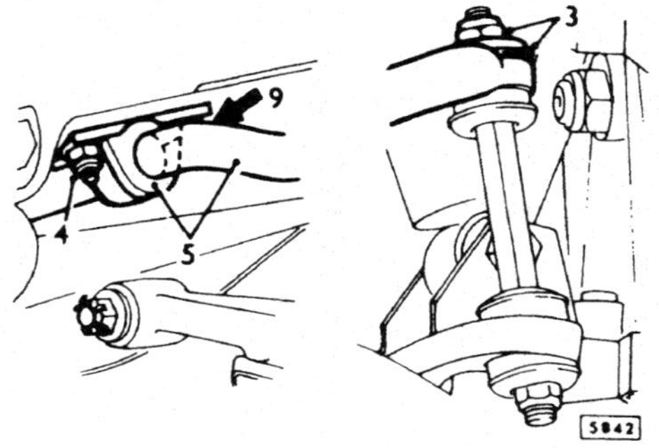

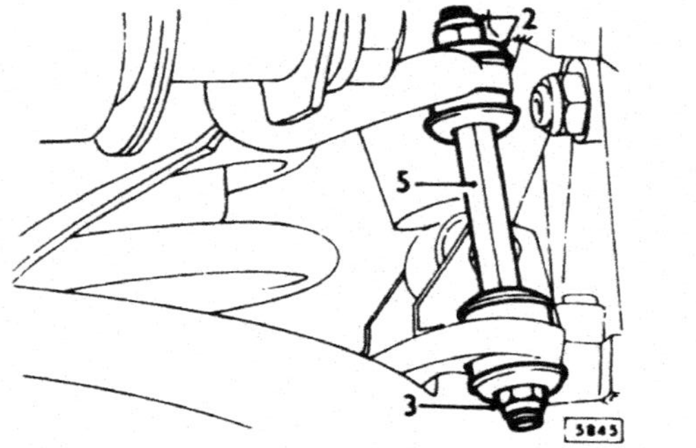

ANTI-ROLL BAR LINK

Remove and refit **60.10.02**

Removing
1 Jack up front of car and rest on stands.
2 Remove self locking nut, special washer and rubber pad securing end of anti-roll bar to anti-roll bar link.
3 Remove self locking nut, special washer and rubber pad securing anti-roll bar link to anti-roll bar support bracket.
4 Release upper nut on link at opposite end of anti-roll bar.
5 Lift link clear and recover two spacer tubes, two rubber pads and special washers.

Refitting
6 Check condition of rubber pads, renew if damaged in any way.
7 Reverse operations 2 to 4 inclusive, but do not fully tighten nuts.
8 Lower car on to wheels.
9 Fully tighten self locking nuts at top and bottom of link, torque 14 to 18 lb.ft. (2,0 to 2,5 kgm.).

ANTI-ROLL BAR LINK BUSHES

Remove and refit **60.10.03**

Removing
1 Remove anti-roll bar links – 60.10.02.

Refitting
2 Renew rubber pads and refit anti-roll bar links.

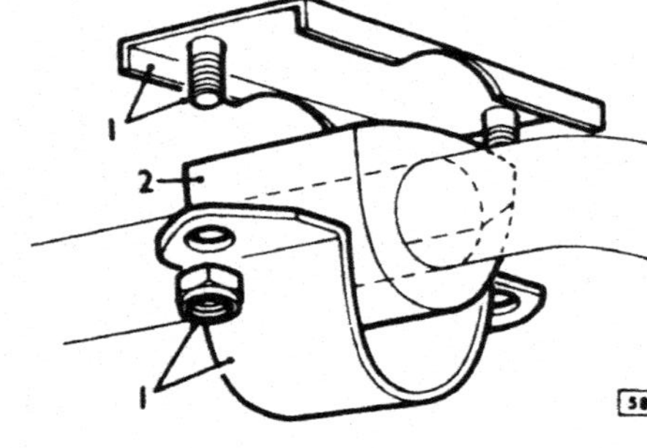

ANTI-ROLL BAR RUBBERS

Remove and refit **60.10.04**

Removing
1 Remove nuts and setscrews securing anti-roll bar brackets to chassis members and remove keeper plates.
2 Remove rubbers from around anti-roll bar.

Refitting
NOTE: Fitting of bushes will be greatly facilitated if a proprietary rubber lubricant or a solution of twelve parts water to one part of liquid soap is used.

3 Reverse operations 1 and 2 ensuring that each rubber protrudes an equal amount each side of its respective keeper plate, the split in rubbers must face to rear of car.
CAUTION: All nuts and setscrews must be tightened with full weight of car on the suspension; premature failure of rubber bushes may occur if this precaution is not taken.

FRONT SUSPENSION RIDING HEIGHT

Check and Adjust **60.10.18**

1 Check that car is full of petrol, oil and water, and that tyre pressures are correctly adjusted.
2 Position car with front wheels on slip plates.
3 Press downwards on front bumper to depress car and slowly release. Lift front bumper and slowly release.
4 Measure distance between centre of outer headlight and ground at both sides of car area. Obtain values for dimension 'A', right and left hand. Correct height is 24 5/8 in. (611 mm.) minimum.
5 If necessary, fit or remove packing rings beneath springs to achieve this dimension; see operation 60.20.01. Packing rings are 1/8 in. (3,18 mm.) thick, and vary the riding height by 5/16 in. (7,93 mm.).

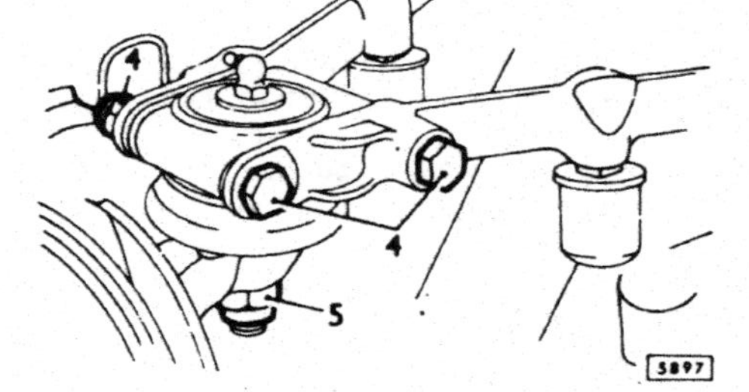

BALL JOINT – UPPER

Remove and refit **60.15.02**

Service tool: Steering joint taper separator JD.24.

The upper wishbone ball joint cannot be dismantled and if worn, the complete assembly must be replaced.

Removing
1 Jack up car beneath lower wishbone.
2 Remove road wheel.
3 Tie stub axle carrier to cross member turret to prevent strain on front brake caliper hose.
4 Remove two nuts, bolts and plain washers securing ball joint to upper wishbone levers.
NOTE: Take careful note of fitted positions of bolts and also positions of packing piece and shims; these control castor angle.
5 Remove self locking nut and plain washer securing ball joint to stub axle carrier.
6 Use taper separator tool JD.24 to extract ball joint from stub axle carrier.

Refitting
CAUTION: Bolts securing upper ball joints in upper wishbone must be fitted from front of car towards rear.
7 Reverse operations 1 to 6 inclusive, ensuring that packing piece and shims are positioned as noted in operation 4. Fit ball joint to stub axle carrier before securing to wishbone.
8 **Check castor angle** – 57.65.04.
9 **Check camber angle** – 57.65.05.
10 **Check front wheel alignment** – 57.65.07.

BALL JOINT LOWER

Service tool: Steering joint taper separator JD.24.

Adjust **60.15.04**

1 Jack up front of car and place on stands.
2 Remove front wheel/s.
3 Place jack beneath front spring seat pan and raise sufficient to relieve stub axle carrier of spring pressure.
4 Remove self locking nut and washer securing steering tie rod ball joint. Separate tie rod from steering arm using service tool JD.24.
5 Lift hub and stub axle carrier assembly to reveal any free play in lower ball joint.
6 Bend back tab washers, remove four screws securing ball pin cap to stub axle carrier.
7 Detach ball pin cap, shims and socket from stub axle carrier.
8 Clean and examine all parts for wear. **CAUTION: In order to obtain correct adjustment of ball joint it is necessary to shim to correct clearance. Excessive wear on ball pin and sockets must not be adjusted by shims. Worn parts must be renewed.**
9 Remove shims one by one until ball pin is tight in its socket with screws fully tightened. **NOTE**: Shims are available in .002 in. (,05 mm.) and .004 in. (,10 mm.) thicknesses.
10 Remove screws, ball pin cap, shims and socket. Add shims to the value of .004 in. to .006 in. (,10 mm. to ,15 mm.).
11 Lightly grease ball pin and socket. Refit socket ball pin cap and new tab washers. Refit and tighten screws; torque to 15 to 20 lbs.ft. (2,1 to 2,75 kgm.).
12 When correctly adjusted, hub and stub axle carrier can be pivoted with a very slight drag.
13 Turn up tab washers and charge joint with correct grease.
14 Reverse operations 1 to 4 inclusive.

BALL JOINT – LOWER

Overhaul **60.15.13**

Service tool. Steering joint taper separator JD.24.

Removing
1 Jack up front of car and place stand beneath spring seat pan. Lower car to firmly locate on stand.
2 Remove road wheel.
3 Remove self locking nut and washer securing steering tie rod ball joint. Separate rod from steering arm using service tool JD.24.
4 Disconnect flexible brake hose, and immediately plug to prevent ingress of dirt and loss of fluid.
5 Remove two nuts, bolts and plain washers securing upper ball joint to upper wishbone levers. **NOTE**: Take careful note of fitted position of bolts and also position of packing piece and shims; these control castor angle.
6 Support hub and stub axle carrier assembly and using service tool JD.24 separate upper ball joint from upper wishbone.
7 Remove self locking nut and washer and using service tool JD.24 separate lower ball joint from wishbone, draw assembly from car.
8 Remove retaining ring and withdraw rubber gaiter.
9 Withdraw retainer from top of ball pin.
10 Tap back tab washers and unscrew four setscrews securing ball pin cap to stub axle carrier.
11 Remove cap, shims, lower ball pin socket, ball pin and spigot.

Overhaul
12 Clean and inspect all components. **CAUTION: In order to obtain correct adjustment of ball joint it is necessary to shim to correct clearance. Excessive wear on ball pin and sockets must not be adjusted by shims. Worn parts must be renewed.**

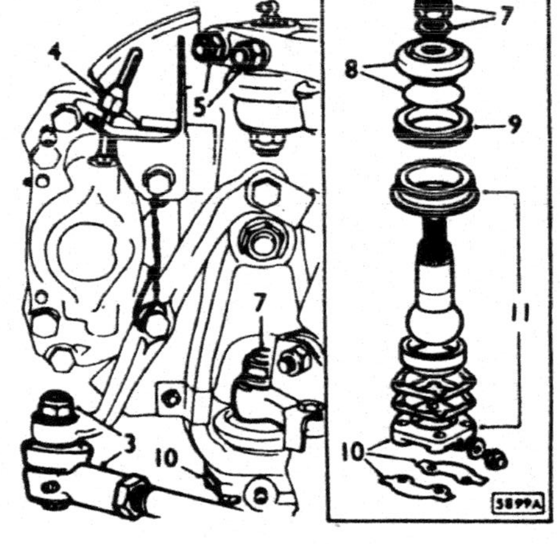

13 Fit spigot, ball pin, socket, shims, ball pin cap and screws. Remove shims one by one until the ball pin is tight in its socket with screws fully tightened.
14 Remove screws, ball pin cap, shims and socket. Add shims to the value of .004 in. to .006 in. (,10 mm. to ,15 mm.).
15 Lightly grease ball pin and socket. Refit socket, ball pin cap and new tab washers. Refit and tighten screws. Ball pin should now be slightly stiff in socket.

Refitting
CAUTION: Bolts securing upper ball joint in upper wishbone must be fitted from front of car towards rear.
16 Reverse operations 1 to 9 inclusive, fitting upper ball joint to stub axle carrier before securing to wishbone. Tighten ball joint nut to 45 to 55 lbf.ft. (6,23 to 7,60 kgf.m.), and upper ball joint to wishbone bolts and nuts to 26 to 32 lbf.ft. (3,60 to 4,42 kgf.m.).
17 Bleed brakes – 70.25.02.
18 Check front wheel alignment – 57.65.01.
19 Check castor angle – 57.65.04.
20 Check camber angle – 57.65.05.

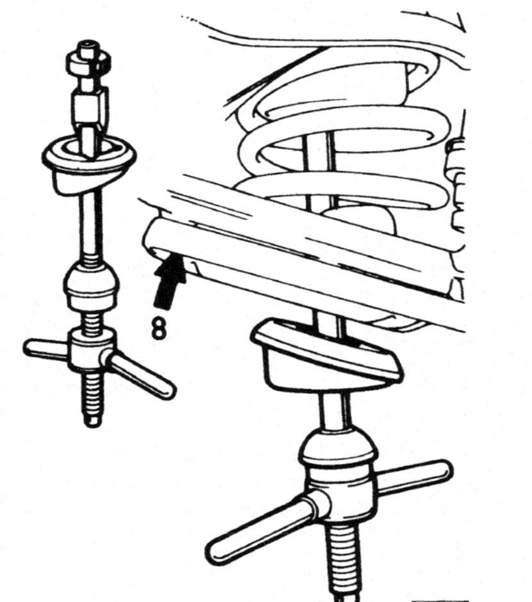

FRONT SPRING

Remove and refit 60.20.01

Service tools: Spring compressor tool JD.6F, or JD.6D and adaptor JD.6D-1 with spring locating pegs JD.6E-6.

Removing

1 Jack up front of car and place on stand.
2 Remove road wheel.
3 Fit spring compressor tool JD.6D with adaptor JD.6D-1 and compress spring sufficiently to relieve load on seat pan fastening.
4 Remove four setscrews and washers and two nuts, bolts and washers securing spring seat pan to lower wishbone.
5 Slacken spring compressor tool and remove, together with seat pan, spring and spacers.
NOTE: Record position of packers to assist during replacement.

Refitting

6 Remove handle nut and adaptors from spring compressor and offer threaded bar up through spring turret. Secure at top end.
7 Assemble spring, packing and seat pan as noted in operation 5, and lift up into spring turret, retain with handle nut and adaptors of spring compressor.

WARNING: A MAXIMUM OF THREE PACKERS MAY BE FITTED IN THE SPRING PAN AND TWO PACKERS ON THE CROSS MEMBER.

8 Fit pilot bolts to holes nearest centre line of car on forward and rear limbs of wishbone or insert locating pegs JD.6E-6 in two tapped holes.
NOTE: A jack may be used beneath lower ball joint to assist with location of spring pan on pilot bolts.
9 Compress spring, locating seat pan on pilot bolts, and tighten until setscrews and nuts, bolts and washers can be fitted in outer location.
10 Remove pilot bolts and fit two setscrews and washers.
11 Remove spring compressor.
12 Fit road wheel and remove stands.
13 Check front suspension riding height – 60.10.18.

WARNING: A MAXIMUM OF THREE PACKERS MAY BE FITTED IN THE SPRING PAN AND TWO PACKERS ON THE CROSS MEMBER.

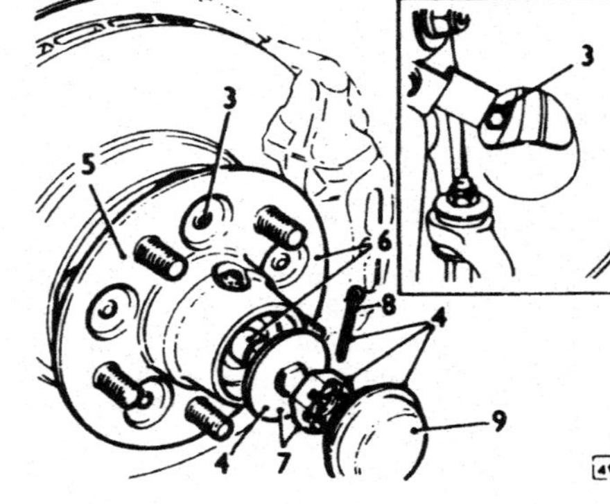

FRONT HUB ASSEMBLY

Remove and refit 60.25.01

Removing

1 Jack up front of car and place on stands.
2 Remove road wheel.
3 Through aperture in disc shield remove five bolts and washers holding hub assembly to brake disc.
4 Remove hub grease cap, extract split pin, and remove nut and washer from stub axle.
5 Withdraw hub by hand.

Refitting

6 Pack hub with specified grease and refit to stub axle.
7 Fit bearing, nut and washer to stub axle and tighten nut to give endfloat of .002 in. to .006 in. (0,05 mm. to 0,15 mm.).
NOTE: End float is measured by fitting a dial test indicator with the button against the hub.
8 Fit new split pin.
9 Refit grease cap. Ensure that vent hole in grease cap is clear.
10 Reverse operations 1 to 3 inclusive.

FRONT HUB BEARINGS

Remove and refit 60.25.14

Removing

1 Remove front hub assembly – 60.25.01, operations 1 to 5.
2 Extract grease seal.
3 Withdraw inner bearing race.
4 Drift bearing cups from hub, grooves are provided in the abutment shoulders for this purpose.

Refitting

5 Tap replacement cups into position, ensuring that they are seated square to abutments.
6 Lubricate large bearing race and fit to cup.
7 Fit grease seal.
8 Fit front hub assembly 60.25.01, operations 6 to 10.

FRONT HUB GREASE SEAL

Remove and refit 60.25.15

Removing

1 Remove front hub assembly – 60.25.01, operations 1 to 5.
2 Extract grease seal.

Refitting

Reverse operations 1 and 2, using suitable 'bell-piece' and tapping seal squarely into position.

FRONT HUB STUB AXLE

Remove and refit **60.25.22**

Service tool: Steering joint taper separator JD.24.

Removing

1 Jack up front of car and place stand beneath spring seat pan. Lower car to firmly locate on stand.
2 Remove road wheel.
3 Remove self-locking nut and washer securing steering tie rod ball joint. Separate rod from steering arm using tool JD.24.
4 Disconnect flexible brake hose from caliper and immediately plug hose to prevent ingress of dirt and loss of fluid.
5 Remove two nuts, bolts and plain washers securing upper ball joint to upper wishbone levers.
NOTE: Take careful note of fitted position of bolts and also position of packing piece and shims; these control castor angle.
6 Remove self-locking nut and washer and separate lower ball joint from wishbone; draw assembly from car.
7 Break locking wire and remove two bolts and spring washers securing steering arm and brake caliper to stub axle carrier.
NOTE: Record number of shims fitted between steering arm and brake caliper. Recover large plain washer from between disc shield and caliper.
8 Draw brake caliper from stub axle carrier.
9 Remove grease cap, split pin and castellated nut securing hub assembly to stub axle; draw assembly clear.
10 Remove nyloc nut and plain washer securing stub axle to stub axle carrier.
11 Support stub axle carrier and drift out stub axle.

Refitting

CAUTION: Bolts securing upper ball joint in upper wishbone must be fitted from front of car towards rear.

12 Reverse operations 1 to 11, fitting shims removed in operation 7 between steering arm and brake caliper.

Torque bolts to:
Stub axle nut 80 to 90 lbs.ft. (11,1 to 12,4 kg.m.).
Steering arm 49 to 55 lbs.ft. (6,75 to 7,6 kg.m.).
Brake caliper 50 to 60 lbs.ft. (7,0 to 8,3 kg.m.).

13 Wire lock brake caliper bolts.
14 Bleed brakes – 70.25.02.
15 Check front wheel alignment – 57.65.01.
16 Check castor angle – 56.65.04.
17 Check camber angle – 57.65.05.

NOTE: Stiffer stub axles of increased diameter, and modified carriers to accommodate them, were introduced on 1977 series cars. These parts may be fitted to earlier cars, using existing hubs, but new bearings, etc. Part numbers required are as follows:

Vertical link, R.H.	CAC 1100
Vertical link, L.H.	CAC 1101
Stub axle shaft	CAC 1102
Hub bearing, inner	C 45709
Hub bearing, outer	C 45710
Hub oil seal	C 45711
Special washer	CAC 1099
'Dee' washer	C 45724
Nut retainer	C 45726

FRONT HUB STUB AXLE CARRIER

Remove and refit **60.25.23**

Service tool: Steering joint taper separator JD.24.

Removing

1 Remove front hub stub axle – 60.25.22.
2 Remove two nyloc nuts securing clamps at bottom of disc shields, remove attachment plate and rear disc shield.
3 Remove one bolt, spring and plain washer securing steering arm and forward disc shield.
4 Remove self locking nut and washer and separate upper ball joint from stub axle carrier, using separator JD.24.
5 Remove retaining ring and withdraw rubber gaiter.
6 Withdraw retainer from top of ball pin.
7 Tap back tab washers and unscrew four setscrews securing ball pin cap to stub axle carrier.
8 Remove cap, shims, lower ball pin socket, ball pin and spigot.

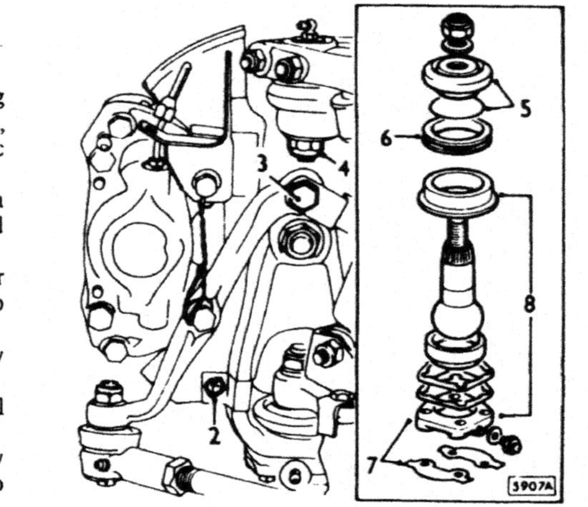

Refitting

CAUTION: In order to obtain correct adjustment of the ball joint it is necessary to shim to the correct clearance. Excessive wear on ball pin and socket must not be adjusted by shims. Worn parts must be renewed.

9 Fit spigot, ball pin, socket, shims, ball pin cap and screws. Remove shims one by one until the ball pin is tight in its socket with screws fully tightened.
10 Remove screws, ball pin cap, shims and socket. Add shims to the value of .004 in. to .006 in. (,10 mm. to ,15 mm.).

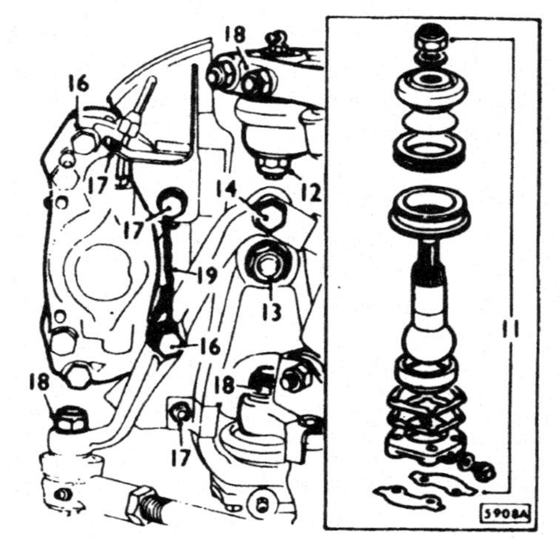
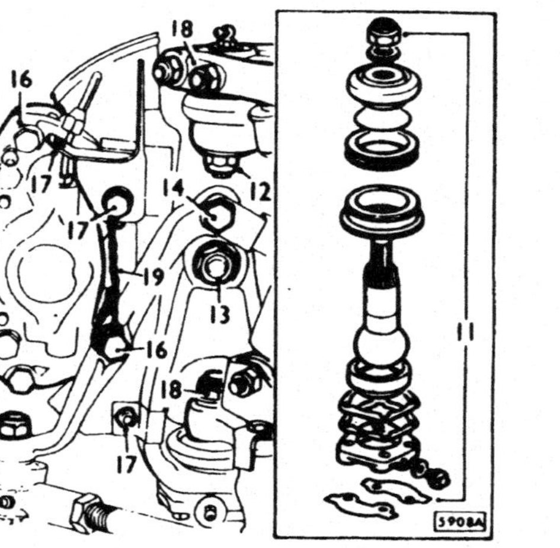

11 Lightly grease ball pin and socket. Refit socket, ball pin cap and new tab washers. Refit and tighten screws. Ball pin should now be slightly stiff in socket.
12 Fit upper ball joint to stub axle carrier and secure using one nyloc nut and washer.
13 Fit stub axle and secure using new nyloc nut and plain washer.
14 Assemble forward end of steering arm to its location and **loosely** secure using one bolt, plain and spring washer.
15 Fit hub to stub axle.
16 Locate brake caliper on stub axle carrier, and secure with long bolt and spring washer through steering arm. Fit shims removed in Operation 7 – 60.25.22, between steering arm and caliper.
17 Locate disc shields and secure using clamps, nyloc nuts and upper caliper bolt. Fit large plain washer between disc shield and caliper, refit flexible brake hose.

Torque bolts to:
Stub axle nut 80 to 90 lb.ft. (11,1 to 12,4 kg.m.).
Steering arm 49 to 55 lb.ft. (6,75 to 7,6 kg.m.).
Brake caliper 50 to 60 lb.ft. (7,0 to 8,3 kg.m.).

18 Fit stub axle carrier to wishbones and steering tie rod.
19 Wire lock brake caliper bolts.
20 Bleed brakes – 70.25.02.
21 Check front wheel alignment – 57.65.01.
22 Check castor angle – 57.65.04.
23 Check camber angle – 57.65.05.

FRONT HUB STUDS

Remove and refit **60.25.29**

Removing
1 Remove front hub – 60.25.01.
2 Using power press and suitable mandrel, press stud/s from hub.

Refitting
3 Use power press and suitable mandrel to press stud/s into hub.
4 Refit front hub – 60.25.01.

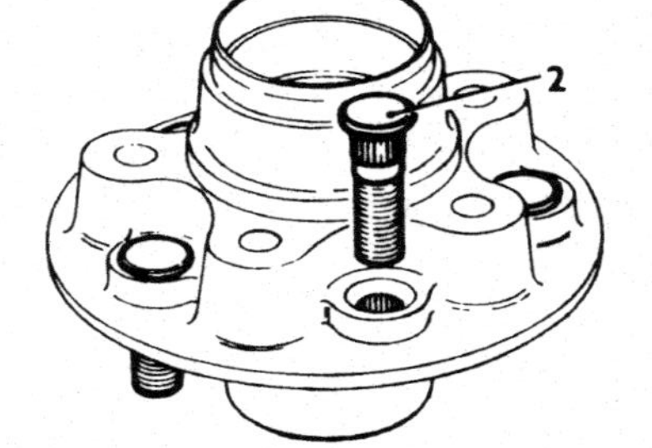

FRONT DAMPER

Remove and refit **60.30.02**

Removing
1 Beneath bonnet, remove locknut, nut, outer washer, buffer and inner washer from damper front mounting.
2 Jack up front of car and place on stands.
3 Remove road wheel.
4 Remove self locking nut and bolt from bottom mounting.
5 Draw damper from car.

Refitting
Reverse operations 1 to 5 inclusive.

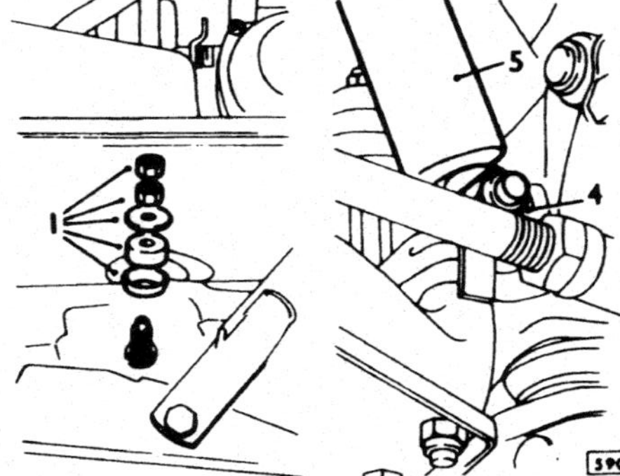

BUMP STOP

Remove and refit **60.30.10**

Removing
1 Jack up front of car and place on stands.
2 Remove road wheel.
3 Remove two plain nuts and spring washers securing bump stop.
4 Manoeuvre bump stop clear through coils of spring, prising coils carefully apart with bar if necessary.

Refitting
Reverse operations 1 to 4 inclusive.

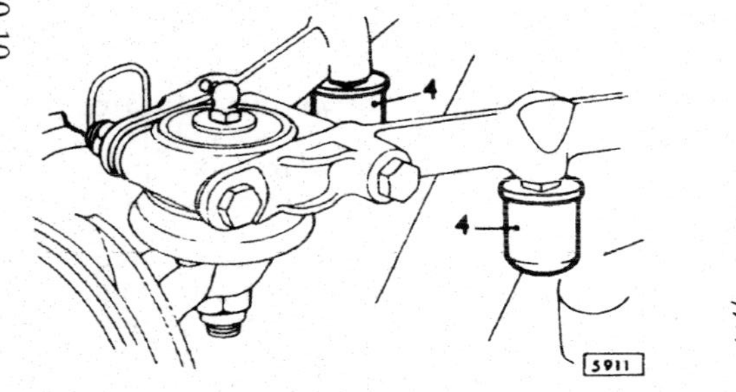

REBOUND STOPS

Remove and refit **60.30.14**

NOTE: Rebound stops must only be replaced as a pair; uneven loads will be placed on upper wishbone if this is not done.

Removing
1 Jack up front of car and place stand beneath spring seat pan.
2 Lower car on to stand.
3 Remove road wheel.
4 Unscrew rebound stops from upper wishbone.

Refitting
Reverse operations 1 to 4 inclusive, tightening stops to 8 to 10 lbf.ft. (1,11 to 1,38 kgf.m.).

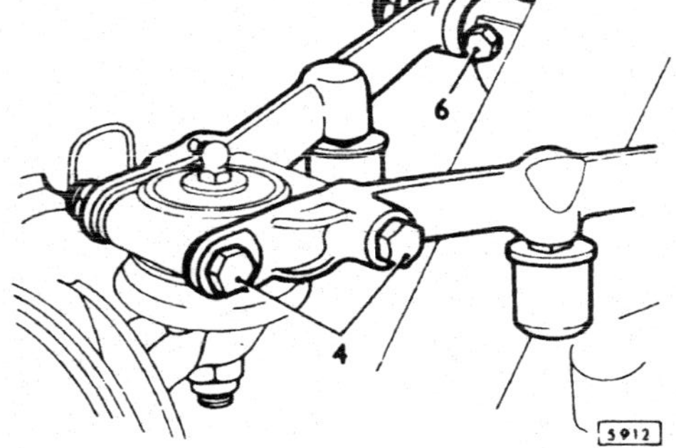

WISHBONE – UPPER

Remove and refit **60.35.01**

Removing
1 Jack up front of car and place stand beneath spring seat pan.
2 Lower car on to stand.
3 Remove road wheel.
4 Remove two nuts, bolts and plain washers securing upper ball joint to upper wishbone levers.
NOTE: Take careful note of fitted position of bolts and also position of packing piece and shims, these control castor angle.
5 Tie stub axle carrier to road spring turret to prevent damage to brake flexible hose.
6 Remove two bolts, special washers and nyloc nuts securing upper wishbone fulcrum shaft to road spring turret.
NOTE: Take careful note of position of shims as these control camber angle.
7 Manoeuvre wishbone assembly clear of damper unit.

Refitting
8 Reverse operations 1 to 7 inclusive. No washers are fitted under nuts of fulcrum shaft bolts; tighten these nuts to 49 to 55 lbf.ft. (6,78 to 7,60 kgf.m.) and tighten nuts removed in operation 4 to 26 to 32 lbf.ft. (3,60 to 4,42 kgf.m.).
9 Check front wheel alignment – 57.65.01.
10 Check castor angle – 57.65.04.
11 Check camber angle – 57.65.05.

WISHBONE – LOWER

Remove and refit **60.35.02**

Service tools. Steering joint taper separator JD.24. Spring compressor tool JD.6D and adaptor JD.6D-1. Spring plate locating pegs JD.6E-6.

Removing
1 Remove front suspension unit 60.35.05. Invert unit.
2 Remove self locking nut and washer securing steering tie rod ball joint. Separate rod from steering arm using tool JD.24.
3 Remove three bolts, nuts and washers securing steering rack to front suspension cross member.
4 Remove front spring – 60.20.01.
5 Remove two nuts, bolts and plain washers securing upper ball joint to upper wishbone levers.
NOTE: Take careful note of fitted position of bolts and also position of packing piece and shims; these control castor angle.
6 Remove self locking nut and washer, and separate lower ball joint from wishbone. Recover anti-roll bar support bracket and damper unit mounting.
7 Remove split pin at fulcrum shaft nut and remove nut and plain washer.
8 Drift fulcrum shaft from cross member and recover two washers.

Refitting
9 Reverse operations 1 to 8 inclusive.
CAUTION: Do not fully tighten fulcrum shaft nut until full weight of car is on suspension.
10 Fully tighten fulcrum shaft nut to 32 to 50 lbf.ft (4,43 to 6,91 kgf.m.) and fit new split pin.
11 Check front wheel alignment – 57.65.01.
12 Check castor angle – 57.65.04.
13 Check camber angle – 57.65.05.

FRONT SUSPENSION

Remove and refit 60.35.05

Service tools: Engine support bracket MS.53.

Removing

1 Disconnect battery earth lead – 86.15.20.
2 Remove air cleaners – 19.10.01.
3 Remove locknut, nut, plain washer, rubber and cup securing upper end of each shock absorber.
4 Using a suitable syringe, drain oil from power assisted steering pump; discard oil and replace cap on reservoir.
5 Disconnect inlet and outlet hoses from power assisted steering pump; plug or tape connections to prevent ingress of dirt.
6 Remove nuts securing engine mountings to mounting brackets.
7 Remove nuts securing crossbeam rear mountings.
8 Remove self locking nut securing each anti-roll bar link to anti-roll bar, withdraw cup washers and rubbers.
9 Turn steering wheel until lower steering column universal joint pinch bolt is accessible.
10 Remove self locking nut and pinch bolt.
11 Turn steering wheel until road wheels are in straight ahead position.
12 Disconnect wiring harness from horns. Remove setscrews securing earthing strap.
13 Release harness from retaining clips.
14 Remove self locking nuts and plain washers from front pivot bolts.

WARNING: DO NOT ATTEMPT TO REMOVE FRONT PIVOT BOLTS AT THIS STAGE.

15 In driver's footwell, slacken both upper steering column universal joint pinch bolts.
CAUTION: Do not turn steering wheel after slackening pinch bolts.
16 Slide lower steering column universal joint off pinion housing splines.
17 Remove front wheel nave plates and slacken wheel securing nuts.
18 Fit engine support bracket MS.53(A) to engine front lifting eyes. Adjust links until engine is just supported.
19 Position gear selector lever in 'P' and apply handbrake.
20 Locate trolley jack beneath centre of front suspension crossbeam and raise car.
21 Support car on suitable stands; DO NOT lower jack.

WARNING: STANDS SHOULD BE POSITIONED UNDER FRONT JACKING POINTS: ENSURE CAR IS SAFELY SUPPORTED.

22 Remove front wheels.
23 Disconnect brake flexible hose from each caliper; plug or tape connections to prevent ingress of dirt.
24 Ensure that brake hoses are clear of suspension.
25 Withdraw front pivot bolts noting fitted positions of washers.
26 Carefully lower jack ensuring that suspension assembly remains correctly located on support tool.
NOTE: If further attention is required to suspension unit, transfer to work bench by using adequate lifting tackle. Do not attempt to place in position by hand.

Refitting

27 Position suspension assembly on trolley jack.
28 Raise jack, ensure that shock absorber, rear mounting and engine mounting studs are correctly located.
29 Fit front pivot bolts, washers and nuts; DO NOT tighten nuts at this stage.
30 Fit suspension rear mounting and engine mounting securing nuts and washers; DO NOT tighten nuts at this stage.
31 Reconnect brake flexible hoses to calipers.

WARNING: ENSURE PIPES ARE ROUTED CORRECTLY AND ARE NOT KINKED, TWISTED OR DAMAGED. SUSPECT PIPES MUST BE RENEWED.

continued

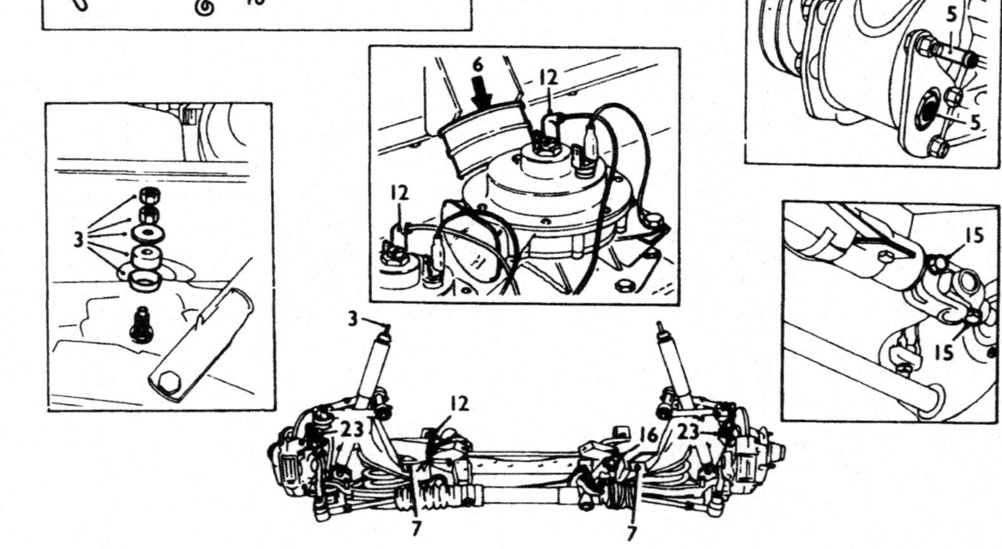

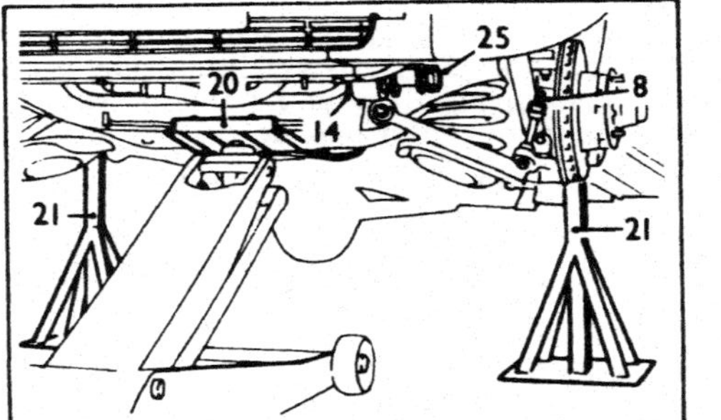

32 Fit cup, rubber, plain washer and nut to upper end of each shock absorber; **DO NOT tighten nuts or fit locknuts at this stage.**
33 Remove engine support bracket.
34 Refit road wheels.
35 Remove stands; lower car.
36 Tighten wheel securing nuts; refit nave plates.
37 Tighten shock absorber securing nuts; fit locknuts and tighten nuts to 27 to 32 lbf.ft. (3,74 to 4,42 kgf.m.)
38 Fit lower steering column universal joint on pinion housing splines.
39 Refit lower steering column universal joint pinch bolt and nut. Tighten nut to 14 to 18 lbf.ft. (1,94 to 2,48 kgf.m.).

WARNING: WHEN CARRYING OUT THIS OPERATION, REFER TO 57.40.02, ITEM 16.

40 Ensure road wheels are in straight ahead position and steering wheel boss is in horizontal plane.
41 Tighten upper steering column universal joint pinch bolts to 14 to 18 lbf.ft. (1,94 to 2,48 kgf.m.).
42 Tighten nuts securing front pivot bolts to 95 to 115 lbf.ft. (13,14 to 15,91 kgf.m.).
43 Tighten engine mounting and suspension rear mounting nuts to 14 to 18 lbf.ft. (1,94 to 2,48 kgf.m.).
44 Connect anti-roll bar links to anti-roll bar. Tighten nuts to 14 to 18 lbf.ft. (1,94 to 2,48 kgf.m.).
45 Fit cup washers, rubbers and nuts.
46 Route wiring harness through retaining clips.
47 Connect wiring harness to horns.
48 Reverse operations 1 to 5.

CAUTION: Engine must NOT be started unless steering pump reservoir is filled.

49 Bleed brakes – 70.25.02.
50 Run engine and turn steering from lock to lock several times to bleed power assisted steering system.
51 Check/top up oil level in power assisted steering pump reservoir.
52 Repeat item 50 if necessary.

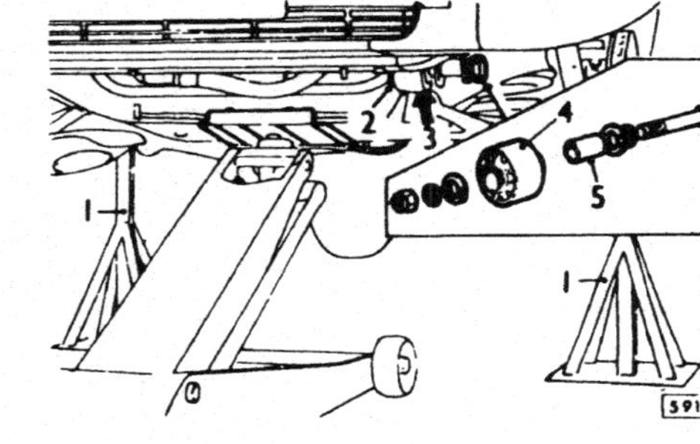

SUSPENSION UNIT MOUNTING BUSH

Remove and refit **60.35.06**

NOTE: A worn or damaged bush infers that undue strain has been thrown upon the apparently satisfactory opposite number. Bushes must therefore be changed as a pair.

Removing
1 Raise front of car and support body on stands.
2 Remove self locking nut securing one mounting bolt and drift bolt clear of bush.
NOTE: Record position of plain and special washers, and securing bracket if fitted.
3 Slacken clamping nut and bolt securing relevant mounting bush eye.
4 Tap mounting bush clear of eye.
5 Remove sleeve from mounting bush.

Refitting
6 Reverse operations 1 to 5 inclusive. Tighten clamping nut to 25 to 30 lbf.ft (3,46 to 4,14 kgf.m.) and main nut to 95 to 115 lbf.ft (13,14 to 15,91 kgf.m.).
7 Repeat operations 1 to 6, inclusive on opposite mounting bush.

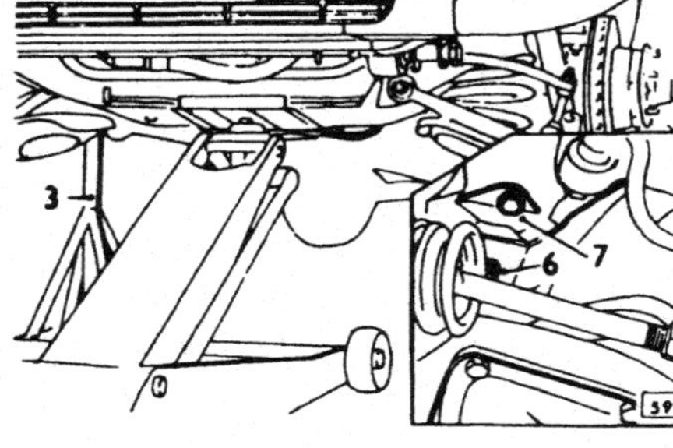

SUSPENSION UNIT MOUNTING – REAR

Remove and refit **60.35.07**

NOTE: A worn or damaged mounting infers that undue strain has been thrown on the apparently satisfactory opposite number. Mountings must therefore be changed as a pair.

Removing
1 Remove front exhaust pipe – 30.10.09.
2 Slacken self locking nuts securing mounting bolts.
3 Raise front of car and support body on stands.
4 Remove both front wheels.
5 Locate trolley jack to support front suspension unit crossbeam.
6 Remove self locking nuts and washers securing suspension unit to mountings.
7 Carefully lower rear of suspension unit sufficient to remove two special setscrews and lockwashers securing each mounting to body sub-frame.

Refitting
NOTE: Mountings are offset.

8 Position mountings and secure to body sub-frame using special setscrews and lockwashers. Tighten to 22 to 26 lbf.ft. (3,04 to 3,59 kgf.m.).
9 Raise rear of suspension unit and secure to mountings using two self locking nuts and plain washers. Tighten to 14 to 18 lbf.ft. (1,94 to 2,48 kgf.m.).
10 Reverse operations 1 to 5 inclusive.

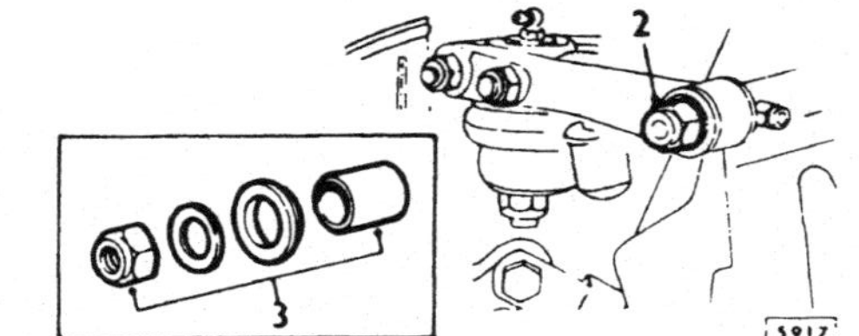

WISHBONE – UPPER

Overhaul **60.35.08**

1 Remove upper wishbone – 60.35.01.

Dismantling
2 Remove self locking nut at each end of fulcrum shaft and recover plain washers and bushes.
3 Using a press and suitable mandrel, remove bushes from wishbone arms.

Reassembling
4 Using a press and suitable mandrel, fit new bushes to wishbone arms. Ensure each bush is central in arm.
CAUTION: New bushes must be coated with Esso Process Oil 'L' before they are pressed in to wishbone arms.
5 Assemble wishbone arms to fulcrum shaft, using new bushes, and retain with plain washers and self locking nuts.
CAUTION: Do not fully tighten at this stage.
6 Fit upper wishbone.
7 Torque to 45 to 55 lb.ft. (6,25 to 7,6 kg.m.).

WISHBONE – LOWER

Overhaul **60.35.09**

1 Remove lower wishbone – 60.35.02, operations 1 to 8.

Dismantling

2 Using a press and suitable mandrel, remove bushes from wishbone arms.

Reassembling

3 Using a press and suitable mandrel fit new bushes to wishbone arms, ensure each bush is central in arm.
CAUTION: New bushes must be coated with Esso Process Oil 'L' before they are pressed in to wishbone arms.

4 Refit lower wishbone – 60.35.02, operations 9 to 13.

Notes

ACCIDENTAL DAMAGE

The dimensional drawing below is provided to assist in assessing accidental damage. A component suspected of being damaged should be removed from the car and cleaned off, the dimensions should then be checked and compared with those given in the illustration.

DIMENSION

A 0.62 to 0.64 in. (15,75 to 16,26 mm.)
B 20.45 to 20.47 in. (519,43 to 519,94 mm.)
C 5.93 to 5.95 in. (150,62 to 151,13 mm.)
D 10.632 to 10.642 in. (270,05 to 270,31 mm.)
E 6.12 to 6.13 in. (155,45 to 155,70 mm.)

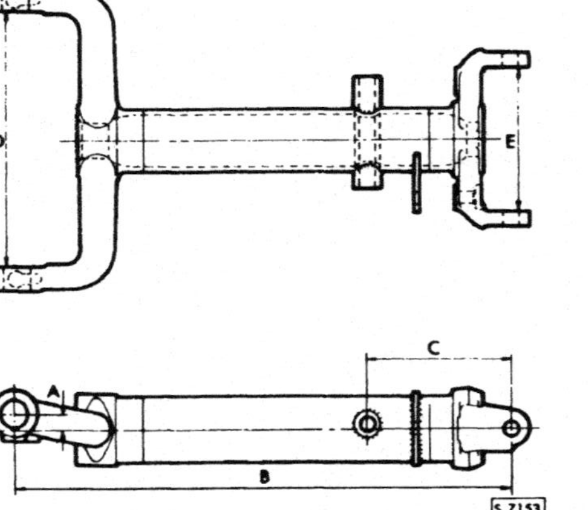

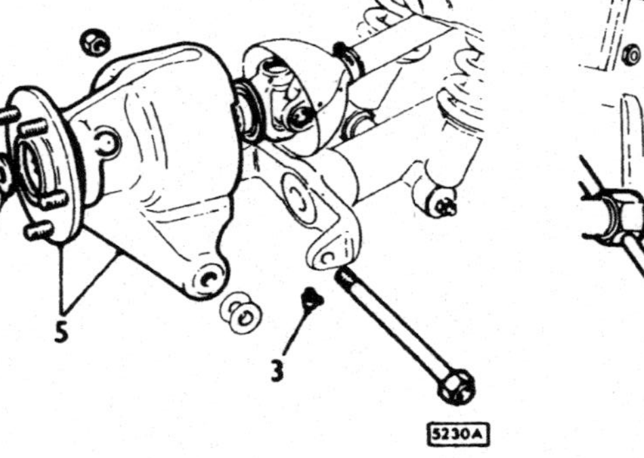

REAR HUB AND CARRIER ASSEMBLY

Remove and refit **64.15.01**

Service tools: Hub puller JD.1D, Dummy shaft JD.14. Thread protector JD.1C/7.

Removing

1 Remove rear road wheel.
2 Place stand under rear of car.
3 Remove fulcrum shaft grease nipple from hub carrier.
4 Withdraw split pin, remove castellated nut and plain washer from splined end of half-shaft and fit thread protector JD.1C/7 over end of shaft.
5 Fit hub puller, JD.1D, to rear hub and secure. Withdraw hub and carrier from half shaft. Remove hub puller from hub and carrier and recover thread protector.
6 Recover spacer from half shaft. Examine inner oil seal track and renew if necessary.
7 Remove one nut from outer wishbone fulcrum shaft and using a hide mallet, drift out shaft. Remove hub and carrier assembly from car. Temporarily secure retaining washers and shims using adhesive tape.

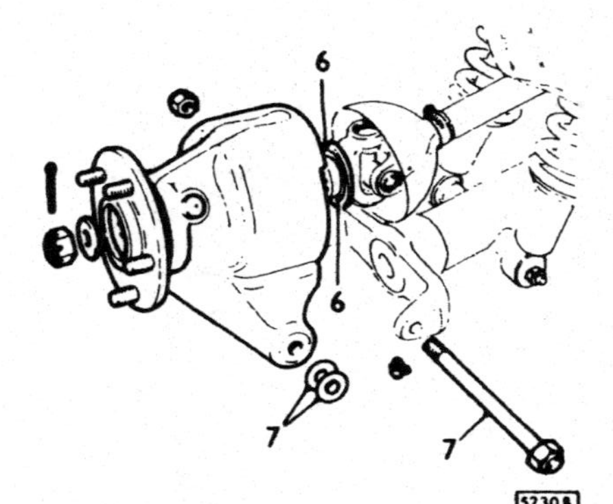

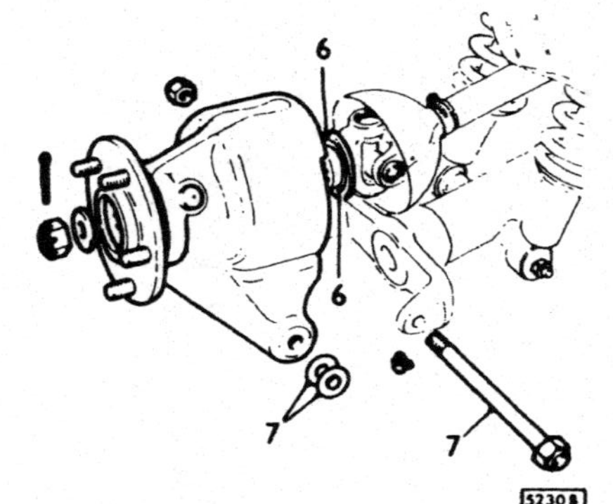

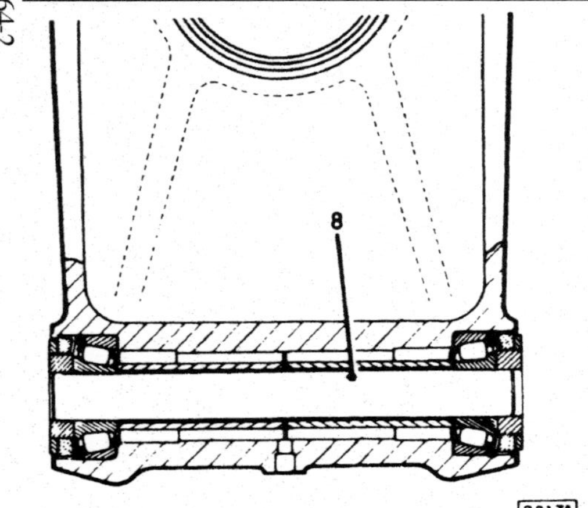

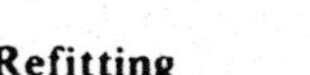

Refitting

8 Fit dummy shaft tool number JD.14 to hub carrier fulcrum.

9 Fit hub carrier to wishbone, positioning shims removed between carrier and wishbone.

10 Replace outer wishbone fulcrum shaft, displacing dummy shaft.

11 Secure shaft with nut. Torque to 97 – 107 lb.ft. (13,4 – 14,8 kg.m.). Refit grease nipple.

12 If necessary fit oil seal track to half shaft splined flange. Refit spacer.

13 Thoroughly clean and de-grease splines of half shaft and bore of hub.

14 Using a small brush sparingly apply Loctite 'Stud Lock' to outer two thirds of half shaft splines.

15 Assemble hub carrier to half shaft.

16 Fit washer and secure hub carrier assembly with castellated nut. Torque to 100 to 120 lb.ft. (13,8 to 16,6 kg.m.). Lock using new split pin.

17 Check, and if necessary, adjust hub bearing end float 64.15.13.

18 Remove stands.

19 Refit road wheel.

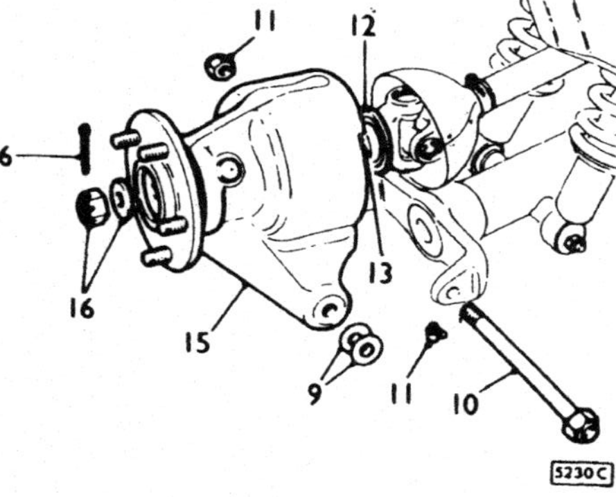

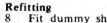

REAR HUB AND CARRIER ASSEMBLY

Overhaul **64.15.07**

Service tools: Master spacer JD.15, Dummy shaft JD.14, Press tool JD.16C, Hand press SL.14, Press tool JD.20A, Tool JD.20A-1, Adaptor JD.16C-1.

Dismantling

1 Remove rear hub and carrier assembly see 64.15.01, operations 1 to 9.

2 Prise out oil seal retainers from fulcrum shaft housing and remove seals, dummy shaft, bearings, distance tubes and shims.

3 Mount hub carrier in vice and drift out bearing cups from fulcrum shaft housing.

4 Transfer hub carrier to press and remove hub assembly from carrier.

5 Drift out inner hub bearing cup, with seal and bearing, from hub carrier.

6 Drift out outer bearing cup.

7 Fit hand press SL.14 with adaptors JD.16C-1 to hub and pull outer bearing from hub.

8 Remove oil seal track from hub shaft and clean and inspect all parts.
NOTE: When inspecting components, pay particular attention to oil seal tracks, when a minute score can considerably shorten oil seal life. For further details on inspection of seals and bearings refer to 'General Fitting Instructions', Group 07.

Reassembling

9 Replace outer oil seal track on hub shaft.

10 Press outer bearing cone into position on hub shaft and grease bearing with 70 cc of Retinax 'A'.

11 Press outer and inner cups of bearings into hub carrier, using tool JD.20A with adaptor JD.20A-1.

12 Drift new outer oil seal into position in hub carrier and lower carrier on to hub shaft and outer bearing.

13 Place inner bearing into position for fitting.

14 Place master spacer JD.15 in position as shown and press bearing on to hub shaft.

15 Transfer hub and carrier assembly to vice, set up dial gauge and spacer JD.15 as shown and measure end float, lifting carrier by using two screwdrivers as levers.

16 Select spacer to be fitted on drive shaft.
NOTE: Master spacer has a diameter of length 'A' equivalent to a spacer of 0.15 in. (3,81 mm.). Calculate the spacer required to give end float of .001 to .003 in. (,025 to ,076 mm.). Spacers are supplied in thicknesses of .109 to .151 in. (2,77 to 3,84 mm.) in steps of .003 in. (,076 mm.) and are lettered A to R (less letters I, N and O).

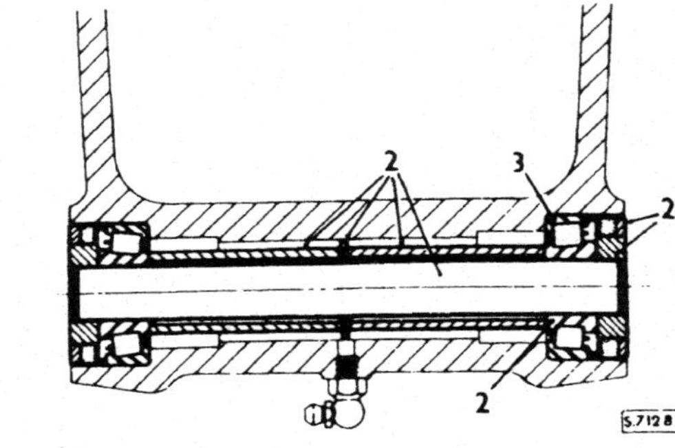

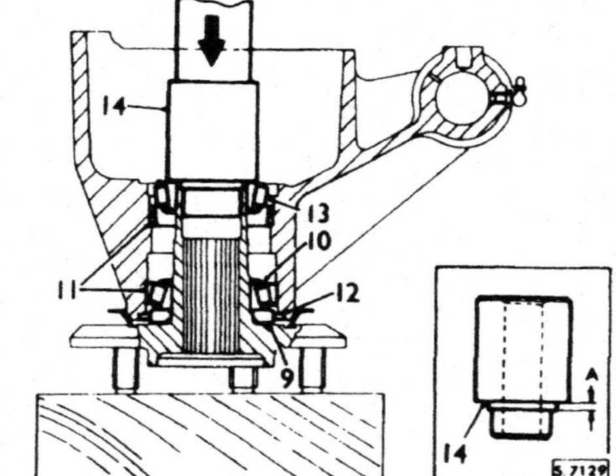

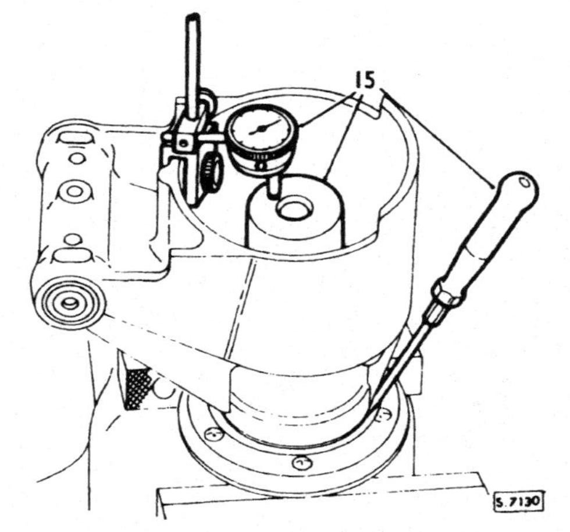

SPACER LETTER	THICKNESS inches	mm
A	0.109	2,77
B	0.112	2,85
C	0.115	2,92
D	0.118	3,00
E	0.121	3,07
F	0.124	3,15
G	0.127	3,23
H	0.130	3,30
J	0.133	3,38
K	0.136	3,45
L	0.139	3,53
M	0.142	3,61
P	0.145	3,68
Q	0.148	3,76
R	0.151	3,84

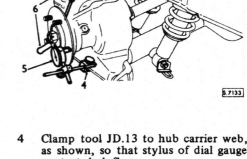

For example, assume end-float to be .026 in. (,66 mm.). Subtract required nominal end float of .002 in. (,050 mm.) from measured end float giving .024 in. (,61 mm.). Since special collar is .150 in. (3,81 mm.) thick, the thickness of the spacer to be fitted will be .150 in.–.024 in., i.e. .126 in. (3,20 mm.). The nearest spacer is .127 in. (3,23 mm.) so letter G spacer should be fitted in place of special collar.

17 Remove adaptor and fit new inner bearing oil seal to hub carrier.
18 Fit fulcrum shaft bearing cups to hub carrier and insert one bearing.
19 Secure fulcrum shaft vertically in suitably protected jaws of vice and slide bearing in hub carrier over shaft.
20 Replace distance tubes and shims as removed in operation 2, adding 0.010 in. (0,25 mm.) extra shims. (One extra 0.003 in. [0,076 mm.] shim and one extra 0.007 in. [0,178 mm.] shim.)
21 Fit second bearing over fulcrum shaft, remove hub assembly from vice and replace oil seal tracks outside bearings.
22 Place a large washer (e.g. inner fork thrust washer) next to one oil seal track.
23 Cover exposed plain length of fulcrum shaft with suitable temporary spacers, fit nuts and tighten to 97 to 107 lbf.ft. (13,4 to 14,8 kgf.m.).
24 Apply pressure to fulcrum shaft at large washer end, turning it to settle

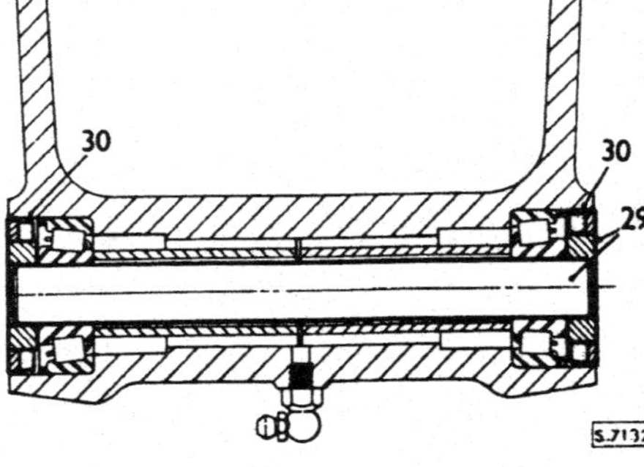
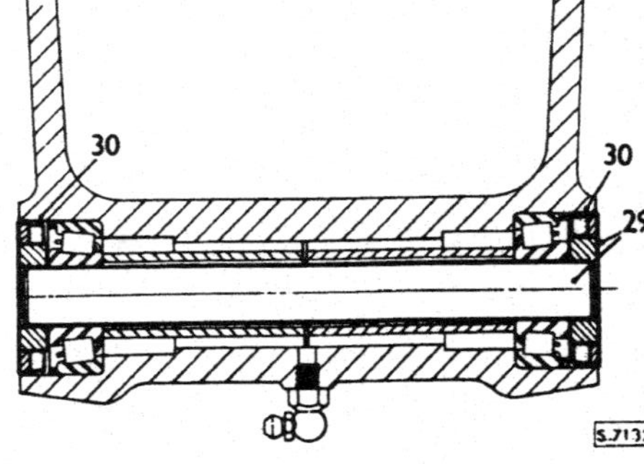

taper rollers and using feeler gauge measure minimum distance between large washer and hub carrier.
25 Apply pressure to opposite end of fulcrum shaft and measure maximum distance between washer and hub carrier.
NOTE: End play of fulcrum shaft in hub carrier is now obtained by subtracting measurement obtained in operation 24 from that in 25. This end play must be replaced by a preload of 0.002 in. (0,05 mm.) by removing shims, to a total thickness of 0.002 in. (0,05 mm.) more than the end play, from between spacer tubes:
For example:
Assume end play found in operation 24 to be .010 in. (,25 mm.).
Therefore shims to the value of
.010 + .002 in. = .012 in.
(,25 + ,05 mm. = ,30 mm.)
must be removed to give correct preload.
26 Release nut from large washer end of fulcrum shaft and detach spacers, washer, oil seal track and bearing.
27 Remove one spacer tube and extract shims to thickness established to give preload.
28 Replace spacer tube, pack fulcrum shaft housing with grease and replace bearing and oil seal track.

S.7132

29 Push out fulcrum shaft by inserting dummy shaft and detach temporary spacers from fulcrum shaft. Check that oil seal tracks are in position.
30 Press new oil seals into fulcrum shaft housings and secure with oil seal retainers.
31 Replace rear hub and carrier assembly, see 64.15.01, operations 10 to 17.

REAR HUB BEARING END-FLOAT

Check and adjust **64.15.13**

NOTE: End float is controlled by a spacer located next to the universal joint on the hub shaft. Spacers are available in thickness from 0.109 in. (2,77 mm.) to 0.151 in. (3,84 mm.) in 0.003 in. (0,076 mm.) steps. End float is normally 0.001 to 0.003 in. (0,026 to 0,076 mm.) and **must** be rectified if it exceeds 0.005 in. (0,127 mm.) by changing the spacer for a thicker one.

Service tools: Hub remover JD.1D. Thread protector JD.1C-7. Backlash gauge JD.13.

Checking
1 Raise car and place on stands.
2 Remove rear road wheel.
3 Tap hub towards car.

S.7133

4 Clamp tool JD.13 to hub carrier web, as shown, so that stylus of dial gauge contacts hub flange.
5 Note reading of dial gauge.
6 Using two levers between hub and hub carrier boss, press hub outwards. Take care not to damage water thrower. Note altered reading on dial gauge.
NOTE: The difference between dial gauge readings in operations 5 and 6 represents end float of hub bearings. If this exceeds 0.005 in. (0,127 mm.) refer to 'Adjust' below. Otherwise proceed with operation 7.
7 Remove clamp tool and dial gauge.
8 Refit wheel.
9 Remove car from stands.

Adjusting
10 Remove split pin, nut and washer from end of drive shaft.
11 Remove fulcrum shaft grease nipple from hub carrier.
12 Place thread protector JD.1C/7 on end of drive shaft.
13 Fit hub puller JD.1D to rear hub and secure. Withdraw hub and carrier from drive shaft and remove hub puller and thread protector.
14 Remove spacer from drive shaft and measure thickness with micrometer.
NOTE: A simple calculation will now give the thickness of spacer required to reduce end float to specified 0.001 to 0.003 in. (0,026 to 0,076 mm.) i.e. If end float measured in operations 5 and 6 was 0.007 in. (0,203 mm.) a replacement spacer will need to be 0.005 in. (0,127 mm) thicker than that removed to reduce end float to .002 in. (0,051 mm.).

continued

As spacers are supplied in 0.003 in. (0,075 mm.) steps of thickness, a spacer 0.006 in. (0,152 mm.) thicker would be used, reducing end-float to 0.001 in. (0,026 mm.).

15 Clean dried 'Loctite' from drive shaft splines.
16 Place selected spacer on drive shaft.
17 Apply Loctite 'Stud Lock' to outer two thirds of drive shaft splines, using a small brush.
18 Enter drive shaft in hub and drift hub on to shaft.
19 Replace washer, tighten nut to 100 to 120 lbf.ft. (13,83 to 16,6 kgf.m.) and fit new split pin.
20 Replace grease nipple.
21 Repeat operations 3 to 6, to re-check end float.
22 Carry out operations 7 to 9.

REAR HUB OIL SEALS

Remove and refit 64.15.15

The degree of dismantling required to change rear hub oil seals is extensive; full rear hub overhaul procedu.e should therefcre be carried out, see 64.15.07 and all oil seals, including outer wishbone fulcrum oil seals changed. Renew grease content of both hub and fulcrum bearing assemblies.

REAR HUB WHEEL STUDS

Remove and refit 64.15.26

Removing

1 Remove rear hub and carrier assembly-- 64.15.01.
2 Support hub carrier and press out hub using handpress and suitable mandrel.
3 Prise old oil seals from hub.
4 Draw outer bearing and oil seal track from hub.
5 Use a narrow, sharp cold chisel to open peening securing water thrower. Remove thrower.
6 Support hub, and file or grind staking from faulty stud/s.
7 Unscrew stud/s from hub flange.

Refitting

8 Screw new stud/s into hub and stake in four places to back of flange.
9 Fit water thrower to hub and use blunt cold chisel to peen over flange in three or four places.
10 Press oil seal track and outer bearing race on to hub.
11 Press new outer and inner oil seals into hub.
12 Fit hub into hub carrier and pack with suitable grease.
13 Locate inner bearing over hub and press into position.
14 Refit rear hub and carrier assembly.

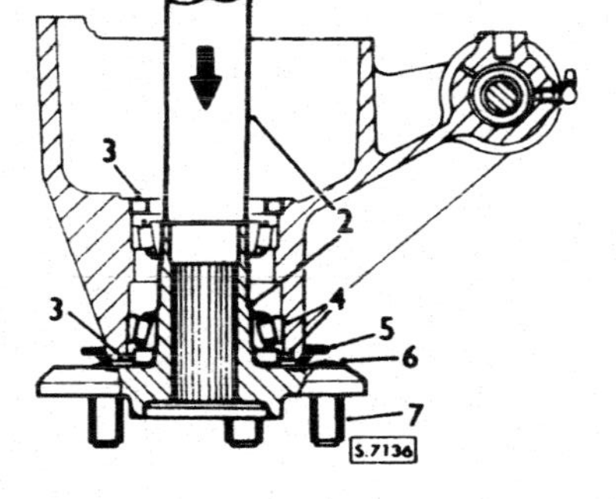
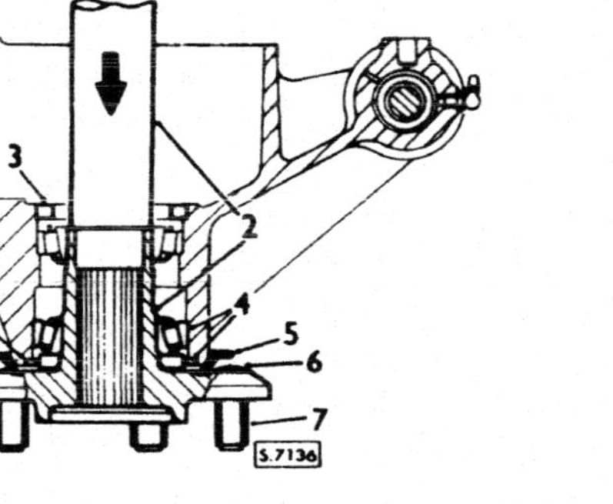

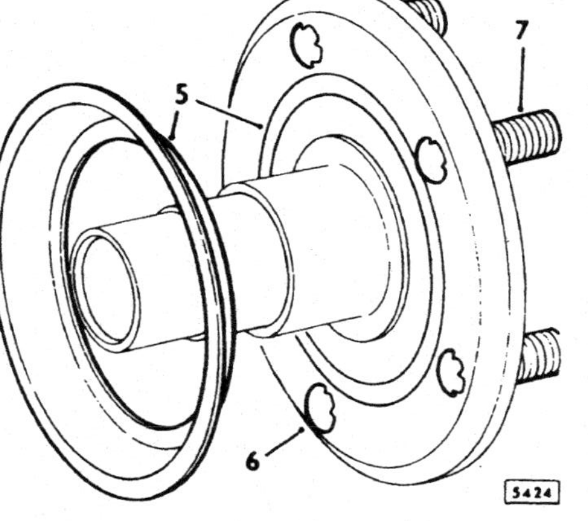

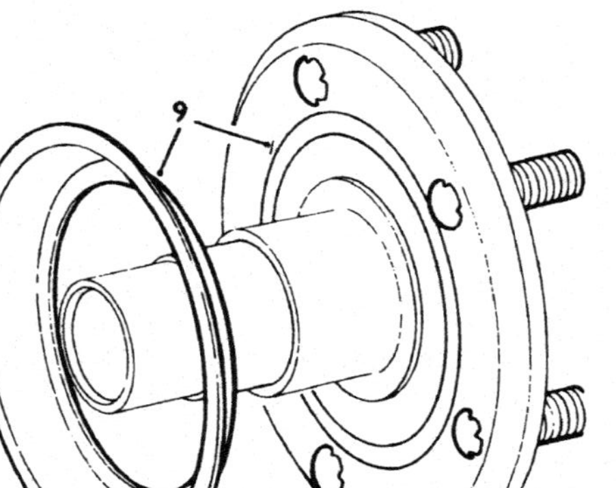

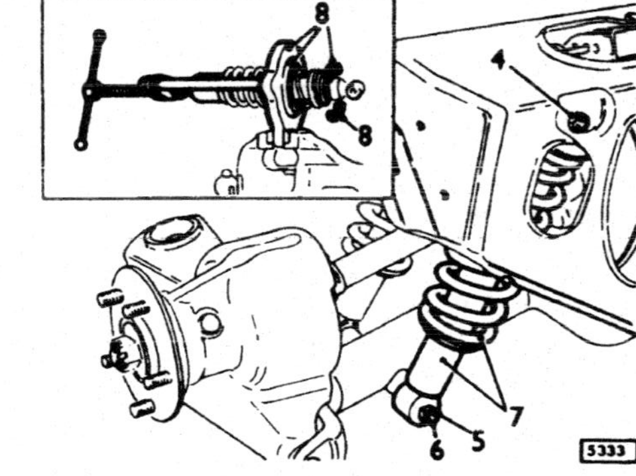

REAR ROAD SPRINGS

Remove and refit 64.20.01

Service tools: Handpress SL.14, Adaptor JD.11B.

Removing

NOTE: Rear springs can be removed with rear suspension fitted to car.

1 Remove rear road wheel.
2 Support rear of car on stands.
3 Place jack to support wishbone.
4 Remove self-locking nut and bolt securing top of hydraulic damper to suspension unit cross beam.
5 Remove washers and nuts securing hydraulic dampers to wishbone.
6 Drift out damper mounting pin. Recover spacer at forward end of mounting pin tube.
7 Withdraw hydraulic damper and road spring assembly.
8 Using tools SL.14 and JD.11B compress road spring until collets and spring seat can be removed.
9 Release spring pressure and withdraw hydraulic damper from road spring.

Refitting

Reverse operations 1 to 9 inclusive.

REAR SUSPENSION UNIT

Remove and refit 64.25.01

Removing

1 Remove rear road wheels – 74.20.07.
2 Place stands beneath car, forward of radius arm anchor points.
3 Release 'C' clamps securing tail pipe and silencers to rear intermediate pipes.
4 Release 'C' clamps securing rear intermediate pipes to front silencer assemblies.
5 Manoeuver intermediate pipes from rear of suspension unit, after disengaging pipe mounting pin from rubber mounting.
6 Place suitably sized block of wood between each exhaust pipe trim and rear bumper to support rear silencer and tail pipe assembly in fitted position.
7 Remove special bolt and spring washer securing each radius arm safety strap to body.
8 Remove locking wire and bolts securing radius arms; remove safety straps.
9 Disconnect brake pipe hose from body mounting bracket, plug ends to prevent ingress of dirt.
10 Remove self locking nuts and bolts securing propeller shaft rear flange to differential pinion flange.
11 Fully release hand brake.
12 Remove split pin, washer, and clevis pin securing handbrake cable to caliper actuating lever.
13 Slide protective rubber boot from brake outer cable.
14 Remove outer cable from trunnion on opposite lever.
15 Release outer brake cable from securing spring; secure cable away from suspension unit.
16 Position jack beneath tie plate of rear suspension unit.
17 Remove eight self locking nuts and bolts, and four nuts securing mounting bracket to body.
18 Lower jack to remove suspension unit.

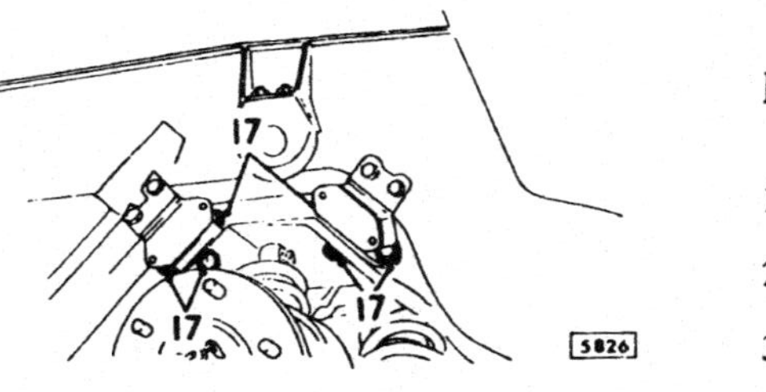

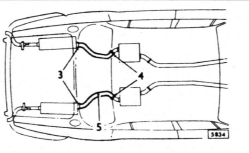

Refitting

19 Reverse operations 1 to 18 inclusive.
NOTE: Before refitting radius arms to body, it is advisable to wire brush spigot mounting and lightly smear it with waterproof grease. Wire lock radius arm bolt to safety strap.
Tighten following fixings to stated torque levels:
Radius arm and safety strap to body.
40 to 45 lb.ft. (5,5 to 6,2 kg.m.)
Safety strap to body.
27 to 32 lb.ft. (3,75 to 4,4 kg.m.).
Vee mounting fixings
14 to 18 lb.ft. (2,0 to 2,5 kg.m.).
20 Bleed brakes – 70.25.02.
21 Adjust handbrake – 70.35.10.

REAR SUSPENSION UNIT

Overhaul 64.25.06

The rear suspension unit is an assembly comprising individual units, the removal, refitting and overhaul of each being covered elsewhere in this Manual.
For this reason, an overhaul procedure is not given for the rear suspension unit assembly proper, although it is advisable to check all bushes, fulcrum bearings and oil seals for damage or leakage whenever the unit is removed from the car.

REAR SUSPENSION HEIGHT

Check 64.25.12

1 Ensure radiator topped up with coolant.
2 Ensure engine sump filled to correct level with specified lubricant.
3 Ensure tyre pressures correct.

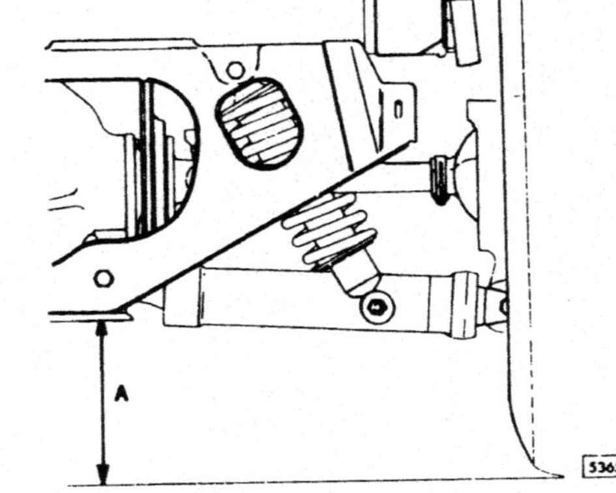

4 Note contents of fuel tanks by switching on ignition and switching from one tank to another.
NOTE: Fuel tanks hold a total of 22 Imperial gallons (26 U.S. gallons or 100 litres).
5 Calculate ballast weights required to represent difference between weight of fuel tank contents and weight of full tanks.
NOTE: Full fuel tanks total approximately 176 lb. (80 kg.).
6 Place ballast weights required in centre of luggage compartment floor.
7 Roll car forward three lengths on perfectly level surface.
8 Measure distance between lower surface of rear cross member and ground at both sides of car. (Dimension A must be 7.45 ± .25 in. (189 mm. ± 6,4 mm.).)

If dimension is not correct, check all bushes and bearing points of rear suspension. If no cause discovered, rear road springs must be changed.
Remove all four springs and change as complete set, see operation 64.20.01.

REAR SUSPENSION CAMBER ANGLE

Check and adjust 64.25.18

Service tool: Setting links JD.25.

Checking

1 Set car on level surface.
2 Ensure tyre pressures correct.
3 Hook one end of setting link, tool JD.25, in lower hole of rear mounting, depress body until other end of setting link can be slid over outer wishbone fulcrum nut. Repeat on other side of car.
4 Set camber gauge against each rear tyre and read off camber angle. The correct reading should be ¾° + ¼° negative. If these limits are not met, note deviation and adjust camber angle, see operations 6 to 15 inclusive. If result satisfactory continue with operation 5.
5 Remove setting links.

Adjust

6 Remove setting links.
7 Jack up rear of car and place stands to support body.
8 Remove road wheel.
9 Remove lower wishbone outer fulcrum grease nipple.
10 Release clip securing inner universal joint cover. Slide cover clear of joint.
11 Remove four steel locknuts securing half shaft flange to brake disc.
12 Separate half shaft from disc to enable shims to be fitted.
NOTE: Addition of one shim .020 in. (,5 mm.) will alter camber position ¼°.
13 Add or remove shims as required.
14 Reverse operations 6 to 12 inclusive.
15 Repeat operation 4.

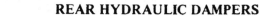

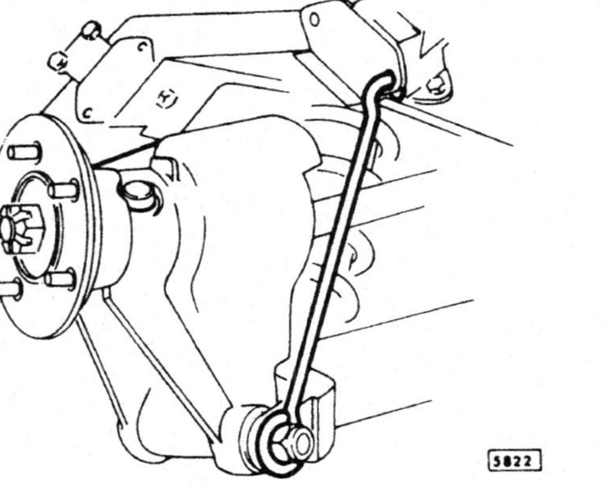

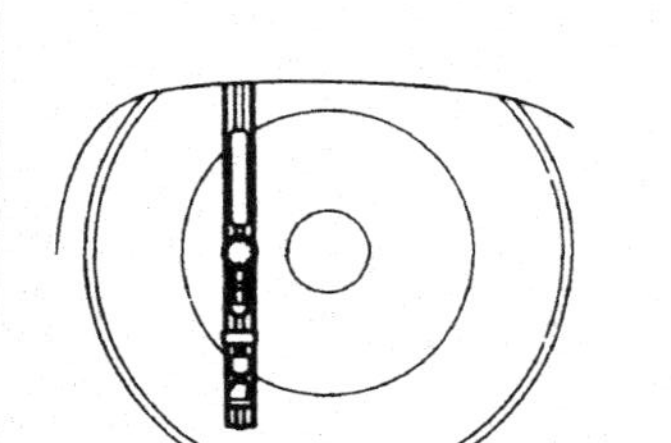

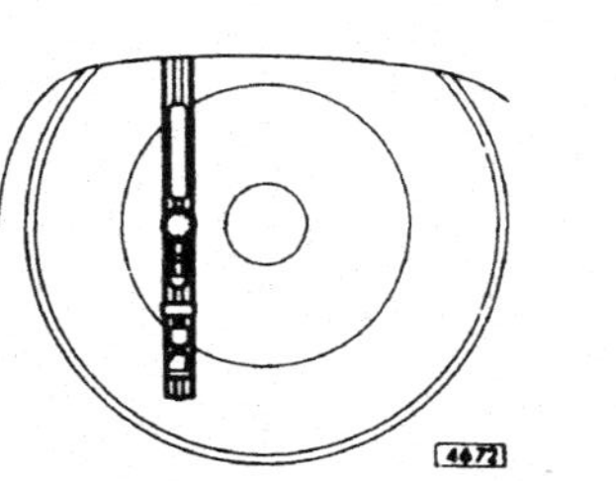

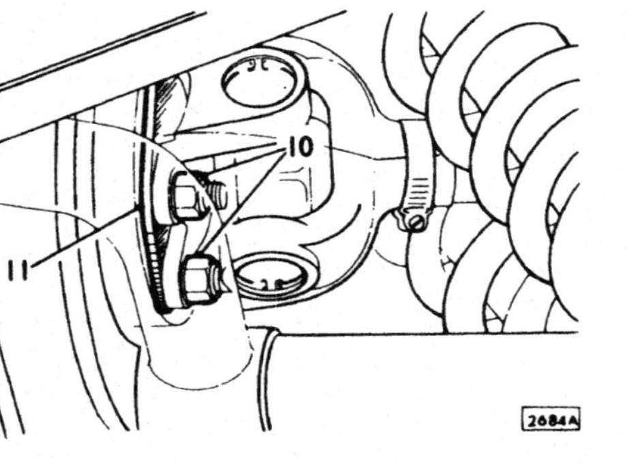

REAR HYDRAULIC DAMPERS

Remove and refit 64.30.01

Service tools: Handpress SL.14, Adaptor JD.11B.

Removing

NOTE: Rear hydraulic dampers can be removed with rear suspension unit fitted to car.

1 Remove rear road wheel.
2 Support rear of car on stand.
3 Place jack to support wishbone.
4 Remove self-locking nut and bolt securing top of hydraulic damper to suspension unit cross beam.
5 Remove washers and nuts securing hydraulic dampers to wishbone.
6 Drift out damper mounting pin. Recover spacer at forward end of mounting pin tube.
7 Withdraw hydraulic damper and road spring assembly.
8 Using tools SL.14 and JD.11B compress road spring until collets and spring seat can be removed.
9 Release spring pressure and withdraw hydraulic damper from road spring.

Refitting

NOTE: Hydraulic dampers fitted to this car are of the gas pressurized type and therefore need not be exercised before installation.

Reverse operations 1 to 9 inclusive.

BUMP STOP

Remove and refit 64.30.15

Removing

1 Remove rear road wheel – 74.20.01.
2 Remove two self-locking nuts and washers and detach bump stop.

Refitting

Reverse operations 1 and 2, tightening nuts to 8 to 10 lbf.ft. (1,11 to 1,38 kgf.m.).

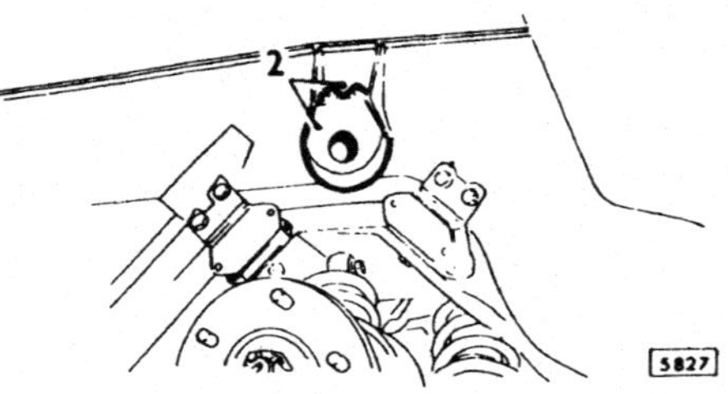

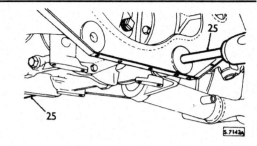

WISHBONE

Remove and refit 64.35.15

Service tool: Dummy shaft JD.14.

Removing

1 Remove rear road wheel.
2 Support rear of car on stands forward of radius arms.
3 Remove one self-locking nut from outer fulcrum shaft, drift out shaft and remove.
4 Fit dummy shaft JD.14 to hub carrier assembly. Retain shims and oil seal retaining washers at each side of fulcrum with adhesive tape.
5 Raise hub and drive shaft clear of wishbone and suspend with strong wire from cross beam.
6 Remove 6 bolts and nuts securing bottom tie plate to crossbeam.
7 Remove locking wire and unscrew radius arm retaining bolt from body.
8 Detach forward end of radius arm from mounting on body.
9 Remove 8 setscrews securing bottom tie plate to inner fulcrum brackets.
10 Remove nuts and washers securing dampers to wishbone.
11 Drift out damper mounting pin. Recover spacer and tie-down bracket.
12 Remove rear nut from inner fulcrum shaft.
13 Drift fulcrum shaft forward to free wishbone from inner fulcrum. Remove wishbone and radius arm.
14 Collect oil seals, distance washers and bearings.
15 Remove bolt securing radius arm to wishbone; discard tab washer.
16 Remove grease nipples from wishbone ends. Clean and inspect all parts.

Refitting

17 Smear needle bearing cage with grease and press into wishbone inner fulcrum boss, engraved face outwards.
18 From opposite end of boss, press in second needle bearing cage, again with engraved face outwards.
19 Fit grease nipple.
20 Insert bearing tube.
21 Repeat 17, 18, 19 and 20 for other boss.

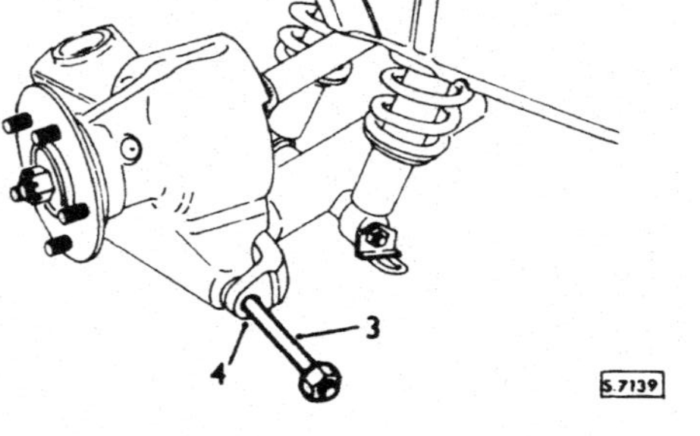

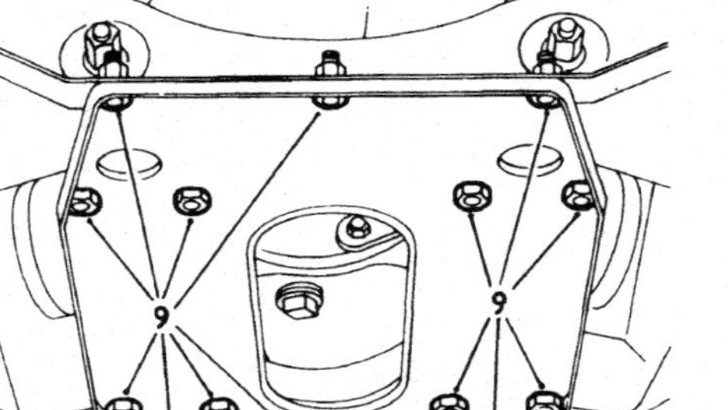
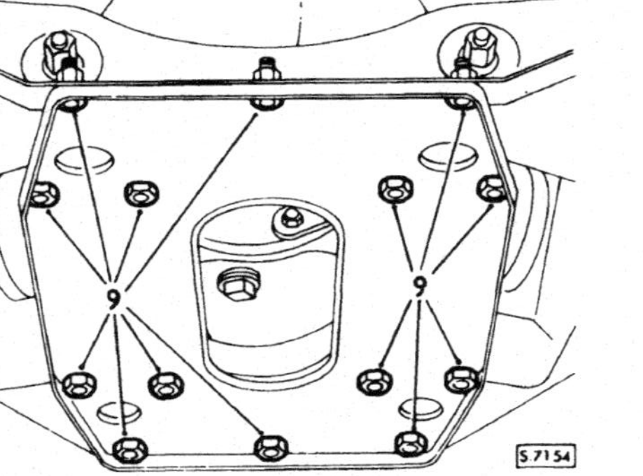

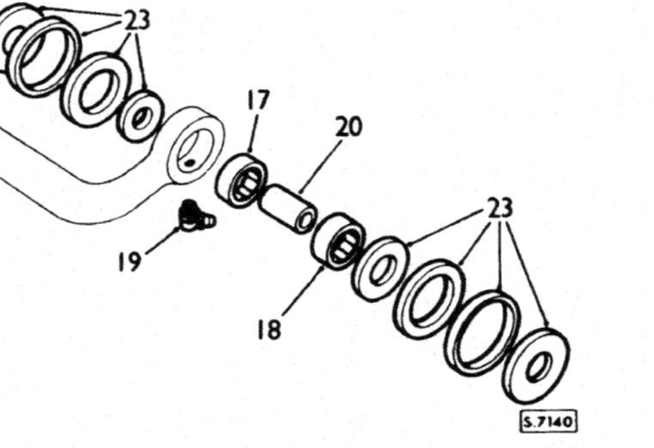

22 Attach radius arm to wishbone. Fit new tab washer and tighten nut to 60 to 70 lbf.ft. (8,30 to 9,68 kgf.m.).
23 Smear four outer thrust washers, inner thrust washers, new oil seals and oil seal retainers with grease and place into position on wishbone.
24 Offer up wishbone to inner fulcrum mounting bracket with radius arm bracket towards front of suspension unit.
NOTE: Take great care not to displace any of the fulcrum bearing components.
25 Carefully enter dummy shaft, tool JD.14, from each end to retain bearing assemblies and locate wishbone with mounting bracket.
26 Smear fulcrum shaft with grease and gently drift it through fulcrum to chase out dummy shafts.
NOTE: It is advisable to maintain a slight reaction pressure on dummy shafts as they emerge from fulcrum. This ensures that thrust washers are not knocked out of position. Should this happen, fulcrum shaft, dummy shaft and wishbone must be removed, and installation operations 23 to 26 repeated.
27 Fit self-locking nut to fulcrum shaft. Tighten to torque of 45 to 50 lbf.ft. (6,2 to 6,9 kgf.m.).
28 Raise wishbone and replace damper mounting pin, spacer and tie-down bracket. Tighten nuts to 32 to 36 lbf.ft. (4,45 to 4,95 kgf.m.).
29 Raise radius arm, clean and lightly grease spigot, replace bolt, tighten to 40 to 45 lbf.ft. (5,5 to 6,2 kgf.m.) and wire lock.
30 Remove wire suspending hub assembly from cross beam.
31 Remove adhesive tape attaching shims and washers to hub carrier, fit new seals, replace retainers and shims, and line up with wishbone.
32 Chase out dummy shaft with fulcrum shaft and tighten self locking nuts to 97 to 107 lbf.ft. (13,4 to 14,8 kgf.m.).
33 Replace bottom tie plate and insert 8 setscrews.
34 Replace 6 bolts and nuts and tighten all 14 bolts and setscrews to 14 to 18 lbf.ft. (1,94 to 2,48 kgf.m.).

35 Replace rear road wheel.
36 Remove car from stands.
37 Check rear suspension camber angle, see 64.25.18.
38 Grease wishbone bearings.

WISHBONE BEARINGS

Remove and refit 64.35.16

Procedures for removal and refitting the wishbone outer fulcrum bearings are given in Rear hub and carrier assembly – remove and refit – 64.15.01, and overhaul – 64.15.07. The wishbone inner fulcrum bearings are covered in Wishbone – remove and refit – 64.35.15.

WISHBONE OIL SEALS

Remove and refit 64.35.17

Follow procedure given under Wishbone - remove and refit – 64.35.15.

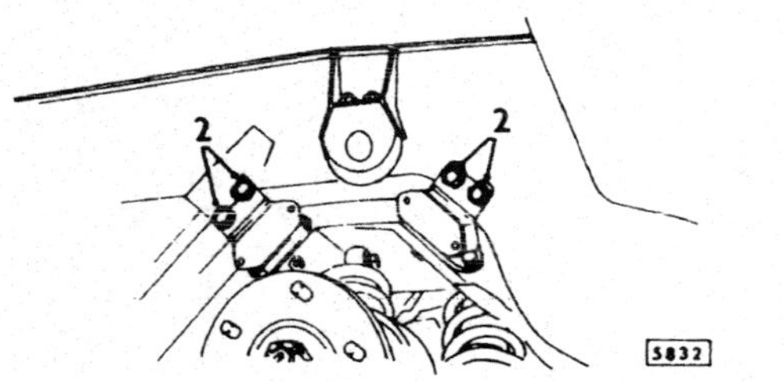

MOUNTING BRACKET

Remove and refit 64.35.20

Removing
1 Remove rear suspension unit – 64.25.01.
2 Remove two self locking nuts and bolts securing each mounting bracket to body.

Refitting
3 Fit new rear suspension rubber mountings to body with cut-away end of flange upwards.
4 Secure bracket using bolts and self locking nuts. Tighten to torque of 27 to 32 lb.ft. (3,75 to 4,4 kg.m.).
5 Refit rear suspension unit.

INNER FULCRUM BRACKET (ONE)

Remove and refit 64.35.21

Service tools: Dummy shaft JD.14.

Removing
1 Remove adjacent rear road wheel.
2 Support rear of car on stands forward of radius arms.
3 Remove 14 bolts and setscrews securing bottom tie plate to cross beam and inner fulcrum brackets.
4 Detach forward end of radius arm from mounting on body.
5 Remove bolt securing anti-roll bar link to radius arm and raise link clear of arm.
6 Remove nuts and washers securing damper to wishbone.
7 Drift out damper mounting pin; recover spacer and tie down bracket.
8 Suspend hub and drive shaft assembly from cross beam with string wire.
9 Remove rear nut from inner fulcrum shaft.
10 Drift fulcrum shaft forward to free wishbone from inner fulcrum.
11 Collect oil seals, distance washers and bearings.
12 Tap spacer tube from between lugs of fulcrum bracket.
13 Remove locking wire from two setscrews securing fulcrum bracket to final drive unit. Remove setscrews and withdraw fulcrum bracket, noting position and number of shims at each attachment point.

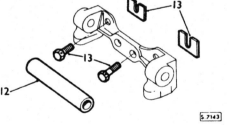

Refitting
14 Position fulcrum bracket against final drive unit and locate loosely with two setscrews.
15 Replace shims removed in operation 13 between bracket and final drive unit.
16 Tighten mounting setscrews to 60 to 65 lbf.ft. (8,30 to 8,98 kgf.m.) and wire lock.
17 Replace spacer tube between lugs of fulcrum bracket.
18 Clean, inspect and grease wishbone bearings, thrust washer etc. Refit with new oil seals.
19 Offer up wishbone to fulcrum bracket lugs and locate with dummy shafts, tool number JD.14. Take great care not to displace any component during this operation.
20 Drift dummy shafts from fulcrum bracket with fulcrum shaft. Restrain dummy shafts to prevent spacers or thrust washers dropping out of position.
21 Tighten fulcrum shaft nut to 45 to 50 lbf.ft. (6,23 to 6,91 kgf.m.).
22 Remove wire suspending hub assembly from cross beam.
23 Replace damper lower mounting shaft, refitting spacer and tie-down bracket. Tighten nuts to 32 to 36 lbf.ft. (4,43 to 4,97 kgf.m.).
24 Clean spigot on body, raise radius arm and replace bolt. Tighten to 40 to 45 lbf.ft. (5,54 to 6,22 kgf.m.) and wire lock bolt.
25 Bolt anti-roll bar link to radius arm and tighten.
26 Replace bottom tie plate and tighten bolts and setscrews to 14 to 18 lbf.ft. (1,94 to 2,48 kgf.m.).
27 Replace road wheel.
28 Remove car from stands.

RADIUS ARM

Remove and refit 64.35.28

Removing

1 Jack up rear of car and support on stands forward of radius arm anchor points.
2 Remove rear road wheel.
3 Remove special bolt and spring washer securing safety strap to body.
4 Remove locking wire and bolt securing radius arm to body; remove safety strap.
5 Remove self-locking nut and flat washer securing forward damper assembly lower mounting pin.
6 Drift mounting pin to rear of wishbone clearing damper assembly mounting boss and spacer.
7 Recover spacer and swing damper assembly to centre line of car.
8 Turn down tab washer and remove bolt securing radius arm to wishbone; remove radius arm.
9 Examine radius arm bushes and replace as necessary.

Refitting

NOTE: Prior to fitting radius arm to body spigot wirebrush spigot and smear with waterproof grease.

10 Reverse operations 1 to 9.
Tighten following fixings to stated torque settings.
Radius arm to wishbone 60 to 70 lb.ft. (8,3 to 9,7 kg.m.).
Fit new tab washer.
Radius arm to body 40 to 45 lb.ft. (5,5 to 6,2 kg.m.).
Safety strap to body 27 to 32 lb.ft. (3,75 to 4,4 kg.m.).
Damper assembly lower retaining nut 32 to 36 lb.ft. (4,4 to 5,0 kg.m.).
11 Wire lock radius arm and safety strap retaining bolt.

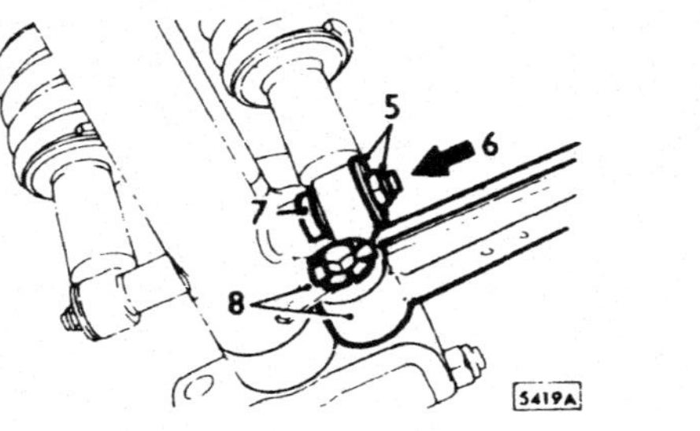

RADIUS ARM BUSHES

Remove and refit 64.35.29

Service tool: Mandrel JD.21.

Removing

1 Remove radius arm – 64.35.28, operations 1 to 9.
2 Use mandrel tool JD.21 and press front bush from housing.
3 Use mandrel tool JD.21 and press rear bush from housing.

Refitting

4 Press new bush into rear bush housing so that bush is central in radius arm.
5 Use mandrel and press new bush into front bush housing so that holes in bush rubber are in line with centre line of radius arm. Press bush into radius arm until bush ring is flush with bush housing. When pressing bush, have small hole in bush core upwards.
6 Refit radius arm – 64.35.28, operations 10 and 11.

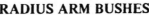

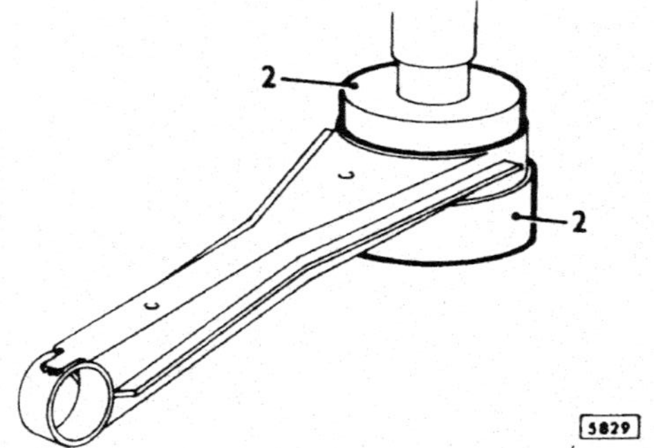

ADDITIONAL MAINTENANCE OPERATIONS – ALL VEHICLES

Brake System – Preventive Maintenance

In addition to the periodical inspection of brake components it is advisable as the car ages and as a precaution against the effects of wear and deterioration to make a more searching inspection and renew parts as necessary.

It is recommended that:

1 Disc brake pads, hoses and pipes should be examined at intervals no greater than those laid down in the Passport to Service.

2 Under normal operating conditions brake fluid should be changed completely every 18 months or 18,000 miles (30,000 km) whichever is the sooner.

3 All fluid seals in the hydraulic system should be renewed and all flexible hoses should be examined and renewed if necessary every three years or 36,000 miles (60,000 km) whichever is the sooner. At the same time the working surfaces of the pistons and the bores of the master cylinder, wheel cylinders and other slave cylinders should be examined and new parts fitted where necessary.

Care must always be taken to observe the following:

a At all times use the recommended brake fluid.

b Never leave fluid in unsealed containers; it absorbs moisture quickly and can be dangerous if used in the braking system in this condition.

c Fluid drained from the system or used for bleeding is best discarded.

d The necessity for absolute cleanliness when carrying out any operations on the braking system cannot be over-emphasized.

BRAKE SYSTEM – EARLY CARS

Description **70.00.00**
The brake system consists of the following main components.

1. Pedal box.
2. Servo unit.
3. Tandem master cylinder.
4. Pressure differential warning actuator (P.D.W.A.) – fitted only to models exported to some European Countries.
5. Four disc brake assemblies.
6. Two handbrake calipers.

The above components provide the car with a braking system in which the front and rear caliper assemblies are totally independent of each other. Thus, in the event of a brake line fracture or a partial loss of brake fluid, one pair of brake calipers will at all times be operative.

Pressure Differential Warning Actuator
The purpose of the P.D.W.A. Unit fitted to certain models is to monitor front and rear brake line pressures and give visual warning to the driver should there be an undue fall in either of the pressures.

Operation
On application of the brake pedal, the servo unit which is directly coupled to the master cylinder, transfers increased pedal pressure to the master cylinder primary piston 'A', causing the piston to move forward and close the tipping valve 'B'. Movement of the primary piston upon the primary spring 'C' and front brake line pressure force the secondary piston 'D' forward, which in turn closes the secondary piston valve 'E' and so providing rear brake line pressure.

On cars fitted with a **P.D.W.A.**, front and rear braking pressures enter the unit at ports 'F' and 'G', act on either end of the shuttle valve 'H' and then travel to front and rear calipers via ports 'J' and 'K'. Should a fall in front or rear braking pressure occur the resultant imbalance upon the shuttle valve causes its displacement, which in turn operates the switch 'L' and illuminates the warning light on the drivers facia panel.

In order to reset the displaced shuttle valve the cause of fall in brake line pressure must first be established and rectified. During bleeding of the brake system, which follows rectification, a special procedure must be observed in order to reset the shuttle valve.

On cars not fitted with a **P.D.W.A.** Unit the brake pressures travel direct to front and rear calipers.

Brake pressure, entering the calipers 'M' force the pistons (two per rear caliper and three per front caliper) out and clamp the disc between the brake pads. On releasing the brake pedal the piston seals retract pistons into the caliper, sufficient for brake pads to be in a relaxed position. This operation also provides automatic adjustment for brake lining wear.

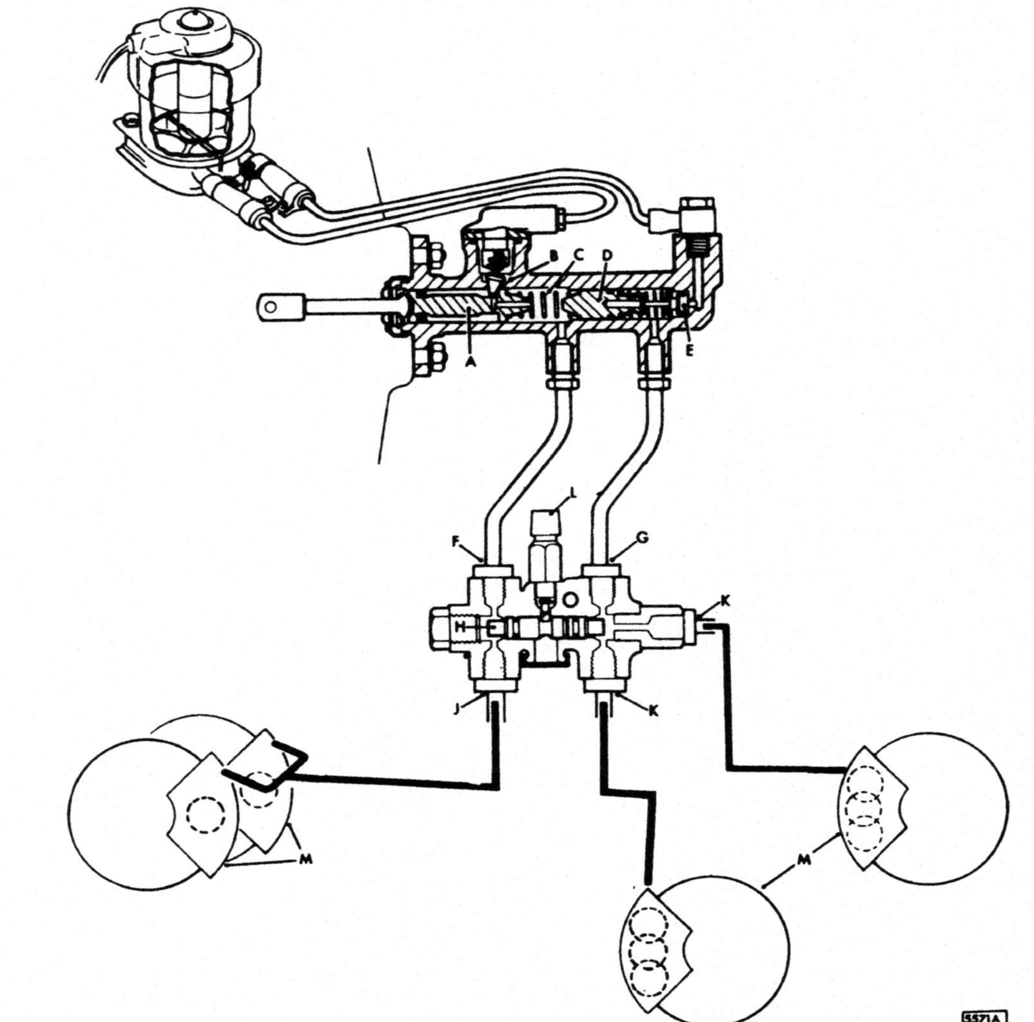

BRAKE SYSTEM – LATER CARS

Description **70.00.00**

The brake system now fitted to all cars differs from earlier systems in the following respects.

1. One system common to all cars.
2. A pressure differential warning actuator (P.D.W.A.), with an automatic resetting capability.
3. A four piston front caliper.
4. A new tandem master cylinder.
5. Metrication of brake system.

Common System

The system now common to all cars contains the following main components.

1. Pedal Box.
2. Servo Unit.
3. Tandem Master Cylinder.
4. Pressure Differential Warning Actuator.
5. Four disc brake assemblies.
6. Two Handbrake Calipers.

Pressure Differential Warning Actuator

The revised P.D.W.A. unit differs from its predecessor in that it possesses an automatic resetting capability.

The previous recommendation for resetting the shuttle valve required that certain precautions be observed during bleeding of the brakes. This is no longer necessary with the new P.D.W.A. unit as resetting is achieved during the normal bleeding procedure.

Metrication

Metrication does not apply to the following brake components.

1. Rear Calipers.
2. Handbrake Calipers.
3. Feed pipes from rear Threeway Connector to Rear Calipers.
4. Threeway Connector.

The revised brake system can be identified by the plastic adaptors which secure the reservoir hoses to the master cylinder.

A guide to the identification of metric components is included in General Fitting Instructions, Section 07, under the sub-heading "Hydraulic Fittings – Metrication".

CLEANING SOLVENTS

WARNING: NEVER USE METHYLATED SPIRITS (DENATURED ALCOHOL) FOR CLEANING PURPOSES. USE ONLY CASTROL/GIRLING BRAKE CLEANING FLUID.

SYMPTOM AND DIAGNOSIS CHART FOR HYDRAULIC BRAKE SYSTEM

SYMPTOM	DIAGNOSIS	ACTION
FADE	Incorrect pads. Overloaded vehicle. Excessive braking. Oil hydraulic fluid.	Replace the pads. Decrease vehicle load or renew hydraulic fluid as necessary.
SPONGY PEDAL	Air in system. Badly lined pads. Weak master cylinder mounting.	Check for air in the system, and bleed if necessary. Check the master cylinder mounting, pads and discs and replace as necessary.
LONG PEDAL	Discs running out pushing pads back. Distorted damping shims. Misplaced dust covers.	Check that the disc run out does not exceed 0.004 in. (0,1 mm.) Rotate the disc on the hub. Check the disc/hub mounting faces.
BRAKES BINDING	Handbrake incorrectly adjusted. Seals swollen. Seized pistons. Servo faulty.	Check and adjust handbrake linkage. Check for seized pistons, repair or replace as necessary. Refer to Servo check and test – 70.50.03.
HARD PEDAL – POOR BRAKING	Incorrect pads. Glazed pads. Pads wet, greasy or not bedded correctly. Servo unit inoperative. Seized caliper pistons. Defective shock absorbers causing wheel bounce.	Replace the pads or if glazed, lightly rub down with rough sandpaper. Refer to Servo check and test, if servo is faulty. Check caliper for damage and repair as necessary. Fit new shock absorbers.
BRAKES PULLING	Seized pistons. Variation in pads. Unsuitable tyres or pressures. Defective shock absorbers. Loose brakes. Greasy pads. Faulty discs, suspension or steering.	Check tyre pressures; check for seized pistons, greasy pads or loose brakes; then check suspension, steering and repair or replace as necessary. Fit new shock absorbers.
FALL IN FLUID LEVEL	Worn disc pads. External leak. Leak in servo unit.	Check the pads for wear and for hydraulic fluid leakage. Refer to Servo check and test – 70.50.03.
DISC BRAKE SQUEAL – PAD RATTLE	Worn retaining pins. Worn discs. Worn pads.	Renew the retaining pins, or discs. Fit new pads.
UNEVEN OR EXCESSIVE PAD WEAR	Disc corroded. Disc badly scored. Incorrect friction pads.	Check the disc for corrosion or scoring and replace if necessary. Fit new pads with correct friction material.
BRAKE WARNING LIGHT ILLUMINATED (WITH HAND-BRAKE RELEASED)	Fluid level low, combination valve or P.D.W.A. unit operated. Short in electrical warning circuit.	Top up reservoir. Check for leaks in system and pads for wear. Check electrical circuit.

IMPORTANT NOTE
Before commencing the following operations you are advised to familiarise yourself with the information in Section 07 – General Fitting Instructions. Pay especial regard to the notes on Unified and Metric unions, nuts and adaptors.

WARNING: THROUGHOUT THE FOLLOWING OPERATIONS ABSOLUTE CLEANLINESS MUST BE OBSERVED TO PREVENT GRIT OR OTHER FOREIGN MATTER CONTAMINATING THE BRAKE SYSTEM. IF THE SYSTEM IS TO BE FLUSHED OR CLEANED THROUGH, ONLY GIRLING BRAKE CLEANER MUST BE USED. BRAKE SYSTEM COMPONENTS MUST BE WASHED IN GIRLING BRAKE CLEANER, AND ALL TRACES OF CLEANER REMOVED BEFORE REASSEMBLY.
ALL BRAKE SYSTEM RUBBER COMPONENTS MUST BE DIPPED IN CLEAN BRAKE FLUID AND ASSEMBLED USING THE FINGERS ONLY.

BRAKE FLUID
DURING OPERATIONS WHICH NECESSITATE THE HANDLING OF BRAKE FLUID, EXTREME CARE MUST BE OBSERVED; BRAKE FLUID MUST NOT BE ALLOWED TO CONTACT THE CAR PAINTWORK. IN INSTANCES WHERE THIS HAS OCCURRED THE CONTAMINATED AREA MUST IMMEDIATELY BE CLEANED, USING A CLEAN CLOTH AND WHITE SPIRIT. THIS SHOULD BE FOLLOWED BY WASHING THE AREA WITH CLEAN WATER. METHYLATED SPIRIT (DENATURED ALCOHOL) MUST NOT BE USED TO CLEAN THE CONTAMINATED AREA.

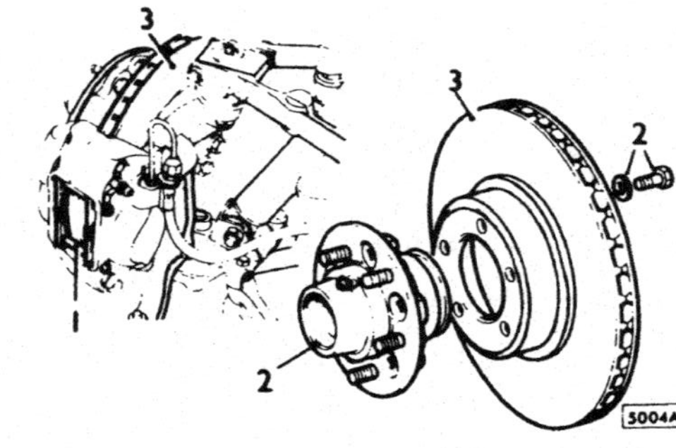

FRONT DISC

Remove and refit (early cars with 3-piston calipers) 70.10.10

Removing
1. Remove brake caliper friction pads – 70.40.02.
2. Remove front hub – 60.25.01.
3. Remove disc assembly, sliding from caliper jaws and withdrawing over stub axle.

Refitting
4. Reverse operations 2 and 3.
5. Check brake disc for 'run out', clamp dial test indicator to stub axle carrier and position indicator against disc face, setting reading to zero. 'Run out' must not exceed 0.004 in. (0,10 mm.).
6. Refit brake caliper friction pads.

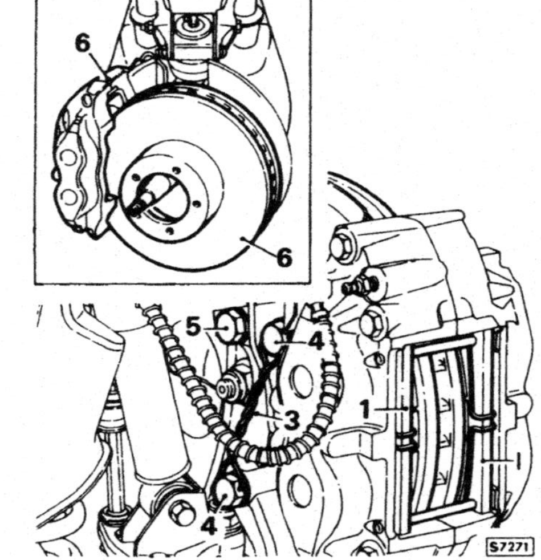
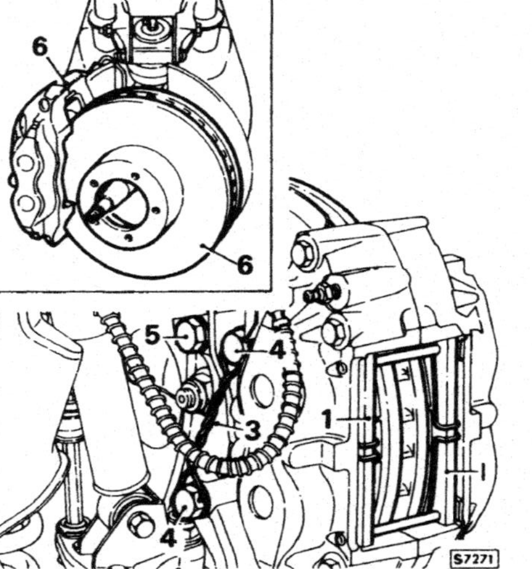

FRONT DISC

Remove and refit (cars with 4-piston calipers) 70.10.10

Removing
1. Remove brake caliper friction pads, see 70.40.02.
2. Remove front hub, see 60.25.01.
3. Remove locking wire from caliper mounting bolts.
4. Remove caliper mounting bolts, recover and note position of shims located between steering arm and caliper.
5. Slacken bolt securing steering arm to hub carrier.
6. Gently easing caliper aside remove disc.

Inspection
7. Examine disc for cracks and heavy scoring, light scratches and scoring are not detrimental and may be ignored. If doubt exists a new disc should be fitted.

Refitting
8. If original disc is refitted reverse operations 1 to 6 and ensure caliper mounting bolts are torqued to 55 lb. ft. (7,5 kg.m.).
9. If new disc is fitted reverse operations 2 to 6 ensuring mounting bolts are not wire locked.
10. Check gap between caliper abutments and disc face. Gap on opposite sides of disc may differ by up to 0.010 in. (0,25 mm.) but gap on upper and lower abutment on same side of disc should be same.
11. If disc is not central in caliper carry out operations 12 – 14. If disc is central proceed to operation 15.
12. Remove one caliper mounting bolt and add or withdraw shim required to centralise disc, refit caliper bolt.
13. Repeat operation 12 on remaining caliper mounting bolt.
14. Repeat operation 10.
15. Torque caliper mounting bolts to 55 lb. ft. (7,5 kg. m.) wire lock bolts.
16. Refit brake friction pads.

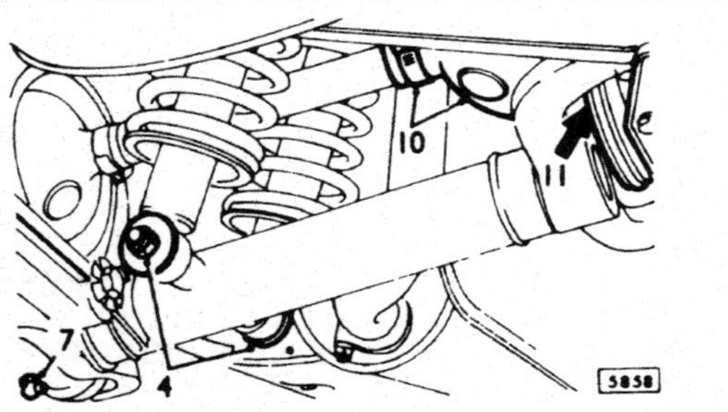

REAR DISCS

Remove and refit **70.10.11**

Removing

1. Place car on ramp, remove road wheel adjacent to brake disc to be removed.
2. Place rear of car on stands.
3. Remove brake caliper – 70.55.03.
4. Remove shock absorber lower fulcrum pin, recover distance piece and washers.
5. Remove locking wire securing radius arm locking bolt.
6. Remove radius arm locking bolt.
7. Remove hub fulcrum shaft grease nipple.
8. Place support blocks below hub.
9. Lower radius arm from spigot anchor point.
10. Release clip securing inner universal joint cover, slide cover clear of joint.
11. Remove nuts securing universal joint to brake disc.
12. Tap disc mounting bolts towards final drive unit.
13. Separate universal joint from brake disc, collect camber angle shims held on disc mounting bolts.
14. Jack up car sufficiently to allow removal of brake disc, lift out disc.

NOTE: Do not disturb shims mounted between final drive flange and brake disc.

Inspection

NOTE: The condition of discs are a vital factor in efficient functioning of the brakes.
Examine surface of disc, which should be smooth. Scratches and light scoring are not detrimental after normal use. Should doubt exist a new disc should be fitted.

Refitting

15. Locate new disc on mounting bolts.
16 Reverse operations 11 to 13.
17. Check disc for run out, clamp dial test indicator to suspension unit cross beam, position indicator rod against disc face and set reading to zero. Run out must not exceed 0.004 in. (0,10 mm.).
18. Offer brake caliper to mounting and secure with mounting bolts. Torque to 49 to 55 lb. ft. (6,7 to 7,6 kg. m.).
19. Check caliper centralization on brake disc. Dimensions between faces of disc and caliper abutments are to be equal within 0.010 in. (0,25 mm.). To adjust (if necessary) remove caliper and disc assembly, adding or withdrawing shims located between disc and axle unit output flange. Note thickness of shims added or withdrawn during this operation.
NOTE: On completion of centralization operation, (if necessary) add or withdraw a Camber Angle shim, to size of centralization shim used in adjustment. e.g. If a 0.06 in. (2,15 mm.) shim was **ADDED** to centralization shims in operation 19, **WITHDRAW** same size shim from camber angle shims. If shims were **WITHDRAWN** in operation 19 **ADD** same size shim to camber angle shims. This operation corrects camber angle to that prior to the caliper centralization operation.

NOTE: Prior to fitting radius arm to body spigot, wire brush spigot and smear with grease.

20. Reverse operations 5 to 10.
21. Wire lock caliper mounting bolts.

NOTE: Before refitting brake friction pads check pads for wear. Minimum thickness 0.125 in. (3,17 mm.).

22. Fit brake friction pads to caliper – 70.40.03.
23. Refit handbrake caliper – 70.55.04.
24. Fit brake feed pipe to caliper, tighten connector at three way union.
25. Refit suspension unit tie plate.
26. Bleed brakes – 70.25.02.
27. Refit road wheel.
28. Check and if necessary adjust camber angle – 64.25.18.

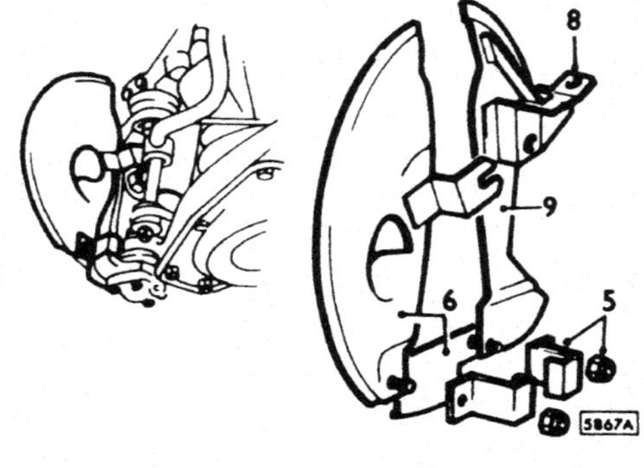

DISC SHIELDS – FRONT

Remove and refit **70.10.18**

Removing

1. Remove road wheel.
2. Slacken upper bolt securing steering arm to stub axle carrier.
3. Remove locking wire securing caliper mounting bolts.
4. Remove upper caliper mounting bolt.
5. Remove clips securing lower, secondary and main shield assemblies to lower portion of stub axle carrier.
6. Withdraw lower and main shields from disc assembly.
7. Remove brake feed pipe between flexible pipe and caliper. Plug exposed ends to prevent ingress of dirt and loss of fluid.
8. Remove locknut securing brake hose union to secondary shield assembly; withdraw hose from securing bracket.
9. Withdraw shield from disc assembly.

Refitting

10. Reverse operations 2 to 9, ensure brake hose is not twisted when securing to secondary shield bracket. Fit new self locking nuts to lower shield securing studs. Tighten steering arm bolt and caliper securing bolt to 50-60 lb. ft. (6,91 – 8,30 kg. m.).
11. Refit road wheel.
12. Bleed brakes – 70.25.02.

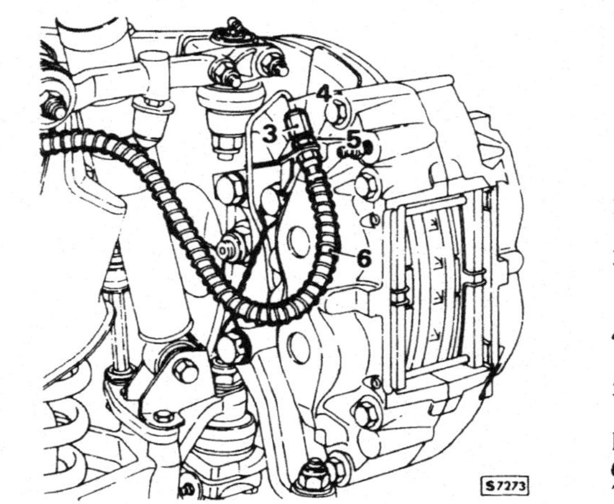

HOSES

General fitting and removal instructions 70.15.00

Removing
1. Clean unions of hose to be removed.
2. Ensure pipe sealing plugs are at hand.
3. Fully release unions securing fluid pipes to hose ends.
4. Withdraw pipe unions from hose ends, plug pipes to prevent loss of fluid and ingress of dirt.
5. Remove locknuts securing hose ends to mounting brackets.
6. Remove hose from car.

Inspection
7. After thoroughly cleaning hose examine for any signs of deterioration or damage. If doubt exists a new hose must be fitted.
8. Thoroughly clean bore of hose by feeding compressed air into one end of hose.

Refitting
9. Reverse operations 3 to 5.
10. Bleed brakes, see 70.25.02.

THREE WAY CONNECTOR (FRONT) – EARLY CARS ONLY

Remove and refit 70.15.33

Removing
1. Remove air cleaner (right hand drive cars only) – 10.10.01.
2. Slacken union nuts securing pipes to three way connector.
3. Remove nut and bolt securing connector to wing valance, recover flat washers and spacer.
4. Disengage pipes from connector, plug ends of pipe to prevent loss of fluid.
5. Lift connector from car.

Refitting
6. Reverse operations 1 to 5.
7. Bleed brakes – 70.25.02.

THREE WAY CONNECTOR – REAR

Remove and refit 70.15.34

Removing
1. Disconnect three feed pipe unions at connector, plug pipes to prevent loss of fluid and ingress of dirt.
2. Remove nut and bolt securing three way connector to suspension unit, collect spacer and connector.

Refitting
3. Reverse operations 1 and 2.
4. Bleed brakes – 70.25.02.

PIPES

General fitting and removal instructions 70.20.00

Removing
1. Clean unions of pipe to be removed.
2. Ensure pipe sealing plugs are at hand.
3. Fully release pipe unions.
4. Withdraw pipe from car, plug open end of pipe remaining on car.

Inspection
5. Thoroughly clean bore of pipe by feeding compressed air into one end.
6. After thoroughly cleaning pipe examine for any sign of fracture or damage. If doubt exists, a new pipe must be fitted.

Refitting
7. Reverse operations 3 to 6.
8. Bleed brakes – 70.25.02.

BRAKES – BLEED

Bleed 70.25.02

Bleeding the brake system is not a routine maintenance operation and should only be necessary when air has contaminated the fluid, or a part of the system has been disconnected.

On early cars fitted with a plain pressure differential warning actuator (P.D.W.A.) the following additional precautions must be observed when bleeding the system.

a. Only a light pedal pressure is required.
b. Brake pedal should not be fully depressed.
c. Never check "feel" of pedal until system is fully bled.

NOTE: The above precautions do not apply to later models which are fitted with the revised P.D.W.A. unit (see brake description – later cars).

Bleeding
1. Ensure fluid reservoir is topped up with fluid of correct specification.
2. Attach bleeder tube to left hand rear bleed screw, immerse open end of tube in small jar partially filled with clean brake fluid.
3. Position gear selector in neutral and run engine at idling speed.
4. Slacken left hand rear bleed screw.
5. Operate brake pedal through full stroke until fluid issuing from tube is free of air bubbles.

NOTE: The fluid level in reservoir must be checked at regular intervals and topped up as necessary.

6. Keep pedal fully depressed and close bleed screw.
7. Repeat operations, 2, 4, 5 and 6 on right hand rear brake.
8. Continue operations, 2, 4, 5 and 6 on remaining front brakes.
9. Check tighten all bleed screws and fit protective caps.
10. Top up reservoir as necessary.
11. Apply normal working load to brake pedal for several minutes, if pedal moves or feels spongy further bleeding of system is required.
12. When brake pedal "feel" is satisfactory release handbrake; brake warning light should extinguish. If brake warning light remains illuminated carry out remaining operation.

Early cars with a plain P.D.W.A.
13. Carry out P.D.W.A. check and reset operation – 70.25.08.

Later cars fitted with P.D.W.A. incorporating automatic resetting.
14. Operate brake pedal using heavy foot pressure, warning light should extinguish, if light remains illuminated carry out P.D.W.A. check operation – 70.25.08.

PRESSURE DIFFERENTIAL WARNING ACTUATOR

Check and reset **70.25.08**

Check

NOTE: Before commencing check and reset procedure ensure that car is adequately chocked and cars with automatic transmission have selector lever in 'P' or 'N' position.

1. Switch on ignition and start engine, brake warning light illuminates. If light fails to illuminate fit new bulb.
2. Release handbrake, if warning light remains illuminated carry out operation 3.
3. Check brake reservoir fluid level, top up as necessary. If warning light remains illuminated carry out remaining operation.
4. Disconnect electrical connector from P.D.W.A. switch, if warning light goes out P.D.W.A. has operated, if warning light remains illuminated check for 'short' in electrical circuit of brake warning circuit.

NOTE: If warning light goes out in operations 1 to 3, P.D.W.A. has not operated.

Reset

The following operations are only necessary on cars fitted with early P.D.W.A. unit, and should only be carried out following rectification of defect causing displacement of shuttle valve, or in conjunction with brake system bleeding procedure.

1. Ensure fluid in brake system reservoir is at correct level.
2. Switch on ignition and run engine.
3. Attach bleed tube to FRONT right hand caliper bleed nipple and position free end in suitable container.
4. Apply gentle pressure to brake pedal.
5. Slacken bleed screw and slowly increase brake pedal pressure until P.D.W.A. resets, and warning light goes OFF.

CAUTION: Immediately P.D.W.A. resets stop increasing brake pedal pressure. A further increase in pressure could trip P.D.W.A. in opposite direction. If warning light comes ON immediately after going OFF the P.D.W.A. has tripped in opposite direction and operation 5 must be repeated for left hand REAR caliper.

6. Hold pedal stationary while bleed screw is tightened.
7. Repeat operations 3 – 6 as necessary until warning light remains OFF.
8. Switch off ignition, apply handbrake, refit bleed screw covers and check system for leaks.
9. Top up reservoir if necessary.

CAUTION: Brake fluid emitted from system during above checks must NOT be put back into system.

PRESSURE DIFFERENTIAL WARNING ACTUATOR

Remove and refit **70.25.13**

Removing

1. Disconnect battery – 86.15.20.

Right hand drive cars only

2. Remove air cleaner cover and element.

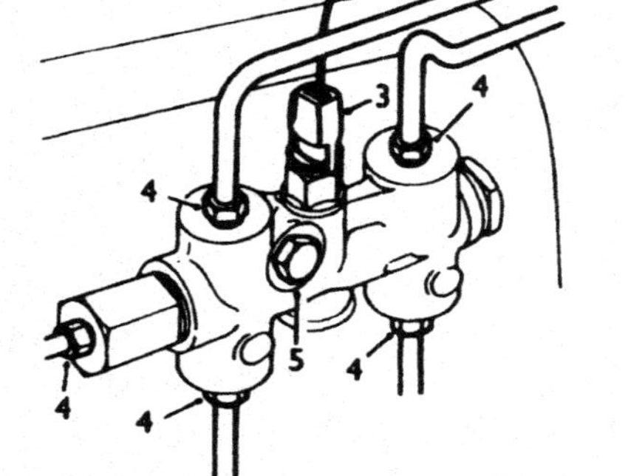

All cars

3. Disconnect electrical lead from P.D.W.A. switch.
4. Disconnect all feed pipes from P.D.W.A. plug pipes and P.D.W.A. unions to prevent loss of fluid and ingress of dirt.
5. Remove nut and bolt securing P.D.W.A. to wing valance.
6. Lift P.D.W.A. unit from car.

Refitting

7. Reverse operations 1 to 6.
8. Bleed brakes – 70.25.02.

PRESSURE DIFFERENTIAL WARNING ACTUATOR

Overhaul **70.25.14**

NOTE: Overhaul of the P.D.W.A. Unit is not possible, and the following test should be carried out at intervals detailed in Group 10, page 10.03.

Operational check

1 Ensure car is adequately chocked.
2 Check brake fluid level and top-up if necessary.
3 Ensure gear selector lever is in 'N' neutral or 'P' (Park). Check that with ignition on and handbrake applied "Brake Warning" light is illuminated.
4 Run engine at idle speed and release handbrake.
5 Apply heavy foot pressure to brake pedal.

NOTE: The brake pedal should be fully depressed and kept fully applied throughout operations 6 to 8.

6 Release any brake caliper bleed nipple, ensure ejected fluid is collected in a jar or waste rag.
7 "Brake Warning" light should illuminate.
8 Close bleed nipple.
9. Release and re-apply foot pressure to brake pedal.
10 "Brake Warning" light should extinguish.
11 Switch off engine and apply handbrake.
12 Top-up brake fluid reservoir.
13 Should warning light fail to illuminate during operation 6, repeat operations 4 to 12. A new P.D.W.A. Unit is required if warning light fails to illuminate during repeat operation.

BRAKE SYSTEM – FLUSH

Drain, Flush and Bleed **70.25.17**

Service Tool: Brake piston retractor tool 64932392

Draining

1 Slacken all road wheel nuts.
2 Jack up front of car and place on stands.
3 Jack up rear of car and place on stands.
4 Remove all road wheels.
5 Attach bleeder tube to rear left hand caliper bleed screw with open end of tube in suitable container.
6 Slacken bleed screw.
7 Operate brake pedal slowly through full stroke, until 'rear' brake section of fluid reservoir is drained and fluid ceases to issue from bleed tube.
8 Remove rear left hand caliper friction pads – 70.40.03.

WARNING: DO NOT OPERATE BRAKE PEDAL WHILE FRICTION PADS ARE REMOVED.

9 Using special tool 64932392, lever pistons into bores expelling remaining trapped fluid into container.
10 Replace friction pads.

NOTE: It is not necessary to replace retaining pins and clips at this time.

11 Close bleed screw.
12 Discard expelled fluid.
13 Repeat operations 5 to 12 on right-hand rear and front calipers.

Flushing
14 Fill fluid reservoir with Castrol/Girling brake flushing fluid.
15 Attach bleeder tube to rear left-hand caliper bleed screw with open end of tube in container.
16 Slacken bleed screw.
17 Operate brake pedal slowly through full stroke, until clear flushing fluid issues from tube.

NOTE: The fluid level in the reservoir must be checked at regular intervals and topped u,) as necessary.

18 Close bleed screw and operate pedal two or three times.
19 Repeat operations 15 to 18 on remaining rear and front calipers.
20 Carry out operations 5 to 10 on rear brake calipers.
21 Secure rear friction pads with retaining pins and clips.
22 Repeat operations 5 to 10 on front brake calipers.
23 Secure front friction pads with retaining pins, clips and anti-chatter springs.
24 Close bleed screws on front and rear calipers.
25 Discard expelled flushing fluid.

Refilling
26 Fill brake reservoir with new brake fluid of correct specification.
27 Bleed brakes – 70.25.02.

NOTE: Prior to closing bleed screw during the bleeding of each caliper, check that issuing brake fluid is completely free of flushing fluid.

28 Refit road wheels to car.
29 Remove stands.

TANDEM MASTER CYLINDER

Remove and refit **70.30.08**

Removing

Early Cars
1 Disconnect reservoir to master cylinder pipes at banjo connector and tipping valve cover. Plug pipes to prevent loss of fluid.

Later Cars
2 Slacken clips securing reservoir hoses to adaptors on master cylinder.
3 Ensuring hose sealing plugs are at hand slide hoses from adaptors, fit plugs to hose ends.

All Cars
4 Disconnect master cylinder fluid delivery pipes, plug pipes to prevent ingress of dirt.
5 Remove nuts and washers securing master cylinder to servo unit.

Early Cars
6 Withdraw vacuum pipe support strap from mounting stud.

Later Cars
7 Remove reservoir hose guide plate from mounting stud.
8 Lift master cylinder from mounting studs.

Refitting
9 Reverse operations 1 to 8, as applicable.
10 Bleed brakes – 70.25.01.

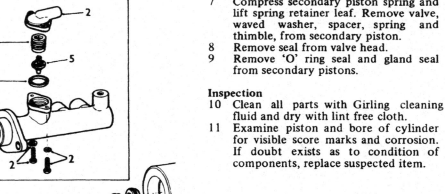

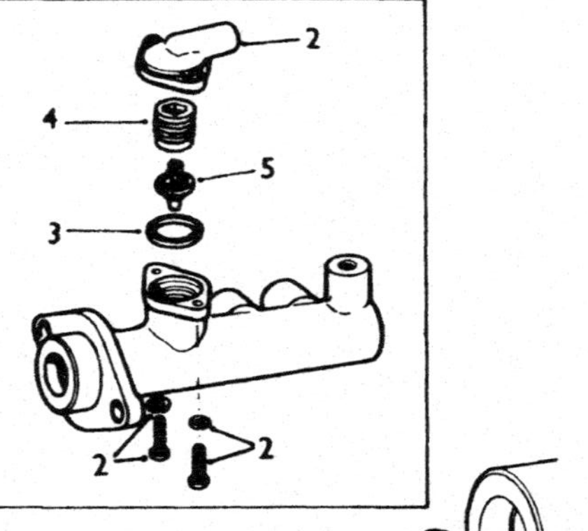

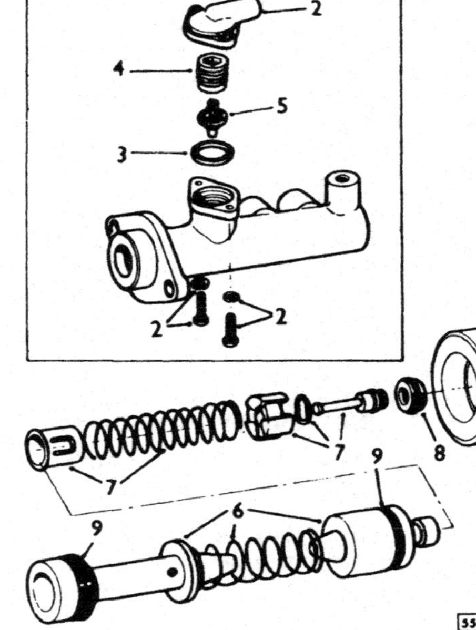

TANDEM MASTER CYLINDER – EARLY CARS

Overhaul **70.30.09**

1 Remove master cylinder – 70.30.08.

NOTE: Overhaul of the master cylinder should be carried out with the work area, tools and hands in a clean condition.

Dismantling
2 Remove Phillips head screws and spring washers securing tipping valve cover, lift off cover.
3 Remove tipping valve seal.
4 Remove tipping valve retaining nut.
5 Depress primary piston into cylinder bore and remove tipping valve.
6 Remove primary piston, spring and secondary piston assembly from master cylinder. It may prove necessary to feed compressed air into master cylinder front inlet port.
7 Compress secondary piston spring and lift spring retainer leaf. Remove valve, waved washer, spacer, spring and thimble, from secondary piston.
8 Remove seal from valve head.
9 Remove 'O' ring seal and gland seal from secondary pistons.

Inspection
10 Clean all parts with Girling cleaning fluid and dry with lint free cloth.
11 Examine piston and bore of cylinder for visible score marks and corrosion. If doubt exists as to condition of components, replace suspected item.

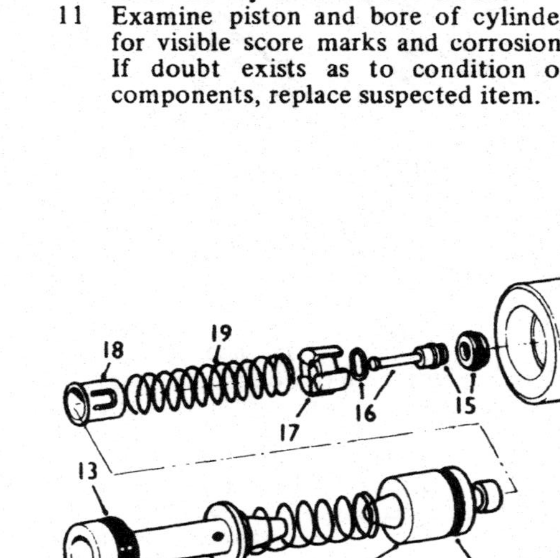

Re-assembling
12 Lubricate all parts with clean brake fluid.
13 Fit gland seal (groove facing forwards) to primary piston.
14 Fit 'O' ring seal to secondary piston.
15 Fit valve seal (smallest diameter leading) to valve head.
16 Position waved washer on valve stem, spring to flare away from valve head.
17 Fit valve spacer (legs first) to valve stem.
18 Position spring retainer over valve stem (keyhole first).
19 Place secondary spring over valve stem and spring washer.

continued

20 Position valve assembly, spring end leading over secondary piston extension ('O' ring seal).
21 Compress secondary spring and position spring retainer over piston extension.
22 Turn down spring retainer leaf behind extension.
23 Lubricate cylinder bore and plunger seals with clean brake fluid.
24 Insert secondary piston, (valve leading), primary spring and primary piston (cone leading) into cylinder bore.
25 Depress primary piston in cylinder bore and fit tipping valve assembly.
26 Secure tipping valve with retaining nut, torque to 35 – 40 lb. ft. (4,84 – 5,53 kg. m.):
27 Fit tipping valve seal and cover, secure with Phillips head screws and spring washers.
28 Refit master cylinder – 70.30.08.

TANDEM MASTER CYLINDER – LATER CARS

Overhaul 70.30.09

1 Remove master cylinder – 70.30.08.

NOTE: Overhaul of the master cylinder should be carried out with the work area, tools and hands in a clean condition.

Dismantling

2 Carefully prise reservoir hose adaptors from sealing grommets.
3 Using suitable screwdriver, lever sealing grommets from master cylinder.
4 Press primary piston into bore of cylinder and withdraw secondary piston stop pin from forward grommet housing.
5 Remove circlip.
6 Tap flange end of cylinder on wooden block to remove primary piston and spring, secondary piston and spring. It may prove necessary to feed compressed air into cylinder front delivery port.

NOTE: Once the piston assemblies are withdrawn the appropriate piston and spring must be kept together. In the event of the springs being mixed, the secondary piston spring can be easily identified; it being slightly thicker and longer than the primary spring.

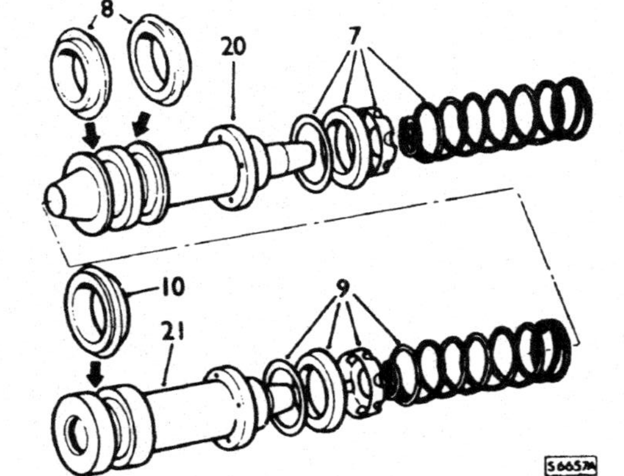

7 Remove spring, spring seat, recuperating seal and washer from secondary piston.
8 Carefully prise seals from rear of secondary piston.
9 Remove spring, spring seat, recuperating seal and washer from primary piston.
10 Carefully prise seal from rear of primary piston.
11 Discard all old seals and associated items that will be replaced by those contained within service kit.

Inspection

12 Clean all parts with Girling cleaning fluid and dry with lint-free cloth.
13 Examine piston and bore of cylinder for visible score marks and corrosion. If doubt exists as to condition of components, replace suspect item.

Re-assembling

WARNING: TO HELP PREVENT DAMAGE IT IS ESSENTIAL THAT GENEROUS AMOUNTS OF CLEAN BRAKE FLUID ARE USED AT ALL STAGES OF SEAL ASSEMBLY.

14 Carefully fit inner seal of secondary piston in locating groove, ensure seal lip faces forwards.
15 Fit remaining seal in locating groove, ensure seal lip faces towards primary piston, i.e. in opposite direction to seal fitted in operation 14.
16 Fit washer, recuperating seal, spring seat and spring over forward end of secondary piston.
17 Carefully fit rear seal of primary piston in locating groove, ensure seal lip faces forward, i.e. away from circlip.
18 Fit washer, recuperating seal, spring seat and spring over forward end of primary piston.
19 Generously lubricate bore of master cylinder with clean brake fluid.

WARNING: ADHERENCE TO THE FOLLOWING INSTRUCTION IS VITALLY IMPORTANT. FAILURE TO COMPLY WILL RESULT IN DAMAGED PISTON SEALS.

20 Secure master cylinder in vice and generously lubricate piston seals in new brake fluid. Offer secondary piston assembly to cylinder till recuperating seal rests centrally in mouth of cylinder. Ensuring seal is not trapped, slowly rotate and rock piston assembly whilst GENTLY introducing piston into cylinder bore. Once recuperating seal enters bore of cylinder SLOWLY push piston into bore in one continuous movement.
21 Repeat operations 19 and 20 with primary piston and spring.
22 Pressing piston into bore of cylinder, fit circlip.
23 Press primary piston into bore of cylinder to full extent, fit secondary piston stop pin.
24 Fit sealing grommets to master cylinder.
25 Lubricate hose adaptors with brake fluid and press into sealing grommets.
26 Refit master cylinder – 70.30.08.

FLUID RESERVOIR – MASTER CYLINDER

Remove and refit 70.30.16

Removing

1 Disconnect battery – 86.15.20.
2 Remove reservoir cap and float assembly (cap turns independently of terminal block).
3 Slacken clips securing hoses to reservoir.
4 Place suitable container beneath reservoir hoses.
5 Slide hoses clear of reservoir and allow fluid to drain into container.
6 Plug hose ends to prevent ingress of dirt.
7 Remove nuts, bolts and flat washers securing reservoir to mounting bracket, Lift off reservoir.
8 Remove reservoir filter element.

Refitting

9 Reverse operations 1 to 8.
10 Bleed brakes – 70.25.02.

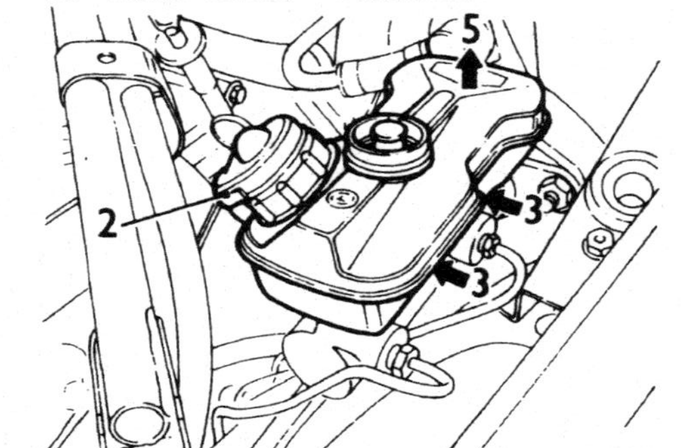

NOTE: 1977 and later cars, except L.H.D. cars for Norway, Sweden and Finland, are fitted with fluid reservoirs attached directly to the master cylinder, as shown.

FLUID RESERVOIR – LATER CARS

Remove and refit **70.30.16**

Removing

1 Disconnect battery, see 86.15.20.
2 Remove reservoir cap and switch assembly.
3 Detach two spring clips and withdraw two retaining pins.
4 Place suitable container in position to catch fluid.
5 Pull reservoir vertically away from master cylinder.
6 Fit closing plugs to grommets in master cylinder ports.

Refitting

7 Prise grommets from master cylinder ports.
8 Inspect ports for complete cleanliness and fit new grommets, lubricating them with brake fluid before insertion.
9 Press replacement reservoir into position.
10 Replace retaining pins and spring clips.
11 Fill reservoir to bottom of neck with recommended fluid (Castrol-Girling Universal Brake and Clutch Fluid).
12 Re-connect battery, see 86.15.20.
13 Bleed brakes, see 70.25.02.

PEDAL BOX

Remove and refit **70.35.03**

Removing

1 Disconnect battery – 86.15.20.
2 Disconnect four brake fluid pipes from master cylinder, tape or plug pipes to prevent loss of fluid and ingress of dirt.

3 Peel cover from brake reservoir cap and disconnect leads from fluid level indicator switch.
4 Remove two nuts, flat washers and bolts securing brake fluid reservoir to mounting bracket, carefully lift reservoir from car.
5 Slacken clip securing brake vacuum hose to servo adaptor, slide hose from adaptor.

Left Hand Drive Cars – Manual Transmission Only

6 Remove banjo bolt securing clutch slave cylinder hose to clutch master cylinder, recover copper washers and Tape-up banjo union and master cylinder outlet.
7 Remove self locking nut securing slave cylinder hose to pedal box position hose clear of servo assembly.

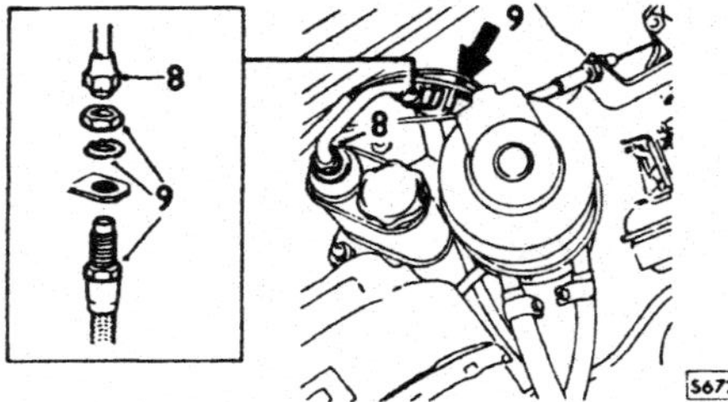

Right Hand Drive Cars – Manual Transmission Only

8 Release nuts securing clutch feed pipe to master cylinder and slave cylinder hose, remove pipe from car. Tape-up open ends of pipe and master cylinder.
9 Remove locknut securing slave cylinder hose to reservoir mounting bracket, disengage hose from bracket and tape-up open end of hose.
10 Remove self-locking nut (adjacent to clutch pedal housing) securing steering column lower mounting bracket to pedal box.

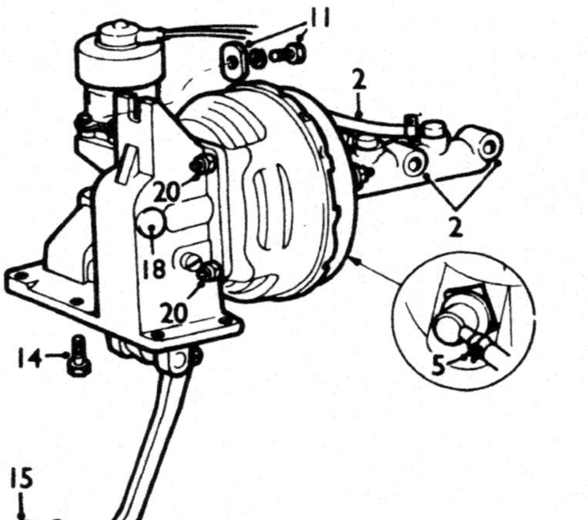

All Cars

11 Remove bolt, oval washer and spacer securing upper portion of pedal box to bulkhead.
12 Position drivers seat to rear as far as possible, remove seat cushion – 76.70.02, and lift out footwell carpets.
13 Remove brake stop light switch – 86.65.51.
14 Remove five bolts (right hand drive cars), six bolts (left hand drive cars), flat washers and spring washers securing pedal box base to bulkhead, recover clips retaining footwell noise absorbing mats.
15 Remove rubber pad from brake pedal.

Manual Transmission Cars only

16 Remove nut and spring washer securing clutch pedal to operating lever, lift pedal from lever.

All Cars

17 Carefully raise servo unit, pedal box and master cylinder, draw complete assembly forward and lift from car.
18 Prise two rubber sealing plugs from sides of pedal box.
19 Remove split pin, washer and clevis pin securing brake pedal lever to servo operating rod.
20 Remove nuts securing pedal box to servo unit. If reservoir bracket is mounted on servo studs, lift off bracket and recover spacers. Detach pedal box from servo unit.

Refitting

21 Reverse operations 1 to 20; fit new split pin to servo rod clevis pin.
22 Bleed clutch (manual transmission cars) – 33.15.01.
23 Bleed brakes – 70.25.02.

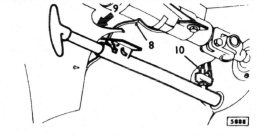

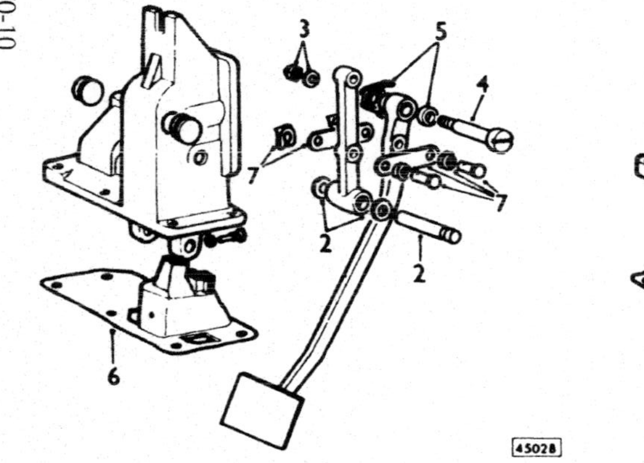

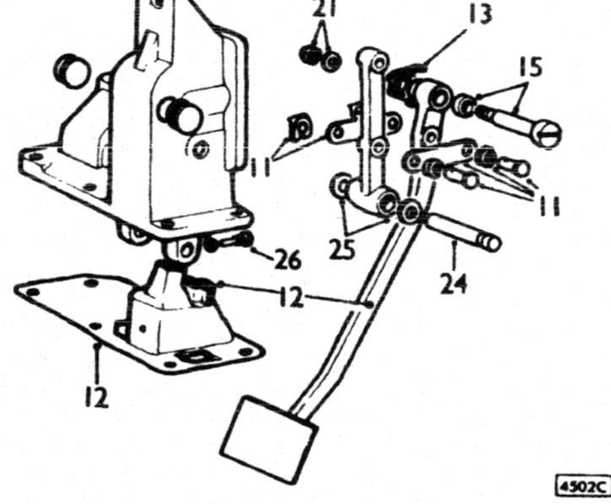

PEDAL BOX

Overhaul 70.35.04

1 Remove pedal box – 70.35.03.

Dismantling

2 Carefully drift lower pivot shaft from pedal box, recover nylon washers from either side of lever boss.

3 Remove self locking nut and flat washer securing pedal lever upper pivot shaft.

4 Using narrow drift, carefully remove upper pivot shaft from lever and pedal box.

5 Withdraw pedal lever assembly from box, recover nylon washers and return spring.

6 Remove rubber boot by turning boot inside out and withdrawing over upper portion of levers.

7 Remove retaining clips, clevis pins and spring washers securing link arms to pedal levers.

Inspection

8 Clean all pedal lever components.

9 Examine pivot shafts, clevis pins, bushes and thrust washers for wear, should doubt exist as to condition a new component must be fitted.

Re-assembling

10 Slightly coat pivot shafts and thrust washers with grease.

11 Fit link arms to pedal lever, secure with clevis pins, spring washers and retaining clips.

12 Slide rubber boot over pedal levers, ensure that hole with side extensions fits over long pedal lever.

13 Position pedal lever return spring over extended boss of long lever, raise neck of rubber boot and locate spring hook over lever.

14 Position pedal box in vice.

15 Locate upper pivot shaft in one side of pedal box, enter shaft sufficient to allow nylon washer to locate on threaded portion of shaft.

16 Enter lever assembly into box, ensure return spring leg locates in guide channel.

17 Align pedal lever upper boss with upper shaft.

18 Enter shaft into boss, adjust nylon washer to locate over shaft.

19 Position second nylon washer between pedal box and extended boss of pedal lever.

20 Carefully push upper shaft fully home.

21 Position flat washer over shaft and secure with new locknut.

22 Check operation of pedal lever, ensure lever operates freely.

23 Align small lever pivot boss with pedal box shaft mountings.

24 Ensuring groove in lower pivot shaft will align with retaining pin locating hole, enter shaft in box.

25 Locate nylon washers on either side of lever boss and push pivot shaft fully home.

26 Align pivot shaft groove with retaining pin hole, test fit retaining pin.

27 Check condition of servo/pedal box gasket and if necessary fit new gasket.

28 Refit pedal box.

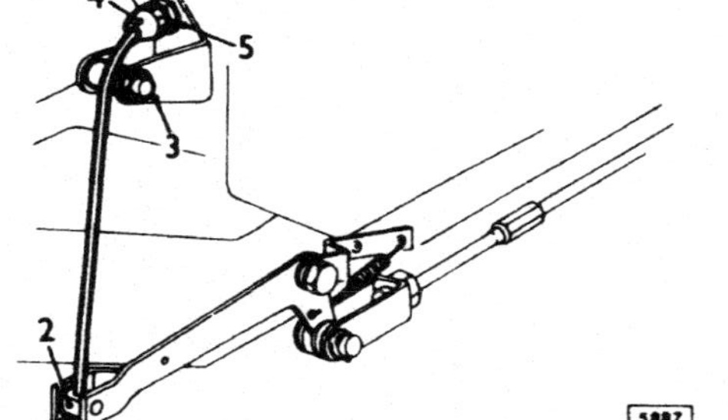

HANDBRAKE LEVER ASSEMBLY

Remove and refit 70.35.08

Removing

1 Disconnect battery – 86.15.20.

2 Disconnect handbrake operating cables at bell crank lever.

3 Remove split pin, washer and clevis pin securing nylon roller to mounting bracket, withdraw roller.

4 Remove protective cover from nut securing nylon roller mounting bracket.

5 Remove nut securing roller mounting bracket.

6 Remove drivers side dash liner – 76.46.11.

7 Remove steering column trim cover.

8 Peel back trim covering handbrake mounting bracket securing bolts.

9 Remove bolts securing handbrake assembly to footwell side panel.

10 Noting terminal locations detach electrical leads from handbrake warning switch.

NOTE: If new handbrake assembly is to be fitted, remove warning switch from old handbrake. Fit and adjust warning switch to new handbrake assembly – 86.65.46.

Refitting

11 Reverse operations 1 to 9, fit new split pins to all clevis pins.

HANDBRAKE CABLE

Adjust 70.35.10

Adjusting

1 Set handbrake fully off.

2 Slacken front yoke locknut.

3 Remove split pins, flat washer and clevis pin securing yoke to bell crank lever.

4 Check handbrake calipers are "fully off".

5 Turn back yoke on adjuster rod, to a point, that when yoke is connected to handbrake lever a slight amount of slack is apparent within the cable.

NOTE: Should cable be adjusted so that all slack is removed, binding of the handbrake caliper may result.

6 Reconnect yoke to handbrake bell crank lever, secure clevis pin with new split pin.

7 Tighten yoke locknut.

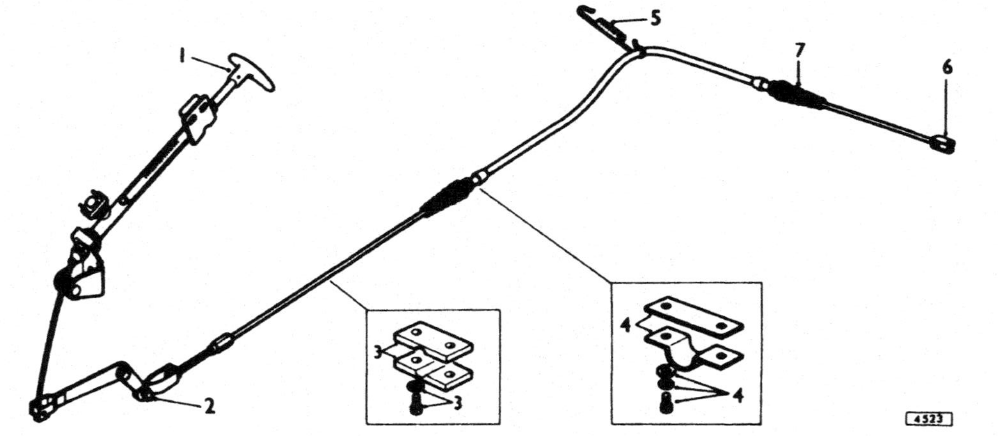

HANDBRAKE CABLE ASSEMBLY

Remove and refit 70.35.16

Removing
1 Set handbrake fully off.
2 Remove split pin, flat washer and clevis pin securing front yoke to bell crank lever.
3 Remove guide securing handbrake inner cable to underside of car body.
4 Remove guide securing outer cable to underside of car body.
5 Release guide spring from outer cable.
6 Remove split pin, flat washer and clevis pin securing rear yoke to handbrake caliper operating lever.
7 Slide rubber grommet clear of opposite handbrake lever; detach cable from lever.
8 Remove cable from car.

Refitting
9 Reverse operations 1 to 8, fit new split pins to clevis pins.
10 Check handbrake and adjust if necessary – 70.35.10.

BRAKE PADS – FRONT

Remove and refit 70.40.02

Service Tool: Brake piston retractor tool 64932392

Removing
1 Remove road wheel.

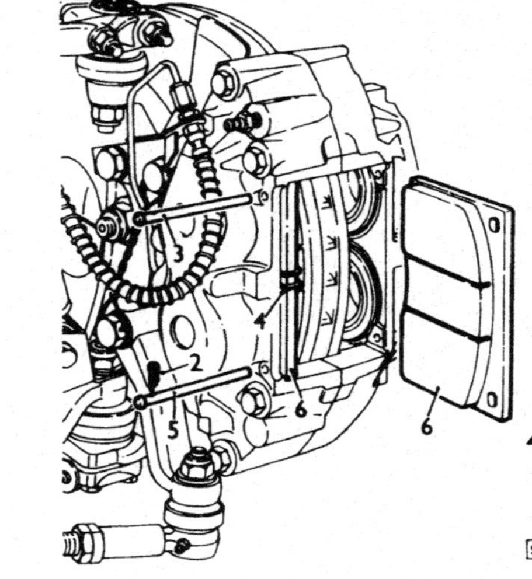

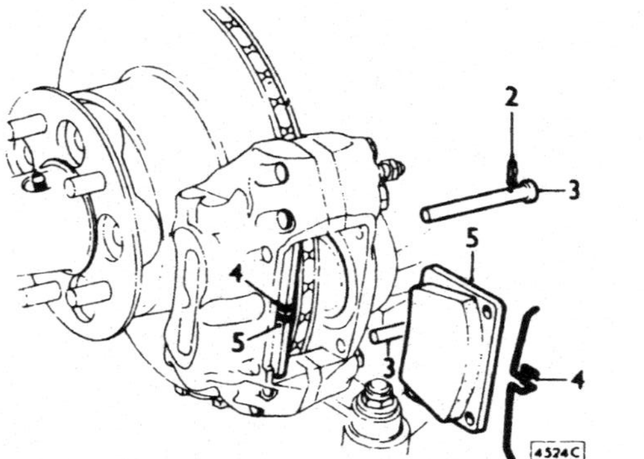

2 Remove clips securing retaining pins.
3 Remove retaining pins.
4 Recover anti-chatter springs.
5 Withdraw worn pads.

Refitting

NOTE: It is advisable to reduce level of brake fluid in reservoir before fitting new pads.

If thickness of any pad is less than 0.125 in. (3,17 mm.) new pads MUST be fitted.

6 Lever pistons into cylinder bores using service tool 64932392.
7 Fit new brake pads to caliper.
8 Fit retaining pins.
9 Secure retaining pins with clips.
10 Fit anti-chatter springs.
11 Refit road wheel.
12 Top up brake fluid reservoir.
13 Run engine and apply brake pedal several times until pedal feels solid.

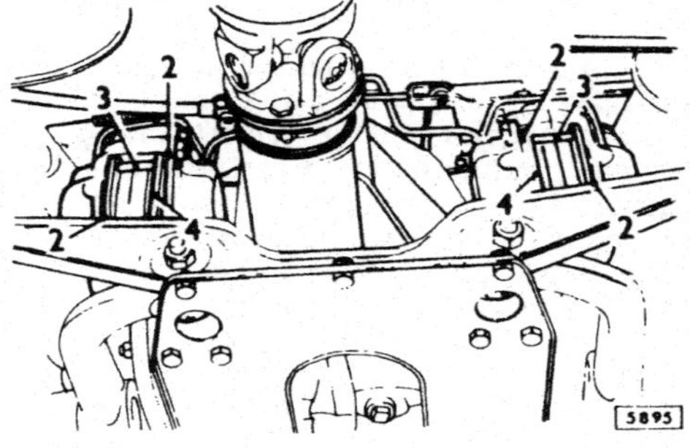

BRAKE PADS – REAR

Remove and refit 70.40.03

Service Tool: Brake piston retractor tool 64932392

Removing
1 Jack up rear of car and place on stands, or raise car on ramp.
2 Remove clips securing friction pad mounting pins.
3 Remove mounting pins.
4 Withdraw friction pads.

Refitting

NOTE: Prior to fitting new brake pads reduce level of brake fluid in reservoir to prevent ejection.

If thickness of any pad is less than 0.125 in. (3,17 mm.) new pads MUST be fitted.

5 Using service tool 64932392 lever pistons into cylinder bores.
6 Fit new brake pads, locate with mounting pins, ensuring upper mounting pin enters caliper from centre line of car and lower mounting pin enters caliper from wheel side of car.
7 Fit retaining clips to pad mounting pins.
8 Top up brake fluid reservoir.
9 Remove stands.
10 Run engine and apply brake pedal several times until pedal feels solid.

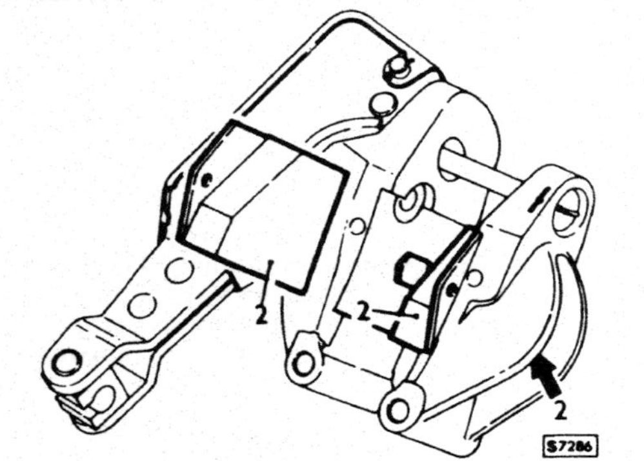

HANDBRAKE PADS

Remove and refit **70.40.04**

Removing

1 Remove handbrake caliper – 70.55.04.
2 Remove nut and spring washer securing pads to brake pad carriers, remove pads.

Refitting

3 Holding one pad carrier, wind remaining one out two or three turns.
4 Fit new brake pads to carrier using new nut and spring washer.
5 Refit handbrake caliper.
6 Operate handbrake several times to adjust pads to correct clearance.

SERVO ASSEMBLY

Remove and refit **70.50.01**

Removing

1 Remove pedal box – 70.35.03.
2 Remove nuts securing master cylinder to servo unit.
3 Detach master cylinder and vacuum pipe support bracket from servo unit.
4 Prise vacuum pipe connector from servo, recover rubber sealing washer.

Refitting

5 Reverse operations 1 to 4, fit new sealing rubber to vacuum pipe connector.

BRAKE SERVO – CHECK AND TEST PROCEDURE

70.50.05

The following tests on the vacuum system should only be carried out with the hydraulic braking system in a satisfactory condition.

Servo Test and Check

1 Jack up front of car and confirm one wheel turns freely. Start engine, allow vacuum to build up and apply brake pedal several times. It should be possible to rotate wheel immediately pedal is released. If brakes bind a defective servo unit is indicated.
2 With engine running apply brake pedal several times and check operation of pedal. If response is sluggish, check condition of vacuum hoses and servo unit air filter.
3 Switch off engine and operate brake pedal several times to evacuate vacuum in system. Hold a light foot pressure on pedal and start engine. If servo is operating correctly, pedal will fall under existing foot pressure. If pedal remains stationary a leaking vacuum system is indicated.

SERVO ASSEMBLY

Overhaul **70.50.06**

The servo assembly is a sealed unit and overhaul is not possible, should the operation of the servo unit deteriorate to an extent where braking efficiency is affected, a replacement unit must be fitted.

NON RETURN VALVE

Remove and refit **70.50.15**

Removing

1 Slacken clips securing vacuum hoses to non return valve.
2 Pull hoses from non-return valve, lift valve from car.

Refitting

3 Prior to refitting, blow through valve to test one way action.
4 Ensuring arrow stamped on barrel of valve points away from manifold vacuum hose, fit valve to hoses.
5 Fully tighten hose securing clips.

FRONT CALIPER

Remove and refit **70.55.02**

Removing

1 Slacken feed pipe union at caliper and disconnect feed pipe union at support bracket; plug pipe to prevent loss of fluid and ingress of dirt.
2 Remove locking wire securing caliper mounting bolts.
NOTE: Do not under any circumstances remove four setbolts securing two halves of caliper.
3 Remove caliper mounting bolts, note position and number of shims located between steering arm and caliper.
4 Withdraw caliper from disc.

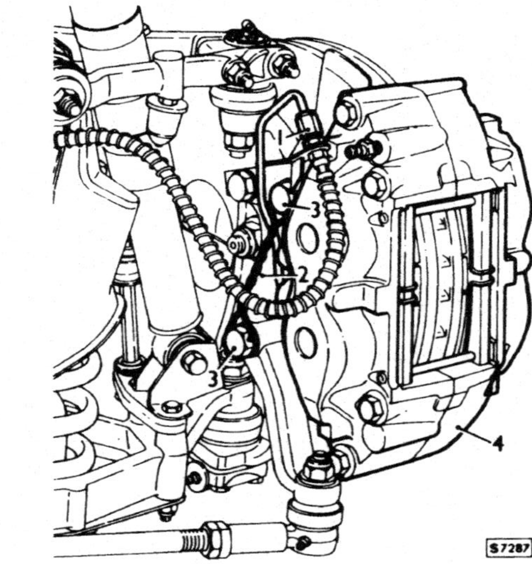

Refitting

5 If new caliper is to be fitted, reverse operations 3 and 4 and carry out caliper/disc centralisation – 70.10.10 operations 10 to 14. If no adjustment is necessary reverse operations 2 and 3.
6 Where original caliper is refitted reverse operations 1 to 5. In either case tighten caliper mounting bolts to 50 to 60 lb. ft. (7,0 to 8,3 kgf. m.).
7 Bleed brakes – 70.25.02.

REAR CALIPER

Remove and refit **70.55.03**

Removing
1 Remove handbrake caliper – 70.55.04.
2 Slacken caliper feed pipe union at three way connector.
3 Disconnect feed pipe at caliper, swing pipe clear of caliper, plug holes to prevent ingress of dirt and loss of fluid.
4 Remove brake friction pads – 70.40.03.
5 Remove lock wire securing caliper mounting bolts.
CAUTION: Under no circumstances must caliper be split by removing four set bolts securing two halves of caliper.
6 Remove caliper mounting bolts.
7 Slide caliper around brake disc and withdraw through gap exposed by removal of tie plate.

Refitting
8 Offer caliper to mountings, fit mounting bolts and torque to 49 – 55 lbs. ft (6,7 – 7,6 kg.m.).
9 Check caliper is central of disc. Adjust as necessary, by adding or withdrawing brake disc shims – 70.10.11.
NOTE: If adjustment carried out, camber angle must be checked as a final operation – 64.25.18.
10 Wire lock caliper mounting bolts.
NOTE: Prior to fitting friction pads, check pads for wear. Minimum thickness being 0.125 in. (3,17 mm.).
11 Reverse operation 1 to 4.
12 Bleed brakes – 70.25.02.

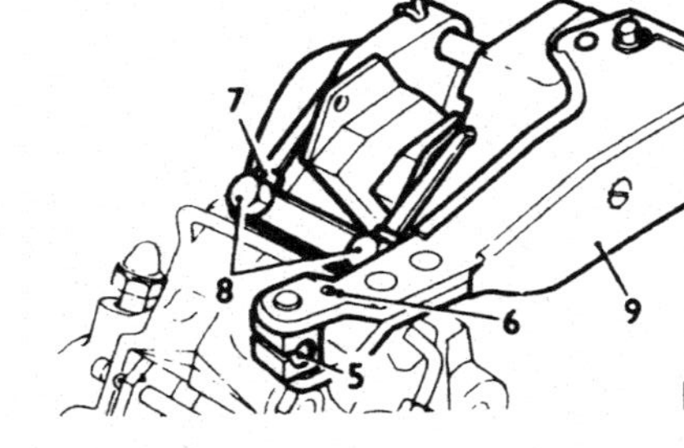

HANDBRAKE MECHANISM

Remove and refit **70.55.04**

Removing
1 Place car on ramp.
2 Remove nuts and bolts securing tie plate to suspension unit, lift off tie plate.
3 Place handbrake fully off.
4 Remove split pin and clevis pin securing handbrake cable to caliper operating lever.
5 Detach handbrake cable from remaining operating lever.
6 Unclip return spring from handbrake operating lever.
7 Turn down locking tabs securing handbrake caliper mounting bolts.
8 Remove mounting bolts, tab washer and retraction lever.
9 Slide caliper around brake disc and withdraw through gap exposed by removal of tie plate.

Refitting
10 If new pads are fitted, or mechanism overhauled, adjust caliper. Holding one pad carrier, rotate remaining one to give a dimension of 0.75 in. (19,05 mm.) between pad surfaces.
11 Reverse operations 7 to 9.
12 Operate actuating lever until adjuster ratchet ceases to click, this adjusts pads to correct clearance.
13 Reverse operations 1 to 6.

BRAKE CALIPER – FRONT – EARLY CARS

Overhaul **70.55.13**

Service Tool: Piston Clamp 18G72

1 Remove front friction pads – 70.40.02.
2 Remove front caliper – 70.55.02.
3 Thoroughly clean caliper using Girling brake cleaner.

Dismantling
CAUTION: Under no circumstances must the caliper halves be separated.
4 Fit piston clamp to caliper, retaining two OUTBOARD pistons in position.
5 Carefully feed compressed air into caliper fluid inlet port, expelling large inboard piston.

7 6 8 5 5054A

6 Remove piston and dust seal from caliper.
7 Remove dust seal from piston.

WARNING: EXTREME CARE MUST BE TAKEN NOT TO DAMAGE THE CYLINDER BORE WHEN EXTRACTING SEAL
8 Carefully prise seal from recess in cylinder wall.

Inspection
9 Using Girling brake cleaner thoroughly clean piston, cylinder bore and seal groove.
10 Examine piston and cylinder bore for signs of corrosion or scratches. Should doubt exist as to condition, a new component must be fitted.

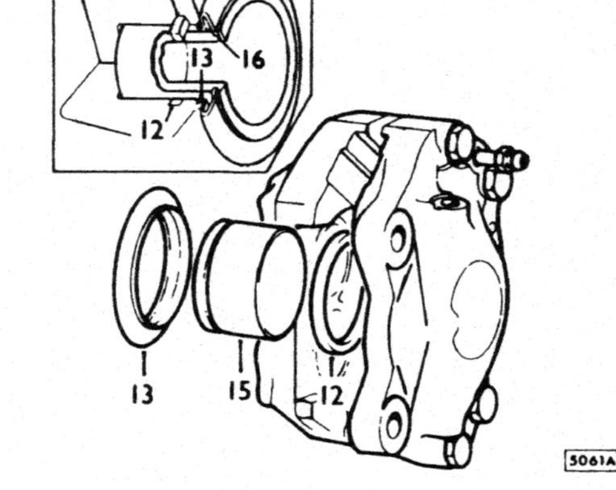

Assembling
11 Coat new seal in Girling Disc brake lubricant.
12 Using 'fingers' ONLY fit new seal to recess in cylinder bore.
13 Locate dust cover in outer groove in cylinder bore.
14 Coat piston in clean disc brake lubricant.
15 Enter piston into cylinder bore through dust seal.
16 Locate dust seal in groove in piston.
17 Release piston clamp and refit to retain large INBOARD Piston in location in cylinder bore.
18 Repeat operations 5 to 15 on remaining two small pistons held in caliper.
19 Fit piston clamp to outboard pistons and press fully home.
20 Refit caliper to car.

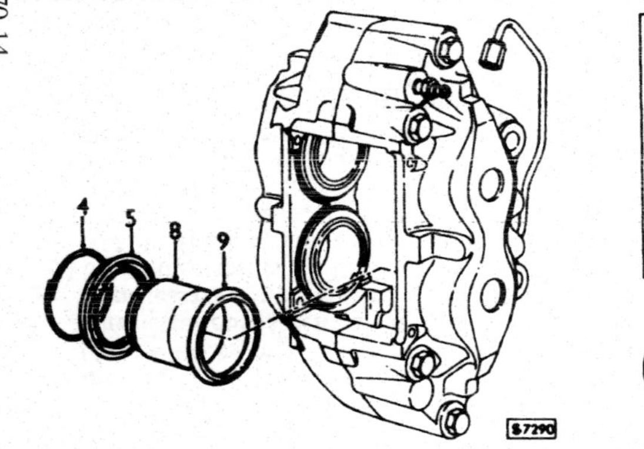

BRAKE CALIPER – FRONT – LATER CARS

Overhaul **70.55.13**

Service Tool: 18G672 Piston Clamp

1 Remove front friction pads, see 70.40.

2 Remove front caliper, see 70.55.02.
3 Thoroughly clean caliper with Girling brake cleaner.

Dismantling
CAUTION: Under no circumstances must caliper halves be separated.
4 Remove spring clips securing piston dust covers.
5 Remove covers from pistons.
6 Fit piston clamp to any half of caliper.
7 To expel pistons carefully feed compressed air into caliper fluid inlet port.
8 Remove pistons from caliper. **WARNING: EXTREME CARE MUST BE TAKEN NOT TO DAMAGE CYLINDER BORE WHEN EXTRACTING SEALS.**
9 Carefully prise seals from recess in cylinder wall.

Inspection
10 Using Girling brake cleaner thoroughly clean piston, cylinder bore and seal groove.
11 Examine piston and cylinder bore for signs of corrosion or scratches. Should doubt exist as to condition a new component must be fitted.

Assembling
12 Coat new seals in Girling brake disc lubricant.
13 Using fingers ONLY fit new seals to recess in cylinder bore.
14 Coat piston in clean disc brake lubricant.
15 Enter pistons into cylinder bores.
16 Fit new dust covers over pistons.
17 Push pistons fully home.
18 Locate dust cover over rim in caliper, secure with spring clips.
19 Release piston clamp and fit to opposite half of caliper.
20 Repeat operations 5 to 18 on remaining two pistons.
21 Refit caliper to car.

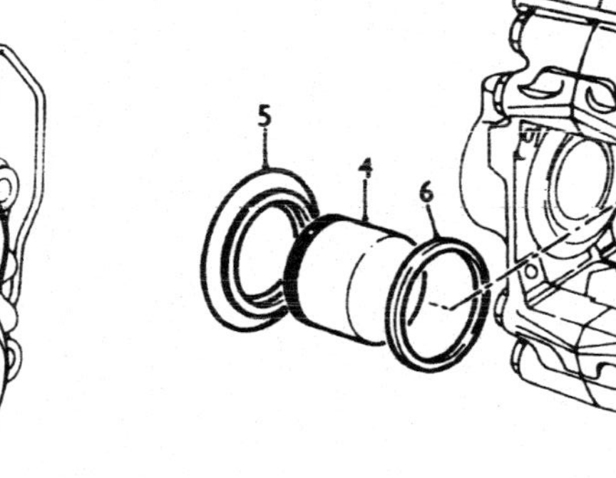

BRAKE CALIPER – REAR

Overhaul **70.55.14**

Service Tool: Piston Clamp 18G672

1 Remove rear brake caliper – 70.55.03.
2 Thoroughly clean caliper using Girling cleaning fluid.

Dismantling
CAUTION: Under no circumstances must the caliper halves be separated.
3 Fit piston clamp to retain one piston in location.
4 Carefully feed compressed air into caliper fluid inlet port expelling one piston.
5 Remove dust seal from piston and caliper cylinder bore. **WARNING: EXTREME CARE MUST BE TAKEN NOT TO DAMAGE THE CYLINDER BORE WHEN EXTRACTING SEAL.**
6 Carefully prise seal from recess in cylinder bore.

Inspection
7 Using Girling Brake cleaner thoroughly clean piston, cylinder bore and seal recess.

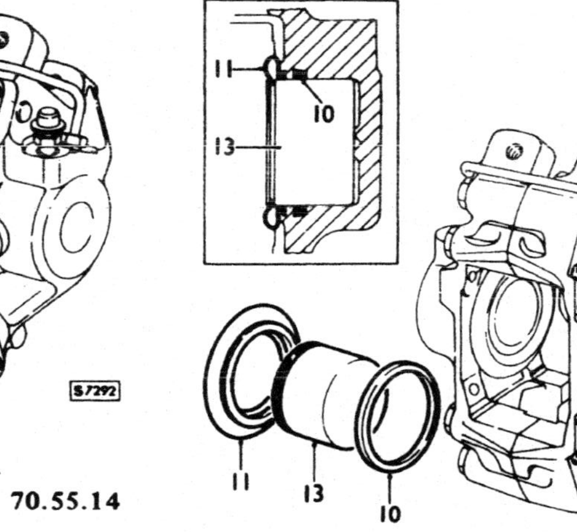

8 Examine piston and cylinder for signs of corrosion or scratches. Should doubt exist as to condition, a new component must be fitted.

Assembly
9 Coat new seal with Girling disc brake lubricant.
10 Using 'fingers' ONLY fit new seal to recess in cylinder bore.
11 Locate dust cover in outer groove in cylinder bore.
12 Coat piston in clean disc brake lubricant.
13 Enter piston into cylinder bore through dust seal.
14 Locate dust seal into groove in piston.
15 Release piston clamp and fit to opposite side of caliper to press 'serviced' piston fully home.
16 Repeat operations 4 to 15 on remaining cylinder piston.
17 Remove piston clamp.
18 Refit rear brake caliper to car.

ALIGNMENT CHECK

Service tool – Body alignment jig
L.W.B. adaptor plates for use with jig 700;
J700 – 1148. S700 – 1111.

Data Check **76.10.01**

NOTE: The datum line is established by positioning the car (unladen, correct tyre pressures and fuel tanks full) on a flat surface and rolling the car forward approximately 40 ft. (12 m.). The datum line being 13.12 in. (33,3 cm.) above ground level at front and 13.31 in. (33,8 cm.) at rear, each measurement being taken through the centre line of wheel hubs.

The following measurements are also applicable for 2 door cars.

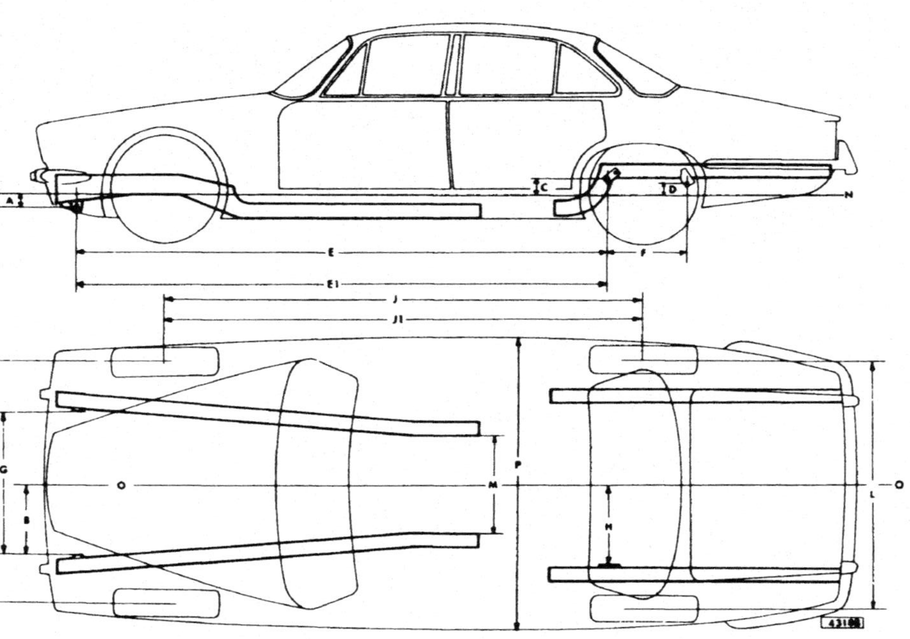

Symbol	Measurement taken from	Inches	Centimetres
	All cars		
A	Front suspension mounting point to datum line.	3.05	7,7
B	Inner face of front suspension mounting point to centre line of car.	15.56	39,0
C	Rear suspension front lower mounting point to datum line.	4.54	11,5
D	Rear suspension rear lower mounting point to datum line	4.34	11,0
	Short wheel base cars only		
E	Front suspension front mounting point to rear suspension front lower mounting point.	116.54	296,0
	Long wheel base cars only		
E1	Front suspension front mounting point to rear suspension front lower mounting point.	120.54	306,1
	All cars		
F	Rear suspension front lower mounting point to rear suspension rear lower mounting point.	13.06	33,05
G	Distance between inner faces of front suspension mounting points.	31.12	79,04
H	Distance between inner face of rear suspension front mounting bracket and centre line of car	19.53	49,7
	Short wheel base cars only		
J	Wheel base	108.97	276,4
	Long wheel base cars only		
J1	Wheel base	112.87	288,5
	All cars		
K	Track (front)	58.0	147,0
L	Track (rear)	58.66	149,1
M	Distance between inner faces at rear of front chassis members.	13.43	34,1
N	Horizontal datum line.	–	–
O	Centre line of car.	–	–
P	Overall width of car.	69.6	176,3

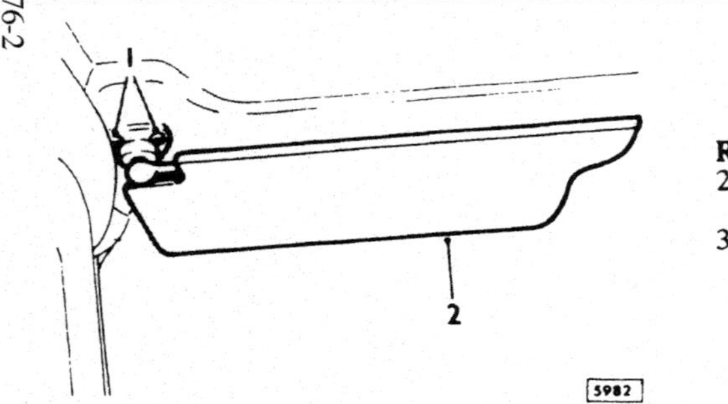

SUN VISORS

Remove and refit 76.10.47

Removing

1 Remove two screws securing visor bracket to headlining trim rail.
2 Lift off visor.

Refitting

Reverse operations 1 and 2.

INTERIOR MIRROR

Remove and refit 76.10.51

Removing

1 Remove screws securing mirror arm to headlining trim rail, lift off mirror.
NOTE: It is possible to detach mirror arm from mounting bracket by applying tension to mirror arm until arm disengages from socket in mounting bracket.

Refitting

2 Fit mirror arm to headlining trim rail, secure with screws.
3 If mirror detached at socket, position arm ball in socket mouth and strike rear of ball with heel of hand.

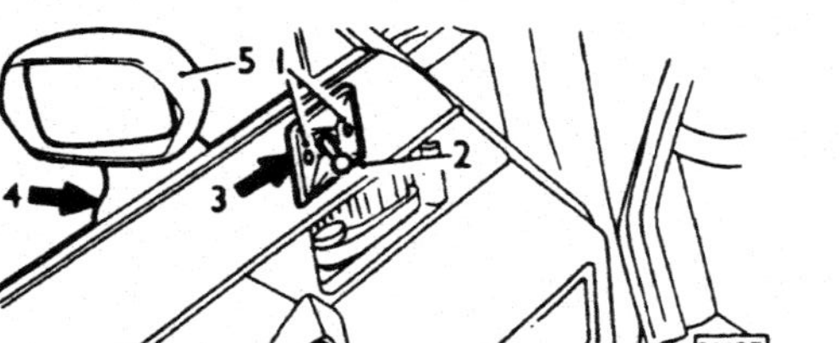

EXTERIOR MIRROR (REMOTE CONTROLLED)

Remove and refit 76.10.52

Removing

1 Remove two screws securing adjusting lever surround to door trim.
2 Partially withdraw adjusting lever and surround from trim.
3 Slacken grub screw securing surround to adjusting lever, withdraw surround from lever.
4 Remove two screws securing mirror to door.
5 Remove mirror and mounting pad, carefully withdrawing adjusting cable through door.

Refitting

Reverse operations 1 to 5

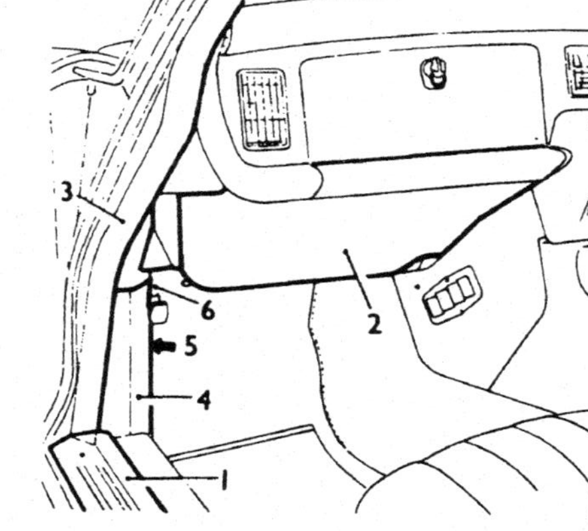

FRONT TRIM CASING

Remove and refit 76.13.01

Removing

1 Remove door sill tread plate – 76.76.01.
2 Remove underscuttle casing – 76.46.11.
3 Release 8 in. (200 mm.) of draught welting.
4 Peel trim from lip of door aperture.
5 Remove two screws securing trim casing to side of foot well.
6 Disengage trim casing from air vent regulator control and lift casing from car.

Refitting

7 Reverse operations 1 to 6; apply suitable sealing compound to area of trim covering draught welting locating lip.
8 Check operation of fresh air control.

'A' POST TRIM CASING

Remove and refit 76.13.07

Removing

1 Remove facia crash roll – 76.46.04.
2 Remove screw securing trim casing to mounting plate.
3 Slacken nut securing trim casing mounting plate to screen rail.

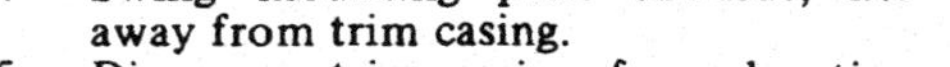

4 Swing mounting plate inwards, i.e. away from trim casing.
5 Disengage trim casing from locating clip and lift from car.

Refitting

Reverse operations 1 to 5.

'B' POST TRIM CASING – FOUR DOOR CARS

Remove and refit 76.13.08

Removing

1 Prise interior light cover from 'B' Post.
2 Carefully prise trim casing from 'B' Post.

Refitting

Reverse operations 1 and 2.

CANTRAIL CRASH ROLL – FOUR DOOR CARS

Remove and refit **76.13.10**

Removing
1 Remove screws securing coat hook to cantrail, lift off hook.
2 Prise cantrail complete with crash roll from roof rail.

Refitting
Reverse operations 1 and 2.

CANTRAIL CRASH ROLL – TWO DOOR CARS

Remove and refit **76.13.10**

Removing
1 Disconnect battery – 86.15.20.
2 Remove interior light – 86.45.04.
3 Remove rear quarter crash roll – 76.13.15.
4 Remove rear passenger grab handle – 76.58.30.
5 Remove rear parcel shelf – 76.67.06.
6 Remove two screws located in interior light aperture securing cantrail to roof rail.
7 Carefully disengage cantrail securing clips from roof rail.

Refitting
Reverse operations 1 to 7.

REAR QUARTER TRIM CASING – TWO DOOR CARS

Remove and refit **76.13.14**

Removing
1 Remove rear seat squab – 76.70.38.
2 Remove door sill tread plate – 76.76.01.
3 Release 8 in. (200 mm.) of draught welting from rear door of aperture.

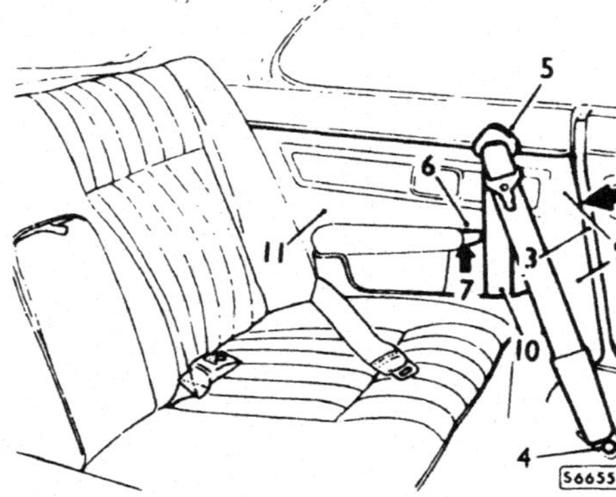

4 Remove bolt securing seat belt lower anchorage plate to sill, note position of washers, spacers and spring.
5 Unclip plastic casing covering seat belt upper anchorage plate, remove belt securing anchor plate to body.
6 Remove screw securing chrome bezel to front of armrest, slide bezel forward and disengage from armrest.
7 Remove screw exposed by removal of bezel.
8 Peel trim from lip of door aperture.
9 Prise edges of trim casing from body.
10 Feed seat belt through guide aperture in trim casing.
11 Lift casing from car.

Refitting
Reverse operations 1 to 11.

REAR QUARTER CRASH ROLL – TWO DOOR CARS

Remove and refit **76.13.15**

Removing
1 Remove rear quarter trim casing – 76.13.14.
2 Remove two screws securing crash roll to body.
3 Push crash roll forward and disengage from locating pegs.
4 Raise crash roll and lift from car.

Refitting
Reverse operations 1 to 4.

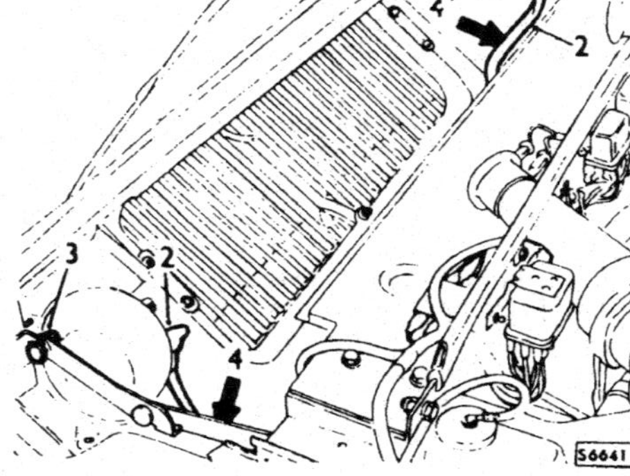

BONNET

Remove and refit **76.16.01**

Removing
1 Disconnect battery – 86.15.20.
2 Disconnect cables feeding headlamps at snap connectors.
3 Remove nut and bolt securing bonnet stay to bonnet.
4 Remove six bolts, spring washers and flat washers securing bonnet to hinges, lift bonnet from hinges.

Refitting
5 Fit bonnet to hinges, do not fully tighten securing bolts.
6 Close bonnet and centralise if necessary.
7 Open bonnet and fully tighten securing bolts.
8 Reverse operations 1 to 3.

BONNET HINGES

Remove and refit **76.16.12**

Removing
1 Remove bonnet – 76.16.01.
2 Remove bonnet assist springs – 76.16.13.
3 Remove lower grille – 76.55.06.
4 Remove four bolts from inside wheel arch securing sides of front apron panel to body.

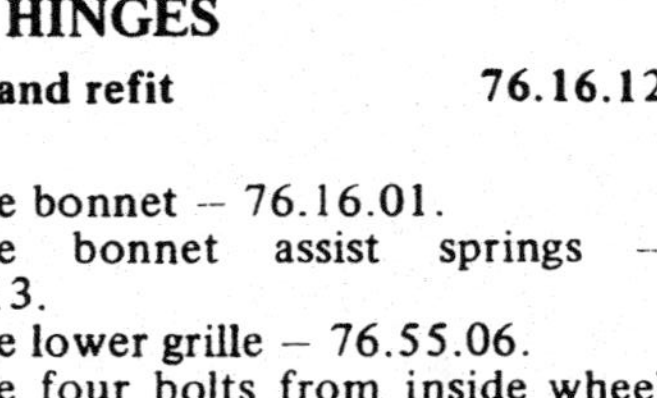
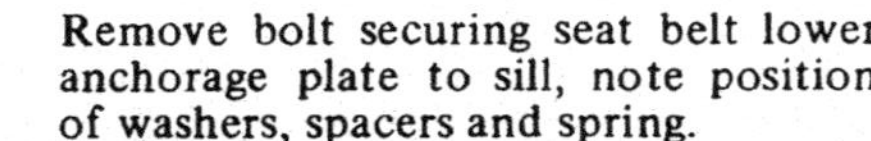

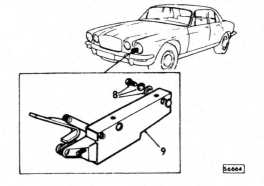

5 Remove three screws securing underside of apron panel to body.
6 Carefully withdraw apron panel from car.
7 Remove radiator – 26.40.04.
8 Remove three bolts, flat washers and star washers securing hinge and bumper mounting bracket to subframe.
9 Remove bonnet hinge and humper mounting bracket from subframe.

Refitting
Reverse operations 1 to 9. Cover with underseal bolts securing mounting bracket assembly and area where bracket enters subframe.

BONNET ASSIST SPRING

Remove and refit **76.16.13**

Removing
1 Remove front bumper – 76.22.08.
2 Open bonnet and remove nut and bolt securing stay to bonnet, allow bonnet to fully open.

continued

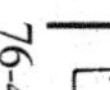

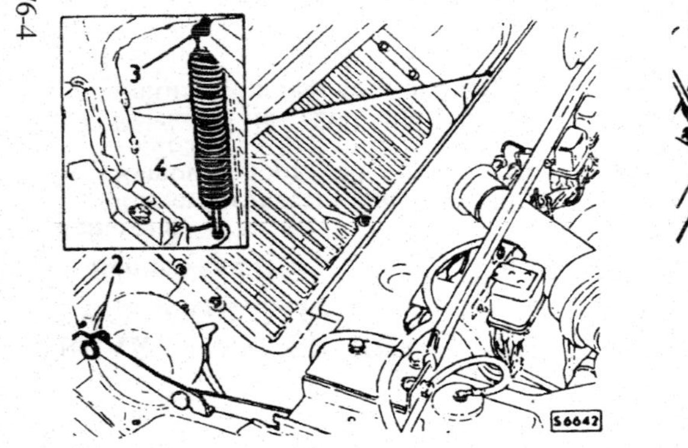

3 Using suitable screwdriver, unhook spring from upper fixing point.
4 Unhook spring from lower fixing point and lift from car.

Refitting
Reverse operations 1 to 4.

BONNET LOCK ADJUST

Adjusting **76.16.20**

1 Slacken locknut at base of striker peg.
2 Rotate peg in or out as required until bonnet, in lock position is flush and central with surrounding bodypanels.
3 Tighten peg locknut.

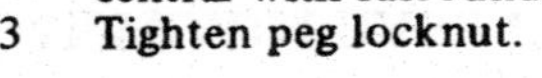

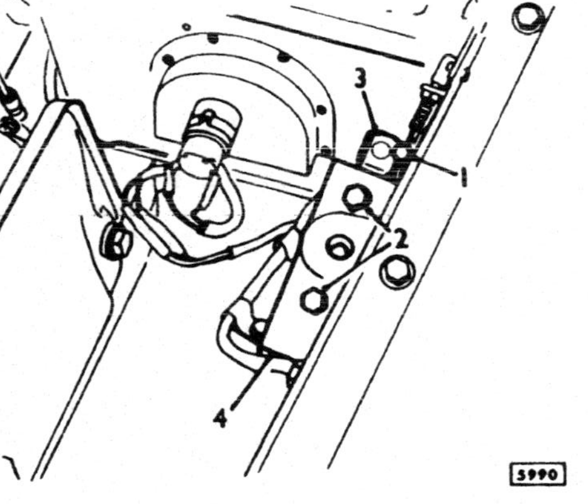

BONNET LOCK

Remove and refit **76.16.21**

Removing
1 Slacken clamping nut securing operating cable to bonnet lock release lever.
2 Remove two bolts securing lock assembly to mounting plate.
3 Slide release lever free of operating cable.
4 Withdraw lock assembly from mounting plate.

Refitting
5 Reverse operations 1 to 4.
6 Check and if necessary adjust bonnet cable – 76.16.28.

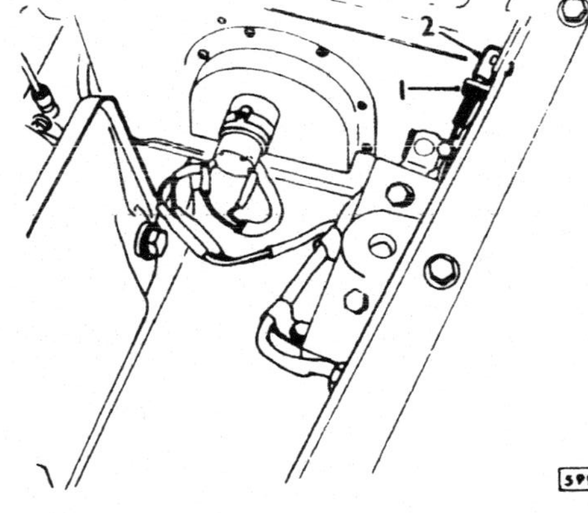

BONNET LOCK CONTROL CABLE

Adjust **76.16.28**

1 Slacken adjuster locknut.
2 Turn adjuster sleeve to a point that when release handle is operated, bonnet lock catch is aligned with locking peg lower guide hole. A slight amount of slack should be apparent within operating cable when catch is in fully locked position.

BONNET LOCK CONTROL CABLE

Remove and refit **76.16.29**

Removing
1 Slacken clamp screw securing operating cable to bonnet lock.

Long control cable only
2 Remove two screws securing cable adjuster bracket to wing valance.

All cables
3 Pull inner cable free from catch lever and push into outer cable.
4 Remove driver's underscuttle casing – 76.46.11.
5 Grasp section of inner cable protruding beyond operating lever and withdraw from outer cable.

Refitting
NOTE: Prior to fitting cable to car ensure clamping end of cable is clean and firmly bound.
6 Feed cable in hole in operating lever and locate in outer cable.
7 Ensuring operating lever is fully closed feed inner cable through outer till cable protrudes at locking catch end.
8 Locate inner cable in hole in locking catch lever, feed cable through hole to full extent.

Long control cable only
9 Secure cable adjuster bracket to wing valance.

All cables
10 Tighten inner cable clamping bolt.
11 Check and if necessary adjust bonnet lock control cable – 76.16.28.

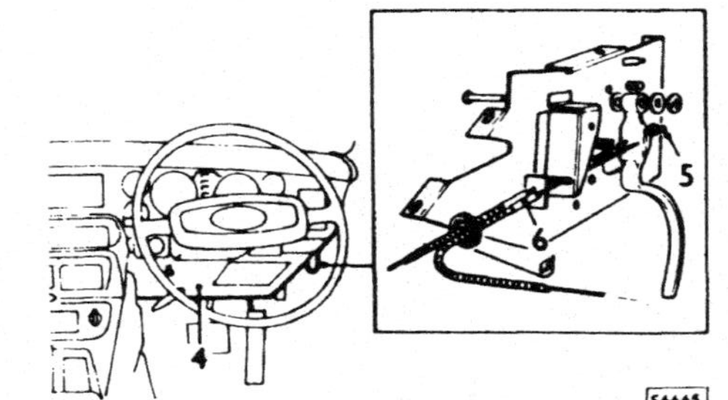

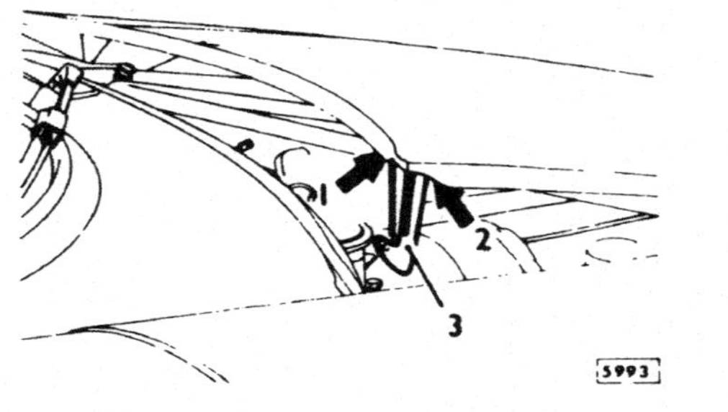

BONNET SAFETY CATCH

Remove and refit **76.16.34**

Removing
1 Remove spring retainer securing clevis pin.
2 Remove clevis pin.
3 Withdraw safety catch, spring and spacers.

Refitting
Reverse operations 1 to 3.

BOOT LID

Remove and refit **76.19.01**

Removing
1 Disconnect battery – 86.15.20.
2 Disconnect plastic straps securing electric cables to boot lid hinge.
3 Disconnect electric cables at connectors.
4 Remove two bolts, spring washers and flat washers securing hinge mounting bracket to boot lid.
5 Supporting disconnected end of boot lid, remove two bolts, spring washers and flat washers securing opposite hinge mounting bracket to boot lid.
6 Lift boot lid from car.

Refitting
7 Refit boot lid to hinge mounting brackets, do not fully tighten securing bolts.
8 Adjust position of boot lid (if required) so lid is central in luggage aperture and closes with push effort only.
9 Fully tighten boot lid securing bolts.
10 Reconnect electric cables to snap connectors.
11 Secure cable to hinge with plastic strips.
12 Reconnect battery.

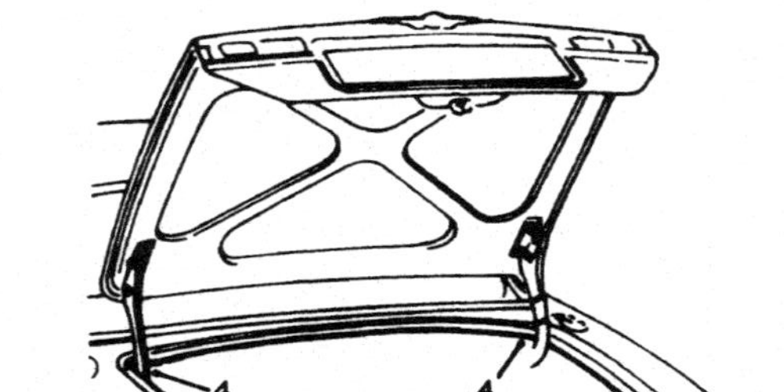

BOOT LID SEAL

Remove and refit **76.19.06**

Removing
1 Release both ends of seal from boot sill cover plate.
2 Pull remaining seal from boot mouth edging.

Refitting
3 Position both ends of seal central of boot sill cover plate. Fit seal ends under cover plate.
4 Locate and fit corners of seal to boot mouth edging.
5 Secure remaining seal to boot mouth edging.

BOOT LID HINGE

Remove and refit **76.19.07**

Removing
1 Remove boot lid – 76.19.01
2 Remove four bolts securing hinge assembly to luggage compartment, lift out hinge.
3 Remove two nuts, spring washers and flat washers securing boot lid mounting to hinge.
4 Repeat operations 2 and 3 on opposite hinge assembly.

Refitting
Reverse operations 1 to 4.

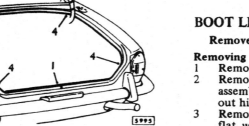

BOOT LID LOCK

Remove and refit **76.19.11**

Removing
1 Open boot lid.
2 Release clip securing latch mechanism control link rod to lock lever, detach link rod from lock lever.
3 Remove three screws securing latch mechanism to boot lid, withdraw latch mechanism from boot lid.

Refitting
Reverse operations 1 to 3.

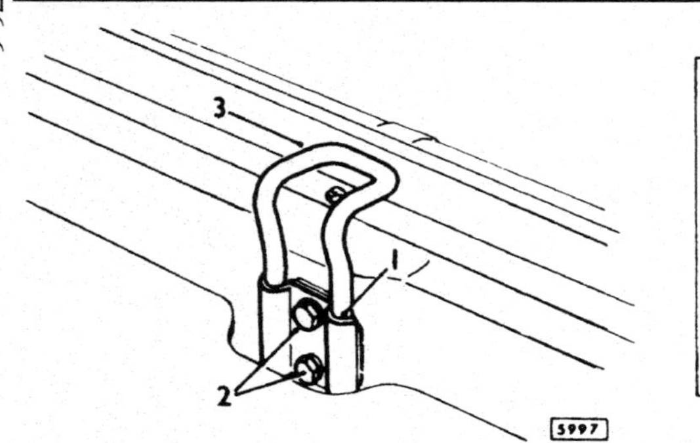

BOOT LID LOCK STRIKER

Remove and refit 76.19.12

Removing

1 Mark striker legs along top face of clamp plate for reference when re-fitting.
2 Slacken two bolts securing striker clamp plate to boot sill.
3 Slide striker free from clamp.

Refitting

4 Locate striker behind clamp plate aligning scribed marks to top face of clamp plate.
5 Tighten clamp plate locking bolts.
6 Close boot lid, adjust striker should more than a push effort be required.

FRONT UNDERRIDER

Remove and refit 76.22.01

Removing

1 Remove bolt and spring washer securing bottom of underrider to hinge mounting bracket.
2 Remove two bolts securing top of underrider to bumper, recover nuts, flat washers and spring washers.

Refitting

Reverse operations 1 and 2; ensure underrider top mounting bracket lays under buffer rubber mounting pad.

REAR OVERRIDER

Remove and refit 76.22.02

Removing

1 Remove bolt, flat washer and spring washer securing overrider to bumper assembly.

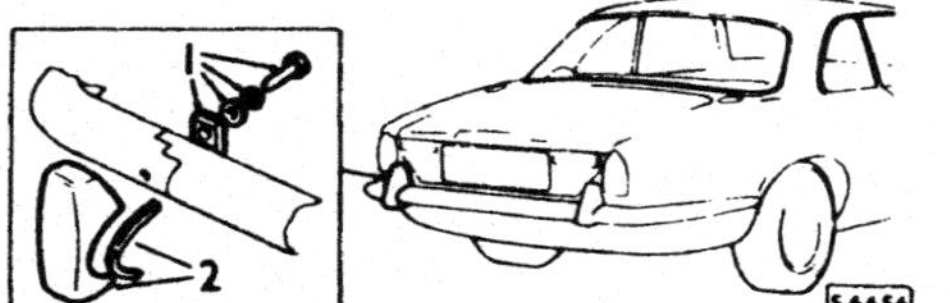

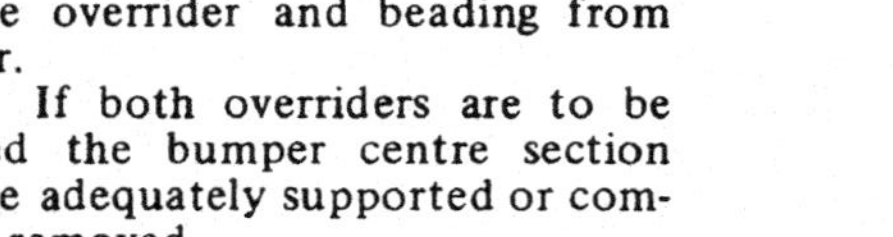

2 Remove overrider and beading from bumper.
NOTE: If both overriders are to be removed the bumper centre section must be adequately supported or completely removed.

Refitting

Reverse operations 1 and 2.

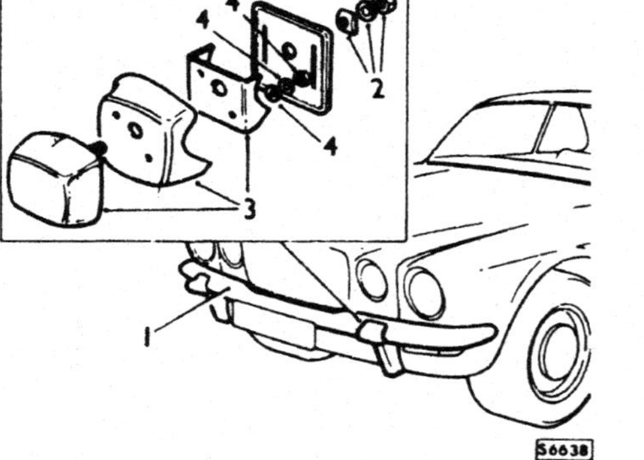

FRONT BUFFER

Remove and refit 76.22.07

Removing

1 Remove front bumper – 76.22.08.
2 Remove nut, spring washer and flat washer securing buffer assembly and rubber skirt to bumper.
3 Withdraw buffer assembly from bumper, recover rubber pad fitted between buffer mounting and bumper.
4 Remove two nuts, spring washers and flat washers securing buffer to mounting bracket, lift buffer from mounting bracket.

Refitting

Reverse operations 1 to 4.

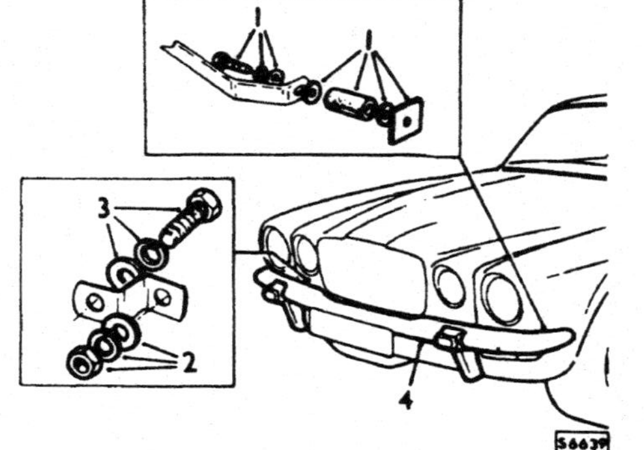

FRONT BUMPER

Remove and refit 76.22.08

Removing

1 Remove bolts located in front wheel arch securing sides of bumper to front wing support stay, recover flat washer and rubber spacer fitted between bumper and wing.
2 Remove two nuts, flat washers and spring washers securing front of bumper to bonnet hinge brackets.
3 Remove bolt and spring washer securing underrider to bonnet hinge bracket.
4 Lift bumper from car, recover washers on front mounting studs.

Refitting

Reverse operations 1 to 4.

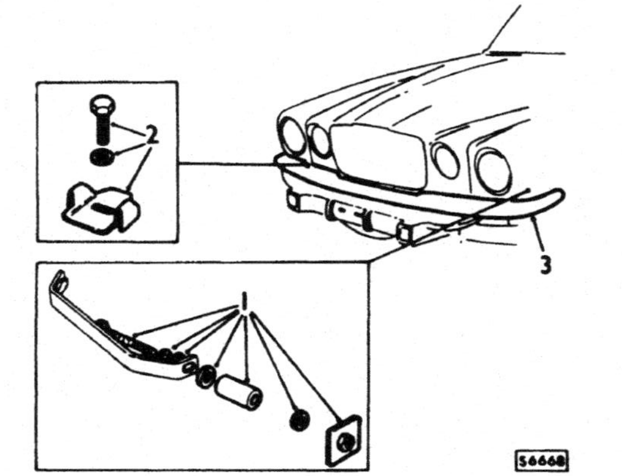

FRONT BUMPER

Cars to U.S.A. Federal specification only

Remove and refit 76.22.08

Removing

1 Remove bolt in either front wheel arch securing sides of bumper to wing support stay, recover flat washers, rubber spacers and securing plates fitted between bumper and wing.
2 Remove two bolts securing front of bumper to bonnet hinge bracket, recover plastic surrounds.
3 Lift bumper from car.

Refitting

Reverse operations 1 to 3.

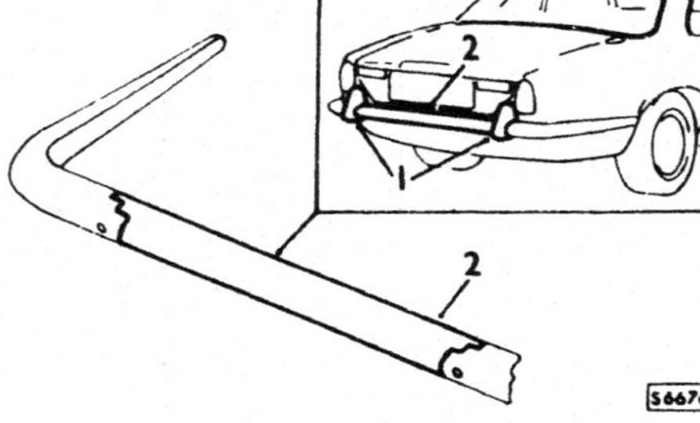

REAR BUMPER CENTRE SECTION

Remove and refit 76.22.12

Removing

1 Remove rear overriders – 76.22.02.
2 Lift bumper centre section from car.

Refitting

Reverse operations 1 and 2.

REAR BUMPER CENTRE SECTION

Cars to U.S.A. Federal speciiication only

Remove and refit 76.22.12

Removing

1 Remove rear bumper assembly – 76.22.16.
2 Remove nut and spring washer securing side sections to centre blade.
3 Detach side sections and recover plastic beading located between mating faces of sections.

Refitting

Reverse operations 1 to 3.

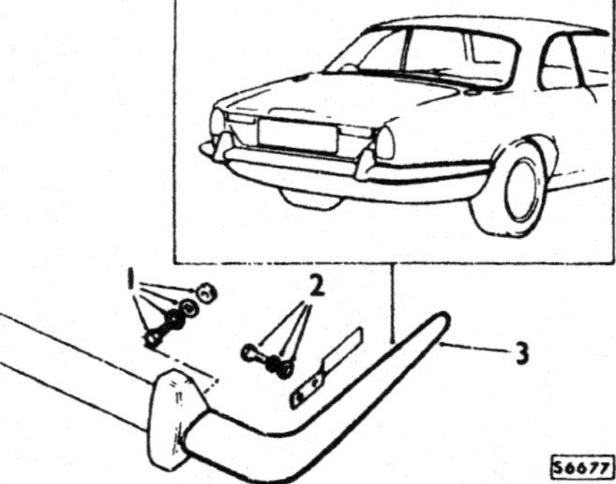

REAR BUMPER SIDE SECTION

Remove and refit 76.22.13

Removing

1 Remove rear overriders – 76.22.16.
2 Remove two bolts, flat washers and spring washers securing side section to car.
3 Remove bumper side section from car.

Refitting

Reverse operations 1 to 3.

REAR BUMPER SIDE SECTION

Cars to U.S.A. Federal specification only

Remove and refit 76.22.13

Removing

1 Remove three bolts securing side section to mounting brackets, recover flat and spring washers.

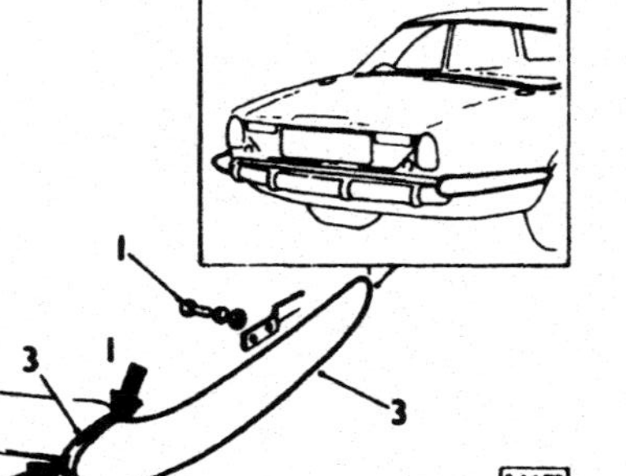

2 Remove nut and spring washer securing side section to centre blade.
3 Lift side section from car; recover plastic beading located between mating faces of sections.

Refitting

Reverse operations 1 to 3.

REAR BUMPER

Remove and refit 76.22.15

Removing

1 Remove four bolts and flat washers securing bumper assembly to side mounting brackets.
2 Supporting bumper, remove two bolts, flat washers and spring washers securing bumper to rear mountings.
3 Lift bumper from car.

Refitting

Reverse operations 1 to 3.

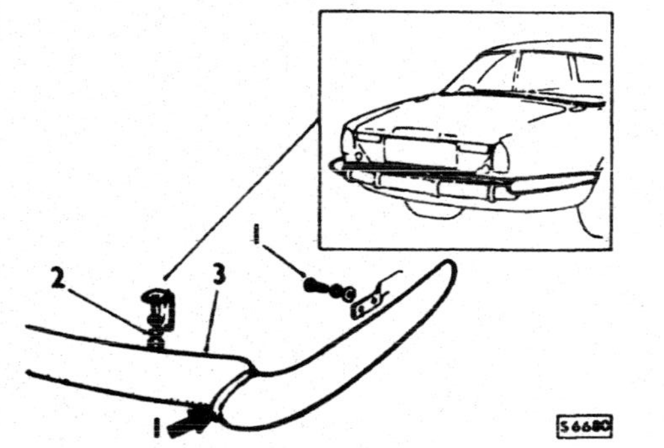

REAR BUMPER

Cars to U.S.A. Federal specification only

Remove and refit **76.22.15**

Removing

1 Remove six bolts securing side sections to bumper assembly mounting brackets to bumper assembly mounting brackets, recover flat and spring washers.
2 Remove four nuts and spring washers securing centre blade to mounting brackets.
3 Lift bumper assembly from car.

Refitting

Reverse operations 1 to 3.

ENERGY ABSORBING BEAM – FRONT

Cars to U.S.A. Federal specification only

Remove and refit **76.22.26**

Removing

1 Remove front beam cover – 76.22.28.
2 Remove self locking nuts securing beam mounting bolts.

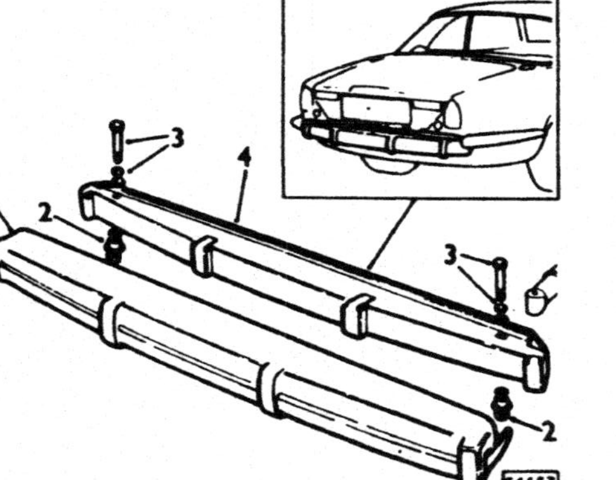

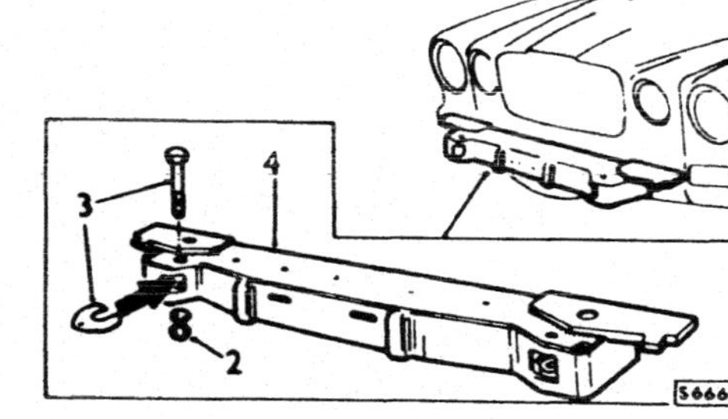

3 Noting quantity and relative position of beam adjustment shims remove bolts securing beam to struts, recover shims.
4 Lift beam from struts.

Refitting

Reverse operations 1 to 4.

ENERGY ABSORBING BEAM – REAR

Cars to U.S.A. Federal specification only

Remove and refit **76.22.27**

Removing

1 Removing rear energy absorbing beam cover – 76.22.29.
2 Remove self locking nuts securing beam mounting bolts, recover guide tubes and adjusting shims, position and location of shims should be noted.
3 Withdraw beam mounting bolts and flat washers.
4 Lift beam from car.

Refitting

Reverse operations 1 to 4.

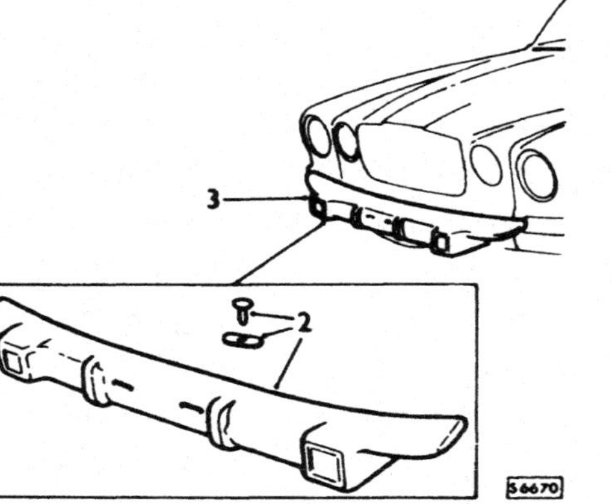

ENERGY ABSORBING BEAM COVER – FRONT

Cars to U.S.A. Federal specification only

Remove and refit **76.22.28**

Removing

1 Remove front bumper – 76.22.08.
2 Prise off clips and remove oval washers securing cover to beam.
3 Lift cover from beam

Refitting

Reverse operations 1 to 3.

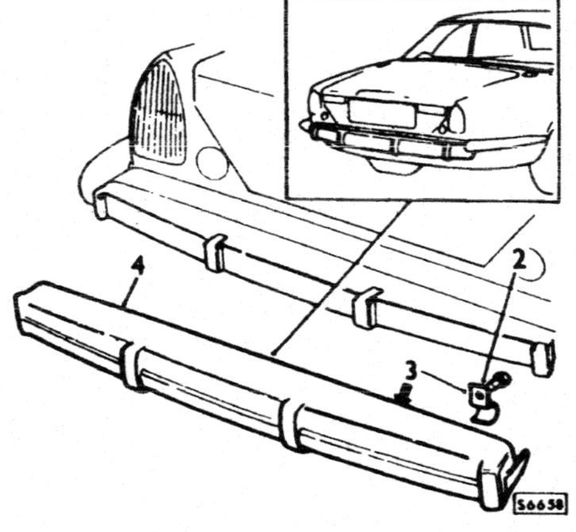

ENERGY ABSORBING BEAM COVER – REAR

Cars to U.S.A. Federal specification only

Remove and refit **76.22.29**

Removing

1 Remove rear bumper assembly – 76.22.15.
2 Slacken six bolts securing underside of cover to inner face of energy absorbing beam.
3 Disengage locating clips from beam cover.
4 Peel cover from beam.

Refitting

Reverse operations 1 to 4.

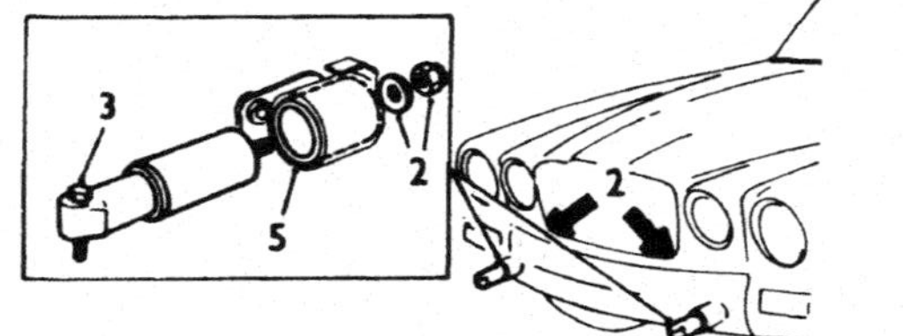

ENERGY ABSORBING STRUT – FRONT

Cars to U.S.A. Federal specification only

Remove and refit 76.22.31

Removing

1 Remove front energy absorbing beam – 76.22.26.
2 Open bonnet and remove nut and flat washer securing strut to mounting tube.
3 Position energy absorbing beam mounting bolt in strut locating hole.
4 Gently tapping bolt head with hammer remove strut from mounting tube.

Inspection

5 Examine rubber sleeve in strut mounting tube for any signs of damage or deterioration.
6 Reposition strut in mounting tube and check for any radial movement. If rubber sleeve is damaged or radial movement between strut and sleeve exists a new rubber sleeve must be fitted.

Refitting

Reverse operations 1 to 4.

ENERGY ABSORBING STRUT – REAR

Cars to U.S.A. Federal specification only

Remove and refit 76.22.32

Removing

1 Remove rear energy absorbing beam – 76.22.27.
2 Remove tail pipe and rear silencer – 30.10.22.

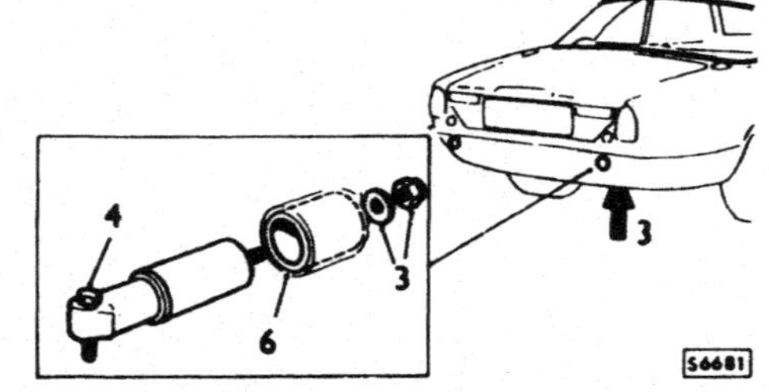

3 Remove nut securing strut to mounting tube, recover flat washer.
4 Position energy absorbing beam mounting bolt in strut locating hole.
5 Gently tapping bolt head with hammer, remove strut from mounting tube.

Inspection

6 Examine rubber sleeve in strut mounting tube for signs of damage or deterioration.
7 Reposition strut in mounting tube and check for any radial movement.
If rubber sleeve is damaged or radial play between strut and sleeve exists, a new sleeve must be fitted.

Refitting

Reverse operations 1 to 5.

CONSOLE ASSEMBLY

Remove and refit 76.25.01

Removing

NOTE: Throughout the following operation where electrical leads are detached from switches etc., a note as to their position should be made.

1 Disconnect battery – 86.15.20.
2 Remove console side trim casings – 76.25.02.
3 Pull off heater and ventilation control knobs.
4 Withdraw panel sufficiently to allow access to centre shelf securing screws. Care must be taken not to damage fibre optic elements.

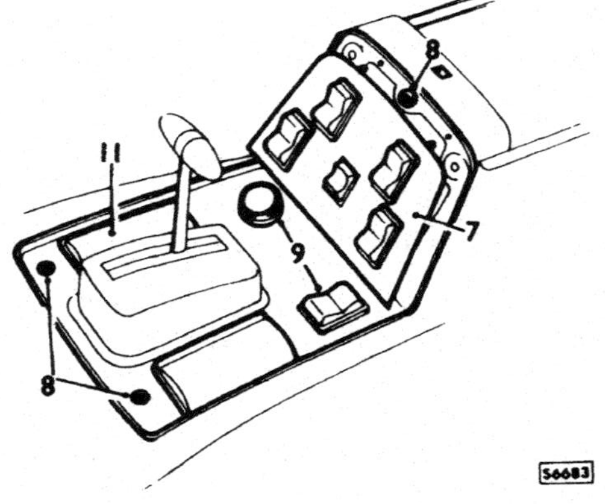
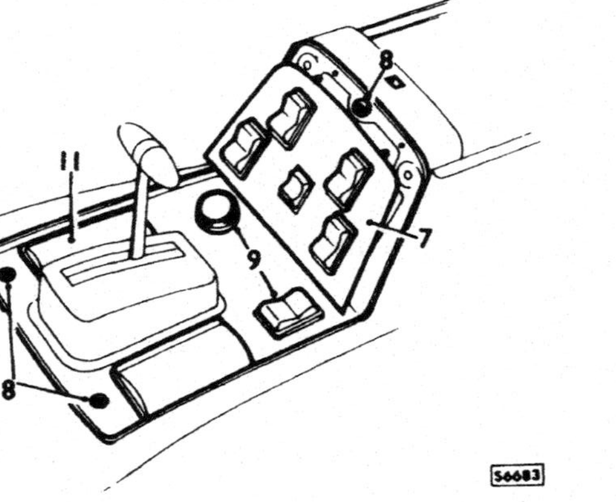

5 Remove four screws securing centre shelf to console and facia.
6 Detach temperature air sensor pipe from centre shelf, position tray clear of console.
7 Prise window switch panel from console top finisher. Care must be taken not to disconnect leads feeding window lift switches.
8 Remove three screws securing top finisher to console.
9 Raise top finisher and detach leads from cigar lighter and door lock switch.
10 Feed window switch panel and switches through aperture in top finisher.
11 Lift finisher from console.
12 Remove front seat cushions – 76.70.02.
13 Adjust front seats to fully forward position.
14 Remove two screws securing pedestal which mounts rear window operating switches.
15 Raise pedestal and detach leads feeding window operating switches, lift pedestal and switches from car.
16 Remove two screws securing rear of console to transmission tunnel.
17 Disconnect multi-pin connector exposed by removal of pedestal.
18 Raise rear of console and remove two screws securing electrical loom to air duct assembly.
19 Slide console slightly to rear of car.
20 Release electrical loom from clips located at front underside of console.
21 Feed radio and ventilation panel through aperture in front of console.
22 Slide console away from facia, disengaging air duct pipes from air outlets.
23 Raise console over gear selector and lift from car.

Refitting

24 Reverse operations 1 to 23.
25 Check operation of all switches mounted on console.

CONSOLE SIDE CASING

Remove and refit 76.25.02

Removing

1 Remove two screws securing side casing to ventilation outlets.
2 Lift casing from car.

Refitting

3 Reverse operations 1 and 2, ensure that ventilation outlet louvres direct air into footwell when refitting side casing.

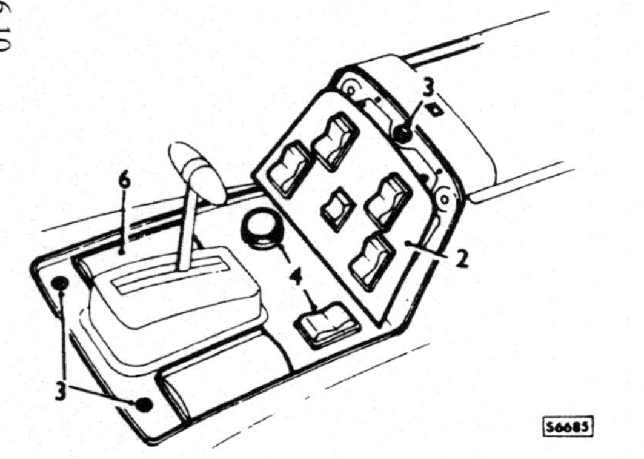

AUTOMATIC TRANSMISSION SELECTOR QUADRANT

Remove and refit 76.25.08

Removing

1 Disconnect battery – 86.15.20.
2 Prise window switch panel from console top finisher position panel forward of finisher.
3 Remove three screws securing top finisher to console.
4 Raise top finisher and detach leads feeding electric door lock switch and cigar lighter, note position of leads feeding door lock switch.
5 Taking care not to detach leads from window operating switches feed complete switch panel through aperture in top finisher.

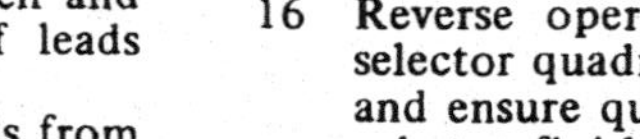

6 Lift finisher panel from console.
7 Remove four nuts and washers securing quadrant cover to mounting plate.
NOTE: Position of cable clips cover illumination bulb at snap connector.
8 Detach cable feeding quadrant cover illumination bulb at snap connector.
9 Unscrew left and right hand sections of selector lever handle.
10 Withdraw quadrant cover over selector lever.
11 Noting location, detach electrical leads from reverse switch, inhibitor switch and seat belt warning switch (U.S.A./Canada only).
12 Remove split pin and washer securing transmission operating cable to selector quadrant lever, detach cable from mounting.
13 Remove forward lock nut securing operating cable to quadrant extension bracket.
NOTE: Position of quadrant bracket on mounting studs should be marked for reference when refitting.
14 Remove three bolts and washers securing quadrant assembly to transmission tunnel cover.
15 Remove quadrant assembly from car.

Refitting

16 Reverse operations 7 to 15. If new selector quadrant is to be fitted check and ensure quadrant is central of console top finisher before fully tightening quadrant securing bolts.
17 Check gear selector cable adjustment – see operation 44.15.08.
18 Reverse operations 1 to 6.

FRONT DOOR – FOUR DOOR CARS – TWO DOOR CARS

Remove and refit 76.28.01

Removing

1 Disconnect battery – 86.15.20.
2 Remove door trim casing – 76.34.01.
3 If radio speaker fitted, remove four screws securing speaker to door, noting position detach leads from speaker unit, lift speaker from door.

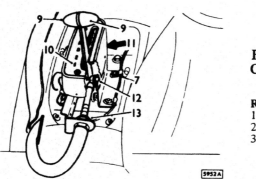

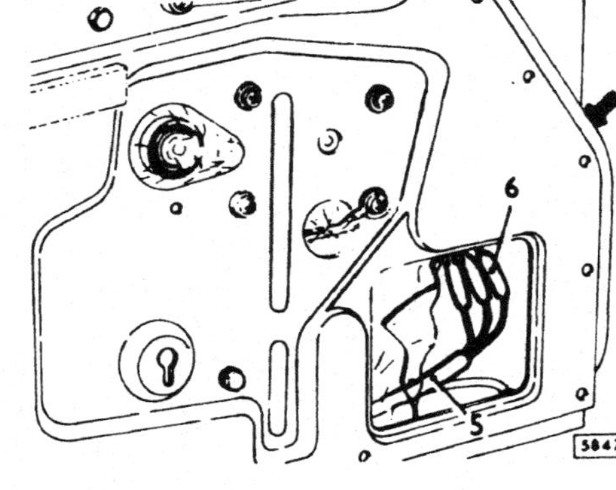

4 Recover loom located in speaker mounting aperture.
5 Noting position of each electrical lead, detach leads from snap connectors.
6 Prise loom protective cover from forward face of door and 'A' post.
7 Withdraw loom and radio speaker cables through hole in forward face of door.
8 Adequately supporting door, remove bolts securing door to hinges.
9 Remove door from hinges recover packing pieces located between hinges and door.

Refitting

10 Fit bolts in hinges and place packing pieces over bolts, ensure door earthing strap is located behind one door securing bolt.
11 Fit door to hinges, do not fully tighten bolts.
12 Close door to correctly position and align with surrounding body.
13 Open door and fully tighten door mounting bolts.
14 Reverse operations 1 to 7.
15 Check operation of central door lock system and window fit.

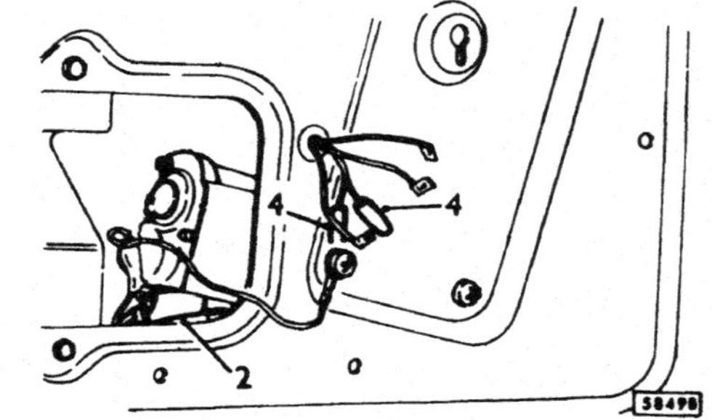

REAR DOOR – FOUR DOOR CARS

Remove and refit 76.28.02

Removing

1 Remove rear door trim casing – 76.34.04.
2 Locate cable loom inside door casing, noting position, separate cables at snap connectors.
3 Prise loom protective cover from forward face of door.
4 Withdraw loom and radio speaker cables through hole in forward face of door.
5 Ensuring door is adequately supported remove six bolts securing door to hinges.
6 Lift door from car.

Refitting

7 Fit bolts on hinges, ensure door earthing strap is located behind head of top inner hinge securing bolt.
8 Offer door to hinges, slightly tighten securing bolts.
9 Close door, ensure door fully closes and locks.
10 Tighten door mounting bolts.
11 Reverse operations 1 to 4.

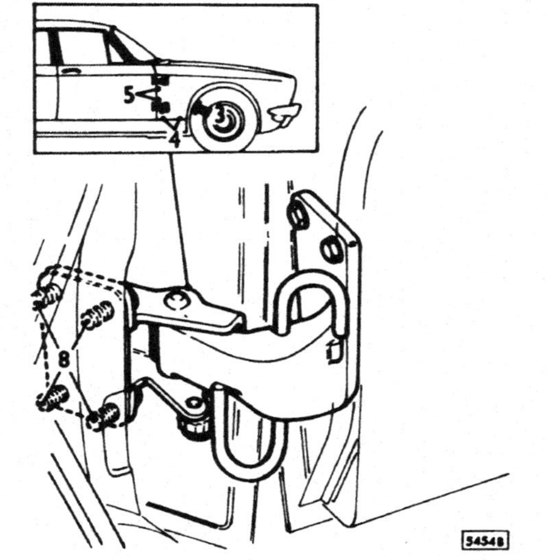

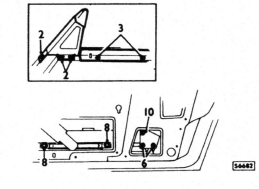

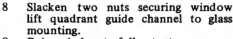

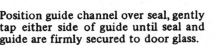

FRONT DOOR HINGE – FOUR DOOR CARS

DOOR HINGE – TWO DOOR CARS

Remove and refit **76.28.42**

Removing

1 Remove door – 76.28.01.
2 Jack up front of car and position wheels on full left or right lock.
3 Remove five bolts and washers securing wheel arch diaphragm panel to wing and 'A' post, remove panel from car.
4 Remove two bolts located inside wheel arch securing lower section of wing to sill.
5 Remove two bolts between door hinges securing wing to 'A' post, recover door earthing strap fitted behind top bolt.
6 Remove bolts, flat washers and spring washers securing top edge of wing to valance.
7 Using suitable size wedge separate lower portion of wing from body.
8 Remove eight bolts securing upper and lower hinges to 'A' post, lift hinges from car.

Refitting

Reverse operations 1 to 8; seal wheel arch diaphragm panel with underseal.

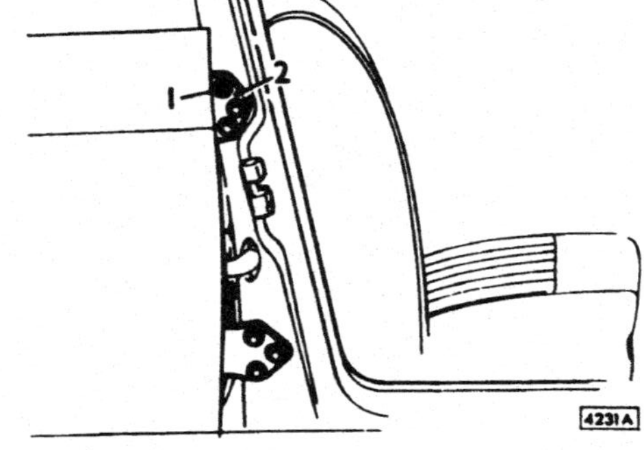

REAR DOOR HINGES – FOUR DOOR CARS

Remove and refit **76.28.43**

Removing

NOTE: Throughout the following operation the door should be adequately supported in the closed position.

1 Remove bolts securing hinges to door and B.C. post, recover door earthing strap fitted to top hinge securing bolts.
2 Lift hinges from door.

Refitting

3 Reverse operations 1 and 2.
4 Open and close door, checking door closes without undue effort.

FRONT DOOR GLASS – FOUR DOOR CARS

Remove and refit **76.31.01**

Removing

1 Remove front door quarter light – 76.31.28.
2 Slide door glass forward and disengage lift motor operating arm from guide channel.
3 Withdraw glass from door.
4 Remove guide channel and seal from door glass.

Refitting

5 Locate new guide channel seal in correct fitted position over door glass.

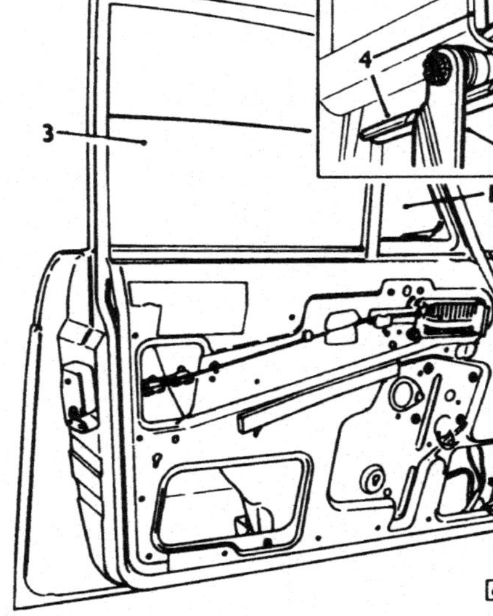

6 Position guide channel over seal, gently tap either side of guide until seal and guide are firmly secured to door glass.
7 Position glass in door casing.
8 Locate guide channel over lift motor operating arm.
9 Refit quarter light to door.

DOOR GLASS – TWO DOOR CARS

Remove and refit **76.31.01**

Removing

1 Remove door crash roll – 76.34.17.
2 Remove three screws securing glass bezel/guide to front of door, lift bezel/guide from door.
3 Remove five screws securing crash roll retaining plate, lift plate from door.
4 Prise free anti-rattle pads fitted between door frame and glass.
5 Remove nuts and bolts retaining lower portion of polythene sheet to door, position sheet clear of window lift mechanism.
6 Lower window sufficient to allow access to four screws securing window mounting plate.
7 Slacken four screws securing window mounting plate to lift of mechanism.

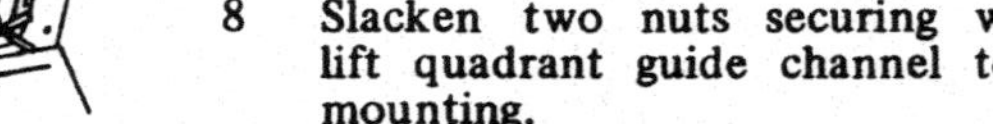

8 Slacken two nuts securing window lift quadrant guide channel to glass mounting.
9 Raise window to full extent.
10 Remove two screws securing glass to mounting plate.
11 Remove rubber grommet sealing glass to door shut face.
12 Carefully ease glass from mounting plate and lift from door.

Refitting

13 Position glass between mounting plates.
14 Refit glass retaining screws, do not fully tighten screws.
15 Lower glass to allow access to mounting plate securing screws.
16 Slightly tighten mounting plate securing screws.
17 Raise glass to full extent.
18 Refit door glass front guide.
19 Close door and adjust glass to obtain a 9/32" (7 mm.) clearance between drip rail and glass edge.
20 Open door and fully tighten mounting plate securing screws.
21 Lower glass and fully tighten mounting plate securing screws.
22 Fully tighten window lift guide securing nuts.
23 Resecure lower portion of polythene sheet.
24 Refit grommet to door shut face.
25 Refit glass door anti-rattle pads.
26 Refit crash roll mounting plate.
27 Refit crash roll and trim casing.

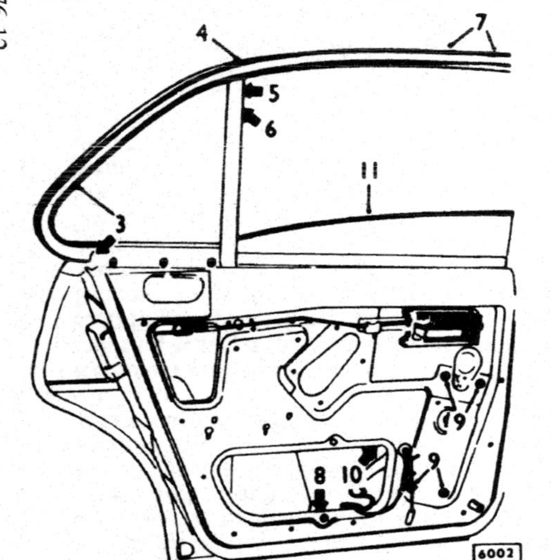

REAR DOOR GLASS – FOUR DOOR CARS

Remove and refit 76.31.02

Removing

1. Remove rear door trim casing – 76.34.03.
2. Prise chrome trim free from door glass frame.
3. Remove screw securing inner chrome trim to door glass frame, prise trim from frame.
4. Release rubber seal from door glass frame.
5. Lower door glass and release upper portion of felt channel fitted to quarter light.
6. Remove screws exposed by removal of felt channel.
7. Remove two screws, adjacent to B.C. Post securing vertical door glass frame to top glass frame and gently tap top glass frame free, lift frame from door.
8. Remove screws securing glass buffer stop to door panel, lift buffer stop from door.
9. Remove screw securing window lift mechanism to door panel.
10. Disengage window lift arm from glass guide bracket.
11. Withdraw glass from door.
12. Remove guide bracket and seal from glass.

Refitting

14. Locate new seal in correct position over glass.
15. Position lift arm guide bracket over seal, using mallet gently tap either side of guide until seal and guide are firmly secured to glass.
16. Reverse operations 1 to 11.

NOTE: IMPROVED RETENTION OF BOTTOM CHANNEL TO DOOR GLASS (4-DOOR CARS ONLY).

Insecurity of attachment of bottom channel to door glass may be rectified as follows:

1. Cut the Everseal strip (Part No. BD 47937) to make it 38 to 50 mm (1½ to 2 in) shorter than the bottom channel.
2. Thoroughly clean mating surfaces of channel, Everseal strip and door glass.
3. Fit the Everseal strip midway in the channel i.e. with 19 to 25 mm (¾ to 1 in) between each end of the strip and the end of the channel.
4. Replace bottom channel, complete with strip, on door glass.
5. Fill the ends of the channel with Dow Corning Silastik 732 or a similar silicone sealant, using a hand-gunned cartridge. Allow time for sealant to cure before refitting door glass.

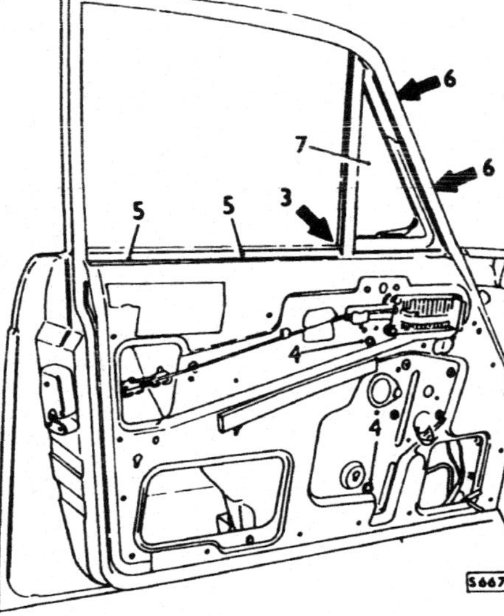

FRONT DOOR QUARTER LIGHT – FOUR DOOR CARS

Remove and refit 76.31.28

Removing

1. Remove front door trim casing – 76.34.01.
2. Lower door glass to full extent.
3. Prise free chrome beading along base of quarter light.
4. Remove two bolts securing quarter light support leg to door panel.
5. Remove screws securing glass weather-strip to door, lift weatherstrip from door.
6. Remove two screws securing quarter light to angled section of door glass frame.
7. Manoeuvre quarter light assembly free from door.

Refitting

Reverse operations 1 to 7, apply suitable sealing compound between quarter light and chrome beading.

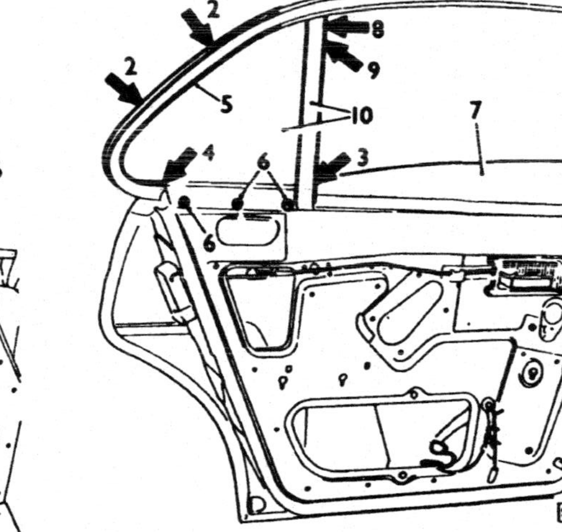

REAR DOOR QUARTER LIGHT – FOUR DOOR CARS

Remove and refit 76.31.31

Removing

1. Remove rear door trim casing – 76.34.04.
2. Prise chrome trim free from quarter light frame.
3. Prise chrome beading from base of quarter light.
4. Remove screw securing inner chrome trim to door glass frame, prise trim from quarter light frame.
5. Release section of door seal fitted to quarter light frame.
6. Remove three screws securing base of quarter light to door.
7. Lower door glass to full extent.
8. Release upper portion of felt channel fitted to quarter light.
9. Remove screws exposed by removal of quarter light felt channel.
10. Prise chrome trim from quarter light vertical post, lift quarter light from door.

Refitting

Reverse operations 1 to 10, using suitable sealing compound, seal area between base of quarter light and chrome beading.

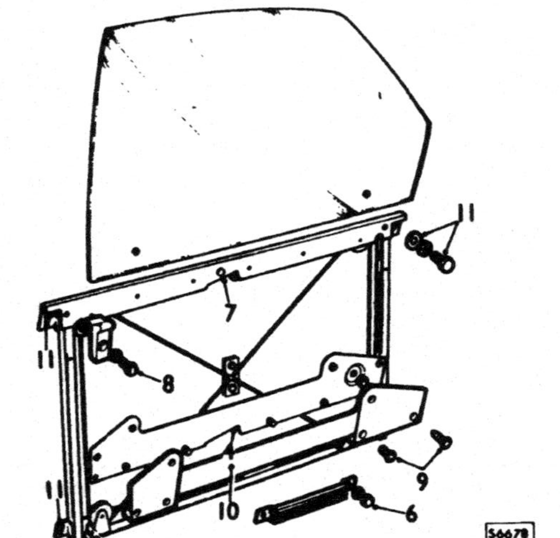

DOOR GLASS CARRIER ASSEMBLY – TWO DOOR CARS

Remove and refit **76.31.40**

Removing

1 Remove door glass – 76.31.01.
2 Remove screws securing chrome beading and weatherstrip to door, lift weatherstrip from door.
3 Raise glass carrier to full extent.
4 Disengage tensator spring from glass carrier plate.
5 Lower carrier plate sufficient to allow access to guide channel which locates lift motor quadrant.
6 Remove two nuts securing guide channel to glass carrier, slide channel from lift motor quadrant, lift guide from door.
7 Disengage tensator spring assembly from spigot mounting, lift spring assembly from door.
8 Remove two screws securing nylon anti-rattle pads to top corners of pulley mechanism frame, lift pads from door.
9 Position glass carrier to allow access to four setscrews securing carrier plates.
10 Remove four setscrews securing carrier plates, separate outer plate from inner and withdraw from door.
11 Remove four setscrews securing corners of pulley mechanism frame to door, recover washers located between frame and door panel.
12 Withdraw glass carrier and pulley assembly from door.

Refitting

13 Refit glass carrier and pulley assembly in door.
14 Position washers between frame and door panel.
15 Refit four setscrews securing pulley frame to door panel, do not fully tighten setscrews.
16 Refit tensator spring assembly on mounting spigot.
17 Fully tighten pulley frame securing screws.
18 Refit glass outer carrier plate, ensure that long setscrews secure outer ends of carrier plates. Do not fully tighten setscrews.
19 Locate guide channel on lift motor quadrant and secure to carrier plates. Do not fully tighten securing nuts.
20 Refit nylon anti-rattle pads to pulley frame.
21 Refit chrome beading and weatherstrip to door.
22 Raise glass carrier plate to full extent.
23 Unreel tensator spring and locate in recess on glass carrier plate.
24 Refit door glass.

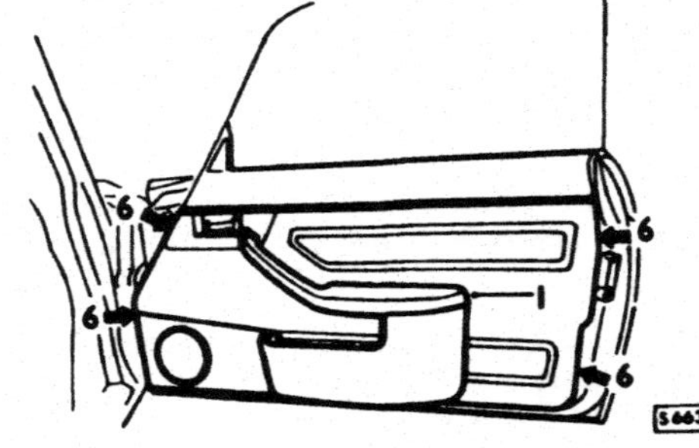

FRONT DOOR TRIM CASING – FOUR DOOR CARS
DOOR TRIM CASING – TWO DOOR CARS

Remove and refit **76.34.01**

Removing

1 Remove door armrest – 76.34.22.

Cars fitted with manual operated windows

2 Remove screw securing chrome bezel and operating handle to window lift mechanism, withdraw operating handle from door.

Four door cars fitted with remote controlled mirror

3 Remove screws securing adjusting lever surround to trim casing.
4 Partially withdraw surround from trim casing.
5 Slacken grub screw securing surround to adjusting lever, withdraw surround from lever.

All Cars

6 Carefully prise trim casing fixing clips from crash roll.

7 Slide upper portion of casing from crash roll.

Refitting

Reverse operations 1 to 7.

REAR DOOR TRIM CASING – FOUR DOOR CARS

Remove and refit **76.34.04**

Removing

1 Remove rear door armrest – 76.34.23.
2 Prise trim securing clips from door panel.
3 Disengage upper section of trim casing from crash roll.
4 Lift casing from door.

Refitting

Reverse operations 1 to 4.

DOOR CRASH ROLL

Remove and refit **76.34.17**

Removing

1 Remove door trim casing – 76.34.01.

Cars fitted with remote controlled mirror

2 Remove screws securing adjusting lever surround to crash roll.
3 Partially withdraw adjusting lever and surround from crash roll.
4 Slacken grub screw securing surround to adjusting lever, withdraw surround from lever.

All Cars

5 Remove four screws securing crash roll to door.
6 Disengage crash roll from locating pegs and lift from door.

Refitting

Reverse operations 1 to 6.

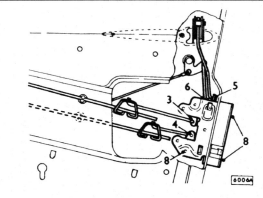

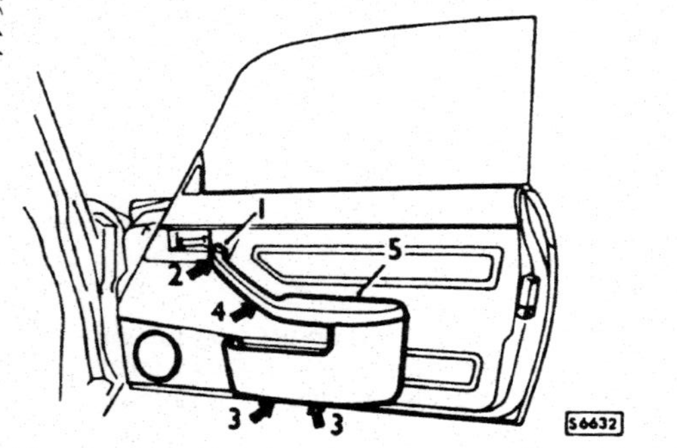

FRONT DOOR ARMREST – FOUR DOOR CARS

DOOR ARMREST – TWO DOOR CARS

Remove and refit 76.34.22

Removing

1 Prise chrome shroud from armrest door pull.
2 Remove screw securing door pull to casing, recover shroud retaining clip.
3 Remove four screws securing underside of armrest pocket to door casing.
4 Remove screw securing underside of armrest pad to door casing.
5 Disengage armrest and pocket locating pegs from door casing, lift armrest from floor.

Refitting

Reverse operations 1 to 5.

REAR DOOR ARMREST – FOUR DOOR CARS

Remove and refit 76.34.23

Removing

Cars fitted with speaker units to armrest

1 Disconnect battery – 86.15.20

All Cars

2 Remove screws securing underside of armrest to door.
3 Disengage armrest locating pegs from door panel.

Cars fitted with speaker units to armrest

4 Slightly withdraw armrest from door and disconnect speaker feed cables at snap connectors.

All Cars

5 Lift armrest from door.

Refitting

Reverse operations 1 to 5.

DOOR LOCK

Adjust 76.37.01

WARNING: IF ANY OF THE FOLLOWING SYMPTOMS BECOME EVIDENT, IMMEDIATE REMEDIAL ACTION MUST BE TAKEN AS OUTLINED BELOW:–

A Door fails to fully close.
B Door fails to open on operation of inside handle.
C Door opens upon initial movement of inside handle.
D Door fails to lock upon operation of inside lock lever.
E Door fails to open with inside lock lever in unlocked position.

1 Remove door trim casing. Front – 76.84.01. Rear – 76.34.04.
NOTE: When symptoms A, B or C are evident, proceed as follows:–
2 Squeeze inside handle link rod spring connector and slightly operate handle, release spring connector. Close door and check for evidence of symptoms A B or C.
3 Continue operation 2 adjusting link rod to left or right of spring connector until door fully closes and opens. Check that inside handle opens door when handle is threequarters operated.
NOTE: If symptoms D or E are evident, proceed as follows:–
4 Squeeze spring connector joining lock lever link rods, slightly operate lock lever and release spring connector. Close door and check for evidence of symptoms D or E.
5 Continue operation 4 adjusting link rod to left or right of spring connector until door locks with lever in rear position and opens with lever in forward position.
6 Refit door trim casing.

FRONT DOOR LOCK – FOUR DOOR CARS

DOOR LOCK – TWO DOOR CARS

Remove and refit 76.37.12

Removing

1 Remove door trim casing – 76.34.01.
2 Ensure window is fully closed.
3 Release spring clip securing inside handle remote control rod to latch lever mechanism, detach rod from lever.
4 Release spring clip securing inside lock lever remote control rod to latch lever mechanism, detach rod from lever.
5 Release spring clip securing outside door handle remote control rod to latch lever mechanism, detach rod from lever.
6 Release spring clip securing key lock remote control rod to latch lever mechanism detach rod from lever.

Four door cars only

7 Remove screw securing lower section of window channel to door casing.

All Cars

8 Remove four screws securing latch outer unit and latch mechanism to door shut face, recover latch mechanism from behind window channel.

Refitting

9 Check inside lock lever and corresponding lever on latch mechanism are in forward position.
10 Ensure latch outer unit is in open position.
11 Offer latch mechanism and outer unit to door shut face, secure with Phillips head screws.
12 Connect inside and outside handle/lock remote control rods to latch mechanism levers, secure with retaining clips.
13 Check operation of inside and outside door operating mechanism in "lock" and "unlocked" position, adjust as necessary – 76.37.01.

Four door cars only

14 Secure lower section of window channel to door.

All Cars

15 Refit door trim casing.

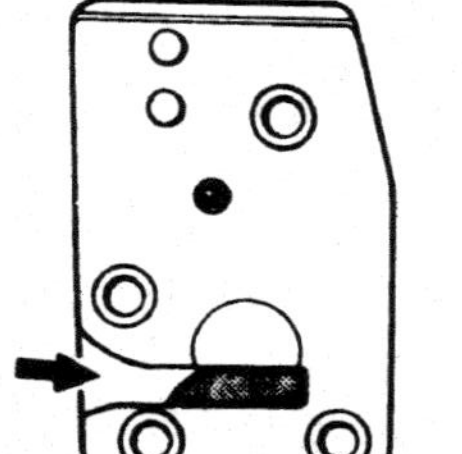

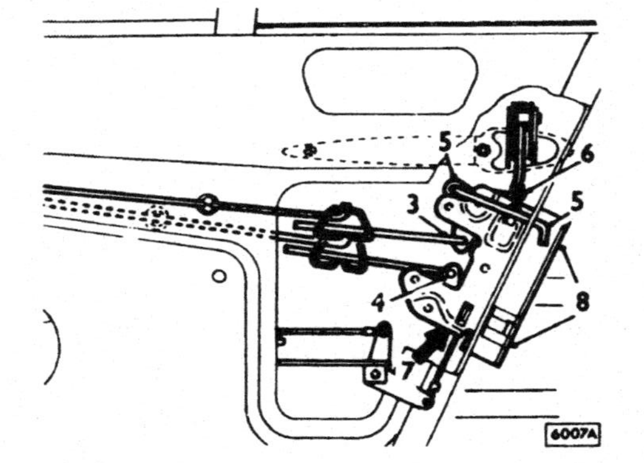

REAR DOOR LOCK – FOUR DOOR CARS

Remove and refit 76.37.13

Removing
1 Ensure window is fully closed.
2 Remove rear door trim casing – 76.34.04.
3 Release spring clip securing inside handle remote control rod to latch lever mechanism, detach rod from door.
4 Release spring clip securing inside lever lock remote control rod to latch lever mechanism, detach rod from lever.
5 Prise child safety link from latch lever mechanism, withdraw operating link from door shut face.
6 Release spring clip securing outside handle remote control rod to latch lever mechanism detach rod from lever.
7 Release spring clip securing solenoid remote control rod to latch lever mechanism, detach rod from lever.
8 Remove four screws securing latch outer unit and latch mechanism to door shut face, recover latch mechanism from inside door.

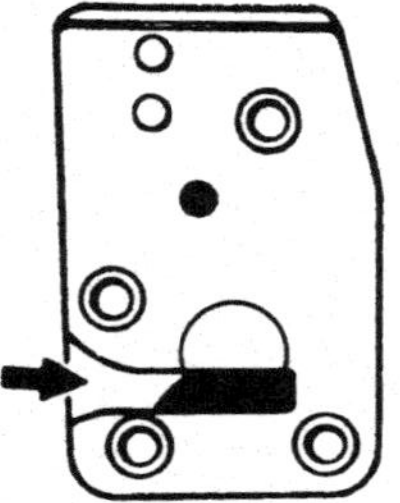

Refitting
9 Check inside lock lever and corresponding lever on latch mechanism are in forward position.
10 Ensure latch outer unit is in open position.
11 Reverse operations 3 to 8.
12 Check operation of inside and outside door operating mechanism in "lock" and "unlocked" position, adjust as necessary – 76.37.01.
13 Refit door trim casing.

FRONT DOOR LOCK STRIKER PLATE – FOUR DOOR CARS

Remove and refit 76.37.23

Removing
1 Disconnect battery – 86.15.20.
2 Remove rear door courtesy light switch mounting plate. Disconnect courtesy switch cable at connector.

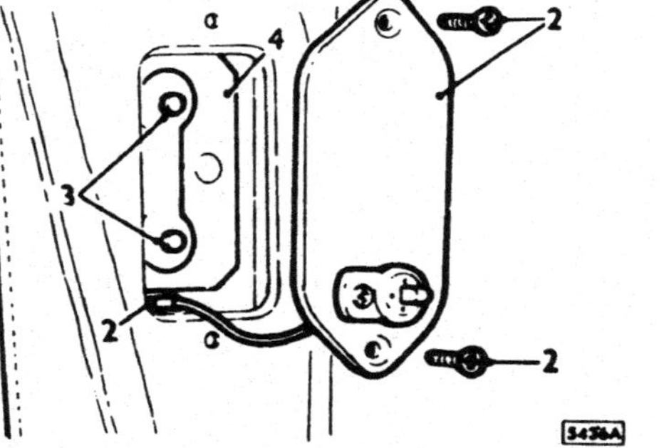

3 Remove screws securing striker and striker plate to B.C. Post shut face.
4 Withdraw striker assembly through rear of B.C. Post.

Refitting
5 Coat striker unit front face with waterproof sealing compound.
6 Fit striker assembly to B.C. Post shut face, do not fully secure retaining screws.
7 Adjust striker plate – 76.37.27.
8 Reconnect courtesy light switch cable.
9 Secure courtesy light switch mounting plate of B.C. Post.
10 Reconnect battery.

DOOR LOCK STRIKER PLATE – TWO DOOR CARS

Remove and refit 76.37.23

Removing
1 Remove rear window lift motor – 87.25.02.
2 Remove two screws securing striker to door shut face.
3 Withdraw striker from inside rear quarter body panel.

Refitting
4 Reverse operations 1 to 3.
5 Adjust striker plate – 76.37.27.

REAR DOOR LOCK STRIKER PLATE – FOUR DOOR CARS

Remove and refit 76.37.24

Removing
1 Remove rear seat squab – 76.70.38.
2 Carefully peel back 'D' post trim fabric and adhesive tape covering striker plate access hole.
3 Remove screws securing striker and retaining plate to 'D' post shut face, recover striker from inside 'D' post.

Refitting
4 Coat striker unit front face with waterproof sealing compound.
5 Fit striker assembly to 'D' post shut face, do not fully secure retaining screws.
6 Adjust striker plate – 76.37.27.
7 Cover striker plate access hole with adhesive tape.
8 Secure trim fabric to 'D' post with suitable adhesive.
9 Refit rear seat squab.

DOOR LOCK STRIKER

Adjust 76.37.27

1 Slacken setscrews securing striker plate to body.
2 Re-position striker and tighten setscrews.
3 Close door. Door should close with minimum push effort.
4 Continue operation 2 until door closes as described in operation 3.

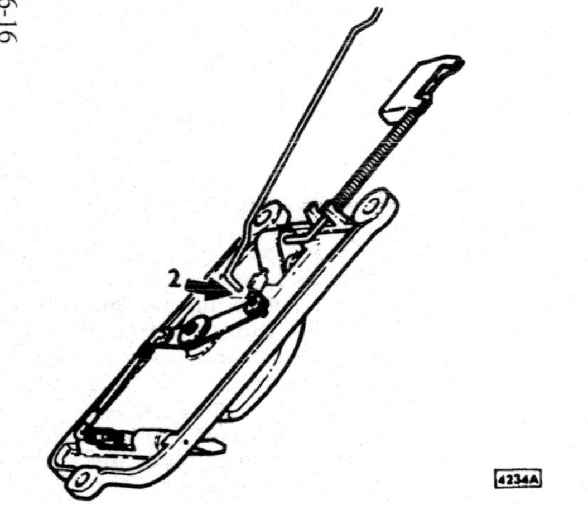

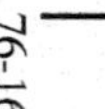

DOOR LOCK REMOTE CONTROL

Remove and refit **76.37.31**

Removing

1 Remove door inside handle – 76.58.18.
2 Release spring clip securing remote control link to door lock, detach control rod from lock lever.

Refitting

Reverse operations 1 and 2.

DOOR SEAL

Remove and refit **76.40.01**

Removing

1 Pull seal from locating guide.
2 Remove all traces of dirt from seal locating guide.

Refitting

3 If available, coat locating edge of new seal in soft soap.
4 Locate corners and ends of seal in guide.
5 Secure remainder of seal in guide.

DRIP MOULDING BEADING – FOUR DOOR CARS

Remove and refit **76.43.11**

Removing

1 Remove rivet securing beading centre bezel to 'BC' post, lift bezel from car.
2 Remove screw securing beading centre clip to 'BC' post.
3 Commencing at beading join, prise beading sections from drip moulding. Push end section of rear beading down to disengage retaining clip from drip moulding.
4 Lift beading sections from car.

Refitting

5 Lightly coat edge of drip moulding with sealing compound.
NOTE: If new beading sections are to be fitted, set a slight twist in length of beading, this helps retain beading in position during refitting.
6 Locate rear beading retaining clip in end of drip moulding, press remainder of beading on to moulding.
7 Locate leading end of front beading on front of drip moulding, press remainder of beading on to moulding.
8 Fit centre clip over beading join and secure with screw to 'BC' post.
9 Position bezel over beading join, clip and secure with rivet to 'BC' post.

DRIP MOULDING BEADING – TWO DOOR CARS

Remove and refit **76.43.11**

Removing

1 Carefully prise door seal from underside of beading centre clip.
2 Remove screw securing centre clip to drip moulding; prise clip from drip moulding.
3 Commencing at centre join, carefully prise beading sections from drip moulding.

Refitting

4 Lightly coat edge of drip moulding with sealing compound.
NOTE: If new beading sections are to be fitted set a slight twist in the length of the beading, this helps to retain beading in position during refitting.
5 Locate trailing end of rear beading in drip moulding, press remainder of beading on to moulding.
6 Locate leading end of front beading in drip moulding, press remainder of beading on to moulding.
7 Refit clip over beading join and secure with screw.
8 Reseal door seal to underside of clip.

WINDSCREEN FINISHER

Remove and refit Left hand – 76.43.39
Right hand – 76.43.40

Removing

Cars to U.S.A. Federal specification only

1 Remove two nuts located under screen rail trim securing retaining plates to screen finisher.
2 Prise retaining plates from screen finishers.

All Cars

3 Prise free chrome strips covering join in screen finishing strips.
4 Prise finishing strips from windscreen rubber surround.

Refitting

Reverse operations 1 to 4.

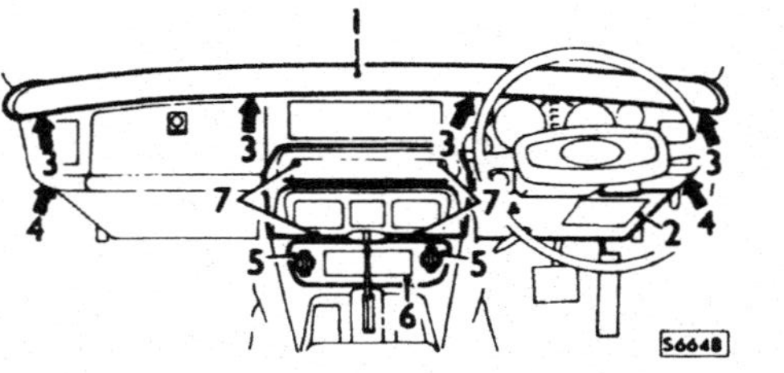

FACIA PANEL

Remove and refit **76.46.01**

Removing

1 Remove crash roll – 76.46.04.
2 Remove drivers under scuttle casing – 76.46.11.
3 Remove four screws securing facia to screen rail.
4 Remove two nuts and washers securing outer ends of facia to lower mounting brackets.
5 Pull off heater and ventilation control knobs.
6 Withdraw radio panel forward sufficient to allow access to centre tray securing screws. Care must be taken not to damage fibre optic elements.
7 Remove four screws securing centre shelf to console.
8 Detach temperature air sensor pipe from centre tray and position tray clear of facia.
9 Remove two nuts, flat washers and spring washers securing facia to heater unit.
10 Slacken clamp screws securing ignition and light switch shrouds.
11 Withdraw shrouds and mounting clamps from switches, detach fibre optics from rear of shrouds and switches.
12 Slacken steering column upper mounting bolts, care must be taken not to fully remove bolts.
13 Remove three screws securing indicator switch assembly shroud, lift off shroud.
14 Ease facia panel forward and disconnect three electrical block connectors feeding instruments.
15 Disconnect speedometer cable from rear of speedometer.
16 Carefully lift facia assembly from car, it should be noted that facia air vent ducting is removed with facia assembly.

Refitting

NOTE: For ease of refitting air vent ducts to demister outlets, slacken four nuts securing demister outlets to screen rail.
Reverse operations 1 to 15.

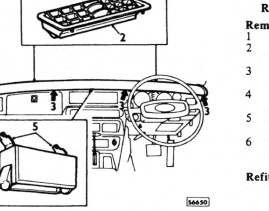

FACIA CRASH ROLL

Remove and refit **76.46.04**

Removing

1 Disconnect battery – 86.15.20.
2 Prise demister air direction vents from crash roll.
3 Remove four screws securing front of crash roll to screen rail.
4 Prise map light from housing in crash roll.
5 Detach lucars from map light.
6 Lift crash roll from car.

Refitting

Reverse operations 1 to 6.

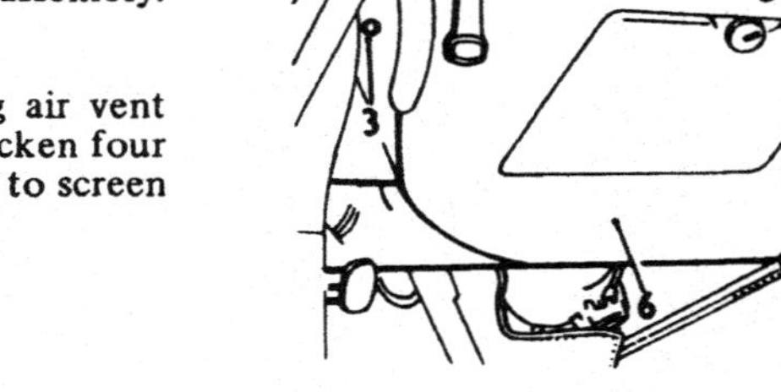

DRIVER'S UNDER SCUTTLE CASING

Remove and refit **76.46.11**

Removing

1 Disconnect battery – 86.15.20.
2 Unscrew locking ring securing speedometer trip to under scuttle casing.
3 Remove two screws securing casing and quarter panel to facia support bracket.
4 Lower top of casing sufficient to allow access to rheostat.
5 Noting position detach leads from rheostat.
6 Withdraw under scuttle casing and quarter panel from car.

Refitting

Reverse operations 1 to 6.

PASSENGER'S UNDER SCUTTLE CASING

Remove and refit **76.46.15**

Removing

1 Open glove box.
2 Remove two screws, located adjacent to glove box lid hinges securing under scuttle casing to facia.

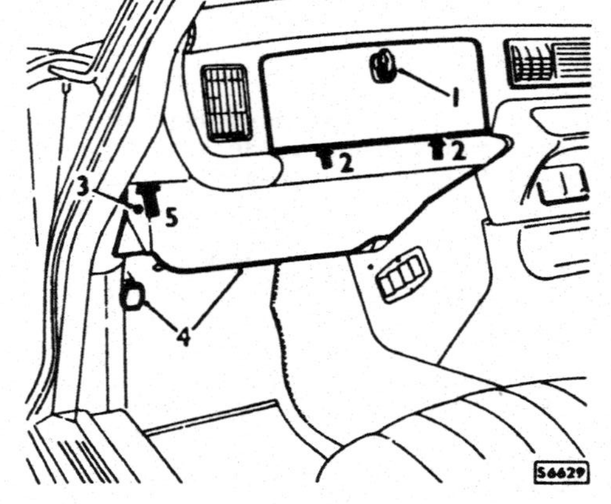

3 Remove two screws securing casing past footwell fresh air control, lift casing from car.
4 Manoeuvre under scuttle casing past footwell fresh air control, lift casing from car.
5 Remove quarter panel from car.

Refitting

Reverse operations 1 to 5.

FACIA VENEER

Remove and refit **76.46.14**

Removing

1 Remove facia panel – 76.46.01.
2 Place clean cloth over suitable work surface.
3 Lay facia on cloth and stand on top edge in upright position.
4 Remove tape securing air ducting to air vent outlets, slide ducting from vents.
5 Release spring clips securing side air vents to facia, withdraw air vents from facia.
6 Remove four Philips head screws securing centre air vent to facia, withdraw air vent from facia.
NOTE: Location and colour of electrical leads feeding instruments should be noted before commencing with the following operations.

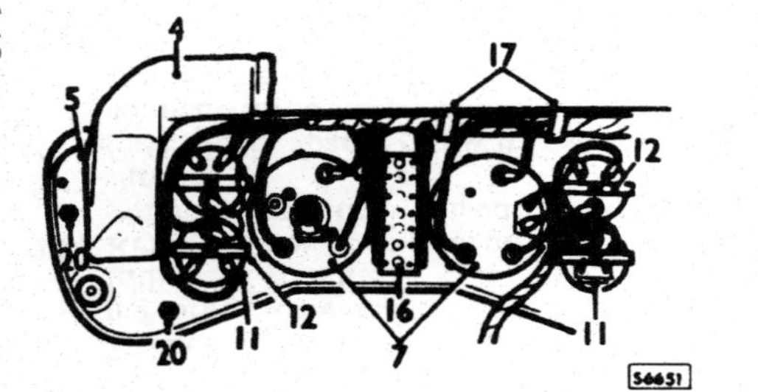

7 Detach electrical leads from rear of speedometer and tachometer.
8 Withdraw bulbs and holders from speedometer and tachometer.
9 Carefully prise warning light cluster cover from facia.
10 Rotate speedometer and tachometer anti-clockwise sufficient to align locating pegs with recess in facia back plate, withdraw gauges from facia.
11 Detach electrical leads feeding four auxiliary gauges.
12 Remove nuts securing auxiliary gauges retaining bars, slide bars from locating pins.
13 Withdraw gauges from facia.
14 Detach electrical leads secured to facia backplate.
15 Remove four screws securing warning light cluster to facia.
16 Withdraw warning light cluster and electrical harness from facia.
17 Release main electrical harness from retaining clips, remove loom from facia.
18 Remove glove box lid – 76.52.02.
19 Remove six screws securing glove box liner to facia, withdraw liner from facia.
20 Remove four nuts and flat washers securing crash padding to facia, withdraw padding from facia.
21 Remove Philips head screw securing facia veneer to backplate, remove veneer from backplate.

Refitting

Reverse operations 1 to 21.

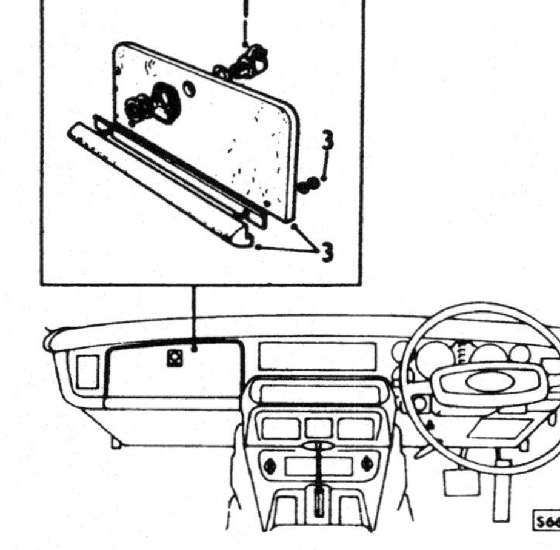

GLOVE BOX LID

Remove and refit 76.52.02

Removing

1 Remove glove box lid lock – 76.52.08.
2 Remove two screws securing sliding stay to lid.
3 Remove two plastic nuts securing lid to crash padding; remove lid.

Refitting

Reverse operations 1 to 4.

GLOVE BOX

Remove and refit 76.52.03

Removing

1 Remove passenger's under scuttle casing – 76.46.11.
2 Remove six screws securing glove box to facia.

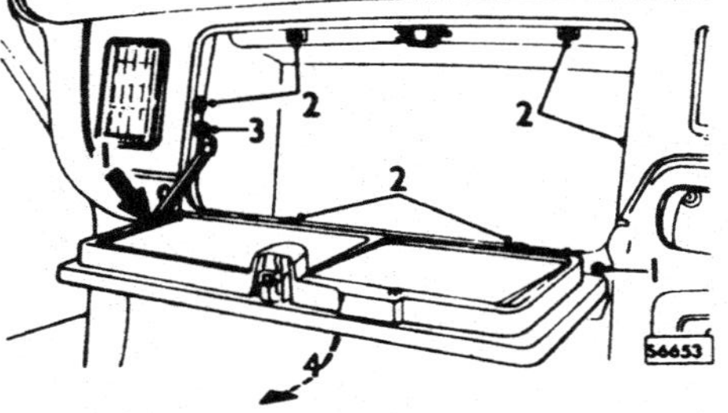

3 Slacken two screws securing sliding link bracket to facia.
4 Remove glove box from rear of facia through aperture exposed by removal of under scuttle casing.

Refitting

Reverse operations 1 to 4.

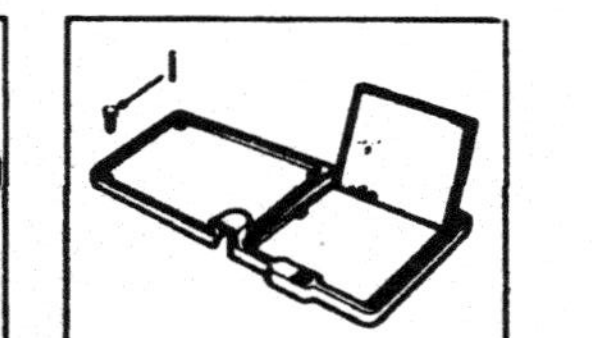
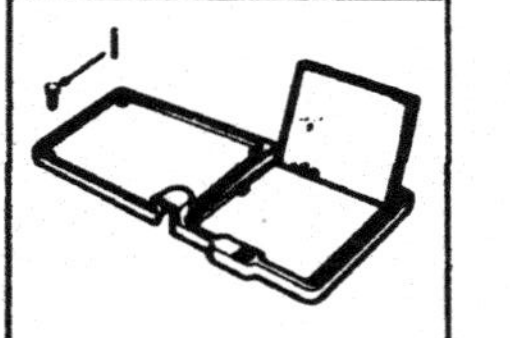
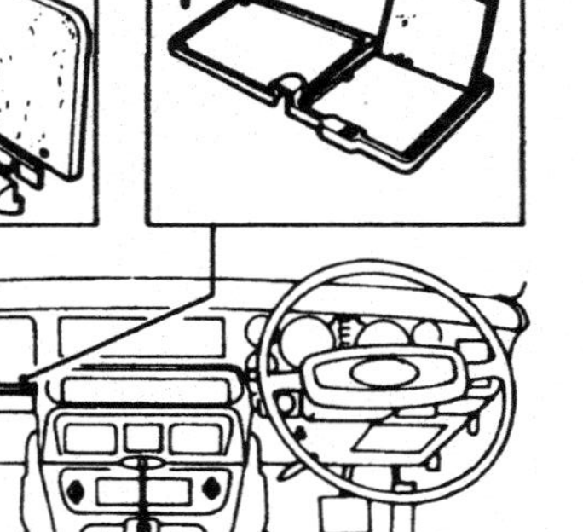
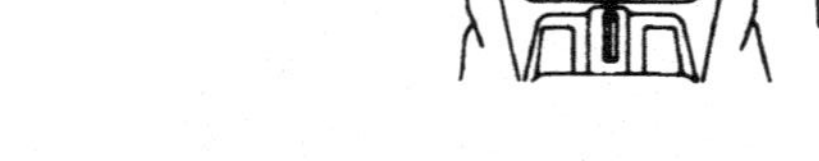

GLOVE BOX LID LOCK

Remove and refit 76.52.08

Removing

1 Remove six screws securing mirror and tray liner to glove box lid, lift liner from lid.
2 Remove two screws securing lock retaining plate, remove plate.
3 Unscrew lock retaining ring, recover lock, lock handle and mounting plate.

Refitting

4 Reverse operations 2 and 3, do not fully tighten lock retaining ring.
5 Offer lock to catch and adjust as necessary, fully tighten locking ring.
6 Refit glove box lid liner.

RADIATOR GRILLE

Remove and refit 76.55.03

Removing

1 Remove two nuts and Philips head screws securing grille to bonnet, recover oval and flat washers.
2 Withdrawing evenly, remove grille from bonnet.

Refitting

3 Reverse operations 1 and 2, ensure grille is central of aperture before tightening securing nuts.

RADIATOR CENTRE BAR

Remove and refit 76.55.04

Removing

1 Remove two nuts securing upper section of centre bar to retaining plate, lift plate from centre bar studs.
2 Remove nut securing lower section of centre bar to radiator grille, lift centre bar from grille.

Refitting

3 Reverse operations 1 and 2, prior to tightening upper securing nuts ensure centre bar is vertical.

RADIATOR FRONT LOWER GRILLE

Remove and refit **76.55.06**

Removing

1 Remove two screws located behind spotlights securing lower grille to apron.
2 Raise lower section of grille and disengage locating pegs from apron, lift grille from car.

Refitting

Reverse operations 1 and 2.

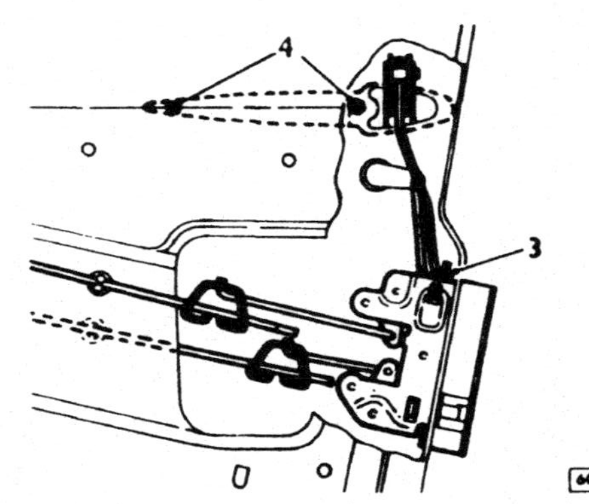

DOOR OUTSIDE HANDLE – FOUR DOOR CARS

Remove and refit **76.58.01**

Removing

1 Remove door trim casing – Front 76.34.01. Rear 76.34.04.
2 Ensure door glass is in fully closed position.
3 Release spring clip securing push button link rod to latch lever mechanism, detach rod from lever.
4 Remove two nuts securing handle to door, withdraw handle and link rod from door.
5 Recover gasket fitted between handle and door.

Refitting

Reverse operations 1 to 5, fit new handle mounting gasket.

DOOR OUTSIDE HANDLE – TWO DOOR CARS

Remove and refit **76.58.01**

Removing

1 Remove door glass.
2 Release spring clip securing push button link rod to latch lever mechanism, detach rod from lever.
3 Remove two nuts securing handle to door, withdraw handle and link rod from door.
4 Recover gasket fitted between handle and door.

Refitting

Reverse operations 1 to 4, fit new handle mounting gasket.

DOOR PUSH BUTTON

Remove and refit **76.58.12**

Removing

1 Remove door outside handle 76.58.01.
2 Remove two screws securing push button lever mechanism to door handle.
3 Disengage rear of mechanism mounting plate from handle, recover push button spring.
4 Operate push button and withdraw from button surround guide.

Refitting

5 Re-locate push button in guide channel.
6 Position return spring over operating button.
7 Locate mechanism mounting plate over return spring, compress spring and secure rear of mounting plate in locating recess.
8 Fit two screws securing mounting plate to door handle.
9 Refit handle to door.

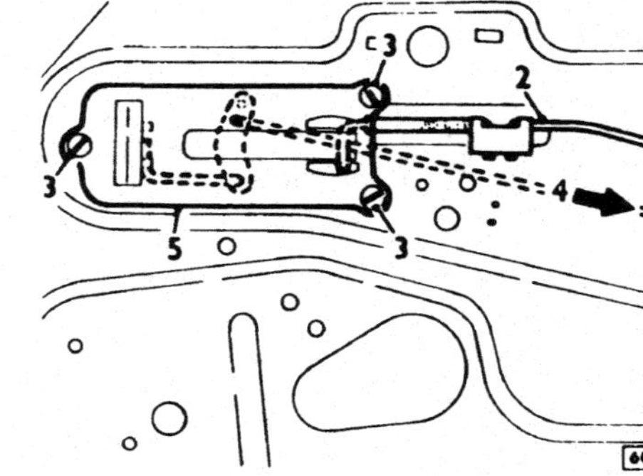

DOOR INSIDE HANDLE

Remove and refit **76.58.18**

Removing

1 Remove door crash roll 76.34.17.
2 Disconnect long section of outer link rod at nylon block connector.
3 Remove setscrews securing door inside handle to door casing.
4 Squeezing lower portion of rear link connector, slide link rod and connector free of adjoining link.
5 Withdraw inside handle from door.

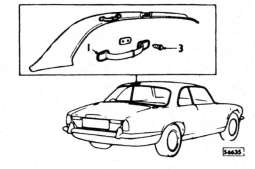

Refitting

6 Ensure locking lever and corresponding lever on latch mechanism are in open position.
7 Reverse operations 2 to 5.
8 Check operation of inside locking lever in door 'locked' and 'open' position, adjust as necessary – 76.37.01.
9 Check automatic door locking system operates satisfactory.
10 Refit door trim casing.

GRAB HANDLE – TWO DOOR CARS

Remove and refit **76.58.30**

Removing

1 Prise chrome shrouds from ends of grab handle ensuring not to damage cantrail trim.
2 Manoeuvre shrouds along grab handle to allow access to securing screws.
3 Remove two screws securing grab handle to cantrail, lift grab handle from car.

Refitting

Reverse operations 1 to 3.

HEADLINING

Remove and refit **76.64.01**

WARNING: THIS OPERATION SHOULD NOT BE ATTEMPTED BY PERSONS KNOWN TO BE ALLERGIC TO GLASS FIBRE (FIBREGLASS). SHOULD SKIN AREAS DEVELOP A RASH OR IF ITCHING OCCURS, WASH AFFECTED AREA WITH WATER AND SEEK MEDICAL ADVICE IMMEDIATELY. ALWAYS WEAR GLOVES, FACE MASK AND GOGGLES WHEN HANDLING HEADLINING.

NOTE: A strip of 'Velcro' approximately 12 ins. (30,4 cm.) long and 2 ins. (5 cm.) wide should be used to assist in removing and refitting of headlining.

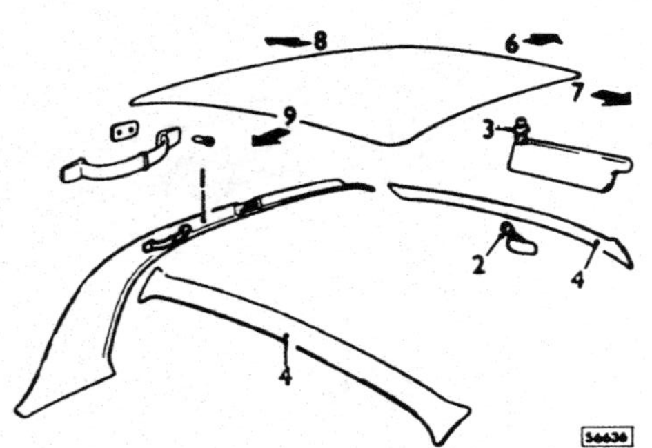

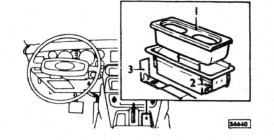

Removing

1. Remove cantrail crash roll – 76.13.10.
2. Remove interior mirror – 76.10.51.
3. Remove sun visors – 76.10.47.
4. Prise backlight and windscreen upper trim panels free from roof rail.
5. Attach 'Velcro' strip to headlining.
6. Pull headlining forward and carefully disengage rear of headlining from locating recess.
7. Move headlining to right and disengage left hand side of headlining from locating recess.
8. Move headlining to left disengaging right hand side of headlining from locating recess.
9. Pull headlining to rear and withdraw from car.

Refitting

CAUTION: Ensure outer edge of headlining is of equal thickness. Thick sections must be trimmed with sharp knife. Failure to observe this warning will result in extreme difficulty when refitting.

10. Fit rear right hand corner of headlining in locating recess.
11. Position right hand side of headlining in locating recess.
12. Attach 'Velcro' strip to headlining.
13. Move headlining to rear and locate in recess.
14. Move headlining to left and locate in recess.
15. Move headlining forward and locate in screen rail.
16. Reverse operations 1 to 4.

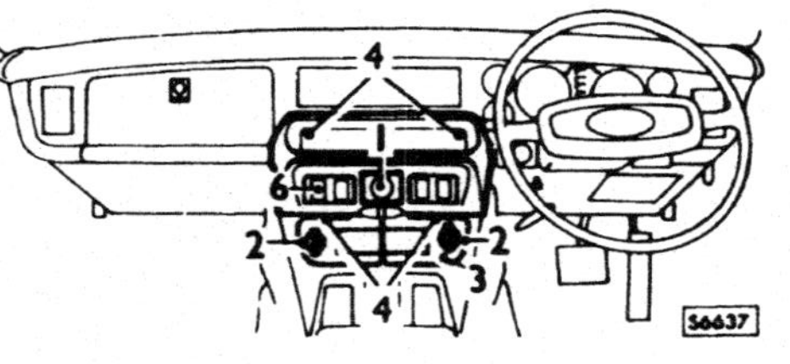

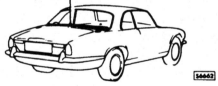

CENTRE PARCEL SHELF

Remove and refit **76.67.03**

Removing

1. Remove clock – 88.15.07.
2. Pull off heater and ventilation control knobs.
3. Withdraw radio panel forward sufficient to allow access to centre tray securing screws. Care must be taken not to damage fibre optic elements.
4. Remove four screws securing centre tray to console.
5. Detach temperature air sensor pipe from tray.
6. Remove switches fitted to tray – see items 6 to 8 operation 86.65.06.

Refitting

Reverse operations 1 to 6.

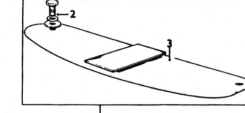

REAR PARCEL SHELF

Remove and refit **76.67.06**

Removing

1. Remove rear passenger squab – 76.70.38.
2. Remove two bolts and four washers securing parcel shelf, slide shelf forward and disengage from locating peg.
3. Lift parcel shelf from car.

Refitting

Reverse operations 1 to 3.

FRONT ASHTRAY

Remove and refit **76.67.13**

Removing

1. Open ashtray cover and withdraw ash container.
2. Remove two screws securing ash container holder to console.
3. Withdraw holder and securing bracket from console.

Refitting

4. Slightly secure bracket with one screw to holder unit.
5. Fit holder and bracket to console, turn bracket securing screw, do not fully tighten.
6. Align unsecured portion of bracket with hole in holder. Fit remaining bracket securing screw.
7. Fully tighten bracket securing screws.
8. Fit ash container to holder.

REAR ASHTRAY

Remove and refit **76.67.14**

Removing

1. Open ashtray.
2. Push ashtray down against spring pressure and lift from holder.

Refitting

Reverse operations 1 and 2.

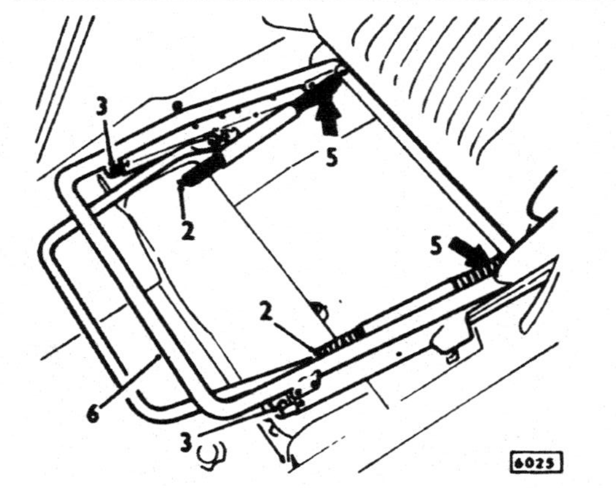

FRONT SEAT

Remove and refit 76.70.01

Removing
1 Remove seat cushion – 76.70.02.
2 Unlock seat runners, return springs from forward runner supports.
3 Remove two nuts, spring washers and spacers securing front runners to mounting brackets.
4 Slide seat forward to full extent.
5 Remove nuts and spring washers securing rear of runners to mounting bracket.
6 Remove seat assembly from car.

Refitting
Reverse operations 1 to 6.

FRONT SEAT CUSHION

Remove and refit 76.70.02

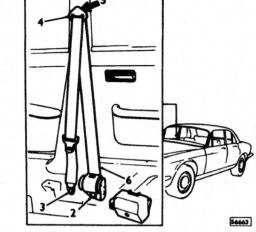

Removing
1 Disconnect battery (USA/Canada only) – 86.15.20.
2 Remove Philips head screw securing front of cushion to bracket, remove bracket from under side of cushion.
3 Position squab in reclining position.
4 Raise front of cushion and pull forward, on cars fitted with seat belt alarm, disconnect electrical connector feeding seat detector switch fitted to under side of cushion.
5 Lift cushion from support assembly.

Refitting
Reverse operations 1 to 5.

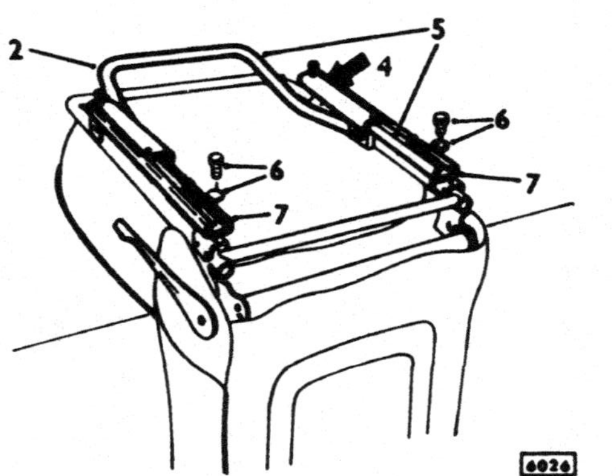

FRONT SEAT RUNNERS AND ADJUSTER ASSEMBLY

Remove and refit 76.70.24

Removing
1 Remove front seat – 76.70.01.
2 Raise seat adjuster bar and push seat runner to opposite end of runner guide.
3 Repeat operation 2 on opposite runner.
4 Remove screws securing front of adjuster assembly to seat frame.
5 Raise adjuster bar and slide seat runners to opposite end of runner guides.
6 Remove screws securing rear of adjuster assembly to seat frame.
7 Remove adjuster assembly from seat frame.

Refitting
Reverse operations 1 to 7.

HEADREST

Fit 76.70.29

1 Remove headrest guide blanking plug from front seat squab.
2 Locate headrest slide in guide.
3 Adjust headrest to required height.

REAR SEAT CUSHION

Remove and refit 70.70.37

Removing
1 Adjust front seats to fully forward position.
2 Remove screw either side of transmission tunnel securing cushion to seat pan cross member.
3 Draw seat forward and remove from car.

Refitting
Reverse operations 1 to 3.

REAR SEAT SQUAB

Remove and refit 76.70.38

Removing
1. Remove rear seat cushion – 76.60.37.
2 Remove two screws and flat washers securing lower section of squab to rear of seat pan.
3 Push squab upwards and disengage rear of squab from retaining clips.
4 Remove squab from car.

Refitting
Reverse operations 1 to 4.

REAR SEAT ARMREST

Remove and refit 76.70.39

Removing
1 Remove rear seat squab.
2 Remove four bolts and flat washers securing armrest to seat squab frame.
3 Remove six clips securing armrest trim to squab frame.
4 Withdraw armrest from squab.

Refitting
Reverse operations 1 to 4.

5
4
3
2
6
56663

FRONT SEAT BELT – FOUR DOOR CARS

Remove and refit 76.73.10

Removing
1 Place front seat in fully forward position with squab upright.
2 Remove screws securing reel assembly cover to sill, (unclip cover on later cars), lift cover from car.
3 Remove screws securing belt retaining strap to sill, lift strap from car.
4 Remove bolt securing reel assembly to sill.
5 Remove bolt adjacent to belt reel securing belt lower fixing to sill, recover spacers and washers fitted between lug and sill.
6 Press upper fixing cover upwards and release from belt lug.
7 Pull cover clear of lug and remove bolt securing upper lug to 'BC' post, recover spacers and washers fitted between lug and 'BC' post.
8 Lift belt from car.

Refitting
Reverse operations 1 to 8.

FRONT SEAT BELT – TWO DOOR CARS

Remove and refit **76.73.10**

Removing
1 Remove rear quarter trim casing – 76.13.14.
2 Remove bolt securing reel assembly to body, lift reel assembly from car.

Refitting
Reverse operations 1 and 2.

REAR SEAT BELT

Remove and refit **76.73.18**

Removing

Two door cars
1 Remove rear quarter trim casing – 76.13.14.

Four door cars
2 Remove rear seat squab – 76.70.38.

All Cars
3 Noting position of lug on buckle assembly remove bolt, flat washer and spacer securing lug to rear of seat pan, lift buckle assembly from car.
4 Unclip belt reel cover and withdraw over seat belt clip fastener.
5 Fully unwind belt from reel assembly and retain in unwound position.
6 Remove bolt securing reel assembly to body, lift seat belt from car.

Refitting
Reverse operations 1 to 6.

SILL TREAD PLATE

Remove and refit **76.76.01**

Removing
1 Remove screws securing tread plate to sill.
2 Remove tread plate and packing piece from sill.

Refitting
Reverse operations 1 and 2.

WINDSCREEN GLASS AND SEALING RUBBER

Remove and refit **76.81.01**

Service tool – JD.23

Removing
1 Remove windscreen finisher – 76.43.39.
2 Prise end of rubber insert free and withdraw from windscreen seal.
3 Using suitable thin bladed instrument, insert tool between windscreen and seal. Run tool around periphery of windscreen to break seal in locating groove.
4 Strike inside top section of windscreen with palm of hand and disengage edge of screen from seal locating groove. Continue striking windscreen along periphery until screen is completely disengaged from surrounding seal.
5 Remove windscreen from car.
6 Pull seal from windscreen aperture, discard seal.
7 Remove excess amounts of sealing compound from windscreen seal locating edge.

Refitting
NOTE: Refitting will be assisted, especially in cold conditions, if the sealing rubber is warmed to about 50°C (120°F) before fitment.
8 Remove 'A' post trim casings – 76.13.07.
9 Apply sealing compound to windscreen seal locating edge.
10 Ensure smooth side of new seal faces towards interior of car, with join at bottom of windscreen fit seal to windscreen aperture. If seal appears to be too long, feed excess length first into top corners of 'A' posts and then, if any excess remains, into bottom corners of 'A' posts.
11 Apply soft soap solution to channel in seal to assist fitting of windscreen.
12 Position lower edge of windscreen in seal locating channel.
13 Locate special tool JD.23 fitted with right angled adaptor in lower corner of windscreen locating channel.

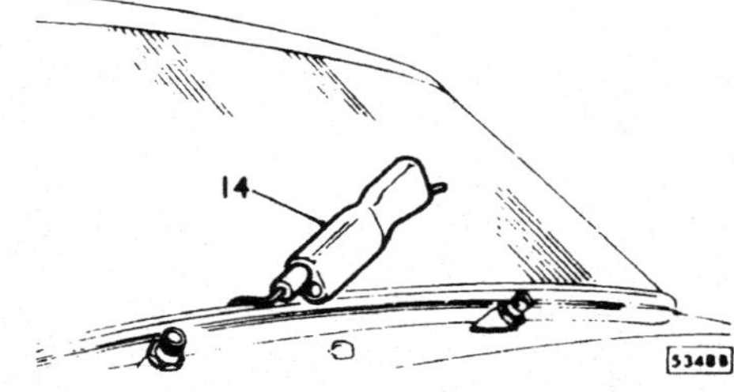

14 Drive special tool JD.23 around periphery of screen locating outer section of seal guide channel over windscreen edge.
15 Ensure windscreen is fully located in seal guide channel.
16 Using suitable pressure gun, inject sealing compound between outer face of windscreen and seal guide channel.
17 Fit rubber insert to special tool JD.23 fitted with square end adaptor.
18 Ensuring rounded side of insert faces outwards, locate rubber insert in windscreen seal.
19 Fit windscreen finisher to seal.
20 Replace 'A' post trim casings 76.13.07.

HEATED BACKLIGHT

Remove and refit 76.81.11

Service Tool – JD.23

Removing

1 Disconnect battery – 86.15.20.
2 Remove rear seat squab – 76.70.38.
3 Remove two screws and four flat washers securing rear parcel shelf. Slide parcel shelf forward and disengage from locating peg.
4 Remove parcel shelf from car.
5 Prise ends of backlight lower trim panel free from parcel shelf securing points, remove panel from car.
6 Unclip rear sections of left and right hand crash roll.
7 Using thin bladed instrument prise backlight upper trim from headlining.
8 Disconnect Lucar connector at right hand side of backlight.
9 Remove screw securing backlight earthing strap.
10 Remove backlight finisher – 76.43.39.
11 Prise end of rubber insert free and withdraw from backlight seal.
12 Using suitable thin bladed instrument, insert tool between backlight and seal. Run tool around periphery of backlight to brake seal in locating groove.
13 Strike inside top section of backlight with palm of hand and disengage edge of screen from seal locating groove. Continue striking backlight along periphery until screen is completely disengaged from surrounding seal.
14 Remove backlight from car.
15 Pull seal from backlight aperture, discard seal.
16 Remove excess amounts of sealing compound from backlight seal locating edge.

Refitting

17 Apply sealing compound to backlight seal locating edge.
18 Ensure smooth side of new seal faces towards interior of car with join at bottom of aperture. Fit seal to backlight aperture.
19 Ensuring backlight electrical connections are flush with glass, position lower edge of backlight in seal locating channel.
20 Locate special tool JD.23 fitted with right angled adaptor in lower corner of backlight locating channel.
21 Drive special tool JD.23 around periphery of backlight locating outer section of seal guide channel over backlight edge.
22 Ensure backlight is fully located in seal guide channel.
23 Using suitable pressure gun, inject sealing compound between outer face of backlight and seal guide channel.
24 Fit rubber insert to special tool JD.23 fitted with square end adaptor.
25 Ensuring rounded disc of insert faces outwards, locate rubber insert in backlight seal.
26 Blend backlight electrical connections 180° to lay flush along seal and rear pillar.
27 Connect Lucar connector to backlight right hand electrical connector.
28 Secure backlight earthing strap with set screw.
29 Reconnect battery and check operation of backlight.
30 Reverse operations 2 to 7.
31 Fit chrome finisher to backlight seal.

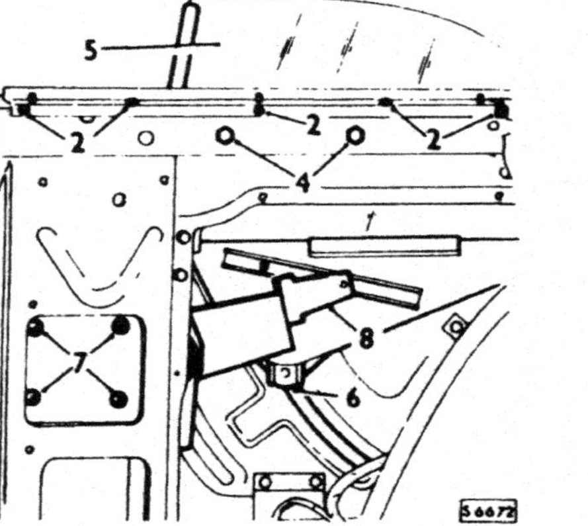

REAR QUARTER GLASS – TWO DOOR CARS

Remove and refit 76.81.19

Special Tool – TMT.13166

Removing

1 Remove rear quarter crash roll – 76.13.15.
2 Remove five screws securing crash roll mounting to quarter panel.
3 Peel plastic cover from glass housing aperture and lay in seat pan.
4 Remove two bolts and washers securing glass buffer to quarter panel, lift buffer from panel.
5 Lower rear glass to half open position.
6 Fit special tool TMT.13166 in glass guide channel, ensure tool is flush with glass carrier plate.
7 Remove four set screws securing window lift motor to quarter panel.
8 Supporting window lift motor, remove special tool, manoeuvre lift motor to rear and disengage quadrant arm from glass guide channel.
9 Withdraw lift motor from housing and lay in seat pan.
10 Pull rear quarter glass into fully closed position.
11 Disengage glass guide rollers from carrier plate.
12 Withdraw glass rear quarter panel.

Refitting

NOTE: If fitting new glass, smear grease in guide channel which locates lift motor quadrant.

13 Reverse operations 1 to 12.

REAR QUARTER GLASS CARRIER – TWO DOOR CARS

Remove and refit 76.81.31

Removing

1 Remove rear quarter glass – 76.81.19.
2 Remove two bolts and flat washers securing glass carrier to lower mounting bracket.
3 Remove bolt and flat washer securing glass carrier to side mounting bracket.

continued

4 Remove two Philips head screws securing upper section of glass carrier to quarter panel.
5 Lower glass carrier and disengage upper section from chrome beading.
6 Withdraw carrier from quarter panel.

Refitting

NOTE: If new carrier is to be fitted remove glass buffer guide from old carrier to fit to new carrier. Smear grease in guide channels.

7 Reverse operations 1 to 6.

HEATING AND VENTILATION

Description 80.00.00

The car heating and ventilating system consists of selective ducting and a water heated matrix through which fresh air can be forced, either by the passage of the car through the air or by twin, three speed blower fans. The ducts channel air as required by the driver or passengers in front and rear compartments.

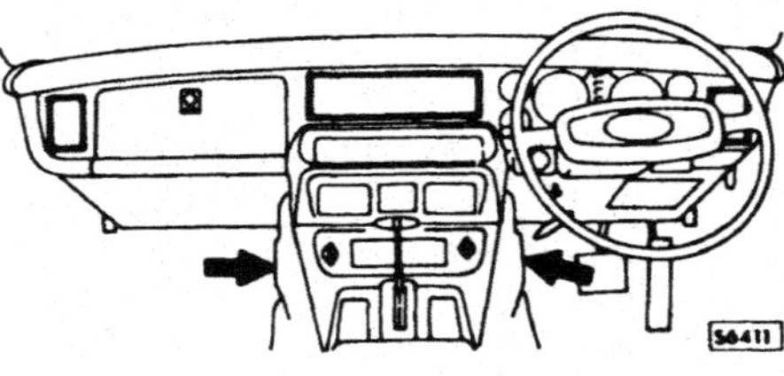

(a) **To the driver and front passenger compartment**
Face level outlets at either end of the facia, manually opened and closed and adjusted for direction of delivery.
Face level outlet in the centre of the facia, the end sections of which can be adjusted for direction of delivery.
One outlet at each side of the centre console directing air into driver's and passenger's footwells.

(b) **To the windscreen**
Adjustable vents, situated at the base of the windscreen, provide demisting and defrosting.

(c) **To the rear passenger compartment**
Manually controlled louvered outlets into each rear compartment footwell.
A manually opened and closed directional outlet in the rear of the console.

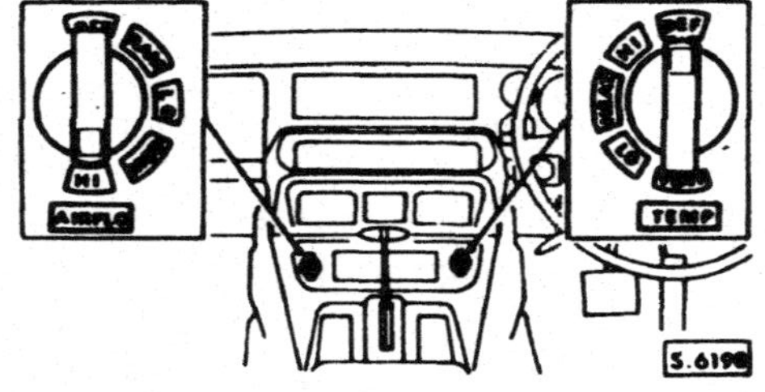

Heater Controls

All heater controls are operated either by vacuum supplied by the engine or by mechanical linkage. With the engine switched off, a supply tank will provide sufficient vacuum for approximately six complete operations.

The control switches operate as follows:-

Left hand Switch 'AIRFLO'

OFF
When the switch is set in this position, the heating and ventilating system is inoperative.

RAM
When the switch is set in this position, air is forced into the car by its forward movement, then routed and heated as determined by the position of the right hand switch, **'TEMP'**.

LO–MED–HI
When the switch is set to any of these positions the twin blower fans run at the selected speed to boost the air flow into the car. Air is again routed and heated as determined by the right hand switch, **'TEMP'**.

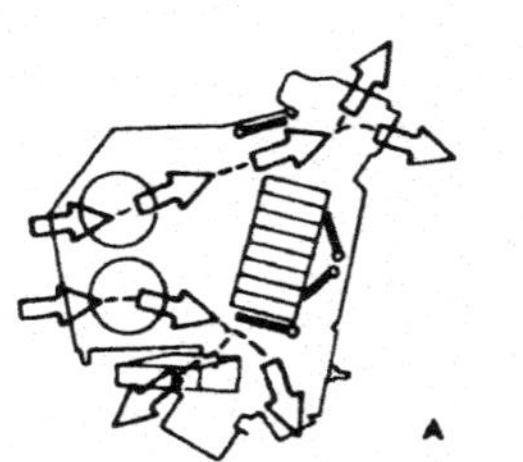

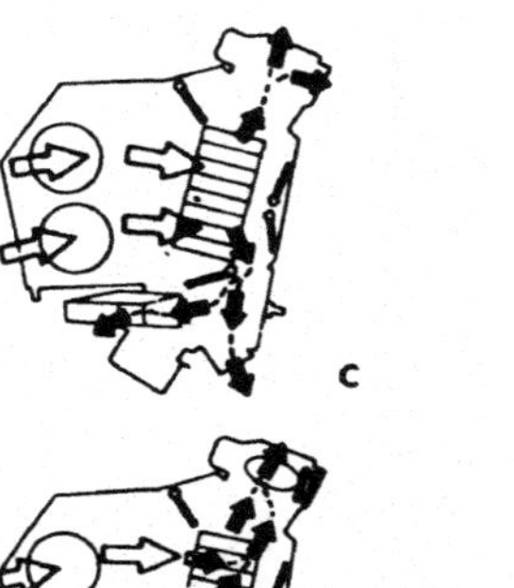

Right hand Switch 'TEMP'

A. VENT
When the switch is set to this position, unheated fresh air is delivered from the face level outlets across the facia, at a delivery rate determined by the position of the left hand switch. Individual outlets can be controlled as required. Movement of the knurled control knob beneath each of the side facia outlets can be used to regulate airflow. A small proportion of the airflow is bled to windscreen outlets for demist purposes.

B. LO
When the switch is set to this position the hot water supply to the heater matrix is switched on and the centre facia outlet is closed. A flap is mechanically positioned to deliver air at the minimum temperature. The airflow is as follows:-
(a) Majority of air is delivered to footwell outlets and rear compartment.
(b) Small proportion of air to facia end outlets and to windscreen.
The air delivered to the facia and windscreen is, while warm, always cooler than the air delivered to the footwell. The volume of air to the windscreen may be increased by closing both facia end outlets.

C. HI
The temperature of the air delivered is progressively increased to a maximum as the switch is rotated to 'HI'. Airflow from the facia end and windscreen outlets is always cooler than that delivered to the footwell.

D. DEF
When the switch is set to this position, air flow at maximum temperature is distributed 90% to windscreen and facia end outlets and 10% to footwell and rear passenger compartment. The facia end outlets may be aimed to defrost the side windows or closed to concentrate airflow at the windscreen.

OPERATION

COLD WEATHER

To obtain heating and demisting

(a) Set the **'TEMP'** control between 'LO' and **'HI'**, to give the desired temperature, and allow a short period to elapse to permit the heater matrix to warm up.
(b) Set the **'AIRFLO'** control to give the desired volume of air delivery.
(c) Set the facia end outlets as desired. For maximum demist effect, close both outlets.
(d) Set the rear compartment outlets as desired.

To obtain rapid demisting or defrosting
(a) Set the **'TEMP'** control to **'DEF'** and allow a short period to elapse to permit the heater matrix to warm up.
(b) Close the facia end outlets, or direct them to defrost side windows as required.
(c) Set the **'AIRFLO'** control to **'HI'**.
(d) Close the rear compartment outlets.

HOT WEATHER

To obtain fresh air ventilation

(a) Set the **'TEMP'** control to **'VENT'**.
(b) Set the **'AIRFLO'** control to give desired volume of air delivery.
(c) Set the facia end and centre outlets as desired.
(d) Set the rear compartment outlets as desired.

To obtain rapid demisting

(a) **Set the 'TEMP' control to 'LO'**.
(b) Set the **'AIRFLO'** control to **'HI'**.
(c) Close the facia end outlets, or direct air flow at side windows if desired.
(d) Close the rear compartment outlets.

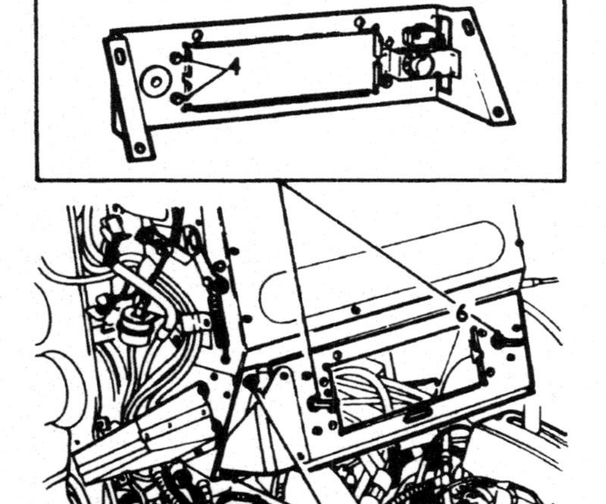

HEATER CONTROLS

Remove and refit 80.10.02

Removing
1 Disconnect battery -- 86.15.20.
2 Remove centre console – 76.25.01.
3 Remove two bolts, two nuts and associated shakeproof washers securing mounting plate to heater unit.
4 Remove three screws securing vacuum switches to mounting plate.
5 Note positions of vacuum pipes and disconnect from switches.
6 Remove circlip from shaft of temperature control.
7 Remove mounting plate from studs.
8 Note position of cables and pipes on vacuum switch, and micro switches before disconnecting.
9 To change micro switch(es) remove secure screws and nuts as necessary.
NOTE: Ensure replacement switches are of correct pattern.
10 To change vacuum switch remove two screws securing mounting bracket.

Refitting
Reverse operations 1 to 10.

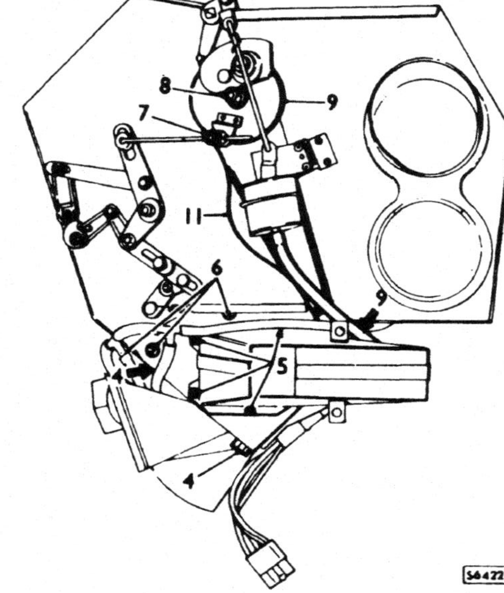
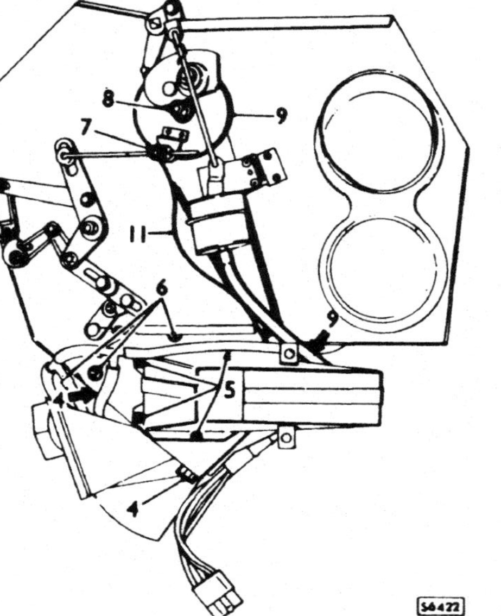

HEATER TEMPERATURE CONTROL CABLE ASSEMBLY

Remove and refit 80.10.05

Removing
1 Disconnect battery – 86.15.20.
2 Remove centre console – 76.25.01.
3 Remove right hand dash liner 76.46.11.
4 Remove nut and set screw securing radio/heater controls mounting panel to heater unit L.H. side.
5 Remove four drive screws securing R.H. footwell outlet duct.
6 Remove three drive screws securing R.H. footwell and rear outlet assembly.
NOTE: One screw is located behind control mounting panel and will require use of a right angle star headed screwdriver.
7 With temperature control knob in vent position, loosen flap link operating rod locking nut on main drive wheel.
8 Remove nut and washer from fulcrum of main drive wheel.
9 Lift jockey pulleys against spring tension and remove main drive wheel from its fulcrum.
10 Ease radio/heater control panel and R.H. footwell outlet assembly away from heater unit.
11 Remove bowden cable by releasing locking screw on driving bollard and removing nipples from main driving wheel.

Refitting
12 Fit replacement cable to drive bollard such that cable is wound around drum 2½ times i.e. three strands of wire should be seen adjacent to locking screw on bollard.
13 Ensure cable can be locked by washer under locking screw. DO NOT TIGHTEN.
14 With temperature control knob in 10 o'clock position, and cable passing round jockey pulleys such that upper strand leaving bollard passes around forward pulley, stretch cable ends to fullest extent horizontally. Adjust cable until nipples are level with each other.
15 Tighten locking screw on bollard ensuring that turns of cable are secured beneath washer.
16 Fit nipples into main drive wheel ensuring cable ends do not cross.
17 Refit radio/heater control panel and R.H. footwell outlet assembly to heater unit.
18 Keeping cable taut, refit main driving wheel to fulcrum and secure with nut and washer.
Note: It may be necessary to lift jockey pulleys against spring. Upper by-pass flap drive lever must also be pushed upwards to allow location of wheel on shaft.
19 Reset flap operating mechanism as laid down in procedure for flap link adjustment in general section.
20 Reverse operations 1 to 5.

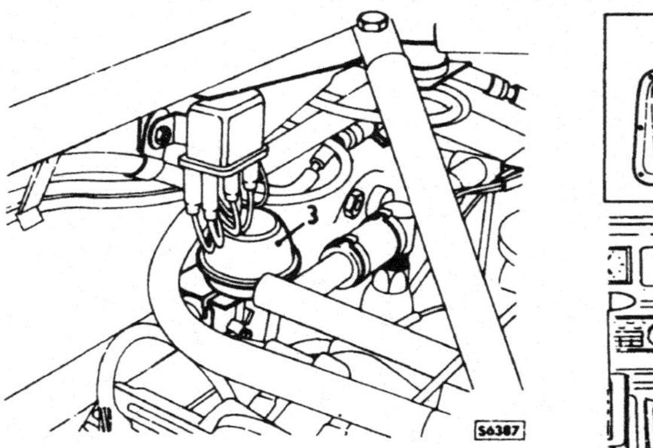

HEATER WATER VALVE

Remove and refit **80.10.16**

Removing

1 Drain coolant from system – 26.10.01. **NOTE**: Conserve coolant if anti-freeze is in use.
2 Release hose clips and withdraw hose from unit.
3 Remove vacuum tube from connector and detach unit.

Refitting

Reverse operations 1 to 3.

NOTE: Water valves are sealed units and must be replaced if faulty.

AIR DIRECTION BOX REMOTE CONTROL

Remove and refit **Left and Right hand – 80.10.31**

Removing

1 Withdraw two screws and one shrouded nut securing parcel shelf.
2 Remove shelf.

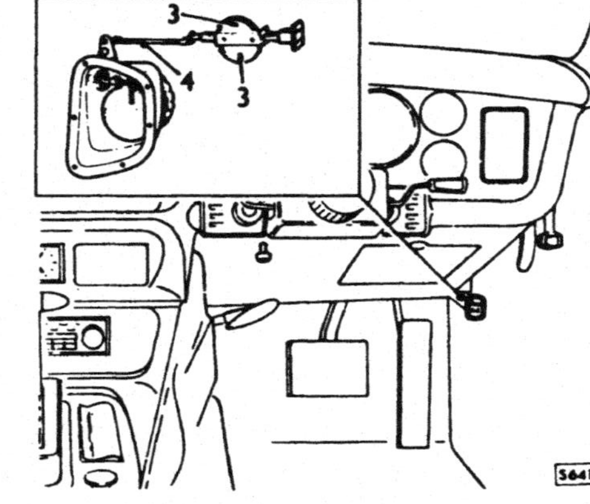

3 Withdraw two screws securing control handle assembly.
4 Unclip operating arm from control handle assembly.

Refitting

Reverse operations 1 to 4.

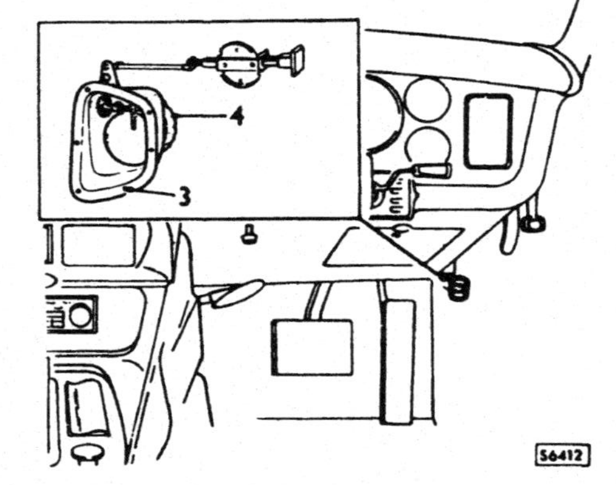

AIR DIRECTION BOX

Remove and refit **Left and Right hand – 80.10.32**

Removing

1 Remove air direction box remote control – 80.10.31.
2 Remove lower body side front trim pad – 76.13.01
3 Withdraw five screws securing air direction box.
4 Remove air direction box.

Refitting

Reverse operations 1 to 4

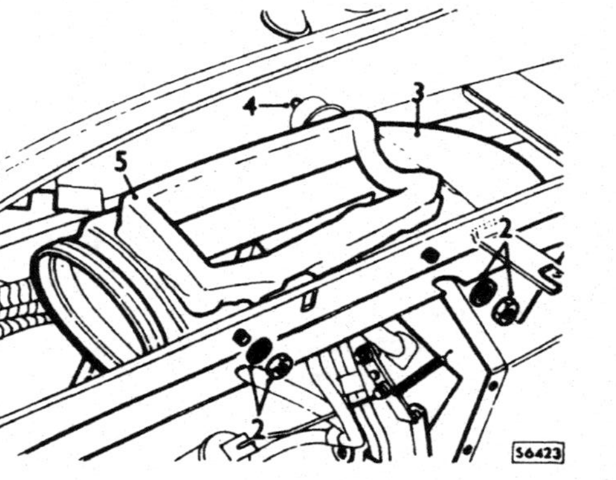

DEMISTER FLAP AND ACTUATOR ASSEMBLY

Remove and refit **80.10.37**

Removing

1 Remove crash roll – 76.46.04.
2 Remove two nuts securing assembly to screen rail.
3 Disconnect plastic ducting from assembly.
4 Disconnect vacuum tube from actuator.
5 Lift assembly away from screen rail.

Refitting

Reverse operations 1 to 5.

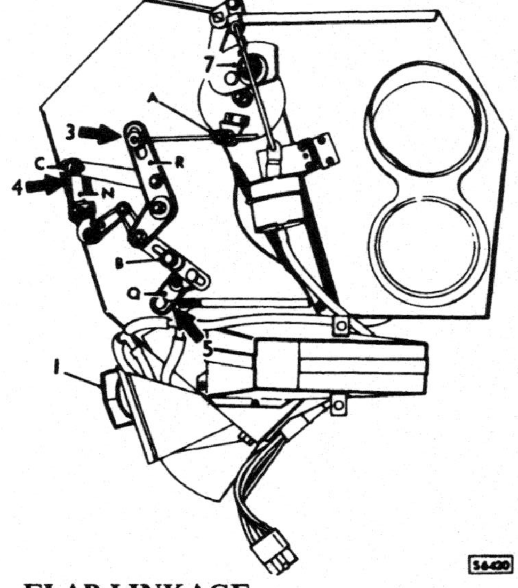

FLAP LINKAGE

Adjust **80.10.41**

In order to obtain correct adjustment of heater mechanism following procedure should be adopted.

1 Turn temperature control knob to vent.
2 Slacken locking screws, **'A'**, **'B'** and **'C'**.
3 Rotate lever **'R'** into fully clockwise position and hold in place using firm finger pressure. Tighten locking screw **'A'**.
4 Press lever operating flap **'N'** to fully clockwise position using finger pressure and tighten.
5 Turn temperature control knob to defrost. Using a screwdriver placed in slotted end of adjusting link, apply pressure in order to push lever operating flap **'Q'** into fully clockwise position. Tighten locking screw **'B'**.
6 Check that detent loads at either end of knob travel are acceptable. If not, some adjustment is possible by adjusting position of driving link pivot in lever **'R'**. However this should not normally be necessary.

continued

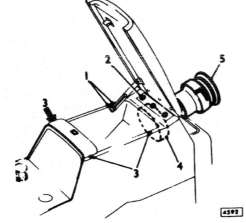

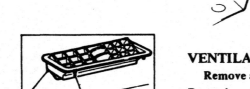

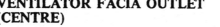

7 The eccentric pivot on upper flap actuating cam is adjustable through about 180°. This gives an adjustment of upper level temperature of 10°C in mid heat position. Turning nut clockwise increases face level temperature, turning it anti-clockwise reduces face level temperature. With eccentric pivot in mid position and with R.H. knob in horizontal position, there should be a gap of about 0.25 ins. (6,35 mm.) between flap and body of unit. This can only be checked with upper ducting removed.

DEMISTER DUCT OUTLETS

Remove and refit **80.15.02**

Removing

1 Insert blade of narrow thin tool between edge of demister outlet grille and surround. Carefully lever apart.
2 Grille and surround are retained in place by nylon friction bushes.

Refitting

3 Place surround and grille in position and press firmly.

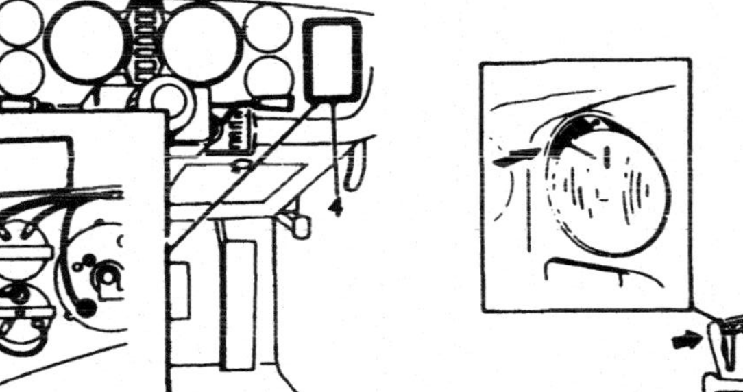

VENTILATOR (REAR)

Remove and refit **80.15.10**

Removing

1 Lift console glove box lid and remove two screws securing lid retaining bar.
2 Withdraw three screws securing hinge plate to glove box.
3 Withdraw three screws securing glove box liner.
4 Insert hand under glove box liner and grip bayonet locking ring of air vent assembly. Exert pressure on front of vent assembly and rotate anti-clockwise until locking ring releases.
5 Remove air vent assembly.

Refitting

Reverse operations 1 to 5

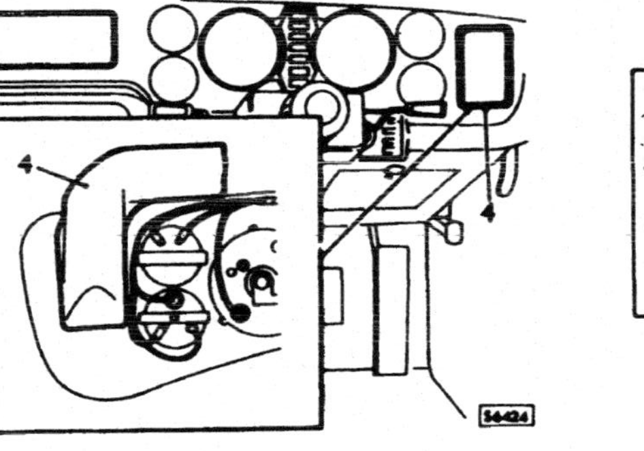

VENTILATOR FACIA OUTLETS

Remove and refit **Left – 80.15.22**
Right – 80.15.23

Removing

1 Disconnect battery – 86.15.20.
2 Remove facia – 76.46.01.
3 Unclip outlet at rear of facia.
4 Withdraw outlet assembly from ducting and facia.

Refitting

Reverse operations 1 to 4.

VENTILATOR FACIA OUTLET (CENTRE)

Remove and refit **80.15.24**

Removing

1 Disconnect battery – 86.15.20.
2 Remove facia – 76.46.01.
3 Withdraw four retaining screws.
4 Remove outlet assembly.

Refitting

Reverse operations 1 to 4

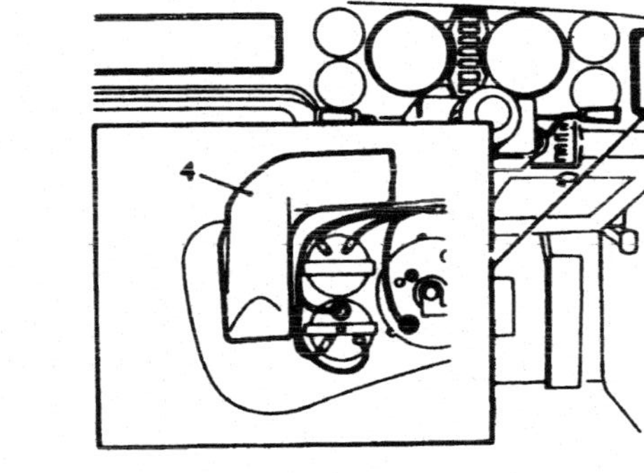

FRESH AIR INTAKE

NOTE: With air conditioning fitted but inoperative, fresh air will not be available at facia adjustable outlets with fans switched ON. Facia outlets will only deliver air at the selected temperature.

An additional fresh air supply is available to driver and passenger. A grille located in the outer headlamp embellisher (1) admits air which is ducted via the wings (2) to outlets in the scuttle side panels (3) beneath the parcel tray. These outlets are controlled by a three position lever marked 'PULL AIR' (4). The louvre outlets can be rotated to direct air as required. Air flow will depend upon the speed at which the car is moving and position of selector lever.

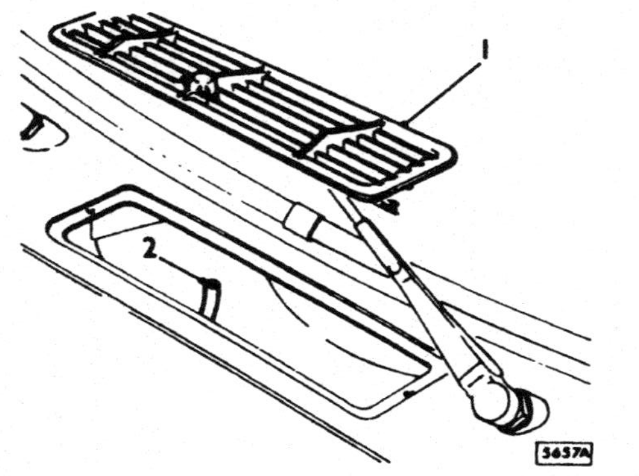

FRESH AIR INTAKE

Remove and refit Scuttle – 80.15.29

Removing

1 Insert screwdriver under edge of intake and carefully lever away from nylon friction bush. Take care not to damage paintwork.
2 Disconnect windscreen washer capillary tube from washer jet.

Refitting
Reverse operations 1 and 2.

FRESH AIR INTAKE

Remove and refit Headlamp – 80.15.29

Removing
1 Withdraw screw retaining headlamp embellisher.
2 Clear grille of road dirt, insects etc.

Refitting
Reverse operations 1 and 2.

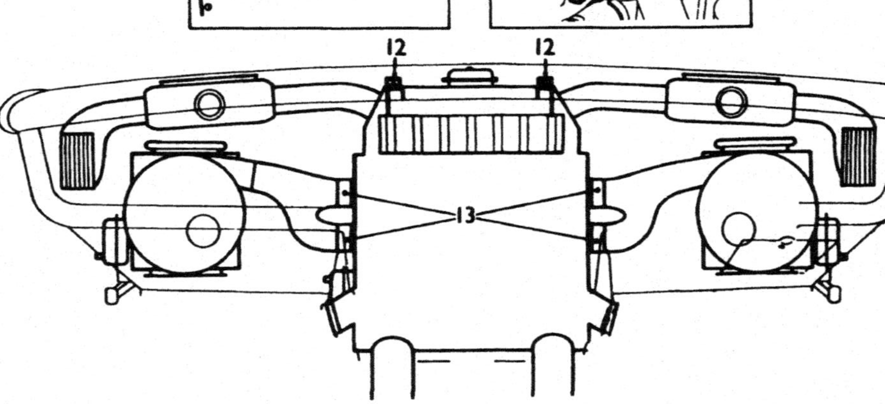

HEATER UNIT

Remove and refit 80.20.01

Removing
1 Disconnect battery – 86.15.20.
2 Drain cooling system – 26.10.01.
3 Remove facia crash roll – 76.46.04.
4 Remove driver's side dash liner – 76.46.11.
5 Remove passenger's side dash liner – 76.46.11.
6 Remove glove compartment liner – 76.52.03.
7 Remove centre parcel shelf – 76.67.03.
8 Remove centre console – 76.25.01.
9 Remove facia – 76.46.01.
10 Disconnect coolant hoses at heater matrix bulkhead connectors in engine compartment.
Note: Retain metal washer and sponge collar.
11 Remove two large retaining nuts from centre of bulkhead in engine compartment.
12 Remove two retaining nuts from centre of top rail.
13 Remove four bayonet connected stub pipes from sides of unit.
14 Locate vacuum connectors and clearly mark all tubes before disconnecting.
15 Disconnect electrical multi-pin connectors either side of unit. Note positions for refitting purposes.
16 Ease unit forward and left from car.
NOTE: Transmission selector should be in '1' position on automatic cars, or 4th, 2nd or Reverse gear on manual gearbox cars.

CAUTION: Great care must be exercised when lifting unit not to damage relay box. The unit must not be supported on these components.

Refitting
17 Offer unit up to mounting position and ease heater connectors through bulkhead apertures.
NOTE: Ensure sponge backing is in position.
18 Loosely fit retaining nuts, ensuring that pipes, speedometer cables and electrical harness are not trapped before tightening.
19 Re-connect vacuum pipes as marked in operation 14.
20 Re-connect electrical multi-pin plugs and sockets as noted in operation 17.
21 Refit bayonet connected stub pipes to unit. Connect, turn clockwise until pipes are locked.
22 Ensure drain tubes from unit are located through grommets in side of transmission tunnel.
23 Refit facia.
24 Ensure pliable ducting is correctly located on facia and crash roll air vents.
25 Refit centre console.
26 Refit centre parcel shelf.
27 Refit scuttle casings.
28 Refit crash roll.
29 Re-connect water hoses in engine compartment.
NOTE: Ensure sponge collars and metal washers are in place before connecting heater pipes.
30 Fill cooling system – 26.10.01.
31 Re-connect battery.

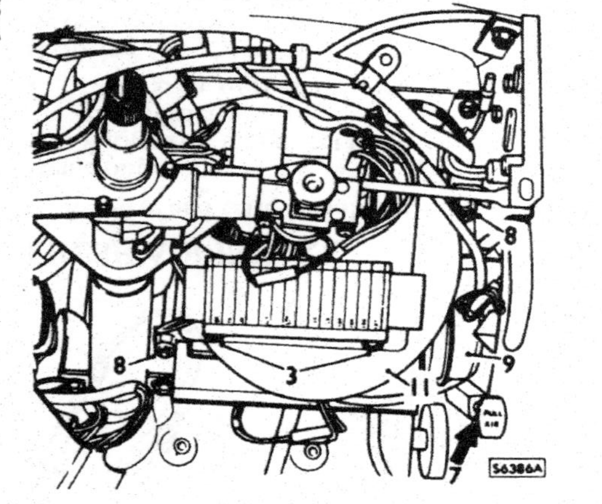

HEATER MOTOR ASSEMBLY

The blower fans are heavy duty motors with metal impellors attached. Speed variation is controlled by resistance units wired in series. Air flow control flaps are operated by a vacuum actuator mounted on the side of the inlet duct.

Remove and refit **Right hand unit – 80.20.15**

Removing

1 Disconnect battery – 86.15.20.
2 Remove right hand dash liners – 76.46.11

R.H. Drive

3 Remove four nuts retaining fuse block mounting panel to assembly case. Lay fuse block on one side.

L.H. Drive

4 Remove glove box liner – 76.52.03.

All cars

5 Pull pliable air duct from stub pipes at side of heater unit.
6 Remove front body side trim pads.
7 Withdraw two screws securing fresh air pull mounting bracket.
8 Remove two nuts retaining assembly from mounting posts.
9 Disconnect vacuum tube from actuator.
10 Disconnect electrical harness at snap connectors.
11 Ease fan motor unit from car.

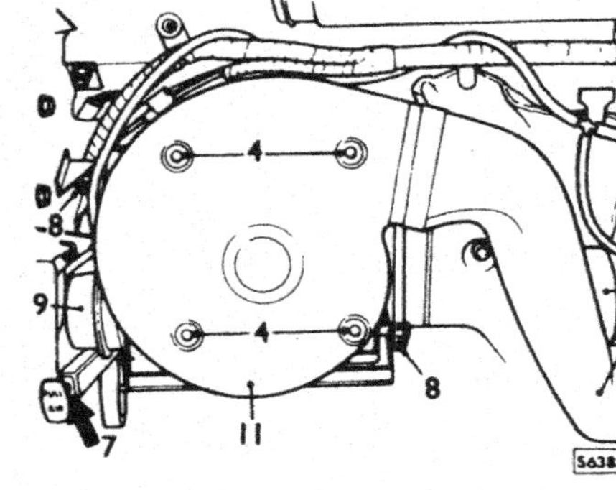

HEATER MOTOR ASSEMBLY

Remove and refit **Left hand unit – 80.20.15**

Removing

1 Disconnect battery – 86.15.20.
2 Remove left hand dash liner – 76.46.11.

R.H. Drive

3 Remove glove box liner – 76.52.03.

L.H. Drive

4 Remove four nuts retaining fuse block mounting panel to assembly case. Lay fuse block on one side.

All cars

5 Pull pliable air ducts from stub pipes at side of heater unit.
6 Remove front body side trim pad.
7 Withdraw two screws securing fresh air pull mounting bracket.
8 Remove two nuts retaining assembly from mounting posts.
9 Disconnect vacuum pipes from actuator.
10 Disconnect electrical harness at snap connectors.
11 Ease fan motor unit from car.

Refitting

Reverse operations 1 to 11.

NOTE: To refit assemblies successfully it is necessary to apply vacuum to the actuator, closing the top air flap. This simplifies insertion of the top flap and flange into its aperture and seal.

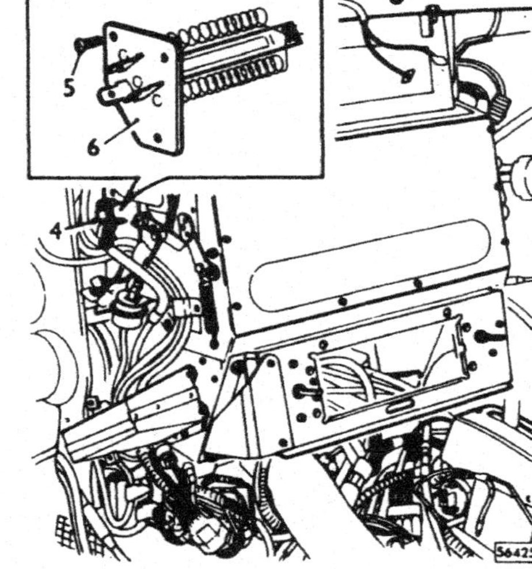

MOTOR RESISTANCE UNIT

Remove and refit **Left hand drive cars – 80.20.17**

Removing

1 Disconnect battery – 86.15.20.
2 Remove driver's side dash liner – 76.46.11.
3 Remove driver's side centre console side casing – 76.25.02.
4 Note position of cables at resistance unit and disconnect lucars.
5 Withdraw three crosshead screws.
6 Withdraw unit from heater unit case.

Refitting

Reverse operations 1 to 6.

Remove and refit **Right hand drive cars – 80.20.17**

Removing

1 Disconnect battery – 86.15.20.
2 Remove glove compartment liner – 76.52.03.
3 Note position of cables at resistance unit and disconnect lucars.
4 Withdraw three crosshead screws.
5 Withdraw resistance unit from heater case.

Refitting

Reverse operations 1 to 5.

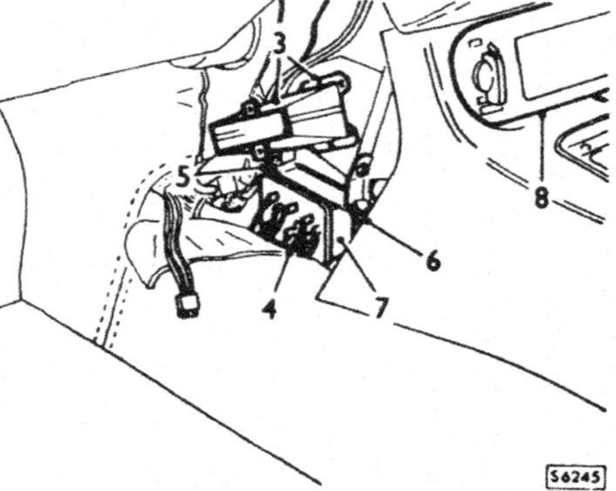

MOTOR RELAYS

Remove and refit **80.20.19**

Removing

1 Disconnect battery – 86.15.20.
2 Remove left hand centre console side casing – 76.25.02.
3 Withdraw four screws and remove footwell air outlet duct.
4 Note positions of cables at lucar connectors on relay box.
5 Disconnect cables at lucar connectors.
6 Remove securing nuts and washers and recover relay unit.

Refitting

Reverse operations 1 to 6.

NOTE: Ensure earth strap tag is replaced under relay box securing nut.

BLOWER ASSEMBLY

Overhaul 80.20.20

1 Disconnect battery – 86.15.20.
2 Remove blower assembly – 82.25.13/14.

Dismantling
3 Withdraw three self tapping screws from air inlet casing.
4 Part air inlet casing and motor assembly and disconnect electrical connections at lucars.
NOTE: It is recommended at this stage that positions of various components are marked either with paint or scriber. One cable lucar has a raised projection which matches the aperture in motor casing. This assists in ensuring connections are replaced correctly and direction of rotation of motor is not altered.
5 Unscrew three bolts securing fan motor mounting bracket to outlet duct.
6 Release nut and bolt securing motor mounting clip and remove motor fan bracket.
7 Using appropriate Allen key, remove impellor fan motor shaft, note position of shaft for reassembling.
NOTE: Blowers are handed for rotation and impeller operation, ensure correct motor and impeller are fitted if replacement is necessary.

Reassembling
Reverse operations 1 to 7.
NOTE: Ensure that impeller does not foul outlet duct, and that motor mounting clip does not obscure lucar connector spades.

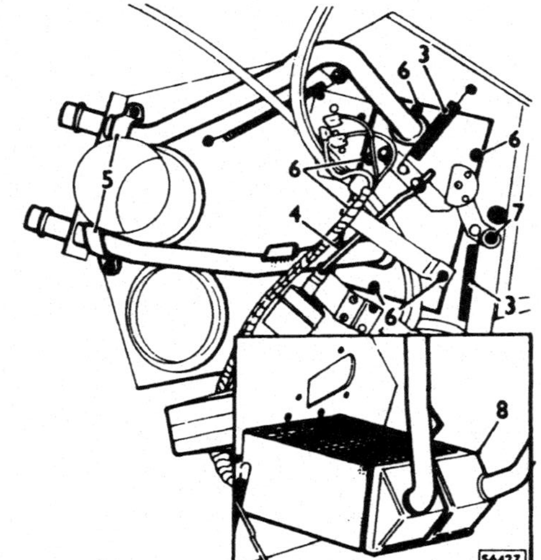

HEATER MATRIX

Remove and refit 80.20.29

Removing
1 Remove heater unit – 80.20.01.
2 Using scriber or thin brush and white paint mark positions of all control rods, knobs and cams.
3 Disconnect tensioning springs from heater matrix control flap operating arms.
4 Disconnect operating rods.
5 Remove two clips and screws securing inlet and outlet pipes to heater unit case.
6 Withdraw six screws securing heater matrix cover plate.
7 Withdraw one screw securing cam and operating arm to footwell outlet flap shaft and remove arm.
8 Withdraw matrix from side of heater unit with steady straight pull. Care must be taken not to damage inlet and outlet pipes.

Refitting
Reverse operations 1 to 8.

NOTE: Ensure sponge shock absorbing pads are refitted correctly when replacing matrix.

DEFROST AND DEMIST SYSTEM

Test 80.30.01

1 **Purpose**
To ensure that the heating system is functioning correctly in the 'Defrost' mode, and that adequate airflow is maintained in the heat mode to ensure that the windscreen remains mist-free.

2 **Method**
(a) Set L.H. Control to fan speed 'HI'.
(b) Set R.H. Control to 'Defrost'.
(c) Close end of dash outlets
(d) Start engine and run for 7 minutes at 1500 r.p.m.
(e) During the running period measure the airflow from each screen outlet using checking ducts and velometer. Ensure that the centre dash outlet is closed and that it seals satisfactorily. The velocity from the screen outlets should be:-

1500 f.p.m. (7,62 m/s) (Minimum)

(f) Also during the running period turn the R.H. Control to 'Heat', and open end of dash outlets. Using the screen outlet and end of dash checking ducts measure the resulting air velocity. These should be:-

Minimum Velocity (f.p.m.)

Screen	End of dash
450 (2,29 m/s)	650 (3,30 m/s)

(g) At the end of 7 minutes running at 1500 r.p.m. check that the water temperature gauge indicates 'Normal'. Using mercury in glass thermometers also check that the following minimum screen outlet temperatures are achieved.

Plenum Inlet		Screen Outlet (minimum)	
°C	°F	°C	°F
10	50	54	129.2
12	53.6	55	131
14	57.2	55.5	131.9
16	60.8	56.5	133.7
18	64.4	57	134.6
20	68	58	136.4
22	71.6	58.5	137.3
24	72.5	59.5	139.1

HEATER UNIT

Test 80.30.05

1 **Warm up and heat pick up on vent and water valve operation**
Turn the R.H. Knob to vent and the L.H. Knob to high. Start the engine and warm up, run at 1000 r.p.m. In this condition the inlet flaps should be open and the centre outlet flap open.
With a thermometer placed in the air stream issuing from the centre vent, ensure that as the engine reaches normal operating temperatures, the air temperature does not rise above 5°C higher than it was in the engine cold state.

2 **Defrost mode**
Turn the R.H. Knob to defrost.
The centre vent should close as should the upper mixing flap. The airflow to the footwell will be cut off apart from a small bleed.
At this point the defrost schedule can be operated if so desired. This will also check that the upper-mixing flap is operating.

3 **Fan speeds**
Check that high, medium and low speeds can be obtained by rotating the L.H. Knob.

4 **Temperature range**
By rotating the R.H. Knob ensure that the air temperature changes between hot and ambient over the heating range.

5 **Ram and off**
On the road check that air flows from the vent when the L.H. Knob is in the Ram position, but is cut off in the Off position.

6 **Heater matrix – flow test and descale**
If insufficient heat is available, and no fault exists in fans, water valve, flaps or controls, measure rate of coolant flow through heater matrix at 1000 rev/min.
Flow rate of less than 1.7 gal/min (7.7 litres/min) indicates obstruction of coolant passages.

continued

Equipment required: $\frac{5}{8}$ in (16 mm) bore hose at least 5 ft (1,6 m) long.
Water supply, controlled by tap.
One 2 gallon (or 10 litre) capacity container.
Stop watch.

NOTE: All tests must be completed with the engine cold, i.e. with the thermostats closed. Should the engine temperature rise sufficiently to open the thermostats, the engine must be stopped and allowed to cool before the tests are continued.

1 Drain coolant; conserve for refill, see 26.10.01.
2 Disconnect hose from heater matrix outlet stub pipe (this hose connects to water pump intake). Plug open end of hose.
3 Connect $\frac{5}{8}$ in (16 mm) bore hose to heater stub pipe, and place other end in 2 gallon (or 10 litre) container.
4 Refill cooling system with water, leaving hose from supply tap in header tank.
5 Start engine, run at 1000 rev/min with 'defrost' selected on heater control. Adjust water supply to keep header tank filled.
6 When water from heater matrix is free from air, measure time required to fill the 2 gallon (or 10 litre) container. Stop engine. If the time to fill a 1 gallon container is more than 1 min 11 secs, or for a 10 litre container more than 1 min 18 secs, heater matrix is obstructed and must be cleared as detailed below.
7 Disconnect hose from heater matrix output stub pipe, unplug car hose and refit to stub pipe.
8 Add one pint of Ferroclene to header tank, top up system with water and replace both filler caps.
9 Start engine and run at 1000 rev/min for 15 minutes.
10 Stop engine and drain, see 16.10.01. Continue flushing system (operations 5 and 6 of 26.10.01) for at least 30 minutes to remove all traces of Ferroclene which would otherwise cause internal corrosion.
11 Repeat operations 2 to 6 above. If necessary, repeat operations 7 to 10.
12 Refill, using coolant conserved in operation 1 above.

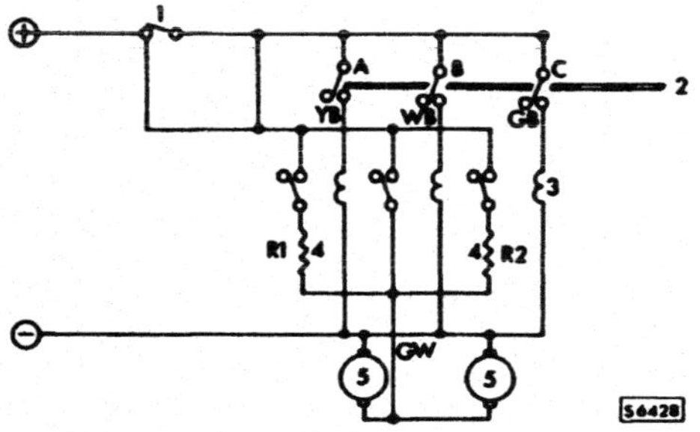

S6428

KEY TO WIRING DIAGRAM

1 Ignition Switch.
2 Cam Operated Switches.
3 Relays – Motor Speed.
4 Resistors – Motor Speed.
5 Fan Motors.

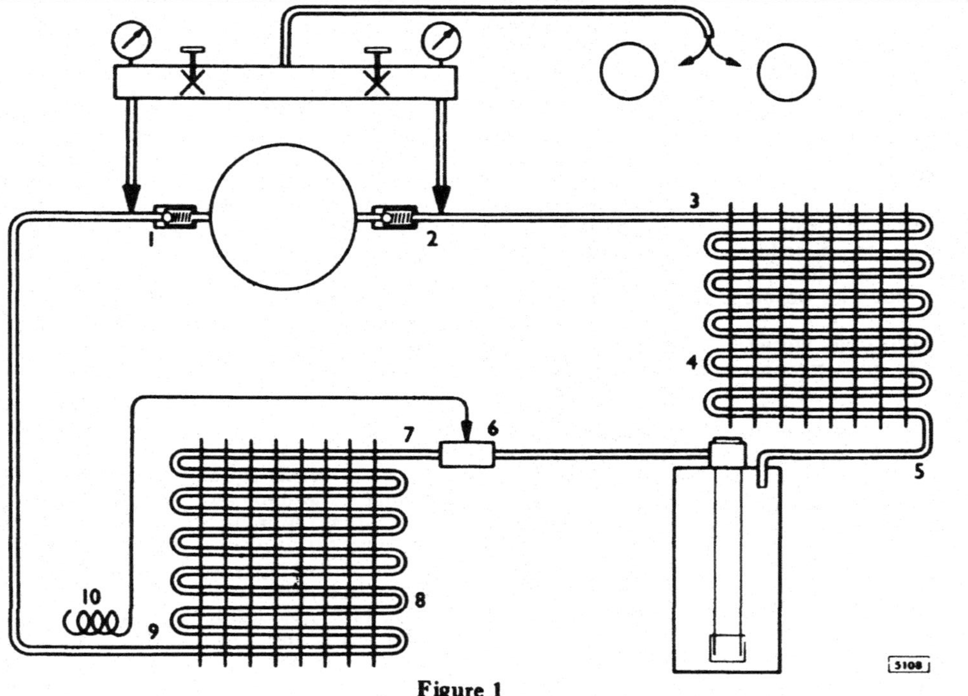

Figure 1

AIR CONDITIONING SYSTEM

System description 82.00.00

The air conditioning system is comprised of the following components:

1 Compressor with magnetic clutch.
2 Condenser.
3 Combined receiver/drier unit.
4 Combined evaporator coil, expansion valve, heater coil and control system.
5 Blower motors.
6 Temperature sensing devices (thermistors) to compare in car and ambient temperatures.

The refrigeration cycle is best described with reference to figures 1 and 2. The refrigerant used is to specification R.12 (refrigerant 12) which is a halogenated hydrocarbon (dichlorodifluoromethane).
The heart of the automobile refrigerant system is the compressor. Its purpose is two fold; to raise the pressure of the refrigerant vapour and correspondingly raise its temperature.

The suction side of the compressor, point 1, pulls in superheated refrigerant vapour. The compression cycle occurs between 1 and 2 of figure 1, work being done on the vapour to raise its pressure and add heat. The fact that heat is added is shown by point 2 on figure 2 being to the right of point 1. The pressure difference is given by the vertical axis of figure 2. The high pressure, high temperature vapour is delivered to a fin and tube construction condenser located in front of the engine coolant radiator where heat flow takes place from the high temperature vapour to the surrounding air. As the refrigerant passes through the condenser, heat transfer and a reduction in temperature takes place, the gas giving up its latent heat and condensing to a cool liquid. However, the length of the condenser is selected so that further heat loss takes place, sub-cooling the refrigerant liquid to ensure complete condensation. In figure 2 these conditions are shown between points 3 and 5. At point 3 condensation commences, passes through a wet vapour state, and is complete at point 4. The sub-cooling is shown taking place between points 4 and 5.

The high pressure liquid now passes to the receiver/drier, a reservoir for the liquid content of the system. The receiver/drier incorporates a filter and a limited capacity dehydrating element to remove traces of moisture from the refrigerant.

Two forms of receiver/drier are fitted, the pot-type unit of earlier cars being replaced in 1976 Series cars incorporating twin electric cooling fans by a horizontal unit, located above the car radiator. This type of unit is fitted to all 1978 Series cars.

From the receiver/drier, liquid refrigerant passes to the expansion valve and evaporator unit point 6 of figure 1.

The expansion valve is the dividing point in the system, a step change from a high pressure area into a low through a small metering orifice. The metering orifice is protected by a gauze filter in the inlet union of the expansion valve. The orifice size is controlled by the temperature at the outlet from the evaporator unit and by the inlet pressure to the expansion valve. A quantity of liquid refrigerant passes the expansion valve orifice and expands suddenly as it enters the low pressure area. As the liquid passes through the coils of the evaporator unit heat transfer takes place from the car interior air to the liquid causing it to boil.

The length of the evaporator coil is so chosen that the liquid refrigerant has completely vapourised at approximately three quarters through, the remaining length serving to absorb more heat and super-heat the vapour. This ensures that no liquid refrigerant reaches the compressor, and that as much heat as possible is absorbed from the car interior. The temperature sensing

continued

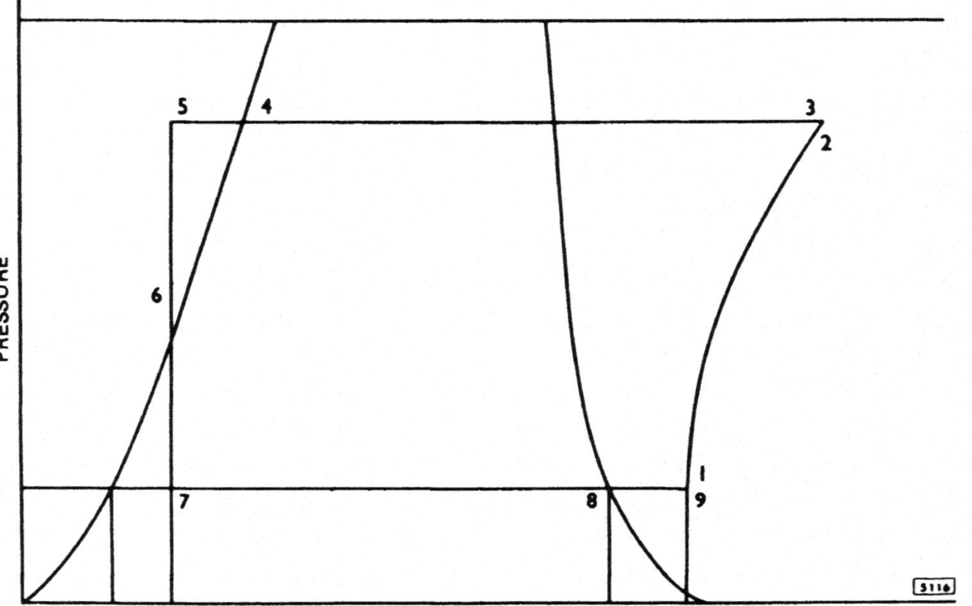

Figure 2

capillary of the expansion valve is fitted at the outlet of the evaporator. The capillary senses the outlet gas temperature and sets the expansion valve to meter the supply of cold liquid to the input of the evaporator.

For example, should the outlet pipe temperature fall, the expansion valve closes, cutting off the flow of liquid refrigerant until the temperature rises to the preset level. The super-heated vapour is then drawn to the suction side of the compressor, point 1 of figure 1, and the cycle continues. Later cars incorporate a fuel cooler in the vapour return pipe to the compressor.

Moisture from air passing over the matrix of the evaporator unit condenses on to the cool fins and drains from the evaporator via rubber tubes. Use of the air conditioning system can therefore result in a pool of water beneath the vehicle after parking. This is completely normal and does not indicate malfunction of the system.

It can be seen that ice formation is possible upon the fins of the evaporator unit. Anti-icing of the coil, and control of the vehicle interior temperature is provided by the thermostat. The capillary senses the temperature of the evaporator coil, and via a switch, de-energises the compressor clutch when the temperature falls to the preset level. This stops the flow of refrigerant and allows the coil to heat up until the thermostat switch re-closes. The compressor clutch then engages to re-start the cycle.

Component description

Compressor

The compressor utilizes three double acting pistons disposed axially around the compressor drive shaft. The pistons are actuated by a swash plate pressed on to the shaft. A magnetic clutch is used to drive the compressor shaft. When current passes through the clutch coil, the armature clutch plate assembly, keyed to the compressor shaft, is drawn rearwards against the belt driven pulley that is free wheeling upon the same shaft. This locks pulley and armature plate together to drive the compressor. When current ceases to flow, springs in the armature plate draw the clutch face from the pulley. The compressor comes to rest and the pulley continues to free wheel.

Condenser

The condenser is a copper tube and aluminium fin heat transfer unit, fitted forward of the engine coolant radiator. The condenser transfers heat from the refrigerant flowing through it to the airstream drawn through it by the engine cooling fans.

Receiver/Drier

The receiver/drier is a cylindrical tank that serves as a reservoir for the refrigerant. The liquid refrigerant is fed in, and is drawn out, via a screen and filter. The outlet tube has a sight glass fitted through which it can be determined by observing the refrigerant condition, whether there is adequate refrigerant in the system. A cloth sac filled with moisture absorbing granules is located inside the tank. This retains any traces of moisture that may be present in the refrigerant.

Expansion Valve

The expansion valve controls the flow of refrigerant through the evaporator coil to achieve optimum cooling efficiency. To do this, the valve senses the outlet pipe temperature and inlet pipe pressure and increases or decreases the flow of refrigerant liquid to maintain the outlet temperature constant.

Evaporator

The evaporator is a tube and fin heat exchanger into which the liquid refrigerant is metered. The air content of the vehicle, when forced over the fins by the recirculating blower fans, gives up its heat to boil the refrigerant.

Air conditioning heater/cooler unit and Automatic temperature sensing and control system

Automatic control is achieved by comparing car interior temperature and the temperature selected. This comparison provides an error signal to the air conditioning control unit, demanding an increase or decrease in car interior temperature. When the selected temperature is reached, the control unit will maintain it. Air from the car interior is drawn over the in-car sensor (thermistor) through an aspirator tube which leads to the L.H. fan ducting. The desired air temperature is selected on the L.H. control knob.

The error signal is detected across a Wheatstone Bridge circuit; two arms of which are fixed resistors, one arm contains the in-car thermistor and the fourth arm the temperature selection potentiometer. An error signal will be detected if car interior temperature is above or below that set on the temperature selection potentiometer. The error signal is amplified, and via relays, switches the servo motor to run clockwise or anti-clockwise. The position of the servo motor cam shaft directly determines the heating or cooling effect of the air conditioning system. Full heating and full cooling, are at opposite extremes of cam shaft travel.

The ambient thermistor in the Wheatstone Bridge circuit modifies the effect of the in-car thermistor. The result is a slightly colder interior temperature on hot days, and vice versa. A potentiometer driven by the servo motor is connected into the bridge circuit, modifying dynamic response. This provides control system damping, preventing excessive fluctuations in discharge air temperature.

It is important to note that the performance of the thermistors is influenced by the temperature of the wires leading to the sensor units; the wires must not be located close to or touching the clock, radio, heater casing or any other possible source of heat.

The servo motor shaft mounted cams control seven functions:-

1 Air discharge temperature – The cam shaft moves blend flaps to vary air flow progressively from full cold to full heat. The cams are set to provide cooler air at head level, than to foot level, when the unit is in the low-medium heating mode. This prevents stuffiness at head level.

2 Fan speeds – The cam shaft alters fan speed progressively to increase air flow at full cold or full heat positions. Four fan speeds are available on cooling, three on heating. On low heating or cooling the cam shaft selects a low fan speed, preventing noise and excessive air movement.

3 Mode – The cam shaft controls a vacuum switch so that the distribution of air in the car is automatically controlled by a vacuum operated flap. Cold air is distributed from the face level vents, and hot air is distributed mainly from foot level vents with a bleed of air from screen vents.

4 Fresh/Recirculated Air – To improve performance the cam shaft selects recirculated air on maximum cooling. Fresh air is selected for all other requirements.

5 Water Valve – On maximum cold, the cam shaft controls a second vacuum switch to switch off the water valve controlling flow through the heater block.

6 Water Thermostat – A thermostat is fitted to prevent the system operating until engine water is hot enough to produce warm air. When on cooling mode the cam shaft overrides this switch, and allows the system to operate immediately.

7 Evaporator thermostat – A thermostat is fitted to prevent icing of the evaporator. Under conditions where icing would be impossible and maximum cooling performance is required, the thermostat is overriden by the cam-shaft.

Manual Controls

1 Temperature selection potentiometer – This provides for the selection of interior temperature from 65°F (18°C) to 85°F (29°C) approximately.

B Mode Switch –

1 Off – The system is switched 'off' and the fresh air intake is closed.

2 Auto – The system operates automatically.

3 Hi Auto and Lo Auto – These switch positions select a fixed high or low fan speed independently from that selected by the automatic control.

4 Defrost – The switch directs 90% air flow to the screen by closing the lower heater flap and opening the bleed flap to the screen outlets. At the same time an additional resistor is switched into the Wheatstone Bridge circuit to ensure that the servo motor cam shaft runs to full heat position.

Method of Temperature Variation

All air passes through the fans and evaporator matrix. In the evaporator air is cooled and dehumidified. After leaving the evaporator, four blend flaps control the degree of heat added by the heater matrix. On maximum cold all air by-passes the heater matrix, and on maximum heat all air passes through the heater. Intermediate temperatures are obtained by varying the mixtures of cooled and heater air. One pair of blend flaps control the air to the car interior upper level, and another pair control the temperature to the lower level.

GENERAL SECTION

This section contains safety precautions, general information, good practice and standards that must be followed when working upon the air conditioning system. A fault finding and rectification section is included

SAFETY PRECAUTIONS

The air conditioning equipment is manufactured for use only with Refrigerant 12 (dichlorodifluoromethane) and extreme care must be taken NEVER to use a methylchloride refrigerant.

The chemical reaction between methylchloride and the aluminium parts of the compressor will result in the formation of products which burn spontaneously on exposure to air, or decompose with violence in the presence of moisture. The suitable refrigerant is supplied under the following trade names:

FREON 12
ARCTON 12
ISCEON 12

or any refrigerant to specification 12.

Goggles and gloves must be worn while working with the refrigerant.

WARNING: EXTREME CARE SHOULD BE EXERCISED IN HANDLING THE REFRIGERANT. LIQUID REFRIGERANT AT ATMOSPHERIC PRESSURE BOILS AT −29°C (−20°F) SERIOUS DAMAGE OR BLINDNESS MAY OCCUR IF REFRIGERANT IS ALLOWED TO CONTACT THE EYES.

FIRST AID: IF REFRIGERANT SHOULD CONTACT THE EYES OR SKIN, SPLASH THE EYES, OR AFFECTED AREA WITH COLD WATER FOR SEVERAL MINUTES. DO NOT RUB. AS SOON AS POSSIBLE THEREAFTER, OBTAIN TREATMENT FROM A DOCTOR OR EYE SPECIALIST.

GENERAL INFORMATION

Torque levels to be used when tightening all pipe connection nuts are as follows:

	Torque loading	
	lbf ft	kgf m
Nuts on 0.38 in (9,5 mm) dia. pipes	11 to 13	1,52 to 1,80
Nuts on 0.50 in (12,7 mm) dia. pipes	15 to 20	2,10 to 2,76
Nuts on 0.63 in (16 mm) dia. pipes	21 to 27	2,90 to 3,73

GOOD PRACTICE

1 The protective sealing plugs must remain in position on all replacement components and hoses until immediately before assembly.
2 Any part arriving for assembly without sealing plugs in position must be returned to the supplier as defective.
3 It is essential that a second backing spanner is always used when tightening all joints. This minimises distortion and strain on components or connect-pipes.
4 Components must not be lifted by connecting pipes, hoses or capillary tubes.
5 Care must be taken not to damage fins on condenser or evaporator matrices. Any damage must be rectified by the use of fin combs.
6 Before assembly of tube and hose joints, use a small amount of clean new refrigerant oil on the sealing seat.
7 Refrigerant oil for any purpose must be kept very clean and capped at all times. This will prevent the oil absorbing moisture.
8 Before assembly the condition of joints and flares must be examined. Dirt and even minor damage can cause leaks at the high pressures encountered in the system.
9 Dirty end fittings can only be cleaned using a clean cloth wetted with alcohol.
10 After removing sealing plugs and immediately before assembly, visually check the bore of pipes and components. Where ANY dirt or moisture is discovered, the part must be rejected.
11 All components must be allowed to reach room temperature before sealing plugs are removed. This prevents condensation should the component be cold initially.
12 Before finally tightening hose connections ensure that the hose lies in the correct position, is not kinked or twisted, and will not be trapped by subsequent operations e.g. closing bonnet, refitting battery.
13 Check hose is correctly fitted in clips or strapped to subframe members.
14 The Frigidaire compressor must be stored horizontally and sump down. It must not be rotated before fitting and charging. Do not remove the shipping plate until immediately before assembly. Always use new 'O' ring seals beneath union housing plate, and in those pipe joints which incorporate them.
15 Components or hoses removed must be sealed immediately after removal.
16 AFTER A SYSTEM HAS BEEN OPENED TWICE THE RECEIVER/DRIER MUST BE RENEWED.

FAULT FINDING CHART 1

Direct access to the air conditioning unit is very limited. The following checks are designed to be carried out with the minimum of test equipment and confined to those areas that are readily accessible. The sequence must be strictly adhered to, each check is based on the satisfactory result of the previous test. The standard cable colour code is used to identify leads and terminal connections referred to in the tests.

Before commencing checks, run engine until normal running temperature is reached, this also ensures that sufficient vacuum is available for tests. For cooling tests the engine must be running for compressor clutch to operate.

Note

1 The voltages quoted in the chart are nominal, assuming an actual 12 volts in the system.
2 This procedure applies only for ambient temperatures between 65°F (18.3°C) – 85°F (29.4°C) which is the controlled range of the unit. At higher temperatures it will not be possible to set a heating mode.
3 Actuators have been tested for operations down to 8 ins. (20.32 cms) of mercury. Check vacuum level of system, and upstream of suspect valves, before rejecting valves.

Equipment Required

1 Voltmeter, capable of covering 0–13 volts D.C.
2 Continuity tester.
3 Ohmmeter capable of covering 0–20K ohms.
4 Vacuum gauge, (not essential) to check vacuum level.

TEST 1:

AIR CONDITIONING CONTROL KNOB POSITIONS — **L.H. 75°** — **R.H. 'OFF'**

ITEM	CORRECT OPERATION	FAULT SYMPTOM	CHECK	RESULT	ACTION
1–1	BLOWERS 'OFF'	AIR FLOW AT OUTLETS	1–1–1 Single relay NY terminals for voltage	(a) 'O' Volts	Change switch 'C'
				(b) 12 Volts	Change relay
1–2	FRESH AIR FLAPS CLOSE. RECIRCULATION FLAPS OPEN	RECIRCULATION FLAP CLOSED	1–2–1 Disconnect vacuum line at bottom of solenoid valve	(a) No vacuum	Blockage in supply line
				(b) Vacuum	1–2–2
			1–2–2 Disconnect vacuum line at solenoid valve outlet	(a) No Vacuum	1–2–3
				(b) Vacuum	1–2–4
			1–2–3 Check voltage at 'K' terminal of solenoid	(a) 12 Volts	Change solenoid
				(b) 'O' Volts	Trace circuit from solenoid to switch 'C'
		ONE SIDE CLOSED	1–2–4 Pull open flap by hand	(a) Not possible	Mechanical link fault
				(b) Possible	1–2–5
			1–2–5 Check vacuum at actuator inlet	(a) No Vacuum	Blockage in line to solenoid valve
				(b) Vacuum	Actuator flap linkage fault

TEST 2:

CONTROL KNOB POSITIONS — **L.H. 75°** — **R.H. 'DEFROST'**

ITEM	CORRECT OPERATION	FAULT SYMPTOM	CHECK	RESULT	ACTION
2–1	BLOWERS TO HIGH SPEED	BLOWERS 'OFF'	2–1–1 Check voltages at fan motor connectors	(a) Voltage NOT 'O' Volts	Blower electrical fault-change
				(b) 'O' Volts	2–1–2
			2–1–2 Check voltages at triple relay, GS lead and terminal	(a) 12 Volts	Switching O.K.
				(b) 10 Volts (Break in GS line(s) relay to blower connections)	2–1–10
				(c) 5 Volts	2–1–7
				(d) 'O' Volts	2–1–3
			2–1–3 Check voltage at NW lead on triple relay	(a) 'O' Volts	Electrical fault in main supply
				(b) 12 Volts	2–1–4

ITEM	CORRECT OPERATION	FAULT SYMPTOM	CHECK	RESULT	ACTION
			2–1–4 Check voltage at NY lead on single relay	(a) 'O' Volts	Break in NY or switch fault
				(b) 12 Volts	2–1–5
			2–1–5 Check earth resistance at single relay	(a) High resistance	Earth contact loose
				(b) Low resistance	2–1–6
			2–1–6 Check Y terminal on single relay	(a) 'O' Volts	Replace single relay
				(b) 12 Volts	Resistor assembly fault. Check Y & GS connections
		BLOWERS AT LOW SPEED ONLY (2–1–2c)	2–1–7 Check earth resistance at B.U. lead on triple relay	(a) High resistance	Break in B.U. or Switch fault in switch D, or poor earth at 'D'
				(b) Low resistance	2–1–8
			2–1–8 Check voltage at BG lead on triple relay	(a) 'O' Volts	Break in BG lead to switch 'A'
				(b) 12 Volts	2–1–9
			2–1–9 Check voltage at relay terminal 'R'	(a) 'O' Volts	Replace relay
				(b) 12 Volts	Fault in resistor assembly or connection to harness lead 'R'
		BLOWERS AT MED 2 SPEED (2–1–2b)	2–1–10 Check voltage at BW lead, triple relay	(a) 'O' Volts	Break in BW line to hand control
				(b) 12 Volts	Replace relay
2–2	HOT AIR TO SCREEN	NO AIR TO SCREEN (AIR TO FOOT LEVEL ONE/BOTH SIDES)	2–2–1 Check vacuum at 'T' piece under crash roll (green line)	(a) Vacuum	Vacuum switch fault on hand control
				(b) No vacuum	
		COLD AIR FOOT LEVEL, COLD AIR SCREEN	2–2–2 Check air at outlets	(a) Servo has not traversed	See Test 5
				(b) Water valve failure	See Test 6–4
		COLD AIR FOOT LEVEL OR COLD AIR SCREEN	2–2–3 Check air at outlets		Mechanical link or flap fault See Test 6

TEST 3:

CONTROL KNOB POSITIONS — L.H. HEATING MODE (HIGHER THAN AMBIENT) — R.H. AUTO-HI

ITEM	CORRECT OPERATION	FAULT SYMPTOM	CHECK	RESULT	ACTION
3–1	BLOWER SPEED HIGH	BLOWERS OFF	3–1–1 Listen to blowers		Water temperature switch faulty or harness break in N & NY lines
3–2	SCREEN FLAPS CLOSE AIR TO FOOT LEVEL	HIGH FLOW AT SCREEN OR COLD AIR TO FOOT LEVEL	3–2–1 Check vacuum at 'T' piece under crash roll (green line)	(a) Vacuum	Actuator fault or flap mechanical failure
				(b) No vacuum	Faulty vacuum switch 'C' or line blocked

TEST 4:

CONTROL KNOB POSITIONS — L.H. 85° — R.H. AUTO-LO

ITEM	CORRECT OPERATION	FAULT SYMPTOM	CHECK	RESULT	ACTION
4–1	BLOWERS TO LOW SPEED	BLOWERS OFF	4–1–1 Check voltage at NY lead on single relay	(a) 'O' Volts	Break in NY lead
				(b) 12 Volts	4–1–2
			4–1–2 Check earth resistance at single relay	(a) High resistance	Earth contact loose
				(b) Low resistance	4–1–3
			4–1–3 Check voltage at Y terminal on single relay	(a) 'O' Volts	Replace relay
				(b) 12 Volts	Resistor assembly fault
		BLOWERS AT MED 1 (8.5 V)			Switch 'D' faulty

TEST 5:

AMPLIFIER/SERVO RESPONSE

ITEM	CORRECT OPERATION	FAULT SYMPTOM	CHECK	RESULT	ACTION
5–1	SERVO TRAVERSE MOVE LEFT HAND KNOB BOTH WAYS		5–1–1 Check that servo traverses (listen for servo motor)	(a) Movement	Test 6
				(b) No movement	5–1–2
			5–1–2 Check voltage at P & PR connector and move L.H. control	(a) Voltage changes ± 12 Volts	Servo motor, condenser, wiring, disconnected
				(b) Both voltages at 12 volts	Replace amplifier

ITEM	CORRECT OPERATION	FAULT SYMPTOM	CHECK	RESULT	ACTION
				(c) Both leads at earth potential	5–1–3
				(d) One or both leads open circuit	Line break in RP leads
				(e) PR Terminal at constant 12 Volts (Continuous heating)	Switch off unit to to 5–1–5
			5–1–3 Check amplifier supply at fuse (N line)	(a) 'O' Volts	Harness break N Line
				(b) 12 Volts	5–1–4
			5–1–4 Disconnect ambient sensor lead 'U' and check resistance of servo socket at No. 7 (U) to No. 4 (W)	(a) Open circuit	Temperature selector disconnected
				(b) O–2K	Amplifier
			5–1–5 Switch OFF unit. Check resistance between amplifier fuse and IN-CAR sensor lead WR	(a) High resistance	Switch A fault
				(b) Low resistance	5–1–6
			5–1–6 Check resistance between amplifier socket No. 3 (N) and No. 7 (U)	(a) Open circuit	Break in harness or sensor fault
				(b) 14K ohms	5–1–7
		R Terminal at constant 12V (Constant cooling)	5–1–7 Check resistance between amplifier socket No. 7 (U) and No. 4 (W). Rotate L.H. control	(a) No variation	Temperature selector faulty
				(b) Variation	5–1–8
			5–1–8 Check resistance between amplifier socket No. 5 (G) and 8(Y) and between No. 8(Y) and 9(0)	(a) 0 or Open circuit	Feed back potentiometer or harness fault
				(b) Up to 2K ohms	Amplifier fault
TEST 6:					
AUTOMATIC FUNCTIONS					
6–1	Limit cooling & heating	Servo will not traverse			Servo could be damaged See Test 5

ITEM	CORRECT OPERATION	FAULT SYMPTOM	CHECK	RESULT	ACTION
6–2	REFRIGERATION SYSTEM	OUTLET TEMPERATURE INCREASES	6–2–1 Check voltage and fuse in NY lead	(a) 'O' Volts	Break in NY lead Fuse blown
				(b) 12 Volts	6–2–2
			6–2–2 Check voltage at clutch terminal	(a) 'O' Volts	Servo switch lead break GN
				(b) 12 Volts	Clutch fault loss of refrigerant
	Full cooling	LOW FLOW RATE DESPITE HIGH SPEED	6–2–3 Check air flow at outlets	(a) Evaporator blockage	Ranco thermostat fault
				(b) Icing in matrix	
6–3	FRESH AIR/HIGH SPEED Full cooling	FANS NOT AT HIGH SPEED & RECIRCULATION FLAPS CLOSED	6–3–1 Check voltage in servo WG lead	(a) 'O' Volts	Servo switch fault
				(b) 12 Volts	Test 2–1
		FANS NOT AT HIGH SPEED & RECIRCULATION FLAPS OPEN	6–3–2 Test 2–1	(a) Fault condition	Rectify as 2–1
				(b) No fault	Harness break WG lead
		FANS AT HIGH SPEED AND RECIRCULATION FLAPS CLOSED	6–3–3 Test 1–2	(a) Fault condition	Rectify as 1–2
				(b) No fault	Break in Servo branch of K lead
6–4	WATER VALVE Full cooling	WATER PIPES FEEL HOT (Valve open)	6–4–1 Check vacuum at actuator	(a) Vacuum	Actuator or valve fault
				(b) No vacuum	Servo valve fault
	Full heating	AIR NOT HOT (Valve closed)	6–4–2 Check vacuum at actuator	(a) Vacuum	Servo valve fault
				(b) No vacuum	Actuator or valve sticking
6–5	WATER THERMOSTAT BYPASS (Disconnect Thermostat leads) Full cooling	BLOWERS OFF			Harness break N or NY Servo switch fault
	Heating mode	BLOWERS ON			Servo switch fault
6–6	BLOWERS MED 1 and MED 2 Full Heating	BLOWERS NOT ON MED 1	6–6–1 Check voltage at triple relay BY lead	(a) 12 Volts	6–6–2
				(b) 'O' Volts	6–6–3
			6–6–2 Check voltage at triple relay U lead	(a) 'O' Volts	Relay fault
				(b) 12 Volts	Lead or resistance unit fault

ITEM	CORRECT OPERATION	FAULT SYMPTOM	CHECK	RESULT	ACTION
	Traverse full heating to full cooling	NO INTERMEDIATE FAN SPEEDS – MED 1 and MED 2 OFF	6–6–3		NY Lead break, or Servo switch fault
		MED 2 MISSING	6–6–4		BE lead break in servo limb or MED 2 switch fault
6–7	FACE FLAP (MODE)– Full cooling	NO AIR TO FACE LEVEL	6–7–1 Check vacuum at servo vacuum valve S9	(a) Vacuum	Blockage or actuator fault
				(b) No vacuum	Servo vacuum valve fault
	Full heating	AIR TO FACE LEVEL	6–7–2 Check vacuum at servo vacuum valve S9	(a) Vacuum	Servo valve fault
				(b) No vacuum	Blockage or actuator fault
6–8	INCORRECT AIR TEMPERATURES AND AIR DISTRIBUTION				
		6–8–1 If above tests are satisfactory			Blend flap fault
		6–8–2 Full cooling			Ensure flaps are seated – readjust linkage as necessary
		6–8–3 Full heating			

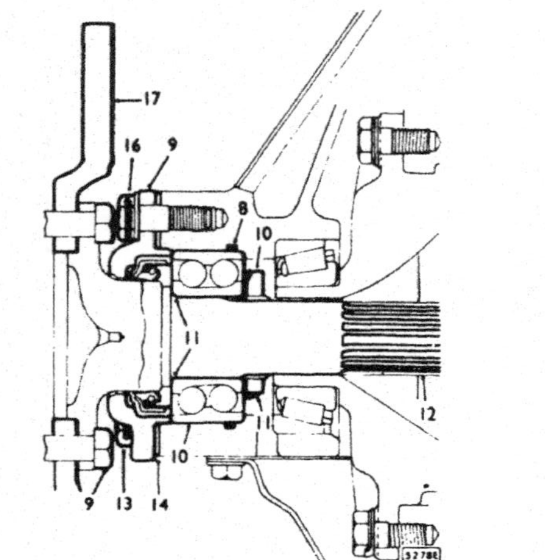

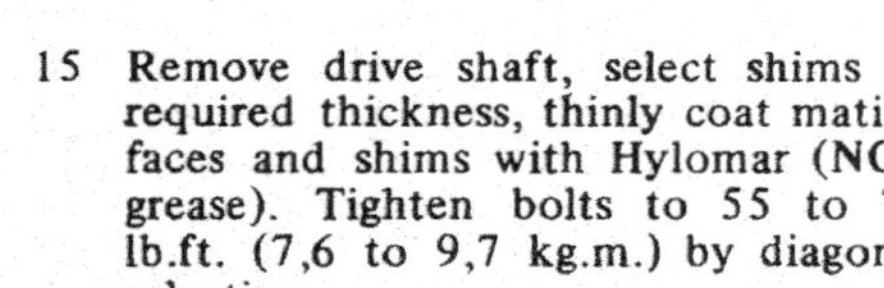

15 Remove drive shaft, select shims of required thickness, thinly coat mating faces and shims with Hylomar (**NOT** grease). Tighten bolts to 55 to 70 lb.ft. (7,6 to 9,7 kg.m.) by diagonal selection.
16 Wire lock five securing bolts to tension in clockwise direction.
17 Fit discs to drive shaft flanges, using shims removed in operation 3 between disc and flange.
18 Fit caliper to mounting bracket using two bolts and lockwashers.
19 Fit distance tubes (oversize nuts) to disc studs and secure using four nuts. Use feeler gauges to ensure disc central between jaws of caliper. If necessary add to or remove from shim pack between drive flange and disc.
20 Reverse operations 1 and 2.

FINAL DRIVE UNIT

Remove and refit 51.25.13

Service tool: Dummy shaft JD.14.

Removing
1 Removing rear suspension unit, see 64.25.01.
2 Invert unit and place on workbench.

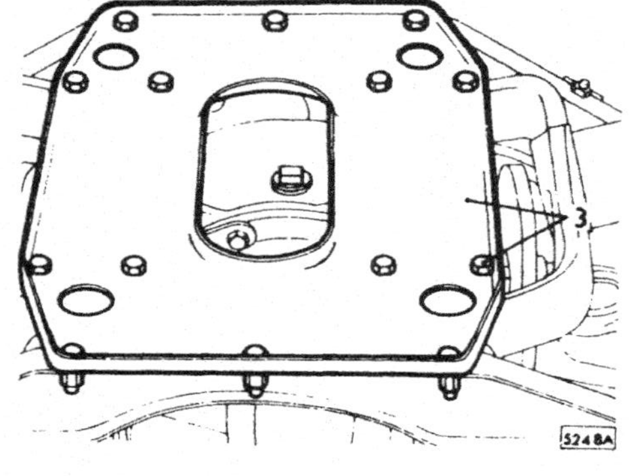

3 Remove 14 bolts and setscrews securing bottom tie plate to crossbeam and inner fulcrum brackets.
4 Remove nuts and washers securing dampers to wishbone.
5 Drift out damper mounting pins; recover spacers and tie-down brackets.
6 Slacken clips securing inner universal joint shrouds and displace shrouds outwards.
7 Remove four self locking nuts securing drive shaft inner universal joint to brake disc and output flange on one side.
8 Remove nut from inner wishbone fulcrum shaft.
9 Drift out shaft, collecting spacers, seals and bearings for wishbone pivots.
10 Remove drive shaft, hub and wishbone assembly from rear suspension.
11 Remove camber shims from drive shaft flange studs at brake disc.
12 Repeat operations 7 and 11 on opposite side assembly.
13 Tap spacer tubes from between lugs of fulcrum brackets.
14 Turn suspension assembly over on bench.
15 Disconnect brake feed pipes at calipers. Seal ports and ends of pipes.
16 Release brake return springs at hand-brake levers.
17 Cut locking wire and remove bolts attaching final drive to crossbeam.
18 Lift suspension crossbeam off final drive unit.

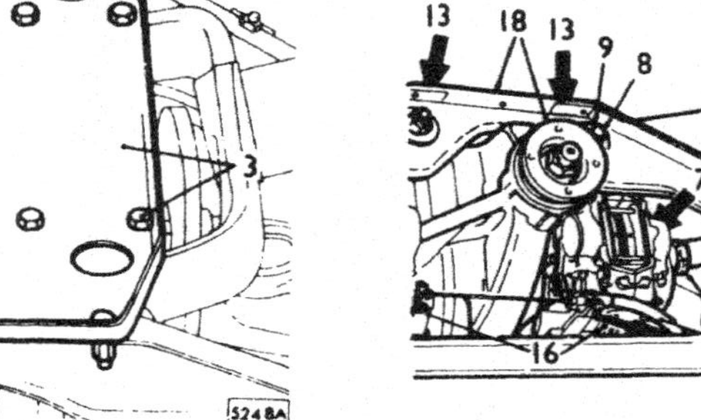

19 Invert final drive unit.
20 Remove locking wires from setscrews securing fulcrum brackets to final drive unit. Remove setscrews and remove brackets, noting position and number of shims at each attachment point.
21 Cut locking wires from caliper mounting bolts; remove bolts and calipers.
22 Remove brake discs, noting number of shims between discs and flanges.

Refitting
23 Replace shims and disc on one drive shaft flange; secure with two nuts.
24 Replace caliper, tighten mounting bolts and check centering and run-out of disc.
25 Correct centering of disc, if necessary, to within ± 0.010 in. (0,25 mm.) by transferring shims from one side of disc to the other.
26 Tighten caliper bolts to 49 to 55 lbf.ft. (6,77 to 7,60 kgf.m.) and wire lock.
27 Repeat operations 24 to 27 on opposite side.
28 Remove nuts from both discs.
29 Place crossbeam over final drive, align, replace bolts, tighten to 70 to 77 lbf.ft. (9,68 to 10,64 kgf.m.) and wire lock.
30 Slacken brake feed pipes at centre union.
31 Unseal brake pipes and ports, align pipes and tighten union nuts to 6.3 to 7 lbf.ft. (0,88 to 0,96 kgf.m.).
32 Replace handbrake lever return springs.
33 Invert assembly on bench.
34 Position fulcrum brackets against final drive unit and locate each bracket loosely with two setscrews.
35 Replace shims removed in operation 20 between brackets and final drive unit.
36 Tighten setscrews to 60 to 65 lbf.ft. (8,30 to 8,98 kgf.m.) and wire lock.
37 Refit camber shims, removed in operation 11, to drive shaft studs on one side.
38 Replace drive shaft on studs, and fit nuts loosely, then tighten to 49 to 55 lbf.ft. (6,78 to 7,60 kgf.m.).
39 Replace spacer tube between lugs of fulcrum bracket.
40 Clean, inspect and grease wishbone bearings, thrust washers etc. Refit with new oil seals.
41 Offer up wishbone fulcrum bracket lugs and locate with dummy shafts, tool No. JD.14. Take great care not to displace any component during this operation.
42 Drift dummy shafts from fulcrum bracket with fulcrum shaft. Restrain dummy shafts to prevent spacers or thrust washers dropping out of position.
43 Tighten fulcrum shaft nut to 45 to 50 lbf.ft. (6,23 to 6,91 kgf.m.).
44 Reposition and secure drive shaft shroud.
45 Line up damper lugs with wishbone bosses and replace damper shaft, including spacer and tie-down bracket. Tighten nuts to 32 to 36 lbf.ft. (4,43 to 4,97 kgf.m.).
46 Repeat operations 31 to 39 on opposite side.
47 Replace bottom tie plate and tighten bolts and setscrews to 14 to 18 lbf.ft. (1,94 to 2,48 kgf.m.).
48 Replace rear suspension unit, see 64.25.01.
49 Check rear wheel camber, see 64.25.18.
50 Bleed brakes, see 70.25.02.
51 Check final drive oil level and top up as necessary.

Defective expansion valve

Check

Carry out checks as for partial restriction of expansion valve.

Correction

As for partial restriction of expansion valve.

Evaporator coil blocked with ice

Check

Thermostat sensor not in contact with fins of evaporator.
Thermostat setting.
Expansion valve.

Correction

Reposition sensor to touch fins.
Reposition thermostat to lower level.
Renew expansion valve.

Excessive refrigerant charge

Check

Observe charging manifold gauge readings. If both suction and discharge pressure readings are unusually high for the prevailing ambient temperature this indicates the possibility of the system being overfilled. Ensure centre hose of charging manifold pointing in safe direction, and slowly open pressure side valve to bleed off some refrigerant.
If the gauge pressures fall, this confirms excessive refrigerant charge.

Correction

Continue to slowly bleed off refrigerant until both gauge readings are approximately normal.

CAUTION: Keep close watch on receiver/drier sight glass during this operation. Any bubbles appearing will indicate that too much refrigerant has been removed.

Very high heat load

Check

Very hot or humid day.
Vehicle heater is switched off.
All windows and doors are closed.

Correction

Ensure heater is switched off and that all air vents, windows, and doors are closed.

Loose capillary tube connection at evaporator coil outlet

Check

Observe suction side of compressor connector union housing for severe frosting or icing.

Correction

If icing is heavy, check that expansion valve capillary coil is in correct contact and clamped to evaporator outlet pipe. Tighten clip as necessary. Do not overtighten to damage capillary coil.
Replace expansion valve – 82.25.01.

Restrictions in high pressure side

Check

For restriction in condenser, receiver/drier, and hoses connecting these units.
Any restriction or partial blockage will create a drop in temperature at the point of restriction. This temperature drop will be obvious to the touch, and in some cases frost or sweating may occur at that point.

Correction

Replace component or hose affected.

Insufficient air over condenser

Check

That the condenser matrix is not damaged or obstructed.
Vehicle radiator matrix is not damaged.
Cooling fan runs continually while air conditioning system is on.
Direction of rotation of fan.

Correction

Blow out matrices with compressed air. Use hose if necessary to soften caked mud.
Dress deformed finning.
Check wiring to fan and replace fan if wiring correct.

Unusually hot running engine

Check

Engine cooling system.
Ensure radiator blind (if fitted) is not in operation.

Air or non-condensable gas in system

Check

If all other methods fail to reduce head pressure to a satisfactory level, check for air in the system.
Pour cold water over condenser to accelerate condensing action.
If there is excessive refrigerant in system the pressure will momentarily fall.
Air in the system will not condense. The pressure will therefore remain high.

Correction

Sweep (purge) the system – 82.30.07.
Change receiver/drier unit.

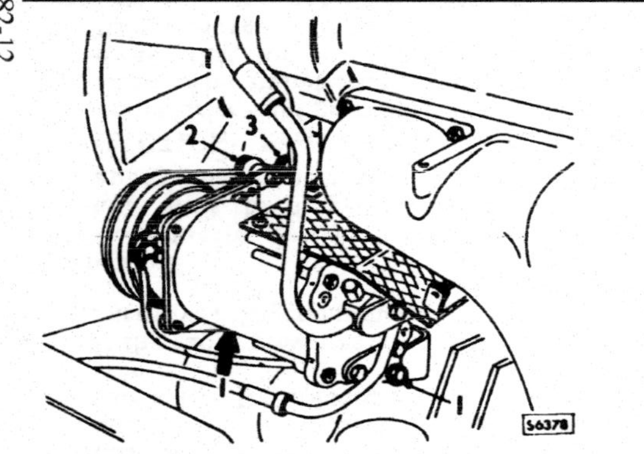

COMPRESSOR DRIVE BELT

Adjustment **82.10.01**

1 Slacken compressor mounting bolts on front and rear flanges.
2 Slacken adjusting link mounting bolts.
3 Slacken adjusting link locknut.
4 Adjust belt tensioning nut; correct tension is as follows:
A load of 6.4 lb (2.9 kg) must give a total belt deflection of 0.17 in (4.32 mm) when applied at mid point of belt.
5 Reverse operations 1 to 3.

COMPRESSOR DRIVE BELT

Remove and refit **82.10.02**

Removing
1 Remove power steering/water pump drive belt – 26.20.07.
2 Slacken compressor drive belt – 82.10.01.
3 Remove compressor drive belt.

Refitting
4 Reverse operations 1 to 3.
5 Adjust compressor drive belt – 82.10.01.

COMPRESSOR OIL LEVEL

Check **82.10.14**

There is no way to check oil level while the compressor is installed but the level should not change throughout normal service. However, owing to the fact that oil is normally in suspension and comes to rest whenever the system is shut down, that oil within a component removed is lost to the total quantity.

In order to compensate for this loss, a specific quantity of oil is to be added for each component replaced; the quantity relating to each component will be given in the relevant procedure. If oil has been lost from the system owing to accident damage depressurisation or incorrect depressurisation procedure, the component must be removed from the installation to check oil level – 82.10.20.

COMPRESSOR

Remove and refit **82.10.20**

WARNING: BEFORE COMMENCING WORK ON THIS OPERATION REFER TO GENERAL SECTION – 82.00.00. DO NOT OPERATE COMPRESSOR UNTIL SYSTEM IS CORRECTLY CHARGED.

NOTE: Ensure that suitable clean, dry male and female sealing caps are to hand.

Removing
1 Disconnect battery – 85.15.20.
2 Withdraw two drive screws securing hot air duct to cam covers (not necessary on U.S.A. Federal specification engines).
3 Withdraw two setscrews and remove exhaust manifold heat shield. (Not necessary on U.S.A. Federal emission specification engines).
4 Remove air pump – 17.25.07 (if fitted).
5 Remove compressor heat shield.
6 Remove electrical connectors from clutch.
7 Depressurise air conditioning system – 82.30.05.
8 Remove compressor drive belt – 82.10.02.
9 Remove setscrew and spring washer securing valve and union assembly housing to rear of compressor.

NOTE: IMMEDIATELY seal all connection orifices using clean, dry caps. Recover 'O' ring seals.

10 Remove nuts, bolts and spring washers from front and rear mounting flanges.
11 Keeping compressor horizontal, sump down, lift from engine compartment.
12 Drain oil from compressor sump into a suitable clean container and accurately measure quantity.

CAUTION: If oil shows any sign of contamination, system must be swept – 82.30.07 and receiver/drier unit replaced – 82.17.01.

13 Drain oil if any from replacement compressor.

NOTE: Following manufacturers instructions transfer parts from defective compressor to replacement.

14 If replacement compressor contained oil on receipt, refill with clean refrigerant oil equal in quantity to that removed in operation 12. If replacement compressor contained no oil, refill with clean refrigerant oil equal in quantity to that removed in operation 12, **PLUS** 1 oz. (29 g).

NOTE: This compensates for oil lost by retention in freshly drained unit - 82.10.14.

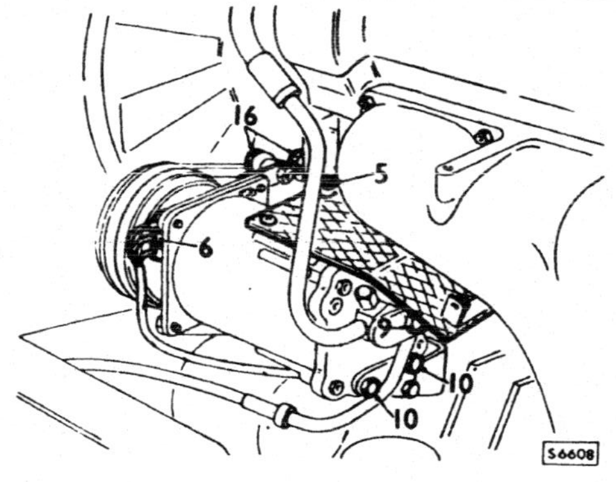

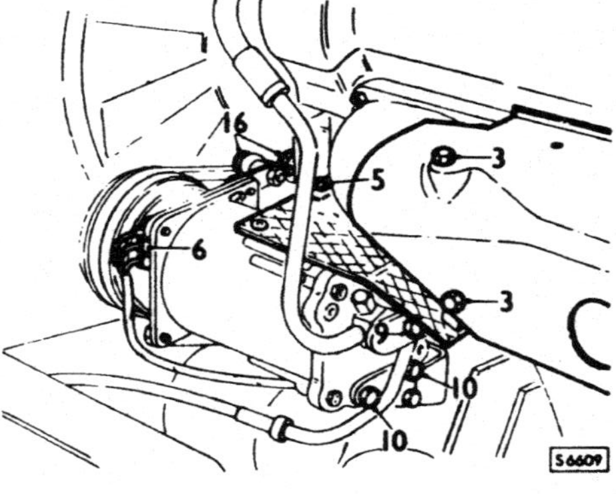

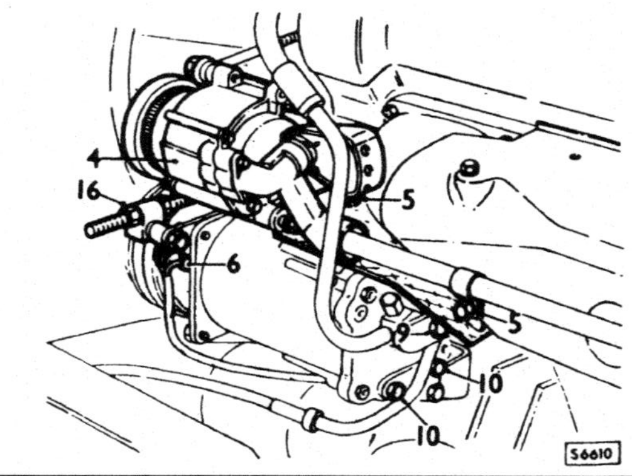

Refitting

15 Place compressor in position, sump down and loosely secure nuts, bolts and spring washers.
16 Refit compressor drive belt and adjust tension – 82.10.01.
17 Tighten all mounting bolts.
18 Remove shipping plate from rear of compressor, transfer to defective compressor.

NOTE: Use 'O' ring seals removed in operation 9 beneath shipping plate.

19 Remove sealing plugs from valve and union housing assembly, and secure to rear of replacement compressor using one setscrew and spring washer to a torque of **10** lb.ft. – 25 lb.ft. (1,4 kg.m – **2,4** kg.m).

NOTE: Ensure replacement 'O' ring seals are not displaced.

20 Refit electrical connection to clutch.
21 Reconnect battery.
22 Charge air conditioning system – 82.30.08.

CAUTION: **After charging, cycle clutch in and out 10 times by selecting OFF-LO AUTO-OFF on mode selector switch with engine running. This ensures that pulley faces and clutch plate are correctly bedded in before a high demand is made upon them.**

CONDENSER UNIT

Remove and refit – without twin electric fans 82.15.07

Removing

The condenser is mounted forward of the radiator and is accessible after raising the bonnet.

1 Depressurise the system – 82.30.05.
2 Disconnect hoses and unions.

NOTE: Hoses and unions must be sealed immediately with clean blanking caps.

3 Withdraw 2 Phillips head screws from retaining straps to front top cross member.
4 Lift unit from locating spigots in radiator mounting cradle.

Refitting

5 Reverse operations 2 to 4.
6 Charge system – 82.30.08.

CONDENSER UNIT

Remove and refit – with twin electric fans 82.15.07

Removing

1 Remove receiver drier unit – 82.17.01.
2 Disconnect wiring on radiator top rail at Lucars.
3 Remove two setscrews, washers and self locking nuts securing fan cowl to radiator top rail.
4 Remove setscrews and bolts securing radiator top rail.
5 Detach air intake ram pipe coupling (if fitted) and lift off top rail.
6 Disconnect refrigerant pipes from condenser and plug ends immediately with clean blanking caps.
7 Remove two nuts from condenser top supports and lift condenser from bottom spigot mountings.

Refitting

8 Reverse operations 1 to 7, including recharging system after replacing receiver drier unit.

LEAK TESTING

The condenser unit can be tested for leaks whilst removed from car.

1 Seal off outlet pipe union with suitable cap, nut and sealing disc.
2 Connect a small refrigerant container to condenser inlet union with flexible hose.
3 Open container valve and allow a quantity of refrigerant to enter condenser.
4 Pass leak detector around condenser tubes. Pay particular attention to U bends at each end of condenser unit.
5 Replace defective unit with new unit.

RECEIVER DRIER UNIT

Servicing

If the drying agent in the receiver drier unit becomes completely saturated with water the unit must be replaced. If the system is allowed to remain open for a long period, or even a short time in very humid conditions, the drier unit must be changed. DO NOT REMOVE the protective sealing caps from a new unit until it has been fitted and is ready for coupling to pipe unions.

CAUTION: **It is of the utmost importance that water is not allowed in the system. Refrigerant '12' is a hydrocarbon containing chlorine and fluorine halogens. The hydrogen in water, can under certain temperature conditions, hydrolize with chlorine and fluorine to produce hydrochloric and hydrofluoric acids. These acids will attack the copper tubing and polished surfaces within the air conditioning system.**

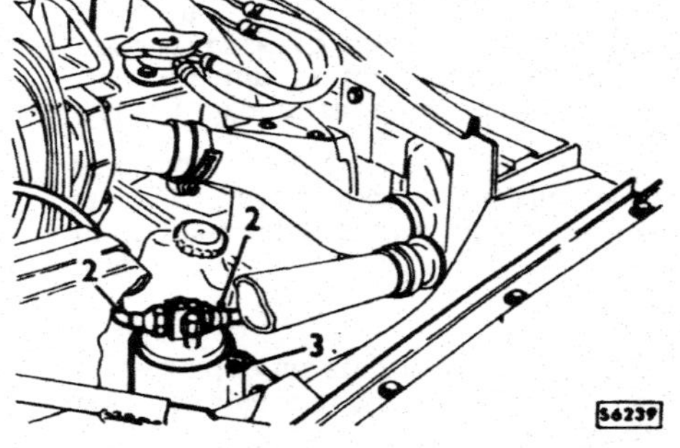

RECEIVER DRIER UNIT

Remove and refit – without twin electric fans 82.17.01

Removing

1 Evacuate system, see 82.30.06, to ensure that all moisture is withdrawn.
2 Disconnect pipe lines.

NOTE: Blank off unions and pipe lines with clean dry caps.

3 Slacken three screws and nuts on retaining bracket and withdraw unit.

Refitting

4 Reverse operations 2 and 3.
5 Charge system – 82.30.08.

RECEIVER DRIER UNIT

Remove and refit – with twin electric fans 82.17.01

Removing

1 Evacuate system, see 82.30.06, to ensure that all moisture is withdrawn.
2 Release union nuts at ends of receiver drier unit, detach pipes and immediately plug their ends.
3 Remove four Phillips head screws and lift off receiver drier.

Refitting

4 Reverse operations 2 to 4.
5 Charge system – 82.30.08.

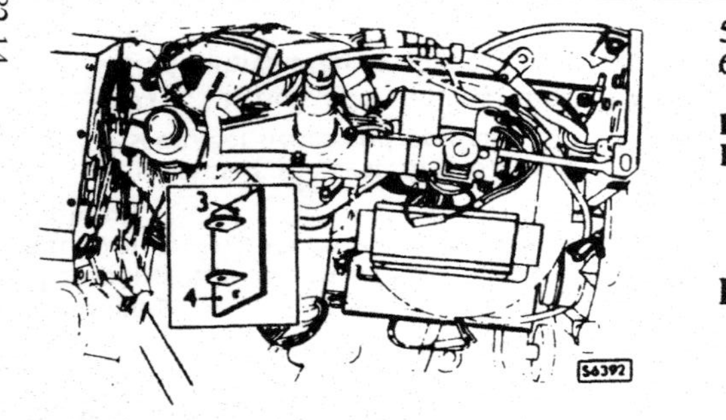

AMBIENT TEMPERATURE SENSOR

Remove and refit **82.20.02**

Removing

1 Disconnect battery – 86.15.20.
2 Remove right hand blower motor assembly – 82.25.13.
3 Withdraw two screws securing sensor.
4 Remove sensor from blower motor assembly.

Refitting

Reverse operations 1 to 4.

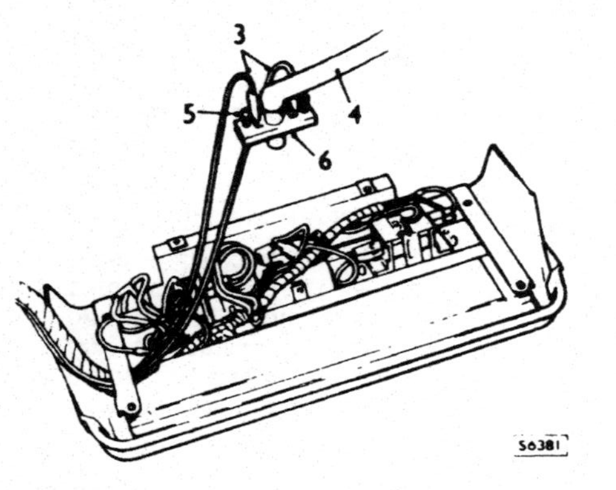

IN-CAR TEMPERATURE SENSOR

Remove and refit – early cars (sensor in console) **82.20.03**

Removing

1 Disconnect battery – 86.15.20.
2 Remove centre tray – 76.67.03.
3 Disconnect cables from sensor.
4 Remove air tube.
5 Withdraw two screws securing sensor.
6 Remove sensor from centre tray.

Refitting

Reverse operations 1 to 6.

IN-CAR TEMPERATURE SENSOR

Remove and refit – later cars (sensor at crash roll) **82.20.03**

Removing

1 Remove fascia crash roll, see 76.46.04.
2 Separate Lucars at sensor.
3 Detach elbow from sensor.
4 Withdraw sensor and aspirator tube.

Refitting

Reverse operations 1 to 4, ensuring that tubes and elbow are correctly fitted and seals are intact around crash roll and screen vents, to prevent access of hot air to sensor.

BLOWER MOTOR POWER RELAY

Remove and refit **82.20.06**

Removing

1 Disconnect battery – 86.15.20.
2 Remove left hand cheek and air vent assembly from centre console.
3 Remove relay by exerting straight pull downwards to disconnect from mounting block.

Refitting

Reverse operations 1 to 3.

TEMPERATURE SELECTOR

Remove and refit **82.20.10**

Removing

1 Disconnect battery – 86.15.20.
2 Pull off temperature selector and mode selector operating knobs.
3 Remove radio aperture escutcheon.
4 Remove centre console – 76.25.01

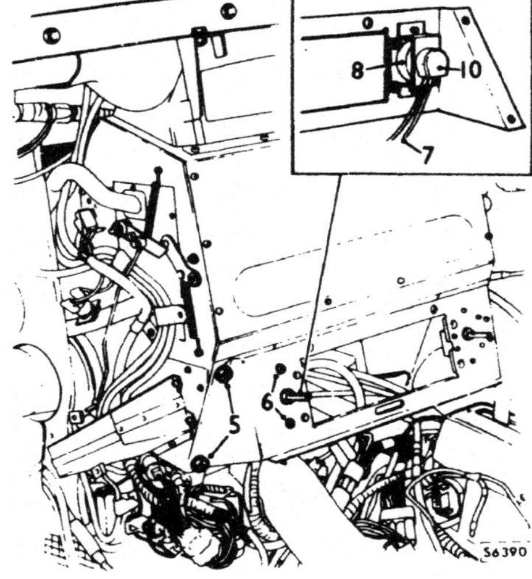

5 Remove four nuts and washers securing selector mounting bracket to heater/cooler unit.
6 Withdraw two Phillips head screws retaining selector and mounting bracket.
7 Disconnect electrical cables at snap connectors.
8 Note position and remove nylon limit stop from operating shank.
9 Remove nut and shakeproof washer from selector.
10 Withdraw selector from mounting.

NOTE: Retain locating washer from between selector and mounting.

Refitting

Reverse operations 1 to 10.

MODE SELECTOR

Remove and refit **82.20.11**

Removing

1 Disconnect battery – 86.15.20.
2 Pull off temperature selector and mode selector operating knobs.
3 Remove radio aperture escutcheon.

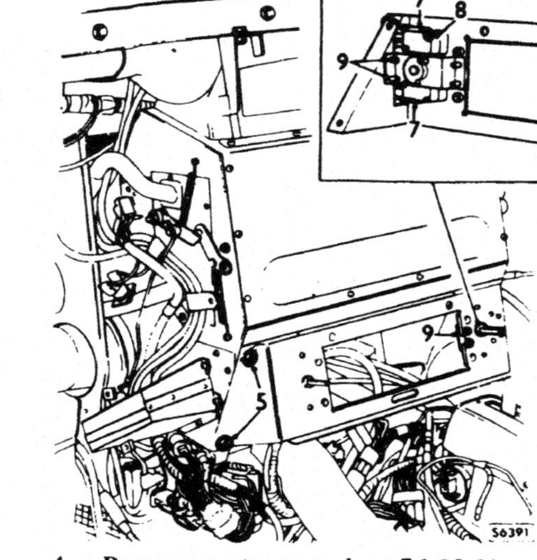

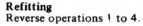

4 Remove centre console – 76.25.01.
5 Remove four nuts and washers securing selector mounting bracket to heater/cooler unit.
6 Note position of vacuum pipes and mark clearly before removing.
7 Note position of cables, disconnect at lucar connectors.
8 Note positions of switches, remove two screws and nuts securing each pair of switches. Retain distance pieces for refit operation.
9 Withdraw four Phillips head screws retaining operating cam mounting bracket.
10 Remove two Phillips head screws from vacuum switch retaining bracket.

NOTE: If replacement items are fitted care must be taken to ensure that only correct replacements are used and that individual items are replaced in correct position.

Refitting

11 Insert new selector unit into mounting bracket. Ensure locating washer is in position.

NOTE: When refitting cams ensure that vacuum switch operating rod is pressed back to allow camshaft into position.

PROCEDURE FOR FLAP LINK ADJUSTMENT 82.20.17

NOTE: When adjustment procedure is in progress the main system tension spring "**Must not be connected**". Only bottom by-pass spring may be connected during adjustment.

1 Ensure top heater flap adjuster, and bottom by-pass adjustable link are free to move.
2 Place link system in FULL COLD position b/ rotating servo-motor clockwise. Appiy slight pressure to main link ensuring bottom heater flap only is sealed. (Check for correct sealing by applying slight anti-clockwise pressure to defrost lever – there should be no resultant movement).

3 When in FULL COLD position apply pressure to top heater flap in clockwise direction ensuring that flap seals. Lock top heater flap adjuster. Check that both heater flaps close together by moving main link.
4 Place link system in "full heat" position by rotating servo motor anti-clockwise. Top heater flap should just make contact with casing. Maintain this position, seal bottom by-pass flap with link, and lock.
5 With main linkage system now adjusted, rotate main link to ensure flaps seal at each end of travel, and check that link system moves freely.
6 Attach main system tension spring to linkage, check that bottom by-pass flap seals correctly.

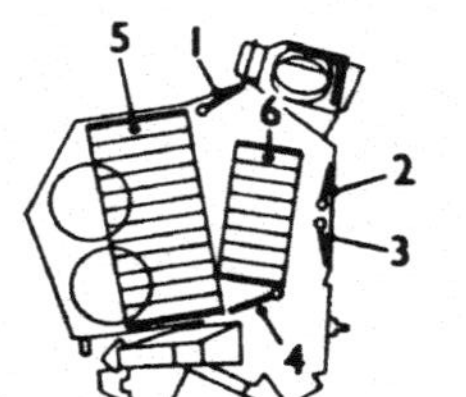

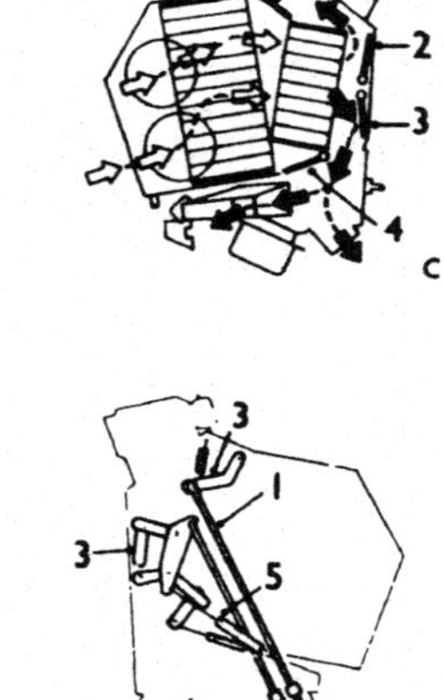

KEY TO DIAGRAMS

A. **FLAP LOCATION**
1 Top By-Pass Flap.
2 Top Heater Flap.
3 Bottom Heater Flap.
4 Bottom By-Pass Flap.
5 Evaporator Matrix.
6 Heater Matrix.

B. **FULL COLD CONDITION**
1 Flap Open (Cool Air).
2
3 Flaps Closed (No Hot Air).
4 Flap Open (Cool Air).

C. **FULL HEAT CONDITION**
1 Flap Closed (No Cool Air).
2
3 Flaps Open (Heated Air).
4 Flap Closed (No Cool Air).

D. **FLAP OPERATING RODS**
1 Adjusting Rods.
2 Adjusters (On Servo Unit).
3 Operating Linkage For Flaps.
4 Main Tension Spring.

THERMOSTAT

Remove and refit 82.20.18

Removing
1 Disconnect battery – 86.15.20.
2 Remove right hand console side casing – 76.25.02.
3 Remove right hand dash liner – 76.46.11.
4 Withdraw two screws securing thermostat to support bracket on heater/cooler unit.
5 Disconnect cables at lucars after noting positions.
6 Carefully remove thermostat by pulling capillary tube from heater/cooler unit.

Refitting
Reverse operations 1 to 6.

NOTE: If a replacement is fitted, ensure capillary is formed to exact dimensions of unserviceable item. When refitting capillary probe section ensure that it makes contact with evaporator matrix.

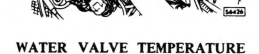

THERMOSTAT

Adjust 82.20.19

NOTE: Adjustment of the thermostat may be necessary if air flow through the evaporator is reduced by the formation of ice on the evaporator fins. Raising the thermostat operating temperature will prevent ice formation.

1 Remove R.H. side casing from central console, to gain access to thermostat.
2 Carefully remove nickel plated spring-on cover at bottom of thermostat.
3 Turn adjusting screw to vary operating temperatures of thermostat; clockwise rotation of the screw raises the operating temperatures, one full turn of the screw causing a temperature change of approximately 3°C (5½°F).
4 Reverse operations 1 and 2.

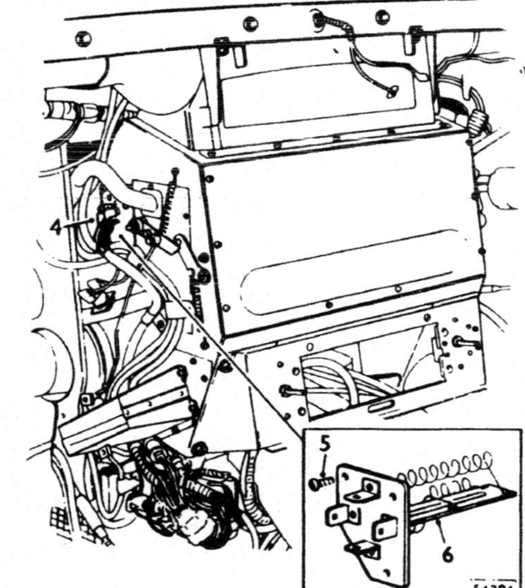

BLOWER MOTOR RESISTANCE UNIT

Remove and refit – Left-hand drive cars 82.20.26

Removing
1 Disconnect battery, see 86.15.20.
2 Remove driver's side underscuttle casing, see 76.46.11.
3 Remove driver's side centre console cheek and air vent, see 76.25.02.
4 Note position of cables at resistance unit and disconnect Lucars.
5 Withdraw three crosshead screws.
6 Withdraw unit from heater/cooler unit case.

Refitting
Reverse operations 1 to 6.

BLOWER MOTOR RESISTANCE UNIT

Remove and refit – Right-hand drive cars 82.20.26

Removing
1 Disconnect battery – 86.15.20.
2 Remove glove compartment liner – 76.52.03.
3 Note position of cables at resistance unit and disconnect Lucars.
4 Withdraw three crosshead screws.
5 Withdraw resistance unit from heater/cooler unit case.

Refitting
Reverse operations 1 to 5.

BLOWER MOTOR RELAY BOX

Remove and refit 82.20.27

Removing
1 Disconnect battery – 86.15.20.
2 Remove left hand centre console cheek and air vent – 76.25.02.
3 Withdraw four screws and remove footwell air outlet duct.
4 Note positions of cables at lucar connectors on relay box.
5 Disconnect cables at lucar connectors.
6 Remove securing nuts and washers and recover relay unit.

Refitting
Reverse operations 1 to 5.

NOTE: Ensure earth strap tag is replaced under relay box securing nut.

WATER VALVE TEMPERATURE SWITCH

Remove and refit 82.20.29

Removing
1 Disconnect battery – 86.15.20.
2 Remove left side dash liner – 76.46.11.
3 Remove glove box liner – 76.25.03 (R.H. Drive cars).
4 Disconnect cables at Lucars on switch.
5 Withdraw two securing screws and remove switch.

Refitting
Reverse operations 1 to 4.

WATER VALVE

Remove and refit **82.20.33**

Removing

1 Drain coolant – 26.10.01
2 Disconnect heater hoses at water valve.
3 Withdraw securing screw and remove water valve from mounting bracket.

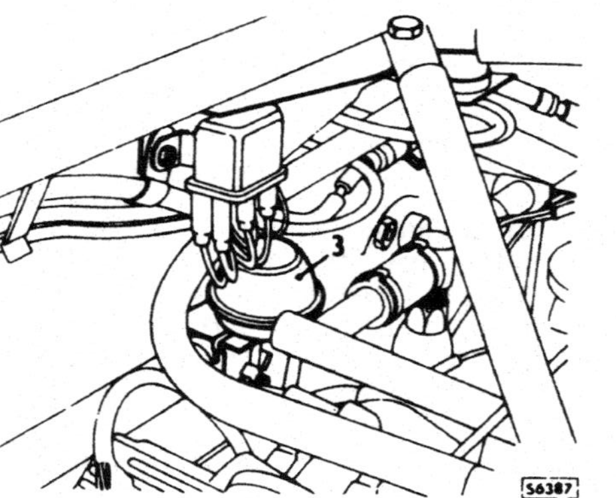

Refitting

Reverse operations 1 to 3,

EXPANSION VALVE

Remove and refit **82.25.01**

Removing

1 Lift bonnet.
2 Evacuate air conditioning system – 82.30.05.
3 Release clip securing thermal bulb to outlet pipe.
4 Disconnect hose unions and seal with clean blanking caps.
5 Remove valve by unscrewing union nut.

NOTE: To avoid straining joint or pipe ensure that valve is held firmly whilst union nut is unscrewed.

6 Retrieve gauze filter from valve and replace with new item.

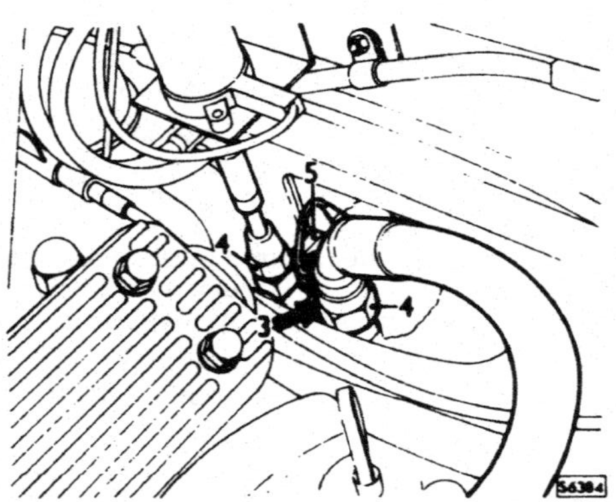

Refitting

7 Reverse operations 1 to 6.
8 Charge system – 82.30.08.

BLOWER ASSEMBLY

Remove and refit – Right-hand unit **82.25.13**

The blower fans are heavy duty motors with metal impellors attached. Speed variation is controlled by resistance units wired in series. The right hand unit has the ambient temperature sensor mounted in the inlet duct. Air flow control flaps are operated by a vacuum actuator mounted on the side of the inlet duct.

Removing

1 Disconnect battery – 86.15.20.
2 Remove right hand under dash liner – 76.46.11.

R.H. Drive

3 Remove glove box liner – 76.52.03.

L.H. Drive

4 Remove four nuts retaining fuse block mounting panel to assembly case. Lay fuse block to one side.

All cars

5 Insert suitable wedge into bottom air flap to retain top air flap closed.
6 Disconnect Lucars from ambient temperature sensor.
7 Pull pliable air duct from stub pipes at side of heater/cooler unit.
8 Remove front body side trim pads.
9 Withdraw two screws securing fresh air pull mounting bracket.
10 Remove two nuts retaining assembly, from mounting posts.
11 Disconnect vacuum tube from actuator.
12 Disconnect electrical harness at snap connectors.
13 Ease fan motor unit from car.

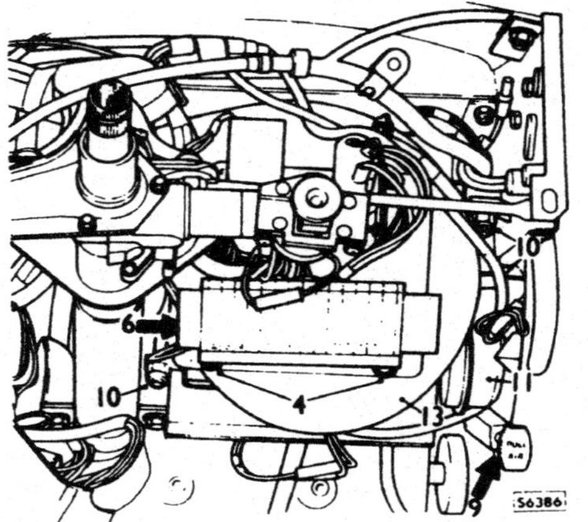

Refitting

Reverse operations 1 to 13.

NOTE: To refit assemblies successfully it is necessary to apply vacuum to the actuator, closing the top air flap. This simplifies insertion of the top flap and flange into its aperture and seal. An alternative method is to insert a suitable wedge into bottom air flap.

BLOWER ASSEMBLY

Remove and refit – Left-hand unit **82.25.14**

Removing

1 Disconnect battery, see 86.15.20.
2 Remove left-hand dash liner, see 76.46.11.

R.H. Drive

3 Remove glove box liner – 76.52.03.

L.H. Drive

4 Remove four nuts retaining fuse block mounting panel to assembly case. Lay fuse block to one side.

All cars

5 Insert suitable wedge into bottom air flap to retain top air flap closed.
6 Pull pliable air ducts from stub pipes at side of heater/cooler unit.
7 Remove front body side trim pad.
8 Withdraw two screws securing fresh air pull mounting bracket.
9 Remove two nuts retaining assembly from mounting posts.
10 Disconnect vacuum pipes from actuator.
11 Disconnect electrical harness at snap connectors.
12 Ease fan motor unit from car.

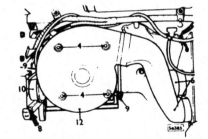

Refitting

Reverse operations 1 to 12.

NOTE: To refit assemblies successfully it is necessary to apply vacuum to the actuator, closing the top air flap. This simplifies insertion of the top flap and flange into its aperture and seal. An alternative method is to insert a suitable wedge into bottom air flap.

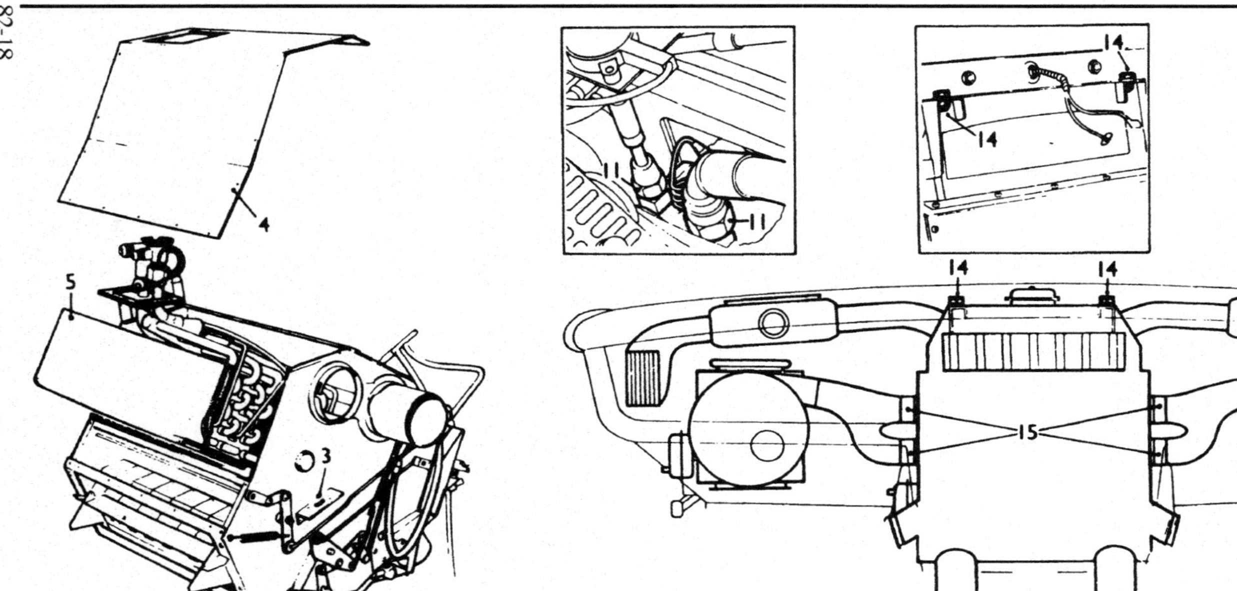

EVAPORATOR UNIT

Remove and refit **82.25.20**

Removing

1 Disconnect battery – 86.15.20
2 Remove heater/cooler unit – 82.25.21.
3 Remove thermostat unit by disconnecting electrical harness at Lucar connectors, removing two retaining screws and pulling capillary from matrix.
4 Remove back plate, retained by twelve self tapping screws and two setscrews.

NOTE: Care must be taken not to deform or crack the capillary attached to the expansion valve.

5 Carefully pull evaporator unit from heater/cooler case.

Refitting

Reverse operations 1 to 5.

AIR CONDITIONING HEATER/ COOLER UNIT

Remove and refit **82.25.21**

Removing

Water condensate is discharged from the evaporator assembly through drain pipes. This condensate drains from the evaporator case soon after the car stops and the blowers switched off, creating a pool under the car. This is a natural condition and needs no investigation.

1 Disconnect battery, see 86.15.20.
2 Depressurise air conditioning system, see 82.30.05.
3 Drain cooling system, see 26.10.01.
4 Remove crash roll, see 76.46.04.
5 Remove driver's side dash liner, see 76.46.11.
6 Remove passenger's side dash liner, see 76.46.11.
7 Remove glove compartment liner, see 76.52.03.
8 Remove centre parcel shelf, see 76.67.03.
9 Remove centre console, see 76.25.01.
10 Remove fascia, see 76.46.01.
11 Disconnect air conditioning hoses at bulkhead connectors to expansion valve fitment in engine compartment.
12 Disconnect coolant hoses at heater matrix bulkhead connectors in engine compartment.

NOTE: Retain metal washer and sponge collar.

13 Remove two large retaining nuts from centre of bulkhead in engine compartment.
14 Remove two retaining nuts from centre of top rail.
15 Remove four bayonet connected stub pipes from sides of unit.
16 Locate four vacuum connectors and clearly mark all tubes before disconnecting.
17 Disconnect electrical multi-pin connectors either side of unit. Note positions for refitting purposes.
18 Ease unit forward and lift from car.

Refitting

19 Offer unit up to mounting position and ease valves, capillary tube and heater connectors through bulkhead apertures.

NOTE: Ensure sponge backing is in position.

20 Loosely fit retaining nuts, ensuring that pipes, speedometer cables, and electrical harness are not trapped before tightening.
21 Reconnect vacuum pipes as marked in operation 16.
22 Reconnect electrical multi-pin plugs and sockets as noted in operation 17.
23 Refit bayonet connected stub pipes to unit. Connect, turn clockwise until are locked.
24 Ensure drain tubes from unit are located through grommets in side of transmission tunnel.
25 Refit fascia.
26 Ensure pliable ducting is correctly located on fascia and crash roll air vents.
27 Refit centre console.
28 Refit centre parcel shelf.
29 Refit scuttle casings.
30 Refit crash roll.
31 Reconnect water and air conditioning hoses in engine compartment.

NOTE: Ensure sponge collars and metal washers are in place before connecting heater pipes.

32 Fill cooling system – 32.30.08.
33 Charge air conditioning system – 32.30.08.
34 Reconnect battery.

Leak Test

While unit is removed from car.

1 Seal outlet union with suitable cap nut and sealing disc.
2 Connect small capacity refrigerant container to inlet union with suitable length of hose.
3 Open container valve and allow a quantity of refrigerant into evaporator.
4 Pass leak detector along all accessible joints and tubes.
5 **A defective unit must be replaced with a new unit. Defective unit must be returned to manufacturer.**

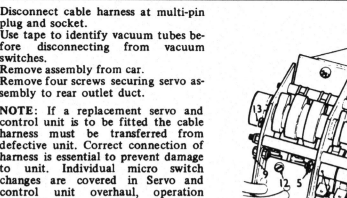

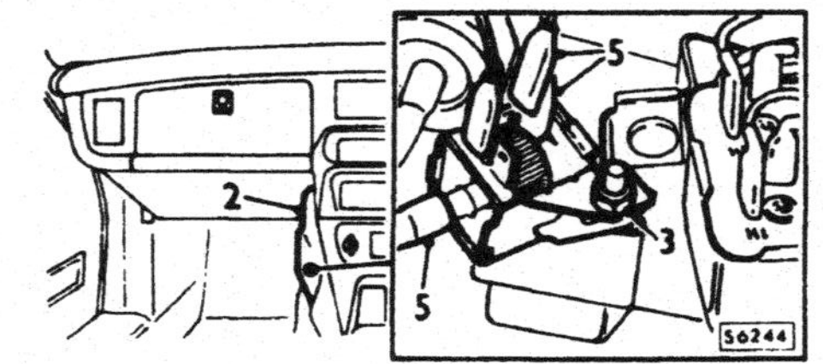

VACUUM SOLENOID

Remove and refit 82.25.23

Removing
1 Disconnect battery – 86.15.20.
2 Remove left hand console cheek and air vent.
3 Remove retaining nut from vacuum solenoid mounting bracket.
4 Note positions of cables and vacuum tubes, mark clearly to assist in refitting operation.
5 Remove vacuum tubes and cables.

Refitting
Reverse operations 1 to 5.

SERVO AND CONTROL UNIT

Remove and refit 82.25.24

Removing
1 Disconnect battery – 86.15.20.
2 Remove centre console.
3 Lay centre oddments tray and switch panel to one side, do not disconnect cables.
4 Remove air conditioning controls mounting bracket from front of heater/cooler unit, secured by four nuts and washers. Lay bracket to one side, do not disconnect cables or vacuum tubing.
5 Remove footwell air inlet duct by withdrawing four screws.
6 Withdraw three screws, one at front of heater/cooler unit and two at side, securing rear outlet duct and servo mounting corner section of heater/cooler unit.
7 Disconnect two flap operating rods from cam followers. Mark rods to facilitate correct refitting.
8 Disconnect cable harness at multi-pin plug and socket.
9 Use tape to identify vacuum tubes before disconnecting from vacuum switches.
10 Remove assembly from car.
11 Remove four screws securing servo assembly to rear outlet duct.

NOTE: If a replacement servo and control unit is to be fitted the cable harness must be transferred from defective unit. Correct connection of harness is essential to prevent damage to unit. Individual micro switch changes are covered in Servo and control unit overhaul, operation 82.25.25.

Refitting
Reverse operations 1 to 11.

NOTE: Ensure all pipeline and cable runs are refitted in original positions and that pipelines are not kinked or trapped.

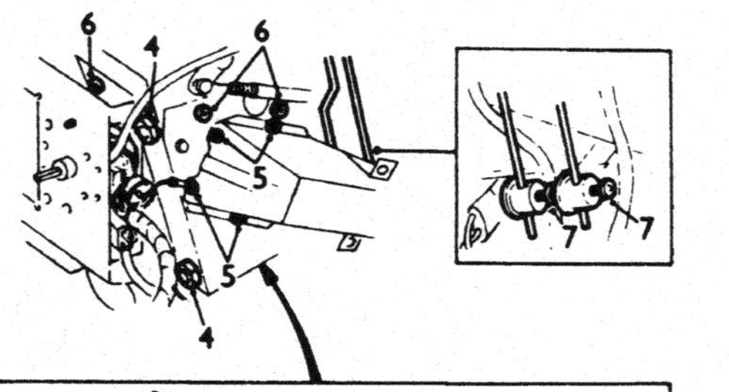

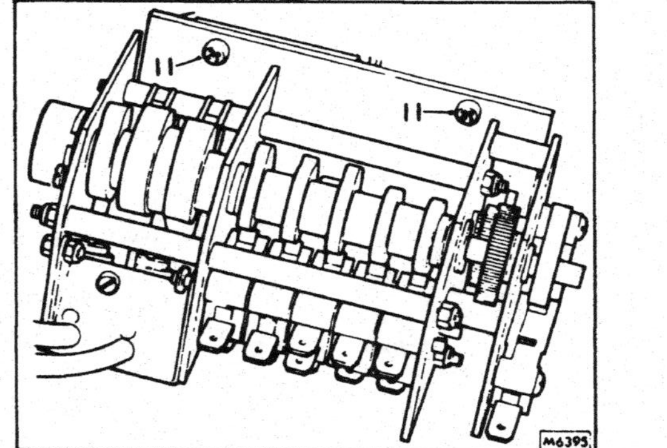

SERVO AND CONTROL UNIT ASSEMBLY

Overhaul 82.25.25

CAUTION: No attempt must be made to dismantle servo motor from gearbox. 12 volts must never be applied direct to motor connections. The motor will overrun limit switches and could strip gear assembly. Do not attempt to dismantle cam shaft assembly.

1 Disconnect battery – 86.15.20.
2 Remove servo motor and control unit – 82.25.24.

Dismantling

Recirculation and Ranco override micro switches;

3 Remove two securing screws and take switch from end plate.

Other micro switches

4 Remove recirculation micro switch – operation 3.
5 Ease friction washers from ends of micro switch locating rods.
6 Push rods through micro switch pack and remove.
7 Ease micro switch pack from assembly.

Vacuum switches

8 Carry out operations 4 and 5.
9 Remove two screws and nuts retaining vacuum switch mounting bracket.
10 Pull bracket from assembly.
11 Remove nut and screw clamping switch mounting plates together.
12 Remove plates to free switches.

Feed back potentiometer

13 Withdraw two screws. Note position of cables if fitting a replacement component. Cables are soldered to contacts.

NOTE: Ensure replacement potentiometer is fitted exactly as item replaced.

Re-assembling
14 Re-assembling is the reverse of dismantling in all cases.

NOTE: When refitting micro switches ensure that adhesive sponge backed tape is replaced between all switches.

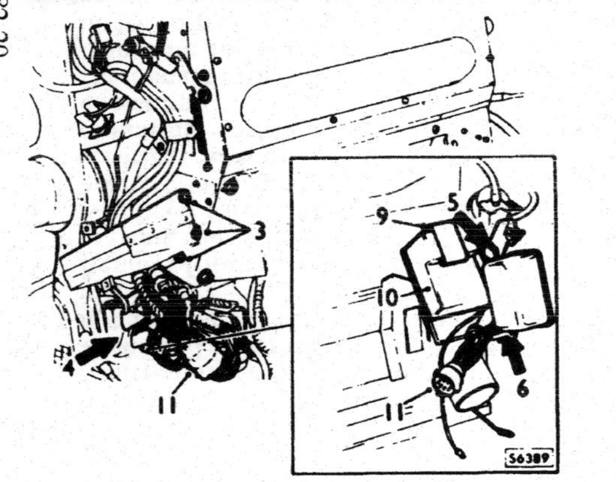

AMPLIFIER UNIT

Remove and refit 82.25.29

Removing
1 Disconnect battery – 86.15.20.
2 Remove left hand console cheek and air vent.
3 Withdraw four retaining screws from air outlet duct and remove duct.
4 Disconnect cables from relay box, note cable positions to assist in refitting operation.
5 Remove nut retaining vacuum solenoid and relay box.
6 Slacken other nut retaining relay box.
7 Swing relay box clear of access to amplifier unit.
8 Remove radio/air conditioning control switch escutcheon.
9 Release amplifier retaining clip with flat bladed screwdriver.
10 Manipulate amplifier from beneath heater/cooler unit.
11 Disconnect amplifier cable harness at multi-pin plug/socket and earth connector.

Refitting
Reverse operations 1 to 11.

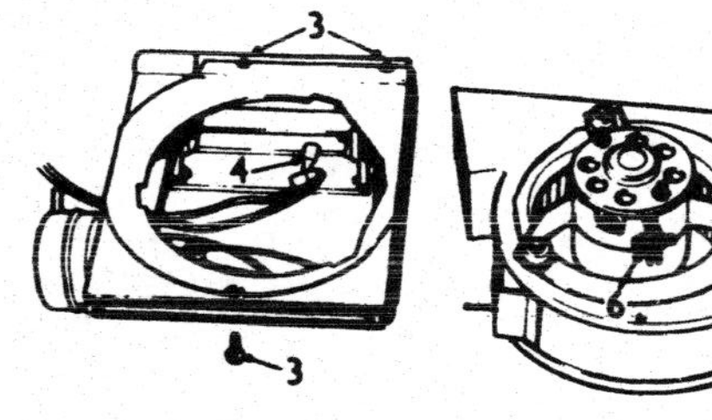

BLOWER ASSEMBLY

Overhaul 82.25.30

1 Disconnect battery – 86.15.20.
2 Remove blower assembly. Right hand 82.25.13. Left hand – 82.25.14.

Dismantling
3 Withdraw three self tapping screws from air inlet casing.
4 Part air inlet casing and motor assembly and disconnect electrical connections at Lucars.

NOTE: It is recommended at this stage that positions of various components are marked either with paint or scriber. One cable Lucar has a raised projection which matches the aperture in motor casing. This assists in ensuring connections are replaced correctly and direction of rotation of motor is not altered.

5 Unscrew three bolts securing fan motor mounting bracket to outlet duct.
6 Release nut and bolt securing motor mounting clip and remove motor fan bracket.
7 Using appropriate Allen key remove impellor fan motor shaft, note position on shaft for reassembling.

NOTE: Blowers are handed for rotation and impeller operation, ensure correct motor and impeller are fitted if replacement is necessary.

Re-assembling
Reverse operations 1 to 7.

NOTE: Ensure that impeller does not foul outlet duct, and that motor mounting clip does not obscure Lucar connector spades.

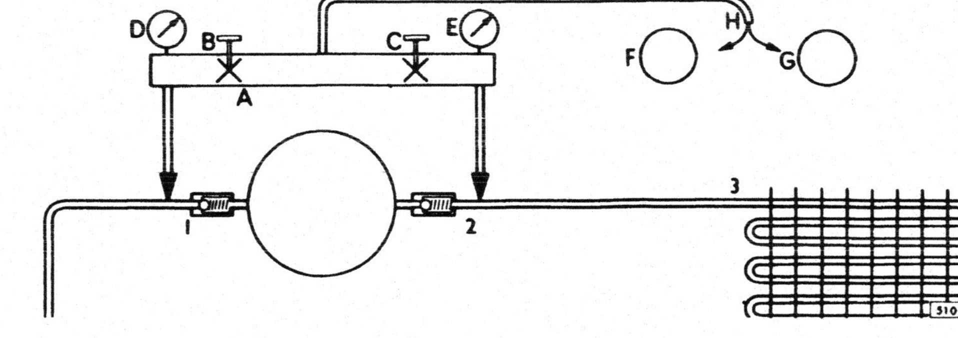

CHARGING AND TESTING EQUIPMENT

Fit and remove 82.30.01

The charging and testing equipment consists of a charging manifold A fitted with two stop valves B and C and two pressure gauges D and E, a vacuum pump F, and a supply of refrigerant gas, G.

One gauge is a compound type, reading both vacuum and positive pressure, and is connected to the suction side of the union housing; the other is a high pressure gauge and is connected to the delivery side.

WARNING: FOR SAFETY REASONS, THE ACCURACY OF BOTH GAUGES MUST BE CHECKED AT FREQUENT INTERVALS.

The stop valves enable either suction or delivery hoses, or both, to be connected to the centre port of the manifold. The centre hose H can be connected either to a vacuum pump or to a supply of refrigerant. Two hose connectors must be fitted with depressers to operate the Schrader valves. The equipment should be fitted with a means of accurately weighing the refrigerant container during the charging process.

Fitting
1 To fit the charging manifold to the air conditioning system, remove the protective sealing caps from the Schrader valves on compressor.
2 Ensure both manifold stop valves are fully closed (screwed in).
3 Quickly fit hose connectors to correct Schrader valves. The gauges will display system pressures on suction and delivery sides.

Removing
4 To remove the equipment from the vehicle, **quickly** unscrew each connector in turn. This ensures that the Schrader valves are held open for the shortest possible time.
Refit the valve sealing caps.

AIR CONDITIONING SYSTEM

Depressurise **82.30.05**

Depressurising the system means that the system is vented until the refrigerant remaining is at atmospheric pressure. The system is then resealed to prevent air contaminating the components.

The procedure **MUST** be carried out before any connection is released.

It is very important that the method used is **EXACTLY** as described. Too rapid venting entrains the compressor lubricating oil and necessitates refilling to the correct level.

WARNING: NO SMOKING. POINT THE VENT HOSE IN A SAFE DIRECTION.

1 Remove protective cap from the discharge Schrader valve.
2 Using a piece of hose approximately 36 in. (910 mm) long, fitted with a suitable connector, vent the system by **SLOWLY** screwing the hose connector on to the discharge Schrader valve.
3 If oil is seen escaping or if the vented gas becomes dense and white, **IMMEDIATELY** slow the flow rate by unscrewing the hose.
4 As the flow rate falls, the hose connector can be screwed further on to the union.
5 When no further gas escapes, and the hose connector is fully home, **IMMEDIATELY** unscrew it as quickly as possible.
6 Refit protective sealing cap.

AIR CONDITIONING SYSTEM

Evacuate **82.30.06**

The system is evacuated by removing all residual gas or air after depressurisation and/or repair using a vacuum pump. Evacuation must be carried out before charging, as the ability of the system to hold a high vacuum is a measure of its tightness: the vacuum also assists in drawing in the charge of refrigerant. The evacuation process serves to boil off any moisture in the system if ambient temperature is high enough. In conditions of low ambient temperature the purging method of system cleansing must be used before charging.

Any sign of a rapid fall in vacuum indicates a serious leak. This must be found and rectified **IMMEDIATELY**, as air is being drawn in through the leak.

Follow the procedure given under leak test before proceeding. The procedure given here refers to the evacuation of an old system. The method for a new system is similar, but **no** decrease in vacuum is permitted.

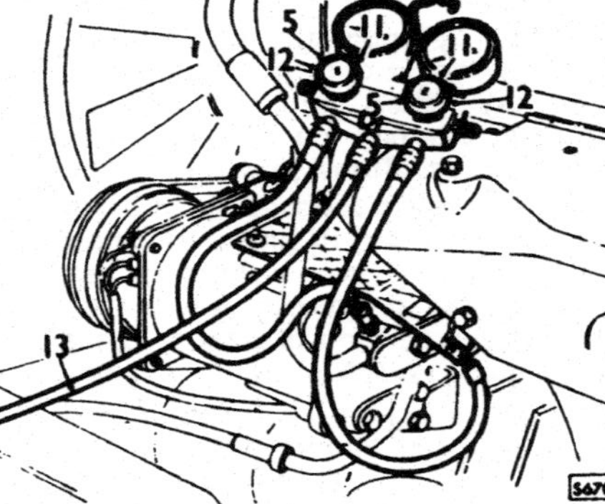

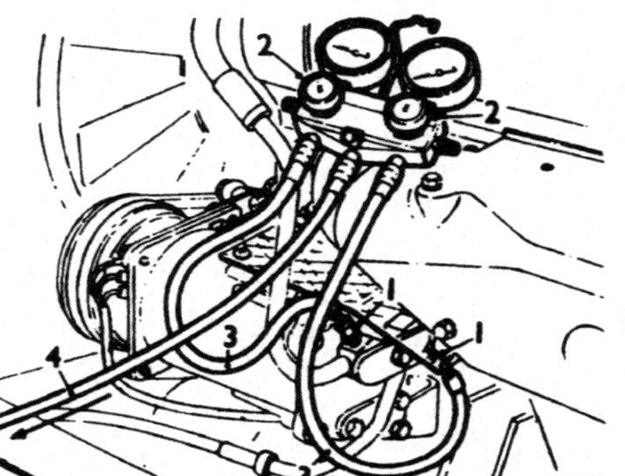

1 Remove both protective caps from the Schrader valves.
2 Ensure both manifold stop valves are fully closed (screwed in).
3 **Quickly** fit hose connectors to correct Schrader valves.
4 Fit centre hose of charging manifold to vacuum pump connection.
5 Fully open both valves of charging manifold.
6 Start vacuum pump.
7 Wait until a vacuum of 28 in. Hg. (50.8 Torr) has been drawn, or when the maximum that can be achieved with the prevailing barometric conditions is obtained.
8 Close both valves on charging manifold.
9 Switch off vacuum pump and wait 20 minutes.
10 A very slight pressure rise may occur due to the slow evaporation of liquid refrigerant or moisture entrained in the compressor oil.
11 If the vacuum holds satisfactorily, switch on vacuum pump, open both charging manifold valves and allow the pump to pull on the system for a further 20 minutes.
12 Fully close both charging manifold valves.
13 Switch off vacuum pump.
14 Disconnect centre hose from vacuum pump connection.

The air conditioning system is now ready for charging.

AIR CONDITIONING SYSTEM

Sweep (Purge) 82.30.07

The sweeping, or purging, operation given below may be used in addition to, and following, evacuation as a method of removing the last traces of moisture if ambient temperature is low.

The operation must be carried out if the system has inadvertently been left open for longer than a few minutes on a humid day. The operation must also be carried out if moisture is suspected in the system following the diagnosis of a fault.

The receiver/drier **MUST** be replaced immediately after the purging operation and before the final evacuation operation commences.

1 Evacuate system – 82.30.06.
2 Disconnect vacuum connection from pump and connect to refrigerant supply.
3 Open refrigerant supply valve.
4 To purge length of hose, slightly crack centre connector at charging manifold; retighten connection.
5 Slowly open the suction side valve on charging manifold and allow ½ lb. to 1 lb. (0,23 kg. to 0,45 kg.) of gas to enter system.
6 Close suction side valve on charging manifold.
7 Close refrigerant valve.
8 Leave for 10 minutes.
9 Disconnect hose from refrigerant supply.
10 Open both valves on charging manifold to allow refrigerant to escape slowly from system. **IMMEDIATELY** flow stops, reconnect hose to refrigerant supply.
11 Close suction side valve of charging manifold.
12 Loosen hose connection at suction side of charging manifold.
13 Open refrigerant supply valve slowly and allow gas to pass through entire system and escape at charging manifold for about 5 seconds.

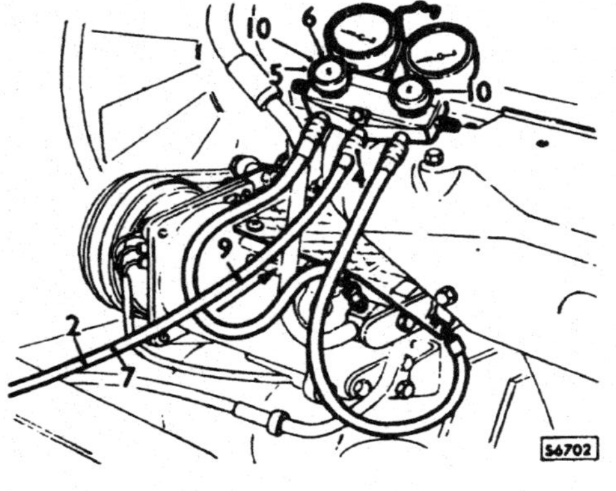

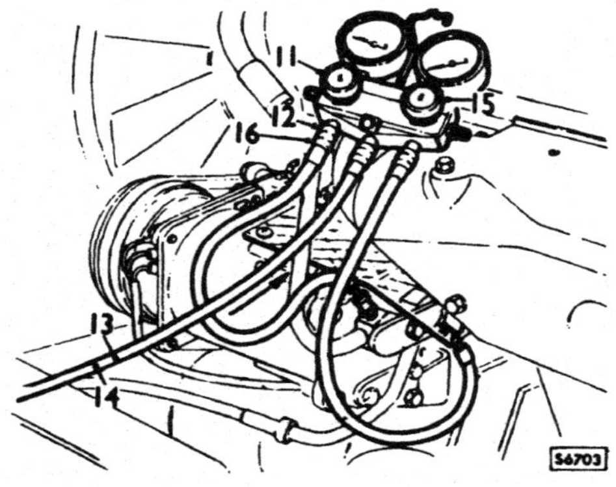

14 Close refrigerant supply valve.
15 Close valve at pressure side of charging manifold.
16 Tighten suction side hose connection while gas still flows.
17 If system is being purged to remove excess moisture, change receiver/drier before proceeding to evacuation and charging. If system is being purged owing to low ambient temperature, evacuate and charge immediately.

AIR CONDITIONING SYSTEM

Charge 82.30.08

Charging the air conditioning system is the process of adding a specific quantity of refrigerant to the circuit. Before attempting the charging operation the system **MUST** have been evacuated and, if necessary, swept (purged) immediately beforehand. No delay between evacuation and charging procedures is permissible. Great care must be taken to charge correctly, as under charging will result in very inefficient operation, and over charging will result in very high pressures and possible damage to components.

1 Evacuate the system – 82.30.06.
2 Connect centre hose of charging manifold to supply of refrigerant. The supply available must be at least 7.2 lb. (3,3 kg.) weight.
3 Open refrigerant supply valve.
4 Purge centre hose by momentarily cracking connection at manifold block; retighten connector.
5 Record weight of refrigerant supply source.
6 Open both valves on charging manifold and allow refrigerant source pressure to fill vacuum in system.
7 Between ½ lb. to 1 lb. (0,23 kg. and 0,45 kg.) weight will enter the system. Record quantity.

NOTE: The quantity drawn in will vary with ambient temperature.

8 Close pressure side valve on manifold block.
9 Ensure all clear and start vehicle engine. Run engine at 1500 r.p.m.
10 Set air conditioning system blower speed control to '**FAST**'.

NOTE: This engages compressor clutch to start system circulation, and runs blower motors at fast speed to heat evaporator coil. Vapour will be turned to liquid in the condenser and stored in the receiver drier.

11 Control flow of refrigerant with suction side valve on charging manifold, and allow a total weight (including operation 7) of 3½ lb ± 2ozs. (1,58 kg. ± 0,028 kg.) refrigerant to enter system.
12 Close suction side valve.

NOTE: Alternatively, observe sight glass on receiver/drier until sight glass clears, and no bubbles or foam are visible.

Re-open suction valve for 2 to 5 minutes (2 mins. if ambient temperature low, 5 minutes if high).
This will allow an additional ¼ lb. (0,11 kg.) of refrigerant to enter the system.

13 Run system for 5 minutes, observing sight glass.
14 If foaming very slight, switch off engine.

NOTE: It is normal for there to be slight foaming if ambient air temperature is 70°F (21°C) or below.

15 Close refrigerant supply valve; disconnect hose.
16 Quickly disconnect hoses from Schrader valves on union block.
17 Fit protective sealing caps.
18 Switch on engine and check function of air conditioning system.
19 Switch off engine; flush engine compartment and interior of vehicle with shop compressed air line.
20 Conduct a leak test on installation.

AIR CONDITIONING SYSTEM

Leak test **82.30.09**

The system shall show no leaks when tested by a detector with high sensitivity ideally of 1 lb. (0,45 kg.) in 32 years. Exceptions are the receiver/drier sight glass and uncapped Schrader valves, which must show no leakage when tested by a detector with sensitivity of 1 lb. (0,45 kg.) in 15 years.

Do not smoke while conducting the leak tests.

For safety reasons the discharge pressure gauge on the charging manifold must be checked at frequent intervals.

The testing area must be well ventilated, but free from draughts.

The system must be operated at high pressure before leak testing. As compressor discharge pressures are variable with ambient temperature the following procedure must be used.

Pressurising

1 Remove Schrader valve protective sealing cap from discharge connector at compressor.
2 Ensure both valves are charging manifold closed.
3 **Quickly** screw pressure hose from charging manifold block on to union.
4 If necessary blank off condenser.
5 Set heater control to full hot, fast fan.
6 Set air conditioning controls to full cold.
7 Start engine and allow discharge pressure to reach 225 lb/sq.in. (15,76 bars).
Under no circumstances allow the pressure to rise above 250 lb/sq.in. (17,58 bars).

CAUTION: Do not allow engine to overheat

8 When pressure reaches 225 lb/sq.in. (15,76 bars) turn off engine.
9 Continue with Testing.

Testing

1 All joints and fittings shall be free of excess oil to eliminate the possibility of false readings caused by refrigerant absorption in the oil. For this reason any joint tightened to eliminate leakage should be cleared with compressed air to remove refrigerant vapour.
2 Since refrigerant vapour is heavier than air, the detector probe must be moved in the area below the joint tested.
3 The detector probe must be held for at least 3 seconds closer than .250 in. (6,4 mm.) to the joint tested.
4 The detector should be cleared with uncontaminated air before each usage.
5 False readings may occur if the detectors are used in atmospheres where solvents or volatile compounds containing halides (Fluorine, Bromine, Chlorine or Iodine) are present e.g. Trichlorethylene.

Cigarette smoke and exhaust fumes may also cause false readings.

6 If the exact location of a leak is in doubt, liquid soap solution should be brushed on to the area and the position of the bubble observed.
7 The detector probe should be held at the air conditioning outlets with the system off and the fans turned on and off quickly to flow a small quantity of air. The procedure will find any leaks in the evaporator coil. The car body must be cleared of refrigerant before the test.

AIR CONDITIONING – TEST OPERATION 82.30.11

NOTE: During the following tests windows should be closed and footwell fresh air vents shut 'off'.

Warm up and check operation of Thermostatic cut out and low speed override. R.H. control to 'auto'.

With the engine cold turn the L.H. knob to full heat. Start the engine and run at 1000 r.p.m. If after any previous running the camshaft has turned to the cold position the servo will operate for a few seconds and then shut down. As the water temperature reaches 40°C the system will start up, the centre outlet will close if not already closed, and the fans will slip up to speed 2. This can be checked by turning the R.H. knob to low when a drop in speed should be noticed.

Sequence of operation check. R.H. control to 'auto'

With the engine warm turn the L.H. knob to 65°. Operate the cigar lighter or other heat source and hold the heated unit about 1" below the sensor inlet hole, which is situated below the centre parcel shelf. The unit should then go through the following sequence in approximately 20 seconds.

1 Blower speeds will drop to low.
2 Temperatures will decrease, the upper temperature dropping more quickly than the footwell temperature.
3 After approximately 10 seconds the centre outlet flap will open.
4 Approximately 1 second after this the fan speeds will shift up to a medium 1.
5 A further 1 second later the fan speed will shift up to medium 2.
6 Another 1 second later the fan speeds will shift to maximum, at the same time the fresh air vents will close and the recirculating flaps will open. The rush of air into the air boxes will be felt along the bottom edge of the lower trim panels. Turn the R.H. knob to 'LO' which should cause the fan speeds to drop. Return R.H. knob to auto setting.

On some cars in which the servo action is fairly fast the separation of the fan speeds may not be discernable.

Aspiration and intermediate position check

Remove the heat source from the sensor. Within ten minutes, depending upon ambient conditions, the unit should shift off recirculation and the blowers will drop to one of the intermediate speeds. This test can be carried out on the road since thermistor aspiration will be better and hence the test will be performed more quickly. In certain high ambient conditions the system will be reluctant to come off recirculation, in which case the intermediate modes can be checked by inching the servo through these positions. This is done by turning the L.H. knob slightly clockwise until the servo motor is heard to operate, and then returning it to a lower position to stop the servo motor at the desired position.

Defrost and Fan vibration check

Turn the R.H. knob to defrost. The centre outlet flap should close and the screen outlets open. Air to the footwells should be cut off leaving air to the upper ducts only. The fans should shift to maximum speed and hot air should issue from the upper ducts. Fan vibration is best assessed under these conditions. Tests in accordance with the defrost schedule can be carried out at this point if desired.

Outlet Vent valve check

Check that air can be cut off from the outer face level vents by rotating the wheels beneath the outlets.

Settled mid range and HI speed override check

Set the R.H. knob to auto. Set the L.H. knob to 75° and wait for the unit to settle. The fans should now be on low speed. Turn the R.H. knob to HI. Maximum fan speeds should now be engaged.

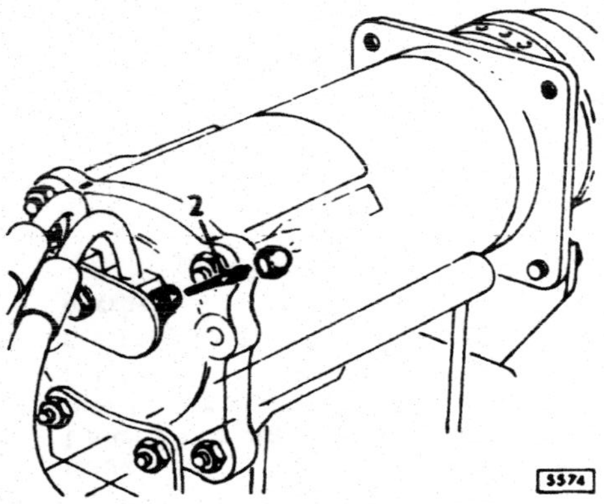

CHARGING VALVE CORE

Remove and refit 82.30.12

A possible reason for very slow charging is a bent or damaged Schrader valve depressor. Do not attempt to straighten. The valve core must be replaced.

If excessive leakage is detected from the Schrader valve cores at the rear of the compressor, use a soap solution to ensure that the valve core itself is at fault. If the valve core is leaking replace it by following this procedure. Ensure replacement clean dry valve core is to hand before commencing operation.

Removing

1. Depressurise the system – 82.20.05.
2. Remove valve core using a Schrader removing tool.

Refitting

3. Insert new valve into union and ensuring threads not crossed, screw home.

   NOTE: Do not overtighten.

4. Charge the system – 82.30.08.

DEFROST AND DEMIST TESTS

82.30.15

Purpose

To ascertain that the heating/air conditioning system is functioning correctly in the 'Defrost' mode, and that adequate airflow is maintained in the heat mode to ensure that the windscreen remains mist-free.

Method

a. Set the Control to '85°'.
b. Set R.H. Control to 'Defrost'.
c. Close end of dash outlets.
d. Start engine and run for 7 minutes at 1500 r.p.m.
e. During the running period measure the airflow from each screen outlet using checking ducts and velometer. Ensure that the centre dash outlet is closed and that it seals satisfactorily. The velocity from the screen outlets should be:–

   1550 f.p.m.

   Also during the running period turn the R.H. control to 'HI' and open end of dash outlets. Using the screen outlet and end of dash checking ducts measure the resulting air velocity. This should be:

   Minimum velocity (f.p.m.)

Screen	End of dash
500	850

At the end of 7 minutes running at 1500 r.p.m. check that the water temperature gauge indicates 'Normal'. Using mercury in glass thermometers check that the following minimum screen outlet temperatures are achieved.

Plenum Inlet		Screen outlet (minimum)	
°C	°F	°C	°F
10	50	54	129.2
12	53.6	55	131
14	57.2	55.5	131.9
16	60.8	56.5	133.7
18	64.4	57	134.6
20	68	58	136.4
22	71.6	58.5	137.3
24	75.2	59.5	139.1

Conclusions

If the above minimum requirements are met then it can be assumed that:–

a. The thermostats are opening correctly.
b. The water valve is opening fully.
c. The flaps and linkages are correctly adjusted for the heating mode.
d. The fans give adequate airflow at maximum speed.

If the above criteria are not met the causes may be related to:–

Thermostats

The water temperature gauge will not achieve 'Normal' position within 7 minutes and the air outlet temperature remains low. The thermostat(s) must be removed and checked for sticking open.

Water Valve

The temperature gauge reads 'Normal' but the air outlet temperature remains low. Check that the vacuum operated water valve is subjected to at least 8½" (21,6cms) Hg of vacuum. If the valve is under adequate vacuum, change the valve. However if the vacuum is low, check that vacuum is being supplied to the whole system, that the water valve vacuum actuator is operational and that the water valve vacuum switch is operational (See that the supply from the switch to valve is not pinched or trapped).

Flaps and Linkages

Inadequate flap sealing will result in low air velocity at the screen outlets. Check that the centre facia flap closes fully on 'Defrost' and that only a small air bleed to the footwells occurs. These leaks can be detected by hand and may be rectified by adjusting the linkage. Excessive airflow from the screen outlets in the heat mode may be caused by the demist control flap sticking open.

Blowers

If following flap inspection the air flow is still low, investigations should be carried out into the blower assemblies. Check that full voltage is being received on maximum speed and that the units are correctly wired for rotation. If all is correct the only remaining procedure is to change the fan assembly.

AIR CONDITIONING EQUIPMENT

Preliminary tests 82.30.16

The following check must be carried out to ensure that the system is basically functional. These checks may also be used to ensure satisfactory operation after any rectification has been done. If the system proves unsatisfactory in any way refer to fault finding.

1 Check blower fans are giving air flow expected in relation to control switch position. Check that air delivered is equal at both outlets.
2 Check that compressor clutch is operating correctly, engaging and releasing immediately control switch is set to an 'ON' position.

NOTE: The engine must be running and the thermostat control set fully cool.

3 Check radiator cooling fan starts operating when compressor clutch engages.

NOTE: The engine must be running for this check.

4 Check that the compressor drive belt is correctly adjusted and is not slipping at higher engine speeds, at idle speed, or on sudden acceleration of the engine, with the compressor clutch engaged.
5 Observe sight glass on receiver/drier and check for frothing or bubbles with engine running at 1000 r.p.m. Slowly increase engine speed and repeat check at 1800 r.p.m.

NOTE: It is normal for there to be slight foaming if ambient air temperature is below 70°F (21°C).

6 Check for frosting on connector union housing, the region around the suction part is normally cold, and slight frosting is permissible.
7 Check by feel along pipe lines for sudden temperature changes that would indicate blockage at that point.
8 Place a thermometer in the air outlet louvres. Run the vehicle on the road and note drop in temperature with air conditioning system switched on or off.
9 Ensure condenser matrix is free of mud, road dirt, leaves or insects that would prevent free air flow. If necessary clear the matrix.
10 If the foregoing checks are not met satisfactorily, refer to rectification and fault finding procedures.

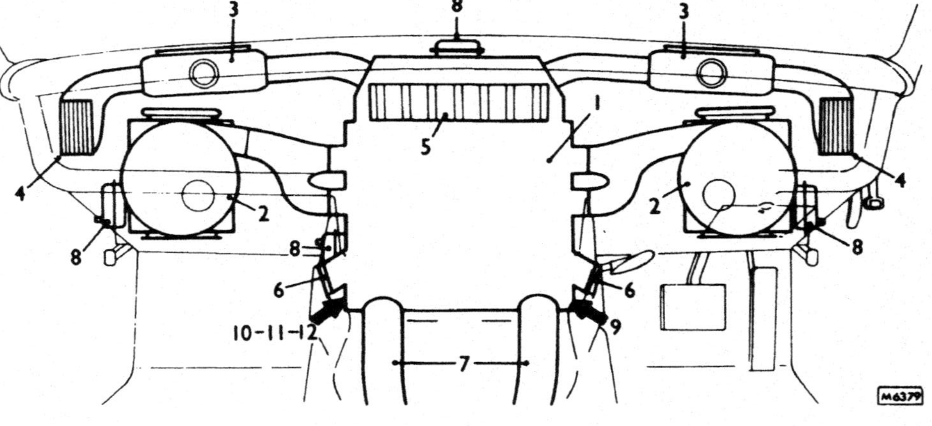

KEY TO INTERNAL AIR CONDITIONING LOCATION PROGRAM

1 Air conditioning heater/cooler unit.
2 Blower motor assembly.
3 Demist flap units.
4 Facia end air outlet.
5 Face level facia air outlet.
6 Footwell air outlet.
7 Rear seat air outlet duct.
8 Vacuum actuator.
9 Servo control unit.
10 Amplifier unit.
11 Blower motor relays.
12 Vacuum solenoid.

Notes

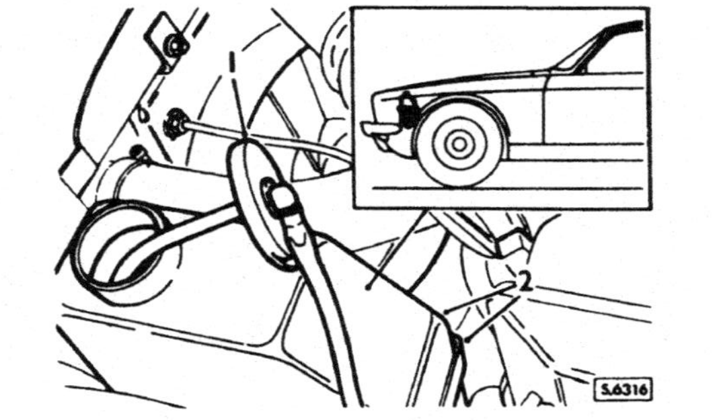

WASHER RESERVOIR

Remove and refit – Early Cars 84.10.01

Removing

1 Pull plastic cap from neck of reservoir; withdraw cap, feed tube and filter complete from reservoir.
2 Withdraw reservoir from bracket.

Refitting

Reverse operations 1 and 2.

NOTE: It is recommended that only soft water mixed with a proprietary cleaning fluid to the correct proportions is used when filling washer system. This will minimise the formation of deposits that affect the performance of the system.

WASHER RESERVOIR

Remove and refit – Cars fitted with headlamp washers – see 84.20.01

WASHER RESERVOIR BRACKET

Remove and refit 84.10.02

Removing

1 Remove reservoir – 84.10.01.
2 Withdraw two set screws and remove bracket.

Refitting

Reverse operations 1 and 2.

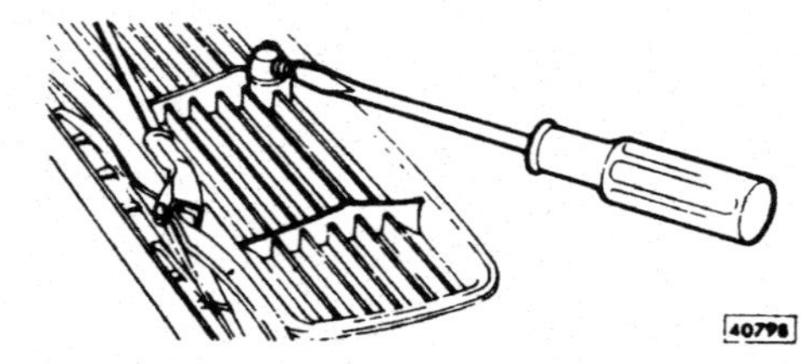

WASHER JETS

Remove and refit 84.10.09

Removing

1 With a screwdriver remove jet.
2 To clean jet use thin wire to clear hole of any deposits.
3 Operate washer with jets removed to flush nozzle.

Refitting

Replace jets and ensure that washer fluid strikes windscreen within wiper arc.

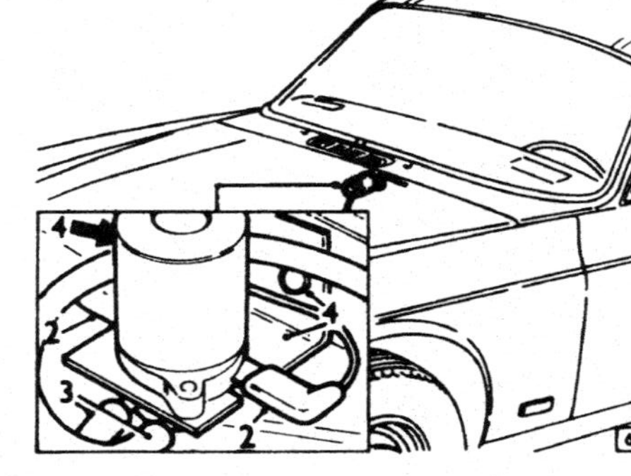
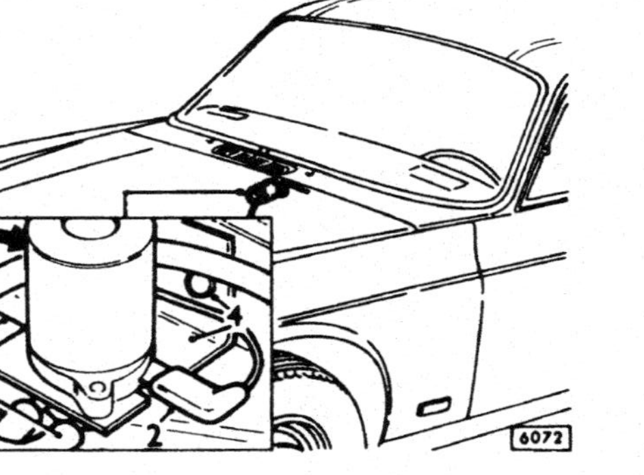

WINDSCREEN WASHER PUMP

Remove and refit 84.10.21

Removing

1 Disconnect battery – 86.15.20.
2 Disconnect cables from Lucar connectors on pump.
3 Withdraw washer tubes from adapters.
4 Withdraw two setscrews and remove pump complete with bracket.

Refitting

Reverse operations 1 to 4.

WINDSCREEN WASHER PUMP

Remove and refit – Later Cars 84.10.21

Removing

1 Open bonnet.
2 Note fitted position of leads; disconnect leads from pump.
3 Carefully prise washer tubing from pump nozzles.
4 Remove screws securing washer and tubing retaining clip to valance; withdraw pump.

Refitting

Reverse operations 1 to 4; ensure tubing is not kinked or twisted.

NOTE: Fitting of tube will be facilitated if ends of tube are warmed immediately prior to refitting.

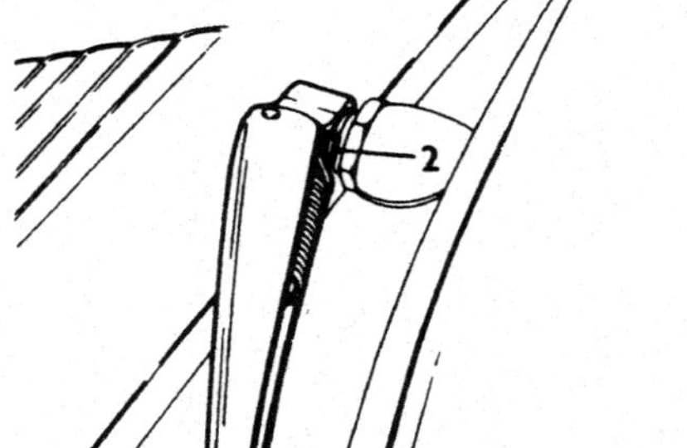

WIPER ARMS

Remove and refit – L.H. 84.15.02
– R.H. 84.15.03

Removing

1 Note angle of parked windscreen wiper arm.
2 Lift spring clip and withdraw wiper arm from spindle.

Refitting

3 Check condition of wiper arm spindle spline.
4 Coat spline with water proof grease.
5 Press arm on to spindle at angle noted in operation 1.
6 Operate wipers and re-locate arm if necessary.

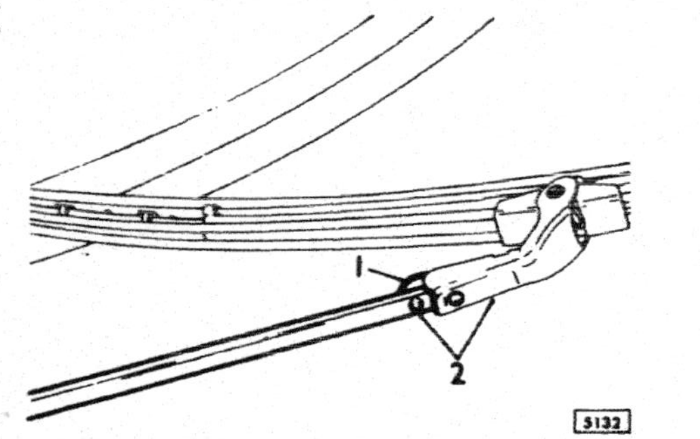

WIPER BLADES

Remove and refit 84.15.05

Removing

1 Hold blade in one hand and with thumb nail of the other hand depress spring clip.
2 Press wiper arm towards windscreen to disengage dimple from blades, slide blade from arm.

Refitting

3 Press blade straight on to wiper arm until dimple engages spring clip.

WIPER MOTOR

Remove and refit 84.15.12

Removing

1 Disconnect and remove battery – 86.15.01.
2 Withdraw wiper arms from spindles – 84.15.02.
3 Disconnect cable rack conduit from motor.

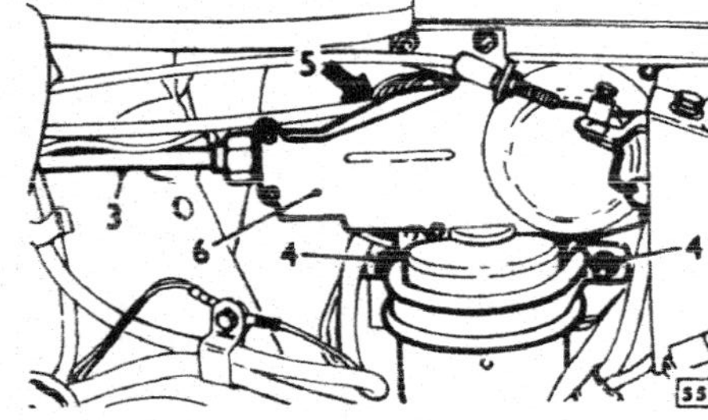

4 Remove two retaining nuts and washers from motor clamp.
5 Tilt motor towards engine and withdraw cable connectors.
6 Remove motor and drive as complete assembly, drawing rack drive from conduit.

Refitting

7 Operate wipers to check swept arc of wiper arms.
8 Reverse operations 1 to 6.

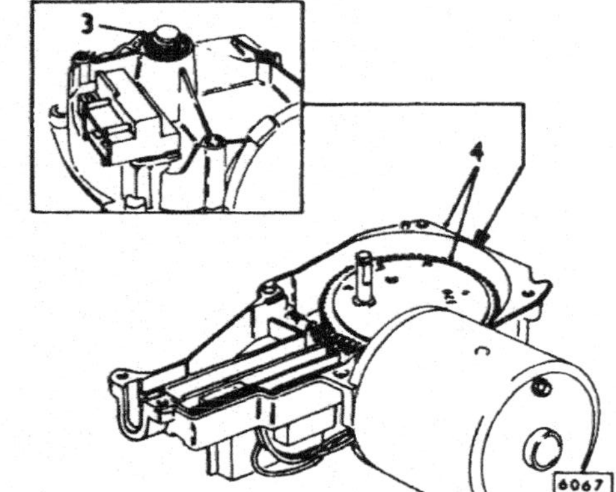

WIPER MOTOR GEAR ASSEMBLY

Remove and refit 84.15.14

Removing

1 Remove wiper motor – 84.15.12.
2 Remove rack drive cable – 84.15.24.
3 Remove circlip and washer on gear assembly shaft.
4 Mark and note position of gear assembly in relation to a chosen point on housing.

Refitting

Reverse operations 1 to 4.

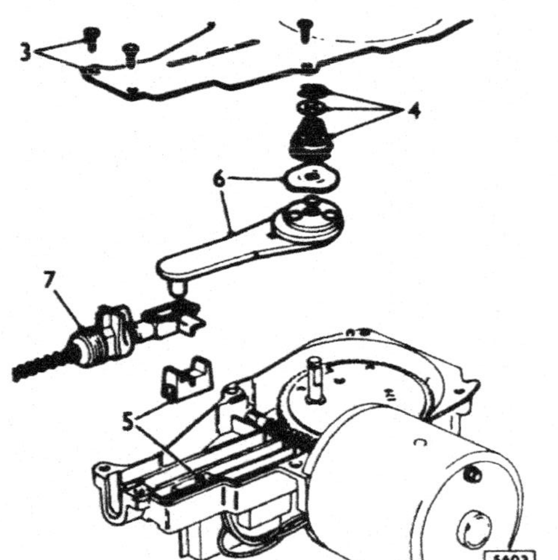

WINDSCREEN WIPER RACK DRIVE

Remove and refit 84.15.24

Removing

1 Disconnect battery – 86.15.20.
2 Remove wiper motor – 84.15.12.
3 Remove cover plate by withdrawing five hexagon headed set screws and earth lead.
4 Carefully remove circlip, washer and conical spring.
5 Mark position of slider block in relation to terminal limit switch assembly.

NOTE: Ensure that during this operation the gear assembly is not removed.

6 Remove friction plate and connecting rod.
7 Withdraw rack drive cable.

Refitting

Reverse operations 1 to 7.

NOTE: Ensure that rack drive, slider block and limit switch assembly is re-assembled in the same position as noted at 5.

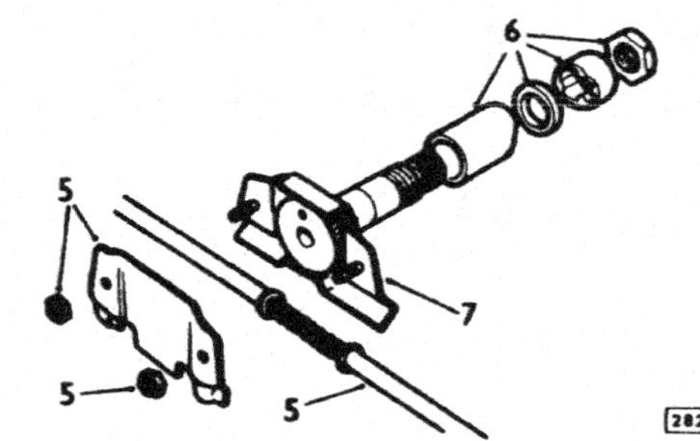

WHEEL BOXES

Remove and refit – L.H. 84.15.28
– R.H. 84.15.29

Removing

1 Disconnect and remove battery – 86.15.01.
2 Remove screen rail facia – 76.46.04.
3 Remove wiper motor – 84.15.12.
4 Remove demister flap/actuator assembly – 80.10.37.
5 Remove two nuts retaining wheel box back plate and release drive conduit.
6 Remove nuts securing the wheel box(es) to the scuttle and remove the chrome distance pieces and sealing rings.
7 Remove wheel boxes.

Refitting

8 Smear waterproof grease on splines before refitting wiper arms.
9 Reverse operations 1 to 7.

NOTE: When refitting ensure that flared sections of drive rack conduit locate with slots in cover plate.

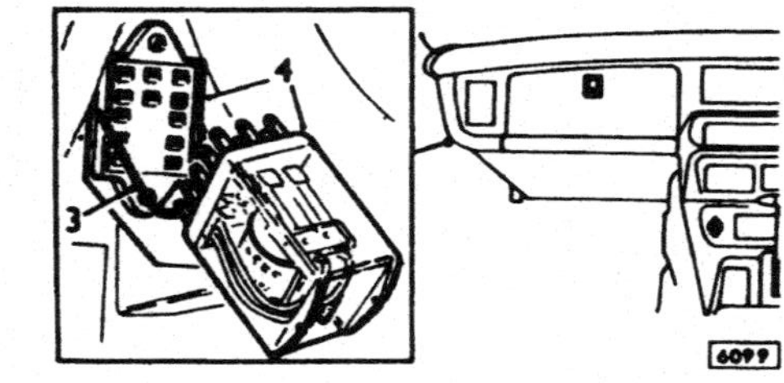

WINDSCREEN WIPER MOTOR RELAY

Remove and refit **84.15.32**

Removing

1 Disconnect battery – 86.15.20.
2 Drop passenger seat side dash casing – 76.46.11.
3 Release relay securing spring clip.
4 Pull relay unit from base connector block.

Refitting

Reverse operations 1 to 4.

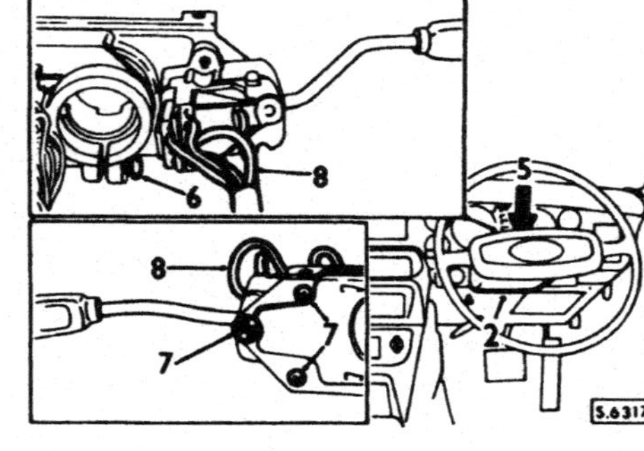

WINDSCREEN WASHER/WIPER SWITCH

Remove and refit **84.15.34**

Removing

1 Disconnect battery – 86.15.20.
2 Remove steering wheel lower shroud.
3 Remove steering wheel – 57.60.01.
4 Remove drivers side dash casing – 76.46.11.
5 Remove steering wheel upper shroud.
6 Slacken clinch bolt and pull switch assembly from upper steering column.
7 Remove two screws and spire washer retaining switch.
8 Disconnect harness at multi pin connector and earth lead at snap connector.

Refitting

Reverse operations 1 to 8.

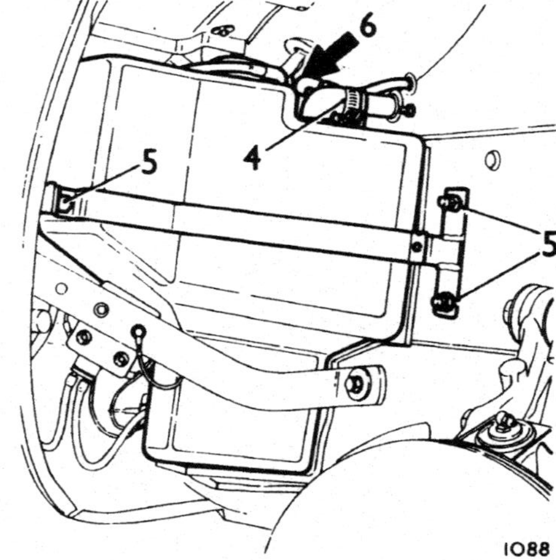
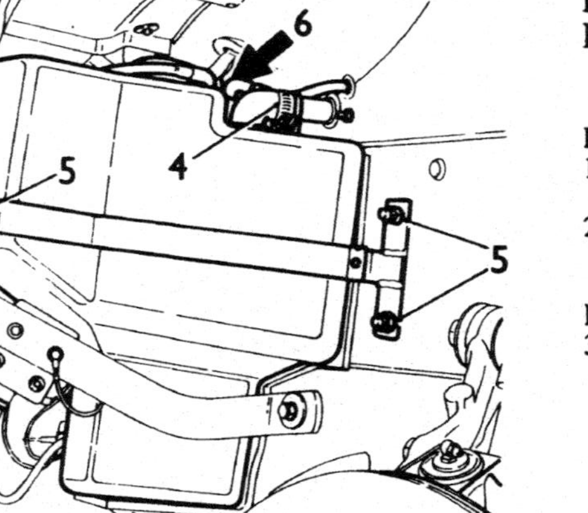

HEADLAMP WASHER RESERVOIR

Remove and refit **84.20.01**

NOTE: This reservoir supplies both windscreen and headlamp washing systems.

Removing

1 Raise front of car and place on stands.
2 Remove L.H. front wheel.
3 Remove three screws and detach stoneguard; collect sealing strips.
4 Slacken hose clip securing rubber elbow to filler neck.
5 Remove three screws securing mounting strap assembly, detach mounting strap and lower reservoir until screws attaching manifold assembly to reservoir are accessible.
6 Remove four screws securing manifold assembly; withdraw reservoir from pipes.

Refitting

7 Reverse operation 1 to 6, ensuring that tubes and filters enter lowest section of reservoir.

HEADLAMP WASHER RESERVOIR BRACKET

Remove and refit **84.20.02**

Removing

1 Remove headlamp washer reservoir, see 84.20.01.
2 Remove screw securing bracket to wheel arch.

Refitting

3 Reverse operations 1 and 2.

HEADLAMP WASHER JETS

Remove and refit **84.20.09**

Removing

1 Open bonnet.
2 Carefully prise tubes from jets.
3 Restraining jets by hand outside car, detach nut securing each pair of jets to headlamp panel.
4 Remove jets; collect rubber washers.

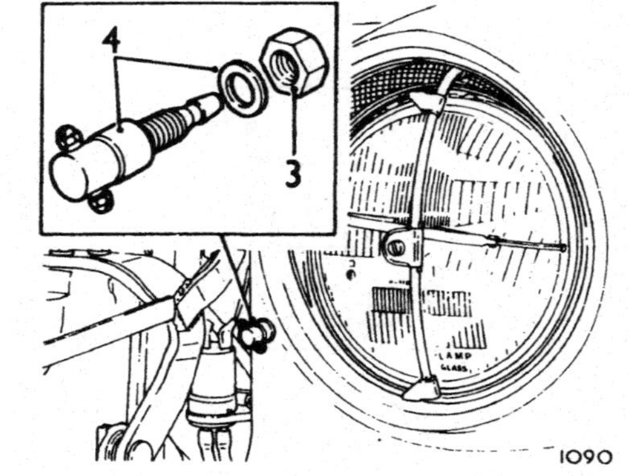

Refitting

5 Reverse operations 1 to 4.

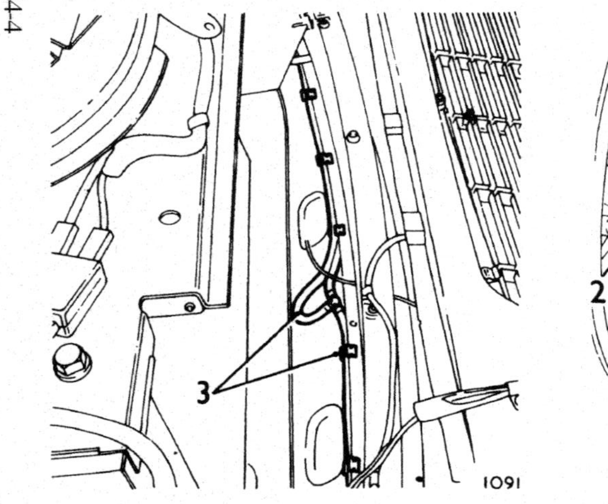

HEADLAMP WASHER TUBES

Remove and refit 84.20.15

Removing
1 Open bonnet.
2 Carefully prise washer tubes from jets and pump.
3 Separate washer tubes from six spring clips attaching them to flange below lower grille and remove tubes from car.

Refitting
4 Reverse operations 1 to 3.

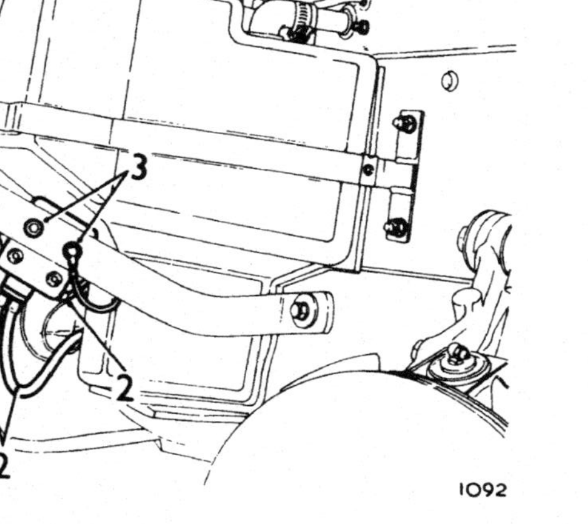

HEADLAMP WASHER PUMP

Remove and refit 84.20.21

Removing
1 Remove L.H. front wheel. Support front of car on stands.
2 Carefully prise both tubes from washer pump and detach both Lucars.
3 Unbolt pump from attachment plate on bumper support arm.

Refitting
4 Reverse operations 1 to 3.

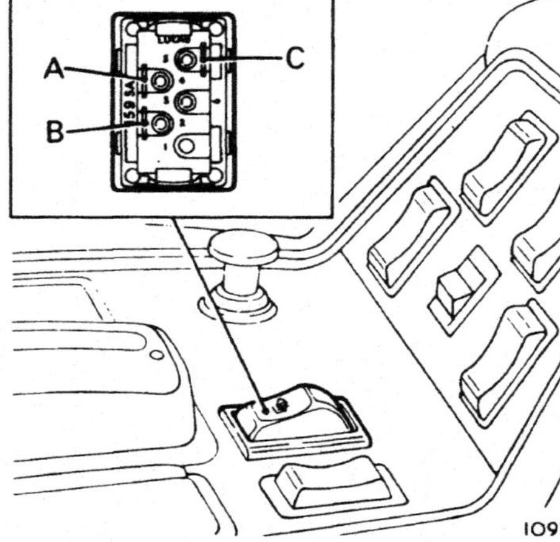

A – Green/red
B – Green
C – Green/brown

HEADLAMP WIPER AND WASHER SWITCH

Remove and refit 84.20.27 (86.65.67)

Removing
1 Disconnect battery, see 86.15.20.
2 Remove three screws securing top panel to console.
3 Raise top panel, detach Lucars at washer switch and remove switch from panel.

Refitting
4 Connect leads to new switch as shown, through aperture in panel.
5 Press switch into panel aperture; replace top panel on console.
6 Reverse operations 1 and 2.

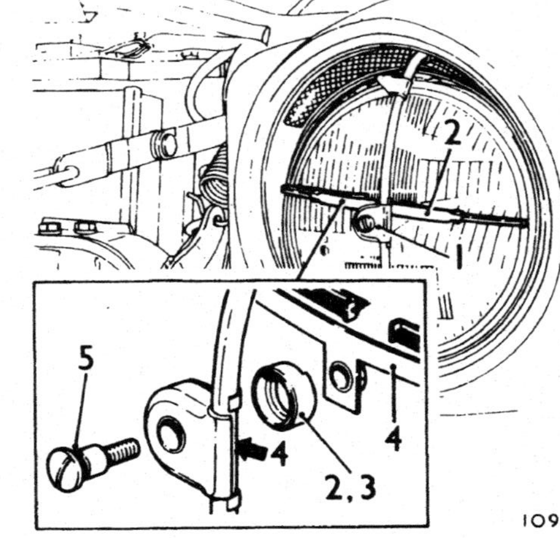

HEADLAMP WIPER ARM

Remove and refit 84.25.02

Removing
1 Restrain wiper arm by hand and remove pivot screw.
2 Press wiper arm towards headlamp glass and withdraw. Collect spacing cup.

Refitting
3 Fit spacing cup to wiper arm at forward face of pivot.
4 Position wiper arm against drive boss.
5 Check that 'O' ring is fitted to pivot screw and insert screw. Do not tighten at this stage.
6 Turn wiper blades to 'parked' position (in line with drive tube) and fully tighten screw, restraining wiper arm by hand.

HEADLAMP WIPER MOTOR

Remove and refit 84.25.12

Removing

1 Disconnect battery, see 86.15.20.
2 Remove four self-tapping screws securing cover plate to rack drive.
3 Remove nylon channel and lift rack drive peg from cross-head.
4 Remove bolts and nuts securing motor clip to mounting plate.
5 Disconnect leads and remove motor. Collect pad from between motor and bracket.

Refitting

6 Reverse operations 1 to 5.

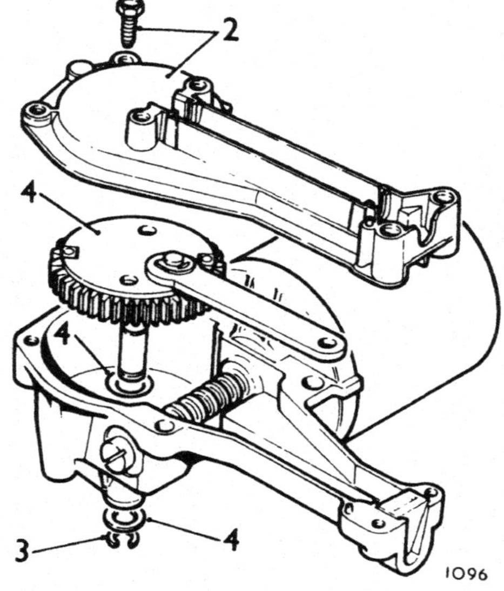

HEADLAMP WIPER MOTOR GEAR

Remove and refit 84.25.17

Removing

1 Remove headlamp wiper motor, see 84.25.12.
2 Remove two self-tapping screws securing gear cover-plate to gear housing.
3 Detach external circlip from gear spindle.
4 Remove gear; collect plain and conical washers.

Refitting

5 Place conical spring washer on gear spindle with outer diameter contacting gear.
6 Reverse operations 1 to 4.

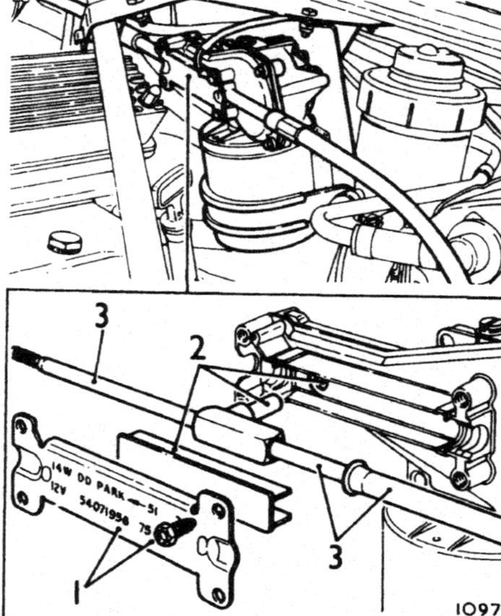

HEADLAMP WIPER RACK

Remove and refit 84.25.24

Removing

1 Remove four self-tapping screws securing cover plate to rack drive at motor.
2 Remove nylon channel and lift out rack drive from cross-head.
3 Carefully withdraw rack drive cables from conduits.

Refitting

4 Reverse operations 1 to 3.

Align wiper blades correctly in 'parked' position, see 84.25.02.

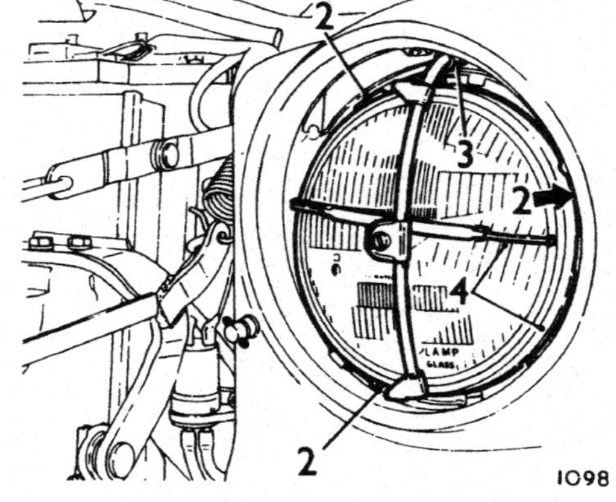

HEADLAMP WIPER WHEEL BOXES AND RACK TUBES

Remove and refit 84.25.27

Removing (each side)

1 Remove outer headlight rim finisher, see 86.40.01.
2 Remove three screws securing headlight rim and rack tube.
3 Ease rim and tube forward and slacken collet nut.
4 Draw rim assembly away from tube, allowing wiper blades to rotate as rack is withdrawn.

Refitting

5 Reverse operations 1 to 4.

Align wiper blades correctly in 'parked' position, see 84.25.02.

Notes

SYMPTOM AND DIAGNOSIS CHART

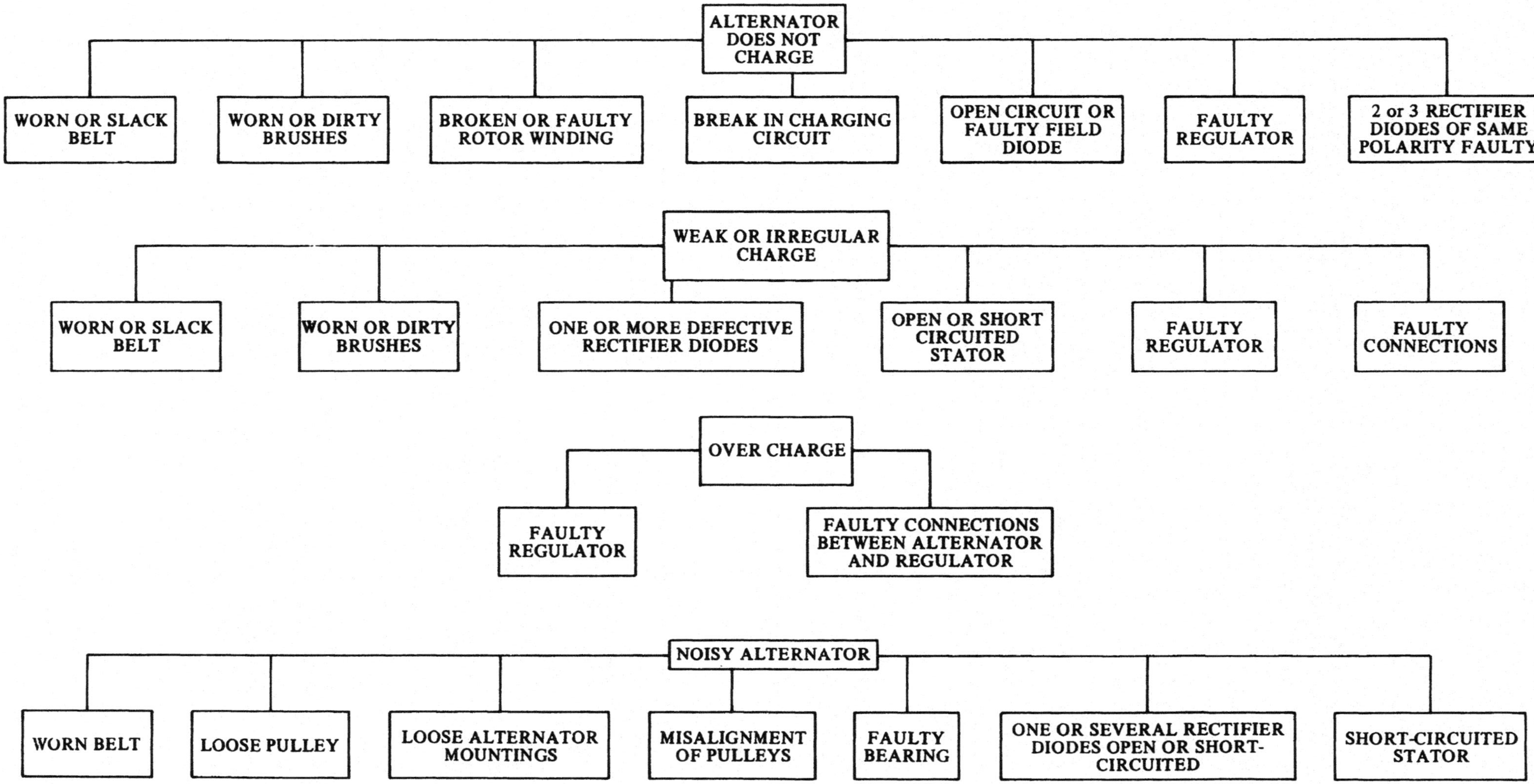

ALTERNATOR DOES NOT CHARGE

- WORN OR SLACK BELT
- WORN OR DIRTY BRUSHES
- BROKEN OR FAULTY ROTOR WINDING
- BREAK IN CHARGING CIRCUIT
- OPEN CIRCUIT OR FAULTY FIELD DIODE
- FAULTY REGULATOR
- 2 or 3 RECTIFIER DIODES OF SAME POLARITY FAULTY

WEAK OR IRREGULAR CHARGE

- WORN OR SLACK BELT
- WORN OR DIRTY BRUSHES
- ONE OR MORE DEFECTIVE RECTIFIER DIODES
- OPEN OR SHORT CIRCUITED STATOR
- FAULTY REGULATOR
- FAULTY CONNECTIONS

OVER CHARGE

- FAULTY REGULATOR
- FAULTY CONNECTIONS BETWEEN ALTERNATOR AND REGULATOR

NOISY ALTERNATOR

- WORN BELT
- LOOSE PULLEY
- LOOSE ALTERNATOR MOUNTINGS
- MISALIGNMENT OF PULLEYS
- FAULTY BEARING
- ONE OR SEVERAL RECTIFIER DIODES OPEN OR SHORT-CIRCUITED
- SHORT-CIRCUITED STATOR

CHECK EACH ITEM IN TURN AND RECTIFY IF NECESSARY BEFORE PROCEEDING TO NEXT ITEM

FUSE NO.	CABLE COLOURS on 3.4L and 4.2L cars	PROTECTED CIRCUITS	FUSE MAX CONTIN-UOUS	RATING AMPS FUSING CURRENT	LOCATION OF FUSE	FUSE COLOURS LUCAS	FUSE COLOURS TDC 78
1	Red/Yellow	Fog lamps (if fitted)	10	20	Main fuse box	Blue on yellow	Orange/violet
2	Brown to Brown/Orange	Hazard warning switch	8	15	Main fuse box	Light brown	Orange/green
3	Brown to Purple	Map and interior lights, cigar lighter, clock and boot light	17	35	Main fuse box	White	White/sky blue
4	White to Green (2)	Instrument and transmitters, fuel pumps, reverse lamps and overdrive controls (if fitted)	8	15	Main fuse box	Light brown	Orange/green
5	White/Pink to Green	Direction indicator system	8	15	Main fuse box	Light brown	Orange/green
6	White/Pink to Green (2)	Stop lamps, horn relay windings, screen washer and battery cooling system	17	35	Main fuse box	White	White/sky blue
7	Red/Blue	Panel lights	8	15	Main fuse box	Light brown	Orange/green
8	Red/Slate to Red (2)	L.H. sidelamp and tail lamp	8	15	Main fuse box	Light brown	Orange/green
9	Red/Orange to Red (2)	R.H. sidelamp and tail lamp and cigar lighter illumination	8	15	Main fuse box	Light brown	Orange/green
10	Brown (2) to Brown/White (2)	Air conditioning or heater motors	25	50	Main fuse box	Yellow	Yellow/sky blue
11	White/Pink to Light Green (2)	Windscreen wiper system	10	20	Main fuse box	Blue on yellow	Orange/violet
12	Link to Light Green	Air conditioning (if fitted)	8	15	Main fuse box	Light brown	Orange/green
	Blue/White	Headlamp main beam, inner and outer, RH	12	25	Small box on radiator top rail	Pink	Orange/white
	Blue/Red	Headlamp dipped beam, RH	5	10	Small box on radiator top rail	Pale blue	Orange/black
	Blue/White	Headlamp main beam, inner and outer, LH	12	25	Small box on radiator top rail	Pink	Orange/white
	Blue/Red	Headlamp dipped beam, LH	5	10	Small box on radiator top rail	Pale blue	Orange/black
	IN LINE FUSES						
	Purple/Brown	Horn relay	17	35	Harness on RH of bulkhead	White	White/sky blue
	White/Black	Heated rear window	17	35	Clipped below main fuse box	White	White/sky blue
	White/Pink	Radio. Fuse varies according to type of radio fitted, and may be 1½ to 2, 1.6 or 5 amp: also protects aerial motor relay windings, if fitted	–	–	In console		
	Brown/Purple	Aerial motor relay (if fitted)	5	10	Under boot floor on rear wall, near centre line car.	Pale blue	Orange/black
	Red/Orange	Rear fog guard lamps (if fitted)	5	10	Normally in console, but position may vary	Pale blue	Orange/black

ALTERNATOR

Description 86.10.00

The Lucas alternators – types 18-, 20-, or 25-ACR, fitted according to specification of car, are high output three phase machines which produce current at idling speed.

The heatsink – rectifier, terminal block assembly can be removed complete. There are six silicon diodes connected to form a full wave rectifier bridge circuit, and three silicon diodes which supply current to the rotor winding. Individual diodes cannot be removed from the heatsink assemblies. Regulation is by a Lucas control unit mounted in the slip ring end bracket. There is no provision for adjustment in service.

Individual connectors are used to connect external wiring to the alternator. The alternators main negative terminals are connected internally to the body of the machine.

Surge Protection Device

The surge protection device is a special avalanche-diode, fitted to the outer-face of the slip-ring end bracket (not to be confused with a suppression capacitor, similarly fitted in the end bracket). The avalanche-diode is connected between terminal 'IND' and frame and its purpose is to protect the regulator from damage by absorbing high transient voltages which occur in the charging system due to faulty cable connections, or when certain switching devices are operated. (The surge protection device is intended to provide limited protection for the regulator under normal working conditions and therefore the service precaution not to disconnect any of the charging system cables, particularly those at the battery, while the engine is running, should still be observed).

Alternative high output alternators, the Motorola 9AR 2512P and 9AR 2533P are fitted to some later cars; instructions for their overhaul, which differ in some details from those for Lucas alternators, are given in the appropriate sections of the manual.

CAUTION: No part of the charging circuit should be connected or disconnected while the engine is running.

When using electric-arc welding equipment in the vicinity of the engine take the following precautions to avoid damage to the semi-conductor devices used in the alternator and control box, and also the ignition system.

Disconnect battery earthed lead.

Disconnect alternator output cables.

Disconnect ignition and amplifier unit.

ALTERNATOR

Test (in situ) Lucas alternators only 86.10.01

(a) Output Test

Equipment required: A moving coil ammeter or multi-range test meter on range 0–75 amperes.

This test should be carried out with the alternator at normal temperature. Run cold engine at 3000 rev/min for 3–4 minutes.

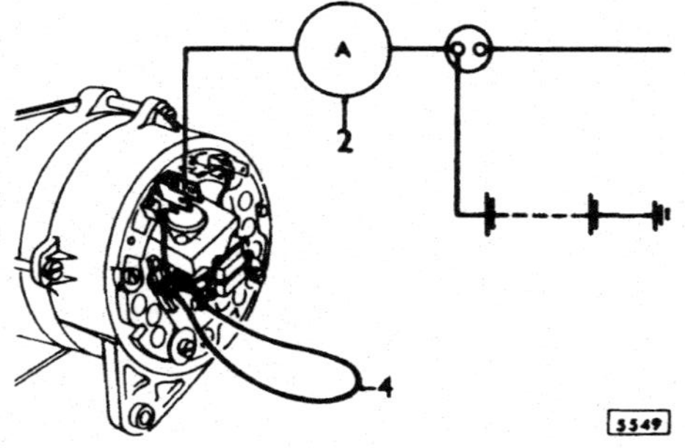
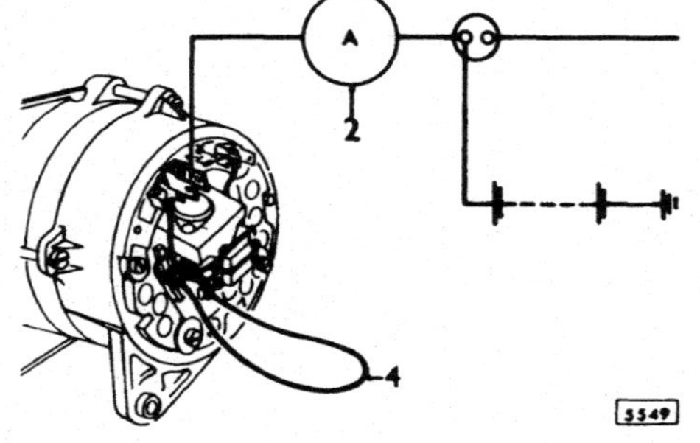

1 Disconnect battery earth lead.
2 Connect ammeter in series with alternator main output cable and starter solenoid.
3 Remove connectors from alternator. Remove moulded end cover and remake connectors.
4 Connect jumper lead to short out the 'F' and '–' terminals of the control unit.

(This makes regulator inoperative by effectively linking 'F' green lead to alternator frame).

5 Re-connect battery earth lead.
6 Switch on all vehicle lighting, headlights on main beam. Switch on ignition and check warning light is on.
7 Start engine, slowly increase speed to 3000 rev/min. Ammeter reading should equal maximum rated output of 66 amperes (45 amperes for 18 ACR alternator).

(b) Voltage Drop Test (in situ)

Equipment required: A moving coil voltmeter multi-range test meter on 0–30 volt range.

To check for high resistance in the charging circuit.

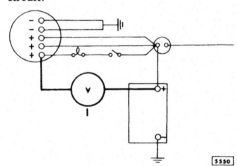

1 Connect voltmeter between battery + VE terminal and alternator main output terminal.
2 Switch on all vehicle lighting, headlights on main beam.
Start engine and run at 3000 rev/min.
Note voltmeter reading. Stop engine.

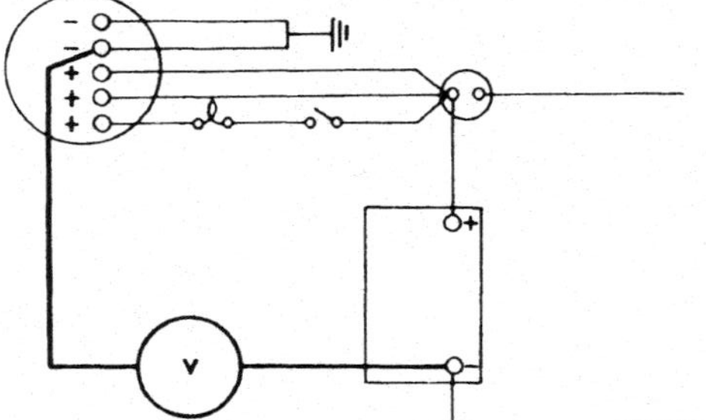

3 Transfer voltmeter connections to battery earth and alternator negative terminal.
4 Repeat operation 2. Note voltmeter reading.
5 Voltage should not exceed 0.5 volts for positive side. Higher readings indicate high resistance in the circuit.

(c) Control Unit Test

Equipment required: A moving coil ammeter and moving coil voltmeter or multi-range test meters.

Circuit wiring must be in good condition, and all connections clean and secure. The battery must be in a well charged condition or be temporarily replaced by a charged unit.

1 Connect ammeter in series with starter solenoid and alternator main output cable.
2 Connect voltmeter between battery terminals.
3 Start engine and run at 3000 rev/min until the ammeter reads less than 10 amperes. Voltmeter reading should be between 13.6 volts and 14.4 volts.
4 An unstable reading or a reading outside the specified limits indicates a faulty control unit.

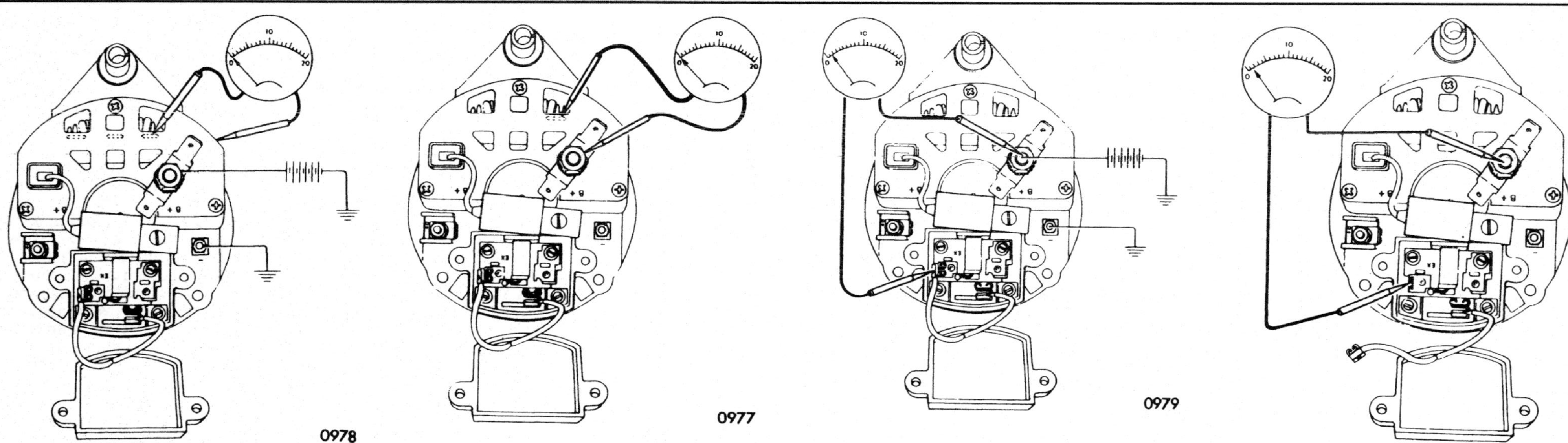

ALTERNATOR

Test (in situ) Motorola alternators

86.10.01

Equipment required: Voltmeter and ammeter, field rheostat.

NOTE: Before commencing tests ensure that battery is fully charged. If not, disconnect battery before recharging it.

Never disconnect battery, alternator or regulator with engine running.

Do not earth field winding (terminal marked EX, connected to regulator by green lead).

On cars fitted with air conditioning it is advisable to remove alternator from vehicle before carrying out tests 1 and 3 and to substitute bench tests for tests 4, 5 and 6.

Always disconnect battery when removing or refitting alternator.

Test 1

Ignition switched OFF. Check of stator windings. Check voltage on one of the three phases of stator windings, accessible to a probe from voltmeter passing through ventilation hole as shown.

Connect voltmeter first between phase and earth, then between winding and positive terminal, observing correct polarity.

Indication of any reading other than zero on voltmeter shows defective positive rectifier diode, necessitating changing of diode bridge, see 86.10.08

Test 2

Ignition switched OFF. Check of battery connections. Check voltage at B + terminal on alternator and at battery positive terminal. Voltage should be the same at both points. If voltage at B + terminal is lower than battery voltage, or fluctuates, check for broken wires, faulty connections or corroded terminals.

Test 3

Ignition ON, engine not running. Check of field circuit.

Check voltage at slip ring, by touching probe of voltmeter on field terminal 'EX' with regulator attachment screws removed.

If voltmeter reading is higher than 2 volts, field circuit is defective; remove brush holder by detaching green regulator lead from field terminal 'EX' and remove two setscrews, with washers, securing brush holder to alternator. Check that brushes are free to slide, undamaged and not excessively worn; new brushes protrude by approximately 0.35 in. (9 mm.) from the brush holder, and complete brush holder must be renewed if either brush protrudes by less than 0.15 in. (4 mm.). Ensure that brush leads are not frayed and are securely attached to brushes, and that slip rings are clean. If in doubt, refer to 86.10.14 and check brushes electrically.

If voltmeter reads zero, check connections to regulator, ignition switch and ignition indicator lamp.

Also check regulator circuit by detaching its green lead from field EX terminal and measuring voltage across field windings, which should not exceed 2 volts. If this voltage is between 8 and 12 volts, alternator is defective. If correct proceed to test 5.

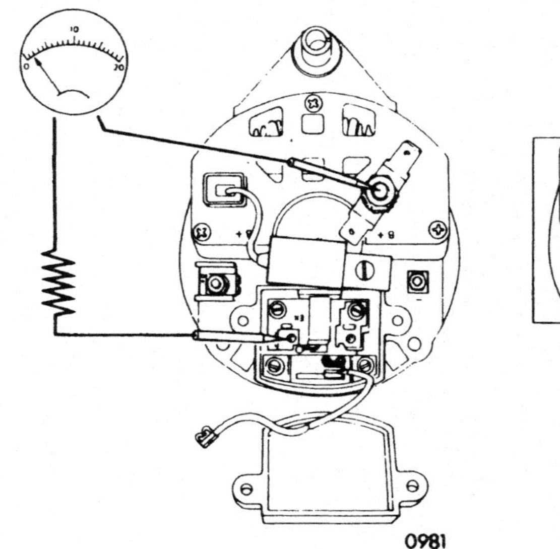

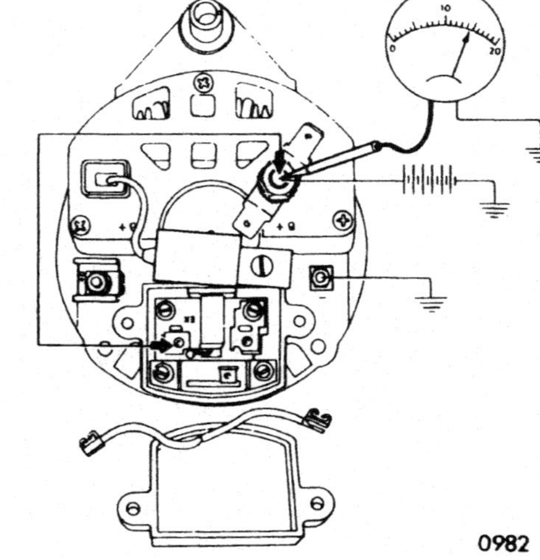

Test 4
Ignition ON, engine running faster than idle. Further check of field circuit.
If incorrect readings were obtained in Test 3, retest field circuit by disconnecting regulator from field terminal EX and connecting ammeter between this terminal and output terminal B +. If meter indicates current less than 1 amp, recheck brushes, leads and slip rings.
CAUTION: Use a field rheostat in series with ammeter, so that excessive current which could flow if field is shorted will not damage ammeter.

Test 5
Ignition ON, engine running faster than idle.
Check of output voltage.
Check voltage both at output terminal (B +) and at positive terminal of battery. Correct voltage at both points is 14.2 volts ± 0.5 volts, at 25°C (77°F).
If difference between battery voltage and voltage at B + terminal is more than 0.3 volts check wiring and terminals for corrosion or breaks.

Test 6
Field lead disconnected, regulator disconnected, output terminal shorted to field terminal, ignition on, engine running at fast idle. Regulator and diodes check.
With alternator connected as specified above and shown in diagram, check voltage between output terminal B + and earth.
It voltage rises to 14 to 16 volts in this test, but did not reach 14 volts in test 5, regulator is defective. Replace by new regulator.
If output voltage does not rise, and field circuit has been found satisfactory in tests 3 or 4, then either alternator stator or rectifier diodes are defective. Remove alternator for further attention, see 86.10.02.

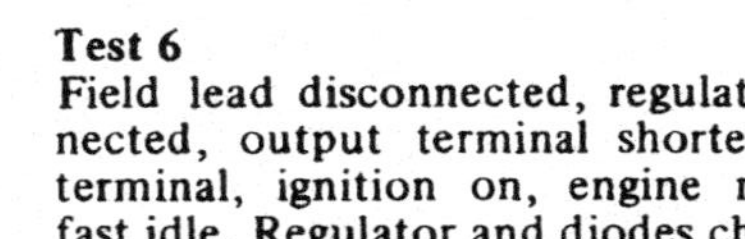

ALTERNATOR

Remove and refit (Lucas or Motorola) 86.10.02

Removing
1 Disconnect battery – 86.15.20.
2 Drain coolant – 26.10.01.
3 Remove remote header tank – 26.15.01.
4 Slacken air conditioning compressor mounting bolts (if fitted).
5 Slacken compressor drive belt adjuster trunnion retaining nut.
6 Slacken compressor drive belt adjustment and locknuts.
7 Adjust compressor as near to engine block as practicable without kinking air conditioning hoses.
8 Withdraw adjusting arm securing bolt from alternator end frame.
9 Disconnect alternator cables from lucar connections.
10 Withdraw alternator mounting bolts.
11 Ease alternator past compressor and clear of engine compartment, taking great care not to damage or disturb air conditioning pipes.

Refitting
12 Reverse operations 7 to 10.
13 Tighten adjusting nut to obtain an alternator belt tension as follows:
A load of 3.2 lbs. (1,45 kg) applied at midpoint of lower portion of belt will give a deflection of .15 ins. (4,0 mm).
14 Tighten adjuster locknut and alternator securing bolts.
15 Reverse operations 1 to 7.

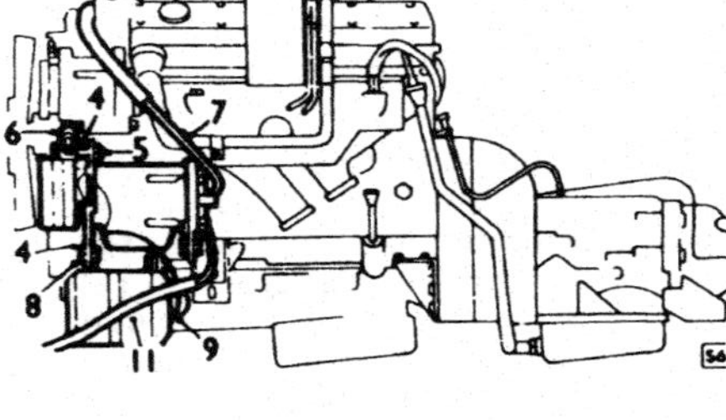

ALTERNATOR DRIVE BELT

Remove and refit 86.10.03

Removing
1 Remove water pump/power steering pump drive belt – 57.20.02.
2 Remove air conditioning compressor drive belt – 82.10.02.
3 Slacken alternator mounting bolt.
4 Slacken adjusting link securing bolt.
5 Slacken trunnion block securing bolt.
6 Slacken adjusting link locking nut.
7 Slacken adjusting nut.
8 Remove drive belt.

Refitting
9 Ease belt over crankshaft pulley and alternator pulley.
10 Adjust drive belt – 86.10.05/2.
11 Reverse operations 1 and 2.
12 Tighten all locknuts, mounting bolts and nuts.

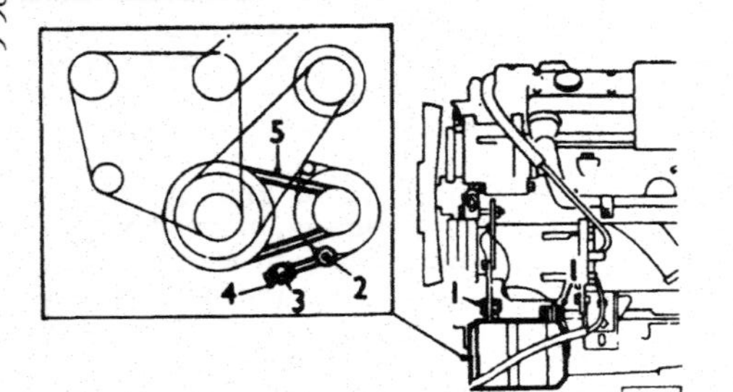

ALTERNATOR DRIVE BELT

Adjustment (Lucas or Motorola) **86.10.05**

1 Slacken alternator mounting bolt.
2 Slacken adjusting link securing bolt.
3 Slacken trunnion block securing bolt.
4 Slacken adjusting link locking nut.
5 Adjust belt tension with adjusting nut. Belt tension – 3.2 (1,45 kgs) .15 in. (3,8 mm).
6 Tighten all securing nuts and bolts.

ALTERNATOR – LUCAS 18 ACR

Overhaul **86.10.08**

Dismantling

1 Withdraw two retaining screws and remove moulded slip ring end cover.
2 Note positions of stator winding connections to rectifier connecting pins.
3 Using thermal shunt and light weight soldering iron (25 watt) unsolder connections.
4 Note position of cable connectors to rectifier plates.
5 Disconnect cables.
6 Withdraw three hexagon headed screws securing brushbox and regulator to slip ring end bracket.
7 Remove brushbox moulding and regulator assembly.
8 Slacken rectifier securing nut and remove rectifier.

Brushgear

9 Renew brush and spring assemblies if brushes are worn to 0.312 in. (8 mm).
10 Check brush spring pressure with push type spring gauge to end of brush. Spring pressure should be 9-13 oz/f (255-368 g or 2.5-3.6 N) when brush is flush with moulding.

Slip rings

If necessary clean slip rings with petrol moistened cloth or very fine glass paper.

NOTE: Do not use emery cloth or similar abrasive.

Further dismantling

11 Withdraw three through bolts.
12 Separate alternator into its major components.
(a) Slip ring end bracket.
(b) Drive end bracket, totor, fan and pulley.
(c) Stator laminations and windings.

13. Separate rotor from drive end bracket by removing pulley, fan and shaft key. Press rotor shaft from bearing.
14 Inspect bearings and if satisfactory pack with grease, Shell Alvania 'RA'.

NOTE: To pack slip ring end bearing with grease it is first necessary to remove slip ring moulding.

Bearings

Slip ring end.

15 Unsolder field windings from slip ring moulding.
16 Remove slip ring moulding.
17 Press bearing from shaft.

Drive end.

18 Remove circlip and retaining plate from drive end bearing.
19 Press out bearing.

Reassembly

Reverse operations 1 to 19.

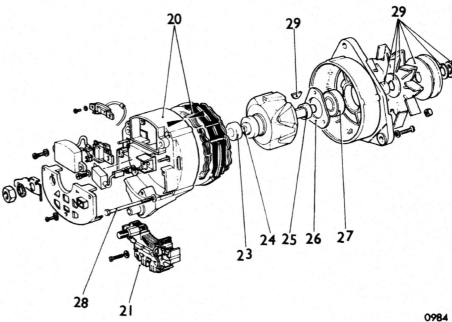

ALTERNATOR – MOTOROLA 9AR 2512 P AND 9AR 2533 P

Overhaul 86.10.08

Dismantling

1 Detach nut, shakeproof washer and connector blade from B + terminal at end cover.
2 Remove setscrew and washer securing capacitor to alternator case, separate lucar and detach capacitor.
3 Withdraw three screws and remove moulded rear cover.
4 Remove two setscrews and washers, separate two Lucars and detach regulator.
5 Remove two setscrews and washers and lift out brush holder.
6 Clamp pulley, unscrew pulley nut and remove small washer, pulley, fan and large washer from alternator spindle.
7 Extract Woodruff key from spindle and remove spacer.
8 Remove four through-bolts; collect washers and square trapped nuts.
9 If casing halves do not readily separate, clamp alternator spindle in protected jaws of vice and draw off rear housing, with stator and diode bridge. Rear bearing will remain on spindle.
CAUTION: Take care to avoid damage to stator and windings by rotor.
10 Remove alternator spindle from vice and draw off front housing. Collect short spacer adjacent to rotor.
11 If necessary, remove front bearing from housing by withdrawing three screws securing retaining plate and pressing out bearing.
12 If necessary, draw rear bearing off alternator spindle, using an extractor reacting against spindle end.
13 Mark position of stator ring in rear housing to ensure that it is correctly replaced.
14 Unsolder leads of three phase windings and D + (red) lead from diode bridge.
CAUTION: Avoid transmitting excessive heat to diodes by incorporating a thermal shunt by using long-nosed pliers to grip each terminal as wire is unsoldered.
15 Withdraw two setscrews and lift out diode bridge. Collect washers.
16 Lift housing off stator, detach two terminals from housing and remove D + lead complete.
17 Extract O-ring from bearing housing.
NOTE: To remove diode bridge with a minimum of dismantling, carry out operations 1, 2, 3, 14 and 15 only.
Refer to 86.10.14 for details on inspection and bench testing.

Reassembling

18 Fit new O-ring into recess in rear bearing housing.
19 Replace D + (red) lead assembly in rear housing, securing it with two setscrews and washers at lucar carrier and bolt and nut at D + terminal. Thread loose end of lead through hole below D + terminal.
20 Place stator and coils in marked position with three leads passing back through housing. Rest stator, with housing on top of it, on non-abrasive surface.
21 Lower diode bridge, with terminals and capacitor fitted, into position in housing, with three leads passing through gaps between fins. Secure with two setscrews and washers, trapping capacitor connector under RH setscrew.
22 Using long-nosed pliers (as a thermal shunt) to grip each terminal in turn and prevent excess heat reaching diode, solder three phase winding leads and D + lead to diode bridge. Do not overheat diode bridge.
23 If required, press new bearing on to rear end of rotor spindle.
24 Press spindle and bearing into position in rear housing.
25 Place short spacer over front end of spindle, ensuring that its larger inside diameter is next to rotor.
26 If necessary, press new front bearing into front housing and secure with retaining plate; apply Loctite to screw threads and to tapped holes in plate.
27 Press front housing into position and insert four through-bolts with plain washers under heads.
28 Coat threads of through-bolts and trapped nuts with Loctite and tighten to 3.6 lbf.ft. (0,5 kgf.m.).

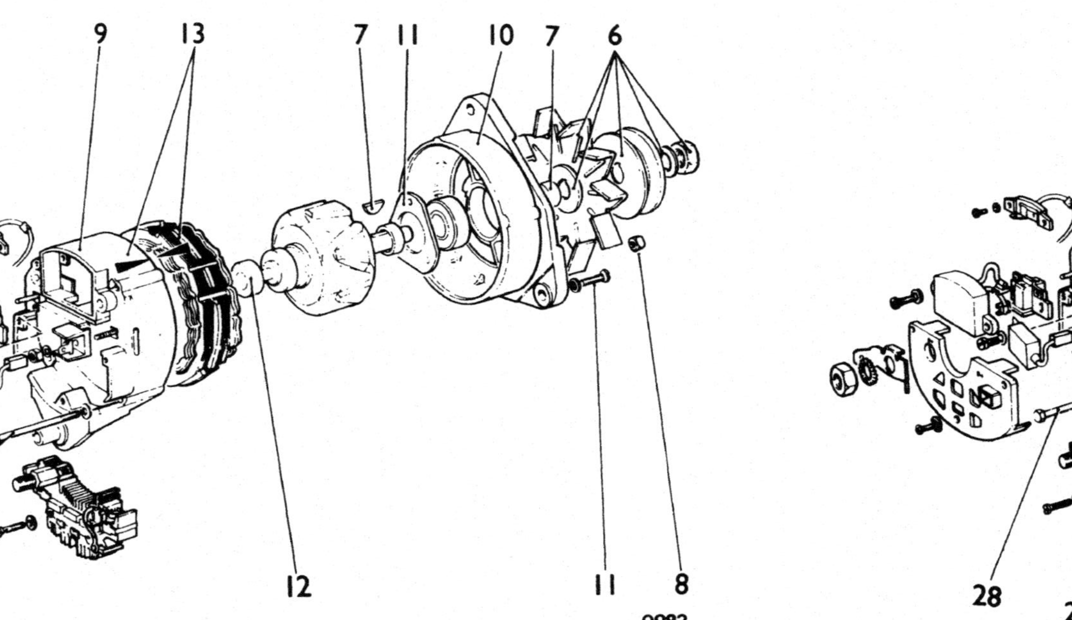

29 Place plain spacer over spindle, insert Woodruff key and replace large washer, fan, pulley, small washer and nut on spindle.
Tighten nut to 29 lbf.ft. (4.0 kgf.m.).
30 Reverse operations 1 to 5.

ALTERNATOR

Inspection and testing (Lucas alternators) 86.10.14

Brush Gear and Slip Ring Inspection
The serviceability of the brushes is gauged by the length protruding beyond the brush moulding in the free position. This amount should exceed 0.3 ins. (8 mm). If renewal is necessary care must be taken to replace the leaf spring at the side of the inner brush.
The surface of the slip rings should be smooth and free from grease or dirt. Servicing is confined to cleaning with a petrol moistened cloth or finest grade glass-paper.

NOTE: Emery cloth or similar abrasive must not be used. The slip rings cannot be machined.

(a) Brush Replacement
1 Remove the small screws securing the brush retaining plates and regulator cables.
2 Replace brushes with new units and refit brush retaining plates and regulator cables.
3 Brush spring pressure should be checked with a push type spring tension gauge. This should indicate 9–13 ozs. (255–368 grammes) when brush face is flush with the moulding.

(b) ROTOR
Testing

Equipment required: An ohmmeter, or a 12-volt battery and ammeter. A 110-volt a.c. supply and a 15 watt test lamp.

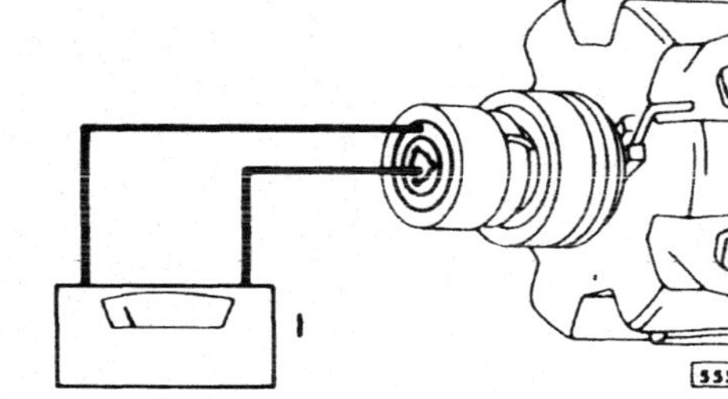

1 Connect the ohmmeter between the slip rings. Resistance should be 3.2 ohms. at 20°C.

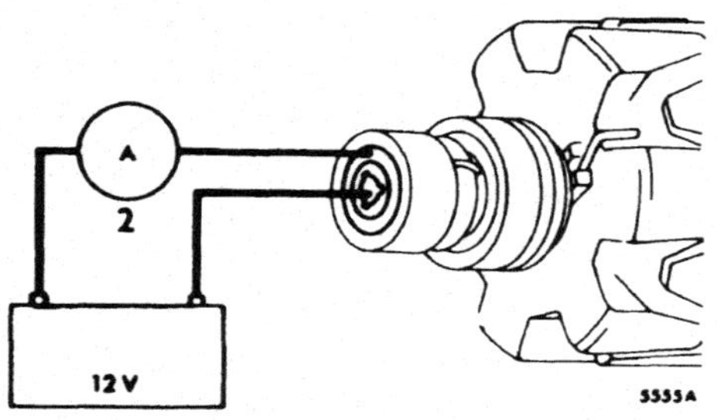

2 Alternatively connect ammeter and battery between slip rings, the ammeter should read approximately 3 amperes.

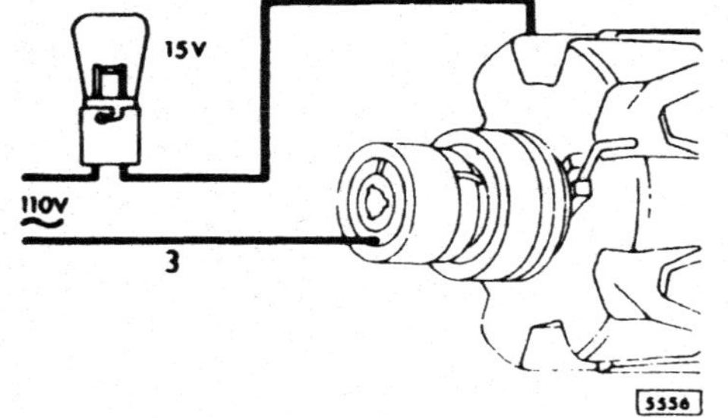

3 To test for defective insulation between slip rings and rotor poles connect the 110 volt supply and 15 watt test lamp between slip rings and rotor poles in turn. If the lamp lights, the coil is earthed to the rotor core. A replacement rotor, slip ring assembly should be fitted.

(c) STATOR
Testing

Equipment required: A 12-volt battery and 36 watt test lamp. A 110-volt a.c. supply and a 15 watt test lamp.

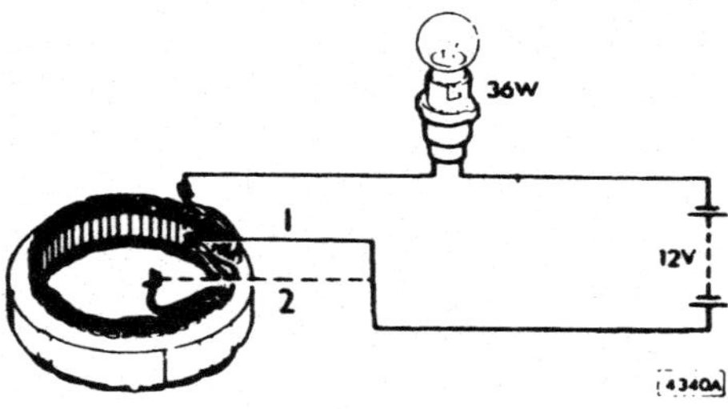

1 Check continuity of stator windings between any pair of wires by connecting in series a 12 volt battery and test lamp of not less than 36 watts. Failure of the test lamp to light means that part of the stator winding is open-circuit and a replacement stator must be fitted.

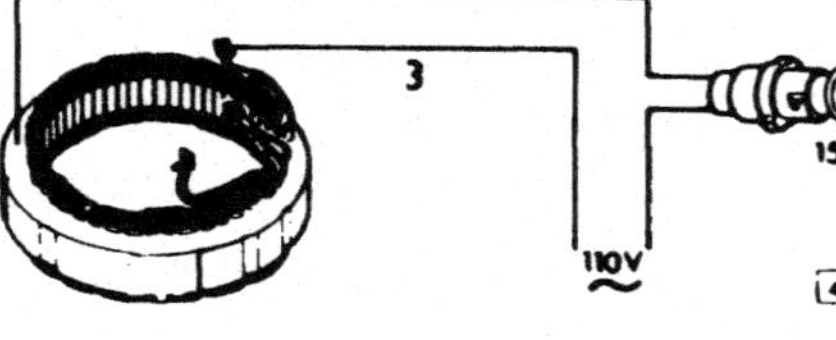

2 Test stator insulation with 110 volt test lamp. Connect test leads to laminated yoke and any one of the three stator cables. If the lamp lights, the stator coils are earthed. A replacement stator must be fitted.

(d) DIODES
Testing

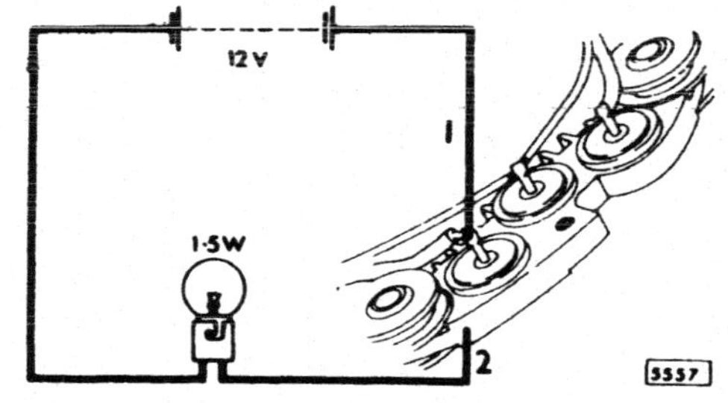

1 Connect one battery terminal to the heatsink under test.
2 Connect the other battery terminal in series with the test lamp and each diode pin in turn.
3 Reverse connections to heatsinks and diode pins. The lamp should light in one direction only. Should the lamp light in both tests, or not light at all the diode is defective and a new rectifier heatsink assembly must be fitted.

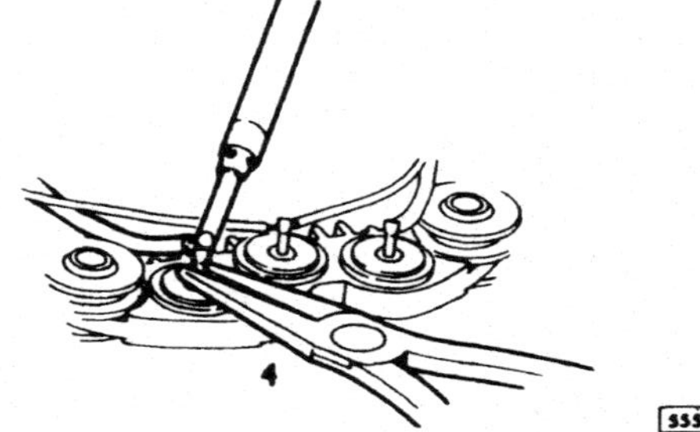

4 To prevent damage to diode assemblies during soldering operations it is important that a thermal shunt is used.

NOTE: Only 'M' grade 45–55 tin lead solder should be used.

Inspection and testing (Motorola 9 AR 2533 alternator) 86.10.14

Brush Gear and Slip Ring Inspection

Equipment required. Compressor spring testing gauge, range up to 250 g (½ lb.) 12 volt supply, test probes and indicator bulb, ohmmeter.

1 Remove alternator from car – 86.10.02.
2 Remove brush holder by carrying out operations 4 and 5 of Alternator overhaul, dismantling – 86.10.08.
3 Measure length of brushes protruding from housing; if either brush measures less than 4 mm. (0.15 in.) complete brush holder must be renewed.
4 Using push-type spring tension gauge, measure load required to press each brush face in turn flush with housing. If either reading is less than 120 g (4¼ oz.) complete brush holder must be renewed.
5 Using 12 volt supply, bulb and test probes, touch field lucar terminal (EX) with one probe and the adjacent brush with the other. Bulb should light and remain lit without flickering when brush is moved in holder.
6 Repeat operation 5 on second brush and negative terminal plate. Again, bulb should light and remain lit without flickering when brush is moved.
7 Touch each brush with one probe; bulb must not light or even flicker when brushes are moved.
NOTE: If failure is recorded in any of the tests made in operations 3 to 7 above, complete brush holder assembly must be renewed. Separate brushes and springs, etc., are not supplied as spares.

ROTOR

Testing

8 Connect ohmmeter in series with probes and touch each slip ring with one probe. Ohmmeter should record a resistance of between 3.8 and 5.2 ohms.
9 Touch alternator casing with one probe and each slip ring in turn with the other probe. Ohmmeter should indicate infinite resistance.

NOTE: Incorrect reading in operations 8 and 9 indicate defective wiring in field coils or between coils and slip rings; a low reading in operation 8 would imply shorting of the field coils, a high reading a wire breakage. Indication of any current flow in operation 9 implies a breakdown of insulation.
Rotor assembly must be removed for further inspection. Refer to operations 6 to 10 in 86.10.08 for removal, 10 and 11 below for further inspection and 24 to 29 in 86.10.08 for replacement of rotor in alternator casing.

10 Clean slip ring with a lint-free petrol-soaked cloth; wipe off any petrol adhering to rotor.
11 Using micrometer, measure diameter of both slip rings. Limits of diameter of newly fitted rings are 1.244 to 1.240 in. (31,6 to 31,5 mm.) for both rings, and rotor may not be refitted if diameter of either ring is less than 1.226 in. (31,15 mm.).
NOTE: Replacement of worn slip rings on Motorola alternators is possible but it is most strongly urged that this work should be entrusted to specialists equipped with the special tools required for the fitting and machining of slip rings.

STATOR

Testing

12 Visually inspect the portion of stator coils which can be seen through regulator housing for signs of damage due to overheating.
13 Check stator insulation by use of ohmmeter, touching one probe on alternator casing and the other on to each phase winding in turn. The phase windings are accessible to a probe through ventilation holes in rear moulded cover. If any current is shown to flow the stator insulation is defective and it must be removed – 86.10.08 operations 6 to 17.

DIODES

Testing

Equipment required: 12 V. supply, test probes and indicator bulb.

14 Remove diode bridge – 86.10.08, operations 1, 2, 3, 14 and 15.
15 Check positive diodes by connecting probe from indicator bulb to each phase terminal in turn, the second probe being in contact with terminal B +. Then reverse probes. Indicator bulb should only light in one direction of circuit; it it lights in both, diode is shorted, and if it does not light in either direction, diode is in open circuit. Complete diode bridge must then be renewed. Individual diodes are not supplied as spares.
CAUTION: Complete circuits for shortest possible time to avoid damage to diodes.
16 Check negative diodes similarly, but touching second probe on diode bridge, and again reversing probes. Indications should be as for operation 15.
17 Check field diodes by holding one probe in contact with D + terminal and second probe on each phase terminal, in turn. Then reverse probes and repeat. Indications should again be as in operation 15.

CONTROL UNIT

Remove and refit (Lucas 18ACR Alternators only) 86.10.26

Removing

1 Disconnect battery – 86.15.20.
2 Remove alternator – 86.10.02.
3 Remove alternator end cover by withdrawing two retaining screws.
4 Unsolder stator winding connections at rectifier diodes.
CAUTION: It is essential to use a thermal shunt and a lightweight soldering iron.

5 Note position of cables at rectifier plates and disconnect.
6 Remove three hexagon headed screws securing brush moulding and regulator to slip ring end bracket.
7 Remove brush gear and regulator from alternator.

Refitting

Reverse operations 1 to 7.

CONTROL UNIT

Remove and refit (Lucas 20ACR alternator) 86.10.26

Removing

1 Disconnect battery, see 86.15.20.
2 Remove alternator, see 86.10.02.
3 Remove alternator end cover by withdrawing two retaining screws.
4 Withdraw two retaining screws and remove brush gear moulding.
5 Disconnect control unit cables from brush retaining plates and '+' and output terminals.
6 Withdraw control unit retaining screw and remove unit.
NOTE: Retain insulating spacer from beneath control unit mounting flange.

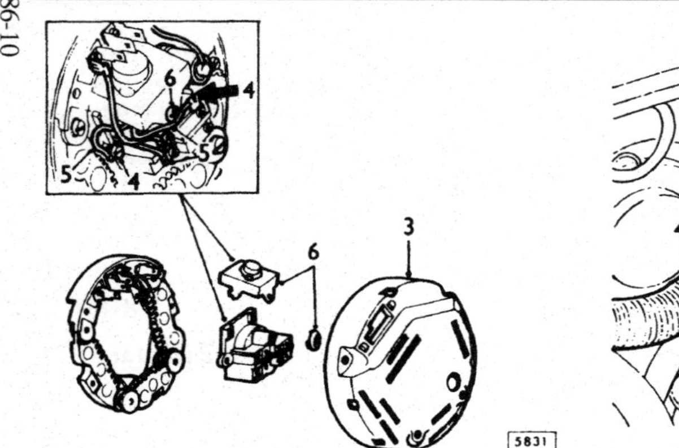

Refitting
Reverse operations 1 to 6.

NOTE: The aluminium casing of the control unit must not make contact with the alternator body; this would cause the field circuit to be fully switched on and the alternator to supply maximum output regardless of battery condition.

BATTERY 86.15.00

WARNING: THE BATTERY FITTED TO THIS VEHICLE HAS SPECIAL TOPPING UP FACILITIES. WHEN BATTERY CHARGING IS CARRIED OUT THE VENT COVER SHOULD BE LEFT IN POSITION ALLOWING GAS TO ESCAPE OR FLOODING OF ELECTROLYTE WILL RESULT.

Description
The battery is a special high performance type and is located in the engine compartment.

Data
Battery type: Lucas 12 volt 66 AH Pacemaker CP11.

BATTERY

Remove and refit 86.15.01

Removing
1 Ease back battery terminal covers, slacken pinch bolts and disconnect battery leads.
2 Disconnect snap connectors to battery cooling fan.
3 Slacken retaining bolts (these are hinged and fixed to battery tray).
4 Withdraw cooling inlet pipe from grommet fixing.
5 Release positive battery lead from clip on cooling jacket.
6 Ease battery and cooling jacket forward until clear of scuttle and lift jacket clear of battery.
7 Lift battery clear of car.

Refitting
Reverse operations 1 to 7. Smear terminals with petroleum jelly before re-connecting battery leads.

NOTE: The battery must be kept level at all times to prevent spillage of electrolyte, consequent damage to vehicle finish, and possible personal injury.

BATTERY

Test 86.15.02

It is NOT possible to test this battery with a high rate discharge meter, due to the location of the intercell connectors. The battery top must not be drilled in an attempt to locate the connectors. Check the specific gravity of the electrolyte in each cell using an hydrometer. A variation of more than 40 points (0.040) in any cell reading means that the battery is suspect and should be removed for testing by a battery agent. If possible prove the battery by substitution.

State of Charge – S.G. Readings
1 Lift and tilt the battery vent cover to one side.
2 Insert the hydrometer into each cell through the filling tube and note the readings.

	SPECIFIED GRAVITY READINGS CORRECTED TO 60°F (15°C)	
STATE OF CHARGE	CLIMATES NORMALLY Below 77°F (25°C)	CLIMATES NORMALLY Above 77°F (25°C)
FULLY CHARGED	1.270 – 1.290	1.210 – 1.230
70% CHARGED	1.230 – 1.250	1.170 – 1.190
DISCHARGED	1.100 – 1.120	1.050 – 1.070

Electrolyte Temperature Correction
For every 18°F (10°C) below 60°F (15°C) subtract 0.007.
For every 18°F (10°C) above 60°F (15°C) add 0.007.

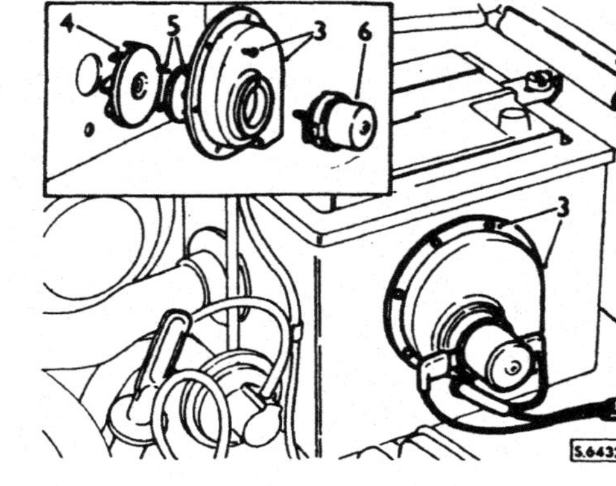

BATTERY COOLING FAN MOTOR

Remove and refit 86.15.03

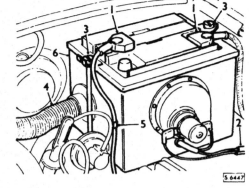

Removing
1 Disconnect battery – 86.15.20.
2 Remove battery cooling jacket – 86.15.01., Operations 1 to 6.
3 Withdraw seven securing screws and remove cooling fan assembly from cooling jacket.
4 Remove nylon impeller by carefully levering away from spindle with two screwdrivers, keeping impeller square to spindle.
5 Withdraw two screws from keep plate.
6 Remove motor from mounting grommet to duct.

Refitting
7 Spin motor to check that spindle and armature shaft are not distorted.
8 Reverse operations 5 and 6.
9 Carefully press impeller into position, using not more than 6 kg (14 lb) force on impeller.
10 Refit 'fir tree' retention piece in slot in armature shaft.
11 Reverse operations 1 to 3.
12 Connect 12-volt supply, and check for quiet running and absence of vibration.

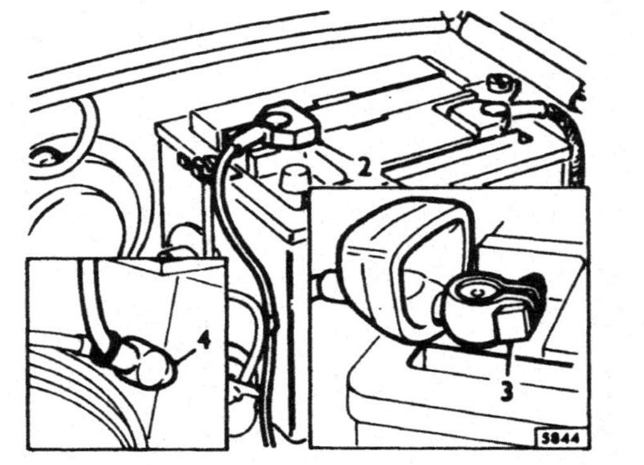

BATTERY LEAD – POSITIVE

Remove and refit 86.15.17

Removing
1 Raise bonnet.
2 Lift plastic cover from terminal on battery post.
3 Release clamp bolt and remove terminal from battery post.
4 Remove lead from terminal post located on upper right hand engine sub-frame member.

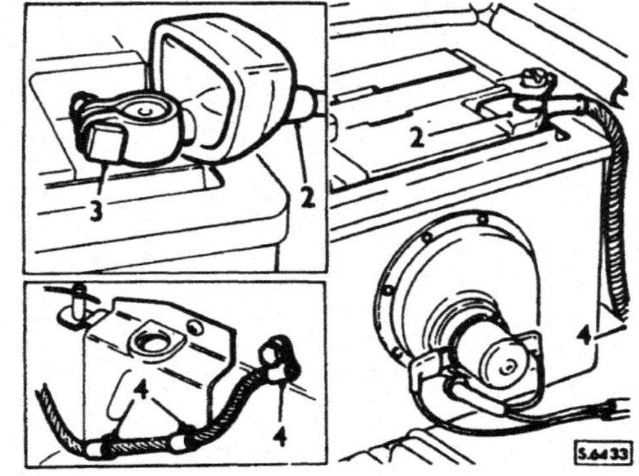

3 Release clamp bolt and remove terminal from battery post.
4 Remove lead from bulkhead, secured by two clips, setscrew and washer.

Refitting
Reverse operations 1 to 4.

NOTE: Ensure that all connections are clean and metal to metal. Protect the battery terminal with a smear of petroleum jelly. Tighten all fixings.

Refitting
Reverse operations 1 to 4.

NOTE: Ensure that all connections are clean and metal to metal. Protect the battery terminal with a smear of petroleum jelly. Tighten all fixings.

BATTERY LEAD – NEGATIVE

Remove and refit 86.15.19

Removing
1 Raise bonnet.
2 Lift plastic cover from terminal on battery post.

BATTERY TERMINALS

Disconnect 86.15.20

1 Ease back terminal insulated cover.
2 Slacken clamp bolt.
3 Lift connector from terminal post.

Reconnect
Reverse operations 1 to 3.

ELECTRICALLY OPERATED WINDOWS AND DOOR LOCKS

Description 86.25.00

The electrically operated window lift system comprises four motors, drivers and passengers control panels, relay and thermal overload cut out. The electrically operated door lock circuit comprises of a solenoid for each door lock, thermal overload relay, two relays and a selector switch mounted in the centre console escutcheon.

Operation
With the window lift master switch ON, operation of any of the centre 'off' two pole switches will cause the associated window lift motor to run in the selected direction. Selections can only be made on one switch at a time; the driver's window switch has first priority, followed by the front passenger's window switch, then the rear windows from the front panel, before the rear windows from the rear panel switches. The circuit is arranged so that the operation of each switch isolates the subsequent circuit, thus preventing operation of more than one motor at a time and protecting the circuit from an overload condition.

Fault conditions i.e. sticking windows, or overload will result in excessive current consumption causing the thermal cut out to operate. The cut out will reset after a short interval allowing normal operation of window lift motors to be resumed. If the condition persists a detailed examination of the system is required.

The door lock selector switch is of the centre 'off' rocker variety, operation in one direction locks the doors from inside, preventing access from outside when the car is occupied. An opposite selection on the switch will open the door locks. The door lock solenoids will remain in the last selected position when the switch is returned to the off position. Manual operation of the conventional door handles from inside the car will over-ride the door lock solenoids.

NOTE: Rapidly repeated operation of the door locks, or prolonged depression of any switch in either direction, will result in an overload condition, causing the thermal cut-out to operate, isolating the door lock solenoid circuit. A short wait is necessary before the thermal cut-out automatically resets.

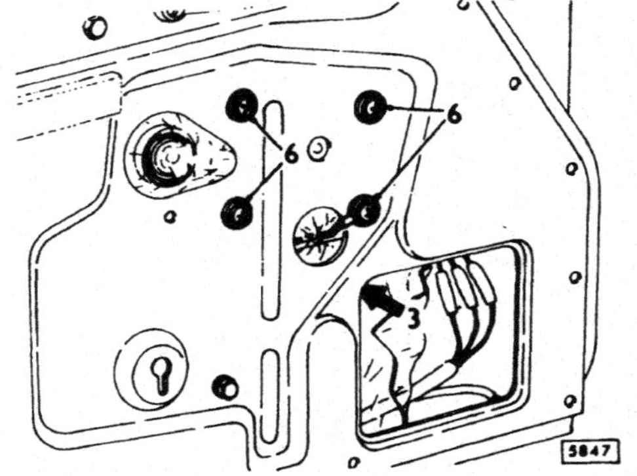

WINDOW LIFT MOTOR – FRONT

Remove and refit – 4 Door cars 86.25.01

Removing
1 Disconnect battery – 86.15.20.
2 Remove the door casing and arm rest – 76.34.01.
3 Disconnect the cables from motor at plug and socket connection.
4 Remove top bolt securing glass channel to door inner panel.
5 Remove four pan-headed setscrews and detach regulator mechanism from door panel.
6 Slide mechanism towards hinge face of door to clear the regulator arm roller from channel.
7 Lift regulator arm to pass the outer side of glass channel.
8 Remove the assembly through aperture in door inner panel.
9 Withdraw three setscrews and washers from regulator.

Refitting
Reverse operations 1 to 9.

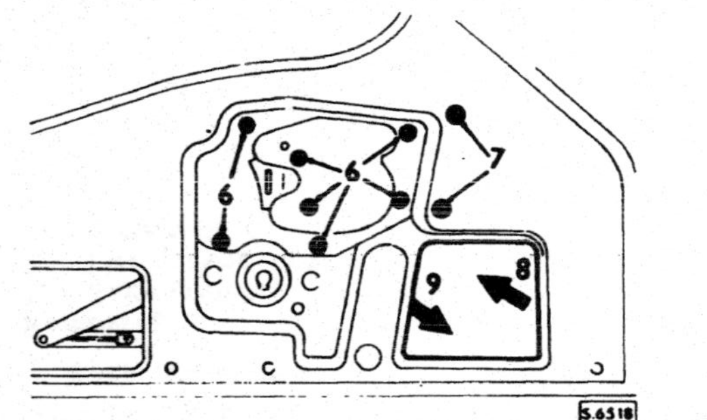

WINDOW LIFT MOTOR – FRONT

Remove and refit – 2 Door cars **86.25.01**

Removing

CAUTION: Before disengaging regulator from motor ensure that lifting arm and quadrant of regulator are clamped firmly together. This prevents spring from disengaging suddenly and causing possible damage or injury.

1 Remove arm rest and door trim panel.
2 Lower window to approximately 1 inch above door.
3 Disconnect battery – 86.15.20.
4 Remove two nuts securing window lift arm bobbin channel.
5 Slide channel off bobbin.
6 Remove seven set screws and 1 drive screw from regulator mounting plate.
7 Remove two set screws from motor mounting bracket.
8 Disconnect electrical cables.
9 Withdraw motor and regulator assembly through aperture.

Refitting
Reverse operations 1 to 9.

NOTE: If fitting a replacement motor, it should be noted that a right hand door window lift assembly has a left hand motor and vice versa.

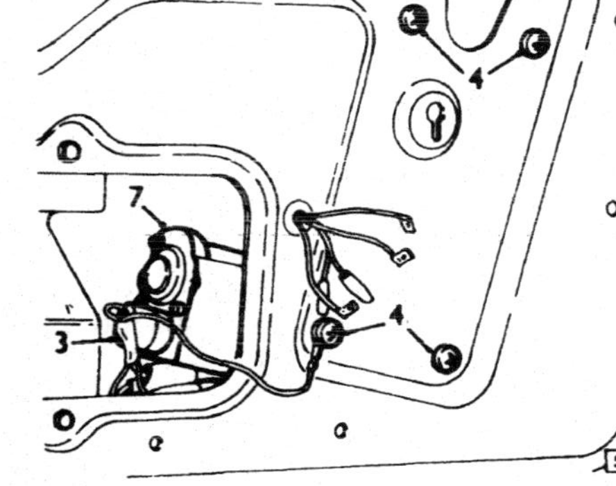

WINDOW LIFT MOTOR – REAR

Remove and refit – 4 Door cars **86.25.02**

Removing
1 Remove door casing and arm rest – 76.34.04.
2 Disconnect battery – 86.15.20.
3 Disconnect cables from motor at plug and socket connection.
4 Remove four pan-headed setscrews and detach regulator mechanism from door panel.
5 Adjust position of door until regulator arm can be removed from channel. Withdraw regulator through aperture in door.
6 If it is necessary, remove glass in order to withdraw regulator.
7 Withdraw three setscrews and washers and detach motor from regulator.
The motor is sealed during manufacture. Faulty units must be replaced, no service repair being possible.

Refitting
Reverse operations 1 to 7.

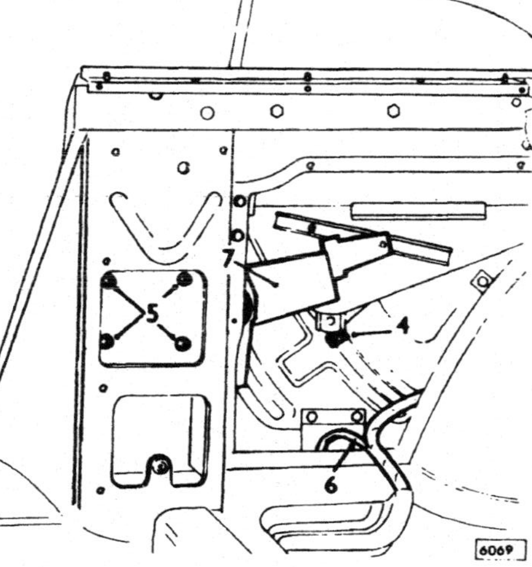

WINDOW LIFT MOTOR – REAR

Remove and refit – 2 Door cars **86.25.02**

Removing

CAUTION: Before disengaging regulator from motor ensure that lifting arm and quadrant of regulator are clamped firmly together. This prevents spring from disengaging suddenly and causing possible damage or injury.

1 Remove rear compartment side trim – 76.13.14.
2 Lower window until approximately horizontal.
3 Disconnect battery – 86.15.20.
4 Fit special tool JD47 to window guide channel.
5 Remove four set screws securing regulators to body side panel.
6 Disconnect cables.
7 Withdraw window motor and regulator assembly through aperture.

Refitting
Reverse operations 1 to 7

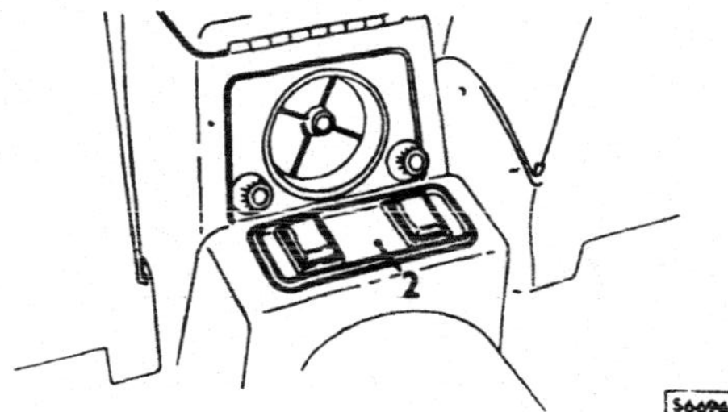

REAR SWITCH PANEL WINDOW LIFT SWITCH(ES)

Remove and refit **86.25.12**

Removing
1 Disconnect battery – 86.15.20.
2 Lever mounting panel from rear of centre console.
3 Carefully note position of cables and orientation of switch.
4 Disconnect cables
5 Depress locating tags and push switch through panel.

Refitting
Reverse operations 1 to 5.

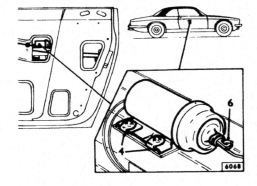

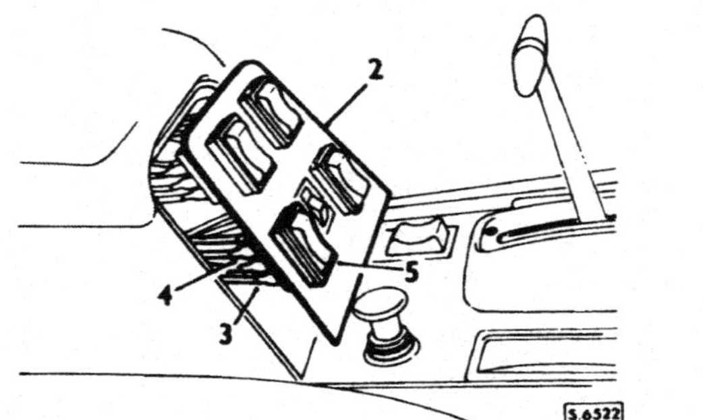

FRONT SWITCH PANEL WINDOW LIFT SWITCH(ES)

Remove and refit 86.25.13

Removing
1 Disconnect battery – 86.15.20.
2 Lever switch mounting panel from centre console.
3 Note position of cables and orientation of switch in panel.
4 Disconnect cables.
5 Depress locating tags and push switch through panel.

Refitting
Reverse operations 1 to 5.

NOTE: Care must be taken to ensure correct refitting of cables.

DOOR LOCK SELECTOR SWITCH

Remove and refit 86.25.14

Removing
1 Disconnect battery – 86.15.20.
2 Lever drivers window lift switch panel from centre console.

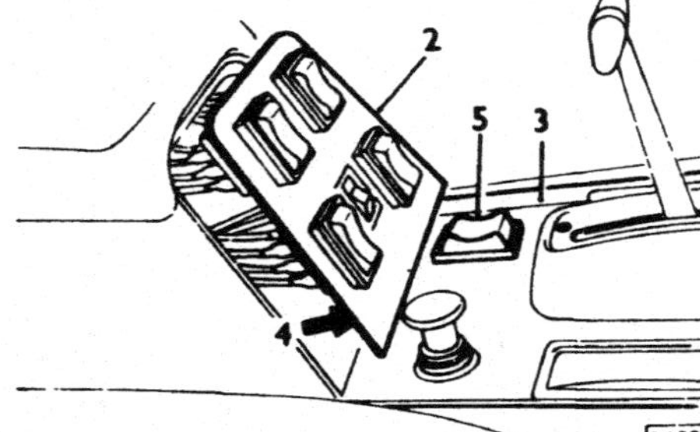

3 Remove two drive and one setscrew from centre console escutcheon.
4 Lift escutcheon, note position of cables and disconnect.
5 Depress locating tags and push switch through panel.

Refitting
Reverse operations 1 to 5.

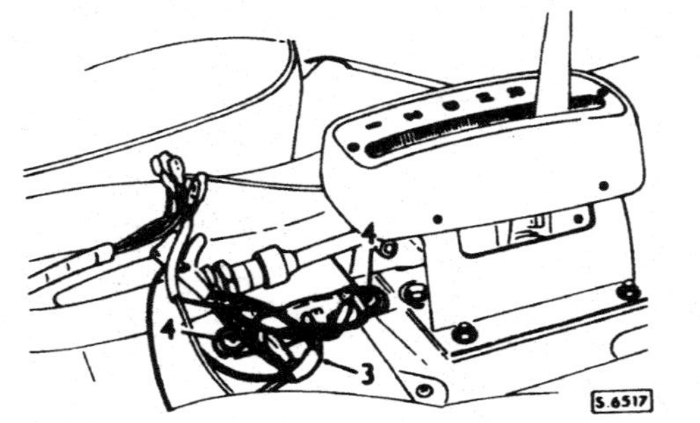

WINDOW LIFT RELAY

Remove and refit 86.26.28

Removing
1 Disconnect battery – 86.15.20.
2 Remove centre console escutcheon.
3 Note position of cables and disconnect.
4 Withdraw two retaining screws and remove relay from bracket attached to transmission selector quadrant.

Refitting
Reverse operations 1 to 4.

NOTE: Cylindrical 26RA relay is fitted to later cars.

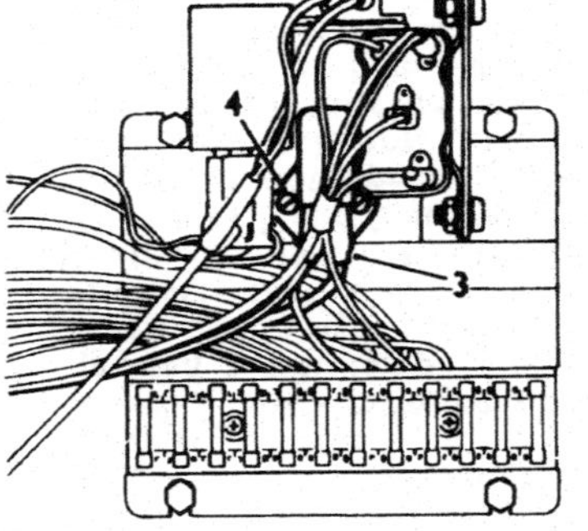

CIRCUIT BREAKERS

Remove and refit 86.25.31

Removing
1 Remove facia crash roll, see 76.46.04.
2 Remove driver's side dash liner, see 76.46.11.
3 Note position of cables and disconnect at Lucars on relevant circuit breaker.
4 Withdraw two screws securing unit to mounting plate.

Refitting
Reverse operations 1 to 4.

NOTE: Cylindrical 26RA relay replaces type illustrated on later cars.

DOOR LOCK SOLENOIDS

Remove and refit 86.25.32

Removing
1 Raise window to fully closed.
2 Disconnect battery – 86.15.20.
3 Remove arm rests and door trim – 76.34.01.

4 Remove two setscrews securing solenoid to door stretcher.
5 Disconnect cables at snap connectors.
6 Unhook solenoid operating piston from door lock push rod and remove from door.

Refitting
Reverse operations 1 to 6.

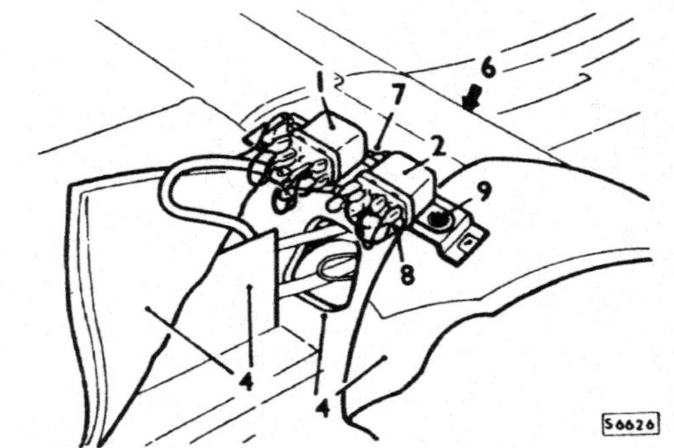

DOOR LOCK SOLENOID RELAYS

Remove and refit 86.25.33

Removing
1 Reconnect battery – 86.15.20.
2 Push left hand front seat forward to its full extent.
3 Remove rear seat cushion.

continued

4 Carefully pull carpet and sound insulation material away from transmission tunnel and front of box section supporting rear seat cushion.
5 Support relays through aperture in front of cross member.
6 Remove two screws from rear outside face of cross member which secure relay assembly.
7 Manoeuvre relay assembly through aperture.
8 Disconnect suspect relay harness at Lucar connectors.
9 Remove two nuts and shakeproof washers securing relay to bracket.

Refitting
Reverse operations 1 to 9.

Wiring delays – relay assembly

Connect cable harness to relay lucar connectors as in chart. Note shorting links.

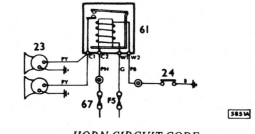

RELAY	TERMINAL	CABLE COLOUR
'1'	C1	ORANGE/RED
		BLACK
	C4	BLACK
	C2	BROWN/BLUE
		BROWN/BLUE
	W1	BLACK
		BLACK
	W2	ORANGE/RED
'2'	C1	ORANGE/GREEN
		BLACK
	C4	BLACK
	C2	BROWN/BLUE
	W1	BLACK
	W2	ORANGE/GREEN

HORNS

Description 86.30.00

Twin horns are fitted, mounted one each side of the engine block on early cars, and beneath the front bumper on later cars. Both horns operate simultaneously and are energised by a relay. The relay is connected to the battery through the ignition and switch so that the horns will only operate with ignition switched 'ON'.

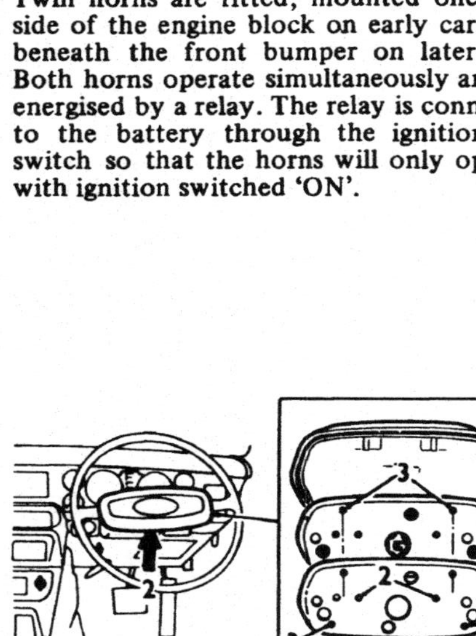

HORN PUSH

Remove and refit 86.30.01

Removing
1 Disconnect battery – 86.15.20.
2 Withdraw two screws from behind push and lift push from steering wheel.
3 Withdraw four screws from push backplate.
4 Ease trim pad from push and recover push contact unit.

Refitting
Reverse operations 1 to 4. Do not overtighten screws removed in operation 2.

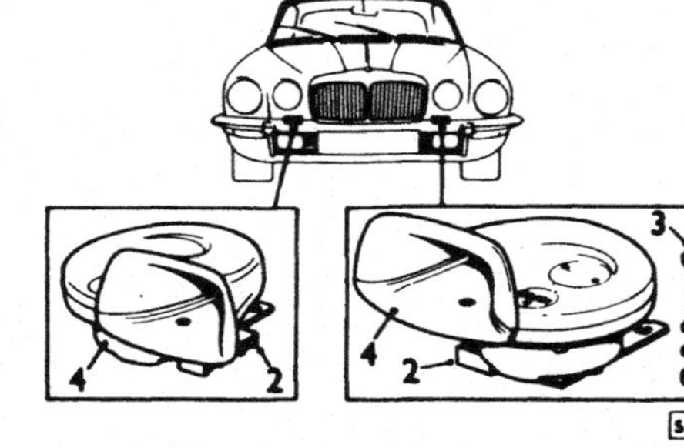
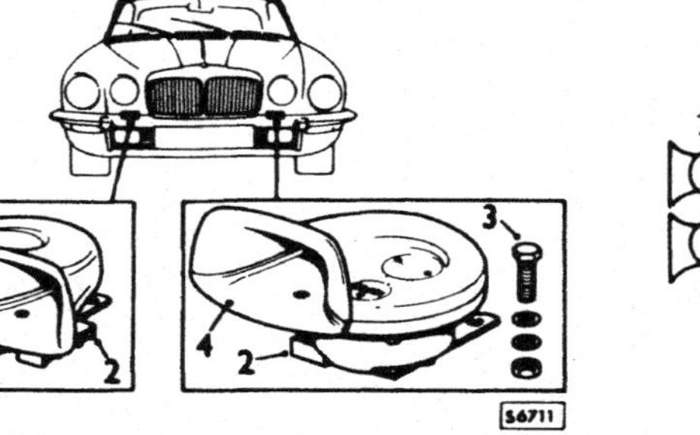

HORNS

Remove and refit 86.30.09

Removing
1 Disconnect battery – 86.15.20.
2 Disconnect wiring at Lucar connectors.
3 Withdraw retaining bolt and washers.
4 Remove horn.

Refitting
Reverse operations 1 to 4.

HORN RELAY CIRCUIT

Check in situ 86.30.17

1 Switch ignition 'ON'.

NOTE: Avoid leaving ignition 'On' for extended periods.

2 With ignition 'On', a 12V test lamp between W1 and earth should light up. If lamp does not light check Fuse No.1. Horn push on, test lamp on W2 – if test lamp fails to light an unserviceable relay is indicated.
3 If relay operates when horn push is pressed a test lamp between C1 and earth should light up. Failure to do so indicates that relay contacts are inoperative or fuse No.4 unserviceable.
4 If checks 1 and 2 are satisfactory and horns do not operate substitute test lamp for each horn in turn. If lamp lights, horn units are unserviceable. If lamp does not light, further investigation of the horn harness will be required.

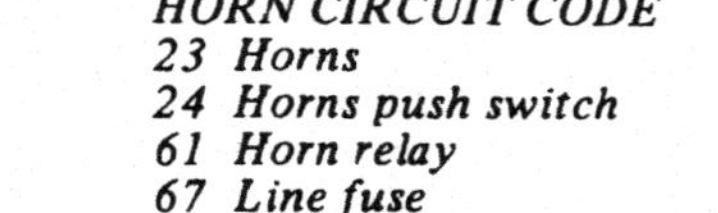

HORN CIRCUIT CODE
23 Horns
24 Horns push switch
61 Horn relay
67 Line fuse

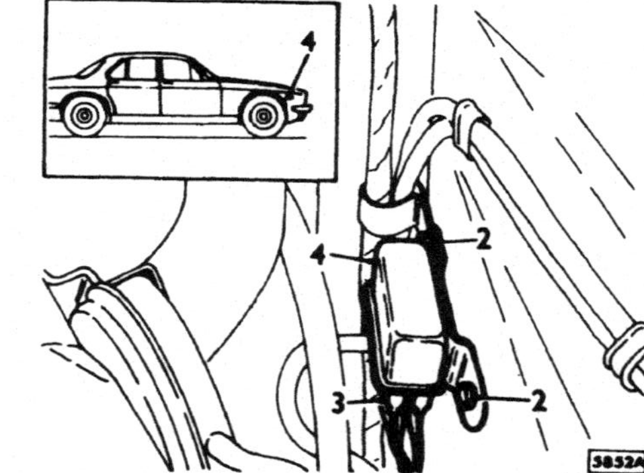

HORN RELAY

Remove and refit 86.30.18

Removing
1 Disconnect battery – 86.15.20.
2 Remove two securing nuts and lock washers.
3 Disconnect cables from lucar connectors. Note positions of cables.
4 Remove relay.

NOTE: Later cars are fitted with cylindrical relays in place of rectangular relay shown. Ensure that Lucars are correctly connected.

Refitting
Reverse operations 1 to 4. Ensure that cables are re-connected correctly – refer to wiring diagram if in doubt.

THE IGNITION SYSTEM 86.35.00

General
The ignition system comprises of a conventional high tension coil and distributor providing high tension sparking to a plug in each cylinder head. The distributor is a Lucas type 22D6 on early cars and type 45D6 on later cars.

A ballast resistor is fitted in the ignition coil circuit and has a similar resistance to that of the coil. This reduces the inductive resistance of the coil primary winding resulting in better high speed performance of the ignition coil. The coil fitted with this system is not interchangeable with normal 6 or 12 volt coils, and performance testing of the coil must be carried out in conjunction with the ballast resistor in circuit.

4.2 litre cars to Emission 'A' specification, this is, cars intended for use in North America, Canada, Sweden, Japan and Australia (the latter only after 1st January 1976) are equipped with Lucas Opus ignition systems, in which mechanical contact-breakers are replaced by electronic triggering devices.

The distributor, which is Lucas type 45DE6 (or 43DE6, for California only) differs externally from a mechanical contact-breaker unit by the presence of a rectangular block containing oscillator and amplifier, attached to its side by three setscrews, two of which serve as hinge pins for cover retaining clips; the third setscrew is adjacent to the clamp plate screw. Distributor cap and centrifugal advance mechanism are identical with those of 45D6 distributor.

A vacuum advance capsule is fitted only to 45DE6 distributors; it is retained to the oscillator and amplifier housing by a roll pin and operates in the usual manner, advancing ignition by rotating a moveable base plate carrying the electronic pick up unit, which replaces the fixed contact point of a mechanical contact breaker.

An additional component which is essential for the correct functioning of the Opus system is a drive resistor, wired in conjunction with the transistor in the amplifier. It is located on the coil mounting plate stud adjacent to the distributor, and shares its power supply with the ballast resistor (for the coil) to which it is connected by a white lead.

IGNITION SYSTEM DATA

Distributor – Type 22D6 or 45D6 (clockwise rotation viewed on driven end)

Compression ratio	'L', 'S' or 'H'.
Distributor contact breaker gap	0.014 in.–0.016 in. (0,36–0,41 mm.)
Spark plug type	Champion N11Y
Spark plug gap	0.025 in. (0,64 mm.)
Ignition timing (static)	
'S' comp. ratio	8° B.T.D.C.
'H' comp. ratio	8° B.T.D.C.
'L' comp. ratio (USA/Canada only)	8° B.T.D.C.

Distributor – Type 45DE6 or 43DE6

As above for Type 22D6 or 45D6 except air gap of 0.014 in.–0.016 in. (0,36–0,41 mm.) replaced contact breaker gap.

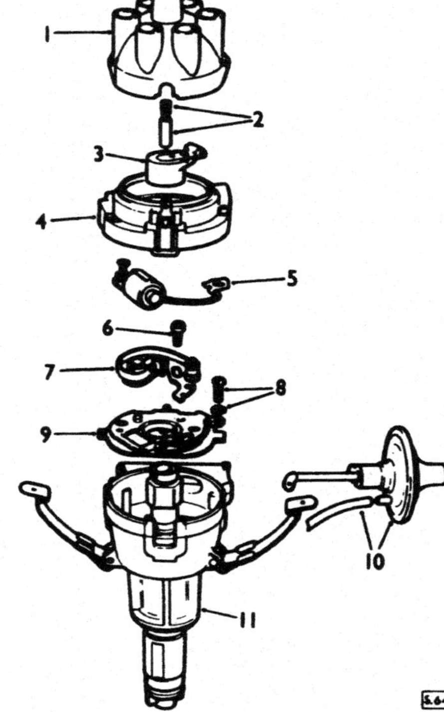
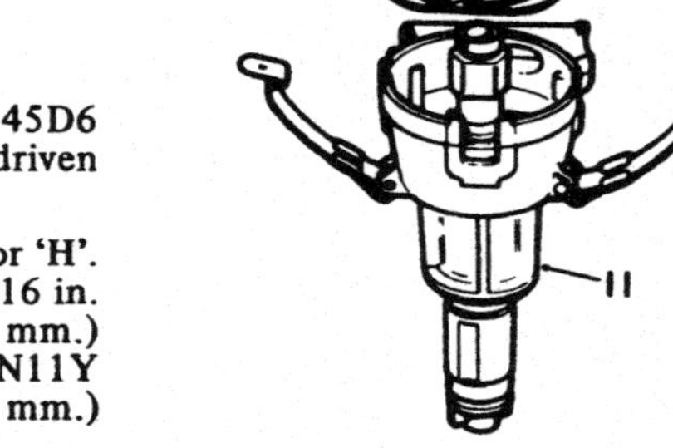

KEY TO DISTRIBUTOR DIAGRAM (22D6 and 45D6)

1. Distributor cap.
2. Centre contact.
3. Rotor arm.
4. Waterproof cap and L.T. connector.
5. Condenser.
6. Contact breaker set retaining screw.
7. Contact breaker set.
8. Contact breaker set carrier plate retaining screws and shakeproof washers.
9. Contact breaker set carrier plate.
10. Vacuum operated capsule and vacuum line.
11. Distributor body.

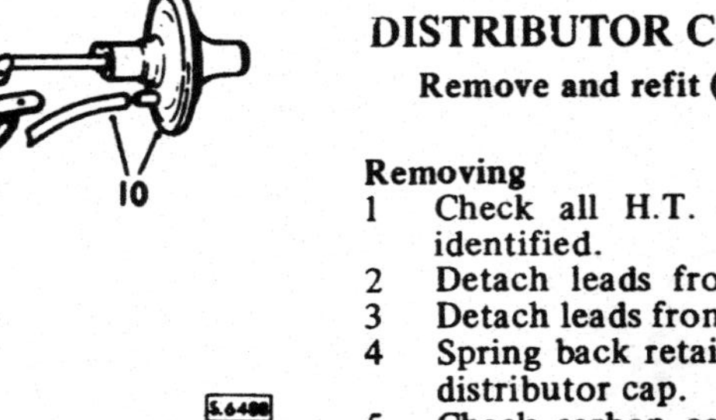

DISTRIBUTOR CAP

Remove and refit (all distributors) 86.35.10

Removing
1. Check all H.T. leads are adequately identified.
2. Detach leads from spark plugs.
3. Detach leads from H.T. coil.
4. Spring back retaining clips and lift off distributor cap.
5. Check carbon contact is in good condition and moving freely against spring.

Refitting
Reverse operations 1 to 5.

CONDENSER (22D6 & 45D6 distributors only)

Remove and refit 86.35.12

Removing
1. Disconnect battery – 86.15.20.
2. Remove distributor cap – 85.35.10/2.
3. Remove rotor arm – 86.35.16/2.

continued

4 Withdraw crosshead screw securing condenser to contact mounting plate.
5 Remove nut securing contact arm to mounting post.
6 Lift off waterproof contact cover.
7 Remove condenser cable end from post and remove condenser.

Refitting
Reverse operations 1 to 7.

CONTACT BREAKER GAP (22D6 & 45D6 distributors only)

Adjust 86.35.14

1 Disconnect battery – 86.15.20.
2 Remove distributor cap – 86.35.10.
3 Remove rotor arm – 86.35.16.
4 Turn engine until contacts show maximum opening (as operating heel is on high point of cam).
5 Check gap is between 0.014 in. to 0.016 in. (0,35 – 0,44 mm) with feeler gauge. If not, slacken contact plate securing screw.
6 Insert screwdriver into slot between fixed and moving contact plates and adjust gap to correct limits.
7 Tighten fixed contact plate securing screw and recheck gap.
8 Refit rotor arm and distributor cap.

IGNITION TIMING

Adjust (45DE6 and 43DE6 distributors only) 86.35.15

1 Remove distributor cap.
2 Remove flashover shield.
3 Rotate engine until rotor arm approaches No. 6 (front) cylinder segment in distributor cap.
4 Slowly rotate engine until ignition timing scale on crankshaft damper is at the appropriate number of degrees (see 'General Data') at pointer on lower left-hand side of timing chain cover.
5 Slacken distributor pinch bolt and rotate distributor body so that pick-up is lined up with nearest ferrite rod in the timing rotor.
6 Switch on ignition.
7 Position distributor cap end of centre high tension lead approximately 0.025 in. (0,64 mm.) from a good earth point on the engine and rotate distributor body slowly until a spark between high tension lead and ground occurs.
8 Tighten distributor pinch bolt.
9 Switch off ignition.
10 Check ignition timing by repeating operations 3 to 7.
11 Refit flashover shield, distributor cap and centre high tension lead.
12 Check advance and retard characteristics by means of suitable electronic equipment.
13 If necessary, carry out an exhaust emission test.

ROTOR ARM

Remove and refit 86.35.16

Removing
1 Spring back retaining clips and lift off distributor cap.
2 Lift off rotor arm.

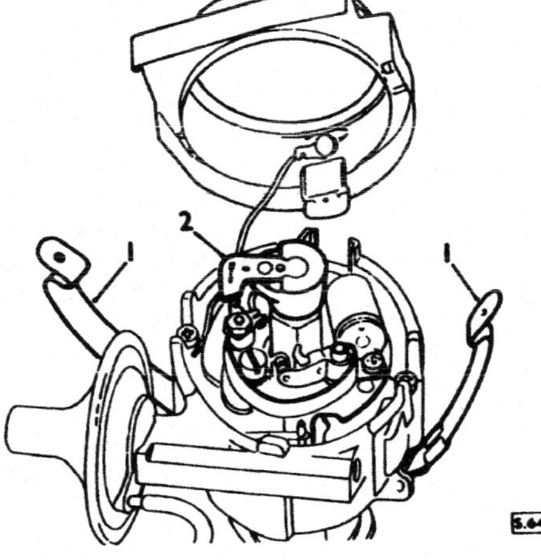

Refitting
3 Inject a few drops of thin machine oil into rotor arm spindle.
4 Replace rotor arm, ensure keyway engaged and rotor pushed fully home.
5 Refit distributor cap.

ELECTRONIC TIMING ROTOR

Remove and refit 86.35.17

Removing
1 Disconnect battery – 86.15.20.
2 Remove distributor cap – 86.35.10.
3 Remove rotor arm – 86.35.16.
4 Detach external circlip beneath rotor.
5 Lift timing rotor off distributor shaft; collect washer and O-ring.

Refitting
6 Place timing rotor on distributor shaft, ensuring that master projection at its lower end engages with master recess in shaft.
7 Fit new O-ring over shaft and replace washer.
8 Reverse operations 1 to 4.

PICK-UP MODULE

Remove and refit 86.35.18

NOTE: The pick up module is not supplied as a separate item, but as a sub-assembly, wired to the amplifier unit. To remove and refit this sub-assembly see 86.35.30.

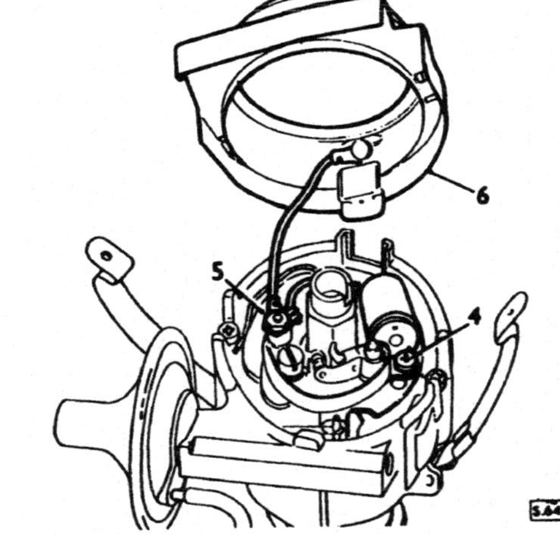

WATERPROOF COVER AND L.T. CONNECTOR

Remove and refit 86.35.19

Removing
1 Disconnect battery – 86.15.20.
2 Remove distributor cap – 86.35.10.
3 Remove rotor arm – 86.35.16.
4 Withdraw crosshead screws securing condenser to contact mounting plate.
5 Remove nut securing contact arm to contact mounting post.
6 Lift off waterproof contact cover.

Refitting
Reverse operations 1 to 6.

DISTRIBUTOR

Remove and refit, 22D6 distributor 86.35.20

Removing

1 Disconnect battery – 86.15.20.
2 Spring back retaining clips and remove distributor cap.
3 Disconnect low tension wire from distributor.
4 Disconnect vacuum pipe.
5 Withdraw setscrew plain and spring washer from retaining plate and withdraw distributor.

NOTE: Do not disturb clamp plate pinch bolt.

Refitting

Reverse operations 1 to 5.

NOTE: If clamp plate has been slackened and it is necessary to re-time ignition refer to 'General Specification Data' section 05, for relevant figures.

DISTRIBUTOR

Remove and refit, 45D6, 45DE6 and 43DE6 distributors 86.35.20

Follow operating procedure detailed above for 22D6 distributor (omitting operation 4 for 43D6 distributor) but retime ignition after refitting, even if clamp plate has not been slackened. Refer to 'General Specification Data', section 05, for static setting figure and 86.35.15 for details of timing setting.

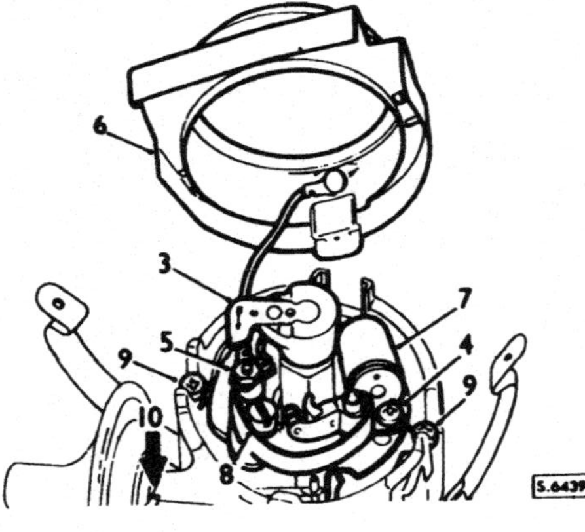

DISTRIBUTOR

Overhaul, 22D6 distributor 86.35.26

Dismantling

1 Disconnect battery – 86.15.20.
2 Remove distributor – 86.35.20
3 Lift off rotor arm.
4 Withdraw crosshead screw securing condenser to contact mounting plate.
5 Remove nut securing contact arm to contact assembly mounting post.
6 Lift off waterproof cover.
7 Remove condenser.
8 Withdraw securing screw and remove contact set.
9 Withdraw two screws and remove contact breaker base plate by lifting advance capsule operating arm from spigot and lifting plate from distributor body.
10 Using a pin punch .073 in. (1,85 mm) in diameter drive out roll pin securing vacuum unit to distributor body.

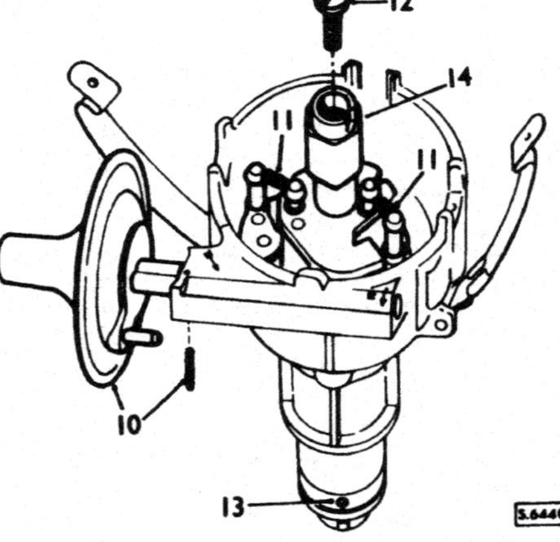

11 Remove advance weight springs.
12 Remove cam fixing screw from top of shaft, lift out cam assembly and auto-advance weights.

NOTE: Mark position of offset driving tongues in relation to rotor arm, keyway in shaft.

13 Clamp shank of distributor and drive out mills pin from driving dog using pin punch 0.187 in. (4,76 mm) diameter.
14 Remove shaft and action plate assembly from distributor body.

Reassembling

15 Apply clean engine oil to shaft and insert shaft and action plate assembly into distributor body.
16 Ensure thrust washer is fitted to shaft between driving dog and distributor shank.
17 If fitting a new driving dog it is necessary to carry out the following procedure.
(a) Position dog on shaft with driving tongues in correct position in relation to rotor arm keyway.
(b) Insert a 0.005 in. (0,12 mm) feeler gauge between thrust washer and driving dog.
(c) Using hole in driving dog as a guide pass 0.187 in. (4,76 mm) drill through shaft and other side of driving dog.
(d) Remove feeler gauge and insert 0.187 in. (4,76 mm) diameter mills pin
(e) Lightly rivet both ends of pin.
18 Smear auto advance mechanism with 'Rocol' grease.
19 Reverse operations 3 to 12.
20 Apply a few drops of Ragosine Molybdenised non-creep oil to top of shaft. Smear cam with clean engine oil. Apply one drop of clean engine oil to contact breaker pivot post and felt oiler pad of vacuum unit operating rod.
21 Set contact breaker gap to 0.014 in. – 0.016 in. (0,36 – 0,4 mm) – 86.35.14.
22 Clean distributor cap with soft clean cloth, check carbon brush and spring and refit cover.
23 Refit distributor.

DISTRIBUTOR

Overhaul 45D6 distributor 86.35.26

Dismantling

1 Disconnect battery – 86.15.20.
2 Remove distributor – 86.35.20.
3 Lift off rotor arm.
4 Withdraw Phillips head screw securing condenser to base plate.
5 Remove low tension and condenser leads from contact assembly mounting post.
6 Remove condenser.
7 Withdraw securing screw and remove contact set.
8 Withdraw low tension lead and grommet from locating hole on distributor body.
9 Withdraw earth lead from base plate.
10 Remove screws and shakeproof washers securing vacuum capsule, push actuating rod downwards to disengage.
11 Lever base plate upwards.
12 Clamp shank of distributor and drive out dowel pin from drive dog using pin punch 0.187 in. (4,76 mm.) diameter.
13 Withdraw drive dog and thrust washer.
14 Remove shaft and action plate assembly from distributor body.
15 Remove and discard 'O' ring.

continued

Reassembling

NOTE: If distributor shaft, action plate or spindle bush are found to be excessively worn, these components must be renewed together as a complete unit.

16 Apply clean engine oil to shaft and insert shaft and action plate assembly into distributor body.
17 Ensure thrust washer is fitted to shaft between driving dog and distributor shank.
18 To fit a new drive dog, carry out items 19 to 23.
19 Position dog on shaft with driving tongues in correct position relative to keyway in rotor arm.
20 Insert a 0.005 in. (0,12 mm.) feeler gauge between thrust washer and drive dog.
21 Using hole in drive dog as a guide, pass 0.187 in. (4,76 mm.) drill through shaft and other side of dog.
22 Remove feeler gauge and insert 0.187 in. (4,76 mm.) diameter dowel pin.
23 Lightly rivet both ends of pin.
24 Smear automatic advance mechanism with Rocol MP oil.
25 Reverse operations 3 to 11.
26 Sparingly apply clean engine oil to felt pad in top of cam. Apply oil sparingly through two apertures in contact breaker base plate.
   NOTE: Do not oil felt pad fitted to contact breaker.
27 Smear Shell Retinax 'A' grease on working surface of cam.
28 Set contact breaker gap to 0.014 ins.– 0.016 in. (0,35 mm.–0,40 mm.) – 86.35.14.
29 Clean distributor cap with clean, soft cloth, check carbon brush and spring for free movement; refit cover.
30 Refit distributor.

DISTRIBUTOR

Overhaul, 45DE6 and 43DE6 Distributors 86.35.26

Dismantling

1 Disconnect battery – 86.15.20.
2 Remove distributor – 86.35.20.
3 Lift off rotor arm.
4 Remove plastic anti-flash shield and lift out felt pad (if fitted) from distributor shaft. Do not remove flanged nylon bush.
5 Carefully remove two screws, with washers and lock washers, securing pick up to movable plate.
6 Remove two long screws and spring washers securing amplifier housing to distributor body.
7 Holding amplifier housing, remove its third retaining screw and spring washer from beneath housing.
8 Holding distributor body in one hand and amplifier housing in the other, carefully disengage vacuum advance unit link from pin in movable plate.
   NOTE: This operation does not apply to 43DE6 distributors.
9 Ease grommet from distributor wall and remove amplifier housing and pick up, with connecting lead. Collect spring clips.
10 Tap out roll pin securing vacuum advance unit (45DE6 distributor only) and withdraw unit.
11 Remove external circlip from distributor shaft.
12 Carefully withdraw timing rotor, and remove washer and O-ring from it.
13 Remove two Phillips-head screws and lift out base plate, with movable plate attached to it.
14 Detach springs from centrifugal advance unit. Take great care to avoid distorting them, and note the positions of the two different springs.
   NOTE: Further dismantling of unit is not recommended.

Assembling

15 Lubricate moving surfaces of centrifugal advance mechanism with Rocol M.P. or similar molybdenised grease.
16 Refit springs as removed in operation 14, again using great care to avoid distorting them.
   NOTE: If either spring should be accidentally distorted it must not be refitted, as emission control could be affected; renew both springs.
17 Smear movable plate pin of 45DE6 distributor with molybdenised grease and replace sub-assembly of plates in distributor body. Secure with two Phillips-head screws.
   NOTE: It is possible to replace sub-assembly 180° out of position. This is of no consequence on 43DE6 distributor, but inspect through hole for advance link in 45DE6 body to ensure that pin is correctly located to pick up link.
18 Replace two spring clips removed in operation 9 in C-shaped lugs on distributor body.
19 45DE6 distributors only. Replace vacuum advance unit in amplifier housing and secure with roll pin.
20 45DE6 distributor only; ensure that lower grommet is in position in amplifier housing, and that lead to pick up is outside top of housing. Holding housing in one hand and distributor body in the other, rotate movable plate fully clockwise and carefully hook advance link over pin; this operation is not visible.
21 Fit grommets fully into slots in amplifier housing and distributor body and replace three screws and spring washers securing housing to body. Tighten screws evenly.
22 Carefully replace timing rotor on distributor shaft, ensuring that large master projection engages with large slot in shaft.
23 Place new O-ring over shaft and secure rotor with washer and circlip.
24 Place pick up in position, and insert two screws, with washers and lock washers. Do not fully tighten screws.
25 Adjust pick up air gap. – 86.35.31.
26 Insert felt pad, if removed in operation 4.
27 Lubricate with a few drops of engine oil on pad (or nylon bush) and through apertures to lubricate centrifugal advance unit; apply one drop only to each of the two D-shaped holes at movable plate pivot.
28 Replace anti-flash cover, with recesses adjacent to spring clips.
29 Press rotor on to the shaft and ensure that it is fully engaged with slot.
30 Replace cover.

THE IGNITION SYSTEM

Checking 86.35.29

CAUTION: Ignition coils normally operated with ballast resistors should not be connected direct to full battery voltage without the ballast resistor in circuit.

EQUIPMENT REQUIRED:
DC Moving coil voltmeter
0-26V Scale
Hydrometer
Ohmmeter
H.T. Jumper lead

Preliminary procedure.

(a) **BATTERY** 86.35.29/1

Test

It is NOT possible to test this battery with a high rate discharge meter, due to the location of the intercell connectors. The battery top must not be drilled in an attempt to locate the connectors. Check the specific gravity of the electrolyte in each cell using an hydrometer. A variation of more than 40 points (0.040) in any cell reading means that the battery is suspect and should be removed for testing by a battery agent. If possible prove the battery by substitution.

State of Charge – S.G. Readings

1 Lift and tilt the battery vent cover to one side.

2 Insert the hydrometer into each cell through the filling tube and note the readings.

	SPECIFIC GRAVITY READINGS CORRECTED TO 60°F (15°C)	
STATE OF CHARGE	CLIMATES NORMALLY Below 77°F (25° C)	CLIMATES NORMALLY Above 77°F (25°C)
FULLY CHARGED	1.270 – 1.290	1.210 – 1.230
70% CHARGED	1.230 – 1.250	1.170 – 1.190
DISCHARGED	1.100 – 1.120	1.050 – 1.070

Electrolyte Temperature Correction

For every 18°F (10°C) below 60°F (15°C) subtract 0.007
For every 18°F (10°C) above 60°F (15°C) add 0.007

(b) Ensure that spark plugs are checked and that fuel is available before commencing tests on the ignition system.
(c) Check all electrical connections for security and cleanliness.
(d) **Check supply to 'SW' or '+ve' coil terminal.**

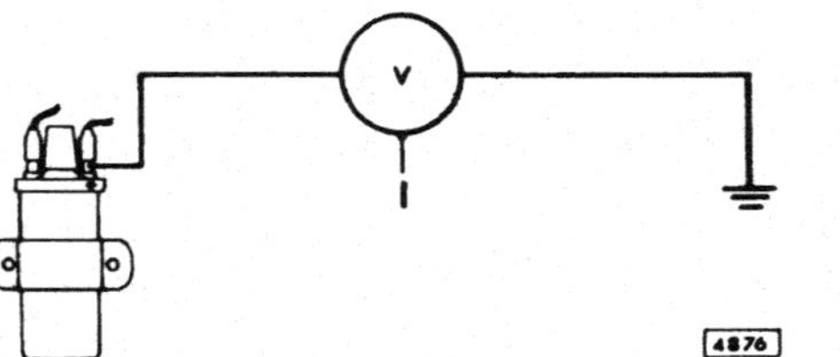

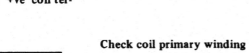

1 Connect voltmeter between coil and earth. Black lead to a good earth and Red lead to the 'SW' (+ve) terminal of the coil.
2 Close distributor contact points, switch on ignition. Meter will register battery voltage*, if the supply line is in order.

* With ballasted ignition system meter reading will be approximately 6 volts.

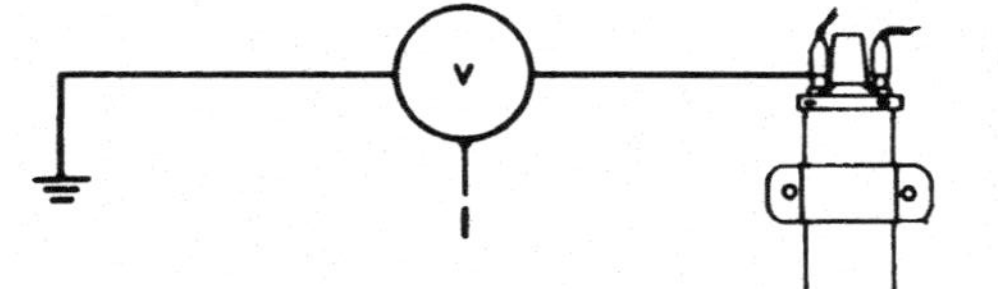

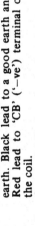

Check coil primary winding 86.35.29/2

1 Connect voltmeter between coil and earth. Black lead to a good earth and Red lead to 'CB' ('–ve') terminal of the coil.
2 Open distributor contact points and switch on ignition. Meter will read battery volts, if primary winding is satisfactory.
A zero reading* may indicate open-circuited primary winding, short-circuited capacitor or the 'CB' ('–ve') line is earthed.

* With ballasted ignition system may also indicate open-circuit or short to earth on the ballast resistor.

Check distributor contacts and CB Earth 86.35.29/3

1 Leave voltmeter as in – 86.35.29/2.
2 Switch on ignition, close distributor contacts. Meter should read zero, if circuit is satisfactory.
A high reading indicates poor C.B. earth or dirty contact points.

Check coil secondary winding and capacitor 86.35.29/4

1 Disconnect H.T. cable from coil at the distributor.
2 Hold free end about 0.25 in. (6 mm) from engine block. Switch on ignition, flick the contact points. A good H.T. spark between the cable end and engine block indicates that the circuit is satisfactory.
No spark probably indicates that the H.T. cable is broken, (check with jumper H.T. cable), or faulty capacitor. Proceed to 86.35.29/5.

Check capacitor by substitution 86.35.29/5

1 Disconnect existing capacitor at the contact breaker.
2 Connect test capacitor between L.T. terminal of the distributor and a good earth.
3 Hold free end of H.T. cable 0.25 in. (6mm) from engine block. Switch on ignition, flick open contact points.
If a good H.T. spark is produced, the original capacitor is probably faulty. No spark indicates that the coil secondary winding is faulty.

Check rotor arm insulation 86.35.29/6

1 Hold free end of H.T. cable about 0.125 in. (3 mm) from rotor arm electrode.
2 With ignition on, flick open contact points. No spark proves that the insulation of the rotor arm is satisfactory.

Check contact point gap setting 86.35.29/7

1 Rotate engine until contacts are open to widest extent.
2 Correct gap should be 0.014 in. – 0.016 in. (0,35 mm – 0,40 mm). Check gap with all camp lobes.

Visual check of H.T. cables and Distributor cover 86.35.29/8

1 **H.T. cables should be clean. Remove oil and grease deposits. Worn or perished cables should be replaced.**
2 Distributor cover should be clean inside and out.
3 H.T. carbon brush should move freely against spring pressure in its holder. Ensure brush makes contact with the rotor arm.
4 If distributor cover electrodes are badly pitted, the cover should be replaced. Excessive carbon deposits on the electrodes must be removed.

OPUS IGNITION SYSTEM

Check 86.35.29/9

Before checking ignition system to locate cause of misfiring or failure to start, ensure that fuel supply is satisfactory.
CAUTION; The two following precautions MUST be observed or damage may be caused to the ignition system.

1 Never connect white leads with blue or black sleeve to positive supply.
2 Always ensure that ignition is 'OFF' when setting air gaps at timing rotor with feeler gauge.

TRAINING SYSTEM IN CAR TO LOCATE CAUSE OF MISFIRE

Check in the order given below, correcting any fault found before proceeding with the next test.

1 Check all connections. Ensure HT leads are a tight fit inside chimneys and ascertain all LT connections are clean and tight.
2 Test spark plugs and check gaps.

continued

3 Check HT leads. Inspect for sign of tracking, broken or damaged cables etc.
4 Check distributor cover for signs of tracking inside and out. Clean and examine HT brush, electrodes etc.
5 Check rotor arm for tracking.
6 Check pick-up/timing rotor air gap (ensure ignition is switched off).
7 Check coil chimney for signs of tracking etc.
8 Substitute ignition coil.
9 Substitute amplifier unit.

TESTING TO LOCATE CAUSE OF FAILURE TO START.

Equipment required: D.C. Moving coil voltmeter, 0-20V scale, hydrometer, ohmmeter and H.T. jumper lead.
Refer to adjoining chart and check each item in turn, rectifying any fault found before proceeding to the next item.

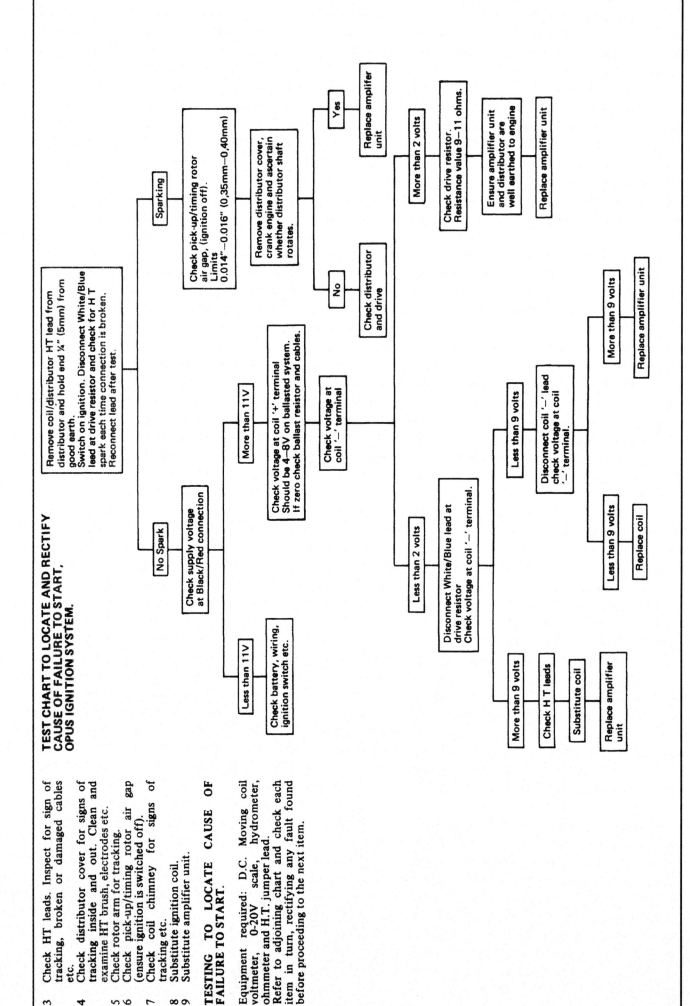

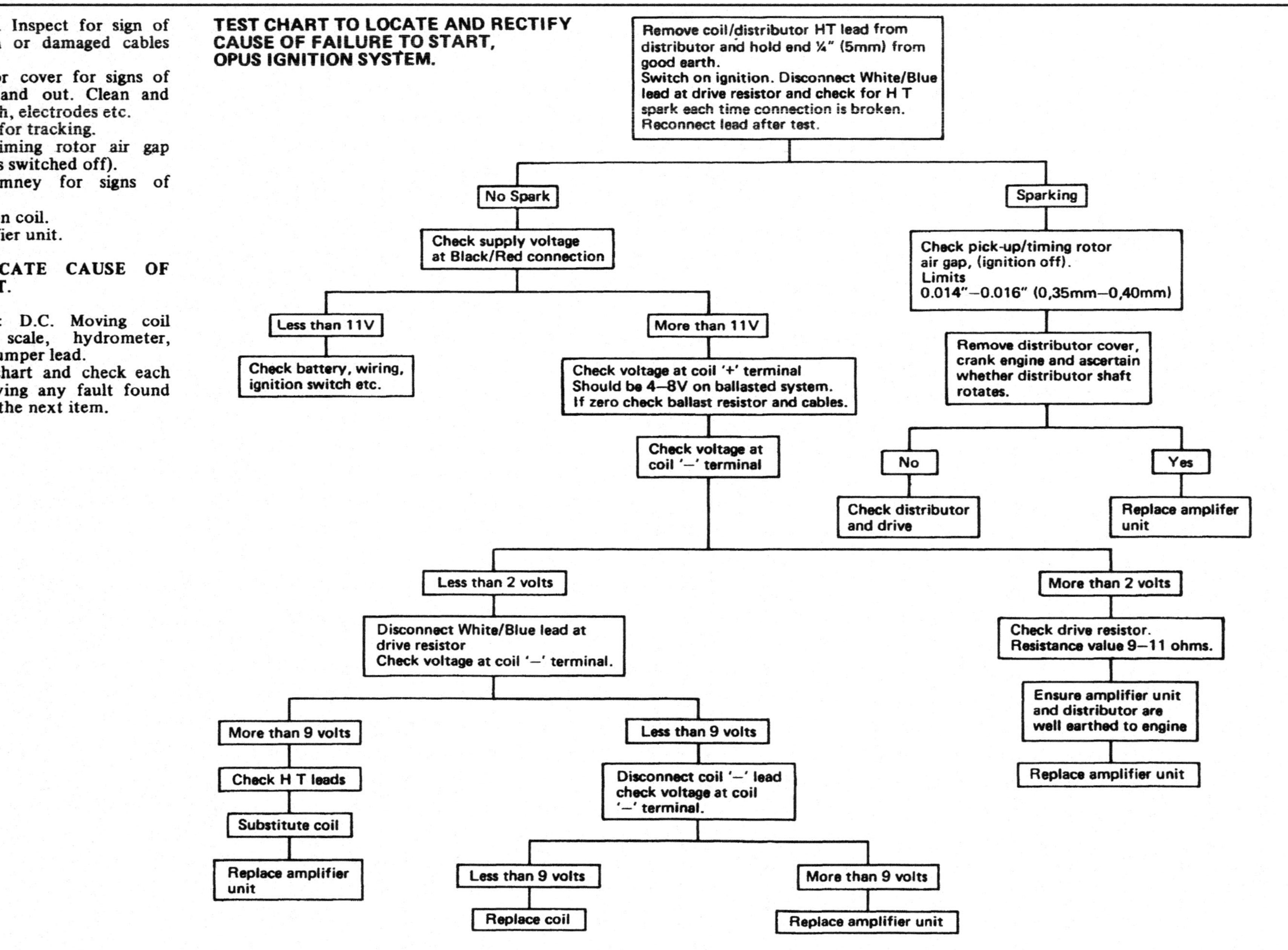

AMPLIFIER UNIT

Remove and refit **86.35.30**

Removing
1 Disconnect battery – 86.15.20.
2 Remove distributor – 86.35.20.
3 Lift off rotor arm.
4 Remove plastic anti-flash shield.
5 Carefully remove two screws, with washers and lock washers, securing pick up to movable plate.
6 Remove two long screws and spring washers securing amplifier housing to distributor body.
7 Holding amplifier housing, remove its third retaining screw and spring washer from beneath housing.
8 45DE6 distributor only; hold distributor body in one hand and amplifier housing in the other and carefully disengage vacuum advance unit link from pin in movable plate.
NOTE: 43DE6 distributors are not fitted with vacuum advance.
9 Ease grommet from distributor wall and remove amplifier unit and pick up, with connecting lead.

Refitting
10 45DE6 distributor only; ensure that lower grommet is in position in amplifier housing, and that lead to pick up is outside top of housing. Holding housing in one hand and distributor body in the other, rotate movable plate fully clockwise and carefully hook advance link over pin; this operation is not visible.
11 Fit grommets fully into slots in amplifier housing and distributor body and replace three screws and washers securing housing to body. Tighten screws evenly.
12 Place pick up in position and secure with two screws, finger tight.
13 Adjust pick up air gap. – 86.35.31.
14 Reverse operations 1 to 4.

DISTRIBUTOR PICK UP GAP

Adjust 45DE6 and 43DE6 distributors **86.35.31**

1 Disconnect battery – 86.15.20.
2 Remove distributor cap.
3 Remove rotor arm.
4 Remove flashover shield.
5 By means of feeler gauges check that gap between timing rotor and pick-up is 0.014–0.016 in. (0,35–0,44 mm.). To adjust, slacken pick-up securing screws.
6 Insert screwdriver into notch at base of pick-up and adjust gap to correct limit.
7 Tighten pick-up securing screws and recheck gap.
8 Refit flashover shield, rotor arm and distributor cap after wiping each with a clean dry nap-free cloth.
9 Reconnect battery.

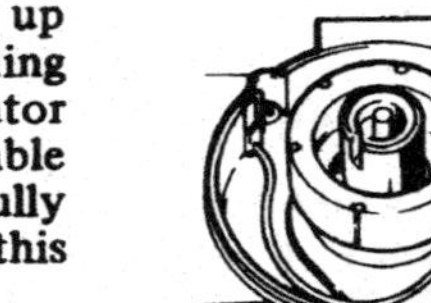

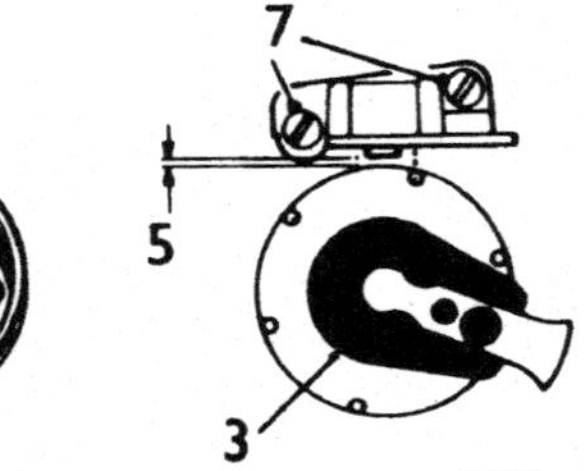

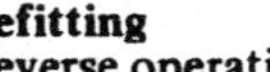

1207

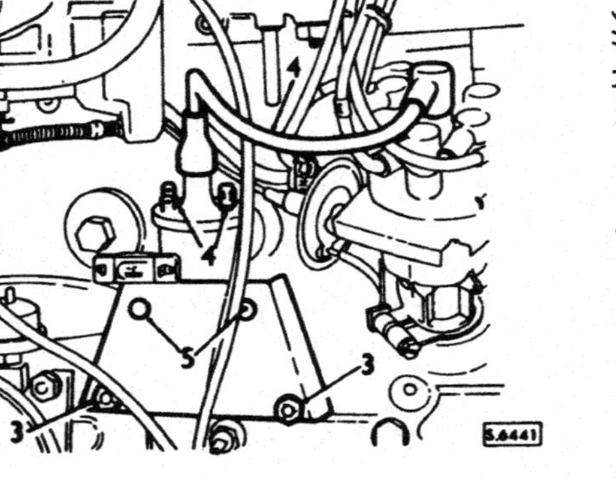

IGNITION COIL

Remove and refit **86.35.32**

Removing
1 Disconnect battery → 86.15.20.
2 Remove air cleaner cover for access.
3 Withdraw two bolts securing coil mounting plate to engine block.

NOTE: Recover spacers from behind plate.

4 Note positions of cables and disconnect at lucars and centre H.T. connector.
5 Remove nuts and washer securing coil to mounting plate.

Refitting
Reverse operations 1 to 5.

BALLAST RESISTOR

Remove and refit **86.35.33**

Removing
1 Disconnect battery – 86.15.20.
2 Remove air cleaner cover for access.
3 Withdraw two bolts securing mounting plate to engine block.

NOTE: Recover spacers from behind plate.

4 Note positions of cables and disconnect at lucars.
5 Remove nut and washer securing resistor to mounting plate.

Refitting
Reverse operations 1 to 5.

BALLAST RESISTOR/ STARTER RELAY

Remove and refit **86.35.34**

Removing
1 Disconnect battery – 86.15.20.
2 Note connections and pull connectors from relay.
3 Release two setscrews securing relay and recover plain washers and spring washers.

Refitting
Reverse operations 1 to 3, fitting earth tag beneath lower screw.

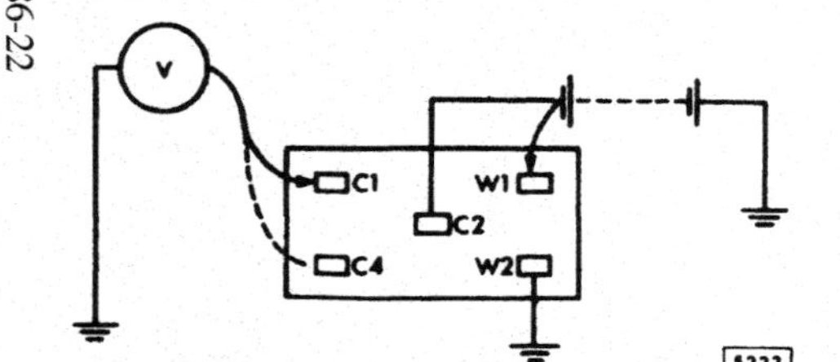

BALLAST RESISTOR/STARTER RELAY

Test (in situ) **86.35.35**

If starter motor does not operate when ignition key turned initially, check as follows.

1 Pull cable from 'C2' and 'C4' connectors on relay and short together. Starter motor should operate showing relay at fault. If starter does not operate, no supply in brown cable or starter motor at fault, or broken earth connection to relay; although manual transmission cars have 'W2' connected directly to earth, connection on automatic transmission cars is via inhibitor switch on gear selector.

Relay removed

1 Apply 12V as shown, 12V should appear on both 'C1' and 'C4'.

IGNITION PROTECTION RELAY

Remove and refit **86.35.36**

Removing

1 Disconnect battery, see 86.15.20.
2 Remove driver's side dash liner, see 76.46.11.
3 Remove direction/hazard warning flasher unit by lifting out of connector block.
4 Remove four nuts securing fuse box mounting panel and ease panel down to full extent.
5 Remove two screws, nuts and shakeproof washers securing relay to mounting bracket.

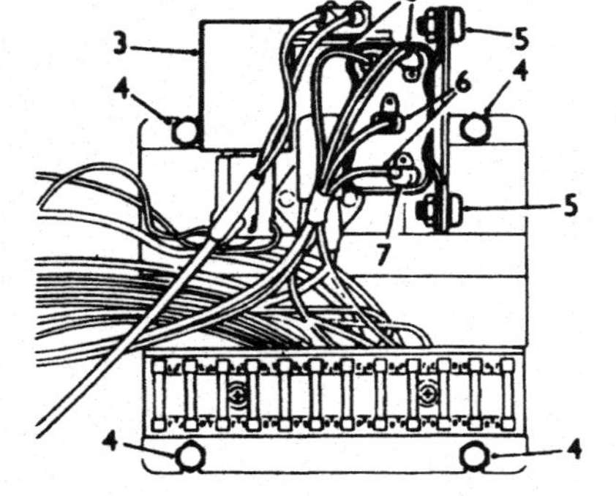

6 Note carefully position of cables.
7 Disconnect cables at Lucar connectors.

Refitting

Reverse operations 1 to 7.
NOTE: Later cars are fitted with cylindrical type 26RA relay.

IGNITION DRIVE RESISTOR

Remove and refit **86.35.37**

Removing

1 Disconnect battery – 86.15.20.
2 Remove air cleaner cover for access.
3 Withdraw two bolts securing coil mounting plate to engine block.
NOTE: Recover spacers from behind plate.
4 Note position of cables and disconnect at lucars.
5 Remove nut and washers securing resistor to mounting plate.

Refitting

6 Reverse operations 1 to 5.
NOTE: On L.H.D. cars it may be found more convenient to remove and refit resistor from beneath car, in which case operation 2 is not necessary.

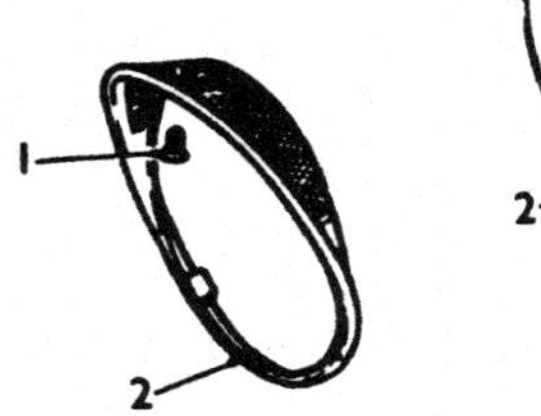

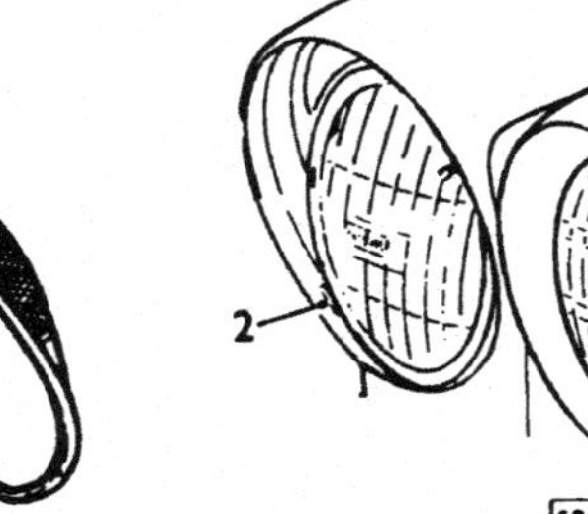

HEADLIGHT RIM FINISHER

Remove and refit **86.40.01**

Removing

1 Remove top retaining screw.
2 Pull finisher away from two retaining lugs at lower edge.

Refitting

Reverse operations 1 and 2.
Check that finisher clears headlight retaining rim.

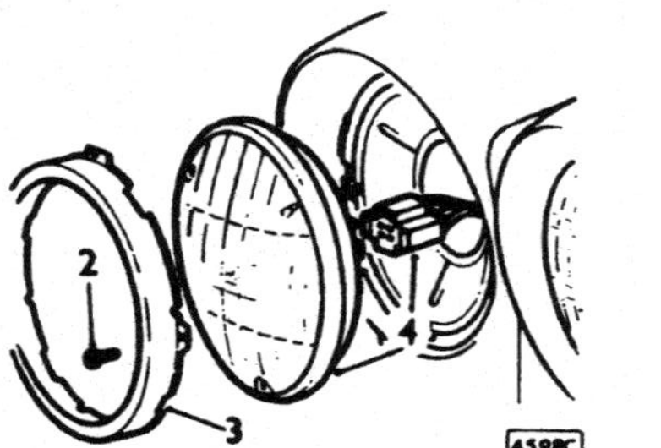

HEADLIGHT ASSEMBLY (OUTER)

Remove and refit **86.40.02**

Removing

1 Remove headlight rim finisher – 80.40.01.
2 Remove three cross head screws.
3 Withdraw headlight retaining rim.
4 Withdraw headlight and disconnect adaptor at rear of sealed beam unit.

Refitting

Reverse operations 1 to 4.
NOTE: Do not disturb two beam setting screws.

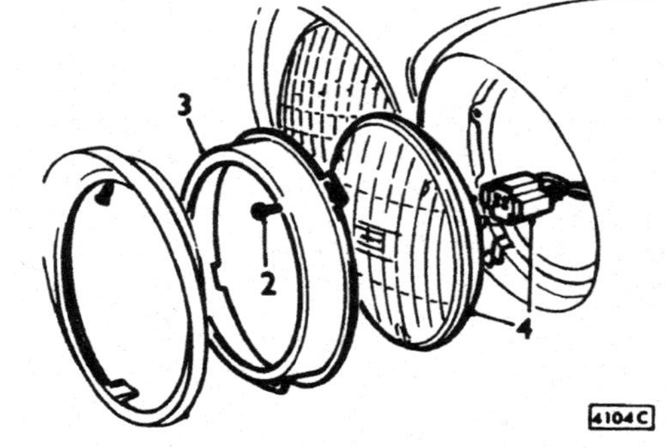

HEADLIGHT ASSEMBLY (INNER)

Remove and refit **86.40.03**

Removing

1 Remove headlight rim finisher – 80.40.01.
2 Slacken three cross head screws.
3 Rotate headlight retaining rim anti-clockwise until it can be withdrawn.
NOTE: Do not disturb and disconnect adaptor at rear of unit.
4 Withdraw headlight and disconnect adaptor at rear of unit.
5 Non sealed beam unit – proceed as operations 1 to 4 then release bulb containing spring clips.
NOTE: There is a raised locating piece that registers with a groove in the bulb backplate.

Refitting

Reverse operations 1 to 5.

HEADLIGHT ALIGNMENT

86.40.18

Headlight beam setting' should only be carried out by qualified personnel, and with approved beam setting apparatus.

Adjustment

1 Remove headlight rim finisher – 86.40.01.

Outer Headlight

2 Turn top screw anti-clockwise to lower the beam, clockwise to raise the beam.

3 Turn side screw anti-clockwise to move beam to left, clockwise to move beam right.

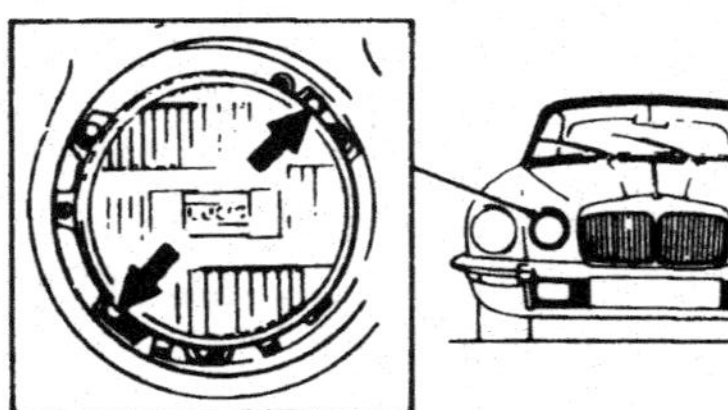

Inner Headlight

4 The adjustment screws are set diagonally opposite each other. The upper screw is for vertical alignment, the lower screw for horizontal alignment. Operations 2 and 3 refer.

5 Replace headlight rim finishers, see 86.40.01, and re-check alignment to ensure that settings have not been disturbed.

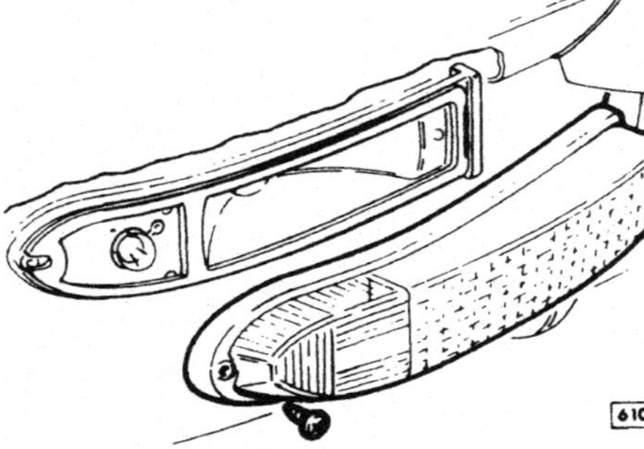

SIDE/FLASHER LAMP LENS

Remove and refit **86.40.24**

Removing

1 Withdraw crosshead screw retaining lens.

2 Lift lens until locating flange can be easily withdrawn from slot.

Refitting

Reverse operations 1 and 2.

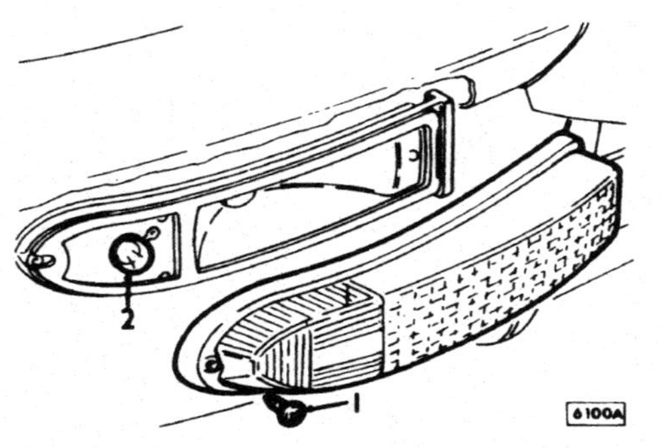

SIDE/FLASHER LAMP BULBS

Remove and refit **86.40.25**

Removing

1 Remove lens – 86.40.24.

2 Withdraw bulb by pressing against spring tension and turning anti-clockwise until it releases from locating slots.

Refitting

Reverse operations 1 and 2.

NOTE: Replacement bulbs must be of correct size.

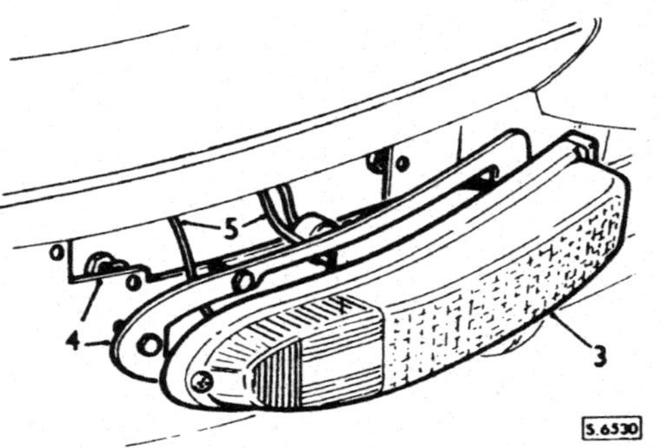

SIDE/FLASHER ASSEMBLY

Remove and refit **86.40.26**

Removing

1 Disconnect battery – 86.15.20.

2 Withdraw two screws and remove moulded cable harness cover from related wing valance.

3 Remove lens – 86.40.24.

4 Remove four screws, nuts and shakeproof washers (or plug fasteners on later cars) securing assembly.

5 Disconnect cables at snap connectors on wing valance.

6 Secure draw string/cable to harness and pull cables through channel.

7 Untie draw string/cable and recover assembly.

Refitting

Reverse operations 1 to 7.

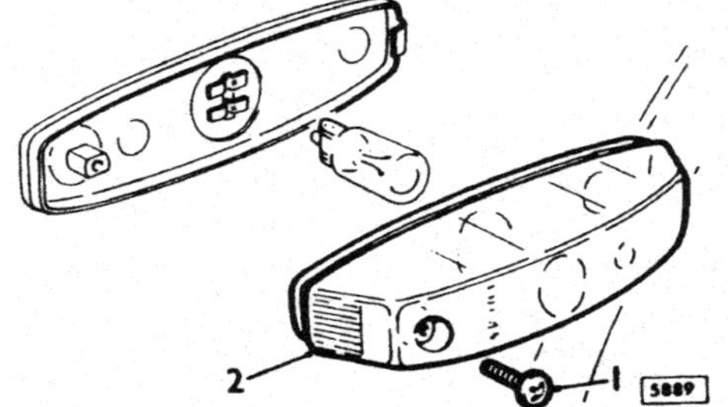

FRONT FLASHER REPEATER LENS

Remove and refit **86.40.51**

Removing

1 Withdraw one crosshead securing screw.

2 Remove lens.

Refitting

Reverse operations 1 and 2.

FRONT FLASHER REPEATER BULB

Remove and refit **86.40.52**

Removing

1 Remove lens – 86.40.51.

2 Withdraw bulb.

Refitting

Reverse operations 1 and 2.

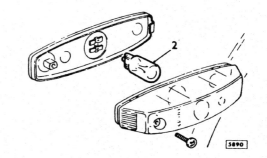

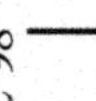

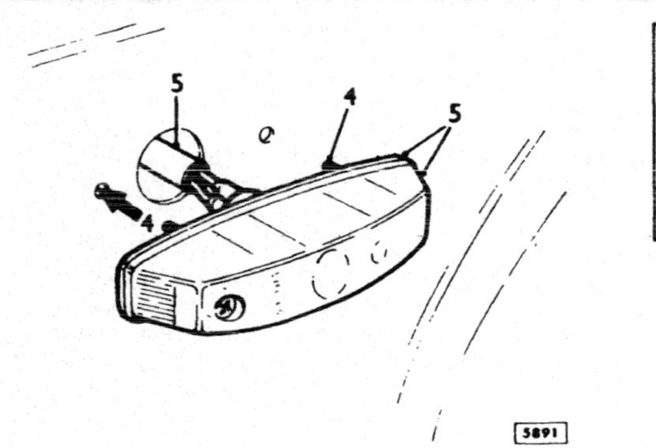

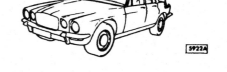

FRONT FLASHER REPEATER ASSEMBLY

Remove and refit **86.40.53**

Removing

1 Disconnect battery earth lead – 86.15.20.
2 Remove lens – 86.40.51.
3 Remove bulb.
4 Remove two nuts and lock washer from captive retaining bolts.
5 Disconnect cables from snap connectors.
Check condition of seals while assembly is removed from car.

Refitting

Reverse operations 1 to 5.

SIDE MARKER LENS

Remove and refit **Front – 86.40.57**
Rear – 86.40.62

Removing

1 Withdraw one crosshead retaining screw.
2 Remove lens, note retaining clip.

Refitting

Reverse operations 1 and 2.

SIDE MARKER BULB

Remove and refit **Front – 86.40.58**
Rear – 86.40.63

Removing

1 Remove lens – 86.40.57.
2 Withdraw bulb.

Refitting

Reverse operations 1 and 2.

SIDE MARKER ASSEMBLY

Remove and refit **Front – 86.40.59**

Removing

1 Disconnect battery – 86.15.20.
2 Remove retaining nuts and lockwashers from captive retaining bolts inside wheel arch.
3 Disconnect cables from snap connectors.
4 Check condition of seals while assembly is removed from car.

Refitting

Reverse operations 1 to 4.

SIDE MARKER ASSEMBLY

Remove and refit **Rear – 86.40.64**

Removing

1 Disconnect battery – 86.15.20.
2 Remove lens – 86.40.57.
3 Remove two retaining screws.
4 Disconnect cables from snap connector.

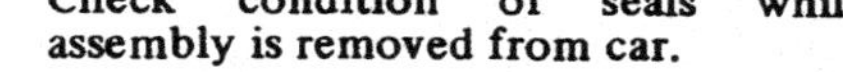

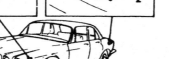

5 Check condition of seals while assembly is removed from car.

Refitting

Reverse operations 1 to 5.

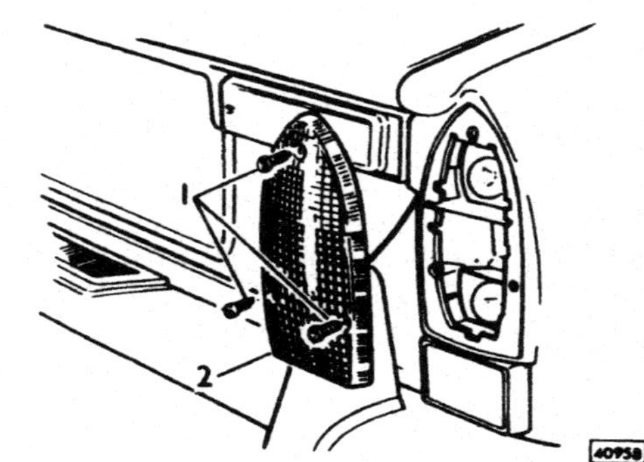

TAIL/STOP/FLASHER LIGHTS LENS

Remove and refit **86.40.68**

Removing

1 Withdraw 3 cross head screws.
2 Remove lens.

Refitting

Reverse operations 1 and 2, inspect rubber seal for damage.

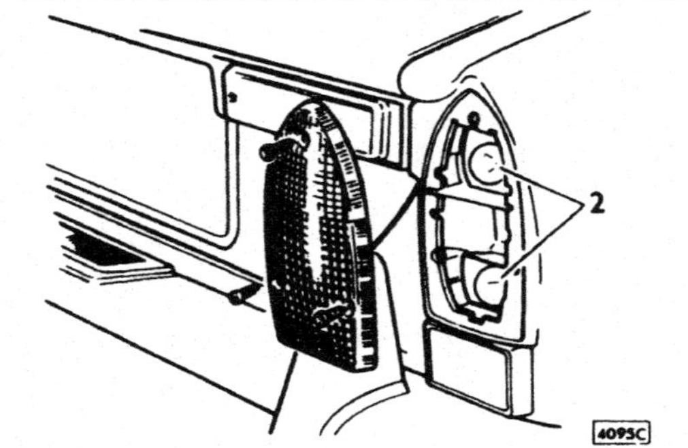

TAIL/STOP/FLASHER LIGHTS BULB

Remove and refit **86.40.69**

Removing

1 Remove lens – 86.40.68.
2 Remove bulb.

Refitting

Reverse operations 1 and 2.

TAIL/STOP/FLASHER LIGHT ASSEMBLY

Remove and refit **L.H. – 86.40.70**
R.H. – 86.40.71

Removing

1 Remove lens – 86.40.68.
2 Remove bulb – 86.40.69.

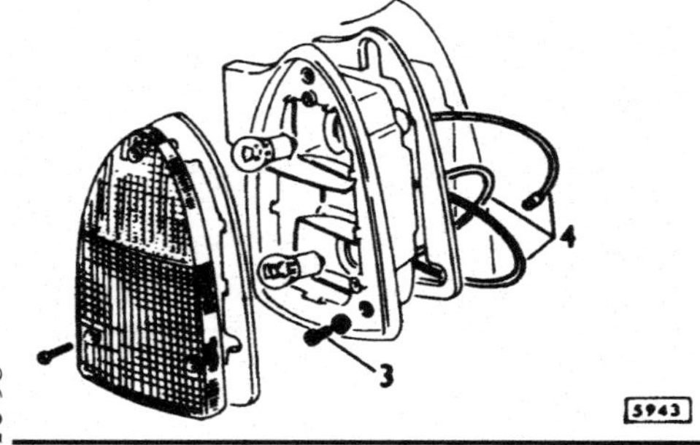

3 Withdraw three slotted screws and washers.
4 Withdraw assembly and disconnect cables at snap connectors.

Refitting

Reverse operations 1 to 4.

NUMBER PLATE LAMP LENS

Remove and refit **86.40.84**

Removing

1 Disconnect battery – 86.15.20.
2 Remove two screws securing lens to number plate lamp.
3 Open boot and disconnect pigtail lead at snap connector.
4 Remove lens and bulb assembly by feeding leads through lamp assembly.

Refitting

Reverse operations 1 to 4.

NUMBER PLATE LAMP BULB

Remove and refit **86.40.85**

Removing

1 Remove two screws securing lens and bulb assembly.

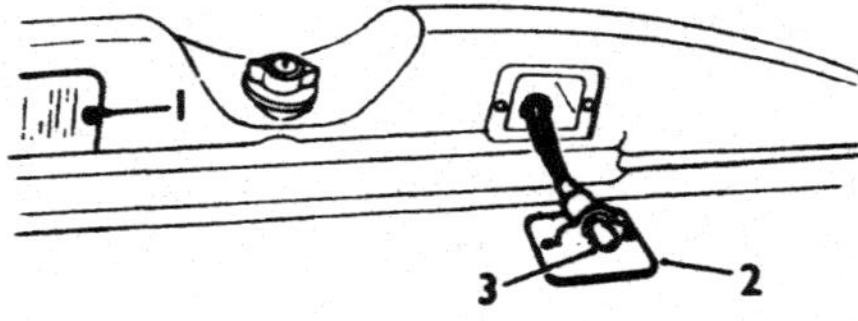

2 Ease lens away from lamp assembly.
3 Remove bulb.
NOTE: It is only necessary to exert a straight pull as lamp bulb is of capless type.

Refitting

Reverse operations 1 to 3.

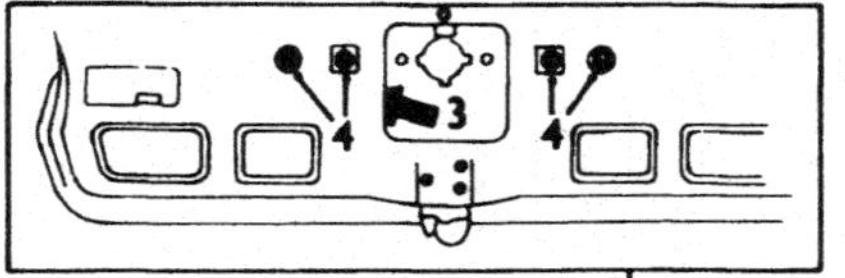

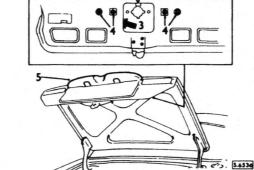

NUMBER PLATE LAMP ASSEMBLY

Remove and refit **86.40.86**

Removing

1 Disconnect battery – 86.15.20.
2 Open boot.
3 Disconnect all cables at snap connectors.
4 Remove four nuts, plain and shakeproof washers.
5 Remove assembly from boot rim.

Refitting

Reverse operations 1 to 5.

REVERSE LAMP LENS

Remove and refit **86.40.89**

Removing

1 Withdraw two screws retaining lens.
2 Remove lens – examine seal for condition.

Refitting

Reverse operations 1 and 2, ensuring that gasket is refitted with drain hole at bottom.

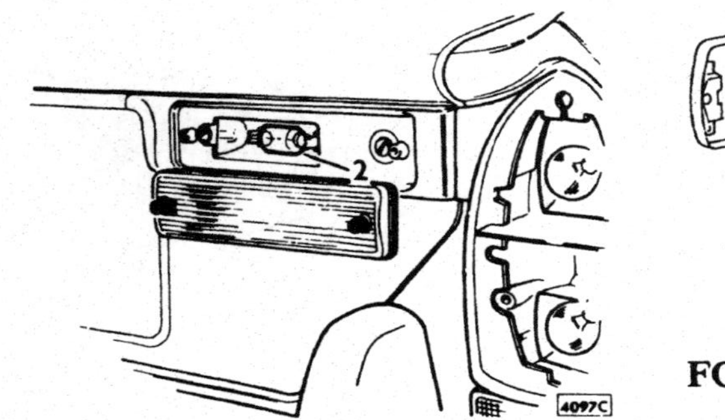

REVERSE LAMP BULB

Remove and refit **86.40.90**

Removing
1 Remove lens – 86.40.89.
2 Remove bulb.

Refitting
Reverse operations 1 and 2.

REVERSE LAMP ASSEMBLY

Remove and refit **86.40.91**

Removing
1 Remove lens – 86.40.89.
2 Remove bulb – 86.40.90.
3 Withdraw two retaining screws.
4 Disconnect cables at snap connectors.

Refitting
Reverse operations 1 to 4.

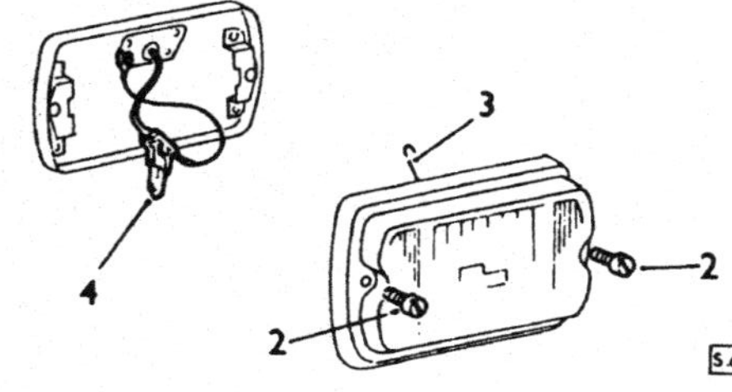

FOG/SPOTLIGHT BULB

Remove and refit **86.40.94**

Removing
CAUTION: Under no circumstances should bulbs in these units be touched with bare hands; if any dirt or grease is present on the glass it must be removed using a lint-free cloth dipped in methylated spirits.

1 Disconnect battery – 86.15.20.
2 Remove two screws retaining beam unit.
3 Move bulb retaining clip to one side.
4 Remove bulb holder from beam unit.
5 Using cloth or glove pull bulb from holder.

Refitting
Reverse operations 1 to 5.

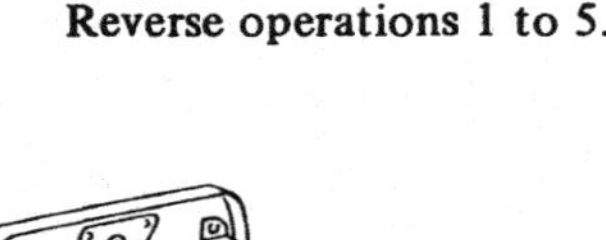

FOG/SPOTLIGHT BEAM/LENS UNIT

Remove and refit **86.40.95**

Removing
1 Disconnect battery – 86.15.20.
2 Remove two screws retaining beam unit.
3 Move bulb retaining clip to one side.
4 Remove bulb holder from beam unit.
5 Remove rubber retaining washers from beam unit retaining screws and separate beam and lens units.

Refitting
Reverse operations 1 to 5.

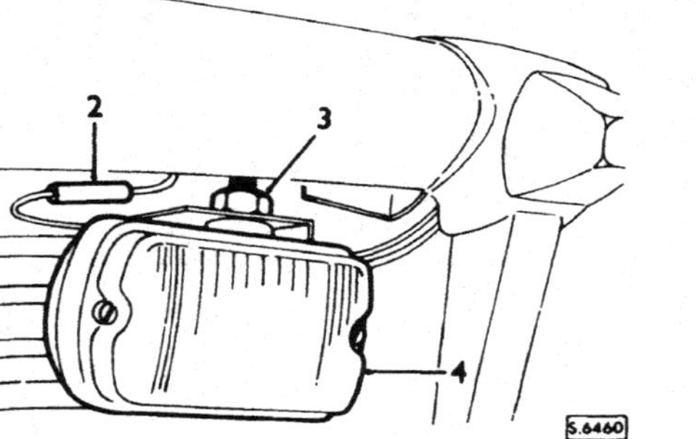

FOG/SPOTLIGHT ASSEMBLY

Remove and refit **86.40.96**

Removing
1 Disconnect battery – 86.15.20.
2 Disconnect cable at snap connector.
3 Remove nut, plain and shakeproof washer securing assembly to mounting bracket.
4 Remove assembly.

Refitting
Reverse operations 1 to 4.

ROOF LAMP BULB

Remove and refit – 2 Door cars **86.45.01**

Removing
1 Disconnect battery – 86.15.20.

2 Carefully lever interior light assembly from cantrail.
3 Withdraw bulb from spring retainer contacts.

Refitting
Reverse operations 1 to 3.
NOTE: Fit 6 watt bulbs only to Brycrest lamps. 10 watt bulbs may be fitted to Hella lamps.

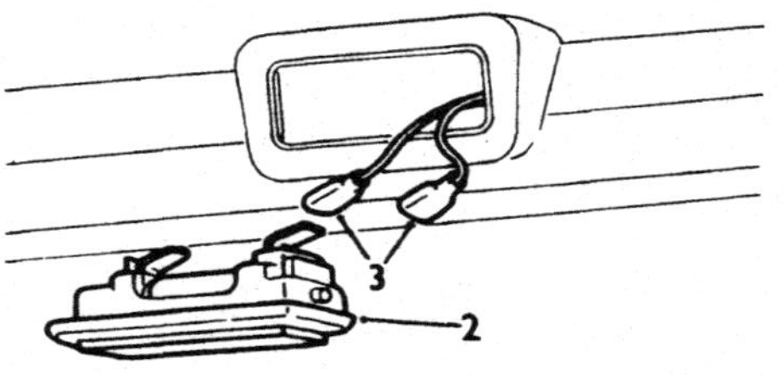

ROOF LAMP ASSEMBLY

Remove and refit – 2 Door cars **86.45.02**

Removing
1 Disconnect battery – 86.15.20.
2 Carefully lever interior light assembly from cantrail.
3 Disconnect cables at lucar connectors.

Refitting
Reverse operations 1 to 3.

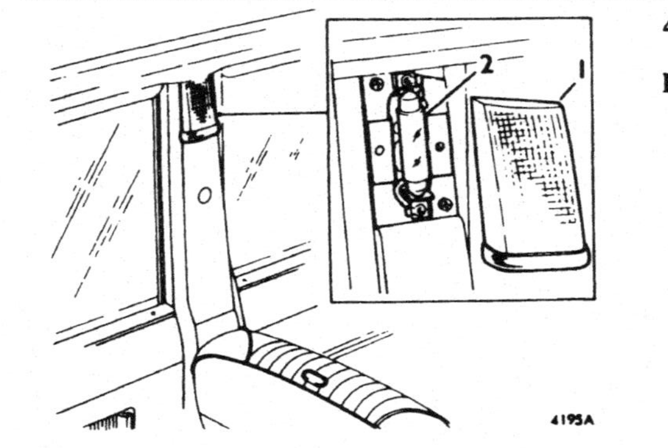

DOOR POST LAMP BULB

Remove and refit – 4 Door cars **86.45.03**

Removing
1 Pull off lens and cover assembly.
2 Withdraw pendent-type bulb from holder.

Refitting
Reverse operations 1 and 2.

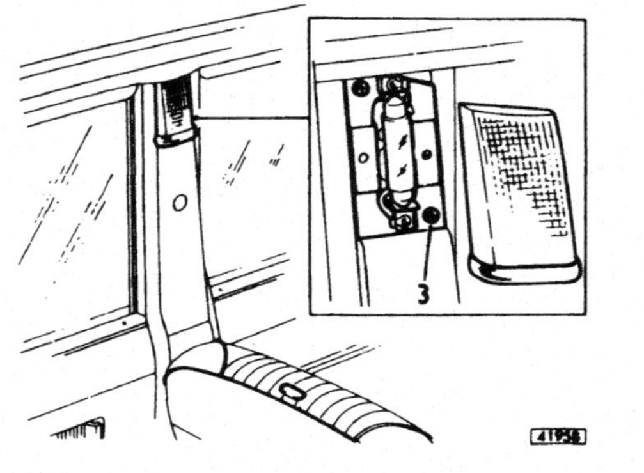
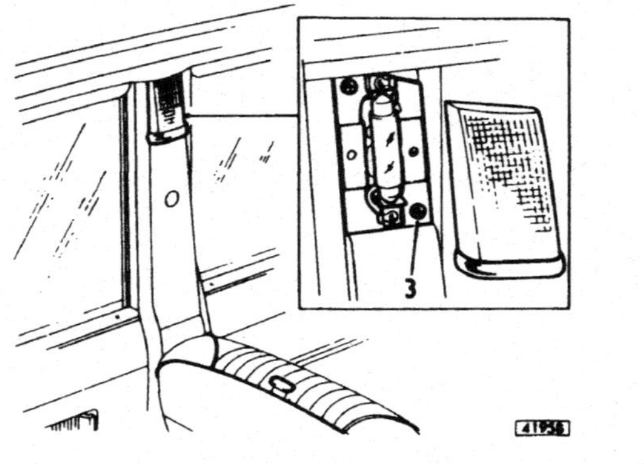

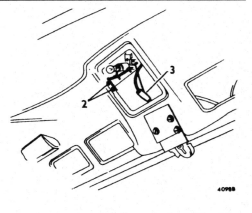

DOOR POST LAMP ASSEMBLY

Remove and refit – 4 Door cars **86.45.04**

Removing
1 Remove lens – 86.45.03.
2 Remove bulb – 86.45.03.
3 Withdraw two retaining screws.
4 Disconnect cables from snap connectors.

Refitting
Reverse operations 1 to 4, ensuring that connectors are fully covered by insulating sleeves.

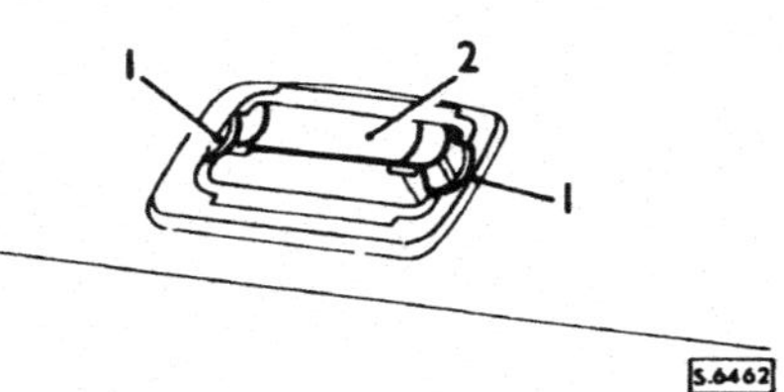

MAP LIGHT BULB

Remove and refit **86.45.09**

Removing
1 Withdraw bulb holder by exerting pressure on side clips and pulling holder downwards.
2 Withdraw bulb, pendent type.

Refitting
Reverse operations 1 and 2.

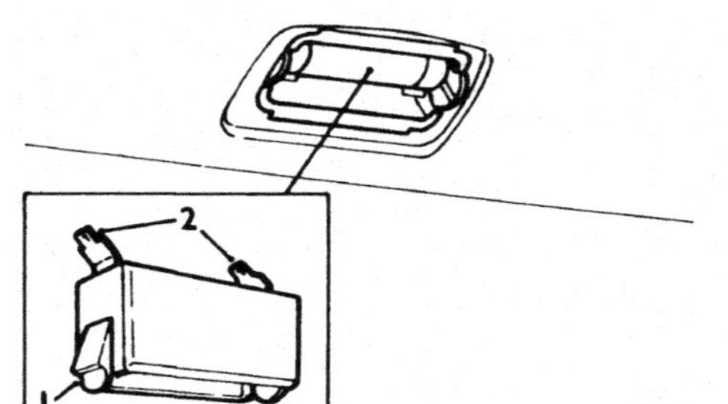

MAP LIGHT ASSEMBLY

Remove and refit **86.45.10**

Removing
1 Remove bulb holder – 86.45.09.
2 Disconnect cables from connectors.

Refitting
Reverse operations 1 and 2.

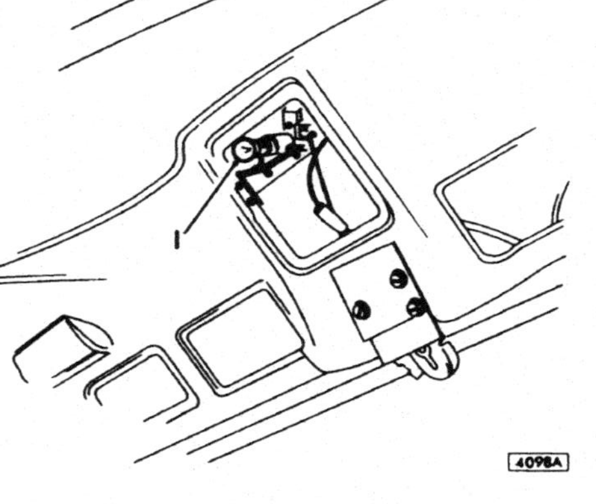

LUGGAGE COMPARTMENT LIGHT BULB

Remove and refit **86.45.15**

Removing
1 Open luggage compartment.
2 Access to bulb is through aperture in luggage compartment lid.
3 Remove bulb.

Refitting
Reverse operations 1 to 3, using Wotan 6253 bulb.

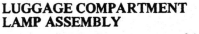

LUGGAGE COMPARTMENT LAMP ASSEMBLY

Remove and refit **86.45.16**

Removing
1 Disconnect battery earth lead – 86.15.20.
2 Withdraw two screws retaining bracket.
3 Disconnect cable from snap connectors.

Refitting
Reverse operations 1 to 3.

NOTE: On later cars the mounting differs from that illustrated, to improve switch operation.

FIBRE OPTIC ILLUMINATION SYSTEM

Description

Consists of a centralised light source (opticell) feeding localised illumination via fibre elements and diffuser lens units to specific areas. Control switches illuminated in this way are as follows:
1 Ignition switch, (one element).
2 Lighting switch, (one element).
3 Heater/Air conditioning control switches, (two elements to each control).

Failure of the light source will result in loss of illumination at all the above consumer units.

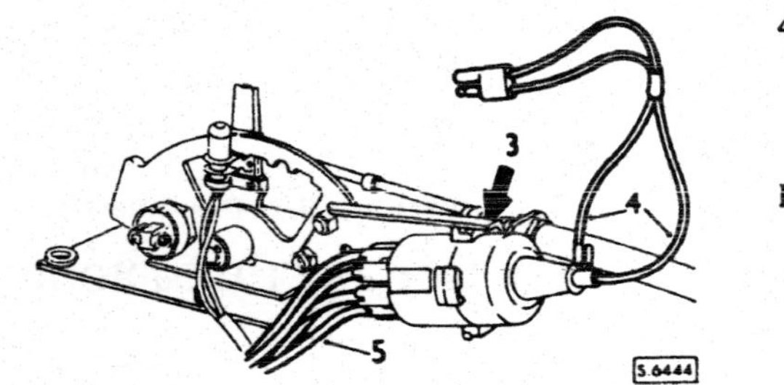

OPTICELL

Remove and refit **86.45.27**

Removing
1 Disconnect battery – 86.15.20.
2 Remove centre console escutcheon and window lift switch panel.
3 Withdraw two screws securing opticell to transmission selector quadrant.
4 Disconnect fibre elements by pulling each from opticell lens hood.
5 Disconnect cables.

Refitting
Reverse operations 1 to 5; ensure that all unused light outputs are blanked to prevent light leakage in console.

OPTICELL BULB

Remove and refit **86.45.28**

Removing
1 Disconnect battery – 86.15.20.
2 Remove centre console escutcheon and window lift switch panel.
3 Pull bulb holder from opticell reflector.
4 Withdraw miniature bayonet capped bulb from holder.
NOTE: Replace with bulb of correct type if necessary (Wotan 6253).

Refitting
Reverse operations 1 to 4.

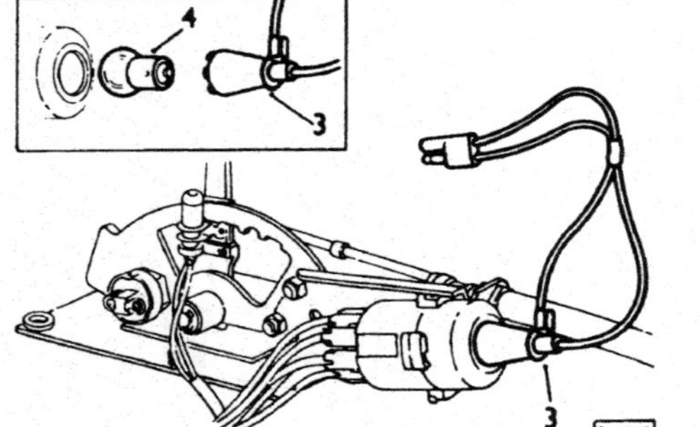

S.6539

PANEL SWITCH ILLUMINATION BULB

Remove and refit **86.45.31**

Removing
1 Disconnect battery – 86.15.20.
2 Drop centre oddments tray;
   (a) Pull off air conditioning/heater control knobs and radio aperture escutcheon.
   (b) Withdraw four screws centre oddments tray.
   (c) Lift tray forward.
3 Pull bulb holder from lamp holder/diffuser.
4 Remove miniature bayonet capped bulb from holder.

Refitting
Reverse operations 1 to 4.

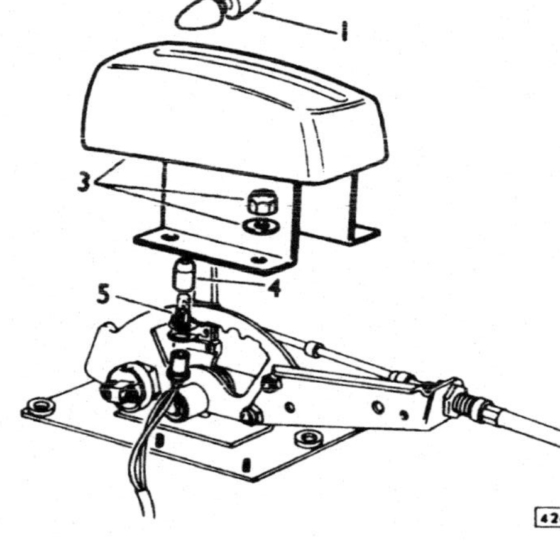
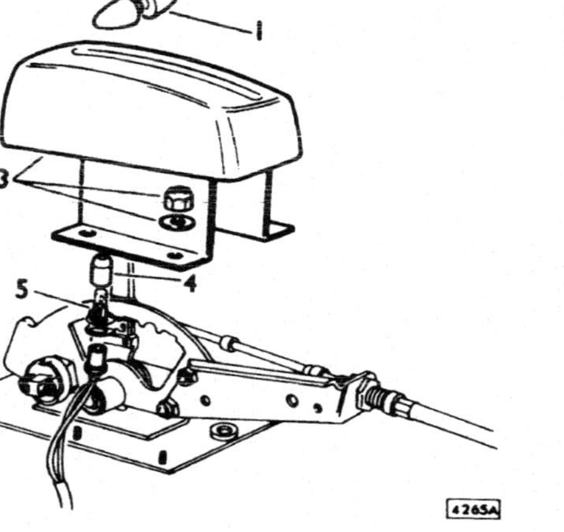

TRANSMISSION INDICATOR BULB

Remove and refit **86.45.40**

Removing
1 Remove transmission selector quadrant control knob.
2 Remove window lift switch panel escutcheon and console escutcheon.
3 Remove four retaining nuts from transmission selector cover.
4 Remove bulb shroud.
5 Withdraw bulb.

Refitting
Reverse operations 1 to 5.

S.6535

SPEEDOMETER ILLUMINATION BULB

Remove and refit **86.45.49**

Removing
1 Disconnect battery – 86.15.20.
2 Remove speedometer – 88.30.01.
3 Pull bulb holder from back of speedometer and remove bulb.

Refitting
Reverse operations 1 to 3.

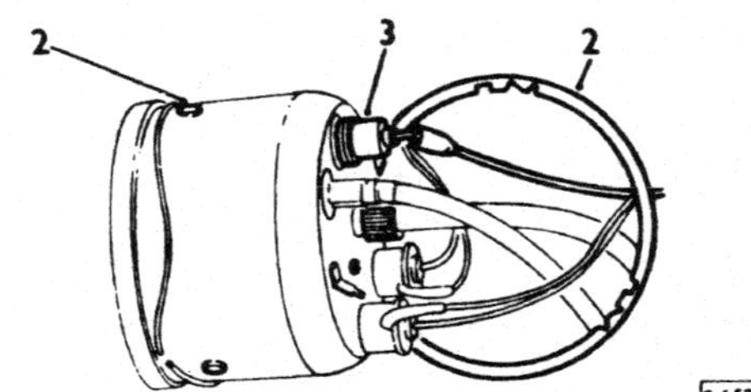

REVOLUTION COUNTER ILLUMINATION BULB

Remove and refit **86.45.53**

Removing
1 Disconnect battery – 86.15.20.
2 Remove revolution counter – 88.30.21.
3 Pull bulb holder from back of instrument and remove bulb.

Refitting
Reverse operations 1 to 3.

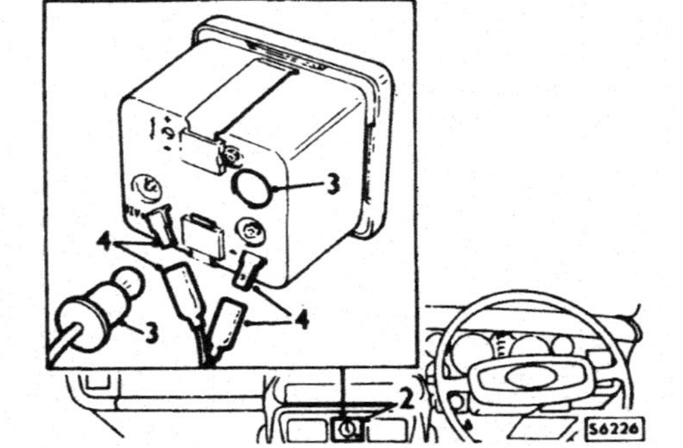

CLOCK ILLUMINATION BULB

Remove and refit 86.45.54

Removing
1 Disconnect battery – 86.15.20.
2 Drop centre oddments tray.
3 Pull bulb holder from clock case.
4 Remove bulb from holder.

Refitting
Reverse operations 1 to 4.

WARNING LIGHT CLUSTER

Remove and refit 86.45.62

Removing
1 Disconnect battery – 86.15.20.
2 Remove facia – 76.46.01.
3 Remove cluster legend plate, retained in position by spigots in nylon friction bushes.

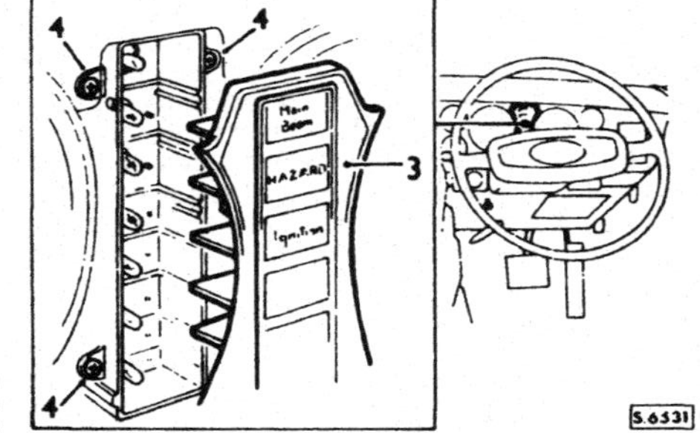

4 Withdraw four screws from front of cluster.
5 Release 'P' Clip securing cable harness to back of facia.
6 Remove cluster from facia.

Refitting
Reverse operations 1 to 6; do not omit gasket, to prevent leakage of light.

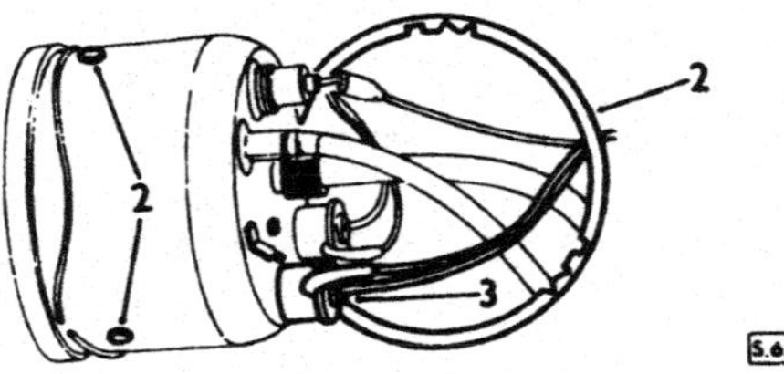

FLASHING INDICATOR BULB

Remove and refit 86.45.63

Removing
1 Disconnect battery – 86.15.20.
2 Remove speedometer or revolution counter as appropriate.
3 Pull bulb holder from back of instrument and remove bulb.

Refitting
Reverse operations 1 to 3.

CHOKE WARNING BULB 86.45.71
DEMIST WARNING BULB 86.45.82

Remove and refit

Carry out operation 86.45.63.

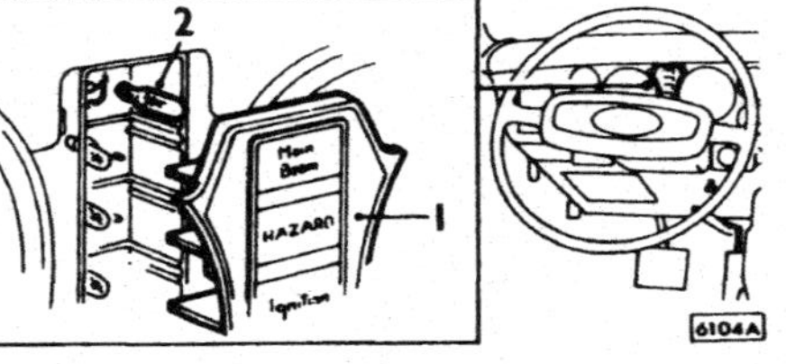

MAIN BEAM WARNING LIGHT BULB 86.45.65
HAZARD WARNING LIGHT BULB 86.45.68
IGNITION WARNING LIGHT BULB 86.45.64
PARKING BRAKE WARNING BULB 86.45.67
BRAKE WARNING LIGHT BULB 86.45.69
OIL PRESSURE WARNING LIGHT BULB 86.45.66
SEAT BELT WARNING LIGHT BULB 86.45.75

Remove and refit

Removing
1 Disconnect battery.
2 Remove warning light cluster legend bearing lens cover plate (retained by locating spigots in nylon friction bushes).
3 Remove defective bulb.
NOTE: The bulbs used in this unit are of capless design and only require a straight pull to remove them from holder.

Removing
Reverse operations 1 to 3; do not omit gasket, to prevent leakage of light.

HAZARD/TURN SIGNAL FLASHER UNIT

Remove and refit 86.55.12

Removing
1 Remove drivers side dash liner.
2 Grip unit firmly and withdraw by a straight pull from its mounting socket.

Refitting
Reverse operations 1 and 2.

HEADLIGHT RELAY

Remove and refit 86.55.17

Removing
1 Disconnect battery – 86.15.20.
2 Note positions of cables and disconnect at lucars.
3 Withdraw two screws securing relay. Recover spacers and washers.

Refitting
Reverse operations 1 to 3.
NOTE: Reversal of blue/white and blue/red leads at Lucars provides dipped beam flashing (legally required in Italy).

SEAT BELT WARNING AND SEQUENTIAL START SYSTEM ON EARLIER 4.2 LITRE CARS

86.57.00

NOTE: The sequential start system is not fitted to later cars, as it is no longer required by law, but is replaced by a seat belt warning system as shown in a later issue of the wiring diagram.
Some earlier cars are fitted with a sequential start interlock and seat belt warning system that prevents engine starting unless the correct sequence of operations has been carried out.

To start the car carry out the following sequence of operations:

1 Sit in car.
2 Ensure handbrake is applied.
3 Ensure selector lever is in 'N' or 'P' position (Automatic Gearbox) or that change speed lever is in Neutral (Manual Gearbox).
4 Extend and fasten seat belt.
5 If a front seat passenger is to be carried ensure passenger's seat belt is correctly fastened.
6 Using manual choke if necessary, start engine with ignition in normal way.

Deviation from this sequence will prevent the engine starting. Additional audible warning will be given by a high pitched buzz, whilst a warning light in the central cluster gives visual indication of the error. These warnings are activated if either front seat belt is unfastened while the engine is running.

It is possible for a passenger to leave the car when it is stopped with the engine running. There will be warnings as the passenger seat belt is unfastened but these will operate for approximately 7 seconds only. If the driver leaves the car with the engine running (e.g. to open garage doors) warnings will operate when a gear is selected after re-entering the car.

NOTE: If there are no front seat occupants it is possible to reach into the car and start the engine, for service or test purposes. However, the belts of occupied seats must be correctly fastened before a gear is selected. Failure to do so will activate warning signals.

SEAT BELT WARNING BUZZER/ CONTROL UNIT

Remove and refit **86.57.01**

Removing

1 Disconnect battery – 86.15.20.
2 Remove passenger side dash liner – 76.46.11.
3 Remove glove box liner – 76.52.03.
4 Withdraw nut and washer securing unit to bracket on blower motor case.

Refitting

Reverse operations 1 to 4.

SEAT BELT WARNING AND SEQUENTIAL START SYSTEM

Testing **86.57.15**

The following test procedure is divided into two sections:–

1 A function check of the system that requires no special equipment and designed to indicate if more intensive fault finding is required.
2 A test procedure using special equipment designed to prove the logic sequence of the Sequential start unit, the continuity of the electrical harness and the operation of associated switches.

TEST 1:

	PROCEDURE	RESULT
1.	(a) Occupant(s) seated (b) Ignition 'ON' (c) Forward or reverse gear selected	Audio/Visual warning – Car will not start.
2.	(a) Occupant(s) seated (b) Gear selector in 'NEUTRAL' (c) Ignition 'ON' (d) 'START' selection made	Audio/Visual warning – Car will not start.
3.	(a) Belts fastened (b) Occupant(s) seated (c) Gear selector in 'NEUTRAL' (d) Ignition 'ON' (e) 'START' selection made	Audio/Visual warning – Car will not start.
4.	(a) Belts fastened (b) Occupant(s) seated (c) Ignition 'ON' (d) Forward or reverse gear selected	Audio/Visual warning – Car will not start.
5.	(a) Occupant(s) seated (b) Belts fastened (c) Ignition 'ON' (d) Start selection made	Car will start.
6.	(a) Occupant(s) seated (b) Belts fastened (c) Ignition 'ON' (d) Ignition 'OFF' (e) Ignition 'ON' (f) Start selection made	Car will start.
7.	(a) Ignition 'ON' (b) Start selection made **Note**: This allows an unoccupied car to be started for service and test purposes. The transmission should be in NEUTRAL or PARK and Handbrake 'ON'	Car will start.

continued

TEST 2:

Equipment required – Smiths sequence simulator and harness test box.

1 Remove passenger side dash liner – 76.46.11.
2 Remove glove box liner – 76.52.03.
3 Disconnect harness connector from sequential start unit.
4 Insert connector of simulator harness into unit.
5 Connect harness test lead into harness connector removed from unit in (3).
6 Connect negative supply lead of test box to good earth point on car.
7 Connect positive supply lead of test box to positive terminal of car battery. **NOTE**: Ensure connection is firmly fixed. Battery lamp indicates correct connection. In the following test matrix ● shows lamp or buzzer 'ON'. Switches once pressed remain so until indicated otherwise.

NOTE: Harness checks are powered by car supply circuits.

8 If unit fails any operation in test 2 it must be changed – 86.57.01.
9 Harness check failures must be investigated further for unserviceable components i.e. switches and connections.
10 Remove test equipment.
11 Refit glove box liner.
12 Refit dash liner.

Step No.	Switches operated on test box	Ignition Lamp	Start Lamp	Seat Belt Warning Lamp	Buzzer	Test Function
1.	Ignition switch ON – Start Button pressed (1-17)	●	●			'No driver' start
2.	Drivers seat switch ON	●	●	●	●	Restart circuit
3.	Ignition switch OFF					Ignition OFF does not reset latches
4.	Ignition switch ON	●	●	●	●	
5.	Drivers seat belt switch ON	●	●			Normal start logic
6.	Passenger seat switch ON	●	●	●	●	
7.	Passenger belt switch ON	●	●			
8.	Supply to 5 volts	●	●			Logic memory remains 'held' during start
9.	Supply to 11 volts	●	●			
10.	Passenger belt switch to OFF	●	●	●	●	Resets logic and Seat switch delay
11.	Passenger seat switch to OFF	●	●	After 7.7 sec. delay		
12.	Drivers belt switch to OFF	●	●	●	●	Resets logic and seat switch delay
13.	Drivers seat switch to OFF	●	●	After 7.7 sec. delay		
14.	Ignition switch to OFF					Check restart latch unlatches
15.	Drivers seat switch to ON					
16.	Ignition switch to ON	●		●	●	
17.	Select gear switch to 'in gear' and ensure start switch is UP	●		●	●	Transmission switch input functions
18.	Drivers seat switch to OFF	●		After 7.7 sec. delay		
19.	Press door push switch	●			●	Check door switch operates buzzer
20.	Release door push switch	●				

Step No.	Switches operated on test box	Ignition Lamp	Start Lamp	Seat Belt Warning Lamp	Buzzer	Test Function
21.	Passenger belt switch ON	●				Passenger side reverse logic
22.	Passenger seat switch ON	●		●	●	
23.	Passenger belt switch OFF	●		●	●	
24.	Passenger belt switch ON	●				
25.	Drivers belt switch ON	●				Drivers side reverse logic
26.	Drivers seat switch ON	●		●	●	
27.	Drivers belt switch OFF	●		●	●	
28.	Drivers belt switch ON	●				
29.	Drivers seat switch OFF and Passengers seat switch OFF	●		Wait max: seat delay		Seat switch logic lockout check
30.	Drivers seat switch ON and Passengers seat switch ON	●				
31	All switches to OFF					

Step No.	Check	Action	Battery	Ignition	Start	Gear Switch	Seats	Belts
1.	Power Supply	Ignition ON	●	●				●
2.	Gear/Transmission Switch	Select Gear	●	●		●		●
3.	Seat switch	Press down seats	●	●			●	●
4.	Belt switch	Fasten belts	●	●				
5.	Start switch	Start car	●	●				●
6.		All switches OFF	●					●

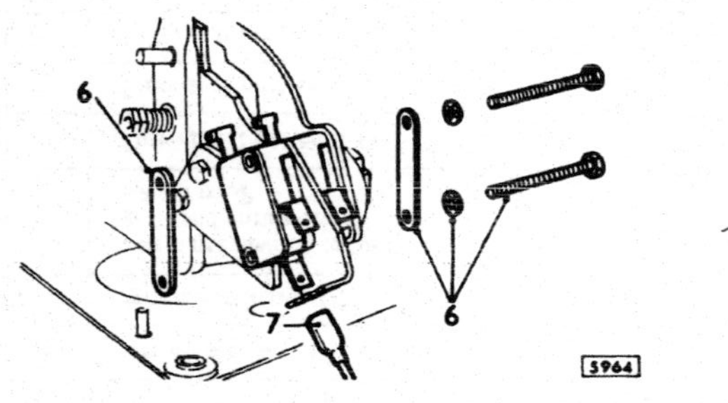

SEAT BELT WARNING GEAR BOX SWITCH

Remove and refit **86.57.19**

Removing

1 Disconnect battery – 86.15.20.
2 Remove electric window lift control panel.
3 Remove transmission selector hand-grip.
4 Withdraw four screws retaining console centre panel and ashtrays.
5 Withdraw four bolts retaining transmission selector cover.
6 Withdraw two bolts and keep plates from automatic transmission inhibitor switch and gearbox switch.
7 Disconnect seat belt warning harness from Lucar connector on gearbox switch.

Refitting

8 Reconnect cables to gearbox switch.
9 Fit switches to bracket, do not tighten retaining bolts and plates to fullest extent.
10 Reconnect battery leads – 86.15.20.
11 With ignition switch on and seat belts loose, set gearbox switch to operate buzzer alarm when any forward or reverse drive selection is made.
12 Tighten retaining bolts.
13 Test operation of gearbox switch to ensure switch has not moved.
14 Reverse operations 2 to 5.

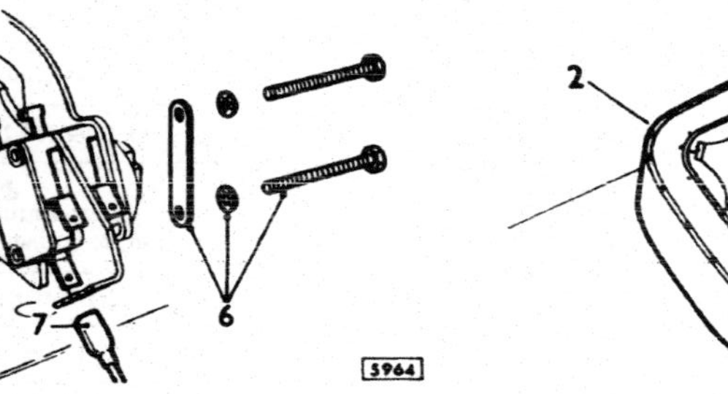

SEAT SWITCH

Remove and refit – Driver's 86.57.21
– Passenger's 86.57.23

Removing

1 Disconnect battery – 86.15.20.
2 Remove passenger seat cushion – 76.70.01.
3 Disconnect cable connector located beneath seat.
4 Slacken seat diaphragm using special tool (Nitool).
5 Withdraw two switch retaining screws and washers.
6 Remove seat switch.

Refitting

Reverse operations 1 to 6.

BELT SWITCHES (when fitted)

Remove and refit – Driver's 86.57.25
– Passenger's 86.57.27

Removing

1 Disconnect battery – 86.15.20.
2 Remove seat cushion – 76.70.01.

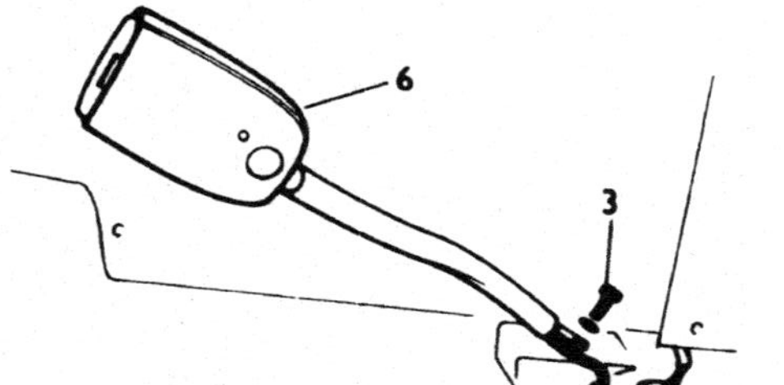

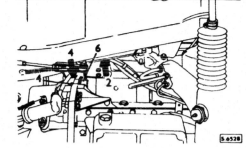

3 Withdraw seatbelt anchorage bolt – 76.70.01.
4 Slacken two screws retaining transmission tunnel side trim.
5 Lift side trim slightly and pull seat belt harness and connector clear.
6 Disconnect cable connector and remove belt complete with its harness.

Refitting

Reverse operations 1 to 6.

KEY WARNING SYSTEM

Description **86.58.00**

U.S.A. market

This system is designed to discourage leaving the ignition key in the lock with the vehicle unattended. While it should discourage theft, it is not a comprehensive anti-theft device.

The system is actuated by opening the driver's door when the ignition key is still in the lock; when the system is actuated a buzzer provides an audible warning.

The system is cancelled when the ignition key is removed from the steering lock or when the driver's door is closed.

The driver's door switch in the circuit controls the electrical supply to the key warning circuit and the key light circuit.

The key switch is built into the steering column lock unit. Failure of the switch would necessitate the replacement of the steering column lock.

The same buzzer is used for the seat belt warning system and is an integral part of the timer module.

STARTER MOTOR

Remove and refit **86.60.01**

Removing

1 Disconnect battery – 86.15.20.
2 Disconnect starter motor cables at terminal post (thick cable) and at lucar snap connector, (red/white braid covered cable).
3 Remove air cleaner – 19.10.01.
4 Remove two mounting bolts.
5 Pull starter from housing.
6 Retrieve spigot plate.

Refitting

Reverse operations 1 to 6.
NOTE: Ensure spigot plate is correctly positioned over locating spigots between starter motor drive end plate and bell housing.

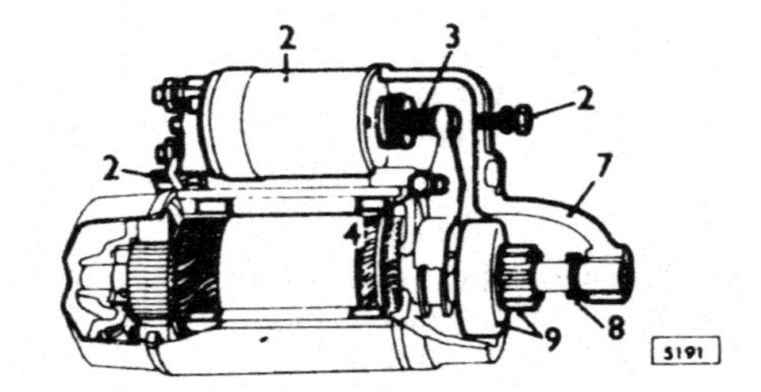

STARTER MOTOR ROLLER CLUTCH DRIVE UNIT

Remove and refit **86.60.05**

Removing

1 Remove starter motor – 86.60.01.
2 Remove solenoid complete with bridge strap (copper link).
3 Remove solenoid unit from drive end fixing bracket.
4 Remove engagement lever pivot pin.
5 Withdraw through bolts, but do not remove end bracket or commutator end cover.
6 Mount starter motor vertically in a vice, (drive end uppermost).
7 Withdraw drive end fixing bracket.
8 Remove jump ring from groove on drive shaft.
9 Remove collar and drive unit from shaft.

Refitting

10 Reverse operations 3 to 9.
Tightening torques:
Through bolts 8.0 lb.ft. (1,1 kg.m.).
Solenoid unit fixing bolts 4.5 lb.ft. (0,62 kg.m.).
(a) Smear all moving parts of drive unit liberally with grease.
Shell SB.2628 (Home and cold climate countries).
Retinax 'A' (Hot climate countries).

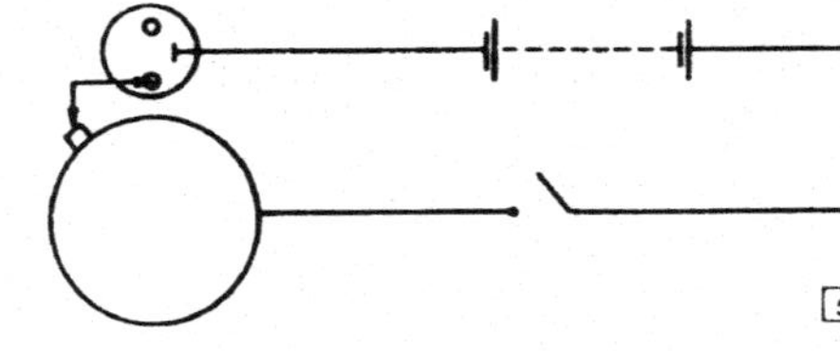

11 Connect solenoid terminal 'STA' to starter motor casing.
12 Connect a 6 volt supply between solenoid operating 'Lucar' terminal and starter motor casing.

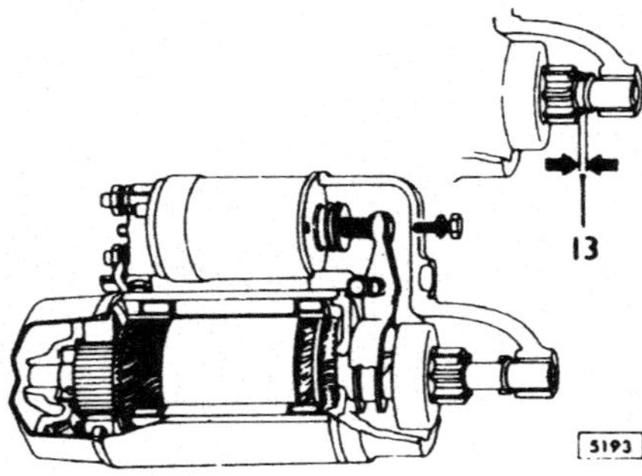

13 With solenoid energised and drive assembly now in engaged position, press pinion lightly back towards armature to take up any slack in drive operating mechanism and then set position of eccentric pivot pin to obtain 0.005 in. to 0.015 in. (0,127 mm. to 0,381 mm.) clearance between pinion and thrust collar.
14 Apply sealing compound and tighten locknut.
15 Refit bridge strap (copper link).
16 Refit starter motor – 86.60.01.

STARTER MOTOR SOLENOID UNIT

Remove and refit **86.60.08**

Removing

1 Remove starter motor — 86.60.01.
2 Remove link connecting solenoid to yoke terminal.
3 Remove two fixings, withdraw solenoid from bracket. Collect gasket.
4 Release plunger from top of drive engagement lever.

Refitting

Reverse operations 1 to 4 inclusive.

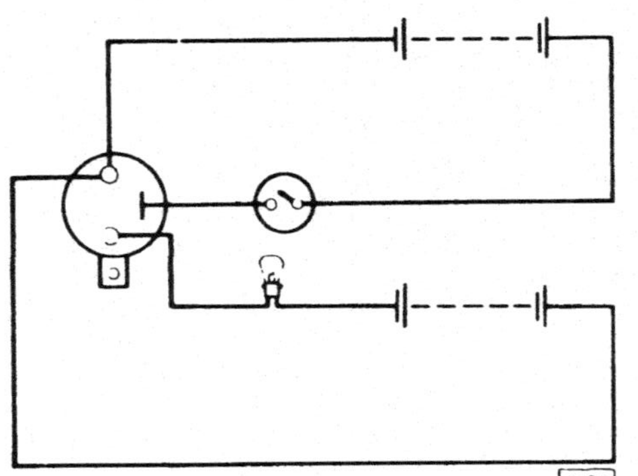

STARTER MOTOR SOLENOID UNIT

Test **86.60.09**

The following checks assume that the pinion travel has been correctly set.

1 Remove bridge strap connecting solenoid to motor.
2 Connect a 12 volt D.C. supply, with switch between solenoid 'Lucar' and large terminal 'STA'.
DO NOT CLOSE SWITCH
3 Connect a separately energised 60 watt test lamp across solenoid main terminals.
4 Close switch. Solenoid should be heard to operate, and lamp should light with full brilliance.
5 Open switch. Lamp should go out.

STARTER MOTOR

Overhaul **86.60.13**

Dismantling

1 Disconnect battery – 86.15.20.
2 Remove starter motor – 86.60.01.
3 Remove nut, plain and spring washers securing starter to solenoid connecting link.
4 Remove two bolts and spring washers securing solenoid to fixing bracket.
5 Lift terminal end of solenoid clear of connecting link and remove solenoid body.
6 Remove piston by pushing against spring and lifting from drive engagement lever.
7 Remove end cap seal.
8 Remove Spire retaining ring and bearing bush using chisel to remove some of claws on retaining ring.
NOTE: Discard Spire ring and provide new item for reassembly procedure.
9 Remove two through bolts and spring washers.
10 Remove commutator end cover by partially withdrawing cover and disengaging two field coil brushes from brush box.
11 Withdraw yoke and field coil assembly.
12 Remove mounting bracket from armature roller clutch drive and lever assembly by removing spire ring and pivot pin from drive engagement lever. Discard used spire ring.
13 Remove roller clutch drive and lever assembly from armature shaft by driving thrust collar from jump ring with tubular drift.

14 **Renewing brushes**
NOTE: Brushes which are worn to approximately 0.375 in. (9,5 mm.) in length must be renewed.
(a) Note which field coil conductor is fitted with long and short brush flexible connectors.
(b) Cut worn brush flexible connectors from field coils.
(c) Using resin cored solder, solder new brushes in position.
(d) Replace brushes in moulding.
NOTE: Ensure brushes are positioned exactly as originally fitted.
(e) Check push spring pressure with push type spring pressure gauge. Press on brush until it protrudes 0.062 in. (1,5 mm.) from moulding spring pressure should be 36 oz. (10.0 N).

15 Check individual components as detailed under relevant sub-headings below.

Reassembling

16 Inspect all components for wear and replace as necessary. Inspect commutator and clean with petrol soaked cloth. To remove burnt spots or grooving use a flat fine glass paper surface.
Always clean with petrol soaked cloth after rubbing down.
NOTE: Do not undercut insulation between segments.

17 Reverse operations 3 to 13.
NOTE: Torque figures for reassembly are as below:
Through bolts 8.0 lb.ft. (10,84Nm).
Solenoid unit fixing bolts 4.5 lb.ft. (6,10 Nm).
Solenoid terminal nuts 3.0 lb.ft. (4,1 Nm).

18 On completion of reassembling procedure drive spire ring on to armature shaft to a position which provides a maximum clearance between retaining ring and bearing bush shoulder of 0.010 in. (0,25 mm.).

Commutator cleaning

19 Clean the commutator if not scored with a petrol-moistened cloth.
Worn commutators should be cleaned with fine glass-paper or mounted in a lathe and a fine cut taken with a sharp tool. Finally polish with very fine glass-paper. DO NOT UNDERCUT INSULATORS BETWEEN SEGMENTS.
NOTE: Armatures must not be skimmed below a minimum diameter of 1.5 in (38 mm). Replace if below this limit.

Armature – checking

20 Armature conductors lifted from risers indicate overspeeding. Carefully resolder conductors or replace armature. Check clutch operation.
Armatures showing signs of fouling indicate worn bearings or un-true shaft.
Renew armature or bearings as required.
No attempt should be made to machine an untrue shaft.

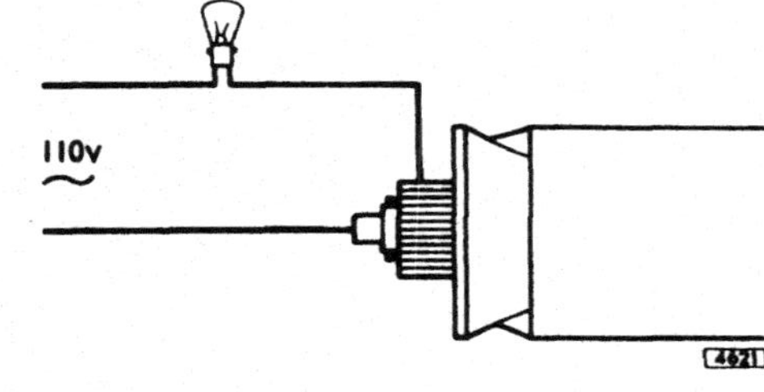

Armature insulation test

21 Connect a 110V a.c. 15W test lamp between any one of the commutator segments and the shaft.
If lamp lights renew armature.

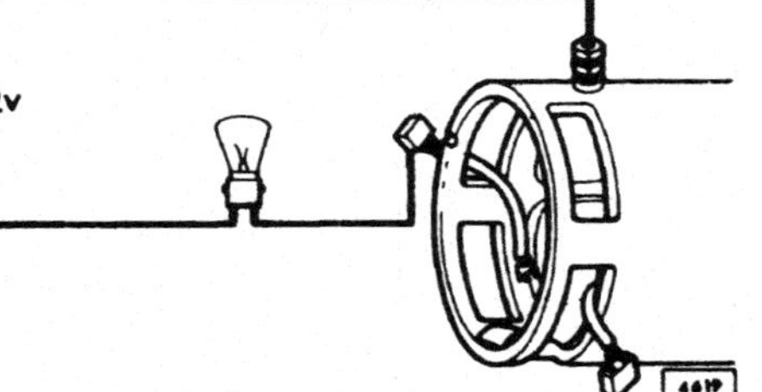

Field coil – Test

22 Check continuity of winding by connecting a 12 volt test lamp and battery between the terminal post and each brush (with the armature removed).
An open circuit is indicated if lamp does not light.
Replace faulty coils.

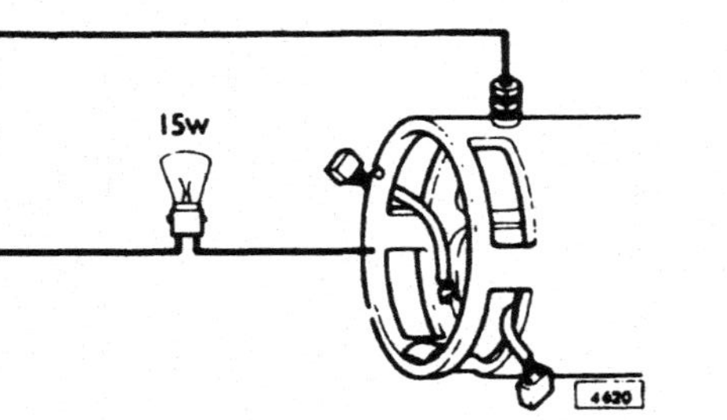

23 Check coil insulation with a 100 volt a.c. 15 watt test lamp connected between the terminal post and a clean part of the yoke.
Renew field coils if bulb is illuminated.

24 To replace field coils, unscrew the four pole shoe retaining screws using a wheel-operated screwdriver.
Remove coils, pole shoes and insulation pieces.
Fit new coils over shoes, and replace in yoke, taking care that the taping around the coils is not trapped between the shoes and yoke.
Locate shoes by lightly tightening the screws, fit insulation pieces, and finally tighten screws with wheel-screwdriver.

Bearing – replacement

25 Replace bearings if excessive side play of shaft is evident.
Bushes in intermediate and drive end brackets should be pressed out, commutator end bracket bush must be withdrawn with a withdrawal tool.
Soak bushes in clean engine oil for 24 hours before refitting. Refit by using a shouldered polished mandrel, 0.0005 in. (0,013 mm.) greater in diameter than shaft.
NOTE: **Porous bronze bushes must not be reamed out after fitting.**

Roller clutch drive – Checking

26 Check that pinion is free to move on shaft splines, and clutch assembly operates correctly. Replace faulty or sticking units.

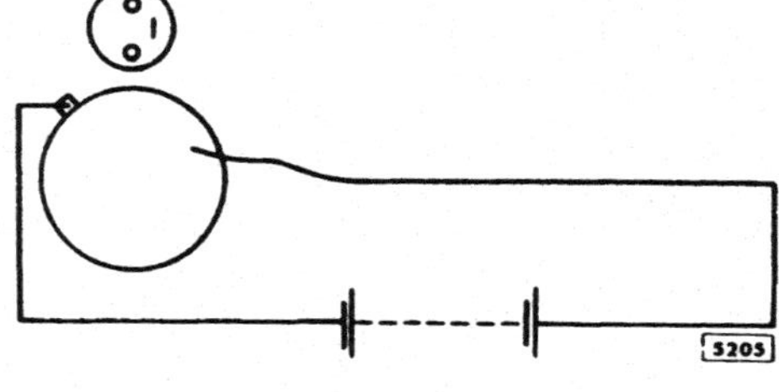

Pinion Movement Setting

27 After re-assembly of the starter (cranking) motor pinion movement must be reset as follows:
Connect the 'Lucar' solenoid terminal in series with a switch to a 10 volt battery.
Connect other battery terminal to starter yoke.
Close switch. (This throws the drive assembly forward into the engage position). Measure the distance between pinion and thrust washer on armature shaft extension.
NOTE: Pinion should be pressed lightly towards armature to take up any slack in engagement linkage. Correct setting should be 0.005 in. to 0.015 in. (0,127 mm. to 0,381 mm.).
To adjust, slacken the eccentric pin securing nut and turn pin until correct setting is obtained.
NOTE: Arc of adjustment is 180° and the head of the arrow on the pivot pin should be set only between the arrow heads on the drive end casting.
Tighten securing nut to retain pin position after setting.

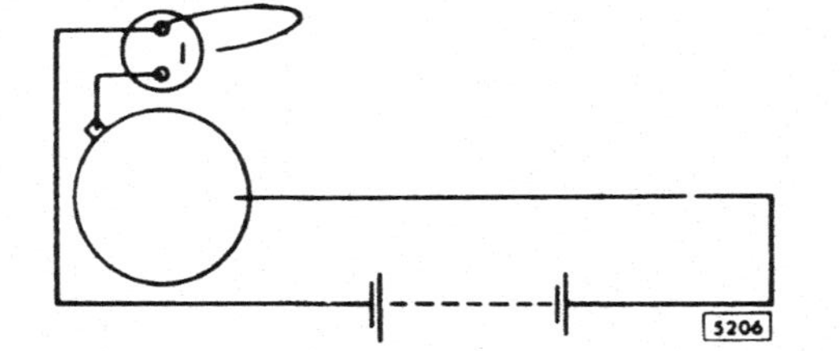

STARTER MOTOR

Bench Testing 86.60.14

The following bench tests will determine if the fault is with the motor or solenoid unit.

1 Clamp motor in vice.
2 Connect a 12 volt battery, using heavy duty cables, to the motor frame and motor terminal.
3 Check that motor operates under light running conditions. If necessary equipment is available check light running current and speed against figures stated under "Performance Data".
4 If starter motor fails test, dismantle for overhaul.
If starter operates check or replace solenoid unit as follows: –
5 Transfer cable from motor terminal to main solenoid terminal.
6 Fit jumper lead and touch to Lucar solenoid connector.
7 If motor does not operate, solenoid or solenoid contacts are faulty. Check and replace as necessary.

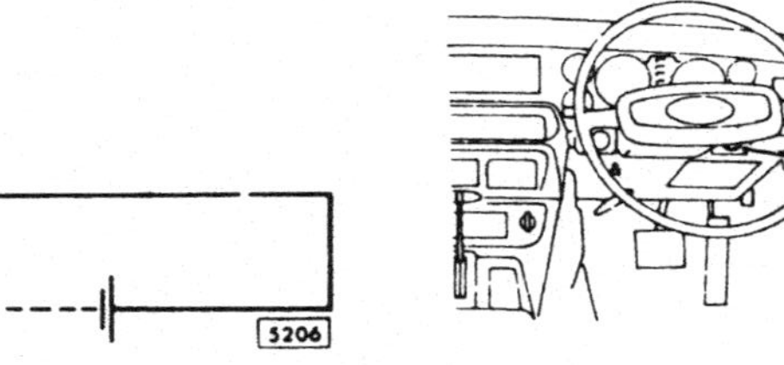

IGNITION SWITCH

Remove and refit 86.65.03

Removing
1 Disconnect battery, see 86.15.20.
2 Remove driver's side dash liner, see 76.46.11.
3 Pull retaining ring from rear of ignition/steering lock mechanism, and remove retaining screw on later cars.
4 Disconnect switch from harness at multi-pin connector plug.

Refitting
5 Reconnect switch to harness.
6 Push retaining ring over lock mechanism ensuring that locating segment is correctly positioned.
Reverse operations 1 and 2.

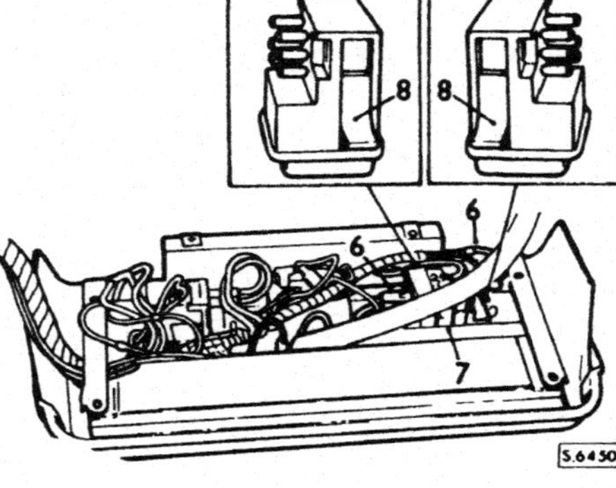
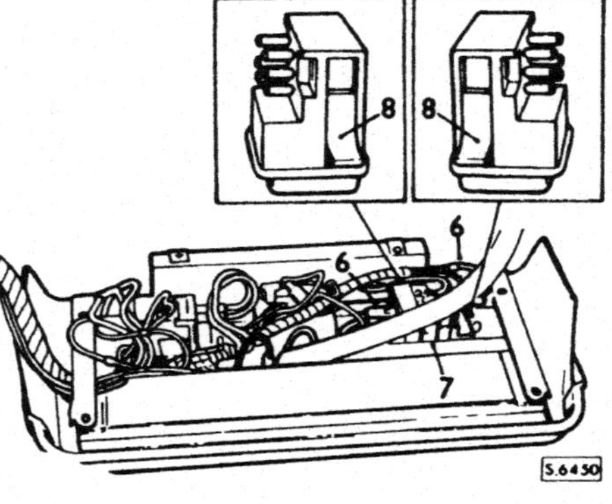
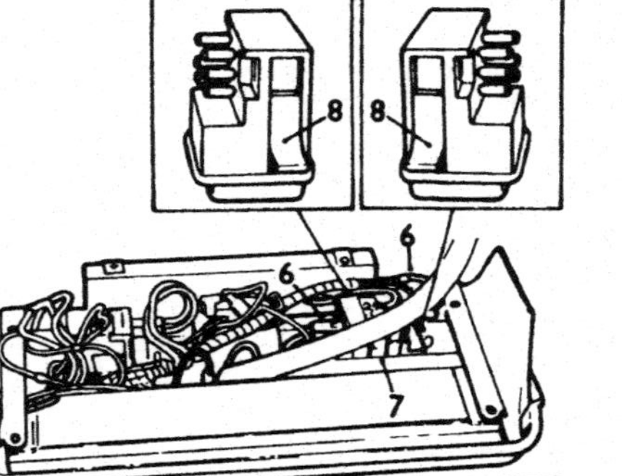

PANEL SWITCHES

Remove and refit 86.65.06

FUEL TANK SWITCH 86.65.39

BACKLIGHT HEATER SWITCH 86.65.37

MAP LIGHT SWITCH 86.65.24

INTERIOR LIGHT SWITCH 86.65.13

Removing
1 Disconnect battery – 86.15.20.
NOTE: On later cars it is only necessary to lever switch mounting panel from surround.
2 Remove heater/air condition control knobs.
3 Pull radio escutcheon forward.
4 Withdraw four screws from centre oddments tray.
5 Pull oddments tray forward.
6 Note cable positions and disconnect from related pair of switches.
7 Remove pair of switches and mounting panel from oddments tray.
8 Depress spring retaining clips at top and bottom of switch and push through mounting panel.

Refitting
Reverse operations 1 to 8.

INSTRUMENT PANEL LIGHTING RHEOSTAT

Remove and refit 86.65.07

Removing
1 Disconnect battery – 86.15.20.
2 Withdraw two screws and drop dash casing.
3 Depress spring loaded pip on rheostat centre shaft and remove control knob.
4 Unscrew retaining ring.
5 Remove rheostat heat shield by sliding out from under lock nut.
6 Disconnect cables at lucars on rheostat case.
7 Withdraw rheostat from dash casing.

Refitting
Reverse operations 1 to 7.

MASTER LIGHTING SWITCH

Remove and refit 86.65.09

Removing
1 Disconnect battery – 86.15.20.
2 Remove drivers side dash liner – 76.46.11.
3 Slacken two screws retaining switch legend plate.
4 Remove control knob by inserting pin through access hole and depressing retaining pin while pulling knob.

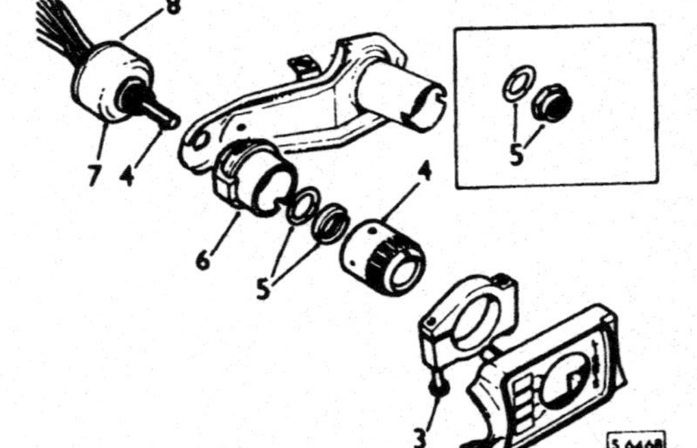

5 Unscrew switch retaining bezel.
6 Remove switch shroud.
7 Push switch through mounting plate.
8 Disconnect switch at multi pin plug and socket.

Refitting
Reverse operations 1 to 8.

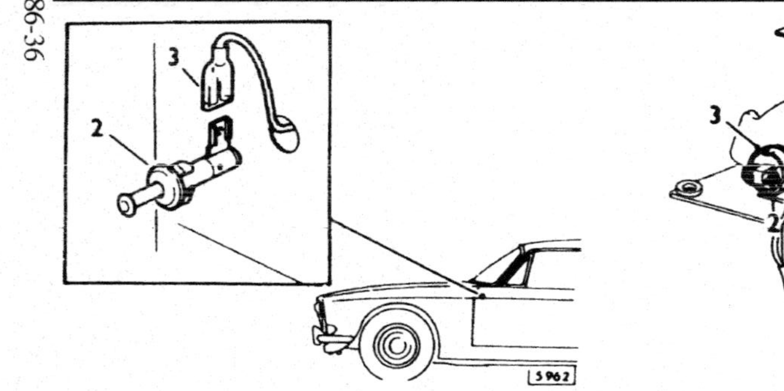
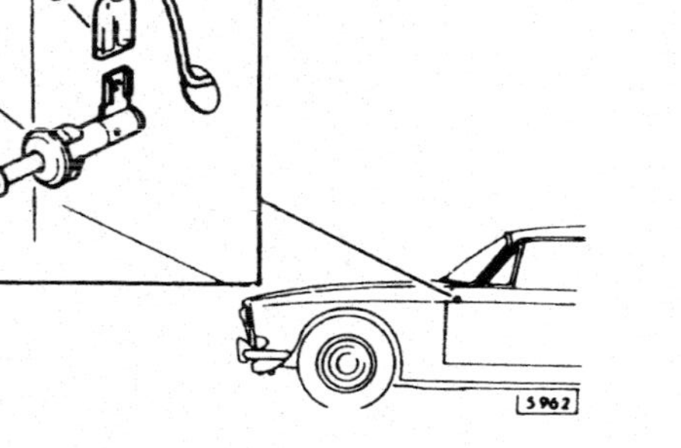

DOOR PILLAR SWITCH

Remove and refit – 4 Door cars 86.65.15

Removing
1 Disconnect battery - 86.15.20.
2 Using screwdriver or other suitable tool, lever switch from door pillar. Care must be taken not to damage paintwork.
3 Disconnect cable from lucar connector on switch.
4 Secure cable to prevent it pulling back into door pillar cavity.

Refitting
Reverse operations 1 to 4.
NOTE: A different type of switch from that illustrated is fitted to later cars.

REVERSE LIGHT SWITCH

Remove and refit 86.65.20

Removing
1 Carry out operation 86.57.19, items 1 to 5.
2 Disconnect cables from reverse light switch.
3 Withdraw reverse light switch, retain washer and spacers.

Refitting
4 When refitting reverse light switch ensure that operating plunger protrudes through mounting plate by an amount sufficient for cam to operate switch when reverse is selected.
5 Reverse operations 1 and 2.

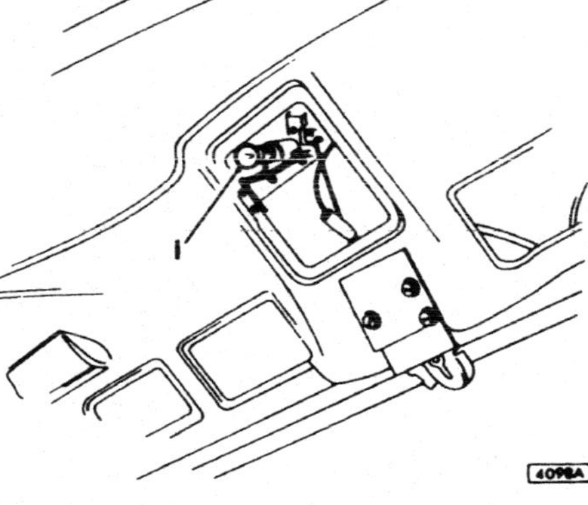

LUGGAGE COMPARTMENT LIGHT SWITCH

Remove and refit 86.65.22

The switching device for the luggage compartment illumination is an integral part of the boot light assembly. Removal and refitting is detailed under 86.45.16. No servicing is possible to this unit; defective units must be renewed.

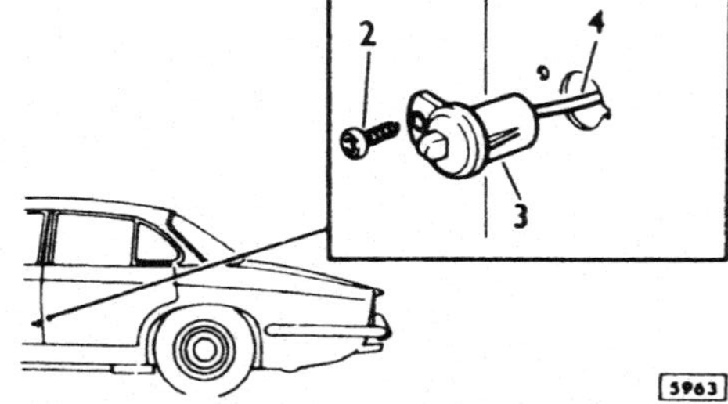

DOOR PILLAR SWITCH (Key alarm)

Remove and refit 86.65.27

NOTE: This type of switch is used on both two- and four-door versions of Series 2 cars. Early-type switch shown.
1 Disconnect battery, see 86.15.20.
2 Withdraw retaining screw from switch.
3 Withdraw switch from door pillar.
4 Disconnect cables from lucar connectors on switch.

Refitting
Reverse operations 1 to 4.

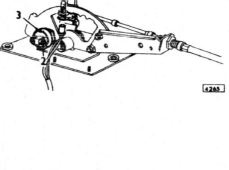

OIL PRESSURE SWITCH

Remove and refit 86.65.30

Removing
1 Disconnect battery – 86.15.20.
2 Disconnect cable from connector on top of switch.
3 Withdraw switch by unscrewing from manifold.

Refitting
Reverse operations 1 to 3.
NOTE: Installation torque must not exceed 240 lbf in (2,76 kgf m).

WINDSCREEN WASHER/WIPER SWITCH

Remove and refit 86.65.41

Removing
1 Disconnect battery – 86.15.20.
2 Remove steering wheel lower shroud.
3 Remove steering wheel – 57.60.01.

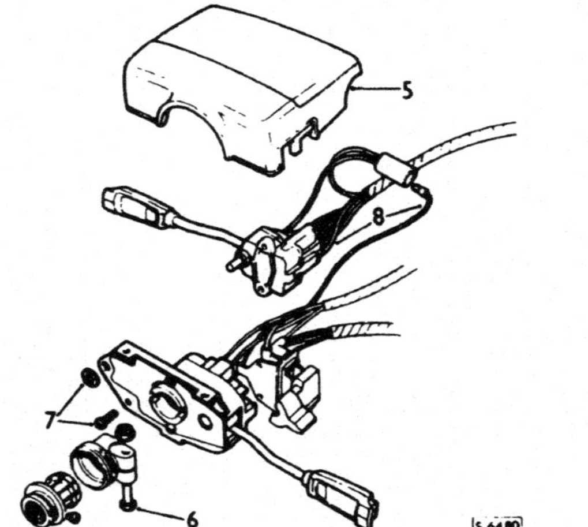

4 Remove driver's side dash liner, see 76.46.11.
5 Remove steering wheel upper shroud.
6 Slacken clinch bolt and pull switch assembly from upper steering column.
7 Remove two screws and spire washer retaining switch.
8 Disconnect harness at multi pin connector and earth lead at snap connector.

Refitting
Reverse operations 1 to 8.

HANDBRAKE WARNING LIGHT SWITCH

Remove and refit 86.65.45

Removing
1 Disconnect battery – 86.15.20.
2 Remove driver's side centre console side cheek, see 76.25.02.
3 Remove driver's side dash liner, see 76.46.11.
4 Withdraw two bolts and washers securing hand brake mounting bracket.
5 Pull trim from side of footwell to reveal handbrake warning switch.
6 Disconnect cables from lucars on switch.
7 Note number of threads above lock nut and slacken nut.
8 Unscrew switch from handbrake pull mounting tube.

Refitting
9 Reverse operations 6, 7 and 8, ensuring that black lead is fitted to forward Lucar.
10 Re-connect battery – 86.15.20.
11 Operate handbrake to ensure correct operation of warning light. Adjust as necessary.
12 Reverse operations 1 to 5.

HANDBRAKE WARNING SWITCH

Adjustment 86.65.46

1 Pull footwell side casing carpet to one side and clear of handbrake control.
2 Slacken locknut.
3 With handbrake in the 'OFF' position screw in switch unit until warning light just goes out. Ensure switch is mounted lengthwise on the handbrake control rod.
4 Tighten locknut.
5 Function the handbrake to ensure that switch operates correctly. Adjust as necessary.
6 Replace carpet.

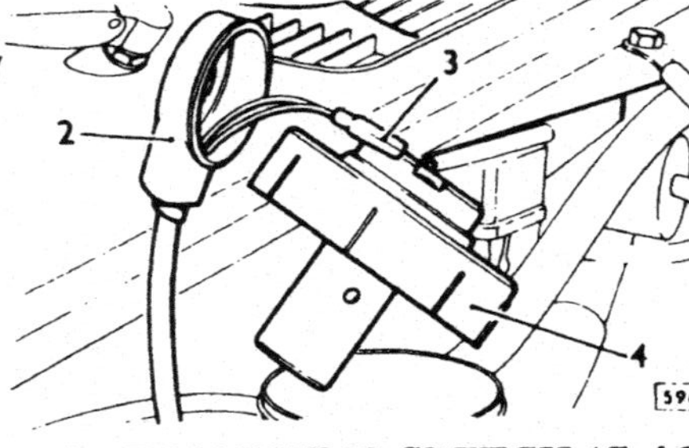
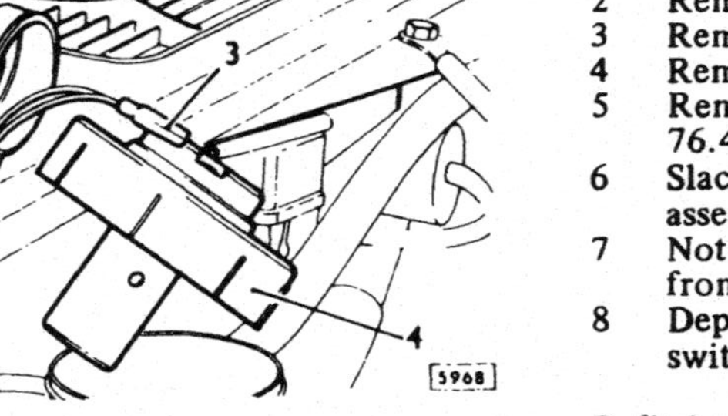

BRAKE WARNING SWITCH (fluid level)

Remove and refit 86.65.49

Removing
1 Disconnect battery – 86.15.20.
2 Ease back rubber cover on the lid of brake fluid reservoir.
3 Disconnect cables at lucar connectors.
4 Unscrew reservoir lid.
NOTE: No servicing is possible on this unit. Defective units must be changed.

Refitting
Reverse operations 1 to 4.
NOTE: Early type reservoir and switch illustrated.

HAZARD WARNING SWITCH

Remove and refit 86.65.50

Removing
1 Disconnect battery – 86.15.20.

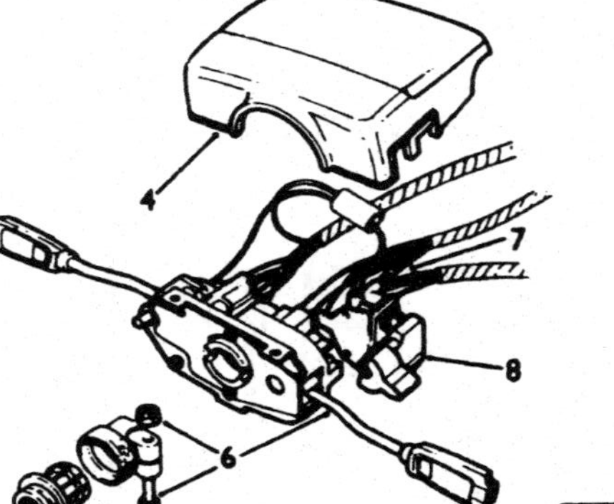

2 Remove steering column lower shroud.
3 Remove steering wheel – 57.60.01.
4 Remove steering column upper shroud.
5 Remove driver's side dash liner, see 76.46.11.
6 Slacken clinch bolt and pull switch assembly from upper steering column.
7 Note positions of cables and disconnect from lucars on back of switch.
8 Depress nylon retaining tags and push switch through mounting plate.

Refitting
Reverse operations 1 to 8.

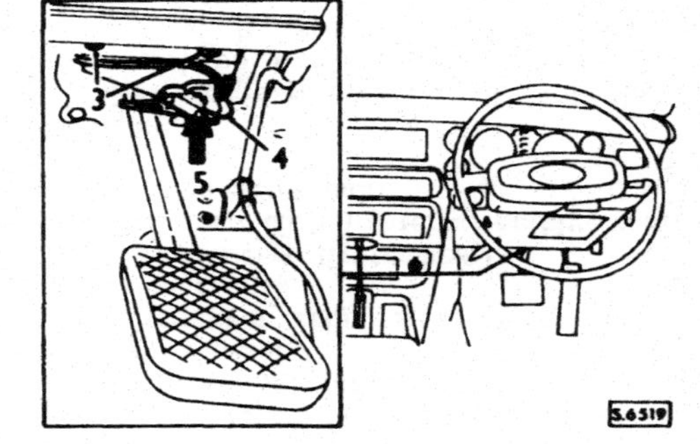

STOP LIGHT SWITCH

Remove and refit 86.65.51

Removing
1 Disconnect battery – 86.15.20.
2 Remove driver's side dash liner, see 76.46.11.
3 Withdraw one bolt and one dowel bolt securing switch mounting plate.
NOTE: Ensure position of dowel bolt is noted to facilitate correct refitting.
4 Disconnect cables at lucar connectors on switch.
5 Remove two screws and keep plate securing switch to mounting plate.
NOTE: Mark switch position before removing to ensure correct positioning during refitting.

Refitting
6 Reverse operations 1 to 5, ensuring leads are routed clear of pedals, etc.
7 Check operation of switch, adjust as necessary.

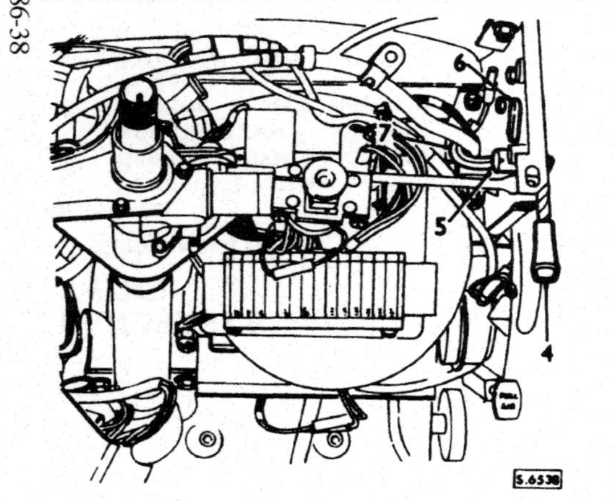

CHOKE WARNING LIGHT SWITCH (Not fitted to later cars)

Remove and refit 86.65.53

Removing

1 Disconnect battery – 86.15.20.
2 Remove driver's side dash liner, see 76.46.11.
3 Remove nut and spring washer securing choke cable outer casing to facia bracket.
4 Pull choke handle illumination bulb holder from choke handle.
5 Remove nut securing choke cable nipple to choke handle and secure choke cable to one side.
6 Withdraw two securing screws from micro switch, recover keep plate.
7 Disconnect cables at cable connectors.

Refitting

Reverse operations 1 to 7.

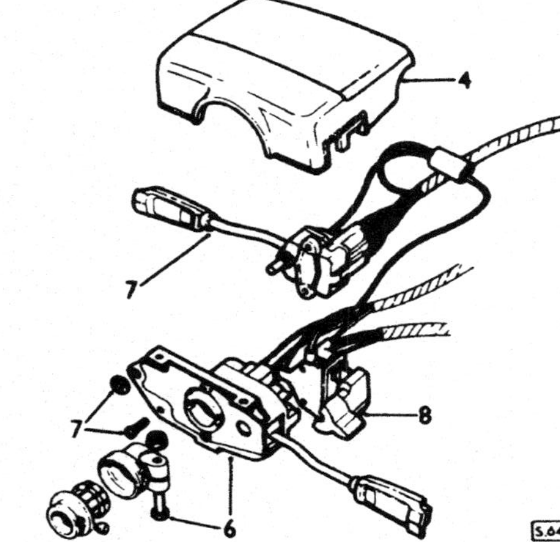

DIRECTION/HEADLIGHT FLASHER SWITCH

Remove and refit 86.65.55

Removing

1 Disconnect battery – 86.15.20.
2 Remove steering column lower shroud.
3 Remove steering wheel – 57.60.01.
4 Remove steering column upper shroud.
5 Remove drivers side dash liner – 76.46.11.
6 Slacken clinch bolt and pull switch assembly from upper steering column.
7 Remove two screws and spire washer securing windscreen washer/wiper switch to assembly and lay switch to one side.
8 Remove two screws securing hazard warning switch mounting bracket to assembly and lay switch and bracket to one side.
9 Recover remainder of assembly.
CAUTION: No attempt must be made to separate Direction/Headlight/Flasher switch from mounting bracket. Faulty items are changed as complete assemblies.

Refitting

Reverse operations 1 to 9.

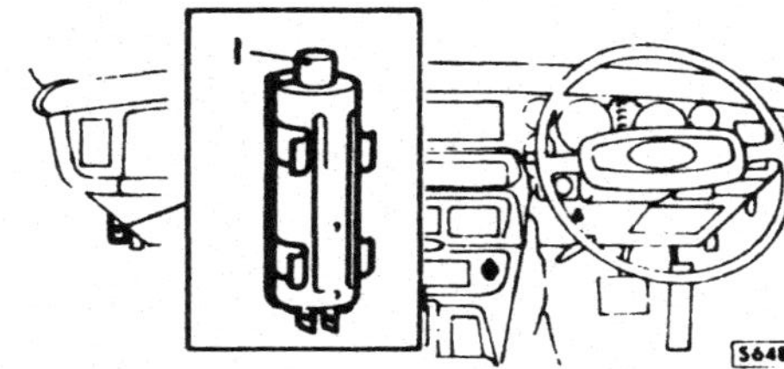

FUEL CUT-OFF INERTIA SWITCH

Remove and refit (see 19.22.09) 86.65.58
Reset 86.65.59

An inertia sensitive switch is fitted in the electrical supply to the fuel pumps. Should the car be subjected to heavy impact forces, the switch opens, isolating the fuel pumps, ensuring fuel is not pumped into a potentially dangerous situation.

The switch is located above the fresh air pull on the passenger side of the car. The switch can be reset by inserting finger through access point in top of switch cover, and pressing button (1) in top of switch.

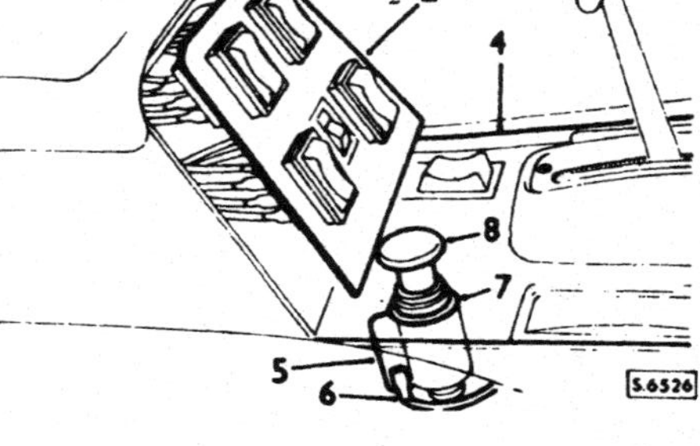

CIGAR LIGHTER ASSEMBLY

Remove and refit 86.65.60

Removing

1 Disconnect battery – 86.15.20.
2 Lever off electric window switch panel.
3 Withdraw four screws retaining transmission console trim panel.
4 Lift panel away from console.
5 Press together the sides of cigar lighter bulb assembly and remove from cigar lighter bezel.
6 Disconnect cable from cigar lighter connector.
7 Unscrew cigar lighter bezel.
8 Withdraw cigar lighter assembly from console escutcheon.

Refitting

Reverse operations 1 to 8. Note that radial position of lighter socket is critical, to avoid shorting to window lift relay.

The following pages contain details of:

COMPONENT LOCATION

WIRING DIAGRAMS

To assist in identification and location, the symbols and cable colour codes are given below. A master key to location and wiring diagrams is given with the component location chart. Extracts from this master key are given with the appropriate systems diagram.

CABLE COLOUR CODE

N. Brown	**P. Purple**	**W. White**
U. Blue	**G. Green**	**Y. Yellow**
R. Red	**L. Light**	**B. Black**
K. Pink	**S. Slate**	**O. Orange**

When a cable has two colour code letters, the first denotes the Main Colour and the second the Tracer Colour.

SYMBOLS USED

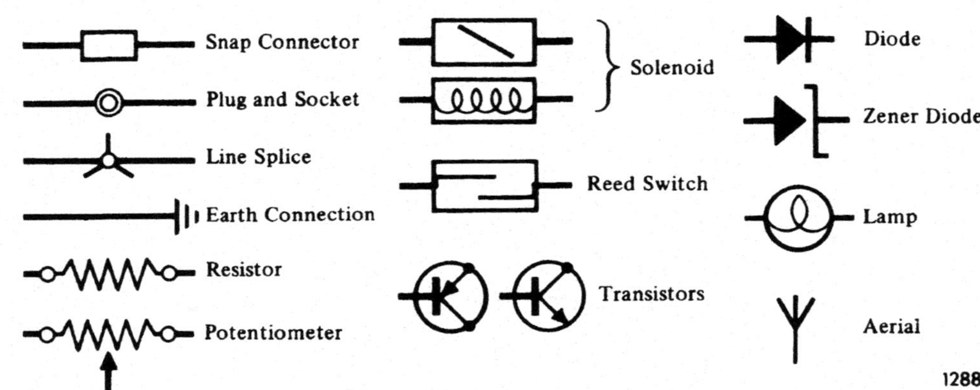

LAMP BULBS

LAMP FUNCTION	PART NUMBER	WATTS	TYPE
Outer Headlight (Main and dipped beam)	–	See local Dealer	Sealed Beam
Inboard main beam only	–	See local Dealer	Sealed Beam
Front/rear flasher lamps	GLB 382	21	Bayonet
Front flasher/side lamp	GLB 380	5/21	Bayonet
Side lamp	GLB 207	5	Bayonet
Stop/tail lamp	GLB 380	21	Bayonet
Reverse lamp	11740	21	Festoon
Number plate lamp	RTC 533	6	Capless
Side marker lamp	GLB 989	5	Bayonet
Map/interior lamps	12273	10	Festoon
Luggage compartment lamp	GLB 989	5	Bayonet
Warning lamps	GLB 286	1.2	Miniature capless
Instrument lamps	GLB 987	2.2	Bayonet
Cigar lighter	GLB 643	22	Miniature bayonet
Automatic transmission selector illumination	GLB 988	5	
Fibre optic light source	GLB 989	5	Bayonet
Catalyst/EGR warning lamp	GLB 281	2	

FUSES

FUSE No.	PROTECTED CIRCUITS	PART NUMBER	CURRENT CAPACITY
1	Fog lamps (if fitted)	GFS 420	20A
2	Hazard warning	GFS 415	15A
3	Map/interior lamps, cigar lighter, electric aerial (if fitted), clock, seat belt warning lamp	GFS 435	35A
4	Panel lights	GFS 415	15A
5	Direction indicators	GFS 415	15A
6	Reversing lights	GFS 435	35A
7	Panel switches, cigar lighter illumination, number plate lamp, luggage compartment lamp, fibre optic unit, gear selector illumination	GFS 415	15A
8	Side/tail lamps (LH)	GFS 415	15A
9	Side/tail lamps (RH)	GFS 415	15A
10	Air conditioning motor	GFS 450	50A
11	Windscreen wipers, air conditioning relay and clutch, windscreen washer, horn relay winding, cooling fan relay winding	GFS 450	50A
12	Heated back light	GFS 435	35A
	Headlamp (main beam)	GFS 425	25A
	Headlamp (dipped beam)	GFS 410	10A

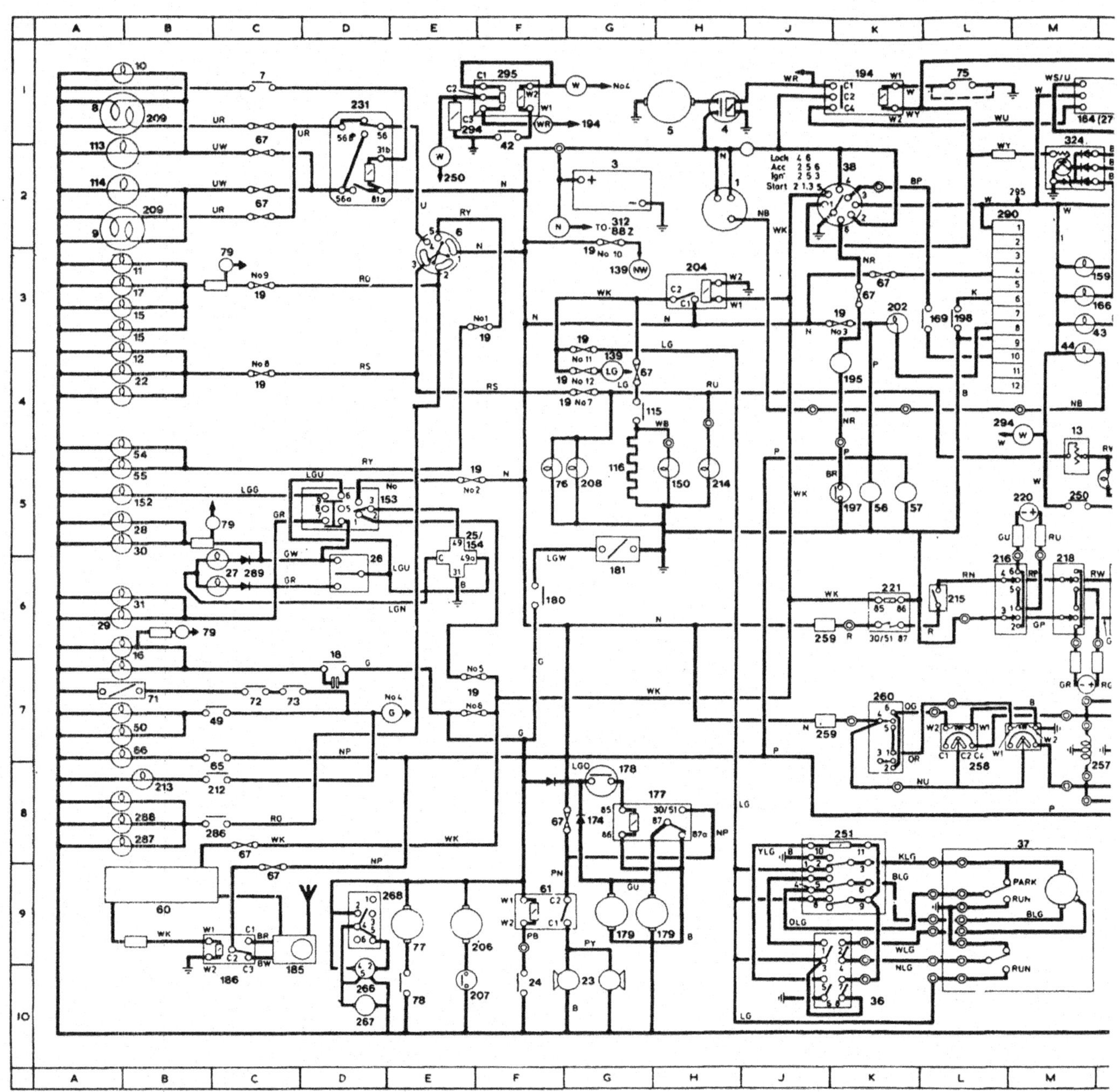

COMPONENT	No.
Alternator	1
Aerial motor	185
Aerial motor relay	186
Air conditioning ambient sensor	265
Air conditioning amplifier	261
Air conditioning blower	33
Air conditioning blower relay	189
Air conditioning blower resistor	188
Air conditioning compressor clutch	190
Air conditioning control switch	192
Air conditioning/Heater (to)	139
Air conditioning in-car sensor	264
Air conditioning servo	262
Air conditioning temperature selector	327
Air conditioning thermostat	191
Air conditioning vacuum valve	263
Air conditioning water temperature sensor	47
Air flow meter	311
Air temperature sensor (part of 311)	297
Altitude switch	325
* Anti-run on valve	195
* Anti-run on valve oil pressure switch (Early cars)	197
* Auto gearbox kickdown solenoid	181
* Auto gearbox kickdown pressure switch	180
Auto gearbox selector lamp	76
Auto gearbox start inhibit switch	75
Ballast resistor	164
* Base drive resistor (part of 164) (Later cars)	279
Battery	3
Battery condition indicator	146
Battery cooling fan	206

COMPONENT	No.
Battery cooling fan thermostat	207
* Blocking diode – brake warning	256
Blocking diode – direction indicators	289
Blocking diode – inhibit incorrect – polarity	315
Boot light	66
Boot light switch	65
Brake differential pressure switch	160
Brake failure warning light	323
Brake fluid level switch	182
Brake fluid level warning light	159
* Choke control illumination	214
* Choke warning light	213
* Choke control warning light switch	212
Cigar lighter	57
Cigar lighter illumination	208
Clock	56
Cold start injectors	300
Cold start relay (Part of 312)	299
Coolant temperature sensor	305
Direction indicator switch	26
Direction indicator warning light	27
Distributor	40
Door lock solenoid	257
Door lock solenoid relay	258
Door lock switch	260
Door switch RH	21
Door switch LH	22
Door switch (buzzer alarm)	169
* EGR warning switch } See Service	277
* EGR warning lamp } Interval	278
* EGR diode } Counter	284

COMPONENT	No.
Extra air valve	317
Fibre optics illumination lamp	255
Flasher unit (part of 154)	25
Flasher lamp RH front	28
Flasher lamp LH front	29
Flasher lamp RH rear	30
Flasher lamp LH rear	31
Fog lamp RH	54
Fog lamp LH	55
* Fuel cut off valve	294
* Fuel cut off relay	295
Fuel gauge	34
Fuel gauge tank unit	35
Fuel injection control unit (E.C.U.)	293
Fuel injection main relay	312
Fuel injection – pressure sensor	318
Fuel pump	41
Fuel pump relay (part of 312)	314
Fuel pump solenoid	205
Fuel tank change-over switch	140
Fuse box	19
Handbrake switch	165
Handbrake warning lamp	166
Hazard warning flasher unit (includes 25)	154
Hazard warning lamp	152
Hazard warning switch	153
Headlamp dip switch	7
Headlamp dip beam	209
Headlamp inner RH	113
Headlamp inner LH	114
Headlamp outer RH	8
Headlamp outer LH	9

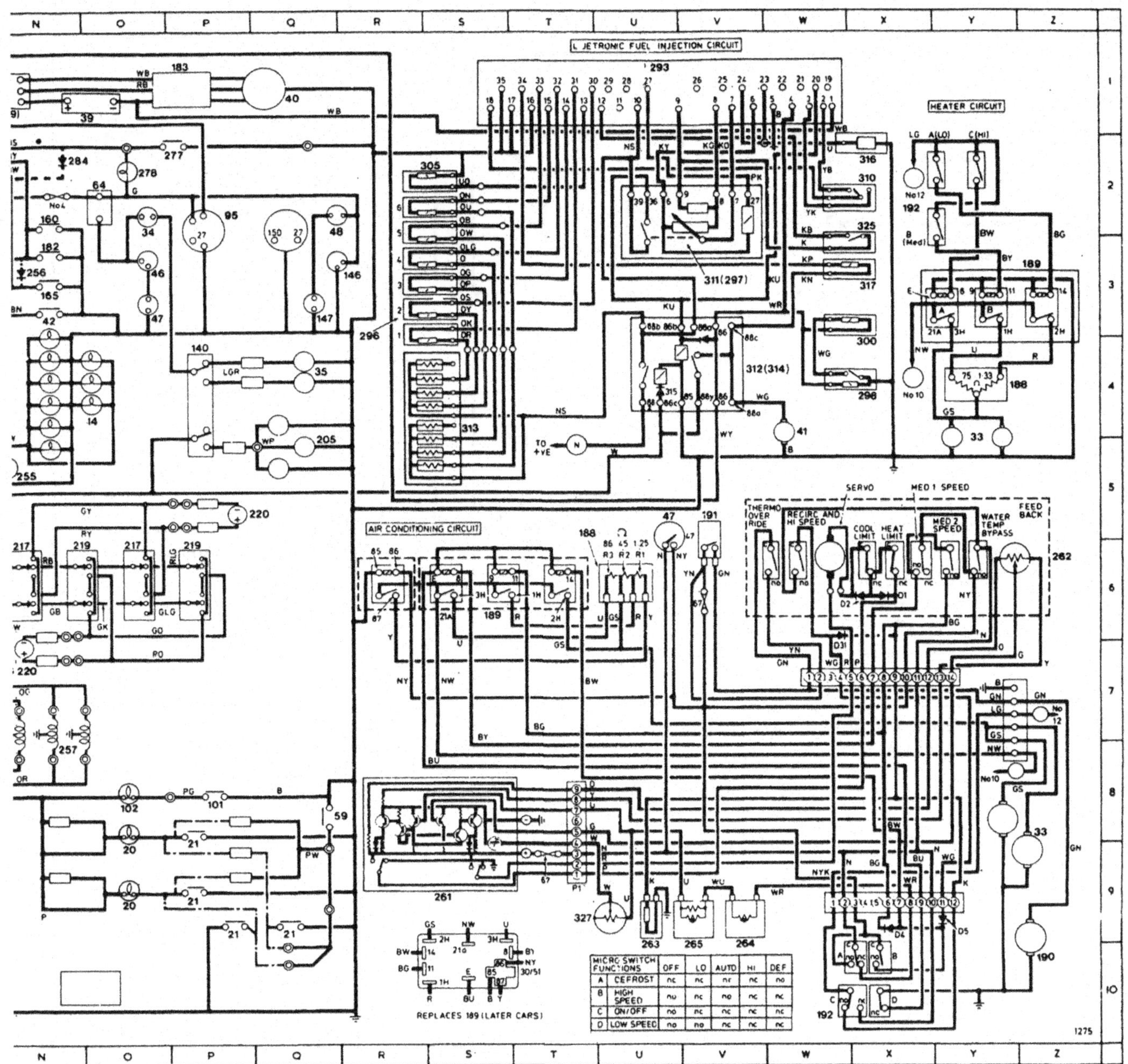

COMPONENT	No.
Headlamp pilot lamp (see sidelamp)	11
Headlamp relay	231
Headlamp washer pump (Scandinavia only)	267
Headlamp washer/wiper switch (Scandinavia only)	268
Headlamp wiper motor (Scandinavia only)	266
Horn	23
Horn push	24
Horn relay	61
Ignition amplifier	183
Ignition coil	39
Ignition protection relay	204
Ignition switch	38
Ignition warning lamp	44
Inertia switch	250
Injectors	296
Injector power resistors	313
Interior light	20
Interior light rear	111
Interior light switch	59
Inverter	324
Line fuse	67
Main beam warning light	10
Main light switch	6
Map light	102
Map light switch	101
Number plate lamp	15
Oil pressure gauge	48
Oil pressure switch (for 43 or 295)	42
Oil pressure transmitter (for 48)	147
Oil pressure warning lamp	43
Overdrive control switch	72
Overdrive gearbox switch	73

COMPONENT	No.
Overdrive solenoid	71
Oxygen (lambda) sensor	316
Oxygen (lambda) sensor warning lamp (see Service Interval Counter*)	
Panel lamps	14
Panel lamps rheostat	13
Radiator cooling fan diode	174
Radiator cooling fan motor	179
Radiator cooling fan relay	177
Radiator cooling fan thermostat	178
Radio	60
Rear fog guard lamp	288
Rear fog guard switch	286
Rear fog guard warning lamp	287
Rear window demist switch	115
Rear window demist unit	116
Rear window demist warning lamp	150
Reverse lamps	50
Reverse lamps switch	49
Revolution counter	95
* Seat belt sequential start unit (Early cars)	245
Seat belt switch — driver	198
* Seat belt switch — passenger	199
Seat belt warning control unit (Later cars)	290
* Seat belt warning gearbox switch (Early cars)	201
Seat belt warning lamp	202
* Seat switch — driver (Early cars)	244
* Seat switch — passenger (Early cars)	200
Side lamp RH or (Headlamp pilot lamp)	11
Side lamp LH or (Headlamp pilot lamp)	12
* Service Interval Counter Switch	277

COMPONENT	No.
* Service Interval Counter warning light †	278
Starter motor	5
Starter solenoid	4
Starter solenoid/ballast resistor relay	194
Stop lamps	16
Stop lamp switch	18
Tail lamp RH	17
Tail lamp LH	22
Thermal circuit breaker	259
Thermotime switch	298
Throttle switch	310
Trailer socket	79
* Unilateral parking light switch (Early cars)	254
Voltage stabiliser	64
Water temperature gauge	46
Water temperature transmitter for gauge	47
Window lift master switch	215
Window lift motor	220
Window lift safety relay	221
Window lift switch RH front	216
Window lift switch LH front	218
Window lift switch RH rear	217
Window lift switch LH rear	219
Windscreen washer pump	77
Windscreen washer switch	78
Windscreen wiper motor	37
Windscreen wiper relay	251
Windscreen wiper switch	36

† SIC operates EGR/Catalyst or F1 oxygen sensor warning light

*See 86—41

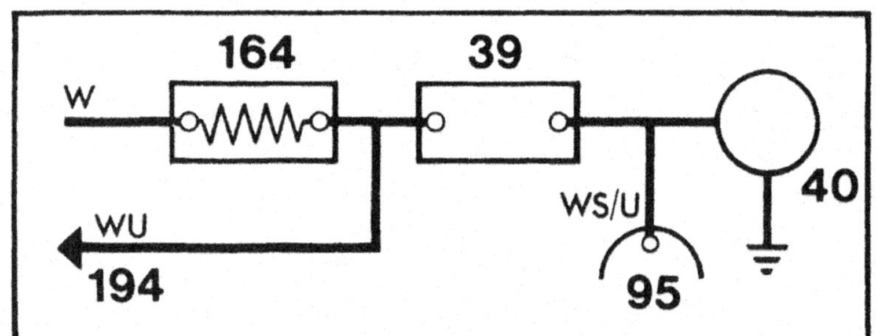

3.4 and 4.2 cars fitted with Ballast Ignition and Carburetters

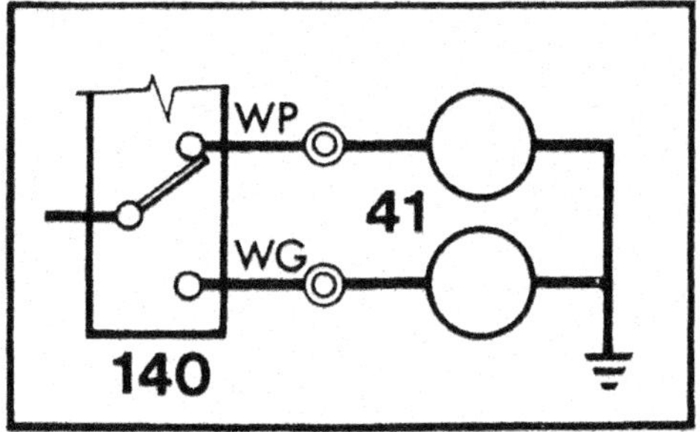

Part of Fuel Changeover switch
(cars fitted with carburetters)

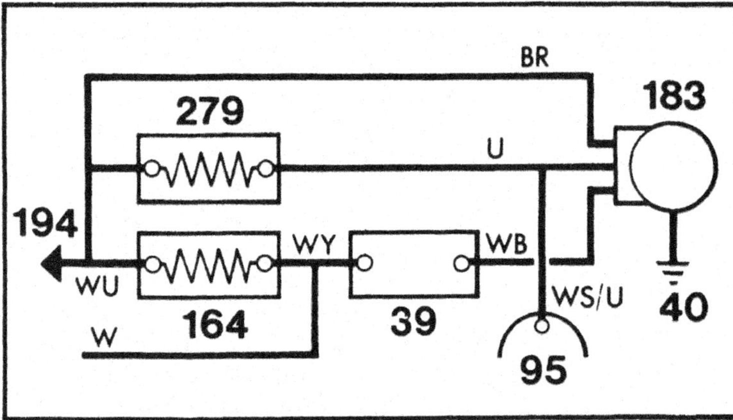

4.2 cars fitted with Ballast Ignition and Electronic Ignition and Carburetters

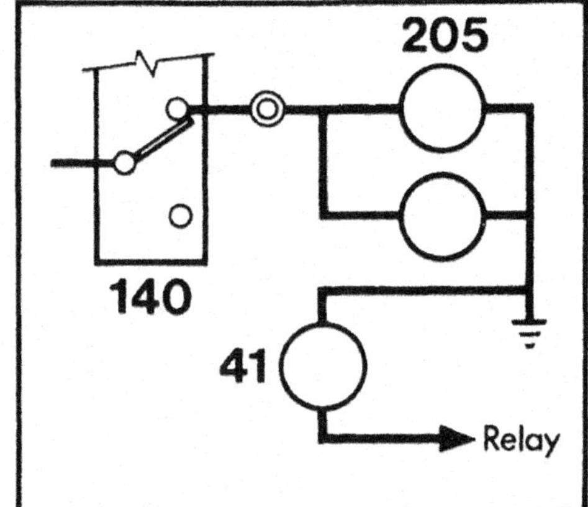

Part of Fuel Changeover switch
(cars fitted with Fuel injection)
(Early cars)

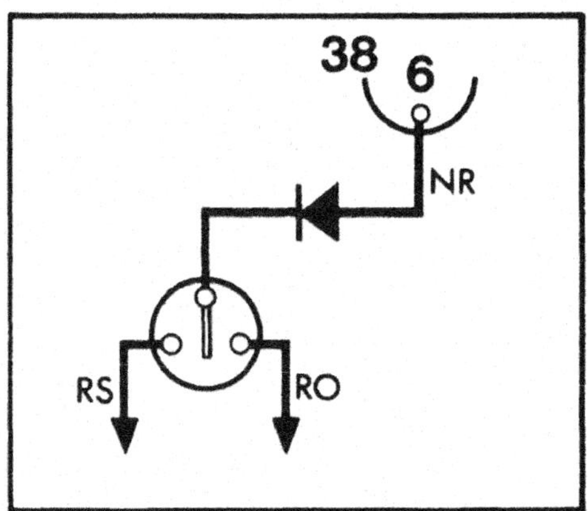

Unilateral Parking Light System
(Early cars)

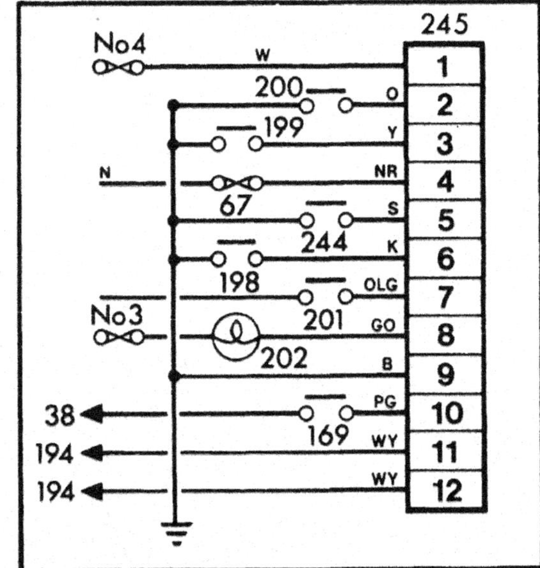

Sequential Start Control Unit
(Early cars)

CIRCUIT VARIATIONS

180, 181 } Borg Warner Model 12

198, 199, 200, 201, 244, 245 } Replaced by 290 (Later cars)

254 Early cars only

256 Replaced by 324

325 if fitted

195, 197, 212, 213, 214 } Carburetter cars

266, 267, 268 } Scandinavia only

314, 299 } Part of 312

297 Part of 311

277, 278, 284 } Service interval counter and warning light show when EGR/Catalyst and (later cars) Oxygen sensor require servicing

279 Electronic ignition for carburetters, Part of 164 for fuel injection

86-41

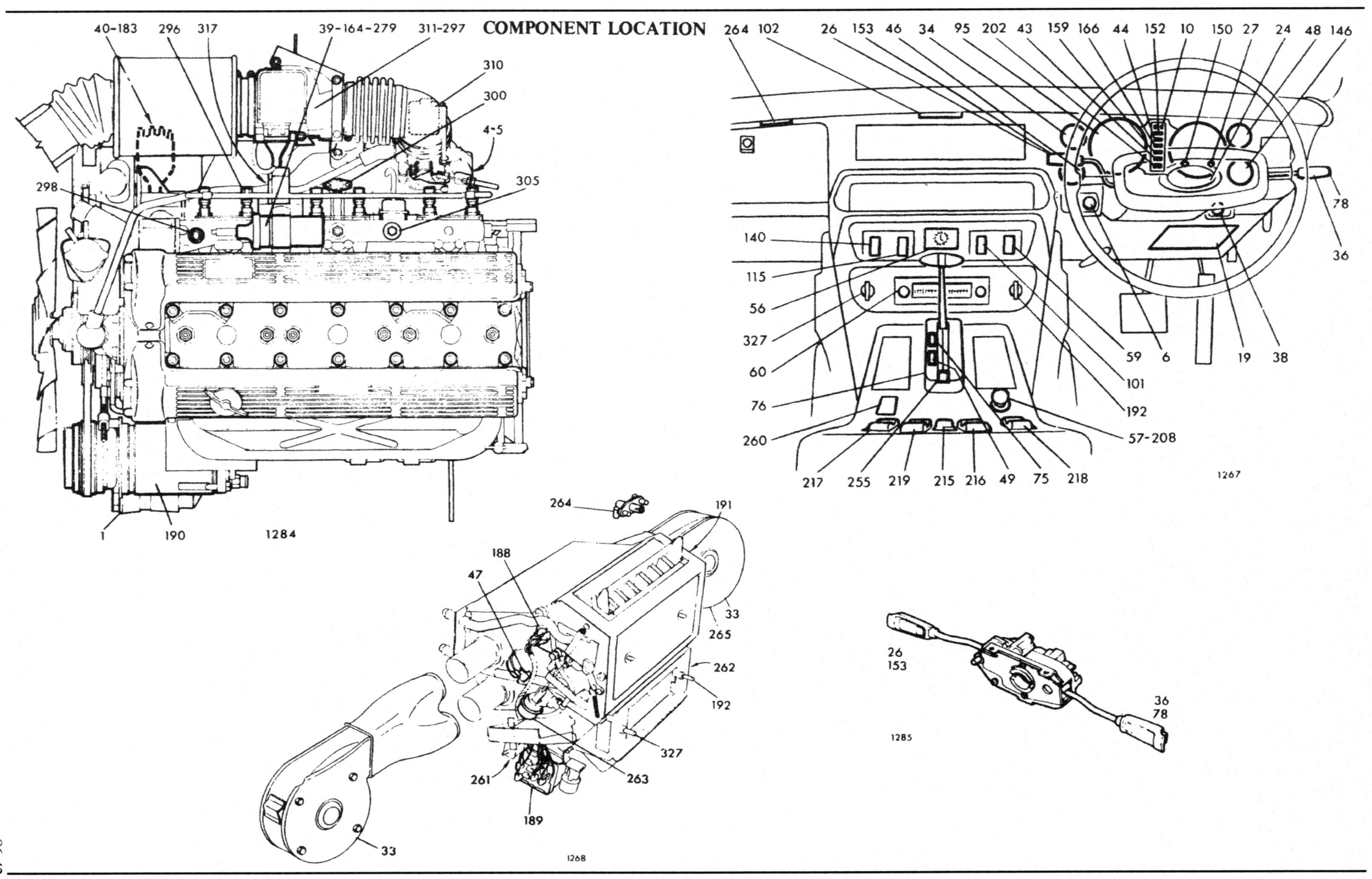
40-183
296
317
39-164-279
311-297
310
300
4-5
305
298
1
190
1284
264
102
26
153
46
34
95
202
43
159
166
44
152
10
150
27
24
48
146
78
36
140
115
56
327
60
76
260
217
255
219
215
216
49
75
218
57-208
192
101
59
6
19
38
1267
264
191
188
47
33
265
262
192
327
263
261
189
33
1268
26
153
36
78
1285

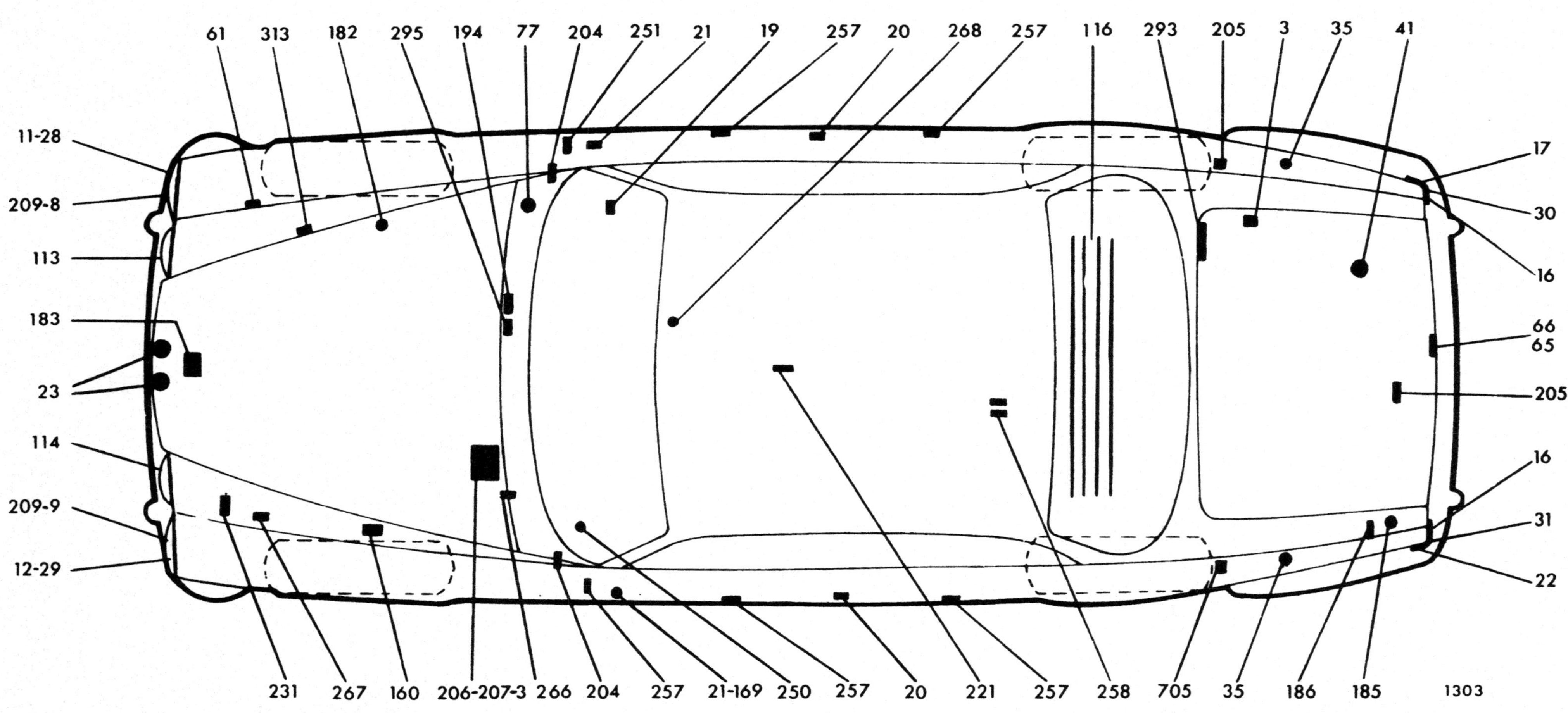
61
313
182
295
194
77
204
251
21
19
257
20
268
257
116
293
205
3
35
41
11-28
209-8
113
183
23
114
209-9
12-29
17
30
16
66
65
205
16
31
22
231
267
160
206-207-3
266
204
257
21-169
250
257
20
221
257
258
705
35
186
185
1303

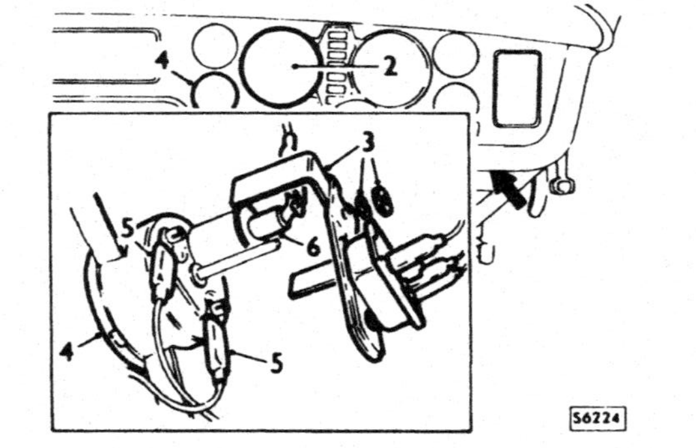

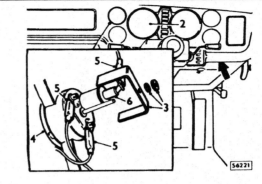

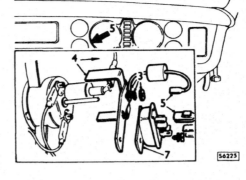

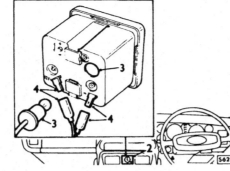

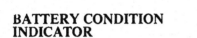

BATTERY CONDITION INDICATOR

Remove and refit **88.10.07**

Removing

1 Disconnect battery – 86.15.20.
2 Remove tachometer – 88.30.21.
3 Remove finger nut and lock washer from battery condition indicator and voltage stabiliser retaining bracket.
4 Withdraw indicator from fascia.
5 Disconnect cables at lucar connectors on rear of instrument.
6 Withdraw instrument lighting bulb holder.

Refitting

Reverse operations 1 to 6.

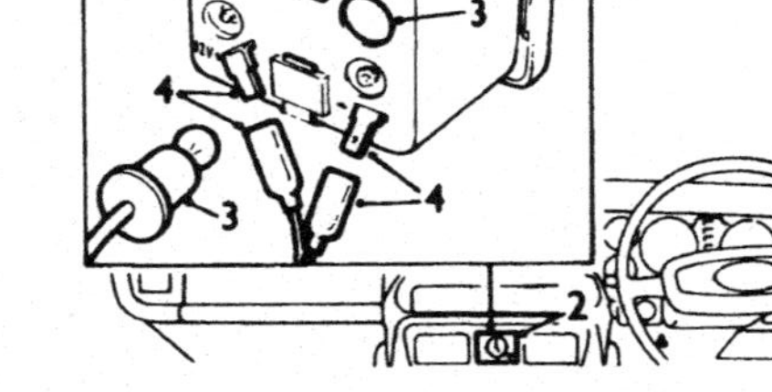

CLOCK

Remove and refit **88.15.07**

Removing

1 Disconnect battery – 86.15.20.
2 Lever clock from aperture.
3 Pull clock illumination bulb holder from back of clock.
4 Note positions of lucar connectors and disconnect cables.

Refitting

Reverse operations 1 to 4.

VOLTAGE STABILISER

Remove and refit **88.20.26**

Removing

1 Disconnect battery – 86.15.20.
2 Remove tachometer – 88.30.21.

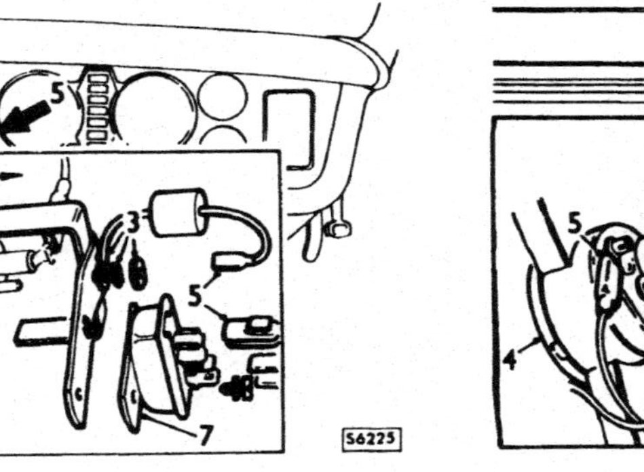

3 Remove finger nut, lock washer, and suppressor connector from battery condition meter retaining bracket.
4 Remove retaining bracket from battery condition meter.
5 Through tachometer aperture, note position of lucars on stabiliser and disconnect electrical connections.
6 Recover stabiliser and bracket.
7 Withdraw retaining screw and remove stabiliser from securing clip.

Refitting

Reverse operations 1 to 7.

OIL PRESSURE GAUGE

Remove and refit **88.25.01**

Removing

1 Disconnect battery – 86.15.20.
2 Remove tachometer – 88.30.21.
3 Remove finger nut and lockwasher from oil pressure gauge retaining bracket.
4 Withdraw instrument from fascia.

5 Disconnect cables at lucar connectors on back of instrument.
6 Withdraw instrument lighting bulb holder.

Refitting

Reverse operations 1 to 6.

OIL PRESSURE TRANSMITTER

Remove and refit **88.25.07**

Removing

1 Disconnect battery – 86.15.20.
2 Disconnect cable at lucar connector.
3 Remove transmitter with correct size spanner.
CAUTION: No pressure should be exerted on the capsule.

Refitting

Reverse operations 1 to 3.

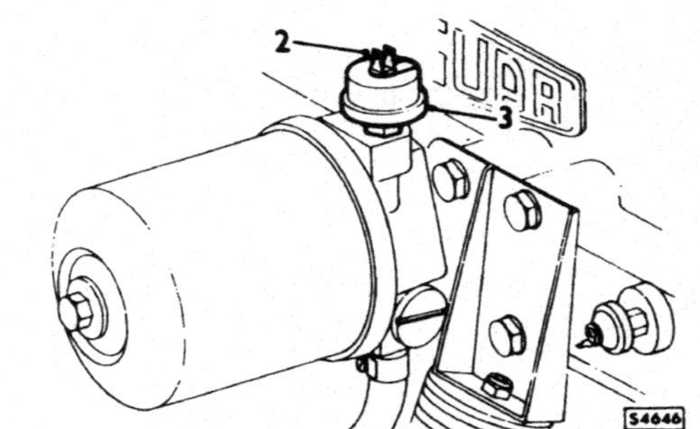

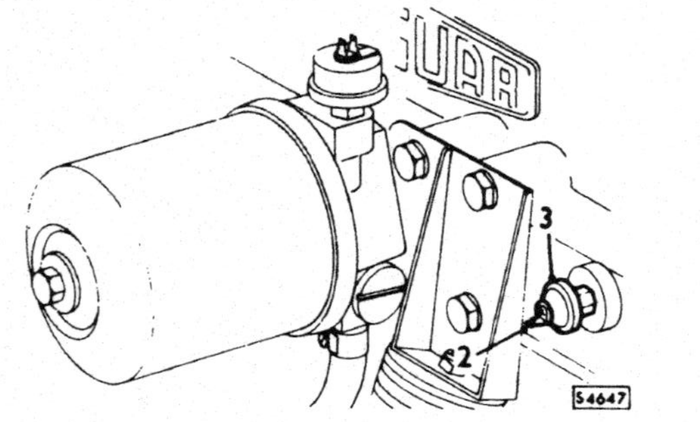

OIL PRESSURE WARNING SWITCH

Remove and refit **88.25.08**

Removing
1 Disconnect battery – 86.15.20.
2 Disconnect cable from lucar connector.
3 Remove oil pressure switch.

Refitting
Reverse operations 1 to 4.
CAUTION: Care must be taken not to overtighten switch.

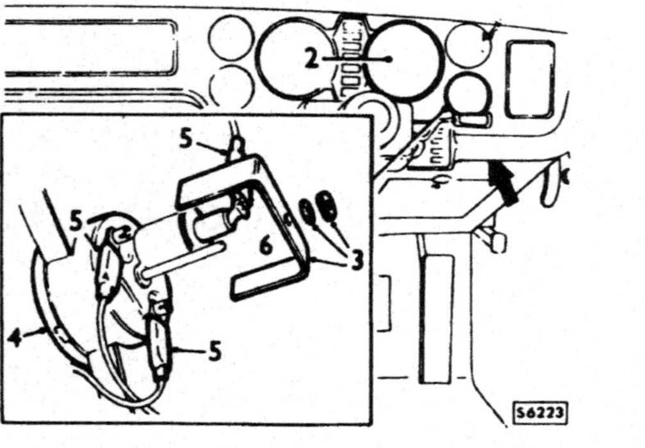

COOLANT TEMPERATURE GAUGE

Remove and refit **88.25.14**

Removing
1 Disconnect battery – 86.15.20.
2 Remove speedometer – 88.30.01.
3 Remove finger nut and lock washer from coolant temperature gauge retaining bracket.
4 Withdraw indicator from fascia.
5 Disconnect cables at lucar connectors on rear of instrument.
6 Withdraw instrument lighting bulb holder.

Refitting
Reverse operations 1 to 6.

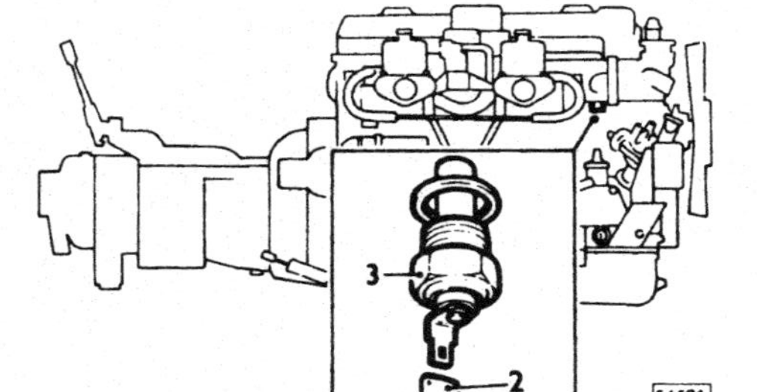

COOLANT TEMPERATURE TRANSMITTER

Remove and refit **88.25.20**

Removing
1 Disconnect battery – 86.15.20.
2 Disconnect cable at connector on transmitter.
3 Withdraw transmitter.

Refitting
4 Reverse operations 1 to 3.
5 Top up coolant.

FUEL GAUGE

Remove and refit **88.25.26**

Removing
1 Disconnect battery – 86.15.20.

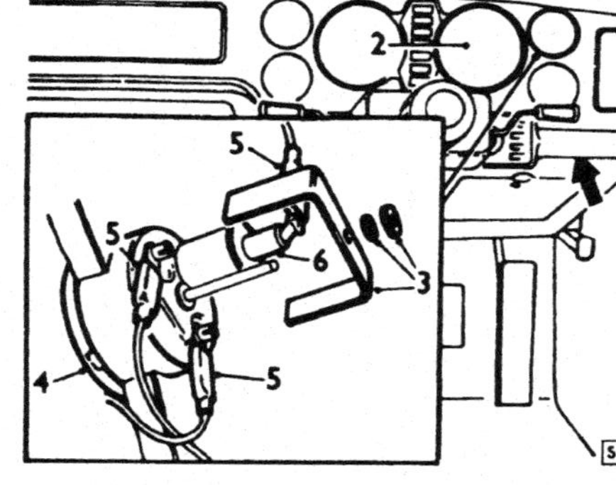

2 Remove speedometer – 88.30.01.
3 Remove finger nut and lock washer from fuel gauge retaining bracket.
4 Withdraw indicator from fascia.
5 Withdraw instrument lighting bulb holder.

Refitting
Reverse operations 1 to 6.

FUEL TANK UNIT

Remove and refit (Early cars) **88.25.32**

Removing
1 Disconnect battery – 86.15.20.
2 Drain fuel tank – 19.55.02.
3 Jack up car rear end.

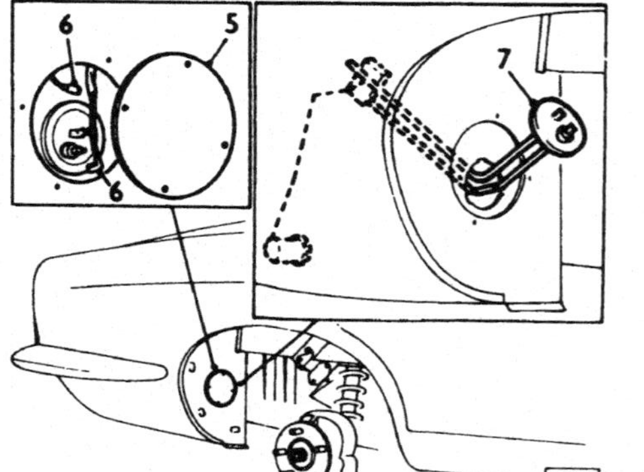

4 Remove wheel.
5 Remove cover plate.
6 Disconnect lucar connectors.
7 Remove tank unit by pressing on mounting plate and turning anti-clockwise.

Refitting
Reverse operations 1 to 7.
WARNING: TANK UNIT SEAL SHOULD BE REPLACED BY A NEW SEAL EVERY TIME THIS OPERATION IS CARRIED OUT.

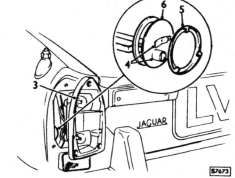

Remove and refit (Later cars with submerged fuel pumps) **88.25.32**

Removing
1 Disconnect battery – 86.15.20.
2 Drain fuel tank – 19.55.02.
3 Remove stop/tail/flasher lights assembly. (See 86.40.70 (L.H.) and 86.40.71 (R.H.).
4 Disconnect lucar connectors.
5 Release tank unit by pressing on mounting plate and turning retaining ring anti-clockwise.
6 Withdraw unit rearwards from tank.

Refitting
Reverse operations 1 to 6.

WARNING: TANK UNIT SEAL SHOULD BE REPLACED BY A NEW SEAL EVERY TIME THIS OPERATION IS CARRIED OUT.

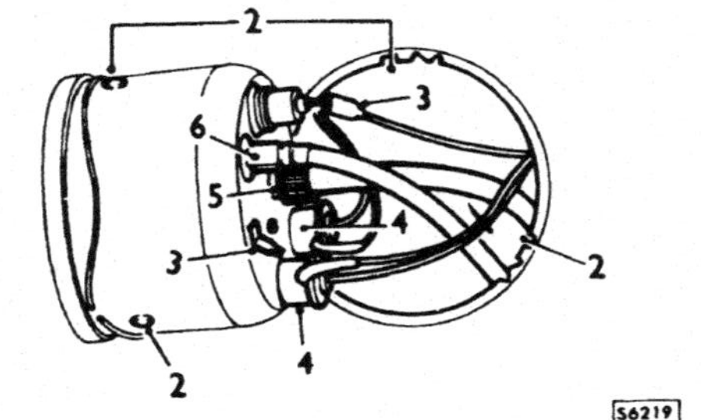

SPEEDOMETER

Remove and refit 88.30.01.

Removing

1. Disconnect battery – 86.15.20.
2. Exert pressure on rim of speedometer, turn anti-clockwise until instrument releases from locking tabs and withdraw from fascia.
3. Note cable positions and disconnect at lucars on back of instrument.
4. Withdraw bulb holders.
5. Unscrew speedometer drive cable.
6. Turn speedometer trip reset connector anti-clockwise until it releases and pull off.

Refitting

Reverse operations 1 to 6.

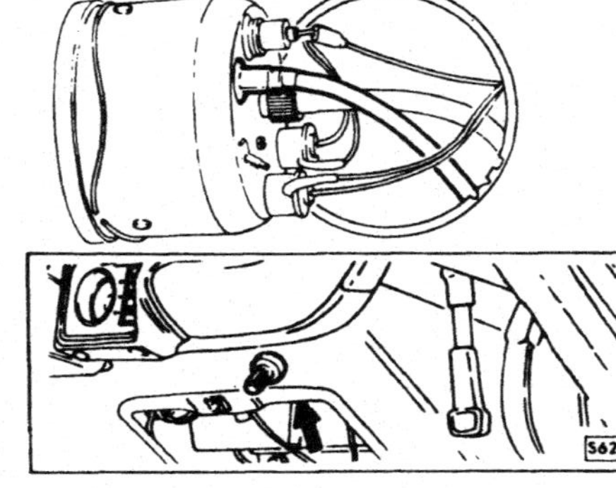

SPEEDOMETER TRIP RESET

Remove and refit 88.30.02

Removing

1. Disconnect battery – 86.15.20.
2. Remove retaining ring from speedometer trip reset knob in drivers side dash casing.
3. Remove speedometer – 88.30.01.
4. Withdraw trip reset cable bayonet connector from back of speedometer.

Refitting

Reverse operations 1 to 4.

NOTE: When refitting speedometer trip reset it is advisable to remove fuse block access panel to assist in location of lower end of reset cable through mounting bracket.

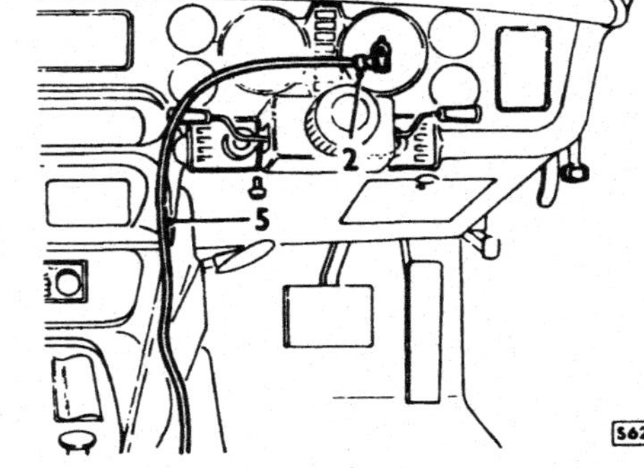
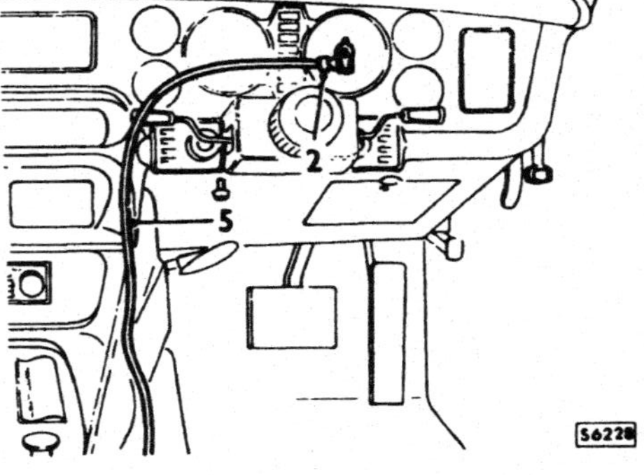

SPEEDOMETER CABLE ASSEMBLY

Remove and refit 88.30.06

Removing

1. Remove speedometer – 88.30.01.
2. Disconnect cable at right angle drive on gearbox – 88.30.16.
3. Remove revolution counter (tachometer) – 88.30.21.
4. Remove console side casing – 76.25.02.
5. Release clips.
6. Remove drive cable complete.

Refitting

Reverse operations 1 to 6.

NOTE: Clips should be replaced in exactly the same position. No extreme angles in cable run, and lubrication carried out before installation.

SPEEDOMETER CABLE – INNER

Remove and refit 88.30.07

Removing

1. Remove speedometer – 88.30.01.
2. Remove inner cable.
3. If cable is broken the gearbox end will have to be disconnected to retrieve other half.

Refitting

Reverse operations 1 to 3. Lubricate cable before refitting.

NOTE: (a) Lubrication should not be excessive, oil should never be used. Use only T.S.D. 119 or equivalent.

(b) The inner cable should only project by 3/8 in. (9,52 mm.) from outer casing at the instrument end to ensure correct engagement at point of drive.

S6229

SPEEDOMETER RIGHT ANGLE DRIVE – INSTRUMENT

Remove and refit 88.30.15

Removing

1. Remove speedometer – 88.30.01.
2. Unscrew knurled retaining ring withdraw drive.

Refitting

Reverse operations 1 and 2.

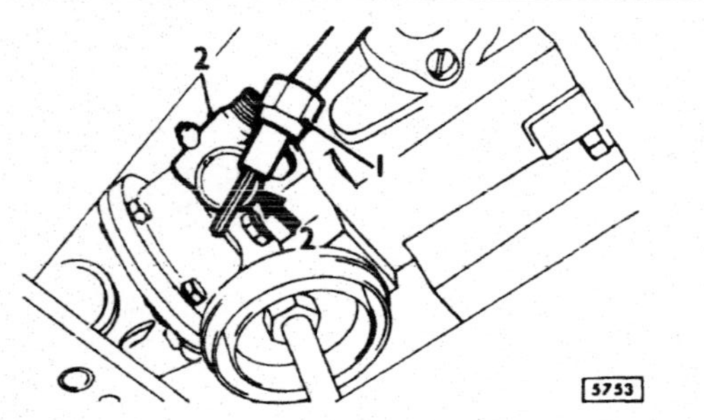

SPEEDOMETER RIGHT ANGLE DRIVE GEARBOX

Remove and refit **88.30.16**

Removing
1 Disconnect speedometer drive cable.
2 Remove right angle drive by unscrewing knurled retaining ring nut.

Refitting
Reverse operations 1 and 2.

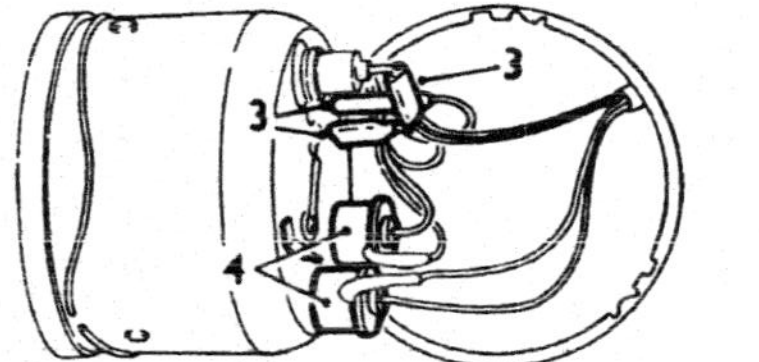

REVOLUTION COUNTER (TACHOMETER)

Remove and refit **88.30.21**

Removing
1 Disconnect battery – 86.15.20.
2 Exert pressure on rim of instrument and turn anti-clockwise until retaining studs release from locking ring.
3 Disconnect cables from lucars/ connectors on back of instrument.
NOTE: Take note of cable positions.
4 Pull bulb holder from instrument case.

Refitting
Reverse operations 1 to 4.

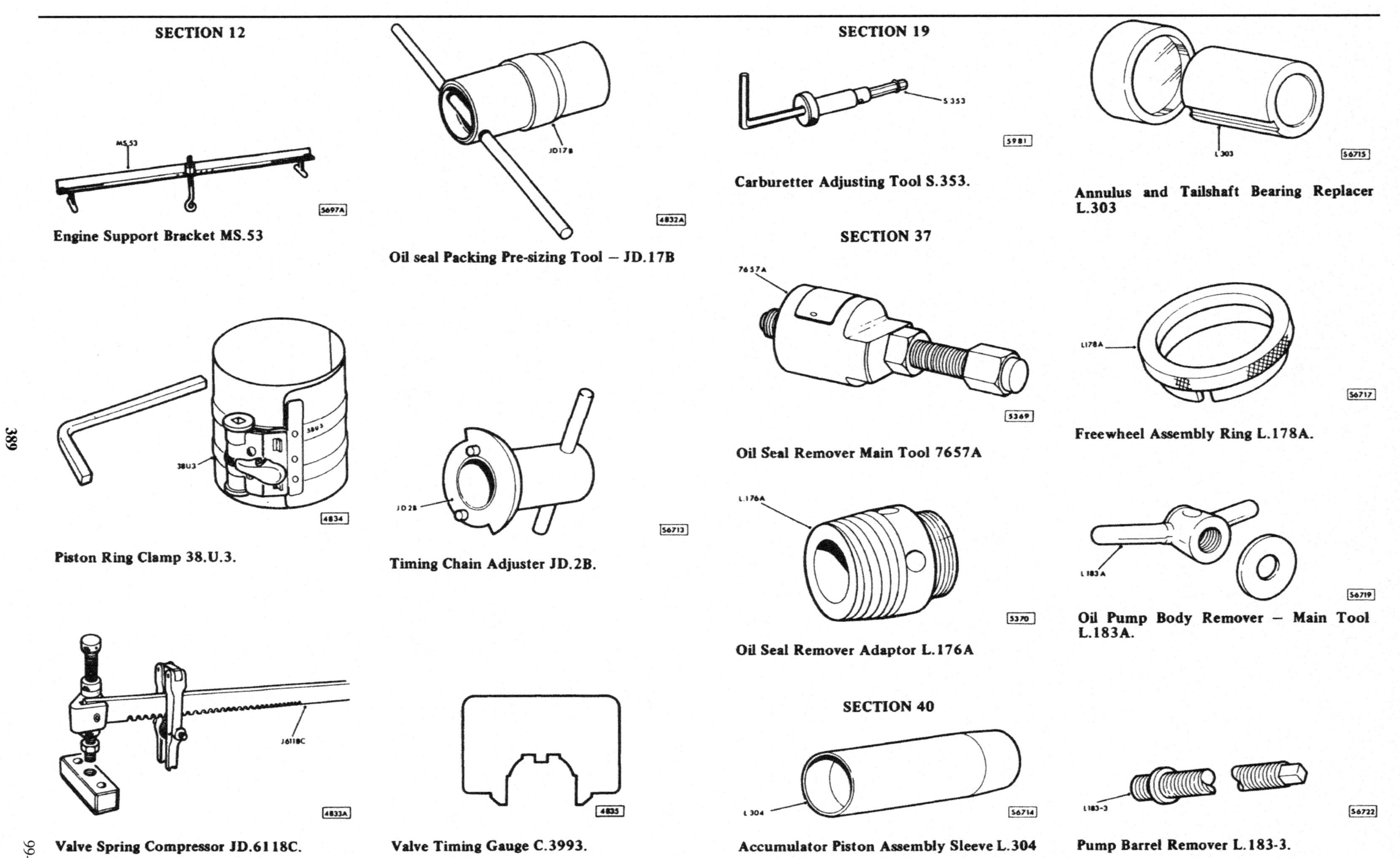

SECTION 12

Engine Support Bracket MS.53

Oil seal Packing Pre-sizing Tool – JD.17B

Piston Ring Clamp 38.U.3.

Timing Chain Adjuster JD.2B.

Valve Spring Compressor JD.6118C.

Valve Timing Gauge C.3993.

SECTION 19

Carburetter Adjusting Tool S.353.

Annulus and Tailshaft Bearing Replacer L.303

SECTION 37

Oil Seal Remover Main Tool 7657A

Freewheel Assembly Ring L.178A.

Oil Seal Remover Adaptor L.176A

Oil Pump Body Remover – Main Tool L.183A.

SECTION 40

Accumulator Piston Assembly Sleeve L.304

Pump Barrel Remover L.183-3.

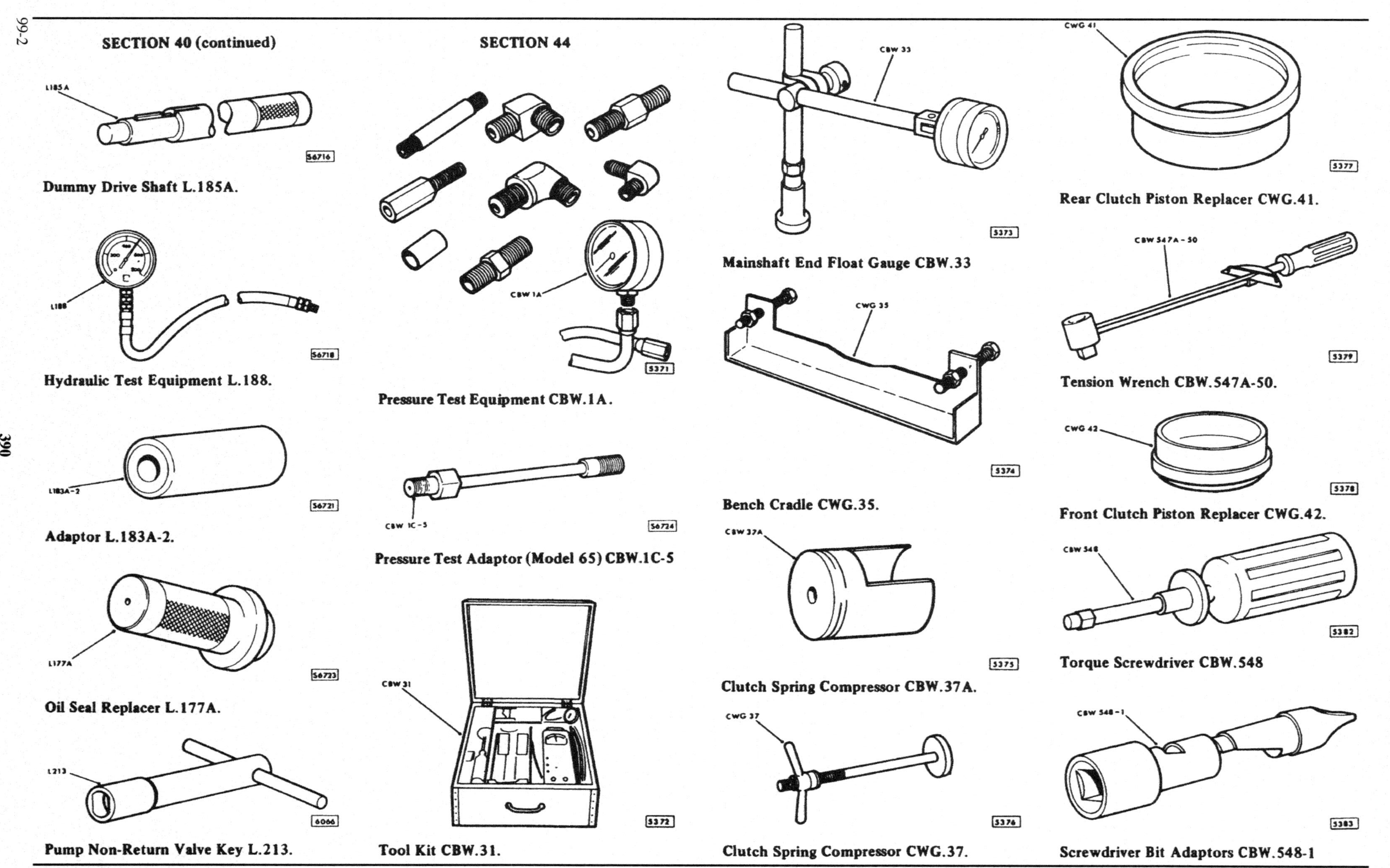

SECTION 40 (continued)

Dummy Drive Shaft L.185A.

Hydraulic Test Equipment L.188.

Adaptor L.183A-2.

Oil Seal Replacer L.177A.

Pump Non-Return Valve Key L.213.

SECTION 44

Pressure Test Equipment CBW.1A.

Pressure Test Adaptor (Model 65) CBW.1C-5

Tool Kit CBW.31.

Mainshaft End Float Gauge CBW.33

Bench Cradle CWG.35.

Clutch Spring Compressor CBW.37A.

Clutch Spring Compressor CWG.37.

Rear Clutch Piston Replacer CWG.41.

Tension Wrench CBW.547A-50.

Front Clutch Piston Replacer CWG.42.

Torque Screwdriver CBW.548

Screwdriver Bit Adaptors CBW.548-1

SECTION 44 (continued)

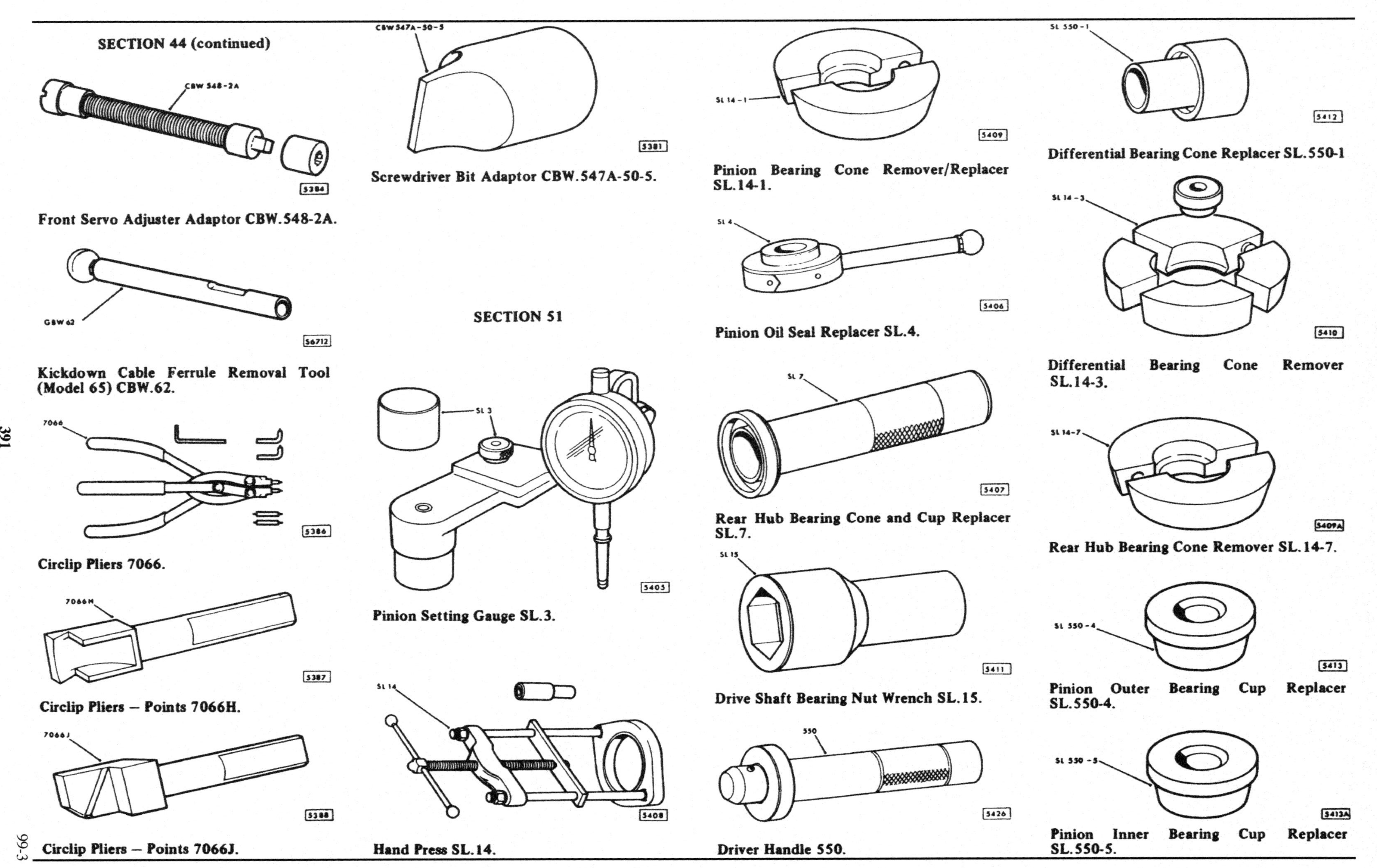

Front Servo Adjuster Adaptor CBW.548-2A.

Kickdown Cable Ferrule Removal Tool (Model 65) CBW.62.

Circlip Pliers 7066.

Circlip Pliers – Points 7066H.

Circlip Pliers – Points 7066J.

Screwdriver Bit Adaptor CBW.547A-50-5.

SECTION 51

Pinion Setting Gauge SL.3.

Hand Press SL.14.

Pinion Bearing Cone Remover/Replacer SL.14-1.

Pinion Oil Seal Replacer SL.4.

Rear Hub Bearing Cone and Cup Replacer SL.7.

Drive Shaft Bearing Nut Wrench SL.15.

Driver Handle 550.

Differential Bearing Cone Replacer SL.550-1

Differential Bearing Cone Remover SL.14-3.

Rear Hub Bearing Cone Remover SL.14-7.

Pinion Outer Bearing Cup Replacer SL.550-4.

Pinion Inner Bearing Cup Replacer SL.550-5.

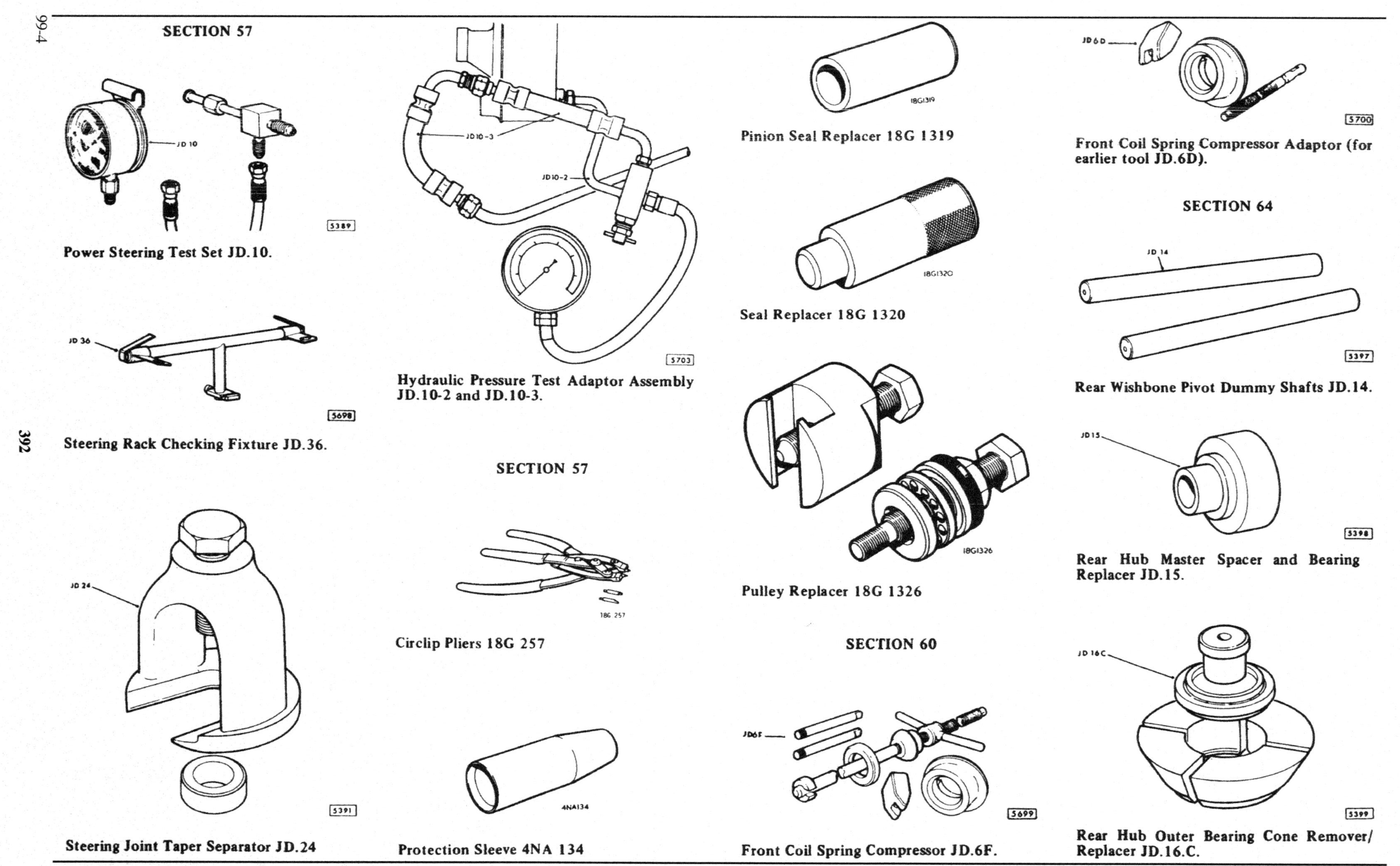

SECTION 57

Power Steering Test Set JD.10.

Steering Rack Checking Fixture JD.36.

Steering Joint Taper Separator JD.24

Hydraulic Pressure Test Adaptor Assembly JD.10-2 and JD.10-3.

SECTION 57

Circlip Pliers 18G 257

Protection Sleeve 4NA 134

Pinion Seal Replacer 18G 1319

Seal Replacer 18G 1320

Pulley Replacer 18G 1326

SECTION 60

Front Coil Spring Compressor JD.6F.

Front Coil Spring Compressor Adaptor (for earlier tool JD.6D).

SECTION 64

Rear Wishbone Pivot Dummy Shafts JD.14.

Rear Hub Master Spacer and Bearing Replacer JD.15.

Rear Hub Outer Bearing Cone Remover/ Replacer JD.16.C.

SECTION 64 (continued)

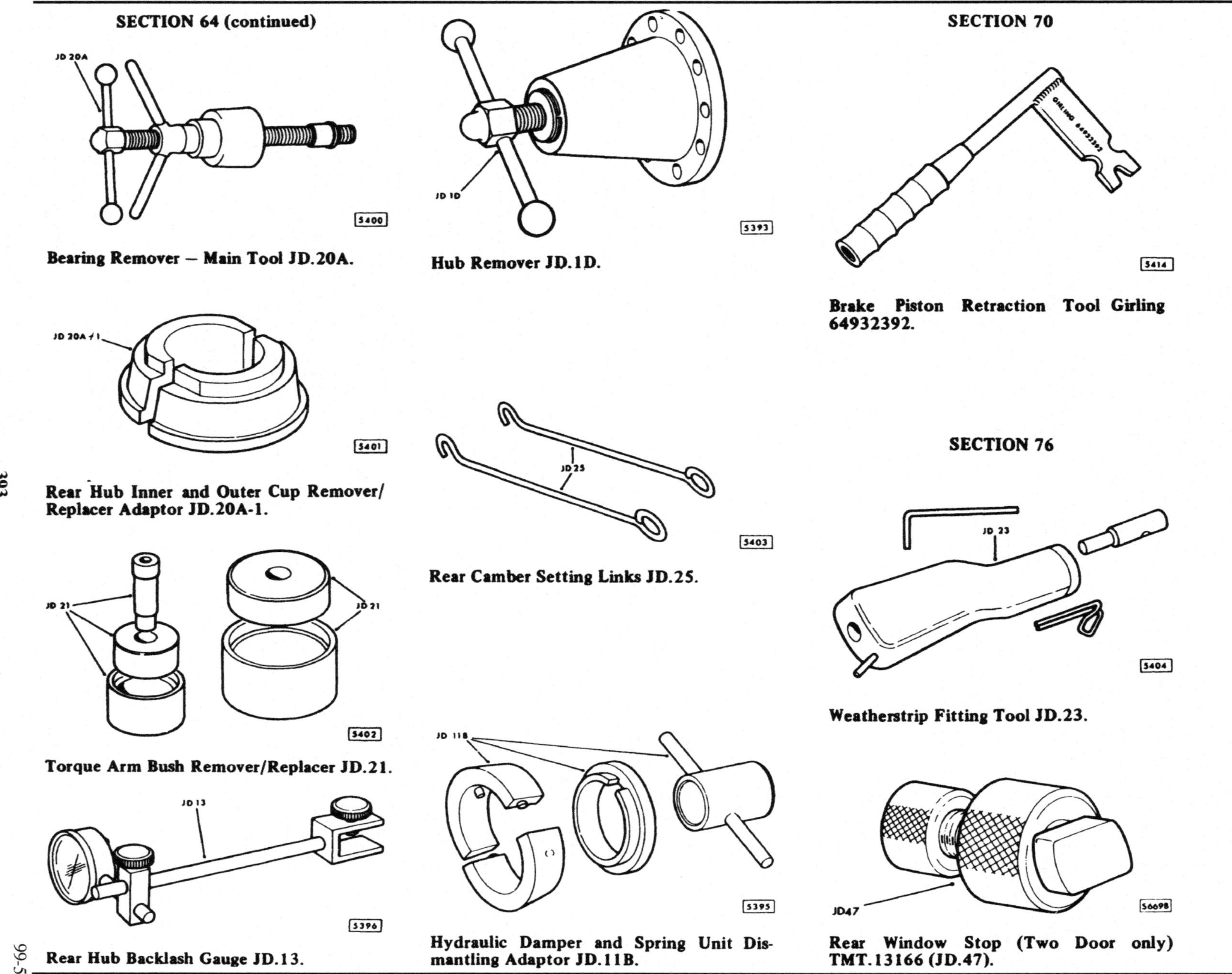

Bearing Remover – Main Tool JD.20A.

Rear Hub Inner and Outer Cup Remover/ Replacer Adaptor JD.20A-1.

Torque Arm Bush Remover/Replacer JD.21.

Rear Hub Backlash Gauge JD.13.

Hub Remover JD.1D.

Rear Camber Setting Links JD.25.

Hydraulic Damper and Spring Unit Dismantling Adaptor JD.11B.

SECTION 70

Brake Piston Retraction Tool Girling 64932392.

SECTION 76

Weatherstrip Fitting Tool JD.23.

Rear Window Stop (Two Door only) TMT.13166 (JD.47).

Distributed by Brooklands Books Ltd., PO Box 146,
Cobham, Surrey KT11 1LG, England
Phone: 01932 865051 Fax: 01932 868803
e-mail: info@brooklands-books.com web-site: www.brooklands-books.com

Printed and bound in Great Britain by
Marston Book Services Ltd, Oxfordshire

ISBN: 9781855200302 Ref: J585WH Pub No. E188/4 6T5/2489

Printed by Printforce, United Kingdom